AN INTRODUCTION TO
PSYCHOLOGI SCIENCE

AN INTRODUCTION TO
PSYCHOLOGICAL
SCIENCE

SECOND CANADIAN EDITION

MARK KRAUSE
Southern Oregon University

DANIEL CORTS
Augustana College

STEPHEN SMITH
University of Winnipeg

DAN DOLDERMAN
University of Toronto

 Pearson

EDITORIAL DIRECTOR: Claudine O'Donnell
ACQUISITIONS EDITOR: Darcey Pepper
MARKETING MANAGER: Leigh-Anne Graham
PROGRAM MANAGER: Madhu Ranadive
PROJECT MANAGER: Kimberley Blakey
DEVELOPMENTAL EDITOR: Lise Dupont
MEDIA DEVELOPER: Tiffany Palmer
PRODUCTION SERVICES: Cenveo® Publisher Services
PERMISSIONS PROJECT MANAGER: Kathryn O'Handley

PHOTO PERMISSIONS RESEARCH: Integra Publishing Services, Inc.
TEXT PERMISSIONS RESEARCH: Integra Publishing Services, Inc.
ART DIRECTOR: Alex Li
INTERIOR DESIGNER: Anthony Leung
COVER DESIGNER: Anthony Leung
COVER IMAGE: Keren Su/The Image Bank/Getty Images
VICE-PRESIDENT, CROSS MEDIA AND PUBLISHING SERVICES: Gary Bennett

Pearson Canada Inc., 26 Prince Andrew Place, Don Mills, Ontario M3C 2T8.

978-0-13-462070-1

1   17

Library and Archives Canada Cataloguing in Publication

Krause, Mark A. (Mark Andrew), 1971-, author
    An introduction to psychological science / Mark Krause, Daniel Corts, Stephen Smith, Dan Dolderman. — Second Canadian edition.

Includes bibliographical references and index.
ISBN 978-0-13-462070-1 (llv)

    1. Psychology—Textbooks. I. Corts, Daniel Paul, 1970-, author
II. Smith, Stephen D. (Stephen Douglas), 1974-, author III. Dolderman, Dan, 1972-, author IV. Title.

BF121.K73 2017   150   C2016-906938-9

*For Andrea and Finn. Both of you fuel
my passion and motivation for this endeavor.
I cannot thank you enough.*

Mark Krause

---

*To Kim, Sophie, and Jonah, for your patience,
understanding, and forgiveness during all
the hours this project has occupied me.*

Dan Corts

---

*To my brilliant wife, Jenn, and our hilarious
children, Oliver and Clara. Thank you for putting
up with me.*

Stephen Smith

---

*To my children, Alexandra, Kate, and Geoff,
who love this world so deeply. And to my mother,
who has had a huge impact on my life.*

Dan Dolderman

Brief Contents

1 Introducing Psychological Science   1

2 Reading and Evaluating Scientific Research   29

3 Biological Psychology   71

4 Sensation and Perception   125

5 Consciousness   180

6 Learning   227

7 Memory   270

8 Thought and Language   313

9 Intelligence Testing   349

10 Lifespan Development   385

11 Motivation and Emotion   439

12 Personality   490

13 Social Psychology   531

14 Health, Stress, and Coping   578

15 Psychological Disorders   614

16 Therapies   653

Contents

About the Authors   xvii
About the Canadian Authors   xvii
From the Authors   xviii
Content and Features   xxi
For Instructors   xxvi
Acknowledgments   xxviii

1   Introducing Psychological Science   1

Module 1.1 The Science of Psychology   2

The Scientific Method   3

Hypotheses: Making Predictions   3 • Theories: Explaining Phenomena   4 • The Biopsychosocial Model   5

Building Scientific Literacy   6

Working the Scientific Literacy Model: Planning When to Study   7

Critical Thinking, Curiosity, and a Dose of Healthy Skepticism   8

■ **MYTHS IN MIND Abducted by Aliens!**   9

Summary   10

Module 1.2 How Psychology Became a Science   11

Psychology's Philosophical and Scientific Origins   12

Influences from the Ancients: Philosophical Insights into Behaviour   12 • Influences from Physics: Experimenting with the Mind   13 • Influences from Evolutionary Theory: The Adaptive Functions of Behaviour   13 • Influences from Medicine: Diagnoses and Treatments   15 • The Influence of Social Sciences: Measuring and Comparing Humans   16

The Beginnings of Contemporary Psychology   18

Structuralism and Functionalism: The Beginnings of Psychology   18 • The Rise of Behaviourism   19 • Radical Behaviourism   20 • Humanistic Psychology Emerges   21 • The Brain and Behaviour   21 • The Cognitive Revolution   21 • Social and Cultural Influences   23

Emerging Themes in Psychology   24

Psychology of Women   24 • Comparing Cultures   25 • The Neuroimaging Explosion   25 • The Search for the Positive   26 • Psychology in the Real World   26

Summary   28

2   Reading and Evaluating Scientific Research   29

Module 2.1 Principles of Scientific Research   30

Five Characteristics of Quality Scientific Research   31

Scientific Measurement: Objectivity   31 • Scientific Measurement: Reliability, and Validity   32 • Generalizability of Results   33 • Sources of Bias in Psychological Research   34

Working the Scientific Literacy Model: Demand Characteristics and Participant Behaviour   35

Techniques That Reduce Bias   36 • Sharing the Results   37

■ **PSYCH@ The Hospital: The Placebo Effect**   37

Replication   38

Five Characteristics of Poor Research   39

Summary   41

Module 2.2 Scientific Research Designs   42

Descriptive Research   43

Case Studies   43

Working the Scientific Literacy Model: Case Studies as a Form of Scientific Research   44

Naturalistic Observation   45 • Surveys and Questionnaires   46

Correlational Research   47

■ **MYTHS IN MIND Beware of Illusory Correlations**   48

Experimental Research   49

The Experimental Method   49 • The Quasi-Experimental Method   50 • Converging Operations   50

Summary   51

Module 2.3 Ethics in Psychological Research   53

Promoting the Welfare of Research Participants   54

Weighing the Risks and Benefits of Research   54 • Obtaining Informed Consent   55 • The Right to Anonymity and Confidentiality   56 • The Welfare of Animals in Research   56

Working the Scientific Literacy Model: Animal Models of Disease   57

REBs for Animal-Based Research   59

Ethical Collection, Storage, and Reporting of Data   59

Summary   61

Module 2.4 A Statistical Primer   62

Descriptive Statistics   63

Frequency   63 • Central Tendency   63 • Variability   65

Hypothesis Testing: Evaluating the Outcome of a Study   66

Working the Scientific Literacy Model: Statistical Significance   68

Summary   70

3   Biological Psychology   71

Module 3.1 Genetic and Evolutionary Perspectives on Behaviour   72

Heredity and Behaviour   73

The Genetic Code   73 • Behavioural Genomics: The Molecular Approach   75 • Behavioural Genetics: Twin and Adoption Studies   75

■ **MYTHS IN MIND Single Genes and Behaviour**   76

Gene Expression and Behaviour   78

Evolutionary Insights into Human Behaviour   79

Evolutionary Psychology   80

Working the Scientific Literacy Model: Hunters and Gatherers: Men, Women, and Spatial Memory   81

Sexual Selection and Evolution   83

■ **BIOPSYCHOSOCIAL PERSPECTIVES** Sexual
Selection and the Colour Red   84
Summary   86

Module 3.2 How the Nervous System Works:
Cells and Neurotransmitters   88
Neural Communication   89
The Neuron   89
■ **MYTHS IN MIND We Are Born with All the
Brain Cells We Will Ever Have**   90
Glial Cells   91 • The Neuron's Electrical System:
Resting and Action Potentials   91
The Chemical Messengers: Neurotransmitters and
Hormones   93
Types of Neurotransmitters   94 • Drug Effects
on Neurotransmission   95 • Hormones and the
Endocrine System   96
**Working the Scientific Literacy Model: Testosterone
and Aggression**   97
Neurons in Context   99
Summary   100

Module 3.3 Structure and Organization
of the Nervous System   101
Divisions of the Nervous System   102
The Central Nervous System   102 • The Peripheral Nervous
System   102
The Brain and Its Structures   104
The Hindbrain: Sustaining the Body   104 • The Midbrain:
Sensation and Action   105 • The Forebrain: Emotion, Memory,
and Thought   106 • The Cerebral Cortex   108 • The
Four Lobes   108 • Left Brain, Right Brain: Hemispheric
Specialization   111
■ **PSYCH@ The Gym**   111
The Changing Brain: Neuroplasticity   112
**Working the Scientific Literacy Model: Neuroplasticity and
Recovery from Brain Injury**   113
Summary   115

Module 3.4 Windows to the Brain: Measuring and
Observing Brain Activity   116
Insights from Brain Damage   117
Lesioning and Brain Stimulation   117
Structural and Functional Neuroimaging   119
Structural Neuroimaging   119 • Functional Neuroimaging   120
**Working the Scientific Literacy Model: Functional
MRI and Behaviour**   122
Summary   124

4 Sensation and Perception   125

Module 4.1 Sensation and Perception at a Glance   126
Sensing the World Around Us   127
Stimulus Thresholds   129 • Signal Detection   130 • Priming
and Subliminal Perception   131
■ **MYTHS IN MIND Setting the Record Straight on
Subliminal Messaging**   131
Perceiving the World Around Us   132
Gestalt Principles of Perception   132
**Working the Scientific Literacy Model: Backward
Messages in Music**   134
Attention and Perception   136
Summary   137

Module 4.2 The Visual System   139
The Human Eye   140
How the Eye Gathers Light   140 • The Structure of
the Eye   141 • The Retina: From Light to Nerve
Impulse   142 • The Retina and the Perception of
Colours   144 • Common Visual Disorders   145
Visual Perception and the Brain   146
The Ventral Stream   148
Working the Scientific Literacy Model: Are Faces Special? 148
The Dorsal Stream   151 • Depth Perception   152
■ **PSYCH@ The Artist's Studio**   153
Summary   155

Module 4.3 The Auditory and Vestibular Systems   156
Sound and the Structures of the Ear   157
Sound   157 • The Human Ear   157
The Perception of Sound   160
Sound Localization: Finding the Source   160 • Theories of
Pitch Perception   160 • Auditory Perception and the
Brain   161 • The Perception of Music   162
**Working the Scientific Literacy Model: The Perception
of Musical Beats**   162
The Vestibular System   164
Sensation and the Vestibular System   164 • The Vestibular
System and the Brain   165
Summary   165

Module 4.4 Touch and the Chemical Senses   167
The Sense of Touch   168
Feeling Pain   169
Working the Scientific Literacy Model: Empathy and Pain   171
Phantom Limb Pain   172
The Chemical Senses: Taste and Smell   173
The Gustatory System: Taste   173 • The Olfactory System:
Smell   175
Multimodal Integration   176
What *Is* Multimodal Integration?   176 • Synesthesia   177
Summary   178

5 Consciousness   180

Module 5.1 Biological Rhythms of Consciousness:
Wakefulness and Sleep   181
What Is Sleep?   182
Biological Rhythms   182 • The Stages of Sleep   184
Why Do We Need Sleep?   186
Theories of Sleep   186 • Sleep Deprivation and Sleep
Displacement   187
Theories of Dreaming   190
The Psychoanalytic Approach   190 • The Activation–
Synthesis Hypothesis   190
**Working the Scientific Literacy Model: Dreams,
REM Sleep, and Learning**   191
Disorders and Problems with Sleep   193
Insomnia   193 • Nightmares and Night Terrors   194
• Movement Disturbances   194 • Sleep Apnea   195
• Narcolepsy   196 • Overcoming Sleep Problems   196
Summary   197

Module 5.2 Altered States of Consciousness: Hypnosis,
Mind-Wandering, and Disorders of Consciousness   199

Hypnosis   200
Theories of Hypnosis   200 • Applications of Hypnosis   201

■ **MYTHS IN MIND Recovering Lost Memories through Hypnosis**   **202**

Mind-Wandering   203
What Is Mind-Wandering?   203 • Mind-Wandering and the Brain   203 • The Benefits of Mind-Wandering   204

Disorders of Consciousness   205
Working the Scientific Literacy Model: Assessing Consciousness in the Vegetative State   **207**
Summary   210

Module 5.3 Drugs and Conscious Experience   211
Physical and Psychological Effects of Drugs   212
Short-Term Effects   212 • Long-Term Effects   213

Commonly Abused "Recreational" Drugs   215
Stimulants   215 • Hallucinogens   217 • Marijuana   218

■ **BIOPSYCHOSOCIAL PERSPECTIVES Recreational and Spiritual Uses of *Salvia Divinorum***   **219**
Working the Scientific Literacy Model: Marijuana, Memory, and Cognition   **219**
Opiates   221

Legal Drugs and Their Effects on Consciousness   222
Sedatives   222 • Prescription Drug Abuse   222 • Alcohol   224 • Why Are Some Drugs Legal and Others Illegal?   224

■ **PSYCH@ University Parties**   **224**
Summary   226

6 Learning   **227**

Module 6.1 Classical Conditioning: Learning by Association   228
Pavlov's Dogs: Classical Conditioning of Salivation   229
Evolutionary Function of the CR   231 • Classical Conditioning and the Brain   231

Processes of Classical Conditioning   233
Acquisition, Extinction, and Spontaneous Recovery   233 • Stimulus Generalization and Discrimination   234

Applications of Classical Conditioning   235
Conditioned Emotional Responses   235 • Evolutionary Role for Fear Conditioning   236 • Conditioned Taste Aversions   237

Working the Scientific Literacy Model: Conditioning and Negative Political Advertising   **239**
Drug Tolerance and Conditioning   241
Summary   242

Module 6.2 Operant Conditioning: Learning through Consequences   244
Basic Principles of Operant Conditioning   245
Reinforcement and Punishment   245 • Positive and Negative Reinforcement and Punishment   247 • Shaping   248 • Applying Operant Conditioning   248

Processes of Operant Conditioning   249
Primary and Secondary Reinforcers   249 • Discrimination and Generalization   250 • Delayed Reinforcement and Extinction   251 • Reward Devaluation   251

Reinforcement Schedules and Operant Conditioning   252
Schedules of Reinforcement   252

■ **PSYCH@ Never Use Multiline Slot Machines**   **254**
Working the Scientific Literacy Model: Reinforcement and Superstition   **255**
Applying Punishment   256 • Are Classical and Operant Learning Distinct Events?   257

Summary   258

Module 6.3 Cognitive and Observational Learning   260
Cognitive Perspectives on Learning   261
Latent Learning   261 • S-O-R Theory of Learning   262

Observational Learning   262
Processes Supporting Observational Learning   263

■ **MYTHS IN MIND Is Teaching Uniquely Human?**   **264**
Imitation and Mirror Neurons   265
Working the Scientific Literacy Model: Linking Media Exposure to Behaviour   **265**

■ **BIOPSYCHOSOCIAL PERSPECTIVES Violence, Video Games, and Culture**   **268**
Summary   269

7 Memory   **270**

Module 7.1 Memory Systems   271
The Atkinson-Shiffrin Model   272
Sensory Memory   273 • Short-Term Memory and the Magical Number 7   274 • Long-Term Memory   275
Working the Scientific Literacy Model: Distinguishing Short-Term from Long-Term Memory Stores   **276**
The Working Memory Model: An Active STM System   279
The Phonological Loop   280 • The Visuospatial Sketchpad   280 • The Episodic Buffer   281 • The Central Executive   281 • Working Memory: Putting the Pieces Together   281

Long-Term Memory Systems: Declarative and Nondeclarative Memories   282
Declarative Memory   282 • Nondeclarative Memory   283

The Cognitive Neuroscience of Memory   283
Memory at the Cellular Level   283 • Memory, the Brain, and Amnesia   284 • Stored Memories and the Brain   285

Summary   287

Module 7.2 Encoding and Retrieving Memories   288
Encoding and Retrieval   289
Rehearsal: The Basics of Encoding   289 • Levels of Processing   290 • Retrieval   290
Working the Scientific Literacy Model: Context-Dependent Memory   **291**
State-Dependent Memory   294 • Mood-Dependent Memory   294

Emotional Memories   295
Flashbulb Memories   296

■ **MYTHS IN MIND The Accuracy of Flashbulb Memories**   **297**

Forgetting and Remembering   298
The Forgetting Curve: How Soon We Forget …   298 • Mnemonics: Improving Your Memory Skills   298
Summary   301

Module 7.3 Constructing and Reconstructing Memories   302

How Memories Are Organized and Constructed   303
The Schema: An Active Organization Process   303
**Working the Scientific Literacy Model: How Schemas
Influence Memory**   **303**
■ **BIOPSYCHOSOCIAL PERSPECTIVES Your
Earliest Memories**   **305**
Memory Reconstruction   306
The Perils of Eyewitness Testimony   306
■ **PSYCH@ Court: Is Eyewitness Testimony Reliable?**   **308**
Imagination and False Memories   308 • Creating False
Memories in the Laboratory   309 • The Danger of False
Remembering   310
Summary   312

8   Thought and Language   **313**

Module 8.1   The Organization of Knowledge   314
Concepts and Categories   315
Classical Categories: Definitions and Rules   315 • Prototypes:
Categorization by Comparison   315 • Networks and
Hierarchies   316
**Working the Scientific Literacy Model: Priming and
Semantic Networks**   **318**
Memory, Culture, and Categories   319
Categorization and Experience   319 • Categories, Memory,
and the Brain   320
■ **BIOPSYCHOSOCIAL PERSPECTIVES Culture and
Categorical Thinking**   **321**
■ **MYTHS IN MIND How Many Words for Snow?**   **322**
Categories and Culture   322
Summary   323

Module 8.2   Problem Solving, Judgment,
and Decision Making   324
Defining and Solving Problems   325
Problem-Solving Strategies and Techniques   325 • Cognitive
Obstacles   326
■ **PSYCH@ Problem Solving and Humour**   **327**
Judgment and Decision Making   328
Conjunction Fallacies and Representativeness   328
• The Availability Heuristic   329 • Anchoring and Framing
Effects   330 • Belief Perseverance and Confirmation Bias   331
**Working the Scientific Literacy Model: Maximizing and
Satisficing in Complex Decisions**   **332**
Summary   335

Module 8.3   Language and Communication   336
What Is Language?   337
Early Studies of Language   337 • Properties of
Language   338 • Phonemes and Morphemes: The Basic
Ingredients of Language   339 • Syntax: The Language
Recipe   339 • Pragmatics: The Finishing Touches   340
The Development of Language   341
Infants, Sound Perception, and Language Acquisition   341
• Producing Spoken Language   342 • Sensitive Periods for
Language   342 • The Bilingual Brain   343
Genes, Evolution, and Language   344
**Working the Scientific Literacy Model: Genes
and Language**   **344**
Can Animals Use Language?   346
Summary   348

9   Intelligence Testing   **349**

Module 9.1   Measuring Intelligence   350
Different Approaches to Intelligence Testing   351
Intelligence and Perception: Galton's Anthropometric
Approach   351 • Intelligence and Thinking: The Stanford–
Binet Test   352 • The Wechsler Adult Intelligence
Scale   353 • Raven's Progressive Matrices   355
The Checkered Past of Intelligence Testing   356
IQ Testing and the Eugenics Movement   356 • The Race and
IQ Controversy   357 • Problems with the Racial Superiority
Interpretation   358
**Working the Scientific Literacy Model: Beliefs about
Intelligence**   **358**
Summary   361

Module 9.2   Understanding Intelligence   362
Intelligence as a Single, General Ability   363
Spearman's General Intelligence   363 • Does G Tell Us
the Whole Story?   364
Intelligence as Multiple, Specific Abilities   365
The Hierarchical Model of Intelligence   365
**Working the Scientific Literacy Model: Testing for Fluid
and Crystallized Intelligence**   **366**
Sternberg's Triarchic Theory of Intelligence   368
■ **MYTHS IN MIND Learning Styles**   **369**
Gardner's Theory of Multiple Intelligences   369
■ **PSYCH@ The NFL Draft**   **370**
The Battle of the Sexes   371
Do Males and Females have Unique Cognitive Skills?   372
Summary   373

Module 9.3   Biological, Environmental,
and Behavioural Influences on Intelligence   374
Biological Influences on Intelligence   375
The Genetics of Intelligence: Twin and Adoption
Studies   375 • The Heritability of Intelligence   375
• Behavioural Genomics   376
**Working the Scientific Literacy Model: Brain Size and
Intelligence**   **377**
Environmental Influences on Intelligence   379
Birth Order   379 • Socioeconomic Status   380
• Nutrition   380 • Stress   381 • Education   381
• The Flynn Effect: Is Everyone Getting Smarter?   381
Behavioural Influences on Intelligence   382
Brain Training Programs   383 • Nootropic Drugs   383
Summary   384

10   Lifespan Development   **385**

Module 10.1   Physical Development from
Conception through Infancy   386
Methods for Measuring Developmental Trends   387
Patterns of Development: Stages and Continuity   387
Zygotes to Infants: From One Cell to Billions   388
Fertilization and Gestation   388 • Fetal Brain
Development   388 • Nutrition, Teratogens, and Fetal
Development   390
**Working the Scientific Literacy Model: The Long-Term
Effects of Premature Birth**   **392**

■ **MYTHS IN MIND** Vaccinations and Autism   394

Sensory and Motor Development in Infancy   394

• Motor Development in the First Year   396

Summary   399

Module 10.2 Infancy and Childhood: Cognitive
and Emotional Development   400

Cognitive Changes: Piaget's Cognitive
Development Theory   401

The Sensorimotor Stage: Living in the Material World   401
• The Preoperational Stage: Quantity and Numbers   402
• The Concrete Operational Stage: Using Logical
Thought   403 • The Formal Operational Stage: Abstract
and Hypothetical Thought   403

Working the Scientific Literacy Model: Evaluating Piaget   404

Complementary Approaches to Piaget   405

Social Development, Attachment, and
Self-Awareness   406

What *Is* Attachment?   407 • Types of Attachment   407
• Development of Attachment   409 • Self Awareness   409

Psychosocial Development   412

Development across the Lifespan   412 • Parenting
and Prosocial Behaviour   413 • Parenting and
Attachment   414

Summary   415

Module 10.3 Adolescence   417

Physical Changes in Adolescence   418

Emotional Challenges in Adolescence   419

Emotional Regulation during Adolescence   420

**Working the Scientific Literacy Model: Adolescent
Risk and Decision Making**   420

Cognitive Development: Moral Reasoning
vs. Emotions   422

Kohlberg's Moral Development: Learning Right from Wrong   422

■ **BIOPSYCHOSOCIAL PERSPECTIVES** Emotion
and Disgust   424

Social Development: Identity and Relationships   425

Who Am I? Identity Formation during Adolescence   425
• Peer Groups   425 • Romantic Relationships   426

Summary   427

Module 10.4 Adulthood and Aging   428

From Adolescence through Middle Age   429

Emerging Adults   429 • Early and Middle Adulthood   429
• Love and Marriage   431 • Parenting   432

Late Adulthood   433

Happiness and Relationships   433 • The Eventual
Decline of Aging   434

■ **PSYCH@ The Driver's Seat**   435

**Working the Scientific Literacy Model: Aging and
Cognitive Change**   436

Summary   438

11 Motivation and Emotion   439

Module 11.1 Hunger and Eating   440

Physiological Aspects of Hunger   442

Food and Reward   443

Psychological Aspects of Hunger   445

Attention and Eating   445 • Eating and Semantic
Networks   446 • Eating and the Social Context   446

Disorders of Eating   448

Anorexia and Bulimia   448

**Working the Scientific Literacy Model: The Effect
of Media Depictions of Beauty on Body Image**   450

Summary   451

Module 11.2 Sex   452

Human Sexual Behaviour: Psychological Influences   453

Psychological Measures of Sexual Motivation   453

■ **Human Sexual Behaviour: Physiological
Influences**   455

Physiological Measures of Sex   455 • Sexual Orientation:
Biology and Environment   456 • Transgender and Transsexual
Individuals   458

■ **PSYCH@ Sex Ed**   459

Human Sexual Behaviour: Cultural Influences   460

Sex and Technology   461

Working the Scientific Literacy Model: Does Sex Sell?   462

Summary   464

Module 11.3 Social and Achievement Motivation   465

Belonging and Love Needs   466

Belonging Is a Need, Not a Want   467 • Love   467
• Belonging, Self-Esteem, and Our Worldview   468

**Working the Scientific Literacy Model: Terror
Management Theory and the Need to Belong**   468

Achievement Motivation   470

Self-Determination Theory   471 • Extrinsic and Intrinsic
Motivation   472 • A Continuum of Motivation   472
• Cultural Differences in Motivation   473

Summary   475

Module 11.4 Emotion   476

Physiology of Emotion   477

The Initial Response   477 • The Autonomic Response:
Fight or Flight?   478 • The Emotional Response:
Movement   479 • Emotional Regulation   479

Experiencing Emotions   479

**Working the Scientific Literacy Model: The Two-Factor
Theory of Emotion**   481

Expressing Emotions   484

Emotional Faces and Bodies   484 • Culture, Emotion,
and Display Rules   486 • Culture, Context,
and Emotion   487

Summary   489

12 Personality   490

Module 12.1 Contemporary Approaches to Personality   491

The Trait Perspective   492

Early Trait Research   492 • The Five Factor Model   493
• Openness   494 • Conscientiousness   495
• Extraversion   495 • Agreeableness   495
• Neuroticism   495

Beyond the Big Five: The Personality of Evil?   496

Honesty–Humility   496 • The Dark Triad   496 • Right-Wing
Authoritarianism   497

**Working the Scientific Literacy Model: Right-Wing
Authoritarianism at the Group Level**   497

Personality Traits over the Lifespan   499

Temperaments   499 • Is Personality Stable over
Time?   499 • Personality Traits and States   500

Behaviourist and Social-Cognitive
Perspectives   501
The Behaviourist Perspective   501 • The Social-Cognitive
Perspective   502
Summary   503

Module 12.2 Cultural and Biological Approaches
to Personality   505
Culture and Personality   506
Universals and Differences across Cultures: The
Big Five   506 • Personality Structures in Different
Cultures   506 • Comparing Personality Traits between
Nations   507
■ BIOPSYCHOSOCIAL PERSPECTIVES How Culture
Shapes Our Development: Cultural Differences
in the Self   507
How Genes Affect Personality   508
Twin Studies   509
Working the Scientific Literacy Model: From Molecules to
Personality   510
The Role of Evolution in Personality   511
Animal Behaviour: The Evolutionary Roots of
Personality   511 • Why There Are So Many Different
Personalities: The Evolutionary Explanation   512
■ MYTHS IN MIND Men Are from Mars,
Women Are from Venus   513
The Brain and Personality   514
Extraversion and Arousal   514 • Contemporary Research:
Images of Personality in the Brain   515 • Extraversion   515
• Neuroticism   515 • Agreeableness   515
• Conscientiousness   515 • Openness to Experience   515
Summary   516

Module 12.3 Psychodynamic and Humanistic
Approaches to Personality   518
The Psychodynamic Perspective   519
Assumptions of Psychodynamic Theories   519 • Unconscious
Processes and Psychodynamics   520 • The Structure of
Personality   520 • Defence Mechanisms   521 • Personality
Development: The Psychosexual Stages   522 • The Oral Stage
(0–18 Months)   523 • The Anal Stage (18 Months–3 Years)   523
• The Phallic Stage (3–6 Years)   523 • The Latency Stage
(6–13 years)   524 • The Genital Stage   524 • Exploring the
Unconscious with Projective Tests   525
Working the Scientific Literacy Model: Perceiving
Others as a Projective Test   526
Alternatives to the Psychodynamic Approach   527
Analytical Psychology   527 • The Power of Social
Factors   528 • Humanistic Perspectives   528
Summary   529

13 Social Psychology   531
Module 13.1 The Power of the Situation:
Social Influences on Behaviour   532
The Person and the Situation   533
Mimicry and Social Norms   534 • Group Dynamics: Social
Loafing and Social Facilitation   535 • Groupthink   536
The Asch Experiments: Conformity   537
Working the Scientific Literacy Model: Examining
Why People Conform: Seeing Is Believing   538
The Bystander Effect: Situational Influences
on Helping Behaviour   541

Social Roles and Obedience   544
The Stanford Prison Study   544 • Obedience to Authority:
The Milgram Experiment   546
Summary   549

Module 13.2 Social Cognition   551
Person Perception   552
Thin Slices of Behaviour   553 • Self-Fulfilling Prophecies
and Other Consequences of First Impressions   553
The Self in the Social World   554
Projecting the Self onto Others: False Consensus
and Naive Realism   554 • Self-Serving Biases and
Attributions   555 • Ingroups and Outgroups   556
Stereotypes, Prejudice, and Discrimination   557
■ MYTHS IN MIND Are Only Negative Aspects of
Stereotypes Problematic?   558
Prejudice in a Politically Correct World   558
Working the Scientific Literacy Model: Explicit versus
Implicit Measures of Prejudice   559
■ PSYCH@ The Law Enforcement Academy   561
Improving Intergroup Relations   562
Summary   563

Module 13.3 Attitudes, Behaviour, and Effective
Communication   564
Changing People's Behaviour   565
Persuasion: Changing Attitudes through Communication   565
Using the Central Route Effectively   566
Make It Personal   567
Working the Scientific Literacy Model: The Identifiable
Victim Effect   568
Value Appeals   570 • Preaching or Flip-Flopping? One-Sided
vs. Two-Sided Messages   570 • Emotions in the Central
Route   570
Using the Peripheral Route Effectively   572
Authority   572 • Liking   572 • Social
Validation   572 • Reciprocity   572 • Consistency   573
The Attitude–Behaviour Feedback Loop   574
Cognitive Dissonance   574 • Attitudes and Actions   575
Summary   576

14 Health, Stress, and Coping   578
Module 14.1 Behaviour and Health   579
Smoking   580
Working the Scientific Literacy Model: Media Exposure
and Smoking   580
Efforts to Prevent Smoking   581
Obesity   582
Defining Healthy Weights and Obesity   583 • Genetics and
Body Weight   584 • The Sedentary Lifestyle   584 • Social
Factors   585 • Psychology and Weight Loss   585
■ BIOPSYCHOSOCIAL PERSPECTIVES Ethnicity,
Economics, and Obesity   585
Psychosocial Influences on Health   586
Poverty and Discrimination   586 • Family and Social
Environment   587 • Social Contagion   587
Summary   588

Module 14.2 Stress and Illness   590
What Causes Stress?   591
Stress and Performance   592

Physiology of Stress   593
   The Stress Pathways   594 • Oxytocin: To Tend
   and Befriend   594
**Working the Scientific Literacy Model: Hormones,
Relationships, and Health**   **596**
Stress, Immunity, and Illness   597
   Stress, Personality, and Heart Disease   598
   ■ **MYTHS IN MIND Stress and Ulcers**   **599**
   Stress, Food, and Drugs   599 • Stress, the Brain, and
   Disease   599
Summary   601

Module 14.3 Coping and Well-Being   602
Coping   603
   Positive Coping Strategies   603 • Optimism and
   Pessimism   603 • Resilience   604 • Biofeedback   605
   • Meditation and Relaxation   605
   ■ **PSYCH@ Church**   **607**
   Exercise   608
Perceived Control   609
**Working the Scientific Literacy Model: Compensatory
Control and Health**   **610**
Summary   612

15 Psychological Disorders   614
Module 15.1 Defining and Classifying Psychological
Disorders   615
Defining Abnormal Behaviour   616
   What Is "Normal" Behaviour?   617 • Psychology's Puzzle:
   How to Diagnose Psychological Disorders   617 • Critiquing
   the DSM   618 • The Power of a Diagnosis   619
**Working the Scientific Literacy Model: Labelling
and Mental Disorders**   **619**
   ■ **BIOPSYCHOSOCIAL PERSPECTIVES Symptoms,
   Treatments, and Culture**   **621**
Applications of Psychological Diagnoses   622
   The Mental Disorder Defence (AKA the Insanity Defence)   622
Summary   623

Module 15.2 Personality and Dissociative Disorders   624
Defining and Classifying Personality Disorders   625
   Borderline Personality   625 • Narcissistic
   Personality   626 • Histrionic Personality   626
**Working the Scientific Literacy Model: Antisocial
Personality Disorder**   **626**
The Biopsychosocial Approach to
Personality Disorders   629
   Psychological Factors   629 • Sociocultural
   Factors   629 • Biological Factors   629
Dissociative Identity Disorder   630
   Types of Dissociative Disorders   630 • Is Dissociative Identity
   Disorder "Real?"   630
Summary   631

Module 15.3 Anxiety, Obsessive–Compulsive, and
Depressive Disorders   633
Anxiety Disorders   634
   Varieties of Anxiety Disorders   634
Working the Scientific Literacy Model: Specific Phobias   **635**
   The Vicious Cycle of Anxiety Disorders   637 • Obsessive–
   Compulsive Disorder (OCD)   637

Mood Disorders   639
   Types of Mood Disorders   639 • Cognitive Aspects
   of Depression   639 • Biological Aspects of
   Depression   640 • Sociocultural and Environmental Influences
   on Mood Disorders   641 • Suicide   641
   ■ **PSYCH@ The Suicide Helpline**   **642**
Summary   643

Module 15.4 Schizophrenia   644
Symptoms and Types of Schizophrenia   645
   Stages of Schizophrenia   645 • Symptoms of
   Schizophrenia   645 • Common Sub-Types of
   Schizophrenia   646
   ■ **MYTHS IN MIND Schizophrenia Is Not a Sign of
   Violence or of Being a "Mad Genius"**   **647**
Explaining Schizophrenia   648
   Genetics   648 • Schizophrenia and the Nervous System   648
**Working the Scientific Literacy Model: The
Neurodevelopmental Hypothesis**   **649**
   Environmental and Social Influences on
   Schizophrenia   650   Culture and Schizophrenia   651
Summary   652

16 Therapies   653
Module 16.1 Treating Psychological Disorders   654
Barriers to Psychological Treatment   655
   Stigma about Mental Illness   655 • Gender Roles   656
   • Logistical Barriers: Expense and Availability   656
   • Involuntary Treatment   656
Mental Health Providers and Settings   657
   Mental Health Providers   657 • Inpatient Treatment and
   Deinstitutionalization   658 • The Importance of Community
   Psychology   659
   ■ **PSYCH@ The University Mental Health
   Counselling Centre**   **659**
Evaluating Treatments   660
   Empirically Supported Treatments   660
**Working the Scientific Literacy Model: Can Self-Help
Treatments Be Effective?**   **661**
Summary   663

Module 16.2 Psychological Therapies   664
Insight Therapies   665
   Psychoanalysis: Exploring the Unconscious   665 • Modern
   Psychodynamic Therapies   666 • Humanistic–Existential
   Psychotherapy   666 • Evaluating Insight Therapies   667
Behavioural, Cognitive, and Group Therapies   668
   Systematic Desensitization   668
**Working the Scientific Literacy Model: Virtual Reality
Therapies**   **669**
   Aversive Conditioning   671 • Cognitive–Behavioural
   Therapies   671 • Mindfulness-Based Cognitive
   Therapy   672 • Group and Family Therapies   673 • Evaluating
   Cognitive–Behavioural Therapies   673
Summary   674

Module 16.3 Biomedical Therapies   676
Drug Treatments   677
   Antidepressants   677
   ■ **MYTHS IN MIND Antidepressant Drugs
   Are Happiness Pills**   **678**

Working the Scientific Literacy Model: Is St. John's Wort Effective? 679

Mood Stabilizers 680 • Antianxiety Drugs 680 • Antipsychotic Drugs 680 • Evaluating Drug Therapies 681

Technological and Surgical Methods 682

Focal Lesions 683 • Electroconvulsive Therapy 683 • Repetitive Transcranial Magnetic Stimulation 683 • Deep Brain Stimulation 684

Summary 685

Glossary 686

References 701

Name Index 752

Subject Index 766

About the Authors

Dr. Mark Krause received his Bachelor's and Master's degrees at Central Washington University, and his PhD at the University of Tennessee in 2000. He completed a postdoctoral appointment at the University of Texas at Austin where he studied classical conditioning of sexual behaviour in birds. Following this, Krause accepted a research fellowship through the National Institute of Aging to conduct research on cognitive neuroscience at Oregon Health and Sciences University. He has conducted research and published on pointing and communication in chimpanzees, predatory behaviour in snakes, the behavioural and evolutionary basis of conditioned sexual behaviour, and the influence of testosterone on cognition and brain function. Krause began his teaching career as a doctoral candidate and continued to pursue this passion even during research appointments. His teaching includes courses in general psychology, learning and memory, and behavioural neuroscience. Krause is currently a professor of psychology at Southern Oregon University, where his focus is on teaching, writing, and supervising student research. His spare time is spent with his family, cycling, reading, and enjoying Oregon's outdoors.

Dr. Daniel Corts discovered psychology at Belmont University where he received his B.S. He completed a PhD in Experimental Psychology at the University of Tennessee in 1999 and then a post-doctoral position at Furman University for one year where he focused on the teaching of psychology. He is now professor of psychology at Augustana College in Rock Island, IL where he has taught for over 15 years. His research interests in cognition have led to publications on language, gesture, and memory, and he has also published in the area of college student development. Corts is increasingly involved in applied work, developing programming and assessments related to K-12 educational programming and teacher preparation. Corts is enthusiastic about getting students involved in research and has supervised or coauthored over 100 conference presentations with undergraduates. Corts has served as the local Psi Chi advisor for a dozen years and has served on the Board of Directors for several years, including his current term as President. In his spare time, he enjoys spending time with his two children, travelling, camping, and cooking.

About the Canadian Authors

Dr. Stephen Smith received his Bachelor of Arts and Science in Psychology and Political Science from the University of Lethbridge, and his M.A. and PhD in Psychology from the University of Waterloo. After graduating in 2004, he completed a postdoctoral fellowship in the Affective Neuroscience Laboratory at Vanderbilt University in Nashville, TN. Smith is now an Associate Professor of Psychology at the University of Winnipeg. His research focuses on how emotion, attention, and movement interact, and on how these processes are performed by the nervous system. He has published research about emotional processing in patients with different types of brain damage, how emotion affects our perception of time, and, using neuroimaging, how emotions influence the activity of cells in both the brain and the spinal cord. Smith's teaching includes introductory psychology, physiological psychology, and third- and fourth-year courses in cognitive neuroscience. In his spare time, he loves to travel, read, play hockey, and spend time with his wife and two young children.

Dr. Dan Dolderman received his Bachelor of Arts, M.A., and PhD from the University of Waterloo. He has taught psychology at the University of Toronto (St. George campus) since 2002 and is now a Senior Lecturer. Dolderman's research is in the area of environmental psychology. He is actively involved in promoting environmentally sustainable behaviours and has presented his research in numerous public and government settings. He has published research papers on these topics as well as on the dynamics of human relationships. His teaching includes introductory psychology, environmental psychology, and positive psychology. In his spare time, he enjoys meditating, camping, and spending time with his three children.

From the Authors

Welcome to the second Canadian edition of *An Introduction to Psychological Science*. It is a great privilege for us to offer an updated and revised version of our textbook. Much has happened in psychology (and the world) since the first Canadian edition and we are excited to present the latest and greatest that our field has to offer. Of course, equally (if not more) important to keeping up with the science is ensuring that our readers find our book accessible, interesting, and hopefully inspiring. To do this, we re-read the first Canadian edition from the perspective of someone new to psychology. By taking this perspective, we were able to identify parts of the book that needed reworking. This exercise also reaffirmed our belief that scientific literacy is important and should be promoted. We need science and critical thinking skills now more than ever.

Scientific literacy is more than simply memorizing lists of scientific terms and famous names; rather, it is the ability to encounter, understand, and evaluate scientific as well as non-scientific claims. Scientific literacy comprises four interrelated components:

1. **Knowledge:** What do we know about a phenomenon?
2. **Scientific explanation:** How does science explain the psychological process we are examining?
3. **Critical thinking:** How do we interpret and evaluate all types of information, including scientific reporting?
4. **Application:** How does research apply to our own lives and to society?

To make scientific literacy the core of our text and MyPsychLab, we developed content and features with the model shown in the graphic as a guide. The competencies that surround the scientific literacy core represent different knowledge or skill sets we want to work toward during the course. The multidirectional nature of the arrows connecting the four supporting themes for scientific literacy demonstrates the interrelatedness of the competencies, which span both core-level skills, such as knowing general information (e.g., terms, concepts), and more advanced skills, such as knowing how to explain phenomena from a scientific perspective, critical thinking, and application of material.

An Introduction to Psychological Science presents students with a model for scientific literacy; this model forms the core of how this book is written and organized. We believe a scientific literacy perspective and model will prove useful in addressing two course needs we often hear from instructors—to provide students with a systematic way to categorize the overwhelming amount of information they are confronted with, and to cultivate their curiosity and help them understand the relevance, practicality, and immense appeal of psychological science.

Psychological science is in a privileged position to help students hone their scientific literacy. It is both a rigorous scientific discipline and a field that studies the most complex of all phenomena: the behavioural, cognitive, and biological basis of behaviour. With this focus on behaviour, one can rightly argue that psychology resides at the hub or core of numerous other scientific disciplines; it also shares connections with neuroscience, education, and public health, to name a few linkages. From this perspective, the knowledge acquired by studying psychological science should transfer and apply to many other fields. This is great news when you consider that psychology is one of the few science courses that many undergraduates will ever take.

In the second Canadian edition of this textbook, we have continued our emphasis on helping the reader organize and assess their thinking and learning about the material. Each module includes learning objectives of increasing depth (knowing, understanding, analyzing, and applying) as well as quiz items that assess learning at each level. We have also included interactive materials using the REVEL platform (found in the e-version of this book). Together, these tools should help make the concepts relevant to readers' lives; this, in turn, should improve retention of the course material.

We would like to thank the many instructors and students who have helped us craft this model and apply it to our discipline, and we look forward to your feedback. Please feel free to contact us and share your experiences with the second Canadian edition of *An Introduction to Psychological Science*.

Mark Krause
krausema@sou.edu

Dan Corts
danielcorts@augustana.edu

Stephen Smith
s.smith@uwinnipeg.ca

Dan Dolderman
doldermanuoft@gmail.com

What's New in the Second Canadian Edition?

Writing the first Canadian edition of *An Introduction to Psychological Science* gave us a new appreciation for how important Canadian researchers have been to the study of psychological science. Although Canada is a relatively small country (in terms of population and the number of research institutions), Canadian researchers have made incredibly important contributions to a number of areas of psychology. These important contributions are again highlighted in the second Canadian edition. We have also continued to focus on issues that are of particular relevance to Canadians, including bilingualism, environmental psychology, and the experiences of first- and second-generation immigrants to Canada.

As Introductory Psychology professors ourselves, we had a chance to use the first edition of our textbook in our own classes. The second edition of our textbook provides us with an opportunity to (1) add new, cutting-edge material to the discussion of different areas of our field, and (2) expand on topics that our own students have found particularly interesting. In fact, several of the changes to this edition of the book are a result of feedback and discussions with students in Winnipeg and Toronto (as well as a few *much-appreciated* emails from students at other institutions).

Each chapter of the second edition of this textbook has been updated to reflect the latest discoveries in psychology. Indeed, we have added new topics to all 16 chapters in the book. For example:

- Chapter 1, Introducing Psychological Science, includes a new section entitled Emerging Themes in Psychology. Here, we highlight five current themes that are found in modern psychology: (1) the psychology of women, (2) cross-cultural psychology, (3) neuroimaging research, (4) positive psychology, and (5) applied psychology. Our hope is that this section will prime readers to look for these themes as they read through the other modules of the book. Chapter 1 also contains new information showing the benefits of distributed (spaced) learning and provides students with specific suggestions for improving their academic performance.

- Chapter 2, Reading and Evaluating Scientific Research, discusses the "replication crisis" in psychology and examines its implications for our field of study. We also include new information about the role that qualitative research can play in psychology, with a Canadian-based study of "friends with benefits" serving as the running example.

- Chapter 3, Biological Psychology, includes a new Working the Scientific Literacy Model section on the role of testosterone in social aggression. We also updated our discussion of sex difference in spatial cognition and streamlined several sections related to evolutionary psychology.

- Chapter 4, Sensation and Perception, includes a new section on the vestibular system as well as a new Working the Scientific Literacy Model section on the ability to follow musical beats. This chapter also contains new content related to two topics that have garnered significant attention in the past year: The Great Dress Debate (about the dress that appears white and gold to some and black and blue to others) and Autonomous Sensory Meridian Response (ASMR), a recently identified example of atypical multimodal integration.

- Chapter 5, Consciousness, includes a new section on mind-wandering (replacing meditation, which is now discussed elsewhere). We have also added material related to the effect of caffeine on circadian rhythms, the role of social isolation in drug dependence, and the societal effects of legalizing drugs. We have also provided updated information about the legal status of some drugs including *Salvia divinorum*.

- Chapter 6, Learning, includes new information explaining how the unconditioned response (UR) and conditioned response (CR) aren't always identical. We have also added a new section on how operant conditioning is used in casino settings, and have highlighted how multi-line slot machines often produce losses that are disguised as wins. We also streamlined the applications of classical conditioning section in an effort to provide clearer examples of these principles.

- Chapter 7, Memory, includes new information about emotion and memory. We have also revamped our explanations of several concepts and have provided clearer examples of the differences in overlapping concepts (e.g., short-term memory and working memory).

- Chapter 8, Thought and Language, includes a new Working the Scientific Literacy Model section on semantic priming. We have also added a new section on the relationship between problem solving and the interpretation of humour.

- Chapter 9, Intelligence Testing, includes updated and reorganized material on a number of topics including multiple intelligences, the hierarchical model of intelligence, and the interactions between beliefs and intelligence-test scores.

- Chapter 10, Lifespan Development, underwent extensive reorganization. It includes new information about fetal alcohol syndrome as well as updated information about several topics including the development of theory of mind and obstacles to healthy relationships in adulthood.

- Chapter 11, Motivation and Emotion, includes a number of new sections. We have added content about semantic networks and food cravings, terror management theory and its role in Canadian and American elections, how bicultural individuals are affected by intrinsic and extrinsic motivation, and brain networks related to emotional perception and regulation. We have also added sections related to two issues that have received a great deal of attention in the past year: (1) the challenges affecting transgender and transsexual individuals, and (2) the controversies surrounding Ontario's "Sex Ed" curriculum (which received national attention).

- Chapter 12, Personality, includes a new discussion of Bandura's social-cognitive theory as well as more refined discussions of several topics including an examination of right-wing authoritarianism and the stability of personality traits across the lifespan.

- Chapter 13, Social Psychology, includes new information about the brain regions involved with implicit prejudice as well as updated information about the identifiable victim effect.

- Chapter 14, Health, Stress, and Coping, includes updated statistics to several sections of Module 14.1 (Behaviour and Health). We have also added information about individual zones of optimal performance to our discussion of stress and added new information to our discussion of meditation.

- Chapter 15, Psychological Disorders, includes updated statistics related to different psychological disorders. We have also added new information about the neuroscience of antisocial personality disorder, genetics and depression, and identifying and helping individuals who are considering suicide. Several sections of this chapter were also reorganized to improve clarity.

- Chapter 16, Therapies, includes new information about the effects of St. John's wort, an herbal remedy for depression, on neurotransmitter systems in the brain. We have also updated sections related to the efficacy of antidepressants, and the use of electroconvulsive therapy and repetitive transcranial magnetic stimulation as treatments for depression.

We believe that these changes (among the many others made to the book) have allowed us to achieve our goal for the second Canadian edition: to provide readers with a thorough description of the field of psychology while also highlighting the importance of scientific literacy and the biopsychosocial model of human behaviour. We hope that you, the reader, feel the same. Enjoy the book!

Content and Features

Modules

Chapters are divided into modules to make it easier for students to organize content as well as to self-test and review their learning at regular intervals. For instructors, the modular content makes it easy to customize their delivery based on their preferred syllabus.

Module 2.1 Principles of Scientific Research

Learning Objectives

2.1a Know ... the key terminology related to the principles of scientific research.

2.1b Understand ... the five characteristics of quality scientific research.

2.1c Understand ... how biases might influence the outcome of a study.

2.1d Apply ... the concepts of reliability and validity to examples.

2.1e Analyze ... whether anecdotes, authority figures, and common sense are reliably truthful sources of information.

Does listening to classical music make you smarter? In January 1998, Governor Zell Miller of Georgia placed a $105 000 line in his state budget dedicated to purchasing classical music CDs for children (Sack, 1998). He even paid the conductor of the Atlanta Symphony to select optimal pieces for this CD. Apparently, Georgia's well-meaning governor and state legislature believed that providing young children with classical music would make them smarter. There were many reasons to believe this assumption might be true, starting with the observation that most people we know who listen to classical music seem intelligent and sophisticated. At around the same time that Georgia took this step, consumers were being bombarded with advertisements about "the Mozart effect," the scientific finding that listening to Mozart improves intelligence. Suddenly the classical sections at music stores were dusted off and moved to the front of the store, with signs drawing customers' attention to the intelligence-boosting effects of the CDs. Parents were told

that it was never too early to start their children on a Mozart program, even as fetuses residing in the womb. In fact, part of the Georgia budget, as well as the budget in some other U.S. states, was dedicated to handing out classical CDs along with hospital birth certificates. Eventually, the enthusiasm toward the Mozart effect died down after other scientists were unable to replicate the results. It turns out that the hype surrounding the Mozart effect was based on the results of one study (Rauscher et al., 1993). In this study, the twelve adult participants who listened to Mozart performed better than other adults on a test of spatial ability. These (temporary) differences in spatial intelligence were then inflated by the popular press to mean intelligence in general (a big difference!). Based on a single study, companies created a multi-million dollar industry, and the state of Georgia spent an extra $105 000.

This example is not meant to demonize the media or to mock Governor Miller. Rather, it highlights the need for

30

Learning Objectives

Learning Objectives are organized around an updated Bloom's taxonomy that aims to guide students to higher-level understanding. Summaries of the key points related to these objectives are provided at the end of each module. Objectives are listed at four levels of increasing complexity: know, understand, apply, and analyze.

Module Summaries

The major terms, concepts, and applications of the modules are reviewed in the Module Summaries. The summaries also return to and address the original Learning Objectives from the beginning of the module and include application questions. **Answers to end-of-module and end-of-chapter assessments can be found in the Instructor's Manual.**

Module 2.1 Summary

2.1a Know ... the key terminology related to the principles of scientific research.

anecdotal evidence
appeal to authority
appeal to common sense
convenience samples
demand characteristics
double-blind study
ecological validity
falsifiable
generalizability
Hawthorne effect
objective measurements
operational definitions
peer review
placebo effect
population random sample
reliability
replication
sample
single-blind study
social desirability
validity
variable

2.1b Understand ... the five characteristics of quality scientific research.

These characteristics include that (1) measurements are objective, valid, and reliable; (2) the research can be generalized; (3) it uses techniques that reduce bias; (4) the findings are made public; and (5) the results can be replicated. For example, objective, valid, and reliable measurements make it possible for other scientists to test whether they could come up with the same results if they followed the same procedures. Psychologists typically study samples of individuals; their goal is usually to describe principles that generalize to a broader population. Single- and double-blind procedures are standard ways of reducing bias. Finally, the process of publishing results is what allows scientists to share information, evaluate hypotheses that have been confirmed or refuted, and, if needed, replicate other researchers' work.

2.1c Understand ... how biases might influence the outcome of a study.

Demand characteristics affect how participants respond in research studies—understandably, they often attempt to portray themselves in a positive light, even if that means not answering questions or behaving in a fully truthful manner. Researchers can also influence the outcomes of their own studies, even unintentionally.

2.1d Apply ... the concepts of reliability and validity to examples.

Try this activity to see how well you can apply these concepts.

Apply Activity

Read the following descriptions and determine whether each scenario involves an issue with reliability or validity.

1. Dr. Williams is performing very standard physiological recording techniques on human participants. Each morning he checks whether the instruments are calibrated and ready for use. One day he discovers that although the instruments are still measuring physiological activity, their recordings are not as sensitive as on previous testing days. *Would this affect the reliability or validity of his research? Explain.*

2. Dr. Nielson uses a behavioural checklist to measure happiness in the children he studies at an elementary school. Every time he and his associates observe the children, they reach near-perfect agreement on what they observed. Another group of psychologists observes the same children in an attempt to identify which children are energetic and which seem tired and lethargic. It turns out that the same children whom Dr. Nielson identifies as happy, using his checklist, are also the children whom the second group of psychologists identify as energetic. *It appears there may be a problem with Dr. Nielson's measure of happiness. Do you think it is a problem of reliability or validity? Explain.*

2.1e Analyze ... whether anecdotes, authority figures, and common sense are reliably truthful sources of information.

To evaluate evidence, you should ask several questions. First, is someone supplying anecdotal evidence? As convincing as a personal testimony may be, anecdotal evidence is not sufficient for backing any claim that can be scientifically tested. Second, is support for the claim based on the words or endorsement of an authority figure? Endorsement by an authority figure is not necessarily a bad thing, as someone who is an authority at something should be able to back up the claim. But the authority of the individual alone is not satisfactory, especially if data gathered through good scientific methods do not support the claim. Finally, common sense also has its place in daily life, but by itself is insufficient as a final explanation for anything. Explanations based on good scientific research should override those based on common sense.

and the data examined, they can be used to inform more sophisticated future studies that ask "why" and "how" that phenomenon occurs.

These descriptions can be performed in different ways. **Qualitative research** *involves examining an issue or behaviour without performing numerical measurements of the variables.* In psychology, qualitative research often takes the form of interviews in which participants describe their thoughts and feelings about particular events or experi-

Key Terms

Key Terms are defined within the narrative, helping students place them in context, and are then listed again within the Module Summaries. A complete glossary is also included at the end of the text.

REVEL™

Fully digital and highly engaging, REVEL offers an immersive learning experience designed for the way today's students read, think, and learn. Enlivening course content with media interactives and assessments, REVEL empowers educators to increase engagement with the course, and to better connect with students: **pearsonhighered.com/revel.**

Most of the billions of cells in the human body include a nucleus that houses most of our genetic code (some additional DNA is located in a cellular structure called the mitochondrion). **Genes** *are the basic units of heredity; they are responsible for guiding the process of creating the proteins that make up our physical structures and regulate development an physiological processes throughout the life span.* Genes are organized along **chromosomes**, *which are large molecules in the cellular nucleus that include the structures shaped like a double helix that are lined with all of the genes an individual inherits.* Humans have approximately 30,000 genes distributed across 23 pairs of chromosomes, half contributed by the mother and half from the father (see Figure 3.1).

Figure 3.1   Chromosomes and the DNA Molecule

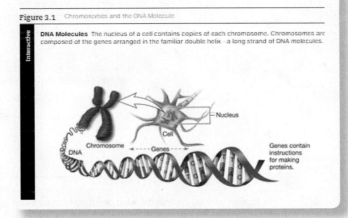

DNA Molecules The nucleus of a cell contains copies of each chromosome. Chromosomes are composed of the genes arranged in the familiar double helix — a long strand of DNA molecules.

Module Quizzes and REVEL End-of-Chapter Quizzes

Quizzes appear in the text at the conclusion of modules and also appear at the end of chapters in REVEL. These quizzes contain multiple-choice questions that enable students to assess their comprehension and better prepare for exams. Like the Learning Objectives, the Module Quizzes assess understanding at the four levels of Bloom's taxonomy and are marked accordingly. **Answers to quizzes can be found in the Instructor's Manual.**

Module 2.1a Quiz:

Five Characteristics of Quality Scientific Research

Know . . .

1. The degree to which an instrument measures what it is intended to measure is known as _____.
   A. validity
   B. generalizability
   C. verifiability
   D. reliability

2. When psychologists question how well the results of a study apply to other samples or perhaps other situations, they are inquiring about the _____ of the study.
   A. validity
   B. generalizability
   C. verifiability
   D. reliability

Understand . . .

3. In a single-blind study, the participants do not know the purpose of the study or the condition to which they are assigned. What is the difference in a double-blind study?
   A. The researcher tells the participants the purpose and their assigned conditions in the study.

B. The participants also do not know when the actual study begins or ends.
   C. The researcher also does not know which condition the participants are in.
   D. The participants know the condition to which they have been assigned, but the researcher does not.

Apply . . .

4. Dr. Rose gives a standardized personality test to a group of psychology majors in January and again in March. Each individual's score remains nearly the same over the two-month period. From this, Dr. Rose can infer that the test is _____.
   A. reliable
   B. generalizable
   C. objective
   D. verified

Scientific Explanation

How can science explain it?

This element of scientific literacy encompasses a basic understanding of research methodology and thinking about problems within a scientific framework. *An Introduction to Psychological Science* integrates and reinforces key research methodology concepts throughout the book. This interweaving of methodology encourages students to continue practising their scientific thinking skills.

Module 2.1   Principles of Scientific Research

LuckyBusiness/Getty Images

∨ Learning Objectives

2.1a Know . . . the key terminology related to the principles of scientific research.

2.1b Understand . . . the five characteristics of quality scientific research.

2.1c Understand . . . how biases might influence the outcome of a study.

2.1d Apply . . . the concepts of reliability and validity to examples.

2.1e Analyze . . . whether anecdotes, authority figures, and common sense are reliably truthful sources of information.

Module Opening Vignettes

Each module opens with a short vignette emphasizing the personal and societal relevance of certain topics to be covered.

Does listening to classical music make you smarter? In January 1998, Governor Zell Miller of Georgia placed a $105 000 line in his state budget dedicated to purchasing classical music CDs for children (Sack, 1998). He even paid the conductor of the Atlanta Symphony to select optimal pieces for this CD. Apparently, Georgia's well-meaning governor and state legislature believed that providing young children with classical music would make them smarter. There were many reasons to believe this assumption might be true, starting with the observation that most people we know who listen to classical music seem intelligent and sophisticated. At around the same time that Georgia took this step, consumers were being bombarded with advertisements about "the Mozart effect," the scientific finding that listening to Mozart improves intelligence. Suddenly the classical sections at music stores were dusted off and moved to the front of the store, with signs drawing customers' attention to the intelligence-boosting effects of the CDs. Parents were told

that it was never too early to start their children on a Mozart program, even as fetuses residing in the womb. In fact, part of the Georgia budget, as well as the budget in some other U.S. states, was dedicated to handing out classical CDs along with hospital birth certificates. Eventually, the enthusiasm toward the Mozart effect died down after other scientists were unable to replicate the results. It turns out that the hype surrounding the Mozart effect was based on the results of one study (Rauscher et al., 1993). In this study, the twelve adult participants who listened to Mozart performed better than other adults on a test of spatial ability. These (temporary) differences in spatial intelligence were then inflated by the popular press to mean intelligence in general (a big difference!). Based on a single study, companies created a multi-million dollar industry, and the state of Georgia spent an extra $105 000.

This example is not meant to demonize the media or to mock Governor Miller. Rather, it highlights the need for

30

Myths in Mind

Many commonly held beliefs people have about behaviour before taking a psychology course are half-truths or outright falsehoods. This feature sets the record straight in a concise and informative way. The selected examples are likely to have personal relevance to many readers and deal with important scientific issues.

Myths in Mind
Beware of Illusory Correlations

Chances are you have heard the following claims:

- Crime and emergency room intakes suddenly increase when there is a full moon.
- Opposites attract.
- Competitive basketball players (and even gamblers) get on a "hot streak" where one success leads to the next.

Many common beliefs such as these are deeply ingrained in our culture. They become even more widely accepted when they are repeated frequently. It is difficult to argue with a hospital nurse or police officer who swears that full-moon nights are the busiest and craziest of all. The conventional, reserved, and studious man who dates a carefree and spirited woman *confirms* that opposites attract. And, after Kyle Lowry has hit a few amazing jump shots for the Raptors, of course his chances of success just get better and better as the game wears on.

But do they? Each of these three scenarios is an example of what are called **illusory correlations**—*relationships that really exist only in the mind, rather than in reality*. It turns out that well-designed studies have found no evidence that a full moon leads to, or is even related to, bizarre or violent behaviour (Lilienfeld & Arkowitz, 2009). People who are attracted to each other are typically very similar (Buston & Emlen, 2003). Also, although some games may be better than others, overall the notion of a "hot streak" is not a reality in basketball or in blackjack (Caruso et al., 2010; Gilovich et al., 1985).

Why do these illusory correlations exist? Instances of them come to mind easily and are more memorable than humdrum examples of "normal" nights in the ER, perfectly matched couples, and all of the times Kyle Lowry missed a shot, even in his best games. However, just because examples are easy to imagine, it does not mean that this is what typically occurs.

Biopsychosocial Perspectives

To emphasize the complexity of scientific explanations, students are reminded throughout each chapter that behaviour includes biology, individual thoughts and experiences, and the influence of social and cultural factors.

BIOPSYCHOSOCIAL PERSPECTIVES
Recreational and Spiritual Uses of *Salvia Divinorum*

Salvia divinorum is an herb that grows in Central and South America. When smoked or chewed, salvia induces highly intense but short-lived hallucinations. Use of this drug also leads to *dissociative experiences*—a detachment between self and body (Surnall et al., 2011). An exploration of salvia reveals a great deal about how cultural views affect how drugs are perceived. A single drug could be described as recreational, addictive, and a scourge to society in one culture, yet highly valued and spiritually significant to another.

Test what you know about this drug:

True or False?

1. Sale of salvia is prohibited by the Canadian government.
2. Very few young people in Canada who use drugs have tried

3. *False.* There is no scientific evidence that salvia has healing properties. Whether one agrees with this statement, however, depends on who is asked. Among the Mazateca people of Mexico, salvia is used in divine rituals in which an individual communicates with the spiritual world. Shamans of the Mazateca people use salvia for spiritual healing sessions. They believe the drug has profound medicinal properties.

Drugs such as salvia and ayahuasca raise important questions about the effects of drugs and our view toward them. Although a given drug usually has standard, reliable effects on brain chemistry, the subjective experience it provides, the purposes it is used for, and people's attitudes toward the drug may vary widely depending on the cultural

Psych@

The "Psych@" feature reveals an everyday, personally relevant application of psychological science. The content of these features is geared toward issues and concerns that many university students care about.

PSYCH@
The Hospital: The Placebo Effect

The demand effect that we know the most about is the **placebo effect**, *a measurable and experienced improvement in health or behaviour that cannot be attributable to a medication or treatment*. This term comes from drug studies, in which it is standard procedure for a group, unbeknownst to them, to be given an inactive substance (the placebo) so that this group can be compared to a group given the active drug. What often happens is that people in the placebo group report feeling better because they have the expectation that the drug will have an effect on their brain and body. This effect has been reported time and again—not just with drugs, but with other medical treatments as well. Why do people receiving a placebo claim to feel better? The initial explanation was that the patients' expectations caused them to simply convince themselves they feel better (i.e., it is "all in their head"). Other research noted that many people who are given a placebo show physiological evidence of relief from

pain and nausea (Hrobjartsson & Gotzsche, 2010). Research conducted at the Rotman Research Institute in Toronto suggests that both of these explanations have merit. Helen Mayberg and colleagues (2002) found that people responding to placebos showed increased activity in several regions of the frontal lobes. This activity may relate to the participants creating a new "mental set" of their current state; in other words, creating the belief that their pain was going to decrease. Interestingly, these researchers also noted a decrease in activity in a number of other brain regions that might represent changes in the sensitivity of pain pathways. These results suggest that there are multiple ways for placebos to affect our responses to pain. Placebos are an important part of experimental research in psychology and related fields, so it is important to recognize their potential influence on how research participants respond.

In recent years, an increasing number of instructors have begun to focus on telling students how psychological science fits within the scientific community. Psychology serves, in essence, as a hub science. Through this emphasis on scientific literacy in psychology, students begin to see the practicality and relevance of psychology and become more literate in the fields that our hub science supports.

Critical Thinking

Can we critically evaluate the evidence?

Many departments are focusing to an increasing extent on the development of critical thinking, as these skills are highly sought after in society and the workforce. Critical thinking is generally defined as the ability to apply knowledge, use information in new ways, analyze situations and concepts, and evaluate decisions. To develop critical thinking, the module objectives and quizzes are built around an updated Bloom's taxonomy. Objectives are listed at four levels of increasing complexity: know, understand, apply, and analyze. The following features also help students organize, analyze, and synthesize information. Collectively, these features encourage students to connect different levels of understanding with specific objectives and quiz questions.

Working the Scientific Literacy Model

Planning When to Study

To develop your scientific literacy skills, in every module (beginning with Chapter 2) we will revisit this model and its four components as they apply to a specific psychological topic—a process we call *working the scientific literacy model*. This will help you to move beyond simply learning the vocabulary of psychological research toward *understanding* scientific explanations, thinking critically, and discovering applications of the material. In order to demonstrate how these sections of the book will work, let's use an example that will be familiar to many: planning study time for your different classes.

What do we know about timing and studying?

In the first stage of the Scientific Literary Model, we attempt to gather the available knowledge about the topic that we're investigating, in this case the fact that students differ on how they attempt to remember information for exams. Many students use what is called *massed learning*—they perform all of their studying for an exam in one lengthy session. Another approach is *spaced* or *distributed learning*—having shorter study sessions, but spreading them out over several days. Which technique do you prefer? If you use the massed learning technique (most students prefer it . . . or end up using it because they've left studying until the last minute), it is likely because it *seems* easier and it may even give you the sense that it is more effective than distributed learning. Actually, the two strategies are not equally effective; more than 100 years of memory research has shown us that distributed learning is the better of the two (Cepeda et al., 2006; Edwards, 1917).

ies, providing strong evidence in favour of distributed learning (Delaney et al., 2010; Dempster, 1988). Although there is no single explanation for this effect, one factor is particularly relevant for students. When information is learned in one massed session, it begins to feel repetitive. This leads the learners to pay less attention to the material than they would in distributed learning sessions, when some of the material may have been forgotten (Ausubel, 1966). As a result, people learning in a distributed fashion are more likely to pay attention to the material than massed learners, a tendency that would obviously improve performance.

Can we critically evaluate this evidence?

In the third stage of the Scientific Literacy Model, we examine the limitations of the studies discussed earlier; we also look for alternative explanations for the results. The most obvious criticism of this research is that results from laboratory-based studies may not reflect how memory works in a real educational setting. This is a valid concern—researchers don't want their effects to be isolated to the laboratory. Luckily, a number of researchers have applied the knowledge and techniques developed by earlier researchers to *applied psychology* studies in the classroom. In one study, elementary school children were taught scientific information about food charts (Gluckman et al., 2014). Each child received four lessons about this topic. One group received all four lessons on a Monday ("massed learning condition"). A second group received two lessons on a Monday and two lessons on a Tuesday ("clumped learning group"). The third group received one lesson per day from Monday through Thursdays ("distributed learning group"). All groups were tested one

Working the Scientific Literacy Model

Working the Scientific Literacy Model, introduced in Chapters 1 and 2, and then featured in each module in the remaining chapters, fully integrates the model of scientific literacy. Core concepts are highlighted and students are walked through the steps of knowledge gathering, approaching the problem from a scientific standpoint, using critical thinking, and revealing applications.

Application

Why is this relevant?

Psychology is a highly relevant, modern science. To be scientifically literate, students should relate psychological concepts to their own lives, making decisions based on knowledge, sound methodology, and skilled interpretation of information.

For Instructors

SCIENTIFIC LITERACY is a key course goal for many introductory psychology instructors.

Learning science is an active process. How do we help instructors model scientific literacy in the classroom and online in a way that meets the needs of today's students?

Organization

Instructors consistently tell us one of the main challenges they face when teaching the introductory psychology course is organizing engaging, current, and relevant materials to span the breadth of content covered. How do we help organize and access valuable course materials?

REVEL™

Educational technology designed for the way today's students read, think, and learn.

When students are engaged deeply, they learn more effectively and perform better in their courses. This simple fact inspired the creation of REVEL: an immersive learning experience designed for the way today's students read, think, and learn. Built in collaboration with educators and students nationwide, REVEL is the newest, fully digital way to deliver respected Pearson content.

REVEL enlivens course content with media interactives and assessments—integrated directly within the authors' narrative—that provide opportunities for students to read about and practice course material in tandem. This immersive educational technology boosts student engagement, which leads to better understanding of concepts and improved performance throughout the course.

Learn more about REVEL
http://www.pearsonhighered.com/revel/

MyPsychLab

MyPsychLab offers students useful and engaging self-assessment tools, and it provides instructors with flexibility in assessing and tracking student progress. For instructors, MyPsychLab is a powerful tool for assessing student performance and adapting course content to students' changing needs, without requiring instructors to invest additional time or resources to do so.

Instructors and students have been using MyPsychLab for more than 13 years. To date, more than 600 000 students have used MyPsychLab. During that time, three white papers on the efficacy of MyPsychLab have been published. Both the white papers and user feedback show compelling results: MyPsychLab helps students succeed and improve their test scores. One of the key ways MyPsychLab improves student outcomes is by providing continuous assessment as part of the learning process. Over the years, both instructor and student feedback have guided numerous improvements

to this system, making MyPsychLab even more flexible and effective.

Pearson is committed to helping instructors and students succeed with MyPsychLab. To that end, we offer a Psychology Faculty Advisor Program designed to provide peer-to-peer support for new users of MyPsychLab. Experienced Faculty Advisors help instructors understand how MyPsychLab can improve student performance. To learn more about the Faculty Advisor Program, please contact your local Pearson representative.

MyPsychLab Video Series

The MyPsychLab Video Series is a comprehensive and cutting-edge series featuring 17 original 30-minute videos covering the most recent research and utilizing the most up-to-date film and animation technology. Multiple choice and short answer essay questions are provided within MyPsychLab so episodes can be assigned as homework.

MyPsychLab Study Plan

Students have access to a personalized study plan, based on Bloom's taxonomy, that arranges content from less complex thinking (such as remembering and understanding) to more complex critical thinking (such as applying and analyzing). This layered approach promotes better critical thinking skills and helps students succeed in the course and beyond.

Learning Catalytics

Learning Catalytics is a "bring your own device" student engagement, assessment, and classroom intelligence system. It allows instructors to engage students in class with real-time diagnostics. Students can use any modern, web-enabled device (smartphone, tablet, or laptop) to access it.

Writing Space

Better writers make great learners—who perform better in their courses. To help you develop and assess concept mastery and critical thinking through writing, we created Writing Space.

It's a single place to create, track, and grade writing assignments, provide writing resources, and exchange meaningful, personalized feedback with students, quickly and easily, including auto-scoring for practice writing prompts. Plus, Writing Space has integrated access to Turnitin, the global leader in plagiarism prevention.

Instructor's Manual

The Instructor's Manual includes suggestions for preparing for the course, sample syllabi, and current trends and strategies for successful teaching. Each chapter offers integrated teaching outlines, lists the key terms for each chapter for quick reference, and provides an extensive bank of lecture launchers, handouts, and activities, as well as suggestions for integrating third-party videos and web resources. The electronic format features click-and-view hotlinks that allow instructors to quickly review or print any resource from a particular chapter. This resource saves prep work and helps maximize classroom time. Chapter and module quiz answers can also be found in the Instructor's Manual.

Standard Lecture PowerPoint Slides

Standard Lecture PowerPoint Slides are available online at **www.pearsoncanada.ca/highered**, with a more traditional format with excerpts of the text material, photos, and artwork.

Assessment

Instructors consistently tell us that assessing student progress is a critical component to their course and one of the most time-consuming tasks. Vetted, good-quality, easy-to-use assessment tools are essential. We have been listening and we have responded by creating the absolutely best assessment content available on the market today.

Test Bank

The Test Bank contains more than 3000 questions, many of which were class-tested in multiple classes at both 2-year and 4-year institutions across the country prior to publication. Item analysis is provided for all class tested items. All questions have been thoroughly reviewed and analyzed line-by-line by a development editor and a copy editor to ensure clarity, accuracy, and delivery of the highest-quality assessment tool. The test bank for the second Canadian edition was also extensively reviewed by a professional psychometrician with over ten years of experience teaching university psychology. Most conceptual and applied multiple-choice questions include rationales for each correct answer and the key distractors. The item analysis helps instructors create balanced tests, while the rationales serve both as an added guarantee of quality and as a time-saver when students challenge the keyed answer for a specific item.

The Test Bank also comes with Pearson MyTest, a powerful assessment generation program that helps instructors easily create and print quizzes and exams. Questions and tests can be authored online, providing instructors with the ultimate in flexibility and the ability to efficiently manage assessments wherever and whenever they want. Instructors can easily access existing questions and then edit, create, and store them using simple drag-and-drop and Word-like controls. The data for each question identifies its difficulty level and the text page number where the relevant content appears. In addition, each question maps to the text's major section and Learning Objective. For more information, go to **www.PearsonMyTest.com**.

Acknowledgments

We cannot fathom completing a project like this without the help and support of many individuals. Through every bit of this process have been our families and we thank you for your love, patience, and support. Although our children will be disappointed that this book is not about the Montreal Canadiens or sea creatures, we hope that they'll read and enjoy this book one day. Our extended families, particularly Peggy Salter, also provided immense support and helped our children feel loved even when we had to work late to finish this book. In addition, our departments have been wonderfully understanding and helpful, offering advice with their various specializations, providing examples and tips, reviewing drafts, and tolerating our occasional absences.

The second Canadian edition of this book would not exist without the hard work and dedication shown by a number of people involved with first edition. Our original Developmental Editor, Johanna Schlaepfer, went above and beyond the call of duty to ensure that the final product was something we could all be proud of. The first edition also benefited from the guidance of Matthew Christian (the Acquisitions Editor at the time); Safa Ali; and Michelle Di Nella, Steve's former lab coordinator and unofficial "solver of all problems."

The second edition of this book was again a team effort. Our Developmental Editor, Lise Dupont, showed superhuman patience. Laura Neves provided amazing copy editing and helped turn our mad scribblings into a coherent book. We are also indebted to Darcey Pepper (Acquisitions Editor) and to everyone on the Productions and Permissions side of things: Kathryn O'Handley and Kimberley Blakey at Pearson Canada, Vastavikta Sharma at Cenveo Publisher Services, and Vignesh Sadhasivam at Integra Software Services Pvt. Ltd. Dr. Leanne Stevens of Dalhousie University deserves a separate tip-of-the-hat for her work linking the REVEL interactivities and assessments with the text of the book. We would also like to thank the entire Pearson sales team for promoting this book as well as the supplements team for editing the MyPsychLab and other online materials.

The second Canadian edition of this book benefitted from conversations with a number of colleagues. Danielle Gaucher from the University of Winnipeg was immensely helpful in making suggestions for the new feature on Women in Psychology (Module 1.2). Pauline Pearson from the University of Winnipeg helped us clarify a number of points related to perceptual constancies (Module 4.2). Dan Smilek from the University of Waterloo (and Steve's former soccer teammate) was kind enough to read through and edit the new section on mind-wandering (Module 5.2). Doug Williams from the University of Winnipeg provided us with a number of fantastic ideas that ended up influencing several new sections in Chapters 6 (Learning).

Finally, we would like to thank the many reviewers and students who carefully read over the first Canadian edition and/or earlier versions of chapters from the second edition of this book. We are very grateful that you shared your expertise in the field of psychology, and in teaching, to help bring this book to life.

We value feedback from both instructors and students, and we are sure that we will need it for our Third Canadian Edition. Please do not hesitate to offer suggestions or comments by writing to Steve Smith (s.smith@uwinnipeg.ca) or Dan Dolderman (doldermanuoft@gmail.com).

List of Reviewers

Jeffrey Adams, Trent University

Kimberly Burton, Marianapolis College

Stephanie Denison, University of Waterloo

Stephane Gaskin, Concordia University and Dawson College

Peter Graf, University of British Columbia

Rick Healey, Memorial University of Newfoundland

Thom Herrmann, University of Guelph

Karsten A. Loepelmann, University of Alberta

Alison Luby, University of Toronto

Laura MacKay, Capilano University

Stacey L. MacKinnon, University of Prince Edward Island

Jamal K. Mansour, Simon Fraser University

Diano Marrone, Wilfrid Laurier University

Katherine McGuire, University of New Brunswick, Saint John

Geoffrey S. Navara, Trent University

Jeffrey Nicol, Vancouver Island University

Peter Papadogiannis, University of Guelph-Humber

JDA Parker, Trent University

Tony Robertson, Vancouver Island University

Biljana Stevanovski, University of New Brunswick

Cheryl Techentin, Mount Royal University

Jennifer Tomaszczyk, University of Waterloo

Randal Tonks, Camosun College

Christine D. Tsang, Huron University College at Western

Ashley Waggoner Denton, University of Toronto

Susan G. Walling, Memorial University of Newfoundland

Stacey Wareham-Fowler, Memorial University of Newfoundland

Doug Williams, University of Winnipeg

Ross Woolley, Langara College

Chapter 1
Introducing Psychological Science

1.1 The Science of Psychology

- The Scientific Method 3
- Module 1.1a Quiz 6
- Building Scientific Literacy 6
  Working the Scientific Literacy Model: Planning When to Study 7
- Module 1.1b Quiz 9
- Module 1.1 Summary 10

1.2 How Psychology Became a Science

- Psychology's Philosophical and Scientific Origins 12
- Module 1.2a Quiz 17
- The Beginnings of Contemporary Psychology 18
- Module 1.2b Quiz 24
- Emerging Themes in Psychology 24
- Module 1.2c Quiz 27
- Module 1.2 Summary 28

Module 1.1 The Science of Psychology

Everett Collection

 Learning Objectives

1.1a Know . . . the key terminology of the scientific method.

1.1b Understand . . . the steps of the scientific method.

1.1c Understand . . . the concept of scientific literacy.

1.1d Apply . . . the biopsychosocial model to behaviour.

1.1e Apply . . . the steps in critical thinking.

1.1f Analyze . . . the use of the term *scientific theory*.

Almost everyone has misinterpreted someone else's meaning in a conversation. You could misinterpret someone leaning closer to you as flirting when really you were just talking too softly. You could mistake someone's tone of voice as being annoyed when that person was actually talking loudly to be heard over other people in the room. We also frequently misjudge other people's attitudes and personalities. The unfriendly and arrogant person at work might actually turn out to be a shy person who dislikes crowded social events. In all of these situations, we make inferences about another person based on the different cues they provide us. But how do we decide which cues are important? Are they really the right cues to be using when we want to explain other people's behaviour?

The situation is even more complicated in the wired world of the 21st century, with everyone plugged in to email, online gaming, and social networking sites like Facebook and Twitter. How do you interpret someone's behaviour or intentions when

all you have to go by is words on a screen and cartoon-like happy faces? How much information do you need to (safely) disclose in order for other people to understand you? These questions highlight the complexity of human behaviour as well as some of the challenges involved in trying to understand it. In this textbook, we will examine many different aspects of behaviour—from basic brain and perception functions to memory to social behaviours. But all of these chapters have the same central theme: the quest to understand why and how we behave the way we do.

Focus Questions

1. How can the human mind, with its quirks and imperfections, conduct studies on itself?

2. How can scientific and critical thinking steer us toward a clearer understanding of human behaviour and experience?

≫ One of the reasons psychology is such an exciting field is that it is easy to see how this field of study relates to your own life. Although chemistry and physics both have a profound effect on our lives, it is sometimes difficult to link formulas and diagrams with real life experiences. Psychology is visceral—we *feel* emotions, we *take in* sensations, and we *produce* behaviours such as thoughts and actions. Psychology is you.

A more official definition of **psychology** *is the scientific study of behaviour, thought, and experience, and how they can be affected by physical, mental, social, and environmental factors.* This definition shows you that psychology involves a number of overlapping areas of investigation. Some of the overarching goals of psychology include:

- to understand how different brain structures work together to produce our behaviour
- to understand how nature (genetics) and nurture (our upbringing and environment) interact to make us who we are
- to understand how previous experiences influence how we think and act
- to understand how groups—family, culture, and crowds—affect the individual
- to understand how feelings of control can influence happiness and health
- to understand how each of these factors can influence our well-being and could contribute to psychological disorders

Critically, these points are not independent of one another. As we will discuss later in this module, every topic in psychology could be examined from a biological, cognitive (thinking), or sociocultural perspective. As you progress through this book, you will begin to understand the different factors that influence *your* thoughts, actions, and feelings. Psychology can help you see the world in a different way. And, just as important, psychology can help you understand why *other people* behave the way they do. All of the factors that influence you also influence other people in one way or another. By understanding these influences, you can gain a better understanding—and acceptance—of the people around you.

Importantly, our knowledge of human behaviour isn't just a series of opinions. Every topic that we will discuss is based on the hard work of scientists who meticulously tested their ideas in laboratories and in the "real world." This text includes many references (e.g., Eastwood et al., 2016) to reinforce this fact. The science of psychology would be nothing without the scientific method.

The Scientific Method

What exactly does it mean to be a scientist? A person who haphazardly combines chemicals in test tubes may look like a chemist, but he is not conducting science; a person who dissects a specimen just to see how it looks may appear to be a biologist, but this is not science either. In contrast, a person who carefully follows a system of observing, predicting, and testing *is* conducting science, whether the subject matter is chemicals, physiology, human memory, or social interactions. In other words, whether a field of study is a science, or a specific type of research is *scientific*, is based not on the subject but on the use of the scientific method. The **scientific method** *is a way of learning about the world through collecting observations, developing theories to explain them, and using the theories to make predictions.* It involves a dynamic interaction between hypothesis testing and the construction of theories, outlined in Figure 1.1.

HYPOTHESES: MAKING PREDICTIONS Scientific thinking and procedures revolve around the concepts of a hypothesis and a theory. Both guide the process and progress of the sciences; however, it is important to differentiate between these terms. A **hypothesis** (plural: hypotheses) *is a testable prediction about processes that can be observed and measured.* A hypothesis can be supported or rejected—you cannot *prove* a hypothesis because it is always possible that a future experiment could show that it is wrong or limited in some way. This support or rejection occurs after scientists have tested the hypothesis. For a hypothesis to be

Figure 1.1 The Scientific Method

Scientists use theories to generate hypotheses. Once tested, hypotheses are either confirmed or rejected. Confirmed hypotheses lead to new ones and strengthen theories. Rejected hypotheses are revised and tested again, and can potentially alter an existing theory.

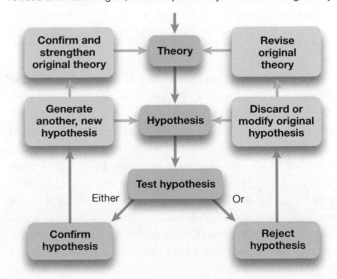

"All swans are white" is a falsifiable statement. A swan that is not coloured white will falsify it. Falsification is a critical component of scientific hypotheses and theories.

Ellie Rothnie/Alamy Stock Photo

testable, it must be **falsifiable**, meaning that *the hypothesis is precise enough that it could be proven false.* This precision is also important because it will help future researchers if they try to replicate the study (i.e., reproduce the findings) to determine if it the results were due to chance (see Module 2.1 for a more in-depth discussion of replication).

These requirements are regularly broken by people claiming to be scientific. For example, astrologers and psychics are in the business of making predictions. An astrologer might tell you, "It's a good time for you to keep quiet or defer important calls or emails." This type of statement is impossible to test. If you keep quiet and nothing happens to you, is that due to you following the horoscope or to the fact that you hid from the world? Horoscopes make *very* general predictions—typically so much so that you could easily find evidence for them if you looked hard enough, and perhaps stretched an interpretation of events a bit. In contrast, a good scientific hypothesis is stated in more precise terms that promote testability, such as the following:

> People become less likely to help a stranger if there are others around.
>
> Cigarette smoking causes cancer.
>
> Exercise improves memory ability.

Each of these hypotheses can be confirmed or rejected through scientific testing. An obvious difference between science and astrology is that scientists are eager to test hypotheses such as these, whereas astrologers would rather you just take their word for it. We acknowledge that astrology is an easy target for criticism. In fact, it is often referred to as **pseudoscience**, *an idea that is presented as science but does not actually utilize basic principles of scientific thinking or procedure.* Incidentally, a 2005 Gallup poll found that 25% of Canadians (17% of males and 33% of females) believe that the position of the stars in the sky can affect a person's behaviour.

THEORIES: EXPLAINING PHENOMENA In contrast to hypotheses, a **theory** *is an explanation for a broad range of observations that also generates new hypotheses and integrates numerous findings into a coherent whole.* In other words, theories are general principles or explanations of some aspect of the world (including human behaviours), whereas hypotheses are specific predictions that can test the theory or, more realistically, specific parts of that theory. Theories are built from hypotheses that are repeatedly tested and confirmed. Similar to hypotheses, an essential quality of scientific theories is that they can be supported *or* proved false with new evidence. If a hypothesis is supported, it provides more support for the theory. In turn, good theories eventually become accepted explanations of behaviour or other phenomena (i.e., they can be used to generate *new* hypotheses). However, if the hypothesis is not supported by the results of a well-designed experiment, then researchers may have to rethink elements of the theory. Figure 1.1 shows how hypothesis testing eventually leads back to the theory from which it was based, and how theories can be updated with new evidence. This process helps to ensure that science is *self-correcting*—bad ideas typically do not last long in the sciences.

The term *theory* is often used very casually, which has led to some persistent and erroneous beliefs about scientific theories. The following points clarify some common misperceptions.

- **Theories are not the same as opinions or beliefs.** Yes, it is certainly true that everyone is entitled to their own beliefs. But the phrase "That's just *your* theory" is confusing the terms "opinion" and "theory." A theory can help scientists develop testable hypotheses; opinions do not need to be testable, or even logical.

- **All theories are not equally plausible.** Groups of scientists might adopt different theories for explaining the same phenomenon. For example, several theories have been proposed to explain why people become depressed. This does not mean that anyone can throw their hat into the ring and claim equal status for his or her theory (or belief). A good theory can explain previous research and can lead to even more testable hypotheses.

- **The quality of a theory is not related to the number of people who believe it to be true.** According to a 2009 poll, only 61% of Canadians (and only 39% of Americans) believe in the theory of evolution by natural selection (Angus Reid Public Opinion, 2012), despite the fact that it is the most plausible, rigorously tested theory of biological change and diversity.

Testing hypotheses and constructing theories are both part of all sciences. Importantly, each science, including psychology, has its own unique way of approaching its complex subject matter as well as its own unique set of challenges. In the case of psychology, we must remember that behaviour can occur on a number of different levels, including the activity of cells in different parts of the brain, thought processes such as language and memory, and sociocultural processes that shape daily life for millions of people. Therefore, psychology examines the individual as a product of multiple influences, including biological, psychological, and social factors.

THE BIOPSYCHOSOCIAL MODEL Because our thoughts and behaviours have multiple influences, psychologists adopt multiple perspectives to understand them. The **biopsychosocial model** *is a means of explaining behaviour as a product of biological, psychological, and* *sociocultural factors* (see Figure 1.2). Biological influences on our behaviour involve brain structures and chemicals, hormones, and external substances such as drugs. Psychological influences involve our memories, emotions, and personalities, and how these factors shape the way we think about and respond to different people and situations. Finally, social factors such as our family, peers, ethnicity, and culture can have a huge effect on our behaviour. Importantly, none of these levels of analysis exists on its own. In fact, these levels influence each other! The firing of brain cells can influence how we think and remember information; this, in turn, can affect how we interact with family members or how we respond to social situations like a concert. But, these influences can occur in the other

Figure 1.2 The Biopsychosocial Model

Psychologists view behaviour from multiple perspectives. A full understanding of human behaviour comes from analyzing biological, psychological, and sociocultural factors.

PERSPECTIVE	FOCUS	EXAMPLES
Biological	Genes, brain anatomy and function, and evolution	Genetics of behaviour and psychological disorders Brain-behaviour relationships Drug effects
Psychological	Behaviour, perception, thought, and experience	Language Memory Decision making Personality
Sociocultural	Interpersonal relationships, families, groups, societies, and ethnicities	Attraction Attitudes and stereotypes Conformity

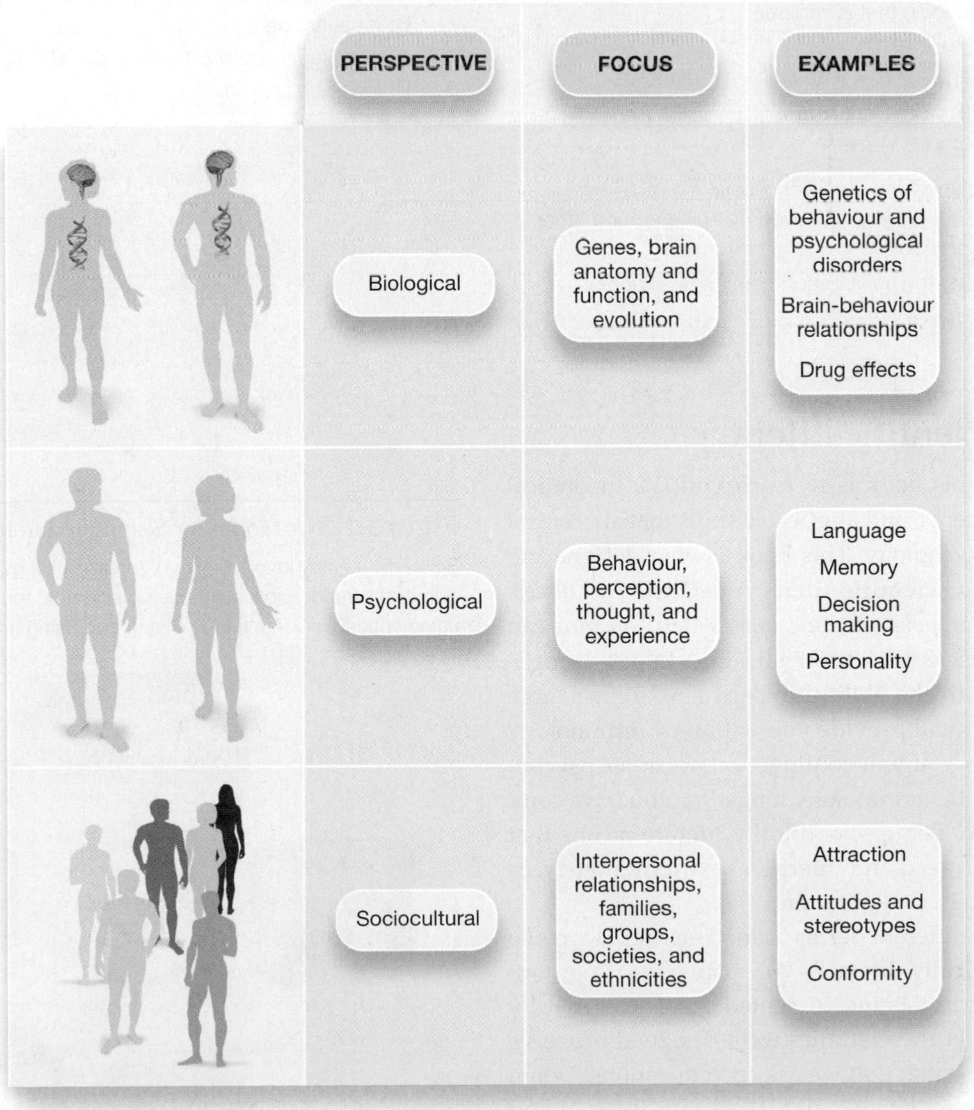

direction as well. Social situations can affect how we think (e.g., getting annoyed by the crowded hallway at your university), which, in turn, can trigger the release of chemicals and hormones in your brain.

The take-home message of this section is that almost every moment of your life is occurring at all three levels; psychologists have taken up the exciting challenge of trying to understand them. Indeed, behaviour can be fully explained only if multiple perspectives—and their interactions—are investigated. This "systems perspective" will become particularly apparent as you read about psychological research that tackles complex topics.

Module 1.1a Quiz:

The Scientific Method

Know . . .

1. A testable prediction about processes that can be observed and measured is referred to as a(n)_____.
   A. theory
   B. hypothesis
   C. opinion
   D. hunch

Understand . . .

2. A theory or prediction is falsifiable if
   A. it is based on logic that is incorrect.
   B. it is impossible to test.
   C. it is precise enough that it could be proven false.
   D. it comes from pseudoscience.

Apply . . .

3. How would you apply the biopsychosocial model to a news report claiming that anxiety is caused by being around other people who are anxious?
   A. Recognize that the news report considers all portions of the biopsychosocial model.

B. Recognize that psychologists do not regard biological factors when it comes to anxiety.
C. Recognize that the only effective treatment of anxiety must be drug-based.
D. Recognize that the news report only considers one portion of the biopsychosocial model.

Analyze . . .

4. The hypothesis that "exercise improves one's ability to remember lists of words" is a scientific one because
   A. it cannot be confirmed.
   B. it cannot be rejected.
   C. it makes a specific, testable prediction.
   D. it can be proven.

Building Scientific Literacy

A major aim of this book is to teach you the theoretical foundations, concepts, and applicable skills that are central to the field of psychology. This book is also designed to help you develop **scientific literacy**, *the ability to understand, analyze, and apply scientific information.* As you can see in Figure 1.3, scientific literacy has several key components, starting with the ability to learn new information. Certainly this text will provide you with new terminology and concepts, but you will continue to encounter psychological and scientific terminology long after you have completed this course. Being scientifically literate means that you will be able to read and interpret new terminology, or know where to go to find out more.

Memorizing different terms is not enough to make someone scientifically literate. We also have to examine whether the ideas being presented were scientifically tested, and whether those studies were designed properly. It is absolutely essential that we ask such questions. Doing so allows us to separate the information that we *should* find convincing from the information that we should view with

---

Figure 1.3 A Model for Scientific Literacy

Scientific literacy involves four different skills: gathering knowledge about the world, explaining it using scientific terms and concepts, using critical thinking, and applying and using information.

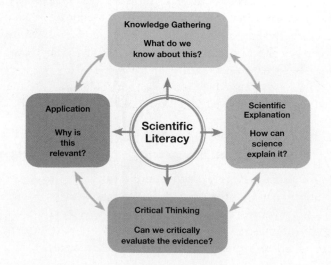

caution. It will also allow you to better analyze the information presented to you by politicians, corporations, and the media; this will make it more difficult for these groups to influence your behaviour. Finally, we want to be able to apply the results of scientific studies to different situations; in other words, to *generalize* the results. Generalization shows us that the studies conducted in universities and hospitals can provide insight into behaviours that extend far beyond the confines of the lab.

Working the Scientific Literacy Model

Planning When to Study

To develop your scientific literacy skills, in every module (beginning with Chapter 2) we will revisit this model and its four components as they apply to a specific psychological topic—a process we call *working the scientific literacy model*. This will help you to move beyond simply learning the vocabulary of psychological research toward *understanding* scientific explanations, thinking critically, and discovering applications of the material. In order to demonstrate how these sections of the book will work, let's use an example that will be familiar to many: planning study time for your different classes.

What do we know about timing and studying?

In the first stage of the Scientific Literacy Model, we attempt to gather the available knowledge about the topic that we're investigating, in this case the fact that students differ on how they attempt to remember information for exams. Many students use what is called *massed learning*—they perform all of their studying for an exam in one lengthy session. Another approach is *spaced* or *distributed learning*—having shorter study sessions, but spreading them out over several days. Which technique do you prefer? If you use the massed learning technique (most students prefer it . . . or end up using it because they've left studying until the last minute), it is likely because it *seems* easier and it may even give you the sense that it is more effective than distributed learning. Actually, the two strategies are not equally effective; more than 100 years of memory research has shown us that distributed learning is the better of the two (Cepeda et al., 2006; Edwards, 1917).

How can science explain the effect of timing on study success?

In the second stage of the Scientific Literacy Model, we examine whether the information that is available about a topic has been tested in scientific studies. In a typical study of massed vs. distributed learning, participants are asked to remember lists of words or concepts. The stimuli are presented multiple times. What varies, however, is *when* these presentations occur. In some conditions, the stimuli are presented in a single session (a massed schedule). In other conditions, the studying is spread out across multiple time periods (a spaced or distributed schedule). As early as 1885, Herman Ebbinghaus, a German psychologist, found that his ability to learn sets of nonsense syllables (e.g., wej) was superior if he spread his learning over three days rather than trying to learn the lengthy list in one sitting. Similar patterns of results have been found in hundreds of other studies, providing strong evidence in favour of distributed learning (Delaney et al., 2010; Dempster, 1988). Although there is no single explanation for this effect, one factor is particularly relevant for students. When information is learned in one massed session, it begins to feel repetitive. This leads the learners to pay less attention to the material than they would in distributed learning sessions, when some of the material may have been forgotten (Ausubel, 1966). As a result, people learning in a distributed fashion are more likely to pay attention to the material than massed learners, a tendency that would obviously improve performance.

Can we critically evaluate this evidence?

In the third stage of the Scientific Literacy Model, we examine the limitations of the studies discussed earlier; we also look for alternative explanations for the results. The most obvious criticism of this research is that results from laboratory-based studies may not reflect how memory works in a real educational setting. This is a valid concern—researchers don't want their effects to be isolated to the laboratory. Luckily, a number of researchers have applied the knowledge and techniques developed by earlier researchers to *applied psychology* studies in the classroom. In one study, elementary school children were taught scientific information about food charts (Gluckman et al., 2014). Each child received four lessons about this topic. One group received all four lessons on a Monday ("massed learning condition"). A second group received two lessons on a Monday and two lessons on a Tuesday ("clumped learning group"). The third group received one lesson per day from Monday through Thursday ("distributed learning group"). All groups were tested one week after their last lesson. As can be seen in Figure 1.4, the distributed learning group retained much more information than the other two groups. Similar patterns of results have been found in studies with middle school children (Sobel et al., 2011) and undergraduate students at an Ontario university (Kapler et al., 2015), suggesting that the laboratory studies of the benefits of distributed learning generalize to the so-called real world.

Figure 1.4 Massed versus Distributed Learning

In a study by Gluckman and colleagues (2014), groups of students learned information in one long session (massed learning), two sessions per day on two consecutive days (clumped learning), or spread across four days (distributed learning). A test one week later found that the distributed learning group retained much more information than the other groups.

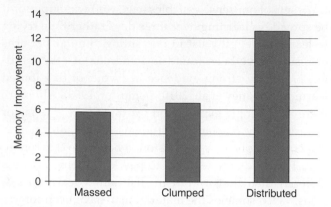

Source: Information is derived from Table 1 of Gluckman et al. (2014), Spacing Simultaneously Promotes Multiple Forms of Learning in Children's Science Curriculum, Applied Cognitive Psychology, 28, p. 270, Wiley Online Library.

Why is this finding relevant?

In the final stage of the Scientific Literacy Model, we attempt to apply the results to situations outside of the laboratory. The information about distributed learning is being presented in the first module of this textbook for a reason: Psychology students should benefit from psychology research. Now that you know that retention is improved if you study over the course of a few days rather than in one long session, you can alter your own study schedule. The benefits to your grades could be substantial. Distributed learning has also proven useful in many clinical contexts, such as helping people improve their memory abilities after suffering a traumatic brain injury (Hillary et al., 2003). Sometimes simple experiments can have widespread implications; that's something to remember.

Now that you have read this feature, we hope you understand how scientific information fits into the four components of the model. But there is still much to learn about working the model: In the next section, we will describe critical thinking skills and how to use them.

CRITICAL THINKING, CURIOSITY, AND A DOSE OF HEALTHY SKEPTICISM People are confronted with more information on a daily basis than they have been at any other point in our history. Some of it is credible and can be used to help guide your decisions or behaviour. But we also must deal with claims—often made by people trying to sell you things—that are not always true.

"This political party will not base its positions on public opinion polls."

"These remedies were developed by ancient cultures and have been used for centuries."

"Join now and find your soul mate."

Misinformation sometimes seems far more abundant than accurate information, which is why it is important to develop critical thinking skills.

Refer to Figure 1.3. As the model shows, critical thinking is an important element of scientific literacy. **Critical thinking** *involves exercising curiosity and skepticism when evaluating the claims of others, and with our own assumptions and beliefs.* Critical thinking does not mean being negative or arbitrarily critical; rather, it means that you intentionally examine knowledge, beliefs, and the means by which conclusions were obtained.

Critical thinking involves cautious skepticism. We are constantly being told about amazing products that help us control body weight, improve thinking and memory, enhance sexual performance, and so on. As consumers, there will always be claims we really hope to be true. But as critical thinkers, we meet these claims with a good dose of skepticism (e.g., *Is there sound evidence that this diet helps people to achieve and maintain a healthy weight?*). Being skeptical can be challenging, especially when it means asking for evidence that we may not want to find. Often the great products or miracle cures that we have always hoped for really *are* "too good to be true." Being curious *and* skeptical leads you to ask important questions about the science underlying such claims. Doing so leads us to search for and evaluate evidence, which is never a bad thing.

Importantly, the ability to think critically can be learned and developed, although most of us need to make a conscious effort to do so (Halpern, 1996). Research points to a core set of habits and skills for developing critical thinking:

1. Be curious. Simple answers are sometimes too simple, and common sense is not always correct (or even close to it). *Example:* Giving your brain some time to rest after having a stroke (a form of brain damage) *hinders* rather than helps your recovery (see Module 3.3).
2. Examine the nature and source of the evidence; not all research is of equal quality. *Example:* Some studies use flawed methods or, in the case of an infamous study linking vaccines and autism, were performed by someone who would benefit financially if the results told a particular story (see Module 2.3).
3. Examine assumptions and biases. This includes your own assumptions as well as the assumptions of those making the claims. *Example:* Research examining the impact of human behaviour on climate change may be biased if it is funded by oil companies (see Module 2.2).
4. Avoid overly emotional thinking. Emotions can tell us what we value, but they are not always helpful when it comes to making critical decisions. *Example:* you may have strong responses when hearing about differences in the cognitive abilities of males and females

Myths in Mind
Abducted by Aliens!

Independent reports of alien abductions often resemble events and characters depicted in science fiction movies.

Occasionally we hear claims of alien abductions, ghost sightings, and other paranormal activity. Countless television shows and movies, both fictional and documentary based, reinforce the idea that these types of events can and do occur. Alien abductions are probably the most far-fetched stories, yet many people believe they occur or at least regard them as a real possibility. What is even more interesting are the extremely detailed accounts given by purported alien abductees. However, physical evidence of an abduction is always lacking. So what can we make of the validity of alien abduction stories?

Scientific and critical thinking involve the use of the **principle of parsimony**, which states that *the simplest of all competing explanations (the most "parsimonious") of a phenomenon should be the one we accept.* Is there a simpler explanation for alien abductions? Probably. Psychologists who study alien abduction cases have discovered some interesting patterns. First, historical reports of abductions typically spike just after the release of science fiction movies featuring space aliens. Details of the reports often follow specific details seen in these movies (Clancy, 2005). Second, it probably would not be too surprising to learn that people who report being abducted are prone to fantasizing and having false memories (vivid recollection and belief in something that did not happen; Lynn & Kirsch, 1996; Spanos et al., 1994). Finally, people who claim to have been abducted are likely to experience sleep paralysis (waking up and becoming aware of being unable to move—a temporary state that is not unusual) and hallucinations while in the paralyzed state (McNally et al., 2004). You can likely see how these three factors could explain reports of alien abductions. Following the principle of parsimony typically leads to real, though sometimes less spectacular, answers—although these answers might leave the so-called "abductees" feeling alienated.

(see Module 3.1); however, it is important to put those aside to examine the studies themselves.

5. Tolerate ambiguity. Most complex issues do not have clear-cut answers. *Example:* Psychologists have identified a number of factors leading to depression, but no single factor *guarantees* that a person will suffer from this condition (see Module 15.3).

6. Consider alternative viewpoints and alternative interpretations of the evidence. *Example:* It is clear that we require sleep in order to function properly; however, there are several theories that can explain the functions that sleep serves (see Module 5.1).

Using these critical-thinking skills might seem difficult at first. However, with some practice, they will soon seem like a natural way of viewing the world. They will also help you see through some rather unbelievable stories.

Module 1.1b Quiz:
Building Scientific Literacy

Know . . .

1. Someone who exercises curiosity and skepticism about assumptions and beliefs is using _____.
   - **A.** critical thinking
   - **B.** a hypothesis
   - **C.** pseudoscience
   - **D.** the biopsychosocial model

Understand . . .

2. Scientific literacy does *not* include _____.
   - **A.** gathering knowledge
   - **B.** accepting common sense explanations
   - **C.** critical thinking
   - **D.** applying scientific information to everyday problems

Apply . . .

3. Paul is considering whether to take a cholesterol-reducing medicine that has been recommended by his physician. He goes to the library and learns that the government agency that oversees medications—Health Canada—has approved the medication after dozens of studies had been conducted on its usefulness. Which aspect of critical thinking does this *best* represent?
   - **A.** Paul has examined the nature and source of the evidence.
   - **B.** Paul was simply curious.
   - **C.** Paul did not consider alternative viewpoints.
   - **D.** Paul was avoiding overly emotional thinking.

Module 1.1 Summary

1.1a   Know . . . the key terminology of the scientific method.

biopsychosocial model
critical thinking
falsifiable
hypothesis
principle of parsimony
pseudoscience
psychology
scientific literacy
scientific method
theory

1.1b   Understand . . . the steps of the scientific method.

The basic model in Figure 1.1 guides us through the steps of the scientific method. Scientific theories generate hypotheses, which are specific and testable predictions. If a hypothesis is confirmed, new hypotheses may stem from it, and the original theory receives added support. If a hypothesis is rejected, the original hypothesis may be modified and retested, or the original theory may be modified or rejected.

1.1c   Understand . . . the concept of scientific literacy.

Scientific literacy refers to the process of how we think about and understand scientific information. The model for scientific literacy was summarized in Figure 1.3. Working the model involves answering a set of questions:

What do we know about a phenomenon?

How can science explain it?

Can we critically evaluate the evidence?

Why is this relevant?

You will see this model applied to concepts in each chapter of this text. This includes gathering knowledge, explaining phenomena in scientific terms, engaging in critical thinking, and knowing how to apply and use your knowledge.

1.1d   Apply . . . the biopsychosocial model to behaviour.

This is a model we will use throughout the text. As you consider each topic, think about how biological factors (e.g., the brain and genetics) are influential. Also consider how psychological factors such as thinking, learning, emotion, and memory are relevant. Social and cultural factors complete the model. These three interacting factors influence our behaviour.

1.1e   Apply . . . the steps in critical thinking.

To be useful, critical thinking is something not just to memorize, but rather to use and apply. Remember, critical thinking involves (1) being curious, (2) examining evidence, (3) examining assumptions and biases, (4) avoiding emotional thinking, (5) tolerating ambiguity, and (6) considering alternative viewpoints. Try applying these steps in the activity below.

Apply Activity

Practise applying critical thinking skills to the following scenario.

Magic Mileage is a high-tech fuel additive that actually increases the distance you can drive for every litre by 20%, while costing only a fraction of the gasoline itself!! Wouldn't you like to cut your fuel expenses by one-fifth? Magic Mileage is a blend of complex engine-cleaning agents and a patented "octane-booster" that not only packs in extra kilometres per litre but also leaves your engine cleaner and running smooth while reducing emissions!

1. How might this appeal lead to overly emotional thinking?
2. Can you identify assumptions or biases the manufacturer might have?
3. Do you have enough evidence to make a judgment about this product?

1.1f   Analyze . . . the use of the term *scientific theory*.

As you read in this module, the term *theory* is often used very casually in the English language, sometimes synonymously with *opinion*. Thus, it is important to analyze the scientific meaning of the term and contrast it with the alternatives. A scientific theory is an explanation for a broad range of observations, integrating numerous findings into a coherent whole. Remember, theories are not the same thing as opinions or beliefs, all theories are not equally plausible, and, strange as it may sound, the quality of a scientific theory is not determined by the number of people who believe it to be true.

Module 1.2 How Psychology Became a Science

Nagib/Shutterstock

Learning Objectives

1.2a Know . . . the key terminology of psychology's history.

1.2b Understand . . . how various philosophical and scientific fields became major influences on psychology.

1.2c Apply . . . your knowledge to distinguish among the different specializations in psychology.

1.2d Analyze . . . how the philosophical ideas of empiricism and determinism are applied to human behaviour.

When we try to imagine the earliest investigations of human behaviour, we rarely think about axe wounds to the head. As it turns out, we should. The ancient Egyptians were a fierce military force for several centuries. The wealth accumulated during these military campaigns filled the palaces of the pharaohs with gold and jewels and allowed them to construct massive monuments like the pyramids. But one side effect of having many battles was that members of the Egyptian army also suffered many injuries, including some to the head. Although the primitive medical knowledge of the time condemned most brain-injured patients to death, some did in fact survive and attempted to return to their normal lives. However, as one might expect when someone has suffered an axe (khopesh) wound to the head, such attempts were not always successful. Similar problems had likely occurred in earlier times, but what makes ancient Egypt stand out is that military

*doctors noticed—and documented—*patterns *that emerged in their patients. As noted in the Edwin Smith papyrus (obviously named after the American discoverer, not the Egyptian authors), damage to different parts of the brain resulted in different types of impairments ranging from problems with vision to problems with higher-order cognitive abilities. Although primitive by modern standards, this initial attempt to link a brain-based injury to a change in behaviour marked the first step toward our modern study of psychology.*

Focus Questions

1. Why did it take so long for scientists to start applying their methods to human thoughts and experience?

2. What has resulted from the application of scientific methods to human behaviour?

》 Psychology has long dealt with some major questions and issues that span philosophical inquiry and scientific study. For example, psychologists have questioned how environmental, genetic, and physiological processes influence behaviour. They have wrestled with the issue of whether our behaviour is determined by external events, or if we have free will to act. Psychology's search for answers to these and other questions continues, and in this module we put this search into historical context and see how these questions have influenced the field of psychology as it exists today.

Psychology's Philosophical and Scientific Origins

Science is more than a body of facts to memorize or a set of subjects to study. Science is actually a philosophy of knowledge that stems from two fundamental beliefs: empiricism and determinism.

Empiricism *is a philosophical tenet that knowledge comes through experience.* In everyday language, you might hear the phrase "Seeing is believing," but in the scientific sense, empiricism means that knowledge about the world is based on careful observation, not on common sense or speculation. Whatever we see or measure should be observable by anyone else who follows the same methods. In addition, scientific theories must be logical explanations of how the observations fit together. Thus, although the empiricist might say, "Seeing is believing," thinking and reasoning about observations are just as important.

Determinism *is the belief that all events are governed by lawful, cause-and-effect relationships.* This is easy enough when we discuss natural laws such as gravity—we probably all agree that if you drop an object, it will fall (unless it is a helium balloon). But does the lawfulness of nature apply to the way we think and act? Does it mean that we do not have control over our own actions? This interesting philosophical debate is often referred to as *free will versus determinism.* While we certainly feel as if we are in control of our own behaviours—that is, we sense that we have free will—there are compelling reasons (discussed later in this book) to believe that some of our behaviours are determined. The level of determinism or free will psychologists attribute to humans is certainly debated, and to be a psychologist, you do not have to believe that every single thought, behaviour, or experience is determined by natural laws. But psychologists certainly do recognize that behaviour is determined by both internal (e.g., genes, brain chemistry) and external (e.g., cultural) influences.

Psychological science is both empirical and deterministic. We now know that behaviour can only be understood by making observations and testing hypotheses. We also know that behaviour occurs at several different levels ranging from cells to societies. However, this modern knowledge did not appear overnight. Instead, our understanding of why we behave the way we do is built upon the hard work, creativity, and astute observational powers of scientists throughout history dating (at least) as far back as the ancient Mediterranean societies of Egypt, Greece, and Rome.

INFLUENCES FROM THE ANCIENTS: PHILOSOPHICAL INSIGHTS INTO BEHAVIOUR As you read in the opening section of this module, ancient Egyptian doctors noticed that damage to different brain areas led to vastly different impairments. While such an observation marked the first recorded linking of biology and behaviour, it was not the only important insight to come out of ancient societies.

In ancient Greece, the physician Hippocrates (460–370 BCE) developed the world's first personality classification scheme. The ancient Greeks believed that four *humours* or fluids flowed throughout the body and influenced both health and personality. These four humours included blood, yellow bile, black bile, and phlegm (theories were a bit gross in ancient times). Different combinations of these four humours were thought to lead to specific moods and behaviours. Galen of Pergamon (127–217), arguably the greatest of the ancient Roman physicians, refined Hippocrates's more general work and suggested that the four humours combined to create *temperaments,* or emotional and personality characteristics that remained stable throughout the lifetime. Galen's four temperaments (each related to a humour) included:

- *Sanguine* (blood), a tendency to be impulsive, pleasure-seeking, and charismatic;
- *Choleric* (yellow bile), a tendency to be ambitious, energetic, and a bit aggressive;
- *Melancholic* (black bile), a tendency to be independent, perfectionistic, and a bit introverted; and
- *Phlegmatic* (phlegm), a tendency to be quiet, relaxed, and content with life.

Although such a classification system is primitive by modern standards, the work of Hippocrates and Galen moved the understanding of human behaviour forward by attempting to categorize different types of personalities; we will see much more scientifically rigorous attempts to do the same thing later in this book (see Module 12.1). However, the golden age of Greek and Roman thought came to a crashing halt in the latter parts of the fourth century; this was the beginning of the Dark Ages. Although some discoveries were made about human anatomy during this period, few notable advances in the study of behaviour were made over the next one thousand years.

Psychology also did not immediately benefit from the scientific revolution of the 1500s and 1600s. Once the scientific method started to take hold around 1600, physics, astronomy, physiology, biology, and chemistry all experienced unprecedented growth in knowledge and technology. But it took psychology until the late 1800s to become scientific. Why was this the case? One of the main reasons was *zeitgeist*, a German word meaning "spirit of the times." **Zeitgeist** *refers to a general set of beliefs of a particular culture at a specific time in history.* It can be used to understand why some ideas take off immediately, whereas other perfectly good ideas may go unnoticed for years.

The power of zeitgeist can be very strong, and there are several ways it prevented psychological science from emerging in the 1600s. Perhaps most important is that people were not ready to accept a science that could be applied to human behaviour and thought. To the average person of the 1600s, viewing human behaviour as the result of predictable physical laws was troubling. Doing so would seem to imply the philosophy of **materialism**: *the belief that humans, and other living beings, are composed exclusively of physical matter.* Accepting this idea would mean that we are nothing more than complex machines that lack a self-conscious, self-controlling soul. The opposing belief, *that there are properties of humans that are not material (a mind or soul separate from the body),* is called **dualism**.

Although most early thinking about the mind and behaviour remained philosophical in nature, scientific methods were generating great discoveries for the natural sciences of physics, biology, and physiology. This meant that the early influences on psychology came from the natural and physical sciences. (Figure 1.5 provides a timeline that summarizes some of the major events in the history of psychology.)

INFLUENCES FROM PHYSICS: EXPERIMENTING WITH THE MIND   The initial forays into scientific psychology were conducted by physicists and physiologists. One of the earliest explorations was made by Gustav Fechner (1801–1887), who studied sensation and perception (see Module 4.1). As a physicist, Fechner was interested in the natural world of moving objects and energy. He turned his knowledge to psychological questions about how the physical and mental worlds interact. Fechner coined the term **psychophysics**, *which is the study of the relationship between the physical world and the mental representation of that world.*

As an example of psychophysical research, imagine you are holding a one-pound (0.45 kg) weight in your right hand and a five-pound (2.27 kg) weight in your left hand. Obviously, your left hand will feel the heavier weight, but that is not what interested Fechner. What if a researcher places a quarter-pound weight (113 g) in each hand, resting on top of the weight that is already there? Fechner wanted to know which of the quarter-pound weights would be perceived as heavier. Oddly enough, although both weigh the same amount, the quarter-pound weight in

your right hand will be more noticeable than the quarter-pound weight added to your left hand, almost as if it were heavier (see Figure 1.6). Through experiments like these, Fechner demonstrated basic principles of how the physical and mental worlds interact. In fact, he developed an equation to precisely calculate the *perceived* change in weight, and then extended this formula to apply to changes in brightness, loudness, and other perceptual experiences. This work served as the foundation for the modern study of perception.

INFLUENCES FROM EVOLUTIONARY THEORY: THE ADAPTIVE FUNCTIONS OF BEHAVIOUR   Around the same time Fechner was doing his experiments, Charles Darwin (1809–1882) was studying the many varieties of plants and animals found around the world. Darwin noticed that animal groups that were isolated from one another often differed by only minor variations in physical features. These variations seemed to fine-tune the species according to the particular environment in which they lived, making them better equipped for survival and reproduction. Darwin's theory of evolution by *natural selection* was based on his observations that the genetically inherited traits that contribute to survival and reproductive success are more likely to flourish within the breeding population (i.e., useful traits will be passed on to future generations). These specific traits differ across locations because different traits will prove beneficial in different environments. This theory explains why there is such a diversity of life on Earth.

Darwin's theory also helps to explain human (and animal) behaviour. As Darwin pointed out in *The Expression*

Charles Darwin proposed the theory of natural selection to explain how evolution works.

Figure 1.5 Major Events in the History of Psychology

ca. 1500 BCE: Ancient Egyptian doctors describe behavioural impairments caused by brain damage.

ca. 430 BCE–216 AD: Greek and Roman physicians develop the four humours and four temperaments theories of personality and behaviour.

Late 1700s: Franz Mesmer develops techniques to treat mental illness, including the use of hypnosis.

Around 1850: Gustav Fechner pioneers the study of psychophysics.

1859: Darwin publishes *On the Origin of Species* introducing his theory of natural selection.

1861: Physician Paul Broca discovers a brain area associated with the production of speech, now known as Broca's area, establishing that regions of the brain are specialized to serve different functions.

1879: Wilhelm Wundt establishes the first psychological laboratory in Leipzig, Germany, and two years later he establishes the first journal in psychology.

1880s: Francis Galton introduces and develops the study of anthropometrics.

1885: Hermann Ebbinghaus begins his scientific study of memory.

1890: William James, founder of the functionalist approach, publishes *Principles of Psychology*.

1891: James Mark Baldwin founds the first psychology laboratory in the British Commonwealth at the University of Toronto.

1892: The American Psychological Association (APA) is established.

AMERICAN PSYCHOLOGICAL ASSOCIATION

1949: Donald Hebb publishes *The Organization of Behavior*, focusing research into the mechanisms of memory.

1939: The Canadian Psychological Association is founded.

CANADIAN PSYCHOLOGICAL ASSOCIATION   SOCIÉTÉ CANADIENNE DE PSYCHOLOGIE

1938: B. F. Skinner writes the *Behavior of Organisms*, which furthers the cause of behaviourism.

1936: Kurt Lewin authors *Principles of Topological Psychology*, which introduces the social psychological formulation that the behaviour of individuals is influenced by their social environment.

1934: Wilder Penfield founds McGill University's Montreal Neurological Institute. While there, Penfield uses electrical stimulation to map out the neural underpinnings of movement and touch.

1913: John B. Watson writes "Psychology as the Behaviorist Views It," establishing behaviourism as the primary school of thought in American psychology.

1912: Max Wertheimer establishes the field of gestalt psychology.

1911: Edward Thorndike demonstrates the basic principles of instrumental learning, forming the basis for the study of operant conditioning.

1905: Alfred Binet develops the first intelligence test.

Early 1900s: Ivan Pavlov demonstrates the basic principles of classical conditioning.

1900: Sigmund Freud writes *The Interpretation of Dreams*, a key book in the development of psychoanalysis.

1951: Carl Rogers writes *Client-Centered Therapy*, which helps establish humanistic psychology.

1952: The first *Diagnostic and Statistical Manual of Mental Disorders*, now in its fifth edition, is published by the American Psychiatric Association.

1967: Ulrich Neisser publishes *Cognitive Psychology*, which introduces a major new subfield of psychology.

1971: B. F. Skinner publishes *Beyond Freedom and Dignity*, stirring controversy over radical behaviourism.

1978: Herbert Simon wins the Nobel Prize in economics for research in cognitive psychology (there is no Nobel Prize dedicated to psychology).

1980s–early 1990s: Brain-imaging techniques such as magnetic resonance imaging become mainstream methods for studying brain anatomy and function in human subjects.

1990: The Canadian Society for Brain, Behaviour, and Cognitive Science is established.

CSBBCS SCSCCC

1990s: U.S. President George H. W. Bush proclaims the 1990s to be "The Decade of the Brain," and there is unprecedented growth in neuroscience and biological psychology.

2003: The Human Genome Project is completed.

Figure 1.6 The Study of Psychophysics

Gustav Fechner studied relationships between the physical world and our mental representations of that world. For example, Fechner tested how people detect changes in physical stimuli.

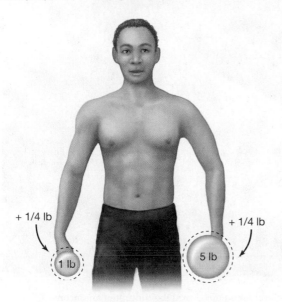

detected by examining the surface of the skull. Although it seems silly now, there was a logic behind phrenology. Its supporters believed that different traits and abilities were distributed across different regions of the brain (e.g., "combativeness" was located at the back of the brain behind the ears). If a person possessed a particular trait or ability, then the brain area related to that characteristic would be larger in the same way that the muscles in your arms would be larger if your job required you to lift things. Larger brain areas would cause bumps on a person's head in the same way that a muscular arm could cause the fabric of a shirt to stretch. So, by measuring the bumps on a person's head, proponents of phrenology believed that it would be possible to identify the different traits that an individual possessed. Phrenology continued to gather supporters for nearly a century before being abandoned by serious scientists. You may have encountered images of the phrenological map of the skull (see Figure 1.7).

The other approach to localization entailed the study of brain injuries and the ways in which they affect behaviour. This work had a scientific grounding that phrenology

of the Emotions in Man and Animals (1872), behaviour is shaped by natural selection, just as physical traits are (see Module 3.1). Over the course of millions of years of evolution, a certain range of behaviours helped our ancestors survive and reproduce. The modern behaviours that we engage in every day—memory, emotions, forming social bonds, and so on—were the same behaviours that allowed our ancestors to flourish over the course of our species' history. The same principle applies to other species as well. Darwin's recognition that behaviours, like physical traits, are subject to hereditary influences and natural selection was a major contribution to psychology.

INFLUENCES FROM MEDICINE: DIAGNOSES AND TREATMENTS Medicine contributed a great deal to the biological perspective in psychology. It also had a considerable influence on the development of **clinical psychology**, *the field of psychology that concentrates on the diagnosis and treatment of psychological disorders.* A research topic that impacted both fields was the study of *localization of brain function*, the idea that certain parts of the brain control specific mental abilities and personality characteristics.

In the mid-1800s, localization was studied in two different ways. The first was *phrenology*, which gained considerable popularity for more than 100 years thanks to physicians Franz Gall (1758–1828) and Johann Spurzheim (1776–1832). Gall, Spurzheim, and their followers believed that the brain consisted of 27 "organs," corresponding to mental traits and dispositions that could be

Figure 1.7 A Phrenology Map

Early scholars of the brain believed that mental capacities and personalities could be measured by the contours, bumps, and ridges distributed across the surface of the skull.

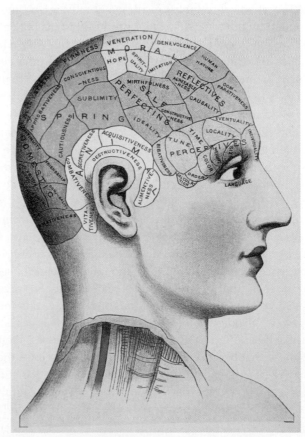

Classic Image/Alamy Stock Photo

lacked. There were many intriguing cases described by physicians of the 1800s. For example:

- Physician Paul Broca found that a patient who had difficulties producing spoken language had brain damage in an area of the left frontal lobes of brain (near his left temple).

- Prussian physician Karl Wernicke found that damage to another area in the left hemisphere led to problems with speech *comprehension.*

- Doctors in Vermont described a railroad employee who became impulsive and somewhat childlike after suffering damage to part of his frontal lobes.

These compelling clinical cases provided early brain researchers with new information about the roles of different brain areas, findings that are still relevant today.

Of course, the influence of the medical perspective was not isolated to studies of the localization of brain function. Additional medical influences on psychology came from outside of mainstream practices. Franz Mesmer, an 18th-century Austrian physician practising in Paris, believed that prolonged exposure to magnets could redirect the flow of metallic fluids in the body, thereby curing disease and insanity. Although his claim was rejected outright by the medical and scientific communities in France, some of his patients seemed to be cured after being lulled into a trance. Modern physicians and scientists attribute these "cures" to the patients' belief in the treatment—what we now call *psychosomatic medicine.*

The medical establishment eventually grew more intrigued by the trances Mesmer produced in his patients, naming the phenomenon *hypnosis* (see Module 5.2). This practice also caught the attention of an Austrian physician named Sigmund Freud (1856–1939), who began to use hypnosis to treat his own patients. Freud was particularly interested in how hypnosis seemed to have cured several patients of *hysterical paralysis*—a condition in which an individual loses feeling and control in a specific body part, despite the lack of any known neurological damage or disease. These experiences led Freud to develop his famous theory and technique called *psychoanalysis.*

Psychoanalysis *is a psychological approach that attempts to explain how behaviour and personality are influenced by unconscious processes.* Freud acknowledged that conscious experience includes perceptions, thoughts, a sense of self, and the sense that we are in control of ourselves. However, he also believed in an unconscious mind that contained forgotten episodes from early childhood as well as urges to fulfill self-serving sexual and aggressive impulses. Freud proposed that because these urges were unconscious, they could exert influence in strange ways, such as restricting the use of a body part (psychosomatic or hysterical paralysis). Freud believed hypnosis played a valuable role in his

Mary Evans Picture Library / Alamy Stock Photo

Sigmund Freud developed the concept of an unconscious mind and its underlying processes in his theory of psychoanalysis.

work. When a person is hypnotized, dreaming, or perhaps medicated into a trancelike state, he thought, the psychoanalyst could have more direct access into the individual's unconscious mind. Once Freud gained access, he could attempt to determine and correct any desires or emotions he believed were causing the unconscious to create the psychosomatic conditions.

Although Freud did not conduct scientific experiments, his legacy can be seen in some key elements of scientific psychology. First, many modern psychologists make inferences about unconscious mental activity, just as Freud had advocated (although not all of them agree with the specific theories proposed by Freud). Second, the use of medical ideas to treat disorders of emotions, thought, and behaviour—an approach known as the *medical model*—can be traced to Freud's influence. Third, Freud incorporated evolutionary thinking into his work; he emphasized how physiological needs and urges relating to survival and reproduction can influence our behaviour. Finally, Freud placed great emphasis on how early life experiences influence our behaviour as adults—a perspective that comes up many times in this text. So, although people often mock some of his theories, Freud's impact on modern psychology is deserving of respect.

THE INFLUENCE OF SOCIAL SCIENCES: MEASURING AND COMPARING HUMANS A fifth influential force came out of the social sciences of economics, sociology, and anthropology. These disciplines developed statistical methods for measuring human traits, which soon became relevant to the emerging field of psychology. An early pioneer in measuring perception and in applying statistical analyses to the study of behaviour was Sir Francis Galton.

Galton was also influential in the study of individual differences between people. He noticed that great achievement tended to run in families; as a result, Galton came to believe that heredity (genetics) could explain the physical and psychological differences found in a population. After all, Galton's cousin—some guy named Charles Darwin—was a great naturalist, his uncle Erasmus was a celebrated physician and writer, and Galton himself was no slouch (he began reading as a 2-year-old child, and was a fan of Shakespeare by age 6). To Galton, it seemed natural that people who did better in scholarship, business, and wealth were able to do so because they were *better* people (genetically speaking).

To support his beliefs, Galton developed ways of measuring what he called *eminence*—a combination of ability, morality, and achievement. One observation supporting his claim for a hereditary basis for eminence was that the closer a relative, the more similar the traits. Galton was one of the first investigators to scientifically take on the question of **nature and nurture relationships**, *the inquiry into how heredity (nature) and environment (nurture) influence behaviour and mental processes.* Galton came down decidedly on the nature side, seemingly ignoring the likelihood that nurturing influences such as upbringing and family traditions, rather than biological endowments, could explain similarities among relatives.

Galton's beliefs and biases led him to pursue scientific justification for *eugenics*, which literally translates as "good genes." He promoted the belief that social programs should encourage intelligent, talented individuals to have children, whereas criminals, those with physical or mental disability, and non-White races should not receive such encouragement (see Module 9.1). The eugenics movement was based largely on what the researchers wanted to believe was true, not on quality research methods. It ultimately led to the mistreatment of many individuals, particularly immigrants and the descendants of slaves who were not of Galton's own demographic group. It also influenced the thinking of Adolf Hitler, with chilling consequences.

In modern times, biological and genetic approaches to explaining behaviour are thriving (and, thankfully, eugenics has vanished). With the advent of new brain-imaging techniques, this area of psychology— *biological psychology—* is poised to provide new and important insights into the underlying causes of our behaviour.

Module 1.2a Quiz:

Psychology's Philosophical and Scientific Origins

Know . . .

1. In philosophical terms, a materialist is someone who might believe that
   A. money buys happiness.
   B. species evolve through natural selection.
   C. personality can be measured by feeling for bumps on the surface of the skull.
   D. everything that exists, including human beings, is composed exclusively of physical matter.

Understand . . .

2. According to Sigmund Freud, which of the following would be the most likely explanation for why someone is behaving aggressively?
   A. They are acting according to psychophysics.
   B. There is something going on at the unconscious level that is causing them to behave this way.
   C. Their cigars are missing and someone's got to pay.
   D. The environment is determining their behavioural response.

Apply . . .

3. Jan believes that all knowledge is acquired through careful observation. Jan is probably _____.
   A. an empiricist

B. a supporter of eugenics
C. a clinical psychologist
D. a phrenologist

Analyze . . .

4. Francis Galton made a significant contribution to psychology by introducing methods for studying how heredity contributes to human behaviour. Which alternative explanation did Galton overlook when he argued that heredity accounts for these similarities?
   A. The primary importance of the nature side of the nature-versus-nurture debate
   B. The fact that people who share genes live together in families, so they tend to share environmental privileges or disadvantages
   C. A materialistic account of behaviour
   D. The concept of dualism, which states that the mind is separate from the body

The Beginnings of Contemporary Psychology

Before psychology became its own discipline, there were scientists working across different fields who were converging on a study of human behaviour. By modern standards, Darwin, Fechner, and others had produced psychological research but it was not referred to as such because the field had not yet fully formed. Nevertheless, progress toward a distinct discipline of psychology was beginning.

By the late 1800s, the zeitgeist had changed so that the study of human behaviour was acceptable. Ideas flourished. Most importantly, researchers began to investigate behaviour in a number of different ways. You will see this breadth as you read the rest of this module. We will include references to other modules (e.g., see Module 6.1) to illustrate that the history that you are reading in this module had a direct effect on the modern understanding of behaviour that you will read about in the rest of this textbook.

STRUCTURALISM AND FUNCTIONALISM: THE BEGINNINGS OF PSYCHOLOGY Most contemporary psychologists agree that Wilhelm Wundt (1832–1920) was largely responsible for establishing psychology as an independent scientific field. Wundt established the first laboratory dedicated to studying human behaviour in 1879 at the University of Leipzig, where he conducted numerous experiments on how people sense and perceive. His primary research method was *introspection*, meaning "to look within." Introspection required a trained volunteer to experience a stimulus and then report each individual sensation he or she could identify. For example, if the volunteer was given a steel ball to hold in one hand, he would likely report the sensations of cold, hard, smooth, and heavy. To Wundt, these basic sensations were the mental "atoms" that combined to form the molecules of experience. Wundt also developed *reaction time* methods as a way of measuring mental effort. In one such study, volunteers watched an apparatus in which two metal balls swung into each other to make a clicking sound. The volunteers required about one-eighth of a second to react to the sound, leading Wundt to conclude that mental activity is not instantaneous, but rather requires a small amount of effort measured by the amount of time it takes to react. What made Wundt's work distinctly psychological was his focus on measuring mental events and examining how they were affected by his experimental manipulations.

Wundt's ideas made their way to the United States and Canada through students who worked with him. However, whereas Wundt's research often attempted to link a person's perceptions with concepts such as free will (a philosophy known as *voluntarism*), many of his students wanted to move psychological research in a different direction (Rieber & Tobinson, 1980). One student,

German scientist Wilhelm Wundt is widely credited as the "father" of experimental psychology.

Edward Titchener, adopted the same method of introspection used by Wundt to devise an organized map of the structure of human consciousness. His line of research, **structuralism**, *was an attempt to analyze conscious experience by breaking it down into basic elements, and to understand how these elements work together*. Titchener chose the term *elements* deliberately as an analogy with the periodic table in the physical sciences. He believed that mental experiences were made up of a limited number of sensations, which were analogous to elements in physics and chemistry. According to Titchener, different sensations can form and create complex compounds, just like hydrogen and oxygen can combine to form water—H_2O—or the hydroxide ion—OH^-. The challenge for psychologists was to determine which elements were grouped together during different conscious experiences and to figure out what caused these specific groupings to occur (Titchener, 1898).

The same year Wundt set up his first laboratory, an American scholar named William James (1842–1910) set out to write the first textbook in psychology, *The Principles of Psychology*, which was eventually published in 1890. Trained as a physician, James combined his knowledge of physiology with his interest in the philosophy of mental activity. Among his many interests, he sought to understand how the mind functions. In contrast to structuralism, which looks for permanent, unchanging elements of thought, James was influenced by Darwin's evolutionary

William James was a highly influential American psychologist who took a functionalist approach to explaining behaviour.

principles; he preferred to examine behaviour in context and explain how our thoughts and actions help us adapt to our environment. This led to the development of **functionalism,** *the study of the purpose and function of behaviour and conscious experience.* According to functionalists, in order to fully understand a behaviour, one must try to figure out what purpose it may have served over the course of our evolution. These principles are found today in the modern field of *evolutionary psychology*, an approach that interprets and explains modern human behaviour in terms of forces acting upon our distant ancestors (see Module 3.1). According to this approach, our brains and behaviours have been shaped by the physical and social environment that our ancestors encountered. Over the next century, this idea was extended to a number of subfields in psychology ranging from the study of brain structures to the study of social groups. Indeed, regardless of their research area, most psychologists are still fascinated by the question, *What function does the behaviour we're investigating serve?* In other words, *why* do we behave the way we do?

During the early years of psychology, the pioneers of this field were trying to find a way to use the methods and instruments of the natural sciences to understand behaviour. Although some of their techniques fell out of favour, by the beginning of the 20th century it was clear that the discipline of psychology was here to stay. With that sense of permanence in place, the second generation of psychologists could focus on refining the subject matter and the methods, and on turning psychology into a widely accepted scientific field.

THE RISE OF BEHAVIOURISM   Early in the 20th century, biologists became interested in how organisms learn to anticipate their bodily functions and responses. One of the first to do so was Professor Edwin Twitmyer (1873–1943), an American psychologist interested in reflexes. His work involved a contraption with a rubber mallet that would regularly tap the patellar tendon just below the kneecap; this, of course, causes a kicking reflex in most individuals. To make sure his volunteers were not startled by the mallet, the contraption would ring a bell right before the mallet struck the tendon. As is often the case in experiments, the technology failed after a number of these bell-ringing and hammer-tapping combinations: The machine rang the bell, but the hammer did not come down on the volunteer's knee. But the real surprise was this—the volunteer's leg kicked anyway! How did that happen? Because the sound of the bell successfully predicted the hammer, the ringing soon had the effect of the hammer itself, a process now called *classical conditioning* (see Module 6.1). The study of conditioning would soon become a focus of **behaviourism,** *an approach that dominated the first half of the 20th century of North American psychology and had a singular focus on studying only observable behaviour, with little to no reference to mental events or instincts as possible influences on behaviour.*

Twitmyer's research was coolly received when he announced his findings at the American Psychological Association meeting. Not a single colleague bothered to ask him a question. The credit for discovering classical conditioning typically goes to a Russian physiologist named Ivan Pavlov (1849–1936). Pavlov, who won the 1904 Nobel Prize for his research on the digestive system, noticed that the dogs in his laboratory began to salivate when the research technician entered the room and turned

Ivan Pavlov (on the right) explained classical conditioning through his studies of salivary reflexes in dogs.

on the device that distributed the meat powder (food). Importantly, salivation occurred *before* the delivery of food, suggesting that the dogs had learned an association between the technician and machine noises and the later appearance of food. This observation quickly led to more focused research on mechanisms of learning; the principles of learning that Pavlov and others identified provided a foundation for the behaviourist movement.

In North America, behaviourism was championed by John B. Watson, a researcher at Johns Hopkins University in Baltimore (1878–1958). As research accumulated on the breadth of behaviours that could be conditioned, Watson began to believe that all behaviour could ultimately be explained through conditioning. This emphasis on learning also came with stipulations about what could and could not be studied in psychology. Watson was adamant that only observable changes in the environment and behaviour were appropriate for scientific study. Methods such as Wundt's introspection, he said, were too subjective to even consider:

> *Psychology as the behaviorist views it is a purely objective natural science. Its theoretical goal is the prediction and control of behavior. Introspection forms no essential part of its methods. (Watson, 1913, p. 158)*

In the diplomatic world of science, this statement was akin to carving "Wundt sucks!" in a park bench. Watson believed so much in the power of experience (and so little in the power of genetics) that he was certain he could engineer a personality however he wished, if given enough control over the environment. Perhaps his most famous statement sums it up:

> *Give me a dozen healthy infants, well-formed, and my own specified world to bring them up in and I'll guarantee to take any one at random and train him to become any type of specialist I might select—doctor, lawyer, artist, merchant-chief and, yes, even beggar-man and thief, regardless of his talents, penchants, tendencies, abilities, vocations, and race of his ancestors. (John Broadus Watson, Behaviorism. Chicago: University of Chicago Press. p. 82, 1930.)*

After a rather public indiscretion involving a female graduate student (due to his wife's social status, his extramarital affair appeared on the front page of the Baltimore newspapers; Fancher, 1990), Watson was dismissed from his university job. But, he quickly found his new career—as well as his fortune—in advertising. Most advertisers at the time just assumed they should inform people about the merits of a product. Watson and his colleagues applied a scientific approach to advertising and discovered a consumer's knowledge about the product really was not that important, so long as he or she had positive emotions associated with it. Thus, Watson's company developed ads that employed behaviourist principles to form associations between a product's brand image and positive emotions.

If Pavlov's dogs could be conditioned to salivate when they heard a tone, what possibilities might there be for conditioning humans in a similar way? Modern advertisers want the logos for their brands of snacks or the trademark signs for their restaurants to bring on a specific craving, and some salivation along the way. And so, from beer commercials with scantily clad women dancing at parties, to car commercials with high-intensity music and vistas of the Cabot Trail, and from impossibly cute kittens playing with toilet paper rolls to giant billboards of bunnies and hippos pitching telecommunications products, the influence of John B. Watson and his colleagues on modern advertising is felt every day.

RADICAL BEHAVIOURISM   The study of learning was not limited to classical conditioning. As early as 1905, psychologists such as Edward Thorndike (1874–1949) had shown that the frequency of different behaviours could be changed based on whether or not that behaviour led to positive consequences or "satisfaction" (Thorndike, 1905). Taking up the reins from Thorndike was B. F. Skinner (1904–1990), another behaviourist who had considerable influence over North American psychology for several decades (see Module 6.2).

In Skinner's view, known as *radical behaviourism*, the foundation of behaviour was how an organism responded to rewards and punishments. This theory is logical in many ways—we tend to repeat actions that are rewarded (e.g., studying for exams leads to better grades, so we study for other exams) and avoid actions that lead to punishment (e.g., if you vomit after eating a 2L container of ice cream, you will be unlikely to do so again . . . for a while). In order to identify the principles of reward and

B. F. Skinner revealed how rewards affect behaviour by conducting laboratory studies on animals.

punishment, Skinner opted to use a tightly controlled experimental setup involving animals such as rats and pigeons. Typically, these studies occurred with animals held in small chambers in which they could manipulate a lever to receive rewards. The experimenter would control when rewards were available, and would observe the effects that changing the reward schedule had on the animals' behaviour. You might ask what this work had to do with human behaviour. The behaviourists believed that the principles of reward and punishment could apply to all organisms, both human and nonhuman. Indeed, Watson explicitly stated that behaviourist psychology "recognizes no line between man and brute" (Watson, 1913, p. 158).

HUMANISTIC PSYCHOLOGY EMERGES Psychology, by the mid-20th century, was dominated by two perspectives, behaviourism and Freudian psychoanalytic approaches, which had almost entirely removed free will from the understanding of human behaviour. To the behaviourists, human experience was the product of a lifetime of rewards, punishments, and learned associations. To the psychoanalysts, human experience was the result of unconscious forces at work deep in the human psyche. From both perspectives, the individual person was merely a product of forces that operated *on* her, and she had little if any control over her own destiny or indeed, even her own choices, beliefs, and feelings.

In contrast to these disempowering perspectives, a new movement of psychologists arose, which emphasized personal responsibility; free will; and the universal longing for growth, meaning and connection, and which highlighted the power that individuals possessed to shape their own consciousness and choose their own path through life. This new perspective, **humanistic psychology**, *focuses on the unique aspects of each individual human, each person's freedom to act, his or her rational thought, and the belief that humans are fundamentally different from other animals.* Among the many major figures of humanistic psychology were Carl Rogers (1902–1987) and Abraham Maslow (1908–1970). Both psychologists focused on the positive aspects of humanity and the factors that lead to a productive and fulfilling life. Humanistic psychologists sought to understand the *meaning* of personal experience. They believed that people could attain mental well-being and satisfaction through gaining a greater understanding of themselves, rather than by being diagnosed with a disorder or having their problems labelled. Both Rogers and Maslow believed that humans strive to develop a sense of self and are motivated to personally grow and fulfill their potential (see Module 12.3). This view stands in particular contrast to the psychoanalytic tradition, which originated from a medical model and, therefore, focused on illnesses of the body and brain. The humanistic perspective also contrasted with behaviourism in proposing that humans

had the freedom to act and a rational mind to guide the process.

THE BRAIN AND BEHAVIOUR The behaviourists and humanists were not the only researchers attempting to understand human abilities. Many neurologists, surgeons, and brain scientists were also focused on these questions. Notable among them was Donald Hebb (1904–1985), a Canadian neuroscientist working at the Montreal Neurological Institute. Hebb conducted numerous studies examining how cells in the brain change over the course of learning. He observed that when a brain cell consistently stimulates another cell, metabolic and physical changes occur to strengthen this relationship. In other words, cells that fire together wire together (Hebb, 1949; see Module 7.1). This theory, now known as *Hebb's Law*, demonstrated that memory—a behaviour that we can measure and that affects so many parts of our lives—is actually related to activity occurring at the cellular level (Brown & Milner, 2003; Cooper, 2005). It also reinforced the notion that behaviour can be studied at a number of different levels ranging from neurons (brain cells) to the entire brain. (Later research, discussed in Module 7.3, has noted that memory is related to social factors as well.)

Further evidence for the relationship between the brain and everyday behaviours came from the stimulating work of Wilder Penfield (1891–1976), founder and original director of the Montreal Neurological Institute. Along with his colleague, Herbert Jasper, Penfield developed a surgical procedure to help patients with epilepsy. This procedure involved removing cells from the brain regions where the seizures began; doing so would prevent the seizures from spreading to other areas of the brain. However, before operating, Penfield needed to find a way to map out the functions of the surrounding brain regions so that he could try to avoid damaging areas that performed important functions such as language. To do this, Penfield electrically stimulated each patient's brain while the patient was under local anesthetic (i.e., was awake, and therefore conscious). The patient was then able to report the sensations he experienced after each burst of electricity. Based on several patients' reports, Penfield was able to create precise maps of the sensory and motor (movement) cortices in the brain (Penfield & Jasper, 1951; Todman, 2008). Importantly, his work also showed that people's subjective experiences can be represented in the brain (see Module 3.3). This insight suggested that the simple learning model put forth by the behaviourists was not a complete representation of our complex mental world.

THE COGNITIVE REVOLUTION Although behaviourism dominated psychology in the United States and Canada throughout the first half of the 20th century, the view that observable behaviours were more important than thoughts and mental imagery was not universal.

Montreal Gazette/The Canadian Press

Donald Hebb made significant contributions to our understanding of memory and the brain.

Figure 1.8 The Whole Is Greater Than the Sum of Its Parts

The Gestalt psychologists emphasized humans' ability to see whole forms. For example, you probably perceive a sphere in the centre of this figure, even though it does not exist on the page.

with the structuralist goal of breaking experience into its individual parts. For example, if Wundt or Titchener were to hand you an apple, you would not think, "Round, red, has a stem …"; you would simply think to yourself, "This is an apple." Gestalt psychologists argued that much of our

In Europe, psychologists retained an emphasis on thinking, and ignored the North Americans' cries to study only what could be directly observed. The European focus on thought flourished through the early 1900s, long before psychologists in North America began to take seriously the idea that they could study mental processes, even if they could not directly see them. Thus, it was the work of European psychologists that formed the basis of the cognitive perspective. Early evidence of an emerging cognitive perspective concerned the study of memory. The German psychologist Hermann Ebbinghaus (1850–1909) collected reams of data on remembering and forgetting (see Module 7.2). British psychologist Frederick Bartlett (1886–1969) found that our memory was not like a photograph. Instead, our cultural knowledge and previous experiences shape what elements of an event or storyline are judged to be important enough to remember.

Another precursor to cognitive psychology can be seen in the early to mid-1900s movement of **Gestalt psychology**, *an approach emphasizing that psychologists need to focus on the whole of perception and experience, rather than its parts* (see Module 4.1). (*Gestalt* is a German word that refers to the complete form of an object; see Figure 1.8.) This contrasts

Montreal Gazette/The Canadian Press

Wilder Penfield, founder of the world-famous Montreal Neurological Institute, used electrical stimulation of the brain to discover how movement and touch were represented in the brain. Like Hebb's, many of his discoveries are still taught in psychology and neuroscience classes throughout the world.

thinking and experience occur at a higher, more organized level than Wundt emphasized; they believed that Wundt's approach to understanding experience made about as much sense as understanding water only by studying its hydrogen and oxygen atoms.

In the 1950s and 1960s—around the time that there was increasing interest in humanistic psychology—the scientific study of cognition was becoming accepted practice in North American psychology. The invention of the computer gave psychologists a useful analogy for understanding and talking about the mind (the *software* of the brain). Linguists such as Noam Chomsky argued that grammar and vocabulary were far too complex to be explained in behaviourist terms; the alternative was to propose abstract mental processes. There was a great deal of interest in memory and perception as well, but it was not until 1968 that these areas of research were given the name "cognitive psychology" by Ulrich Neisser (1928–2012). **Cognitive psychology** *is a modern psychological perspective that focuses on processes such as memory, thinking, and language.* Thus, much of what cognitive psychologists study consists of mental processes that are inferred through rigorous experimentation.

SOCIAL AND CULTURAL INFLUENCES   The vast majority of behaviourist and cognitive psychology research focuses on an individual's responses to some sort of stimulus. Missing from this equation, however, is that fact that people often have to respond to stimuli or events in the presence of other people. The effects of other people on one's behaviour have not been lost on psychologists; indeed, the recognition of this influence can be found in the very early years of psychology. An American psychologist, Norman Triplett (1861–1931), conducted one of the first formal experiments in this area, observing that cyclists ride faster in the presence of other people than when riding alone. Triplett published the first social psychology research in 1898, and a few social psychology textbooks appeared in 1908.

Despite the early interest in this field, studies of how people influence the behaviour of others did not take off until the 1940s. The events in Nazi-controlled Germany that led up to World War II contributed to the development of this new perspective in psychology. Images from the Holocaust highlighted the need to learn about the role that social factors play in human behaviour. Researchers (and the general public) wanted to understand how normal individuals could be transformed into brutal prison camp guards, how political propaganda affected people, and how society might address issues of stereotyping and prejudice (see Module 13.1). This research evolved into what is now known as **social psychology**, *the study of the influence of other people on our behaviour.*

However, psychologists also noted that not *all* people responded to social groups or the presence of others in the same way. While some people were transformed into prison camp guards in World War II, others objected and joined resistance movements. These individual differences were observable in normal, everyday life as well: Some

Social psychologists are often inspired to study human behaviours observed in real-world events. Some of these behaviour are heart-warming—others are not.

people are talkative and outgoing while others are quiet. These observations led to the development of **personality psychology**, *the study of how different personality characteristics can influence how we think and act.*

Although it's easy to think of social psychology (the effect of external factors) and personality psychology (the effect of internal traits) as being distinct, in reality, your personality and the social situations you are in interact. This relationship was most eloquently described by Kurt Lewin (1890–1947), the founder of modern social psychology. Lewin suggested that behaviour is a function of the individual and the environment, or, if you're a fan of formulas (and who isn't?), B = f{I,E}. What Lewin meant was that all behaviours could be predicted and explained through understanding how an individual with a specific set of traits would respond in a context that involved a specific set of conditions. Take two individuals as an

example: One tends to be quiet and engages in solitary activities such as reading, whereas the other is talkative and enjoys being where the action is. Now put them in a social situation, such as a large party at a university dorm or a small get-together at a friend's house. How will the two behave? Given the disparity between the individuals and between the two environments, we would suspect that very different behaviours would emerge for these two individuals in the different settings. The outgoing person may have a wonderful time at the big party, while the quiet person desperately tries to find someone to talk to or pretends to be fascinated by something on his phone. But, at the smaller get-together, the quieter person will likely be much more relaxed, while the outgoing person might be bored. Neither behaviour is *better*, but they are *different*. These outcomes illustrate the essence of Lewin's formulation of social psychology.

Module 1.2b Quiz:

The Beginnings of Contemporary Psychology

Know . . .

1. _____ was the study of the basic components of the mind, while _____ examined the role that specific behaviours may have served in our species' evolution.

   A. Structuralism; functionalism
   B. Behaviourism; functionalism
   C. Functionalism; structuralism
   D. Humanism; structuralism

Understand . . .

2. A distinct feature of behaviourism is its

   A. search for the deeper meaning of human existence.
   B. search for patterns that create a whole that is greater than its parts.
   C. use of introspection.
   D. exclusive emphasis on observable behaviour.

Apply . . .

3. Gwen is in search of the deeper meaning of her life, and would like to learn more about her potential as a human being. Which of the following types of psychologists would likely be most useful to her?

   A. Humanistic
   B. Cognitive
   C. Behaviourist
   D. Social

4. The Gestalt psychologists, with their focus on perception and experience, are closely linked to modern-day _____ psychologists.

   A. developmental
   B. social
   C. cognitive
   D. evolutionary

Emerging Themes in Psychology

The history of psychology is not over, of course. All of the fields discussed in the previous section of this module continue today. Indeed, psychology is expanding, examining new topics and using new research tools to provide interesting insights into human behaviour. In this section, we highlight five trends or topics that are becoming particularly prominent in psychology. This *is not* an exhaustive list of "hot topics." Instead, it is a list of important themes that are currently influencing the course of modern psychology.

PSYCHOLOGY OF WOMEN After reading earlier sections of this module, many readers might assume that psychology is the exclusive domain of older white men, many sporting impressive beards. In fact, this module *does* have photographs of nine prominent male psychologists (five with beards). There *were* female psychologists teaching and performing research during the early stages of the history of psychology. Indeed, Anna Freud (1895–1982) and Karen Horney (1885–1952) made groundbreaking contributions to our understanding of personality. The 1960s saw a dramatic shift in both the role of women in society and in the study of the psychology of women. Until then, many people believed that the male domination of society was due to innate differences between the sexes that made men better leaders; women were thought to be more agreeable and emotional. However, pioneering research from psychologists such as Sandra Bem began to change these views. Researchers began examining how sex differences in power were due in large part to the rampant sexism in politics, the business world, academia, and the home (Bem & Bem, 1973). They also examined how stereotypes could affect women's beliefs about their own abilities (Bem, 1981, 1993). This research led to changes that helped promote greater equality between the sexes. This important work continues today, with new generations of female *and male* psychologists working to promote equality.

Studies of the psychology of women also examine important issues such as women's health, violence toward women, and experiences that are unique to females (e.g., pregnancy). However, this field is not meant to appear "man hating" or exclusive. In fact, many researchers are interested in differences between the sexes and how they influence social behaviour. For instance, in Module 14.2, you will read about the research of Shelly Taylor, who examined sex differences in response to stress. She found that while males *in general* produce a "fight or flight" response to stress, females are more likely to seek out social supports, a tendency she called the "tend and befriend" response (Taylor et al., 2000). Although a complete description of the psychology of women requires its own course, the purpose of this section is to highlight this topic for readers so that they will see how important these types of questions can be for understanding human behaviour, and so that they can better appreciate the obstacles that many of these early researchers faced.

COMPARING CULTURES In addition to studying differences between the sexes, researchers have performed numerous studies examining how human behaviour differs across cultures. *Cross-cultural psychology* is the field that draws comparisons about individual and group behaviour among cultures; it helps us understand the role of society in shaping behaviour, beliefs, and values. Many cross-cultural studies compare the responses of North American research participants (generally psychology students like you) to those of individuals in non-Western countries such as China or Japan. However, Western countries with high immigration rates like Canada and the U.S. also provide researchers with the opportunity to compare the responses and experiences of first- and second-generation Canadians (Abouguendia & Noels, 2001; Gaudet et al., 2005). This type of research

Photograph Provided by Daryl Bem

Pioneering researchers such as Sandra Bem began the systematic study of the psychology of women.

therefore allows us to examine how people respond when being pulled in different directions by family history and the culture of their current country of residence. Such comparisons are also being performed using brain imaging, demonstrating that our social and cultural experiences can also be embedded in our brain tissue (Losin et al., 2010).

THE NEUROIMAGING EXPLOSION Although it has been possible to detect brain activity using sensors attached the scalp since the late 1920s, the use of brain imaging to study behaviour became much more common in the early 1990s. It was at this time that a technique known as *functional magnetic resonance imaging (fMRI)* was developed. fMRI allows us to reliably detect activity throughout the entire brain and to depict this activity on clear three-dimensional images (see Module 3.4). Initially, fMRI was used to examine relatively straightforward behaviours such as visual perception. However, it quickly became the "go to" tool for researchers interested in understanding the neural mechanisms for cognitive behaviours such as memory, emotion, and decision-making. This field, which combines elements of cognitive psychology and biopsychology is known as *cognitive neuroscience.*

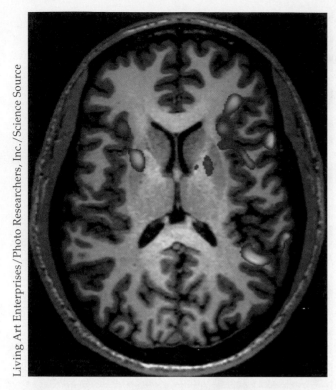

fMRIs allow us to reliably detect activity throughout the entire brain and to depict this activity in clear three-dimensional images.

As fMRI became accessible, researchers in other fields of psychology began to incorporate it into their studies. Psychologists studying social behaviours ranging from racism to relationships use fMRI in their experiments; this new field is known as *social neuroscience.* Neuroimaging has also been used to study personality traits and consumer behaviour. In fact, it is difficult to find an area not touched by the development of neuroimaging technologies.

THE SEARCH FOR THE POSITIVE Another rapidly growing area of psychology involves promoting human strengths and potentials. Rather than focusing on pathologies or negative events such as rejection, the goal of *positive psychology* is to help people see the good in their lives by promoting self-acceptance and improving social relationships with others. The eventual goal of this field is to help people experience feelings of happiness and fulfillment; in short, to help them flourish (Seligman & Csikszentmihalyi, 2000).

Positivity has been linked with improvements in some cognitive abilities (Fredrickson, 2003) and to changes in neural pathways associated with controlling your attention (Tang et al., 2010). In fact, researchers are only beginning to understand the potential benefits of positive thinking. Elements of positive psychology can be found in a number areas of psychological study, ranging from our motivation to achieve (Module 11.3) to techniques for coping with stress and psychological disorders (Modules 14.3 and 16.2).

PSYCHOLOGY IN THE REAL WORLD Finally, it is important to remember that psychology research isn't limited to the laboratory. Although many researchers are interested in the basic mechanisms of human behaviour,

Psychologists work in a number of applied settings. For example, researchers from a number of provinces are involved in important anti-bullying research. These studies are used to influence policies of provincial agencies and local school boards.

many others apply psychological science in different settings. *Applied psychology* can take place in schools, in the workplace, in the military, or in a number of other settings. For example, researchers at Memorial University in Newfoundland are performing research that will lead to improvements in how children are interviewed in the legal arena (Eastwood et al., 2016; Snook et al., 2014); researchers at the University of Alberta, University of Victoria, Queen's University, and Simon Fraser University examine other areas of psychology in the law, ranging from psychopathy to eyewitness testimony (Douglas et al., 2009; Lindsay et al., 2008). Psychologists across the country have come together to help develop anti-bullying policy and educational initiatives (http://www.prevnet.ca/). *Industrial/organizational psychologists* at the University of Guelph, University of Waterloo, and St. Mary's University, among others, apply psychological research to the workplace, helping to ensure that the work environment is fair for all employees. *Human factors psychologists* help to ensure that our interactions with technologies ranging from computer programs to airplane cockpits are intuitive and efficient. And, psychologists are also involved in

the promotion of environmentally sustainable behaviours, searching for factors that influence attitudes toward the environment and for ways to transform our society into one that works *with* nature, rather than against it (Hirsh & Dolderman, 2007; Nisbet & Gick, 2008). In short, psychological science affects every aspect of our society, even if we don't realize or appreciate it.

In conclusion, the trends that emerged during the formative years of psychology laid the foundation for the modern perspectives and theories we see today. Psychology is now a clearly established discipline—there are established venues such as professional organizations and journals to disseminate the results of psychological research. Although modern technology, such as brain imaging and computing, would astound psychology's founders, it is likely that they would find the results of modern research absolutely relevant to their own interests. It is also likely that they would be enthusiastic about the increasing levels of collaboration between the different areas of psychology, and about the current zeitgeist of treating human behaviour as a complex system with biological, psychological, and sociocultural components.

Module 1.2c Quiz:

Emerging Themes in Psychology

Know . . .

1. Cognitive neuroscience examines

   A. what computers can tell us about different cognitive functions.

   B. how functions like memory differ across cultures.

   C. how different brain areas are involved with different cognitive abilities.

   D. how the brains of different animals can help us understand evolutionary forces on behaviour.

Apply . . .

2. Which is NOT an example of applied psychology?

   A. Calculating how many words participants can remember from a lengthy list

   B. Examining whether the wording of questions influences the reports of people who witnessed a crime

   C. Testing ways to promote recycling in the workplace

   D. Examining different techniques to improve relations between police and the community

Module 1.2 Summary

1.2a   Know . . . the key terminology of psychology's history.

behaviourism
clinical psychology
cognitive psychology
determinism
dualism
empiricism
functionalism
Gestalt psychology
humanistic psychology
materialism
nature and nurture relationships
personality psychology
psychoanalysis
psychophysics
social psychology
structuralism
zeitgeist

1.2b   Understand . . . how various philosophical and scientific fields became major influences on psychology.

The philosophical schools of determinism, empiricism, and materialism provided a background for a scientific study of human behaviour. The first psychologists were trained as physicists and physiologists. Fechner, for example, developed psychophysics, whereas Titchener looked for the elements of thought. Darwin's theory of natural selection influenced psychologist William James's idea of functionalism—the search for how behaviours may aid the survival and reproduction of the organism.

1.2c   Apply . . . your knowledge to distinguish among the different specializations in psychology.

Apply Activity

Apply your knowledge to distinguish among different specializations in psychology. You should be able to read a description of a psychologist on the left of Table 1.1 and match her or his work to a specialization on the right.

1.2d   Analyze . . . how the philosophical ideas of empiricism and determinism are applied to human behaviour.

Psychology is based on empiricism, the belief that all knowledge—including knowledge about human behaviour—is acquired through the senses. All sciences, including psychology, require a deterministic viewpoint. Determinism is the philosophical tenet that all events in the world, including human actions, have a physical cause. The deterministic view is also essential to the sciences. Applying determinism to human behaviour has been met with resistance by many because it appears to deny a place for free will.

Table 1.1 Areas of Specialization within Psychology

1. I am an academic psychologist who studies various methods for improving study habits. I hope to help people increase memory performance and become better students. I am a(n) _____.

2. My work focuses on how the presence of other people influences an individual's acceptance of and willingness to express various stereotypes. I am a(n) _____.

3. I have been studying how childrearing practices in Guatemala, Canada, and Cambodia all share some common elements, as well as how they differ. I am a(n) _____.

4. I am interested in behaviours that are genetically influenced to help animals adapt to their changing environments. I am a(n) _____.

5. I help individuals identify problem areas of their lives and ways to correct them, and guide them to live up to their full potential. I am a(n) _____.

a. social psychologist
b. cross-cultural psychologist
c. cognitive psychologist
d. humanistic psychologist
e. evolutionary psychologist

Chapter 2
Reading and Evaluating Scientific Research

2.1 Principles of Scientific Research

- Five Characteristics of Quality Scientific Research 31
  Working the Scientific Literacy Model: Demand Characteristics and Participant Behaviour 35
- Module 2.1a Quiz 39
- Five Characteristics of Poor Research 39
- Module 2.1b Quiz 40
- Module 2.1 Summary 41

2.2 Scientific Research Designs

- Descriptive Research 43
  Working the Scientific Literacy Model: Case Studies as a Form of Scientific Research 44
- Module 2.2a Quiz 46
- Correlational Research 47
- Module 2.2b Quiz 49
- Experimental Research 49
- Module 2.2c Quiz 51
- Module 2.2 Summary 51

2.3 Ethics in Psychological Research

- Promoting the Welfare of Research Participants 54
  Working the Scientific Literacy Model: Animal Models of Disease 57
- Module 2.3a Quiz 59
- Ethical Collection, Storage, and Reporting of Data 59
- Module 2.3b Quiz 60
- Module 2.3 Summary 61

2.4 A Statistical Primer

- Descriptive Statistics 63
- Module 2.4a Quiz 66
- Hypothesis Testing: Evaluating the Outcome of a Study 66
  Working the Scientific Literacy Model: Statistical Significance 68
- Module 2.4b Quiz 69
- Module 2.4 Summary 70

Module 2.1   Principles of Scientific Research

Miodrag Gajic/E+/Getty Images

 ## Learning Objectives

2.1a Know . . . the key terminology related to the principles of scientific research.

2.1b Understand . . . the five characteristics of quality scientific research.

2.1c Understand . . . how biases might influence the outcome of a study.

2.1d Apply . . . the concepts of reliability and validity to examples.

2.1e Analyze . . . whether anecdotes, authority figures, and common sense are reliably truthful sources of information.

Does listening to classical music make you smarter? In January 1998, Governor Zell Miller of Georgia placed a $105 000 line in his state budget dedicated to purchasing classical music CDs for children (Sack, 1998). He even paid the conductor of the Atlanta Symphony to select optimal pieces for this CD. Apparently, Georgia's well-meaning governor and state legislature believed that providing young children with classical music would make them smarter. There were many reasons to believe this assumption might be true, starting with the observation that most people we know who listen to classical music seem intelligent and sophisticated. At around the same time that Georgia took this step, consumers were being bombarded with advertisements about "the Mozart effect," the scientific finding that listening to Mozart improves intelligence. Suddenly the classical sections at music stores were dusted off and moved to the front of the store, with signs drawing customers' attention to the intelligence-boosting effects of the CDs. Parents were told

that it was never too early to start their children on a Mozart program, even as fetuses residing in the womb. In fact, part of the Georgia budget, as well as the budget in some other U.S. states, was dedicated to handing out classical CDs along with hospital birth certificates. Eventually, the enthusiasm toward the Mozart effect died down after other scientists were unable to replicate the results. It turns out that the hype surrounding the Mozart effect was based on the results of one study (Rauscher et al., 1993). In this study, the twelve adult participants who listened to Mozart performed better than other adults on a test of spatial ability. These (temporary) differences in spatial intelligence were then inflated by the popular press to mean intelligence in general (a big difference!). Based on a single study, companies created a multi-million dollar industry, and the state of Georgia spent an extra $105 000.

This example is not meant to demonize the media or to mock Governor Miller. Rather, it highlights the need for greater scientific literacy in our society. The researchers did not make any unethical claims, the media were trying to present an interesting science-based story to their audience, and Governor Miller wanted to improve the well-being of the children in his state. But, because of a lack of scientific literacy and critical thinking, these events have now become a cautionary tale.

Focus Questions

1. We hear claims from marketers and politicians every day, but how can we evaluate them?

2. Can we evaluate evidence even if we are not scientists?

》 This chapter might be the most important one in the book. It will give you the training to become a critical consumer of scientific claims that are made by the media, corporations, politicians, and even scientists. Every time you open a news website, you encounter scientific topics such as how certain foods are linked with cancer risks or psychological issues, or you read about wonder drugs that will improve your grades. Some of this research is fantastic, but some is not. The goal of this chapter is to help you separate the good from the questionable, and to show you that asking tough questions about how research was designed and conducted is never a bad thing. Doing so prevents you from being tricked and manipulated . . . and from spending $105 000 on Mozart CDs.

What makes science such a powerful technique for examining behaviour? Perhaps the single most important aspect of scientific research is that it strives for objectivity. *Objectivity* assumes that certain facts about the world can be observed and tested independently from the individual who describes them (e.g., the scientist). Everyone— not just the experts—should be able to agree on these facts given the same tools, the same methods, and the same context. Achieving objectivity is not a simple task, however.

As soon as people observe an event, their interpretation of it becomes *subjective*, meaning that their knowledge of the event is shaped by prior beliefs, expectations, experiences, and even their mood. A scientific, objective approach to answering questions differs greatly from a subjective one. Most individuals tend to regard a scientific approach as one that is rigorous and demands proof. In this module, we will discuss the key elements of this scientific approach, and how it can help us understand human behaviour.

Five Characteristics of Quality Scientific Research

During the past few centuries, scientists have developed methods to help bring us to an objective understanding of the world. The drive for objectivity influences how scientific research is conducted in at least five ways. Quality scientific research meets the following criteria:

1. It is based on measurements that are *objective, valid,* and *reliable.*
2. It can be *generalized.*
3. It uses techniques that *reduce bias.*
4. It is made *public.*
5. It can be *replicated.*

As you will soon read, these five characteristics of good research overlap in many ways, and they will apply to any of the methods of conducting research that you will read about in this textbook.

SCIENTIFIC MEASUREMENT: OBJECTIVITY   The foundation of scientific methodology is the use of **objective measurements**, *the measure of an entity or behaviour that, within an allowed margin of error, is consistent across instruments and observers*. In other words, the way that a quality or a behaviour is measured must be the same regardless of who is doing the measuring and the exact tool being used. For example, weight is measured in pounds or kilograms. One kilogram in St. John's is the same as one kilogram in Victoria—researchers don't get to choose how much mass a kilogram is worth. Similarly, your weight will be the same regardless of whether you're using the scale in your bathroom or the scale in the change room at the gym. However, your weight *will* vary slightly from scale to scale—this is the margin of error mentioned in the definition. Scientists in a given field have to agree upon how much variability is allowable. Most people will be comfortable if their weight differs by one or two kilograms depending on the scale being used. But, if you weigh 70 kg on one scale and 95 kg on the other, then you know one of your measurement tools is inaccurate.

In this example, weight would be considered a **variable**, *the object, concept, or event being measured*. Variables are a key part of the research described in all of the chapters in this book ranging from perceptual processes, to learning and memory, to how we interact with each other, and so on. Each of these variables can be described and measured. For most of psychology's history, measurements involved observations of behaviour in different situations or examinations of how participants responded on a questionnaire or to stimuli presented on a computer. However, as technology advanced, so did the ability to ask psychological questions in new and interesting ways. High-tech equipment, such as functional magnetic resonance imaging (fMRI), allows researchers to view the brain and see which areas are activated while you perform different tasks such as remembering words or viewing emotional pictures. Other physiological measures might involve gathering samples of blood or saliva, which can then be analyzed for enzymes, hormones, and other biological variables

Figure 2.1 Operational Definitions

A variable, such as the level of intoxication, can be operationally defined in multiple ways. This figure shows operational definitions based on physiology, behaviour, and self-report measures.

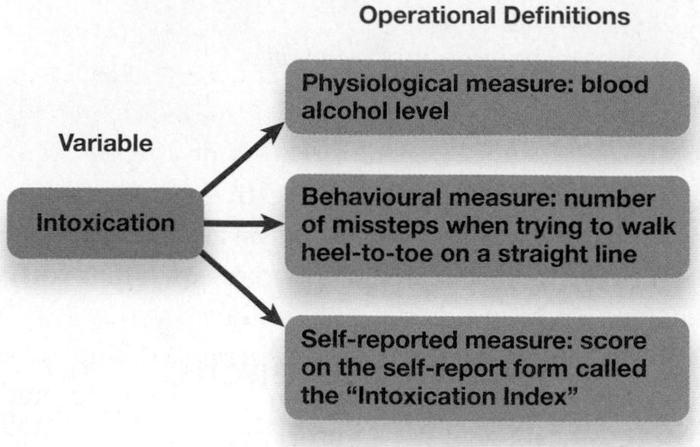

Operational Definitions

Variable

Intoxication

Physiological measure: blood alcohol level

Behavioural measure: number of missteps when trying to walk heel-to-toe on a straight line

Self-reported measure: score on the self-report form called the "Intoxication Index"

that relate to behaviour and mental functioning. With this greater number of measurement options, it's now possible to examine the same variable (e.g., anxiety) using a number of different techniques. Doing so strengthens our ability to understand the different elements of behaviour.

Regardless of the specific experimental question being asked, any method used by a researcher to measure a variable needs to include carefully defined terms. This isn't always as easy as it sounds. How would you define personality, shyness, or cognitive ability? This is the type of question a researcher would want to answer very carefully, not only for planning and conducting a study, but also when sharing the results of that research. In order to do so, researchers must decide upon a precise definition that other researchers can understand. These **operational definitions** *are statements that describe the procedures (or operations) and specific measures that are used to record observations* (Figure 2.1). For example, depression could be operationally defined as "a score of 20 or higher on the Beck Depression Inventory" (Beck & Steer, 1977), with the measure being a common and widely accepted clinical questionnaire.

The concept of operational definitions would have been helpful when the Georgia legislators considered implementing a state-wide program based on the Mozart effect. They should have asked, "How do the researchers define the outcome of their study? Do they mean listening to classical music makes you *smarter*, or just that it helps you remember better? Do they claim the effect is permanent, or does it occur only while listening to Mozart?" If these elected officials had examined the science behind the Mozart effect, they would have found that the results were based primarily on studies of adults (not infants) and led to a small effect on spatial reasoning abilities, not overall intelligence. In fact, subsequent studies by a different

group of researchers found the same type and size of effect after participants listened to a recording of a Stephen King horror novel, a result that companies producing Mozart-effect CDs clearly did not share with consumers. These conclusions make a very strong argument *against* investing the time, money, and effort in writing policy that relies so heavily on the Mozart effect. They also provide an important lesson to anyone making policy decisions that involve human behaviour: thoroughly examine the existing research literature *before* you make any decisions.

SCIENTIFIC MEASUREMENT: RELIABILITY, AND VALIDITY Once researchers have defined their terms, they then turn their attention toward the tools they plan to use to measure their variable(s) of interest. The behavioural measurements that psychologists make must be valid and reliable. **Validity** refers to *the degree to which an instrument or procedure actually measures what it claims to measure.* This seems like a simple task, but creating valid measures of complex behaviours is quite challenging. To go back to the depression example, researchers cannot simply ask people a few questions and then randomly decide that one score qualifies as depressed while another does not. Instead, for the measure to be valid, a particular score would have to differentiate depressed and non-depressed people in a way that accurately maps onto how these people actually feel (i.e., a depressed person would score differently than a non-depressed person). The creation of valid measures is therefore quite time-consuming and requires a great deal of testing and revising before the final product is ready for use.

In addition to being valid, a measurement tool must also be reliable. A measure demonstrates **reliability** *when it provides consistent and stable answers across multiple observations and points in time.* There are actually a number of different types of reliability that affect psychological research (see Figure 2.2). *Test-retest reliability* examines whether scores on a given measure of behaviour are consistent across test sessions. If your scores on a test of depression vary widely each time you take the test, then it is unlikely that your test is reliable. *Alternate-forms reliability* is a bit more complicated. This form of reliability examines whether different forms of the same test produce the same results. Why would you need multiple forms of a test? In many situations, a person will be tested on multiple occasions. For instance, individuals with brain damage might have their memory tested soon after they arrive at the hospital and then at one or more points during their rehabilitation. If you give these individuals the exact same test, it is possible that any improvement is simply due to practice. By having multiple versions of a test that produce the same results (e.g., two equally difficult lists of words as stimuli for memory tests), researchers and hospital

Figure 2.2 Test-Retest and Alternate-Forms Reliability

Test-retest reliability assumes that if the same test is taken at two or more different times, the scores will be similar. Alternate-forms reliability assumes that if a person completed different versions of the same test (e.g., Version A and Version B), her scores would be similar.

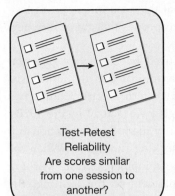

Test-Retest
Reliability
Are scores similar
from one session to
another?

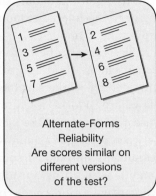

Alternate-Forms
Reliability
Are scores similar on
different versions
of the test?

workers can test individuals on multiple occasions and know that their measurement tools are equivalent.

A third type of reliability takes place when observers have to score or rate a behaviour or response. For example, psychologists might be interested in the effects of nonverbal behaviour when people interact, so they might videotape participants solving a problem and then have trained raters count the number of touches or the amount of eye contact that occurred during the experiment. As another example, participants might write down lengthy, open-ended responses to an experimenter's questions; these responses would then be rated on different variables by laboratory personnel. The catch is that more than one person must do the rating; otherwise it is impossible to determine if the responses were accurately measured or if the results were due to the single rater. Having more than one rater allows you to have *inter-rater reliability,* meaning that the raters agree on the measurements that were taken. If you design an experiment with clear operational definitions and criteria for the raters, then it is likely that you will have high inter-rater reliability.

Reliability and validity are essential components of scientific research. In addition, it is usually very important that your results are not limited to a small group of people in a single laboratory. Instead, it is ideal for these results to relate to other groups and situations—in other words, to be generalizable.

GENERALIZABILITY OF RESULTS Although personal testimony can be persuasive and (sometimes) interesting, psychologists are primarily interested in understanding behaviour *in general.* This involves examining trends and patterns that will allow us to predict how *most people* will respond to different stimuli and situations.

Generalizability *refers to the degree to which one set of results can be applied to other situations, individuals, or events.* For example, imagine that one person you know claimed that a memory-improvement course helped her raise her grades. How useful is the course? Based on this information, you might initially view the course favourably. However, upon further reflection, you'd realize that a number of other factors could have influenced your friend's improvement, not the least of which is that she is suddenly paying more attention to her grades! At this point, you would wisely decide to wait until you've heard more about the course before investing your hard-earned money. But, if you found out that several hundred people in your city had taken the same course and had experienced similar benefits, then these results will appear more likely to predict what would happen if you or other people took the course. They are generalizable.

As you can see from this example, one way to increase the possibility that research results will generalize is to study a large group of participants. By examining and reporting an average effect for that group, psychologists can get a much better sense of how individuals are *likely* to behave. But how large of a group is it possible to study? Ideally, it would be best to study an entire **population**, *the group that researchers want to generalize about.* In reality, the task of finding all population members, persuading them to participate, and measuring their behaviour is impossible in most cases. Instead, psychologists typically study a **sample**, *a select group of population members.* Once the sample has been studied, then the results may be generalized to the population as a whole.

It is important to note that how a sample is selected will determine whether your results are generalizable. If your sample for the memory-improvement course was limited to middle-aged male doctors in Edmonton, it would be difficult to generalize those results to all Canadians. Instead, researchers try to use a **random sample**, *a sampling technique in which every individual of a population has an equal chance of being included.* If you wanted to study the population of students at your school, for example, the best way to obtain a true random sample would be to have a computer generate a list of names from the entire student body. Your random sample—a subset of this population—would then be identified, with each member of the population having an equal chance of being selected regardless of class standing, gender, major, living situation, and other factors. Of course, it isn't always possible to use random sampling. This is particularly true if you are hoping that your results generalize to a large population or to all of humanity. In these cases, researchers often have to settle for **convenience samples**, *samples of individuals who are the most readily available*—for example, Introductory Psychology students.

Ariel Skelley/Blend Images/Getty Images

In a random sample, all members of a population (e.g., Winnipeggers) would be equally likely to be selected to be part of a study. This type of sampling is not always possible. Instead, many psychologists test their hypotheses using a convenience sample, such as psychology students.

In addition to generalizing across individuals, psychological research should generalize across time and location. Research should ideally have high **ecological validity**, *meaning that the results of a laboratory study can be applied to or repeated in the natural environment.* Sometimes this connection doesn't seem obvious, such as computer-based studies testing your ability to pay attention to different stimuli on a computer screen, but such seemingly artificial situations are assessing human abilities that are used in very common situations such as driving or finding a friend in a crowded classroom.

Although generalizability and ecological validity are important qualities of good research, we need to be careful not to *over-generalize*. For example, results from a convenience sample of university students might not predict how a group of elderly people would do on the same task. Conversely, in the Mozart effect example that began this module, most of the studies involved adults, yet companies and politicians assumed—with very little evidence—that the results would generalize to children, including infants. Therefore, scientific literacy also involves thinking critically about when it is *appropriate* to generalize results to other groups, times, and locations.

SOURCES OF BIAS IN PSYCHOLOGICAL RESEARCH
Of course, generalizability is only important if the experiment itself was conducted without bias. While creating objective, reliable, and valid measures is important in quality research, various types of bias can be unintentionally introduced by the researchers; this is known as a *researcher bias*. For instance, the experimenter may treat participants in different experimental conditions differently, thus

making it impossible to know if any differences were due to the experimental manipulation being tested or were instead due to the experimenter's behaviour. It is also possible for the participants, including animals, to introduce their own bias; these effects are known as *subject biases* or *participant biases*. Sometimes this bias will involve a participant trying to figure out what the experimenters are testing or trying to predict the responses that the researchers are hoping to find.

Bias can also be introduced by the act of observation itself. A wonderful example of this tendency was provided by workers at the Western Electric Company's Hawthorne Works, a Chicago-area factory in the 1920s. Researchers went to the factory to study the relationship between productivity and working conditions. When the researchers introduced some minor change in working conditions, such as an adjustment to the lighting, the workers were more productive for a period of time. When they changed another variable in a different study— such as having fewer but longer breaks—productivity increased again. What was not obvious to the researchers was that *any* change in factory conditions brought about increased productivity, presumably because the changes were always followed by close attention from the factory supervisors (Adair, 1984; Parsons, 1974). The results were due to the participants noticing that they were being observed rather than to the variables being manipulated. In honour of these observations, a *behaviour change that occurs as a result of being observed* is now known as the **Hawthorne effect**.

In most psychological research, the participants are aware that they are being observed. This presents a different form of problem, however. *Participants may respond in ways that increase the chances that they will be viewed favourably by the experimenter and/or other participants,* a tendency known as **social desirability** (or *socially desirable responding*). This type of bias is particularly relevant when the study involves an interview in which the researcher has face-to-face contact with the volunteers. As a result, many researchers now collect data using computers; this allows the participants to respond with relative anonymity, thereby reducing the desire to appear likeable.

In these situations, the participants can look for feedback—intentional or unintentional—and then adapt their responses to be consistent with what they think is expected of them. The potential biasing effects of social desirability show us a challenge faced by many psychologists: the need to limit the effect that they have on the results of their own study so that the results are due to the variables being studied rather than to the participants responding to cues from the researcher. As you will read in the next section, this challenge is not as simple as it appears.

Hawthorne Works Museum of Morton College.

The Hawthorne Effect, named after the Western Electric Company's Hawthorne Works in Chicago, states that individuals sometimes change their behaviour when they think they are being observed.

Working the Scientific Literacy Model

Demand Characteristics and Participant Behaviour

Results of psychological studies *should* provide uncontaminated views of behaviour. In reality, however, people who participate in psychological studies typically enter the research environment with a curiosity about the subject of the study. Researchers need to withhold as much detail as possible (while still being ethical) to get the best, least biased results possible.

What do we know about how bias affects research participants?

When studying human behaviour, a major concern is **demand characteristics**, *inadvertent cues given off by the experimenter or the experimental context that provide information about how participants are expected to behave.* Early psychologists often thought of the people being tested as "subjects." This term, still commonly used, assumes that individuals taking part in an experiment will follow instructions (within reason) and will not put too much thought into why certain stimuli are being presented or certain experimental manipulations are occurring. This view changed in the 1950s and 1960s, when psychologists began applying the scientific method to more cognitive topics. Researchers quickly realized that people are active participants in psychological experiments (Orne, 1962). These participants examine their environment and attempt to understand *why* certain stimuli and procedures are being used. As part of this attempt to "figure out" the study, participants will look to the behaviour of other people in that setting, including the experimenters. Sometimes, the actions, tone of voice, body language, or facial expressions of the experimenter can bias participants' responses. These demand characteristics can range from very subtle to obvious influences on the behaviour of research participants (Orne, 1962).

How can science test the effects of demand characteristics on behaviour?

Some classic examples of how demand characteristics can influence results come from the research of Rosenthal and colleagues. In one study, researchers told teachers in 18 different classrooms that a group of children had an "unusual" potential for learning, when in reality they were just a random selection of students (Rosenthal & Jacobson, 1966). After eight months of schooling, the children singled out as especially promising showed significant gains not just in grades, but in intelligence test scores, which are believed to be relatively stable. Why would this occur if the students were randomly selected? The best explanation is that the observers (i.e., teachers) assumed those students would do well, and were therefore more likely to pay attention to those students and to give them positive and encouraging feedback. These positive experiences with the teachers likely motivated these students to improve themselves. In other words, the students changed their behaviour patterns in order to match up with the expectations of the teachers. It is easy to see how similar experimenter effects could occur in psychological research studies.

Experimenter bias can even be found when people work with animals. When research assistants were told they were handling "bright" rats, it appeared that the animals learned significantly faster than when the assistants were told they were handling "dull" rats. Because it is unlikely that the rats were influenced by demand characteristics—they were not trying to give the researchers what they wanted—the most likely explanation for this difference is that researchers made subtle changes in how they treated the animals, and in how they observed and recorded behaviour (Rosenthal & Fode, 1963).

How can we critically evaluate the issue of bias in research?

This issue of bias in research is very difficult to overcome. Very few researchers intentionally manipulate their participants; however, as you have read, many times these influences are subtle and accidental. In most cases, experimenters (often graduate students and undergraduate research assistants) complete rigorous training and follow careful scripts when explaining experimental procedures to participants. These precautions help reduce experimenter effects. Additionally, many studies include interviews or questionnaires at the end of the study asking participants what they thought the experiment was about. This information can then be used by the experimenters to determine if the data from that participant are due to the experimental manipulation or to demand characteristics.

One way to evaluate whether participants' expectations are influencing the results is to create an additional manipulation in which the researchers give different groups of participants different expectations of the results. If the groups then differ when performing the same task, then some form of demand characteristic, in this case from the participant, might be influencing performance. Of course, it is not always practical to include an additional group in a study, and, when doing clinical research, manipulating expectations might not be ethical. But when researchers begin performing research on new topics or with new research methods, testing for demand characteristics would be a wise decision.

Why is this relevant?

Demand characteristics and other sources of bias all have the potential to compromise research studies. Given the time, energy, and monetary cost of conducting research, it is critical that results are as free from contamination as possible. The science of psychology involves the study of a number of very sensitive topics; the results are often used to help policymakers make better-informed decisions. Producing biased results will therefore have negative effects upon society as a whole. Demand effects are particularly problematic when studying clinical populations or when performing experiments with different types of clinical treatments. The results of these studies affect what we know about different patient populations and how we can help them recover from their different conditions. Biased results could therefore affect the health care of vulnerable members of our society.

The fact that demand characteristics can alter results is of particular importance for researchers investigating new drug treatments for different conditions. Patients enter treatment programs (and experiments) with a number of expectations. It turns out these expectations can produce their own unique effects.

TECHNIQUES THAT REDUCE BIAS Although biases can be a threat to the validity and reliability of psychological research, experimenters have established a number of techniques that can reduce the impact of subject and researcher biases. One of the best techniques for reducing subject bias is to provide anonymity and confidentiality to the volunteers. *Anonymity* means that each individual's responses are recorded without any name or other personal information that could link a particular individual to specific results. *Confidentiality* means that the results will be seen only by the researcher. Ensuring anonymity and confidentiality are important steps toward gathering honest responses from research participants. Participants are much more likely to provide information about sensitive

PSYCH@

The Hospital: The Placebo Effect

The demand effect that we know the most about is the **placebo effect**, *a measurable and experienced improvement in health or behaviour that cannot be attributable to a medication or treatment.* This term comes from drug studies, in which it is standard procedure for a group, unbeknownst to them, to be given an inactive substance (the placebo) so that this group can be compared to a group given the active drug. What often happens is that people in the placebo group report feeling better because they have the expectation that the drug will have an effect on their brain and body. This effect has been reported time and again—not just with drugs, but with other medical treatments as well. Why do people receiving a placebo claim to feel better? The initial explanation was that the patients' expectations caused them to simply convince themselves they feel better (i.e., it is "all in their head"). Other research noted that many people who are given a placebo show physiological evidence of relief from pain and nausea (Hrobjartsson & Gotzsche, 2010). Research conducted at the Rotman Research Institute in Toronto suggests that both of these explanations have merit. Helen Mayberg and colleagues (2002) found that people responding to placebos showed increased activity in several regions of the frontal lobes. This activity *may* relate to the participants creating a new "mental set" of their current state; in other words, creating the belief that their pain was going to decrease. Interestingly, these researchers also noted a decrease in activity in a number of other brain regions that might represent changes in the sensitivity of pain pathways. These results suggest that there are multiple ways for placebos to affect our responses to pain. Placebos are an important part of experimental research in psychology and related fields, so it is important to recognize their potential influence on how research participants respond.

issues like their sexual history, drug use, or emotional state if they can do so confidentially and anonymously.

In a related issue, participant anxiety about the experiment—which often leads to changes in how people respond to questions—can be reduced if researchers provide full information about how they will eventually use the data. Many people assume that psychologists are "analyzing them"; in fact, if you mention at your next family gathering that you're taking a psychology course, it is almost certain that someone will make a joke about this. If volunteers know that the data will *not* be used to diagnose psychiatric problems, affect their grades, or harm them in some other way, then their concerns about the study will be less likely to affect their performance.

Another source of bias in psychological research involves participants' expectations of the effects of a treatment or manipulation. We saw this tendency in the discussion of the placebo effect earlier. The critical element of the placebo effect is that the participants believe the pill or liquid they are consuming is actually a drug. If they knew that they were receiving a sugar pill instead of a pain medication, they would not experience any pain relief. Therefore, it is important that experiments involving drugs (recreational or therapeutic) utilize what are known as *blind* procedures. In a **single-blind study**, *the participants do not know the true purpose of the study, or else do not know which type of treatment they are receiving (for example, a placebo or a drug).* In this case, the subjects are "blind" to the purpose of the study. Of course, a researcher can introduce bias as well. This bias is not going to be overt. It is unlikely that a researcher will laugh and call the placebo group "suckers" and then play Pink Floyd albums and Spongebob cartoons for the people in the drug condition. But the researcher might unintentionally treat individuals in the two conditions differently, thus biasing the results. In order to eliminate this possibility, researchers often use a technique known as a **double-blind study**, *a study in which neither the participant nor the experimenter knows the exact treatment for any individual.* To carry out a double-blind procedure, the researcher must arrange for an assistant to conduct the observations or, at the very least, the researcher must not be told which type of treatment a person is receiving until after the study is completed.

Double-blind procedures are also sometimes used when researchers are testing groups that differ on variables such as personality characteristics or subtle demographic factors such as sexual orientation. If the experimenter knows that a participant has scored high on a test of psychopathy, she might treat him differently than she treated a person who scored low on the same test. Keeping the experimenter (and participants) blind to these results allows the research to remain objective. Therefore, researchers should use these techniques whenever possible.

SHARING THE RESULTS   Once a group of researchers has designed and conducted an objective experiment that is free of bias, it is important to communicate their findings to other scientists. Psychology's primary mode of communication is through academic journals. Academic journals resemble magazines in that they are usually soft-bound periodicals with a number of articles by different authors (online formats are typically available as well). Unlike magazines, however, journal articles represent primary research or reviews of multiple studies on a single topic. When scientists complete a piece of research, they may write a detailed description of the theory, hypotheses, measures, and results and submit the article for possible publication. You will not find journals or research books in your average mall bookstore because they are too technical and specialized for the general market (and are not exactly page-turners), but you will find thousands of them in your university library.

However, only a fraction of the journal articles that are written eventually get published. Rather, before research findings can be published, they must go through **peer review**, *a process in which papers submitted for publication in scholarly journals are read and critiqued by experts in the specific field of study*. In the field of psychology, peer review involves two main tasks. First, an editor receives the manuscript from the researcher and determines whether it is appropriate subject matter for the journal (for example, an article on 17th-century Italian sculpture would not be appropriate for publication in the *Journal of Cognitive Neuroscience*, which is focused on biological explanations for memory, thinking, language, and decision making). Second, the editor sends copies of the manuscript to a select group of peer reviewers—"peer" in this case refers to another professional working within the same field of study. These reviewers critique the methods and results of the research and make recommendations to the editor regarding the merits of the research. In this process, the editors and reviewers serve as gatekeepers for the discipline, which helps increase the likelihood that the best research is made public.

REPLICATION Once research findings have been published, it is then possible for other researchers to build upon the knowledge that you have created; it is also possible for researchers to double check whether or not your results simply occurred by chance (which does happen). Science is an ongoing and self-correcting process. The finest, most interesting published research study can quickly become obsolete if it cannot be replicated. **Replication** *is the process of repeating a study and finding a similar outcome each time.* As long as an experiment uses sufficiently objective measurements and techniques, and if the original hypothesis was correct, then similar results *should* be

achieved by later researchers who perform the same types of studies.

Results are not always replicated in subsequent investigations, however. Psychology, like many other scientific fields, is experiencing what the media call a "replication crisis." In 2015, the influential journal *Science* published a paper describing the efforts of a group of researchers—known as the Open Science Collaboration (OSC)—to replicate 100 studies that had been published in three well-known journals (OSC, 2015). Although one would hope that the vast majority of these studies would replicate, the results showed the opposite. Depending upon the statistical cut-offs used, only 36 to 47% of the studies were successfully replicated. This result was quite upsetting for most psychologists, as it implied that our field has some serious methodological problems. However, before assuming that psychology should be tossed aside, it is worth thinking about this issue in more detail. Psychology, like all sciences, has a publication bias in which successful and novel results are published and studies that showed no effects are not. Indeed, this bias is why replication is so important—it helps us determine if these published studies are simply statistical flukes. However, if a single replication attempt is unsuccessful, which result should we believe—the original published experiment or the failed attempt to replicate it? This dilemma was not only pointed out by critics of the original OSC paper (Gilbert et al., 2016), but was noted by some of the OSC researchers themselves. The solution appears to involve performing the same study a number of times to see if it generally produces similar results. Such a strategy was used by the Many Labs Project (MLP). (It is unclear why these replication teams give themselves catchy "squad names.") These researchers performed the same studies over 30 times and found that 10 of the 13 studies they critiqued were replicable (Klein et al., 2014). Regardless of the specific number of studies that can be replicated, however, these efforts send an important message to both researchers and students: replication is important and makes science better.

Incidentally, researchers have had a difficult time replicating the Mozart effect (Steele et al., 1997), the example describing at the beginning of this module. These results likely had Georgia Governor Zell Miller singing the blues.

Module 2.1a Quiz:

Five Characteristics of Quality Scientific Research

Know . . .

1. The degree to which an instrument measures what it is intended to measure is known as _____.

    A. validity

    B. generalizability

    C. verifiability

    D. reliability

2. When psychologists question how well the results of a study apply to other samples or perhaps other situations, they are inquiring about the _____ of the study.

    A. validity

    B. generalizability

    C. verifiability

    D. reliability

Understand . . .

3. In a single-blind study, the participants do not know the purpose of the study or the condition to which they are assigned. What is the difference in a double-blind study?

    A. The researcher tells the participants the purpose and their assigned conditions in the study.

    B. The participants also do not know when the actual study begins or ends.

    C. The researcher also does not know which condition the participants are in.

    D. The participants know the condition to which they have been assigned, but the researcher does not.

Apply . . .

4. Dr. Rose gives a standardized personality test to a group of psychology majors in January and again in March. Each individual's score remains nearly the same over the two-month period. From this, Dr. Rose can infer that the test is _____.

    A. reliable

    B. generalizable

    C. objective

    D. verified

Five Characteristics of Poor Research

In the preceding section, you read about for the characteristics of quality research. It is generally safe to assume that the opposite characteristics detract from the quality of research. Good research uses valid, objective measures; poor research uses measures that are less valid, less reliable, and, therefore, less likely to be replicable. However, other issues must also be scrutinized if you hear someone make a scientific-sounding claim. Most claims are accompanied by what might sound like evidence, but evidence can come in many forms. How can we differentiate between weak and strong evidence? Poor evidence comes most often in one of five varieties: untestable hypotheses, anecdotes, a biased selection of available data, appeals to authority, and appeals to (so-called) common sense.

Perhaps the most important characteristic of science is that its hypotheses are testable. For a hypothesis to be testable, it must be **falsifiable**, meaning that *the hypothesis is precise enough that it could be proven false.* If a hypothesis is not falsifiable, that means that there is no pattern of data that could possibly prove that this view is wrong; instead, there is always a way to reinterpret the results to make the hypothesis match the data. If you cannot disconfirm a hypothesis, then there is no point in testing it. There are very few examples of unfalsifiable hypotheses in modern psychology. However, early personality work by Freud did suffer from this problem (although, to be fair, he wasn't trying to create a testable theory). Briefly, Freud believed that our personality consisted of three components: the id (which was focused on pleasure), the superego (which was based on following rules), and the ego (which attempted to balance the two opposing forces). Although this theory provided wonderful metaphors for behaviour, it is impossible to test. If a person does not behave in the predicted fashion, the analyst can simply say that the other personality component (e.g., the id) was more involved at that moment. There would be no way to prove him wrong. Luckily, researchers have built upon Freud's pioneering work and have created much more scientific (and falsifiable) theories of personality.

A second characteristic of poor research is the use of **anecdotal evidence**, *an individual's story or testimony about an observation or event that is used to make a claim as evidence.* For example, a personal testimonial on a product's webpage might claim that a man used subliminal weight-loss recordings to lose 50 pounds in six months. But there is no way of knowing whether the recordings were responsible for the person's weight loss; the outcome could have been due to any number of things, such as a separate physical problem or changes in food intake and lifestyle that had nothing to do with the subliminal messages. In fact, you do not even know if the anecdote itself is true: The "before" and "after" photos could easily be doctored. Therefore, we must be wary of such anecdotal claims. If they are not backed up by a peer-reviewed scientific study, then we should view the claims with caution.

Figure 2.3 Data Selection Bias

People with a particular political or economic agenda can still make claims that appear scientific if they perform a biased selection of the available data. Groups opposed to the idea that human activity is playing a role in global warming often point to published research supporting their view. However, when one examines *all* of the data on global warming, it appears that negative findings make up less than 1% of the results, suggesting that these individuals are full of hot air.

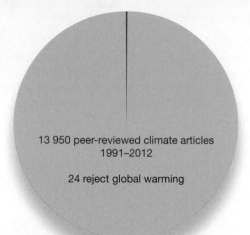

13 950 peer-reviewed climate articles
1991–2012

24 reject global warming

Source: 1991-2012 Pie Chart, Retrieved from http://www.jamespowell.org. Reprinted with permission of James Powell.

However, we still need to be careful even if a scientific claim is backed up by published data. It is possible that some individuals—particularly politicians and corporations—might present only the data that support their views. A beautiful example of this *data selection bias* is shown in the debate over whether human behaviour is a major cause of climate change. A climate-change denier could point out that 24 peer-reviewed scientific studies cast doubt on whether human behaviour is a cause of global warming. Twenty-four sounds like a large body of research. However, James Powell, a member of the U.S. National Science Board,

carefully examined all of the climate-change data from 1991–2012 and found 13 926 papers supporting this view (see Figure 2.3). Therefore, a very selective slice of the data would present one (biased) result, but a thorough and scientific representation of the data would present an entirely different view of the same issue.

The fourth kind of questionable evidence is the **appeal to authority**—*the belief in an "expert's" claim even when no supporting data or scientific evidence is present.* Expertise is not actually evidence; "expert" describes the person making the claim, not the claim itself. It is entirely possible that the expert is mistaken, dishonest, or misquoted. True experts are good at developing evidence, so if a claim cites someone's expertise as evidence, then you should see whether the expert offers the corresponding data to support the claim. It is not unusual for people to find that an expert's claim actually has no evidence backing it, but rather that it is simply an opinion. It is also possible that that the experts have a hidden agenda or a conflict of interest, such as when scientists funded by the oil industry produce research that says human behaviour has no effect on the climate.

Finally, the evidence may consist of an **appeal to common sense**, *a claim that appears to be sound, but lacks supporting scientific evidence.* For example, many people throughout history assumed the world was the stationary centre of the universe. The idea that the Earth could orbit the sun at blinding speeds was deemed nonsense—the force generated would seemingly cause all the people and objects to be flung into space!

In addition to common sense, beliefs can originate from other potentially unreliable sources. For example, *appeals to tradition* ("We have always done it this way!") as well as their opposite, *appeals to novelty* ("It is the latest thing!"), can lead people to believe the wrong things. Claims based on common sense, tradition, or novelty may be worthy of consideration, but whether something is true cannot be evaluated by these standards alone. Instead, what we need is careful and objective testing. What we need is science.

Module 2.1b Quiz:

Five Characteristics of Poor Research

Know . . .

1. Claiming that something is true because "it should be obvious" is really just _____.
   A. anecdotal evidence
   B. an appeal to common sense
   C. an appeal to authority
   D. generalizability

Understand . . .

2. Appeals to authority do not qualify as good evidence because
   A. they always lack common sense.
   B. authority figures are quite likely to distort the truth.

   C. authority does not mean that there is sound, scientific evidence.
   D. authority is typically based on anecdotal evidence.

Apply . . .

3. Ann is convinced that corporal punishment (e.g., spanking) is a good idea because she knows a child whose behaviour improved because of it. Whether or not you agree with her, Ann is using a flawed argument. Which type of evidence is she using?
   A. Anecdotal
   B. Objective
   C. Generalizable
   D. Authority-based

Module 2.1 Summary

2.1a   Know . . . the key terminology related to the principles of scientific research.

anecdotal evidence
appeal to authority
appeal to common sense
convenience samples
demand characteristics
double-blind study
ecological validity
falsifiable
generalizability
Hawthorne effect
objective measurements
operational definitions
peer review
placebo effect
population random sample
reliability
replication
sample
single-blind study
social desirability
validity
variable

2.1b   Understand . . . the five characteristics of quality scientific research.

These characteristics include that (1) measurements are objective, valid, and reliable; (2) the research can be generalized; (3) it uses techniques that reduce bias; (4) the findings are made public; and (5) the results can be replicated. For example, objective, valid, and reliable measurements make it possible for other scientists to test whether they could come up with the same results if they followed the same procedures. Psychologists typically study samples of individuals; their goal is usually to describe principles that generalize to a broader population. Single- and double-blind procedures are standard ways of reducing bias. Finally, the process of publishing results is what allows scientists to share information, evaluate hypotheses that have been confirmed or refuted, and, if needed, replicate other researchers' work.

2.1c   Understand . . . how biases might influence the outcome of a study.

Demand characteristics affect how participants respond in research studies—understandably, they often attempt to portray themselves in a positive light, even if that means not answering questions or behaving in a fully truthful manner. Researchers can also influence the outcomes of their own studies, even unintentionally.

2.1d   Apply . . . the concepts of reliability and validity to examples.

Try this activity to see how well you can apply these concepts.

Apply Activity

Read the following descriptions and determine whether each scenario involves an issue with reliability or validity.

1. Dr. Williams is performing very standard physiological recording techniques on human participants. Each morning he checks whether the instruments are calibrated and ready for use. One day he discovers that although the instruments are still measuring physiological activity, their recordings are not as sensitive as on previous testing days. *Would this affect the reliability or validity of his research? Explain.*

2. Dr. Nielson uses a behavioural checklist to measure happiness in the children he studies at an elementary school. Every time he and his associates observe the children, they reach near-perfect agreement on what they observed. Another group of psychologists observes the same children in an attempt to identify which children are energetic and which seem tired and lethargic. It turns out that the same children whom Dr. Nielson identifies as happy, using his checklist, are also the children whom the second group of psychologists identify as energetic. *It appears there may be a problem with Dr. Nielson's measure of happiness. Do you think it is a problem of reliability or validity? Explain.*

2.1e   Analyze . . . whether anecdotes, authority figures, and common sense are reliably truthful sources of information.

To evaluate evidence, you should ask several questions. First, is someone supplying anecdotal evidence? As convincing as a personal testimony may be, anecdotal evidence is not sufficient for backing any claim that can be scientifically tested. Second, is support for the claim based on the words or endorsement of an authority figure? Endorsement by an authority figure is not necessarily a bad thing, as someone who is an authority at something should be able to back up the claim. But the authority of the individual alone is not satisfactory, especially if data gathered through good scientific methods do not support the claim. Finally, common sense also has its place in daily life, but by itself is insufficient as a final explanation for anything. Explanations based on good scientific research should override those based on common sense.

Module 2.2   Scientific Research Designs

Andersen Ross / Blend Images / Getty Images

 ## Learning Objectives

2.2a   Know . . . the key terminology related to research designs.

2.2b   Understand . . . what it means when variables are positively or negatively correlated.

2.2c   Understand . . . how experiments help demonstrate cause-and-effect relationships.

2.2d   Apply . . . the terms and concepts of experimental methods to research examples.

2.2e   Analyze . . . the pros and cons of descriptive, correlational, and experimental research designs

Can your attitude affect your health? This is the old question of "mind over matter," and psychologist Rod Martin from Western University in London, ON, thinks the answer is definitely yes. He says that if you can laugh in the face of stress, your psychological and physical health will benefit. Martin has found several interesting ways to build evidence for this argument (Martin, 2002, 2007). For example, he developed a self-report instrument that measures sense of humour. People who score high on this measure—those who enjoy a good laugh on a regular basis—appear to be healthier in a number of ways. As interesting as this evidence is, it simply illustrates that humour and health are related—there is no guarantee that one causes the other. To make such a claim, researchers would have to use the experimental method, one of the many research designs discussed in this module.

Focus Questions

1.   What are some of the ways researchers make observations?

2.   Do some research techniques provide stronger evidence than others?

》   Psychologists always begin their research with a *research question*, such as "What is the most effective way to study?", "What causes us to feel hungry?", or "How does attitude affect health?" In most cases, they also make a prediction about the outcome they expect—the hypothesis. Psychologists then create a **research design**, *a set of methods that allows a hypothesis to be tested.* Research designs influence how investigators (1) organize the stimuli used to test the hypothesis, (2) make observations, and (3) evaluate the results. Because several types of designs are available, psychologists must choose the one that best addresses the research question and that is most suitable to the subject of their research. Before we examine different research designs, we should quickly review the characteristics that all of them have in common.

- *Variables.* A variable is a property of an object, organism, event, or something else that can take on different values. How frequently you laugh is a variable that could be measured and analyzed.

- *Operational definitions.* Operational definitions are the details that define the variables for the purposes of a specific study. For sense of humour, this definition might be "the score on the Coping Humour Scale."

- *Data.* When scientists collect observations about the variables of interest, the information they record is called data. For example, data might consist of the collection of scores on the Coping Humour Scale from each individual in the sample.

These characteristics of research designs are important regardless of the design that is used. However, a number of other factors will guide the researchers as they select the appropriate research design for their topic of interest.

Descriptive Research

The beginning of any new line of research must involve descriptive data. Descriptive research answers the question of "what" a phenomenon is; it describes its characteristics. Once these observations have been performed and the data examined, they can be used to inform more sophisticated future studies that ask "why" and "how" that phenomenon occurs.

These descriptions can be performed in different ways. **Qualitative research** *involves examining an issue or behaviour without performing numerical measurements of the variables.* In psychology, qualitative research often takes the form of interviews in which participants describe their thoughts and feelings about particular events or experiences (Madill & Gough, 2008). For example, researchers at St. Francis Xavier University in Nova Scotia performed a qualitative study of how males and females experienced "friends with benefits" relationships (Weaver et al., 2011). As you likely know, "friends with benefits" refers to sexual activity that occurs between partners who do not view the relationship as being romantic. In this study, the researchers performed a semi-structured interview with 16 female and 10 male students. Although the interview contained six primary questions that would be asked over the course of the meeting, the interviews varied widely from person to person, as each individual had a different experience

with their friends-with-benefits relationship. In this case, the fact that the researchers weren't restricted to numerical data helped them answer their research question.

Quantitative research, on the other hand, *involves examining an issue or behaviour by using numerical measurements and/or statistics.* The majority of psychological studies are quantitative in nature. These designs can involve complex manipulations (discussed later in this module); but, it is also possible to perform more descriptive studies using numbers. For instance, if you wanted to examine friends with benefits quantitatively, you could conduct an interview or survey in which participants provided specific responses to questions (e.g., "On a scale of 1 (sad) to 7 (happy), how did you feel when your friends-with-benefits relationship ended?").

Here are a few other examples of descriptive research questions:

- How many words can the average 2-year-old speak?

- How many hours per week does the typical university student spend on homework?

- What proportion of the population will experience depression or an anxiety disorder at some point in their lives?

As you can see, research questions can address the appearance of a behaviour, its duration or frequency, its prevalence in a population, and so on. To answer these questions, researchers usually gather data using one or more of the following designs: *case studies*, *naturalistic observation*, and *surveys and questionnaires*.

CASE STUDIES   A **case study** *is an in-depth report about the details of a specific case.* Rather than developing a hypothesis and then objectively testing it on a number of different individuals, scientists performing a case study describe an individual's history and behaviour in great detail. Of course, case studies are not performed on just anyone. They are generally reserved for individuals who have a very uncommon characteristic or have lived through a very unusual experience.

Perhaps the most famous case study in psychology (and neurology) is that of Phineas Gage (1823–1860). Gage was a foreman working for the Rutland and Burlington Railroad Company in the northeastern U.S. state of Vermont. On September 13, 1848, 25-year-old Gage was helping his crew blast through a rocky outcrop near the town of Cavendish and was involved in an accident that caused an iron rod to be propelled upwards underneath Gage's eye and through his head. According to the original medical report of the incident (Harlow, 1848; available online for interested readers), the iron rod was found 25 m away, suggesting that it was travelling very quickly as it tore through Gage's brain.

Amazingly, Gage survived the accident, although his physical recovery took most of a year (Bigelow, 1850;

Phineas Gage proudly holding the tamping iron that nearly killed him, and that made him one of the most famous names in the history of psychology and neuroscience. The information learned from case studies of Gage led to hundreds of subsequent scientific studies that have helped researchers learn a great deal about the frontal lobes of the brain. Interestingly, over the course of a few years, Gage slowly recovered enough of his self-control to hold down different jobs, including one as a long-distance stagecoach driver in South America (Macmillan, 2008); however, he never did recover all of his self-control. Had doctors paid more attention to this partial recovery, it would have been one of the first reported cases of the brain's ability to compensate and repair itself after injury.

Harlow, 1849). However, it quickly became apparent that Gage's injuries were not limited to physical damage; his mental state had also been affected. Reports indicate that while he had been a reputable citizen prior to the accident, afterward he became much more impulsive, inconsiderate, indecisive, and impatient. Harlow (1868) reported that Gage's friends claimed that the changes were so pronounced that he "was no longer Gage." The doctors treating Gage rightfully concluded that these sudden changes were due to the brain damage that he had suffered. Examination at the time of the accident—which involved Dr. Harlow sticking his finger into the hole in Gage's head—suggested that this damage was located in the frontal lobes of the brain, a region now known to be involved in a number of complex behaviours including decision making and emotional regulation (see Modules 8.2 and 11.4). Because Gage's case was documented in a series of detailed case-study reports, it was possible for future doctors and researchers to use this information to gain a better understanding of the role of the frontal lobes and the problems that emerge when this brain area is damaged.

The case of Phineas Gage is obviously quite striking. However, although case studies tell us a lot about an individual's condition, is it really science? Different researchers have different opinions about the merit of such reports, with some viewing them as important scientific contributions and others viewing them as simply interesting stories.

Working the Scientific Literacy Model

Case Studies as a Form of Scientific Research

Case studies allow the clinician or researcher to present more details about an individual than would be possible in a research report involving a number of participants; however, this detail comes at a price. Is a thorough description of a single individual still a form of science or is it simply an example of anecdotal evidence?

What do we know about using case studies as a form of scientific research?

Case studies have been a form of psychological research for over a century. Freud used case studies of unique patients when he initially described many of his theories of personality and development. Case studies have also been critical for our understanding of the brain. Phineas Gage was just one of many unique neurological patients who have taught us how different areas of the brain influence particular behaviours. In each situation, the researchers described their patient in great detail so the case study could improve the treatment of similar patients in the future.

Case studies can also be useful in describing symptoms of psychological disorders and providing detailed descriptions about specific successes or failures in their treatment. One recently published example of a case study did both (Elkins & Moore, 2011). The authors of this study described the experience of a certain type of anxiety disorder and the steps used in therapy to treat the anxiety over a 16-week period. They were able to document how and when changes occurred and the effects of the treatment on other aspects of the individual's life. This level of detail would not be available if the authors had not focused on a single case. However, as case studies only describe a single individual, there is no guarantee that the findings can be generalized to other people and situations.

How can science test the usefulness of case studies?

Although it is tempting to view case studies as simply being descriptions of an individual, they can also serve another important scientific function: They can be used to test an existing hypothesis. For example, until a couple of years ago, researchers thought that the amygdala—a fear centre in the brain—was essential for emotional information to grab our attention (e.g., the way your attention is almost always drawn to a spider walking across your ceiling). It made sense that a fear centre would be a necessary part of a fear response. Brain-imaging studies showed that this structure was active when these types of images were displayed to healthy participants. But, what would happen if someone with no amygdala on either side of her brain was put in this situation? A case study with one such patient (there are fewer than 300 worldwide) found that her attention was still grabbed by emotional stimuli (Tsuchiya et al., 2009). This told researchers that their models of how emotion and attention work together were too simplistic, and forced them to look at other brain structures that could be influencing these processes. In other words, the case study was used not to generate hypotheses, but to actually test an existing scientific theory.

How can we critically evaluate the role of case studies in research?

The above section demonstrates that case studies can help guide our understanding of existing scientific theories. Case studies can also be used to help scientists form hypotheses for future research studies. Take Phineas Gage, for example. Although there are very few, if any, other reports of individuals experiencing a tamping rod shooting through their frontal lobes, patients who suffered damage to the frontal lobes after car accidents and strokes have noted impairments similar to those suffered by Gage. Specifically, these individuals became more impulsive and risk-prone than they had been before their accident (Bechara et al., 1994; Damasio, 1994). Researchers have also created lesions similar to Phineas Gage's in animal subjects (e.g., laboratory rats) and observed similar tendencies (Quirk & Beer, 2006).

Researchers can also use computer simulations to model the effects of this form of brain damage. In one study—cheekily entitled "Spiking Phineas Gage"—Brandon Wagar and Paul Thagard (2004) of the University of Waterloo created a computerized neural network that used both cognitive and emotional information to produce simple decisions. After the network "learned" the task, the researchers altered its parameters so that the frontal lobe node of the network did not function properly. As predicted, this network's responses quickly became more dependent upon emotional impulses, just like patients with frontal-lobe damage such as Phineas Gage.

Why is this relevant?

These studies demonstrate that case studies are not simply anecdotes that scientists tell each other when they sit around the campfire. The case study of a single patient who somehow survived a terrifying brain injury has stimulated hundreds of scientific research papers leading to improvements in our understanding of how the brain works. Fittingly, such information will be essential in the treatment of any modern-day Phineas Gages. As you continue reading this textbook, you'll be introduced to a number of unique individuals whose stories have informed and guided psychological science for over a century. Without them, our understanding of topics ranging from vision to memory to language to emotions would not be as sophisticated as it has become. These topics would also lack the story-like narratives that make psychology so compelling.

Of course, case studies are often limited to individuals with unique conditions or experiences. They cannot be used to answer all types of research questions. For instance, there are times when a researcher might be interested in how groups of people or animals behave in environments outside of the controlled laboratory setting or interview room. In these situations, an entirely different form of descriptive research is necessary to examine psychological behaviours.

NATURALISTIC OBSERVATION   An alternative form of descriptive research is to observe people (or animals) in their natural settings. When psychologists engage in such **naturalistic observations**, *they unobtrusively observe and record behaviour as it occurs in the subject's natural environment.* The key word here is "unobtrusively"; in other words, the individuals being observed shouldn't know that they are being observed. Otherwise, the mere act of observation could change the participants' behaviours (imagine how your conversations with friends would change if you knew a psychologist was listening and taking notes). Most students have seen television programs about scientists in search of chimpanzees in a rain forest or driving a Range Rover in pursuit of a herd of elephants. This certainly is a form of observation, but there is more to it than just watching animals in the wild. When a scientist conducts naturalistic observation research, she is making systematic observations of specific variables according to operational definitions. By having a very precise definition of what a variable is and how it will be measured, researchers using naturalistic observations can ensure that their results are objective and that different people observing the same environment would score the behaviours in the same way (e.g., two observers would both call the same movement by a chimpanzee a grooming behaviour).

Although it may appear that naturalistic observation is only useful for animal studies or nature programs on TV, there have been a number of interesting human-focused naturalistic observation studies conducted as well. For example, a study conducted by psychologists at Carleton University in Ottawa measured the behaviour of spectators at youth hockey games (Bowker et al., 2009). These researchers were specifically interested in the types of comments made by spectators—the intensity of the remarks, who made them (male vs. female), and who they were directed toward (players, other spectators, or everyone's favourite target, the referees), among other variables. They also examined whether the observed trends changed depending upon whether the game was in a highly competitive or a more recreational league. The researchers found that females made more comments than males; these comments were largely positive and directed toward the players. Males tended to make more negative comments as well as directions on how to improve play (e.g., "Skate faster!"). Both female and male spectators made more negative comments when watching competitive, as opposed to recreational, leagues; these comments were largely directed toward the referees. Based on these observations, which involved five observers attending 69 hockey games, the researchers concluded that the behaviour of spectators is not as negative and unsettling as is often reported in the media (Bowker et al., 2009).

Thus, naturalistic observations can occur anywhere that behaviours occur, be it in "nature," in a hockey rink, or even in a bar (Graham & Wells, 2004). The key point is that the researchers must pay attention to specific variables and use operational definitions. However, naturalistic observations may not always provide researchers with the specific types of information they are after. In these cases, researchers may need to adopt a different research strategy in order to describe a given behaviour.

SURVEYS AND QUESTIONNAIRES Another common method of descriptive research used by psychologists is **self-reporting**, *a method in which responses are provided directly by the people who are being studied, typically through face-to-face interviews, phone surveys, paper and pencil tests, and web-based questionnaires.* These methods allow researchers to assess attitudes, opinions, beliefs, and abilities.

Despite the range in topics and techniques, their common element is that the individuals speak for themselves. Surveys and questionnaires are still a method of observation, but the observations are provided by the people who are being studied rather than by the psychologist.

Although this method initially sounds simple, the creation of objective survey and questionnaire items is extremely challenging. Care must be taken not to create biased questions that could affect the results one way or another. If you're interested in studying emotional sensitivity, you can't ask, "Given that men are drooling pigs, how likely are they to notice someone is unhappy?" Similarly, if you're studying a subject that some individuals might not want to openly discuss, it is important to develop questions that touch on the issue without being too off-putting. For example, asking people, "How depressed are you?" and giving them a 7-point scale might not work, as some respondents might not want to state that they are depressed. But, questionnaires can tap into the symptoms of depression by asking questions about energy levels, problems with sleeping, problems concentrating, and changes in one's mood. The researchers could then use the responses for these questions to determine if a respondent was depressed.

This leads to an important question: How do researchers figure out if their questions are valid? For clinical questionnaires, the researchers can compare results to a participant's clinical diagnosis. For questionnaires examining other phenomena, researchers perform a large amount of pretesting in order to calculate *norms*, or average patterns of data. Almost all of the questionnaires that you will encounter as a psychology student will have undergone prior testing to establish norms and to confirm that the research tool is both valid and reliable. This testing will involve hundreds or even thousands of participants; their efforts help ensure that self-report measures such as questionnaires are a useful tool in psychology's quest to understand different behaviours.

Module 2.2a Quiz:

Descriptive Research

Know . . .

1. When psychologists observe behaviour and record data in the environment where it normally occurs, they are using _____.
   A. case studies
   B. naturalistic observation
   C. the supervisory method
   D. artificial observation

2. Any property of an organism, event, or something else that can take on different values is called _____.
   A. an operational definition
   B. data
   C. a variable
   D. a case study

Apply . . .

3. A psychologist is completing a naturalistic observation study of children's aggressive behaviour on a playground. She says that aggression is "any verbal or physical act that appears to be intended to hurt or control another child." She then goes on to list specific examples. It appears that the psychologist is attempting to establish a(n)
   A. good relationship with the children.
   B. variable.
   C. observational definition.
   D. operational definition.

Correlational Research

Psychologists performing descriptive research almost always record information about more than one variable when they are collecting data. In these situations, the researchers may look for an association among the variables. They will ask whether the variables tend to occur together in some pattern, or if they tend to occur at opposite times. **Correlational research** *involves measuring the degree of association between two or more variables.* For example, consider these two questions:

- What is the average education level of Canadians over the age of 30?

- What is the average income of Canadians over the age of 30?

These two questions ask for different types of information, but their answers may be related. Is it likely that people with higher education levels also tend to have higher income levels? By asking two or more questions—perhaps through a survey—researchers can start to understand the associations among variables.

Correlations can be visualized when presented in a graph called a *scatterplot*, as shown in Figure 2.4. In scatterplot (a), you can see the data for education and income. Each dot represents one participant's data; when you enter dots for all of the participants, you often see a pattern emerge. In this case, the dots show a pattern that slopes upward and to the right, indicating that people with higher education levels tend to have a higher average income. That correlation is not surprising, but it illustrates one of the two main characteristics that describe correlations:

- *Direction:* The pattern of the data points on the scatterplot will vary based on the relationship between the variables. If correlations are *positive* (see Figure 2.4a), it means that the two variables change values in the same direction. So, if the value of one variable increases, the value of the other variable also tends to increase, and if the value of one variable decreases, the value of the other variable decreases. For example, education levels and average income both tend to rise and fall together, with educated people tending to be wealthier. In contrast, if correlations are *negative* (see Figure 2.4b), it means that as the value of one variable increases, the value of the other variable tends to decrease. For instance, if you get a lot of sleep, you are less likely to be irritable; but, if you don't get much sleep, then you will be more likely to be irritable.

- *Magnitude* (or strength): This refers to how closely the changes in one variable are linked to changes in another variable (e.g., if variable A goes up one unit, will variable B also go up one unit?). This magnitude is described in terms of a mathematical measure called

Figure 2.4 Correlations Are Depicted in Scatterplots

Here we see two variables that are positively correlated (a) and negatively correlated (b). In the example of a zero correlation (c), there is no relationship between the two variables.

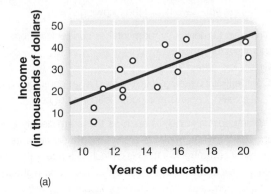

(a)

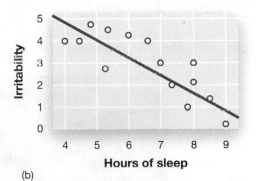

(b)

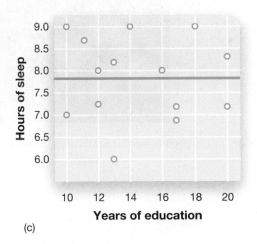

(c)

the *correlation coefficient.* A correlation coefficient of zero means that there is no relationship between the two variables (see Figure 2.4c). A coefficient of +1.0 means that there is a very strong positive correlation between the variables (+1.0 is the most positive correlation coefficient possible). A coefficient of −1.0 means that there is a very strong negative correlation between the variables (−1.0 is the most negative correlation coefficient possible). Importantly, +1.0 and −1.0 coefficients have an equal magnitude or strength; however, they have a different direction.

Myths in Mind

Beware of Illusory Correlations

Chances are you have heard the following claims:

- Crime and emergency room intakes suddenly increase when there is a full moon.
- Opposites attract.
- Competitive basketball players (and even gamblers) get on a "hot streak" where one success leads to the next.

Many common beliefs such as these are deeply ingrained in our culture. They become even more widely accepted when they are repeated frequently. It is difficult to argue with a hospital nurse or police officer who *swears* that full-moon nights are the busiest and craziest of all. The conventional, reserved, and studious man who dates a carefree and spirited woman *confirms* that opposites attract. And, after Kyle Lowry has hit a few amazing jump shots for the Raptors, of course his chances of success just get better and better as the game wears on.

But do they? Each of these three scenarios is an example of what are called **illusory correlations**—*relationships that really exist only in the mind, rather than in reality*. It turns out that well-designed studies have found no evidence that a full moon leads to, or is even related to, bizarre or violent behaviour (Lilienfeld & Arkowitz, 2009). People who are attracted to each other are typically very similar (Buston & Emlen, 2003). Also, although some games may be better than others, overall the notion of a "hot streak" is not a reality in basketball or in blackjack (Caruso et al., 2010; Gilovich et al., 1985).

Why do these illusory correlations exist? Instances of them come to mind easily and are more memorable than humdrum examples of "normal" nights in the ER, perfectly matched couples, and all of the times Kyle Lowry missed a shot, even in his best games. However, just because examples are easy to imagine, it does not mean that this is what typically occurs.

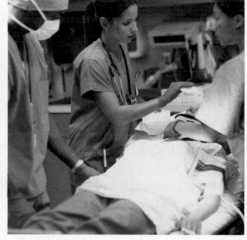

Shutterstock

Florian Franke/Corbis

Contrary to *very* popular belief, a full moon is statistically unrelated to unusual events or increased emergency room visits.

You will encounter many correlations in this text, and it will be important to keep in mind the direction of the relationship—whether the variables are positively or negatively associated. One key point to remember is that the correlation coefficient is a measure of association only—*it is not a measure of causality*. In other words, correlation does not equal causation. This is an extremely important point!

In many cases, a correlation gives the *impression* that one variable causes the other, but that relationship cannot be determined from correlational research. For example, we noted in the beginning of the module that a sense of humour is associated with good health—this is a positive correlation. But this does not mean that humour *is responsible for* the good health. Perhaps good health leads to a better sense of humour. Or perhaps neither causes the other, but rather a third variable causes both good health and good sense of humour. This possibility is known as the **third variable problem**, *the possibility that a third, unmeasured variable is actually responsible for a well-established correlation between two variables*. Consider the negative correlation between sleep and irritability shown in scatterplot (b) of Figure 2.4. Numerous third variables could account for this relationship. Stress, depression, diet, and workload could *cause* both increased irritability and lost sleep. As you can see, correlations must be interpreted with caution.

Module 2.2b Quiz:

Correlational Research

Know . . .

1. Which of the following correlation coefficients shows the strongest relationship between two variables?

   A. +.54

   B. −.72

   C. +10.1

   D. +.10

Understand . . .

2. What does it mean to say that two variables are negatively correlated?

   A. An increase in one variable is associated with a decrease in the other.

   B. An increase in one variable is associated with an increase in the other.

   C. A decrease in one variable is associated with a decrease in the other.

   D. The two variables have no relationship.

Analyze . . .

3. Imagine Dr. Martin finds that sense of humour is positively correlated with psychological well-being. From this, we can conclude that

   A. humour causes people to be healthier.

   B. health causes people to be funnier.

   C. people who have a good sense of humour tend to be healthier.

   D. people who have a good sense of humour tend to be less healthy.

Experimental Research

Experimental designs improve on descriptive and correlational studies because they are the only designs that can provide strong evidence for cause-and-effect relationships. Like correlational research, experiments have a minimum of two variables, but there are two key differences between correlational research and experiments: the random assignment of the participants and the experimenter's control over the variables being studied. As you will see, these unique features are what make experimental designs so powerful.

THE EXPERIMENTAL METHOD Imagine you were conducting an experiment testing whether seeing photographs of nature scenes would reduce people's responses to stressful events. You carefully created two sets of images—one of peaceful images of the B.C. rain forests, Lake Louise, Algonquin Park in Ontario, and rugged Maritime coastlines—and another of neutral images such as houses. When the first two participants arrive at the laboratory for your study, one is wearing a t-shirt supporting a local environmental organization and the other is wearing a t-shirt emblazoned with an oil sands company logo. Which participant gets assigned to the nature scene condition and which gets assigned to the neutral condition? If you are conducting an objective, unbiased study, the answer to this question is that either participant is equally likely to be assigned to either condition. Indeed, a critical element of experiments is **random assignment**, *a technique for dividing samples into two or more groups in which participants are equally likely to be placed in any condition of the experiment*. Random assignment allows us to assume the two groups will be roughly equal (Figure 2.5).

If we assigned anyone who looked like they were nature lovers to the nature scene condition, then our

Figure 2.5 Elements of an Experiment

If we wanted to test whether exposure to nature-related images causes a reduction in stress (as is assumed by people who have nature scenes as their computer's wallpaper), we would first need to randomly assign people in our sample to either the experimental or control condition. The dependent variable, the stress levels, would be measured following exposure to either nature-related or neutral material. To test whether the hypothesis is true, the average stress scores in both groups would be compared.

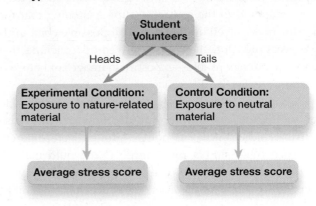

Hypothesis: Nature causes a reduction in stress.

experiment might not be telling us about the effects of the images. Instead, some other **confounding variable**—*a variable outside of the researcher's control that might affect or provide an alternative explanation for the results*—could potentially enter the picture. In our example, the variables of political awareness or tendency to be "outdoorsy" might play an even larger role in the study than the stimuli you worked so hard to create. Randomly assigning participants to the different experimental conditions also allows the researcher to assume that other sources of variability such as mood and personality are evenly spread across the different conditions. This allows you to infer that any differences between the two groups are because of the variable you are testing.

In this experiment, we are manipulating one variable (the types of images being viewed) and measuring another variable (stress response). *The variable that the experimenter manipulates to distinguish between two or more groups is* known as the **independent variable**. The participants cannot alter these variables, as they are controlled by the researcher. In contrast, the **dependent variable** *is the observation or measurement that is recorded during the experiment and subsequently compared across all groups.* The levels of this variable are dependent upon the participants' responses or performance. In our example, the type of images being viewed is the independent variable and the participants' stress response is the dependent variable.

This experiment is an example of a **between-subjects design**, *an experimental design in which we compare the performance of participants who are in different groups.* One of these groups, the **experimental group**, *is the group in the experiment that receives a treatment or the stimuli targeting a specific behaviour,* which in this specific example would be exposure to nature scenes. The experimental group always receives the treatment. In contrast, the **control group** *is the group that does not receive the treatment or stimuli targeting a specific behaviour; this group therefore serves as a baseline to which the experimental group is compared.* In our example, the control group would not be exposed to nature photographs. What if the experimental group showed reduced stress compared to the control group? Assuming that the experiment was well designed and all possible confounds were accounted for, the researchers could conclude that the independent variable—exposure to images of nature—is responsible for the difference.

A between-subjects design allows the researcher to examine differences between groups; however, it is also open to criticism. What if the two groups were different from each other simply by chance? That would make it more difficult to detect any differences caused by your independent variable. In order to reduce this possibility,

researchers often use **within-subjects designs**, *an experimental design in which the same participants respond to all types of stimuli or experience all experimental conditions.* In the experiment we've discussed in this section, a within-subjects design would have involved participants viewing all of the images from one condition (e.g., nature photographs) before being tested, and then viewing all of the images from the other condition (e.g., neutral photographs) before being tested again. In this case, the order of the conditions would be randomly assigned for each participant.

As you can see, designing an experiment requires the experimenter to make many decisions. However, in some cases, some of these decisions are taken out of the researchers' hands.

THE QUASI-EXPERIMENTAL METHOD   Random assignment and manipulation of a variable are required for experiments. They allow researchers to make the case that differences between the groups originate from the independent variable. In some cases, though, random assignment is not possible. **Quasi-experimental research** *is a research technique in which the two or more groups that are compared are selected based on predetermined characteristics, rather than random assignment.* For example, you will read about many studies in this text that compare men and women. Obviously, in this case one cannot flip a coin to randomly assign people to one group or the other. Also, if you gather one sample of men and one sample of women, they could differ in any number of ways that are not necessarily relevant to the questions you are studying. As a result, all sorts of causes could account for any differences that would appear: genetics, gender roles, family history, and so on. Thus, quasi-experiments can point out relationships among pre-existing groups, but they cannot determine what it is about those groups that leads to the differences.

CONVERGING OPERATIONS   An underlying theme of this module has been that each method of studying behaviour has benefits as well as limitations (see Table 2.1). For example, naturalistic observation research allows

Table 2.1 Strengths and Limitations of Different Research Designs

Method	Strengths	Limitations
Case studies	Yields detailed information, often of rare conditions or observations	Focus on a single subject limits generalizability
Naturalistic observation	Allows for detailed descriptions of subjects in environments where behaviour normally occurs	Poor control over possibly influential variables
Surveys/questionnaires	Quick and often convenient way of gathering large quantities of self-report data	Poor control; participants may not answer honestly, written responses may not be truly representative of actual behaviour
Correlational study	Shows strength of relationships between variables	Does not allow researcher to determine cause-and-effect relationships
Experiment	Tests for cause-and-effect relationships; offers good control over influential variables	Risk of being artificial with limited generalization to real-world situations

psychologists to see behaviour as it normally occurs, but it makes experimental control very difficult—some would argue impossible. Conversely, to achieve true random assignment while controlling for any number of confounding variables and outside influences, the situation may be made so artificial that the results of an experiment do not apply to natural behaviour. Luckily, psychologists do not have to settle on only one method of studying behaviour.

Most interesting topics have been studied using a variety of possible designs, measures, and samples. In fact, when a theory's predictions hold up to dozens of tests using a variety of designs—a perspective known as *converging operations*—we can be much more confident of its accuracy, and are one step closer to understanding the many mysteries of human (and animal) behaviour.

Module 2.2c Quiz:

Experimental Research

Know . . .

1. If each participant in an experiment has an equal chance of being assigned to the experimental group or the control group, we can assume that this study involves _____.

   A. a correlational design

   B. a quasi-experimental design

   C. the random assignment of participants

   D. the experimental selection of participants

Understand . . .

2. A researcher sets up an experiment to test a new antidepressant medication. One group receives the treatment and the other receives a placebo. The researcher then measures depression using a standardized self-report measure. What is the independent variable in this case?

   A. Whether the individuals scored high or low on the depression measure

   B. Whether the individuals received the treatment or a placebo

   C. Whether the individuals were experiencing depression before the study began

   D. Whether the individuals' depression decreased or increased during the study period

Apply . . .

3. A researcher compares a group of Conservatives and a group of Liberals on a measure of beliefs about poverty. What makes this a quasi-experimental design?

   A. The researcher is comparing pre-existing groups, rather than randomly assigning people to them.

   B. You cannot be both a Conservative and a Liberal at the same time.

   C. There are two independent variables.

   D. There is no operational definition for the dependent variable.

Analyze . . .

4. A researcher is able to conduct an experiment on study habits in his laboratory and finds some exciting results. What is one possible limitation of using this method?

   A. Results from laboratory experiments do not always generalize to real-world situations.

   B. Experiments do not provide evidence about cause-and-effect relationships.

   C. It is not possible to conduct experiments on issues such as study habits.

   D. Laboratory experiments do not control for confounding variables.

Module 2.2 Summary

2.2a Know . . . the key terminology related to research designs.

between-subjects design
case study
confounding variable
control group
correlational research
dependent variable
experimental group
illusory correlations
independent variable
naturalistic observation
qualitative research
quantitative research
quasi-experimental research
random assignment

research design
self-reporting
third variable problem
within-subjects design

2.2b Understand . . . what it means when variables are positively or negatively correlated.

When two or more variables are positively correlated, their relationship is direct—they increase or decrease together. For example, income and education level are positively correlated. Negatively correlated variables are inversely related—as one increases, the other decreases. Substance abuse may be inversely related to cognitive performance— higher levels of substance abuse are often associated with lower cognitive functioning.

2.2c Understand . . . how experiments help demonstrate cause-and-effect relationships.

Experiments rely on randomization and the manipulation of an independent variable to show cause and effect. At the beginning of an experiment, two or more groups are randomly assigned—a process that helps ensure that the two groups are roughly equivalent. Then, researchers manipulate an independent variable; perhaps they give one group a drug and the other group a placebo. At the end of the study, if one group turns out to be different, that difference is most likely due to the effects of the independent variable.

2.2d Apply . . . the terms and concepts of experimental methods to research examples.

* Here are two examples for practice.

Apply Activity

1. Dr. Vincent randomly assigns participants in a study to exercise versus no exercise conditions and, after 30 minutes, measures mood levels. In this case, exercise level is the _____ variable and mood is the _____ variable.

2. Dr. Harrington surveyed students on multiple lifestyle measures. He discovered that as the number of semesters that university students complete increases, their anxiety level increases. If number of semesters and anxiety increase together, this is an example of a(n) _____ correlation. Dr. Harrington also found that the more time students spent socializing, the less likely they were to become depressed. The increase in socializing and decrease in depression is an example of a(n) _____ correlation.

2.2e Analyze . . . the pros and cons of descriptive, correlational, and experimental research designs.

Descriptive methods have many advantages, including observing naturally occurring behaviour and providing detailed observations of individuals. In addition, when correlational methods are used in descriptive research, we can see how key variables are related. Experimental methods can be used to test for cause-and-effect relationships. One drawback is that laboratory experiments might not generalize to real-world situations.

Module 2.3 Ethics in Psychological Research

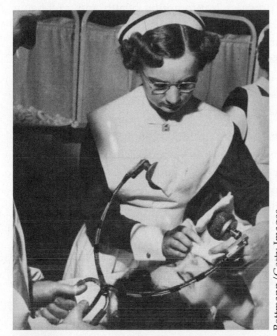

Bettmann/Getty Images

Learning Objectives

2.3a Know . . . the key terminology of research ethics.

2.3b Understand . . . the importance of reporting and storing data.

2.3c Understand . . . why animals are often used in scientific research.

2.3d Apply . . . the ethical principles of scientific research to examples.

2.3e Analyze . . . the role of using deception in psychological research.

In the early 1950s, the United States' Central Intelligence Agency (CIA) became involved in the field of psychology. After hearing that their enemies in the Soviet Union, China, and North Korea had tried to use mind-control techniques—including mind-altering drugs—on U.S. prisoners of war, the CIA felt it had no choice but to research these techniques themselves. Project MKUltra began. After recruiting former Nazi scientists who had studied torture and "brainwashing" during World War II (and who had been prosecuted as war criminals), the CIA secretly poured tens of millions of dollars into research laboratories at hospitals and universities in order to study mind-control techniques that would alter people's personalities, memories, and ability to control themselves while being interrogated. At least one of these institutions was in Canada.

Scottish psychiatrist Donald Ewen Cameron used CIA funds (as well as $500 000 from the Canadian government) to perform terrifying experiments at the Allan Memorial Institute of McGill University from 1957 to 1964. Patients

who were admitted to the institute for fairly minor problems such as anxiety disorders or depression were—without giving proper consent or being informed of the reason for the "treatment"—subjected to manipulations that can only be called torture. These patients received drugs that caused temporary paralysis or even coma, electroconvulsive therapy set at more than 30 times the recommended strength, constant noises, and even looped tapes repeating messages (Klein, 2007). These treatments led to amnesia, confusion, and anxiety; participants in these programs were never the same (Collins, 1988).

Project MKUltra was officially ended in 1973. The experiments are now generally accepted as being among the most unethical studies in the history of science. In the 1980s, the Canadian government paid $100 000 to each of the 127 victims of Cameron's unauthorized research program. For several decades, the CIA's interrogation manual referred to "studies at McGill University" (McCoy, 2006).

Focus Questions

1. Which institutional safeguards are now in place to protect the well-being of research participants?

2. Does all research today require that people be informed of risks and consent to participate in a study?

» The topics that psychologists study deal with living, sensing organisms, which raises a number of ethical issues that must be addressed before any study begins. These concerns include protecting the physical and mental well-being of participants, obtaining consent from them, and ensuring that their responses remain confidential. The procedures discussed in the next section have been developed as protections for participants; they are critical not only to ensure the individual well-being of the study participants, but also to maintain a positive and trustworthy image of the scientists who conduct research.

Promoting the Welfare of Research Participants

The CIA mind-control research program certainly is an extreme case—extreme in the harm done to the volunteers, the disregard for their well-being, and its secretive nature. Today, most research with human participants involves short-term, low-risk methods, and there are now ethical guidelines and procedures for ensuring the safety and well-being of all individuals involved in research. In Canada, all institutions that engage in research with humans, including colleges and universities, are required to have a **research ethics board (REB)**, *a committee of researchers and officials at an institution charged with the protection of human research participants.* (If you read a research report from an American institution, they will refer to Institutional Review Boards [IRBs]; these are the same thing as REBs.) REBs help ensure that researchers abide by the ethical rules set out in the *Tri-Council Policy Statement: Ethical Conduct for Research Involving Humans (2nd edition)*, a set of requirements created by the Government of Canada's Panel of Research Ethics. The REBs are intended to protect individuals in two main ways: (1) The committee weighs potential risks to the volunteers against the possible benefits of the research, and (2) it requires that volunteers agree to participate in the research (i.e., they give informed consent).

WEIGHING THE RISKS AND BENEFITS OF RESEARCH The majority of psychological research, such as computer-based studies of perception or questionnaires studying personality traits, involves minimal exposure to physical or mental stress. Even so, great care is taken to protect participants. Some research involves more risk, such as exposing individuals to brief periods of stress, inducing a negative mood, asking about sensitive topics, or even asking participants to engage in brief periods of exercise. Some studies have even exposed humans to the virus that causes the common cold, or made small cuts to the skin to study factors that affect healing. The benefits that this type of research provides in promoting health and well-being must be weighed against the short-term risks to the people who consent to participate in these studies.

It must be stressed that physical risks are rare in psychological research. More common are measures that involve possible cognitive and emotional stress. Here are a couple of examples:

- *Mortality salience.* In this situation participants are made more aware of death, which can be done in a number of ways. For example, participants may be asked to read or write about what happens to a human body after death.

- *Writing about upsetting or traumatic experiences.* People who have experienced recent trauma such as the death of a loved one or being laid off from a long-term job might be asked to write about that experience in great detail, sometimes repeatedly.

Another source of risk is related to the fact that some studies ask participants to provide the experimenter with sensitive and/or personal information. Think about all the topics in psychology that people might want to keep to themselves: opinions about teachers or supervisors, a history of substance abuse, criminal records, medical records, Internet search history, and so on. Disclosing this information is a potential threat to a person's reputation, friends, and family. Psychologists must find ways to minimize these risks so that participants do not suffer any unintended consequences of participating in psychological research.

Indeed, everyone involved in the research process—the researcher, the REB, and the potential volunteer—must determine whether the study's inherent risks are worth what can potentially be learned if the research goes forward. Consider again the stressors mentioned previously:

- *Mortality salience.* The stress tends to be short term, and psychologists learn how decisions are influenced by recent events in a person's life, such as the loss of a loved one or experiencing a major natural disaster. These decisions range from making charitable donations to voting for or against going to war.

- *Writing about upsetting experiences.* Although revisiting a stressful experience can be difficult, researchers learn how coping through expression can help emotional adjustment and physical health. In fact, participants who write about stress tend to be healthier—emotionally and physically—than those who write about everyday topics (such as describing their dorms or apartments).

These stressful situations have potential benefits that can be applied to other people. The psychologists who undertake such research tend to be motivated by several factors—including the desire to help others, the drive to satisfy their intellectual curiosity, and even their own livelihood and employment. The REB serves as a third party that weighs the risks and benefits of research without being personally invested in the outcome. Under today's standards, there is no chance that the CIA mind-control studies would have been initiated, except in secrecy outside of the public process of science. The danger to the participants in that study—*victims* might be a better term—far outweighed any scientific benefit gained from the experiments, even if the participants had known what they were getting into. Today, it is mandatory that research participants be informed of any risks to which they may be exposed and willfully volunteer to take part in a study.

OBTAINING INFORMED CONSENT In addition to weighing the risks versus the benefits of a study, researchers must ensure that human volunteers truly are *volunteers*. This may seem redundant, but it is actually a tricky issue. Recall that the human subjects in the CIA mind-control studies were volunteers only in the sense that they voluntarily sought treatment from the researchers. But did they volunteer to undergo procedures that were very close to being torture? Had the men and women known the true nature of the study, it is doubtful that any would have continued to participate. Currently, participants and patients have much more protection than they did in the 1950s and 1960s. Before any experimental procedures begin, all participants must provide **informed consent**: *A potential volunteer must be informed (know the purpose, tasks, and risks involved in the study) and give consent (agree to participate based on the information provided) without pressure.*

To be truly informed about the study, volunteers should be told, at minimum, the following details (see also Figure 2.6):

- The topic of the study
- The nature of any stimuli to which they will be exposed (e.g., images, sounds, smells)
- The nature of any tasks they will complete (e.g., tests, puzzles)
- The approximate duration of the study
- Any potential physical, psychological, or social risks involved
- The steps that the researchers have taken to minimize those risks

Ethical practices often involve resolving conflicting interests, and in psychological research the main conflict

Figure 2.6 Informed Consent

Research participants must provide informed consent before taking part in any study. As shown here, the participant must be made aware of the basic topic of the study as well as any possible risks.

Informed Consent Statement

You are invited to participate in a research study assessing your attitudes and behaviours related to alcohol. We ask that you read this document before agreeing to participate in this study. Although the legal drinking age is 19, participants do not need to be of age, nor do they need to be regular drinkers. Participants must be at least 18 years of age and be willing to anonymously share opinions about alcohol. The study takes 30 minutes to complete. There are no risks associated with this study.

If you agree to be in this study, you will be asked to complete a survey and rate 40 statements about alcohol and alcohol use in your life. You may refuse to answer any questions and may withdraw from the study without penalty at any time. This research project has been reviewed and approved by the Research Ethics Board.

Thank you for your time.

___ I give consent to participate in this study

Participant Signature: _____ Date: _____

___ I do not wish to participate in this study

is between the need for informed consent and the need for "blinded" volunteers. (Recall from Module 2.1 that in the best experimental designs the participants do not know exactly what the study is about, because such information may lead to subject bias.) Consider the mortality salience example. If a researcher told a participant, "We are going to test how a recent stressor you have experienced has affected your behaviour," then the experiment probably would not work. In these cases, researchers use **deception**—*misleading or only partially informing participants of the true topic or hypothesis under investigation.* In psychological research, this typically amounts to a "white lie" of sorts. The participants are given enough information to evaluate their own risks. In medical research situations, however, deception can be much more serious. For example, patients who are being tested with an experimental drug may be randomly chosen to receive a placebo. Importantly, in both cases, the deception is only short-term; once the experiment is over, the participants are informed of the true nature of the study and why deception was necessary. Additionally, if a treatment was found to be effective for the experimental group, it will often be made available to participants in the control group at the end of the experiment. This helps to ensure that anyone who *could* benefit from the study *does* benefit from the study.

Once participants are informed, they must also be able to give consent. Again, meeting this standard is trickier than it sounds. To revisit the mind-control studies, the patients were emotionally vulnerable people seeking help from a noted psychiatrist (Dr. Cameron was the president of both the Canadian and American Psychiatric Associations) at a world-class university. They were not told of the treatments they would receive; in some cases, the patients were not informed that they were part of a study at all! Clearly, informed consent was not provided by these research participants. Based on the ethical issues arising from this and many other disturbing studies, modern psychological (and psychiatric and neurological) research includes the following elements in determining whether full consent is given:

- *Freedom to choose.* Individuals should not be at risk for financial loss, physical harm, or damage to their reputation if they choose not to participate.
- *Equal opportunities.* Volunteers should have choices. For example, if the volunteers are introductory psychology students seeking course credit, they must have non-research alternatives available to them for credit should they choose not to participate in a study.
- *The right to withdraw.* Volunteers should have the right to withdraw from the study, at any time, without penalty. The right to give informed consent stays with the participants throughout the entire study.
- *The right to withhold responses.* Volunteers responding to surveys or interviews should not have to answer any question that they feel uncomfortable answering.

Usually, these criteria are sufficient for ensuring full consent. Sometimes, however, psychologists are interested in participants who cannot give their consent that easily. If researchers are studying children or individuals with mental disabilities, some severe psychiatric disorders, or certain neurological conditions, then a third party must give consent on behalf of the participant. This usually amounts to a parent or next-of-kin and, of course, all the rules of informed consent still apply.

After participating in the research study, participants must undergo a full **debriefing**, *meaning that the researchers should explain the true nature of the study, and especially the nature of and reason for any deception.* Although the debriefing of subjects might sound like some kind of military term, it is actually a very important part of the scientific process. You've already read how it is used when deception (or a placebo) is part of a study. But, even in more straightforward experiments, debriefing is necessary to ensure that the participants understand why their time and effort was necessary. This results in the participants leaving the experiment better-informed about your topic of study as well as about the many considerations involved in creating a psychology experiment. In short, it helps them become more scientifically literate.

THE RIGHT TO ANONYMITY AND CONFIDENTIALITY

A final measure of protection involves anonymity and confidentiality. *Anonymity* means that the data collected during a research study cannot be connected to individual participants. In many cases, volunteers can respond on a survey or through a computer-based experimental task without recording their name. This setup is ideal because it reduces both methodological problems (socially desirable responding) and the social risks to participants. If pure anonymity is not possible—for example, when a researcher must watch the participant perform a task—then confidentiality is a reasonable substitute. *Confidentiality* includes at least two parts. First, researchers cannot share specific data or observations that can be connected with an individual. Second, all records must be kept secure (for example, in a password-protected database or locked filing cabinet) so that identities cannot be revealed unintentionally.

THE WELFARE OF ANIMALS IN RESEARCH Many people who have never taken a psychology course view psychology as the study of *human* behaviour, possibly because most psychological research does involve humans. But research with animals is just as important to psychological science for a number of reasons. The simplest and perhaps most obvious is that the study of psychology *does include* the behaviour of animals. However, the most significant reason is that scientists can administer treatments to animals that could never be applied to humans, such as lesioning (damaging) specific areas of the brain in order to examine the resulting behavioural impairments. In addition, genetic research requires species with much shorter life spans than our own so that several successive generations can be observed. Finally, scientists can manipulate the breeding of laboratory animals to meet the needs of their experimental procedures. Selective breeding allows researchers to study highly similar groups of subjects, which helps control for individual differences based on genetic factors.

These forms of animal-based experimentation have improved our understanding of a number of different areas of behaviour. The research area that has benefited most from the use of animal subjects is the study of different brain-related diseases. This leads to an ethical dilemma, however: Is it ethically acceptable to create disease-like symptoms in animals if it could lead to discoveries that could help thousands—or sometimes millions—of people?

Many psychologists use animals in their research, so ethical codes have been extended to cover nonhuman species.

Working the Scientific Literacy Model

Animal Models of Disease

MPTP (1-methyl-4-phenyl-1,2,3,6-tetrahydropyridine) was accidentally discovered in 1976 by a 23-year-old chemistry graduate student who was attempting to create MPPP, a synthetic drug that produces morphine-like effects. Three days after injecting himself with what he thought would be a pleasure-inducing drug, he began to show symptoms of Parkinson's disease, including tremors and difficulties initiating movements. Six years later, seven young people in Santa Clara County, California, were diagnosed with Parkinson's disease, which typically develops in older adults. Again, these individuals had injected doses of MPPP that were contaminated with MPTP. Based on these cases, neurologists realized that the compound MPTP could prove useful as a model of Parkinson's disease (Langston et al., 1983). Animals receiving injections of MPTP quickly develop Parkinsonian symptoms; it is therefore possible to use these animals to test possible treatments of this disorder. MPTP is now the toxin most frequently used for animal models of Parkinson's disease (Blesa et al., 2012). This leads to interesting questions, however. Are animal models valid and useful tools for researchers trying to find treatments and cures for diseases? Is this process ethical?

What do we know about animal models of diseases?

MPTP is just one of hundreds of techniques for modelling different diseases. There are animal models for Alzheimer's disease, depression, schizophrenia, autism, stroke, Huntington's disease, epilepsy, and drug addiction, among many others (Nestler & Hyman, 2010; Virdee et al., 2012). Not all diseases or conditions can be modelled in the same way, however. Depending upon the underlying cause of the disorder and the brain areas that are likely involved, there are at least four methods scientists can use to create an animal model. First, if a disease is associated with a specific brain area, researchers could anesthetize an animal and remove or damage that part of its brain. Brain damage could also occur by introducing a toxic substance, as occurred in the MPTP patients. Second, scientists could introduce a substance that increased or decreased the levels of certain brain chemicals known as *neurotransmitters* in the brain (see Module 3.2). Parkinson's disease is caused by a loss of the neurotransmitter dopamine; therefore, a drug that reduced dopamine levels could simulate the symptoms of Parkinson's. Third, researchers could create animal models of certain disorders by altering the environments of the animals. For instance, placing animals in an environment that is physically or socially stressful can cause them to behave similarly to individuals with anxiety disorders (Willner et al., 1987). Finally, scientists can manipulate the genetic make-up of animals. While earlier research was limited to selectively breeding animals so that they became more prone to a disease, it is now possible to directly alter the genetic codes of animals so that particular traits and physical structures are altered (Spires-Jones & Knafo, 2012). However, despite the enormous possibilities associated with animal models, these techniques are only as good as the scientists who use them.

How can science test animal models of diseases?

The primary goal of developing animal models of a neurological condition, such as the MPTP model of Parkinson's disease, is to simulate the characteristics of a disease so that researchers can test possible treatments without harming humans. Although this may sound unethical at first, there is a logic behind the use of animal models. In order to find treatments for a disease, scientists need a very large number of individuals with the disease to use as test subjects. Any given treatment that is currently available to humans underwent testing with thousands—sometimes tens of thousands—of animals in order to test different chemical compounds and doses to ensure that the side effects of the treatment did not outweigh its benefits. There are simply not enough people with some diseases for this type of trial-and-error testing to occur. Any study that could take place would require the cooperation of universities and hospitals across the world. And, if that single attempt did not work, it would be difficult to find patients who had not already been tested to use in subsequent treatment attempts. Therefore, the use of animal models was a product of necessity.

Importantly, animal models are not developed in a random fashion. Instead, each animal model of a disease must have the following characteristics (Dzirasa & Covington III, 2012). First, it must share the same physiological and behavioural features of the disease as appear in humans. An animal model of depression would not be accepted if the animals were energetic and playful; instead, the animals' behaviours must resemble the behaviours of humans with depression. Second, both the animal model and the "real" disorder must involve similar brain structures; otherwise, researchers would be comparing apples and oranges. Third, the tests used to measure the behaviours must be valid. For depressed humans, laboratory tests often involve questionnaires or computer-based tests; these are obviously not useful research methods when testing rats or mice. Instead, the researcher must use an indirect test to try to tap into the same underlying symptom. For example, one symptom of depression is *anhedonia*, the tendency to get less pleasure out of life than one previously did. To test anhedonia in rats, scientists use a sucrose preference test, a task in which rats have the opportunity to seek out a pleasurable taste (sugar!) if they are motivated to do so. The assumption is that "depressed" rats, just like depressed humans, would be less likely to seek out such stimuli (Cryan et al., 2002).

How can we critically evaluate these models?

The easiest criticism of animal models of disease is that animal brains are not human brains. Human brains are obviously more complex; therefore, how valid is it to assume that treatments that change an animal's behaviour will benefit humans? And, if this isn't guaranteed, is it ethical to use animal subjects in this way? A second criticism is that researchers are only beginning to understand the specific brain areas involved with a number of different conditions. Oftentimes, a large number of interacting brain areas are involved with a disorder. So, if we are unclear of the biology involved in the human version of the disease, how accurate can the resulting animal models really be? Additionally, it is fairly easy to test the validity of animal models of neurological diseases that have clear, observable symptoms (e.g., Parkinson's disease and epilepsy); animals modelling epilepsy will have seizures that you can see. However, models of psychological conditions like depression and schizophrenia present a greater challenge, as the symptoms are often thought-based and subjective. The rat can't explain what he is seeing or feeling. Instead, the researchers must infer that these mental states are occurring (in one form or another) in the animal subjects being tested. Finally, is an animal with limited cognitive abilities even *capable* of serving as a model for a disorder that involves impairments of higher-order cognitive abilities (Nestler & Hyman, 2010)? For example, how can you tell if a laboratory rat is having a hallucination?

These are all valid criticisms and highlight the importance of meeting the conditions of a good model discussed in the previous section. Our confidence in an animal model will also increase if other lines of research produce similar results. So, if brain-imaging tests in humans find problems in the same brain areas being manipulated in an animal model, that model will become more valid. Through the use of converging operations—using multiple research methods to analyze the same question—it is possible to create effective animal models.

Why is this relevant?

Anyone who has watched an elderly relative become a shadow of his or her former self as a result of a neurological disease such as Alzheimer's or Parkinson's disease can likely understand the usefulness of animal models. It is impossible to perform large-scale research investigating these disorders and their possible treatment without the use of these experiments. Therefore, the animals used in these studies are helping to reduce the suffering of millions of people around the world. Whether you agree that it is appropriate to use animals in this fashion is a personal decision that you will have to make on your own. It is important to note that the researchers who perform this type of research also think about these issues. They certainly don't take their ethical responsibilities lightly; every university and research hospital has extremely strict requirements for the treatment of laboratory animals and the well-being of all animals is monitored by laboratory technicians and veterinarians. Importantly, all of these activities are closely monitored by the institution's REB.

REBS FOR ANIMAL-BASED RESEARCH Many ethical standards for animal research were developed at the same time as those for human research. In fact, hospitals and universities have established committees responsible for the ethical treatment of animals, which are in some ways similar to REBs that monitor human research. To be sure, there are differences in standards applied to human research and animal research. For example, we obviously do not ask for informed consent from animals. Nevertheless, similar procedures have been put in place to ensure that risk and discomfort are managed in a humane way, and that the pain or stress an animal may experience can be justified by the potential scientific value of the research.

Three main areas of ethical treatment are emphasized by researchers and animal welfare committees. The first is the basic care of laboratory animals—that is, providing appropriate housing, feeding, and sanitation for the species. The second is minimization of any pain or discomfort experienced by the animals. Third, although it is rare for a study to *require* discomfort, when it is necessary, the researchers must ensure that the pain can be justified by the potential benefits of the research. The same standards apply if animals are to be sacrificed for the research.

Module 2.3a Quiz:

Promoting the Welfare of Research Participants

Know . . .

1. The Research Ethics Board (REB) is the group that determines
   A. whether a hypothesis is valid.
   B. whether the benefits of a proposed study outweigh its potential risks.
   C. whether a study should be published in a scientific journal.
   D. whether animal research is overall an ethical practice.

Understand . . .

2. Which of the following is *not* a requirement for informed consent?
   A. Participants need to know the nature of the stimuli to which they will be exposed.
   B. Participants need to understand any potential physical, psychological, or social risks involved in the research.
   C. Participants need to have a face-to-face meeting with the researcher before volunteering.
   D. Participants need to know the approximate duration of the study.

Analyze . . .

3. In a memory study, researchers have participants study a list of words and then tell them it was the wrong list and that they should forget it. This deception is meant to see how effectively participants can forget something they have already studied. If the researchers plan to debrief the participants afterward, would this design meet the standards of an ethical study?
   A. No, it is not okay to mislead individuals during the course of a study.
   B. Yes, given that the participants are not at risk and that they will be debriefed, this seems to be an ethical study.
   C. No, because the researchers should not debrief the participants.
   D. Yes, because the participants fully understood all aspects of the study.

Ethical Collection, Storage, and Reporting of Data

Ethical research does not end when the volunteers go home. Researchers have continuing commitments to the participants, such as the requirement to maintain the anonymity, confidentiality, and security of the data. Once data are reported in a journal or at a conference, they should be kept for a reasonable amount of time—generally, three to five years is acceptable. The purpose of keeping data for a lengthy period relates to the public nature of good research. Other researchers may request access to the data to reinterpret it, or perhaps examine the data before attempting to replicate the findings. It might seem as though the confidentiality requirement conflicts with the need to make data public, but this is not necessarily true. For example, if the data are anonymous, then none of the participants will be affected if and when the data are shared.

In addition to keeping data safe, scientists must be honest with their data. Some researchers experience great external pressure to obtain certain results. These pressures may relate to receiving tenure at a university; gaining funding from a governmental, industrial, or nonprofit agency; or providing evidence that a product (for example, a medical treatment for depression) is effective.

Unfortunately, cases of *scientific misconduct* sometimes arise when individuals fabricate or manipulate their data to fit their desired results. For instance, in 1998, British researcher Andrew Wakefield and his colleagues published a paper in the highly influential medical journal *The Lancet* describing a link between the vaccine for measles, mumps, and rubella and the incidence rate of autism (Wakefield et al., 1998). The response was immediate—many concerned parents stopped having their children vaccinated out of fear that their kids would then develop autism. Panic was increased by sensationalistic media reports of the study as well as by an anti-vaccine media campaign launched by celebrity personality (and, apparently, amateur developmental neurobiologist) Jenny McCarthy. Vaccine rates plummeted. However, autism rates did not change; what did change were the incidence rates of the diseases the vaccines would have prevented. Hundreds of preventable deaths occurred because children were not vaccinated. Then something interesting happened: Numerous institutions in several different countries reported that they were unable to replicate Wakefield's results. As his data received more attention, it became clear that some of it had been manipulated to fit his theory. Additional investigations uncovered the fact that Wakefield planned to develop screening kits to test for stomach problems associated with the vaccine; in other words, he had a financial motivation for creating a controversy related to the vaccine. Luckily, such cases of misconduct seem to be rare and, as occurred in this instance, other scientists are likely to find that the study cannot be replicated in such instances.

The chances of fraudulent data being published can also be decreased by requiring researchers to acknowledge any potential conflicts of interest, which might include personal financial gain from an institution or company that funded the work. If you look at most published journal articles, you will see a footnote indicating which agency or organization provided the funds for the study. This annotation is not just a goodwill gesture; it also informs the public when there is the *potential* for a company or government agency to influence research. Incidentally, the CIA was not mentioned in any published work resulting from the mind-control studies discussed at the beginning of this module. Dr. Cameron's family destroyed all of his papers upon his death in 1967.

Module 2.3b Quiz:

Ethical Collection, Storage, and Reporting of Data

Understand . . .

1. Researchers should store their data after they present or publish it because
   A. other researchers may want to examine the data before conducting a replication study.
   B. other researchers may want to reinterpret the data using different techniques.
   C. the process of informed consent requires it.
   D. both a and b are true.

Apply . . .

2. After completing a naturalistic observation study, a researcher does not have quite enough evidence to support her hypothesis. If she decides to go back to her records and slightly alters a few of the observations to fit her hypothesis, she is engaged in _____.
   A. informed forgery
   B. scientific misconduct
   C. correcting the data
   D. ethical behaviour

Module 2.3 Summary

2.3a   Know . . . the key terminology of research ethics.

debriefing
deception
informed consent
research ethics board (REB)

2.3b   Understand . . . the importance of reporting and storing data.

Making data public allows scientific peers as well as the general public to have access to the details of research studies. This information includes details about participants, the procedures they experienced, and the outcome of the study. Furthermore, the requirement that data be stored allows fellow researchers to verify reports as well as to examine the study for any possible misconduct. Fortunately, such cases are rare.

2.3c   Understand . . . why animals are often used in scientific research.

First, many research questions that affect medical and public health cannot be answered without animal testing. Second, obvious ethical considerations may not allow such research to be conducted on human subjects. Third, by working with animal models, scientists can control genetic and environmental variables that cannot be controlled with humans.

2.3d   Apply . . . the ethical principles of scientific research to examples.

For practice, read the following two scenarios and identify why they may fail to meet ethical standards.

Apply Activity

1. Dr. Nguyen wants to expose individuals first to a virus that causes people to experience colds, and then to varying levels of exercise to test whether exercise either facilitates or inhibits recovery. She is concerned that people will not volunteer if they know they may experience a cold, so she wants to give them the informed consent form after completing the study.
2. Researchers set up a study on sexuality that involves answering a series of questions in an online survey. At the end of each page of the survey, the software checks whether all of the questions are answered; it will not continue if any questions are left blank. Students cannot advance to the end of the survey and receive credit for participation until they answer all the questions.

2.3e   Analyze . . . the role of using deception in psychological research.

It is often the case that fully disclosing the purpose of a study before people participate in it would render the results useless. Thus, specific details of the study are not provided during informed consent (although all potential risks are disclosed). When deception of any kind is used, researchers must justify that the benefits of doing so outweigh the costs.

Module 2.4   A Statistical Primer

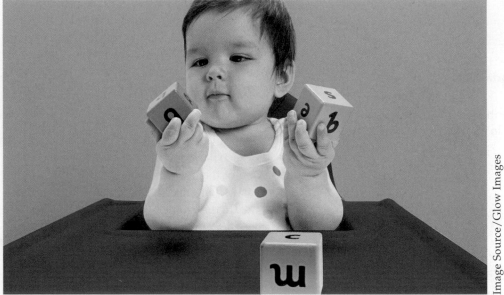

Image Source/Glow Images

Learning Objectives

2.4a Know . . . the key terminology of statistics.

2.4b Understand . . . how and why psychologists use significance tests.

2.4c Apply . . . your knowledge to interpret the most frequently used types of graphs.

2.4d Analyze . . . the choice of central tendency statistics based on the shape of the distribution.

Would you be surprised to learn that even infants and toddlers can think about probability, the foundation of statistics? Dr. Allison Gopnik (2010) writes about some interesting experiments showing just how statistically minded young children are. For example, consider the illustration below. If a researcher reached in and randomly selected five balls, would you be more surprised if they were all red or all white? Given that the white balls outnumber the red, you would be much more surprised if the researcher pulled out five red balls. Interestingly, infants show the same response. In another experiment, Gopnik's research team placed blue or yellow blocks into a fancy contraption. Yellow blocks appeared to make the machine light up

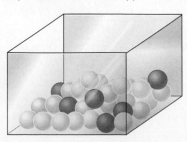

two out of three times (67% of the time), whereas the blue blocks only seemed to work two out of six times (33% of the time). When asked to "make the machine light up," preschoolers

selected the yellow blocks, which had a higher probability of working. If eight-month-olds and preschoolers can think statistically, adults should also be able to do so!

Focus Questions

1. How do psychologists use statistics to describe their observations?

2. How are statistics useful in testing the results of experiments?

》 Statistics initially seem scary to a lot of people. But, they don't have to be. Statistics can be boiled down to two general steps. First, we need to organize the numbers so that we can get a "big picture" view of the results; this process is helped by the creation of tables or graphs. Second, we want to test to see if any differences between groups or between experimental conditions are meaningful. Once these steps have been completed, it is possible to determine whether the data supported or refuted our hypothesis. In order to keep statistics simple, this module is organized around these two general steps.

Descriptive Statistics

Once research data have been collected, psychologists use **descriptive statistics**, *a set of techniques used to organize, summarize, and interpret data.* This gives you the "big picture" of the results. In most research, the statistics used to describe and understand the data are of three types: *frequency, central tendency,* and *variability.*

FREQUENCY Imagine that you asked a group of students who had just taken the Graduate Record Exam (GRE), a standardized test taken by people who want to go to graduate school, how well they did on the exam. Assuming they were honest, you would likely find scores ranging from the 300s up to the high 600s. What you would want to know is (1) whether some scores occurred more often than others and (2) whether all of the scores were clumped in the middle or more evenly spaced across the whole range. These two pieces of information make up the data's *distribution;* the examination of the distribution is a useful first step when analyzing data. Figure 2.7 depicts these data in the form of a *histogram,* a type of *bar graph.* As with most bar graphs, the vertical axis of this graph shows the **frequency**, *the number of observations that fall within a certain category or range of scores.* These graphs are generally very easy to interpret: The higher the bar, the more scores that fall into the specific range. For example, if you look on the horizontal axis in Figure 2.7, you will see a column of test scores corresponding to people who scored around 500 on the test. Looking over to the vertical axis, you will see there were four individuals in that range. It is

usually easy to describe the distribution of scores from a histogram. By examining changes in frequency across the horizontal axis—basically by describing the heights of the bars—we can learn something about the variable.

Histograms are a nice and simple way to present data and are excellent for providing researchers and students with an initial idea of what the data look like. But, they are not the only way to depict results of an experiment. Sometimes it is easier to answer questions about the distribution of the data if we present the same information using a smooth line called a *curve.* Sometimes a distribution is a symmetrical *curve,* as it is with our GRE scores. In this case, the left half is the mirror image of the right half. This is known as a **normal distribution** (sometimes called *the bell curve*), *a symmetrical distribution with values clustered around a central, mean value.*

Many variables wind up in a normal distribution, such as the scores on most standardized tests. Other variables have what is known as a skewed distribution, like the ones shown in Figure 2.8. You've likely encountered skewed distributions in your own life. Imagine a situation in which the grades on a school assignment were incredibly high, with only a few people performing poorly. In this case, the curve would show a **negatively skewed distribution**, *a distribution in which the curve has an extended tail to the left of the cluster.* However, what if the test were extremely difficult, like a calculus exam written by a professor with a mean streak? In this case, most people in the course would have low scores, with only a few stellar students getting As. These results would produce a **positively skewed distribution**, *a distribution in which the long tail is on the right of the cluster.* Although researchers generally prefer to have normally distributed data, skewed results are quite common. Most of the time, skews occur because there is an upper or lower limit to the data. For example, a person cannot take less than 0 minutes to complete a quiz, so a curve depicting times to complete a quiz cannot continue indefinitely to the left, beyond the zero point. In contrast, just one person could take a very long time to complete a quiz, causing the right side of the curve to extend far to the right.

CENTRAL TENDENCY When examining data, it is often useful to look at where the scores seem to cluster together. When we do this, we are estimating **central tendency**, *a measure of the central point of a distribution.* Although we naturally assume that the central tendency is "the average," there are actually three different measures of central tendency used in psychology. The first measure is known as the **mean**, *the arithmetic average of a set of numbers.* This is the measure of central tendency that we are most familiar with as it is used for class averages and in most sports (e.g., batting average in baseball or goals-against average in hockey). A second measure of central tendency is the

Figure 2.7 Graphing Psychological Data

The frequency of standardized test scores forming a normal curve.

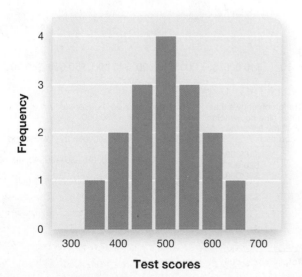

Figure 2.8 Skewed Distributions

Negatively skewed distributions have an extended tail to the left (as in the left graph below). Positively skewed distributions have an extended tail to the right (as in the right graph below).

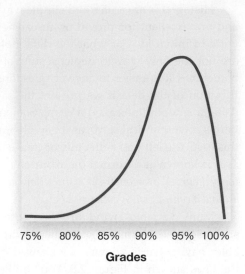

Grades

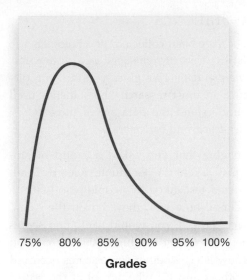

Grades

median, *the 50th percentile—the point on the horizontal axis at which 50% of all observations are lower, and 50% of all observations are higher.* The third and final measure of central tendency is the **mode**, *which is the category with the highest frequency (that is, the category with the most observations).*

At first glance, it might seem silly to have three different methods of measuring the central tendency of your data. Indeed, when the data are normally distributed as they are in Figure 2.9, the mean, median, and mode are identical. The mean is $30 000, which is exactly in the centre of the histogram. The same can be said for the median; again, it is $30 000, with half of the incomes less than $30 000 and half more than $30 000. Likewise, the mode is the same as the mean and median—$30 000 has the highest frequency, which, as seen in Figure 2.9, is 3. So, if the three measures of central tendency are equal, which do we use? If the data are normally distributed, researchers generally use the mean. But, if the data are skewed in some way, then researchers need to think about which measure is best. The measure used *least* is the mode. Because it provides less information than the mean or the median, the mode is typically only used when dealing with categories of data. For example, when you vote for a candidate, the mode represents the candidate with the most votes, and (in most cases) that person wins.

When the data are not a perfectly symmetrical curve, the mean, median, and mode produce different values. If the histogram spreads out in one direction—in Figure 2.10, it is positively skewed—we are usually better off calculating central tendency by using the median. This is because extreme values (positive or negative) will have a large effect on the mean, but will not affect the median. In other words, when you start to add extremely wealthy

households to the data set, the tail extends to the right and the mean is pulled in that direction. The longer the tail, the more the mean is pulled away from the centre of the

Figure 2.9 Central Tendency in Symmetrical Distributions

This symmetrical histogram shows the annual income of nine randomly sampled households. Notice that the mean, median, and mode are all in the same spot—this is a characteristic of normal distributions.

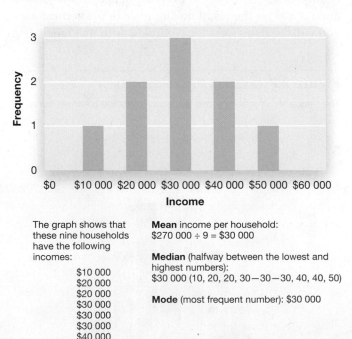

Income

The graph shows that these nine households have the following incomes:

$10 000
$20 000
$20 000
$30 000
$30 000
$30 000
$40 000
$40 000
$50 000

Total = $270 000

Mean income per household:
$270 000 ÷ 9 = $30 000

Median (halfway between the lowest and highest numbers):
$30 000 (10, 20, 20, 30—30—30, 40, 40, 50)

Mode (most frequent number): $30 000

Figure 2.10 Central Tendency in a Skewed Distribution

The mean is not always the ideal measure of central tendency. In this example, the mode and the median are actually more indicative of how much money most people make.

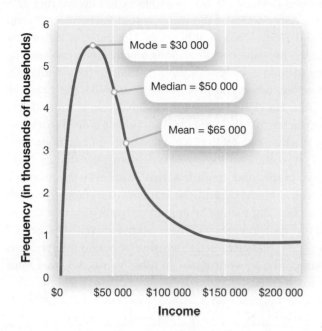

Figure 2.11 Visualizing Variability

Imagine that these curves show how two classes fared on a 20-point quiz. Both classes averaged scores of 15 points. However, the students in one class (depicted in red) scored much more similarly to one another compared to students in another class (depicted in black), whose scores showed greater variability. The class represented by the black line would have a higher standard deviation.

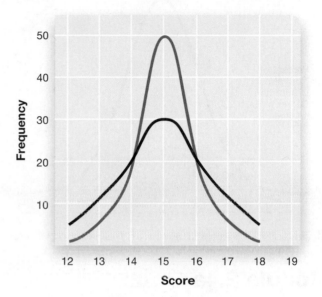

curve. By comparison, the median stays relatively stable, so it is a better choice for describing central tendency when dealing with skewed data. For instance, if you added Bill Gates's annual income (approximately $11.5 billion dollars—for a net worth over $72 billion) to the list of nine incomes in Figure 2.10, the mean annual income becomes just over $1.5 billion. If you take the median of those ten incomes, the central tendency is $30 000. Looking at those data, which measure seems most consistent with the "big picture" of the results?

VARIABILITY Measures of central tendency help us summarize a group of individual cases with a single number by identifying a cluster of scores. However, this information only tells us part of the story. As you can see in Figure 2.11, scores can differ in terms of their **variability**, *the degree to which scores are dispersed in a distribution*. In other words, some scores are quite spread out while others are more clustered. High variability means that there are a larger number of cases that are closer to the extreme ends of the continuum for that set of data (e.g., a lot of excellent students *and* a lot of poor students in a class). Low variability means that most of the scores are similar (e.g., a class filled with "B" students). Variability can be caused by measurement errors, imperfect measurement tools, differences between participants in the study, or characteristics of participants on that given day (e.g., mood, fatigue levels). All data sets have some variability. But, if information about variability is not provided by the researcher, it is impossible to understand how well the measure of central

tendency—the single score representing the data—reflects the entire data set. Therefore, whenever psychologists report data from their research, their measures of central tendency are almost always accompanied by measures of variability.

One calculation that allows researchers to link central tendency and variability is known as the **standard deviation**, *a measure of variability around the mean*. Think of it as an estimate of the *average distance from the mean*. A large standard deviation would indicate that there is a lot of variability in the data and that the values are quite spread out from the mean. A small standard deviation would indicate the opposite.

Standard deviations allow investigators to see how different scores relate to the mean and to each other. Perhaps the best way to understand the standard deviation is by working through an example. In a standard intelligence test, there is a normal distribution (a bell curve) with a mean of 100 and a standard deviation of 15 (see Module 9.1). Based on what you've read in this module, you would infer that 100 is the mid-point of the curve when these data are graphed. But, how much of the data is included in each standard deviation? As you can see in Figure 2.12, researchers have found that approximately 68% of the data are found within one standard deviation of the mean—34% above the mean (between 100 and 115) and 34% below the mean (between 85 and 100). This makes intuitive sense—we would expect a fairly large proportion of the scores to

Figure 2.12 Standard Deviations in a Normal Distribution

In a normal curve, most of the data are clustered within one standard deviation of the mean. Over 95% of the data in a normal distribution are found within two standard deviations of the mean.

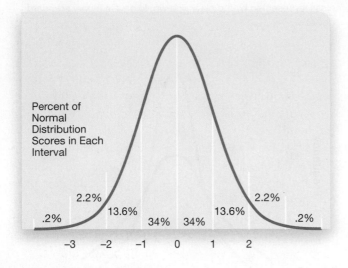

Percent of Normal Distribution Scores in Each Interval

.2% 2.2% 13.6% 34% 34% 13.6% 2.2% .2%

-3 -2 -1 0 1 2

be grouped near the average score. As we move further away from the average score, each standard deviation would make up less and less of the data, because really high or really low scores are relatively rare. So, the next standard deviation in our example makes up roughly 27% of the data—13.5% of the scores would fall between 70 and 85 and 13.5% would fall between 115 and 130. When you add the two standard deviations together, you can see that they include over 95% of the IQ scores in the population. Therefore, when you hear about people like the physicist Stephen Hawking, whose IQ is estimated to be around 160, you can see that these are rare individuals indeed (comprising less than one-tenth of a percent of the population).

This section of the module demonstrates that by making a graph and reporting two numbers—the measure of central tendency and the standard deviation—you can provide a "big picture" summary of your data that almost anyone can understand. That's Step 1 of statistics. Step 2 uses these measures to test whether or not your hypothesis is supported by your data—in other words, whether your project worked.

Module 2.4a Quiz:

Descriptive Statistics

Know . . .

1. The _____ always marks the 50th percentile of the distribution.
   A. mean
   B. median
   C. mode
   D. standard deviation

2. The _____ is a measure of variability around the mean of a distribution.
   A. mean deviation
   B. median
   C. mode
   D. standard deviation

Apply . . .

3. Dr. Lee taught two sections of Introductory Psychology. The mean score for both classes was 70%. However, the standard deviation was 15% for the first class and 5% for the second class. What can we infer about Dr. Lee's two classes?

A. There was more variability in the test scores of the first class.
B. The mode would equal the mean in the first class but not in the second class.
C. There was more variability in the second class than in the first class.
D. The mean, median, and mode would all be equal in the second class.

Analyze . . .

4. In a survey of recent graduates, your university reports that the mean salaries of the former students are positively skewed. What are the consequences of choosing the mean rather than the median or the mode in this case?

A. The mean is likely to provide a number that is lower than the largest cluster of scores.
B. The mean is likely to provide a reliable estimate of where the scores cluster.
C. The mean is likely to provide a number that is higher than the largest cluster of scores.
D. The mean provides the 50th percentile of the distribution, making it the best choice to depict this cluster of scores.

Hypothesis Testing: Evaluating the Outcome of a Study

After researchers have described their data, the next step is to test whether the data support their hypothesis. In order to do this, researchers analyze data using a **hypothesis test**—*a statistical method of evaluating whether differences*

among groups are meaningful, or could have been arrived at by chance alone. What scientists are essentially trying to do is determine if their experimental manipulation is the cause of any difference between groups or between conditions. However, the ability to tease out these differences is affected by the concepts discussed earlier in this module—specifically, the measure of central tendency for the

Figure 2.13 Testing a Simple Hypothesis

To conduct an experiment on whether texting reduces loneliness, students would be randomly assigned to either text-messaging or no-text-messaging groups. Their average scores on a loneliness scale would then be compared.

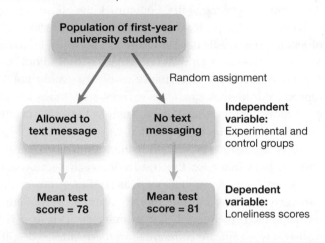

Figure 2.13 shows us the key elements of such an experiment. Individuals are sampled from the population and randomly assigned to either the experimental or control group. The independent variable consists of the two groups, which includes texting or no texting. The dependent variable is the outcome—in this case, loneliness (as measured by a valid questionnaire), with larger scores indicating greater loneliness. As you can see, the mean loneliness score of the group who could text message is three points below the mean of the group who did not text message (78 vs. 81, respectively). So, based on this information, are you willing to say that texting causes people to feel less lonely? Or have we left something out?

What we do not know from the diagram is the variability of test scores. On the one hand, it is quite possible that the scores of the two groups look like the graphs on the left in Figure 2.14. In that situation, the means are three points apart and the standard deviation is very small, so the curves have very little overlap. In this case, it is fairly easy to detect differences between the groups; the "signal" is easy to pick out from the "noise." On the other hand, the scores of each group could have a broad range and therefore look like the graphs on the right. In that case, the group means are three points apart, but the groups overlap so much—the standard deviations are very high—that they seem virtually identical. In this case, the "noise"—the variability within each of the two groups—is so large that it is difficult to detect the "signal," the differences between the two groups.

How, then, would researchers know if the difference in scores is meaningful? "Meaningful" seems like a vague term; as we have already discussed, science requires precise definitions. In order to address this problem, psychologists perform analyses that rely on the concept of *statistical significance*.

groups being measured as well as the variability of data in each of the groups. The difference in the central tendency for the two groups represents a "signal" that we are trying to detect, similar to a voice in a loud room. The variability represents the "noise," the outside forces that are making it difficult to detect the signal.

To make this discussion more concrete, let's use an example of a behaviour that almost everyone performs: texting. Let's say that we wanted to test whether text messaging reduces feelings of loneliness in first-year university students. For three days, randomly selected students who regularly send text messages are assigned to one of two groups: those who can text and those who cannot. After three days, the students fill out a survey measuring how lonely they have felt. The diagram in

Figure 2.14 How Variability Affects Hypothesis Testing

(a) The means (represented by M) differ between the two groups, and there is little overlap in the distribution of scores. When this occurs, the groups are much more likely to be significantly different. (b) Even though the means differ, there is much overlap between the distributions of scores. It is unlikely that these two means would be significantly different.

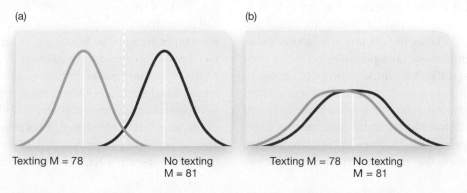

Working the Scientific Literacy Model

Statistical Significance

Statistical significance is a concept that implies that *the means of the groups are farther apart than you would expect them to be by random chance alone.* It was first proposed in 1925 by Ronald Fisher, an English statistician working at an agricultural research station east of London (U.K.). Statistical significance quickly became a key component of research in many disciplines. However, it has also been a source of some surprisingly intense arguments (Cohen, 1994).

What do we know about statistical significance?

Statistical significance testing is based on the researcher making two hypotheses. The **null hypothesis** *assumes that any differences between groups (or conditions) are due to chance.* The **experimental hypothesis** *assumes that any differences are due to a variable controlled by the experimenter.* The goal of researchers is to find differences between groups that are so large that it is virtually impossible for the null hypothesis to be true; in other words, they are not due to chance. The probability of the results being due to chance is known as a *p-value.* Lower *p*-values (e.g., $p = 0.01$ as opposed to $p = 0.45$) indicate a decreased likelihood that your results were a fluke, and therefore an increased likelihood that you had a great idea and designed a good experiment.

So, how do we find the *p*-value? The specific formulas used for these calculations will vary according to how the experiment is set up. But, they all involve a measure of central tendency (usually the mean) and a measure of variability (usually the standard deviation). These numbers are then used in statistical tests that will produce a *p*-value.

What can science tell us about statistical significance?

When Fisher first presented the idea of significance testing, he noted that scientists needed to establish a fairly conservative threshold for rejecting the null hypothesis (i.e., for deciding that the results were significant). He correctly thought that if it were quite easy for researchers to find a significant result, it would increase the likelihood that results labelled as being significant were actually due to chance. If enough of these false positives occurred, then the entire idea of significance would soon become meaningless. Fisher therefore recommended that researchers use $p < 0.05$ as the cut-off point (this value was consistent with earlier statistical techniques, so his decision was likely an attempt to compromise with other statisticians; Stigler, 2008). If a *p*-value were less than 0.05, then there was less than a 5% chance that the results were due to chance. This *p*-value quickly became the standard in a number of fields, including psychology.

Of course, just because a particular value is widely accepted does not mean that scientists can stop using their critical thinking skills. Sometimes the consequences of having a false positive are quite severe, as in the case of testing new medicines for a disease. It would be tragic to make claims about a wonder drug only to find out that the results were due to a chance result that could not be reproduced. In such cases, researchers sometimes use an even more conservative *p*-value, such as requiring results to be less than 0.01 (i.e., $p < 0.01$).

It is also worth noting that when testing small sample sizes, it is difficult for the results to reach significance. But, some types of research, such as studies of rare brain-damaged patients, have a limited number of potential participants. It therefore becomes more difficult to detect statistically significant differences in these studies despite the fact that the groups do appear to differ when you look at graphs of the data (Bezeau & Graves, 2001). In these cases, significance testing might not be the best statistical tool for analyzing the data. Luckily, significance testing is not the only technique available.

Can we critically evaluate the use of statistical significance testing in research?

Although significance testing has been a potent tool for researchers in the social sciences for almost a century, it does have some detractors. American psychologist Paul Meehl (1967) subtly described significance testing as "a potent but sterile intellectual rake who leaves in his merry path a long train of ravished maidens but no viable scientific offspring" (p. 265). Although this description may be a touch dramatic, there *are* at least two concerns related to significance testing. The first is the problem of multiple comparisons. If a "fluke" result can occur approximately 5% of the time, the more tests you perform for your experiment, the greater the likelihood that one of them is due to chance. In order to cope with this problem, researchers generally use a stricter acceptable *p*-value; as the number of comparisons increases, researchers decrease the *p*-value (i.e., make it more conservative). This makes it more difficult to produce significant results, but does help ensure that the results are not due to chance. A second problem is the fact that as you increase the number of participants in your study, it becomes easier to find significant effects. At first blush, this doesn't seem like a valid concern. Having more participants means that you are sampling a larger portion of the population of interest. Isn't that a good thing? The answer is yes, of course it is. But, if you sample thousands of people—as often happens in medical studies tracking potential lifestyle causes of diseases—extremely small differences will still be statistically significant. The media provides almost daily reports of different foods increasing or decreasing the risk of particular diseases. Before totally altering your lifestyle, it is best to look up the original report to see if the difference was large, or was simply due to the fact that the sample size was in the thousands.

As an alternative to significance testing, Jacob Cohen (1988) developed a technique known as *power analysis*, whose goal is to calculate *effect sizes*. Rather than saying that a difference is significant, which is essentially a yes–no decision, effect sizes tell the researcher whether the difference is statistically small or large. So, instead of an experiment supporting or disproving a theory, effect sizes allow the researcher to adjust how much they believe that their hypothesis is true (Cohen, 1994).

Why is this relevant?

Statistical significance gives psychology researchers a useful standard for deciding if the differences between groups (or experimental conditions) are meaningful. Having established criteria for deciding if an effect is significant is important, because it means that all researchers are using standardized tools. If different research groups were using different criteria for deciding that effects were "real," then it would be nearly impossible for that research area to move forward—people would be speaking different languages. Significance testing makes sure that everyone is on the same page, statistically speaking. However, as noted above, there are alternative methods for examining data. Effect sizes are becoming commonplace in many areas of psychology; an increasing number of academic journals now require researchers to calculate *both* statistical significance *and* effect sizes, thus giving readers an even more detailed picture of the data.

A final point is that, although statistical significance tells us that results are meaningful, there is still a possibility that the results were due to chance. It is only through replication—having other laboratories repeat the experiments and produce similar results—that we can become confident that a difference is meaningful. Many scientists now make their stimuli and data available to other researchers in order to encourage this process. This move toward openness and replication is itself quite significant.

Module 2.4b Quiz:

Hypothesis Testing: Evaluating the Outcome of a Study

Understand . . .

1. A hypothesis test is conducted after an experiment to
   A. determine whether the two groups in the study are exactly the same.
   B. determine how well the two groups are correlated.
   C. see if the groups are significantly different, as opposed to being different due to chance.
   D. summarize the distribution using a single score.

Analyze . . .

2. Imagine an experiment where the mean of the experimental group is 50 and the mean of the control group is 40. Given that the two means are obviously different, is it still possible for a researcher to say that the two groups are not significantly different?
   A. Yes, the two groups could overlap so much that the difference was not significant.
   B. Yes, if the difference was not predicted by the hypothesis.
   C. No, because the two groups are so far apart that the difference must be significant.
   D. No, in statistics a difference of 10 points is just enough to be significant.

Module 2.4 Summary

2.4a Know . . . the key terminology of statistics.

central tendency
descriptive statistics
experimental hypothesis
frequency
hypothesis test
mean
median
mode
negatively skewed distribution
normal distribution
null hypothesis
positively skewed distribution
standard deviation
statistical significance
variability

2.4b Understand . . . how and why psychologists use significance tests.

Significance tests are statistics that tell us whether differences between groups or distributions are meaningful. For example, the averages of two groups being compared may be very different. However, how much variability there is among individuals within each of the groups will determine whether the averages are significantly different. In some cases, the averages of the two groups may be different, yet not statistically different because the groups overlap so much. This possibility explains why psychologists use significance tests—to test whether groups really are different from one another.

2.4c Apply . . . your knowledge to interpret the most frequently used types of graphs.

Take a look at Figure 2.15, a histogram showing the grades from a quiz in a statistics course, and then answer the following questions.

1. What is the shape of this distribution? Normal, negatively skewed, or positively skewed?
2. What grade range is the mode for this class?
3. How many people earned a grade in the "B" range (between 80 and 89)?

2.4d Analyze . . . the choice of central tendency statistics based on the shape of the distribution.

Although the mean is the most commonly used measure of central tendency, it is not always the best method for describing a set of data. For example, incomes are positively skewed. Suppose one politician claims the mean income level is $40 000, while the other claims that the median income level is $25 000. Which politician is giving the more representative measure? It would seem that the median would be a more representative statistic because it is not overly influenced by extremely high scores.

Figure 2.15 Application Activity

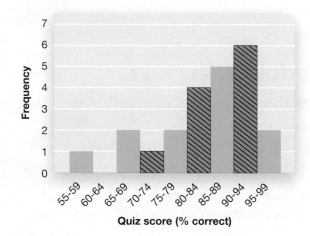

Chapter 3
Biological Psychology

3.1 Genetic and Evolutionary Perspectives on Behaviour

- Heredity and Behaviour 73
- Module 3.1a Quiz 79
- Evolutionary Insights into Human Behaviour 79
  Working the Scientific Literacy Model: Hunters and
  Gatherers: Men, Women, and Spatial Memory 81
- Module 3.1b Quiz 86
- Module 3.1 Summary 86

3.2 How the Nervous System Works: Cells and Neurotransmitters

- Neural Communication 89
- Module 3.2a Quiz 93
- The Chemical Messengers: Neurotransmitters and Hormones 93
  Working the Scientific Literacy Model: Testosterone and Aggression 97
- Module 3.2b Quiz 99
- Module 3.2 Summary 100

3.3 Structure and Organization of the Nervous System

- Divisions of the Nervous System 102
- Module 3.3a Quiz 104
- The Brain and Its Structures 104
  Working the Scientific Literacy Model:
  Neuroplasticity and Recovery from Brain Injury 113
- Module 3.3b Quiz 114
- Module 3.3 Summary 115

3.4 Windows to the Brain: Measuring and Observing Brain Activity

- Insights from Brain Damage 117
- Module 3.4a Quiz 118
- Structural and Functional Neuroimaging 119
  Working the Scientific Literacy Model: Functional MRI and Behaviour 122
- Module 3.4b Quiz 123
- Module 3.4 Summary 124

Module 3.1   Genetic and Evolutionary Perspectives on Behaviour

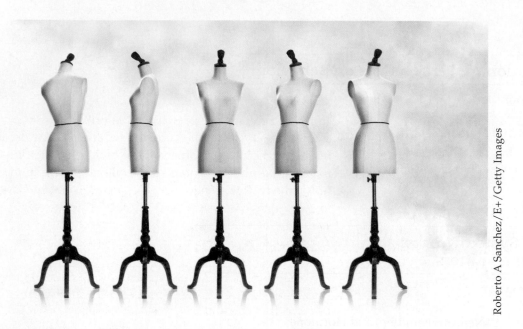

Roberto A Sanchez/E+/Getty Images

 ## Learning Objectives

3.1a Know . . . the key terminology related to genes, heredity, and evolutionary psychology.

3.1b Understand . . . how twin and adoption studies reveal relationships between genes and behaviour.

3.1c Apply . . . your knowledge of genes and behaviour to hypothesize why a trait might be adaptive.

3.1d Analyze . . . claims that scientists have located a specific gene that controls a single trait or behaviour.

3.1e Analyze . . . explanations for cognitive gender differences that are rooted in genetics.

Psychologist Martie Haselton has given new meaning to the phrase dress for success. *She is not talking about professional advancement, however; rather, she is referring to success in attracting a mate. Dr. Haselton is an evolutionary psychologist—she studies how human behaviour has evolved to solve problems that relate to survival and reproductive success. As part of her work, she has discovered that the clothes people choose are related to sexual motivation in some subtle ways.*

In one project, Dr. Haselton and her colleagues invited female volunteers to the laboratory to participate in a study about personality, sexuality, and health. The young women were not given any specific directions about what to wear and during their visit to the laboratory they agreed to be

photographed. Later, male and female volunteers viewed the photographs to judge whether they thought the women in the photos had dressed to look attractive. It turns out that women were rated as having dressed more attractively when they were in their peak level of fertility of the menstrual cycle (Durante et al., 2008; Haselton et al., 2007). The researchers suggested that wearing such clothing during the fertile phase of the menstrual cycle was an attempt to be noticed by a potential mate (although the women in the study might disagree).

Of course, evolutionary psychologists are quick to point out that females are not alone in "signalling" their receptiveness for sexual activity. Males provide numerous—if not more obvious—examples. Indeed, body building, flaunting material assets, and other public displays of strength and status are common male strategies for attracting mates. Researchers must ask themselves this question: Is this behaviour just a coincidence? Or is this how the evolutionary forces that allowed our species to survive for hundreds of thousands of years are influencing our behaviour in the modern world? Evolutionary psychologists like Dr. Haselton are building evidence to argue that how we dress and how we send many other signals can be explained by evolutionary principles, a topic we explore in this module.

Focus Questions

1. How is human behaviour influenced by genetic factors?

2. How has evolution played a role in modern-day human behaviour?

》 A question that underlies a great deal of psychological inquiry is "Why do we behave the way we do?" In some situations, you might be tempted to say that your behaviour was a reaction to someone else or to the situation that you were in. In others, you might say that you *interpreted* a situation in a particular way, and that led to a particular response. You might also say that you just reacted "naturally," which implies that your behaviour is sometimes hard-wired. According to the biopsychosocial model of psychology, all three explanations can be valid in some situations. Therefore, to fully understand why you behave the way you do, it is necessary to understand the forces that influence each of these factors that affect our behaviour. In the current module, we will focus on genetic and evolutionary explanations; however, it is important to remember that almost everything you do—or anyone else does—is due to biological, cognitive (psychological), and social factors.

Heredity and Behaviour

Examples of genetic influences on physical traits easily come to mind because we tend to share our eye colour, facial characteristics, stature, and skin colouration with our parents. But research has made it clear that behaviours are influenced by genes just as physical characteristics are; indeed, the two are often related. Genetics has an influence on the brain, just as it has an influence on eye colour, and changes in brain functions lead to changes in behaviour. Therefore, although a discussion of genetics may seem unrelated to how you think or feel, the work of genes—both during development and during everyday life—has a dramatic effect on your behaviour.

THE GENETIC CODE   Given that genetics can influence so many aspects of our lives, it is important to review some of this field's basic concepts. Our genetic code isn't hidden in the darkest corners of our brains. Instead, it is found in the nucleus of most of the billions of cells in the human body. This genetic material is organized into **genes**, *the basic units of heredity; genes are responsible for guiding the process of creating the proteins that make up our physical structures and regulate development and physiological processes throughout the lifespan.*

Genes are composed of segments of **DNA (deoxyribonucleic acid)**, *a molecule formed in a double-helix shape that contains four nucleotides: adenine, cytosine, guanine, and thymine* (see Figure 3.1). These nucleotides are typically abbreviated using the first letter of their names—A, C, G, and T. Each gene is a unique combination of these four nucleotides. For example, a gene may consist of sequences of nucleotides such as AGCCTAATCGATGCGCCA . . . and so on. These sequences of nucleotides (i.e., these genes) represent the instructions or code used to create the thousands of different proteins found in the human body. These proteins specify which types of molecules to produce and when to produce them. Genes also contain information about which environmental factors might influence whether the genes become active ("expressed") or not. Together, this information makes up an individual's

Figure 3.1 DNA Molecules

The nucleus of a cell contains copies of each chromosome. Chromosomes are composed of the genes arranged in the familiar double helix—a long strand of DNA molecules.

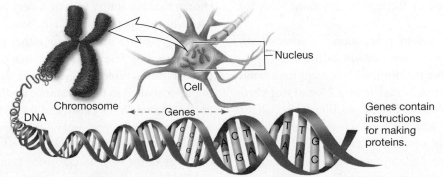

Source: Lilienfeld, Scott O.; Lynn, Steven J; Namy, Laura L.; Woolf, Nancy J., *Psychology: From Inquiry To Understanding,* 2nd Ed., ©2011. Reprinted And Electronically Reproduced By Permission Of Pearson Education, Inc., New York, NY.

Figure 3.2 Human Chromosomes

Human DNA is aligned along 23 paired chromosomes. Numbers 1–22 are common to both males and females. Chromosome 23 is sex linked, with males having the XY pattern and females the XX pattern.

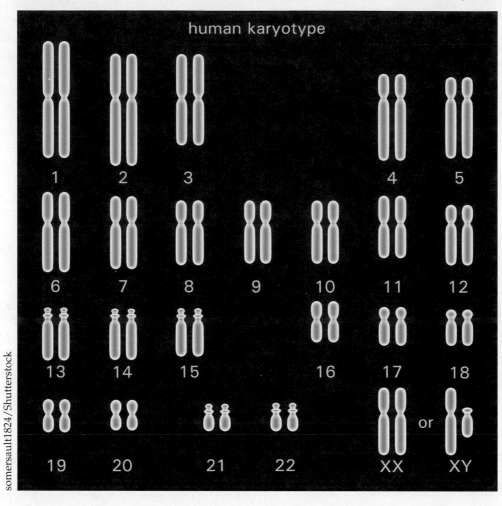

genotype, *the genetic makeup of an organism—the unique set of genes that comprise that individual's genetic code.*

The result is an organism's **phenotype**, *the physical traits and behavioural characteristics that show genetic variation, such as eye colour, the shape and size of facial features, intelligence, and even personality.* This phenotype develops because of differences in the nucleotide sequencing of A, C, G, and T, as well as through interactions with the environment.

Genes are organized in pairs along **chromosomes**, *structures in the cellular nucleus that are lined with all of the genes an individual inherits.* Humans have approximately 20 000–25 000 genes distributed across 23 pairs of chromosomes, half contributed by the mother and half by the father (see Figure 3.2). (In some cases, an extra chromosome—a *trisomy*—is present, thus altering the genetic make-up as well as the phenotype of the individual. The most common chromosomal abnormality is Down Syndrome, a trisomy on the 21st chromosome, although many others exist.)

If two corresponding genes at a given location on a pair of chromosomes are the same, they are referred to as *homozygous*. If the two genes differ, they are *heterozygous*. Whether a trait is expressed depends on which combination of pairs is inherited. In order to make these abstract concepts more concrete, let's look at an example that affects everyone: our sense of taste. Researchers have shown that the ability to taste a very bitter substance called phenylthiocarbamide (PTC) is based on which combination of genes we inherit from either parent (the genotype; see Figure 3.3). The test for whether you can taste PTC (the phenotype) is typically performed by placing a small tab of paper soaked in the substance on the tongue. Some people are "tasters"; they cringe at the bitter taste of PTC. Others—the "non-tasters"—cannot taste anything other than the tab of paper. Those who are tasters inherited at least one copy of the *dominant* gene for tasting (abbreviated capital "T") from either parent. People can also inherit a *recessive* copy of this gene (t). Those who report tasting PTC are either homozygous dominant (TT) or heterozygous (Tt).

Figure 3.3 Genetic Inheritance

Whether someone tastes the bitter compound PTC depends on which copies of the gene he or she inherits. Shown here is the statistically probable outcome of two heterozygous (Tt) parents with four children.

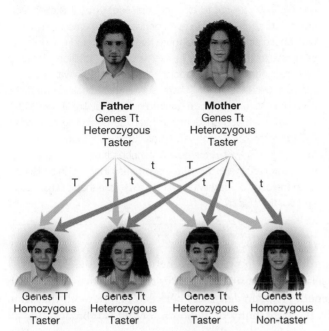

Father
Genes Tt
Heterozygous
Taster

Mother
Genes Tt
Heterozygous
Taster

Genes TT
Homozygous
Taster

Genes Tt
Heterozygous
Taster

Genes Tt
Heterozygous
Taster

Genes tt
Homozygous
Non-taster

Source: Data from Influence of life stress on depression: Moderation by a polymorphism in the 5-HTT gene by Caspi, A., et al., *Science*, 301, 386–389. 2003.

Non-tasters are homozygous recessive (tt)—they inherited a recessive copy of the gene from both parents. Those who are tasters may find foods such as Brussels sprouts, cauliflower, and cabbage to be unpleasant, or at least too bitter to eat, as these foods contain PTC.

In this example, the genotype represents what was inherited (i.e., tt, Tt, or TT). The phenotype represents the physical and behavioural manifestation of that genotype that occurs through interactions with the environment (i.e., being a taster or a non-taster for this *specific* sensation—note that non-tasters in this context might have normal responses to other tastes). As you will see, this attempt to link genes to behaviour is a rapidly growing area of research in psychology and medicine.

As geneticists continue to unravel different parts of the entire human genome, it is becoming increasingly clear that simple examples like the taster/non-taster trait provide only a glimpse of what knowledge might soon be available to us. Indeed, in recent years, an entirely new field has developed that attempts to identify the genes involved with specific behaviours: behavioural genomics.

BEHAVIOURAL GENOMICS: THE MOLECULAR APPROACH Although researchers have suggested that genetics play a role in many abilities and behaviours, until

recently it has not been possible to determine *how* traits are inherited. To make this determination, researchers now go straight to the source of genetic influence—to the genes themselves. **Behavioural genomics** *is the study of DNA and the ways in which specific genes are related to behaviour.* The technology supporting behavioural genomics is relatively new, but once it became available, researchers initiated a massive effort to identify the components of the entire human genome—the *Human Genome Project.* This project, which was completed in 2003, resulted in the identification of approximately 20 000–25 000 genes. Imagine the undertaking: determining the sequences of the billions of A, C, G, and T nucleotides making up the genes, including where each gene begins and ends, and how they are all arranged on the chromosomes. The Human Genome Project itself did not directly provide a cure for a disease or an understanding of any particular behaviour. Instead, it has led to an abundance of new techniques and information about where genes are located, and it opened the door for an entirely new era of research (Plomin & Crabbe, 2000). Indeed, researchers can now compare the genotypes of different groups of people (e.g., depressed and non-depressed individuals) to look for differences that might shed light on the cause of different conditions. For example, in 1997, researchers identified a gene that was found in families prone to Parkinson's disease, a neurological disorder involving tremors and difficulties making movements (Polymeropoulos et al., 1997). Since then, a number of mutations that are linked to Parkinson's have been identified including *SNCA, Parkin, PINK1, DJ1,* and *LRRK2* (Klein & Schlossmacher, 2006).

However, we must be cautious in our interpretation of such discoveries. Like any approach to answering scientific questions, behavioural genomic research does have its limitations. For example, although a single gene has been identified as a risk factor for Alzheimer's disease, not everyone who inherits it develops the disease. The same is true for many other conditions. This is a common misconception about genes and behaviour.

BEHAVIOURAL GENETICS: TWIN AND ADOPTION STUDIES Although behavioural genomics studies can identify genes related to behaviours, they don't tell us how sensitive these genes are to environmental factors like stress, family life, or socioeconomic status. These questions are examined using a complementary field known as **behavioural genetics**, *the study of how genes and the environment influence behaviour.* Behavioural genetic methods applied to humans typically involve comparing people of different levels of relatedness, such as parents and their offspring, siblings, and unrelated individuals, and measuring resemblances for a specific trait of interest. The group that has provided the most insight into the genetic effects on behaviour is twins.

Myths in Mind

Single Genes and Behaviour

Enter the phrase "scientists find the gene for" into your favourite Internet search engine and you will wind up with more hits than you would ever have time to sift through. Although it is true that behaviour, both normal and abnormal, can be traced to individual genes, typically *combinations* of genes influence behaviour. When it comes to complex characteristics such as personality or disorders like Alzheimer's disease and schizophrenia, there is very little chance that any single gene could be responsible for them (Duan et al., 2010). A person's intelligence and his predisposition to alcoholism, anxiety, shyness, and depression are all examples of traits and conditions with genetic links, but they all involve multiple genes.

Another misconception is that a single gene can affect only one trait. In reality, the discovery that a particular gene predisposes someone to alcoholism does not mean that this gene is *only* relevant to alcohol addiction; it most likely affects other traits as well. For example, genes that are present in people who abuse alcohol are also more likely to be found in individuals who have a history of other problems such as additional forms of drug dependence and antisocial behaviour. In other words, these different behaviours may share some characteristics, and the gene may be related to that "shared genetic liability" (Dick, 2007).

So, when you encounter a headline beginning "Scientists find gene for . . . ," don't read it as "Scientists found THE gene for. . . ." It is likely that the news describes the work of scientists who found another one of the many genes involved in a disorder or, in the case of Alzheimer's disease, a gene that is a risk factor and *not* the sole cause.

Twins present an amazing opportunity to conduct natural experiments on how genes influence behaviour. One method commonly used in twin studies involves comparing identical and fraternal twins. **Monozygotic twins** *come from a single ovum (egg), which makes them genetically identical (almost 100% genetic similarity).* An ideal comparison group, **dizygotic twins** (fraternal twins) *come from two separate eggs fertilized by two different sperm cells that share the same womb; these twins have approximately 50% of their genetics in common.* Researchers around the world have studied the genetic and environmental bases of behaviour by comparing monozygotic twins, dizygotic twins, non-twin siblings, and unrelated individuals. The assumption underlying these studies is that if a trait is genetically determined, then individuals with a greater genetic similarity will also have a greater similarity for that trait. Researchers have also examined these different groups in **longitudinal studies**, *studies that follow the same individuals for many years, often decades.* For example, one twin study determined the degree to which anxiety and depression are influenced by genetics in children and adolescents. It was far more likely for both monozygotic twins to show anxiety or depressive symptoms than for both dizygotic twins to do so; thus, these results demonstrate the influential role that genes play in depression (Boomsma et al., 2005).

Behavioural geneticists use twin studies to calculate **heritability**—*a statistic, expressed as a number between zero and one, that represents the degree to which genetic differences between individuals contribute to individual differences in a behaviour or trait found in a population.* A heritability of 0 means that genes do not contribute to individual differences in a trait, whereas a heritability of 1.0 indicates that genes account for all individual differences in a trait. It is important to point out that heritability scores do *not* simply reflect how much genetics contributes to the trait itself. Rather, heritability scores tell us the degree to which genetics explain *differences* between people with that trait. So, the heritability of having a tongue is 0 because we all have a tongue (i.e., there are no differences to explain). But, the taste sensitivity of that tongue differs based on genetics and on the foods you were exposed to while growing up.

Top: Creatas Images/Thinkstock/Getty Images bottom: Martin Harvey/Alamy Stock Photo

Identical twins are genetically the same, whereas fraternal twins are no more closely related than full siblings from different pregnancies. However, fraternal twins do share much of the same prenatal and postnatal environment if they are reared together. Researchers assume, then, that if the identical twins are more similar on a given trait than fraternal twins, this difference is due to genetics. But, it is *possible* that identical twins are treated more similarly than are fraternal twins (so they have more nature *and* more nurture in common). How would this affect your interpretation of twin studies?

Taste will therefore have a heritability score somewhere between 0 and 1.

Heritability estimates are rarely, if ever, an extreme value of 0 or 1.0. Instead, genetics and environmental influences (e.g., family life) both account for some of the differences in our behaviour. For instance, the estimated heritability found in the study on depression and anxiety described earlier was approximately .76 for 3-year-old identical twin pairs (Boomsma et al., 2005). This tells us that 76% of individual differences in depression and anxiety at age 3 can be attributed to genetic factors in the population that was studied. However, depression and anxiety can also obviously be influenced by our different life experiences. It should not be a surprise to learn that heritability estimates for these behaviours change as we age. In the Boomsma and colleagues (2005) study, the heritability of anxiety and depression went from .76 at age 3 to .48 at age 12 for the identical twin pairs. This change is likely due to the fact that an individual's peer group and social life can have a larger effect on one's emotional well-being during the "tween" and teen-aged years than they would during the toddler years (when family is the main non-genetic factor). This finding should serve as a reminder that the environment never stops interacting with genes.

Behavioural geneticists also study adopted children to estimate genetic contributions to behaviour. The adopted family represents the *nurture* side of the continuum, whereas the biological family represents the *nature* side. On the one hand, if adopted children are more like their biological parents than their adoptive parents on measures of traits such as personality and intelligence, we might conclude that these traits have a strong genetic component. On the other hand, if the children are more like their adoptive, genetically *un*related parents, a strong case can be made that environmental factors outweigh the biological predispositions. Interestingly, young adopted children are more similar to their adoptive parents in intelligence levels than they are to their biological parents. By the time they reach 16 years, however, adopted adolescents score more similarly to their biological parents than their adoptive parents in tests of intelligence, suggesting that some genes related to intelligence do not exert their influence(s) on behaviour until later on in development (Plomin et al., 1997). Compare this finding to that from the study described in the preceding paragraphs: For intelligence, heritability seems to increase with age, whereas the opposite is true for depression and anxiety.

Although heritability estimates provide important information about the different effects of "nature" and "nurture" on different behaviours, we have to be cautious about how we generalize this information. Heritability estimates are limited to the population being studied. We cannot make definitive statements about the heritability of depression in Brazil based on the results of a study conducted in Canada (although we can use the Canadian study to generate hypotheses about what we *think* we would find if we performed the same study in Brazil). This is because any estimate of heritability is affected by (1) the amount of genetic variability within the group being studied and (2) the variability in the environments that members of that group might be exposed to. For example, people from an isolated village in the Amazon rain forest would likely not have much variability in their genetics because they would not have a lot of contact with outside groups. In contrast, many Canadians have diverse genetic backgrounds. Therefore, the individual differences in the Amazon village would most likely be due to environmental factors; this would lead to a lower heritability estimate for this group. This is not to say that one way of life is better than another—but we need to be mindful of these differences in genetic and environmental variability so that we don't incorrectly assume that North American genetic studies generalize to the entire world.

Heritability estimates can vary with age. The heritability of depression and anxiety decreases with age whereas the heritability of intelligence increases with age.

Ale Ventura/PhotoAlto Agency RF Collections/Getty Images

Steve Debenport/E+/Getty Images

GENE EXPRESSION AND BEHAVIOUR The fact that heritability estimates change over time based on our different experiences shows us that nature and nurture interact to produce behaviour. What these estimates don't tell us is *how* that interaction occurs in our bodies and brains. Recent advances in our understanding of genetics and the human genome have begun to shed light on some of these relationships.

Almost every cell in our bodies contains the same genes, the basic unit of heredity. But, only some of these genes are active, leading to the production of proteins (or other gene products like ribosomal RNA); the other genes are inactive and do not influence protein production. Of the approximately 20 000–25 000 genes in the human genome, between 6000 and 7000 are active in the human brain. These genes influence the development of different brain structures, the production of chemicals that allow brain cells to communicate with each other, and the refinement of connections between cells that allow large-scale brain networks to form (French & Pavlidis, 2011). The expression of these genes is influenced by genetics, environmental factors that influence the chemical make-up of the cells, or a combination of the two.

If some genes fail to be activated (or *expressed*) properly, people may be at a greater risk for developing brain-related disorders. For example, Dan Geschwind and colleagues (2011) found that children with autism had less gene expression in several regions of the brain. This decrease in gene expression was linked to problems with language, decision making, and understanding other people's emotions. Researchers are now investigating ways to alter gene expression in order to treat different brain disorders such as Parkinson's disease and Alzheimer's disease.

Importantly, gene expression is a lifelong process (Champagne, 2010). Factors such as diet, stress level, and sleep can influence whether genes are turned on or off. This study of *changes in gene expression that occur as a result of experience and that do not alter the genetic code* is known as **epigenetics**. Studies with mice have shown that increased maternal licking and grooming (the rodent equivalent of cuddling) led to an increase in the expression of the *GR* gene in the hippocampus (Francis et al., 1999). This gene influences stress responses and can affect how well (or poorly) individuals respond to novel situations. Low levels of licking and grooming led to decreased *GR* expression and a larger stress response (Weaver et al., 2004). Similar effects have been observed in humans. Decreased GR expression was noted in a recent study of childhood abuse victims who later committed suicide, demonstrating

Eric Isselee/123RF

Epigenetics research suggests that grooming not only influences social bonds, but can also affect the expression of genes.

the power of these gene–environment interactions. Indeed, there is increasing evidence that epigenetics plays a role in a number of psychological disorders (Labrie et al., 2012).

The fact that gene expression can be influenced by the environment is an example of the *social* part of the *biopsychosocial model* of behaviour discussed throughout this textbook—nurture can influence nature. Some researchers have speculated that gene expression could also be influenced by the culture in which one lives. Culture, family, and other social bonds all influence how we respond— both psychologically *and* biologically—to different situations and stimuli. Therefore, these sociocultural factors have the potential to influence whether or not certain genes are expressed (Richardson & Boyd, 2005).

Although many of the changes in gene expression do not alter the genetic code, some do get passed on from generation to generation. Chemically induced changes in the expression of genes in the amygdala and hippocampus— structures related to emotion and memory—have been shown to influence anxiety-related behaviours for *three generations* of rats (Skinner et al., 2008)! Licking and grooming have similarly been shown to affect both gene expression and maternal behaviours across three generations (Champagne et al., 2003). Therefore, how you behave now could have lasting effects on the genetic codes of your grandchildren.

Module 3.1a Quiz:
Heredity and Behaviour

Know . . .

1. The chemical units that provide instructions on how specific proteins are to be produced are called _____.
   A. chromosomes
   B. genes
   C. genomic
   D. autosomes

Understand . . .

2. A person who is homozygous for a trait
   A. always has two dominant copies of a gene.
   B. always has two recessive copies of a gene.
   C. has identical copies of the gene.
   D. has different copies of the gene.

Apply . . .

3. If a researcher wanted to identify how someone's life experiences could affect the expression of specific genes and thus put that person at risk for developing depression, she would most likely use which of the following methods?
   A. Behavioural genetics
   B. A comparison of monozygotic and dizygotic twins in different parts of the world
   C. An adoption study
   D. Epigenetics

Analyze . . .

4. Imagine you hear a report about a heritability study that claims trait X is "50% genetic." Which of the following is a more accurate way of stating this?
   A. Fifty percent of individual differences of trait X within a population are due to genetic factors.
   B. Only half of a population has the trait.
   C. Half of that trait is dependent upon genetics.
   D. More than 50% of similarities of trait X within a population are due to genetic factors.

Knowing about genes gives us some idea as to why individuals differ. But, they don't tell the whole story. We also need to examine how some traits or physical characteristics enhanced our ancestors' ability to survive and to pass on these genes to future generations, including us.

Evolutionary Insights into Human Behaviour

On December 27, 1831, a young Charles Darwin began his voyage on the HMS *Beagle,* a ship tasked to survey the coastline of South America. Darwin's (self-funded) position was to act as a naturalist, examining the wildlife, flora, and geology of the areas the ship visited. This five-year voyage, which included additional stops in Australia and South Africa, exposed Darwin to a vast number of species and eventually led to him developing one of the most important (and controversial) theories in human history.

While travelling among the different Galápagos Islands (900 km west of modern-day Ecuador), Darwin made a number of important observations. First, he identified fossils from several extinct species. This discovery highlighted the fact that not all species were able to survive in this environment. But, some species *did* have characteristics that allowed them to flourish. Second, he noticed small differences between the same species of birds and turtles living on different islands. These differences meshed quite well with the particular environments the animals lived in. From these observations, Darwin deduced that the species that were a good "fit" for their environment survived while other species did not.

The challenge for Darwin was to find a way to explain this observation. Looking at the individual animals, he saw a number of small differences similar to the differences you'd see between people in your classroom. Some individuals had traits that would enhance their ability to survive such as speed and strength. These individuals would likely get enough food to eat and would be able to find mates. Individuals without these traits would be less likely to mate. If this pattern continued, there would be more offspring with the favourable traits (strength and speed) than without those characteristics. Darwin developed these observations into his theory of **natural selection**, *the process by which favourable traits become increasingly common in a population of interbreeding individuals, while traits that are unfavourable become less common* (see Figure 3.4).

Although genes had not yet been discovered, they lay at the heart of Darwin's theories. When animals mate, each parent provides half of the offspring's genetic material. The genes of some animals would combine in such a way to produce traits favourable to that setting (i.e., they were adaptive) and the genes of other animals would combine in less useful ways. Because the adaptive or fit animals were more likely to survive and reproduce, these traits—and therefore these genes—would be more likely to be passed on to future generations. This process is known as **evolution**, *the change in the frequency of genes occurring in an interbreeding population over generations.*

Evolution is not a continuous process, however. If an animal is perfectly adapted for its environment, then there is no evolutionary pressure for change to occur. Let's call that version 1.0 of the animal. But what if some pressure

Figure 3.4 How Traits Evolve

Evolution through natural selection requires both that a trait be heritable (i.e., be passed down through reproductive means) and that certain individuals within a breeding population have a reproductive advantage for having the trait.

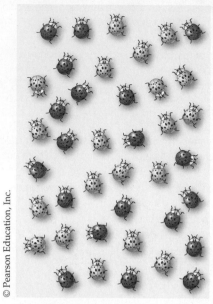 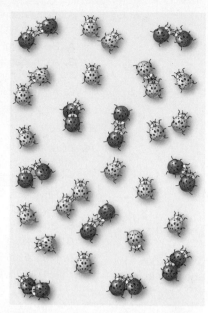 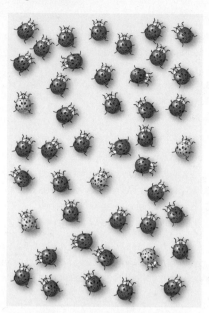

© Pearson Education, Inc.

Suppose colouration is a genetically inherited trait in lady bugs.

Suppose a bird that preys on these lady bugs can see the yellow ones better. This brings about a survival and reproductive advantage to red lady bugs that have red-coloured offspring.

Genes for red colouration should spread through the population because natural selection favours red lady bugs over yellow lady bugs.

such as a change in the climate or the availability of food occurs? In this case, a given trait might be advantageous in that specific environment and specific point in time. Individuals with that trait would survive; those without it might not. Through natural selection, this trait would eventually become common within that species and may in the future serve other functions and interact with the environment in novel ways. Let's call this version 2.0 of the animal. When the next environmental pressure occurred, a subset of version 2.0 of the animal would possess traits to make them more evolutionarily fit than the other version 2.0 animals. This subset would survive and reproduce, eventually leading to version 3.0 of the animal. While this description is over-simplified, it does illustrate a key point: Any modern species is based upon version after version after version of species that were fit for their particular environment and time.

EVOLUTIONARY PSYCHOLOGY Darwin suggested that humans followed a similar evolutionary path, changing and adapting over the course of thousands of generations. He was correct—there is now fossil evidence showing that many branches of our ancestral family tree died out, likely because their physical and mental characteristics were not fit for their environment. What separated our species, *Homo sapiens*, from other animals was that our ancestors had (1) larger frontal lobes than other species (see

Figure 3.5) and (2) had brains with more folds, thus allowing for more brain cells to be squeezed inside their skulls. These adaptations allowed our ancestors to form plans, solve problems, make quick decisions, and control our attention and actions (Stuss, 2011). As a result, they were able to think their way out of different challenges such as changes to the environment or food supply. They also were able to communicate this knowledge using symbolic representations of objects and ideas, as shown in carvings and cave paintings (Chase & Dibble, 1987); this allowed them to pass on knowledge from generation to generation, just as they passed on their genes.

Although all of this makes intuitive sense to us now, in the second half of the 19th century, Darwin's theories met with considerable opposition. By stating that animals evolved over time based on environmental pressures, Darwin was challenging the view that animals had been created "as is" by an all-knowing deity. By stating that all humans had common ancestors that evolved into modern people, Darwin was demonstrating that all people—regardless of ethnicity or economic status—were essentially equal. This view was not popular in Victorian England, where the aristocracy looked at the working class with disdain and where the English felt that they had the right to colonize non-Caucasian countries such as India and parts of Africa. However, over time, Darwin's ideas became accepted in almost all scientific circles. Today, a

Figure 3.5 The Prefrontal Cortex in Different Species

Human brains have much more space dedicated to the frontal lobes, particularly the prefrontal cortex, than any other species. This brain area is related to many of our higher cognitive functions like problem solving and decision making.

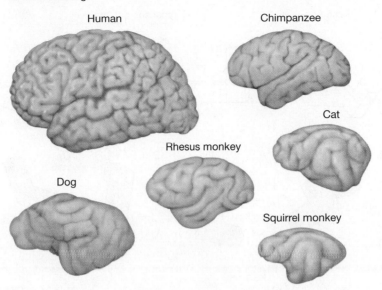

Human

Chimpanzee

Cat

Rhesus monkey

Dog

Squirrel monkey

Source: Based on Fuster, J.M., *The Prefrontal Cortex: Anatomy, Physiology, and Neuropsychology of the Frontal Lobe*, 2nd edition. New York: Raven Press, 1989.

modern branch of psychology known as **evolutionary psychology** *attempts to explain human behaviours based on the beneficial function(s) they may have served in our species' development.*

Hunters and Gatherers: Men, Women, and Spatial Memory

Evolutionary psychologists are now attempting to link evolutionarily useful behaviours that were performed by our ancestors with our own modern cognitive abilities. One notable area of investigation is the study of differences in male and female cognitive abilities.

What do we know about the sex differences in spatial memory?

Evolutionary psychologists hypothesize that male and female brains will differ in some ways because males and females have had to solve a different set of problems in order to survive and reproduce. Specifically, due to their size and strength, males were traditionally responsible for tracking and killing animals. These responsibilities would require males to travel over long distances without becoming lost. Females, due to the fact that they cared for children, remained closer to home and instead

spent time foraging for berries and edible plants. Males' responsibilities would favour individuals with good spatial skills; females' responsibilities would favour memory for the location of objects (e.g., plants). The question, then, is whether the abilities that were adaptive for males and females over the course of our species' evolution are still present today (Silverman & Eals, 1992). Put another way, will modern males and females show performance differences on different tests of spatial abilities that are consistent with their historic roles as hunter (males) and gatherer (females)? This is the logic behind the **hunter-gatherer theory**, *which explicitly links performance on specific tasks to the different roles performed by males and females over the course of our evolutionary history.*

How can science test sex differences and spatial memory?

One sex difference that has been reported involves solving the mental rotation task. In this task, participants see a three-dimensional image. They are then shown several additional figures, one of which is a rotated version of the original image. The task is to identify the rotated figure as quickly and as accurately as possible. To make this task more concrete, try the examples shown in Figure 3.6.

Research shows that males are generally able to perform this task more quickly than females, and with greater accuracy. A possible reason for this difference is that it is influenced by testosterone levels, which are

Figure 3.6 Mental Rotation Task

Instructions: Take a close look at standard object #1. One of the three objects to the right of it is the same. Which one matches the standard? Repeat this with standard object #2 and the three comparison shapes to the right of it.

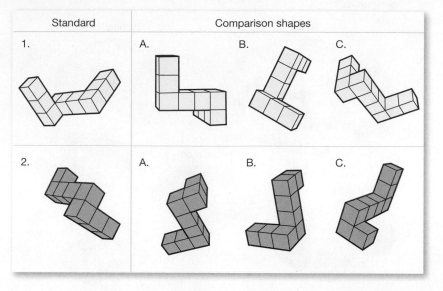

Answers: 1. A; 2. B

Source: Lilienfeld, Scott O.; Lynn, Steven J; Namy, Laura L.; Woolf, Nancy J., *Psychology: From Inquiry to Understanding*, 2nd Ed., ©2011, pp.344. Reprinted and Electronically reproduced by permission of Pearson Education, Inc., New York, NY.

typically higher in males. In fact, researchers have found that males with high testosterone levels were better at solving the task than males with low levels of testosterone (Hooven et al., 2004). These studies suggests that there is a biological (and possibly evolutionary) explanation for the male advantage in performing this specific task.

Researchers have also found that females outperform males on different types of spatial tasks, specifically, tests involving memory for the spatial *location* of objects (see Figure 3.7). In addition to laboratory-based tests, females outperformed men in experiments conducted in natural settings. In one study, women were able to locate specific plants more quickly than were men and also made fewer mistakes in identifying them (New et al., 2007). This advantage *may* be due to females' evolutionary role as a gatherer rather than as a hunter.

Can we critically evaluate this evidence?

Although sex differences on different forms of spatial abilities have been observed in a number of conditions (Voyer et al., 2004), there are some points worth considering. The first is that an overall sex difference does not mean that *all* males will be better at mental-rotation tasks than *all* females. There is a great deal of variability *within* each group on almost all cognitive and perceptual abilities. It is better to think of the sex differences in mental rotation and spatial

location tasks in terms of overlapping curves whose average scores differ slightly rather than as one sex being superior to the other on that cognitive ability. A second issue is whether these differences occur across cultures. Although the roles of hunter and gatherer were likely present in most ancient cultures due to females' need to be with young children, there are much greater differences in modern cultures. Some cultures have very strict sex roles that could influence the education and abilities of males and females. Would culture influence the size of the sex differences on tests like the mental-rotation task? As it turns out, the answer is no. The male advantage in the mental-rotation task has been observed across 40 different countries, suggesting that the finding is not restricted to Canadian universities (Silverman et al., 2007). However, although these results support the hypothesis that the differences on tasks like the mental-rotation task are biological in origin, they *do not necessarily show* that these differences are due to the evolutionary roles of hunter and gatherer. Additionally, while evolutionary psychology presents possible explanations, it is more likely that they are only *one of many* factors influencing your behaviour. Remember the biopsychosocial model!

Why is this relevant?

The hunter-gatherer hypothesis shows us that the behaviours of our ancestors might have had an effect on the abilities of modern humans. The physical and cognitive

Figure 3.7 Spatial Location Memory Task

In this task, participants are asked to remember the location of specific items.

Source: Republished with permission of Springer Science, from The Hunter-Gatherer Theory of Sex Difference in Spatial Abilities: Data from 40 Countries, Irwin Silverman; Jean Choi; Michael Peters, 36, and 2007; permission conveyed through Copyright Clearance Center, Inc.

characteristics that made males evolutionarily fit likely differed slightly from the characteristics that benefited females. Males with good spatial skills and females with good location memory would have been more successful than individuals who did not have those abilities. But, while males and females differ on some skills, the differences are generally quite small, with many females outperforming males on spatial tasks. Therefore, it is important to be careful about over-interpreting the results of these studies.

Natural selection suggests that some traits make an individual more likely to survive and therefore to reproduce. The question is how do these individuals let others know that they possess these traits? In other words, how do they convince someone to mate with them? According to Darwin (1871), certain traits or adaptations will have evolved to help some individuals increase their chances of mating while others do not. How this works varies from species to species.

SEXUAL SELECTION AND EVOLUTION In some species, members of one sex (usually males) compete for access to the other sex (usually females). For instance, some deer and caribou literally lock horns in violent fights known as *rutting.* The winner of the fight is much more likely to mate with females than is the loser. Similar examples occur in many primate species. Here, a dominant male—often referred to as the *alpha male*—intimidates other males and is more likely to mate with multiple females than are the subordinate males. These are examples of **intrasexual selection**, *a situation in which members of the same sex compete in order to win the opportunity to mate with members of the opposite sex.* Intrasexual selection is evolutionarily advantageous because the animals most likely to become dominant are the strongest and/or smartest, and therefore the most fit for that time and place. If this trend continues across many generations, the species as a whole will become stronger and smarter (i.e., more evolutionarily "fit").

A second form of sexual selection is known as **intersexual selection**, *a situation in which members of one sex select a mating partner based on their desirable traits.* In the animal kingdom, we see numerous examples of males attempting to attract the attention of females. For instance, many male birds display bright feathers and perform intricate dances or songs to attract females. This might seem cute, but this has a darker function as well. Brightly coloured birds must be fast and aware of their surroundings (i.e., evolutionarily fit). Otherwise, that glorious plumage, which also attracts

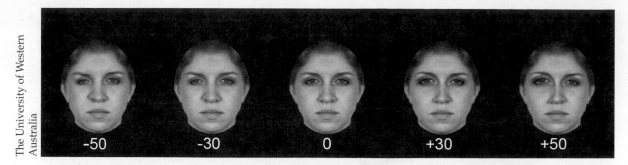

The University of Western Australia

Facial Symmetry and Attraction Which face do you prefer of these five? You likely chose the middle face because it has the highest level of symmetry. People can detect this quality without even having to study the faces very closely.

predators, would turn them into someone's lunch rather than into someone's mate. Therefore, the brightly coloured birds that *do* survive must have physical and mental characteristics that should be passed on to future generations.

Humans also have characteristics that enhance mating success. On average, heterosexual women prefer men who are taller (6′0 or 1.83 m), with good posture, and who are not very hairy (Buss, 2003; Dixson et al., 2010). Heterosexual men prefer women who are slightly shorter than them,

have full lips, high cheekbones, and a small chin. A number of experiments have shown that people rate symmetrical faces as being more attractive than asymmetrical faces (Gangestad et al., 1994; Rhodes, 2006). Overall, people tend to prefer partners who appear healthy. An evolutionary psychologist would suggest that such individuals would also be more likely to be fertile and to possess good genes.

Importantly, not all elements of intersexual selection are the gift (or curse) of our genes. Men often present cues

BIOPSYCHOSOCIAL PERSPECTIVES
Sexual Selection and the Colour Red

Most of us have had the experience of seeing a woman in a red dress walk into a room and turn everyone's head. A number of studies have found that the colour red has a powerful effect on people's behaviour and judgments of beauty. For instance, when black-and-white photographs of women are presented on a red background, these women are rated as being more attractive than when the same images are presented on a white background (Elliot & Niesta, 2008). Researchers in France have found that males tip waitresses more generously when the women are wearing a red shirt (Guéguen & Jacob, 2012a), have a red ornament in their hair (Jacob et al., 2012), or are wearing red (rather than pink or brown) lipstick (Guéguen & Jacob, 2012b). So why does the colour red have these effects? This question has a one-word answer: SEX. Women who are wearing red clothes are perceived to be more interested in having sex than women wearing other colours. This perception occurs even when the same woman is shown in identical t-shirts whose colour has been digitally altered (Guéguen, 2012); it is not affected by the attractiveness of the female model.

Of course, some of these results may be due to social factors. The colour red is related to sex in many cultures (e.g., "red light districts"). To test this hypothesis, researchers tested individuals in a remote village in Burkina Faso (in Western Africa). Importantly, in this village, the colour red had negative associations—death, bad luck, and sickness—and no sexual connotations. The participants viewed black-and-white photographs of women surrounded by either a red or a blue border. Consistent

with North American and European studies—and contrary to their cultural norms—the women with the red borders were rated as being more attractive (Elliot et al., 2013).

Evolutionary psychologists are quick to point out that red is associated with sexual receptivity in many animals, including humans. Female baboons and chimpanzees—species that are evolutionarily close to humans—have redder chests and genitals when they are near ovulation than at other times of their cycles (Deschner et al., 2004; Dixson, 1983). This blushing appears to be linked to estrogen levels, which open up the blood vessels of these regions (Setchell & Wickings, 2004). In these species, males respond to the red swellings with copulation attempts (Waitt et al., 2006). These researchers also found that male rhesus monkeys (*Macaca mulatta*) spent more time looking at red-enhanced photographs of female anogenital regions than at other images. In humans, sexual interest is associated with flushing in the face, neck, and upper chest (Changizi, 2009). Anthropological research has shown that women have used lipstick and rouge to mimic these vascular changes (and thus appear more attractive to potential mates) for over 10 000 years (Low, 1979).

Of course, it is important to point out that women wearing red are *not* necessarily indicating their willingness to have sex! These data are trends across the population and do not predict individual people's behaviour. But, it does show how evolutionary psychology can provide a new perspective on everyday behaviours.

that highlight their masculinity, such as wearing clothes that display their muscles. They also attempt to appear large and athletic, particularly when around potential mates. For example, if an attractive woman walks by a group of men, they tend to stand up straight to appear taller and healthier, and thus more attractive (this makes for wonderful people-watching at bars). Evolutionary psychologists suggest that this behaviour is an attempt to appear more genetically fit than their competitors; doing so would suggest to potential mates that their offspring would be similarly fit. Women also attempt to highlight attractive elements of their physique. At the beginning of this module, you learned that women dress more attractively when they are ovulating. As noted in the Biopsychosocial Perspectives box on page 84, some of these clothing selections might actually be tapping into other primal impulses.

Of course, there are other qualities we look for in a potential partner, particularly when it comes to long-term mates. But what are these qualities, and do members of other cultures value similar characteristics? Buss (1989) conducted a survey of more than 10 000 people from 37 different cultures to discover what they most valued in a long-term partner. Across this broad sample, both men and women agreed that love, kindness, commitment, character, and emotional maturity were important. However, there were some interesting differences. Women valued men with strong financial prospects, status, and good health whereas men placed a greater emphasis on physical beauty, youth, and other characteristics that relate to reproduction. Other investigators have found similar sex differences (see Figure 3.8). Researchers in the United States showed yearbook photographs to heterosexual male and female research participants. Along with the photographs, participants were provided with information about each individual's socioeconomic status (SES), a measure of their financial status. SES had a much greater effect on females' willingness to enter relationships with these individuals than it did for males (Townsend & Levy, 1990b). In a subsequent study, these researchers clothed the same models in outfits that implied high, medium, or low SES. Participants were asked to rate their willingness to engage in different types of relationships with this person ranging from "Coffee and conversation" to "Sex only" to "Marriage." Clothing, the indicator of SES, had a much larger effect on females than males, particularly when the model was not physically attractive. Men were much more willing to engage in "Sex only" relationships regardless of SES or attractiveness (Townsend & Levy, 1990a).

How can we explain this difference? According to evolutionary psychologists, this difference might be due

Figure 3.8 Sex Differences in the Minimum Acceptable Earning Level for Different Types of Relationships

Females place a much higher value on economic stability than do males, particularly for long-term relationships. This result may be due to the fact that females can produce a limited number of offspring and therefore need to ensure that a mate has enough resources to ensure their survival. Evolutionary psychology is not necessarily romantic.

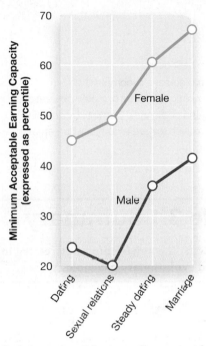

Source: From Evolution, traits and the stages of human courtship: Qualifying the parental investment model, *Journal of Personality*, 58, 97–116 by Douglas T. Kenrick, Edward K. Sadalla, Gary Groth, Melanie R. Trost. Copyright © 1990 John Wiley & Sons, Inc. Reproduced with permission of John Wiley & Sons, Inc.

to the resources required to raise offspring. Females have a limited number of eggs, and thus a finite number of opportunities to pass on their genes to another generation. If a female became pregnant and had a baby, she would require resources to help raise the child, particularly when the child is quite young and it is difficult for the woman to bring in her own resources. Therefore, it would make sense that females would be attracted to males who can provide these resources; this sometimes means mating with someone who is older and more established in life (Trivers, 1972). In contrast, men have a seemingly infinite amount of sperm and have fewer limits on the number of people they could theoretically impregnate. Given that their evolutionary impulse is to pass on their genes to as many offspring as possible, it makes sense for them to be attracted to young, healthy women who are likely able to reproduce (Buss, 1989). Oddly, these motivations don't appear in many love songs.

Module 3.1b Quiz:

Evolutionary Insights into Human Behaviour

Know . . .

1. For a trait to evolve, it must have a(n) _____ basis.
   A. learned
   B. social
   C. heritable
   D. developmental

Apply . . .

2. Evolution is best defined as
   A. a gradual increase in complexity.
   B. a change in gene frequency over generations.
   C. solving the challenge of survival by adapting.
   D. a progression toward a complex human brain.

Analyze . . .

3. Evolutionary psychologists have made some claims that sex differences in cognitive abilities are genetically determined. Which of the following is *not* an alternative explanation for such claims?
   A. Hormone levels affect performance.
   B. Sociocultural history affects performance.
   C. Different educational experiences affect performance.
   D. Technological limitations prevent the accurate study of sex differences.

Module 3.1 Summary

3.1a   Know . . . the key terminology related to genes, heredity, and evolutionary psychology.

behavioural genetics
behavioural genomics
chromosomes
dizygotic twins
DNA (deoxyribonucleic acid)
epigenetics
evolution
evolutionary psychology
genes
genotype
heritability
hunter-gatherer theory
intersexual selection
intrasexual selection
longitudinal studies
monozygotic twins
natural selection
phenotype

3.1b   Understand . . . how twin and adoption studies reveal relationships between genes and behaviour.

Both methods measure genetic, environmental, and interactive contributions to behaviour. Twin studies typically compare monozygotic twins (genetically identical) and dizygotic twins (full siblings sharing the prenatal environment). Adoption studies compare adopted children to their adoptive and biological parents. These designs allow researchers to determine heritability, a number between 0 and 1 that estimates the degree to which individual differences in a trait (in a given population) are due to genetic factors. A heritability of 1.0 would mean that genes contribute to 100% of individual differences. A heritability of 0 would mean that genes have no effect on individual differences. Many human characteristics, including intelligence and personality, have heritability estimates typically ranging between .40 and .70.

3.1c   Apply . . . your knowledge of genes and behaviour to hypothesize why a trait might be adaptive.

Apply Activity

Try putting yourself in an evolutionary psychologist's position and answer the following two questions.

1. Many evolutionary psychologists claim that men are more interested in a mate's physical attractiveness and youth, whereas women are more interested in qualities that contribute to childrearing success, such as intelligence and wealth. If this is the case, then who do you think would express more jealousy over sexual infidelity—men or women?

2. Researchers (Cramer et al., 2008) asked volunteers to rate how upset they would be by sexual infidelity in a mate and then they plotted the results in the graph shown in Figure 3.9. Do their results confirm your hypothesis?

Figure 3.9 Men's and Women's Reactions to Infidelity

Men find sexual infidelity more distressing than do women, regardless of how a question is framed.

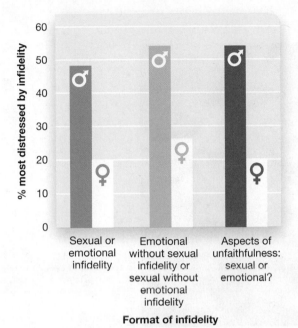

Source: Copyright 2008 From Sex differences in subjective distress to unfaithfulness: Testing competing evolutionary and violation of infidelity expectations hypotheses, *The Journal of Social Psychology* 148 (4): 389–405. by Robert Ervin Cramera, Ryan E. Lipinskia, John D. Meteerb, Jeremy Ashton Houskac. Reproduced by permission of Taylor & Francis LLC, (http://www.tandfonline.com).

3.1d Analyze . . . claims that scientists have located a specific gene that controls a single trait or behaviour.

Most psychological traits, as well as disorders such as Alzheimer's disease, involve multiple genes, some of which may not yet have even been discovered. (See the Myths in Mind feature.)

3.1e Analyze . . . explanations for cognitive gender differences that are rooted in genetics.

The Working the Scientific Literacy Model feature summarized research showing that males have an advantage when it comes to a specific mental rotation task. Given that this is a relatively consistent sex difference, high testosterone levels are associated with better performance on the task, and the male advantage has been found cross-culturally, it seems plausible that this difference has a genetic basis. In future chapters we will return to issues related to sex-based differences in cognitive abilities (see Module 9.2).

Module 3.2 How the Nervous System Works: Cells and Neurotransmitters

Rod Williams/Nature Picture Library

Learning Objectives

3.2a Know . . . the key terminology associated with nerve cells, hormones, and their functioning.

3.2b Understand . . . how nerve cells communicate.

3.2c Understand . . . the ways that drugs and other substances affect the brain.

3.2d Understand . . . the roles that hormones play in our behaviour.

3.2e Apply . . . your knowledge of neurotransmitters to form hypotheses about drug actions.

3.2f Analyze . . . the claim that we are born with all the nerve cells we will ever have.

A bite from an Australian species of snake called the taipan can kill an adult human within 30 minutes. In fact, it is recognized as the most lethally venomous species of snake in the world (50 times more potent than the also fatal venom of the king cobra). The venom of the taipan is **neurotoxic,** *meaning that it specifically attacks cells of the nervous system. These cells are involved with more than just "thinking"—in fact, networks of nervous system cells working together are critical for basic life functions like breathing and having a heartbeat. A direct attack on these cells, therefore, spells trouble. In the case of the taipan, its bite first leads to drowsiness followed by difficulties controlling one's head and neck muscles. Victims then experience progressive difficulty with swallowing, followed by tightness of the chest and paralysis of breathing. If enough venom was injected and treatment is not available, coma and death occur. All of this happens because of damage to the cells that will be discussed in this module—cells that work together to produce the complex human behaviours we engage in every day.*

Incidentally, not all snake venom attacks the nervous system. The venom found in most rattlesnakes in North America is not neurotoxic (although you still shouldn't hug one). Instead, it damages tissue in the vicinity of the bite as well as those tissues it reaches within the bloodstream, particularly the heart. Although this is not exactly comforting news, it should at least allow you to enjoy nature without being afraid that a snake will attack your nervous system's cells. That's what spiders are for . . .

Focus Questions

1. Which normal processes of nerve cells are disrupted by a substance like snake venom?

2. What roles do chemicals play in normal nerve cell functioning?

When we think of cells, we often imagine looking at plants or earthworms through a microscope in high-school biology class. Although thrilling, this activity likely seems to be the furthest thing from the study of behaviour. However, cells—particularly cells in the nervous system—play an incredibly important role in absolutely everything you do, from moving and sensing to thinking and feeling. Understanding how cells function and communicate with each other as part of networks will help you better understand topics discussed in later modules, such as how we learn (Modules 6.1, 6.2, and 7.1), how different drugs (both clinical and recreational) work (Modules 5.3 and 16.3), and how stress affects our bodies and brains (Module 14.2). This module therefore serves as a building block that will deepen your understanding of almost all of the behaviours that make you "you."

Neural Communication

The human body is composed of many different types of cells. Psychologists are most interested in **neurons**, *one of the major types of cells found in the nervous system, that are responsible for sending and receiving messages throughout the body.* Billions of these cells receive and transmit messages every day, including while you are asleep. Millions of them

are firing as a result of you reading these words. In order to understand how this particular type of cell can produce complex behaviours, it is necessary to take a closer look at the structure and function of the neuron.

THE NEURON The primary purpose of neurons is to "fire," to receive input from one group of neurons and to then transmit that information to other neurons. Doing so allows single neurons to work together as part of networks involving thousands (and sometimes millions) of other cells; this will eventually lead to some form of behaviour. To that end, neurons are designed in such a way that there are parts of the cell specialized for receiving incoming information *from* other neurons and parts of the cell specialized for transmitting information *to* other neurons.

All neurons have a **cell body** (also known as the *soma*), *the part of a neuron that contains the nucleus that houses the cell's genetic material* (see Figure 3.10). Genes in the cell body synthesize proteins that form the chemicals and structures that allow the neuron to function. The activity of these genes can be influenced by the input coming from other cells. This input is received by **dendrites**, *small branches radiating from the cell body that receive messages from other cells and transmit those messages toward the rest of the cell.* At any given point in time, a neuron will receive

Figure 3.10 A Neuron and Its Key Components

Each part of a nerve cell is specialized for a specific task.

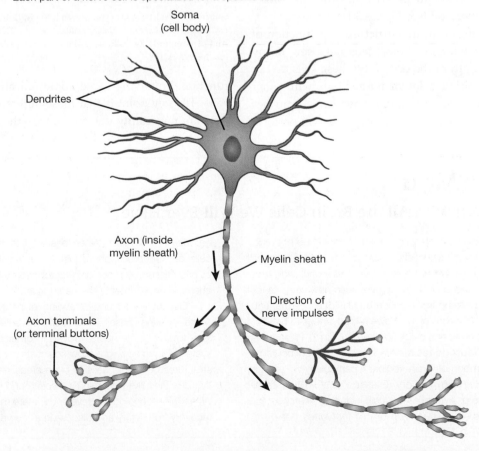

Soma
(cell body)

Dendrites

Axon (inside
myelin sheath)

Myelin sheath

Direction of
nerve impulses

Axon terminals
(or terminal buttons)

input from several other neurons (sometimes over 1000 other neurons!). These impulses from other cells will travel across the neuron to the base of the cell body known as the *axon hillock*. If the axon hillock receives enough stimulation from other neurons, it will initiate a chemical reaction that will flow down the rest of the neuron.

This chemical reaction is the initial step in a neuron communicating with other cells (i.e., influencing whether other cells will fire or not). The activity will travel from the axon hillock along a tail-like structure that protrudes from the cell body. This structure, the **axon**, *transports information in the form of electrochemical reactions from the cell body to the end of the neuron*. When the activity reaches the end of the axon, it will arrive at *axon terminals*, bulb-like extensions filled with vesicles (little bags of molecules). These vesicles contain **neurotransmitters**, *the chemicals that function as messengers allowing neurons to communicate with each other*. The impulse travelling down the axon will stimulate the release of these neurotransmitters, thus allowing neural communication to take place. Many different types of neurotransmitters exist, and each can have a number of different functions—something we will explore in more detail later in this module.

Although all neurons are designed to transmit information, not all neurons perform the same function. *Sensory neurons* receive information from the bodily senses and bring it toward the brain, often via the spinal cord. In contrast, *motor neurons* carry messages away from the brain and spinal cord and toward muscles in order to control their flexion and extension (see Figure 3.11).

Within the brain itself, the structure and function of neurons varies considerably. Some cells have few if any dendrites extending from the cell body; these cells do not perform tasks requiring a lot of interactions with other neurons. In contrast, some neurons have huge branches of dendrites. Obviously, these latter neurons will perform

Figure 3.11 Sensory and Motor Neurons

Sensory neurons carry information toward the spinal cord and the brain, whereas motor neurons send messages to muscles of the body. The interneuron links the sensory and motor neurons. This is the pathway of a simple withdrawal response to a painful stimulus.

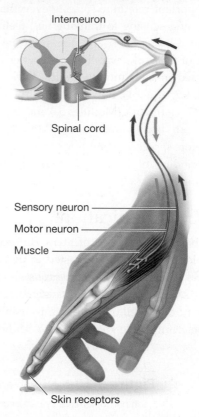

Interneuron

Spinal cord

Sensory neuron

Motor neuron

Muscle

Skin receptors

Source: Lilienfeld, Scott O.; Lynn, Steven J; Namy, Laura L.; Woolf, Nancy J., *Psychology: From Inquiry To Understanding,* 2nd Ed., ©2011. Reprinted And Electronically Reproduced By Permission Of Pearson Education, Inc., New York, NY.

functions involving more communication between neurons. The key point is that these differences between neurons are not simply due to chance—they have a purpose.

Myths in Mind

We Are Born with All the Brain Cells We Will Ever Have

For decades, neuroscience taught us that nerves do not regenerate; in other words, scientists believed that we are born with all of the brain cells we will ever have. This conclusion made perfect sense because no one had ever seen new neurons form in adults, and severe neurological damage is often permanent.

In the past 15 years or so, however, advances in brain science have challenged this belief (Wojtowicz, 2012). Researchers have observed **neurogenesis**—*the formation of new neurons*—in a limited number of brain regions, particularly in a region critical for learning and memory (Eriksson et al., 1998; Tashiro et al., 2007). The growth of a new cell, including neurons, starts with **stem cells**—*a unique type of cell that does not have a*

predestined function. When a stem cell divides, the resulting cells can become part of just about anything—bone, kidney, or brain tissue. The deciding factor seems to be the stem cell's chemical environment (Abematsu et al., 2006).

Our increased understanding of neurogenesis has raised some exciting possibilities—perhaps scientists can discover how to trigger the neural growth in other parts of the nervous system. Doing so might allow scientists to repair damaged brain structures or to add cells to brain areas affected by degenerative diseases like Parkinson's disease and Alzheimer's disease. When this technology is developed, there may finally be hope for recovery from injury and disease in all nerve cells.

The physical structure of a neuron is related to the function it performs.

GLIAL CELLS Although neurons are essential for our ability to sense, move, and think, they cannot function without support from other cells. This support comes from different types of cells collectively known as *glia* (Greek for "glue"). **Glial cells** *are specialized cells of the nervous system that are involved in mounting immune responses in the brain, removing waste, and synchronizing the activity of the billions of neurons that constitute the nervous system.* Given that glial cells perform so many different support functions, it should come as no surprise to learn that they outnumber neurons in the brain by a ratio of approximately 10 to 1.

A critical function served by certain glial cells is to insulate the axon of a neuron. These glial cells form a white substance called **myelin**, *a fatty sheath that insulates axons from one another, resulting in increased speed and efficiency of neural communication.* In an unmyelinated axon, the neural impulse decays quickly and needs to be regenerated along the axon; the myelin protects the impulse from this decay, thus reducing how often the impulse needs to be regenerated. The speed difference between axons with and without myelin is substantial. Axons without myelin transmit information at speeds ranging from 0.5 to 10 m/s (metres per second); myelinated axons transmit information at speeds of up to 150 m/s (Hartline & Coleman, 2007; Hursh, 1939). For obvious reasons, most neurons in the brain have myelin.

When the myelin sheath is damaged, the efficiency of the axon decreases substantially. For instance, *multiple sclerosis* is a disease in which the immune system does not recognize myelin and attacks it—a process that can devastate the structural and functional integrity of the nervous system. When myelin breaks down in multiple sclerosis, it impairs the ability of the affected neurons to transmit information along their axons. As a result, groups of brain structures that normally fire together to produce a behaviour can no longer work as a functional network (Rocca et al., 2010; Shu et al., 2011). It would be similar to trying to drive a car that is missing a wheel. The specific symptoms associated with multiple sclerosis differ depending upon where in the brain the myelin damage occurred. Numbness or tingling sensations could be caused by the disruption of sensory nerve cell signals that should otherwise reach the brain. Problems with voluntary, coordinated movement could be due to the breakdown of myelin that supports motor nerves. The important point is that damage to a small group of axons can lead to impairments in the functioning of large networks of brain areas (Rocca et al., 2012).

As you can see, each part of an individual neuron and glial cell performs an important function. Ultimately, however, it is the activity of networks of nerve cells that allows messages to be transmitted within the brain and the rest of the body. This activity involves the most important function a neuron can perform: to fire.

THE NEURON'S ELECTRICAL SYSTEM: RESTING AND ACTION POTENTIALS Neural activity is based on changes in the concentrations of charged atoms called *ions*. When a neuron is not transmitting information, the outside of the neuron has a relatively high concentration of positively charged ions, particularly sodium and potassium, while the interior of the axon has fewer positively charged ions as well as a relatively high concentration of negatively charged chloride ions. This difference in charge between the inside and outside of the cell leaves the inside of the axon with a negative charge of approximately -70 millivolts (-70 mV; see the first panel of Figure 3.12). This *relatively stable state during which the cell is not transmitting messages* is known as its **resting potential**.

Importantly, this seemingly stable resting state involves a great deal of tension. This is because of two forces, the *electrostatic gradient* and the *concentration gradient*. Don't let these technical terms scare you: the electrostatic gradient

Figure 3.12 Electrical Charges of the Inner and Outer Regions of Nerve Cells

The inner and outer environments of a nerve cell at rest differ in terms of their electrical charge. During the resting potential, there is a net negative charge. When a nerve cell is stimulated, generating an action potential, positively charged ions rush inside the cell membrane. After the cell has fired, the positively charged ions are channelled back outside the nerve cell as it returns to a resting state.

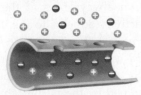
Resting potential.

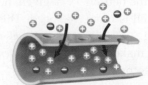
Positively charged ions rush into the cell during an action potential.

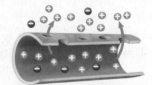
After the nerve has fired, the positively charged ions are pumped back out of the cell.

Source: Lilienfeld, Scott O.; Lynn, Steven J; Namy, Laura L.; Woolf, Nancy J., *Psychology: From Inquiry To Understanding*, 2nd Ed., ©2011. Reprinted And Electronically Reproduced By Permission Of Pearson Education, Inc., New York, NY.

just means that the inside and outside of the cell have different charges (negative and positive, respectively), and the concentration gradient just means that different types of ions are more densely packed on one side of the membrane than on the other (e.g., there are more sodium ions outside the cell than inside the cell). However, most substances have a tendency to move from areas of high concentration to areas of low concentration whenever possible; in other words, substances spread out whenever they can so that they are evenly distributed. So, if small pores (known as *ion channels*) opened up in the neuron's cell membrane, there would be a natural tendency for positively charged sodium ions to rush into the cell.

This is what happens when a neuron is stimulated. The surge of positive ions into the cell changes the potential of the neuron (e.g., changing from –70 mV to –68 mV). These charges flow down the dendrites and cross the cell body to the axon hillock, where the cell body meets the axon. If enough positively charged ions reach the axon hillock to push its charge past that cell's firing threshold (e.g., –55 mV), the neuron will then initiate an **action potential**, *a wave of electrical activity that originates at the beginning of the axon near the cell body and rapidly travels down its length* (see the middle panel of Figure 3.12). When an action potential occurs, the charge of that part of the axon changes from approximately –70 mV to approximately +35 mV; in other words, the cell changes from being negatively to positively charged (see Figure 3.13). This change does not occur along the entire axon at once. Rather, as one part of the axon becomes depolarized, it forces open the ion channels ahead of it, thus causing the action potential to move down the length of the axon as positively charged ions rush through the membrane pores (Hodgkin, 1937). This pattern continues until the action potential reaches the axon terminal.

Of course, if this were the entire story, then all of our neurons would fire once and never fire again because the ion channels would remain open. Luckily for us, there are mechanisms in place to help our neurons return to their resting state (–70 mV) so that they can fire again. At each point of the axon, the ion channels slam shut as soon as the action potential occurs. The sodium ions that had rushed into the axon are then rapidly pumped back out of the cell, returning it to a resting state. This process of removing the sodium ions from the cell often causes the neuron to become *hyperpolarized*; this means that the cell is more negative than its normal resting potential (e.g., –72 mV instead of –70 mV). This additional negativity makes the cell *less* likely to fire. It normally takes 2–3 milliseconds for the membrane to adjust back to its normal resting potential. This *brief period in which a neuron cannot fire is known as a* **refractory period**.

When the action potential reaches the axon terminal, it triggers the release of that cell's neurotransmitters into

Figure 3.13 Time Course and Phases of a Nerve Cell Going from a Resting Potential to an Action Potential

Nerve cells fire once the threshold of excitation is reached. During the action potential, positively charged ions rush inside the cell membrane, creating a net positive charge within the cell. Positively charged ions are then forced out of the cell as it returns to its resting potential.

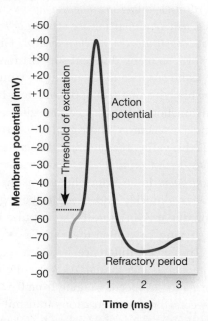

Source: Based on "The Time Course and Phases of a Nerve Cell Going from Resting to Action Potential," adapted from Sternberg, 2004.

the **synapses**, *the microscopically small spaces that separate individual nerve cells*. The cell that releases these chemicals is known as the *presynaptic cell* ("before the synapse") whereas the cell that receives this input is known as the *postsynaptic cell* (or "after the synapse"). The dendrites of the postsynaptic cell contain specialized receptors that are designed to hold specific molecules, including neurotransmitters. Then, this process of neural communication will begin again.

Although this description of an action potential explains how a neuron fires, it does not explain how the nervous system differentiates between a weak and a strong neural response. It would make intuitive sense for a stronger stimulus (e.g., a loud noise) to produce a larger action potential than a weak stimulus (e.g., someone whispering); however, this is not the case. When stimulated, a given neuron always fires at the same intensity and speed. This activity adheres to the **all-or-none principle**: *Individual nerve cells fire at the same strength every time an action potential occurs*. Neurons do not "sort of" fire, or "overfire"—they just fire. Instead, the strength of a sensation is determined by the *rate* at which nerve cells fire as well as by the number of nerve cells that are stimulated. A stimulus is experienced intensely because a greater number of cells are stimulated, and the firing of each cell occurs repeatedly.

Module 3.2a Quiz:

Neural Communication

Know . . .

1. A positive electrical charge that is carried away from the cell body and down the length of the axon is a(n) _____.
   A. refractory period
   B. resting potential
   C. action potential
   D. dendrite

2. Which of the following is a function of glial cells?
   A. Glial cells slow down the activity of nerve cells.
   B. Glial cells help form myelin.
   C. Glial cells suppress the immune system response.
   D. Glial cells contain the nucleus that houses the cell's genetic material.

Understand . . .

3. A neuron will fire when the ions inside the cell body are
   A. in the resting potential.
   B. shifted to a threshold more positive than the resting potential.
   C. shifted to a threshold more negative than the resting potential.
   D. in the refractory period.

4. Sensory and motor nerves differ in that
   A. only sensory neurons have dendrites.
   B. only motor neurons have axons.
   C. sensory neurons carry messages toward the brain, and motor neurons carry information away from the brain.
   D. sensory neurons carry messages away from the brain, and motor neurons carry information toward the brain.

The Chemical Messengers: Neurotransmitters and Hormones

As you read in the first part of this module, the *presynaptic neuron* releases neurotransmitters into the synapse; a fraction of these neurotransmitters will bind to receptors on the *postsynaptic neuron*. This binding can have one of two effects on the postsynaptic cell. If the actions of a neurotransmitter cause the neuron's membrane potential to become less negative (e.g., changing from –70 mV to –68 mV), it is referred to as *excitatory* because it has increased the probability that an action potential will occur in a given period of time. In contrast, if the actions of a neurotransmitter cause the membrane potential to become more negative (e.g., changing from –70 mV to –72 mV), it is referred to as *inhibitory* because it has decreased the likelihood that an action potential will occur. An important factor in determining whether a postsynaptic neuron is excited or inhibited is the type of neurotransmitter(s) binding with its receptors.

Many different types of neurotransmitters have been identified, although most neurons send and receive a limited number of these substances. Each neurotransmitter typically has its own unique molecular shape. A lock-and-key analogy is sometimes used to explain how neurotransmitters and their receptors work: When neurotransmitters are released at the axon terminal, they cross the synapse and fit in a particular receptor of the dendrite like a key in a lock (see Figure 3.14).

After neurotransmitter molecules have bound to postsynaptic receptors of a neighbouring cell, they are released back into the **synaptic cleft**, *the minute space between the axon terminal (terminal button) and the dendrite*. This process is almost as important as the action potential itself. Prolonged stimulation of the receptors makes it more difficult for the cell to return to its resting potential; this is obviously necessary for the neuron to be able to fire again. Therefore, if a neurotransmitter remained latched onto a receptor for long periods of time, it would decrease the number of times that the neurons could fire (i.e., it would make your brain less powerful).

Once neurotransmitters have detached from the receptors and float back into the synapse, they are either

---

Figure 3.14 The Lock-and-Key Analogy for Matching of Neurotransmitters and Receptors

The molecular structures of different neurotransmitters must have specific shapes in order to bind with the receptors on a neuron.

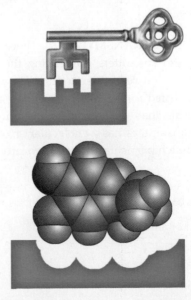

Source: Lilienfeld, Scott O.; Lynn, Steven; Namy, Laura L.; Woolf, Nancy J., *Psychology: From Inquiry To Understanding*, Books A La Carte Edition, 2nd Ed., ©2011. Reprinted and Electronically reproduced by permission of Pearson Education, Inc., New York, NY.

Figure 3.15 Major Events at the Synapse

As the action potential reaches the axon terminals, neurotransmitters (packed into spherically shaped vesicles) are released across the synaptic cleft. The neurotransmitters bind to the postsynaptic (receiving) neuron. In the process of reuptake, some neurotransmitters are returned to the presynaptic neuron via reuptake proteins. These neurotransmitters are then repackaged into synaptic vesicles.

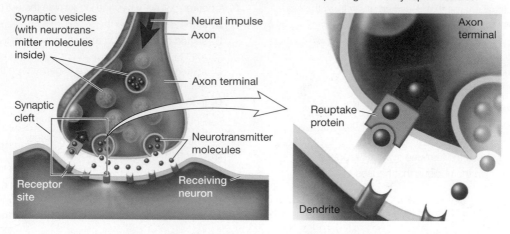

broken down by enzymes or go through **reuptake**, *a process whereby neurotransmitter molecules that have been released into the synapse are reabsorbed into the axon terminals of the presynaptic neuron* (see Figure 3.15). Reuptake serves as a sort of natural recycling system for neurotransmitters. It is also a process that is modified by many commonly used drugs. For example, the class of antidepressant drugs known as selective serotonin reuptake inhibitors (SSRIs), not surprisingly, inhibits reuptake of the neurotransmitter serotonin; in this way, SSRIs such as fluoxetine (Prozac) eventually increase the amount of serotonin available at the synapse. The result is a decrease in depression and anxiety. The process of reuptake occurs for a number of different neurotransmitters released throughout the nervous system.

TYPES OF NEUROTRANSMITTERS   There are literally dozens of neurotransmitters influencing the functioning of your brain as you read this module. The various neurotransmitters listed in Table 3.1 are only a small sample of the chemicals that produce your behaviour. Each of these neurotransmitters has a molecular structure and is designed to match particular types of receptors, similar to how different keys will fit into different locks. These substances also differ in terms of the specific brain areas they target. As a result, different neurotransmitters will have different effects on our behaviour.

The most common neurotransmitters in the brain are *glutamate* and *GABA*. **Glutamate** *is the most common excitatory neurotransmitter in the brains of vertebrates* (Dingledine et al., 1999; Meldrum, 2000). It is involved in a number of processes, including our ability to form new memories (Bliss & Collingridge, 1993; Peng et al., 2011). Abnormal functioning of glutamate-releasing neurons has also been implicated in a number of brain disorders including the triggering of seizures in epilepsy (During & Spencer, 1993) and damage caused by strokes (Hazell, 2007; McCulloch et al., 1991). In contrast, **GABA (gamma-amino butyric acid**, for those of you enraged by acronyms) *is the primary inhibitory neurotransmitter of the nervous system, meaning that it prevents neurons from generating action potentials.* It accomplishes this feat by reducing the negative charge of neighbouring neurons even further than their resting state of −70 mV. When GABA binds to receptors, it causes an influx of negatively charged chloride ions to enter the cell, which is the opposite net effect of what happens when

Table 3.1 Major Neurotransmitters and Their Functions

Neurotransmitter	Some Major Functions
Glutamate	Excites nervous system; memory and autonomic nervous system reactions
GABA (gamma-amino butyric acid)	Inhibits brain activity; lowers arousal, anxiety, and excitation; facilitates sleep
Acetylcholine	Movement; attention
Dopamine	Control of movement; reward-seeking behaviour; cognition and attention
Norepinephrine	Memory; attention to new or important stimuli; regulation of sleep and mood
Serotonin	Regulation of sleep, appetite, mood

a neuron is stimulated. As an inhibitor, GABA facilitates sleep (Tobler et al., 2001) and reduces arousal of the nervous system. Low levels of GABA have been linked to epilepsy, likely because there is an imbalance between inhibitory GABA and excitatory glutamate (Upton, 1994).

Another common neurotransmitter is acetylcholine. **Acetylcholine** *is one of the most widespread neurotransmitters within the body, found at the junctions between nerve cells and skeletal muscles; it is very important for voluntary movement.* Acetylcholine released from neurons connected to the spinal cord binds to receptors on muscles. The change in the electrical properties of the muscle fibres leads to a contraction of that muscle. This link between the nervous system and muscles is known as a *neuromuscular junction.* A number of animals release venom that influences the release of acetylcholine, including the black widow spider (Diaz, 2004) and a number of snakes. Recall the neurotoxic snake venom discussed at the beginning of this module: This toxin disrupts the activity of acetylcholine transmission at the neuromuscular junctions. Different snakes carry slightly different types of neurotoxic venom. Some types of venom block acetylcholine release at the presynaptic terminals, preventing its release into the synapse. Another type of venom blocks the receptors on the postsynaptic cell, preventing acetylcholine from binding to them (Lewis & Gutmann, 2004). Either way, the effects are devastating.

In addition to these effects in neuromuscular junctions, acetylcholine activity in the brain is associated with attention and memory (Drachman & Leavitt, 1974; Himmelheber et al., 2000). Altered levels of this neurotransmitter have also been linked to cognitive deficits associated with aging and Alzheimer's disease (Bartus et al., 1982; Craig et al., 2011). Indeed, several drugs used to reduce the progression of Alzheimer's disease are designed to slow the removal of acetylcholine from the synapse, thus allowing it to have a larger effect on postsynaptic cells (Darvesh et al., 2003). The fact that acetylcholine can influence functions ranging from movement to memory shows us that *where* in the nervous system a neurotransmitter is released can have a dramatic influence on *what* roles that neurotransmitter will serve.

This point is particularly noticeable when one discusses a class of neurotransmitters known as the *monoamines.* This group of brain chemicals includes the well-known neurotransmitters dopamine, norepinephrine, and serotonin. **Dopamine** *is a monoamine neurotransmitter involved in such varied functions as mood, control of voluntary movement, and processing of rewarding experiences.* When reading this definition, you can't help but be stunned by the variety of processes influenced by dopamine. This breadth is due to the fact that dopamine is released by neurons in (at least) three pathways extending to different parts of the brain including areas in the centre of the brain related to movement and to reward responses (Koob & Volkow, 2010; Martinez

& Narendren, 2010; see Module 5.3) and areas in the front third of the brain involved with controlling our attention (Robbins, 2000).

Attention is also influenced by our overall alertness or arousal, a characteristic that is affected by the neurotransmitter norepinephrine. **Norepinephrine** (also known as *noradrenaline*) *is a monoamine synthesized from dopamine molecules that is involved in regulating stress responses, including increasing arousal, attention, and heart rate.* Norepinephrine is formed in specialized nuclei in the bottom of the brain (known as the *brainstem*) and projects throughout the cortex, influencing the activity of a number of different systems ranging from wakefulness to attention (Berridge & Waterhouse, 2003). It also projects down the spinal cord and serves as part of the "fight-or-flight" response to threatening stimuli. Norepinephrine often works alongside *epinephrine* (also known as *adrenaline*), a hormone and neurotransmitter created in the adrenal gland on the kidneys. Both norepinephrine and epinephrine energize individuals to help them become more engaged with a given activity. (Interesting trivia: Epinephrine has its name because the name *adrenaline* was trademarked by a drug company.)

Finally, **serotonin** *is a monoamine involved in regulating mood, sleep, aggression, and appetite* (Cappadocia et al., 2009; Young & Leyton, 2002). It is formed in the brainstem and projects throughout the brain and spinal cord. Serotonin is the neurotransmitter that you are most likely to have heard of due to its critical role in depression. As discussed earlier in this module, many antidepressant medications block the reuptake of serotonin, thus ensuring that this substance remains in the synapse for longer durations. The result is an elevation of mood and a decrease in symptoms of depression and anxiety.

Throughout this section, we have noted that medications (or other substances) can influence the levels of these neurotransmitters as well as how efficiently they bind to their targets. But, as you will see, not all drugs affect neurotransmission in the same way.

DRUG EFFECTS ON NEUROTRANSMISSION Drugs of all varieties, from prescription to recreational, affect the chemical signalling that takes place between nerve cells. **Agonists** *are drugs that enhance or mimic the effects of a neurotransmitter's action.* The well-known drug nicotine is an acetylcholine agonist, meaning that it stimulates the receptor sites for this neurotransmitter. The antianxiety drug alprazolam (Xanax) is a GABA agonist—it causes relaxation by increasing the activity of this inhibitory neurotransmitter. Drugs can behave as agonists either directly or indirectly. A drug that behaves as a *direct agonist* physically binds to that neurotransmitter's receptors at the postsynaptic cells (e.g., nicotine molecules attach themselves to receptors that acetylcholine molecules would normally stimulate). A drug that acts as an *indirect agonist* facilitates

Figure 3.16 Drug Effects at the Synapses

Drugs can act as agonists by facilitating the effects of a neurotransmitter, or as antagonists by blocking these effects.

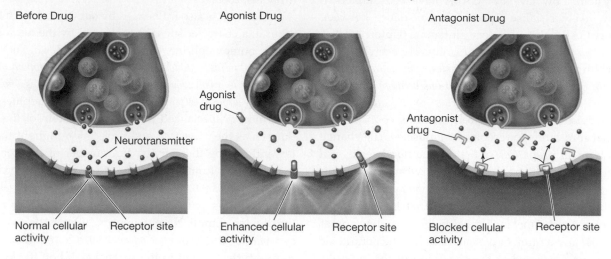

Before Drug

Agonist Drug

Antagonist Drug

Neurotransmitter

Agonist drug

Antagonist drug

Normal cellular activity   Receptor site

Enhanced cellular activity   Receptor site

Blocked cellular activity   Receptor site

the effects of a neurotransmitter, but does not physically bind to the same part of the receptor as the neurotransmitter. For example, a drug that blocks the process of reuptake would be an indirect agonist. A drug that attaches to another binding site on a receptor but does not interfere with the neurotransmitter's binding would also be an indirect agonist.

Drugs classified as **antagonists** *inhibit neurotransmitter activity by blocking receptors or preventing synthesis of a neurotransmitter* (see Figure 3.16). You may have heard of the cosmetic medical procedure known as a Botox injection. Botox, which is derived from the nerve-paralyzing bacterium that causes botulism, blocks the action of acetylcholine by binding to its postsynaptic receptor sites (Dastoor et al., 2007). Blocking acetylcholine could lead to paralysis of the heart and lungs; however, when very small amounts are injected into tissue around the eyes, the antagonist simply paralyzes the muscles that lead to wrinkles. When muscles are not used, they cannot stretch the skin—hence

the reduction in wrinkling when acetylcholine activity is blocked. Because Botox directly binds with acetylcholine receptors and thus prevents acetylcholine from doing so, it is considered a *direct antagonist*. If a chemical reduces the influence of a neurotransmitter *without* physically blocking the receptor, it would be classified as an *indirect antagonist*.

HORMONES AND THE ENDOCRINE SYSTEM Neurotransmitters are not the body's only chemical messenger system. **Hormones** *are chemicals secreted by the glands of the endocrine system.* Generally, neurotransmitters work almost immediately within the microscopic space of the synapse, whereas hormones are secreted into the bloodstream and travel throughout the body. Thus, the effects of hormones are much slower than those of neurotransmitters. With help from the nervous system, the endocrine system contributes to *homeostasis*—the balance of energy, metabolism, body temperature, and other basic functions that keeps the body working properly (see Figure 3.17; see Module 11.1). In other words, the brain triggers activity in the endocrine system which then influences the brain's activity via hormones. This cycle continues as our brain and body attempt to maintain the appropriate energy levels for dealing with the environment.

The brain area that is critical for this brain-endocrine relationship is the **hypothalamus**, *a brain structure that regulates basic biological needs and motivational systems.* The hypothalamus releases specialized chemicals called releasing factors that stimulate the **pituitary gland**—*the master gland of the endocrine system that produces hormones and sends commands about hormone*

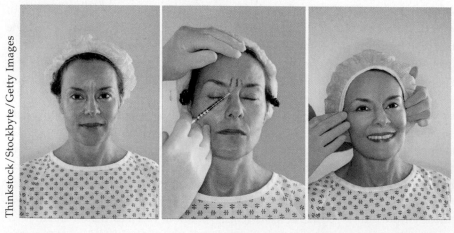

Thinkstock/Stockbyte/Getty Images

Botox injections paralyze muscles, which can increase youthful appearance in areas such as the face. It is a direct antagonist for acetylcholine.

Figure 3.17 The Endocrine System

Glands throughout the body release and exchange hormones. The hypothalamus interacts with the endocrine system to regulate hormonal processes.

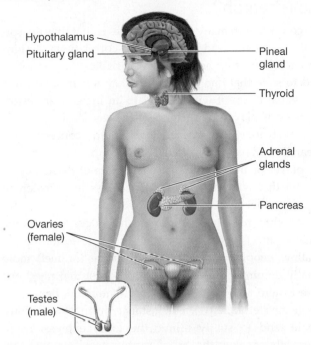

Source: Lilienfeld, Scott O.; Lynn, Steven J; Namy, Laura L.; Woolf, Nancy J., *Psychology: From Inquiry To Understanding*, 2nd Ed., ©2011. Reprinted And Electronically Reproduced By Permission Of Pearson Education, Inc., New York, NY.

production to the other glands of the endocrine system. These hormones can be released by glands throughout the body before finding their way to the brain via the bloodstream.

How we respond to stress illustrates nicely how the nervous and endocrine systems influence each other. In psychological terms, stress is loosely defined as an imbalance between perceived demands and the perceived resources available to meet those demands. Such an imbalance might occur if you suddenly realize your midterm exam is tomorrow at 8:00 A.M. Your resources—time and energy—may not be enough to meet the demand of succeeding on the exam. The hypothalamus, however, sets chemical events in motion that physically prepare the body for stress. It signals the pituitary gland to release a hormone into the bloodstream that in turn stimulates the **adrenal glands**, *a pair of endocrine glands located adjacent to the kidneys that release stress hormones, such as cortisol and epinephrine.* Cortisol and epinephrine help mobilize the body during stress, thus providing enough energy for you to deal with the sudden increase in activity necessary to respond to the stress-inducing situation (see Module 14.2).

Another important chemical is **endorphin**, *a hormone produced by the pituitary gland and the hypothalamus that functions to reduce pain and induce feelings of pleasure.* Endorphins are released into the bloodstream during events such as

Extracts from the seeds of some poppy flowers contain opium. Morphine and one of its derivatives, heroin, can be synthesized from these seeds.

strenuous exercise, sexual activity, or injury. They act on portions of the brain that are attuned to reward, reinforcement, and pleasure, inhibiting the perception of pain and increasing feelings of euphoria (extreme pleasantness and relaxation). Morphine—a drug derived from the poppy plant—binds to endorphin receptors (the term *endorphin* translates to *endogenous [internal] morphine*). Morphine molecules fit into the same receptor sites as endorphins and, therefore, produce the same painkilling and euphoric effects.

The final hormone that will be discussed is perhaps the best known: *testosterone*. This hormone serves multiple functions, including driving physical and sexual development over the long term. Testosterone levels also surge during sexual activity. However, as you will read in the next section, these are not testosterone's only functions.

Working the Scientific Literacy Model

Testosterone and Aggression

Testosterone is one of the main sex hormones produced by the body. In men, it is produced by specialized cells in the testes; in women, it is produced in the ovaries. It can also be secreted by the adrenal cortex on the kidneys (Mazur & Booth, 1998). Because it is related to male sexual development and functioning, this hormone was traditionally targeted as an explanation for why men tend to be more physically aggressive than women. In other words, there was an assumption that testosterone *causes* aggression. Scientific studies paint a slightly more complex picture.

What do we know about testosterone and aggression?

There is a large body of research linking testosterone and aggression. In one experiment, researchers castrated a group of mice, an experience that obviously reduced their testosterone levels. The castrated mice as well as a control group of healthy mice then encountered an aggressive mouse. Although this type of interaction would usually lead to physical fights, the castrated mice showed almost no aggressive response (Beeman, 1947). However, when castrated mice received an injection of testosterone prior to the interaction, they did respond aggressively. This study suggested a causal link between testosterone and aggression. Human research also indicates a similar relationship. High testosterone levels were associated with a history of violent crime (e.g., murder, armed robbery) in both male and female prisoners (Dabbs et al., 1995; Dabbs & Hargrove, 1997). Prisoners who were jailed for less violent crimes had lower testosterone levels. Thus, both animal and human research has historically shown *some* link between testosterone and aggression.

How can science explain the relationship between testosterone and aggression?

Scientific studies show that the relationship between testosterone and aggression is more specific than was once thought. Testosterone appears to be involved with social aggression and dominance rather than with non-social forms of aggression such as hunting or responding to attacks (Eisenegger et al., 2011). Dominance involves an individual striving for or attempting to maintain a high social status. In animals, such a status is often linked with increased access to food and potential mates. In many primate species such as rhesus monkeys, dominance is achieved non-violently through stares, threatening body language, and shouts rather than through physical contact (Higley et al., 1996). It is also associated with higher testosterone levels. In studies with human participants, socially dominant adolescents and adults tended to have higher levels of testosterone (Carré et al., 2009; Rowe et al., 2004).

Testosterone also increased when participants perceived a potential threat to their status. Chimpanzees who anticipate competing for access to food show an elevated testosterone response (Wobber et al., 2010). In humans, several studies have found that competition was linked with increased testosterone, with activities ranging from wrestling and tennis to chess (Booth et al., 1989; Mazur et al., 1992)! Importantly, higher testosterone levels were found for

winners than for losers, again suggesting a link between this hormone and social dominance (Oliveira et al., 2009).

Can we critically evaluate this research?

One concern with many of these studies is that they are correlational. As you read in Module 2.2, correlational designs show a relationship between two variables but cannot be used to state that one causes the other. For instance, it is impossible to say if winning led to an increase in testosterone or if players with higher testosterone levels were more likely to win. In order to deal with this concern, some researchers have manipulated the competitions so that one player or the other wins. The results of these studies showed that winning *leads to* an increase in testosterone (e.g., Schultheiss et al., 2005).

Another question that arises is how does testosterone actually affect behaviour? What does testosterone do to allow people and animals to become (or feel) more socially dominant? Several studies suggest that injections of testosterone lead to less socially minded behaviour (Eisenegger et al., 2011). For instance, in most situations, people tend to subtly mimic the facial expressions of others; this makes the other person feel like they are being understood and increases social bonds. Researchers have found that injections of testosterone decrease facial mimicry (Hermans et al., 2006). Participants who have received testosterone are also more aware of potential threats. When you perceive a happy face, it does not likely cause any alarm. The same is true for people who have received an injection of testosterone (see Figure 3.18). However, when these same individuals view an angry face—which *is* a potential threat—their heart rate increases much more than the heart rates of control participants (van Honk et al., 2001). Together, these studies suggest that testosterone alters behaviours that would promote social bonding, thus making the individual more likely to respond with social aggression.

Why is this relevant?

These studies demonstrate that testosterone is not simply related to aggression. Instead, it is related to *social* aggression. Although this still means that this hormone could be linked with violent crime (which is, in some ways, a form of dominance), social dominance also has an evolutionary purpose. Dominant individuals are more likely to survive (and therefore reproduce) in many species. They would receive better food and access to mates. They would also experience less stress caused by attacks from dominant members of the group. Therefore, although we don't think of social aggression as being as a good thing, testosterone likely helped our ancestors to survive while others did not.

Figure 3.18 Testosterone and Social Threat

Individuals who received an injection of testosterone showed much larger heart rate responses to threatening faces than did control participants. The groups did not differ when viewing non-threatening happy faces.

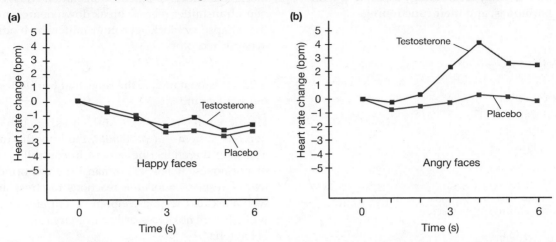

Source: Republished with permission of Elsevier Science, Inc., from The role of testosterone in social interaction. *Trends in Cognitive Sciences*, Vol. 15, No. 6, 2011., by Christoph Eisenegger; Johannes Haushofer; Ernst Fehr. Permission conveyed through Copyright Clearance Center, Inc.

NEURONS IN CONTEXT When reading about neuronal structures, neurotransmitters, and hormones, it is easy to lose sight of how these cells and molecules fit together with discussions of genetics (Module 3.1) and larger brain structures (Module 3.3). In the last few years, a number of genes related to different neurotransmitters have been identified. These genes can influence how the neurotransmitters are formed as well as processes such as reuptake.

These seemingly minor differences in genes can affect neurotransmitter levels and thus how neurons communicate with each other. This alters the networks of neurons firing together in the brain; these networks of structures produce your thoughts, movements, and sensations. So, while a discussion of brain cells seems far removed from the science of behaviour, these brain cells are, in fact, what makes you "you."

Module 3.2b Quiz:

The Chemical Messengers: Neurotransmitters and Hormones

Know . . .

1. A(n) _____ is a drug that blocks the actions of a neurotransmitter.

   A. agonist
   B. antagonist
   C. stop agent
   D. endorphin

Understand . . .

2. To reverse the effects of neurotoxic venom from a snakebite, which of the following actions would likely be most effective?

   A. Give the patient a high dose of dopamine.
   B. Give the patient a substance that would allow the body to resume transmission of acetylcholine.
   C. Give the patient a drug that would increase GABA transmission.
   D. Give the patient an acetylcholine antagonist.

Apply . . .

3. People who experience a *loss* of pain sensation in the middle of exercise are likely having a rush of _____.

   A. adrenaline
   B. norepinephrine
   C. pituitary
   D. endorphin

Analyze . . .

4. People often attribute male aggression to high levels of testosterone. Which of the following statements is an important consideration regarding this claim?

   A. High testosterone levels may be *correlated* with predatory aggression (e.g., hunting behaviours), but may not necessarily be the cause of it.
   B. Testosterone is found exclusively in males and, therefore, is a likely cause of male aggression.
   C. There are multiple types of aggression; testosterone is only linked with social aggression.
   D. Testosterone does not affect aggressive behaviours.

Module 3.2 Summary

3.2a   Know . . . the key terminology associated with nerve cells, hormones, and their functioning.

acetylcholine
action potential
adrenal glands
agonists
all-or-none principle
antagonists
axon
cell body
dendrites
dopamine
endorphin
GABA (gamma-amino butyric acid)
glial cells
glutamate
hormones
hypothalamus
myelin
neurogenesis
neuron
neurotransmitters
norepinephrine
pituitary gland
refractory period
resting potential
reuptake
serotonin
stem cells
synapses
synaptic cleft

3.2b   Understand . . . how nerve cells communicate.

Nerve cells fire because of processes involving both electrical and chemical factors. A stimulated nerve cell goes from resting potential to action potential following an influx of positively charged ions inside the membrane of the cell. As the message reaches the end of the nerve cell, neurotransmitters are released into synapses and bind to neighbouring postsynaptic cells. Depending on the type of neurotransmitter, the effect can be either inhibitory or excitatory.

3.2c   Understand . . . the ways that drugs and other substances affect the brain.

Drugs can be agonists or antagonists. A drug is an agonist if it enhances the effects of a neurotransmitter. This outcome occurs if the drug increases the release of a neurotransmitter, blocks reuptake, or mimics the neurotransmitter by binding to the postsynaptic cell. A drug is an antagonist if it blocks the effects of a neurotransmitter. Antagonists block neurotransmitter release, break down neurotransmitters in the synapse, or block neurotransmitters by binding to post-synaptic receptors.

3.2d   Understand . . . the roles that hormones play in our behaviour.

Hormones have multiple influences on behaviour. The nervous system—in particular, the hypothalamus—interacts with the endocrine system in controlling the release of hormones. A few of humans' many hormonally controlled responses include reactions to stress and pain as well as sexual responses. Some hormones are associated with, though not necessarily a primary cause of, aggressive behaviour.

3.2e   Apply . . . your knowledge of neurotransmitters to form hypotheses about drug actions.

In this module you read about how selective serotonin reuptake inhibitors (SSRIs) slow down the reuptake process to increase the amount of serotonin at the synapse.

Apply Activity

Consider another drug—a monoamine oxidase inhibitor (MAOI).

1. Based on its name, *monoamine oxidase inhibitor*, which neurotransmitters would be affected by such a drug? (See page 95.)
2. If monoamine oxidase is an enzyme that breaks down monoamine transmitters, what would happen if a drug inhibits the enzyme? What effect would this action have on levels of the neurotransmitters (i.e., an overall increase or decrease)?
3. Would the effects of an MAOI resemble those of an SSRI?

3.2f   Analyze . . . the claim that we are born with all the nerve cells we will ever have.

Earlier in this module, a Myths in Mind feature addressed the question of whether we are born with all of the nerve cells we will ever have. Although scientists once believed this to be true, we now know that neurogenesis—the growth of new neurons—takes place in several parts of the brain. One of these regions is the hippocampus, which is involved in learning and memory (see Module 7.1).

Module 3.3 Structure and Organization of the Nervous System

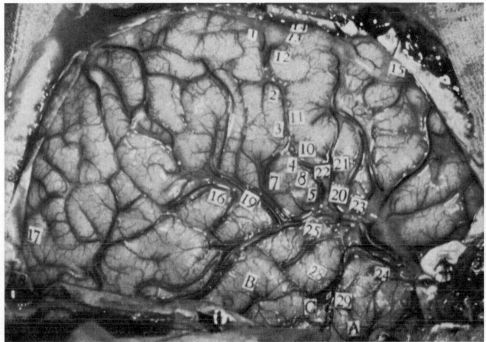

Montreal Neurological Hospital and Institute

Learning Objectives

3.3a Know . . . the key terminology associated with the structure and organization of the nervous system.

3.3b Understand . . . how studies of split-brain patients reveal the workings of the brain.

3.3c Apply . . . your knowledge of brain regions to predict which abilities might be affected when a specific area is injured or diseased.

3.3d Analyze . . . whether neuroplasticity will help people with brain damage.

Some of you may have seen this Canadian Heritage Moment on television: A woman smells toast burning and then collapses to the ground while having a seizure. The scene then changes to a surgical suite. Dr. Wilder Penfield, a doctor at the Montreal Neurological Institute, is electrically stimulating different parts of the woman's brain prior to her surgery to remove the brain tissue causing her seizures. In one scene, she reports that she sees "the most wonderful lights." After another electrical burst, she asks, "Did you pour cold water on my hand, Dr. Penfield?" Then, in the scene's climax, the patient says, "Dr. Penfield! I can smell burnt toast!" By locating the sensation that immediately preceded the woman's seizure, Dr. Penfield was able to deduce the probable source of the woman's seizures.

In addition to showing us that early brain researchers were part scientist and part detective, this Canadian Heritage Moment also makes an important point about the organization of the brain: Different parts of the brain will be related to different functions, including sensations, memories, and emotions. In this module, we will discuss many of

the important brain regions related to the biology of behaviour. (Note: If you haven't seen the video mentioned in this section, you can find it online at https://www.youtube.com/watch?v=mSN86kphL68.)

Focus Questions

1. How do the different divisions of the nervous system work together when you are startled?

2. How does the brain control movement?

» In this module, we translate our knowledge of nerve cells into an understanding of how they work as an integrated system. This section is rich with terminology and can be challenging. As you read through it, try to think about how the different parts of the nervous system apply to your own behaviour and experiences. Doing so will help you remember the terms, and will also show you that many different parts of your nervous system interact when you perform even the simplest of behaviours.

Divisions of the Nervous System

Think about it: billions of cells work together to let you have a personality, feel emotions, dance, enjoy music, and remember all of the ups and downs you experience in life. In addition to these voluntary activities, the nervous system is also involved in a number of involuntary processes like controlling your heart rate, blinking, and breathing. Given these diverse functions, it shouldn't be surprising to hear that the nervous system has a number of divisions that allow these processes to seamlessly take place. We begin our exploration of the nervous system by examining the most basic of these distinctions—the difference between the central and peripheral nervous systems.

THE CENTRAL NERVOUS SYSTEM Look up from this page and examine the objects around you. What are they? Can you use words to describe them? How would you use them? Your ability to think up answers to these questions involves different parts of your central nervous system. The **central nervous system (CNS)** *consists of the brain and the spinal cord* (see Figure 3.19). The human brain is perhaps the most complex entity known. Its capacity to store information is almost limitless. Your personality, preferences, memories, and conscious awareness are all packed into this three-pound structure made up of approximately 100 billion individual neurons. The other part of the CNS, the spinal cord, runs from your neck down to the base of your spine. The spinal cord receives information from the brain and stimulates nerves that extend out into the body; this stimulation produces movements. It also receives information from sensory nerves in the body and transmits it back to the brain (or, in the case of reflexes, organizes rapid movements *without* the help of the brain). These two structures are critical for our survival. But, our ability to move and to sense the outside world would be impossible without another major division of the nervous system.

THE PERIPHERAL NERVOUS SYSTEM Wiggle your fingers. Now feel the edges of this book (or the edge of your computer if you're reading an eText). In both cases, you are sending information from your central nervous system to the nerves in the rest of your body that control movement. You are also receiving sensory input from your body as you interact with your environment. These processes are performed by the **peripheral nervous system (PNS)**, a *division of the nervous system that transmits signals between the brain and the rest of the body and is divided into two subcomponents, the somatic system and the autonomic system*

Figure 3.19 The Organization of the Nervous System

The nervous system can be divided into several different components, each with a specific set of structures and functions.

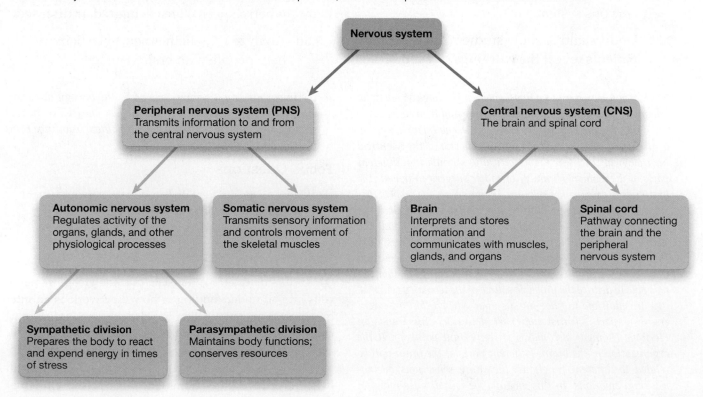

(see Figure 3.20). The **somatic nervous system** *consists of nerves that control skeletal muscles, which are responsible for voluntary and reflexive movement; it also consists of nerves that receive sensory input from the body.* This would be the division of the PNS that is active when you wiggle your fingers or feel the edge of a book. Any voluntary behaviour, such as coordinating the movements needed to reach, walk, or move a computer mouse, makes use of the somatic nervous system.

But, not all behaviours are voluntary. For example, it is unlikely that you can make your heart race or your palms sweat. Responses such as these are often automatic, occurring outside of our conscious control. These behaviours are performed by the **autonomic nervous system**, *the portion of the peripheral nervous system responsible for regulating the activity of organs and glands.* This system includes two subcomponents, one that increases our ability to make rapid responses, and one that helps us return to normal levels of emotional arousal. The **sympathetic nervous system** *is responsible for the fight-or-flight response of an increased heart*

rate, dilated pupils, and decreased salivary flow—responses that prepare the body for action.* If you hear footsteps behind you as you are walking alone or if you barely avoid an accident while driving, then you will experience *sympathetic arousal.* In this process, blood is directed toward your skeletal muscles, heart rate and perspiration increase, and digestive processes are slowed; each of these responses helps to direct energy where it is most needed in case you need to respond. However, if you remained in this heightened state of emotional arousal, you would quickly run out of energy resources. It is therefore important for you to have a system in place that allows your body to quickly return to normal levels of energy use. The **parasympathetic nervous system** *helps maintain homeostatic balance in the presence of change; following sympathetic arousal, it works to return the body to a baseline, nonemergency state.* Generally speaking, the parasympathetic nervous system does the opposite of what the sympathetic nervous system does (see Figure 3.20).

Figure 3.20 The Autonomic Nervous System

The sympathetic and parasympathetic divisions of the autonomic nervous system control and regulate responses of the glands and organs of the body.

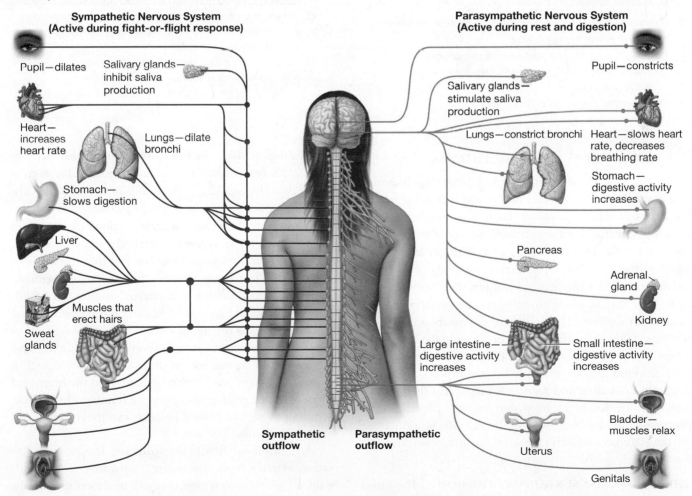

Sympathetic Nervous System
(Active during fight-or-flight response)

Pupil—dilates

Salivary glands—inhibit saliva production

Heart—increases heart rate

Lungs—dilate bronchi

Stomach—slows digestion

Liver

Muscles that erect hairs

Sweat glands

Sympathetic outflow

Parasympathetic Nervous System
(Active during rest and digestion)

Pupil—constricts

Salivary glands—stimulate saliva production

Lungs—constrict bronchi

Heart—slows heart rate, decreases breathing rate

Stomach—digestive activity increases

Pancreas

Adrenal gland

Kidney

Large intestine—digestive activity increases

Small intestine—digestive activity increases

Bladder—muscles relax

Uterus

Genitals

Parasympathetic outflow

Source: Lilienfeld, Scott O.; Lynn, Steven; Namy, Laura L.; Woolf, Nancy J., *Psychology: From Inquiry To Understanding*, Books A La Carte Edition, 2nd Ed., ©2011. Reprinted and Electronically reproduced by permission of Pearson Education, Inc., New York, NY.

So, if you thought you saw a snake beside your foot, you would have a sympathetic nervous system (PNS) response that would increase your heart rate and would send blood toward your leg muscles. Your brain (CNS) would initiate a movement and send that order down the spinal cord (CNS) where it would project out from spinal nerves (PNS) that influence the activity of muscles. Sensory feedback (PNS) from the skin and muscles would travel back to the spinal cord (CNS) and up to the brain (CNS). After some time had passed and you realized that it was actually a stick, not a snake, your parasympathetic

nervous system (PNS) would help you calm down so that you were no longer frightened and no longer using up all of your energy responding to this stimulus.

Although these different parts of the PNS and CNS clearly influence a number of our responses, most of these activities are biologically simple. An exception is the activity that occurs in the brain, a stunningly complex structure made up of hundreds of smaller parts. As most of our behaviour is directed by brain activity, the rest of this module will focus on explaining how the different parts of this biological marvel function, alone and in larger networks.

Module 3.3a Quiz:

Divisions of the Nervous System

Know . . .

1. Which division of the peripheral nervous system is responsible for countering much of the activity associated with the sympathetic nervous system?
   A. Somatic nervous system
   B. Pseudosympathetic nervous system
   C. Central nervous system
   D. Parasympathetic nervous system

2. The central nervous system consists of which of the following?
   A. The brain and the spinal cord
   B. The sympathetic and parasympathetic nervous system
   C. The brain and the nerves controlling digestion and other automatic functions
   D. The somatic and autonomic systems

Understand . . .

3. A major difference between the somatic and autonomic branches of the nervous system is that
   A. the somatic nervous system controls involuntary responses, and the autonomic nervous system controls voluntary movement.
   B. the somatic nervous system is located in the brain, and the autonomic nervous system is located peripherally.
   C. the somatic nervous system controls voluntary movement, and the autonomic nervous system controls involuntary responses.
   D. the somatic nervous system controls sensation, and the autonomic nervous system controls movement.

The Brain and Its Structures

When you look at the brain, you will immediately notice that it appears to be divided into two symmetrical halves known as *cerebral hemispheres.* Each hemisphere contains the same structures, although there are some small differences in the size of these brain areas (Springer & Deutsch, 1998). Within each hemisphere, the structures of the brain are organized in a hierarchical fashion. The human brain, as well as that of other animals, can be subdivided into three main regions: the hindbrain, the midbrain, and the forebrain (Table 3.2). This system of dividing the brain may tempt you to view it as a mass of separate compartments. Keep in mind that the entire brain is composed of highly integrated circuitry and feedback loops. In other words, although the forebrain may perform complex thinking processes like decision making, its activity is influenced by (and influences) structures in the midbrain and the hindbrain.

THE HINDBRAIN: SUSTAINING THE BODY The hindbrain consists of structures that are critical to controlling basic, life-sustaining processes. At the top of the spinal

cord is a region called the **brainstem**, *which is the "stem" or bottom of the brain and consists of two structures: the medulla and the pons* (Figure 3.21). Nerve cells in the medulla connect with the body to perform basic functions such as regulating breathing, heart rate, sneezing, salivating, and even vomiting—all those actions your body does with little conscious control on your part. The fact that the medulla can control all of these activities without us consciously controlling our responses is important—without this ability, our lives would consist of nothing more than sending signals to various organs to ensure that we stayed alive. The pons contributes to general levels of wakefulness, and also appears to have a role in dreaming (see Module 5.1). Due to its connections to other structures in the brain and spinal cord, the pons is also part of a number of networks including those that control balance, eye movements, and swallowing (Nolte, 1999).

An additional hindbrain structure, the *reticular formation*, extends from the medulla upwards to the midbrain, a higher brain region that will be described shortly. The reticular formation influences attention and alertness. When you wake up in the morning, you can thank (in part)

Table 3.2 Major Brain Regions, Structures, and Their Functions

Regions and Structures	Functions
Hindbrain	
Brainstem (medulla and pons)	Breathing, heart rate, sleep, and wakefulness
Cerebellum	Balance, coordination and timing of movements; attention and emotion
Midbrain	
Superior colliculus	Orienting visual attention
Inferior colliculus	Orienting auditory attention
Forebrain	
Basal ganglia	Movement, reward processing
Amygdala	Emotion
Hippocampus	Memory
Hypothalamus	Temperature regulation, motivation (hunger, thirst, sex)
Thalamus	Sensory relay station
Cerebral Cortex	
Occipital lobe	Visual processing
Parietal lobe	Sensory processing, bodily awareness
Temporal lobe	Hearing, object recognition, language, emotion
Frontal lobe	Thought, planning, language, movement

your reticular formation. This structure also communicates with cells in the spinal cord involved with movements related to walking and posture.

The structures in the hindbrain are able to influence a number of different behaviours through their connections to other parts of the brain and spinal cord. They also have dense connections with another hindbrain structure, the

Figure 3.21 The Hindbrain and Midbrain

Structures in the hindbrain are responsible for basic functions that sustain the body. The midbrain includes structures that control basic sensory responses and voluntary movement.

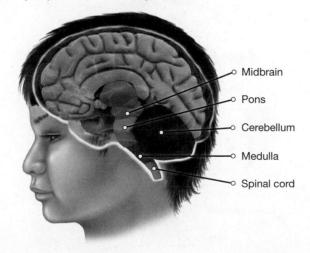

Source: Lilienfeld, Scott O.; Lynn, Steven J; Namy, Laura L.; Woolf, Nancy J., *Psychology: From Inquiry To Understanding*, 2nd Ed., ©2011. Reprinted And Electronically Reproduced By Permission Of Pearson Education, Inc., New York, NY.

cerebellum. The **cerebellum** (Latin for "little brain") *is the lobe-like structure at the base of the brain that is involved in the monitoring of movement, maintaining balance, attention, and emotional responses.* The cerebellum's role in movement has been known for almost two centuries (Flourens, 1824; Schmahmann, 2004). Damage to this structure leads to uncoordinated and jerky movements that interfere with walking, posture, and most limb movements. These symptoms suggest that the cerebellum is involved with coordinating and timing ongoing movements rather than with generating responses on its own (Yamazaki & Tanaka, 2009). However, recent research indicates that these timing functions extend beyond movement. Patients with damage to the cerebellum have difficulty controlling their attention (Schweizer, Alexander, et al., 2007; Schweizer, Oriet, et al., 2007). They also have problems with emotional control, including personality changes and impulsivity, a set of symptoms now known as the *cognitive affective behavioural syndrome* (Schmahmann & Sherman, 1998). The cerebellum is likely able to influence this wide variety of functions because it has dense connections to a number of areas in the forebrain as well as to evolutionarily older structures in the base of the brain like the hypothalamus, a structure related to the autonomic nervous system (Stoodley & Schmahmann, 2010; Zhu et al., 2006). Through these connections, the so-called "little brain" is able to have a big effect on behaviour.

THE MIDBRAIN: SENSATION AND ACTION The cerebellum is not the only neural region involved with both movement and attention. The **midbrain**, which *resides* *just above the hindbrain, primarily functions as a relay station between sensory and motor areas* (Figure 3.21). For example, have you ever detected a sudden movement out of the corner of your eye? This ability to capture your visual attention is influenced by the *superior colliculus* (plural *colliculi*). Of course, your ability to orient your attention is not limited to visual stimuli. How do you respond when someone's phone rings in class? You, quite naturally, pay attention to that new sound and turn your head toward its source (while mentally judging the person's ringtone). This ability to move your auditory attention is influenced by another midbrain structure, the *inferior colliculus* (plural *colliculi*).

Like the hindbrain, structures in the midbrain do not act as independent units; rather, they are part of much larger networks. This concept is powerfully illustrated by the *substantia nigra*. This midbrain area has connections to structures in the forebrain (discussed below); this network of dopamine-releasing cells is involved with the control of movements. Parkinson's disease—a condition marked by major impairments in voluntary movement—is caused by a loss of the dopamine-producing cells in this network.

THE FOREBRAIN: EMOTION, MEMORY, AND THOUGHT
The **forebrain**, *the most visibly obvious region of the brain, consists of all of the neural structures that are located above the midbrain, including all of the folds and grooves on the outer surface of the brain; the multiple interconnected structures in the forebrain are critical to such complex processes as emotion, memory, thinking, and reasoning.* The forebrain also contains spaces called *ventricles* (Figure 3.22). Although the ventricles appear hollow, they are filled with cerebrospinal fluid, a solution that helps to eliminate wastes and provides nutrition and hormones to the brain and spinal cord. Cerebrospinal fluid also cushions the brain from impact against the skull.

Sitting next to the ventricles are the **basal ganglia**, *a group of three structures that are involved in facilitating planned movements, skill learning, and integrating sensory and movement information with the brain's reward system* (Figure 3.23). The basal ganglia form networks that promote and inhibit movements. These two networks interact to allow us to have our different muscles work together in the correct sequence rather than having them "flex" at random times. People who are very practised at a specific motor skill, such as playing an instrument or riding a bicycle, have actually modified their basal ganglia through practice to better coordinate engaging in the activity. Improper functioning of the basal ganglia can lead to movement disorders like Parkinson's disease and Huntington's disease, a condition involving uncontrollable movements of the body, head, and face. The basal ganglia are also affected in people who have Tourette's syndrome—a condition marked by erratic and repetitive facial and muscle movements (called *tics*), heavy eye blinking, and frequent noise making such as grunting, snorting, or sniffing. The excess dopamine

Figure 3.22 The Cerebral Ventricles
Four ventricles in the brain contain cerebrospinal fluid. This provides nutrition and cushioning for many parts of the brain.

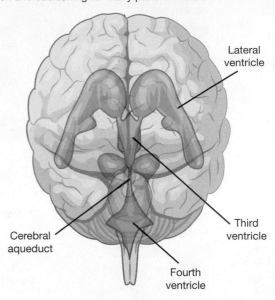

Source: Carlson, Neil R., *Physiology of Behaviour*, 11th ed., ©2013, pp. 29, 72. Reprinted and Electronically reproduced by permission of Pearson Education, Inc., Upper Saddle River, New Jersey.

that appears to be transmitted within the basal ganglia contributes to many of the classic Tourette's symptoms (Baym et al., 2008). Incidentally, contrary to popular belief, the shouting of obscenities (*coprolalia*) is actually relatively uncommon in people with Tourette's syndrome.

Figure 3.23 The Basal Ganglia
The basal ganglia function in both voluntary movement and responses to rewarding stimuli.

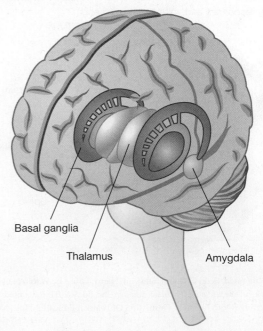

Figure 3.24 The Limbic System

Structures in the limbic system include the hypothalamus, hippocampus, and amygdala, which play roles in regulating motivation, memory, and emotion.

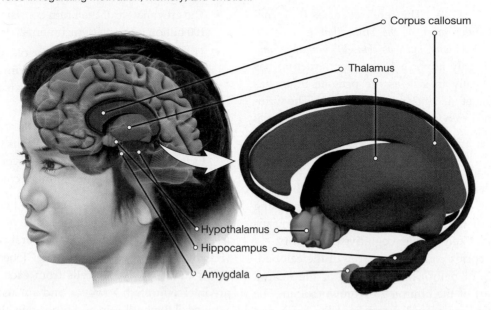

Source: Lilienfeld, Scott O.; Lynn, Steven J; Namy, Laural L.; Woolf, Nancy J., *Psychology: From Inquiry to Understanding*, Books A La Carte Edtion, 2nd Ed., ©2011. Reprinted and Electronically reproduced by permission of Pearson Education, Inc., New York, NY.

Some parts of the basal ganglia are also involved in emotion, particularly experiences of pleasure and reward (Berridge et al., 2009). These structures respond to several different types of rewards including tasty foods like chocolate (Small et al., 2003) and monetary rewards (Elliott et al., 2003; Zald et al., 2004). They also form a network with a nearby structure—the *nucleus accumbens*—whose activity accompanies many kinds of pleasurable experiences, including sexual excitement and satisfying a food craving (Avena et al., 2008). As you will read in Module 5.3, this basal ganglia–nucleus accumbens network is also related to the pleasurable effects caused by some drugs (Uchimura & North, 1990).

Another major set of forebrain structures comprises the **limbic system**, *an integrated network involved in emotion and memory* (Maclean, 1952; see Figure 3.24). One key structure in the limbic system is the **amygdala**, *which facilitates memory formation for emotional events, mediates fear responses, and appears to play a role in recognizing and interpreting emotional stimuli, including facial expressions.* In addition, the amygdala connects with structures in the nervous system that are responsible for adaptive fear responses such as freezing in position when a possible threat is detected; it is also connected to areas responsible for attention, which is why you usually notice when a spider is on your wall. Just below the amygdala is another limbic structure called the hippocampus (Greek for "seahorse"—something it physically resembles if you've had a few drinks). The **hippocampus**

is critical for learning and memory, particularly the formation of new memories (Squire et al., 2007; see Module 7.1).

You already encountered the *hypothalamus* in Module 3.2 when you read about its relationship to the endocrine system, and you will encounter it again in Module 11.1 when you read about its influence on the regulation of hunger and thirst. The hypothalamus serves as a sort of thermostat, maintaining the appropriate body temperature, and it regulates drives such as aggression and sex by interacting with the endocrine system. In fact, regions of the hypothalamus trigger orgasm for both females and males (Meston et al., 2004; Peeters & Giuliano, 2007). Direct electrical stimulation of parts of the hypothalamus can produce intense physical pleasure. In a classic set of studies in the 1950s, Olds (1958) found that rats who could press a lever to stimulate the lateral (outside part) of the hypothalamus did so for hours on end, often forgoing food and sleep in order to repeatedly press the lever. In fact, the rats were willing to cross a painful electrical grid in order to reach the lever so that they could return to stimulating themselves.

Another important, albeit less arousing, forebrain structure is the **thalamus**, *a set of nuclei involved in relaying sensory information to different regions of the brain.* Most of the incoming sensory information, including what we see and hear, is routed through specific nuclei in the thalamus. Different types of information are processed by different nuclei before being sent to more specialized regions of the brain for further processing (Sherman, 2007; Sherman & Guillery, 1996). Many of these regions are found in the outer layer known as the cerebral cortex.

THE CEREBRAL CORTEX The **cerebral cortex** *is the convoluted, wrinkled outer layer of the brain that is involved in multiple higher functions, such as thought, language, and personality.* This highly advanced, complex structure has increased dramatically in size as the primate brain has evolved (Kouprina et al., 2002; see Module 3.1). The wrinkled surface of the brain seems to have solved a biological problem endured by our species, as well as by many other mammals: how to pack more cells (i.e., more computing power) into the same amount of space. Because the skull can only be so large, the brain has countered this constraint by forming a wrinkled surface, thereby increasing the surface area of the cortex. More surface area means more neurons and, likely, greater cognitive complexity.

The cerebral cortex consists primarily of the cell bodies and dendrites of neurons; these parts of the neuron give the outer part of the brain a grey-brown colour. The axons of these neurons extend throughout the brain and allow communication between different neural regions to occur. Most of these axons are wrapped in a white, fatty substance called myelin (see Module 3.2), which helps speed up the transmission of neural impulses. Figure 3.25 shows a slice of the brain revealing contrasting light and dark regions, known as *white matter* and *grey matter*. When you see an image like Figure 3.25, it is easy to underestimate the complexity of the brain and its connections. Just to put this image into perspective:

- The grey matter of the brain consists of approximately 100 billion neurons (Drachman, 2005).

- The white matter of a 20-year-old male brain would extend approximately 176 000 km; for a 20-year-old female brain, it would extend approximately 149 000 km (Marner et al., 2003).

- Healthy adults have between 100 and 500 trillion synapses, or connections between cells (Drachman, 2005). Each of these synapses can fire several times a second. That is a considerable amount of computing power.

THE FOUR LOBES In each cerebral hemisphere, the cortex forms the outer surface of four major areas known as *lobes*: the occipital, parietal, temporal, and frontal lobes (Figure 3.26). Each of the cerebral lobes has a particular set of functions. Nerve cells from each of the four lobes are interconnected, however, and are also networked with regions of the midbrain and hindbrain already described.

The **occipital lobes** *are located at the rear of the brain and are where visual information is processed.* The occipital lobes receive visual information from the thalamus. After processing this information, they send it out along two different visual pathways, one that projects to the temporal lobes and is involved with object recognition and one that projects to the parietal lobes and is involved with using vision to guide our movements (Milner & Goodale, 2006).

Figure 3.25 Grey and White Matter of the Brain

The cerebral cortex includes both grey matter and white matter, which consist of myelinated axons. Also seen here are the ventricles of the brain. These cavities within the brain are filled with cerebrospinal fluid that provides nourishment and exchange of chemicals with the brain as well as its protective structure.

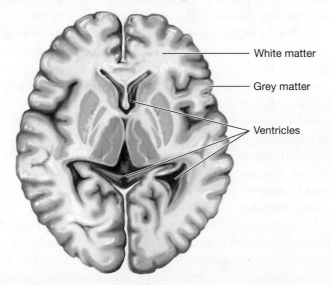

White matter

Grey matter

Ventricles

Figure 3.26 The Four Lobes of the Cerebral Cortex

The cerebral cortex is divided into the frontal, parietal, occipital, and temporal lobes.

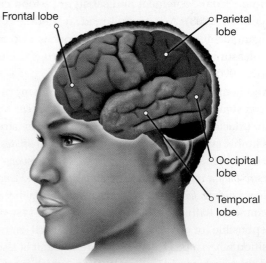

Frontal lobe

Parietal lobe

Occipital lobe

Temporal lobe

Figure 3.27 The Body as Mapped on the Motor Cortex and Somatosensory Cortex

The regions of the motor cortex are involved in controlling specific body parts. The somatosensory cortex registers touch and other sensations that correspond to the body region depicted. Why do you think it is evolutionarily useful to have these two cortices next to each other in the brain?

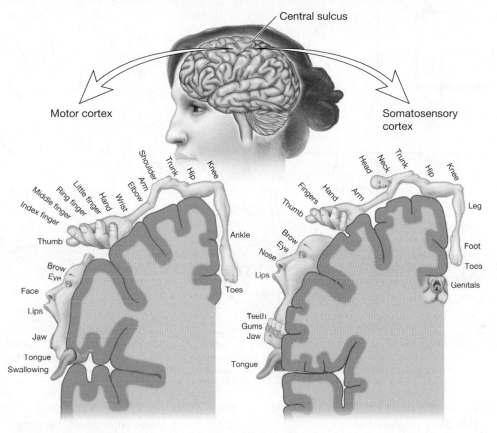

Source: Marieb, Elaine N.; Hoehn, Katja, *Human Anatomy And Physiology*, 7th Ed., ©2007, P.438. Reprinted And Electronically reproduced by permission Of Pearson Education, Inc., New York, NY.

The **parietal lobes** *are involved in our experiences of touch as well our bodily awareness.* At the anterior (front) edge of the parietal lobe is the *somatosensory cortex*—a band of densely packed nerve cells that register touch sensations. The amount of neural tissue dedicated to a given body part in this region is roughly based on the number of sensory receptors present at each respective body region. For instance, the volume of nerve cells in the somatosensory cortex corresponding to the face and hands is proportionally greater than the volume of cells devoted to less sensitive regions like the torso and legs. This is because we acquire more sensory information from our face and hands than we do from most other body parts; very few people use their stomach when trying to identify objects by touch. This difference in the amount of space in the somatosensory cortex allocated to different parts of the body is depicted in Figure 3.27; figures such as this are referred to as a *homunculus* or "little man."

Regions within the parietal lobes also function in performing mathematical, visuospatial, and attention tasks. Damage to different regions of the parietal lobe can lead to specific impairments. For instance, right parietal lobe damage can lead to *neglect*, a situation in which the patient does not attend to anything that appears in the left half of his or her visual field (Heilman & Valenstein, 1979; Hughlings Jackson, 1876/1932); examples of a neglect patient's drawings are shown in Figure 3.28. Neglect can even occur for the left half of the patient's *imagined* visual images (Bisiach & Luzatti, 1978)!

The **temporal lobes** *are located at the sides of the brain near the ears and are involved in hearing, language, and some higher-level aspects of vision such as object and face recognition.* Different sections of the temporal cortex perform different roles. The superior (top) part of the temporal cortex is known as the *auditory cortex*—it is essential for our ability to hear. Damage to this region leads to problems with hearing despite the fact that the patient's ears work perfectly; this condition is known as *cortical deafness* (Mott, 1907). Slightly behind this region, near the back of the temporal lobe, is *Wernicke's area,* which is related to understanding language (Wernicke, 1874). The close proximity of the hearing and language-comprehension areas

Figure 3.28 Unilateral Neglect

Patients with damage to the right parietal lobe sometimes show evidence of neglect, a failure to attend to the left half of their visual field.

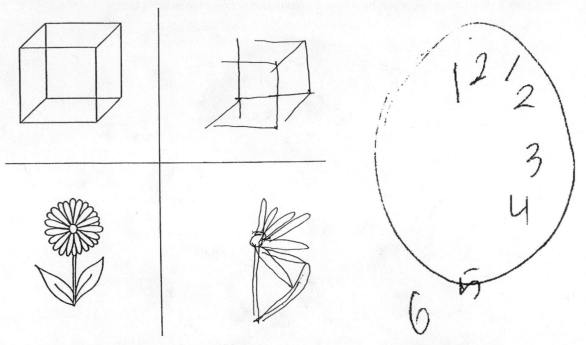

Source: Republished with permission of British Medical Journal (BMJ Publishing Group), from Hemispatial neglect, *J Neurol Neurosurg Psychiatry*, Vol 75, pg 13-21, 2004. Retrieved from http://jnnp.bmj.com/content/75/1/13.abstract?sid=28fd8ac7-acc2-414c-b0b0-e97478852233 by A Parton, P Malhotra, M Husain. Permission conveyed through Copyright Clearance Center, Inc.

makes sense, as these two functions are closely related (see Module 8.3 for a detailed discussion of language).

Some of the structures on the bottom surface of the temporal lobes have a key role in memory. These brain areas send information about the objects being viewed and their location or context to the hippocampus, a forebrain structure discussed above (Diana et al., 2007; Eichenbaum et al., 2007). The hippocampus—which is found in the medial or middle portions of the temporal lobes—then sends output to different brain areas, particularly regions of the frontal lobes, showing again that many different areas of the brain work together to produce almost every behaviour we perform.

The **frontal lobes** *are important in numerous higher cognitive functions, such as planning, regulating impulses and emotions, language production, and voluntary movement* (Goldman-Rakic, 1996). The frontal lobes also allow you to deliberately guide and reflect on your own thought processes. Like the temporal lobes, the frontal lobes can be divided into a number of subsections with specific functions (Miller & Cummings, 2007). A key distinction is between areas related to movement and areas related to the control of our mental lives.

Toward the rear of the frontal lobes is a thick band of neurons that form the *primary motor cortex*, which is involved in the control of voluntary movement. Like the somatosensory cortex discussed above, the primary motor cortex is organized in a homunculus, with different body

areas requiring different amounts of space (see Figure 3.27). Body parts such as the fingers that perform fine-motor control will require more space in the motor cortex than areas like the upper thigh, which does not perform many intricate movements. Importantly, motor areas in the frontal lobes are active not just when moving the corresponding body part, but also when planning a movement. This ability to prepare movements before they are needed would clearly be useful when dealing with threats and likely contributed to our species' survival.

The front two-thirds of the frontal lobes are known as the *prefrontal cortex*. This region, which itself can be divided into a number of subsections, performs many of our higher-order cognitive functions such as decision making and controlling our attention. The prefrontal cortex has connections to many of the other brain areas discussed in this module, and appears to help regulate their activity; these control processes are known as *executive functions*. Such functions are not always necessary; however, when we encounter new situations or need to override our normal responses, the prefrontal cortex is almost always involved (Milner, 1963; Stuss & Knight, 2002).

We would obviously like to find ways to strengthen our executive functions. The Psych@ section on page 111 provides on interesting technique: exercise.

The four lobes of the brain are found in both of our cerebral hemispheres. It is therefore important to have

PSYCH@

The Gym

Somehow, physical exertion, pain, and breaking down and rebuilding muscle end up making people feel better. But the benefits of exercise do not apply just to one's mood: Exercise also affects cognitive activities such as learning and memory. But how?

In recent years, neuroscientists have begun unravelling the mystery of how exercise benefits brain health. Brain imaging studies have revealed that people who engage in regular exercise show improved functioning of the prefrontal cortex compared to non-exercisers. In addition, people who exercise perform better than non-exercisers on tasks involving planning, scheduling, and multitasking (see Davis et al., 2011; Hillman et al., 2008). Animal studies have shown that exercise increases the number of cells in the hippocampus, which is critical for memory, and increases the quantity of brain chemicals that are responsible for promoting cell growth and functioning (Cotman & Berchtold, 2002). But animals are not the only beneficiaries of an exercise program; similar findings have been reported for elderly people who regularly engage in aerobic exercise (Erickson et al., 2011).

Despite the clear benefits associated with exercise, many school curricula have dropped physical education in favour of spending more time on preparation for standardized testing. It is not clear that time away from the gym and the playground is having much benefit. A review of 14 studies—12 conducted in the U.S., one in British Columbia (Ahamed et al., 2007), and one in South Africa—found a "significant positive relationship" between physical activity and academic performance (Singh et al., 2012). This effect may be due to changes in blood flow to the brain, a reduction in stress due to time away from schoolwork, a positive emotional experience associated with play, or, more likely, a combination of several factors. Science is clearly demonstrating that exercise affects the brain basis of learning and memory (Cotman & Berchtold, 2002; Hillman et al., 2008). These results suggest that provincial governments should *increase*, not *decrease*, funding for physical education in schools. I hopefully these studies will help get that ball rolling.

---

some way for these brain regions to communicate with each other. This prevents us from having our left and right hemispheres working against each other. In Figure 3.29, you can see that crossing the midline of the brain is a densely concentrated bundle of nerve cells called the **corpus callosum**, *a collection of neural fibres connecting the two brain hemispheres.* This thick band of fibres allows the right and left hemispheres to communicate with each other. This communication has an added benefit: It allows the two hemispheres to work together to produce some of our behaviours. It also opens up the possibility that each hemisphere will become specialized for performing certain functions.

LEFT BRAIN, RIGHT BRAIN: HEMISPHERIC SPECIALIZATION   Although they appear to be mirror images of each other, the two sides of the cortex often perform very different functions, a phenomenon called *hemispheric specialization.* Speaking in very general terms, the right hemisphere is specialized for cognitive tasks that involve visual and spatial skills, recognition of visual stimuli, and musical processing. In contrast, the left hemisphere is more specialized for language and math (Corballis, 1993; Gazzaniga, 1967, 2000). However, although some hemispheric differences are quite pronounced, many are a matter of degree (Springer & Deutsch, 1998).

Our understanding of hemispheric specialization expanded greatly through work with *split-brain patients.* In the 1960s, physicians hoping to curtail severe epileptic seizures in their patients used a surgical procedure to treat individuals who were not responding to other therapies.

The surgeon would sever the corpus callosum, leaving a patient with two separate cerebral hemispheres. This surgery is not as drastic as it might sound. Patients were remarkably normal after the operation, but several interesting observations were made. One was that split-brain patients responded quite differently to visual input that was presented to either hemisphere alone (Sperry, 1982).

To see how this works, take a look at Figure 3.30. Imagine the person pictured has a split brain. She should be able to match the two objects to her right *and* verbalize the match, because the left side of her visual system perceives the objects and language is processed in the left hemisphere of the brain. In contrast, a visual stimulus presented on the left side of the body would be processed on the right side of the brain. As you can see from Figure 3.30, when the object is presented to the left side of the split-brain patient, the individual does not verbalize which of the objects match, because her right hemisphere is not specialized for language and cannot label the object. If asked to point at the matching object, however, she is able to do so (but only with her left hand, which is controlled by the right hemisphere). Thus, she is able to process the information using her right hemisphere, but cannot articulate it with language.

Today, split-brain studies are extremely rare, as modern epilepsy medications are often sufficient to treat the symptoms of these patients without the need to sever the corpus callosum. However, the insights gained from these patients still inform our understanding of the brain. It must be stressed, however, that many of these differences are a matter of degree rather than being an absolute

Figure 3.29 The Corpus Callosum

The left and right hemispheres of the brain are connected by a thick band of axons called the corpus callosum.

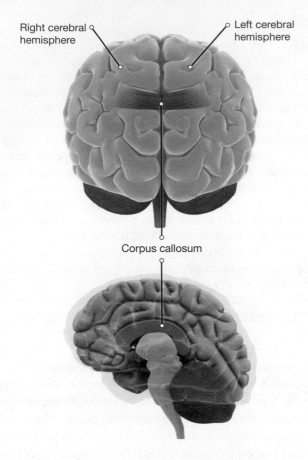

Source: Lilienfeld, Scott O.; Lynn, Steven J; Namy, Laura L.; Woolf, Nancy J., *Psychology: From Inquiry To Understanding*, 2nd Ed., ©2011. Reprinted And Electronically Reproduced By Permission Of Pearson Education, Inc., New York, NY.

one-hemisphere-or-the-other distinction. Indeed, the reality is that most cognitive functions are spread throughout multiple brain regions, with one hemisphere sometimes being superior to the other hemisphere (see Table 3.3).

Before finishing a discussion of the hemispheres, it is also important to point out that the media often misrepresents how hemispheric specialization works. Terms like "left-brained" and "right-brained" are used quite

Table 3.3 Examples of Hemispheric Asymmetries

Left Hemisphere	Right Hemisphere
Language production	Visuospatial skills
Language comprehension	Prosody (emotional intonation)
Word recognition	Face recognition
Arithmetic	Attention (rapid orienting to new stimuli)
Moving the right side of the body	Moving the left side of the body

Figure 3.30 A Split-Brain Experiment

This woman has had a split-brain operation. She is able to verbalize which objects match when they are placed to her right side, because language is processed in the left hemisphere. She cannot verbalize the matching objects on the left, but can identify them by pointing with her left hand (which is controlled by her right hemisphere).

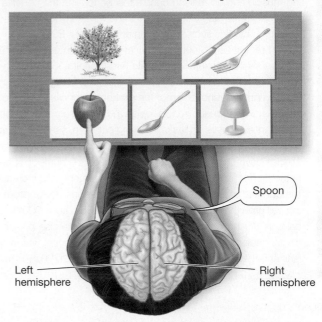

Source: Lilienfeld, Scott O.; Lynn, Steven J; Namy, Laura L.; Woolf, Nancy J., *Psychology: From Inquiry To Understanding*, 2nd Ed., ©2011. Reprinted And Electronically Reproduced By Permission Of Pearson Education, Inc., New York, NY.

frequently, with the assumption that left-brained people are rigid-thinking accountants who spend hours counting their grey suits and right-brained people are creative Bohemian artists who flamboyantly wander from experimental art exhibits to melodramatic poetry readings. There are numerous websites that allow you to test yourself on this dimension. However, while these types of characters undoubtedly exist, the degree to which these personalities are linked to different hemispheres is very limited. In fact, neuroimaging studies of personality traits show that characteristics similar to left- and right-brained people (as measured by the pseudoscientific tests) are distributed across both hemispheres (De Young et al., 2010).

THE CHANGING BRAIN: NEUROPLASTICITY In Module 3.2, you read about *stem cells*, immature cells whose final role—be it a neuron or a kidney cell—is based on the chemical environment in which it develops. In other words, the cell's experience (its environment) influenced its physical structure. While fully formed neurons will never have this type of flexibility, brain cells do have a remarkable property called **neuroplasticity**—*the capacity of the brain to change and rewire itself based on individual experience*. For example, numerous studies have shown that the occipital lobes of people who are blind are used for non-visual purposes (Pascual-Leone et al., 2005). This plasticity was beautifully demonstrated in a brain-imaging study using healthy individuals. All participants underwent brain imaging to determine the areas that became active when they performed tasks related to hearing and touch; during this initial phase, the occipital lobes—a region associated with vision—was not active. These participants were then blindfolded for five days before being scanned again. During the second scan session, brain areas normally dedicated to vision became active during touch and hearing tasks (Pascual-Leone & Hamilton, 2001).

There are numerous other examples of neuroplasticity. For example, experienced musicians develop a greater density of grey matter in the areas of the motor cortex of the frontal lobe as well as in the auditory cortex (Gaser & Schlaug, 2003). Studies of children have found that individuals who practised an instrument regularly for over two years had a thicker corpus callosum in areas connecting the left and right frontal and temporal lobes (Schlaug et al., 2009). Even a seemingly silly skill like learning to juggle can influence the thickness of white-matter pathways connecting different brain areas (Scholz et al., 2009). The key point in all of these studies is that although genetics controls *some* of your brain's characteristics, your brain's connections are not set in stone. What you *do* with (and to) your brain can have a dramatic effect on your brain's connections and thus how your brain functions.

Working the Scientific Literacy Model

Neuroplasticity and Recovery from Brain Injury

The fact that neuroplasticity exists makes it seem like recovery from brain damage should be easy—the remaining brain areas should simply rewire themselves to take over the functions of the damaged brain areas. However, it's not that simple—and we're lucky it isn't.

What do we know about neuroplasticity?

Some animals with relatively simple brains and spinal cords, such as fish and some amphibians, have a lifelong ability to regenerate damaged areas of their central nervous system. If members of these species suffer a brain or spinal cord injury, they will automatically create new tissue to replace the damaged nerves (Sperry, 1951, 1956, 1963, 1968). Humans can do this to a limited degree in the peripheral nervous system as well. This is because chemicals called *trophic factors* (growth factors) can stimulate the growth of new dendrites and axons. However, the ability of the human brain to recover from damage is more limited.

New neurons can form in adulthood, but only in a few regions such as part of the hippocampus (Eriksson et al., 1998). That means we can't simply grow a new brain part whenever we're injured.

Our ability to repair our brains is also limited by the presence of chemicals that actually *inhibit* the growth of new axons around an injured area (Yang & Schnarr, 2008). Why would this occur? Researchers suggest that these inhibitory chemicals prevent the brain from forming incorrect connections between brain areas, a result that might produce even larger behavioural problems than the initial damage itself (Berlucchi, 2011; Kolb et al., 2010). So, if our central nervous system is protecting us against neuroplasticity, how can neuroplasticity be the key to recovering from brain damage?

How can science explain how neuroplasticity contributes to recovery from brain damage?

Although it seems like the brain is preventing its own recovery, there are actually a number of ways that neuroplasticity can work to help patients with brain damage. One possibility is that the same area in the opposite hemisphere will take over some of the functions of the damaged region. Stunning evidence of this phenomenon has been found in studies of Melodic Intonation Therapy (MIT; Norton et al., 2009). Researchers have found that some patients with damage to Broca's area—a part of the left frontal lobe involved with the production of speech—can actually sing using fluent, articulated words, even though they cannot speak those same words (see Figure 3.31). In a study of this technique, patients who had suffered strokes affecting Broca's area underwent intensive MIT sessions. During these sessions the patients would sing long strings of words using just two pitches, while rhythmically tapping their left hand to the melody. You can try this out with the help of Figure 3.32. The patients underwent 80 or more sessions lasting 1.5 hours each day, 5 days per week. Remarkably, this therapy has worked for multiple patients—after these intensive therapy sessions, they typically regain significant language function (Schlaug et al., 2009). The therapy does not "heal" damaged nerve cells in the left hemisphere at Broca's area. Rather, language function is taken over by the corresponding area of the *right* hemisphere.

Another method that the brain uses to repair itself is the reorganization of neighbouring neural regions. In healthy brains, the distinction between most brain areas is not as clear-cut as it appears on textbook diagrams. For instance, it is common for parts of the somatosensory cortex related to the hand to overlap a bit with regions related to the wrist. If one of those somatosensory areas were damaged, there might still be a small number of neurons associated with that body part preserved in other parts of the nearby

Figure 3.31 Brain Specialization

Broca's area and Wernicke's area are associated with different aspects of language function. Damage to Broca's area produces difficulties in generating speech known as *Broca's aphasia.*

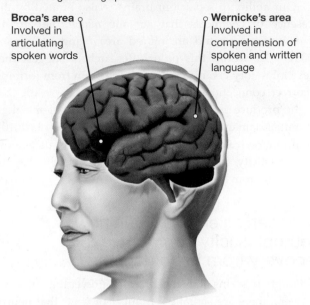

Broca's area
Involved in articulating spoken words

Wernicke's area
Involved in comprehension of spoken and written language

Source: Lilienfeld, Scott O.; Lynn, Steven J; Namy, Laura L.; Woolf, Nancy J., *Psychology: From Inquiry to Understanding,* 2nd Ed., © 2011. Reprinted and electronically reproduced by permission of Pearson Education, Inc., New York, NY.

cortex. When the brain is damaged, it is thought that these preserved neurons attempt to form new connections. Doing so would allow some sensation to return. This process is enhanced if the doctors force the patient to use the affected brain area as much as possible during rehabilitation (Mark et al., 2006). Although it seems cruel, patients must remember to "use it or lose it." In support of this view, research has shown that improvements in a patient's recovery are linked to the reorganization of the affected brain area (Pulvermüller & Berthier, 2008).

Can we critically evaluate this research?

There are obviously limits to the effects of neuroplasticity. If a patient has damage to a large amount of her brain, it will not be possible for her to return to her normal level of functioning. Additionally, plasticity is more likely to be effective in younger people, particularly children, than in

Figure 3.32 Musical Intonation Therapy

During musical intonation therapy, patients are asked to sing phrases of increasing complexity.

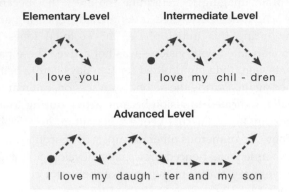

Elementary Level

I love you

Intermediate Level

I love my chil - dren

Advanced Level

I love my daugh - ter and my son

Source: Adapted From Melodic Intonation Therapy, by Nancy Helms-Estabrooks, Marjorie Nicholas, Alisa R. Morgan 1989, Austin, TX: PRO-ED. Copyright 1989 by PRO-ED, Inc. Adapted with permission.

older adults (Kennard, 1942). Therefore, it is important not to over-generalize the results just discussed. It is also possible that results that seem to be due to neuroplasticity are actually due to some other factor, such as changes in hormone levels, the brain's metabolism, or growth factor levels (Knaepen et al., 2010; Sperry, 1968). Although all of these alternative explanations have been tested to some degree in animal studies, it is sometimes difficult to generalize those findings to the human brain. Therefore, much more research is needed before researchers can make any definitive statements about how neuroplasticity helps brain-damaged patients recover.

Why is this relevant?

Each year, 40 000–50 000 Canadians suffer strokes (Heart and Stroke Foundation of Canada, 2013) and over 160 000 suffer traumatic brain injuries (e.g., car accidents; Brain Injury Canada, 2016). Over 55 000 Canadians are living with brain tumours (Brain Tumour Foundation of Canada, 2013). Neuroplasticity will occur, to some degree, in the majority of these individuals. It is what will help people regain some of their abilities and some of their independence. Understanding neuroplasticity will improve the care given to patients. It will also inspire new research and innovative techniques designed to help the brain heal itself (Kim et al., 2010). This research may affect your grandparents or your parents. And eventually, this research may affect you.

Module 3.3b Quiz:

The Brain and Its Structures

Know . . .

1. The ability to hear is based in which of the cerebral lobes?
   A. Frontal
   B. Parietal
   C. Temporal
   D. Hypothalamus

Understand . . .

2. Why would a person who has undergone a split-brain operation be unable to name an object presented to his left visual field, yet be able to correctly point to the same object from an array of choices?

   A. Because his right hemisphere perceived the object, but does not house the language function needed for naming it

   B. Because the image was processed on his left hemisphere, which is required for naming objects

   C. Because pointing is something done with the right hand

   D. Because the right hemisphere of the brain is where objects are seen

Apply . . .

3. Damage to the somatosensory cortex would most likely result in which of the following impairments?

   A. Inability to point at an object

   B. Impaired vision

   C. Impaired mathematical ability

   D. Lost or distorted sensations in the region of the body corresponding to the damaged area

Analyze . . .

4. Which of the following statements best summarizes the results of experiments on exercise and brain functioning?

   A. Both human and animal studies show cognitive benefits of exercise.

   B. Animal studies show benefits from exercise, but the results of human studies are unclear.

   C. Exercise benefits mood but not thinking.

   D. Exercise only benefits older people.

Module 3.3 Summary

3.3a   Know . . . the key terminology associated with the structure and organization of the nervous system.

amygdala
autonomic nervous system
basal ganglia
brainstem
central nervous system (CNS)
cerebellum
cerebral cortex
corpus callosum
forebrain
frontal lobes
hippocampus
limbic system
midbrain
neuroplasticity
occipital lobes
parasympathetic nervous system
parietal lobes
peripheral nervous system (PNS)
somatic nervous system
sympathetic nervous system
temporal lobes
thalamus

3.3b   Understand . . . how studies of split-brain patients reveal the workings of the brain.

Studies of split-brain patients were important in that they revealed that the two hemispheres of the brain are specialized for certain cognitive tasks. For example, studies of split-brain patients showed that the left hemisphere was specialized for language. These studies were carried out before other brain-imaging techniques (see Module 3.4) became available.

3.3c   Apply . . . your knowledge of brain regions to predict which abilities might be affected when a specific area is injured or diseased.

Apply Activity

Review Table 3.2, which summarizes each of the major brain regions described in this module. Then try to answer the following questions.

1. While at work, a woman suffers a severe blow to the back of her head and then experiences visual problems. Which part of her brain has most likely been affected?
2. If an individual has a stroke and loses the ability to produce speech in clear sentences, what part of the brain is most likely to have been damaged?
3. If an individual develops a tumour that affects the basal ganglia, what types of behaviours or abilities are likely to be affected?
4. A man suffers a gunshot wound that slightly damages his cerebellum. What problems might he experience (aside from repeatedly asking himself why someone shot him in the head)?

3.3d   Analyze . . . whether neuroplasticity will help patients with brain damage.

There are many examples of experience changing the structure of the brain. Research suggests that neuroplasticity can also help people recover from brain damage. If the damage is isolated to one cerebral hemisphere, cells in the same region of the opposite hemisphere may be able to take over some of the impaired functions. Additionally, it is possible that some of the cells involved with a function (e.g., sensation of the hand) were undamaged; these remaining cells may form new, stronger connections over the course of rehabilitation.

Module 3.4 Windows to the Brain: Measuring and Observing Brain Activity

Sun Media/Splash News/Newscom

 Learning Objectives

3.4a Know . . . the key terminology associated with measuring and observing brain activity.

3.4b Understand . . . how studies of animals with brain lesions can inform us about the workings of the brain.

3.4c Apply . . . your knowledge of neuroimaging techniques to see which ones would be most useful in answering a specific research question.

3.4d Analyze . . . whether neuroimaging can be used to diagnose brain injuries.

On March 8, 2011, Boston Bruins' (giant) defenceman Zdeno Chara dangerously bodychecked Montreal Canadiens' forward Max Pacioretty into the boards; Pacioretty hit the stanchion, the location where the plexi-glass begins next to the players' bench. Pacioretty lay motionless on the ice for several minutes with many people in the audience concerned for his life. He was taken off the ice on a stretcher while still unconscious and was rushed to the hospital for a neurological exam. He was diagnosed with a fracture of the 4th cervical vertebra (a bone in the neck) but, luckily, no spinal cord damage; he also had a severe concussion (also known as a mild traumatic brain injury). Injuries such as Pacioretty's lead to a number of questions for people interested in the biology of behaviour: How can psychologists and medical personnel acquire clear images of a person's brain for medical or research purposes? Is it possible to map out which brain areas are firing when people are performing a

specific task like viewing photographs or memorizing a list of words? And, can scientists learn anything about the healthy brain by studying patients who have suffered brain damage? These topics will be addressed in the current module.

For those interested, Pacioretty made a full recovery, scoring 33 goals for the Canadiens over the course of the next season. Later that year, he won the Bill Masterton Trophy, handed out by the National Hockey League to the player who provides the best example of perseverance, team spirit, and dedication to hockey. He was very, very lucky.

Focus Questions

1. How can lesions help us learn about the brain?

2. How can we make sense of brain activity as it is actually occurring?

In Module 3.3, you read about different brain areas and their functions. This leads to an obvious question: how did researchers find out what these brains areas do? In this module, we will examine the different methods and tools available to physicians and researchers in their quest to map out the functions of different brain areas.

Insights from Brain Damage

Early studies of the brain often involved case studies. A doctor would note a patient's unique set of symptoms and would then ghoulishly wait for him or her to die so that an autopsy could be performed in order to identify the damaged area. As medical knowledge improved, surgeons began to routinely operate on the brains of patients with neurological problems. This allowed researchers to examine patients before and after brain surgery to see the effect that removing tissue would have on behaviour. However, in each of these cases, insights into the brain were based on individuals who had suffered some sort of trauma or illness. There was no way to test how healthy brains functioned. In the last four decades, advances in brain imaging have changed this, and have allowed researchers to safely measure the brain's activity.

This is not to say that studying patients with brain damage is not scientifically useful. In fact, quite the opposite is true. The only way researchers can truly hope to understand how the brain works is by using a number of different methods to assess its function.

LESIONING AND BRAIN STIMULATION Studies of patients who have suffered brain damage will appear in a number of modules in this book. The logic of this method is that if a person has part of his or her brain damaged and is unable to perform a particular task (e.g., form new memories), then it is assumed that the damaged structure plays a role in that behaviour. One drawback of studying human patients, however, is that the researcher has no control over where the damage occurs. A stroke generally produces widespread damage; rarely will it harm a single area while leaving the rest of the brain totally unaffected. This diffuse damage makes it difficult for brain researchers to perform controlled studies of patients—each patient will have a unique pattern of damage. It is also difficult to isolate the effects of damage to one brain area when several are affected.

In order to gain more experimental control (and a much larger number of subjects), scientists often create brain damage in animals. This process is known as **lesioning**, *a technique in which researchers intentionally damage an area in the brain* (a *lesion* is abnormal or damaged brain tissue). Creating lesions allows the researcher to isolate single brain structures. He or she can then study animals with and without lesions to see how specific behaviours are changed by the removal of that brain tissue. The control subjects are often part of a *sham group,* a set of animals that go through all of the surgical procedures aside from the lesion itself in order to control for the effects of stress, anesthesia, and the annoyance of stitches. An example of the lesion method is found in studies of spatial learning. Researchers hypothesized that the hippocampus was vital for this ability. In order to test this hypothesis, the researchers lesioned the hippocampus on both sides of the brains of one group of rats and performed sham surgery on the other rats. Each rat was then put into the Morris Water Maze (Morris, 1981); this device consists of a container filled with an opaque (non-transparent) fluid (see Figure 3.33). The rat is placed in the water and must swim around until it finds a small

---

Figure 3.33 The Morris Water Maze

Tools like the Morris Water Maze allow researchers to test the effects of brain lesions on behaviours such as spatial memory.

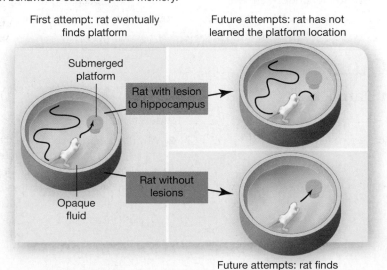

First attempt: rat eventually finds platform

Future attempts: rat has not learned the platform location

Submerged platform

Rat with lesion to hippocampus

Rat without lesions

Opaque fluid

Future attempts: rat finds platform immediately

platform hidden under the fluid. At first, the rat finds the platform by chance; over time, the rat learns the location of the platform and swims to it immediately. However, rats with lesions to the hippocampus show a marked impairment in learning the location of the platform, presumably because the hippocampus is critical for many spatial abilities (Morris et al., 1982). This example demonstrates the power of the lesion method to determine the roles played by specific brain areas.

Less drastic techniques impair brain activity only temporarily; in fact, some can be safely applied to humans. For instance, researchers can study brain functions using **transcranial magnetic stimulation (TMS)**, *a procedure in which an electromagnetic pulse is delivered to a targeted region of the brain* (Bestmann, 2008; Terao & Ugawa, 2002). This pulse interacts with the flow of ions around the neurons of the affected area. The result is a temporary disruption of brain activity, similar to the permanent disruption caused by a brain lesion. This procedure has the advantage that healthy human volunteers can be studied (as opposed to animals or brain-damaged people, many of whom are elderly). TMS has been used to investigate a number of cognitive processes ranging from visual perception (Perini et al., 2012) to arithmetic abilities (Andres et al., 2011) to memory for words and abstract shapes (Floel et al., 2004). In each case, impairments in performance after receiving the TMS "temporary lesion" tell the researcher that the stimulated brain area is likely involved in that cognitive process.

Interestingly, if a weaker electromagnetic pulse is delivered, TMS can also be used to stimulate, rather than temporarily impair, a brain region (Figure 3.34). For example, TMS has been used to increase the activity in the frontal lobes—an area related to planning and inhibiting behaviour—when people were performing a gambling task. This change led the participants to behave in a more cautious, risk-averse manner than when they performed the task without this stimulation (Fecteau et al., 2007). TMS has also been used to stimulate under-active areas associated with depression, suggesting that this tool has

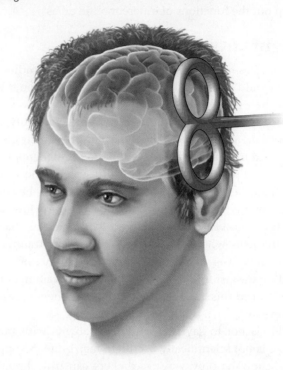

Figure 3.34 Brain Stimulation

Transcranial magnetic stimulation involves targeting a magnetic field to a very specific region of the brain. Depending on the amount of stimulation, researchers can temporarily either stimulate or disable the region.

clinical applications as well (Kluger & Triggs, 2007). In fact, researchers have used this technique to help patients deal with symptoms of disorders ranging from Parkinson's disease (Degardin et al., 2012) to movement problems caused by strokes (Corti et al., 2012; Schlaug et al., 2008).

Although lesion work and TMS allow researchers to understand what happens to the brain when certain regions are removed or inactive, these methods don't provide a picture of the brain's structures or its patterns of activity. Luckily, there have been astonishing advances in structural and functional neuroimaging over the past forty years.

Module 3.4a Quiz:

Insights from Brain Damage

Know . . .

1. The control group in a typical lesion study is called the
    A. metacranial group.
    B. pseudo-incision group.
    C. sham group.
    D. static group.

Understand . . .

2. Why do researchers often use the lesion method instead of studying humans with brain damage?
    A. It is possible to test more subjects using the lesion method.
    B. Brain damage usually differs between patients.
    C. The patients usually only have damage in one specific area.
    D. Both (A) and (B) are true.

Analyze . . .

3. Dr. Cerveau performed a TMS lesion study in her lab. She found that applying a pulse to the parietal lobes prevented people from pressing a keypad in response to a suddenly appearing image. She concluded that the lesion affected attention. Why should we be cautious of her claim?

A. TMS is not a valid method of lesioning brain areas.

B. The TMS lesion covered a large area and may have affected other functions that might have slowed participants' responses.

C. Response times are not a valid measure of how people pay attention.

D. All of the above are valid concerns.

Structural and Functional Neuroimaging

Neuroimaging (or brain imaging) is becoming increasingly important for many fields, particularly for psychology. Being able to examine the brains of living people and to measure neural activity while participants perform different tasks provides an astonishing window into the mind. Neuroimaging has also revolutionized medicine, allowing doctors to see with great precision the size and location of brain injuries. The remainder of this module will focus on the two types of brain scanning: structural and functional neuroimaging.

STRUCTURAL NEUROIMAGING At the beginning of this module, you read about Montreal Canadiens' forward Max Pacioretty's scary injury and his surprising return to the National Hockey League. When Pacioretty first arrived at the hospital, the doctors would obviously have wanted to determine the extent of the damage to his brain. In order to get this information, it was necessary to use **structural neuroimaging**, *a type of brain scanning that produces images of the different structures of the brain.* This type of neuroimaging is used to measure the size of different brain areas and to determine whether any brain injury has occurred.

There are three commonly used types of structural neuroimaging. **Computerized tomography** (or **CT scan**) *is a structural neuroimaging technique in which x-rays are sent through the brain by a tube that rotates around the head.* The x-rays will pass through dense tissue (e.g., grey matter) at a different speed than they will pass through less dense tissue, like the fluid in the ventricles (Hounsfield, 1980). A computer then calculates these differences for each image that is taken as the tube moves around the head and combines that information into a three-dimensional image (see Figure 3.35). As an interesting historical aside, the first commercial CT scanner was created in the early 1970s by EMI (and was called the EMI Scanner), a company also involved in the music industry. This company had enough money to pay for four years of medical-imaging research because they were also the record label of a band known as The Beatles (Filler, 2009).

CT scans were considered state of the art for over a decade. However, in the 1970s and early 1980s, a new form of structural neuroimaging emerged. **Magnetic resonance imaging** (or **MRI**) *is a structural imaging technique in which clear images of the brain are created based on how different neural regions absorb and release energy while in a magnetic field.* Although this sounds confusing, understanding MRIs involves three steps. First, a brain (or other body part) is placed inside a strong magnetic field; this causes the protons of the brain's hydrogen atoms to spin in the same direction. Second, a pulse of radio waves is sent through the brain; the energy of this pulse is absorbed by the atoms in the brain

Figure 3.35 Structural Neuroimaging

Three different types of structural neuroimaging: (a) a CT scan, (b) an MRI scan, and (c) a diffusion tensor imaging scan.

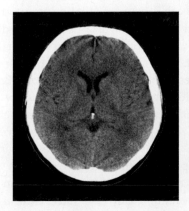
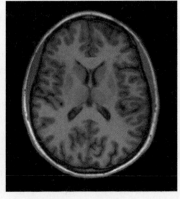
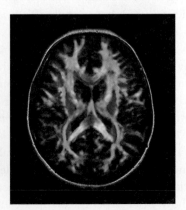

and knocks them out of their previous position (aligned with the magnetic field). Finally, the pulse of radio waves is turned off. At this point, the atoms again become aligned with the magnetic field. But, as they do so, they release the energy they absorbed during the pulse. Different types of tissue—grey matter, white matter, and fluid—release different amounts of energy and return to their magnetic alignment at different speeds. Computers are used to calculate these differences and provide a very detailed three-dimensional image of the brain (Huettel et al., 2009).

As you can see from Figure 3.35, MRIs produce much clearer images than CT scans and are more accurate at detecting many forms of damage including concussions like that suffered by Max Pacioretty (Bazarian et al., 2007). So, why are CT scanners still used? Let's go back to Pacioretty's injury. He was hit into a structure that consisted of a thin pad covering metal and plexi-glass, so the chances of him having metal in his brain were quite slim. But what if a person entered the hospital after a car accident? He might have fragments of metal in his body; these would not react well to a powerful magnet. Therefore, CT scans, aside from being cheap, are a safe first-assessment tool for brain injuries. When the doctors have more information about the patient and his injury, then it is possible that the more accurate MRI will be used.

A final type of structural neuroimaging technique is also the newest. **Diffusion tensor imaging** (or **DTI**) *is a form of structural neuroimaging allowing researchers or medical personnel to measure white-matter pathways in the brain.* Although it is natural to assume that the grey matter—the cell bodies—is the most sensitive part of the brain, white-matter damage has been found in an increasing number of brain disorders (Shenton et al., 2012). This is because most head injuries cause the brain to twist around in the skull. The result is that some of the white-matter pathways connecting different brain areas are torn. A large number of studies have shown that these pathways are damaged in individuals who have suffered concussions (Niogi & Mukherjee, 2010), although it is unclear whether professional and collegiate/university sports leagues are using this technology when making return-to-play decisions for injured athletes (J. K. Johnson et al., 2012).

FUNCTIONAL NEUROIMAGING Although structural images provide useful information about the brain's anatomy, they do not tell us much about the functions of those brain areas. This information is gathered using **functional neuroimaging**, *a type of brain scanning that provides information about which areas of the brain are active when a person performs a particular behaviour.* There are a number of different functional neuroimaging methods available to researchers and physicians. A common trade-off is between *temporal resolution* (how brief a period of time can be accurately measured) and *spatial resolution* (a clear picture of the

brain). Which tool is used depends upon the type of question being asked.

A neuroimaging method with fantastic temporal resolution is an **electroencephalogram** (or **EEG**), *which measures patterns of brain activity with the use of multiple electrodes attached to the scalp.* The neural firing of the billions of cells in the brain can be detected with these electrodes, amplified, and depicted in an electroencephalogram. EEGs measure this activity every millisecond. They can tell us a lot about general brain activity during sleep, during wakefulness, and while patients or research participants are engaged in a particular cognitive activity. EEGs are also used to detect when patients with epilepsy are having a seizure; this would be shown by a sudden spike in activity (neuronal firing) in one or more brain areas (see Figure 3.36). The convenience and relatively inexpensive nature of EEGs, compared to other modern methods, make them very appealing to researchers.

But, how can EEG be used to further our understanding of human behaviour? In most studies, researchers would be interested in how brain responses differ for different types of stimuli, such as happy or fearful faces. EEGs have perfect temporal resolution for this task, but they have a problem: How do you link the EEG output (a bunch of squiggly lines) with your stimuli? To do this, researchers have developed a technique known as *event-related potentials* (or ERPs). ERPs use the same sensors as EEGs; however, a computer takes note of exactly when a given stimulus (e.g., a smiling face) was presented to the participant. The experimenter can then examine the EEG readout for a brief period of time (usually 1–2 seconds) following the appearance of that stimulus. Importantly, the computer can collect the average brain responses for different types of experimental trials; so, if an experiment contained 50 separate stimulus presentations—25 happy faces and 25 fearful faces—the experimenter could collect the *average* pattern of data after each type of stimulus (i.e., there would be one set of squiggly lines for happy faces and one for fearful faces).

Critically, the peaks and valleys of these *waveforms* are not random—each is associated with some sort of process occurring in the brain. For example, initial detection of some sort of visual image could occur after 80–120 ms (Mangun et al., 1993); determining that the image was a face might occur at approximately 170 ms (Bötzel et al., 1995). And, identifying that face as someone you know might occur sometime after 300 ms. Researchers can then look at the size of the peaks and valleys to determine whether there was a difference in the amount of brain activity in response to the different stimulus types (e.g., a peak at 200 ms was higher for fearful than for happy faces). This technique can also have clinical uses. If a patient (e.g., someone with multiple sclerosis) was missing

Figure 3.36 Measuring Brain Activity

The electroencephalogram measures electrical activity of the brain by way of electrodes that amplify the signals emitted by active regions (left). In clinical conditions such as epilepsy (right), specific EEG measurements will spike. This provides the medical team with information about the origin of the seizure.

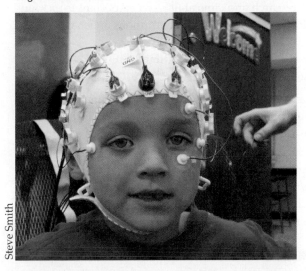 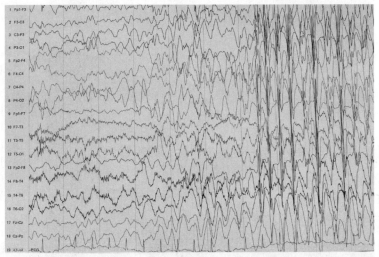

From Figure 2 in Role of EEG in Epilepsy Syndromes in EEG of Common Epilepsy Syndromes by Raj D Sheth, MD. Copyright © 2016 by Raj D Sheth. Used by permission of Medscape LLC.

an expected waveform, the neurologist could conclude that a particular region of her brain was not functioning normally (Ruseckaite et al., 2005).

Although ERPs are very useful for measuring *when* brain activity is occurring, they are much less effective at identifying exactly *where* that activity is taking place. Part of this problem is due to the fact that the skull disrupts the electrical signal from the neurons' firing; this reduces the accuracy of ERP measurements. In order to get around this, some researchers measure the magnetic activity associated with cells firing. This is accomplished by using **magnetoencephalography** (or **MEG**), *a neuroimaging technique that measures the tiny magnetic fields created by the electrical activity of nerve cells in the brain.* Like EEG, MEG records the electrical activity of nerve cells just a few milliseconds after it occurs, which allows researchers to record brain activity at nearly the instant a stimulus is presented (Hamalainen et al., 1993). In a study with happy and fearful faces, MEG could measure when an image was detected and when it was recognized as being a face (Halgren et al., 2000). However, like ERPs, this speed comes with a trade-off; namely, MEGs do not provide a detailed picture of the activity of specific brain areas. So, although its ability to isolate the location of brain activity is slightly better than that of ERPs, it is still difficult to isolate exactly *where* in the brain the activity occurred.

A functional imaging method that *can* show activity of the whole brain is **positron emission tomography** (or **PET**), *a type of scan in which a low level of a radioactive isotope is injected into the blood, and its movement to regions of the brain engaged in a particular task is measured.* This method

works under the assumption that active nerve cells use up energy at a faster rate than do cells that are less active. As a result, more blood will need to flow into those active areas in order to bring more oxygen and glucose to the cells. If the blood contains a radioactive isotope (as in a PET study), more radioactivity will be detected in areas of the brain that were active during that period of time. In most studies, participants will complete separate blocks of trials or even separate scanning sessions for different types of experimental trials. The activity from these sessions is then compared to see which brain areas are more (or less) active in response to different types of stimuli. For instance, researchers at McGill University provided the first evidence that the ventral (bottom) portions of the right hemisphere of the brain were involved with recognizing faces (Sergent et al., 1992).

The greatest strength of PET scans is that they show metabolic activity of the brain. PET also allows researchers to measure the involvement of specific types of receptors (e.g., types of dopamine receptors) in different brain regions while people perform an experimental task (e.g., Woodward et al., 2009). A drawback is that PET scans take a long time to acquire—at least two minutes—which is a problem when you want to see moment-by-moment activity of the brain. The radioactivity of PET also generally limits the participants to men because it is possible that female participants could be in the early stages of pregnancy. In that case, the risks of participating would far outweigh the rewards. Instead, researchers are increasingly turning to a powerful neuroimaging technique with excellent spatial resolution.

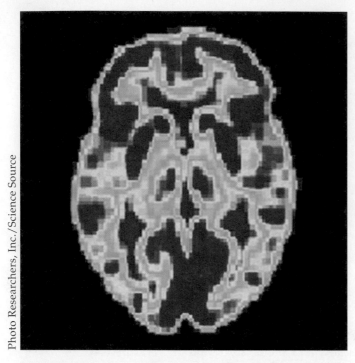

PET scans use radioactive isotopes to help identify which areas of the brain were most active.

Working the Scientific Literacy Model

Functional MRI and Behaviour

Functional magnetic resonance imaging (or **fMRI**) *measures brain activity by detecting the influx of oxygen-rich blood into neural areas that were just active* (Kwong et al., 1992; Ogawa et al., 1992). Like PET scanning, fMRI can produce an accurate image of the functional brain. However, its ease of use (and lack of radioactivity) has quickly made it one of the most influential research tools in modern psychology.

What do we know about fMRI and Behaviour?

If you type in "fMRI" into the PubMed.gov research database, you will see that there have been over 30 000 papers published since this technology was developed 25 years ago. The growth in this field is staggering—there are literally hundreds of fMRI research papers published each year. Researchers are using fMRI to study almost every topic discussed in this book, ranging from sensory processes (Chapter 4) to memory (Chapter 7) to social behaviours (Chapter 13). Importantly, fMRI is also being used to examine clinical issues including psychological disorders (Chapter 15) and disorders of consciousness (e.g., vegetative states, Module 5.3). It is also being used to examine brain activity in neurological patients like Max Pacioretty—psychologists and medical personnel can look at what areas of the brain are active when a person

is performing different tasks such as remembering lists of words. If the patterns of activity deviate from those of healthy individuals, then the investigators can infer that specific brain regions are not working properly. With this surge in fMRI research and clinical use, it is important to examine *how* fMRI links blood flow to descriptions of behaviour.

How can science explain how fMRI is used to examine behaviour?

When a brain area is involved with a particular function, it will use up oxygen. The result is that blood in these areas will be deoxygenated (without oxygen molecules). The body responds by sending in more oxygen-rich blood to replace the deoxygenated blood. Critically, these two types of blood have different magnetic properties. So, by measuring the changing magnetic properties of the blood in different brain areas, it is possible to see which areas were active when the person performed a particular task (Huettel et al., 2009; Magri et al., 2012). When you see pictures of different brain areas "lit up," those colourful areas indicate that more activity occurred in that location during one experimental condition than during another (see Figure 3.37). To continue our example of perceiving faces, researchers could present happy or fearful faces to participants while they were in the fMRI scanner (which is the same machine used for structural MRI scans). After the study, the researchers

Figure 3.37 Functional Magnetic Resonance Imaging
Functional MRI technology allows researchers to determine how blood flow, and hence brain activity, changes as study participants or patients perform different tasks. In this image, the coloured areas depict increases in blood flow to the left and right temporal lobes, relative to the rest of the brain, during a cognitive task.

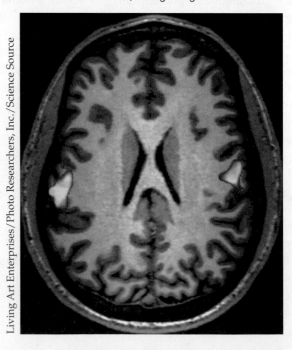

Table 3.4 Common Methods of Functional Neuroimaging

Neuroimaging Method	Advantages	Disadvantages
EEG/ERP	Excellent temporal resolution (measures activity at the millisecond level); inexpensive	Poor spatial resolution (does not give a picture of individual brain structures)
MEG	Excellent temporal resolution (measures activity at the millisecond level)	Poor spatial resolution (does not give a picture of individual brain structures)
PET	Provides a picture of the whole brain (although not as clear as fMRI); allows researchers to examine activity related to specific neurotransmitters (e.g., dopamine)	Very poor temporal resolution (takes at least 2 minutes to scan the brain, often longer); involves radioactive isotopes that limit possible participants; very expensive
fMRI	Excellent spatial resolution (clear images of brain structures)	Temporal resolution is not as good as ERP or MEG (it takes approximately two seconds to scan the whole brain)

could look at the average amount of brain activity that occurred when each participant viewed each type of face. In this case, seeing faces would activate a region in the bottom of the right hemisphere known as the *fusiform gyrus* (Kanwisher et al., 1997; see Module 4.2). Faces expressing fear also would activate the amygdala, and faces expressing happiness activate a wide network of structures in the frontal lobes (M. L. Phillips et al., 1998). Thus, fMRI provides very detailed images of *where* brain activity is occurring. Unfortunately, it can only measure activity at the level of seconds rather than milliseconds; therefore, it lacks the temporal resolution of ERP and MEG (see Table 3.4).

Can we critically evaluate this research?

Although researchers have shown that the activity that we see in fMRI images is actually linked to the firing of neurons (Logothetis et al., 2001), we still need to be cautious when interpreting fMRI data. One reason is that it is correlational in nature. Activity increases or decreases at the same time as different stimuli are perceived; however, we can't definitively show that the activity was *caused* by the stimuli. Also, just because a brain area is *active* while we perform a task does not mean that it is *necessary* for that task. It is possible that a given area that "lights up" on fMRI is a small part of a larger network, or performs a supporting role. Therefore, it is useful to look at research using other methods (if available) to see if similar brain areas were implicated in a given behaviour.

There is an additional reason to be cautious of fMRI data. There is a growing trend for neuroimaging,

particularly fMRI, to be used to explain or justify phenomena that are not easily measured (Satel & Lilienfeld, 2013). Images of brains with areas lit up can be found on almost every major online news site. The problem is that many of the claims made in these stories are overstated (more likely, but not always, by the media than by the scientists). Given the massive connections between brain areas, headlines that suggest that scientists have discovered the "hate centre" or *the* neural structure associated with how someone will vote are misleading. Most brain areas are activated by *many* different situations and stimuli. So, just as you would raise your skeptical eyebrows in response to reports of scientists finding the single gene for a given behaviour (see Module 3.1), you should apply your critical-thinking skills toward claims about scientists identifying the single brain area for any complex process.

Why is this relevant?

It is difficult to overstate how important fMRI has been to psychological science. It has allowed researchers to map out the networks associated with a huge range of topics, thus providing most of the "bio" components of the biopsychosocial model of behaviour. Recently, researchers at Queen's University and the University of Manitoba have found ways to perform fMRI on neurons in the spinal cord (Kornelsen et al., 2013; Stroman, 2005). Thus, it will soon be possible to measure how the *entire* central nervous system responds to different stimuli, an ability that will allow us to gain a more complete understanding of human behaviour.

Module 3.4b Quiz:

Structural and Functional Neuroimaging

Know . . .

1. The brain-imaging technique that involves measuring blood flow in active regions of the brain is called
   A. magnetic resonance imaging.
   B. MEG scan.
   C. PET scan.
   D. transcranial magnetic stimulation.

Understand . . .

2. Which of the following techniques does *not* provide an actual picture of the brain?
   A. PET scan
   B. MRI
   C. Electroencephalogram (EEG)
   D. fMRI

Apply . . .

3. A neuroscientist was interested in identifying the precise brain areas involved when women see photographs of their loved ones. Which functional neuroimaging technique would be the most useful in identifying these regions?

    A. fMRI

    B. MRI

    C. Transcranial magnetic stimulation (TMS)

    D. CT scan

Analyze . . .

4. A drawback of PET scans compared to newer techniques, such as magnetoencephalography, is that

    A. PET is slower, which means it is more difficult to measure moment-to-moment changes in brain activity.

    B. PET is faster, which makes it difficult to figure out how brain activity relates to what someone sees or hears.

    C. PET is too expensive for research use.

    D. PET is slower, and it does not provide a picture of the brain.

Module 3.4 Summary

3.4a Know . . . the key terminology associated with measuring and observing brain activity.

computerized tomography (CT) scan
diffusion tensor imaging (DTI)
electroencephalogram (EEG)
functional magnetic resonance imaging (fMRI)
functional neuroimaging
lesioning
magnetic resonance imaging (MRI)
magnetoencephalography (MEG)
positron emission tomography (PET)
structural neuroimaging
transcranial magnetic stimulation (TMS)

3.4b Understand . . . how studies of animals with brain lesions can inform us about the workings of the brain.

Researchers have learned a great deal from studies of neurological patients; however, because most accidental brain damage is spread out across many structures, it is difficult to determine the effect of damage to *a particular structure*. Lesion studies with animals allow researchers to address this type of question by intentionally damaging a very specific region of the brain. These studies also allow researchers to test far more subjects than they could if they were testing humans with brain damage; therefore, animal lesion studies allow researchers to answer more questions than would otherwise be possible.

3.4c Apply . . . your knowledge of neuroimaging techniques to see which ones would be most useful in answering a specific research question.

Apply Activity

Review Table 3.4, which summarizes each of the major types of functional neuroimaging. Then decide which one should be used to answer each of the following research questions.

1. Lynn was an epilepsy patient seeking treatment. Her seizures did not involve the muscle twitches typical of grand mal seizures. Instead, she would stop talking and stare blankly into the distance for 20–30 seconds (this is known as a petit mal seizure). Her neurologist wanted to use a neuroimaging method to detect when she was having a seizure. Which one should she use?

2. Neil was interested in how dopamine neurons in the brain responded when participants were given rewarding foods like jelly beans versus bland foods. Which functional neuroimaging method should he use to answer his question?

3. Jen wanted to measure the precise brain areas that were active when people experienced pain. Which neuroimaging method would give her this information?

4. Jason was interested in how people pay attention to more than one stimulus at the same time. He wanted to measure brain responses within the first half second after images were flashed on a computer screen. Which method(s) would allow him to answer his research question?

3.4d Analyze . . . whether neuroimaging can be used to diagnose brain injuries.

Several methods for measuring brain activity were covered in this module. A CT scan can provide an initial picture of the brain; this is used most often when a patient first enters the hospital. If a more detailed image is necessary and the patient does not have metal fragments in his body, then MRI is used. If researchers are particularly interested in diagnosing white-matter damage, diffusion tensor imaging (DTI) may be used as well. Additionally, any of the functional imaging methods discussed in this module could show different patterns of activity for individuals with and without brain damage, depending upon the task being performed and the location of the injury.

Chapter 4
Sensation and Perception

4.1 Sensation and Perception At a Glance

- Sensing the World Around Us   127
- Module 4.1a Quiz   132
- Perceiving the World Around Us   132
  Working the Scientific Literacy Model: Backward Messages in Music   134
- Module 4.1b Quiz   137
- Module 4.1 Summary   137

4.2 The Visual System

- The Human Eye   140
- Module 4.2a Quiz   146
- Visual Perception and the Brain   146
  Working the Scientific Literacy Model: Are Faces Special?   148
- Module 4.2b Quiz   154
- Module 4.2 Summary   155

4.3 The Auditory and Vestibular Systems

- Sound and the Structures of the Ear   157
- Module 4.3a Quiz   159
- The Perception of Sound   160
  Working the Scientific Literacy Model: The Perception of Musical Beats   162
- Module 4.3b Quiz   163
- The Vestibular System   164
- Module 4.3c Quiz   165
- Module 4.3 Summary   165

4.4 Touch and the Chemical Senses

- The Sense of Touch   168
  Working the Scientific Literacy Model: Empathy and Pain   171
- Module 4.4a Quiz   173
- The Chemical Senses: Taste and Smell   173
- Module 4.4b Quiz   176
- Multimodal Integration   176
- Module 4.4c Quiz   178
- Module 4.4 Summary   178

Module 4.1 Sensation and Perception at a Glance

Martin Philbey / Redferns / Getty Images

 ## Learning Objectives

4.1a Know . . . the key terminology of sensation and perception.

4.1b Understand . . . what stimulus thresholds are.

4.1c Understand . . . the principles of Gestalt psychology.

4.1d Apply . . . your knowledge of signal detection theory to identify hits, misses, and correct responses in examples.

4.1e Analyze . . . claims that subliminal advertising and backward messages can influence your behaviour.

In December 1985, 18-year-old Ray Belknap shot himself to death in Reno, Nevada. His friend, James Vance, attempted to do the same but survived, his face forever scarred by the shotgun blast. Vance later claimed that his actions were influenced by "subliminal messages" found in the heavy metal music of the band Judas Priest. His family sued the band for damages. The prosecution claimed that when played backwards, the song "Better by You, Better Than Me" contained the phrase "do it." This phrase was allegedly perceived by the two youths, prompting them to attempt suicide. Although this claim seems outlandish, it led to lengthy legal proceedings and received heavy media coverage. It took the work of two Canadian psychologists to demonstrate that these allegations were unfounded. Their research, described later in this module, demonstrates the importance of scientific literacy and provides interesting insights about the abilities—and limitations—of our perceptual systems.

Focus Questions

1. What is the difference between sensation and perception?

2. What are the principles that guide perception?

$\gg$ Sensation and perception are different, yet integrated processes. To illustrate this point, take a look at the Necker cube in Figure 4.1. After staring at it for several seconds, the cube may appear to flip its orientation on the page (the side that looks like an interior wall at the back of the cube can also look like the exterior side of the front of the cube). Although the cube remains constant on the page and in the way it is reflected in the eye, it can be perceived in different ways. The switching of perspectives is a perceptual phenomenon that takes place in the brain.

Figure 4.1 The Necker Cube

Stare at this object for several seconds until it changes perspective.

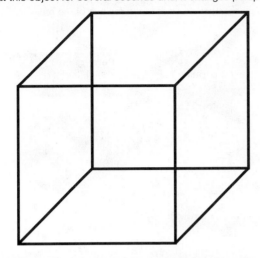

Source: Based on Galanter, E. (1962). Contemporary psychophysics. In R. Brown, E. Galanter, E. H. Hess, & G. Mandler (Eds.), *New Directions in Psychology* (p. 231). New York: Holt, Rinehart, & Winston.

Table 4.1 Stimuli Affecting Our Major Senses and Corresponding Receptors

Sense	Stimuli	Type of Receptor
Vision (Module 4.2)	Light waves	Light-sensitive structures at the back of the eye
Hearing (Module 4.3)	Sound waves	Hair cells that respond to pressure changes in the ear
Touch (Module 4.4)	Pressure, stretching, warming, cooling or piercing of the skin surface	Different types of nerve endings that respond to pressure, temperature changes, and pain
Taste (Module 4.4)	Chemicals on the tongue and in the mouth	Cells lining the taste buds of the tongue
Smell (Module 4.4)	Chemicals contacting mucus-lined membranes of the nose	Nerve endings that respond selectively to different compounds

Sensing the World Around Us

The world outside of the human body is full of light, sound vibrations, and objects we can touch. A walk through campus can be filled with the moving shadows of towering elm trees, the sounds of birds chirping, and the cool crisp air of an autumn morning. In order to make sense of all this information, the body has developed an amazing array of specialized processes for sensing and perceiving the world around us. The process of detecting and then translating the complexity of the world into meaningful experiences occurs in two stages.

The first step is **sensation**, *the process of detecting external events with sense organs and turning those stimuli into neural signals.* At the sensory level, the sound of someone's voice is simply air particles pushing against the eardrum, and the sight of a person is merely light waves stimulating receptors in the eye. All of this raw sensory information is then relayed to the brain, where perception occurs. **Perception** *involves attending to, organizing, and interpreting stimuli that we sense.* Perception includes organizing the different vibrations of the eardrum in a way that allows you to recognize them as a human voice and linking together the stimulation of groups of receptors in the eye into the visual experience of seeing someone walking toward you.

The raw sensations detected by the sensory organs are turned into information that the brain can process through **transduction**, *when specialized receptors transform the physical energy of the outside world into neural impulses.* These neural impulses travel into the brain and influence the activity of different brain structures, which ultimately gives rise to our *internal representation* of the world.

The sensory receptors involved in transduction are different for the different senses (summarized in Table 4.1). The transduction of light occurs when it reaches receptors at the back of the eye; light-sensitive chemicals in the retina then convert this energy into nerve impulses that travel to numerous brain centres where colour and motion are perceived and objects are identified (see Figure 4.2). The transduction of sound takes place in a specialized structure in the ear called the cochlea, where sound energy is converted into neural impulses that travel to the hearing centres of the brain.

The brain's ability to organize our sensations into coherent perceptions is remarkable. All of our senses use the same mechanism for transmitting information in the brain: the action potential (see Module 3.2). As a result, the brain is continually bombarded by waves of neural impulses representing the world in all its complexity; yet, somehow, it must be able to separate different sensory signals from one another so that we can experience distinct sensations—sight, sound, touch, smell, and taste. It accomplishes this feat by sending signals from different sensory organs to different parts of the brain. Therefore, it is not the original sensory input that is most important for generating our perceptions; rather, it is the brain area that processes this information. We see because visual information gets sent to the occipital lobes, which generate our experience of vision. We hear because auditory information gets sent to our temporal lobes, which generate our experience of hearing. This idea, that *the different senses are separated in the brain,* was first proposed in 1826 by the German physiologist Johannes Müller and is known as the **doctrine of specific nerve energies**.

Although this separation seems perfectly logical, it requires that distinct pathways connect sensory organs

Figure 4.2 From Stimulus to Perception

Sensing and perceiving begin with the detection of a stimulus by one of our senses. Receptors convert the stimulus into a neural impulse, a process called transduction. Our perception of the stimulus takes place in higher, specialized regions of the brain.

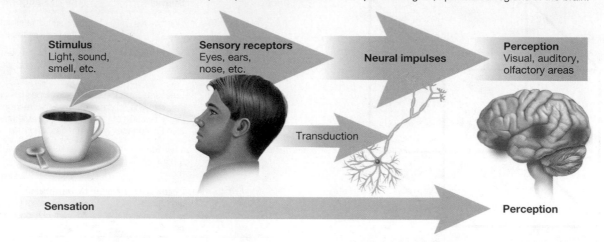

to the appropriate brain structures. Interestingly, these pathways are not fully distinct in the developing brain. Researchers at McMaster University have demonstrated that infants have a number of overlapping sensations (Maurer & Maurer, 1988; Spector & Maurer, 2009). For instance, spoken language elicits activity in areas of the brain related to hearing, but also in brain areas related to vision. This effect does not disappear until age 3 (Neville, 1995). As children age, the pathways in their brains become more distinct, with less-useful connections being pruned away. Thus, perception is a skill that our brains learn through experience.

Experience also influences how we adapt to sensory stimuli in our everyday lives. Generally speaking, our sensory receptors are most responsive upon initial exposure to a stimulus. For example, when you first walk out of a building onto a sidewalk beside a busy street, the sound from the traffic and the bright sunlight initially seem intense. This feeling occurs because both the sensory receptors and brain areas related to perception are extremely sensitive to change. The *orienting response* describes how we quickly shift our attention to stimuli that signal a change in our sensory world.

The flip side of this ability is that we allocate progressively less attention to stimuli that remain the same over time; these unchanging stimuli elicit less activity in the nervous system and are perceived as being less intense over time. So, the sound of traffic or the light outside will seem less intense after a few minutes than it did when you first exited the building. This process is known as **sensory adaptation**, *the reduction of activity in sensory receptors with repeated exposure to a stimulus*. Sensory adaptation provides the benefit of allowing us to adjust to our surroundings and shift our focus to other events that may be important. However, there are also drawbacks to sensory adaptation.

We often get used to listening to loud music in our ear-bud headphones, which can eventually damage the auditory system. We also stop noticing how polluted and loud city life can be, even though both factors can influence our stress levels and overall health (Evans, 2003).

There is a real-world example of sensory adaptation that most of us experience every day. Watch television for 5–10 minutes; but, rather than follow the plot of the show, pay attention to how many times the camera angle changes. Directors change the camera angle (and thus your sensation and perception) every few seconds in order to prevent you from experiencing sensory adaptation. The image on the screen will change from wide-angle shots to close-ups of different actors, and that change stimulates your orienting response, making it difficult for you to look away. Whether this over-exposure to rapidly changing stimuli is having a permanent effect on our

Sensory adaptation is one process that accounts for why we respond less to a repeated stimulus—even to something that initially seems impossible to ignore.

brains—particularly the developing brains of children—is a hotly debated issue in current psychological research (Bavelier et al., 2010; Healy, 2004).

STIMULUS THRESHOLDS How loud does someone have to whisper for you to hear that person? If you touch a railroad track, how sensitive are your fingers to vibrations from a distant train? How does your hearing or sense of touch compare to other people that you know? Are they more or less sensitive? One early researcher, William Gustav Fechner (1801–1887), was fascinated by such questions. Fechner was a German physicist who was interested in vision. In 1839, he developed an eye disorder that forced him to resign from his academic position. He later recovered, but the experience of having impaired vision—and the effects this had on his thoughts and actions—changed the focus of his research. Fechner helped to create **psychophysics**, *the field of study that explores how physical energy such as light and sound and their intensity relate to psychological experience.* A popular approach was to measure the minimum amount of a stimulus needed for detection, and the degree to which a stimulus must change in strength for the change to be perceptible to people.

See if you can estimate human sensory abilities in the following situations (based on Galanter, 1962):

- If you were standing atop a mountain on a dark, clear night, how far away do you think you could detect the flame from a single candle?
- How much perfume would need to be spilled in a three-room apartment for you to detect the odour?

On a clear night, a candle flame can be detected 50 km away. One drop of perfume is all that is needed for detection in a three-room apartment (so no need to douse yourself in perfume or aftershave!). Each of these values represents an **absolute threshold**—that is, *the minimum amount of energy or quantity of a stimulus required for it to be reliably detected at least 50% of the time it is presented* (Figure 4.3). For example, imagine an experimenter asked you to put on headphones and listen for spoken words; however, she manipulated the volume at which the words were presented so that some could be heard and some could not. Your absolute threshold would be the volume at which you could detect the words 50% of the time. But, your absolute threshold might differ from the person beside you—the minimum amount of pressure, sound, light, or chemical required for detection varies among individuals and across the lifespan. There are also large differences across species. The family dog may startle, bark, and tear for the door before you can even detect a visitor's approach, and a cat can detect changes in shadows and light that go unnoticed by humans. There is no magic or mystery in either example: These animals simply have lower absolute thresholds for detecting sound and light.

Figure 4.3 Absolute Thresholds

The absolute threshold is the level at which a stimulus can be detected 50% of the time.

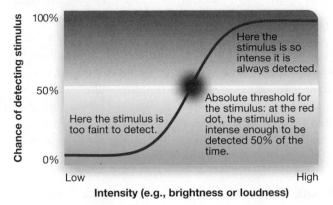

Another measure of perception refers to how well an individual can detect whether a stimulus has changed. A **difference threshold** *is the smallest difference between stimuli that can be reliably detected at least 50% of the time.* When you add salt to your food, for example, you are attempting to cross a difference threshold that your taste receptors can register. Whether you actually detect a difference, known as a *just noticeable difference*, depends primarily on the intensity of the original stimulus. The more intense the original stimulus, the larger the amount of it that must be added for the difference threshold to be reached. For example, if you add one pinch of salt to a plate of french fries that already had one pinch sprinkled on them, you can probably detect the difference. However, if you add one pinch of salt to fries that already had four pinches applied, you probably will not detect much of a difference. Apparently, to your senses, a pinch of salt does not always equal a pinch of salt.

This effect was formalized into an equation by Ernst Weber (1795–1878), a German physician and one of the founders of psychophysics. **Weber's law** *states that the just noticeable difference between two stimuli changes as a proportion of those stimuli.* Imagine you're holding 50 g of candy in your hand. You may not notice if one gram of candy is added; instead, let's say that the just noticeable difference is five grams (i.e., you can tell the difference between 50 g and 55 g of candy). Now let's imagine that your friend hands you 100 g of candy. Again, she starts adding candy to your hand to see when you'll notice a change. Weber's law would suggest that the just noticeable difference would be 10 g. If the just noticeable difference of 50 g is 5 g, and if 100 g is 50 g doubled, then the just noticeable difference of 100 g should be 5 g doubled: 10 g.

The study of stimulus thresholds has its limitations. Whether someone perceives a stimulus is determined by self-report—that is, by an individual reporting that she either did or did not detect a stimulus. But, not all people are equally willing to say they sensed a weak stimulus. Some people may wait until they are 100% certain that a candle was viewed, whereas other people may claim to see a faint candlelight just because they expect to see it. This concept has real-world implications. Think of a radiologist trying to detect tumours in a set of images: If there are differences in the absolute threshold of different radiologists, then one might miss tumours that others would detect. But, this scenario is even more complex—different radiologists might be more or less likely to report seeing a tumour when they are unsure of what they have seen. How do we confirm whether these stimuli were truly perceived or whether the individuals were just guessing?

SIGNAL DETECTION If you are certain that a stimulus exists (e.g., you were hit in the face with a soccer ball), then there is no reason to worry about whether you did or did not perceive something. However, there are many instances in which we must make decisions about sensory input that is uncertain, as in the previous example of a radiologist. It is in these ambiguous situations that signal detection theory can be a powerful tool for the study of our sensory systems. **Signal detection theory** *states that whether a stimulus is perceived depends on both the sensory experience and the judgment made by the subject*. Thus, the theory requires us to examine two processes: a sensory process and a decision process. In a typical signal detection experiment conducted in the laboratory, the experimenter presents either a faint stimulus or no stimulus at all; this is the *sensory process*. The subject is then asked to report whether or not a stimulus was actually presented; this is the *decision process*.

In developing signal detection theory, psychologists realized that there are four possible outcomes (see Figure 4.4). For example, you may be correct that you heard a sound (a *hit*), or correct that you did not hear a sound (known as a *correct rejection*). Of course, you will not always be correct in your judgments. Sometimes you will think you heard something that is not there; psychologists refer to this type of error as a *false alarm*. On other occasions you may fail to detect that a stimulus was presented (a *miss*). By analyzing how often a person's responses fall into each of these four categories, psychologists can accurately measure the sensitivity of that person's sensory systems.

Studies using signal detection theory have shown that whether a person can accurately detect a weak stimulus appears to depend on a number of factors (Green & Swets, 1966). First among these is the sensitivity of a person's sensory organs. For instance, some people can detect tiny differences in the tastes of spicy foods, whereas other people experience them all as "hot." In addition to these objective differences, there are also a number of cognitive and emotional factors that influence how sensitive a person is to various sensory stimuli. These include expectations, level of psychological and autonomic-nervous-system arousal, and how motivated a person is to pay attention to nuances in the stimuli. If you were lost in the woods, your arousal level would be quite high. You would likely be better able to notice the sound of someone's voice, the far-off growl of a bear, or the sound of a car on the road than you would be

Figure 4.4 Signal Detection Theory

Signal detection theory recognizes that a stimulus is either present or absent (by relying on the sensory process) and that the individual either reports detecting the stimulus or does not (the decision process). The cells represent the four possible outcomes of this situation. Here we apply signal detection theory to a man alone in the woods.

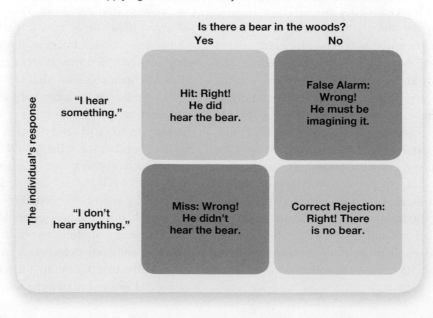

Myths in Mind

Setting the Record Straight on Subliminal Messaging

Do you think that messages presented to you so rapidly that you couldn't consciously see them would still influence your behaviour? In the 1950s, a marketing researcher named James Vicary suggested such persuasion can indeed occur. Vicary claimed that by presenting the messages "Eat popcorn" and "Drink Coca-Cola" on a movie screen, he was able to increase the sales of popcorn and Coke at the theatre. Although later exposed as a hoax, Vicary's claims received a great deal of attention from both the public and the CIA and spawned a huge subliminal self-help industry. But, does *subliminal perception*—meaning perception below the threshold of conscious awareness—really exist? And if so, can it really control our motivations, beliefs, and behaviours?

Numerous companies selling subliminal self-help products would like you to believe so. However, research by Canadian psychologists suggests that these claims may be inaccurate. For example, Merikle and Skanes (1992) tested the usefulness of subliminal weight-loss tapes. Female participants were randomly assigned to one of three experimental conditions: (1) subliminal weight-loss tapes, (2) subliminal tapes for the reduction of dental anxiety, and (3) a wait list (no tapes). The women were weighed before and after a six-week period to see if the tapes affected weight loss. The researchers found no difference between the three groups, suggesting that the tapes were entirely ineffective.

A similar study by American researchers suggests that even if some improvement *were* to occur after participants heard subliminal tapes, these effects may be due to the participants' expectations (Greenwald et al., 1991). In this study, participants were given subliminal cassettes that supposedly improved memory or improved self-esteem. Importantly, the labels on the tapes varied such that half of the participants received the correct cassette–label pairing (e.g., a memory cassette with a memory label) and half received the opposite (e.g., a memory cassette with a self-esteem label). Testing conducted after one month of use showed

no effects based on the content of the cassettes. However, there was a general overall improvement in all conditions, suggesting that simply being in an experiment helped both self-esteem and memory (a result similar to the Hawthorne effect discussed in Module 2.1). Importantly, there was also a trend for participants to believe that the cassettes had produced the desired effect—but this perceived improvement was for the ability that was on the cassette's *label*, not necessarily what the participants *actually heard*. In other words, their *expectations* led them to believe that they had improved an ability even though they hadn't received any subliminal help for that ability (i.e., a placebo effect).

Fuse/Corbis/Getty Images

The allure of subliminal self-help programs is that individuals can improve themselves without putting forth any effort—the subliminal messages will do the changing for the person. Unfortunately, psychological studies suggest that such effects are due more to the individual's expectations than to subliminal perception.

if you were hiking with friends on a familiar trail—even if the surrounding noise level was the same. Why does this difference in sensitivity occur? Is it due to enhanced functioning of your ears (the sensory process) or due to you being more motivated to detect sounds (the decision process)? Research shows that motivational changes are likely to affect the decision process so that you assume that every snapping twig is a bear on the prowl. This change in sensitivity has obvious survival value.

So far, we have described research about stimuli that individuals consciously perceive. What about information that stimulates the sensory organs but is too weak to reach conscious awareness? Could such weak stimuli still influence our behaviour, thoughts, and feelings? How could we

accurately assess such a phenomenon? These questions abound when discussing the myths—and the realities—of subliminal perception.

PRIMING AND SUBLIMINAL PERCEPTION The fact that subliminal self-help tapes are unlikely to turn you into a multilingual genius with washboard abs does not mean that all subliminal perception is a hoax. We can, in fact, perceive subliminal stimuli *under strict laboratory conditions*. Most laboratory-based studies use a technique known as *priming*, in which previous exposure to a stimulus can influence that individual's later responses, either to the same stimulus or to one that is related to it. Indeed, priming by subliminally presented stimuli has been demonstrated time and again in cognitive psychology experiments (Van den Bussche et al., 2009). In this type of study, experimenters often present a word or an image for a fraction of a second. This presentation is then immediately followed by another image, known as a *mask*, which is displayed for a longer period of time. The mask interferes with the conscious perception of the "subliminal" stimulus—the perceivers are often unaware that any stimulus appeared before the mask (e.g., Cheesman & Merikle, 1986). Yet, a number of brain imaging studies have shown that these rapidly presented stimuli do in fact influence patterns of brain activity (Critchley et al., 2000). Thus, it appears that subliminal perception can occur, and it can produce small effects in the nervous system.

It is important to note that subliminal priming is unlikely to create motivations that hadn't previous existed, a grave concern of many people in the 1950s and 1960s. At best, such messages might enhance a motivation or goal that we already have. Erin Strahan and her colleagues at the University of Waterloo examined whether subliminally primed words related to thirst would differentially affect thirsty and non-thirsty viewers (Strahan et al., 2002). They found that after viewing thirst-related subliminal stimuli (the words "thirst" and "dry"), thirsty participants drank more of a beverage and rated it more positively than did non-thirsty participants (who were not influenced by the subliminal words). No group difference was found when the subliminally presented words were not thirst-related. These results demonstrate that although subliminally primed words can activate an *already existing* motivational state, they cannot create a *new* motivational state.

Module 4.1a Quiz:

Sensing the World Around Us

Know . . .

1. _____ is the study of how physical events relate to psychological perceptions of those events.
   A. Sensation
   B. Sensory adaptation
   C. Perception
   D. Psychophysics

Understand . . .

2. The minimum stimulation required to detect a stimulus is a(n) _____, whereas the minimum required to detect the difference between two stimuli is a(n) _____.
   A. just noticeable difference; difference threshold
   B. absolute threshold; difference threshold
   C. difference threshold; absolute threshold
   D. just noticeable difference; absolute threshold

3. Signal detection theory improves on simple thresholds by including the influence of
   A. psychological factors, such as a willingness to guess if uncertain.
   B. engineering factors, such as how well a set of speakers is designed.

   C. whether an individual has hearing or visual impairments.
   D. the actual intensity of the stimulus.

Apply . . .

4. Walking on a crowded downtown sidewalk, Ben thinks he hears his name called, but when he turns around, he cannot find anyone who might be speaking to him. In terms of signal detection theory, mistakenly believing he heard his name is an example of a _____.
   A. hit
   B. miss
   C. bogus hit
   D. false alarm

Analyze . . .

5. Is it reasonable to conclude that subliminal messages have a *strong* effect on behaviour?
   A. No, research shows that they have no effect whatsoever.
   B. No, although research shows they might have mild effects.
   C. Yes, the research shows that subliminal ads are powerful.
   D. Conclusions about subliminal messages have not been reached by psychologists.

Perceiving the World Around Us

The study of thresholds, signal detection, and subliminal perception has given us answers to many basic questions about how we sense and perceive our environment. But, how do we actually form perceptions from all of this sensory information? The attempt to answer this question has a rich history in psychology, taking us back to the first half of the 20th century.

GESTALT PRINCIPLES OF PERCEPTION In 1910, Max Wertheimer was riding on a train from Vienna, Austria, to Frankfurt, Germany. As he stared out the window at the Central European countryside, he noticed that the buildings in the distance appeared to be moving backwards. Wertheimer was intrigued by this obvious illusion, and decided to investigate the experience when he arrived in Frankfurt later that day. That evening, he bought himself a stroboscope, a toy that displayed pictures in rapid succession. He noticed that individual pictures did not move; but, when presented within a fraction of a second of each other, the individual images created the perception of movement. This simple observation had an astounding impact on the study of perception, and led to the development of the Gestalt school of psychology.

Gestalt psychology is an approach to perception that emphasizes that "the whole is greater than the sum of its parts." In other words, the individual parts of an image may have little meaning on their own, but when combined, the whole takes on a significant perceived form. Gestalt psychologists identified several key principles to describe how we organize features that we perceive.

One basic Gestalt principle is that objects or "figures" in our environment tend to stand out against a background. Gestalt psychologists refer to this basic perceptual rule as the *figure–ground* principle. The text in front of you is a figure set against a background, but you may also consider the individual letters you see to be figures against the background of the page. This perceptual tendency is particularly apparent when the distinction between figure and ground is ambiguous, as can be seen in the face–vase illusion in Figure 4.5(a). Do you see a vase or two faces in profile? At the level of sensation, there is neither a vase nor two faces— there is just a pattern. What makes it a perceptual illusion is the recognition that there are two objects, but there is some ambiguity as to which is figure and which is ground. The figure–ground principle applies to hearing as well. When you are holding a conversation with one individual in a crowded party, you are attending to the figure (the voice of the individual) against the background noise (the ground). If the person you are speaking with is uninteresting, you

Animals and insects take advantage of figure–ground ambiguity to camouflage themselves from predators. Can you see the walking stick insect in this photo?

Brian Lasenby/123RF

may attend to the music instead of what he or she is saying to you. In this case, the music would become the figure and the droning voice would become the ground. Exactly which object is the figure and which is the ground at any given moment therefore depends on many factors, including what you are motivated to pay attention to.

Proximity and *similarity* are two additional Gestalt principles that influence perception. We tend to treat two or more objects that are in close proximity to each other as a group. Because of their proximity, people standing next to each other in a photograph are assumed to be a group. Similarity can be experienced by viewing groups of people in uniform, such as two different teams on a soccer field or police facing off against protesters at the 2010 G20 Summit in Toronto. We tend to group together individuals wearing the same uniform based on their visual similarity.

Some other key Gestalt principles are also illustrated in Figure 4.5. *Continuity*, or "good continuation," refers to the perceptual rule that lines and other objects tend to be continuous, rather than abruptly changing direction. The black object snaking its way around the white object is viewed as one continuous object rather than as two separate ones. A related principle, called *closure*, refers to the tendency to fill in gaps to complete a whole object.

It is important to note that Gestalt concepts are not simply a collection of isolated examples. Rather, when put together, they demonstrate an incredibly important characteristic of the perceptual system: we create our own organized perceptions out of the different sensory inputs that we experience. The next time you go outside, look at

Figure 4.5 Gestalt Principles of Form Perception

(a) Figure and ground. (b) Proximity helps us group items together so that we see three columns instead of six rows. (c) Similarity occurs when we perceive the similar dots as forming alternating rows of yellow and red, not as columns of alternating colours. (d) Continuity is the tendency to view items as whole figures even if the image is broken into multiple segments. (e) Closure is the tendency to fill in gaps so as to see a whole object.

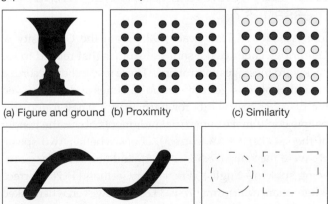

(a) Figure and ground (b) Proximity (c) Similarity

(d) Continuity (e) Closure

Christian Lapid/The Canadian Press

The principle of similarity in action. We perceive groups of police (who are dressed similarly) and protesters, rather than hundreds of individuals.

how we create organized perceptions of architecture, interior design, fashion, and even corporate logos. All of these examples show how much of "you" is in your perceptual experience of the world.

The illusions and figures you have viewed in this section reveal some common principles that guide how we perceive the world. We can take this exploration a step further by discussing the cognitive processes that underlie these principles, a topic that brings us back to the controversial court case discussed at the beginning of this module.

Working the Scientific Literacy Model

Backward Messages in Music

Humans are experts at pattern recognition. This ability to detect patterns is the basis for our ability to understand speech. To newborn babies, speech is a series of nonsense sounds. With experience, we are able to group together different sounds, which leads to the perception of spoken words. But, how sophisticated are these pattern-recognition abilities? This question is central to the issue of backward messages in music.

What do we know about backward messages in music?

The idea that music can contain backward messages has a long history. Fans have reported finding evidence of these messages in a few songs from The Beatles. "Messages" have also been found in 1970s songs by Led Zeppelin and Queen. For example, when Queen's song "Another One Bites the

Dust" is played backwards, some listeners claim to hear "It's fun to smoke marijuana." However, most examples of backward messages are due to *phonetic reversal*, where a word pronounced backwards sounds like another word (e.g., *dog* and *god*). Indeed, in most cases, the bands claim to be unaware that any backward messages exist (although a few bands, such as Pink Floyd, intentionally inserted messages, oftentimes to poke fun at conspiracy theorists).

Importantly, until the 1980s, few people believed that these messages could be *perceived* when the music was played forward (i.e., properly), let alone that these messages could *influence people's behaviour*. This changed with the Judas Priest lawsuit discussed at the beginning of this module. In that case, the prosecution claimed that "backward messages" in the music caused two boys to attempt suicide. Could psychology research explain whether these claims were valid?

How can science explain backward messages?

John Vokey and Don Read (1985) from the University of Lethbridge conducted a series of studies that related to the backward messages controversy. These researchers recorded a number of passages onto audio cassettes and then played the cassettes backwards for participants. They found that people could make superficial judgments about the gender of the speaker (98.9% correct), about whether two speakers were the same (78.5% correct), and about the language being spoken—English, French, or German (46.7% correct, where chance performance is 33.3%). However, when asked to make judgments about the *content* of the backward messages, performance fell to chance levels. Participants were unable to distinguish between nursery rhymes, Christian, satanic, pornographic, or advertising messages (19.1% correct, where chance performance is 20%).

But, what if the participants knew what patterns to listen for? It is a common experience that when a backward message is identified in a song and people are told the message in advance, they are able to identify it. To test whether such expectations could influence perception, Vokey and Read asked participants to listen for specific phrases in the backward messages (these were "phrases" that the researchers had picked out after repeatedly listening to the backward stimuli). When asked to listen for "Saw a girl with a weasel in her mouth" and "I saw Satan," 84.6% of the participants agreed that the phrases were perceivable.

Can we critically evaluate this research?

One concern with Vokey and Read's experiments was that the participants may have been experiencing demand characteristics, producing responses that they thought the experimenter wanted to hear. Such an explanation could easily be tested using more modern technology than was available in the mid-1980s. If participants listened to audio files using headphones and were prompted by a question on a computer rather than by an experimenter, it would help rule out this alternative explanation of the results.

This minor criticism aside, the results do provide a nice demonstration of the fact that our perceptions of the world are influenced both by the stimuli themselves as well as by our own mindset. For example, the centre of Figure 4.6 can be perceived as either the number 13 or the letter B depending upon whether you're reading numbers (12 and 14) or letters (A and C). This is an example of **top-down processing**, *when our perceptions are influenced by our expectations or by our prior knowledge.* Reading "12" and "14" gives us the expectation that the ambiguous stimulus in between them must be "13." In the backward messages experiment, participants used top-down processing to perceive specific phrases.

If the participants were not given any directions from the experimenters and instead simply listened to

Figure 4.6 Top-Down Processing
Is the centre the letter B or the number 13?

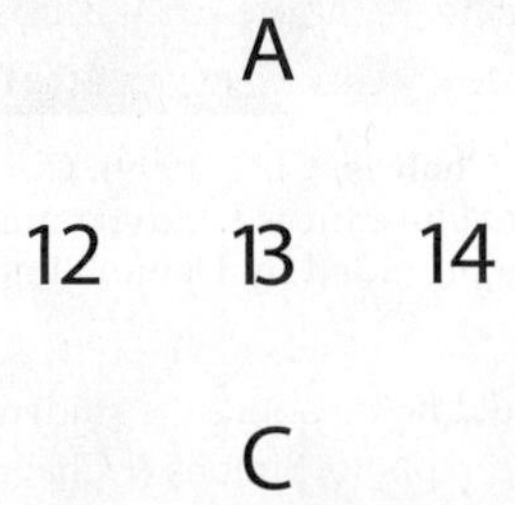

A

12   13   14

C

Figure 4.7 Expectations Influence Perception
Is this a rat or a man's face? People who look at pictures of animals before seeing this image see a rat, whereas those looking at pictures of faces see the image as a man's face.

the music backwards and tried to detect messages based on the different sounds that could be heard, they would be engaging in a different type of processing. **Bottom-up processing** *occurs when we perceive individual bits of sensory information (e.g., sounds) and use them to construct a more complex perception (e.g., a message).* As you might expect, bottom-up processing would occur when you encounter something that is unfamiliar or difficult to recognize.

Top-down and bottom-up processing can be studied using some interesting stimuli, such as the image in Figure 4.7. When you initially looked at this image, you may have seen either a rat or a man. Unless you were surrounded by animals or a lot of people, there was very little to guide your perception of the image—you used bottom-up processing and were just as likely to have thought the image was a rat or a man. However, when people first look at pictures of animals and then look at this ambiguous image, they tend to see the rat first; if they first look at pictures of people, they tend to see the man first. Thus, top-down processes can influence the perception of the image as well. In short, the way we perceive the world is a combination of both top-down and bottom-up processing (Beck & Kastner, 2009).

Incidentally, Vokey and Read were asked to testify in the Judas Priest case in order to explain how their psychology experiments related to the legal proceedings. Judas Priest was found not guilty.

Why is this relevant?

These results suggest that we interpret patterns of stimuli in ways that are consistent with our expectations. Several researchers have demonstrated that it is possible to form a *perceptual set*—a filter that influences what aspects of a scene we perceive or pay attention to. But, focusing on particular patterns of stimuli also means that we are *not* focusing on other patterns; in some cases, we ignore pieces of information that don't fit with our expectations. In the backward messages study, participants had to ignore many different sounds in order to detect the sounds that resembled "Saw a girl with a weasel in her mouth." As we'll see in the next section, sometimes our perceptual sets are so fixed that we fail to notice unexpected objects that are clearly visible . . . and very interesting.

ATTENTION AND PERCEPTION The example of backward messages shows us that what we pay attention to can affect what we perceive. In fact, in many cases, we are *paying attention to more than one stimulus or task at the same time*, a phenomenon known as **divided attention**. Simultaneously playing a video game and holding a conversation involves divided attention; so does using Facebook and Twitter while you are listening to your psychology professor lecture, or attempting to text and drive. Although we often feel that dividing our attention is not affecting our performance, there is substantial evidence from both laboratory and real-world studies telling us otherwise (Pashler, 1998; Stevenson et al., 2013).

In contrast, **selective attention** *involves focusing on one particular event or task*, such as focused studying, driving without distraction, or attentively listening to music or watching a movie. In this case, you are paying more attention to one part of your environment so that you can accurately sense and perceive the information it might provide (e.g., watching the road while driving). While useful, this process comes at a cost—your perception of other parts of your environment suffers (e.g., you don't notice the birds in the trees, or you walk into a fountain in the mall because you're focused on texting). Most of the time, selective attention is quite beneficial; however, there are times when this focus is so powerful that we fail to perceive some very obvious things.

Imagine you are watching your favourite team play basketball. You're a big fan of a particular player and are intently watching his every move. Would you notice if a person in a gorilla suit ran onto the court for a few seconds? Most people would say "yes." However, psychological research suggests otherwise. Missing the obvious can be surprisingly easy—especially if you are focused on just one particular aspect of your environment. For example, researchers asked undergraduate students to watch a video of students dressed in white t-shirts actively moving around while passing a ball to one another. The participants' task was to count the number of times the ball was passed. To complicate matters, there were also students in black t-shirts doing the same thing with another ball; however, the participants were instructed to ignore them. This is a top-down task because the participants selectively attended to a single set of events. The participants in this study found the task very easy; most were able to accurately count the number of passes, give or take a few.

But what if a student wearing a gorilla suit walked through the video, stopped, pounded her chest, and walked off screen? Who could miss that? Surprisingly, about half the participants failed to even notice the gorilla (Simons & Chabris, 1999). This number was even higher in elderly populations (Graham & Burke, 2011). This result is an example of **inattentional blindness**, *a failure to notice clearly visible events or objects because attention is directed elsewhere* (Mack & Rock, 1998). You can imagine how shocked the participants were when they watched the film again without selectively attending to one thing and realized they had completely missed the gorilla. Inattentional blindness shows that when we focus on a limited number of features, we might not pay much attention to anything else.

Inattentional blindness accounts for many common phenomena. For example, people who witness automobile accidents or criminal behaviour may offer faulty or incomplete testimony. In sports, athletes and referees

Top: Simons, D. J., & Chabris, C. F. (1999). Gorillas in our midst: Sustained inattentional blindness for dynamic events. *Perception, 28*, 1059–1074. Figure provided by Daniel Simons; bottom: Photo by Matt Milless.

Do you think you would fail to notice the student in the gorilla suit at a basketball game (top photo, Simons & Chabris, 1999)? In another study of inattentional blindness, researchers discovered that when participants were focused on running after a confederate at night, only 35% of the subjects noticed a staged fight going on right in their pathway, and during the day only 56% noticed (Chabris et al., 2011).

often miss aspects of a game because they are focusing on one area of action (Memmert & Furley, 2007); inattentional blindness decreases as expertise with the game increases (Furley et al., 2010). Interestingly, research conducted at Dalhousie University has shown that stimuli that were not perceived in an inattentional blindness study still influenced performance on later memory tasks, suggesting that these stimuli can in fact influence our perceptual system (Butler & Klein, 2009). Although this doesn't necessarily mean that referees will be haunted by missed calls, it does mean that the refs weren't blind—just inattentionally blind.

Module 4.1b Quiz:

Perceiving the World Around Us

Know . . .

1. Which Gestalt principle refers to the perceptual rule that things that are close together are likely part of the same object or group?
   A. Figure–ground
   B. Proximity
   C. Continuity
   D. Similarity

Understand . . .

2. Failure to notice particular stimuli when paying close attention to others is known as _____.
   A. misattention
   B. divided attention
   C. multitasking
   D. intentional blindness

Analyze . . .

3. While watching television, you see a report about a group of parents complaining that backward messages in music are making their children misbehave. According to research, you would tell these parents that
   A. only backward messages containing emotional information can influence people.
   B. there is no evidence that backward messages can be perceived unless people are told what to listen for.
   C. previous research has shown that backward messages can influence behaviour, but only if they are embedded within music.
   D. researchers have not come to a definitive conclusion about the effects of backward messages.

Module 4.1 Summary

4.1a Know . . . the key terminology of sensation and perception.

absolute threshold
bottom-up processing
difference threshold
divided attention
doctrine of specific nerve energies
inattentional blindness
perception
psychophysics
selective attention
sensation
sensory adaptation
signal detection theory
top-down processing
transduction
Weber's law

4.1b Understand . . . what stimulus thresholds are.

Stimulus thresholds can be either *absolute* (the minimum amount of energy to notice a stimulus) or based on *difference* (the minimum change between stimuli required to notice they are different).

4.1c Understand . . . the principles of Gestalt psychology.

A key principle of Gestalt psychology is that although the individual parts of a stimulus may have little meaning on their own, these parts can be grouped together in ways that are perceived as distinct patterns or objects. For instance, individual stimuli can be grouped together according to principles of figure and ground, proximity, similarity, continuity, and closure.

4.1d Apply . . . your knowledge of signal detection theory to identify hits, misses, and correct responses in examples.

Apply Activity

For practice, consider Figure 4.4, along with this example: Imagine a girl who has seen a scary television program and then while trying to go to sleep, worries about a monster in the closet. Identify which of the four events (A–D) goes within the correct box; that is, identify it as a hit, a miss, a false alarm, or a correct rejection. Warning: For half of these events, you may have to assume there really is a monster in the closet.

Hit:	False alarm:
Miss:	Correct rejection:

A. There is no monster in the closet and the girl is confident that she has not heard anything.

B. There really is a monster in the closet but the girl has not heard it.

C. There really is a monster in the closet and the girl hears it.

D. There is no monster in the closet, but the girl insists that she heard something.

4.1e   Analyze . . . claims that subliminal advertising and backward messages can influence your behaviour.

As you read in the Priming and Subliminal Perception section of this module, we *can* sometimes perceive stimuli below the level of conscious awareness, and this perception can affect our behaviour in some ways. However, as noted in the Myths in Mind feature, research suggests that subliminal advertising has little effect on one's consumer behaviour. Similarly, studies of backward messages in music have shown that individuals typically do not perceive the meaning of these messages *unless they are specifically told what they should listen for,* suggesting that the Devil in heavy metal music is really just top-down processing.

Module 4.2   The Visual System

Facundo Arrizabalaga/EPA/Newscom

Learning Objectives

4.2a Know . . . the key terminology relating to the eye and vision.

4.2b Understand . . . how visual information travels from the eye through the brain to give us the experience of sight.

4.2c Understand . . . the theories of colour vision.

4.2d Apply . . . your knowledge to explain how we perceive depth in our visual field.

4.2e Analyze . . . how we perceive objects and faces.

On Canada Day in 2015, Canadian tennis star Milos Raonic hit a serve that was clocked at 145 mph (233 km/h) against his opponent, German Tommy Haas. At the time, it was the third fastest serve in the 138-year history of the Wimbledon championship. Remarkably, Haas managed to return the serve, although he ended up losing the point to the powerful Canadian. Although spectators were impressed by the skill and athleticism of both athletes on that sunny July afternoon, they were also witness to something equally stunning: the power and complexity of the human visual system.

In order for Haas to return Raonic's serve, he had to identify a yellowish-green tennis ball against a dark green

background, follow the ball as it landed on a light-green grass-court surface, and track its trajectory as it bounced toward him. Doing so required him to be able to perceive different colours, perceive and identify particular objects in his visual field, and perceive motion. Haas' visual system also had to work with his motoric (movement) system so that he could move his racquet (and thus his hand and arm) in order to return the serve.

Although both Raonic and Haas are professional athletes, their exceptional visual abilities did not develop overnight; they are the product of years of training. Vision—and the movements and cognition that go with it—is something we fine-tune with experience.

Focus Questions

1. Which brain areas are involved with identifying your coffee cup versus reaching for your coffee cup?

2. What tricks can artists use to make two-dimensional paintings appear three dimensional?

≫ The world is a visual place to most humans. We use vision to navigate through beautiful landscapes, city centres, and the interiors of buildings. We also use vision to communicate via facial expressions and the written word (such as this text, which you undoubtedly photocopy and tape to your bedroom walls). In this module, we explore how vision works—starting out as patterns of light entering the eye, and ending up as a complex, perceptual experience. We begin with an overview of the basic physical structures of the eye and brain that make vision possible, and then discuss the *experience* of seeing.

The Human Eye

The eye is one of the most remarkable of the human body's physical structures. It senses an amazing array of information, translates that information into neural impulses, and transfers it to the brain for complex perceptual processing.

To ensure that this sequence of events begins correctly, the eye needs specialized structures that allow us to regulate how much light comes in, to respond to different wavelengths of light, to maintain a focus on the most important objects in a scene, and to turn physical energy into action potentials, the method by which information is transmitted in the brain.

HOW THE EYE GATHERS LIGHT The primary function of the eye is to gather light and change it into an action potential. But, "light" itself is quite complex. Although physicists have written vast tomes on the topic of light, for the purposes of human perception, "light" actually refers to radiation that occupies a relatively narrow band of the electromagnetic spectrum, shown in Figure 4.8a. Light travels in waves that vary in terms of two different properties: length and amplitude. The term *wavelength* refers to the distance between peaks of a wave—differences in wavelength correspond to different colours on the electromagnetic spectrum. As you can see from Figure 4.8a, long wavelengths correspond to our perception of reddish colours and short wavelengths correspond to our perception of bluish colours. The different shades of green found in the tennis match described in the opening of this module would represent wavelengths of light in between the wavelengths of red and blue. Interestingly,

Figure 4.8 Light Waves in the Electromagnetic Spectrum

(a) The electromagnetic spectrum: When white light travels through a prism, the bending of the light reveals the visible light spectrum. The visible spectrum falls within a continuum of other waves of the electromagnetic spectrum. (b) Wavelength is measured by distance between the peaks (or the troughs) of the waves.

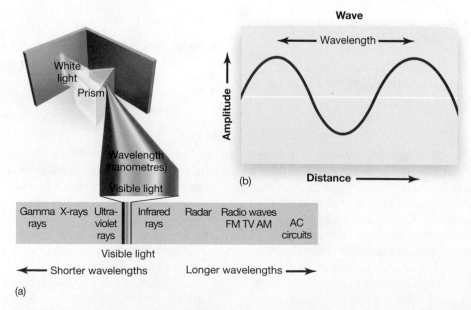

Source: Ciccarelli, Saundra K.; White, J. Noland, *Psychology: An Exploration*, 1st Ed., ©2010, p. 79. Reprinted and Electronically reproduced by permission of Pearson Education, Inc., New York, NY.

some organisms, such as bees, can see ultraviolet light and some reptiles can see infrared light. These interspecies differences are likely due to the different evolutionary demands these species have faced. What pressures do you think led humans to develop their specific visual system? Although no one can answer this question with absolute certainty, some researchers have suggested that our red–green vision allowed us to distinguish between types of edible vegetation (Regan et al., 2001).

Wavelength is not the only characteristic that is important for vision. *Amplitude* refers to the height of a wave (see Figure 4.8b). Low-amplitude waves are seen as dim colours, whereas high-amplitude waves are seen as bright colours. Light waves can also differ in terms of how many different wavelengths are being viewed at once. When you look at a clear blue sky, you are viewing many different wavelengths of light at the same time—but the blue wavelengths are more prevalent and therefore dominate your impression; when our visual angle to the sun changes at dusk, different light frequencies are more apparent, giving the sky a reddish colour. If a large proportion of the light waves are clustered around one wavelength, you will see an intense, vivid colour. If there are a large variety of wavelengths being viewed at the same time, the colour will appear to be "washed out." Figure 4.9 depicts these different characteristics of light—wavelength, amplitude, and purity—as we generally

perceive them. These characteristics of light will be experienced by us as *hue* (colour of the spectrum), *intensity* (brightness), and *saturation* (colourfulness or purity). It is in the eye that this transformation from sensation to perception takes place.

THE STRUCTURE OF THE EYE The eye consists of specialized structures that regulate the amount of light that enters the eye and organizes it into a pattern that the brain can interpret (see Figure 4.10). The **sclera** *is the white, outer surface of the eye* and the **cornea** *is the clear layer that covers the front portion of the eye and also contributes to the eye's ability to focus.* Light enters the eye through the cornea and passes through an opening called the pupil. The **pupil** *regulates the amount of light that enters by changing its size; it dilates (expands) to allow more light to enter and constricts (shrinks) to allow less light into the eye.* The changes in the pupil's size are performed by the **iris**, *a round muscle that adjusts the size of the pupil; it also gives the eyes their characteristic colour.* Behind the pupil is the **lens**, *a clear structure that focuses light onto the back of the eye.* The lens can change its shape to ensure that the light entering the eye is refracted in such a way that it is focused when it reaches the back of the eye. This process is known as *accommodation*. When the light reaches the back of the eye, it will stimulate a layer of specialized receptors that convert light into a message that the brain can then interpret, a process known as *transduction* (see Module 4.1). These receptors are part of a complex structure known as the retina.

The **retina** *lines the inner surface of the back of the eye and consists of specialized receptors that absorb light and send signals related to the properties of light to the brain.* The retina contains a number of different layers, each performing a slightly different function. At the back of the retina are specialized receptors called *photoreceptors*. These receptors, which will be discussed in more depth below, are where light will be transformed into a neural signal that the brain can understand. It may seem strange that light would stimulate the deepest layer of the retina, with the neural signal then turning around and moving forward in the eye (see Figure 4.11); however, there is a reason for this design. Having the photoreceptors wedged into the back of the eye protects them and provides them with a constant blood supply, both of which are useful to your ability to see.

Information from the photoreceptors at the back of the retina is transmitted to the ganglion cells closer to the front of the retina. The ganglion cells gather up information from the photoreceptors; this information will then alter the rate at which the ganglion cells fire. The activity of all of the ganglion cells is then sent out of the eye through the **optic nerve**, *a dense bundle of fibres*

Figure 4.9 Hue, Intensity, and Saturation

Colours vary by hue (colour), intensity (brightness), and saturation (colourfulness or "purity").

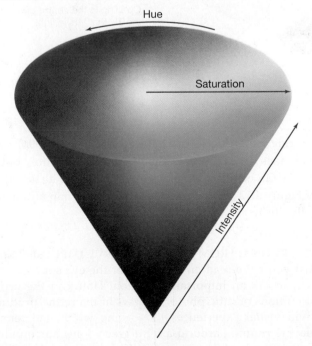

Figure 4.10 The Human Eye and Its Structures

Notice how the lens inverts the image that appears on the retina (see inset). The visual centres of the brain correct the inversion.

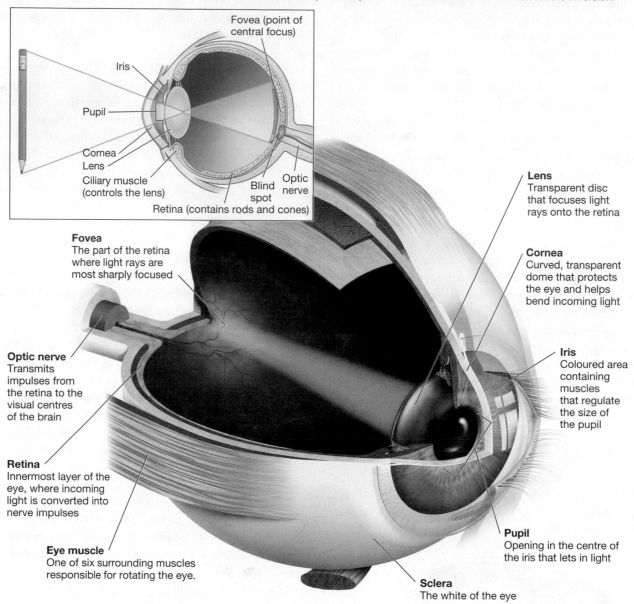

Fovea (point of central focus)

Iris

Pupil

Cornea

Lens

Ciliary muscle (controls the lens)

Blind spot

Optic nerve

Retina (contains rods and cones)

Lens
Transparent disc that focuses light rays onto the retina

Cornea
Curved, transparent dome that protects the eye and helps bend incoming light

Fovea
The part of the retina where light rays are most sharply focused

Optic nerve
Transmits impulses from the retina to the visual centres of the brain

Iris
Coloured area containing muscles that regulate the size of the pupil

Retina
Innermost layer of the eye, where incoming light is converted into nerve impulses

Eye muscle
One of six surrounding muscles responsible for rotating the eye.

Pupil
Opening in the centre of the iris that lets in light

Sclera
The white of the eye

that connect to the brain. This nerve presents a challenge to the brain. Because it travels through the back of the eye, it creates an area on the retina with no photoreceptors, called the *optic disc*. The result is a *blind spot*—a space in the retina that lacks photoreceptors. You can discover your own blind spot by performing the activity described in Figure 4.12.

The blind spot illustrates just how distinct the processes of sensation and perception are. Why do we fail to notice a completely blank area of our visual field? If we consider only the process of sensation, we cannot answer this question. We have to invoke perception: The visual areas of the brain are able to "fill in" the missing

information for us (Ramachandran & Gregory, 1991). Not only does the brain fill in the missing information, but it does so in context. Thus, once the black dot at the right of Figure 4.12 reaches the blind spot, the brain automatically fills in the vacancy with yellow.

THE RETINA: FROM LIGHT TO NERVE IMPULSE Now that you have read an overview of the eye's structures, we can ask an important question: How can the firing of millions of little photoreceptors in the retina produce vivid visual experiences like seeing white-clad tennis players running around a light-green court surrounded by thousands of spectators in different-coloured clothes?

Figure 4.11 Arrangement of Photoreceptors in the Retina

Bipolar and ganglion cells collect messages from the light-sensitive photoreceptors and converge on the optic nerve, which then carries the messages to the brain.

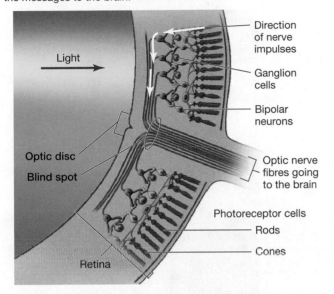

Source: Ciccarelli, Saundra K.; White, J. Noland, *Psychology: An Exploration*, 1st Ed., ©2010, p. 81. Reprinted and Electronically reproduced by permission of Pearson Education, Inc., New York, NY.

The simple answer is that not all photoreceptors are the same. There are two general types of photoreceptors—*rods* and *cones*—each of which responds to different characteristics of light. **Rods** *are photoreceptors that occupy peripheral regions of the retina; they are highly sensitive under low light levels* (see Figure 4.13). This type of sensitivity makes rods particularly responsive to black and grey. In contrast, **cones** *are photoreceptors that are sensitive*

Figure 4.12 Finding Your Blind Spot

To find your blind spot, close your left eye and, with your right eye, fix your gaze on the + in the green square. Slowly move the page toward you. When the page is approximately 6 inches (15 cm) away, you will notice that the black dot on the right disappears because of your blind spot. Not only does the black dot disappear, but its vacancy is replaced by yellow: The brain "fills it in" for you.

Figure 4.13 Distribution of Rods and Cones on the Retina

Cones are concentrated at the fovea, the centre of the retina, while rods are more abundant in the periphery. There are approximately 120 million rods and approximately 6 to 8 million cones in the adult retina.

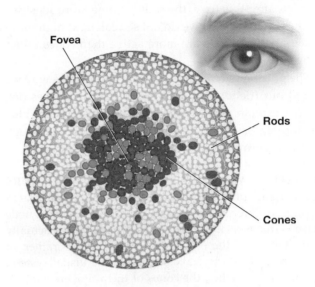

to the different wavelengths of light that we perceive as colour. Cones tend to be clustered around the **fovea**, *the central region of the retina.*

When the rods and cones are stimulated by light, their physical structure briefly changes. This change decreases the amount of the neurotransmitter glutamate being released, which alters the activity of neurons in the different layers of the retina. The final layer to receive this changed input consists of ganglion cells, which will eventually output to the optic nerve. Interestingly, the ratio of ganglion cells to cones in the fovea is approximately one to one; in contrast, there are roughly 10 rods for every ganglion cell. So, all of the input from a cone is clearly transmitted to a ganglion cell whereas the input from a rod must compete with input from other rods (similar to ten people talking at you at the same time). So, cones are clustered in the fovea (i.e., at the centre of our visual field) and have a one-to-one ratio with ganglion cells, while rods are limited to the periphery of the retina and have a ten-to-one ratio with ganglion cells. These differences help explain why colourful stimuli are often perceived as sharp images while shadowy grey images are perceived as being hazy or unclear.

In daylight or under artificial light, the cones in the retina are more active than rods—they help us to detect differences in the colour of objects and to discriminate the objects' fine details. In contrast, if the lights suddenly go out or if you enter a dark room, at first you see next to nothing. Over time, however, you gradually begin to see your surroundings more clearly. **Dark adaptation** *is* *the process by which the rods and cones become increasingly sensitive to light under low levels of illumination.* What is actually happening during dark adaptation is that the photoreceptors are slowly becoming regenerated after having been exposed to light. Cones regenerate more quickly than do rods, often within about ten minutes. However, after this time, the rods become more sensitive than the cones. Indeed, we do not see colour at night or in darkness because rods are more active than cones under low light levels.

The phenomenon of dark adaptation explains why we can find our friends in a dark movie theatre. It does not, however, explain why we perceive the sky as being blue or a stop sign as being red. Luckily, 200 years of vision research has provided answers to such questions.

THE RETINA AND THE PERCEPTION OF COLOURS

Our experience of colour is based on how our visual system interprets different wavelengths on the electromagnetic spectrum (refer back to Figure 4.8). Colour is not actually a characteristic of the objects themselves, but is rather an interpretation of these wavelengths by the visual system. As you learned earlier, the cones of the retina are specialized for responding to different wavelengths of light that correspond to different colours. However, the subjective experience of colour occurs in the brain. Currently, two theories exist to explain how neurons in the eye can produce these colourful experiences.

One theory suggests that three different types of cones exist, each of which is sensitive to a different range of wavelengths on the electromagnetic spectrum. These three types of cones were initially identified in the 18th century by physicist Thomas Young and then independently rediscovered in the 19th century by Hermann von Helmholtz. The resulting **trichromatic theory** (or **Young-Helmholtz theory**) *maintains that colour vision is determined by three different cone types that are sensitive to short, medium, and long wavelengths of light.* These cones respond to wavelengths associated with the colours blue, green, and red. The relative responses of the three types of cones allow us to perceive many different colours on the spectrum (see Figure 4.14) and allow us to experience the vast array of colours seen in environments ranging from flower gardens to dance clubs. For example, yellow is perceived by combining the stimulation of red- and green-sensitive cones, whereas light that stimulates all cones equally is perceived as white. (Note: mixing different wavelengths of light produces different colours than when you mix different colours of paint.) Modern technology has been used to measure the amount of light that can be absorbed in cones and has confirmed that each type responds to different wavelengths. Thus, *some* aspects of our colour vision can be explained by the characteristics of the cones in our retinas.

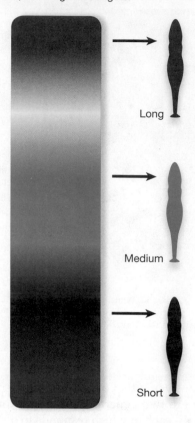

Figure 4.14 The Trichromatic Theory of Colour Vision
According to this theory, humans have three types of cones that respond maximally to different regions of the colour spectrum. Colour is experienced by the combined activity of cones sensitive to short, medium, and long wavelengths.

However, not all colour-related experiences can be explained by the trichromatic theory. For instance, stare at the image in Figure 4.15 for about a minute and then look toward a white background. After switching your gaze to a white background, you will see the colours red, white, and blue rather than green, black, and yellow. How can we explain this tendency to see such a *negative afterimage*, a different colour from the one you actually viewed? In the 19th century, Ewald Hering proposed the **opponent-process theory** of colour perception, *which states that we perceive colour in terms of opposing pairs: red to green, yellow to blue, and white to black.* This type of perception is consistent with the activity patterns of retinal ganglion cells. A cell that is stimulated by red is inhibited by green; when red is no longer perceived (as when you suddenly look at a white wall), a "rebound" effect occurs. Suddenly, the previously inhibited cells that fire during the perception of green are free to fire, whereas the previously active cells related to red no longer do so. The same relationship occurs for yellow and blue as well as for white and black.

Figure 4.15 The Negative Afterimage: Experiencing Opponent-Process Theory

Stare directly at the white dot within the flag and avoid looking away. After about a minute, immediately shift your focus to a white background. What do you see? What colours would you use to create a Canadian flag afterimage?

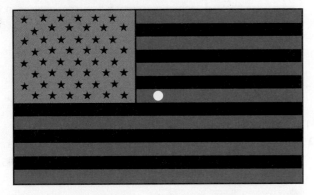

Source: Lilienfeld, Scott O.; Lynn, Steven J; Namy, Laura L.; Woolf, Nancy J., *Psychology: From Inquiry To Understanding*, 2nd Ed., ©2011. Reprinted And Electronically Reproduced By Permission Of Pearson Education, Inc., New York, NY.

The trichromatic and opponent-process theories are said to be complementary because both are required to explain how we see colour. The trichromatic theory explains colour vision in terms of the activity of cones. The opponent-process theory of colour vision explains what happens when ganglion cells process signals from a number of different cones at the same time. Together, they allow us to see the intense world of colours that we experience every day.

COMMON VISUAL DISORDERS Of course, not everyone can see colours. In fact, many people reading this book will have some form of *colour blindness*. Most forms of colour blindness affect the ability to distinguish between red and green. In people who have normal colour vision, some cones contain proteins that are sensitive to red and some contain proteins that are sensitive to green. However, in most forms of colour blindness, one of these types of cones does not contain the correct protein (e.g., "green cones" contain proteins that are sensitive to wavelengths of light that produce the colour red). Most forms of colour blindness are genetic in origin.

There are also visual disorders caused by the shape of the eye itself. Changes to the shape of the eye sometimes prevent a focused image from reaching the photoreceptors in the retina. *Nearsightedness*, or *myopia*, occurs when the eyeball is slightly elongated, causing the image that the cornea and lens focus on to fall short of the retina (see Figure 4.16). People who are nearsighted can see objects that are relatively close up but have difficulty focusing on distant objects. Alternatively, if the length of the eye is shorter than normal, the result is *farsightedness* or *hyperopia*. In this case, the image is focused *behind* the retina. Farsighted people can see distant objects clearly but not those that are close by. Both types of impairments can be corrected with contact lenses or glasses, thus allowing a focused visual image to stimulate the retina at the back of the eye, where light energy is converted into neural impulses.

In the last 20 years, an increasing number of people have undergone laser eye surgery in order to correct near- or farsightedness. In this type of surgery, surgeons use a laser to reshape the cornea so that incoming light focuses on the retina, which produces close to perfect vision. In nearsighted patients, the doctors attempt to flatten the cornea, whereas in farsighted patients the doctors attempt to make the cornea steeper. Although the idea of having a laser fire into your eyes sounds frightening, approximately 95% of the patients who undergo these surgeries report being completely satisfied with the results (Solomon et al., 2009). Seeing is believing.

Figure 4.16 Nearsightedness and Farsightedness

Nearsightedness and farsightedness result from misshapen eyes. If the eye is elongated or too short, images are not centred on the retina.

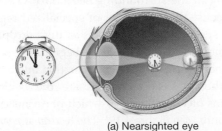

(a) Nearsighted eye

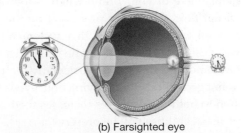

(b) Farsighted eye

Source: Lilienfeld, Scott O.; Lynn, Steven J; Namy, Laural L.; Woolf, Nancy J., *Psychology: From Inquiry to Understanding*, Books A La Carte Edtion, 2nd Ed., ©2011. Reprinted and Electronically reproduced by permission of Pearson Education, Inc., New York, NY.

Module 4.2a Quiz:

The Human Eye

Know . . .

1. Cones are predominantly gathered in a central part of the retina known as the _____.
   A. fovea
   B. photoreceptor
   C. blind spot
   D. optic chiasm

2. Which of the following conditions occurs when the eye becomes elongated, causing the image to fall short of the retina?
   A. Prosopagnosia
   B. Motion parallax
   C. Farsightedness
   D. Nearsightedness

Understand . . .

3. Crystal was at a modern art gallery. After staring at a large, red square (that was somehow worth $20 million), she looked at the wall and briefly saw the colour green. Which theory can explain Crystal's experience?
   A. Opponent-process theory
   B. Hyperopia
   C. Trichromatic theory
   D. Motion parallax

Apply . . .

4. Jacob cannot distinguish between the colours red and green. What structure(s) of the eye is/are most likely not functioning properly?
   A. Rods
   B. Cornea
   C. Cones
   D. Lens

It is important to remember that the initial sensations of light that are processed in the eye itself provide very specific information about the environment that we are viewing. But, in order for this raw sensory information to be perceived, it needs to exit the eye and enter the brain.

Visual Perception and the Brain

Information from the optic nerve travels to numerous areas of the brain. The first major destination is the *optic chiasm*, the point at which the optic nerves cross at the midline of the brain (see Figure 4.17). For each optic nerve, about half of the nerve fibres travel to the same side of the brain (ipsilateral), and half of them travel to the opposite side of the brain (contralateral). As can be seen in Figure 4.17, the outside half of the retina (closest to your temples) sends its optic nerve projections ipsilaterally. In contrast, the inside half of the retina (closest to your nose) sends its optic nerve projections contralaterally. The result of this distribution is that the left half of your visual field is initially processed by the right hemisphere of your brain, whereas the right half of your visual field is initially processed by the left hemisphere of your brain. Although this system might sound like it was designed by someone who had had a few drinks, it serves important functions, particularly if a person's brain is damaged. In this case, having both eyes send *some* information to both hemispheres increases the likelihood that *some* visual abilities will be preserved.

Fibres from the optic nerve first connect with the thalamus, the brain's "sensory relay station." The thalamus is made up of over 20 different nuclei with specialized functions. The *lateral geniculate nucleus (LGN)* is specialized for processing visual information. Fibres from this nucleus send messages to the visual cortex, located in the occipital lobe, where the complex processes of visual perception begin.

How does the visual cortex make sense of all this incoming information? It starts with a division of labour among specialized cells. One set of cells in the visual cortex—first discovered by Canadian David Hubel and his colleague Torsten Wiesel in 1959—are referred to as *feature detection cells*; these cells respond selectively to simple and specific aspects of a stimulus, such as angles and edges (Hubel & Wiesel, 1962). Researchers have been able to map which feature detection cells respond to specific aspects of an image by measuring the firing rates of groups of neurons in the visual cortex in lab animals (Figure 4.18). Feature detection cells of the visual cortex are thought to be where visual input is organized for perception; however, additional processing is required for us to accurately perceive our visual world. From the primary visual cortex, information about different features is sent for further processing in the surrounding secondary visual cortex. This area consists of a number of specialized regions that perform specific functions, such as the perception of colour and movement. These regions begin the process of putting together primitive visual information into a bigger picture.

These specialized areas are the beginning of two streams of vision, each of which performs different visual functions (see Figure 4.19). The *ventral stream* extends from the visual cortex to the lower part of the temporal lobe. The *dorsal stream*, on the other hand, extends from the visual cortex to the parietal lobe. Both streams are essential for our ability to function normally in our visual world.

Figure 4.17 Pathways of the Visual System in the Brain

The optic nerves route messages to the visual cortex. At the optic chiasm, some of the cells remain on the same side and some cross to the opposite side of the brain. This organization results in images appearing in the left visual field being processed on the right side of the brain, and images appearing in the right visual field being processed on the left side of the brain.

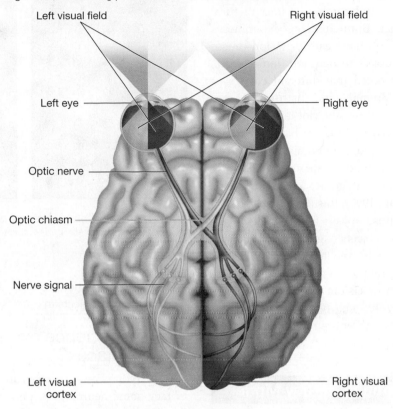

Left visual field

Right visual field

Left eye

Right eye

Optic nerve

Optic chiasm

Nerve signal

Left visual cortex

Right visual cortex

Source: Ciccarelli, Saundra K.; White, J. Noland, *Psychology*, 3rd Ed., ©2012, pp.96. Reprinted and Electronically reproduced by permission of Pearson Education, Inc., New York, NY.

Figure 4.18 Measuring the Activity of Feature Detection Cells

Scientists can measure the activity of individual feature detector cells by inserting a microscopic electrode into the visual cortex of an animal. The activity level will peak when the animal is shown the specific feature corresponding to that specific cell.

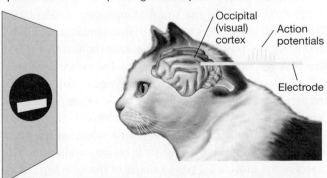

Occipital (visual) cortex

Action potentials

Electrode

Source: Lilienfeld, Scott O.; Lynn, Steven; Namy, Laura L.; Woolf, Nancy J., *Psychology: From Inquiry To Understanding*, Books A La Carte Edition, 2nd Ed., © 2011. Reprinted and Electronically reproduced by permission of Pearson Education, Inc., New York, NY.

Figure 4.19 The Two Streams of Vision

Neural impulses leave the visual centres in the occipital lobe along two different pathways. The ventral (bottom) stream extends to the temporal lobe and the dorsal (top) stream extends to the parietal lobe.

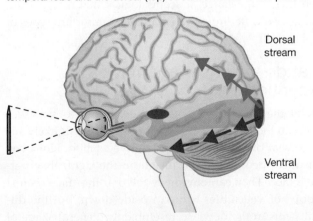

Dorsal stream

Ventral stream

Source: Figure 4.18, p. 139 in *Psychology: From Inquiry to Understanding*, 2nd ed. by Scott O. Lilienfeld, Steven J. Lynn, Laura L. Namy, and Nancy J. Woolf. Copyright © 2011. Printed and electronically reproduced by permission of Pearson Education, Inc., Upper Saddle River, New Jersey.

THE VENTRAL STREAM The ventral stream of vision extends from the visual cortex in the occipital lobe to the anterior (front) portions of the temporal lobe. This division of our visual system performs a critical function: object recognition. Groups of neurons in the temporal lobe gather shape and colour information from different regions of the secondary visual cortex and combine it into a neural representation of an object. Brain imaging experiments have shown that damage to this stream of vision causes dramatic impairments in object recognition (James et al., 2003). Other studies have noted that different categories of objects—such as tools, animals, and instruments—are represented in distinct areas of the anterior temporal lobes (Tranel et al., 1997). Indeed, researchers have identified rare cases where brain-damaged individuals show a striking inability to name items from one category while being unimpaired at naming other categories (e.g., Caramazza & Mahon, 2003; Dixon et al., 1997); this deficit only affects the visual perception of those objects (e.g., a guitar), not the knowledge about those objects (e.g., that a guitar has six strings). But tools, animals, and musical instruments are not the only categories that are represented in distinct areas of the ventral stream of vision. One group of stimuli—possibly the most evolutionarily important one in our visual world—may have an entire region of the brain dedicated to its perception.

Working the Scientific Literacy Model

Are Faces Special?

Faces provide us with an incredible amount of social information. In addition to using faces to identify specific other people, we can use them as a source of important social information, such as someone's emotional state. Other people's faces could therefore give you hints as to how you should respond to them, or to the situation you are both in. Given their importance, it seems logical that faces would be processed differently than many less important types of visual stimuli.

What do we know about face perception?

Look at the painting in Figure 4.20. What do you see? When you look at the image on the left, you will likely see a somewhat dreary bowl filled with vegetables. However, when most people see the image on the right, they perceive a face. They can obviously tell that the "face" is just the bowl of vegetables turned upside down, but the different items in the bowl do resemble the general shape of a face. The Italian artist Guiseppe Archimboldo produced a number of similar paintings in which "faces" could be perceived within other structures. What Archimboldo was

Figure 4.20 Seeing Faces

At left is a painting of turnips and other vegetables by the Italian artist Giuseppe Archimboldo. The image at right is the same image rotated 180 degrees—does it resemble a human face?

Source: *The Vegetable Gardener,* c.1590 (oil on panel), Arcimboldo, Giuseppe (1527–93)/Museo Civico Ala Ponzone, Cremona, Italy/Bridgeman Images.

highlighting was the fact that faces appear to stand out relative to other objects in our visual world.

How can science explain how we perceive faces?

Not everyone sees the faces in Archimboldo's painting. In fact, some neurological patients don't see faces at all. Specific genetic problems or brain damage can lead to an inability to recognize faces, a condition known as *prosopagnosia*, or face blindness. People with face blindness are able to recognize voices and other defining features of individuals (e.g., Angelina Jolie's lips), but not faces. Importantly, these patients tend to have damage or dysfunction in the same general area of the brain: the bottom of the right temporal lobe. So, although prosopagnosia is a relatively rare clinical condition, it does help us understand some basic processes that are involved in perceiving faces.

Brain imaging studies have corroborated the location of the "face area" of the brain (Kanwisher et al., 1997). Using fMRI, researchers have consistently detected activity in this region, now known as the *fusiform face area (FFA)*. The FFA responds more strongly to the entire face than to individual features; unlike other types of stimuli, faces are processed holistically rather than as a nose, eyes, ears, chin, and so on (Tanaka & Farah, 1993). However, the FFA shows a much smaller response when we perceive *inverted* (upside down) faces. In this case, people tend to perceive the individual components of the face (e.g., eyes, mouth, etc.) rather than perceiving the faces as a holistic unit. Figure 4.21 provides an interesting—and somewhat jarring—visual phenomenon demonstrating this difference in our perception of upright and inverted faces.

Figure 4.21 The Face Inversion Effect

After viewing both upside-down faces, you probably noticed a difference between the two pictures. The face on the left probably seemed as a bit "off." Now turn your book upside down and notice how the distortion of one of the faces is amplified when viewed from this perspective. The reason the distorted face didn't seem as bizarre when viewed upside down is that you likely focused on the individual components of Beyoncé's face, none of which are strange on their own. When you viewed the stimuli as upright faces, you would have put the different features together into a more holistic view of Beyoncé's entire face. At this point, the distorted face would definitely not look flawless.

Left: PA Photos/Landov; right: PA Photos/Landov.

Interestingly, the FFA is also active when we perceive images of faces in everyday objects, such as when people see images of Jesus in a piece of toast (Liu et al., 2014). The fact that these illusory perceptions of faces, known as *face pareidolia*, also activate the FFA suggests that this structure is influenced by top-down processing that treats any face-like pattern as a face.

Like many other sensory functions, the ability to perceive faces is dependent upon experience. Researchers at McMaster and Brock Universities have found that early visual input to the right, but not left, hemisphere of the brain is essential for the development of normal face perception (Le Grand et al., 2004, 2005). Our face perception skills also develop as we grow up—adults out-perform children on tests of face recognition (Mondloch et al., 2006) and the fusiform face area does not show special sensitivity to faces until approximately age 10 (Aylward et al., 2005).

Michael Nichols/National Geographic/Getty Images

World-renowned chimpanzee researcher Jane Goodall has face blindness (prosopagnosia). Her sister also has it—there appear to be genetic links to the condition. Despite being face blind, Dr. Goodall and others with this condition use nonfacial characteristics to recognize people, or, in her case, hundreds of individual chimpanzees (Goodall & Berman, 1999).

Can we critically evaluate this evidence?

Although no one doubts that faces are processed by the FFA, there are alternative explanations for these effects. One possibility is that the FFA is being activated by one of the cognitive or perceptual processes that help us perceive faces rather than by the perception of faces themselves. One such process is expertise. We are all experts at recognizing faces. Think of all of the people that you've gone to

school with over the years. Think of all of the entertainers, athletes, and politicians you can recognize. You have the ability to distinguish between thousands of different faces. Canadian psychologist Isabel Gauthier and her colleagues have suggested that face recognition isn't all that special. Instead, the FFA may simply be an area related to processing stimuli that we have become experts at recognizing. To test this hypothesis, she trained undergraduate students to

Figure 4.22 Expertise for Faces and "Greebles"

The images below are Greebles, faceless stimuli used to test whether the FFA responds only to faces (Gauthier & Tarr, 1997). Participants in these studies are taught to classify the Greebles on a number of characteristics such as sex ("male" and "female"). Although this task seems difficult, after several training sessions participants can rapidly make such a decision. These "Greeble experts" also show increased activity in the region of the brain associated with processing faces.

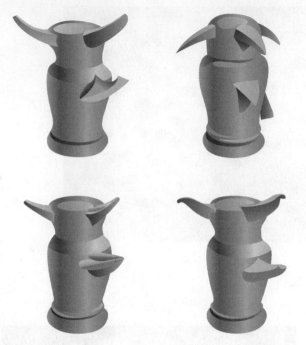

Source: Expertise and the Fusiform Face Area. Reprinted with permission of Dr. Isabel Gauthier.

recognize different types of a novel group of objects called Greebles (see Figure 4.22). Before training, these stimuli did not trigger activity in the FFA; however, after training, this area did become active (Gauthier et al., 1999). Further support for this expertise hypothesis comes from studies of bird and car experts (Gauthier et al., 2000). Both groups showed greater levels of brain activity in the FFA in response to stimuli related to their area of expertise (e.g., cars for car enthusiasts). Although this research doesn't negate the studies showing face-specific processing in this area, it does suggest that more research is necessary to see just how specialized this region of the ventral stream of vision really is.

Why is this relevant?

The fact that a specific brain region is linked with the perception of faces is very useful information for neurologists and emergency room physicians. If a patient has trouble recognizing people, it could be a sign that he has damage to the bottom of the right temporal lobe. Indeed, based on studies of prosopagnosia, tests of face memory are now part of most assessment tools used by doctors and researchers. The fact that fMRI studies corroborate the location of the FFA increases our confidence that such tools are in fact valid.

At this point in the module, we have looked at how we sense visual information and how this information is constructed by our brain-based perceptual system into objects that can influence our behaviour, such as a face or an animal. But, our visual system has even more tricks for us. Somehow, we can identify objects even when they are viewed in different lighting conditions or at different angles—your cat is still your cat, regardless of whether it is noon or midnight. This observation is an example of what is called **perceptual constancy**, *the ability to perceive objects as having constant shape, size, and colour despite changes in perspective.* What makes perceptual constancy possible is our ability to make relative judgments about shape, size, and lightness. For *shape constancy*, we judge the angle of the object relative to our position (see Figure 4.23). *Size constancy* is based on judgments of how close an object is relative to one's position as well as to the positions of other objects. *Colour constancy* allows us to recognize an object's colour under varying levels of illumination. For example, a bright red car is recognized as bright red whether in the shade or in full sunlight.

The phenomenon of colour constancy recently gained international attention during "The Great Dress Debate" of 2015. As you may recall, a photograph of a dress became an international sensation when different people perceived it as being either blue and black or white and gold. A large-scale survey involving over 1400 respondents found that 57% of people perceived the dress as black and blue, 30% saw it as white and gold, 10% saw it as blue and brown, and 10% readily switched between colours (Lafer-Sousa et al., 2015). These striking differences in how different people perceived the dress captured the attention of both the general public and vision experts. Researchers quickly noted that colour constancy was a key factor in determining how the dress was perceived. When we view an object, we naturally try to account for the quality of the surrounding light. If we view something at dawn, our visual system attempts to discount some of the redness of objects because we know that sunrise makes everything appear redder than normal. It turns out that there are individual biases in which types of light people tend to discount. Individuals with a tendency to discount bluish light will perceive the dress as white and gold, whereas individuals who discount yellowish light will perceive the dress as blue and black (Brainard & Hurlbert, 2015; Gegenfurtner et al., 2015). Thus, "the dress" helps us demonstrate that our perceptual biases, along with our previous experiences and expectations, help structure and organize our visual experiences.

Indeed, all types of perceptual constancy are influenced by our previous experience with the objects as well as the presence of other objects that can serve as comparisons. In other words, constancies are affected by top-down processing (see Module 4.1). If we know that a golden retriever is 60 cm tall or that a door is rectangular (or that a dress is blue and black), our visual system will use this knowledge when

Figure 4.23 Perceptual Constancies

(a) Shape constancy: We perceive the door to be a rectangle despite the fact that the two-dimensional outline of the image on the retina is not always rectangular. (b) Colour constancy: We perceive colours to be constant despite changing levels of illumination. (c) Size constancy: the person in the red shirt appears normal in size when in the background. A replica of this individual placed in the foreground appears unusually small because of size constancy.

(a) (b) (c)

Middle: Brian Prawl/Shutterstock;
Right: FORGET Patrick/SAGAPHOTO.COM/
Alamy Stock photo

Source: Lilienfeld, Scott O.; Lynn, Steven J; Namy, Laura L.; Woolf, Nancy J., *Psychology: From Inquiry To Understanding*, 2nd Ed., ©2011. Reprinted And Electronically reproduced by permission Of Pearson Education, Inc., New York, NY.

it organizes our perceptions in the brain. This top-down processing is also important when we have to decide how we plan to interact with the objects we are perceiving, a function performed by the dorsal stream of our visual system.

THE DORSAL STREAM The dorsal stream of vision extends from the visual cortex in our occipital lobe upwards to the parietal lobe. Its function is less intuitive than that of the ventral stream, but is just as important. Imagine looking at your morning cup of coffee sitting on the table you're working at. You immediately recognize that the object is a cup, and that the liquid inside of it is coffee, something you drink. You also decide that it is time to have a sip, thus requiring your arm to move so that your

hand can grasp the mug of caffeinated goodness. Someone with a healthy brain can do this effortlessly. However, someone with damage to the dorsal stream of vision would have great difficulty performing this simple function. How can we explain this impairment?

Leslie Ungerleider and Mortimer Mishkin (1982) suggested that the ventral and dorsal stream of vision could be referred to as the "what" and "where" pathways. The ventral stream identifies the object, and the dorsal stream locates it in space and allows you to interact with it. Although this description is accurate, researchers at Western University have suggested that the function of the "where" pathway is more specific (Goodale et al., 1991; Milner & Goodale, 2006). Their initial research was based

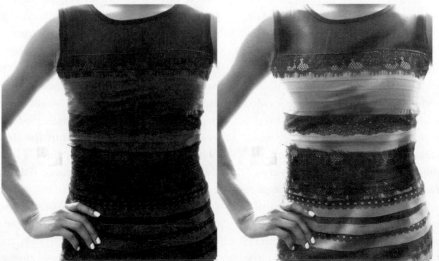

Amina Khan/NSF

Some people see "The Dress" as being blue and black (left); other people see the same dress as being white and gold (right).

Figure 4.24 Testing the Dorsal Stream

Patient D.F. was able to rotate her hand to fit an envelope into a mail slot despite having difficulties identifying either object. Her preserved dorsal stream of vision allowed her to use vision to guide her arm's motions.

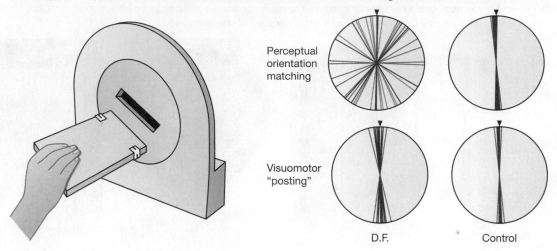

Source: Reprinted by permission from Melvyn A. Goodale.

on studies involving a patient known as "D.F." (in order to preserve patients' anonymity, their names are never provided in research papers). D.F. was a healthy middle-aged woman who suffered damage to her temporal lobe that interfered with the ventral stream of vision. As a result, her ability to recognize objects was severely impaired; indeed, she could not recognize letters or line drawings. However, she could still reach for objects as though she had perfect vision. For instance, when asked to put a letter in a mailbox, she was able to do so, even if the angle of the mail slot was changed by a sneaky researcher (see Figure 4.24). Goodale and colleagues correctly hypothesized that D.F.'s dorsal stream was preserved, and that this pathway was involved with *visually guided movement*. So, the next time you reach out to grab your caffeinated beverage from the table, remember that the "simple" ability to recognize and reach for the object requires multiple pathways in the brain.

DEPTH PERCEPTION   Our ability to use vision to guide our actions is dependent on our depth perception. We need to be able to gauge the distances between different objects as well as to determine where different objects are located relative to each other. Without this ability, it would be difficult to return a tennis serve, drive a car, or even walk through a crowded university hallway. Information related to depth perception can be detected in a number of ways.

Binocular depth cues *are distance cues that are based on the differing perspectives of both eyes.* One type of binocular depth cue, called **convergence**, *occurs when the eye muscles contract so that both eyes focus on a single object.* Convergence typically occurs for objects that are relatively close to you. For example, if you move your fingertip toward your nose, your eyes will move inward and will turn

toward each other. The sensations that occur as these muscles contract to focus on a single object provide the brain with additional information used to create the perception of depth.

One reason humans have such a fine-tuned ability to see in three dimensions is that both of our eyes face forward. This arrangement means that we perceive objects from slightly different angles, which in turn enhances depth perception. For example, choose an object in front of you, such as a pen held at arm's length from your body, and focus on that object with one eye while keeping the other eye closed. Then open your other eye to look at the object (and close the eye you were just using). You will notice that the position of your pen appears to change. This effect demonstrates **retinal disparity** (also called binocular disparity), *the difference in relative position of an object as seen by both eyes, which provides information to the brain about depth.* Your brain relies on cues from each eye individually and from both eyes working in concert—that is, in stereo. Most primates, including humans, have *stereoscopic vision*, which results from overlapping visual fields. The brain can use the difference between the information provided by the left and right eye to make judgments about the distance of the objects being viewed. Species that have eyes with no overlap in their visual field, such as some fish, likely do not require as much depth information in order to survive in their particular environment. These species might also be able to make use of depth information perceived by each eye individually.

Monocular cues *are depth cues that we can perceive with only one eye.* We have already discussed one such cue, called *accommodation*, earlier in this module. During

PSYCH@

The Artist's Studio

Although we often think of painters as being eccentric people prone to cutting off their ears, they are actually very clever amateur vision scientists. Rembrandt (1606–1669) varied the texture and colour details of different parts of portraits in order to guide the viewer's gaze toward the clearest object. The result is that more detailed regions of a painting attract attention and receive more eye fixations than less detailed areas (DiPaola et al., 2011).

In addition to manipulating a viewer's eye movements, painters also use a variety of depth cues to transform their two-dimensional painting into a three-dimensional perception. This use of *pictorial depth cues* is quite challenging, which is why some paintings seem vibrant and multilayered (like nature) while others seem flat and artificial. So what are some strategies that artists use to influence our visual perception?

To understand how artists work, view the painting by Gustave Caillebotte shown in Figure 4.25. In this painting, you will notice that the artist used numerous cues to depict depth:

- *Linear perspective:* Parallel lines stretching to the horizon appear to move closer together as they travel farther away. This effect can be seen in the narrowing of the streets and the converging lines of the sidewalks and the top of the building in the distance. This effect is nicely demonstrated by the illusion in Figure 4.26.
- *Interposition:* Nearby objects block our view of far-off objects, such as the umbrellas blocking the view of buildings behind them.
- *Light and shadow:* The shadow cast by an object allows us to detect both the size of the object and the relative locations of objects. In addition, closer objects reflect more light than far-away objects.
- *Texture gradient:* Objects that are coarse and distinct at close range become fine and grainy at greater distances. In the painting, for example, the texture of the brick street varies from clear to blurred as distance increases.
- *Height in plane:* Objects that are higher in our visual field are perceived as farther away than objects low in our visual field. The base of the main building in the background of the painting is at about the same level as the man's shoulder, but we interpret this effect as distance, not as height.
- *Relative size:* If two objects in an image are known to be of the same actual size, the larger of the two must be closer. This can be seen in the various sizes of the pedestrians.

Interestingly, Harvard neurobiologists recently speculated that Rembrandt suffered from "stereo blindness," an inability to form binocular images (Livingstone & Conway, 2004). He would therefore have had to rely on monocular cues to form the perceptions that led to his innovative depictions of the visual world.

Figure 4.25 Pictorial Depth Cues

Artists make use of cues such as linear perspective, texture gradient, relative size, and others to create the sense of depth.

Source: Sketch for *Paris, a Rainy Day,* 1877 (oil on canvas), pre-restoration (see 181504), Caillebotte, Gustave (1848–94)/Musee Marmottan Monet, Paris, France/Bridgeman Images.

Figure 4.26 The Corridor Illusion

Linear perspective and height in plane create the perception of depth here. The result is that the object at the "back" of the drawing appears to be larger than the one in the foreground; in reality, they are identical in size.

Figure 4.27 Two Monocular Depth Cues

(a) Accommodation. From the top left image light comes from a distant object, and the lens focuses the light on the retina. From the bottom left image the lens changes shape to *accommodate* the light when the same object is moved closer. (b) Motion parallax. As you look out the train window, objects close to you race past quickly and in the opposite direction that you are headed. At the same time, distant objects appear to move slowly and in the same direction that you are travelling.

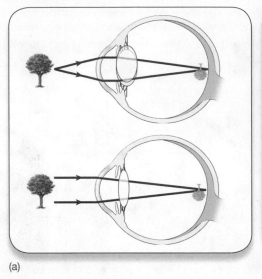

(a)

(b)

Observer movement

accommodation, the lens of your eye curves to allow you to focus on nearby objects. Close one eye and focus on a nearby object, and then slightly change your focus to an object that is farther away; the lens changes shape again so the next object comes into focus (see Figure 4.27a). The brain receives feedback about this movement which it can then use to help make judgments about depth. Another monocular cue is *motion parallax*; it is used when you or your surroundings are in motion. For example, as you sit in a moving vehicle and look out of the passenger window, you will notice objects closer to you, such as the roadside, parked cars, and nearby buildings, appear to move rapidly in the opposite direction of your travel. By comparison, far-off objects such as foothills and mountains in the distance appear to move much more slowly, and in the same direction as your vehicle. The disparity in the directions travelled by near and far-off objects provides a monocular cue about depth.

Module 4.2b Quiz:

Visual Perception and the Brain

Know . . .

1. Also called face blindness, which of the following conditions is the inability to recognize faces?

   A. Prosopagnosia

   B. Farsightedness

   C. Trichromatism

   D. Astigmatism

2. The _____ in the thalamus is where the optic nerves from the left and right eyes converge.

   A. foveal nucleus

   B. occipital nuclei

   C. lateral geniculate nucleus

   D. retinal geniculate nucleus

Understand . . .

3. A familiar person walks into the room. Which of the following choices places the structures in the appropriate sequence required to recognize the individual?

   A. Thalamus, visual cortex, photoreceptors, optic nerve

   B. Visual cortex, thalamus, photoreceptors, optic nerve

   C. Photoreceptors, optic nerve, thalamus, visual cortex

   D. Photoreceptors, thalamus, optic nerve, visual cortex

Apply . . .

4. A patient with brain damage can recognize different objects but is unable to reach out to grasp the object that she sees. This impairment is best explained by the difference between the

   A. primary and secondary visual cortices.
   B. rods and cones.
   C. temporal lobe and the frontal lobes.
   D. ventral and dorsal streams.

Analyze . . .

5. Some people claim that there is a brain area dedicated to the perception of faces. Although there is a great deal of evidence in favour of this claim, what is the best evidence *against* it?

   A. Doctors have yet to find a brain-damaged patient who cannot recognize faces.
   B. The neuroimaging studies of face perception do not show consistent results.
   C. The brain area related to face processing is also active when people see images from categories in which they have expertise.
   D. The brain area related to face processing is equally sensitive to faces that are upright or upside down.

Module 4.2 Summary

4.2a Know . . . the key terminology relating to the eye and vision.

binocular depth cues
cones
convergence
cornea
dark adaptation
fovea
iris
lens
monocular cues
opponent-process theory
optic nerve
perceptual constancy
pupil
retina
retinal disparity
rods
sclera
trichromatic theory (Young-Helmholtz theory)

4.2b Understand . . . how visual information travels from the eye through the brain to give us the experience of sight.

Light is transformed into a neural signal by photoreceptors in the retina. This information is then relayed via the optic nerve through the thalamus and then to the occipital lobe of the cortex. From this location in the brain, neural circuits travel to other regions for specific levels of processing. These include the temporal lobe for object recognition and the parietal lobe for visually guided movement.

4.2c Understand . . . the theories of colour vision.

The two theories reviewed in this module are the trichromatic and opponent-process theories. According to trichromatic theory, the retina contains three different types of cones that are sensitive to different wavelengths of light. Colour is experienced as the net combined stimulation of these receptors. The trichromatic theory is not supported by phenomena such as the negative afterimage. Opponent-process theory, which emphasizes how colour perception is based on excitation and inhibition of opposing colours (e.g., red–green, blue–yellow, white–black), explains this phenomenon. Taken together, both theories help explain how we perceive colour.

4.2d Apply . . . your knowledge to explain how we perceive depth in our visual field.

Apply Activity

For practice, take a look at the accompanying photo. Can you identify at least four monocular depth cues that are present in the image below?

Thinkstock/Getty Images

4.2e Analyze . . . how we perceive objects and faces.

Object perception is accomplished by specialized perceptual regions of the temporal lobe (the ventral stream of vision). Damage to this region can lead to impairments in recognizing specific categories of objects. Facial recognition is a specialized perceptual process, which is supported by evidence from people who are face blind but are otherwise successful at recognizing objects.

Module 4.3 The Auditory and Vestibular Systems

Francey / Shutterstock

Learning Objectives

4.3a Know . . . the key terminology relating to the ear, hearing, and the vestibular system.

4.3b Understand . . . different characteristics of sound and how they correspond to perception.

4.3c Understand . . . how the vestibular system affects our sense of balance.

4.3d Apply . . . your knowledge of sound localization.

4.3e Analyze . . . how musical beats are related to movement.

Imagine watching an action movie like Star Wars: The Force Awakens in a movie theatre with Dolby™ Surround Sound. Your body would feel the powerful vibrations of the sound waves as spaceships enter hyperspace and the characters shoot phaser guns during an exciting battle. Now imagine watching a scary movie with a killer in a Halloween mask chasing a young couple through the woods. The music becomes louder and faster, adding anxiety and emotion to the scene. Now imagine watching these movies with the sound muted. You'll have lost more than the sound waves. . .

Sounds have a dramatic effect on our experience of movies (and to a lesser extent, television). Paramount among these is music. Can you imagine Star Wars without the familiar John Williams theme, or a horror movie without tension-inducing music? The movies would lose their emotional impact almost immediately. This is because music perception

activates regions of the brain related to emotional perception (Bhatara et al., 2011; Gosselin et al., 2005). Indeed, in a novel study, researchers at the Université de Montréal and Concordia University found that patients with damage to the amygdala, an area of the brain related to the experience of fear, were impaired in their ability to recognize that particular pieces of music, such as the theme to Jaws, were scary. Studies such as this imply that in healthy brains, the emotion centres respond during the perception of music in order to help us understand its meaning. They also show us how important the auditory system is to how we experience our world.

Focus Questions

1. How does the auditory system sense and perceive something complex like music?

2. How do we localize sounds in our environment?

Figure 4.28 Characteristics of Sound: Frequency and Amplitude

The frequency of a sound wave (cycles per second) is associated with pitch, while amplitude (the height of the sound wave) is associated with loudness.

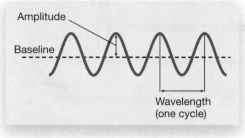

(a) Long-wavelength (low-frequency) sound

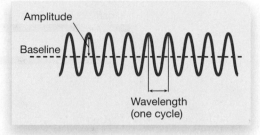

(b) Short-wavelength (high-frequency) sound

Source: Lilienfeld, Scott O.; Lynn, Steven J; Namy, Laura L.; Woolf, Nancy J., *Psychology: From Inquiry To Understanding*, 2nd Ed., ©2011. Reprinted And Electronically Reproduced By Permission Of Pearson Education, Inc., New York, NY.

» In this module we will explore characteristics of sound, the physical structures that support the sensation of sound, and the pathways involved in its perceptual processing. We will also examine how music affects memory and emotion, and how this relationship can influence our behaviour.

Sound and the Structures of the Ear

The function of the ear is to gather sound waves. The function of *hearing* is to extract some sort of meaning from those sound waves; this meaning informs you about the nature of the sound source, such as someone calling your name, a referee's whistle, or a vehicle coming toward you. How do people gain so much information from invisible waves that travel through the air?

SOUND   The function of that remarkably sensitive and delicate device, the human ear, is to detect *sound waves* and to transform them into neural signals. Sound waves are simply changes in mechanical pressure transmitted through solids, liquids, or gases. Sound waves have two important characteristics: frequency and amplitude (see Figure 4.28). *Frequency* refers to wavelength and is measured in hertz (Hz), the number of cycles a sound wave travels per second. **Pitch** *is the perceptual experience of sound wave frequencies.* High-frequency sounds, such as tires screeching on the road, have short wavelengths and a high pitch. Low-frequency sounds, such as those produced by a bass guitar, have long wavelengths and a low pitch. The *amplitude* of a sound wave determines its loudness: High-amplitude sound waves are louder than low-amplitude waves. Both types of information are gathered and analyzed by our ears.

Humans are able to detect sounds in the frequency range from 20 Hz to 20 000 Hz. Figure 4.29 compares the

hearing ranges of several different species. Look closely at the scale of the figure—the differences are of a much greater magnitude than could possibly fit on this page using a standard scale. The comparisons show that mice, for example, can hear frequencies close to five times greater than humans, but have difficulty hearing lower frequencies that we can easily detect.

Loudness—a function of sound wave amplitude—is typically expressed in units called decibels (dB). Table 4.2 compares decibel levels ranging from nearly inaudible to injury inducing. Although we doubt you spend much time beside jet engines, we do suggest wearing earplugs to concerts to protect your ears, even if they don't match your always-stylish "I'm a Belieber" t-shirt.

THE HUMAN EAR   The human ear is divided into outer, middle, and inner regions (see Figure 4.30). The most noticeable part of your ear is the *pinna*, the outer region that helps channel sound waves to the ear and allows you to determine the source or location of a sound. The *auditory canal* extends from the pinna to the eardrum. Sound waves reaching the eardrum cause it to vibrate. Even very soft sounds, such as a faint whisper, produce vibrations of the eardrum. The middle ear consists of three tiny moveable bones called *ossicles*, known individually as the malleus (hammer), incus (anvil), and stapes (stirrup). The eardrum is attached to these bones, so any movement of the eardrum due to sound vibrations results in movement of the ossicles.

The ossicles attach to an inner ear structure called the **cochlea**—*a fluid-filled membrane that is coiled in a snail-like shape and contains the structures that convert sound into neural impulses.* Converting sound vibrations to neural impulses is possible because of hair-like projections that line the *basilar membrane* of the cochlea. The pressing and pulling action of the ossicles causes

Figure 4.29 A Comparison of Hearing Ranges in Different Species

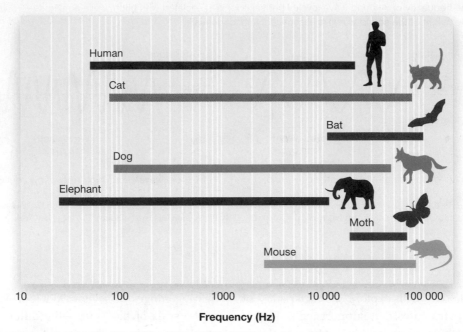

Source: Based on Fay, R.R. (1988) and Warfield, D. (1973).

parts of the basilar membrane to flex. This causes the fluid within the cochlea to move, displacing these tiny hair cells. When hair cells move, they stimulate the cells that comprise the auditory nerves. The auditory nerves are composed of bundles of neurons that fire as a result of hair cell movements. These auditory nerves send signals to the thalamus—the sensory relay station of the brain—and then to the auditory cortex, located within the temporal lobes.

As you might expect, damage to any part of the auditory system will result in hearing impairments. However, recent technological advances are allowing individuals to compensate for this hearing loss. *Cochlear implants* are now quite common and have been used to help tens of thousands of individuals regain some of their hearing. These devices typically consist of a small microphone that detects sounds from the outside world and electronically stimulates parts of the membranes in the cochlea

Table 4.2 Decibel Levels for Some Familiar Sounds

Sound	Noise Level (dB)	Effect
Jet engines (near)	140	We begin to feel pain at about 125 dB
Rock concerts (varies)	110–140	
Thunderclap (near)	120	Regular exposure to sound over 100 dB for more than one minute risks permanent hearing loss
Power saw (chainsaw)	110	
Garbage truck/Cement mixer	100	No more than 15 minutes of unprotected exposure is recommended for sounds between 90 and 100 dB
Motorcycle (25 ft)	88	85 dB is the level at which hearing damage (after eight hours) begins
Lawn mower	85–90	
Average city traffic	80	Annoying; interferes with conversation; constant exposure may cause damage
Vacuum cleaner	70	Intrusive; interferes with telephone conversation
Normal conversation	50–65	Comfortable hearing levels are under 60 dB
Whisper	30	Very quiet
Rustling leaves	20	Just audible

Figure 4.30 The Human Ear

Sound waves travel from the outer ear to the eardrum and middle ear, and then through the inner ear. The cochlea of the inner ear is the site at which transduction takes place through movement of the tiny hair cells lining the basilar membrane. The auditory cortex of the brain is a primary brain region where sound is perceived.

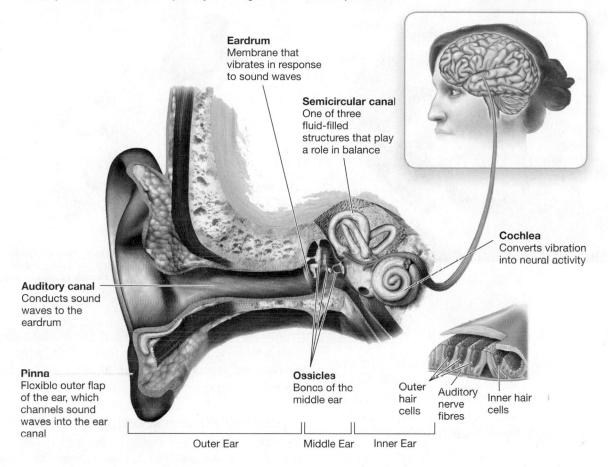

Eardrum
Membrane that vibrates in response to sound waves

Semicircular canal
One of three fluid-filled structures that play a role in balance

Cochlea
Converts vibration into neural activity

Auditory canal
Conducts sound waves to the eardrum

Pinna
Flexible outer flap of the ear, which channels sound waves into the ear canal

Ossicles
Bones of the middle ear

Outer hair cells

Auditory nerve fibres

Inner hair cells

Outer Ear   Middle Ear   Inner Ear

(see Figure 4.31). Although these devices are not a perfect substitute for a normally functioning auditory system, they do allow individuals to hear low-frequency sounds such as those used in human speech. These devices are particularly useful for young children (Fitzpatrick et al., 2011; Peterson et al., 2010), as the brains of children more easily form new pathways in response to the stimulation from the implants.

Module 4.3a Quiz:

Sound and the Structures of the Ear

Know . . .

1. The _____ is the quality of sound waves that is associated with changes in pitch.
   A. frequency
   B. amplitude
   C. pinna
   D. decibel

2. The _____ is a snail-shaped, fluid-filled organ that converts sound waves into neural signals.
   A. ossicle
   B. pinna
   C. cochlea
   D. outer ear

Understand . . .

3. The amplitude of a sound wave determines its loudness; _____ -amplitude sound waves are louder than _____ -amplitude waves.
   A. low; high
   B. short; tall
   C. wide; narrow
   D. high; low

Figure 4.31 A Cochlear Implant

The speech processor and microphone are located just above the pinna. A wire with tiny electrodes attached is routed through the cochlea.

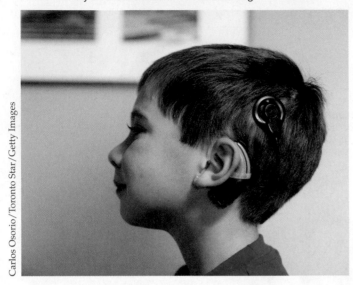

Carlos Osorio/Toronto Star/Getty Images

Figure 4.32 How We Localize Sound

To localize sound, the brain computes the small difference in time at which the sound reaches each of the ears. The brain also registers differences in loudness that reach both ears.

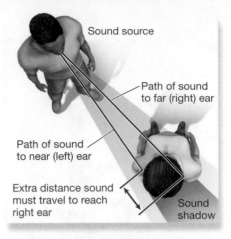

Source: Lilienfeld, Scott O.; Lynn, Steven J; Namy, Laura L.; Woolf, Nancy J., *Psychology: From Inquiry To Understanding*, 2nd Ed., ©2011. Reprinted And Electronically reproduced by permission Of Pearson Education, Inc., New York, NY.

The Perception of Sound

It is quite remarkable that we are able to determine what makes a sound and where the sound comes from by simply registering and processing sound waves. In this section we examine how the auditory system accomplishes these two tasks, starting with the ability to locate a sound in the environment.

SOUND LOCALIZATION: FINDING THE SOURCE Accurately identifying and orienting oneself toward a sound source has some obvious adaptive benefits. Over the course of evolution, failure to do so could result in an organism becoming someone else's dinner, or failing to catch dinner of one's own. Thus, auditory systems have developed to allow organisms, including humans, to orient toward sounds in the environment. This **sound localization**, *the process of identifying where sound comes from*, is handled by parts of the brainstem as well as by a midbrain structure called the *inferior colliculus*.

There are two ways that we localize sound. First, we take advantage of the slight time difference between a sound hitting both ears to estimate the direction of the source. If your friend shouts your name from your left side, the left ear will receive the information a fraction of a second before the right ear. Second, we localize sound by using differences in the intensity in which sound is heard by both ears—a phenomenon known as a *sound shadow* (Figure 4.32). If the source of the sound is to your left, the left ear will experience the sound more intensely than the right because the right ear will be in the sound shadow. Nuclei in the brainstem detect differences in the

times when sound reaches the left versus the right ear (Carr & Konishi, 1990), as well as the intensity of the sound between one side and the other, allowing us to identify where it is coming from.

THEORIES OF PITCH PERCEPTION To explain how we perceive pitch, we will begin in the cochlea and work toward brain centres that are specialized for hearing. How does the cochlea pave the way for pitch perception? One explanation involves the specific arrangement of hair cells along the basilar membrane. Not all hair cells along the basilar membrane are equally responsive to sounds within the 20 to 20 000 Hz range of human hearing. High-frequency sounds stimulate hair cells closest to the ossicles, whereas lower-frequency sounds stimulate hair cells toward the end of the cochlea (see Figure 4.33). Thus, *how we perceive pitch is based on the location (place) along the basilar membrane that sound stimulates*, a tendency known as the **place theory of hearing**.

Another determinant of how and what we hear is the rate at which the ossicles press into the cochlea, sending a wave of activity down the basilar membrane. According to **frequency theory**, *the perception of pitch is related to the frequency at which the basilar membrane vibrates*. A 70-Hz sound stimulates the hair cells 70 times per second. Thus, 70 nerve impulses per second travel from the auditory nerves to the brain, which interprets the sound frequency in terms of pitch (Figure 4.33). However, we quickly reach an upper limit on the capacity of the auditory nerves to send signals to the brain: Neurons cannot fire more than 1000 times per second. Given this limit, how can

Figure 4.33 The Basilar Membrane of the Cochlea and Theories of Hearing

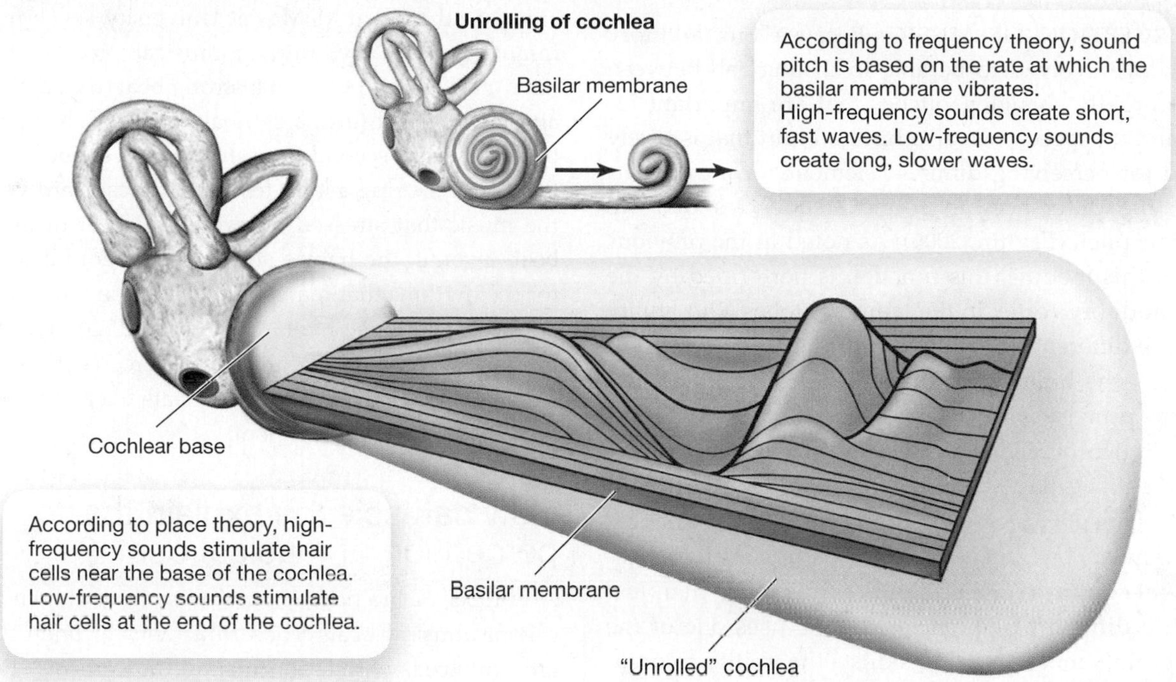

Unrolling of cochlea

Basilar membrane

According to frequency theory, sound pitch is based on the rate at which the basilar membrane vibrates. High-frequency sounds create short, fast waves. Low-frequency sounds create long, slower waves.

Cochlear base

According to place theory, high-frequency sounds stimulate hair cells near the base of the cochlea. Low-frequency sounds stimulate hair cells at the end of the cochlea.

Basilar membrane

"Unrolled" cochlea

Source: "A Cochlear Implant" "Cochlear Implant" (Fig. 3.9, p. 104) from *Psychology*, 3rd edition, by Saundra Ciccarelli & J. Noland White. Copyright © 2012. Printed and electronically reproduced by permission of Pearson Education, Inc., Upper Saddle River, New Jersey.

we hear sounds exceeding 1000 Hz? The answer lies in the *volley principle*. According to the volley principle, groups of neurons fire in alternating (hence the term "volley") fashion. A sound measuring 5000 Hz can be perceived because groups of neurons fire in rapid succession (Wever & Bray, 1930).

Currently, the place, frequency, and volley theories are all needed to explain our experience of hearing. When we hear complex stimuli, such as music, the place, frequency, and volley principles are likely all functioning at the sensory level. However, turning this sensory information into the perception of music, voices, and other important sounds occurs in specialized regions of the brain.

AUDITORY PERCEPTION AND THE BRAIN The **primary auditory cortex** *is a major perceptual centre of the brain involved in perceiving what we hear*. The auditory cortex is organized in very similar fashion to the cochlea. Cells within different areas across the auditory cortex respond to specific frequencies. For example, high musical notes are processed at one end of the auditory cortex, and progressively lower notes are heard as you move to the opposite end (Wang, Lu, et al., 2005). As in the visual system, the primary auditory cortex is surrounded by brain regions that provide additional sensory processing. This *secondary auditory cortex* helps us to interpret complex sounds, including those found in speech and music. Interestingly, the auditory cortices in the two hemispheres of the brain

are not equally sensitive. In most individuals the right hemisphere is able to detect smaller changes in pitch than the left hemisphere (Hyde et al., 2007). Given this fact, it is not surprising that the right hemisphere is also superior at detecting sarcasm, as this type of humour is linked to the tone of voice used (Voyer et al., 2008).

However, we are not born with a fully developed auditory cortex. In order to perceive our complex auditory world, the auditory cortices must *learn* to analyze different patterns of sounds. Researchers have identified a number of different changes in the brain's responses to sounds during the course of development. Brain imaging studies have shown that infants as young as three months of age are able to detect simple changes in pitch (He et al., 2007, 2009). Infants can detect silent gaps in a tone (an ability that may help us learn languages) between the ages of 4 to 6 months (Trainor et al., 2003), and develop the ability to localize sound at approximately 8 months of age (Trainor, 2010). By 12 months of age, the auditory system starts to become specialized for the culture in which the infant is living. Infants who are 10–12 months of age do not recognize sound patterns that are not meaningful in their native language or culture (Werker & Lalonde, 1988); indeed, children in this age group show different patterns of brain activity when hearing culturally familiar and unfamiliar sounds (Fujioka et al., 2011). This brain plasticity explains why many of us have difficulty hearing fine distinctions in the sounds of languages we are exposed to later in life. Interestingly, this fine-tuning of the auditory cortex also influences how we perceive music.

THE PERCEPTION OF MUSIC Because our auditory systems have evolved to be able to distinguish between different rapidly changing pitches that are important for understanding speech, we also have a brain that is nicely designed for perceiving different elements of music, particularly the differences in sound frequencies that we perceive as pitch (Levitin, 2006). As noted in the previous section of this module, this function is performed by the primary auditory cortex in the temporal lobes. Our ability to compare different pitches also uses the secondary auditory cortex, the brain areas immediately in front of and behind the primary auditory cortex (see Zatorre & Zarate, 2010). Both neuroimaging studies and studies with brain-damaged patients have shown that the auditory cortices in the right hemisphere are particularly sensitive to nuances in pitch (Hyde, Peretz, et al., 2008; Johnsrude et al., 2000).

However, music perception requires more than just perceiving different frequencies. It also uses one of the human brain's most amazing skills—the ability to organize information into a coherent structure or pattern.

Working the Scientific Literacy Model

The Perception of Musical Beats

The next time you listen to music, concentrate on what you are thinking and on how your body is responding. Do you find yourself subtly moving with the music? Are you tapping your fingers or feet to the beat? Do you sing (or hum) along to the music? Most people are able to perform some or all of these musical responses, even if they have no musical training. In the last decade, psychologists have begun to unravel the perceptual and neural processes that allow us to do so.

What do we know about the perception of musical beats?

Our brains are pattern-recognition machines. In terms of music, this ability is most clearly shown by our ability to detect metrical structure, or groups of stronger and weaker events that we perceive as musical beats. When we listen to music, most people are able to detect the fact that certain patterns tend to repeat; as a result, our brains begin to expect beats to occur at specific times (Large & Palmer, 2002). This is the basis of our ability to detect musical beats or rhythms. As a result, we can tap our fingers to any song we hear on the radio, from Nicky Minaj to Nickelback.

This ability to detect rhythms or beats appears to be innate—even babies can do it! In one study, babies were exposed to a series of musical beats. Babies showed distinct changes in brain activity when they heard sound files that skipped a beat (Winkler et al., 2008). Interestingly, this ability appears to be linked to motion. In an innovative study conducted at McMaster University, seven-month-old infants heard a two-minute musical piece that did not have a difference between a strong beat (e.g., a bass drum) and a weak beat (e.g., a cymbal). Some of the babies were bounced every second beat and some were bounced every third beat. During a later test, the babies heard versions of the music that stressed every second beat or every third beat. Overall, the babies showed behavioural preferences for the rhythms that matched the beats on which they were bounced (Phillips-Silver & Trainor, 2005). The fact that motion influences how humans perceive musical beats suggests that detection of these beats likely involves brain systems related to movement.

How can science explain the perception of musical beats?

A number of brain imaging studies have shown that perceiving musical beats leads to activity in brain areas that are involved with coordinating movements (Merchant et al., 2015). For example, researchers have shown that individual differences in the ability to detect musical beats are linked to differences in activity in the basal ganglia (Grahn & McAuley, 2009), a group of brain structures in the centre of the brain that are related to the coordination of movement. Additional studies have tried to figure out if the basal ganglia are involved with *discovering* a beat or *maintaining an internal representation* of a beat, an ability that would allow the individual to predict future beats once the rhythm has been discovered. In one study by Jessica Grahn of Western University, brain activity was measured while participants first learned a beat (i.e., discovered a beat) and when participants were familiar with a beat (i.e., maintained an internal representation). Activity in the putamen, one part of the basal ganglia, was much higher when a familiar beat was repeatedly presented to the participants (Grahn & Rowe, 2013).

Importantly, the basal ganglia do not work alone. As with most of our behaviours, detecting musical beats involves a number of brain areas working together as a team. When we perceive beats, there is an increase in connectivity (brain areas firing together) between the basal ganglia and areas of the frontal lobe related to the planning of movements (Grahn & Rowe, 2009). In fact, one study showed that this coordinated brain activity increased as the beat became more noticeable (Chen et al., 2008); however, more research is needed before we draw any definitive conclusions.

Can we critically evaluate this information?

Although the evidence linking the basal ganglia to our ability to maintain a musical beat is compelling, we need to remember that brain imaging experiments show which

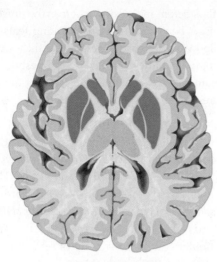

The basal ganglia is a group of structures in the centre of your brain. Activity in this region is related to our ability to detect musical beats.

areas of the brain are *active*; this does not guarantee that these regions are *necessary* for a function to occur. We therefore need evidence from other types of research studies to support this finding. Recently, researchers found that individuals with Parkinson's disease—who have damage to structures that input to the basal ganglia—have difficulty picking out subtle musical beats (Grahn, 2009).

However, it is still possible that previous experience influenced these results to some degree. Almost everyone has heard musical beats; this previous knowledge might influence how we perceive new beats. Although this problem might seem impossible to solve, music researchers have found an interesting solution: play musical beats to animals. To do this, researchers measured the firing rates

of brain cells in monkeys while they listened to repeated beats and random noise. Greater firing occurred in the putamen (basal ganglia) of monkeys when they heard a familiar beat (Barolo et al., 2014). Therefore, there is evidence from multiple types of research studies linking the perception of music to brain areas related to movement, specifically the basal ganglia.

Why is this relevant?

The link between musical beats and movement systems should make intuitive sense to most of you; it's almost impossible to listen to music without moving in some way. Musical beats allows people to synchronize movements with each other, leading to coordinated behaviours ranging from dancing to rocking a baby to sleep. Interestingly, this ability is influenced by culture. Growing up in a given culture leads us to be more familiar with some musical rules and patterns than others; as a result, people from different cultures will have different rhythmic expectations and will therefore be more sensitive to certain musical rhythms (Levitin, 2006).

As you can see, the detection of musical beats influences many aspects of our lives. But, discussing beats in terms of movement systems only tells part of the story. Think about the last time you danced; as you were moving, your body was adjusting its position so that you were (hopefully) able to avoid falling on your face. The body's ability to do so leads us to a discussion of another role played by the structures found within our ears: balance.

Module 4.3b Quiz:

The Perception of Sound

Know . . .

1. The primary auditory cortex is found in which lobe of the brain?
   A. Frontal
   B. Temporal
   C. Occipital
   D. Parietal

Understand . . .

2. _____explains pitch perception when hair cells are stimulated at the same rate that a sound wave cycles.
   A. Place theory
   B. Frequency theory
   C. The volley principle
   D. Switch theory

3. Neurons cannot fire fast enough to keep up with high-pitched sound waves. Therefore, they alternate firing according to the _____.
   A. place theory
   B. frequency theory
   C. volley principle
   D. switch theory

Apply . . .

4. While crossing the street, you know a car is approaching on your left side because
   A. the left ear got the information just a fraction of a second before the right ear.
   B. the right ear got the information just a fraction of a second before the left ear.
   C. the right ear experienced the sound more intensely than the left ear.
   D. both ears experienced the sound at the same intensity.

The vestibular system in the inner ear provides information about the head's movement and spatial orientation. It is crucial for our sense of balance. Sports such as gymnastics and freestyle skiing rely heavily on this system.

The Vestibular System

On February 10, 2014, Canadian freestyle skier Alexandre Bilodeau stood at the top of the moguls course at the Rosa Khudor Extreme Park in Sochi, Russia. His Russian rival, Alexandr Smyshlyaev, had just amazed the crowd by performing a flip *while grabbing his skis* after going over one of the two jumps on the course. Bilodeau needed to put in an almost perfect run if he was to repeat as Olympic gold medallist. As he began the course, Bilodeau maintained his balance while carving perfect turns around the moguls. As his descent continued, he picked up more speed and hurtled toward the first jump, which had caused many of his competitors to fall. Undaunted, he leapt up, performed multiple twists in the air, and landed with his feet again in perfect moguls stance. He continued down the course and picked up even more speed before taunting gravity again with a dazzling display of twists and flips before racing down across the finish line. The gold was his. When we watch breathtaking feats of athleticism like Bilodeau's, it's easy to forget that these abilities rely on our perceptual abilities. In the case of freestyle skiing, the ability to maintain one's balance is related to the activity of two structures in the inner part of the ears.

SENSATION AND THE VESTIBULAR SYSTEM Our sense of balance is controlled, at least in part, by our **vestibular system**, *a sensory system in the ear that provides information about spatial orientation of the head as well as head motion*. This system consists of two groups of structures (see Figure 4.34). The **vestibular sacs** *are structures that influence your ability to detect when your head is no longer in an upright position*. This section of your vestibular system is made up of two parts, the *utricle* ("little pouch") and the *saccule* ("little sac"). The bottom of both of these sacs is lined with cilia (small hair cells) embedded in a gelatinous substance. When you tilt your head, the gelatin moves and causes the cilia to bend. This bending of the cilia opens up ion channels, leading to an action potential.

Your ability to perceive when your head is in motion involves a separate group of vestibular structures. The **semicircular canals** are *three fluid-filled canals found in the inner ear that respond when your head moves in different directions (up-down, left-right, forward-backward)*. Receptors in each of these canals respond to movement along one of these planes. At the base of each of these canals is an enlarged area called the *ampulla*. The neural activity within the ampulla is similar to that of the vestibular sacs—cilia (hair cells) are embedded within a gelatinous mass. When you move your head in different directions, as Alexandre Bilodeau did during his flips, the gelatin moves and causes the cilia to bend. This bending, again, makes an action potential more likely to occur.

Figure 4.34 The Vestibular System

The vestibular system consists of two groups of structures. The vestibular sacs detect our head's position, particularly when it is no longer upright. The semicircular canals—shown in detail on the left—detect when our head is in motion. Both structures send information to nuclei in the brainstem.

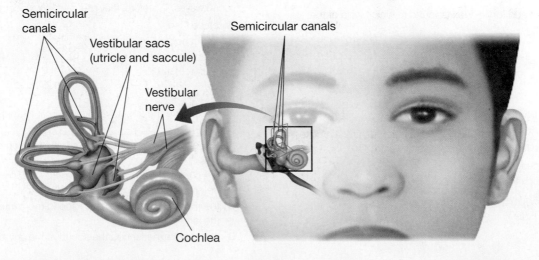

Although it may seem as though the vestibular system would only fire when we moved our heads in different directions, the vestibular sacs and semicircular canals actually provide the brain with a continuous flow of information about the head's position and movement (Tascioglu, 2005). This constant input from the vestibular system allows us to keep our head upright and to maintain our balance. When you have an inner ear infection, this stream of input can be disrupted. The result is dizziness and a loss of balance.

THE VESTIBULAR SYSTEM AND THE BRAIN Of course, for the activity of the vestibular sacs and semicircular canals to have an effect on our perceptual experiences, they need to transmit information from the inner ear to the brain. These two parts of the vestibular system send information along the vestibular ganglion, a large nerve fibre, to nuclei in the brainstem. Vestibular nuclei can then influence activity in a number of brain areas. For instance, the panic we feel when we lean too far back in a chair is likely due to the fact that vestibular nuclei in the brainstem influence the activity of your autonomic nervous system ("fight or flight") as well as the amygdala, an emotion centre of the brain (Petrovich & Swanson, 1997; Carmona et al., 2009). The vestibular nuclei also project to part of the insula, an area of cortex that is folded in the interior of the brain (de Waele et al., 2001; Guldin & Grusser, 1998). This region helps us link together visual, somatosensory, and vestibular information. At times, however, this process goes awry.

Have you ever experienced motion sickness, perhaps when trying to read while in moving vehicle? One reason for this feeling is an inconsistency in the input from your visual and vestibular systems. The visual input (i.e., the words on the page) is not moving, yet your vestibular system is sending signals to your brain saying that your body is in a moving car. The driver, on the other hand, sees (and controls) the movement of the car; he or she therefore has the same movement-related information arriving from both sensory systems.

This link between the vestibular system and other senses brings us back to the example of Alexandre Bilodeau, the freestyle skier discussed earlier in this section. In order to maintain balance, Bilodeau had to receive input from his vestibular sacs and semicircular canals. But, he also needed to have information about kinesthesis, the sense of bodily motion and position (see Module 4.4). Together, this input allowed Bilodeau to maintain his balance while he performed his gravity-defying jumps and to continue skiing around the moguls when he landed. Without these inner ear structures and feedback from his body, Bilodeau's trip to the Sochi Olympics would certainly have been less golden.

Module 4.3c Quiz:

The Vestibular System

Know . . .

1. The structures that detect head motion are known as the _____.
   A. vestibular sacs
   B. ossicles
   C. tympanic membranes
   D. semicircular canals

Apply . . .

2. Mr. Cerveaux went to his doctor to complain about dizziness and problems with balance. Which of the following is NOT a likely explanation for his symptoms?
   A. Mr. Cerveaux might have a tumour affecting his vestibular nerve.
   B. Mr. Cerveaux experienced brain damage that affected his left and right occipital lobes.
   C. Mr. Cerveaux might have an inner ear infection.
   D. Mr. Cerveaux might have had a small stroke (a blockage of a blood vessel in the brain) that damaged his insula.

Module 4.3 Summary

4.3a   Know . . . the key terminology relating to the ear and hearing.

cochlea
frequency theory
pitch
place theory of hearing
primary auditory cortex
semicircular canals
sound localization
vestibular sacs
vestibular system

4.3b   Understand . . . different characteristics of sound and how they correspond to perception.

Sound can be analyzed based on its frequency (the number of cycles a sound wave travels per second) as well as on its amplitude (the height of a sound wave). Our experience of pitch is based on sound wave frequencies. Amplitude corresponds to loudness: The higher the amplitude, the louder the sound.

4.3c Understand . . . how the vestibular system affects our sense of balance.

The vestibular system consists of two components, the vestibular sacs and the semicircular canals. The vestibular sacs note the position of the head relative to the body. The semicircular canals note when the head is in motion. Both structures send information to brain regions that integrate vestibular information with input from other senses; this process allows us to maintain our balance.

4.3d Apply . . . your knowledge of sound localization.

Apply Activity

Get a friend to participate in a quick localization demonstration. Have her sit with her eyes closed, covering her right ear with her hand. Now walk quietly in a circle around your friend, stopping occasionally to snap your fingers. When you do this, your friend should point to where you are standing, based solely on the sound. If her right ear is covered, at which points will she be most accurate? At which points will she have the most errors? Use the principles of sound localization to make your predictions.

4.3e Analyze . . . how musical beats are related to movement.

It seems intuitive that music and movement are related. However, testing this relationship involves critical thinking. Although brain imaging studies in healthy individuals have shown basal ganglia activity when people follow beats, we must remember that this activity does not mean that the basal ganglia are *necessary* for beat perception. However, studies of patients with damage to the basal ganglia, structures in the middle of the brain related to movement, show that these structures *are* likely necessary for us to be able to follow a musical beat. Together, these studies provide a scientific explanation for our ability to tap our fingers to the rhythm of our favourite songs.

Module 4.4   Touch and the Chemical Senses

tuja66/Getty Images

  Learning Objectives

4.4a   Know . . . the key terminology of touch and chemical senses.

4.4b   Understand . . . how pain messages travel to the brain.

4.4c   Understand . . . the relationship between smell, taste, and food flavour experience.

4.4d   Apply . . . your knowledge about touch to describe the acuity of different areas of skin.

4.4e   Apply . . . your knowledge to determine whether you or someone you know is a "supertaster."

4.4f   Analyze . . . how different senses are combined together.

Would you ever describe your breakfast cereal as tasting pointy or round? Probably not. Touch, taste, and smell combine together to make your favourite foods, yet most of us can still identify the separate components associated with what is felt, tasted, and smelled. Individuals with a condition called synesthesia *experience blended perceptions, such that affected individuals might actually hear colours or feel sounds (Cytowic, 1993). For the individuals who experience this condition, even letters or numbers may have a colour associated with them. To illustrate this effect, find the number 2 below:*

5555555555555555555555
5555555555555555555555
5555555555555525555555
5555555555555555555555

People who have a type of synesthesia in which words or numbers have unique colours associated with them find the 2 faster than people without synesthesia because the colours cause the 2 to "pop out" (Blake et al., 2005). In some individuals, even the idea of a number can elicit a colourful response (Dixon et al., 2000). Synesthesia can also involve blending taste and touch, which certainly can influence dining experiences. People may avoid oatmeal because it tastes bland, but can you imagine avoiding a food because it tastes "pointy," or relishing another food because of its delicate hints of corduroy? Synesthesia occurs in an estimated 1 in 500 people. For the 499 others, touch, taste, and smell are distinct senses.

Focus Questions

1. How are our experiences of touch, taste, and smell distinct?

2. What are the different types of sensations that are detected by our sense of touch?

» Generally speaking, vision and hearing are the senses that we seem to be aware of the most and, therefore, have received the most attention from researchers. In this module, we will explore the senses of touch, taste, and smell. Putting them together in a single module is not meant to diminish their importance, however. Our quality of life, and possibly our survival, would be severely compromised without these senses. We will also examine how we combine information from our different senses into vibrant *multimodal* experiences, such as when taste and smell are combined to create a perception of flavour.

The Sense of Touch

The sense of touch allows us to actively investigate our environment and the objects that are in it (Lederman & Klatzky, 2004; Lederman et al., 2007). Using touch, we can acquire information about texture, temperature, and pressure upon the skin. These different forms of stimulation are combined to give us a vivid physical sense of every moment. Imagine you're at a concert. You don't just hear music. You *feel* the vibrations of the bass rippling through you. You *feel* the heat of the crowd. You *feel* other people brushing up against you. And, you *feel* your own body moving to the rhythm of the music. These sensual experiences—which seem so social and so distant from the nervous system—are dependent on the actions of several types of receptors located just beneath the surface of the skin, and also in the muscles, joints, and tendons. These receptors send information to the *somatosensory cortex* in the parietal lobes of the brain, the neural region associated with your sense of touch.

Sensitivity to touch varies across different regions of the body. One simple method of testing sensitivity, or *acuity*, is to use the two-point threshold test shown in Figure 4.35. Regions with high acuity, such as the fingertips, can detect the two separate, but closely spaced, pressure points of the device, whereas less sensitive regions such as the lower back will perceive the same stimuli as only one pressure point. Body parts such as the fingertips, palms, and lips are highly sensitive to touch compared to regions such as the calves and forearm. Research has shown that women have a slightly more refined sense of touch than men, precisely because their fingers (and therefore their receptors) are smaller (Peters et al., 2009). Importantly, the sensitivity of different parts of the body also influences how much space in the somatosensory cortex is dedicated to analyzing each body part's sensations (see Figure 3.27 in Module 3.3). Regions of the body that send a lot of sensory input to the brain such as the lips have taken over large portions of the somatosensory cortex while less sensitive regions like the thigh use much less neural space (see Figure 4.36).

Like vision and hearing, touch is very sensitive to change. Merely laying your hand on the surface of an object does little to help identify it. What we need is an active exploration that stimulates receptors in the hand. **Haptics** *is the active, exploratory aspect of touch sensation and perception*. Active touch involves feedback. For example,

---

Figure 4.35 Two-Point Threshold Device for Measuring Touch Acuity

The more sensitive regions of the body can detect two points even when they are spaced very close together. Less sensitive parts of the body have much larger two-point thresholds.

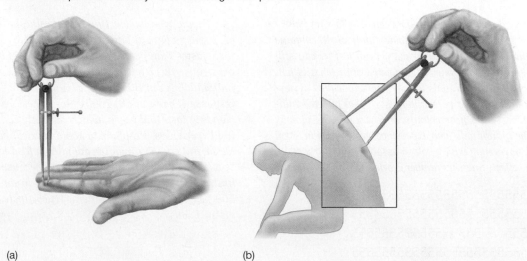

(a)　　　　　　　　　　　　　(b)

Figure 4.36 The Sensory Homunculus

Sensitive areas of the body used to acquire somatosensory information use larger portions of the somatosensory cortex than less sensitive body parts. The amount of cortex used by each body part is represented in the homunculus ("little man") depicted below.

BSIP SA/Alamy Stock Photo

Figure 4.37 The Sense of Kinesthesis

Receptors in muscles and joints send sensory messages to the brain, helping us maintain awareness and control of our movements. Muscle spindles and Golgi tendon organs are sensory receptors that provide information about changes in muscle length and tension.

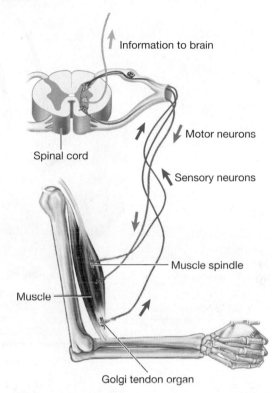

Source: From KALAT. *Biological Psychology*, 10E. © 2009 South-Western, a part of Cengage Learning, Inc. Reproduced by permission. www.cengage.com/permissions

as you handle an object, such as a piece of fruit, you move your fingers over its surface to identify whether any faults may be present. Your fingertips can help you determine whether the object is the appropriate shape and can detect bruising or abnormalities that may make it unsuitable to eat. Haptics allows us not only to identify objects, but also to avoid damaging or dropping them. Fingers and hands coordinate their movements using a complementary body sense called **kinesthesis**, *the sense of bodily motion and position*. Receptors for kinesthesis reside in the muscles, joints, and tendons. These receptors transmit information about movement and the position of your muscles, limbs, and joints to the brain (Figure 4.37). As you handle an object, your kinesthetic sense allows you to hold it with enough resistance to avoid dropping it, and to keep your hands and fingers set in such a way as to avoid letting it roll out of your hands. Touch, therefore, provides us with a great deal of information about our bodies and the world around us.

FEELING PAIN   Of course, not all of the information we receive from our sense of touch is pleasant. **Nociception** *is the activity of nerve pathways that respond to uncomfortable stimulation*. Our skin, teeth, corneas, and internal organs contain nerve endings called *nociceptors*, which are receptors that initiate pain messages that travel to the central nervous system (see Figure 4.38). Nociceptors come in varieties that respond to various types of stimuli—for example, to sharp stimulation, such as a pin prick, or to extreme heat or cold (Julius & Basbaum, 2001).

Two types of nerve fibres transmit pain messages. Fast fibres register sharp, immediate pain, such as the pain felt when your skin is scraped or cut. Slow fibres register chronic, dull pain, such as the lingering feelings of bumping your knee into the coffee table. Although both slow and fast fibres eventually send input to the brain, these impulses first must travel to cells in the spinal cord; the firing of neurons within the spinal cord will influence how this pain is experienced.

The activity of pathways in the spinal cord can explain several interesting characteristics of pain perception, including why you feel better if you rub your toe after stubbing it on your coffee table. One long-held theory of pain perception is the **gate-control theory**, *which explains our experience of pain as an interaction between nerves that transmit pain messages and those that inhibit these messages*. According to this theory, cells in the spinal cord regulate how much pain signalling reaches the brain. The spinal cord serves as a "neural gate" that pain messages must pass through (Melzack & Wall, 1965, 1982). The spinal cord contains small nerve fibres that conduct pain messages

Figure 4.38 Cross-Section of Skin and Free Nerve Endings That Respond to Pain

The nerve endings that respond to pain reside very close to the surface of the skin and, as you are likely aware, are very sensitive to stimulation.

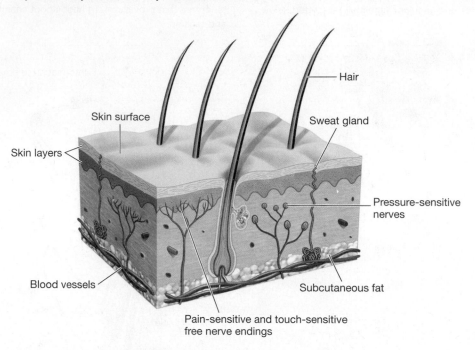

Hair

Skin surface

Sweat gland

Skin layers

Pressure-sensitive nerves

Blood vessels

Subcutaneous fat

Pain-sensitive and touch-sensitive free nerve endings

Source: Ciccarelli, Saundra K.; White, J. Noland, *Psychology*, 3rd Ed., © 2012, pp. 96, 109. Reprinted and electronically reproduced by permission of Pearson Education, Inc., New York, NY.

and larger nerve fibres that conduct other sensory signals such as those associated with rubbing, pinching, and tickling sensations. Stimulation of the small pain fibres results in the experience of pain, whereas the larger fibres inhibit pain signals so that other sensory information can be sent to the brain. Thus, the large fibres close the gate that is opened by the smaller fibres. According to gate-control theory, if you stub your toe, rubbing the area around the toe may alleviate some of the pain because the large fibres carrying the message about touch inhibit the firing of smaller fibres carrying pain signals. Likewise, putting ice on an injury reduces pain by overriding the signals transmitted by the small fibres.

The gate-control theory provided an important first step in our understanding of pain. Updates of this theory have allowed researchers to explain even more pain-related experiences (Melzack & Katz, 2013). Our experience of pain obviously involves input from the spinal cord to the somatosensory cortex—this provides our brain with information about the location of the aversive stimulation. However, pain is not just sensation gone awry. Expectations and memory can both increase (or decrease) your feelings of pain. Attention, too, can influence how painful a stimulus seems. If you focus all of your attention

on the pain, it will feel worse than if you're focusing on something else. Pain is also related to emotions; negative emotions increase the perception of pain (Loggia et al., 2008b). As shown in Figure 4.39, these cognitive, sensory, and emotional factors all interact to influence nociception. This interaction is why the same painful stimulus might rate as a 5/10 on a pain scale one day and as a 7/10 another day—cognitive and emotional factors likely differed between the two days.

This updated view of pain also helps explain why different people produce different pain-related responses. Our response to pain isn't simply, "Ouch!" It involves the feeling of pain, as well as some form of movement and an emotional or stress-related response to being in pain. Many of these responses involve the anterior cingulate gyrus, a brain area above the corpus callosum that forms networks with many structures in the limbic system.

Our discussion thus far has focused on how we perceive pain when it affects our own body. But, how do you feel when you see *someone else* in pain? And, does the pain of other people affect how your own pain feels? Psychology researchers have begun to address these complicated—and fascinating—questions.

Figure 4.39 Multiple Factors Influence Pain-Related Behaviours

Cognitive, sensory, and emotional factors all influence how we experience pain. Importantly, pain also leads to multiple behavioural responses, including stress. This likely explains why different people—including some patient populations—are particularly sensitive to painful stimuli.

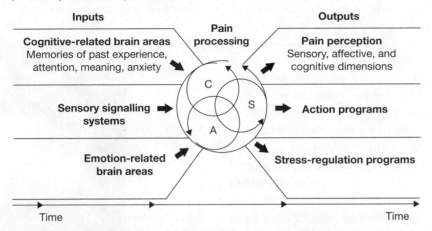

Source: From Pain, *WIREs Cognitive Science*, Vol 4, Issue 1 by Ronald Melzack, Joel Katz. Copyright © 2012 John Wiley & Sons, Inc. Reproduced with permission of John Wiley & Sons, Inc.

Working the Scientific Literacy Model

Empathy and Pain

A running theme of this chapter has been that sensation and perception involve an interaction with your environment. While the term *environment* often makes people think of birds, trees, and buildings, a key part of our environment is other people. Is it possible for one person's somatosensory experiences to influence those of another person?

What do we know about empathy and pain?

We've all seen someone in pain. Sometimes it's a friend stubbing his toe on a chair; other times it's a person rubbing her foot after stepping on a piece of Lego. Our experience of these situations differs a great deal. If we see someone we care about in pain, we experience negative emotions and sometimes even feel pain ourselves. If it is a stranger or someone we don't like, our reaction might be less intense. This leads to several interesting questions. Are we able to feel the pain of others? Under what conditions? And how does the presence of another person influence how we experience pain?

How does science explain the influence of empathy on pain perception?

The power of emotion in the experience of pain is profound. In one study, researchers at McGill University asked participants to immerse their right hand in hot water while viewing emotionally negative videos (disaster scenes) and neutral videos (cityscape scenes). Participants rated the unpleasantness of the pain as being higher when they watched disaster scenes (Loggia et al., 2008a). These results suggest that the emotional component of pain can influence our physical sensations, particularly when it involves seeing the suffering of others.

In another study, these researchers asked participants to feel either high or low levels of empathy for an actor in a video. The researchers then measured the participants' sensitivity to painful heat stimuli while they watched the actor experience similar stimulation. Participants who felt empathy for the actor reported experiencing higher levels of pain than did low-empathy participants. This result suggests that emotionally connecting with someone else in pain can influence our own sensitivity (Loggia et al., 2008b).

Can we critically evaluate the research?

An obvious criticism of research studies involving emotion and the experience of pain is that the participants may simply be reporting what they think the experimenters want to hear. If you were in a study in which someone was manipulating your mood, you would likely be able to predict the hypotheses being tested in that study. It is therefore necessary to find additional support for these self-report experiments. Numerous neuroimaging studies have found that activity in a brain structure called the insula (near the junction of the frontal lobes and the top of the temporal lobes) is related to the awareness of bodily sensations (Wiens, 2005). Activity in the insula also increases when people are performing empathy-related tasks (Fukushima et al., 2011). Thus, there might be a biological link between feeling pain and feeling empathy.

Stronger support comes from studies that show an effect of empathy on pain perception in individuals that are much less likely to be influenced by the experimenter's expectations: mice! When injected with a pain-inducing substance, mice that were tested in pairs showed more pain-related behaviours than did mice that were tested alone. But, this effect only occurred when the mice were cagemates with their test partner (i.e., they knew the other mouse)! Additionally, observing a cagemate in pain altered the mouse's own pain sensitivity, suggesting that these animals are capable of some form of empathy (Langford et al., 2006). Even more remarkable, some male mice refused to show pain responses in the presence of mice they didn't know (a mouse version of acting tough); this effect, not surprisingly, appears to be dependent upon the hormone testosterone (Langford et al., 2011; see Module 3.2). Taken together, these neuroimaging and animal-based studies suggest that our own pain can be dramatically influenced by the pain of those around us.

Why is this relevant?

These studies demonstrate that our sensations, particularly pain, can be influenced by the experiences of other people. Feeling negative emotions or seeing someone else feel pain makes our own pain more unpleasant. Although these studies might seem a bit morbid, they do offer an incredibly important insight that could affect the well-being of many people. If people can influence each other's negative sensations, then it should be possible to influence each other's positive sensations. Just as pain can be "contagious," so too might happiness and well-being.

PHANTOM LIMB PAIN   Astonishingly, it is possible for people to feel pain in body parts that no longer exist. **Phantom limb sensations** *are frequently experienced by amputees, who report pain and other sensations coming from the absent limb*. Amputees describe such sensations as itching, muscle contractions, and, most unfortunately, pain. One explanation for phantom pain suggests that rewiring occurs in the brain following the loss of the limb. After limb amputation, the area of the somatosensory cortex formerly associated with that body part is no longer stimulated by the lost limb. Thus, if someone has her left arm amputated, the right somatosensory cortex that registers sensations from the left arm no longer has any input from this limb. Healthy nerve cells become hypersensitive when they lose connections. The phantom sensations, including pain, may occur because the nerve cells in the cortex continue to be active, despite the absence of any input from the body.

Figure 4.40 A Mirror Box Used in Therapy for People with Limb Amputation

In this case, a woman who has lost her left arm can experience some relief from phantom pain by moving her intact hand, such as by unclenching her fist. In turn, she will experience relief from phantom pain corresponding to her left side.

Source: Lilienfeld, Scott O.; Lynn, Steven J; Namy, Laura L.; Woolf, Nancy J., *Psychology: From Inquiry to Understanding*, 2nd Ed., ©2011, pp.157. Reprinted and Electronically reproduced by permission of Pearson Education, Inc., New York, NY.

One ingenious treatment for phantom pain involves the mirror box (Figure 4.40). This apparatus uses the reflection of the amputee's existing limb, such as an arm and hand, to create the visual appearance of having both limbs. Amputees often find that watching themselves move and stretch the phantom hand, which is actually the mirror image of the real hand, results in a significant decrease in phantom pain and in both physical and emotional discomfort (Ramachandran & Altschuler, 2009).

Researchers have conducted experiments to determine how well mirror box therapy works compared both to a control condition and to mentally visualizing the presence of a phantom hand. Over the course of four weeks of regular testing, the people who used the mirror box had significantly reduced pain compared to a control group who used the same mirror apparatus, except the mirror was covered; they also had less pain than a group who used mental visualization (Figure 4.41; Chan et al., 2007). Notice in Figure 4.40 that everyone was given mirror therapy after the fourth week of the study, and that the procedure seemed to have lasting, positive benefits. No one is sure why mirror box therapy works, but evidence suggests that the short-term benefits are due to how compelling the illusion is; in the long term, this therapy may actually result in reorganization of the somatosensory cortex (Ramachandran & Altschuler, 2009).

Figure 4.41 Mirror Box Therapy Compared to Mental Visualization and a Control Condition

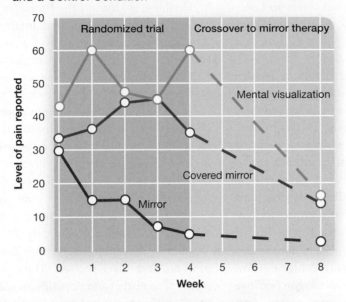

Source: Chan, B. L., et. al., (2006). Mirror Therapy for Phantom Limb Pain, *The New England Journal of Medicine*, 357 (21), 2206, Massachusetts Medical Society, 2007.

Module 4.4a Quiz:

The Sense of Touch

Know . . .

1. The sense associated with actively touching objects is known as ____.
   A. tactile agnosia
   B. haptics
   C. nociception
   D. gestation

2. Phantom limb sensations are
   A. sensations that arise from a limb that has been amputated.
   B. sensations that are not perceived.
   C. sensations from stimuli that do not reach conscious awareness.
   D. sensations from stimuli that you typically identify as intense, such as a burn, but that feel dull.

Understand . . .

3. Nociceptors send pain signals to both the ____ and the ____.
   A. occipital lobe; hypothalamus
   B. cerebellum; somatosensory cortex
   C. somatosensory cortex; anterior cingulate gyrus
   D. occipital lobe; cochlea

Apply . . .

4. A student gently touches a staple to her fingertip and to the back of her arm near her elbow. How are these sensations likely to differ? Or would they feel similar?
   A. The sensation would feel like two points on the fingertip but is likely to feel like only one point on the arm.
   B. The sensations would feel identical because the same object touches both locations.
   C. The sensation would feel like touch on the fingertips but like pain on the elbow.
   D. The sensation would feel like two points on the arm but is likely to feel like only one point on the fingertip.

The Chemical Senses: Taste and Smell

The chemical senses comprise a combination of both taste and smell. Although they are distinct sensory systems, both begin the sensory process with chemicals activating receptors on the tongue and mouth, as well as in the nose.

THE GUSTATORY SYSTEM: TASTE The **gustatory system** *functions in the sensation and perception of taste.* But, what exactly is this system tasting? Approximately 2500 identifiable chemical compounds are found in the food we eat (Taylor & Hort, 2004). When combined, these compounds give us an enormous diversity of taste sensations. The *primary tastes* include salty, sweet, bitter, and sour. In addition, a fifth taste, called *umami*, has been identified (Chaudhari et al., 2000). Umami, sometimes referred to as "savouriness," is a Japanese word that refers to tastes associated with seaweed, the seasoning monosodium glutamate (MSG), and protein-rich foods such as milk and aged cheese.

Taste is registered primarily on the tongue, where roughly 9000 taste buds reside. On average, approximately 1000 taste buds are also found throughout the sides and roof of the mouth (Miller & Reedy, 1990). Sensory neurons that transmit signals from the taste buds respond to different types of stimuli, but most tend to respond best to a particular taste. Our experience of taste reflects an overall pattern of activity across many neurons, and generally comes from stimulation of the entire tongue rather than just specific, localized regions. The middle of the tongue has very few taste receptors, giving it a similar character to the blind spot on the retina (Module 4.2). We do not feel or sense the blind spot of the tongue because the sensory information is filled in, just as we find with vision. Taste receptors replenish themselves every 10 days throughout the life span—the only type of sensory receptor to do so.

Receptors for taste are located in the visible, small bumps (*papillae*) that are distributed over the surface of the tongue. The papillae are lined with taste buds. Figure 4.42 shows papillae, taste buds, and an enlarged view of an individual taste bud and a sensory neuron's dendrites and axon that sends a message to the brain.

The bundles of nerves that register taste at the taste buds send the signal through the thalamus and on to higher-level regions of the brain, including the *gustatory cortex*; this region is located in the back of the frontal lobes and extends inward to the insula (near the top of the temporal lobe). Another region, the *secondary gustatory cortex*, processes the pleasurable experiences associated with food.

Why do some people experience tastes vividly while other people do not? One reason is that the number of taste buds present on the tongue influences the psychological experience of taste. Although approximately 9000 taste buds is the average number found on the human tongue, there is wide variation among individuals. Some people may have many times this number. *Supertasters*, who account for approximately 25% of the population, are especially sensitive to bitter tastes such as those of broccoli and black coffee. They typically have lower rates of obesity and cardiovascular disease, possibly because they tend not to prefer fatty and sweet foods. Figure 4.43 shows the number of papillae, and hence taste buds, possessed by a supertaster compared to those without this ability.

How much of our taste preferences are learned and how much are innate? Like most of our behaviours, there is no simple answer. Human infants tend to prefer the foods consumed by their mothers during gestation (Beauchamp & Mennella, 2009). Soon after starting solid foods, children begin to acquire a taste for the foods prevalent in

Figure 4.42 Papillae and Taste Buds

The tongue is lined with papillae (the bumpy surfaces). Within these papillae are your taste buds, the tiny receptors to which chemicals bind.

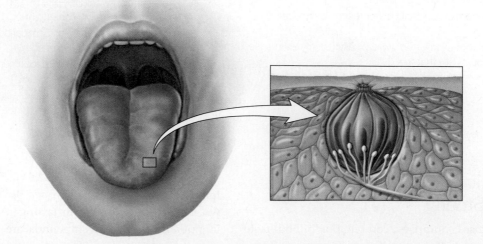

Figure 4.43 Density of Papillae, and Hence Taste Buds, in a Supertaster and in a Normal Taster

Some of the individual differences in taste sensitivity may be due to the number of taste buds found on the tongue. Supertasters (left tongue) have many more taste buds than the average person (right tongue).

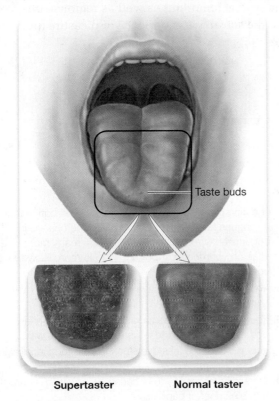

Taste buds

Supertaster   **Normal taster**

Source: Lilienfeld, Scott O.; Lynn, Steven; Namy, Laura L.; Woolf, Nancy J.; *Psychology: From Inquiry To Understanding*, Books A La Carte Edition, 2nd Ed., © 2011. Reprinted and Electronically reproduced by permission of Pearson Education, Inc., New York, NY.

their culture. Would you eat a piece of bread smeared with a sticky brown paste that was processed from wasted yeast from a brewery? This product, called vegemite, is actually quite popular among people in Switzerland, Australia, and New Zealand. People brought up eating vegemite may love it, while most others find it tastes like death. The Masai people of Kenya and Tanzania enjoy eating a coagulated mixture of cow's blood and milk. These foods may sound unappetizing to you. Of course, non-Canadians are often repulsed by poutine, a decadent mixture of french fries, cheese curds, and gravy, so we should be careful not to judge . . . too much.

Closely related to taste is our sense of smell, which senses the chemical environment via a different mode than does taste.

THE OLFACTORY SYSTEM: SMELL The **olfactory system** *is involved in smell—the detection of airborne particles with specialized receptors located in the nose.* Our sensation of smell begins with nasal air flow bringing in molecules that bind with receptors at the top of the nasal cavity. (So, when you smell something, you are actually taking in part of the environment—including other people—into your body.) Within the nasal cavity is the **olfactory epithelium**, *a thin layer of cells that are lined by sensory receptors called cilia*—tiny hair-like projections that contain specialized proteins that bind with the airborne molecules that enter the *nasal cavity* (Figure 4.44). Humans have roughly 1000 different types of odour receptors in their olfactory system, but can identify

Figure 4.44 The Olfactory System

Lining the olfactory epithelium are tiny cilia that collect airborne chemicals, sending sensory messages to the nerve fibres that make up the olfactory bulb.

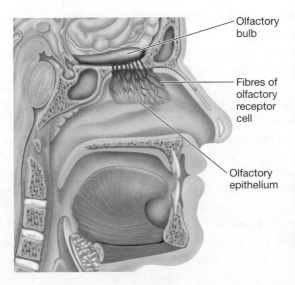

Olfactory bulb

Fibres of olfactory receptor cell

Olfactory epithelium

(a)

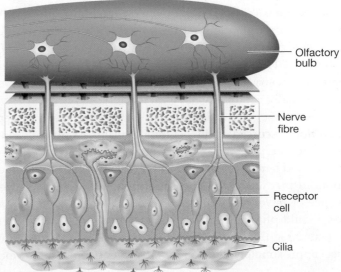

Olfactory bulb

Nerve fibre

Receptor cell

Cilia

(b)

approximately 10 000 different smells. How is this possible? The answer is that it is the *pattern* of the stimulation, involving more than one receptor, which gives rise to the experience of a particular smell (Buck & Axel, 1991). Different combinations of cilia are stimulated in response to different odours.

These groups of cilia then transmit messages directly to neurons that converge on the **olfactory bulb** on the bottom surface of the frontal lobes, *which serves as the brain's central region for processing smells.* (Unlike our other senses, olfaction does not involve the thalamus.) The olfactory bulb connects with several regions of the brain through the olfactory tract, including the limbic system (emotion) as well as regions of the cortex where the subjective experience of pleasure (or disgust) occurs.

Module 4.4b Quiz:

The Chemical Senses: Taste and Smell

Know . . .

1. The bumps that line the tongue surface and house our taste buds are called ___.
   A. epithelia
   B. gustates
   C. the gustatory cortex
   D. papillae

2. Where are the receptor cells for smell located?
   A. The papillae
   B. The olfactory epithelium
   C. The olfactory bulb
   D. The odour buds

Apply . . .

3. After eating grape lollipops, you and a friend notice that your tongues have turned purple. With the change in colour, it is easy to notice that there are many more papillae on your friend's tongue. Who is more likely to be a supertaster?
   A. You are, because you have fewer, and therefore more distinct, papillae.
   B. Your friend is, because she has many more papillae, and therefore many more taste buds, to taste with.
   C. You are, because less dye stuck to your tongue, allowing you to taste more.
   D. It could be either of you because supertasting is unrelated to the number of papillae.

Multimodal Integration

Modules 4.2–4.4 have described our five different, most commonly discussed, sensory systems. After reading about them, it is quite tempting to view the five systems as being distinct from one another. After all, our brains are set up in such a way that it is simple to separate the different senses. Indeed, the doctrine of specific energies stated *in 1826* that our senses are separated in the brain (see Module 4.1). However, this view is at odds with some of our sensory experiences. Many of these experiences are actually combinations of multiple types of sensations, just as they are in individuals with synesthesia, the condition discussed at the beginning of this module. For example, the perceptual experience of flavour combines taste and smell (Small et al., 1997). You have probably noticed that when you have nasal congestion, your experience of flavour is diminished. You may also have noticed a child plugging his nose when he has to eat or drink something that tastes bad. This loss of taste occurs because approximately 80% of our information about food comes from olfaction (Murphy et al., 1977). This link between taste and smell is a perfect example of **multimodal integration**, *the ability to combine sensation from different modalities such as vision and hearing into a single integrated perception.*

WHAT *IS* MULTIMODAL INTEGRATION? Multimodal integration is so much more than simply combining different senses. In fact, it's a form of problem-solving performed by your brain hundreds of times each day. We must decide, almost instantaneously, if two types of sensation should be integrated into a multimodal perception. How do we do this? One factor is whether the different sensations are in a similar location. If you hear a "meow" and see a cat with its mouth open, you infer that the movements of the cat's mouth and the "meow" sound were linked together. We also make use of temporal information. Sensations that occur in roughly the same time period are more likely to be linked than those that are not. If you hear a "meow" five seconds before the cat's mouth moved, you will not likely combine the sound with the sight of the cat (unless you know your cat is a ventriloquist).

Multimodal integration occurs quite naturally—we're often unaware of these perceptions until some outside force interferes with it. You may have experienced watching a television show or YouTube clip in which the movement of the characters' lips didn't match up with the sound of their voices. These perceptions are often annoying because the lag between the image and the sound makes it difficult to combine the two into the expected multimodal perception. In fact, sometimes this mismatch can interfere with perception, even to the point of producing new perceptions that did not actually occur.

This result occurred by accident in a study conducted by Harry McGurk and John MacDonald in 1976. These researchers were investigating language perception in infants and had videos of different actors producing sounds such as /ba-ba/. However, when the sound /ba-ba/ was presented during the video of someone mouthing the sound /ga-ga/, the experimenters noticed that it seemed to produce an entirely different multimodal stimulus: /da-da/. It was as though the movement of the speaker's lips provided the viewer with the expectation of a particular sound; this expectation biased the perception of the presented sounds. This phenomenon is now known as the *McGurk Effect*.

Expectations and multimodal integration can also influence our social interactions. We routinely integrate visual and auditory information when we are speaking with someone. Researchers have found that both women and men rated masculine faces (i.e., tough, rugged faces) as being more attractive when they were matched with a masculine voice (Feinberg et al., 2008). Other studies have shown that heterosexual men preferred viewing female faces that were paired with high-pitched rather than low-pitched voices (Feinberg et al., 2005). Facial expressions of a singer also influence judgments of the emotional content of songs (Thompson et al., 2008). These studies show us that we naturally form auditory expectations when we visually perceive a face.

SYNESTHESIA   If our brains are set up to perceive our senses separately and then combine them only when it seems appropriate (due to location, time, and expectations), how can we explain synesthesia, the condition discussed in the opening of this module? These blended multimodal associations (e.g., chicken that tastes "pointy") do not come and go. Rather, they occur automatically and are consistent over time (Ramachandran & Hubbard, 2003). Why does synesthesia occur?

This question has puzzled scientists since the first reported case of synesthesia in 1812 (Sachs, 1812; Jewanski

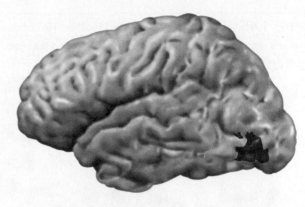

Synesthetes who experience colours when they see letters or numbers have stronger connections between brain areas related to colour (red) and letters/numbers (green).

Source: Figure 4 from Ramachandran, V.S., and Hubbard, E.M. (2001). "Synaesthesia—A window into perception, thought and language." *JCS, 8,* No. 12, pp. 3–34.

et al., 2009). To date, there is still no clear answer. Researchers have noted that synesthesia does run in families (Baron-Cohen et al., 1996). However, the exact genes involved with this condition are still unknown. In fact, researchers at the University of Waterloo found a pair of identical twins, only one of whom had synesthesia (Smilek et al., 2001)!

Neuroimaging studies have provided some insight into this condition. For instance, one research group tested synesthetes who have specific colour perceptions appear whenever they read a number (e.g., every time they see "2", it appears with a yellow border). These researchers found activity in areas of the brain related to colour perception in synesthetes, but not in non-synesthetes (Nunn et al., 2002). More recent studies suggest that the brains of people with synesthesia may contain networks that link different sensory areas in ways not found in other people (Dovern et al., 2012).

A similar cross-wiring of brain networks may explain another unusual example of multimodal integration. **Autonomous sensory meridian response (ASMR)** *is a condition in which specific auditory or visual stimuli trigger tingling sensations in the scalp and neck, sometimes extending across the back and shoulders* (see Figure 4.45). What makes this condition so unusual is that many of the stimuli that trigger ASMR are social in nature, such as whispering or watching someone slowly brush her hair (Barratt & Davis, 2015). Like synesthesia, ASMR appears to be caused by unusual patterns of connections between different brain areas (Smith et al., 2016).

Together, these findings demonstrate a point made repeatedly in this text: Our experiences involve groups of brain areas working together. This point holds for all five of our senses, as well as for their multimodal integration.

Figure 4.45 Autonomous Sensory Meridian Response (ASMR)

Individuals with ASMR experience tingling sensations on the scalp, shoulders, and back when they hear specific auditory and visual stimuli such as someone whispering or performing socially intimate acts such as braiding someone's hair.

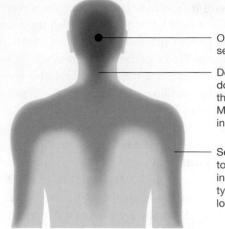

Origin of tingling sensation.

Described as moving downwards, following the line of the spine. Many also feel this in the shoulders.

Sensation may spread to other areas with increasing intensity, typically the limbs and lower back.

Source (right): Barratt EL, Davis NJ. (2014). Autonomous Sensory Meridian Response (ASMR): A flow-like mental state. *PeerJ PrePrints* 2:e719v1 https://doi.org/10.7287/peerj.preprints.719v1.

Module 4.4c Quiz:

Multimodal Integration

Know . . .

1. Multimodal integration involves:

   A. combining sensations from different senses into a single integrated perception.

   B. keeping different sensory inputs separate in the brain.

   C. different sensory inputs competing to see which one will reach conscious awareness.

   D. certain parts of the body being more sensitive to touch than other regions.

Understand . . .

2. The perceptual experience of flavour originates from:

   A. taste cues alone.

   B. olfactory cues alone.

   C. olfactory and taste cues together.

   D. haptic and olfactory cues together.

Apply . . .

3. Lexi is watching a movie with her friends. When one of the characters starts whispering, Lexi experiences a sudden tingling sensation on her scalp and neck. She has never been diagnosed with seizures or any psychological disorder. What condition would you diagnose her with?

   A. Epilepsy

   B. Synesthesia

   C. Autonomous sensory meridian response

   D. McGurk Syndrome

Module 4.4 Summary

4.4a   Know . . . the key terminology of touch and chemical senses.

Autonomous sensory meridian response
gate-control theory
gustatory system
haptics
kinesthesis
multimodal integration
nociception
olfactory bulb
olfactory epithelium
olfactory system
phantom limb sensations

4.4b   Understand . . . how pain messages travel to the brain.

According to gate-control theory, small nerve fibres carry pain messages from their source to the spinal cord, and then up to, among other regions, the anterior cingulate gyrus and somatosensory cortex. However, large nerve cells that register other types of touch sensations (such as rubbing) can override signals sent by small pain fibres.

4.4c   Understand . . . the relationship between smell, taste, and food flavour experience.

Both senses combine to give us flavour experiences. Contact with food activates patterns of neural activity among nerve cells connected to the taste buds, and food odours activate patterns of nerve activity in the olfactory epithelium. The primary and secondary gustatory cortex and the olfactory bulb are involved in the perceptual experience of flavour.

4.4d   Apply . . . your knowledge about touch to describe the acuity of different areas of skin.

Apply Activity

Try creating a two-point threshold device like the one shown earlier in Figure 4.35 by straightening a paper clip and then bending it so the two points are about 5 mm apart. Gently apply them to different parts of the body—your fingertips, elbow, cheek, etc. Which parts of your body are sensitive enough to feel both points, and on which parts does it feel like a single object is touching you? Now try the experiment again with the two points closer together. Can you detect a change in acuity?

4.4e   Apply . . . your knowledge to determine whether you or someone you know is a "supertaster."

Scientists use a very precise measurement system to identify supertasters, but one less complicated way to do so is to dye your tongue by placing a drop of food colouring on it, or by eating or drinking something dark blue or purple. Next, count the number of papillae you can see in a 4 mm circle. You can accomplish this by viewing the dyed portion of your tongue through the punched hole in a sheet of loose-leaf notebook paper. If you can count more than 30 papillae, then chances are you are a supertaster. Of course, if you already know that you do not like bitter vegetables like broccoli or asparagus, then perhaps you would expect to find a high number of papillae.

4.4f   Analyze . . . how different senses are combined together.

Humans have five distinct types of senses. However, that does not mean that these senses always operate independently—they often interact to form more vivid experiences. The flavour of food is an experience that involves both taste *and* smell. Numerous other studies have shown that our visual perception interacts with our auditory system, leading us to be surprised when sounds (such as the pitch of someone's voice) don't match our visual expectations.

Chapter 5
Consciousness

5.1 Biological Rhythms of Consciousness: Wakefulness and Sleep

- What Is Sleep? 182
- Module 5.1a Quiz 186
- Why Do We Need Sleep? 186
- Module 5.1b Quiz 189
- Theories of Dreaming 190

  Working the Scientific Literacy Model: Dreams, REM Sleep, and Learning 191
- Module 5.1c Quiz 193
- Disorders and Problems with Sleep 193
- Module 5.1d Quiz 197
- Module 5.1 Summary 197

5.2 Altered States of Consciousness: Hypnosis, Mind-Wandering, and Disorders of Consciousness

- Hypnosis 200
- Module 5.2a Quiz 202
- Mind-Wandering 203
- Module 5.2b Quiz 205
- Disorders of Consciousness 205

  Working the Scientific Literacy Model: Assessing Consciousness in the Vegetative State 207
- Module 5.2c Quiz 210
- Module 5.2 Summary 210

5.3 Drugs and Conscious Experience

- Physical and Psychological Effects of Drugs 212
- Module 5.3a Quiz 214
- Commonly Abused "Recreational" Drugs 215

  Working the Scientific Literacy Model: Marijuana, Memory, and Cognition 219
- Module 5.3b Quiz 222
- Legal Drugs and Their Effects on Consciousness 222
- Module 5.3c Quiz 225
- Module 5.3 Summary 226

Module 5.1 Biological Rhythms of Consciousness: Wakefulness and Sleep

es/Sylvia Serrado/PhotoAlto/Alamy Stock Photo

⌄ Learning Objectives

5.1a Know . . . the key terminology associated with sleep, dreams, and sleep disorders.

5.1b Understand . . . how the sleep cycle works.

5.1c Understand . . . theories of why we sleep.

5.1d Apply . . . your knowledge to identify and practise good sleep habits.

5.1e Analyze . . . different theories about why we dream.

Smashing through a window in your sleep seems perfectly plausible if it occurs as part of a dream. Mike Birbiglia did just this—but in his case, it was both dream and reality. Birbiglia is a comedian whose show, Sleepwalk with Me, *is full of stories of personal and embarrassing moments, which include jumping through a second-storey window of his hotel room while he was asleep. He awoke upon landing; picked his bloodied, half-naked self up; and went to the hotel front desk to notify personnel of what happened. Perhaps his comedy is just his way of dealing with an otherwise troubling sleep problem—a serious condition called REM behaviour disorder. People with REM behaviour disorder act out their dreams, which clearly has the potential to be very dangerous. In Mike's case, the injury was self-inflicted. Other people with the condition, however, have been known to hit or choke their bed partner. As it turns out, jumping through windows is not entirely uncommon for people with REM behaviour disorder*

(Schenck et al., 2009). In this module, we explore how normal sleep works and we explain how and why sleep disorders, such as Mike Birbiglia's, occur.

Focus Questions

1. How do body rhythms affect memory and thinking?

2. What is REM and how is it related to dreaming?

» **Consciousness** *is a person's subjective awareness, including thoughts, perceptions, experiences of the world, and self-awareness.* Every day we go through many changes in consciousness—our thoughts and perceptions are constantly adapting to new situations. In some cases, when we are paying close attention to something, we seem to be more in control of conscious experiences. In other situations, such as when we are daydreaming, consciousness seems to wander. These changes in our subjective experiences, and the difficulty in defining them, make consciousness one of the most challenging areas of psychological study. We will begin this module by exploring the alternating cycles of consciousness—sleeping and waking.

What Is Sleep?

It makes perfect sense to devote a module to a behaviour that humans spend approximately one-third of their lives doing. What happens during sleep can be just as fascinating as what happens during wakefulness. Psychologists and non-psychologists alike have long pondered some basic questions about sleep, such as "Why do we need sleep?" and "Why do we dream?" But perhaps we should begin with the most basic question: "What is sleep?"

BIOLOGICAL RHYTHMS Life involves patterns—patterns that cycle within days, weeks, months, or years. Organisms have evolved *biological rhythms* that are neatly adapted to the cycles in their environment. For example, bears are well known for hibernating during the cold winter months. Because this behaviour happens on a yearly basis, it is part of a *circannual rhythm* (a term that literally means "a yearly cycle"). This type of rhythm is an example of an *infradian rhythm*, which is any rhythm that occurs over a period of time longer than a day. In humans, the best-known infradian rhythm is the menstrual cycle. However, most biological rhythms occur with a much greater frequency than once a month. For instance,

heart rate, urination, and some hormonal activity occur in 90–120-minute cycles. These more frequent biological rhythms are referred to as *ultradian rhythms.*

However, the biological rhythm that appears to have the most obvious impact upon our lives is a cycle that occurs over the course of a day. **Circadian rhythms** *are internally driven daily cycles of approximately 24 hours affecting physiological and behavioural processes* (Halberg et al., 1959). They involve the tendency to be asleep or awake at specific times, to feel hungrier during some parts of the day, and even the ability to concentrate better at certain times than at others (Lavie, 2001; Verwey & Amir, 2009).

Think about your own circadian rhythms: When are you most alert? At which times of day do you feel the most tired? Night shift workers and night owls aside, we tend to get most of our sleep when it is dark outside because our circadian rhythms are regulated by daylight interacting with our nervous and endocrine (hormonal) systems. One key brain structure in this process is the *suprachiasmatic nucleus* (SCN) of the hypothalamus. Cells in the retina of the eye relay messages about light levels in the environment to the SCN (Hendrickson et al., 1972; Morin, 2013). The SCN, in turn, communicates signals about light levels with the pineal gland (see Figure 5.1). The pineal gland releases a hormone called *melatonin*, which peaks in concentration at nighttime and is reduced during wakefulness. Information about melatonin levels feeds back to the hypothalamus; this feedback helps the hypothalamus monitor melatonin levels so that the appropriate amount of this hormone is released at different times of the day.

Figure 5.1 Pathways Involved in Circadian Rhythms

Cells in the retina send messages about light levels to the suprachiasmatic nucleus, which in turn relays the information to the pineal gland, which secretes melatonin.

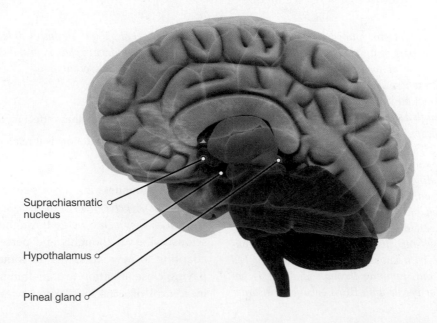

Suprachiasmatic nucleus

Hypothalamus

Pineal gland

But what actually causes us to adopt these circadian rhythms? Why don't we stay awake for days and then sleep all weekend? There are two explanations for our 24-hour rhythms. One is **entrainment**, *when biological rhythms become synchronized to external cues such as light, temperature, or even a clock.* Because of its effects on the SCN-melatonin system, light is the primary entrainment mechanism for most mammals (Rusak, 1979; Wever et al., 1983). We tend to be awake during daylight and asleep during darkness. We're also influenced by the time on our clocks. If you're tired at 8 P.M., you likely try to fight your fatigue until a "normal" bed time such as 10 P.M. Why? Because we've been trained to believe that some times of day are associated with sleep and others are not.

However, not all of our body rhythms are products of entrainment. Instead, some are **endogenous rhythms**, *biological rhythms that are generated by our body independent of external cues such as light.* Studying endogenous rhythms is tricky because it is difficult to remove all of the external cues from a person's world. To overcome this problem, researchers in the 1960s and 1970s asked motivated volunteers to spend extended periods of time (months) in caves or in isolation chambers. For instance, Jürgen Aschoff (1965; Aschoff et al., 1967; Aschoff & Wever, 1962) had participants stay in an underground chamber for four weeks.

He noted that individuals tended to adopt a 25-hour day. Michel Siffre, a French cave expert, remained by himself in a dark cave for much longer durations than Aschoff's participants: two months in 1962 and six months in 1972 (Foer & Siffre, 2008). Whenever he woke up or intended to go to sleep, he called his support team who were stationed at the entrance to the cave. Data from Siffre and a number of his subsequent participants indicated that most people fell into a 24.5-hour circadian rhythm. Although a few participants would briefly enter longer cycles—sometimes as long as 48-hour days—most people possess an endogenous circadian rhythm that is 24–25 hours in length (Lavie, 2001; Mills, 1964).

Although our sleep–wake cycle remains relatively close to 24 hours in length throughout our lives, some patterns within our circadian rhythms do change with age (Caci et al., 2009). As shown in Figure 5.2, researchers have found that we need much less sleep—especially a type called REM sleep—as we move from infancy and early childhood into adulthood. Moreover, people generally experience a change in when they prefer to sleep. In your teens and 20s, many of you have (or will) become night owls who prefer to stay up late and sleep in. When given the choice, most people in this age range prefer to work, study, and play late in the day, and then awake later in the morning (Galambos et al., 2013). Later in

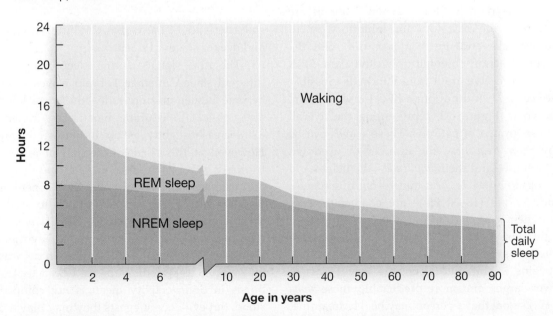

Figure 5.2 Sleep Requirements Change with Age

People tend to spend progressively less time sleeping as they age. The amount of a certain type of sleep, REM sleep, declines the most.

Source: Based on Ontogenetic Development of the Human Sleep–Dream Cycle, *Science*, 152(3722): 604–619. 29 Apr 1966.

adulthood, many of you will find yourselves going to bed earlier and getting up earlier, and you may begin to prefer working or exercising before teenagers even begin to stir. Research shows that these patterns are more than just preferences: People actually do show higher alertness and cognitive functioning during their preferred time of day (Cavallera & Giudici, 2008; Hahn et al., 2012). For instance, researchers at the University of Toronto have found that when older adults (approximately 60–80 years of age) are tested later in the day as opposed to early in the morning, they have a greater difficulty separating new from old information (Hasher et al., 2002) and have a larger variability in their reaction times on a test in which they learned to pair together a digit and a symbol (Hogan et al., 2009). These results have implications for the cognitive testing older patients receive in hospitals; clearly, these individuals will appear healthier if tested in the morning as opposed to later in the day, when their bodies are preparing to go to sleep.

THE STAGES OF SLEEP We have already seen how sleep fits into the daily rhythm, but if we take a closer look, we will see that sleep itself has rhythms. In order to measure these rhythms, scientists use **polysomnography**, *a set of objective measurements used to examine physiological variables during sleep*. Some of the devices used in this type of study are familiar, such as one to measure respiration and a thermometer to measure body temperature. In addition, electrical sensors attached to the skin measure muscle activity around the eyes and other parts of the body. However, sleep cycles themselves are most often defined by the *electroencephalogram* (*EEG*), a device that measures brain activity using sensors attached to the scalp (see Module 3.4).

EEGs detect changes involving the ion channels on neurons. As you read in Module 3.2, ion channels are involved with receiving excitatory and inhibitory potentials from other cells and are also involved with the transmission of an action potential down the axon. Each EEG sensor would receive input from hundreds (possibly thousands) of cells. The output of an EEG is a waveform, like that shown in Figure 5.3, representing the overall activity of these groups of neurons. These waves can be described by their *frequency*—the number of up-down cycles every second—and their *amplitude*—the height and depth of the up-down cycle. *Beta waves*—high-frequency, low-amplitude waves (15–30 Hz)—are characteristic of wakefulness. Their irregular nature reflects the bursts of activity in different regions of the cortex, and they are often interpreted as a sign that a person is alert. As the individual begins to shift into sleep, the waves start to become slower, larger, and more predictable; these *alpha waves* (8–14 Hz) signal that a person may be daydreaming, meditating, or starting to fall asleep. These changes in the

Figure 5.3 EEG Recordings during Wakefulness and Sleep

Brain waves, as measured by the frequency and amplitude of electrical activity, change over the course of the normal circadian rhythm. Beta waves are predominant during wakefulness but give way to alpha waves during periods of calm and as we drift into sleep. Theta waves are characteristic of stage 1 sleep. As we reach stage 2 sleep, the amplitude (height) of brain waves increases. During deep sleep (stages 3 and 4), the brain waves are at their highest amplitude. During REM sleep, they appear similar to the brain waves occurring when we are awake.

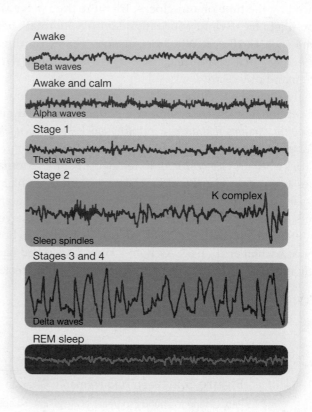

characteristics of the waves continue as we enter deeper and deeper stages of sleep.

The EEG signals during sleep move through four different stages. In stage 1, brain waves slow down and become higher in amplitude—these are known as *theta waves* (4–8 Hz). Breathing, blood pressure, and heart rate all decrease slightly as an individual begins to sleep. However, at this stage of sleep, you are still sensitive to noises such as the television in the next room. After approximately 10 to 15 minutes, the sleeper enters stage 2, during which brain waves continue to slow. As shown in Figure 5.3, stage 2 includes *sleep spindles* (clusters of high-frequency but low-amplitude waves) and *K complexes* (small groups of larger amplitude waves), which are detected as periodic bursts of EEG activity. What these bursts in brain activity mean is not completely understood, but evidence suggests they may play a role in helping maintain a state of sleep and in the process of memory

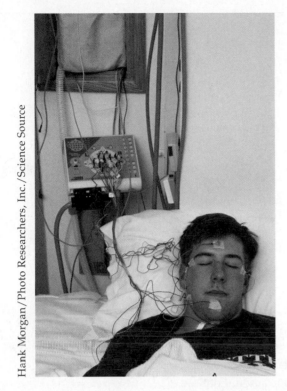

Using physiological recording devices, sleep researchers and doctors can monitor eye movements, brain waves, and other physiological processes.

storage (Fogel et al., 2007; Gais et al., 2002)—a topic we cover more fully later on.

As stage 2 sleep progresses, we respond to fewer and fewer external stimuli, such as lights and sounds.

Approximately 20 minutes later, we enter stage 3 sleep, in which brain waves continue to slow down and assume a new form called *delta waves* (large, looping waves that are high-amplitude and low-frequency—typically less than 3 Hz). The process continues with the deepest stage of sleep, stage 4, during which time the sleeper will be difficult to awaken.

About an hour after falling asleep, we reach the end of our first stage 4 sleep phase. At this point, the sleep cycle goes in reverse and we move back toward stage 2. From there, we move into a unique stage of **REM sleep**— *a stage of sleep characterized by quickening brain waves, inhibited body movement, and rapid eye movements (REM)*. This stage is sometimes known as *paradoxical sleep* because the EEG waves appear to represent a state of wakefulness despite the fact that we remain asleep. The REM pattern is so distinct that the first four stages are known collectively as *non-REM (NREM) sleep*. At the end of the first REM phase, we cycle back toward deep sleep stages and back into REM sleep again every 90 to 100 minutes. (Think back to the beginning of this module: What type of biological rhythm would a 90–100-minute cycle represent?)

The sleep cycle through a typical night of sleep is summarized in Figure 5.4. As shown in the figure, the deeper stages of sleep (3 and 4) predominate during the earlier portions of the sleep cycle, but gradually give way to longer REM periods.

Figure 5.4 Order and Duration of Sleep Stages through a Typical Night

Our sleep stages progress through a characteristic pattern. The first half of a normal night of sleep is dominated by deep, slow-wave sleep. REM sleep increases in duration relative to deep sleep during the second half of the night.

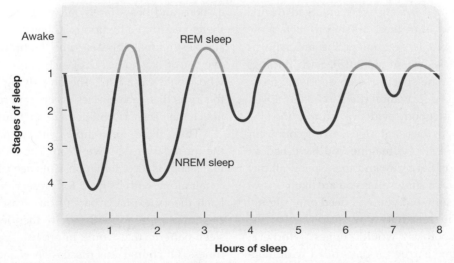

Source: Based on Some Must Watch while Some Must Sleep by W.D. Dement. WC Freeman & Company, 1974.
URL: http://socrates.berkeley.edu/~kihlstrm/ConsciousnessWeb/SleepDreams/images/DementSuccession.JPG.

Module 5.1a Quiz:

What Is Sleep?

Know . . .

1. Large, periodic bursts of brain activity that occur during stage 2 sleep are known as _____.
   A. beta waves
   B. sleep spindles
   C. delta waves
   D. alpha waves

Understand . . .

2. Why is REM sleep known as paradoxical sleep?
   A. The brain waves appear to be those of an awake person but the individual seems to be in a deep sleep.
   B. The brain waves resemble those of a sleeping individual but the person behaves as if he is nearly awake.
   C. The brain wave patterns in REM sleep are totally unlike those produced by brain activity at any other time.
   D. The brain waves resemble those of a sleeping individual and the person seems to be in a very deep sleep.

Apply . . .

3. Which of the following is the most likely order of sleep stages during the first 90 minutes of a night of rest?
   A. Stages 1–2–3–4–1–2–3–4–REM
   B. Stages 1–2–3–4–REM–1–2–3–4
   C. Stages 1–2–3–4–3–2–1–REM
   D. Stages REM–4–3–2–1

Why Do We Need Sleep?

Sleep is such a natural part of life that it is difficult to imagine what the world would be like if there were no such thing. It raises another question: Why do humans and other animals need to sleep in the first place?

THEORIES OF SLEEP   The most intuitive explanation for why we sleep is probably the **restore and repair hypothesis**, *the idea that the body needs to restore energy levels and repair any wear and tear experienced during the day's activities.* Research on sleep deprivation clearly shows that sleep is a physical and psychological necessity, not just a pleasant way to relax. A lack of sleep eventually leads to cognitive decline, emotional disturbances, and impaired functioning of the immune system (Born et al., 1997). It appears that sleeping helps animals, including humans, clear waste products and excess proteins from the brains. In a study using rodents, the researchers found that the pathways of the brain's waste removal system were enlarged during sleep, making the removal of these waste products more efficient. This effect was largest when the animal was sleeping on its side (Lee, Xie, et al., 2015). Such findings may explain why for some species, sleep deprivation can be as dangerous as food deprivation (Rechtschaffen, 1998).

Although there is good evidence supporting the restore and repair hypothesis, it does not account for all the reasons why we sleep. Imagine you have had an unusually active day on Saturday and then spend all day Sunday relaxing. Research shows that you are likely to feel sleepier on Saturday night, but you will need only slightly more sleep after the high-activity day, despite what the restore and repair hypothesis would suggest (Horne & Minard, 1985). The same is true for days filled with mentally challenging activities (De Bruin et al., 2002). Rather than requiring more sleep, it could be that sleep is more efficient after an exhausting day (Montgomery et al., 1987); in other words, more restoring and repairing may go on in the same amount of time.

A second explanation for sleep, the **preserve and protect hypothesis**, *suggests that two more adaptive functions of sleep are preserving energy and protecting the organism from harm* (Berger & Philips, 1995; Siegel, 2005). To support this hypothesis, researchers note that the animals most vulnerable to predators sleep in safe hideaways during the time of day when their predators are most likely to hunt (Siegel, 1995). Because humans are quite dependent upon vision, it made sense for us to sleep at night, when we would be at a disadvantage compared to nocturnal predators.

The quantity of sleep required differs between animal species. Hoofed species like antelope (the species you always see getting killed in nature programs) sleep less than four hours per day, primarily because they have to remain alert in case a predator attacks. Conversely, animals such as lions and bears rarely fall victim to predators and can therefore afford a luxurious 15 hours of sleep per day. (The sleepiest animal appears to be the brown bat. It sleeps an average of 19.9 hours out of each 24 hours . . . because really, who would eat a bat?) The underlying message from this theory is that each species' sleep patterns have evolved to match their sensory abilities and their environment.

Thus, there are complementary theories that answer the question of why we sleep. The amount that any animal sleeps is a combination of its need for restoration and repair along with its need for preservation and protection. Each theory explains part of our reasons for drifting off each night. Importantly, both theories would produce sleep patterns that would improve a species' evolutionary fitness. Of course, this discussion of the reasons for sleep leads to an equally important discussion, particularly for students: What happens when we don't get enough sleep?

SLEEP DEPRIVATION AND SLEEP DISPLACEMENT

Chances are you have experienced disruptions to your sleep due to jet lag or to an "occasional late night" (i.e., life as a student), and we've all had that awful feeling in the spring when we are robbed of a precious hour of slumber by Daylight Savings Time. We don't usually think of time shifts as being anything more than an annoyance. However, researchers have found that switching to Daylight Savings Time in the spring costs workers an average of 40 minutes of sleep and significantly increases work-related injuries on the Monday following the time change (Barnes & Wagner, 2009). The same analysis showed that returning to standard time in the fall produces no significant changes in sleep or injuries. Similar results have been noted for traffic accidents. Stanley Coren at the University of British Columbia found that there was a significant increase in the number of accidents immediately following the "spring forward," but not after the "fall back" (1996a; see Figure 5.5). Coren also looked at accidental deaths unrelated to car accidents (Coren, 1996b). Using U.S. data from 1986–1988, he found a 6.6% increase in accidental deaths in the four days following the "spring forward" of Daylight Savings Time. Importantly, the effects of disrupted sleep aren't limited to clumsiness; a substantial amount of research has shown that it can affect our thinking and decision making as well (Lavie, 2001).

Sleep deprivation *occurs when an individual cannot or does not sleep.* In other words, it can be due to some external factor that is out of your control (e.g., noisy neighbours) or to some self-inflicted factor (e.g., studying, staying up to watch the late hockey game on TV, etc.). Exactly how sleep deprivation affects daily functioning has been the subject of scientific inquiry since 1896, when researchers examined cognitive abilities in people kept awake for 90 consecutive

Figure 5.5 Car Accident Statistics for the Years 1991 and 1992

These data represent the number of car accidents on the Monday before, the Monday immediately after, and the Monday one week after the spring and fall time changes. Note the dramatic increase in accidents immediately following the spring time change, when we lose one hour of sleep. Astute observers will also note that, overall, there were still more accidents in the fall than in the spring (the *y* axes are different in the two graphs); this is likely due to the inclement weather found in many parts of Canada in October. Poor weather and earlier darkness are also the most likely explanations for the spike in accidents one week after the fall shift (green bar). These data are from the Canadian Ministry of Transport (and exclude Saskatchewan, which doesn't observe Daylight Savings Time).

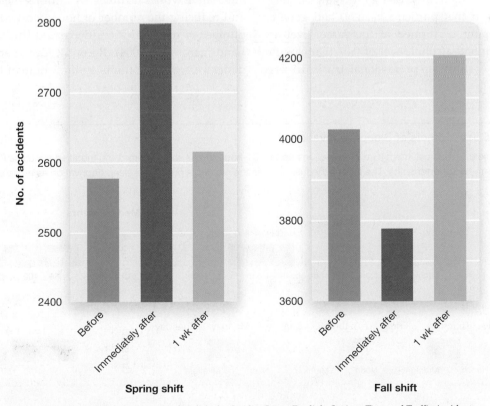

Source: From *The New England Journal of Medicine* by Stanley Coren, Daylight Savings Time and Traffic Accidents, 344 (14), 924. Copyright © 1996 Massachusetts Medical Society. Reprinted with permission from Massachusetts Medical Society.

hours (Patrick & Gilbert, 1896). In almost all of the studies in the past century, the strength of the circadian rhythms was evident; the volunteers generally went through cycles of extreme sleepiness at night, with normal levels of wakefulness in the daytime (especially the afternoon). However, each night saw an increasing level of sleepiness, likely as an attempt by the body to preserve and protect the health of the individual. In addition to feelings of fatigue, researchers have discovered a number of specific impairments resulting from being deprived of sleep. These include difficulties with multitasking, maintaining attention for long periods of time, assessing risks, incorporating new information into a strategy (i.e., "thinking on the fly"), working memory (i.e., keeping information in conscious awareness), inhibiting responses, and keeping information in the correct temporal order (Durmer & Dinges, 2005; Lavie, 2001; Wimmer et al., 1992). Importantly, these deficits also appear after partial sleep deprivation, such as when you don't get enough sleep (Cote et al., 2008). In fact, cognitive deficits typically appear when individuals have less than seven hours of sleep for a few nights in a row (Dinges, 2006; Dinges et al., 2005).

The problems associated with sleep deprivation aren't limited to your ability to think. Research with adolescents shows that for every hour of sleep deprivation, predictable increases in physical illness, family problems, substance abuse, and academic problems occur (Roberts et al., 2009). Issues also arise with your coordination, a problem best seen in studies of driving ability. Using a driving simulator, researchers found that participants who had gone a night without sleeping performed at the same level as people who had a blood-alcohol level of 0.07 (Fairclough & Graham, 1999). A study of professional truck drivers accustomed to long shifts found that going 28 hours without sleep produced driving abilities similar to someone with a blood-alcohol level of 0.1, which is above the legal limit throughout North America (Williamson & Feyer, 2000). Given that sleep deprivation is as dangerous as driving while mildly intoxicated (Dawson & Reid, 1997; Maruff et al., 2005), it is not surprising that it is one of the most prevalent causes of fatal traffic accidents (Lyznicki et al., 1998; Sagberg, 1999).

Sleep deprivation has led to some serious errors in the medical field as well. Medical residents ("residency" is the 2- to 5-year internship performed after completing medical school that precedes becoming a licensed, independent physician) and attending physicians often work through the night at hospitals; in some fields such as Internal Medicine, the doctors often don't even have time for naps. From what you've read in the preceding paragraphs, you can see that this is obviously a recipe for disaster. For instance, researchers at Harvard noted a number of critical errors by medical interns who were tired, including draining the wrong lung, prescribing a medication dose 10 times higher than it should have been, and causing an accidental overdose of benzodiazepines (Landrigan et al., 2004). Exhausted medical interns were also more likely to crash their cars on the way home (Barger et al., 2005) and suffer from job stress and burnout (Chen, Vorona, et al., 2008). These findings have motivated some researchers to investigate potential benefits of alternative work schedules; by limiting the length of shifts and reducing the number of hours worked per week, the number of medical errors decreased by 36% (Figure 5.6; Landrigan et al., 2004). Recently, Canadian medical residents were granted limits on the length of their shifts and

Figure 5.6 The Costly Effects of Sleep Deprivation

The traditional schedule of a medical intern (Group A) requires up to a 31-hour on-call shift, whereas the modified schedule (Group B) divides the 31 hours into two shorter shifts. The latter schedule reduces the effects of prolonged sleep deprivation as measured in terms of medical errors.

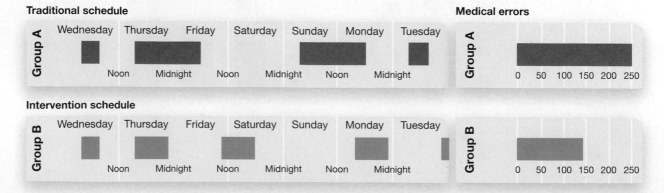

on the number of nights they can be "on call" per month. Perhaps someone was reading psychology research . . . or listening to their lawyers.

Cognitive and coordination errors are not limited to situations involving full or partial sleep deprivation. They can also occur when *the timing* of our sleep is altered. This phenomenon, **sleep displacement**, *occurs when an individual is prevented from sleeping at the normal time although she may be able to sleep earlier or later in the day than usual*. For example, consider a man from balmy Winnipeg who flies to London (U.K.) for a vacation. The first night in London, he may try to go to bed at his usual 12 A.M. time. However, his body's rhythms will be operating six hours earlier—they are still at 6 P.M. Winnipeg time. If he is like most travellers, this individual will experience sleep displacement for three or four days until he can get his internal rhythms to synchronize with the external day–night cycles. **Jet lag** *is the discomfort a person feels when sleep cycles are out of synchronization with light and darkness* (Arendt, 2009). How much jet lag people experience is related to how many time zones they cross and how quickly they do so (e.g., driving versus flying). Also, it is typically easier to adjust when travelling west. When travelling east, a person must try to fall asleep earlier than usual, which is difficult to do. Most people find it easier to stay up longer than usual, which is what westward travel requires.

For someone on a long vacation, jet lag may not be too much of an inconvenience. But imagine an athlete who has to be at her physical best, or a business executive who must remain sharp through an afternoon meeting. For these individuals, it is wise to arrive a week early if possible, or to try to adapt to the new time zone before leaving.

Although jet lag has limited implications for our lives (unless you happen to be a pilot or a flight attendant who crosses oceans several times a month), many people will at some point in their lives have jobs that require shift work. In many hospitals, nurses and support staff rotate across three different 8-hour shifts over the course of a month (e.g., midnight–8 A.M., 8 A.M.–4 P.M., 4 P.M.–midnight). Switching shifts requires a transition similar to jet lag; your day is suddenly altered by several hours. In order to better adapt to these changes, companies and hospitals are increasingly scheduling the shift rotations so that workers are able to stay up later (similar to travelling westward in the jet lag example). This reduces the negative effects on a worker's sleep patterns, which reduces the symptoms of sleep deprivation, thus giving the employer a more alert (and friendlier) employee.

It is important to note that sleep deprivation is not always caused by external factors such as world travel or tough work schedules; in fact, it can be caused by our own behaviours. One possible cause of sleep deprivation is consuming caffeine before bedtime. A 49-day study of five individuals found that consuming caffeine—in this case a double espresso—prior to going to bed delayed their internal clock by 40 minutes (Burke et al., 2015). This shift was twice as large as that caused by exposure to bright lights. (These participants were obviously dedicated and patient people.) A follow-up examination of the cellular mechanisms of this effect found that caffeine influences the levels of cyclic AMP, a molecule involved in the brain's internal clock. The good news is that the effects of caffeine on your circadian rhythms—and the cognitive impairments that go with it—are entirely under your control. The next time you spend an evening at Starbucks with your favourite psychology textbook, order a decaf.

Module 5.1b Quiz:

Why Do We Need Sleep?

Know . . .

1. When does sleep displacement occur?
   A. When an individual tries to sleep in a new location
   B. When an individual is allowed to sleep only at night
   C. When an individual is allowed to sleep, but not at his normal time
   D. When an individual is not allowed to sleep during a controlled laboratory experiment

Understand . . .

2. Sleep may help animals stay safe and conserve energy for when it is needed most. This is known as the _____.
   A. preserve and protect hypothesis
   B. restore and repair hypothesis
   C. REM rebound hypothesis
   D. preserve and repair hypothesis

Apply . . .

3. Jamie reports that it is easier for her to adjust to a new time zone when flying west than when flying east. This occurs because
   A. it is easier to get to sleep earlier than dictated by your circadian rhythms.
   B. it is easier to stay up later than your circadian rhythms expect.
   C. there is more sunlight when you travel west.
   D. there is less sunlight when you travel west.

Theories of Dreaming

It is very difficult to think about sleeping without thinking about dreaming. Dreams are mysterious and have captured our imaginations for most of human history. A study of 1348 Canadian university students found that some patterns emerge when we analyze the *content* of our dreams. Using a statistical technique called factor analysis, researchers found that students' dreams can be reduced to 16 different factors or subtypes. Females tended to have a larger number of negative dreams related to failures, loss of control, and frightening animals. Males, on the other hand, had more positive dreams including those related to magical abilities and encounters with alien life (Nielsen et al., 2003). However, studies such as this one, despite being conducted properly, do not provide insight into the purpose(s) dreams serve in our lives.

THE PSYCHOANALYTIC APPROACH One of the earliest and most influential theories of dreams was developed by Sigmund Freud in 1899. His classic work, *The Interpretation of Dreams,* dramatically transformed the Western world's view of both the function and meaning of dreams. Although many ancient societies performed dream interpretations, most viewed the content of dreams as representing connections to specific gods, as omens (good or bad), or as predictors of the future. In contrast, Freud viewed dreams as an unconscious expression of *wish fulfillment.* He believed that humans are motivated by primal urges, with sex and aggression being the most dominant. Because giving in to these urges is impractical most of the time (not to mention potentially immoral and illegal), we learn ways of keeping these urges suppressed and outside of our conscious awareness. When we sleep, however, we lose the power to suppress our urges. Without this active suppression, these drives are free to create the vivid imagery found in our dreams. This imagery can take two forms. **Manifest content** involves *the images and storylines that we dream about.* In many of our dreams, the manifest content involves sexuality and aggression, consistent with the view that dreams are a form of wish fulfillment. However, in other cases, the manifest content of dreams might seem like random, bizarre images and events. Freud would argue that these images are anything but random; instead, he believed they have a hidden meaning. This **latent content** is *the actual symbolic meaning of a dream built on suppressed sexual or aggressive urges.* Because the true meaning of the dream is latent, Freud advocated *dream work,* the recording and interpreting of dreams. Through such work, Freudian analysis would allow you to bring the previously hidden sexual and aggressive elements of your dreams into the forefront, although it might mean you'd never look at the CN Tower the same way again.

It is difficult to overstate the influence that Freud's ideas have had on our culture's beliefs about dreaming. There is an abundance of books offering insights into interpreting dreams including dictionaries that claim to define certain symbols found in a dream's latent content. However, it is important to note that the scientific support for Freud's work is quite limited. Although his theories are based on extensive interviews with patients, many of these theories are difficult to test in a scientific manner because they cannot be falsified (i.e., there is no way to prove them wrong). Moreover, dream work requires a subjective interpreter to understand dreams rather than using objective measures. Therefore, the analysis of your dream might have more to do with the mindset of the analyst than it does your own hidden demons. Not surprisingly, modern dream research focuses much more on the biological activity of dreaming. These studies focus primarily on REM sleep, when dreams are most common and complex.

THE ACTIVATION–SYNTHESIS HYPOTHESIS Freud saw deep psychological meaning in the latent content of dreams. In contrast, the **activation–synthesis hypothesis** *suggests that dreams arise from brain activity originating from bursts of excitatory messages from the pons, a part of the brainstem* (Hobson & McCarley, 1977). This electrical activity produces the telltale signs of eye movements and patterns of EEG activity during REM sleep that resemble wakefulness; moreover, the burst of activity stimulates the occipital and temporal lobes of the brain, producing imaginary sights and sounds, as well as numerous other regions of the cortex (see Figure 5.7). Thus, the brainstem initiates the *activation* component of the model. The *synthesis* component arises as different areas of the cortex of the brain try to make sense of all the images, sounds, emotions, and memories (Hobson et al., 2000). Imagine having a dozen different people each provide you with one randomly selected word, with your task being to organize these words to look like a single message; this is essentially what your cortex is doing every time you dream. Because we are often able to turn these random messages into a coherent story, researchers assume that the frontal lobes—the region of the brain associated with forming narratives—play a key role in the synthesis process (Eiser, 2005).

The activation–synthesis model, although important in its own right, has some interesting implications. If the cortex is able to provide (temporary) structure to input from the brainstem and other regions of the brain, then that means the brain is able to work with and restructure information while we dream. If that is the case, then is it possible that the neural activity involved with dreaming also influences our ability to learn new information?

Figure 5.7 The Activation–Synthesis Hypothesis of Dreaming

The pons, located in the brainstem, sends excitatory messages through the thalamus to the sensory and emotional areas of the cortex. The images and emotions that arise from this activity are then woven into a story. Inhibitory signals are also relayed from the pons down the spinal cord, which prevents movement during dreaming.

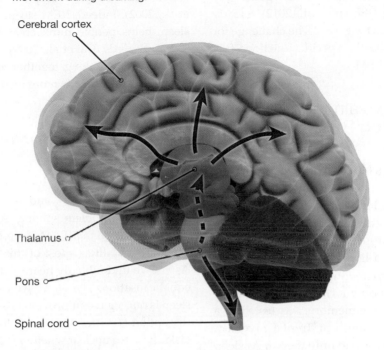

Cerebral cortex

Thalamus

Pons

Spinal cord

Working the Scientific Literacy Model

Dreams, REM Sleep, and Learning

The activation–synthesis model of dreaming suggests that our dreams result from random brainstem activity that is organized—to some degree—by the cortex. Although this theory is widely accepted, it doesn't provide many specifics about the *purpose* of dreams. *Why* do we have these processes occurring and what functions do they serve? Dream researcher Rosalind Cartwright (Cartwright et al., 2006; Webb & Cartwright, 1978) proposed the **problem-solving theory**—*the theory that thoughts and concerns are continuous from waking to sleeping, and that dreams may function to facilitate finding solutions to problems encountered while awake.* This theory suggests that many of the images and thoughts we have during our dreams are relevant to the problems that we face when we are awake. For instance, researchers have found that individuals who are in poor physical health have more dreams about pain, injuries, illnesses, and medical themes than do healthy individuals (King & DeCicco, 2007). Another study showed that the number of threatening images in participants' dreams increased immediately following the September 11 terrorist attacks (Propper et al., 2007). However, although no one doubts

that our daily concerns find their way into our dreams, the problem-solving theory does not explain if (or how) any specific cognitive mechanisms are influenced by dreaming. In contrast, increasing evidence suggests that REM sleep, the sleep stage involved with dreaming, is essential for a number of cognitive functions.

What do we know about dreams, REM sleep, and learning?

Approximately 20–25% of our total sleep time is taken up by REM, or rapid eye movement, sleep. When we are deprived of REM sleep, we typically experience a phenomenon called *REM rebound*—our brains spend increased time in REM-phase sleep when given the chance. If you usually sleep 8 hours but get only 3 hours of sleep on a particular night, you can recover from the sleep deficit the next time you sleep with only the normal 8 hours; however, your time in REM sleep will increase considerably. The fact that our bodies actively try to catch up on missed REM sleep suggests that it may serve an important function.

As discussed earlier in this module, REM sleep produces brainwaves similar to being awake, yet we are asleep (Aserinsky & Kleitman, 1953). This similarity suggests that the types of functions being performed by the brain are likely similar during the two states. Studies with animals have shown that REM sleep is associated with a number of different neurotransmitter systems, all of which influence activity in the brainstem. Projections from the brainstem can then affect a number of different functions, including movement (which is inhibited), emotional regulation (through connections to the amygdala and frontal lobes), and learning (Brown et al., 2012). Clearly REM is not simply about twitching eyes! The challenge for psychologists is to determine the specific functions that are, and are not, affected by REM.

How can science explain the effects of dreams and REM sleep on learning?

In the last 25 years, scientists have performed an extraordinary number of experiments in their attempt to understand how REM sleep (and possibly dreaming) influences our thinking. The results of these studies show that REM sleep affects some, but not all, types of memory. If someone were to give you a list of words to remember and then tested you later, this would be an example of declarative memory (see Module 7.1). The effect of REM sleep disruption on declarative memory was tested in a study conducted by Carlyle Smith at Trent University. Different groups of participants had only their REM sleep disrupted, only their non-REM sleep disrupted, or all of their sleep disrupted. When their memory for the words was tested, there were no differences between the groups, suggesting that REM sleep is not critical for this simple type of memory. However, when researchers gave participants tests that involved a larger number of steps or procedures, a different pattern of results emerged: Being deprived of REM sleep produced large deficits in performance (Smith, 2001).

Several studies have shown that the amount of REM sleep people experience increases the night after learning a new task (Smith et al., 2004). For instance, Mandai and colleagues (1989) found increases in REM sleep in individuals the night following a Morse-code learning task. There was a high correlation between retention levels for the Morse code signals, the number of REM episodes, and the density of the REM activity (i.e., the frequency of eye movements made during REM episodes). In a study directly related to students' lives, Smith and Lapp (1991) measured REM sleep 3–5 days after senior undergraduate students had completed their fall semester final exams. These students had more REM sleep episodes and a greater REM sleep density than they had when they were tested in the summer, when less learning was taking place. They also had higher sleep-density values than age-matched participants who were not in university. These results suggest that REM sleep may help us consolidate or maintain newly learned information.

Research has also demonstrated that REM sleep and dreaming also influence our ability to problem solve. Depriving people of REM sleep reduces their ability to perform a complex logic task (Smith, 1993). This may be due to the fact that our ability to form new associations increases during REM sleep (Stickgold et al., 1999; Walker et al., 2002). Indeed, REM sleep, as opposed to non-REM sleep, helps people think creatively to find associations between words (Cai et al., 2009). REM sleep appears to be involved with linking together steps in the formation of new memories and in reorganizing information in novel ways.

Can we critically evaluate this evidence?

We have to be cautious when we consider the different effects that REM sleep, and perhaps dreaming, have on memory and problem solving. Although there is a great deal of evidence that REM sleep does influence a number of different abilities, most of this research is correlational. As you've undoubtedly heard before, correlation does not equal causation. Therefore, we can't guarantee that REM sleep is *causing* the improvements in memory—just that its disruption *is related to* poor performance on a number of tasks. It is also unclear whether the observed effects are due to dreaming or to some other REM-related function.

In addition to these questions, it is also worth noting that the effects from these studies are not occurring during every period of REM sleep. When it comes to memory, not all REM sleep is created equal. The final few REM periods in the early morning appear to be critical for learning (Smith, 2001). Stickgold and colleagues (2000) found that performance on a visual search task (in which participants tried to find a particular target image that was hidden amongst distracter images, similar to "Where's Waldo?") correlated with the amount of *non*-REM sleep a person had in the early part of the night and the amount of REM sleep in the early morning. Therefore, to say that REM sleep, in general, improves some types of learning is an oversimplification. Further research is needed to understand what makes these early morning windows of REM special. Finally, it is possible that it is dreaming, not REM sleep, that is affecting cognition. However, although dreaming *can* sometimes occur during non-REM sleep, these dreams tend to be less vivid and emotional than REM-based dreams and therefore less likely to affect learning (Suzuki et al., 2004).

Why is this relevant?

Studies of REM sleep and learning show us that the benefits of sleep go beyond restoring and repairing the body. Rather, the effect(s) of REM sleep on our ability to learn new tasks should serve as a wake-up call to all of us. Almost everyone in a university setting is working on a less-than-optimal amount of sleep despite the fact that REM sleep is clearly an important part of our ability to learn. This seems counterproductive. Studying and sleeping every night is a much more effective way to retain information than pulling a frantic all-nighter just before an exam, even if we all feel like we're out of time.

Interestingly, REM sleep is not the only stage of sleep that affects our ability to learn. There is some evidence that the sleep spindles found in stage 2 sleep are involved with learning new movements (Fogel et al., 2007; Peters

et al., 2008). Smith and MacNeil (1994) found that disrupting stage 2 sleep impaired performance on a pursuit-rotor task in which participants tried to move a computer mouse so that the cursor followed an object on the computer screen. However, when participants were asked to move as though the image was in a mirror (so that an object farther away on the screen was closer to their body), REM, and not stage 2 sleep, became essential. The only difference between the two tasks was the cognitive difficulty associated with figuring out which movement to perform (Aubrey et al., 1999). This suggests that the brain has different systems for processing simple and complex movements and that these systems are influenced by different stages of sleep (Smith, 2001).

Module 5.1c Quiz:

Theories of Dreaming

Know . . .

1. The problem-solving theory of dreaming proposes that
   - **A.** dreams create more problems than they solve.
   - **B.** the problems and concerns we face in our waking life also appear in our dreams.
   - **C.** the symbols in our dreams represent unconscious urges related to sex and aggression.
   - **D.** we cannot solve complex moral or interpersonal problems until we have dreamed about them.

Understand . . .

2. The *synthesis* part of the activation–synthesis hypothesis suggests that
   - **A.** the brain interprets the meaning of symbolic images.
   - **B.** the brainstem activates the cortex to produce random images.
   - **C.** the cortex stimulates the brainstem to produce interpretations of dreams.
   - **D.** the brain tries to link together, or make sense of, randomly activated images.

Analyze . . .

3. Scientists are skeptical about the psychoanalytic theory of dreaming because the _____ of a dream is entirely subject to interpretation.
   - **A.** latent content
   - **B.** sleep stage
   - **C.** activation
   - **D.** manifest content

Disorders and Problems with Sleep

Throughout this module, we have seen that sleep is an essential biological and psychological process; without sleep, individuals are vulnerable to cognitive, emotional, and physical symptoms. Given these widespread effects, it should come as no surprise that a lot of research has been directed at improving our ability to diagnose and treat sleep disorders. In the final section of this module, we will discuss some of the more common sleep disorders.

INSOMNIA The most widely recognized sleeping problem is **insomnia**, *a disorder characterized by an extreme lack of sleep*. According to a 2002 Canadian Community Health Survey from Statistics Canada, one in seven Canadian adults (3.3 million people) suffer from insomnia. This number was lowest in the 18–25 age bracket (10%) and

highest in individuals 75 years of age and older (20%) (Statistics Canada, 2003). Although the average adult may need 7 to 8 hours of sleep to feel rested, substantial individual differences exist. For this reason, insomnia is defined not in terms of the number of hours of sleep, but rather in terms of the degree to which a person feels rested during the day. If a person feels that her sleep disturbance is affecting her schoolwork, her job, or her family and social life, then it is indeed a problem. However, for this condition to be thought of as a sleep *disorder*, it would have to be present for three months or more—one or two "bad nights" is unpleasant, but is not technically insomnia.

Although insomnia is often thought of as a single disorder, it may be more appropriate to refer to *insomnias* in the plural. *Onset insomnia* occurs when a person has difficulty falling asleep (30 minutes or more), *maintenance*

Steve Prezant/Glow Images

Insomnia can arise from worrying about sleep. It is among the most common of all sleep disorders.

insomnia occurs when an individual cannot easily return to sleep after waking in the night, and *terminal insomnia* or *early morning insomnia* is a situation in which a person wakes up too early—sometimes hours too early—and cannot return to sleep (Pallesen et al., 2001).

It is important to remember that for a sleep disorder to be labelled insomnia, the problems with sleeping must be due to some internal cause; not sleeping because your roommate snores does not count as insomnia. Sometimes insomnia occurs as part of another problem, such as depression, pain, developmental disorders such as attention deficit hyperactivity disorder (ADHD), or various drugs (Corkum et al., 2014; Schierenbeck et al., 2008); in these cases, the sleep disorder is referred to as a *secondary insomnia*. When insomnia is the only symptom that a person is showing, and other causes can be ruled out, physicians would label the sleep disorder as *insomnia disorder*. If you think back to our earlier discussion of sleep deprivation, you can see why insomnia—despite not seeming serious—can have a profound effect on a person's ability to function in our demanding world. However, it isn't the only disorder that can affect our ability to sleep a full eight hours each night.

NIGHTMARES AND NIGHT TERRORS Although most of our dreams are interesting and often bizarre, some of our dreams really scare us. **Nightmares** *are particularly vivid and disturbing dreams that occur during REM sleep.* They can be so emotionally charged that they awaken the individual (Levin & Nielsen, 2007). Almost everyone—as many as 85% to 95% of adults—can remember having bad dreams that have negative emotional content, such as feeling lost, sad, or angry, within a one-year period (Levin,

1994; Schredl, 2003). Data from numerous studies indicate that nightmares are correlated with psychological distress including anxiety (Nielsen et al., 2000; Zadra & Donderi, 2000), negative emotionality (Berquier & Ashton, 1992; Levin & Fireman, 2002), and emotional reactivity (Kramer et al., 1984). They are more common in females (Nielsen et al., 2006), likely because women tend to have higher levels of depression and emotional disturbances. Indeed, in individuals with emotional disorders, the "synthesis" part of dreaming appears to reorganize information in a way consistent with their mental state, with a focus on negative emotion.

Nightmares, although unpleasant, are a normal part of life. In contrast, 1–6% of children and 1% of adults experience **night terrors**—*intense bouts of panic and arousal that awaken the individual, typically in a heightened emotional state.* A person experiencing a night terror may call out or scream, fight back against imaginary attackers, or leap from the bed and start to flee before waking up. Unlike nightmares, night terrors are not dreams. These episodes occur during NREM sleep, and the majority of people who experience them typically do not recall any specific dream content. Night terrors increase in frequency during stressful periods, such as when parents are separating or divorcing (Schredl, 2001). There is also some evidence linking them to feelings of anxiety, which suggests that for some sufferers, counselling and other means for reducing anxiety may help reduce the symptoms (Kales et al., 1980; Szelenberger et al., 2005).

MOVEMENT DISTURBANCES To sleep well, an individual needs to remain still. During REM sleep, the brain prevents movement by sending inhibitory signals down the spinal cord. A number of sleep disturbances, however, involve movement and related sensations. For example, **restless legs syndrome** *is a persistent feeling of discomfort in the legs and the urge to continuously shift them into different positions* (Smith & Tolson, 2008). This disorder affects approximately 5% to 10% of the population (generally older adults), and occurs at varying levels of severity. For those individuals who are in constant motion, sleep becomes very difficult. They awake periodically at night to reposition their legs, although they often have no memory of doing so. The mechanism causing RLS is unclear; however, there is some evidence that it is linked to the dopamine system and to an iron deficiency (Allen, 2004). Therefore, current treatments are focused on keeping dopamine and iron at normal levels in these patients.

A more common movement disturbance is **somnambulism**, or *sleepwalking, a disorder that involves wandering and performing other activities while asleep.* It occurs during NREM sleep, stages 3 and 4, and is more prevalent during childhood. Sleepwalking is not necessarily indicative of any type of sleep or emotional disturbance, although it may put people in harm's way. People who sleepwalk are not acting out dreams, and they typically do not remember the episode. (For the record, it is not dangerous to wake up a sleepwalker, as is commonly thought. At worst, he or she will be disoriented.) There is no reliable medicine that curbs sleepwalking; instead, it is important to add safety measures to the person's environment so that the sleepwalker doesn't get hurt.

A similar, but more adult, disorder is *sexomnia* or *sleep sex*. Individuals with this condition engage in sexual activity such as the touching of the self or others, vocalizations, and sex-themed talk while in stages 3 and 4 sleep (Shapiro et al., 2003). In the original case report of this disorder (Motet, 1897, described in Thoinot, 1913), a man exposed his genitals to a policeman (that's bad). He was unable to recall the incident afterwards and was sentenced to three months in jail. Other reports are more extreme, including sex with strangers and unwanted contact with sleeping partners (Béjot et al., 2010). The exact cause of sexomnia is unknown, although stress, fatigue, and a history of trauma have all been mentioned as possible factors (Schenck et al., 2007).

Another potentially dangerous condition is *REM behaviour disorder*, which was introduced in the beginning of this module. People with this condition do not show the typical restriction of movement during REM sleep; in fact, they appear to be acting out the content of their dreams (Schenck & Mahowald, 2002). Imagine what happens when an individual dreams of being attacked—the dreamed response of defending oneself or even fighting back can be acted out. Not surprisingly, this action can awaken some individuals. Because it occurs during REM sleep, however, some individuals do not awaken until they have hurt themselves or someone else, as occurred with Mike Birbiglia (Schenck et al., 1989). Unlike sleepwalking and restless legs syndrome, REM behaviour disorder can be treated with medication; benzodiazepines, which inhibit the central nervous system, have proven effective in reducing some of the symptoms associated with this condition (Paparrigopoulos, 2005). However, given the potential side effects of this class of drug, this option should only be taken if the person is a threat to himself or others.

SLEEP APNEA The disorders discussed thus far have focused on changes in the brain that lead to altered thinking patterns (nightmares and night terrors) and movements. In contrast, **sleep apnea** *is a disorder characterized by the temporary inability to breathe during sleep* (*apnea* literally translates to "without breathing"). Although a variety of factors contribute to sleep apnea, this condition appears to be most common among overweight and obese individuals, and it is roughly twice as prevalent among men as among women (Lin et al., 2008; McDaid et al., 2009). In most cases of apnea, the airway becomes physically

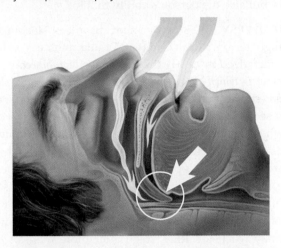

Figure 5.8 Sleep Apnea

One cause of sleep apnea is the obstruction of air flow, which can seriously disrupt the sleep cycle.

Source: Lilienfeld, Scott O.; Lynn, Steven J; Namy, Laura L.; Woolf, Nancy J., *Psychology: From Inquiry to Understanding*, 2nd ed., © 2011. Reprinted and electronically reproduced by permission of Pearson Education, Inc., New York, NY.

obstructed at a point anywhere from the back of the nose and mouth to the neck (Figure 5.8). Therefore, treatment for mild apnea generally involves dental devices that hold the mouth in a specific position during sleep. Weight-loss efforts should accompany this treatment in cases in which it is a contributing factor. In moderate to severe cases, a continuous positive airway pressure (CPAP) device can be used to force air through the nose, keeping the airway open through increased air pressure (McDaid et al., 2009).

In rare but more serious cases, sleep apnea can also be caused by the brain's failure to regulate breathing. This failure can happen for many reasons, including damage to or deterioration of the medulla of the brainstem, which is responsible for controlling the chest muscles during breathing.

You might wonder if disorders that stop breathing during sleep can be fatal. They can be, but rarely are. As breathing slows too much or stops altogether, oxygen levels in the blood rapidly decline, resulting in a gasping reflex and resumed oxygen flow. Actually, gasping may not even result in waking up. A person with sleep apnea may not be aware that he is constantly cycling through oxygen loss and gasping as he sleeps, although it would certainly be noticed by anyone sharing a bed with him. It is often the case that affected individuals discover that they have sleep apnea only after visiting their physician to find a solution for their snoring and fatigue.

Although sleep apnea is serious in its own right, it also leads to a number of other problems. Repeatedly waking up during the night reduces the quality of an individual's sleep and can lead to a mild form of sleep deprivation (Naëgelé et al., 1995). In fact, individuals who suffer from sleep apnea often perform more poorly on tests requiring mental flexibility, the control of attention, and memory (Fulda & Schulz, 2003). Treating sleep apnea will therefore not only improve a person's physical safety and fatigue levels, but also the person's ability to think.

NARCOLEPSY While movement disorders, sleep apnea, and night terrors can all lead to insomnia, another condition is characterized by nearly the opposite effect. **Narcolepsy** *is a disorder in which a person experiences extreme daytime sleepiness and even sleep attacks.* These bouts of sleep may last only a few seconds, especially if the person is standing or driving when she falls asleep and is jarred awake by falling, a nodding head, or swerving of the car. Even without such disturbances, the sleep may last only a few minutes or more, so it is not the same as falling asleep for a night's rest.

Narcolepsy differs from more typical sleep in a number of other ways. People with a normal sleep pattern generally reach the REM stage after more than an hour of sleep, but a person experiencing narcolepsy is likely to go almost immediately from waking to REM sleep. Also, because REM sleep is associated with dreaming, people with narcolepsy often report vivid dream-like images even if they did not fully fall asleep.

Why does narcolepsy occur? Scientists have investigated a hormone called *orexin* that functions to maintain wakefulness. Individuals with narcolepsy have fewer brain cells that produce orexin, resulting in greater difficulty maintaining wakefulness (Nakamura et al., 2011). Luckily, medications are available to treat this condition, thus allowing these individuals to function relatively normally (Mayer, 2012).

OVERCOMING SLEEP PROBLEMS Everyone has difficulty sleeping at some point, and there are many myths and anecdotes about what will help. For some people, relief can be as simple as a snack or a warm glass of milk; it can certainly be difficult to sleep if you are hungry. Others might have a nightcap—a drink of alcohol—in hopes of inducing sleep, although the effects can be misleading.

Alcohol may make you sleepy, but it disrupts the quality of sleep, especially the REM cycle, and may leave you feeling unrested the next day.

Many people turn to drugs (e.g., sedatives) to help them sleep. A number of sleep aids are available on an over-the-counter basis, and several varieties of prescription drugs have been developed as well. For most of the 20th century, drugs prescribed for insomnia included sedatives such as barbiturates (Phenobarbital) and benzodiazepines (e.g., Valium). Although these drugs managed to put people to sleep, several problems with their use were quickly observed. Notably, people quickly developed tolerance to these agents, meaning they required increasingly higher doses to get the same effect, and many soon came to depend on the drugs so much that they could not sleep without them (Pallesen et al., 2001). Even though benzodiazepines are generally safer than barbiturates, the risk of dependence and worsening sleep problems makes them suitable only for short-term use—generally for a week or two. Modern sleep drugs are generally thought to be much safer in the short term, and many have been approved for long-term use as well. However, few modern drugs have been studied in placebo-controlled experiments, and even fewer have actually been studied for long-term use (e.g., for more than a month; Krystal, 2009).

Fortunately, most people respond very well to psychological interventions. By practising good *sleep hygiene—* healthy sleep-related habits—they can typically overcome sleep disturbances in a matter of a few weeks (Morin et al., 2006; Murtagh & Greenwood, 1995). The techniques shown in Table 5.1 are effective for many people who prefer self-help methods, but effective help is also available from psychologists, physicians, and even (sometimes) over the Internet (Ritterband et al., 2009; van Straten & Cuijpers, 2009). So, rather than taking drugs to alter your brain chemistry, it is generally safer to change your sleep hygiene (sleeping routines) if you want to put your sleeping problems to rest.

Table 5.1 Nonpharmacological Techniques for Improving Sleep

1. Use your bed for sleeping only, not for working or studying. (Sexual activity is an appropriate exception to the rule.)

2. Do not turn sleep into work. Putting effort into falling asleep generally leads to arousal instead of sleep.

3. Keep your clock out of sight. Watching the clock increases pressure to sleep and worries about getting enough sleep.

4. Get exercise early during the day. Exercise may not increase the amount of sleep, but it may help you sleep better. Exercising late in the day, however, may leave you restless and aroused at bedtime.

5. Avoid substances that disrupt sleep. Such substances include caffeine (in coffee, tea, many soft drinks, and other sources), nicotine, and alcohol. Illicit drugs such as cocaine, marijuana, and ecstasy also disrupt healthy sleep.

6. If you lie in bed worrying at night, schedule evening time to deal with stress. Write down your worries and stressors for approximately 30 minutes prior to bedtime.

7. If you continue to lie in bed without sleeping for 30 minutes, get up and do something else until you are about to fall asleep, and then return to bed.

8. Get up at the same time every morning. Although this practice may lead to sleepiness the first day or two, eventually it helps set a daily rhythm.

9. If you still have problems sleeping after four weeks, consider seeing a sleep specialist to get tested for sleep apnea, restless legs syndrome, or other sleep problems that may require more specific interventions.

Source: Based on recommendations from the American Psychological Association, 2004.

Module 5.1d Quiz:

Disorders and Problems with Sleep

Know . . .

1. When people do not show the typical restriction of movement during REM sleep, they are experiencing _____.
   - A. somnambulism
   - B. REM behaviour disorder
   - C. insomnia
   - D. restless legs syndrome

2. _____is(are) a condition in which a person's breathing becomes obstructed or stops during sleep.
   - A. Somnambulism
   - B. Night terrors
   - C. Narcolepsy
   - D. Sleep apnea

Apply . . .

3. Which of the following is *not* good advice for improving your quality of sleep?
   - A. Use your bed for sleeping only—not for doing homework or watching TV.
   - B. Exercise late in the day to make sure you are tired when it is time to sleep.
   - C. Avoid drinking caffeine, especially late in the day.
   - D. Get up at the same time every morning to make sure you develop a reliable pattern of sleep and wakefulness.

Module 5.1 Summary

5.1a   Know . . . the key terminology associated with sleep, dreams, and sleep disorders.

activation–synthesis hypothesis
circadian rhythms
consciousness
endogenous rhythms
entrainment
insomnia
jet lag
latent content
manifest content
narcolepsy
night terrors
nightmares
polysomnography
preserve and protect hypothesis
problem-solving theory
REM sleep
restless legs syndrome
restore and repair hypothesis
sleep apnea
sleep deprivation
sleep displacement
somnambulism

5.1b   Understand . . . how the sleep cycle works.

The sleep cycle consists of a series of stages going from stage 1 through stage 4, cycles back down again, and is followed by a REM phase. The first sleep cycle lasts approximately 90 minutes. Deep sleep (stages 3 and 4) is longest during the first half of the sleep cycle, whereas REM phases increase in duration during the second half of the sleep cycle.

5.1c   Understand . . . theories of why we sleep.

Sleep theories include the restore and repair hypothesis and the preserve and protect hypothesis. According to the restore and repair hypothesis, we sleep so that the body can recover from the stress and strain on the body that occurs during waking. Waste products are more efficiently removed from the brain during this time as well. According to the preserve and protect hypothesis, sleep has evolved as a way to reduce activity and provide protection from potential threats, and to reduce the amount of energy intake required. Evidence supports both theories, so it is likely that there is more than one reason for sleep.

5.1d   Apply . . . your knowledge to identify and practise good sleep habits.

Apply Activity

Try completing the Epworth Sleepiness Scale to make sure you are getting enough sleep (Table 5.2). If you score 10 points or higher, you are probably not getting enough sleep. You can always refer to Table 5.1 for tips on improving your sleep.

5.1e   Analyze . . . different theories about why we dream.

Dreams have fascinated psychologists since Freud's time. From his psychoanalytic perspective, Freud believed that the manifest content of dreams could be used to uncover their symbolic, latent content. Contemporary scientists are skeptical about the validity of this approach given the lack of empirical evidence to support it. The activation–

synthesis theory eliminates the meaning of dream content, suggesting instead that dreams are just interpretations of haphazard electrical activity in the sleeping brain that are then organized to some degree by the cortex. Increasing evidence suggests that REM sleep, the sleep stage associated with dreaming, improves our ability to form new procedural (step-by-step) memories and to find solutions to problems.

Table 5.2 Epworth Sleepiness Scale

Use the following scale to choose the most appropriate number for each situation:

0 = would *never* doze or sleep   1 = *slight* chance of dozing or sleeping

2 = *moderate* chance of dozing or sleeping   3 = *high* chance of dozing or sleeping

Situation	Chances of Falling Asleep
Sitting and reading	0 1 2 3
Watching TV	0 1 2 3
Sitting inactive in a public place	0 1 2 3
Being a passenger in a motor vehicle for an hour or more	0 1 2 3
Lying down in the afternoon	0 1 2 3
Sitting and talking to someone	0 1 2 3
Sitting quietly after lunch (no alcohol)	0 1 2 3
Stopped for a few minutes in traffic while driving	0 1 2 3
Your total score	

Source: Reprinted with permission from SLEEP. Sleep Research Society, Darien, IL, USA 2016.

Module 5.2 Altered States of Consciousness: Hypnosis, Mind-Wandering, and Disorders of Consciousness

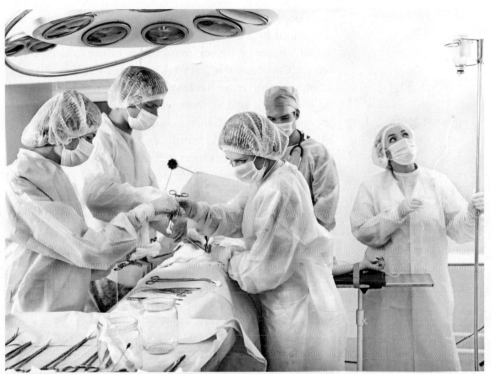

Gennadiy Poznyakov/Fotolia

Learning Objectives

5.2a Know . . . the key terminology associated with hypnosis, mind-wandering, and disorders of consciousness.

5.2b Understand . . . the competing theories of hypnosis.

5.2c Apply . . . your knowledge of hypnosis to identify what it can and cannot do.

5.2d Analyze . . . the effectiveness of using neuroimaging to study mind-wandering.

5.2e Analyze . . . the ability of researchers to detect consciousness in brain-damaged patients.

"Just a moment! I don't like the patient's colour. Much too blue. Her lips are very blue. I'm going to give a little more oxygen. . .. There, that's better now. You can carry on with the operation" (Levinson, 1965, p. 544). If you were undergoing surgery with a local anesthetic and heard this, you would certainly be worried . . . if not panicking. But, what if you had been given general anesthetic so that you were "unconscious"? Presumably, you should be blissfully unaware of the fact that you were turning blue. However, when prompted by an experimenter one month later, 8 of the 10 patients who heard these statements—which were a script read during real surgeries as part of an experiment—were able to report back some

elements of the fake crisis. Four of the patients were able to give an almost verbatim account of what the experimenter said. In other studies, post-operative patients were able to complete word stems (e.g., H O - - -) with words presented under anesthesia (e.g., HORSE, not HOUSE) at levels far above chance (Bonebakker et al., 1996; Merikle & Daneman, 1996). How is this possible? Brain-imaging studies have noted that anesthesia affects more than just activity related to pain and touch; instead, it affects how different areas of the brain work together to form networks (MacDonald et al., 2015). Importantly, anesthesia seems to affect brain networks related to complex thought more than it affects networks related to auditory and visual perception (Boveroux et al., 2010; Liu et al., 2012). This difference may explain why anesthetized patients might, upon coming out of the anesthetic state, use the presented words to complete word stems even though they have no conscious recollection of their presentation.

It is important to note that these studies don't tell us what consciousness is. What these studies do illustrate, however, is that consciousness does not have a simple on/off switch. Instead, there are a number of possible states of consciousness, each with its own abilities and limitations.

Focus Questions

1. How is information perceived in different states of consciousness?

2. Is information processed in the background of our awareness?

》 Philosophers have attempted to understand the mysteries of consciousness for thousands of years. Recently, cognitive neuroscience researchers have used methods ranging from brain imaging to computer modelling to examine how the coordinated activity of groups of brain cells can produce our everyday conscious experiences (Crick, 1994; Ward et al., 2010). Although these investigations have shown great promise, many psychologists use a different strategy to study consciousness: examining situations in which consciousness is altered or impaired. By examining how our abilities and experiences change during altered states of consciousness, we can gain greater insight into our "normal" conscious behaviour. In this module, we will discuss three of these altered states—hypnosis, mind wandering, and disorders of consciousness caused by brain damage.

Hypnosis

The caricature of a hypnotist as an intense-looking bearded man swinging his glistening pocket watch back and forth before an increasingly subdued subject will probably always be around, though it promotes just one of many misunderstandings about hypnosis. **Hypnosis** is actually *a procedure of inducing a heightened state of suggestibility.* According to this definition, hypnosis is *not* a trance, as is often portrayed in the popular media (Kirsch & Lynn, 1998). Instead, the hypnotist simply suggests changes, and the subject is more likely (but not certain) to comply as a result of the suggestion.

Although one could conceivably make suggestions about almost anything, hypnotic suggestions generally are most effective when they fall into one of three categories:

- *Ideomotor suggestions* are related to specific actions that could be performed, such as adopting a specific position.

- *Challenge suggestions* indicate actions that are not to be performed, so that the subject appears to lose the ability to perform an action.

- *Cognitive-perceptual suggestions* involve a subject remembering or forgetting specific information, or experiencing altered perceptions such as reduced pain sensations (Kirsch & Lynn, 1998).

People who have not encountered scientific information about hypnosis are often skeptical that hypnosis can actually occur or are very reluctant to be hypnotized themselves (Capafons et al., 2008; Molina & Mendoza, 2006). It is important to note that hypnotists cannot make someone do something against their will. For example, the hypnotist could not suggest that an honest person rob a bank and expect the subject to comply. Instead, the hypnotist can increase the likelihood that subjects will perform simple behaviours that they have performed or have thought of before, and would be willing to do (in some contexts) when in a normal conscious state.

THEORIES OF HYPNOSIS In the previous section, we discussed the types of behaviours that can and cannot be influenced by hypnosis; in this section, we attempt to uncover how this process actually works. The word *hypnosis* comes from the Greek word *hypno,* meaning "sleep." In reality, scientific research tells us that hypnosis is nothing like sleep. Instead, hypnosis is based on an interaction

Bookstaver / AP Images

Stage hypnotists often use the human plank demonstration with their subjects. They support an audience volunteer on three chairs. To the audience's amazement, when the chair supporting the mid-body is removed, the hypnotized subject does not fall (even when weight is added, as shown in the photo). However, nonhypnotized subjects also do not fall. (Please do not try this at home—there is a trick behind it!)

between (1) automatic (unconscious) thoughts and behaviours and (2) a supervisory system (Norman & Shallice, 1986), sometimes referred to as *executive processing*, which is involved in processes such as the control of attention and problem solving. The roles played by these two pieces of the puzzle differ across theories of hypnosis.

Dissociation theory *explains hypnosis as a unique state in which consciousness is divided into two parts: a lower-level system involved with perception and movement and an "executive" system that evaluates and monitors these behaviours* (Hilgard, 1986; Woody & Farvolden, 1998). It may sound magical, but this kind of divided state is actually quite common. Take any skill that you have mastered, such as driving a car or playing an instrument. When you began, it took every bit of your conscious awareness to focus on the correct movements—you were a highly focused observer of your actions. In this case, your behaviour required a lot of executive processing. After a few years of practice, you can do it automatically while you observe and pay attention to something else. In this case, you require much less executive processing. Although we call the familiar behaviour automatic, part of you is still paying attention to what you are doing in case you suddenly need to change your behaviour. During hypnosis, there appears to be a separation between these two systems. As a result, actions or thoughts suggested by the hypnotist may bypass the evaluation and monitoring system and go directly to the simpler perception and movement systems (Landry & Raz, 2015). In other words, suggestible individuals will experience *less* input from the executive system (Jamieson & Sheehan, 2004; Woody & Bowers, 1994). In support of this view, neuroimaging studies have found reduced activity in the anterior cingulate cortex, a region of the frontal lobe related to executive functions, in hypnotized subjects (McGeown et al., 2009; Raz et al., 2005).

A second approach, **social-cognitive theory**, *explains hypnosis by emphasizing the degree to which beliefs and expectations contribute to increased suggestibility*. This perspective is supported by experiments in which individuals who are not yet hypnotized are told either that they will be able to resist ideomotor suggestions or that they will not be able to resist them. In these studies, people tend to conform to what they have been told to expect—a result that cannot be easily explained by dissociation theory (Lynn et al., 1984; Spanos et al., 1985). Similarly, research on hypnosis as a treatment for pain shows that *response expectancy*— whether the individual believes the treatment will work— plays a large role in the actual pain relief experienced (Milling, 2009).

At this point, there appears to be some evidence in favour of both theories. It is possible that expectations might make some people more likely to enter a hypnotic state, but once they enter it, they act in a way consistent with the dissociation theory. These expectations may be why people are more likely to enter a hypnotic state under the guidance of a hypnotist than with a non-hypnotist. However, the exact relationship (if any) between these two theories remains unclear. This lack of clarity is due to the fact that hypnosis did not receive much scientific attention for most of the 20th century. However, despite the fact that there is not a clear answer as to how hypnosis works, most scientists agree that for *some* individuals hypnosis can be a powerful therapeutic tool.

APPLICATIONS OF HYPNOSIS Although it is used far less frequently than medications or talk-based therapies, hypnosis has been used to treat a number of different physical and psychological conditions. Hypnosis is often used in conjunction with other psychotherapies such as cognitive-behavioural therapy (CBT; see Module 16.2) rather than as a stand-alone treatment. The resulting *cognitive hypnotherapy* has been used as an effective treatment for depression (Alladin & Alibhai, 2007), anxiety (Abramowitz et al., 2008; Schoenberger et al., 1997), eating disorders (Barabasz, 2007), hot flashes of cancer survivors (Elkins et al., 2008), and irritable bowel syndrome (Golden, 2007), among many others (M. R. Nash et al., 2009). Hypnosis is far from a cure-all, however. For example, researchers found that hypnotherapy combined with a nicotine patch is more effective as a smoking cessation intervention than the patch alone. Nonetheless, only one-fifth of the individuals receiving this kind of therapy managed to remain smoke-free for a year (Carmody et al., 2008). Moreover, although some therapists combine hypnotherapy with traditional cognitive behavioural therapy when treating depression, much more research is required before this technique becomes a standard treatment (Alladin, 2012). The best conclusion regarding hypnosis in therapy is that it shows promise, especially when used in conjunction with other evidence-based psychological or medical treatments.

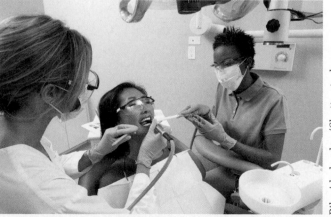

Under hypnosis, people can withstand higher levels of pain for longer periods of time, including the discomfort associated with dental procedures.

Bikeriderlondon/Shutterstock

Myths in Mind

Recovering Lost Memories through Hypnosis

Before the limitations of hypnosis were fully understood, professionals working in the fields of psychology and law regularly used this technique for uncovering lost memories. What a powerful tool this would be for a psychologist—if a patient could remember specifics about trauma or abuse it *could* greatly help the individual's recovery. Similarly, law enforcement and legal professionals could benefit by learning the details of a crime recovered through hypnosis—or so many assumed.

However, as you have read, hypnosis puts the subject into a highly suggestible state. This condition leaves the individual vulnerable to prompts and suggestions by the hypnotist. A cooperative person could certainly comply with suggestions and create a story that, in the end, was entirely false. This has happened time and again. In reality, hypnosis does not improve memory (Kihlstrom, 1997; Loftus & Davis, 2006). Today, responsible psychologists do not use hypnotherapy to uncover or reconstruct lost memories. Police officers have also largely given up this practice. In 2007, the Supreme Court of Canada ruled that testimony based on hypnosis sessions alone cannot be submitted as evidence (*R. v. Trochym*, 2007).

Perhaps the most practical use for hypnosis is in the treatment of pain. If researchers can demonstrate its effectiveness in this application, it may be a preferred method of pain control given painkillers' potential side effects and risk of addiction. What does the scientific evidence say about the use of hypnosis in treating pain? A review of 18 individual studies found that approximately 75% of all individuals experienced adequate pain relief with this approach beyond that provided by traditional analgesics or no treatment (Montgomery et al., 2000). What happened to the other 25%? Perhaps the failure of the treatment in this group is attributable to the fact that some people are more readily hypnotized than others. Indeed, brain-imaging studies suggest that the strength of connections to and from the anterior cingulate gyrus differs between hypnotizable and non-hypnotizable individuals (Cojan et al., 2015); this brain region is involved in both hypnosis *and* the perception of pain (see Module 4.4). In addition, to truly understand pain control, researchers must distinguish among different types of pain. Research has shown that hypnosis generally works as well as drug treatments for *acute pain*, which is the intense, temporary pain associated with a medical or dental procedure (Patterson & Jenson, 2003). The effect of hypnosis on chronic pain is more complicated, as some conditions are due to purely physical causes whereas others are more psychological in nature. For these latter conditions, it is likely that the patient will expect to continue to feel pain regardless of the treatment, thus reducing the effectiveness of hypnosis.

Module 5.2a Quiz:

Hypnosis

Know . . .

1. _____ suggestions specify that certain actions cannot be performed while hypnotized.
   A. Ideomotor
   B. Challenge
   C. Cognitive-perceptual
   D. Dissociation

Understand . . .

2. Dr. Johnson claims that hypnosis is a distinct state of consciousness involving a disconnection between perception and executive processing. It appears that she is endorsing the _____ theory of hypnosis.
   A. social-cognitive
   B. psychoanalytic
   C. dissociation
   D. hypnotherapy

Analyze . . .

3. Which of the following statements best describes the scientific consensus about recovering memories with hypnosis?
   A. Memories "recovered" through hypnosis are highly unreliable and should never be used as evidence in court.
   B. If the memory is recovered by a trained psychologist, then it may be used as evidence in court.
   C. Recovering memories through hypnosis is a simple procedure and, therefore, the findings should be a regular part of court hearings.
   D. Memories can be recovered only in individuals who are highly hypnotizable.

Mind-Wandering

During hypnosis, an individual enters an altered state of consciousness in which he or she is more suggestible than at other times. Although the idea of altered states of consciousness might seem strange to you at first, you actually experience them all the time, possibly even while reading this book. One such example is mind-wandering, an obstacle to your (and everyone else's) ability to work and study.

WHAT IS MIND-WANDERING? Imagine sitting in a large lecture hall listening to an enthusiastic professor talk about European history. Despite the fascinating topic filled with battles and revolutions, after a few minutes, you start to think about a conversation you had with a friend the day before. Then you start to think about the witty remarks you wish you had made, and fantasize about unleashing these comments on people in an argument sometime in the future. Then, suddenly, you are back in your classroom, and see an unfamiliar slide on the screen at the front of the room. Your body was physically present in the classroom for the entire lecture, but your mind was elsewhere. This is an example of **mind-wandering**, *an unintentional redirection of attention from one's current task to an unrelated train of thought* (Mooneyham & Schooler, 2013).

The frequency with which we think about something unrelated to what we are doing is astonishing. This was powerfully demonstrated in an innovative study in which researchers programmed an iPhone "app" that contacted participants at random points during the day (Killingsworth & Gilbert, 2010). Participants were asked, "Are you thinking about something other than what you're currently doing?" The results indicated that mind-wandering occurred in 47% of the samples taken. The frequency of mind-wandering was over 30% for every activity other than sex! The challenge for psychologists is to determine whether—or how much—these lapses of attention affect our ability to work and study.

At first glance, studying the effects of mind-wandering might seem impossible—how you do study the process of *not* paying attention? However, in the past decade, psychologists have conducted a number of studies examining how mind-wandering affects attention and memory (e.g., Kam & Handy, 2014). For instance, several studies have shown that mind-wandering decreases reading comprehension. In one such study conducted at the University of Alberta, participants read either an engaging passage (an excerpt from Anne Rice's *Interview with the Vampire*) or a less interesting passage (an excerpt from William M. Thackeray's *The History of Pendennis*). While reading the assigned passages, participants were occasionally asked whether they were attending to the text. Not surprisingly, the researchers found that for both types of passages, the recall of the material was better when participants were paying attention to the text rather than mind-wandering

(Dixon & Bortolussi, 2013). However, the errors caused by mind-wandering went beyond missing minor details. Participants in this and other experiments often missed major elements of the plot. One study found that mind-wandering participants couldn't identify the villain in a mystery story (Smallwood et al., 2008)! Given these results, it should come as no surprise that mind-wandering is associated with poorer retention of university lecture material (Risko et al., 2012) and with poorer scores on intelligence tests (Mrazek et al., 2012).

Of course, if we spend at least 30% of our time not consciously attending to our current situation, it does make you wonder where your mind wandered off to. Recent brain-imaging studies suggest an interesting destination.

MIND-WANDERING AND THE BRAIN In the late 1990s, Marcus Raichle and his research team made a discovery that would change psychology. While looking at their brain-imaging data, Raichle noticed that a number of brain areas were active. For most scientists, finding brain activity that is consistent with your predictions is a cause for celebration, if not a trip to the campus pub. But Raichle noticed something else in his data. He noticed that across a number of studies, the same pattern of *deactivations* also occurred (Raichle et al., 2001). In other words, a network of brain regions became *less* active when participants performed a task (see Figure 5.9). This network, now known as the **default mode network**, *is a network of brain regions including the medial prefrontal cortex, posterior cingulate gyrus, and medial and lateral regions of the parietal lobe that is most active when an individual is awake but* not *responding to external stimuli*. In other words, the default mode network is more active when a person is paying attention to his internal thoughts rather than to an outside stimulus or task (Raichle, 2015).

The default mode network also appears to be related to mind-wandering; this makes sense given that mind-wandering is often associated with becoming lost in one's own thoughts (Gruberger et al., 2011). In one fMRI study conducted at the University of British Columbia, researchers measured participants' brain activity while they performed a simple (and boring) perceptual task. At different points in the experiment, participants were asked (1) "Where was your attention focused just before the probe [the question]?" and (2) "How aware were you of where your attention was focused?" Activity in the default mode network was more pronounced when participants were not paying attention to the perceptual task. This effect was largest when they weren't aware that they were mind-wandering (Christoff et al., 2009). Importantly, the default mode network wasn't the only group of brain areas found to be active during mind-wandering. A network involving parts of the frontal and parietal lobes also showed increased activity when mind-wandering was occurring

Figure 5.9 The Default Mode Network and Frontoparietal Network

The default mode network (left) is involved with self-related thinking. The frontoparietal network is linked with goal-directed thought and planning. Both are involved with mind-wandering.

Default Mode Network

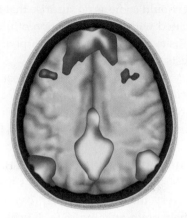

Frontoparietal Network

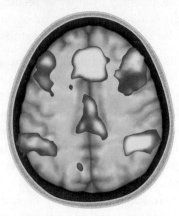

Source: Reproduced with permission of *Annual Review of Neuroscience*, Volume © by Annual Reviews, http://www.annualreviews.org.

(Fox et al., 2015). This *frontoparietal network* is associated with goal-directed thinking such as planning for the future, as well as the control of attention (i.e., "executive functioning"). This pattern of activity is important—the fact that a brain network involved in higher-order thought shows stronger connectivity during mind-wandering suggests that these lapses of attention might actually serve a useful purpose.

THE BENEFITS OF MIND-WANDERING Our minds don't always wander. If you're being chased by a bear, it's unlikely that you'll start daydreaming about your cute classmate. Instead, mind-wandering typically occurs during tasks that are repetitive, don't require much thought, and/or that we've experienced before. If we're not dedicating many mental resources to a given task, we will have more resources to dedicate to mind-wandering (Risko et al., 2012).

It is at this point that the increased activity in the frontal and parietal brain areas becomes important. One function of the frontal lobes is planning future goals and actions. As it turns out, mind-wandering is related to future thinking (Smallwood et al., 2011). In one study, participants completed a simple reaction-time task; at various points in the experiment, they were interrupted and asked what they were thinking about. The experimenters then judged whether the participants' thoughts were focused on the past, the present, or the future. When participants were thinking about the experimental task, their thoughts were (not surprisingly) rated as being focused on the present most of the time (see Figure 5.10). In contrast, when

Figure 5.10 Mind-Wandering about the Future

When participants are paying attention to the task ("On"), their thoughts were judged to be focused on the present situation. When they were mind-wandering ("Off," for "off-task"), they were more likely to be thinking about the future.

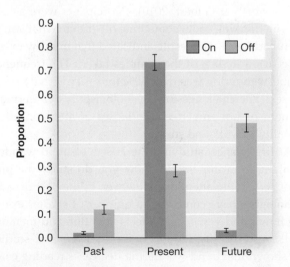

Source: Republished with permission of Elsevier Science, Inc., from Back to the future: Autobiographical planning and the functionality of mind-wandering. *Consciousness and Cognition* 20, 1604-1611, 2011., Benjamin Baird; Jonathan Smallwood; Jonathan W. Schooler. Permission conveyed through Copyright Clearance Center, Inc.

people were mind-wandering, there was a strong tendency to be thinking about the future. This future focus may allow us to think about possible plans of action before we are actually in that situation, an ability that could be quite useful (Baird et al., 2011).

It is important to note that although some studies have shown benefits to mind-wandering, this area of research is still in its initial stages. Most researchers would agree that your performance on most tasks would be improved if they received your full conscious attention. Unfortunately, as you will read in the next section, this is not always possible.

Module 5.2b Quiz:

Mind-Wandering

Know . . .

1. What functions may benefit from mind-wandering?
   A. Thinking about things you plan to do in the near future
   B. Reading comprehension
   C. Thinking about abstract problems
   D. Paying attention to other cars while you are driving

Analyze . . .

2. The default mode network is often active when people are mind-wandering. What can you infer from the activity of *this particular network?*

A. The individual is trying to solve problems that they may encounter in the future.
B. The individual is thinking about problems that a friend is having.
C. The individual is likely thinking about ideas or future plans related to him- or herself.
D. The individual is paying attention to interesting external stimuli such as sounds or smells.

Disorders of Consciousness

In 1990, a Florida woman named Terri Schiavo collapsed to the ground. She had suffered a full cardiac arrest, resulting in massive brain damage due to a lack of oxygen. She would never regain consciousness. After she had been in a coma for almost three months, her diagnosis was changed to a persistent vegetative state. In 1998, her husband asked the hospital to remove her feeding tube because he was sure she wouldn't want to live this way. Her parents fought the decision, claiming part of Terri was still conscious. The ethical and legal battles continued for seven years, and included President George W. Bush cutting his vacation short in order to return to Washington to sign a legal order keeping her alive (Cranford, 2005). Eventually, after the U.S. Supreme Court refused to hear an appeal, her feeding tube was removed for the last time. Terri Schiavo died on March 31, 2005.

The Terri Schiavo case highlights the importance of consciousness in medical decision making. Consciousness can take many forms, all of which vary in terms of how aware a person is of his or her environment. In patients with brain damage, the degree to which a patient is conscious of her surroundings can influence the diagnosis that she receives (G. Lee et al., 2015). Neurologists distinguish between six types of consciousness, ranging from little-to-no brain function up to normal levels of awareness (see Figure 5.11).

The lowest level of consciousness in a person who is still technically alive is known as **brain death**, *a condition in which the brain, specifically including the brainstem, no longer functions* (American Academy of Neurology, 1995). Individuals who are brain dead have no hope of recovery because the brainstem regions responsible for basic life functions like breathing and maintaining the heartbeat do not function (see Figure 5.12).

In contrast to brain death, a **coma** *is a state marked by a complete loss of consciousness.* It is generally due to damage to the brainstem or to widespread damage to both hemispheres of the brain (Bateman, 2001). Patients who are in a coma have an absence of both wakefulness and awareness of themselves or their surroundings (Gawryluk et al., 2010). Some of the patient's brainstem reflexes will be suppressed, including pupil dilation and constriction in response to changes in brightness. Typically, patients who survive this stage begin to recover to higher levels of consciousness within 2–4 weeks, although there is no guarantee that the patient will make a full recovery.

If a patient in a coma improves slightly, the individual may enter a **persistent vegetative state**, *a state of minimal to no consciousness in which the patient's eyes may be open, and the individual will develop sleep–wake cycles without clear signs of consciousness.* For example, vegetative state patients do not appear to focus on objects in their visual field, nor do they track movement. These patients generally do not have damage to the brainstem. Instead, they have extensive brain damage to the grey matter and white matter of both hemispheres, leading to impairments of most functions (Laureys et al., 2004; Owen & Coleman, 2008). The likelihood of recovery from a vegetative state is time dependent. If a patient emerges from this state within the first few months, he or she

Figure 5.11 Disorders of Consciousness

Although more nuanced diagnoses exist, this diagram depicts six key levels of consciousness used in the diagnosis of brain-damaged individuals.

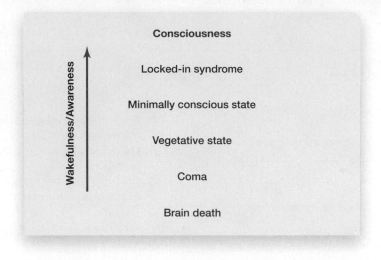

Source: Gawryluk, J. R., D'Arcy, R. C. N., Connolly, J. F., & Weaver, D. F. (2010). Improving the clinical assessment of consciousness with advances in electrophysiological and neuroimaging techniques. *BMC Neurology, 10,* 11. Figure 1, p. 3.

could regain some form of consciousness. In contrast, if symptoms do not improve after three months, the patient is classified as being in a *permanent vegetative state;* the chances of recovery from that diagnosis decrease sharply (Wijdicks, 2006).

Thus far, we have discussed disorders of consciousness as though there were a quick-and-easy tool for diagnoses. While this is definitely true for brain death, distinguishing between other conditions is much more difficult. In fact, misdiagnosis of these disorders is estimated to be as high as 43% (Gawryluk et al., 2010; Schnakers et al., 2009). The challenge, therefore, is to develop or adapt tools that will help neurologists more accurately diagnose these mysterious conditions.

Figure 5.12 Neuroimaging of Brain Death

This positron emission tomography (PET) scan shows the amount of glucose being used by the brain. In a healthy brain, most of the image would be yellow, green, or red, indicating activity. Here, only the tissue surrounding the brain is using glucose, giving the image the appearance of being an empty skull; functionally speaking, it is one.

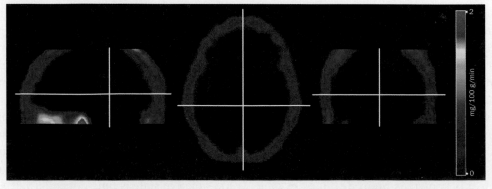

Source: Laureys, S., Owen, A. M., & Schiff, N. D. (2004). Brain function in brain death, coma, vegetative state, and related disorders. *Lancet Neurology, 3,* 537–546. Figure 3, p. 539.

Working the Scientific Literacy Model

Assessing Consciousness in the Vegetative State

Determining a brain-damaged patient's level of consciousness is quite challenging. It also has important implications for the patient's treatment. If she is shown to have some degree of awareness of her situation and/or her environment, then it seems reasonable to get her opinion on matters affecting her treatment. In contrast, if she is unresponsive, then such decisions should be made entirely by the family and the medical team. Everyone wants what is best for the patient, but the tools used to assess consciousness are still a work in progress.

What do we know about the assessment of consciousness in vegetative patients?

The initial assessment of consciousness in severely brain-damaged patients is generally performed at the patient's bedside. Doctors will perform tests of a patient's reflexes (e.g., pupil responses, which involve the brainstem) and examine other simple responses. The most common assessment tool is the Glasgow Coma Scale (GCS), a 15-item checklist for the physician. The GCS measures eye movements—whether they can open at all, open in response to pain, open in response to speech, or open spontaneously without any reason. The next five items on this checklist assess language abilities (e.g., does she use incorrect words?). The final six items measure movement abilities such as whether the patient responds to pain and whether she can obey commands. Scores of 9 or below reflect a severe disturbance of consciousness. (For comparison, individuals suffering from a concussion tend to score between 13 and 15, which is labelled as a mild disturbance.)

Checklists such as the GCS provide a useful initial indicator of a brain-damaged patient's abilities. However, many of the behaviours measured by this and similar assessment tools focus more on overt behaviours (i.e., movements) than on direct indications of awareness. A patient's inability to move may imply a greater disturbance of consciousness than actually exists, thus leading to potential misdiagnoses. Improvements in brain-imaging techniques may prove to be a more sensitive tool for investigating consciousness.

How can science explain consciousness in vegetative patients?

Researchers have argued for some time that *some* patients in a persistent vegetative state can show *some* signs of consciousness. For example, some patients have shown rudimentary responses to language. There have been cases of neurological changes in response to one's name (Staffen et al., 2006), as well as the emotional tone of a speaker's voice (Kotchoubey et al., 2009). However, the most stunning example of consciousness in this patient group was shown by Adrian Owen (now at Western University) and his colleagues (Owen et al., 2006). In their study, a 23-year-old patient in a vegetative state was asked to perform two different mental imagery tasks during an fMRI scan. In one task, she was asked to imagine playing tennis, an activity involving a specific set of movements. In the other task, she was asked to imagine visiting all of the rooms in her house, starting at the front door (this required her to develop a spatial map of her house). Despite not being able to respond to any questions verbally, this patient's brain showed clear evidence of understanding the commands. Imagining playing tennis activated brain areas related to movement; imagining walking through her house activated a spatial network including the parahippocampal gyrus and the parietal lobe. This result provided stunning evidence that the patient did, in fact, have some degree of consciousness.

Owen and his colleagues have performed several subsequent studies with larger groups of patients (Owen, 2013). However, not all patients are able to modify their own brain activity. In a study including 54 patients, only five were able to perform the tennis–house task (Monti et al., 2010). But, one of these patients was able to do something remarkable: He was able to learn to use the tennis–house imagery task to communicate! The experimenters asked him simple questions and told him to imagine playing tennis if he wanted to respond "yes" and to imagine walking through his house if he wanted to respond "no" (see Figure 5.13). Using this technique, he was able to demonstrate that some of his cognitive abilities were preserved. Of course, we must be cautious and remember that this is only one patient among dozens who were tested. The ongoing challenge for researchers is to determine what made the five "fMRI responders" different from the 49 non-responders, and to use that information to help identify other patients who might still retain some degree of consciousness.

Can we critically evaluate this evidence?

The initial neuroimaging studies of consciousness in vegetative state patients are indeed promising. However, there are some important issues that need to be dealt with. First, we mentioned above that up to 43% of patients with disorders of consciousness are misdiagnosed. Given that a small subset of the vegetative state patients were able to modify their brain activity, it is possible that they were not

Figure 5.13 Using fMRI to Communicate with a Vegetative Patient

Results of two sample communication scans obtained from Patient 23 (Panels A and C) and a healthy control subject (Panels B and D) during functional MRI are shown. In Panels A and B, the observed activity pattern (orange) was very similar to that observed in the motor-imagery localizer scan (i.e., activity in the supplementary motor area alone), indicating a "yes" response. In Panels C and D, the observed activity pattern (blue) was very similar to that observed in the spatial-imagery localizer scan (i.e., activity in both the parahippocampal gyrus and the supplementary motor area), indicating a "no" response. The names used in the questions have been changed to protect the privacy of the patient.

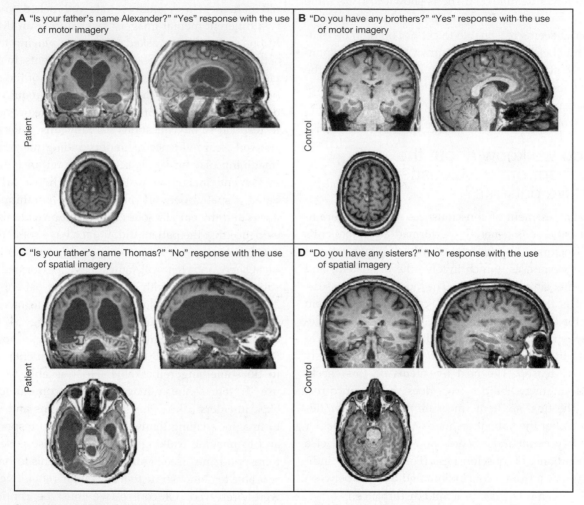

Source: Monti, M.M, et al. (2010). Willful modulation of brain activity in disorders of consciousness. *New England Journal of Medicine, 362*(7), 587. Figure 3 (communication scans).

actually in a vegetative state, but instead had a less severe condition. Second, the researchers are equating language abilities with consciousness; yet, consciousness could take the form of responses to other, non-linguistic stimuli (Overgaard & Overgaard, 2011). This criticism would be particularly important if a vegetative state patient had damage to brain areas related to language comprehension.

We also have to be cautious about the use of PET and fMRI scans in patients with widespread brain damage. Both types of neuroimaging measure characteristics of blood flow in the brain. But, damage to the brain will alter how the blood flows (Rossini et al., 2004); therefore, we need to be careful when comparing patients with healthy controls. One way around this latter concern is to use multiple methods of neuroimaging (Gawryluk et al., 2010). Increasing numbers of research groups are using EEG, which measures neural activity using electrodes attached to the scalp, to search for brain function in vegetative patients (Cruse et al., 2011; Wijnen et al., 2007). Given that distinct brain waves have been identified for sensory detection of a stimulus, the detection of unexpected auditory stimuli, higher-level analysis of stimuli, and semantic (meaning) analysis of language, this technology could provide important insights into the inner worlds of vegetative state patients. Indeed, Canadian researchers have developed the EEG-based Halifax Consciousness

Scanner for this specific purpose (http://mindfulscientific.ca/hcs/).

Why is this relevant?

Neuroimaging investigations of consciousness in vegetative state patients could literally have life-and-death implications. Currently, doctors have a very difficult time determining a patient's level of consciousness if they cannot move or make some sort of response. However, this information influences the decision about whether to remove that patient from life support. If brain imaging could provide insight into the inner world of patients (or, in some cases, lack thereof), it would provide doctors and family members with valuable information that would help them make the right decision for the patient.

There are two other disorders of consciousness that are often diagnosed by neurologists. One is the **minimally conscious state (MCS)**, *a disordered state of consciousness marked by the ability to show some behaviours that suggest at least partial consciousness, even if on an inconsistent basis.* A minimally conscious patient must show *some* awareness of himself or his environment, and be able to reproduce this behaviour. Examples of some behaviours that are tested are following simple commands, making gestures or yes/no responses to questions, and producing movements or emotional reactions in response to some person or object in their environment. When neuroimaging is used, minimally conscious patients show more activity than vegetative patients (see Figure 5.14), including activity in some higher-order sensory and cognitive regions (Boly et al., 2004).

The disorder of consciousness that most resembles the healthy, awake state—at least in terms of awareness—is **locked-in syndrome**, *a disorder in which the patient is aware and awake but, because of an inability to move his or her body, appears unconscious* (Smith & Delargy, 2005). Locked-in syndrome was brought to the attention of most people by the movie *The Diving Bell and the Butterfly*, which depicted Jean-Dominique Bauby's attempts to communicate to the outside world using eye movements. This disorder is caused by damage to part of the pons, the region of the brainstem that sticks out like an Adam's apple. Most patients with locked-in syndrome remain paralyzed. Luckily, new technology is making it easier for these patients to communicate with the outside world.

The final stage of consciousness is the healthy, conscious brain. That's you. Be grateful.

Figure 5.14 Brain Activity in Four Levels of Consciousness

PET images of brain activity found in a healthy conscious brain and the brains of three patients with different types of brain damage. The highlighted red area near the back of the brain (along the midline) is the precuneus and the posterior cingulate cortex; these areas are involved in a number of different functions and use the most energy in the brain.

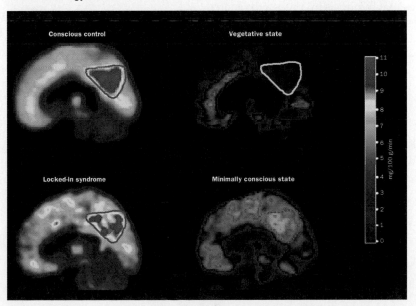

Source: Laureys, S., Owen, A. M., & Schiff, N. D. (2004). Brain function in brain death, coma, vegetative state, and related disorders. *Lancet Neurology, 3,* 537–546. Figure 7, p. 543.

Module 5.2c Quiz:

Disorders of Consciousness

Know . . .

1. _____ is a disorder of consciousness in which an individual may open the eyes and exhibit sleep–wake cycles but show no specific signs of consciousness.
   - **A.** A coma
   - **B.** A persistent vegetative state
   - **C.** Brain death
   - **D.** A minimally conscious state

Understand . . .

2. What is the difference between a persistent vegetative state (PVS) and a minimally conscious state (MCS)?
   - **A.** Nothing—they are both names for the same state.
   - **B.** Someone in an MCS can have conversations, unlike someone in a PVS.
   - **C.** Someone in an MCS has sleep–wake cycles, unlike someone in a PVS.
   - **D.** People in an MCS show at least some behaviours that indicate consciousness, even if on an irregular basis.

Module 5.2 Summary

5.2a   Know . . . the key terminology associated with hypnosis, mind-wandering, and disorders of consciousness.

brain death
coma
default mode network
dissociation theory
hypnosis
locked-in syndrome
mind-wandering
minimally conscious state (MCS)
persistent vegetative state
social-cognitive theory

5.2b   Understand . . . the competing theories of hypnosis.

Dissociation theory states that hypnosis involves a division between a lower-level system involved with perception and movement and an "executive" system that evaluates and monitors these behaviours. In contrast, the social-cognitive theory states that a person's beliefs and expectations about hypnosis heighten his or her willingness to follow suggestions.

5.2c   Apply . . . your knowledge of hypnosis to identify what it can and cannot do.

Apply Activity

Hypnosis could *potentially* work in the following scenarios (answer true or false):

1. Temporarily increasing physical strength
2. Helping someone quit smoking

3. Remembering all of the precise details of a crime scene
4. Recovering a traumatic memory
5. Helping someone relax
6. Reducing pain sensation

5.2d   Analyze . . . the effectiveness of using neuroimaging to study mind-wandering.

Neuroimaging studies have repeatedly shown that two brain networks—the default mode network and the frontoparietal network—are more active when someone is mind-wandering. However, it is important to remember that brain-imaging studies are correlational in nature. The activity in these networks *co-occurs* with mind-wandering, but we cannot say for certain if this activity *causes* mind-wandering.

5.2e   Analyze . . . the ability of researchers to detect consciousness in brain-damaged patients.

Consciousness is difficult to detect using traditional bedside testing because many of these testing tools require movement. Using neuroimaging (specifically fMRI), it has been possible to detect conscious awareness in some patients who are in a vegetative state, as well as in patients who are in a minimally conscious state and those with locked-in syndrome. Although these studies do have some limitations (discussed earlier in this module), the results show that it is an exciting time for neuroscience research in Canada!

Module 5.3 Drugs and Conscious Experience

Nathan Griffith/ Alamy Stock Photo

∨ Learning Objectives

5.3a Know . . . the key terminology related to different categories of drugs and their effects on the nervous system and behaviour.

5.3b Understand . . . drug tolerance and dependence.

5.3c Apply . . . your knowledge to better understand your own beliefs about drug use.

5.3d Analyze . . . the difference between spiritual and recreational drug use.

5.3e Analyze . . . the short- and long-term effects of drug use.

Could taking a drug-induced trip be a way to cope with traumatic stress or a life-threatening illness? A variety of medications for reducing anxiety or alleviating depression are readily available. However, a few doctors and psychologists have suggested that perhaps a 6-hour trip on psychedelic "magic" mushrooms (called psilocybin) could be helpful to people dealing with difficult psychological and life problems. (It would also help them communicate with the sparkling trilingual dragon sighing in the bathtub.)

    In the 1960s, a fringe group of psychologists insisted that psychedelic drugs were the answer to all the world's problems. The outcast nature of this group and the ongoing "war on drugs" prompted mainstream psychologists to shelve any ideas that a psychedelic drug or something similar could be used in a therapeutic setting. However, this perception appears to be changing. Recently, Roland Griffiths from Johns Hopkins University in Maryland has been conducting studies on the possible therapeutic benefits of psilocybin mushrooms. Cancer patients who were experiencing depression volunteered to take

psilocybin as a part of Dr. Griffiths's study. Both at the end of their experience and 14 months later, they reported having personally meaningful, spiritually significant experiences that improved their overall outlook on life (Griffiths et al., 2008). Subsequent studies have shown that psilocybin mushrooms can help reduce the symptoms of tobacco addiction (Johnson et al., 2014) and may even increase openness of one's personality (MacLean et al., 2011). Although these findings are not likely to convince your doctor to give you a bag of magic mushrooms, they do illustrate an important point: most drugs can be used to alter brain chemistry for both medical and recreational purposes. The line between "medicine" and "drug" is a blurry one indeed.

Focus Questions

1. How do we distinguish between recreationally abused drugs and therapeutic usage?

2. What other motives underlie drug use?

》 Every human culture uses drugs. It could even be argued that every *human* uses drugs, depending on your definition of the term. Many of the foods that we eat contain the same types of compounds found in mind-altering drugs. For example, nutmeg contains compounds similar to those found in some psychedelic substances, and chocolate contains small amounts of the same compounds found in amphetamines and marijuana (Wenk, 2010). Of course, caffeine and alcohol—both of which are mainstream parts of our culture—are also drugs. The difference between a drug and a nondrug compound seems to be that drugs are taken because the user has an intended effect in mind. Regardless of why we use them, drugs influence the activity of some elements of our central nervous system, affecting us both physically and psychologically. In this module, we will discuss these physical and psychological effects of drug use. We will then examine how these processes are affected by different classes of drugs.

Physical and Psychological Effects of Drugs

Although we often think of drugs as having a simple effect such as relieving pain or "getting someone high," the reality is actually much more complicated. To truly understand the impact of a drug on how people act and feel, we have to look at both the short-term and the long-term effects of drugs.

SHORT-TERM EFFECTS   Your brain contains a number of different chemical messengers called neurotransmitters (see Module 3.2). These brain chemicals are released by a neuron (the pre-synaptic neuron) into the synapse, the space between the cells. They then bind to receptors on the surface of other neurons (the post-synaptic neurons), thus making these neurons more or less likely to fire. Drugs influence the amount of activity occurring in the synapse. Thus, they can serve as an *agonist* (which enhances or mimics the activity of a neurotransmitter) or an *antagonist* (which blocks or inhibits the activity of a neurotransmitter).

The short-term effects of drugs can be caused by a number of different brain mechanisms including (1) altering the amount of the neurotransmitter being released into the synapse, (2) preventing the reuptake (i.e., reabsorption back into the cell that released it) of the neurotransmitter once it has been released, thereby allowing it to have a longer influence on other neurons, (3) blocking the receptor that the neurotransmitter would normally bind to, or (4) binding to the receptor in place of the neurotransmitter. In all of these scenarios, the likelihood of the postsynaptic neurons firing is changed, resulting in changes to how we think, act, and feel.

Different drugs will influence different neurotransmitter systems. For instance, the "club drug" ecstasy primarily affects serotonin levels, whereas painkillers like

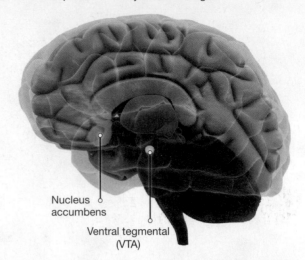

Figure 5.15 Brain Regions Associated with the Effects of Drugs

The nucleus accumbens and ventral tegmental area are associated with reward responses to many different drugs.

Nucleus accumbens

Ventral tegmental (VTA)

OxyContin™ affect opioid receptors. However, the brain chemical that is most often influenced by drugs is dopamine, a neurotransmitter that is involved in responses to rewarding, pleasurable feelings (Volkow et al., 2009). Dopamine release in two brain areas, the *nucleus accumbens* and the *ventral tegmental area*, is likely related to the "high" associated with many drugs (Koob, 1992; see Figure 5.15). These positive feelings serve an important, and potentially dangerous, function: They reinforce the drug-taking behaviour. In fact, the dopamine release in response to many drugs makes them more rewarding than sex or delicious food (Bassareo & Di Chiara, 1999; Di Chiara & Imperato, 1988; Fiorino et al., 1997). This reinforcing effect is so powerful that, for someone who has experience with a particular drug, even the *anticipation* of taking the drug is pleasurable and involves the release of dopamine (Schultz, 2000).

But, the drug–neurotransmitter relationship is not as simple as it would seem. This is because the effects of drugs involve biological, psychological, and social mechanisms. Think about the effects of alcohol. Drinking half a bottle of wine at a party often leads people to be more outgoing, whereas drinking half a bottle at home might cause them to fall asleep on the couch. In each case, the drug was the same: alcohol. But the effects of the drug differed because the situations in which the drug was consumed changed. The setting in which drugs are consumed can also have a more sinister effect: Overdoses of some drugs are more common when they are taken in new environments than when they are taken in a setting that the person often uses for drug consumption (Siegel et al., 1982). When people enter an environment that is associated with drug use, their bodies prepare to metabolize drugs even before they are consumed (i.e., their bodies become braced for the drug's effects). Similar preparations do not occur in new environments, which leads to larger, and potentially fatal, drug effects (see Module 6.1). Another psychological factor that influences drug effects is the person's experience with a drug. It takes time for people to learn to associate taking the drug with the drug's effects on the body and brain. Therefore, a drug might have a much more potent effect on a person the third or fourth time he took it than it did the first time, which is very common with some drugs, such as marijuana. Finally, a person's expectations about the drug can dramatically influence its effects. If a person believes that alcohol will make him less shy, then it is likely that a few glasses of wine will have that effect.

How can we reconcile these psychological effects with the physiological effects discussed above? To do so, we have to remember that the psychological states mentioned above also influence the activity of brain areas. For instance, dealing with novel or stressful situations (e.g., being surrounded by strangers, or your parents arriving home early) often requires input from the frontal lobes; this activity might reduce the impact that drugs are having on a person's behaviour. A similar result can occur when a person has expectations about a drug. This mental set can itself change the activity of different brain areas and can alter the effects of a drug. Thus, the effects of drugs are yet another example of how our biology and psychology interact to create our conscious experiences.

LONG-TERM EFFECTS Importantly, the effects that different drugs will have on us change as we become frequent users. Think about a drug that most of you use: caffeine (found in coffee, tea, and some soft drinks). The first time you had a cup of coffee, you were likely wired and unable to sleep. But, veteran coffee drinkers rarely experience such a large burst of energy; some can even drink coffee before going to bed. This is an example of **tolerance**, *when repeated use of a drug results in a need for a higher dose to get the intended effect.* While tolerance might seem annoying, it is actually the brain's attempt to keep the level of neurotransmitters at stable levels. When receptors are overstimulated by neurotransmitters, as often happens during drug use, the neurons fire at a higher rate than normal. In order to counteract this effect and return the firing rate to normal, some of the receptors move further away from the synapse so that they are more difficult to stimulate, a process known as *down-regulation.*

Tolerance is not the only effect that can result from long-term use of legal or illegal drugs. Another is **physical dependence**, *the need to take a drug to ward off unpleasant physical withdrawal symptoms.* The characteristics of dependence and withdrawal symptoms differ from drug to drug. Caffeine withdrawal can involve head and muscle aches and impaired concentration. Withdrawal from long-term alcohol abuse is much more serious. A person who is dependent on alcohol can experience extremely severe, even life-threatening, withdrawal symptoms including nausea, increased heart rate and blood pressure, and hallucinations and delirium. However, drug dependence is not limited to physical symptoms. **Psychological dependence** *occurs when emotional need for a drug develops without any underlying physical dependence.* Many people use drugs in order to ward off negative emotions. When they no longer have this defence mechanism, they experience the negative emotions they have been avoiding, such as stress, depression, shame, or anxiety. Therefore, treatment programs for addiction often include some form of therapy that will allow users to learn to cope with these emotional symptoms while they are attempting to deal with the physical symptoms of withdrawal.

There is no single cause of drug dependence; instead, consistent with the biopsychosocial model, researchers believe that numerous factors influence whether someone will become dependent upon a drug as well as the severity of that dependence. At the biological level, researchers are attempting to identify the specific genes—or groups of genes—that make someone prone to becoming addicted to different drugs (Foroud et al., 2010). For example, the A1 allele of the *DRD2* gene, which influences the activity of dopamine receptors, is related to reward processing and to being open to new experiences (Peciña et al., 2013); it is also more common in people who are addicted to opioid drugs such as heroin (Clarke et al., 2012). In contrast, researchers at the University of Toronto found that a protective version of the *CYP2A6* gene is more common in people who do *not* smoke; this version of the gene is related to feelings of nausea and dizziness occurring when the person is exposed to smoking (Pianezza et al., 1998). Although we cannot go through a complete list of the genes involved with responses to different drugs, these examples show that scientists are rapidly identifying specific genes related to drug-taking behaviour.

However, genes are obviously not the only cause of drug dependence; researchers are also examining cognitive factors affecting drug-taking behaviour. For example, dependence is influenced by the fact that drugs are often taken in the same situations, such as a cup of coffee to start your day or alcohol whenever you see particular friends. Eventually, taking the drug becomes linked in your memory to that setting or that group of people. When you next see those people or enter that environment, thoughts of the drug will often resurface, making it more likely that you will use, or at least crave, that drug.

Addiction rates are also affected by social factors, such as the culture in which a person lives. For instance, alcoholism rates are lower in religious and social groups that prohibit drinking even though these groups are genetically similar to the rest of the population (Chentsova-Dutton & Tsai, 2007; Haber & Jacob, 2007). Family attitudes toward drugs is a factor as well, as early experiences with different drugs can shape our attitudes toward them and influence how we consume those drugs later in life (Zucker et al., 2008). If a young person first tries wine in a family setting, it will feel much less like a "cool" part of teenage rebellion than if that person first tried the same drink at a high school house party. That initial introduction can alter how that person views alcohol for years to come.

Drug dependence is also influenced by the social support available. The importance of this factor was powerfully demonstrated in a classic (if imperfect) study by Bruce Alexander and his colleagues at Simon Fraser University in 1978. Research in the 1960s and 1970s had shown that rats housed in small cages would eagerly press a lever in order to receive drugs such as morphine; these studies made it appear as though the chemistry of the drugs made them irresistible. However, another possibility existed: perhaps the drug-seeking behaviour was due to the fact that the rats felt isolated, a feeling that mirrors how many drug addicts report feeling. To test this, the researchers gave caged rats access to morphine in a way similar to previous studies. After several weeks of drug consumption, the rats were randomly assigned to different conditions: a caged group that remained isolated or a social group that was able to interact with other rats in what became known as Rat Park. When rats from both conditions were later given the opportunity to press a lever to receive morphine, the isolated rats were much more likely to do so than the social rats. This effect was particularly apparent in females (see Figure 5.16). These findings suggest that a key factor in drug dependence is a feeling of isolation.

Finally, all of these variables interact with a person's personality; individuals with impulsive personality traits are more likely to become addicted to drugs regardless of their early experiences or cultural setting (Lejuez et al., 2010; Perry & Carroll, 2008). Thus, drug dependence does

Figure 5.16 Rat Park: The Effects of Isolation and Gender on Morphine Self-Administration

In the Rat Park study, all rats self-administered morphine for several weeks. They were then randomly divided into two conditions. Rats that were able to socialize with other rats showed much less drug-seeking behaviour than rats that were housed in isolation. This effect was largest in females.

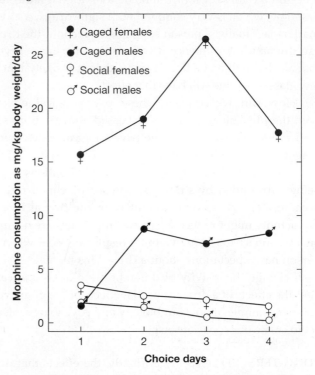

Source: Republished with permission of Springer Science, from The effect of housing and gender on morphine self-administration in rats. Bruce K. Alexander; Robert B. Coambs; Patricia F. Hadaway, 58, 1978. Permission conveyed through Copyright Clearance Center, Inc.

not have a single, simple cause, but is instead influenced by a number of interacting factors, as would be expected by the biopsychosocial model of behaviour.

Module 5.3a Quiz:

Physical and Psychological Effects of Drugs

Know . . .

1. Physical dependence occurs when
   A. an individual will die if he does not continue to use the drug.
   B. an individual desires a drug for its pleasant effects.
   C. an individual has to take the drug to prevent or stop unpleasant withdrawal symptoms.
   D. an individual requires increasingly larger amounts of a substance to experience its effects.

Understand . . .

2. Drug tolerance occurs when
   A. an individual needs increasingly larger amounts of a drug to achieve the same desired effect.
   B. individuals do not pass judgment on drug abusers.

C. an individual experiences withdrawal symptoms.
D. an individual starts taking a new drug for recreational purposes.

Apply . . .

3. Which is NOT a way in which drugs affect neurotransmitter levels?
   A. Binding to receptors that would normally receive the neurotransmitters
   B. Stimulating the release of excess neurotransmitters
   C. Preventing down-regulation from occurring
   D. Preventing neurotransmitters from being reabsorbed into the cell that released them

Table 5.3 The Major Categories of Drugs

Drugs	Psychological Effects	Chemical Effects	Tolerance	Likelihood of Dependence
Stimulants: caffeine, cocaine, amphetamine, ecstasy	Euphoria, increased energy, lowered inhibitions	Increase dopamine, serotonin, norepinephrine activity	Develops quickly	High
Marijuana	Euphoria, relaxation, distorted sensory experiences, paranoia	Stimulates cannabinoid receptors	Develops slowly	Low
Hallucinogens: LSD, psilocybin, DMT, ketamine	Major distortion of sensory and perceptual experiences. Fear, panic, paranoia	Increase serotonin activity; block glutamate receptors	Develops slowly	Very low
Opiates: heroin	Intense euphoria, pain relief	Stimulate endorphin receptors	Develops quickly	Very high
Sedatives: barbiturates, benzo-diazepines	Drowsiness, relaxation, sleep	Increase GABA activity	Develops quickly	High
Alcohol	Euphoria, relaxation, lowered inhibitions	Primarily facilitates GABA activity; also stimulates endorphin and dopamine receptors	Develops gradually	Moderate to high

Commonly Abused "Recreational" Drugs

Thus far, we have discussed some of the ways in which drugs can affect our brain and our behaviour. These drugs are categorized based on their effects on the nervous system. Drugs can speed up the nervous system, slow it down, stimulate its pleasure centres, or distort how it processes the world. Table 5.3 provides an overview of some of the better-known drugs.

Almost all of the drugs discussed in this chapter are known as **psychoactive drugs**, *substances that affect thinking, behaviour, perception, and emotion*. However, not all of them are legal. As you will see, the boundary between illicit recreational drugs and legal prescription drugs can be razor-thin at times. Many common prescription medications are chemically similar, albeit safer, versions of illicit drugs; additionally, many legal prescription drugs are purchased illegally and used in ways not intended by the manufacturer.

STIMULANTS **Stimulants** *are a category of drugs that speed up the activity of the nervous system, typically enhancing wakefulness and alertness.* There are a number of different types of stimulant drugs, ranging from naturally occurring substances such as leaves (cocaine) and beans (coffee) to drugs produced in a laboratory (crystal meth). Additionally, each drug has its own unique effect on the nervous system, influencing the levels of specific neurotransmitters in one of the four ways discussed earlier in this module.

The most widely used—and perhaps abused—stimulant is one that is likely in front of you as you read this: caffeine. Caffeine is not a "recreational" drug *per se;* however, because its neural mechanisms are similar to other stimulants, we will discuss it here. Caffeine can be found in many substances including coffee, tea, many soft drinks, and chocolate. It should come as no surprise that caffeine tends to temporarily increase energy levels and alertness.

It produces these effects by influencing the activity of a brain chemical called *adenosine*. When adenosine binds to its receptors in the brain, it slows down neural activity. In fact, it helps you become sleepy. Caffeine binds to adenosine receptors, but without causing a reduction in neural activity. In other words, it prevents adenosine from doing its job. At the same time, caffeine stimulates the adrenal glands to release adrenaline. This hormone accounts for the burst of energy associated with caffeine. Given that adrenaline is also associated with "fight or flight" responses, it may also explain why many people feel jittery after consuming too much caffeine.

Although no drug is harmless, the withdrawal effects associated with it are far less severe than those found for other stimulants. Depriving yourself of caffeine will typically result in headaches, fatigue, and occasionally nausea; however, these symptoms will usually disappear after two to three days. Other stimulants are not so forgiving.

Cocaine is another commonly abused stimulant. It is synthesized from coca leaves, most often grown in South American countries such as Colombia, Peru, and Bolivia. The people who harvest these plants often take the drug in its simplest form—they chew on the leaves and experience a mild increase in energy. However, by the time it reaches Canadian markets, it has been processed into powder form. It is typically snorted and absorbed into the bloodstream through the nasal passages or, if prepared as crack cocaine, smoked in a pipe. Cocaine influences the nervous system by blocking the reuptake of dopamine in reward centres of the brain, although it can also influence serotonin and norepinephrine levels as well (see Figure 5.17). By preventing dopamine from being reabsorbed by the neuron that released it, cocaine increases the amount of dopamine in the synapse between the cells, thus making the postsynaptic cell more likely to fire. The result is an increase in energy levels and a feeling of euphoria.

Figure 5.17 Stimulant Effects on the Brain

Like many addictive drugs, cocaine and amphetamines stimulate the reward centres of the brain, including the nucleus accumbens and ventral tegmental area. Cocaine works by blocking reuptake of dopamine, and methamphetamine works by increasing the release of dopamine at presynaptic neurons.

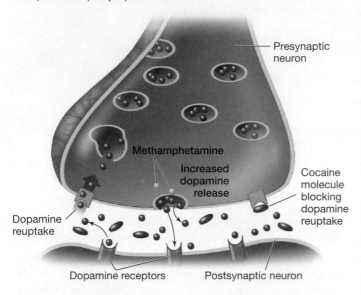

Presynaptic neuron

Methamphetamine

Increased dopamine release

Cocaine molecule blocking dopamine reuptake

Dopamine reuptake

Dopamine receptors   Postsynaptic neuron

Amphetamines, another group of stimulants, come in a variety of forms. Some are prescription drugs, such as methylphenidate (Ritalin) and modafinil (Provigil), which are typically prescribed for attention deficit hyperactivity disorder (ADHD) and narcolepsy, respectively. When used as prescribed, these drugs can have beneficial effects; oftentimes, however, these drugs are used recreationally. Other stimulants, such as methamphetamine, are not prescribed drugs. Methamphetamine, which stimulates the release of dopamine in presynaptic cells (see Figure 5.17), may be even more potent than cocaine when it comes to addictive potential. (*Crystal meth*, a drug made famous by the TV program *Breaking Bad*, is a form of methamphetamine that has undergone additional chemical refinement to remove impurities.) Methamphetamines are also notorious for causing significant neurological and external physical problems. For example, chronic methamphetamine abusers often experience deterioration of their facial features, teeth, and gums, owing to a combination of factors. First, methamphetamine addiction can lead to neglect of basic dietary and hygienic care. Second, the drug is often manufactured from a potent cocktail of substances including hydrochloric acid and farm fertilizer—it is probably not surprising that these components can have serious side effects on appearance and health.

Long-term use of potent stimulants like methamphetamines can actually alter the structure of the user's brain. Compared to non-users, people who have a history of abusing methamphetamine have been shown to have structural abnormalities of cells in the frontal lobes, which reduce the brain's ability to inhibit irrelevant thoughts (Tobias et al., 2010). This ability can be measured through

Advertising Archive/Courtesy Everett Collection

It often comes as a surprise to learn that the very substances that people can become addicted to, or whose possession and use can even land them in prison today, were once ingredients in everyday products. Cocaine was once used as an inexpensive, over-the-counter pain remedy. A concoction of wine and cocaine was popular, and the drug was also added to cough syrups and drops for treating toothaches. Coca-Cola used to contain nine milligrams of cocaine per glass; this practice ceased in 1903 (Liebowitz, 1983).

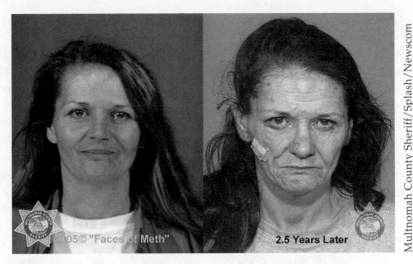

Multnomah County Sheriff/Splash/Newscom

Theresa Baxter was 42 when the picture on the left was taken. The photo on the right was taken 2.5 years later; the effects of methamphetamine are obvious and striking.

the Stroop test (Figure 5.18), which challenges a person's ability to inhibit reading a word in favour of identifying its colour. Methamphetamine abusers had greater difficulty with this task than non-users, and they also had reduced activity in the frontal lobes, likely because of the damage described previously (Salo et al., 2010).

Changes in brain structure have also been noted in chronic users of **ecstasy** (3,4-methylenedioxy-*N*-methyl-amphetamine or MDMA), *a drug that is typically classified as a stimulant, but also has hallucinogenic effects* (Cowan et al., 2008). MDMA was developed in 1912 by the German pharmaceutical company Merck KGaA; it was originally designed as a blood-clotting agent (Meyer, 2013). In the late 1970s, it was rediscovered by a chemist at the Dow chemical company, who described its emotional and sensual effects (Shulgin & Nichols, 1978). In the 1980s, it was labelled a "club drug" because of its frequent appearance at nightclub and rave parties. Ecstasy exerts its influence on the brain by stimulating the release of massive amounts of the neurotransmitter serotonin; it also blocks its reuptake, thereby ensuring that neurons containing serotonin receptors will fire at levels much greater than normal. Ecstasy heightens physical sensations and is known to increase social bonding and compassion among those who are under its influence. Unfortunately, this drug has also been linked to a number of preventable deaths. Heat stroke and dehydration are major risks associated with ecstasy use, especially when the drug is taken at a rave where there is a high level of physical exertion from dancing in an overheated environment. It can also lead to lowered mood two to five days after consumption, as it takes time for serotonin levels to return to normal (Curran & Travill, 1997).

The long-term effects of ecstasy use are difficult to identify because most users of this drug also abuse other illegal substances. That said, recent neuroimaging studies with long-term ecstasy users have highlighted some of the effects this drug can have on the brain (Urban et al., 2012). For instance, several studies have shown that MDMA impairs the sensitivity of many visual regions in the occipital lobe (Oliveri & Calvo, 2003; White et al., 2013). Additionally, recent neuroimaging data show that using ecstasy can produce unique damage (independent of the effects of other drugs) in several areas of the cortex in the left hemisphere (Cowan et al., 2003). Given that the left hemisphere is also critical for language abilities, it should come as no surprise that ecstasy users show slight impairments on language-based tests of memory (e.g., lists of words; Laws & Kokkalis, 2007).

HALLUCINOGENS Hallucinogenic drugs *are substances that produce perceptual distortions.* Depending on the type of hallucinogen consumed, these distortions

Figure 5.18 The Stroop Task

The Stroop task requires you to read aloud the colour of the letters of these sample words. The task measures your ability to inhibit a natural tendency to read the word, rather than identify the colour. Chronic methamphetamine users have greater difficulty with this task than do non-users.

BLUE	**GREEN**	**YELLOW**
PINK	**RED**	**ORANGE**
GREY	**BLACK**	**PURPLE**
TAN	**WHITE**	**BROWN**

may be visual, auditory, and sometimes tactile in nature, such as the experience of crawling sensations against the skin. Hallucinogens also alter how people perceive their own thinking. For example, deep significance may be attached to what are normally mundane objects, events, or thoughts. One commonly used hallucinogen is LSD (lysergic acid diethylamide), which is a laboratory-made (synthetic) drug. A recent study examined brain activity of individuals after they had just taken LSD (Carhart-Harris et al., 2016). These researchers found that the LSD experience involves greater activity in visual areas; this activity strongly correlated with participants' reports of hallucinations. The researchers also noted reduced connectivity between areas in the temporal and parietal lobe; these changes were related to feelings of "losing oneself" and finding "altered meanings." These results show the strong link between brain activity and moment-to-moment experiences.

Hallucinogenic substances also occur in nature, such as psilocybin (a mushroom) and mescaline (derived from the peyote cactus). Hallucinogens can have very long-lasting effects—more than 12 hours for LSD, for example. These drugs may also elicit powerful emotional experiences that range from extreme euphoria to fear, panic, and paranoia. The two most common hallucinogens, LSD and psilocybin, both act on the transmission of serotonin.

Short-acting hallucinogens have become increasingly popular for recreational use. The effects of two of these hallucinogens, ketamine and DMT (dimethyltryptamine), last for about an hour. Ketamine (street names include "Special K" and "Vitamin K") was originally developed as a surgical anesthetic to be used in cases where a gaseous anesthetic could not be applied, such as on the battlefield. It has been gaining popularity among university students as well as among people who frequent dance clubs and raves. Ketamine induces dream-like states, memory loss, dizziness, confusion, and a distorted sense of body ownership (i.e., feeling like your body and voice don't belong to you; Fu et al., 2005; Morgan et al., 2010). This synthetic drug blocks receptors for glutamate, which is an excitatory neurotransmitter that is important for, among other things, memory.

The short-acting hallucinogen known as DMT occurs naturally in such different places as the bark from trees native to Central and South America and on the skin surface of certain toads. DMT is even found in very small, naturally produced amounts in the human nervous system (Fontanilla et al., 2009). The function of DMT in the brain remains unclear, although some researchers have speculated that it plays a role in sleep and dreaming, and even out-of-body experiences (Barbanoj et al., 2008; Strassman, 2001). DMT is used in Canada primarily for recreational purposes. Users frequently report having intense "spiritual" experiences, such as feeling connected to or communicating with divine beings (as well as aliens, plant spirits, and other beings that aren't part of most modern people's version of reality). In fact, its ability to apparently enhance spiritual experiences has been well known in South American indigenous cultures. DMT is the primary psychoactive ingredient in *ayahuasca*, which plays a central role in shamanistic rituals involving contact with the spirit world. An increasing number of Canadians have used another drug, *salvia divinorum*, for similar purposes.

Many psychedelics can have serious negative consequences on users, ranging from memory problems to unwanted "flashbacks" in which the user re-experiences the visual distortions and emotional changes associated with the psychedelic state (Halpern & Pope, 2003). However, as you read in the introduction to this module, some psychedelics are now being used to treat a number of clinical conditions. LSD has been used to help people deal with the anxiety associated with terminal illnesses (Gasser et al., 2015). Psilocybin (magic mushrooms), ayahuasca, and DMT have all been used to help reduce addiction to tobacco and alcohol (Tupper et al., 2015). MDMA (ecstasy) has been used to help people suffering from post-traumatic stress disorder or PTSD (Mithoefer et al., 2011, 2013). Obviously these drugs are generally only used when traditional treatments are ineffective. But, it does demonstrate that the line between "recreational drugs" and "medical drugs" is not as clear cut as we might think.

MARIJUANA Thus far, we have discussed drugs that stimulate the central nervous system and drugs that lead to altered states of consciousness. However, not all drugs neatly fit into these distinct categories. For instance, **marijuana** is *a drug comprising the leaves and buds of the* Cannabis *plant that produces a combination of hallucinogenic, stimulant, and relaxing (narcotic) effects.* These buds contain a high concentration of a compound called tetrahydrocannabinol (THC). THC mimics *anandamide,* a chemical that occurs naturally in the brain and the peripheral nerves. Both anandamide and THC bind to cannabinoid receptors and induce feelings of euphoria, relaxation, reduced pain, and heightened and sometimes distorted sensory experiences (Edwards et al., 2012; Ware et al., 2010). They also stimulate one's appetite (Kirkham, 2009). Although "having the munchies" might seem like a funny side effect for recreational users, it is an incredibly important benefit for cancer sufferers who use medicinal marijuana to counteract the nausea and lack of appetite that occurs following chemotherapy (Machado Rocha et al., 2008).

From the above list, it is clear that marijuana use can affect a number of different behaviours. Missing from this list, however, are the effects that this drug can have on our cognitive abilities.

BIOPSYCHOSOCIAL PERSPECTIVES
Recreational and Spiritual Uses of *Salvia Divinorum*

Salvia divinorum is an herb that grows in Central and South America. When smoked or chewed, salvia induces highly intense but short-lived hallucinations. Use of this drug also leads to *dissociative experiences*—a detachment between self and body (Sumnall et al., 2011). An exploration of salvia reveals a great deal about how cultural views affect how drugs are perceived. A single drug could be described as recreational, addictive, and a scourge to society in one culture, yet highly valued and spiritually significant to another.

Test what you know about this drug:

True or False?

1. Sale of salvia is prohibited by the Canadian government.
2. Very few young people in Canada who use drugs have tried salvia.
3. Salvia has profound healing properties.

Answers

1. *True*. The legal status of salvia changed in February 2016. Previously, it had been listed as a natural product under the control of Health Canada; although technically illegal, regulations controlling salvia were not strictly enforced. However, it is now listed as a Schedule IV drug under the *Controlled Drugs and Substances Act*. It is illegal to sell, cultivate, or transport salvia, although possession of small amounts is still legal. Further details of the change, passed by the Conservative government in 2015, can be found online: www.hc-sc.gc.ca/hc-ps/substancontrol/substan/legal-salvia-statut-eng.php.
2. *False*. The use of salvia is on the rise among North Americans and Europeans, particularly among younger people (Nyi et al., 2010). Approximately 7.3% of Canadians aged 15–24 have tried it (Health Canada, 2010).

3. *False*. There is no scientific evidence that salvia has healing properties. Whether one agrees with this statement, however, depends on who is asked. Among the Mazateca people of Mexico, salvia is used in divine rituals in which an individual communicates with the spiritual world. Shamans of the Mazateca people use salvia for spiritual healing sessions. They believe the drug has profound medicinal properties.

Drugs such as salvia and ayahuasca raise important questions about the effects of drugs and our view toward them. Although a given drug usually has standard, reliable effects on brain chemistry, the subjective experience it provides, the purposes it is used for, and people's attitudes toward the drug may vary widely depending on the cultural context.

Ted Kinsman/Photo Researchers, Inc./Science Source

Salvia divinorum is a type of sage plant that grows naturally in Central and South America. Users of the herb chew or smoke the leaves or combine juices from the leaves with tea for drinking.

Working the Scientific Literacy Model

Marijuana, Memory, and Cognition

No one doubts that marijuana affects a person's thinking and behaviour. That said, descriptions of the exact nature of these effects are often more anecdotal than scientific. The earliest reference to marijuana is found in the ancient Hindu text *Raja Nirghanta*, which translates the drug as "promoter of success," "the cause of the reeling gait," and "the laughter moving" (see Chopra & Chopra, 1957). Indeed, more recent descriptions have noted that marijuana's effects on one's ability to think are both widespread and testable.

What do we know about the effects of marijuana on memory and cognition?

Studies of people under the influence of marijuana have demonstrated a number of different impairments to memory processes (Crean et al., 2011). Several researchers have confirmed that marijuana disrupts short-term memory (Ranganathan & D'Souza, 2006). Studies of long-term memory have indicated that marijuana use was associated with a reduced ability to recall information (Miller et al., 1977) and a greater tendency to commit intrusion errors—adding in words that were not actually on a list of to-be-remembered items (i.e., a "false positive"; Hooker &

Jones, 1987; Pfefferbaum et al., 1977). Marijuana also affects a number of cognitive abilities. Executive functions, such as decision making and the control of attention, are critical for dealing with novel situations and for changing or inhibiting responses to stimuli in the environment. Many executive functions are impaired by THC. For instance, marijuana impairs people's ability to problem solve and to change their strategies while performing a task (Bolla et al., 2002; Pope et al., 2003). It may impair creative thinking and attention as well (Hermann et al., 2007; Kowal et al., 2015).

How can science explain these effects?

Neuroimaging results indicate that the memory and cognitive difficulties experienced by people who smoke marijuana are likely related to changes in the brains of marijuana smokers. A number of studies have noted that reduced performance on memory tests is related to decreases in brain activity in the right frontal lobe (Block et al., 2002; Jager et al., 2007), an area involved with memory retrieval (Tulving et al., 1994). Interestingly, some researchers have found that even when marijuana users and healthy control participants produce the same results on a memory test, their brains generate different patterns of activity. For instance, Kanayama and colleagues (2004) found that participants who had recently smoked marijuana (< 24 hours ago) were able to perform a spatial memory task; but doing so recruited a much more widespread network of brain regions, including several that are not typically associated with memory. This suggests that the brains of marijuana users need to work harder to reach the same level of performance, oftentimes relying on additional brain structures to help out (Jager et al., 2006).

Problems with executive functions can also be explained, at least in part, by differing patterns of brain activity. The inability to inhibit responses on a Stroop task (which was discussed earlier in this module) was related to the fact that marijuana users had less activity than healthy controls in a number of frontal-lobe regions (Eldreth et al., 2004; Gruber & Yurgelun-Todd, 2005). These studies also demonstrated that, similar to the memory studies, the brains of marijuana users had additional activity in areas not typically associated with the task they were performing. In other words, these brains had to find alternative networks to allow them to compensate for the marijuana so that they could still perform the task (Martín-Santos et al., 2010).

Can we critically evaluate this information?

When we look at these data, we have to remember that fMRI activity is correlational. The orange and yellow "lights" in the brain pictures represent areas that are activated at the same time that a person is performing a task; but, it doesn't mean that those areas are causing the person's behaviour. More importantly, we have to think of the participants in drug studies. Many of the people involved in these studies use more than one drug (e.g., marijuana plus alcohol, tobacco, and possibly other drugs). It is therefore difficult to isolate the effects of marijuana *by itself* on cognition.

One way to get around these problems is to look at which areas of the brain are involved with these different abilities and then see if marijuana targets those areas. As it turns out, a receptor sensitive to THC, the cannabinoid (CB1) receptor, is found throughout the hippocampus and in the medial part of the frontal lobes (Pertwee & Ross, 2002; see Figure 5.19). Importantly, stimulating these receptors can lead to impairments in short-term memory and higher-level thinking (Ranganathan & D'Souza, 2006). Thus, there is a cellular-level mechanism that can explain (some of) the odd behaviours that you see when people are smoking up.

Why is this relevant?

Marijuana use seems, to many people, harmless and funny. What's so bad about spending hours getting high, watching cartoons, and eating chips? But, although occasional use hasn't been linked to serious cognitive consequences, recent brain-imaging studies of long-term smokers showed reduced amounts of grey matter (neurons) in memory regions of the temporal lobe (Battistella et al., 2014); there were also fewer white-matter connections involving this brain area (Zalesky et al., 2012). In other words, chronic marijuana use can influence how parts of the brain transmit and receive information. Heavy long-term use of marijuana is also related to a four-point decline in IQ scores (a number that isn't huge, but is still something to think about; Fried et al., 2002). Importantly, the strains of marijuana that are currently available tend to be higher in THC content than the strains available to previous generations of drug users (Hardwick & King, 2008). It is possible, therefore, that the small cognitive deficits found in current studies of long-term marijuana users may be magnified in young people who are just beginning to use this drug.

Marijuana and the Teenage Brain Marijuana use often starts during the teenage years. From a neurological perspective, early drug use is a particular cause for concern (Lubman et al., 2015). The brain develops in a step-by-step fashion, with higher-order cognitive areas—particularly the frontal lobes—developing after other areas have fully matured (Gogtay et al., 2004). As part of this step-by-step development, the white-matter fibres connecting brain regions grow and form new connections while unnecessary synapses are pruned away. Marijuana use during the teenage years has been shown to impair both of these

Figure 5.19 CB1 Receptors in the Brain

The locations of the CB1 receptors, which bind to the active ingredient in marijuana, help explain the diverse effects users often experience. CB1 receptors are found in the frontal lobes (executive functions), hippocampus (memory), and cerebellum (coordination of movement). They are also found in the nucleus accumbens, an area related to the rewarding feeling associated with many drugs.

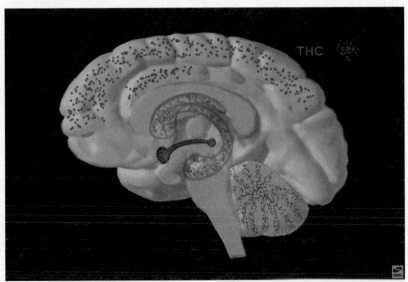

Courtesy of National Institute of Drug Abuse

developmental processes (Gruber et al., 2014). It has also been linked with thinning (i.e., fewer cells) in a number of cortical areas (Mashhoon et al., 2015; Price et al., 2015) and smaller hippocampal volumes (Ashtari et al., 2011).

These changes in the brain's development can affect cognitive abilities. Increasing evidence indicates that the effects of marijuana on memory and executive functions are much larger in people who started taking the drug before the age of 17 (Brook et al., 2008; Pope et al., 2003). In other words, using marijuana during an earlier stage of development can have a much larger effect on a person's future than if the same dose were to be consumed or smoked later in life (Squeglia et al., 2009). These data therefore suggest that prevention programs should specifically target teens to ensure that their cognitive abilities don't go up in smoke.

It is important to note that if you *did* smoke marijuana before the age of 17, your life isn't ruined. It just means that if you continue to frequently use marijuana, you are statistically more likely to have memory and executive functioning programs later in life. It is quite possible that your brain will recover. You can help it bounce back by reducing your consumption of drugs and by engaging in behaviours that help increase the thickness of white-matter pathways in the frontal lobes (e.g., mindfulness training; see Modules 14.3 and 16.2). So, you have a lot of control over what happens to your brain.

Currently, marijuana is the most commonly used recreational drug in Canada. Indeed, survey research suggests that 22% of people aged 15–19 (469 000 Canadian teens) had used marijuana within the year prior to the survey (Statistics Canada, 2013). This high usage rate reflects, in part, the fact that this drug is so readily available. A similar issue is emerging for another class of drugs, opiates, which includes well-known narcotics such as heroin, as well as many commonly abused prescription drugs.

OPIATES   Opiates (*also called narcotics*) *are drugs such as heroin and morphine that reduce pain and induce extremely intense feelings of euphoria.* These drugs bind to endorphin receptors in the nervous system. Endorphins ("endogenous morphine") are neurotransmitters that reduce pain and produce pleasurable sensations—effects magnified by opiates. Naturally occurring opiates are derived from certain species of poppy plants that are primarily grown in Asia and the Middle East (particularly Afghanistan). Opiate drugs are very common in medical and emergency room settings. For example, the drug fentanyl is used in emergency rooms to treat people in extreme pain. A street version of fentanyl, known as "China White," can be more than 20 times the strength of more commonly sold doses of heroin. This drug is so dangerous that in April 2016, British Columbia declared a public health emergency after more than 200 people died from overdoses of the drug. Yet despite the well-publicized dangers, people continue to use it.

Treating opiate addiction can be incredibly challenging. Opiates produce very rapid and powerful "highs";

because the time between injecting or smoking opiates and their physical impact is so short, it is easy for people to mentally link the drug to the pleasurable feeling. This increases the addictiveness of these drugs. People who are addicted to opiates and other highly addictive drugs enter a negative cycle of having to use these drugs simply to ward off withdrawal effects, rather than to actually achieve the sense of euphoria they may have experienced when they started using them. Methadone is an *opioid* (a synthetic opiate) that binds to opiate receptors but does not give the same kind of high that heroin does. A regimen of daily methadone treatment can help people who are addicted to opiates avoid painful withdrawal symptoms as they learn to cope without the drug. In recent years, newer alternatives to methadone have been found to be more effective and need to be taken only a few times per week.

Another opioid, oxycodone (OxyContin), has helped many people reduce severe pain while having relatively few side effects. Unfortunately, this drug, along with a similar product, Percocet, has very high abuse potential. It is often misused, especially by those who have obtained it through illegal means (i.e., without a prescription). Indeed, the abuse of prescription opiates is a growing problem in Canada, particularly among high school students and the elderly (Sproule et al., 2009); this topic will be discussed in more detail later in this module.

Module 5.3b Quiz:

Commonly Abused "Recreational" Drugs

Know . . .

1. _____ are drugs that increase central nervous system activity.
   A. Hallucinogens
   B. Narcotics
   C. Psychoactive drugs
   D. Stimulants

2. Drugs that are best known for their ability to alter normal visual and auditory perceptions are called _____.
   A. hallucinogens
   B. narcotics
   C. psychoactive drugs
   D. stimulants

Apply . . .

3. Which statement about marijuana's effects on memory is *not* true?
   A. Marijuana use led to poorer recall of information and a greater tendency to remember information that hadn't been presented earlier (false alarms).
   B. Marijuana leads to decreased activity in brain areas related to memory retrieval.
   C. Marijuana use led to poorer recall of information and a lower tendency to remember information that hadn't been presented earlier (false alarms).
   D. Areas of the brain not typically involved with memory are active when smokers attempt to recall information.

Legal Drugs and Their Effects on Consciousness

So far we have covered drugs that are, for the most part, produced and distributed illegally. Some prescription drugs can also have profound effects on consciousness and, as a consequence, are targets for misuse.

SEDATIVES Sedative drugs, *sometimes referred to as "downers," depress activity of the central nervous system. Barbiturates* were an early form of medication used to treat anxiety and promote sleep. High doses of these drugs can shut down the brainstem regions that regulate breathing, so their medical use has largely been discontinued in favour of safer drugs. Barbiturates have a high potential for abuse, typically by people who want to lower inhibitions, relax, and try to improve their sleep. (Incidentally, while these agents may knock you out, they do not really improve the quality of sleep. Barbiturates actually reduce the amount of REM sleep.)

Newer forms of sedative drugs, called *benzodiazepines*, include prescription drugs such as Xanax, Ativan, and Valium. These drugs increase the effects of gamma-aminobutyric acid (GABA), an inhibitory neurotransmitter that helps reduce feelings of anxiety or panic. The major advantage of benzodiazepine drugs over barbiturates is that they do not specifically target the brain regions responsible for breathing and, even at high doses, are unlikely to be fatal. However, people under the influence of any kind of sedative are at greater risk for injury or death due to accidents caused by their diminished attention, reaction time, and coordination.

PRESCRIPTION DRUG ABUSE Prescription drugs are commonly abused by illicit users; over 15% of Canadian high school students have reported abusing prescription drugs at some point in their lives (Hammond et al., 2010; Figure 5.20). The prevalence of prescription drug abuse becomes even more extreme when these students enter university. Surveys have shown that as many as 31% of university students sampled have abused Ritalin, the stimulant commonly prescribed as a treatment for ADHD (Bogle & Smith, 2009). A massive number of prescription drugs are available on the market, including stimulants,

Figure 5.20 Frequency of Drug Use among Grade 12 Students

The abuse of prescription and over-the-counter drugs is becoming increasingly common in Canada. In a 2008 nationwide survey, over 15% of Grade 12 students admitted to illegally using these drugs at least once. This figure illustrates how the prevalence of prescription drug abuse compares to that of other frequently abused substances.

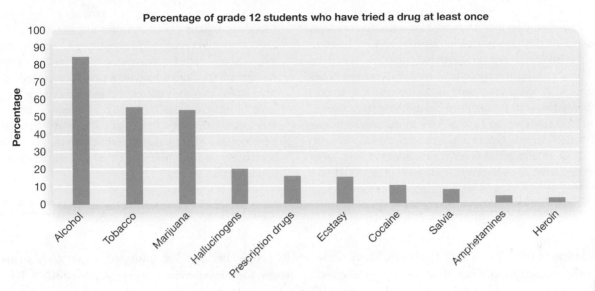

Source: Based on Hammond, D., Ahmed, R., Burkhalter, R., Sae Yang, W., & Leatherdale, S. (2010). Illicit substance use among Canadian youth: Trends between 2002 and 2008. *Canadian Journal of Public Health*, 102, 7-12.

opiates, and sedatives. In 2011, 3.2% of Canadians (approximately 1.1 *million* people) used prescription drugs for nonmedical reasons within the year prior to the survey (Health Canada, 2012). Users typically opt for prescription drugs as their drugs of choice because they are legal (when used as prescribed), pure (i.e., not contaminated or diluted), and relatively easy to get. Prescription drugs are typically taken at large doses, and administered in such a way as to get a quicker, more intense effect—for example, by crushing and snorting stimulants such as Ritalin (see Figure 5.21).

Some of the most commonly abused prescription drugs in Canada are painkillers such as OxyContin. When used normally, OxyContin is a pain-reliever that slowly releases an opioid over the course of approximately 12 hours, thus making it a relatively safe product (Roth et al., 2000). However, crushing the OxyContin tablet frees its opioid component oxycodone from the slow-release mechanism; it can then be inhaled or dissolved in liquid and injected to provide a rapid "high" (Carise et al., 2007). Almost 80% of people entering treatment programs for OxyContin abuse admitted that the drug was not prescribed to them, suggesting that there is a flourishing trade in this drug. Indeed, a recent study of drug users in Vancouver found that OxyContin is quite easy to illegally purchase in Canada (Nosyk et al., 2012); not surprisingly, the number of people entering drug rehabilitation programs for oxycodone abuse is also increasing (Sproule et al., 2009). In order to counteract this trend, Purdue Pharma Canada, the company that makes the drug, has replaced it with a similar substance, OxyNeo, that is more difficult to grind up into a powder. However, this action will likely have little effect on addiction rates—in April 2013, the federal government allowed *six* pharmaceutical companies to begin manufacturing generic (cheaper) versions of the drug.

Curbing prescription drug abuse poses quite a challenge. Approaches to reducing this problem include efforts to develop pain medications that do not act on pleasure and reward centres of the brain. For example, pain can be reduced by the administration of compounds that stimulate cannabinoid receptors in peripheral regions of the nervous system, thereby avoiding the high associated

Figure 5.21 Ritalin and Cocaine

Stimulants like methylphenidate (Ritalin) affect the same areas of the brain as cocaine, albeit with different speed and intensity.

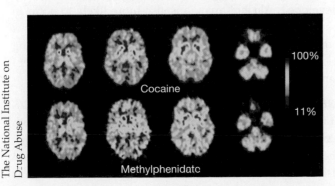

The National Institute on Drug Abuse

PSYCH@

University Parties

Researchers have determined that university students drink significantly more than their peers who do not attend university (Carter et al., 2010). However, although heavy drinking—particularly on the weekend—is often associated with positive emotions (Howard et al., 2015), it can lead to some serious consequences for students. In one study, nearly half of the university student participants binge-drank, one-third drove under the influence, 10% to 12% sustained an injury or were assaulted while intoxicated, and 2% were victims of date rape while drinking (Hingson et al., 2009). Alcohol abuse in our society is widespread, especially during times of celebration (Glindemann et al., 2007), so it might seem as if universities have few options at their disposal

to reduce reckless drinking on campus. Psychologists Kent Glindemann, Scott Geller, and their associates, however, have conducted some interesting field studies in fraternity houses at their U.S. university. For example, in two separate studies, these researchers measured the typical blood-alcohol level at fraternity parties. They then offered monetary awards or entry into a raffle for fraternities that could keep their average blood-alcohol level below 0.05 at their next party. The interventions proved to be successful in both studies, with blood-alcohol levels being significantly reduced from the baseline (Fournier et al., 2004; Glindemann et al., 2007).

---

with stimulation of receptors within the brain. Many communities offer prescription drug disposal opportunities, which helps remove unused drugs from actual or potential circulation. In addition, doctors and other health care professionals are becoming increasingly aware that some individuals seeking prescription drugs are doing so because they are addicted to them.

ALCOHOL   Alcohol can be found in nearly every culture, although some frown on its use more than others. Alcohol use is a part of many cherished social and spiritual rituals, but is also associated with violence and accidents. It has the power to change societies, in some cases for the worse. Several decades ago, "problem drinking" was not an issue for the Carib people of Venezuela, for example. During specific yearly festivals, alcohol was brewed and consumed in limited amounts. In more recent years, the influence of Western civilization has led to the emergence of problems with alcohol abuse and alcoholism in this group of people (Seale et al., 2002). Most societies regard alcohol as an acceptable form of drug use, though they may attempt to limit and regulate its use through legal means. Customs and social expectations also affect usage. For example, drinking—especially heavy drinking—is generally considered more socially acceptable for men than for women.

Alcohol has a number of effects on the brain. It initially targets GABA receptors, and subsequently affects opiate and dopamine receptors. The stimulation of opiate and dopamine receptors accounts for the euphoria associated with lower doses as well its rewarding effects. The release of GABA, an inhibitory neurotransmitter, reduces the activity of the central nervous system, which helps explain the impairments in balance and coordination associated with consumption of alcohol. But if alcohol increases the release of an inhibitory brain chemical, why

do people become *less* inhibited when they drink? The reason for this behaviour is that alcohol inhibits the frontal lobes of the brain. One function of the frontal lobes is to inhibit behaviour and impulses, and alcohol appears to impair the frontal lobe's ability to do so—in other words, it inhibits an inhibitor.

The lowered inhibitions associated with alcohol may help people muster the courage to perform a toast at a wedding, but many socially unacceptable consequences are also associated with alcohol use. Alcohol abuse has been linked to health problems, sexual and physical assault, automobile accidents, missing work or school, unplanned pregnancies, and contracting sexually transmitted diseases (Griffin et al., 2010). These effects are primarily associated with heavy consumption, which can often lead to *alcohol myopia* (Steele & Josephs, 1990). When intoxicated, people often pay more attention to cues related to their desires and impulses (e.g., the attractive-looking person on the couch at the party) and less attention to cues related to inhibiting those desires (e.g., friends telling them to stop drinking, or the lecture about safe sex that they received in their sex-education class). This tendency to focus on short-term rewards rather than long-term consequences is particularly noticeable in underage drinkers whose frontal lobes (which help inhibit behaviour) are not fully developed. Alcohol myopia is also more likely to occur in people with low self-esteem; these individuals may focus on their fear of social rejection and respond by engaging in risky behaviours that they feel will lead to social acceptance (MacDonald & Martineau, 2002).

WHY ARE SOME DRUGS LEGAL AND OTHERS ILLEGAL?   In the November 2012 U.S. election, both Colorado and Washington states voted to legalize marijuana. Colorado Governor John Hickenlooper cautioned users by noting that, "[F]ederal law still says marijuana is an illegal drug, so don't break out the Cheetos or Goldfish [crackers] too quickly." That caveat aside, these votes do suggest that attitudes toward certain drugs are changing in the U.S., which has traditionally been much more conservative than Canada. Indeed, Alaska, Oregon, and the District of Columbia (Washington, D.C.) legalized marijuana possession in November 2014. In Canada, the newly elected government of Justin Trudeau promised to legalize marijuana as well, although the sale of this drug will likely be controlled in a manner similar to alcohol and tobacco. These changes in the legal status of marijuana lead us to an interesting question: Why are some drugs legal and others illegal?

It is relatively easy to understand some decisions, such as making drugs with intense effects (such as opium) illegal, but allowing chemically similar drugs with weaker effects (such as OxyContin) to be legal (at least, with prescriptions). But, some distinctions are less clear. Nicotine is more addictive than THC, the active ingredient in marijuana, yet the sale of tobacco products is legal while the sale of marijuana is not legal in most parts of the world. As you read earlier in this module, alcohol can lead to violence and many risky behaviours; marijuana's most dangerous effects are to the lungs and to short-term memory (and perhaps the waistline). Yet, it is legal to buy alcohol in Canada (and even at gas stations in the U.S.!), while marijuana users in many places risk getting criminal records every time they light up. One possible argument for the difference is that it is easier to tell if people have been drinking than smoking marijuana; for example, police can use a breathalyzer to test if people are drinking and driving, whereas no such test is available for marijuana, even though it also interferes with coordination and attention. As you can see, the decision to legalize or criminalize a drug is not a simple one.

Some countries, such as Portugal, *have* gone ahead and decriminalized drugs. The rationale for doing so was that the "War on Drugs" was not decreasing addiction rates but was costing billions of dollars to fight. Neighboring countries were understandably nervous—if Portugal turned into a drug haven, this activity would undoubtedly affect other Mediterranean nations. However, an examination of drug use in Portugal, Spain, and Italy suggests that decriminalization had little effect on drug use. Between 2001 (the year Portugal decriminalized drugs) and 2007, the number of Portuguese people who reported consuming any recreational drug in the previous 12 months increased 0.3%. These results were almost identical to drug use in Spain and were *lower* than the levels of drug use in Italy, even though drugs were illegal in both of those countries (Hughes & Stevens, 2010).

The purpose of this section is not to promote one drug or another, nor is it to promote any political agenda regarding decriminalization. Rather, this information *should* promote critical thinking and the use of science when making decisions. Today's young people will likely be asked to make legal decisions about a number of drugs ranging from marijuana to several often-abused prescription drugs. Using rigorously controlled experiments to test the physiological and psychological effects of different drugs—and paying attention to the effects of different drug policies in other countries—will help people make informed decisions about whether or not particular substances should be banned.

Module 5.3c Quiz:
Legal Drugs and Their Effects on Consciousness

Know . . .

1. Drugs that depress the activity of the central nervous system are known as _____.
   A. stimulants
   B. sedatives
   C. hallucinogens
   D. GABAs

Apply . . .

2. Research shows that one effective way to decrease problem drinking on a college or university campus is to
   A. hold informative lectures that illustrate the neural effects of drinking.
   B. give up—there is little hope for reducing drinking on campus.
   C. provide monetary incentives for student groups to maintain a low average blood-alcohol level.
   D. threaten student groups with fines if they are caught drinking.

Analyze . . .

3. Why are benzodiazepines believed to be safer than barbiturates?
   A. Barbiturates can inhibit the brain's control of breathing.
   B. Benzodiazepines can be prescribed legally, but barbiturates cannot.
   C. No one misuses benzodiazepines.
   D. Both benzodiazepines and barbiturates are viewed as equally dangerous.

Module 5.3 Summary

5.3a   Know . . . The key terminology related to different categories of drugs and their effects on the nervous system and behaviour.

ecstasy (MDMA)
hallucinogenic drugs
marijuana
opiates
physical dependence
psychoactive drugs
psychological dependence
sedative drugs
stimulants
tolerance

5.3b   Understand . . . drug tolerance and dependence.

Tolerance is a physiological process in which repeated exposure to a drug leads to a need for increasingly larger dosages to experience the intended effect. Physical dependence occurs when the user takes a drug to avoid withdrawal symptoms. Psychological dependence occurs when people feel addicted to a drug despite the absence of physical withdrawal symptoms; this form of dependence is often related to a person's emotional reasons for using a drug (e.g., dealing with stress or negative emotions).

5.3c   Apply . . . your knowledge to better understand your own beliefs about drug use.

One tool that might help you in this regard is the scale in Table 5.4.

Apply Activity

For each item on the left of Table 5.4, circle the number in the column that represents your level of agreement. After you have circled an answer for each item, add up all the circled numbers to find your final score.

5.3d   Analyze . . . the difference between spiritual and recreational drug use.

The difference, such as in the case of salvia, is dependent upon cultural factors, the setting in which the drug is used, and the expectations of the user.

5.3e   Analyze . . . the short- and long-term effects of drug use.

Review Table 5.3 for a summary of short-term effects of the major drug categories. Long-term effects of drug use include tolerance, physical dependence, and psychological dependence. Additionally, long-term use of a number of drugs can change the structure of the brain, leading to permanent deficits in a number of different cognitive and physical abilities.

Table 5.4 What Are Your Beliefs About Drug Use?

	Strongly Disagree	Disagree	Neutral	Agree	Strongly Agree
Marijuana should be legalized.	1	2	3	4	5
Marijuana use among teachers can be just healthy experimentation.	1	2	3	4	5
Personal use of drugs should be legal in the confines of one's own home.	1	2	3	4	5
Daily use of one marijuana cigarette is not necessarily harmful.	1	2	3	4	5
Tobacco smoking should be allowed in high schools.	1	2	3	4	5
It can be normal for a teenager to experiment with drugs.	1	2	3	4	5
Persons convicted for the sale of illicit drugs should not be eligible for parole.	5	4	3	2	1
Lifelong abstinence is a necessary goal in the treatment of alcoholism.	5	4	3	2	1
Once a person becomes drug-free through treatment he can never become a social user.	5	4	3	2	1
Parents should teach their children how to use alcohol.	5	4	3	2	1
Total					

Note: This scale measures permissive attitudes toward substance use and abuse. Higher scores indicate more permissive attitudes.

Source: Reproduced with the permission of Alcohol Research Documentation, Inc. publisher of the Journal of Studies on Alcohol (now the Journal of Studies on Alcohol and Drugs [www.jsad.com]).

Chapter 6
Learning

6.1 Classical Conditioning: Learning by Association

- Pavlov's Dogs: Classical Conditioning of Salivation **229**
- Module 6.1a Quiz **232**
- Processes of Classical Conditioning **233**
- Module 6.1b Quiz **235**
- Applications of Classical Conditioning **235**

  Working the Scientific Literacy Model: Conditioning and Negative Political Advertising **239**
- Module 6.1c Quiz **242**
- Module 6.1 Summary **242**

6.2 Operant Conditioning: Learning Through Consequences

- Basic Principles of Operant Conditioning **245**
- Module 6.2a Quiz **249**
- Processes of Operant Conditioning **249**
- Module 6.2b Quiz **252**
- Reinforcement Schedules and Operant Conditioning **252**

  Working the Scientific Literacy Model: Reinforcement and Superstition **255**
- Module 6.2c Quiz **257**
- Module 6.2 Summary **258**

6.3 Cognitive and Observational Learning

- Cognitive Perspectives on Learning **261**
- Module 6.3a Quiz **262**
- Observational Learning **262**

  Working the Scientific Literacy Model: Linking Media Exposure to Behaviour **265**
- Module 6.3b Quiz **269**
- Module 6.3 Summary **269**

Module 6.1 Classical Conditioning: Learning by Association

Brenda Carson/Fotolia

Learning Objectives

6.1a Know . . . the key terminology involved in classical conditioning.

6.1b Understand . . . how responses learned through classical conditioning can be acquired and lost.

6.1c Understand . . . the role of biological and evolutionary factors in classical conditioning.

6.1d Apply . . . the concepts and terms of classical conditioning to new examples.

6.1e Analyze . . . the use of negative political advertising to condition emotional responses to candidates.

What do you think of when you smell freshly baked cookies? Chances are you associate the smell of cookies with your mother or grandmother, and immediately experience a flood of memories associated with them. These associations form naturally. It is quite unlikely that your grandmother shoved a chocolate chip cookie under your nose and screamed, "Remember me!" Instead, you linked these two stimuli together in your mind; now, the smell of cookies is associated with the idea of grandmother. This ability to associate stimuli provides important evolutionary advantages: It means that you can use one stimulus to predict the appearance of another, and that your body can initiate its response to the second stimulus before it even appears. Although the link between your grandmother and the smell of cookies is not vital to your survival, similar

associations such as the smell of a food that made you sick and a feeling of revulsion just might. Interestingly, we are not the only species with this ability—even the simplest animals (such as the earthworm) can learn by association, suggesting that these associations are in fact critical for survival. In this module, we will explore the different processes that influence how these associations form.

Focus Questions

1. Which types of behaviours can be learned?

2. Do all instances of classical conditioning go undetected by the individual?

» **Learning** *is a process by which behaviour or knowledge changes as a result of experience.* To many people, the term "learning" signifies the activities that students do—reading, listening, and taking tests in order to acquire new information. This process, which is known as *cognitive learning*, is just one type of learning, however. Another way that we learn is by *associative learning*, which is the focus of this module.

Pavlov's Dogs: Classical Conditioning of Salivation

Research on associative learning has a long history in psychology, dating back to Ivan Pavlov (1849–1936), a Russian physiologist and the 1904 Nobel laureate in medicine (for work on digestion, *not* his now-famous conditioning research). Pavlov studied digestion, using dogs as a model species for his experiments. As a part of his normal research procedure, he collected saliva and other gastric secretions from the dogs when they were presented with meat powder. Pavlov and his assistants noticed that as they prepared dogs for procedures, even before any meat powder was presented, the dogs would start salivating. This curious observation led Pavlov to consider the possibility that digestive responses were more than just simple reflexes elicited by food. If dogs salivate *in anticipation* of food, then perhaps the salivary response can also be learned (Pavlov's lab assistants referred to them as "psychic secretions"). Pavlov began conducting experiments in which he first presented a sound from a metronome, a device that produces ticking sounds at set intervals, and then presented meat powder to the dogs. After pairing the sound with the food several times, Pavlov discovered that the metronome could elicit salivation by itself (see Figure 6.1).

Pavlov's discovery began a long tradition of inquiry into what is now called **classical conditioning** or **Pavlovian conditioning**—*a form of associative learning in which an organism learns to associate a neutral stimulus (e.g., a sound) with a biologically relevant stimulus (e.g., food), which results in a change in the response to the previously neutral stimulus (e.g., salivation).* You can think about classical conditioning in mechanical terms—that is, one event causes another. A *stimulus* is an external event or cue that elicits a perceptual response; this occurs regardless of whether the event is important

---

Figure 6.1 Associative Learning

Although much information may pass through the dog's brain, in Pavlov's experiments on classical conditioning an association was made between the clicking sound of a metronome and the food. (Pavlov used a metronome as well as other devices for presenting sounds.)

or not. Some stimuli—such as food, water, pain, or sexual contact—elicit responses instinctively (i.e., without any learning being required). Each of these is an example of an **unconditioned stimulus (US)**, *a stimulus that elicits a reflexive response without learning.* An **unconditioned response (UR)**, on the other hand, *is a reflexive, unlearned reaction to an unconditioned stimulus.* URs could include hunger, drooling, expressions of pain, and sexual responses. Again, you do not need to learn these; they occur fairly automatically. In Pavlov's experiment, meat powder elicited unconditioned salivation in his dogs (see the top panel of Figure 6.2). The link between the US and the UR is, by definition, unlearned. The dog's parents did not have to teach it to salivate when food appeared; this response occurs naturally.

A defining characteristic of classical conditioning is that a neutral stimulus comes to elicit a response. It does so

Figure 6.2 Pavlov's Salivary Conditioning Experiment

Food elicits the unconditioned response of salivation. Before conditioning, the sound of the metronome elicits no response by the dog. During conditioning, the metronome's clicking repeatedly precedes the food. After conditioning, the sound of the metronome alone elicits salivation. Interestingly, the term "conditioning" was actually a translation error. Pavlov initially used the term "condition*al*" stimulus to describe stimuli that were previously unimportant (or neutral) but that later acquired greater significance due to their ability to signal the upcoming occurrence (or, in some cases, nonoccurrence) of a biologically important stimulus. These stimuli can be contrasted with stimuli such as food, which are relevant to an animal's survival and therefore trigger an almost automatic—or "unconditional"—response such as salivating. These terms were mistranslated into English as "conditioned" and "unconditioned."

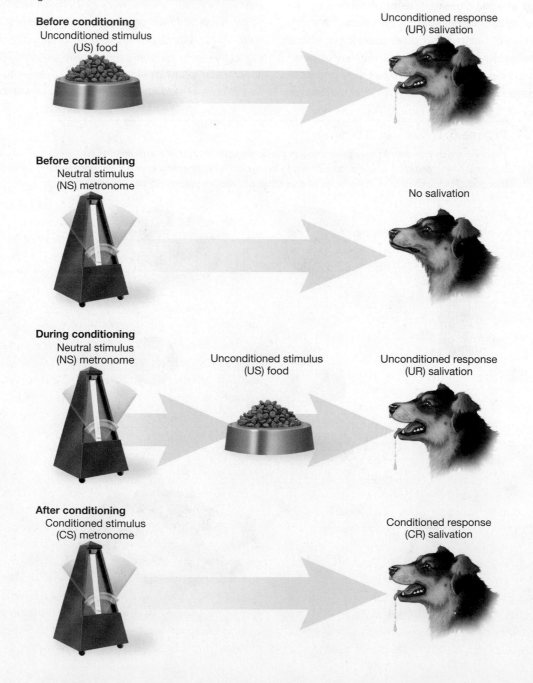

Before conditioning
Unconditioned stimulus (US) food

Unconditioned response (UR) salivation

Before conditioning
Neutral stimulus (NS) metronome

No salivation

During conditioning
Neutral stimulus (NS) metronome

Unconditioned stimulus (US) food

Unconditioned response (UR) salivation

After conditioning
Conditioned stimulus (CS) metronome

Conditioned response (CR) salivation

because the neutral stimulus is paired with, and therefore predicts, an unconditioned stimulus. In Pavlov's experiment, the sound of the metronome was *originally* a neutral stimulus because it did not elicit a response, least of all salivation (see Figure 6.2); however, over time, it began to influence the dogs' responses because of its association with food. In this case, the metronome became a **conditioned stimulus (CS)**, *a once-neutral stimulus that later elicits a conditioned response because it has a history of being paired with an unconditioned stimulus.* A **conditioned response (CR)** *is the learned response that occurs to the conditioned stimulus.* In other words, after being repeatedly paired with the US, the once-neutral metronome clicking in Pavlov's experiment became a conditioned stimulus (CS) because it elicited the conditioned response of salivation. To establish that conditioning has taken place, the metronome's sound (CS) must elicit salivation in the *absence* of food (US; see the bottom panel of Figure 6.2).

A common point of confusion is the difference between a conditioned response and an unconditioned response—in Pavlov's experiment, they are both salivation. What distinguishes the UR from the CR is the stimulus that elicits them. Salivation is a UR if it occurs in response to a US (food). Salivation is a CR if it occurs in response to a CS (the clicking of the metronome). A CS can have this effect only if it becomes *associated* with a US. In other words, a UR is a *naturally occurring* response whereas a CR must be *learned*.

EVOLUTIONARY FUNCTION OF THE CR In Pavlov's original experiments, the response to the signal (after pairings) and to food were exactly the same: salivation. It is important to note that the UR and CR do *not* have to be identical. In Pavlov's study, it made good evolutionary sense to salivate just prior to receiving food. Saliva moisturizes the mouth and is a critical first step in the digestive process. An animal with the ability to prepare in this way would process food more efficiently. Therefore, the CR of salivation served a useful function. Following this line of thinking, what do you think would happen if the US was unpleasant, painful, and potentially life threatening? The answer from an evolutionary perspective is pretty obvious: avoid death and minimize physical damage.

Many animals have an instinct to "freeze" when they are scared. You see this when deer are caught in headlights. They remain motionless—why? The reason is that many of their predators, such as the wolf, have perceptual systems that are quite sensitive to detecting movement; so remaining still has an evolutionary survival advantage. (Highways weren't part of the evolution of deer.) However, if the wolf were to begin to stalk the deer, it should immediately stop freezing and run. So, there are two different defensive responses associated with fear: freezing and fleeing.

Psychologists have spent decades trying to study these defensive responses in the lab (although these experiments

The UR and CR sometimes differ. CRs are often evolutionarily useful behaviours such as the "freezing" response.

used rodents rather than the potentially more dramatic combination of deer and wolves). For instance, many conditioning experiments have studied the ability of rats to associate a cue (e.g., a tone) with a painful electric shock to their feet. Some of the URs to shock include flinching, jumping, and pain. However, once the rat has learned to associate the tone with the shock, the rat's primary learned response to the tone is to "freeze" (the CR). The freezing CR has served many species well for millions of years, so it is the natural response to a fear-inducing signal in the laboratory. The lesson from this experimental situation is that UR and the CR are often quite different responses. The CR has been selected by evolution to be a helpful response.

This example isn't meant to confuse you! Rather, it is to show you that classical conditioning has a dramatic effect on an organism's survival. In other words, conditioning has an evolutionary *function*, and so the CR and the UR are not necessarily the same response.

CLASSICAL CONDITIONING AND THE BRAIN Classical conditioning can occur in extremely simple organisms such as *Aplysia*, a type of sea slug (Hawkins, 1984; Pinsker et al., 1970). Of course, the number of possible conditioned responses is more limited in the sea slug than in humans. But, the fact that both of these species can be classically conditioned suggests that at its heart, classical conditioning is a simple biological process. The connections between specific groups of neurons (or specific axon terminals and receptor sites on neurons) become strengthened during each instance of classical conditioning (Murphy & Glanzman, 1997).

SCS Studio/Corbis/Getty Images

Figure 6.3 Conditioning and Synapses

During conditioning, weak synapses fire at the same time as related strong synapses. The simultaneous activity strengthens the connections in the weaker synapse.

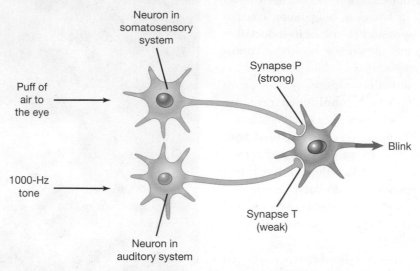

Source: Carlson, Neil R., *Psychology Of Behavior*, 11th ed., Copyright © 2013, pp. 29, 72. Reprinted and electronically reproduced by permission of Pearson Education, Inc., Upper Saddle River, New Jersey.

According to the Hebb Rule (named after Canadian neurologist Donald Hebb; see Module 7.1), when a weak connection between neurons is stimulated at the same time as a strong connection, the weak connection becomes strengthened. So, before conditioning, there may be a strong connection between perceiving a puff of air and a blinking response and a weak connection between a sound (e.g., a metronome) and the blinking response. But, if both networks are stimulated at the same time, the link between the sound and the blinking response would be strengthened. Over repeated conditioning trials, this connection would become strong enough that the sound itself would trigger an eyeblink (see Figure 6.3).

When reading these examples, it's quite easy to think of conditioning as something unrelated to your life. Not many of us undergo eyeblink conditioning. But these principles still apply to your everyday existence. For instance, most of you have received a needle at the doctor's office. In this situation, the needle caused a response of pain. The doctor's office itself did not harm you in any way. But, over time, you may start to feel scared whenever you enter the doctor's office because it has been repeatedly paired with pain. What do you think the US, UR, CS, and CR would be in this situation? In this case, the needle (US) causes pain (UR). The office is the neutral stimulus (NS). Over time, the sights and sounds of the doctor's office could be the CS, because it would trigger the CR (fear). Importantly, as you will read in the next section, the strength of these networks—and thus of the conditioning—will vary depending upon how often and how consistently the CS and the US appear together.

Module 6.1a Quiz:

Pavlov's Dogs: Classical Conditioning of Salivation

Know . . .

1. The learned response to the conditioned stimulus is known as the _____.
   A. unconditioned stimulus
   B. conditioned stimulus
   C. conditioned response
   D. unconditioned response

2. A once-neutral stimulus that elicits a conditioned response because it has a history of being paired with an unconditioned stimulus is known as a(n) _____.
   A. unconditioned stimulus
   B. conditioned stimulus

   C. conditioned response
   D. unconditioned response

Apply . . .

3. A dental drill can become an unpleasant stimulus, especially for people who may have experienced pain while one was used on their teeth. In this case, the pain elicited by the drill is a(n) _____.
   A. conditioned response
   B. unconditioned stimulus
   C. conditioned stimulus
   D. unconditioned response

Processes of Classical Conditioning

Although classically conditioned responses typically involve reflexive actions, there is still a great deal of flexibility in how long they will last and how specific they will be. Conditioned responses may be very strong and reliable, which is likely if the CS and the US have a long history of being paired together. Conditioned responding may diminish over time, or it may occur with new stimuli with which the response has never been paired. We now turn to some processes that account for the flexibility of classically conditioned responses.

ACQUISITION, EXTINCTION, AND SPONTANEOUS RECOVERY Learning involves a change in behaviour due to experience, which can include acquiring a new response. **Acquisition** *is the initial phase of learning in which a response is established*; thus, in classical conditioning, acquisition is the phase in which a neutral stimulus is repeatedly paired with the US. In Pavlov's experiment, the conditioned salivary response was *acquired* with numerous metronome–food pairings (see Figure 6.4). A critical part of acquisition is the predictability with which the CS and the US occur together. In Pavlov's experiment, conditioning either would not occur or would be very weak if food was delivered only sometimes (i.e., inconsistently) when the metronome sound occurred.

Of course, even if a conditioned response is fully acquired, there is no guarantee it will persist forever.

Extinction *is the loss or weakening of a conditioned response when a conditioned stimulus and unconditioned stimulus no longer occur together.* For the dogs in Pavlov's experiment, if the sound of the metronome clicking is presented repeatedly and no food follows, then salivation should occur less and less, until eventually it may not occur at all (Figure 6.4). This trend probably makes sense from a biological perspective: If the sound of the metronome is no longer a reliable predictor of food, then salivation becomes unnecessary. At the neural level, the rate of firing in brain areas related to the learned association decreases over the course of extinction (Robleto et al., 2004). However, even after extinction occurs, a previously established conditioned response can return.

A number of studies have shown that classically conditioned behaviours that had disappeared due to extinction could quickly reappear if the CS was paired with the US again. This tendency suggests that the networks of brain areas related to conditioning were preserved in some form (Schreurs, 1993; Schreurs et al., 1998). Additionally, some animals (and humans) show **spontaneous recovery**, *or the reoccurrence of a previously extinguished conditioned response, typically after some time has passed since extinction.* Pavlov and his assistants noticed that salivation would reappear when the dogs were later returned to the experimental testing room where acquisition and extinction trials had been conducted. The dogs would also salivate again in response to a metronome clicking, albeit

---

Figure 6.4 Acquisition, Extinction, and Spontaneous Recovery

Acquisition of a conditioned response occurs over repeated pairings of the CS and the US. If the US no longer occurs, conditioned responding diminishes—a process called *extinction*. Often, following a time interval in which the CS does not occur, conditioned responding rebounds when the CS is presented again—a phenomenon called *spontaneous recovery*.

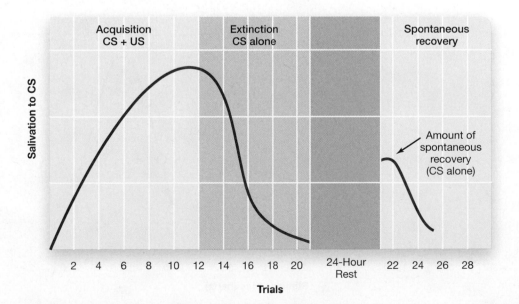

less so than at the end of acquisition (Figure 6.4). Why would salivation spontaneously return after the response had supposedly extinguished? One possibility is that extinction also involves learning something new (Bouton, 1994). In this case, Pavlov's dogs would be learning that the clicking of a metronome indicates that food will *not* appear. It is possible that spontaneous recovery is a case of the animal not being able to retrieve the memory of extinction and thus reverting back to the original memory, the classically conditioned response (Bouton, 2002; Brooks et al., 1999).

Extinction and spontaneous recovery are evidence that classically conditioned responses can change once they are acquired. Further evidence of flexibility of conditioned responding can be seen in some other processes of classical conditioning, including generalization and discrimination.

STIMULUS GENERALIZATION AND DISCRIMINATION Stimulus **generalization** *is a process in which a response that originally occurred for a specific stimulus also occurs for different, though similar, stimuli.* In Pavlov's experiment, dogs salivated not just to the original sound (CS), but also to very similar sounds (see Figure 6.5). At the cellular level, generalization may be explained, at least in part, by the Hebb rule discussed above. When we perceive a stimulus, it activates not only our brain's representation of that item, but also our representations

of related items. Some of these additional representations (e.g., a sound that has a slightly higher or lower pitch than the conditioned stimulus) may become activated at the same time as the synapses involved in conditioned responses. If this did occur, according to the Hebb rule, the additional synapse would become strengthened and would therefore be more likely to fire along with the other cells in the future.

Generalization allows for flexibility in learned behaviours, although it is certainly possible for behaviour to be *too* flexible. Salivating in response to *any* sound would be wasteful because not every sound correctly predicts food. Thus Pavlov's dogs also showed **discrimination**, *which occurs when an organism learns to respond to one original stimulus but not to new stimuli that may be similar to the original stimulus.* In salivary conditioning, the CS might be a 1200-hertz tone, which is the only sound that is paired with food. The experimenter might produce tones of 1100 or 1300 hertz as well, but not pair these with food. This point is critical: If stimuli that are similar to the CS are presented *without* a US, then it becomes *less* likely that these stimuli will lead to stimulus generalization. Instead, these other tones would have their own memory representation in the brain—in which they did *not* receive food. So, stimulus discrimination would occur if salivation was triggered by the target 1200-hertz tone, but was not triggered (or was triggered less) in response to the other tones (Figure 6.5).

Figure 6.5 Stimulus Generalization and Discrimination

A conditioned response may generalize to other similar stimuli. In this case, salivation occurs not just for the 1200-Hz tone used during conditioning, but for other tones as well. Discrimination learning has occurred when responding is elicited by the original training stimulus, but much less so, if at all, for other stimuli.

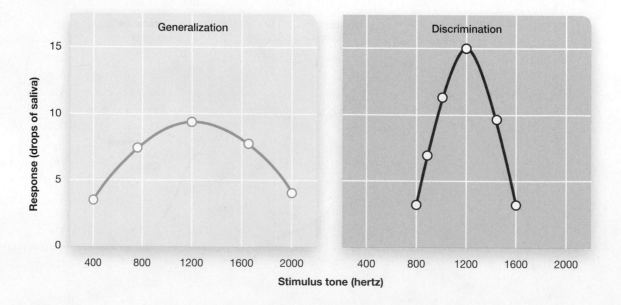

Module 6.1b Quiz:

Processes of Classical Conditioning

Know . . .

1. What is the reoccurrence of a previously extinguished conditioned response, typically after some time has passed since extinction?

A. Extinction

B. Spontaneous recovery

C. Acquisition

D. Discrimination

Understand . . .

2. In classical conditioning, the process during which a neutral stimulus becomes a conditioned stimulus is known as _____.

A. extinction

B. spontaneous recovery

C. acquisition

D. discrimination

Apply . . .

3. Your dog barks every time a stranger's car pulls into the driveway, but not when you come home. Reacting to your car differently is a sign of _____.

A. discrimination

B. generalization

C. spontaneous recovery

D. acquisition

Applications of Classical Conditioning

Now that you are familiar with the basic processes of classical conditioning, we can begin to explore its many applications. Classical conditioning is a common phenomenon that applies to many different situations, including emotional learning, aversions to certain foods, advertising, and responses to drugs.

CONDITIONED EMOTIONAL RESPONSES Psychologists dating back to John Watson in the 1920s recognized that our emotional responses could be influenced by classical conditioning (Paul & Blumenthal, 1989; Watson & Rayner, 1920). These **conditioned emotional responses** *consist of emotional and physiological responses that develop to a specific object or situation*. In one of the most diabolical studies in the history of psychology, Watson and Rayner conditioned an 11-month-old child known as Albert B. (also referred to as "Little Albert") to fear white rats. When they first presented Albert with a white rat, he showed no fear, and even reached out for the animal. Later, while Albert was again in the vicinity of the rat, they startled him by striking a steel bar with a hammer. Watson and Rayner reported that Albert quickly associated the rat with the startling sound; the child soon showed a conditioned emotional response to the rat. In this situation, the US would be the loud noise. The UR would be the feeling of fear elicited by the loud noise. With repeated pairings of the loud noise and the white rat, the white rat—which preceded the onset of the loud noise—would start to trigger fear. In this case, the white rat became the CS and the fear it elicited became the CR. Little Albert not only developed a fear of rats; the emotional conditioning generalized to other white furry objects including a rabbit and a Santa Claus mask.

It should be pointed out that ethical standards in modern-day psychological research would not allow this type of experiment to take place. To make matters worse, it appears that Watson and Rayner did not keep in touch with Little Albert to see if there were any lasting effects from the study. In fact, the fate of Little Albert has been shrouded in mystery for almost a century. One group of researchers examined hospital records and reported that Little Albert passed away as a result of a brain illness (i.e., for reasons unrelated to this study) at the age of 5 (Beck et al., 2009; Fridlund et al., 2012). However, researchers at Grant MacEwan University in Edmonton found evidence suggesting that Little Albert actually lived a long and relatively happy life, although he was not comfortable around furry animals such as dogs (Digdon et al., 2014). More detective work is necessary to address these competing claims. Ironically, in 1928, Watson published a book entitled *Psychological Care of Infant and Child*.

The Watson and Rayner procedure may seem artificial because it took place in a laboratory, but here is a more naturalistic example. Consider a boy who sees his neighbour's cat. Not having a cat of his own, the child is very eager to pet the animal—perhaps a little too eager, because the cat reacts defensively and scratches his hand. The cat may become a CS for the boy, which elicits a fear response. Further, if generalization occurs, the boy might become afraid of all cats. Conditioned emotional responses like these offer a possible explanation for many phobias, which are intense, irrational fears of specific objects or situations (discussed in detail in Module 15.2).

During the past two decades, researchers have made great strides in identifying the brain regions responsible for such conditioned emotional responses. When an organism learns a fear-related association such as a tone predicting the onset of a startling noise, activity occurs in

Watson and Rayner generalized Albert's fear of white rats to other furry, white objects. Shown here, Watson tests Albert's reaction to a Santa Claus mask.

Archives of the History of American Psychology, The Center for the History of Psychology—The University of Akron

the amygdala, a brain area related to fear (LeDoux, 1995; Maren, 2001). If an organism learns to fear a particular location, such as learning that a certain cage is associated with an electrical shock, then context-related activity in the hippocampus will interact with fear-related activity in the amygdala to produce *contextual fear conditioning* (Kim & Fanselow, 1992; Phillips & LeDoux, 1992). Importantly, the neural connections related to conditioned fear remain intact, even after extinction has occurred. Instead, other neurons suppress the activity of the brain areas related to the fear responses (Marek et al., 2013). If the CS is paired with the US again, this suppression will be removed and the fear-conditioned response will quickly reappear.

Neuroimaging has been used to study the brain's responses to fear conditioning in both clinical populations and in healthy control participants. For example, scientists have conducted some fascinating experiments on people diagnosed with psychopathy (the diagnosis of "psychopathy" is very similar to antisocial personality disorder; see Module 15.2). People with this disorder are notorious for disregarding the feelings of others. In one study, a sample of people diagnosed with psychopathy looked at brief presentations of human faces (neutral stimuli) followed by a painful stimulus (the US). The painful stimulus would obviously elicit a pain response (the UR). What *should* have happened is that over repeated pairings, participants would acquire a negative emotional reaction (the CR) to the faces (which are now the CS); but, this particular sample did not react this way. Instead, these individuals showed very little physiological arousal, their emotional brain centres remained quiet, and overall they did not

seem to mind looking at pictures of faces that had been paired with pain (see Figure 6.6; Birbaumer et al., 2005). In contrast, people who showed no signs of psychopathy did not enjoy this experience. In fact, following several pairings between CS and US, the control group showed increased physiological arousal and activity of the emotion centres of the brain, and understandably reported disliking the experience of the experiment.

EVOLUTIONARY ROLE FOR FEAR CONDITIONING A healthy fear response is important for survival, but not all situations or objects are equally dangerous. Snakes and heights probably elicit more fear and caution than butterflies or flowers. In fact, fearing snakes is very common, which makes it tempting to conclude that we have an *instinct* to fear them. In reality, young primates (both human children and young monkeys, for example) tend to be quite curious about, or at least indifferent to, snakes, so this fear is most likely the product of learning rather than instinct.

Psychologists have conducted some ingenious experiments to address how learning is involved in snake fear. For instance, photographs of snakes (the CS) were paired with a mild electric shock (the US). One unconditioned response that a shock elicits is increased palm sweat— known as the skin conductance response. This reaction, part of the fight-or-flight response generated by the autonomic nervous system (Module 3.3), occurs when our bodies are aroused by a threatening or uncomfortable stimulus. Following several pairings between snake photos and shock in an experimental setting, the snake photos alone (the CS) elicited a strong increase in skin

Figure 6.6 Fear Conditioning and the Brain

During fear conditioning, a neutral stimulus (NS) such as a tone or a picture of a human face is briefly presented, followed by an unconditioned stimulus (US), such as a mild electric shock. The result is a conditioned fear response to the CS. A procedure like this has been used to compare fear responses in people diagnosed with psychopathy with control participants. The brain images show that those with psychopathy (right image) showed very little response in their emotional brain circuitry when presented with the CS. In contrast, control participants showed strong activation in their emotional brain centres (left image) (Birbaumer et al., 2005).

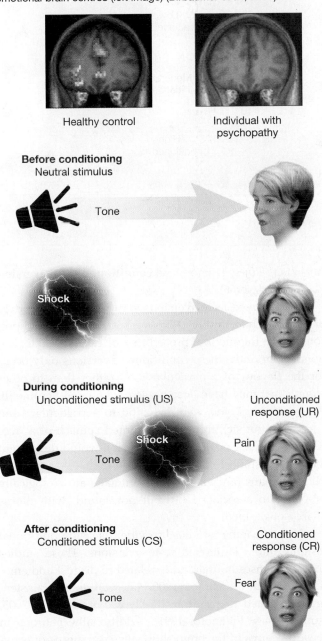

Source: Courtesy of Dr. Herta Flor

conductance response (the CR). For comparison, participants were also shown nonthreatening pictures of flowers, paired with the shock. Much less intense conditioned responding developed in response to pictures of flowers,

even though the pictures had been paired with the shock just as many times as the snake pictures had been paired with the shock (Figure 6.7; Öhman & Mineka, 2001). Thus, it appears we are predisposed to acquire a fear of snakes, but not flowers.

This finding may not be too surprising, but what about other potentially dangerous objects such as guns? In modern times, guns are far more often associated with death or injury than snakes, and certainly flowers. When the researchers paired pictures of guns (the CS) with the shock (US), they found that conditioned arousal to guns among participants was less than that to snake photos, and comparable to that of harmless flowers. In addition, the conditioned arousal to snake photos proved longer lasting and slower to extinguish than the conditioned responding to pictures of guns or flowers (Öhman & Mineka, 2001). However, before completely accepting this finding, it is important to point out that the participants in this study were from Sweden, a country that has relatively little gun violence. It is unclear whether similar results would be found in participants who lived in a location where gun violence was more prevalent.

This caveat aside, given that guns and snakes both have the potential to be dangerous, why is it so much easier to learn a fear of snakes than a fear of guns? One possibility is that over time, humans have evolved a strong predisposition to fear an animal that has a long history of causing severe injury or death (Cook et al., 1986; Öhman & Mineka, 2001). The survival advantage has gone to those who quickly learned to avoid animals such as snakes. The same is not true for flowers (which do not attack humans) or guns (which are relatively new in our species' history). This evolutionary explanation is known as **preparedness**, *the biological predisposition to rapidly learn a response to a particular class of stimuli* (Seligman, 1971).

CONDITIONED TASTE AVERSIONS Another example of an evolutionarily useful conditioned fear response comes from food aversions. Chances are there is a food that you cannot stand to even look at because it once made you ill. This new aversion isn't due to chance; rather, your brain and body have linked the taste, sight, and smell of that food to the feeling of nausea. In this situation, the taste (and often the sight and smell) of the food or fluid serves as the CS. The US is whatever substance in the food or environment happened to make you sick (e.g., some sort of bacteria); this, in turn, leads to the actual sickness (the UR). Aversion is not simply a case of "feeling gross." Instead, it involves both a feeling (and in some species, a facial expression) of disgust *and* a withdrawal or avoidance response. When the CS and US are linked, the taste of the food or fluid soon produces aversion responses (the CR), even in the absence of physical illness (see Figure 6.8). This *acquired dislike or disgust for a food or drink because it was*

Figure 6.7 Biologically Prepared Fear

Physiological measures of fear are highest in response to photos of snakes after the photos are paired with an electric shock—even higher than the responses to photos of guns. Flowers—something that humans generally do not need to fear in nature—are least effective when it comes to conditioning fear responses.

Experimental condition	Conditioned stimulus	Unconditioned stimulus (shock)	Result
Nonthreatening	🌸 →	⚡	Low conditioned fear
Acquired threat	🔫 →	⚡	Moderate conditioned fear
Biological threat	🐍 →	⚡	High conditioned fear

Figure 6.8 Conditioned Taste Aversions

Classical conditioning can account for the development of taste aversions. Falling ill after eating a particular food can result in conditioned feelings of disgust as well as withdrawal responses when you are later re-exposed to the taste, smell, or texture of the food. Conditioned taste aversions are another example of conditioning occurring even though the UR and the CR are not identical responses.

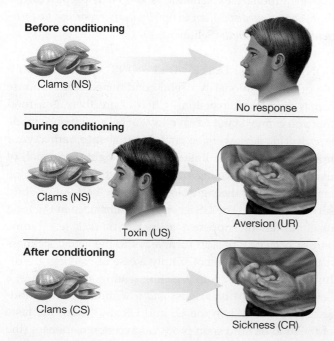

Before conditioning

Clams (NS) → No response

During conditioning

Clams (NS)
Toxin (US) → Aversion (UR)

After conditioning

Clams (CS) → Sickness (CR)

paired with illness is known as **conditioned taste aversion** (Garcia et al., 1966).

Conditioned taste aversions may develop in a variety of ways, such as through illness associated with food poisoning, the flu, medical procedures, or excessive intoxication. Importantly, these conditioned aversions only occur for the flavour of a particular food rather than to other stimuli that may have been present when you became ill. For example, if you were listening to a particular song while you got sick from eating tainted spinach or a two-week-old tuna sandwich, your aversion would develop to the taste of spinach, but not to the song that was playing. Thus, humans (and many other animals) are biologically prepared to associate food, but not sound, with illness (Garcia et al., 1966).

Neuroimaging studies provide us with additional insights into conditioned taste aversions. These studies show responses in brain areas related to disgust and emotional arousal (Yamamoto, 2007) as well as in brainstem regions related to vomiting (Reilly & Bornovalova, 2005; Yamamoto & Fujimoto, 1991). Additionally, neurons in reward centres in the brain show altered patterns of activity to the food associated with illness (Yamamoto et al., 1989). These different brain responses suggest that illness triggers a strong emotional response that causes the reward centres to update their representation of the illness-causing food, thus making that food less rewarding.

Although these studies may explain how some aspects of conditioned taste aversions are maintained, there are still some riddles associated with this phenomenon. For instance, the onset of symptoms from food poisoning may not occur until several hours have passed after the tainted food or beverage was consumed. As a consequence, the interval between tasting the food (CS) and feeling sick (UR) may be a matter of hours, whereas most conditioning happens only if the CS, US, and the UR occur very closely to each other in time. Another peculiarity is that taste aversions are learned very quickly—a single CS–US pairing leading to illness is typically sufficient. These special characteristics of taste aversions are extremely important for survival. The flexibility offered by a long window of time separating food (CS) and the illness (UR), as well as the requirement for only a single exposure, raises the chances of acquiring an important aversion to the offending substance.

One potential explanation for these characteristics involves the food stimuli themselves. Usually, a conditioned taste aversion develops to something we have ingested that has an unfamiliar flavour. Such flavours stick out when they are experienced for the first time and are therefore much easier to remember, even after considerable time has passed. In contrast, if you have eaten the same ham and Swiss cheese sandwich at lunch for years, and you become ill one afternoon after eating it, you will be less prone to develop a conditioned taste aversion. This scenario can be explained by **latent inhibition**, *which occurs when frequent experience with a stimulus before it is paired with a US makes it less likely that conditioning will occur after a single episode of illness* (Lubow & Moore, 1959).

Conditioned taste aversions are a naturally occurring experience. However, conditioned emotional responses are also being created by advertisers to influence our responses. As you will read in the next section, food is not the only stimulus that can make you feel sick.

Working the Scientific Literacy Model

Conditioning and Negative Political Advertising

Some politicians have charisma; you want to like them and believe what they say. Barack Obama (2009–2017) was treated like a rock star when he travelled internationally. Justin Trudeau (2016–) also seems rather well liked. But not everyone has natural charisma. In these cases, politicians need to use advertising and carefully constructed "photo ops" to create emotional responses that can influence voting behaviours. In an ideal world, these advertisements would focus on issues and would highlight the candidates' positive qualities. Unfortunately, the last few decades have seen a dramatic upsurge in a different form of advertising: negative attack ads. In a three-month period during the 2008 U.S. presidential election, Republican John McCain

and Democrat Barack Obama combined for 150,000 negative ads in "battleground states" (Nielsen Research, 2008). This type of advertisement relies on the principles of classical conditioning and, in the process, treats you, the voter, like one of Pavlov's dogs.

What do we know about classical conditioning in negative political advertising?

Negative political advertisements routinely include unflattering images. In the next federal or provincial election, pay attention to the commercials that are sponsored by each party and you will notice a few tricks. First, many images of opponents will be black and white and of poor quality (grainy). This trick is designed to make viewers feel mildly frustrated when viewing the unclear photographs. Second, the images of the attacked politicians will include them expressing a negative emotion. In some, they will be yelling (angry faces trigger a physiological response in people). Others may show facial expressions that appear smug or that suggest the candidate feels contempt toward the person they're looking at (which, in this case, would appear to be *you*). The assumption underlying these attack ads is that if you pair a party leader with imagery that generates unpleasant emotions, then viewers will associate that leader with negative feelings and be less likely to vote for that party.

In this case, the CS would be the attacked politician. The US would be the negative imagery. The UR would be the negative emotional response to the imagery (or unflattering photograph). Eventually, the individuals who constructed the ad hope that simply seeing the attacked person will produce a negative emotional response (CR) along with the thought, "I will not vote for him or her." The question is, "Does this work?"

How can science help explain the role of classical conditioning in negative political advertising?

An attempt to use negative emotions to alter people's opinions of political candidates is similar to a psychology research technique known as *evaluative conditioning*. In an evaluative conditioning study, experimenters pair a stimulus (e.g., a shape) with either positive or negative stimuli (e.g., an angry face; Murphy & Zajonc, 1993). The repeated association of a stimulus with an emotion leads participants to develop a positive or negative feeling toward that stimulus (depending on the emotional pairing; see Figure 6.9). This is precisely what political strategists are attempting to do when they show unpleasant pictures of an opponent and pair it with angry narrators and emotional labels.

In the laboratory, evaluative conditioning works. This phenomenon has been found with visual, auditory,

Figure 6.9 Evaluative Conditioning

In evaluative conditioning, researchers pair an emotional image (e.g., an emotional face) with a previously neutral target image such as a Japanese symbol. The association that (sometimes) forms between the two images can influence participants' later judgments of the target image, leading them to like (if paired with a happy face) or dislike (if paired with angry face) them more than if no conditioning had occurred. Political advertising sometimes uses similar, if less subtle, techniques.

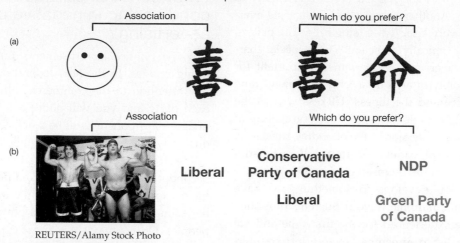

REUTERS/Alamy Stock Photo

olfactory (smell), taste, and tactile (touch) stimuli. It has been used to alter feelings toward objects ranging from snack foods (Lebens et al., 2011), to consumer brands (Walther & Grigoriadis, 2004), to novel shapes (Olson & Fazio, 2001). A number of studies have specifically attempted to use conditioning to create negative attitudes toward products or behaviours (Moore et al., 1982; Zanna et al., 1970), a goal similar to the attack ads you see each election. For instance, Stuart and colleagues (1990) found that associating a new brand of toothpaste with negative pictures decreased evaluations of that product. In all of these cases, the advertisers and sponsoring politicians are assuming that the viewer will associate the negative emotions (UR) with the ad's target (CS) and that this will make the viewer more likely to select an alternative (i.e., the candidate sponsoring the attack ad). In the case of politics, this assumption makes sense—attack ads tend to be effective and are recalled better than other types of political information (Fernandes, 2013).

Can we critically evaluate this information?

A major question that arises from this research is whether producing a negative opinion of one option (be it a brand of toothpaste or a political candidate) automatically means that you also produce a positive opinion of the other option. Oftentimes, we can't tell if the results are due to liking one option or disliking the other option. This question isn't really an issue for U.S.-based studies, as there are only two parties in that country (for now). However, with five political parties running in the next federal election in

Canada, there is a danger that attack ads might produce negative opinions of the target, but still not boost opinions of the party running the ads.

Recent research has examined who is actually influenced by these attack ads. In one U.S.-based study (none have been conducted in Canada), researchers found that negative ads had no effect on donations to political parties. They did, however, increase voter turnout among *partisans,* people who already agreed with the views expressed in the ads (Barton et al., 2016). In other words, although the primary goal of attack ads might be to make undecided voters associate negative emotions with the target of the ads, the actual effect of the ads is to motivate people who already had negative emotions to *act* on those emotions (i.e., to vote).

Of course, politicians also need to be careful not to overstep certain boundaries and inadvertently create sympathy for the target of the negative ads. In October 1993, the Progressive Conservative Party broadcast two television commercials that highlighted the partial facial paralysis of Liberal leader (and future Prime Minister) Jean Chrétien. One ad asked, "Is this a Prime Minister?" Another had a female narrator stating, "I personally would be embarrassed if he were to become the Prime Minister of Canada." The goal of the commercials was not to attack Chrétien's political credentials or experience, which far surpassed those of the other, less experienced, party leaders. Instead, the ads were designed to link the negative emotion associated with physical deformities, and any stigma associated with them, to the Liberal party so that people would feel uneasy about voting Liberal. It didn't work: The public outcry in response to the

Negative ads can backfire if the public views them as overly personal or insensitive. Mocking Jean Chrétien's facial paralysis led to a disastrous outcome for the Progressive Conservative party in the 1993 election.

commercials caused the Conservatives to withdraw the ads after only one day. Indeed, people who saw the ads were inclined to sympathize with Chrétien and feel anger toward Conservative leader Kim Campbell (Haddock & Zanna, 1997). The Liberals won the election handily, with the Conservatives being reduced to two seats in the House of Commons.

Why is this relevant?

Dozens of studies indicate that people are prone to a *third-person effect* whereby they assume that other people are more affected by advertising and mass media messages than they themselves are (Cheng & Riffe, 2008; Perloff, 2002). Thus, there appears to be a disconnect between the power of negative advertising and people's awareness of its effects. It is important to realize that conditioning often occurs without our conscious awareness. Our brains are designed to make associations; it's how we learn. So, by becoming aware of how marketing companies and politicians are using classical conditioning to influence how you vote, you can try to reduce the effect of their manipulation. That way, when you cast your vote, it will hopefully be because of issues you care about and not because of conditioned emotional responses.

Incidentally, the type of evaluative conditioning that occurs with negative political advertising may also work with positive information if it is powerful enough. At the beginning of the 2015 federal election campaign, the Liberal Party was concerned that the much wealthier Conservatives would buy up all of the advertising time during sporting events. To prevent this, they booked some commercial time with sports networks just in case the Blue Jays made the playoffs (Thibedeau, 2015). They did— and although they ended up losing in the second round, their dramatic first-round victory over the Texas Rangers

brought the nation together. Millions of excited Jays fans (jumping up and down after José Bautista's bat flip) got to see frequent commercials featuring Justin Trudeau.

DRUG TOLERANCE AND CONDITIONING In addition to influencing overt behaviours such as salivating and emotional behaviours such as phobias, classical conditioning can influence how the body regulates its own responses to different stimuli. For example, classical conditioning can help explain some drug-related phenomena, such as cravings and tolerance. Cues that accompany drug use can become conditioned stimuli that elicit cravings (Sinha, 2009). For example, a cigarette lighter, the smell of tobacco smoke, or the presence of another smoker can elicit cravings in people who smoke.

Conditioning can also influence drug tolerance, or a decreased reaction that occurs with repeated use of the drug (Siegel et al., 2000). When a person takes a drug, his or her body attempts to metabolize that substance. Over time, the setting and paraphernalia associated with the drug-taking begin to serve as cues (a CS) that a drug (US) will soon be processed by the body (UR). As a result of this association, the physiological processes involved with metabolizing the drug will begin with the appearance of the CS rather than when the drug is actually consumed. In other words, because of conditioning, the body is already braced for the drug before the drug has been snorted, smoked, or injected. This response means that, over time, more of the drug will be needed to override these preparatory responses so that the desired effect can be obtained; this change is referred to as *conditioned drug tolerance.*

This phenomenon can have fatal consequences for drug abusers. Shepard Siegel (1984), a psychologist at McMaster University, conducted interviews with patients who were hospitalized for overdosing on heroin. Over the course of his interviews, a pattern among the patients emerged. Several individuals reported that they were in situations unlike those that typically preceded their heroin injections—for example, in a different environment or even using an injection site (i.e., part of the body) that differed from the usual ritual. As a result of these differences, there were fewer CSs present to trigger the CR, the body's metabolizing activity that braced (or prepared) the drug taker's body for the arrival of the drug. Without this conditioned preparatory response, delivery of even a *normal* dose of the drug can be lethal. This finding has been confirmed in animal studies: Siegel and his associates (1982) found that conditioned drug tolerance and overdosing can also occur with rats. When rats received heroin in an environment different from where they experienced the drug previously, mortality rates were double that of control rats that received the same dose of heroin in their normal surroundings (64% versus 32%).

The examples discussed in this module are only a few of the applications of classical conditioning (Domjan et al., 2004). But, the fact that behaviours ranging from phobias, to voting preferences, to drug tolerance can be explained by classical conditioning shows us that Pavlov's observations of his salivating dogs were really just a drop in the bucket.

Module 6.1c Quiz:
Applications of Classical Conditioning

Know . . .

1. Conditioning a response can take longer if the subject experiences the conditioned stimulus repeatedly before it is actually paired with a US. This phenomenon is known as _____.
   A. preparedness
   B. extinction
   C. latent inhibition
   D. acquisition

2. When a heroin user develops a routine, the needle can become the _____, whereas the body's preparation for the drug in response to the presence of the needle is the _____.
   A. CS; CR
   B. US; UR
   C. US; CR
   D. CS; US

Understand . . .

3. Why are humans biologically *prepared* to fear snakes and not guns?
   A. Guns kill fewer people than do snakes.
   B. Guns are a more recent addition to our evolutionary history.
   C. Snakes are more predictable than guns.
   D. Guns are not a natural phenomenon, whereas snakes do occur in nature.

Apply . . .

4. A television advertisement for beer shows young people at the beach drinking and having fun. Based on classical conditioning principles, the advertisers are hoping you will buy their beer because the commercial elicits
   A. a conditioned emotional response of pleasure.
   B. a conditioned emotional response of fear.
   C. humans' natural preparedness toward alcohol consumption.
   D. a taste aversion to other companies' beers.

Module 6.1 Summary

6.1a   Know . . . the key terminology involved in classical conditioning.

acquisition
classical conditioning (Pavlovian conditioning)
conditioned emotional response
conditioned response (CR)
conditioned stimulus (CS)
conditioned taste aversion
discrimination
extinction
generalization
latent inhibition
learning
preparedness
spontaneous recovery
unconditioned response (UR)
unconditioned stimulus (US)

6.1b   Understand . . . how responses learned through classical conditioning can be acquired and lost.

Acquisition of a conditioned response occurs with repeated pairings of the CS and the US. Once a response is acquired, it can be extinguished if the CS and the US no longer occur together. During extinction, the CR diminishes, although it may reappear under some circumstances. For example, if enough time passes following extinction, the CR may spontaneously recover when the organism encounters the CS again.

6.1c   Understand . . . the role of biological and evolutionary factors in classical conditioning.

Not all stimuli have the same potential to become a strong CS. Responses to biologically relevant stimuli, such as snakes, are more easily conditioned than are responses to stimuli such as flowers or guns, for example. Similarly, avoidance of potentially harmful foods is critical to survival, so organisms can develop a conditioned taste aversion quickly (in a single trial) and even when ingestion and illness are separated by a relatively long time interval.

6.1d   Apply . . . the concepts and terms of classical conditioning to new examples.

Apply Activity

Read the three scenarios that follow and identify the conditioned stimulus (CS), the unconditioned stimulus (US), the conditioned response (CR), and the unconditioned response (UR) in each case. (*Hint:* When you apply the terms CS, US, CR, and UR, a good strategy is to identify whether something is a stimulus (something that elicits) or a response (a behaviour). Next, identify whether the stimulus automatically elicits a response (the US) or does so only after being paired with a US (a CS). Finally, identify whether the response occurs in response to the US alone (the UR) or the CS alone (the CR).)

1. Cameron and Tia went to the prom together. During their last slow dance, the DJ played the theme song for the event. During the song, the couple kissed. Now, several years later, whenever Cameron and Tia hear the song, they feel a rush of excitement.

2. Harry has visited his eye doctor several times due to problems with his vision. One test involves blowing a puff of air into his eye. After repeated visits to the eye doctor, Harry starts blinking as soon as the doctor begins to prepare the instrument.

3. Sarah went to a new restaurant and experienced the most delicious meal she had ever tasted. The restaurant began advertising on the radio, and now every time an ad comes on, Sarah finds herself craving the meal she enjoyed so much.

6.1e   Analyze . . . the use of negative political advertising to condition emotional responses to candidates.

Negative political advertising often uses a form of conditioning known as evaluative conditioning. Negative images, sounds, and/or statements are paired with images of the targeted candidate. The goal is to have viewers link negative emotions with the target. Research has found that this technique can be successful. But, if the images used are deemed cruel or inappropriate, it is possible that viewers will feel negative emotions toward the sponsor of the ad instead.

Module 6.2 Operant Conditioning: Learning through Consequences

Mike Mergen/Bloomberg via Getty Images

 ## Learning Objectives

6.2a Know . . . the key terminology associated with operant conditioning.

6.2b Understand . . . the role that consequences play in increasing or decreasing behaviour.

6.2c Understand . . . how schedules of reinforcement affect behaviour.

6.2d Apply . . . your knowledge of operant conditioning to examples.

6.2e Analyze . . . the effectiveness of punishment on changing behaviour.

Gambling is a multibillion-dollar industry in Canada. According to Statistics Canada, the net revenue from lotteries, video-lottery terminals (VLTs), and casinos was $13.74 billion in 2011. That's an average of $515 per person. Given these huge sums, it is clear that some individuals are spending more than they should on this habit. Psychologists and government officials have invested a considerable amount of time into the development of prevention and treatment programs for gambling addictions. Although these programs have led to addiction rates levelling off in recent years, compulsive gambling is still a problem in Canada. So, what compels people to keep pulling the lever on a slot machine or pressing buttons on a VLT screen when logic would tell them to stop and go home?

Although the answer to this question is complicated (Hodgins et al., 2011), it is clear that reinforcement plays

a role in these behaviours. As you will read in this module, rewarding a behaviour—which happens when someone wins money after pressing the button on a VLT—makes that behaviour more likely to occur again in the future. The effect is larger when the reward doesn't happen every time and isn't predictable—qualities that perfectly describe gambling. The machines aren't the only ones having their buttons pushed.

Focus Questions

1. How do the consequences of our actions—such as winning or losing a bet—affect subsequent behaviour?

2. Many behaviours, including gambling, are reinforced only part of the time. How do the odds of being reinforced affect how often a behaviour occurs?

Table 6.1 Major Differences between Classical and Operant Conditioning

	Classical Conditioning	Operant Conditioning
Target response is . . .	Automatic	Voluntary
Reinforcement is . . .	Present regardless of whether a response occurs	A consequence of the behaviour
Behaviour mostly depends on . . .	Reflexive and physiological responses	Skeletal muscles

›› Very few of our behaviours are random. Instead, people tend to repeat actions that previously led to positive or rewarding outcomes. If you go to a new restaurant and like it, you will eat there again. Conversely, if a behaviour previously led to a negative outcome, people are less likely to perform that action again. If you go to a new restaurant and don't enjoy the meal, then you will likely not eat there again. These types of stimulus-response relationships are known as **operant conditioning**, *a type of learning in which behaviour is influenced by consequences*. The term *operant* is used because the individual *operates* on the environment before consequences can occur. In contrast to classical conditioning, which typically affects *reflexive* responses, operant conditioning involves *voluntary* actions such as speaking or listening, starting and stopping an activity, and moving toward or away from something. Whether and when we engage in these types of behaviours depend on how our unique collection of previous experiences has influenced what we do and do not find rewarding.

Initially, the difference between classical and operant conditioning may seem unclear. One useful way of telling the difference is that in classical conditioning a response is *not* required for a reward (or unconditioned stimulus) to be presented; to return to Pavlov's dogs, meat powder was presented regardless of whether salivation occurred. In classical conditioning, learning has taken place if a conditioned response develops following pairings of the conditioned stimulus and the unconditioned stimulus. In other words, the dogs learned the association between the sound of a metronome and food (as shown by their salivation), but they didn't have to actually *do* anything. In operant conditioning, a response and a consequence are required for learning to take place. Without a response of some kind, there can be no consequence. See Table 6.1 for a summary of differences between operant and classical conditioning.

Basic Principles of Operant Conditioning

The concept of *contingency* is important to understanding operant conditioning; it simply means that a consequence depends upon an action. Earning good grades is generally contingent upon studying effectively. Excelling at athletics is contingent upon training and practice. The consequences of a particular behaviour can be either reinforcing or punishing (see Figure 6.10).

REINFORCEMENT AND PUNISHMENT Reinforcement *is a process in which an event or reward that follows a response increases the likelihood of that response occurring again.* We can

Figure 6.10 Reinforcement and Punishment

The key distinction between reinforcement and punishment is that reinforcers, no matter what they are, increase behaviour. Punishment involves a decrease in behaviour, regardless of what the specific punisher may be. Thus both reinforcement and punishment are defined based on their effects on behaviour.

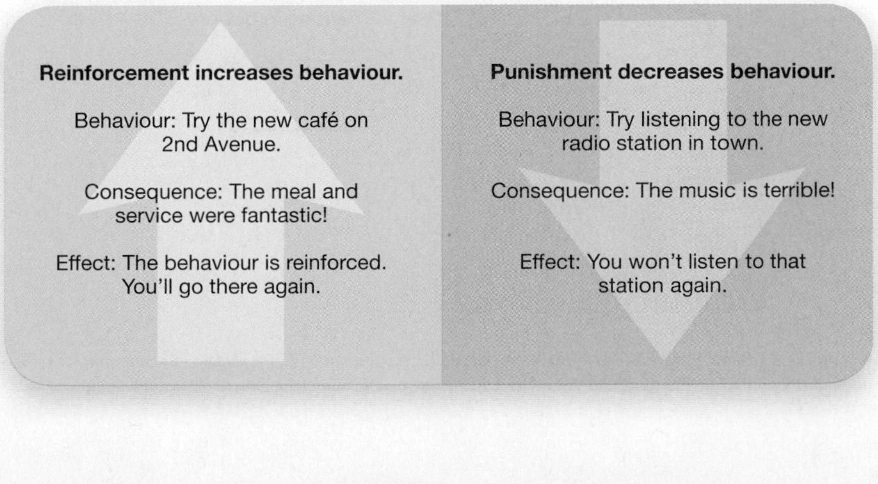

Reinforcement increases behaviour.

Behaviour: Try the new café on 2nd Avenue.

Consequence: The meal and service were fantastic!

Effect: The behaviour is reinforced. You'll go there again.

Punishment decreases behaviour.

Behaviour: Try listening to the new radio station in town.

Consequence: The music is terrible!

Effect: You won't listen to that station again.

Figure 6.11 Thorndike's Puzzle Box and the Law of Effect

(a) Thorndike conducted experiments in which cats learned an operant response that was reinforced with escape from the box and access to a food reward. (b) Over repeated trials, the cats took progressively less time to escape, as shown in this learning curve.

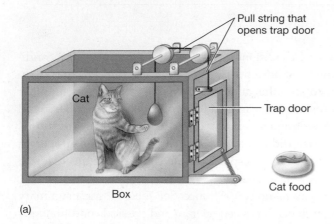

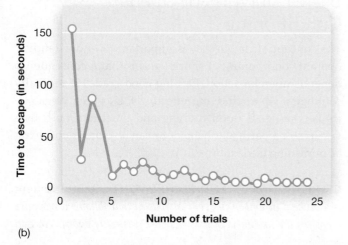

(b)

trace the scientific study of reinforcement's effects on behaviour back to Edward Thorndike, who conducted experiments in which he measured the time it took cats to learn how to escape from puzzle boxes (see Figure 6.11). Thorndike (1905) observed that over repeated trials, cats were able to escape more rapidly because they learned which responses worked (such as pressing a pedal on the floor of the box). From his experiments, Thorndike proposed the **law of effect**—*the idea that responses followed by satisfaction will occur again in the same situation whereas those that are not followed by satisfaction become less likely*. In this definition, "satisfaction" implies either that the animal's desired goal was achieved (e.g., escaping the puzzle box) or it received some form of reward for the behaviour (e.g., food).

Within a few decades of the publication of Thorndike's work, the famous behaviourist B. F. Skinner began conducting his own studies on the systematic relationship between reinforcement and behaviour. Although operant conditioning can explain many human behaviours, most of its basic principles stem from laboratory studies conducted on nonhuman species such as pigeons or rats, which were placed in an apparatus such as the one pictured in Figure 6.12. These *operant chambers*, sometimes referred to as *Skinner boxes*, include a lever or key that the subject can manipulate. Pushing the lever may result in the delivery of a reinforcer such as food. In operant conditioning terms, a **reinforcer** *is a stimulus that is contingent upon a response and that increases the probability of that response occurring again*. (So, a reinforcer would be a stimulus like food, whereas reinforcement would be the changes in the frequency of a behaviour like lever-pressing that occur *as a result of* the food reward.) Researchers use machinery such as operant chambers to help them control and quantify learning. Specifically, researchers record an animal's rate

Figure 6.12 An Operant Chamber

The operant chamber is a standard laboratory apparatus for studying operant conditioning. The rat can press the lever to receive a reinforcer such as food or water. The lights can be used to indicate when lever pressing will be rewarded. The recording device measures cumulative responses (lever presses) over time.

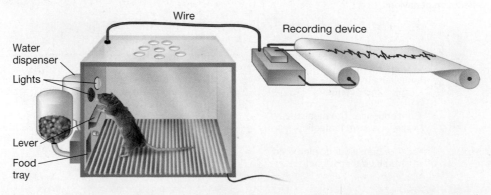

of responding over time (a measure of learning), and typically set a criterion for the number of responses that must be made before a reinforcer becomes available. As you will read later in this module, animals and humans are quite sensitive to how many responses they must make, or how long they must wait, in order to receive a reward.

The discussion thus far has focused on how reinforcement can lead to increased responding; but, decreased responding is also a possible outcome of an encounter with a stimulus. **Punishment** *is a process that decreases the future probability of a response.* Thus, a **punisher** *is a stimulus that is contingent upon a response, and that results in a decrease in behaviour.* Like reinforcers, punishers are defined not based on the stimuli themselves, but rather on their effects on behaviour. In all cases, a punisher—be it yelling, losing money, or going to jail—will make it less likely that a particular response will occur again.

POSITIVE AND NEGATIVE REINFORCEMENT AND PUNISHMENT Thus far, we have differentiated between reinforcement (when a response increases the likelihood that a behaviour will occur again) and punishment (when a response decreases the likelihood that a behaviour will occur again). In both of these cases, it is natural to think of the responses as something that is added to the situation. For instance, a behaviour could be reinforced by giving the animal food. Or, it could be punished by shocking the animal. But, both reinforcement and punishment can be accomplished by *removing* a stimulus as well. In the descriptions that follow, try to remember the following four terms as they are used in operant conditioning:

- Reinforcement: this *increases* the chances of a behaviour occurring again
- Punishment: this *decreases* the chances of a behaviour occurring again
- Positive: this means that a stimulus is *added* to a situation; positive can refer to reinforcement or punishment
- Negative: this means that a stimulus is *removed* from a situation; negative can refer to reinforcement or punishment

These terms can be combined to produce four different subtypes of operant conditioning. For instance, a response can be strengthened because it brings a reward. This form of reinforcement, **positive reinforcement**, *is the strengthening of behaviour after potential reinforcers such as praise, money, or nourishment follow that behaviour* (see Table 6.2). For example, if you laugh at your professor's jokes, the praise will serve as a reward; this will increase the likelihood that your professor will tell more jokes. (Remember: the "positive" in positive reinforcement indicates the *addition* of a reward.) Positive reinforcement can be a highly effective method of rewarding desired behaviours among humans and other species.

Behaviour can also be reinforced by the removal of something that is unpleasant. This form of reinforcement, **negative reinforcement**, *involves the strengthening of a behaviour because it removes or diminishes a stimulus* (Table 6.2). For instance, taking aspirin is negatively reinforced because doing so removes a painful headache. Similarly, studying in order to prevent nagging from parents is also a form of reinforcement as the behaviour, studying, will increase.

Negative reinforcement is a concept that students frequently find confusing because it seems unusual that something aversive could be involved in the context of reinforcement. Recall that reinforcement (whether positive or negative) always involves an increase in the strength or frequency of responding. Also remember that the term "positive" in this context simply means that a stimulus is introduced or increased, whereas the term "negative" means that a stimulus has been reduced or avoided.

But, not all types of negative reinforcement are the same; in fact, negative reinforcement can be further classified into two subcategories. **Avoidance learning** *is a specific type of negative reinforcement that removes the possibility that a stimulus will occur.* Examples of avoidance learning include leaving a sporting event early to avoid crowds and traffic congestion, and paying bills on time to avoid late fees. In these cases, negative situations are avoided. **Escape learning**, on the other hand, *occurs if a response removes a stimulus that is already present.* Covering your ears upon hearing overwhelmingly loud music is one example. You cannot avoid the music, because it is already present, so you

Table 6.2 Distinguishing Types of Reinforcement and Punishment

	Consequence	Effect on Behaviour	Example
Positive reinforcement	Stimulus is added or increased.	Increases the response	A child gets an allowance for making her bed, so she is likely to do it again in the future.
Negative reinforcement	Stimulus is removed or decreased.	Increases the response	The rain no longer falls on you after opening your umbrella, so you are likely to do it again in the future.
Positive punishment	Stimulus is added or increased.	Decreases the response	A pet owner scolds his dog for jumping up on a house guest, and now the dog is less likely to do it again.
Negative punishment	Stimulus is removed or decreased.	Decreases the response	A parent takes away TV privileges to stop the children from fighting.

perform a specific behaviour (covering your ears) to escape the aversive stimulus instead. The responses of paying bills on time to avoid late fees and covering your ears to escape loud music both increase in frequency because they have effectively prevented or removed the aversive stimuli.

In the laboratory, operant chambers such as the one pictured in Figure 6.12 often come equipped with a grid metal floor that can be used to deliver a mild electric shock; responses that remove (escape learning) or prevent (avoidance learning) the shock are negatively reinforced. This highly controlled environment allows researchers to carefully monitor all aspects of an animal's environment while investigating the different contingencies that will cause a behaviour to increase or decrease in frequency.

As with reinforcement, various types of punishment are possible. **Positive punishment** *is a process in which a behaviour decreases in frequency because it was followed by a particular, usually unpleasant, stimulus* (Table 6.2). For example, some cat owners use a spray bottle to squirt water when the cat hops on the kitchen counter or scratches the furniture. Remember that the term "positive" simply means that a stimulus is added to the situation (i.e., no one is claiming that spraying a cat with water is an emotionally positive experience). In these cases, the stimuli are punishers because they decrease the frequency of a behaviour.

Finally, **negative punishment** *occurs when a behaviour decreases because it removes or diminishes a particular stimulus* (Table 6.2). Withholding someone's privileges as a result of an undesirable behaviour is an example of negative punishment. A parent who "grounds" a child does so because this action removes something of value to the child. If effective, the outcome of the grounding will be to decrease the behaviour that got the child into trouble.

SHAPING Although these different forms of reinforcement and punishment make sense in theory, researchers (and parents) have an additional challenge: How do you get animals (or children) to perform the behaviour that you want to reinforce? Rats placed in operant chambers do not automatically go straight for the lever and begin pressing it to obtain food rewards. Instead, they must first learn that lever pressing accomplishes something. Getting a rat to press a lever can be done by reinforcing behaviours that *approximate* (or lead up to) lever pressing, such as standing up, facing the lever, standing while facing the lever, placing paws upon the lever, and pressing downward. This process of *reinforcing successive approximations of a specific operant response* is known as **shaping**. Shaping is done in a step-by-step fashion until the desired response—in this case, lever pressing—is learned. These techniques can also be used to help people develop specific skill sets (e.g., toilet training). A similar process, **chaining**, *involves linking together two or more shaped behaviours into a more complex action or sequence of actions*. When you see an animal

Bork/Shutterstock

Applications of shaping. Reinforcement can be used to shape complex chains of behaviour in animals and humans. (Later attempts to teach the cat to use a bidet were less successful.)

"acting" in a movie, its behaviours were almost certainly learned through lengthy shaping and chaining procedures.

APPLYING OPERANT CONDITIONING It is important to remember that although most studies of operant learning have involved animals, the principles derived from these studies apply to humans as well. In fact, they are found in many different areas of our lives ranging from work and school to interpersonal relationships. For example, the operant conditioning principles that we've reviewed thus far serve as the basis for an educational method called **applied behaviour analysis** (ABA), *which involves using close observation, prompting, and reinforcement to teach behaviours, often to people who experience difficulties and challenges owing to a developmental condition such as autism* (Granpeesheh et al., 2009). People with autism are typically nonresponsive to normal social cues from a very early age. This impairment can lead to a deficit in developing many skills, ranging from basic, everyday ones to complex skills such as language. For example, explaining how to clear dishes from the dinner table to a child with autism could prove difficult. Psychologists who specialize in ABA often shape the desired behaviour using prompts (such as asking the child to stand up, gather silverware, stack plates, and so on) and verbal rewards as each step is completed. These and more elaborate ABA techniques can be used to shape a remarkable variety of behaviours to improve the independence and quality of life for people with autism.

Module 6.2a Quiz:

Principles of Operant Conditioning

Know . . .

1. _____ removes the immediate effects of an aversive stimulus, whereas _____ removes the possibility of an aversive stimulus from occurring in the first place.
   - **A.** Avoidance learning; escape learning
   - **B.** Positive reinforcement; positive punishment
   - **C.** Negative reinforcement; negative punishment
   - **D.** Escape learning; avoidance learning

Understand . . .

2. When children misbehave, they are sometimes told to go to their room. As a result, they no longer get to play with their friends or siblings. How does this consequence affect children's behaviour?
   - **A.** It adds a stimulus in order to decrease bad behaviour.
   - **B.** It takes away a stimulus in order to decrease bad behaviour.
   - **C.** It adds a stimulus in order to increase bad behaviour.
   - **D.** It takes away a stimulus in order to increase bad behaviour.

Apply . . .

3. Lucy hands all of her homework in to her psychology professor on time because she does not want to lose points for late work. This is an example of _____.
   - **A.** negative reinforcement
   - **B.** positive reinforcement
   - **C.** negative punishment
   - **D.** positive punishment

Processes of Operant Conditioning

In the previous section, you read about how the frequency of a behaviour can be increased (reinforcement) or decreased (punishment) by a number of different stimuli or responses. The obvious question, then, is why do some stimuli affect behaviour while others have no influence whatsoever? Is there a biological explanation for this difference?

PRIMARY AND SECONDARY REINFORCERS Reinforcers can come in two main forms. **Primary reinforcers** *consist of reinforcing stimuli that satisfy basic motivational needs—needs that affect an individual's ability to survive (and, if possible, reproduce).* Examples of these inherently reinforcing stimuli include food, water, shelter, and sexual contact. In contrast, **secondary reinforcers** *consist of stimuli that acquire their reinforcing effects only after we learn that they have value.* Money and Facebook "likes" are both examples of secondary reinforcers. They are more abstract and do not *directly* influence survival-related behaviours.

Both primary and secondary reinforcers satisfy our drives, but what underlies the motivation to seek out these reinforcers? The answer is complex, but research points to a specific brain circuit including a structure called the *nucleus accumbens* (see Figure 6.13). The nucleus accumbens becomes activated during the processing of all kinds of rewards, including primary ones such as eating and having sex, as well as "artificial" rewards such as using cocaine and smoking a cigarette. Variations in this area might also account for why individuals differ so much in their drive for reinforcers. For example, scientists have

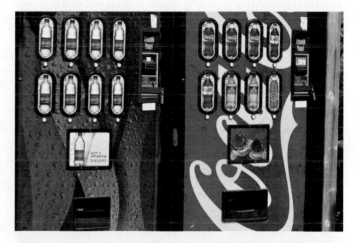

Animals pressing levers in operant chambers to receive rewards may seem artificial. However, if you look around you will see that our environment is full of devices that influence our operant responses.

Top: RisingStar/Alamy Stock Photo; bottom: Richard Goldberg/Shutterstock

Figure 6.13 Reward Processing in the Brain

The nucleus accumbens is one of the brain's primary reward centres.

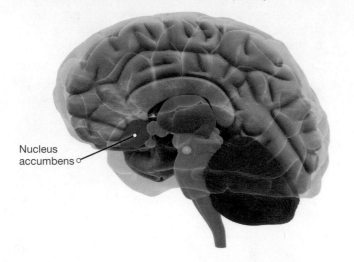

Nucleus
accumbens

discovered that people who are prone to risky behaviours such as gambling and alcohol abuse are more likely to have inherited particular copies of genes that code for dopamine and other reward-based chemicals in the brain (Comings & Blum, 2000). Researchers have also found that individuals who are impulsive, and therefore vulnerable to gambling and drug abuse, release more dopamine in brain areas related to reward, and have trouble removing dopamine from the synapses in these areas (Buckholtz et al., 2010).

Secondary reinforcers also trigger the release of dopamine in reward areas of the brain. A number of neuroimaging experiments have shown that monetary rewards cause dopamine to be released in parts of the basal ganglia (Elliott et al., 2000) as well as in the medial regions of the frontal lobes (Knutson et al., 2003). Some of these areas directly overlap with those involved with primary reinforcers (Valentin & O'Doherty, 2009).

How can dopamine be related to operant conditioning? When a behaviour is rewarded for the first time, dopamine is released (Schultz & Dickinson, 2000); this reinforces these new, reward-producing behaviours so that they will be performed again (Morris et al., 2006; Schultz, 1998). These dopamine-releasing neurons in the nucleus accumbens and surrounding areas help maintain a record of which behaviours are, and are not, associated with a reward. Interestingly, these neurons alter their rate of firing when you have to update your understanding of which actions lead to rewards; so, they are involved with *learning* new behaviour–reward associations as well as with reinforcement itself.

DISCRIMINATION AND GENERALIZATION Once a response has been learned, the individual may soon learn that reinforcement or punishment will occur under only

certain conditions and circumstances. A pigeon in an operant chamber may learn that pecking is reinforced only when the chamber's light is switched on, so there is no need to continue pecking when the light is turned off. This illustrates the concept of a **discriminative stimulus**—*a cue or event that indicates that a response, if made, will be reinforced.* Our lives are filled with discriminative stimuli. Before we pour a cup of coffee, we might check whether the light on the coffee maker is on—a discriminative stimulus that tells us the beverage will be hot and, presumably, reinforcing. There are also numerous social examples of discriminative stimuli. For instance, you might only ask to borrow your parents' car when they show signs of being in a good mood. In this case, your parents' mood (smiling, laughing, etc.) will dictate whether you perform a behaviour (asking to borrow the car). Discriminative stimuli demonstrate that we (and animal subjects) can use cues from our environment to help us decide whether to perform a conditioned behaviour.

The idea of a discriminative stimulus should not be confused with the concept of *discrimination*. **Discrimination** *occurs when an organism learns to respond to one original stimulus but not to new stimuli that may be similar to the original stimulus.* For example, a pigeon may learn that he will receive a reward if he pecks at a key after a 1000-Hz tone, but not if he performs the same action following a 2000-Hz tone. As a result, he won't peck at the key after a 2000-Hz tone. Or, to extend our earlier example, you may quickly learn that your father will lend you the car whereas your mother will not. In this case, the process of discrimination would lead you to perform a behaviour (asking to borrow the car) when you are with your father but not when you are with your mother.

In contrast to discrimination, **generalization** *takes place when an operant response occurs in response to a new stimulus that is similar to the stimulus present during original learning.* In this case, a pigeon who learned to peck a key after hearing a 1000-Hz tone may attempt to peck the key whenever *any* tone is presented. If petting a neighbour's border collie (a type of dog) led to a child laughing and playing with the animal, then he might be more likely to pet other dogs or even other furry animals. In this instance, a specific reinforcement related to an action (petting a *specific* dog) led to a similar behaviour (petting) occurring in other instances (petting *other* dogs).

If you've noticed similarities between discrimination and generalization in operant conditioning and the same processes in classical conditioning (see Module 6.1), you are not mistaken. The same general logic underlies these concepts in both types of conditioning. However, while discrimination and generalization in classical conditioning were due to the strengthening of synapses as a result of simultaneous firing, in operant conditioning, the mechanism appears to be dopamine-secreting neurons.

DELAYED REINFORCEMENT AND EXTINCTION The focus of this module thus far has been on behavioural and biological responses to reinforcement and punishment. In most studies exploring these responses, the reward or punishment occurred immediately following the behaviour. This allows individuals to predict when a reward will occur (Schultz & Dickinson, 2000). But, you know from your own life that rewards are not always immediate. What happens if the reward is delayed, or doesn't occur at all? As early as 1911, Thorndike (the cat imprisoner) noted that reinforcement was more effective if there was very little time between the action and the consequence. Indeed, in a study with pigeons, researchers found that the frequency of responses (pecking a button) decreased as the amount of time between the pecking and the reward (a food pellet) increased (Chung & Herrnstein, 1967). Interestingly, neuroscientists have found that neural activity decreases during this time as well. In fact, delays of as little as half a second decrease the amount of neural activity in dopamine-releasing neurons (Hollerman & Schultz, 1996).

This effect of *delayed reinforcement* influences a number of human behaviours as well. For instance, drugs that have their effect (i.e., produce their rewarding feeling) soon after they are taken are generally more addictive than drugs whose effects occur several minutes or hours after being taken. This difference is due, in part, to the ease with which one can mentally associate the action of taking the drug with reinforcement from the drug (the consequence).

Sometimes, however, a reinforcer is not just delayed; it doesn't occur at all. A pigeon may find that pressing a key in its operant chamber no longer leads to a food reward. You may find that your parents no longer let you borrow the car no matter how nicely you ask. Although both you and the pigeon may persist in your behaviour for a while, eventually you'll stop. This change is known as **extinction**, *the weakening of an operant response when reinforcement is no longer available.* If you lose your Internet connection, for example, you will probably stop trying to refresh your web browser because there is no reinforcement for doing so—the behaviour will no longer be performed. Extinction, like most of the observable behaviours you've

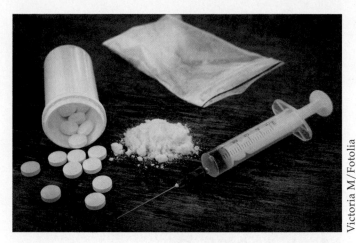

Injecting drugs allows them to enter the bloodstream and therefore the brain more quickly than if they are taken orally. This is one reason why injected drugs are often more addictive than pills.

read about in this module, is related to dopamine. If you expect a reward for your behaviour and none comes, the amount of dopamine being released decreases (Schultz, 1998). Dopamine release will increase again when there is a new behaviour–reward relationship to learn.

Table 6.3 differentiates among the processes of extinction, generalization, and discrimination in classical and operant conditioning.

REWARD DEVALUATION In all of these examples of operant conditioning, the value of the reinforcement remained the same. But, if you think about your own life it quickly becomes apparent that this is not always the case. Food is incredibly rewarding when you are hungry but becomes less so after you have eaten a large meal. Similarly, $100 may seem like a lot of money to a starving student, but would seem less important to a doctor with a high income. If a behaviour is more likely to occur because of reward, what happens when the reward becomes less rewarding?

Scientists have found that behaviours do change when the reinforcer loses some of its appeal (Colwill & Rescorla, 1985, 1990). In a typical experiment, rats are trained to press two different levers, each associated with a different reward (e.g., two different rewarding tastes). If the

Table 6.3 Comparing Discrimination, Generalization, and Extinction in Classical and Operant Conditioning

Process	Classical Conditioning	Operant Conditioning
Discrimination	A CR does not occur in response to a different CS that resembles the original CS.	There is no response to a stimulus that resembles the original discriminative stimulus used during learning.
Generalization	A different CS that resembles the original CS used during acquisition elicits a CR.	Responding occurs to a stimulus that resembles the original discriminative stimulus used during learning.
Extinction	A CS is presented without a US until the CR no longer occurs.	Responding gradually ceases if reinforcement is no longer available.

experimenters pre-feed the animal with one of these two tastes, they will crave it less than the other; in other words, its reward will be devalued compared to the other taste. Researchers consistently find a decrease in the response rate for the "devalued" reward, whereas the other reward remains largely unaffected.

Reward devaluation can also occur by making one of the rewards less appealing. In this version of reward devaluation, one of the reinforcing tastes is paired with a toxin that made the rats feel ill; this obviously reduces its value! (Ideally, this pairing would occur outside of the operant chamber so that the toxin didn't serve as a positive punishment.) The rats would then have the choice of two levers to press, one associated with a rewarding taste and the other associated with the taste that is now less rewarding than before. When these rats were later given the opportunity to choose between the two operant learning tasks, they showed a strong preference for the task whose reward had not been devalued (Colwill & Rescorla, 1985, 1990).

Module 6.2b Quiz:
Processes of Operant Conditioning

Know . . .

1. A basic need such as food may be used as a _____ reinforcer, whereas a stimulus whose value must be learned is a _____ reinforcer.
   - A. primary; continuous
   - B. secondary; shaping
   - C. primary; secondary
   - D. continuous; secondary

Understand . . .

2. The difference between a discriminative stimuli and discrimination (as it applies to operant conditioning) is that
   - A. discrimination tells you when behaviours could be reinforced whereas discriminative stimuli involve an animal responding to some stimuli but not others.
   - B. discriminative stimuli are used only in animal research (which involve simple cues) where discrimination occurs in psychological studies involving human participants.
   - C. discriminative stimuli can only affect behaviour after the process of discrimination has taken place.
   - D. a discriminative stimulus tells you when behaviours could be reinforced whereas discrimination involves responding to some stimuli but not others.

Apply . . .

3. Jack's mother rewarded him for cleaning his messy room by baking him cookies. As a result, Jack cleaned his room every week. However, after few months, Jack's mother stopped rewarding his cleaning behaviour. As a result, Jack didn't clean his room very often. This is an example of _____.
   - A. extinction
   - B. reward devaluation
   - C. discrimination
   - D. Skinner's paradox

4. Jennifer used to love both tequila and vodka (although not mixed together). One night, she drank so much tequila that she felt sick. At a house party the next week, she avoided tequila and drank vodka instead. This is an example of _____.
   - A. extinction
   - B. reward devaluation
   - C. discrimination
   - D. positive reinforcement

Reinforcement Schedules and Operant Conditioning

Think about the last time you did something nice for a friend. How did he or she respond? You may have received a hug. She may have said "Thanks!" and smiled. Regardless, you likely received some positive feedback that made you feel like your behaviour was worth repeating. Now think about the last time you played a sport or a video game. Not every shot would have hit the target, so your behaviour wasn't reinforced each time. But, it was likely reinforced *some of the time.* These real-world examples show you that some behaviours are reinforced more consistently than others. The question that interested

psychologists was "How do these different patterns of reinforcement affect learning?

SCHEDULES OF REINFORCEMENT Operant conditioning occurs, intentionally or unintentionally, in many different areas of our lives. However, the exact timing of the action and reinforcement (or punishment) differs across situations. Typically, a given behaviour is rewarded according to some kind of schedule. These **schedules of reinforcement**—*rules that determine when reinforcement is available*—can have a dramatic effect on both the learning and unlearning of responses (Ferster & Skinner, 1957). Reinforcement may be available at highly predictable or very irregular times. Also, reinforcement may be based on how often someone engages in a behaviour, or on the passage of time.

During **continuous reinforcement**, *every response made results in reinforcement.* As a result, learning initially occurs rapidly. For example, vending machines (should) deliver a snack every time the correct amount of money is deposited. In other situations, not every action will lead to reinforcement; we also encounter situations where reinforcement is available only some of the time. For example, phoning a friend may not always get you an actual person on the other end of the call. In this kind of **partial (intermittent) reinforcement**, *only a certain number of responses are rewarded, or a certain amount of time must pass before reinforcement is available.* Four types of partial reinforcement schedules are possible (see Figure 6.14). These schedules have different effects on rates of responding.

In the descriptions that follow, try to remember the following four terms as they are used in operant conditioning:

- Ratio schedule: This means that the reinforcements are based on the *amount of responding.*

- Interval schedule: This means that the reinforcements are based on the *amount of time between reinforcements, not* the number of responses an animal (or human) makes.

- Fixed schedule: This means that the schedule of reinforcement remains the same over time.

- Variable schedule: This means that the schedule of reinforcement, although linked to an average (e.g., 10 lever presses or 10 seconds), varies from reinforcement to reinforcement.

Figure 6.14 Schedules of Reinforcement

(a) Four types of reinforcement schedule are shown here: fixed ratio, variable ratio, fixed interval, and variable interval. Notice how each schedule differs based on when reinforcement is available (interval schedules) and on how many responses are required for reinforcement (ratio schedules). (b) These schedules of reinforcement affect responding in different ways. For example, notice the vigorous responding that is characteristic of the variable ratio schedule, as indicated by the steep upward trajectory of responding. (c) Real-world examples of the four types of reinforcement schedules.

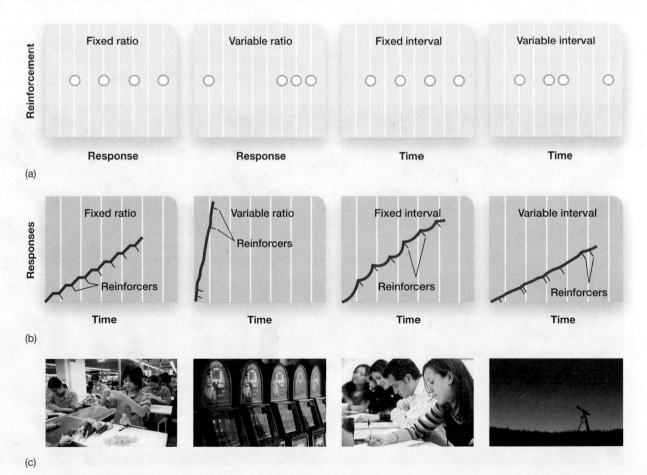

Source: Lilienfeld, Scott O.; Lynn, Steven J; Namy, Laura L.; Woolf, Nancy J., *Psychology: From Inquiry to Understanding*, 2nd Ed., © 2011. Reprinted and electronically reproduced by permission of Pearson Education, Inc., New York, NY.

Photos: bottom left: Li jianbin/Imaginechina/AP Images; bottom centre left: Lightreign/Alamy Stock Photo; bottom centre right: Andresr/Shutterstock; bottom right: Bill Felu/Shutterstock

Keeping these distinctions in mind should help you make sense of the four different reinforcement schedules discussed below.

In a **fixed-ratio schedule**, *reinforcement is delivered after a specific number of responses have been completed*. For example, a rat may be required to press a lever 10 times to receive food. Similarly, a worker in a factory may get paid based on how many items she worked on (e.g., receiving $1 for every five items produced). In both cases, a certain number of responses is required before a reward is given.

In a **variable-ratio schedule**, *the number of responses required to receive reinforcement varies according to an average*. A VR5 (variable ratio with an average of five trials between reinforcements) could include trials that require seven lever presses for a reward to occur, followed by four, then six, then three, and so on. But, the average number of responses required to receive reinforcement would be five. Slot machines at casinos operate on variable-ratio reinforcement schedules. The odds are that the slot machine will not give anything back, but sometimes a player will win a small amount of money. Of course, hitting the jackpot is very infrequent. The variable nature of the reward structure for playing slot machines helps explain why responding on this schedule can be vigorous and persistent. Slot machines and other games of chance hold out the *possibility* that at some point players will be rewarded, but it is unclear how many responses will be required before the reward occurs. The fact that the reinforcement *is* due to the number of times a player responds promotes strong response levels (i.e., more button presses or lever pulls on a slot machine). In animal studies, variable-ratio schedules lead to the highest rate of responding of the four types of reinforcement schedules.

PSYCH@

Never Use Multiline Slot Machines

When casinos first became popular in the middle of the 20th century, people who used slot machines would pull a lever. Wheels with different images or numbers would spin around; if the correct combination of numbers appeared, the player would win a reward (often paired with loud noises and hundreds of coins being dispensed). In modern casinos, the slot machines are computerized. This technology has allowed game designers to add a sinister trick to slot machines: It is now possible for players to bet on several lines (rows) of numbers rather than on just one. These *multiline slot machines* therefore allow the

Multiline video slot machines allow a player to bet on more than one line of numbers and symbols at a time. However, the small "wins" that players experience are often smaller than their overall losses.

frans lemmens / Alamy Stock Photo

player to make multiple bets on each "spin." On the surface, this doesn't seem alarming. But, these machines are using operant conditioning against players. For each line that a player bets on, he or she has to insert money into the machine. So, if a player is betting on nine lines, he would put $9 into the machine. Then the machine "spins" so that the numbers and symbols on each line change. On many of these spins, the player will win, a result that is paired with rewarding celebratory sound effects as well as money. However, the "win" will be for less money than the original total bet (e.g., winning $5 after putting $9 into the machine). In other words, it is a *loss*

that is *disguised as a win* (Dixon et al., 2010). In an interview, one game designer wrote, "[W]e give them a sense of winning but also continue to accrue [their] credits" (Dow Schull, 2012, p. 121). Indeed, gambling researchers at the University of Waterloo have worked out the mathematics for these slot machines and found that players will double their bets only 20% of the time and will win 10x their initial bet (viewed as a "big win" by gamblers) less than 1% of the time (Harrigan et al., 2014). And yet, due to the little rewards on each trial—the losses disguised as wins—gamblers continue to press the buttons. The house always wins in the long run.

In contrast to ratio schedules, interval schedules are based on the passage of time, not the number of responses. A **fixed-interval schedule** *reinforces the first response occurring after a set amount of time passes.* If your psychology professor gives you an exam every four weeks, your reinforcement for studying is on a fixed-interval schedule. In Figure 6.14, notice how the fixed-interval schedule shows that responding drops off after each reinforcement is delivered (as indicated by the tick marks). However, responding increases because reinforcement is soon available again. This schedule may reflect how you devote time to studying for your next exam—studying time tends to decrease after an exam, and then builds up again as another test looms.

The final reinforcement schedule is the **variable-interval schedule**, *in which the first response is reinforced following a variable amount of time.* The time interval varies around an average. For example, if you were watching the nighttime sky during a meteor shower, you would be rewarded for looking upward at irregular times. A meteor may fall on average every 5 minutes, but there will be times of inactivity for a minute, 10 minutes, 8 minutes, and so on.

As you can see from Figure 6.14, ratio schedules tend to generate relatively high rates of responding. This outcome makes sense in light of the fact that in ratio schedules, reinforcement is based on how often you engage in the behaviour (something you have some control over) versus how much time has passed (something you do not control). For example, looking up with greater frequency does not *cause* more meteor activity because a variable-interval schedule is in effect. In contrast, a salesperson is on a variable-*ratio* schedule because approaching more customers increases the chances of making a sale.

One general characteristic of schedules of reinforcement is that partially reinforced responses tend to be very persistent. For example, although people are only intermittently reinforced for putting money into a slot machine, a high rate of responding is maintained and may not decrease until after a great many losses in a row (or the individual runs out of money). The effect of partial

reinforcement on responding is especially evident during extinction. The **partial reinforcement effect** *refers to a phenomenon in which organisms that have been conditioned under partial reinforcement resist extinction longer than those conditioned under continuous reinforcement.* This effect is likely due to the fact that the individual is accustomed to not receiving reinforcement for every response; therefore, a lack of reinforcement is not surprising and does not alter the motivation to produce the response, even if reinforcement is no longer available. We see this effect in many situations ranging from gambling, to cheesy pick-up lines in bars, to the numerous superstitions developed by professional and amateur athletes.

Working the Scientific Literacy Model

Reinforcement and Superstition

It is clear that reinforcement can appear in multiple forms and according to various schedules. What all forms have in common is the notion that the behaviour that brought about the reinforcement will be strengthened. But what happens if the organism is mistaken about what caused the reinforcement to occur—will it experience reinforcement anyway? This raises the topic of superstition.

What do we know about superstition and reinforcement?

Reinforcement is often systematic and predictable. If it is not, then behaviour is eventually extinguished. In some cases, however, it is not perfectly clear what brings about the reinforcement. Imagine a baseball player who tries to be consistent in how he pitches. After a short losing streak, the pitcher suddenly wins a big game. If he is playing the same way, then what happened to change the outcome of the game? Did an alteration in his pre-game ritual lead to the victory? Humans the world over are prone to believing that some ritual or lucky charm will somehow improve their chances of success or survival. Psychologists believe these superstitions can be explained by operant conditioning.

How can science explain superstition?

Decades ago, B. F. Skinner (1948) attempted to create superstitious behaviour in pigeons. Food was delivered every 15 seconds, regardless of what the pigeons were doing. Over time, the birds started engaging in "superstitious" behaviours. The pigeons repeated the behaviour occurring just before reinforcement, even if the behaviour was scratching, head-bobbing, or standing on one foot. A pigeon that happened to be turning in a counterclockwise direction when reinforcement was delivered repeated this seemingly senseless behaviour.

Humans are similarly superstitious. For example, in one laboratory study, psychologists constructed a doll that could spit marbles (Wagner & Morris, 1987). Children were told that the doll would sometimes spit marbles at them and that these marbles could be collected and traded for toys. The marbles were ejected at random intervals, leading several of the children to develop superstitious behaviours such as sucking their thumbs or kissing the doll on the nose.

Psychologists have conducted controlled studies to see whether superstitious behaviours have any effect on performance outcomes. In one investigation, college students, 80% of whom believed in the idea of "good luck," were asked to participate in a golf putting contest in which members of one group were told they were playing with "the lucky ball," and others were told they would be using "the ball everyone has used so far." Those who were told they were using the lucky ball performed significantly better than those who used the ball that was not blessed with good luck (Damisch et al., 2010). These effects also occurred in other tasks, such as memory and anagram games, and participants also showed better performance at tasks if allowed to bring a good luck charm.

Can we critically evaluate these findings?

Superstitious beliefs, though irrational on the surface, may enhance individuals' belief that they can perform successfully at a task. Sometimes these beliefs can even enhance performance, as the golf putting experiment revealed. These findings, however, are best applied to situations where the participant has some control over an outcome, such as taking an exam or playing a sport. People who spend a lot of time and money gambling are known to be quite superstitious, but it is important to distinguish between games of chance versus skill in this setting. "Success" at most gambling games is due entirely, or predominantly, to chance. Thus, the outcomes are immune to the superstitious beliefs of the players.

Superstitions are also prone to the confirmation bias—the tendency to seek out evidence in favour of your existing views and ignore inconsistent information—and the partial reinforcement effect discussed above. If an athlete believes that a superstitious behaviour leads to success, then he or she will notice when the behaviour *does* lead to success. However, given that losing is generally part of being an athlete, there will be times when the behaviour is not reinforced. Given what you've read about the partial reinforcement effect, it is easy to see how a superstitious behaviour could be difficult to change. For instance, former NHL goaltender Patrick Roy was as famous for his many superstitions as he was for his playoff heroics. During every game he would (1) skate backwards toward his net before spinning around at the last minute (which made it appear smaller), (2) talk to his goalposts, (3) thank his goalposts when the puck hit one of them, and (4) avoid touching the blue line and red line when skating off the ice. Roy has the second-highest total of wins for NHL goalies and the most playoff wins in history (151). He won the Stanley Cup four times and was the playoffs's Most Valuable Player three times (an NHL record). But, in addition to his 702 reinforcers, he also lost over 400 games in his impressive career.

Why is this relevant?

Between Skinner's original work with pigeons, and more contemporary experiments with people, it appears that operant conditioning plays a role in the development of some superstitions. Perhaps you have a good luck charm or a ritual you must complete before a game or even before taking a test. Think about what brings you luck, and then try to identify why you believe in this relationship. Can you identify a specific instance when you were first reinforced for this behaviour? Then remember that the superstition is a form of reinforcement, a linking of a behaviour and a response that is formed *in your mind*. Whether a superstition affects your performance is based on whether or not you allow it to.

APPLYING PUNISHMENT   People tend to be more sensitive to the unpleasantness of punishment than they are to the pleasures of reward. Psychologists have demonstrated this asymmetry in laboratory studies with university students who play a computerized game in which they can choose a response that can bring either a monetary reward or a monetary loss. It turns out that the participants found losing money to be about three times as punishing as being rewarded with money was pleasurable. In other words, losing $100 is three times more punishing than gaining $100 is reinforcing (Rasmussen & Newland, 2008).

The use of punishment raises some ethical concerns—especially when it comes to physical means. A major issue

Table 6.4 Punishment Tends to Be Most Effective When Certain Principles Are Followed

Principle	Description and Explanation
Severity	Should be proportional to offence. A small fine is suitable for parking illegally or littering, but inappropriate for someone who commits assault.
Initial punishment level	The initial level of punishment needs to be sufficiently strong to reduce the likelihood of the offence occurring again.
Contiguity	Punishment is most effective when it occurs immediately after the behaviour. Many convicted criminals are not sentenced until many months after they have committed an offence. Children are given detention that may not begin until hours later. Long delays in punishment are known to reduce its effectiveness.
Consistency	Punishment should be administered consistently. A parent who only occasionally punishes a teenager for breaking her curfew will probably have less success in curbing the behaviour than a parent who uses punishment consistently.
Show alternatives	Punishment is more successful, and side effects are reduced, if the individual is clear on how reinforcement can be obtained by engaging in appropriate behaviours.

that is debated all over the world is whether corporal punishment (e.g., spanking) is acceptable to use with children. In fact, more than 20 countries, including Sweden, Austria, Finland, Denmark, and Israel, have banned the practice. It is technically legal to spank a child aged 2–12 in Canada; in a contentious decision, the Supreme Court of Canada (in a 6–3 vote) upheld Section 43 of the *Criminal Code* allowing spanking (Supreme Court of Canada, 2004). Some parents use this tactic because it works: Spanking is generally a very effective punisher when it is used for immediately stopping a behaviour (Gershoff, 2002). However, one reason so few psychologists advocate spanking is because it is associated with some major side effects (Gershoff, 2002; Gershoff & Bitensky, 2007). In a recent review of this research published in the *Canadian Medical Association Journal*, investigators at the University of Manitoba noted that spanking has been associated with poorer parent–child relationships, poorer mental health for both adults and children, delinquency in children, and increased chances of children becoming victims or perpetrators of physical abuse in adulthood (Durrant & Ensom, 2012).

It is also important to note that, while punishment may suppress an unwanted behaviour temporarily, by itself it does not teach which behaviours are appropriate. As a general rule, punishment of any kind is most effective when combined with reinforcement of an alternative, suitable response. Table 6.4 offers some general guidelines for maximizing the effects of punishment and minimizing negative side effects.

ARE CLASSICAL AND OPERANT LEARNING DISTINCT EVENTS? It is tempting to think of behaviour as being due to *either* classical conditioning *or* operant conditioning. However, it is possible, even likely, that a complex behaviour is influenced by both types of learning, each influencing behaviour in slightly different ways. Consider gambling with video lottery terminals (VLTs), the topic of the opening story in this module. As discussed above, slot machines and VLTs use a variable-ratio schedule of reinforcement, a type of operant conditioning that leads to a high response rate. But, the flashy lights, the dinging sounds coming from the machine, and even the chair all serve as conditioned stimuli for the unconditioned response of excitement associated with gambling (Dixon et al., 2014). So, classical conditioning produces an emotional response and operant conditioning maintains the behaviour. Given these forces, should we really be surprised that VLTs are so alluring to people, particular those prone to problem gambling (Clarke et al., 2012; Nicki et al., 2007)?

Module 6.2c Quiz:

Reinforcement Schedules and Operant Conditioning

Know . . .

1. In a _____, the first response occurring after a set amount of time leads to a reward.

  A. fixed-ratio schedule

  B. variable-ratio schedule

  C. fixed-interval schedule

  D. variable-interval schedule

Understand . . .

2. Pete cannot seem to stop checking the change slots of vending machines. Although he usually does not find any money, occasionally he finds a quarter. Despite the low levels of reinforcement, this behaviour is likely to persist due to _____.

  A. escape learning

  B. the partial reinforcement effect

  C. positive punishment

  D. generalization

Apply . . .

3. Frederick trained his parrot to open the door to his cage by pecking at a lever three times. Based on this description, which schedule of reinforcement would he most likely have used?

    A. variable-interval

    B. variable-ratio

    C. fixed-interval

    D. fixed-ratio

Analyze . . .

4. Jeremy regularly spanks his children to decrease their misbehaviour. Which statement is most accurate in regard to this type of corporal punishment?

    A. Spanking is an effective method of punishment and should always be used.

    B. Spanking can be an effective method of punishment but carries risks of additional negative outcomes.

    C. Spanking is not an effective method of punishment, so it should never be used.

    D. The effects of spanking have not been well researched, so it should not be used.

Module 6.2 Summary

6.2a Know . . . the key terminology associated with operant conditioning.

applied behaviour analysis
avoidance learning
chaining
continuous reinforcement
discrimination
discriminative stimulus
escape learning
extinction
fixed-interval schedule
fixed-ratio schedule
generalization
law of effect
negative punishment
negative reinforcement
operant conditioning
partial (intermittent) reinforcement
partial reinforcement effect
positive punishment
positive reinforcement
primary reinforcer
punisher
punishment
reinforcement
reinforcer
schedules of reinforcement
secondary reinforcer
shaping
variable-interval schedule
variable-ratio schedule

6.2b Understand . . . the role that consequences play in increasing or decreasing behaviour.

Positive and negative reinforcement increase the likelihood of a behaviour, whereas positive and negative punishment decrease the likelihood of a behaviour. Positive reinforcement and positive punishment involve adding a stimulus to the situation, whereas negative reinforcement and negative punishment involve removal of a stimulus.

6.2c Understand . . . how schedules of reinforcement affect behaviour.

Schedules of reinforcement can be fixed or variable, and can be based on intervals (time) or ratios (the number of responses). As can be seen in Figure 6.14, variable-ratio schedules produce the most robust learning; reinforcement is linked to the animal's (or human's) response rather than to an amount of time, but the animal never knows how many responses will be necessary for a reward to occur. Variable-interval schedules lead to the slowest rate of learning.

6.2d Apply . . . your knowledge of operant conditioning to examples.

The concepts of positive and negative reinforcement and punishment are often the most challenging when it comes to this material.

Apply Activity

Read the following scenarios and determine whether positive reinforcement, negative reinforcement, positive punishment, or negative punishment explains the change in behaviour.

1. Bill is caught for cheating on multiple examinations. As a consequence, the school principal suspends him for a three-day period. Bill likes being at school and, when he returns from his suspension, he no longer cheats on exams. Which process explains the change in Bill's behaviour? Why?

2. Ericka earns As in all of her math classes. Throughout her schooling, she finds that the personal and social rewards for excelling at math continue to motivate her. She eventually completes a graduate degree and teaches math. Which process explains her passion for math? Why?

3. Automobile makers install sound equipment that produces annoying sounds when a door is not shut

properly, lights are left on, or a seat belt is not fastened. The purpose is to increase proper door shutting, turning off of lights, and seat belt fastening behaviour. Which process explains the behavioural changes these sounds are attempting to make?

4. Hernan bites his fingernails and cuticles to the point of bleeding and discomfort. To reduce this behaviour, he applies a terrible-tasting topical lotion to his fingertips and the behaviour stops. Which process explains Hernan's behavioural change?

6.2e Analyze . . . the effectiveness of punishment on changing behaviour.

Many psychologists recommend that people rely on reinforcement to teach new or appropriate behaviours. The issue here is not that punishment does not work, but rather that there are some notable drawbacks to using punishment as a means to change behaviour. For example, punishment may teach individuals to engage in avoidance or aggression, rather than developing an appropriate alternative behaviour that can be reinforced.

Module 6.3 Cognitive and Observational Learning

Courtesy of Victoria Horner and the Chimpanzee Sanctuary and Wildlife Conservation Trust, Ngamba Island, Uganda

∨ Learning Objectives

6.3a Know . . . the key terminology associated with cognitive and observational learning.

6.3b Understand . . . the concept of latent learning and its relevance to cognitive aspects of learning.

6.3c Apply . . . principles of observational learning outside of the laboratory.

6.3d Analyze . . . the claim that viewing violent media increases violent behaviour.

Are you smarter than a chimpanzee? For years psychologists have asked this question, but in a more nuanced way. More specifically, they have tested the problem-solving and imitative abilities of chimpanzees and humans to help us better understand what sets us apart from, and what makes us similar to, other animals. Chimps and humans both acquire many behaviours from observing others, but imagine if you pitted a typical human preschooler against a chimpanzee. Who do you think would be the best at learning a new skill just by watching someone else perform it? Researchers Victoria Horner and Andrew Whiten asked this question by showing 3- and 4-year-old children how to retrieve a treat by opening a puzzle box, and then they demonstrated the task to chimpanzees as well. But there was one trick thrown in: As they demonstrated the process, the researchers added in some steps that were unnecessary to opening the box. The children and chimps both

figured out how to open it, but the children imitated all the steps—even the unnecessary ones—while the chimps skipped the useless steps and went straight for the treat (Horner & Whiten, 2005).

What can we conclude from these results? Maybe it is true that both humans and chimps are excellent imitators, although it appears the children imitated a little too well, while the chimps imitated in a smarter manner. Clearly, we both share a motivation to imitate—which is a complex cognitive ability and one of the keys to learning new skills.

Focus Questions

1. What role do cognitive factors play in learning?

2. Which processes are required for imitation to occur?

» The first two modules of this chapter focused on relatively basic ways of learning. Classical conditioning occurs through the formation of associations (Module 6.1), and operant conditioning involves changes in behaviour due to rewarding or punishing consequences (Module 6.2). Both types of learning emphasize relationships between stimuli and responses and avoid making reference to the *thinking* part of the learning process. However, since the 1950s, psychologists have recognized that cognitive processes such as thinking and remembering are useful to theories and explanations of how we learn.

Cognitive Perspectives on Learning

Cognitive psychologists have contributed a great deal to psychology's understanding of learning. In some cases, they have presented a very different view from behaviourism by addressing unobservable mental phenomena. In other cases, their work has simply complemented behaviourism by integrating cognitive accounts into even the seemingly simplest of learned behaviours, such as classical and operant conditioning.

LATENT LEARNING   Much of human learning involves absorbing information and then demonstrating what we have learned by performing a task, such as taking a quiz or exam. Learning, and reinforcement for learning, may not be expressed until there is an opportunity to do so. In other words, learning may be occurring even if there is no behavioural evidence of it taking place.

Psychologist Edward Tolman proposed that humans, and even rats, express **latent learning**—*learning that is not immediately expressed by a response until the organism is reinforced for doing so.* Tolman and Honzik (1930) demonstrated latent learning in rats running a maze (see Figure 6.15). The first group of rats could obtain food if they navigated the correct route through the maze. They were given 10 trials to figure out an efficient route to the end of the maze, where food was always waiting. A second group was allowed to explore the maze, but did not have food available at the other end until the 11th trial. A third group (a control) never received food while in the maze. It might seem that only the first group—the one that was reinforced on all trials—would learn how to best shuttle from the start of the maze to the end. After all, it was the only group that was consistently reinforced. This is, in fact, what happened—at least for the first 10 trials. Tolman and Honzik discovered that rats that were finally rewarded on the 11th trial quickly performed as well as the rats that were rewarded on every trial (see Figure 6.15). It appears that this second group of rats was learning after all, but only demonstrated their knowledge when they received reinforcement worthy of quickly running through the maze.

Figure 6.15 Learning without Reinforcement

Tolman and Honzik (1930) placed rats in the start box and measured the number of errors they made in getting to the end box. Rats that were reinforced during the first 10 days of the experiment made fewer errors. Rats that were reinforced on day 11 immediately made far fewer errors, which indicated that they had learned some spatial details of the maze even though food reinforcement was not available during the first 10 trials for this group.

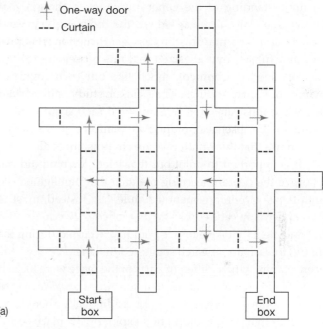

(a)

Source: Ciccarelli, Saundra K.; White, J. Noland, *Psychology: An Exploration*, 1st ed., © 2010, p.79, 81,141. Reprinted and Electronically reproduced by permission of Pearson Education, Inc., New York, NY.

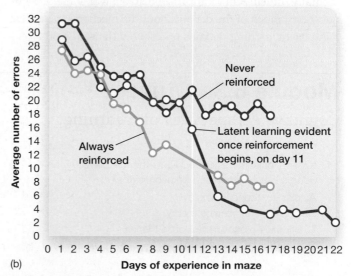

(b)

Source: Adapted from "Degrees of Hunger, Reward and Non-Reward and Maze Learning in Rats" by E. C. Tolman & C. H. Honzik, (1930), *University of California Publications in Psychology*, 4241–4256.

If you put yourself in the rat's shoes—or perhaps paws would be more appropriate—you will realize that humans experience latent learning as well. Consider the layout of a university campus. In the first months of school, new students might wander around the campus to find different classrooms and perhaps the cafeteria, but they would probably leave entire buildings unexplored. Yet, if they were suddenly asked to meet someone in a specific building, they would likely be able to find that location without much problem (i.e., they would not wander aimlessly from building to building in a trial-and-error fashion as though investigating a new environment for the first time). The reason is that they would have formed an understanding of the general area, even though that knowledge wasn't rewarded at the time. Tolman and Honzik assumed that this process held true for their rats, and they further hypothesized that rats possess a *cognitive map* of their environment, much like our own cognitive map of our surroundings. Their classic study is important because it illustrates that humans (and rats) acquire information in the absence of immediate reinforcement and that we can use that information when circumstances allow.

It is important to point out that latent learning did not disprove the operant learning research that highlighted the importance of reinforcement (Module 6.2). Instead, most of the controversy centred on the idea of cognitive maps and the statement that *no* reinforcement had occurred during the first 10 trials. Later research suggested that the rats may have been learning where different parts of the maze were located *in relation* to each other rather than forming a *complete* map of the environment (Whishaw, 1991). Additionally, there is no guarantee that the rats didn't find exploring the maze on the first 10 trials to be rewarding in some way, as rats are naturally curious about their environment. Because it is experimentally difficult, if not impossible, to answer some of these questions, much of the debate about the mechanisms underlying latent learning remains unresolved (Jensen, 2006).

S-O-R THEORY OF LEARNING   Latent learning suggests that individuals engage in more "thinking" than is shown by operant conditioning studies. Instead, cognitive theories of learning suggest that an individual actively processes and analyzes information; this activity influences observable behaviours as well as our internal mental lives. Because of the essential role played by the individual, this early view of cognitive learning was referred to as the *S-O-R theory* (*stimulus-organism-response theory*; Woodworth, 1929).

Stimulus–response (S–R) and S–O–R theorists both agreed that thinking took place; however, they disagreed about the content and causes of the thoughts. S–R psychologists (such as Thorndike) assumed that thoughts were based on the S–R contingencies that an organism had learned throughout its life; in other words, thinking was a form of behaviour. Individual differences in responding would therefore be explained by the different learning histories of the individuals. S–O–R psychologists, on the other hand, assumed that individual differences were based on people's (or animals') cognitive *interpretation* of that situation—in other words, what that stimulus meant to them. In this view, the same stimulus in the same situation could theoretically produce different responses based on a variety of factors including an individual's mood, fatigue, the presence of other organisms, and so on. For example, the same comment to two coworkers might lead to an angry response from one person and laughter from another. The explanation for these differences is the *O* in the S–O–R theory; each person or organism will think about or interpret a situation in a slightly different way.

Module 6.3a Quiz:

Cognitive Perspectives on Learning

Know . . .

1. A theory of learning that highlights the role played by an individual's interpretation of a situation is (the)
   A. classical conditioning theory.
   B. operant conditioning theory.
   C. stimulus-organism-response theory.
   D. individualist theory.

Understand . . .

2. Contrary to some early behaviourist views, _____ suggests that learning can occur without any immediate behavioural evidence.
   A. latent learning
   B. operant conditioning
   C. classical conditioning
   D. desirable difficulties

Observational Learning

The first two modules in this chapter focused on aspects of learning that require direct experience. Pavlov's dogs experienced the clicking sound of the metronome and the food one right after the other, and learning occurred. Rats in an operant chamber experienced the reinforcing consequences of pressing a lever, and learning occurred.

However, not all learning requires direct experience, and this is a good thing. Can you imagine if surgeons had to learn by trial and error? Who on earth would volunteer to be the first patient?

Luckily, many species, including humans, are able to learn new skills and new associations without directly experiencing them. **Observational learning** *involves changes in behaviour and knowledge that result from watching* *others*. Humans have elaborate cultural customs and rituals that spread through observation. The cultural differences we find in dietary preferences, clothing styles, athletic events, holiday rituals, music tastes, and so many other customs exist because of observational learning. Indeed, it is the primary way that adaptive behaviour spreads so rapidly within a population, even in nonhuman species (Heyes & Galef, 1996). For example, cats that observe others being trained to leap over a hurdle to avoid a foot shock learn the same trick faster than cats who did not observe this training (John et al., 1968). A less shocking example involves rats' foraging behaviour. Before setting off in search of food, rats smell the breath of other rats. They will then search preferentially for food that matches the odour of their fellow rats' breath. To humans, this practice may not seem very appealing—but for rats, using breath as a source of information about food may help them survive. By definition, a breathing rat is a living rat, so clearly the food the animal ate did not kill it. Living rats are worth copying. Human children are also very sensitive to social cues about what they should avoid. Curious as they may be, even young children will avoid food if they witness their parents reacting with disgust toward it (Stevenson et al., 2010). However, for observational learning to occur, some key processes need to be in place if the behaviour is to be successfully transmitted from one person to the next.

Even rats have a special way of socially transmitting information. Without directly observing what other rats have eaten, rats will smell the food on the breath of other rats and then preferentially search for this food.

Figure 6.16 Processes Involved in Observational Learning

For observational learning to occur, several processes are required: attention, memory, the ability to reproduce the behaviour, and the motivation to do so.

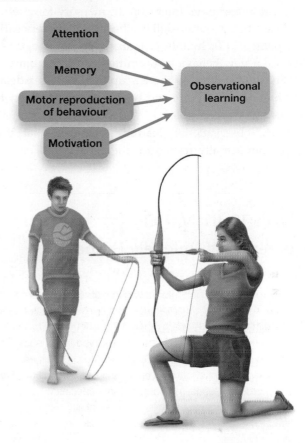

PROCESSES SUPPORTING OBSERVATIONAL LEARNING Albert Bandura (Bandura, 1973; Bandura & Walters, 1963) identified four processes involved in observational learning: *attention* to the act or behaviour, *memory* for it, the *ability to reproduce it*, and the *motivation* to do so (see Figure 6.16). Without any one of these processes, observational learning would be unlikely—or at least would result in a poor rendition of the behaviour.

First, consider the importance of attention. Seeing someone react with a classically conditioned fear to snakes or spiders can result in acquiring a similar fear—even in the absence of any direct experience with snakes or spiders (LoBue et al., 2010). As an example, are you afraid of sharks? It is likely that many of you have this fear, even if you live thousands of kilometres away from shark-infested waters. The fear you see on the faces of people in horror movies and in "Shark Week" documentaries is enough for you to learn this experience. Observational learning can extend to operant conditioning as well. Observing someone being rewarded for certain behaviours facilitates imitation of the same behaviours that bring about rewards.

Second, memory is an important facet of observational learning. When we learn a new behaviour, there is often a delay before the opportunity to perform it arises. If you tuned in to a cooking show, for example, you would need to recreate the steps and processes required to prepare the dish at a later time. Interestingly, memory for how to reproduce a behaviour or skill can be found at a very early age (Huang, 2012). Infants just nine months of age can reproduce a new behaviour (admittedly, a much simpler one than cooking), even if there is up to a one-week delay between observing the act and having the opportunity to reproduce it (Meltzoff, 1988).

Third, observational learning requires that the observer can actually reproduce the behaviour. This can be very challenging, depending on the task. Unless an individual has a physical impairment, learning an everyday task—such as operating a can opener—is not difficult. By comparison, hitting a baseball thrown by a Toronto Blue Jays pitcher requires a very specialized skill set. Research indicates that observational learning is most effective when we first observe, practise immediately, and continue practising and observing soon after acquiring the response. For example, one study found that the optimal way to develop and maintain motor (movement) skills is by repeated observation before and during the initial stages of practising (Weeks & Anderson, 2000). It appears that watching someone else helps us practise effectively, and allows us to see how errors are made. When we see

Myths in Mind
Is Teaching Uniquely Human?

Teaching is a significant component of human culture and a primary means by which information is learned in classrooms, at home, and in many other settings. But are humans the only species with the ability to teach others? Some intriguing examples of teaching-like behaviour have been observed in nonhuman species (Thornton & Raihani, 2010). Prepare to be humbled.

Teaching behaviour was recently discovered in ants (Franks & Richardson, 2006)—probably the last species we might suspect would demonstrate this complex ability. For example, a "teacher" ant gives a "pupil" ant feedback on how to locate a source of food.

Field researchers studying primates discovered the rapid spread of potato-washing behaviour in Japanese macaque monkeys (Kawai, 1965). Imo—perhaps one of the more ingenious monkeys of the troop—discovered that potatoes could be washed in salt water, which also may have given them a more appealing taste. Potato-washing behaviour subsequently spread through the population, especially among the monkeys that observed the behaviour in Imo and her followers.

Transmission of new and unique behaviours typically occurs between mothers and their young (Huffman, 1996). Chimpanzee mothers, for example, actively demonstrate to their young the special skills required to crack nuts open (Boesch, 1991). Also, mother killer whales appear to show their offspring how to beach themselves (Rendell & Whitehead, 2001), a behaviour that is needed for the type of killer whale that feeds on seals that congregate along the shoreline.

In each of these examples, it is possible that the observer animals are imitating the individual who is demonstrating a behaviour. These observations raise the possibility that teaching may not be a uniquely human endeavour.

Primate researchers have documented the spread of potato washing in Japanese macaque monkeys across multiple generations. Monkeys appear to learn how to do this by observing experienced monkeys from their troop.

Is this killer whale teaching her offspring to hunt for seals? Researchers have found evidence of teaching in killer whales and a variety of other nonhuman species.

a model making a mistake, we know to examine our own behaviour for similar mistakes (Blandin & Proteau, 2000; Hodges et al., 2007).

Finally, motivation is clearly an important component of observational learning. On the one hand, being hungry or thirsty will motivate an individual to find out where others are going to find food and drink. On the other hand, a child who has no aspirations to ever play the piano will be less motivated to observe his teacher during lessons. He will also be less likely to practise the observed behaviour that he is trying to learn.

Observational punishment is also possible, but appears to be less effective at changing behaviour than reinforcement. Witnessing others experience negative consequences may decrease your chances of copying someone else's behaviour. Even so, we are sometimes surprisingly bad at learning from observational punishment. Seeing the consequences of smoking, drug abuse, and other risky behaviours does not seem to prevent many people from engaging in the same activities.

IMITATION AND MIRROR NEURONS One of the primary mechanisms that allows observational learning to take place is **imitation**—*recreating someone else's motor behaviour or expression, often to accomplish a specific goal.* From a very young age, infants imitate the facial expressions of adults (Meltzoff & Moore, 1977). Later, as they mature physically, children readily imitate motor acts produced by a model, such as a parent, teacher, or friend. This ability seems to be something very common among humans. However, it is currently unclear what imitation actually is, although a number of theories exist. Some researchers suggest that children receive positive reinforcement when they properly imitate the behaviour of an adult and that imitation is a form of operant learning (Horne & Erjavec, 2007). Others suggest that imitation allows children to gain a better understanding of their own body parts versus the "observed" body parts of others (Mitchell, 1987). Finally, imitation might involve a more cognitive representation of one's own actions as well as the observed actions of someone else (Whiten, 2000). It is likely that all three processes are involved with imitation at different points in human (and some animal) development (Zentall, 2012).

Neuroscientists have provided additional insight into the functions of imitation. In the 1990s, Italian researchers discovered that groups of neurons in parts of the frontal lobes associated with planning movements became active both when a monkey performed an action *and* when it observed another monkey performing an action (di Pellegrino et al., 1992). These cells, now known as *mirror neurons,* are also found in several areas in the human brain and have been linked to many different functions ranging from understanding other people's emotional states to observational learning (Rizzolatti et al., 1996; Rizzolatti & Craighero, 2004). Additionally, groups of neurons appear to be sensitive to the context of an action. In one study, participants viewed a scene of a table covered in a plate of cookies, a teapot, and a cup (see Figure 6.17). In one photo of these items, the setting is untouched. In this case, reaching for the cup of tea would indicate that the person intended to have a sip. In another photo, many of the cookies are gone and the milk container has been knocked over. In this case, reaching for the cup of tea—the identical action as in the previous photo—would indicate that the person was cleaning up the mess. Incredibly, different groups of mirror neurons fired in response to the two images, despite the fact that the identical movement was being viewed (Iacoboni et al., 2005). These results suggest that the mirror neuron system—a key part of our ability to imitate—is sensitive to the purpose or goal of the imitated action.

Working the Scientific Literacy Model

Linking Media Exposure to Behaviour

Imitating behaviours such as opening contraptions with sticks or picking up teacups is fairly harmless. However, not all of the behaviours children see are this innocent. Children (and adults) are exposed to dozens of violent actions in the media, on the Internet, and in computer games every day. If kids are imitating the behaviours they see in other contexts, does this mean that the media are creating a generation of potentially violent people?

What do we know about media effects on behaviour?

In some cases, learning from the media involves direct imitation; in other cases, what we observe shapes what we view as normal or acceptable behaviour. Either way, the actions people observe in the media can raise concerns, especially when children are watching. Given that North American children now spend an average of five hours per day interacting with electronic media, it is no wonder that one of the most discussed and researched topics in observational learning is the role of media violence in developing aggressive behaviours and desensitizing individuals to the effects of violence (Anderson et al., 2003; Huesmann, 2007). So how have researchers tackled the issue?

How can science explain the effect of media exposure on children's behaviour?

One of the first experimental attempts to test whether exposure to violence begets violent behaviour in children was made by Albert Bandura and colleagues (1961, 1963)

Figure 6.17 Grasping Intentions of Mirror Neurons

Watching the same physical action—grabbing the teacup— in these two scenarios will lead to activity in different groups of neurons in the mirror neuron system. This suggests that the mirror neuron system is influenced by the goals of the actions, not just the physical action itself.

Source: From Iacoboni, M., Molnar-Szakacs, I., Gallese, V., Buccino, G., Mazziotta, J. C., and Rizzolatti, G. *PLoS Biol*, 2005, 3, e79. http://dx.doi.org/10.1371/journal.pbio.0030079.g001. Reprinted under open access license.

In a series of studies, groups of children watched an adult or cartoon character attack a "Bobo" doll, while another group of children watched adults who did not attack the doll. Children who watched adults attack the doll did likewise when given the opportunity, in some cases even imitating the specific attack methods used by the adults. The other children did not attack the doll. This provided initial evidence that viewing aggression makes children at least temporarily more prone to committing aggressive acts toward an inanimate object.

Decades of research has since confirmed that viewing aggression is associated with increased aggression and desensitization to violence (Bushman & Anderson, 2007). In one Canadian study, Wendy Josephson (1987) had children aged 7–9 view a violent or nonviolent film before playing a game of floor hockey. Not surprisingly, children who viewed the violent film were more likely to act aggressively (i.e., to commit an act that would be penalized in a real hockey game). As an added twist, in some of the floor hockey games, a referee carried a walkie-talkie that had appeared in the violent film and thus served as a reminder of the violence. This movie-associated cue stimulated more violence, particularly in children who the teachers had indicated were prone to aggression.

Visual images are not the only source of media violence, however. Music, particularly hip hop and rap music (Herd, 2009), has become increasingly graphic in its depictions of violence over the last few decades. Psychologists have found that songs with violent lyrics can lead to an increase in aggressive and hostile thoughts in a manner similar to violent movies (Anderson et al., 2003). In one study, German researchers asked male and female participants to listen to songs with sexually aggressive lyrics that were degrading to women. After listening to this music, the participants were asked to help out with a (staged) taste-preference study by pouring hot chili sauce into a plastic cup for another participant (who was actually a confederate of the experimenters). The researchers found that after listening to aggressive music that degraded women, males poured more hot sauce for a female than for a male confederate; this difference did not occur after listening to neutral music. Female participants did not show this effect. Male participants also recalled more negative and aggressive thoughts. Interestingly, when women listened to lyrics that were demeaning to men, they too recalled more negative and hostile information (Fischer & Greitmeyer, 2006). Thus, the effects of media violence are not limited to the visual domain and can affect both males and females.

Can we critically evaluate this research?

Exposure to violent media and aggressive behaviour and thinking are certainly related to each other. However, at least two very important questions remain. First, does exposure to violence *cause* violent behaviour or desensitization to violence? Second, does early exposure to violence turn children into violent adolescents or adults? Unfortunately, there are no simple answers to either question, due in large part to investigators' reliance on correlational designs, which are typically used for studying long-term effects. Recall that correlational studies can establish only that variables are related, but cannot determine that one variable (media) causes another one (violent behaviour). What is very clear from decades of research is that a positive correlation exists between exposure to violent media and aggressive behaviour in individuals, and that this correlation is stronger than those between aggression and peer influence, abusive parenting, or intelligence (Bushman & Anderson, 2007).

Another concern with these studies is that they aren't really examining *why* people respond aggressively when they see violent imagery. Although there is clearly a role for observational learning, a number of researchers have also suggested that people become desensitized to the violence and thus less likely to inhibit their own violent impulses. Recent brain-imaging studies support this view. In one study, activity in parts of the frontal and parietal lobes showed reductions in activity as people became less sensitive to aggression shown in videos (Strenziok et al., 2011). In another experiment, participants with a low history of exposure to media violence showed more activity in frontal-lobe regions related to inhibiting responses than did participants who had more exposure to media violence and who had a history of aggressive behaviour. These differences were particularly strong when participants had to inhibit responses related to aggression-related words (Kalnin et al., 2011). Although these studies don't definitively explain why media violence affects behaviour, they do point to at least one potential cause.

Why is this relevant?

Clearly then, media violence is a significant risk factor for future aggressiveness. Many organizations have stepped in to help parents make decisions about which type of media their children will be exposed to. The Motion Picture Association of America has been rating movies, with violence as a criterion, since 1968. (Canada does not have a national ratings system; individual provinces each rate movies.) Violence on television was being monitored and debated even before the film industry took this step. Since the 1980s, parental advisory stickers have been appearing on music with lyrics that are sexually explicit, reference drug use, or depict violence. Of course, as you know, these precautions have little effect on what children watch and listen to.

Albert Bandura

In Albert Bandura's experiment, children who watched adults behave violently toward the Bobo doll were aggressive toward the same doll when given the chance—often imitating specific acts that they viewed.

BIOPSYCHOSOCIAL PERSPECTIVES
Violence, Video Games, and Culture

Can pixilated, fictional characters controlled by your own hands make you more aggressive or even violent? Adolescents, university students, and even adults in their thirties and forties play hours of video games each day, many of which are very violent. Also, because video games are becoming so widespread, questions have been raised about whether the correlations between media violence and aggression are found across different cultures. What do you think: Do these games increase aggression and violent acts by players? First, test your knowledge and assumptions and then see what research tells us.

True or False?

1. Playing violent video games reduces a person's sensitivity to others' suffering and need for help.
2. Gamers who play violent video games are less likely to behave aggressively if they are able to personalize their own character.
3. Gamers from Eastern cultures, who play violent video games as much as Westerners, are less prone to video game–induced aggression.
4. Physiological arousal is not affected by violent video games.
5. Male gamers are more likely to become aggressive by playing video games than female gamers.

Answers

1. *True.* People who play violent video games often become less sensitive to the feelings and well-being of others.
2. *False.* Personalizing a character seems to increase aggressive behaviour.
3. *False.* Gamers from both Eastern and Western cultures show the same effects.
4. *False.* Players of violent video games show increased physiological arousal during play. However, it is important to remember that this does not mean that playing these games will necessarily cause someone to become violent.
5. *False.* There are no overall gender differences in aggression displayed by gamers.

SOURCE: These data are from Anderson et al., 2010; Carnagey et al., 2007; and Fischer et al., 2010.

Kids will always find a way to access this type of material. But, providing parents with more information about how these depictions of violence can affect children will hopefully highlight some of the dangers of these images and lyrics, and may inspire them to *talk to* their kids about how violence can be real. Doing so might teach children and adolescents to be better at examining how media violence could be affecting their own behaviour.

Research examining the effects of violent movies, television shows, and music lyrics paints a disturbing picture of the effects of media on aggressive behaviour. Recently, due to a drastic upsurge in their popularity and sophistication, video games have also been labelled with parental advisory stickers. Some violent games, such as Call of Duty (which has sold over 140 million copies worldwide), involve shooting and blowing up the enemy. Other games, such as Grand Theft Auto, allow the player to commit illegal and violent acts. An obvious question is: Are video games related to aggressive behaviour (i.e., observational learning) in the same way that movies are?

Of course, the most important question is whether a regular pattern of playing violent video games *causes* violent behaviour. In 2015, the American Psychological Association issued a report stating that research has shown a consistent link between violent video games and violent behaviour. However, a number of academics disagreed with the methods used to come to these conclusions. Critics also pointed out that violent crime is decreasing in most countries despite the prevalence of video games. The general consensus is that violent video games can lead to aggressive thoughts and behaviours in some people. Whether these games have a long-term effect on behaviour is still unclear.

These data don't mean that you should *never* watch a violent movie or play violent video games. And, you don't need to delete your gangsta rap songs and replace them with a steady diet of Taylor Swift. Rather, these data show you that the media *can* influence your behaviour. It's up to you to become aware of how media violence can lead to (unintentional) observational learning. Doing so will help ensure that your actions are, in fact, your own.

Module 6.3b Quiz:

Observational Learning

Know . . .

1. Observational learning
   A. is the same thing as teaching.
   B. involves a change in behaviour as a result of watching others.
   C. is limited to humans.
   D. is not effective for long-term retention.

2. _____ is the replication of a motor behaviour or expression, often to accomplish a specific goal.
   A. Observational learning
   B. Latent learning
   C. Imitation
   D. Cognitive mapping

Apply . . .

3. Nancy is trying to learn a new yoga pose. To obtain the optimal results, research indicates she should
   A. observe, practise immediately, and continue to practice and to observe others.
   B. observe and practise one time.

C. just closely observe the behaviour.
D. observe the behaviour just one time and then practise on her own.

Analyze . . .

4. Which is the most accurate conclusion from the large body of research that exists on the effects of viewing media violence?
   A. Exposure to violent media directly causes increased aggression and desensitization to violence.
   B. There is a positive correlation between exposure to media violence and aggressive behaviour.
   C. Researchers cannot establish a link between exposure to violent media and either aggression levels or desensitization to violence without first conducting brain-imaging studies.
   D. Viewing aggression is not related to increased aggression and desensitization to violence.

Module 6.3 Summary

6.3a   Know . . . the key terminology associated with cognitive and observational learning.

imitation
latent learning
observational learning

6.3b   Understand . . . the concept of latent learning and its relevance to cognitive aspects of learning.

Without being able to observe learning directly, it might seem as if no learning occurs. However, Tolman and Honzik showed that rats can form cognitive maps of their environment. They found that even when no immediate reward was available, rats still learned about their environment.

6.3c   Apply . . . principles of observational learning outside of the laboratory.

Apply Activity

Based on what you read about in this module, how would you use observational learning in each of these settings?

1. Teaching children how to kick a soccer ball
2. Improving efficiency in a busy office
3. Improving environmental sustainability at a university

Are you simply letting people observe your behaviour, or does your plan involve elements learned in other modules in this chapter (e.g., shaping)?

6.3d   Analyze . . . the claim that viewing violent media increases violent behaviour.

Psychologists agree that observational learning occurs and that media can influence behaviour. Many studies show a correlational (noncausal) relationship between violent media exposure and aggressive behaviour. Also, experimental studies, going all the way back to Albert Bandura's work in the 1960s, indicate that exposure to violent media can at least temporarily increase aggressive behaviour.

Chapter 7

Memory

7.1 Memory Systems

- The Atkinson-Shiffrin Model   272
  Working the Scientific Literacy Model: Distinguishing Short-Term from Long-Term Memory Stores   276
- Module 7.1a Quiz   278
- The Working Memory Model: An Active STM System   279
- Module 7.1b Quiz   281
- Long-Term Memory Systems: Declarative and Nondeclarative Memories   282
- Module 7.1c Quiz   283
- The Cognitive Neuroscience of Memory   283
- Module 7.1d Quiz   286
- Module 7.1 Summary   287

7.2 Encoding and Retrieving Memories

- Encoding and Retrieval   289
  Working the Scientific Literacy Model: Context-Dependent Memory   291
- Module 7.2a Quiz   295
- Emotional Memories   295
- Module 7.2b Quiz   297
- Forgetting and Remembering   298
- Module 7.2c Quiz   300
- Module 7.2 Summary   301

7.3 Constructing and Reconstructing Memories

- How Memories Are Organized and Constructed   303
  Working the Scientific Literacy Model: How Schemas Influence Memory   303
- Module 7.3a Quiz   305
- Memory Reconstruction   306
- Module 7.3b Quiz   311
- Module 7.3 Summary   312

Module 7.1 Memory Systems

Jsemeniuk/E+/Getty Images

Learning Objectives

7.1a Know . . . the key terminology of memory systems.

7.1b Understand . . . which structures of the brain are associated with specific memory tasks and how the brain changes as new memories form.

7.1c Apply . . . your knowledge of the brain basis of memory to predict what types of damage or disease would result in which types of memory loss.

7.1d Analyze . . . the claim that humans have multiple memory systems.

In October 1981, an Ontario man lost control of his motorcycle and flew off an exit ramp west of Toronto. He suffered a severe head injury and required immediate brain surgery in order to treat the swelling caused by the impact. Brain scans conducted after the accident showed extensive damage to the temporal lobes (including the hippocampus) as well as to both frontal lobes and the left occipital lobe. When the man, now known as patient K.C., recovered consciousness, doctors quickly noted that he had severe memory impairments. However, when psychologists from the University of Toronto dug deeper into K.C.'s condition, it became clear that he had retained some memory for general knowledge, but had lost his episodic memory, the memory of his specific experiences (Tulving et al., 1988). Strikingly, K.C. could recall the facts about his life (e.g., where he lived) but could not recall his personal experiences or feelings relating to those facts (e.g., sitting on the steps with friends).

K.C.'s devastating experience helped researchers prove that we have several different types of memory, each involving different networks of brain areas (Rosenbaum et al., 2005). His case also hearkens back to a philosophical question posed by William James (1890/1950) over a century ago: If an *individual were to awaken one day with his or her personal memories erased, would he or she still be the same person?*

Focus Questions

1. How is it possible to remember just long enough to have normal conversations and activities but then to forget them almost immediately?

2. How would damage to different brain areas affect different types of memory?

≫ You have probably heard people talk about memory as if it were a single ability:

- I have a terrible memory!

- Isn't there some way I could improve my memory?

But have you ever heard people talk about memory as if it were several abilities?

- One of my memories works well, but the other is not so hot.

271

Probably not. However, as you will learn in this module, *memory* is actually a collection of several systems that store information in different forms for differing amounts of time (Atkinson & Shiffrin, 1968). One influential model for understanding these different systems, and the different types of memories they involve, can be seen in Figure 7.1.

The Atkinson-Shiffrin Model

In the 1960s, Richard Atkinson and Richard Shiffrin reviewed what psychologists knew about memory at that time and constructed the memory model that bears their name (see Figure 7.1). The first thing to notice about the Atkinson-Shiffrin model is that it includes three memory stores (Atkinson & Shiffrin, 1968). **Stores** *retain information in memory without using it for any specific purpose*; they essentially serve the same purpose as hard drives serve for a computer. The three stores include sensory memory, short-term memory (STM), and long-term memory (LTM), which we will investigate in more detail later. In addition, **control processes** *shift information from one memory store to another*. These are represented by the arrows in the model in Figure 7.1.

An important point illustrated in Figure 7.1 is that our memory systems, although stunningly powerful, are not perfect. We lose, or forget, information at each step of this model. Information enters the sensory memory store through all of the senses (e.g., vision, hearing, etc.), and the control process we call **attention** *selects which information*

Figure 7.1 The Atkinson-Shiffrin Model

Memory is a multistage process. Information flows through a brief sensory memory store into short-term memory, where rehearsal encodes it into long-term memory for permanent storage. Memories are retrieved from long-term memory and brought into short-term storage for further processing.

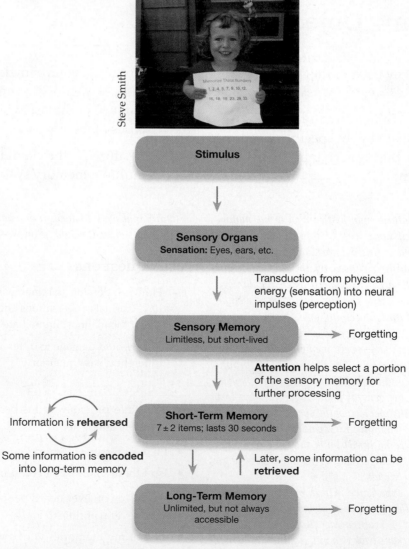

Source: Based on "Human Memory: A Proposed System and Its Control Processes" by in *The Psychology of Learning and Motivation: Advances in Research and Theory*, Vol 2 (pp. 89–195).

will be passed on to STM. This is highly functional: the attention process selects some elements of our environment that will receive further processing and add to our experience and understanding of the world. However, this functionality comes at a cost, because a vast amount of sensory information is quickly forgotten, almost immediately replaced by new input. We selectively narrow the information we receive in STM even further through **encoding**, *the process of storing information in the LTM system.* We retain only some information and lose the rest. **Retrieval** *brings information from LTM back into STM;* this happens when you become aware of existing memories, such as remembering the movie you saw last week. Of course, this process is not perfect—we are sometimes unable to retrieve information when we want to. But, overall, our ability to retrieve information is astonishing. This interplay between remembering and forgetting is a theme that extends across all of the modules in this chapter. In this module, we are primarily concerned with the various types of memory stores, so we will examine each one in detail.

SENSORY MEMORY "What did I just say to you?" This sentence rarely leads to good things. It is generally spoken when one person in a conversation (e.g., a relationship partner) is apparently not paying attention to what another person (e.g., the other relationship partner) is saying. Individuals on the receiving end of this sentence often experience anxiety, if not a sense of doom. Luckily, we have a memory store that can sometimes come to the rescue.

Sensory memory *is a memory store that accurately holds perceptual information for a very brief amount of time*—how brief depends on which sensory system we talk about. **Iconic memory**, *the visual form of sensory memory,* is held for about one-half to one second. **Echoic memory**, *the auditory form of sensory memory,* is held for considerably longer, but still only for about 5–10 seconds (Cowan et al., 1990). It is this form of sensory memory that will allow you to repeat back the words you just heard, even though you may have been thinking about something else.

How much information can be held in sensory memory? This important question has proven very difficult to answer, because sensory memories—particularly visual memories—disappear faster than an individual can report them. George Sperling (1960) devised a brilliant method for testing the storage capacity of iconic memory. In his experiment, researchers flashed a grid of letters on a screen for a fraction of a second (Figure 7.2a), and participants were asked to report what they saw. In the *whole report* condition, participants attempted to recall as many of the letters as possible—the *whole* screen. Participants were generally able to report only three or four of the letters, and these would usually be in the same line. But does this mean that the iconic sensory memory system can only store three or four bits of information at a time? Sperling

Figure 7.2 A Test of Iconic Sensory Memory

Sperling's participants viewed a grid of letters flashed on a screen for a split second, then attempted to recall as many of the letters as possible. In the whole report condition (a), they averaged approximately four items, usually from a single row. However, in the partial report condition (b), participants could usually name *any* row of four items, depending on the row they were cued to recite. This indicated that participants' iconic memory system could store far more than the mere four items they were able to report.

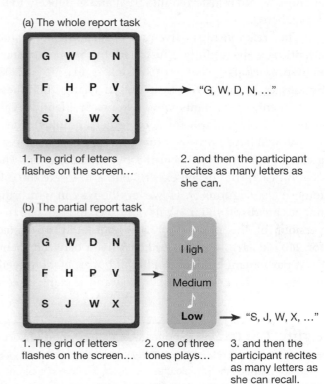

(a) The whole report task

1. The grid of letters flashes on the screen...

2. and then the participant recites as many letters as she can.

(b) The partial report task

1. The grid of letters flashes on the screen...

2. one of three tones plays...

3. and then the participant recites as many letters as she can recall.

thought that it likely had a larger capacity, but hypothesized that the memory of the letters actually faded faster than participants could report them. To test this, in the *partial report* condition, participants were again flashed a set of letters on the screen, but the display was followed immediately by a tone that was randomly chosen to be low, medium, or high (Figure 7.2b). After hearing the tone, participants were to report the corresponding line of letters—bottom, middle, or top. Under these conditions, participants still reported only three or four of the letters, but they reported them from the row indicated by the tone. Because the tone came after the screen went blank, the only way the participants could get the letters right is if all of the letters were (temporarily) stored in sensory memory. Thus Sperling argued that iconic memory could hold all 12 letters as a mental image, but that they would only remain in sensory memory long enough for a few letters to be reported.

But if information in our sensory memory disappears after half a second, then how can we have any continuous perceptions? How can you stare meaningfully into someone's eyes without that person fading away from memory half a second after you look away, just like the letters in Sperling's experiment? The answer is attention. Attention allows us to move a small amount of the information from our sensory memory into STM for further processing. This information is often referred to as being within the "spotlight of attention" (Pashler, 1998). Information that is outside of this spotlight of attention is not transferred into STM and is unlikely to be remembered.

The relationship between sensory memory and attention is beautifully illustrated by a phenomenon known as *change blindness* (Rensink et al., 1997, 2000; Simons & Levin, 1997). In a typical change blindness experiment, participants view two nearly identical versions of a photograph (or some other stimulus); these stimuli will have only one difference between them (e.g., a car is different colours in the two photographs). The goal on each trial of the experiment is to locate the difference (see Figure 7.3). However, the way in which the images are displayed presents quite a challenge. The two versions of the photograph are alternately presented for 240 ms each, with a blank screen in between them. So, a participant would see Photograph 1, blank screen, Photograph 2, blank screen, Photograph 1, blank screen,

and so on. If the item that differs between the two photographs (e.g., the car) is not the focus of attention, people generally fail to notice the change (hence the term *change blindness*). This is likely because the appearance of the blank screen in between the two photographs occupies sensory memory, thus making the memory of the previous photograph less accessible. However, if the participant is paying attention to that changing element (i.e., the "spotlight" of attention is focused on that part of the image), the image of the first version of that item will be transferred into STM when the second, changed version appears on the screen. The difference between the two photographs then becomes apparent.

An obvious question that arises is: Why don't people quickly move their spotlight of attention around so that they can transfer all of their sensory memory into short-term memory? Unfortunately, there is a limit to how much information can be transferred at once (Marois & Ivanoff, 2005).

SHORT-TERM MEMORY AND THE MAGICAL NUMBER 7
Although transferring information from sensory memory into short-term memory increases the chances that this information will be remembered later, it is not guaranteed. This is because **short-term memory (STM)** is *a memory*

Figure 7.3 Change Blindness, Attention, and Sensory Memory

In change blindness, the sensory memory of photograph A disappears before the onset of photograph B, making it difficult to identify the difference between the two pictures. However, if a person is paying attention to the area that differs between the two photographs, then the representation of that part of the first photograph will still be in short-term memory when the second photograph appears, thus making it relatively easy to spot the change. In this example, part of a tree branch disappears in photograph B.

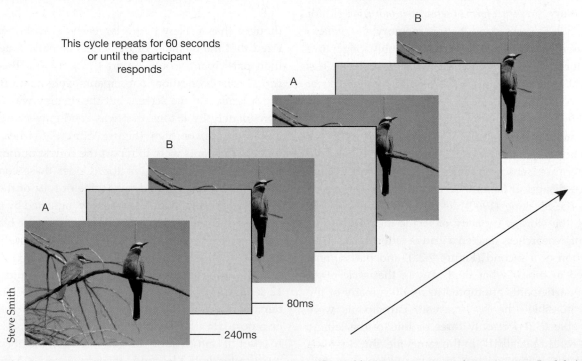

Source: Based on Rensink, R. A., O'Regan, J. K., & Clark, J. J. (1997). To see or not to see: The need for attention to perceive changes in scenes. *Psychological Science, 8,* 368–373. (Figure 1, p. 369).

store with limited capacity and duration (approximately 30 seconds). The capacity of STM was summed up by one psychologist as *The Magical Number Seven, Plus or Minus Two* (Miller, 1956). In his review, Miller found study after study in which participants were able to remember seven units of information, give or take a couple. One researcher made the analogy between STM and a juggler who can keep seven balls in the air before dropping any of them. Similarly, STM can rehearse only seven units of information at once before forgetting something (Nairne, 1996).

This point leads to an important question: What, exactly, is "a unit of information"? The answer is not as straightforward as one might expect. It turns out that, whenever possible, we expand our memory capacity with **chunking**, *organizing smaller units of information into larger, more meaningful units.* These larger units are referred to as *chunks.* Consider these examples:

1. O B T N C H C V N T C N S N C
2. C B C H B O C T V T S N C N N

If we randomly assigned one group of volunteers to remember the first list, and another group to remember the second list, how would you expect the two groups to compare? Look carefully at both lists. List 2 is easier to remember than list 1. Volunteers reading list 2 have the advantage of being able to apply patterns that fit their background knowledge; specifically, they can chunk these letters into five groups based on popular television networks:

1. CBC HBO CTV TSN CNN

In this case, chunking reduces 15 bits of information to a mere five. We do the same thing with phone numbers. We turn the area code (236) into one chunk, the first three numbers (555) into another chunk, and then the final four numbers into one or two chunks depending upon the numbers (e.g., 1867 might be one chunk because it can be remembered as the year Canada became a country, while 8776 could be remembered as two chunks representing the jersey numbers for hockey players Sidney Crosby and P. K. Subban or, if you're not a hockey fan, some other meaningful pattern).

The ability to chunk material varies from situation to situation. If you had never watched television, then the five chunks of information in the example above wouldn't be very meaningful to you. This suggests that experience or expertise plays a role in our ability to chunk large amounts of information so that it fits into our STM. Studies of chess experts have confirmed that this is the case. Whereas most people would memorize the positions of chess pieces on a board individually, chess masters perceive it as a single unit, like a photograph of a scene (Chase & Simon, 1973; Gobet & Simon, 1998). Therefore, they are able to remember the positions of significantly more chess pieces than novices can. Of course, chunking only works when the chess pieces are aligned in meaningful chess positions; when they are randomly placed on the board, the experts' memory advantage disappears (see Figure 7.4). Chunking also allows the chess masters to envision what the board will look like after future moves, again providing them with an edge over novices.

Importantly, this expertise is not necessarily based on some innate talent; it can be learned through intensive practice. The most stunning confirmation of this view comes from the Polgár sisters of Budapest, Hungary (Flora, 2005). Their father, Lázló Polgár, decided before they were born that he was going to raise them to become chess grandmasters. Doing so would confirm his belief that anyone could be trained to become a world-class expert in any field if he or she worked hard enough (he was not a grandmaster himself). Polgár trained his daughters in the basics of chess, and had them memorize games so that they could visualize each move on the board. After thousands of hours of what amounts to "chunking training," the girls (who, luckily, enjoyed chess) rose to the top of the chess world. The eldest daughter, Susan, became the first female to earn the title of Grandmaster through tournament play. The youngest daughter, Sofia, is an International Master. The middle daughter, Judit, is generally thought of as the best female chess player in history.

LONG-TERM MEMORY Not all of the information that enters STM is retained. A large proportion of it is lost forever. This isn't necessarily a bad thing, however. Imagine if every piece of information you thought about remained accessible in your memory. Your mind would be filled with phone numbers, details from text messages, images from billboards and ads on buses, as well as an incredible amount of trivial information from other people (e.g., overhearing the coffee order of the person in front of you). Instead, only a small amount of information from STM is encoded or transformed into a more permanent representation that we can intentionally access later on. Encoding allows information to enter the final memory store in the Atkinson-Shiffrin model. This store, **long-term memory (LTM)**, *holds information for extended periods of time, if not permanently.* Unlike short-term memory, long-term memory has no capacity limitations (that we are aware of). All of the information that undergoes encoding will be entered into LTM.

Once entered into LTM, the information needs to be organized. Researchers have identified at least two ways in which this organization occurs. One way is based on the semantic categories that the items belong to (Collins & Loftus, 1975). The mental representation of *cat* would be connected to and stored near the mental representation of other animals such as *dog* and *mouse.* This model is consistent with the results from an interesting experiment from the 1950s. Participants were asked to remember a list of 60 words that were drawn from four different

Figure 7.4 Chunking in Chess Experts

Chess experts have superior STM for the locations of pieces on a chess board due to their ability to create STM chunks. This advantage only occurs when the pieces are placed in a meaningful way, as they would appear in a game. (a) A depiction of a board with the pieces placed as they would appear in a game (left) and pieces placed in random locations (right). (b) The difference in STM for meaningful vs. randomly placed pieces increased as a function of the test subject's chess experience.

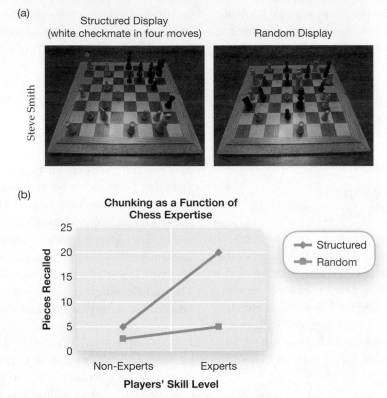

Source: Based on Gobet, F., Lane, P. C. R., Croker, S., Cheng, P. C. H., Jones, G., Oliver, I., and Pine, J. M. (2001). Chunking mechanisms in human learning. *TRENDS in Cognitive Sciences*, 5(6), 236–243. (Figure 1, p. 237).

categories. Although the words were randomly presented, participants recalled them in semantically related groups (e.g., lion, tiger, cheetah . . . guitar, violin, cello, etc.). This research suggests that semantically related items are stored near each other in LTM (see Module 8.1). A second way that LTM is organized is based on the sounds of the word and on how the word looks. This explains part of the **tip-of-the-tongue (TOT) phenomenon**, *when you are able to retrieve similar sounding words or words that start with the same letter but can't quite retrieve the word you actually want* (Brown & McNeil, 1966). What appears to be happening in these situations is that nearby items, or nodes, in your neural network are activated.

Of course, having the information in LTM doesn't necessarily mean that you can access it when you want to. If that were the case, then you would never forget where you put your keys, and no one would be impressed by your knowledge of pop culture trivia. Instead, the likelihood that a given piece of information will undergo retrieval—the process of accessing memorized information and returning it to short-term memory—is influenced by

a number of different factors including the quality of the original encoding and the strategies used to retrieve the information. These important processes are described in depth later in this chapter.

Working the Scientific Literacy Model

Distinguishing Short-Term from Long-Term Memory Stores

The Atkinson-Shiffrin model of memory is very neat and tidy, with different memory stores contained in separate boxes. The problem is that the real world rarely involves 30-second blocks of time filled with 7 ± 2 pieces of information followed by a short break to encode them. Instead, we are often required to use both STM and LTM at the same time. Without this ability, we wouldn't be able to have conversations, nor would we be able to understand paragraphs of text like this one. So, if both STM and LTM are constantly working together, how do we isolate the functions of each memory store?

Figure 7.5 The Serial Position Effect

Memory for the order of events is often superior for original items (the primacy effect) and later items (the recency effect). The serial position effect provides evidence of distinct short-term and long-term memory stores.

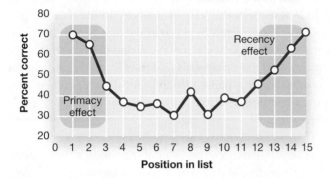

Figure 7.6 Proactive and Retroactive Interference Contribute to the Serial Position Effect

Sam was asked to remember a list of 10 words: happy, train, carrot, water, bus, sky, cat, candy, hike, telephone.

Happy, Train, Carrot, Water

Bus, Sky, Cat

Candy, Hike, Telephone

After hearing the first four words on the list, *proactive interference* made it difficult to remember additional information.

After hearing the last three words, *retroactive interference* made it difficult to remember the preceding words.

As a result, Sam could not recall the words in the middle of the list.

What do we know about short-term and long-term memory stores?

As you'll recall (thanks to your LTM), STM lasts for approximately 30 seconds and usually contains 7 ± 2 units of information; LTM has no fixed time limits or capacity. The distinction between STM and LTM can be revealed with a simple experiment. Imagine a group of people studied a list of 15 words and then immediately tried to recall the words in the list. The serial position curve—the U-shaped graph in Figure 7.5—shows what the results would look like according to the **serial position effect**: *In general, most people will recall the first few items from a list and the last few items, but only an item or two from the middle* (Ebbinghaus, 1885/1913). This finding holds true for many types of information, ranging from simple strings of letters to the ads you might recall after watching the Super Bowl (Laming, 2010; Li, 2010).

The first few items are remembered relatively easily (known as the *primacy effect*) because they have begun the process of entering LTM. The last few items are also remembered well (known as the *recency effect*); however, this is because those items are still within our STM (Deese & Kaufman, 1957). The fate of the items in the middle of the test is more difficult to determine, as they would be in the process of being encoded into LTM. As you have already read, some information is lost during this process.

How can science explain the difference between STM and LTM stores?

The shape of the serial position effect (see Figure 7.5) suggests that there are two different processes at work. But, how do we explain the dip in the middle of the curve? Memory researchers suggest that this dip in performance is caused by two different mechanisms. First, the items that were at the beginning of the list produce **proactive interference**, *a process in which the first information learned (e.g., in a list of*

words) occupies memory, leaving fewer resources left to remember the newer information. The last few items on the list create **retroactive interference**—that is, *the most recently learned information overshadows some older memories that have not yet made it into long-term memory* (see Figure 7.6). Together, these two types of interference would result in poorer memory performance for items in the middle of a list.

In addition to demonstrating behavioural differences between STM and LTM, scientists have also used neuroimaging to attempt to identify the different brain regions responsible for each form of memory. Deborah Talmi and colleagues (2005) at the University of Toronto performed an fMRI experiment in which they asked ten volunteers to study a list of 12 words presented one at a time on a computer screen. Next, the computer screen flashed a word and the participants had to determine whether the word was from their study list. The researchers were mostly concerned about the brain activity that occurred when the volunteers correctly recognized words. When volunteers remembered information from early in the serial position curve, the hippocampus was active (this area is associated with the formation of LTM, as you will read about later). By comparison, the brain areas associated with sensory information—hearing or seeing the words—were more active when people recalled items at the end of the serial position curve. Thus, the researchers believed they had isolated the effects of two different neural systems which, working simultaneously, produce the serial position curve.

Can we critically evaluate the distinction between STM and LTM?

In order to evaluate the idea that the serial-position effect is caused by two interacting memory systems, we need at least two types of tests. First, we need to find evidence that it is possible to change the performance on one test but not the other. Then we need to find medical cases in which brain damage affected one system, but not the other. Together, these findings would support the view that STM and LTM stores can be distinguished from each other.

The fact that it is possible to separately affect the primacy and recency effects was demonstrated in the 1950s and 1960s. When items on a list are presented quickly, it becomes more difficult to completely encode those items into long-term memory. The result is a reduction in the primacy effect; however, STM will still contain the most recently presented items, thus leaving the recency effect unchanged (Murdock, 1962). The recency effect can be reduced by inserting a delay between the presentation of the list and the test. This delay will allow other information to fill up STM; LTM, as shown by the primacy effect, will be unaffected (Bjork & Whitten, 1974).

Evidence from neurological patients also supports the distinction between STM and LTM. STM deficits can occur after damage to the lower portions of the temporal and parietal lobes, as well as to lateral (outside) areas of the frontal lobes (Müller & Knight, 2006). In contrast, damage to the hippocampus will prevent the transfer of memories from STM to LTM (Scoville & Milner, 1957). These patients will have relatively preserved memories of their past, but will be unable to add to them with new information from short-term memory.

Why is this relevant?

The idea of multiple memory stores is theoretically interesting and can explain some of the minor memory problems we all experience (e.g., forgetting parts of a phone number). But, being able to distinguish between STM and LTM has more wide-reaching implications. The fact that it is possible to separate STM and LTM—and that these stores are driven by different brain systems—suggests that you could use simple tests like the serial-position effect to predict where a neurological patient's brain damage had occurred. Many common assessment tools such as the Wechsler Memory Scales (Wechsler, 2009) include tests of both types of memory in order to do just that. Clues uncovered by these initial assessment tests can be used by emergency room physicians and neurologists to assist with their diagnosis and may lead them to request a brain scan for a patient (to look for damage) when they might not otherwise have done so.

The Atkinson-Shiffrin Model provides a very good introduction to the different stages of memory formation. However, memory is much more complex than is implied by this box-and-arrow diagram. There are many instances in which information that we didn't pay much attention to still seems to influence our later behaviour, suggesting that this information entered our memory without us putting effort into encoding it. For instance, children learn new languages and mimic the behaviours of those around them (i.e., exhibit observational learning) without being able to articulate how or why they do it. Additionally, brain-imaging studies have shown that both encoding and retrieval involve complex networks of interacting brain structures. Throughout the rest of this module, we will move beyond the Atkinson-Shiffrin Model to examine more complex and nuanced aspects of human memory. In the next section, we will discuss working memory, a sophisticated form of STM that involves a number of different, complementary, pieces.

Module 7.1a Quiz:

The Atkinson-Shiffrin Model

Know . . .

1. Which elements of memory do not actually store information, but instead describe how information may be shifted from one type of memory to another?
   A. Serial position processes
   B. Recency effects
   C. Primacy effects
   D. Control processes

2. _____ lasts less than a second, whereas _____ holds information for extended periods of time, if not permanently.
   A. Sensory memory; short-term memory
   B. Short-term memory; sensory memory
   C. Sensory memory; long-term memory
   D. Long-term memory; process memory

Apply . . .

3. Chris forgot about his quiz, so he had only 5 minutes to learn 20 vocabulary words. He went through the list once, waited a minute, and then went through the list again in the same order.

Although he felt confident, his grade indicated that he missed approximately half of the words. Which words on the list did he most likely miss, and why?
   A. According to the primacy effect, he would have missed the first few words on the list.
   B. According to the recency effect, he would have missed the last few words on the list.
   C. According to the serial position effect, most of the items he missed were probably in the middle of the list.
   D. According to the primacy effect, he would have missed all of the words on the list.

Analyze . . .

4. Brain scans show that recently encountered items are processed in one area of the brain, whereas older items are stored in a different area. Which concept does this evidence support?
   A. Multiple memory stores
   B. A single memory store
   C. Complex control processes
   D. Retrieval

The Working Memory Model: An Active STM System

Imagine you are driving a car when you hear the announcement for a radio contest—*the 10th caller at 1-800-555-HITS will win an all-expenses paid trip to Costa Rica!* As the DJ shouts out the phone number, panic sets in. You desperately want this prize, but you're driving—and traffic is swarming. What do you do? As you try to pull over to the side of the road as quickly as you can, you will probably try to remember the number by using **rehearsal**, *or repeating information* (in this case, the number) *until you do not need to remember it anymore*. Psychological research, however, demonstrates that remembering is much more than just repeating words to yourself (see Module 7.2). Instead, keeping information like the radio station's phone number available is an active process that is much more complex than one would expect.

According to the Atkinson-Shiffrin model of memory, you would attempt to retain the phone number in STM, possibly transferring it to LTM. This process would go smoothly if no other information entered STM, and if traffic cooperated so that you didn't really have to attend to anything other than the phone number. Of course, the world is rarely that simple. Indeed, in the 1970s, psychologists led by Alan Baddeley suggested that a slightly more complex model of memory was required, one that better explained how memory relates to our moment-to-moment conscious experiences (Baddeley & Hitch, 1974). The result was a theory of **working memory**, *a model of short-term remembering that includes a combination of memory components that can temporarily store small amounts of information for a short period of time.*

A key feature of working memory is that it recognizes that stimuli are encoded simultaneously in a number of different ways, rather than simply as a single unit of information. Indeed, the classic working memory model for short-term remembering can be subdivided into three storage components (Figure 7.7), each of which has a specialized role (Baddeley, 2001; Jonides et al., 2005): the phonological loop, the visuospatial sketchpad, and the episodic buffer. In the example above, the auditory information from the DJ needs to be remembered so that you can win the trip to Costa Rica (phonological loop). Visual information needs to be remembered so that you can keep track of the traffic patterns while you drive (visuospatial sketchpad). And, while you are juggling these bits of information, you are also linking them together into a mental narrative or story about how you had to pull your car over to try to win an exotic vacation (episodic buffer). These storage components are then coordinated by a control centre known as the *central executive*. The central executive helps decide which of the working-memory stores is most important at any given moment (e.g., remembering the phonological information of the phone number). It can also draw from older information that is stored in a relatively stable way to help organize or make sense of the new information.

As you can see, working memory provides a more nuanced model of short-term memory processes than the Atkinson-Shiffrin model (Cowan, 2008). But is all this additional complexity necessary? Below, we will discuss this model in more detail and show how various research findings support this more complex understanding of memory.

Figure 7.7 Components of Working Memory Work Together to Manage Complex Tasks

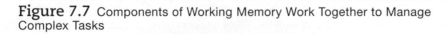

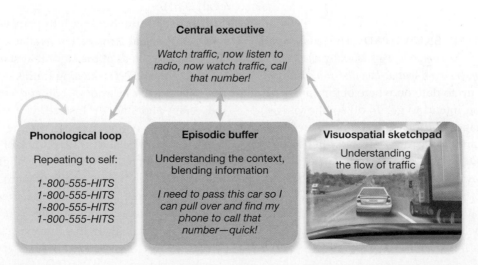

THE PHONOLOGICAL LOOP The **phonological loop** *is a storage component of working memory that relies on rehearsal and that stores information as sounds, or an auditory code.* It engages some portions of the brain that specialize in speech and hearing, and it can be very active without affecting memory for visual and spatial information. At first glance, it appears similar to the STM store of the Atkinson-Shiffrin model; however, a simple experiment will show you how it differs. Earlier in this module, you read about the magical number 7, the finding that the capacity of STM is generally 7 ± 2 items. However, research into the *word-length effect* has shown that people remember more one-syllable words (*sum, pay, bar, . . .*) than four- or five-syllable words (*helicopter, university, alligator, . . .*) in a short-term-memory task (Baddeley et al., 1975). Psychologists have found that working memory can only store as many syllables as can be rehearsed in about two seconds, and that this information is retained for approximately 15 to 30 seconds (Brown, 1958; Peterson & Peterson, 1959). So, in the radio-contest example, you would likely be able to remember the phone number (it can be spoken in under two seconds), but you would need to pull over to use your phone fairly quickly, before the information started to fade away.

Some readers might wonder how the word-length effect and chunking (discussed earlier in this module) can both affect memory. According to early models of chunking, long words like *helicopter* and *alligator* and short words like *bar* and *pay* would all be one chunk, whereas the word-length effect suggests that fewer long words would be remembered. Which view is correct? As it turns out, both *can* be correct, depending upon how memory is tested. If participants are allowed to recall information in any order, chunking appears to be an important factor. If participants have to recall the information in a particular order, then the length of the stimuli limits memory (Chen & Cowan, 2005). In the case of remembering the phone number of the radio station in our example, the order of the numbers would obviously be a critical factor.

THE VISUOSPATIAL SKETCHPAD The **visuospatial sketchpad** *is a storage component of working memory that maintains visual images and spatial layouts in a visuospatial code.* It keeps you up to date on where objects are around you and where you intend to go. To do so, the visuospatial sketchpad engages portions of the brain related to perception of vision and space and does not affect memory for sounds. Just as the phonological store can be gauged at several levels—that is, in terms of the number of syllables, the number of words, or the number of chunks—items stored in visuospatial memory can be counted based on visual features such as shape, colour, and texture. This

Figure 7.8 Working Memory Binds Visual Features into a Single Chunk

Working memory sometimes stores information such as shape, colour, and texture as three separate chunks, like the three pieces of information on the left. For most objects, however, it stores information as a single chunk, like the box on the right.

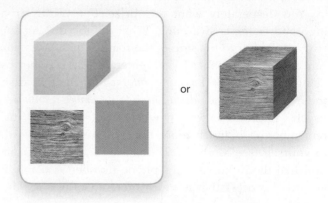

leads to an important question: How are these different visual features processed by the visuospatial sketchpad? Do different types of features (e.g., colour vs. shape) get stored separately, or are they integrated into one "chunk"? For example, would a smooth, square-shaped, red block count as one chunk, or three? Research has consistently shown that a square-shaped block painted in two colours is just as easy to recognize as the same-shaped block painted in one colour (Vogel et al., 2001). Therefore, visuospatial working memory may use a form of chunking. This process of combining visual features into a single unit goes by a different name, however: *feature binding* (see Figure 7.8).

After visual feature binding, visuospatial memory can accurately retain approximately four whole objects, regardless of how many individual features one can find on those objects. Perhaps this is evidence for the existence of a second magical number—four (Awh et al., 2007; Vogel et al., 2001).

To put feature binding into perspective, consider the amount of visual information available to you when you are driving a car, as in the story that started this section. If you are at the wheel, watching traffic, you probably would not look at a car in front of you and remember images of red, shiny, and smooth. Instead, you would simply have these features bound together in the image of the car, and you would be able to keep track of three or four such images without much problem as you glance at the speedometer and then back to the traffic around you. It is also possible that you might group together several cars into one visual chunk (e.g., the six cars you can see directly in front of you); it is likely that our expertise with situations will allow us to alter the size of the chunks in this component of working memory.

THE EPISODIC BUFFER Recent research suggests that working memory also includes an **episodic buffer**—that is, *a storage component of working memory that combines the images and sounds from the other two components into coherent, story-like episodes*. These episodes allow you to organize or make sense of the images and sounds, such as "I was driving to a friend's house when I heard the radio DJ give a number to call."

The episodic buffer is the most recently hypothesized working memory system (Baddeley, 2001). It seems to hold 7 to 10 pieces of information, which may be combined with other memory stores. This aspect of its operation can be demonstrated by comparing memory for prose (words strung into sentences) to memory for unrelated words. When people are asked to read and remember meaningful prose, they usually remember 7 to 10 *more* words than when reading a random list of unrelated words. Some portion of working memory is able to connect the prose with information found in LTM ("knowledge") to increase memory capacity.

THE CENTRAL EXECUTIVE Finally, working memory includes one component that is not primarily used for storing information. Instead, the **central executive** *is the control centre of working memory; it coordinates attention and the exchange of information among the three storage components*. It does so by examining what information is relevant to the person's goals, interests, and prior knowledge and then focusing attention on the working memory component whose information will be most useful in that situation. For example, when you see a series of letters from a familiar alphabet, it is easy to remember the letters by

rehearsing them in the phonological loop. In contrast, if you were to look at letters or characters from a foreign language, you may not be able to convert them to sounds; thus you would assign them to the visuospatial sketchpad instead (Paulesu et al., 1993). Regions within the frontal lobes of the brain are responsible for carrying out these tasks for the central executive.

WORKING MEMORY: PUTTING THE PIECES TOGETHER Thus far, we've talked about the different pieces of working memory as separate functions. In reality, however, these pieces would work together to influence what information you are able to remember. So how do these four components of the working-memory system work for you when you cannot pull your car over immediately to place the 10th call to win the trip to Costa Rica? Most of us would rely on our phonological loop, repeating the number 1-800-555-HITS to ourselves until we can call. Meanwhile, our visuospatial sketchpad is remembering where other drivers are in relation to our car, even as we look away to check the speedometer, the rearview mirror, or the volume knob. Finally, the episodic buffer binds together all this information into episodes, which might include information such as "I was driving to school," "the DJ announced a contest," and "I wanted to pull over and call the station." In the middle of all this activity is the central executive, which guides attention and ensures that each component is working on the appropriate task. So, if a bus suddenly changed lanes in front of you, the central executive would focus more on the visuospatial sketchpad until you were sure that you were safe; then it would again focus on the phonological loop. Thus, although your memories often seem almost automatic, there is actually a lot of work being performed by your working memory.

Module 7.1b Quiz:

The Working Memory Model: An Active STM System

Know . . .

1. Which of the following systems maintains information in memory by repeating words and sounds?

   A. Episodic buffer

   B. Central executive

   C. Phonological loop

   D. Visuospatial sketchpad

2. Which of the following systems coordinates attention and the exchange of information among memory storage components?

   A. Episodic buffer

   B. Central executive

   C. Phonological loop

   D. Visuospatial sketchpad

Apply . . .

3. When Nick looks for his friend's motorcycle in a parking lot, he sees a single object, not two wheels, a seat, and a red body. This is an example of _____.

   A. a phonological loop

   B. feature binding

   C. buffering

   D. proactive interference

Long-Term Memory Systems: Declarative and Nondeclarative Memories

Figure 7.1 at the beginning of this module suggests that humans have just one type of long-term memory (LTM). However, as you read in the story about the neurological patient K.C., LTM has a number of different components. K.C. could learn new skills, draw maps, and remember basic facts. Yet, he was unable to recall specific episodes in his own life (Tulving & Markowitsch, 1998). What do cases like K.C.'s tell us about the organization of LTM?

One way to categorize LTM is based on whether or not we are conscious of a given memory (see Figure 7.9). Specifically, **declarative memories** (or **explicit memories**) *are memories that we are consciously aware of and that can be verbalized, including facts about the world and one's own personal experiences*; an easy way to remember this is that declarative memories are, handily, about things we can *declare*. In contrast, **nondeclarative memories** (or **implicit memories**) *include actions or behaviours that you can remember and perform without awareness*; that is, these are memories about things that we cannot *declare*. But, this initial division only scratches the surface of LTM's complexity. Both declarative and nondeclarative memories have multiple subtypes, each with its own characteristics and brain networks.

DECLARATIVE MEMORY Declarative memory comes in two varieties (Tulving, 1972). **Episodic memories** *are declarative memories for personal experiences that seem to be organized around "episodes" and are recalled from a first-person ("I" or "my") perspective*. Examples of episodic memories would be your first day of university, the party you went to last month, and that time you remember watching the Olympics on TV. **Semantic memories**, on the other hand,

are *declarative memories that include facts about the world*. Examples of semantic memories would include knowing that Fredericton is the capital of New Brunswick, remembering that your mother's birthday is April 6th, and that bananas are (generally) yellow. The two types of memory can be contrasted in an example: Your semantic memory is your knowledge of what a bike is, whereas episodic memory is the memory of a specific time when you rode a bike. It is worth clarifying that both episodic and semantic memory representations *can* be active at the same time. If someone asks you, "Can you ride a bike?", you will likely think of both semantic information about bikes as well as episodic instances in which you rode one. But, there are also instances in which only one type of memory can be active, such as if someone asked you if you had ever piloted a space shuttle. The term "space shuttle" would activate semantic memory but, unless you are one of the ten Canadians who have been in space, it would not activate episodic memories of you flying through the atmosphere.

The case of K.C. provides compelling evidence that semantic and episodic memories are distinct forms of declarative memory. Although K.C. had no specific memories of events that took place in his high school or his house, he did understand that he had attended high school and that he lived in a specific home in Mississauga, ON. However, K.C. is not the only example of the distinction between these types of memory. Studies of older adults have noted that they show similar (but much less severe) impairments to K.C. on memory tests. As people get older, their episodic memory declines more rapidly than their semantic memory (Luo & Craik, 2008). Older people are more likely to forget going on vacation five years ago than they are to forget something like the names of provincial capitals (Levine et al., 2002). Interestingly, they also show

Figure 7.9 Varieties of Long-Term Memory

Long-term memory can be divided into different systems based on the type of information that is stored.

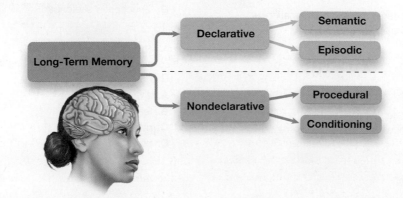

normal performance on a number of tests related to nondeclarative memories.

NONDECLARATIVE MEMORY Nondeclarative memory occurs when previous experiences influence performance on a task that does not require the person to intentionally remember those experiences (Graf & Schacter, 1985). The earliest published report of this form of memory came in 1845 when a British physician named Robert Dunn described the details of a woman with amnesia (Schacter, 1985). This woman learned how to make dresses following her injury, but had no conscious memory of learning to do so. A more pointed example was published in the early 20th century by Claparède (1911/1951). He reported on an amnesic woman who learned not to shake his hand because he had previously stuck her with a pin attached to his palm. In both cases, the behaviours of patients with no conscious memories were altered because of previous experiences, thus suggesting that this previous information was encoded into LTM in some form.

But, nondeclarative memories are not isolated to cases of amnesia. You have thousands of nondeclarative memories in your brain right now. However, these two historical examples provide nice examples of two common forms of nondeclarative memories. The example of a woman being able to sew dresses is an example of a **procedural memory**, a *pattern of muscle movements (motor memory)* such as how to walk, play piano, tie your shoes, or drive a car. We often don't think of the individual steps involved in these behaviours, yet we execute them flawlessly most of the time.

The patient learning not to shake hands with the physician who had a pin attached to his hand is an example of *classical conditioning*, when a previously neutral stimulus (e.g., the sound of a metronome) produces a new response (e.g., salivating) because it has a history of being paired with another stimulus that produces that response (e.g., food). Although these associations can sometimes be consciously recalled, this recollection is not necessary for conditioning to successfully take place (see Module 6.1).

Module 7.1c Quiz:

Long-Term Memory Systems: Declarative and Nondeclarative Memories

Know . . .

1. Memories learned without our awareness of them are known as _____.
   A. semantic memories
   B. episodic memories
   C. nondeclarative memories
   D. declarative memories

2. Memories that can be verbalized, whether they are about your own experiences or your knowledge about the world, are called _____.
   A. nondeclarative memories
   B. procedural memories
   C. conditioned memories
   D. declarative memories

Apply . . .

3. Mary suffered a head injury during an automobile accident and was knocked unconscious. When she woke up in a hospital the next day, she could tell that she was in a hospital room, and she immediately recognized her sister, but she had no idea why she was in the hospital or how she got there. Which memory system seems to be affected in Mary's case?
   A. Semantic memories
   B. Episodic memories
   C. Nondeclarative memories
   D. Working memories

The Cognitive Neuroscience of Memory

Many psychologists who are interested in memory examine it from a biological perspective, examining how the nervous system changes with the formation of new memories. To explore the cognitive neuroscience of memory, we will take a brief look at the neuronal changes that occur as memories are forming and strengthening, and will then examine the brain structures involved in long-term storage. Finally, we will use examples from studies of amnesia and other forms of memory loss to understand how our memory models fit with biological data.

MEMORY AT THE CELLULAR LEVEL Memory at the cellular level can be summed up in the following way: Cells that fire together, wire together. This idea was proposed in the 1940s by Canadian neuroscientist Donald Hebb. Specifically, he suggested that when neurons fire at the same time, it leads to chemical and physical changes in the neurons, making them more likely to fire together again in the future (Hebb, 1949). Later research proved Hebb correct, and demonstrated that changes occur across numerous brain cells as memories are forming, strengthening, and being stored (Lømo, 1966). This process, **long-term potentiation (LTP)**, *demonstrated that there is an enduring increase in connectivity and transmission of neural signals between nerve cells that fire together.*

Figure 7.10 The Hippocampus

The hippocampus resides within the temporal lobe and is critical for memory processes.

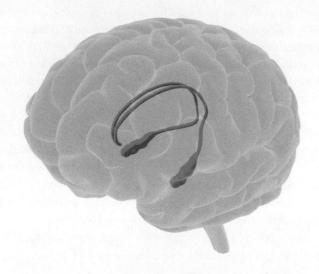

The discovery of LTP occurred when researchers electrically stimulated two neurons in a rabbit's hippocampus—a key memory structure of the brain located in an area called the medial temporal lobes (see Figure 7.10). Stimulation of the hippocampus increased the number of electrical potentials from one neuron to the other. Soon, the neurons began to generate *stronger* signals than before, a change that could last up to a few hours (Bliss & Lømo, 1973). This finding does not mean that LTP *is* memory—no one has linked the strengthening of a particular synapse with a specific memory like your first day of university. In fact, no one has seen LTP outside of a laboratory. But, the strengthening of synapses shown in LTP studies may be one of the underlying mechanisms that allow memories to form.

To see how such microscopic detail relates to memory, consider the very simple case of learning and remembering discussed in a previous module: eyeblink conditioning. Imagine you hear a simple tone right before a puff of air is blown in your eye; you will reflexively blink. After two or three pairings, just the tone will be enough to cause an eye blink—this is an example of classical conditioning (see Module 6.1). At the neural level, the tone causes a series of neurons to respond, and the puff of air causes another series of neurons to respond. With repeated tone and air puff pairings, the neurons that are involved in hearing the tone, and those that control the blinking response, develop a history of firing together. This simultaneous activation provides the opportunity for synapses to become strengthened, representing the first stages of memory.

This relationship is not permanent, however. Lasting memories require **consolidation**, *the process of converting short-term memories into long-term memories in the brain,*

which may happen at the level of small neuronal groups or across the cortex (Abraham, 2006). When neurons fire together a number of times, they will adapt and make the changes caused by LTP more permanent—a process called *cellular consolidation*. This process involves physical changes to the synapse between the cells so that the presynaptic cell is more likely to stimulate a *specific* postsynaptic cell (or group of cells). Without the consolidation process, the initial changes to the synapse (LTP) eventually fade away, and presumably so does the memory. (This process can therefore be summed up with the saying: Use it or lose it.) To demonstrate the distinction between the initial learning and longer-term consolidation, researchers administered laboratory rats a drug that allowed LTP, but prevented consolidation from occurring (by blocking biochemical actions). The animals were able to learn a task for a brief period, but they were not able to form long-term memories. By comparison, rats in the placebo group, whose brains were able to consolidate the information, went through the same tasks and formed long-term memories without any apparent problems (Squire, 1986).

The initial strengthening of synapses (LTP) and longer-term consolidation of these connections allow us to form new memories, thus providing us with an ability to learn and to adapt our behaviour based on previous experiences. However, these processes are not performed in all areas of the brain. Instead, specific structures and regions serve essential roles in allowing us to form and maintain our memories, a fact powerfully demonstrated by the memory deficits of patients with amnesia.

MEMORY, THE BRAIN, AND AMNESIA On August 31, 1953, Henry Molaison was a 27-year-old man with intractable epilepsy. Because his seizures could not be controlled by medications, Mr. Molaison had been referred to Dr. William Scoville, a respected Hartford-based neurosurgeon, for treatment. Dr. Scoville and his colleagues had suggested that removing the areas of Molaison's brain that triggered the seizures would cure, or at least tame, his epilepsy. On September 1, 1953, Henry Molaison underwent a resection (removal) of his medial temporal lobes—including the hippocampus—on both sides of his brain. After that day, he became known to the world as neurological patient H.M.

H.M.'s surgery was successful in that he no longer had seizures. However, as he recovered from his surgery, it became apparent that the procedure had produced some unintended consequences. The doctors quickly determined that H.M. had **amnesia**—*a profound loss of at least one form of memory*. However, not all of his memories were lost; in fact, numerous studies conducted by Brenda Milner of McGill University demonstrated that H.M. retained many forms of memory (Milner, 1962; Scoville & Milner, 1957). He was able to recall aspects of his childhood. He could also remember the names of the nurses who had treated him before the surgery, although he was unable to learn the names of nurses he met afterward. Indeed, H.M. appeared unable to encode new information at all. Therefore, H.M. was experiencing a specific subtype of amnesia known as **anterograde amnesia**, *the inability to form new memories for events occurring after a brain injury.*

H.M.'s anterograde amnesia was not due to problems with his sensory memory or his STM. Both abilities remained normal throughout his life (Corkin, 2002). He was also able to recall details of his past, such as incidents from his school years and from jobs he had held before his surgery; this demonstrates that his LTM was largely intact (Milner et al., 1968). He was also able to form new implicit memories—he was able to learn new skills such as drawing a picture by looking at its reflection in the mirror despite the fact that he had no memory for learning this skill (Milner, 1962). Similar improvements were found for solving puzzles (Cohen et al., 1985). After extensive testing, researchers concluded that H.M.'s amnesia was not due to problems with a particular memory store, but was instead due to problems with one of the control processes associated with those stores. Specifically, H.M. could not transfer declarative memories from STM into LTM.

The fact that H.M.'s brain damage was due to a precise surgical procedure (rather than to widespread damage from an accident like patient K.C.) allowed researchers to pinpoint the area of the brain responsible for this specific memory problem. H.M. was missing the medial temporal lobes of both hemispheres. This damage included the hippocampus and surrounding cortex as well as the amygdala. Based on H.M. and several similar cases, researchers concluded that this region of the brain must be involved with consolidating memories (see Figure 7.11), enabling information from STM to enter and remain in LTM, a process that most of us take for granted.

The hippocampus also appears to be essential for spatial memories such as remembering the layout of your house or recalling the route you would take to get to a friend's apartment. In fact, brain-imaging studies suggest that the size of a person's hippocampus can vary with the amount of spatial information that people are asked to consolidate. Researchers at King's College London (U.K.) examined the brains of taxi drivers in that maze-like city and compared them to the brains of age-matched control participants. The taxi drivers, who were required to undergo extensive training and to memorize most of London, had substantially larger hippocampi than did the control participants (Maguire et al., 2000). This result implies that the demanding memory requirements of that job altered the structure of brain areas related to memory consolidation and spatial memory.

STORED MEMORIES AND THE BRAIN It is important to note that our long-term memories do not just sit on a neurological shelf and collect dust after they have

Researchers in London found that the hippocampi of taxi drivers, who navigate the complex maze of the city, are larger than the hippocampi of non-taxi drivers (Maguire et al., 2000).

Figure 7.11 Damage to the Hippocampus: Disruption of Consolidation

When the hippocampus is damaged, the injury interferes with consolidation, the formation of long-term memories. Such damage does not prevent recall of pre-existing memories, however.

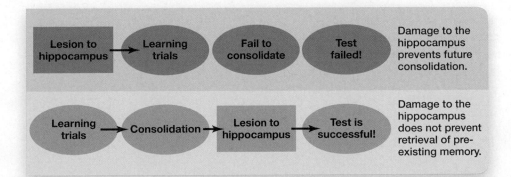

formed. Memory **storage** *refers to the time and manner in which information is retained between encoding and retrieval.* In other words, memory storage is an active process; stored memories can be updated regularly, such as when someone reminds you of an event from years ago, or when you are reminded of information you learned as a child. In this way, memories undergo a process called *reconsolidation,* in which the hippocampus functions to update, strengthen, or modify existing long-term memories (Lee, 2010; Söderlund et al., 2012). These memories then form networks in different regions of the cortex, where they can (sometimes) be retrieved when necessary. These long-term declarative memories are distributed throughout the cortex of the brain, rather than being localized in one region—a phenomenon known as *cross-cortical storage* (Paller, 2004). Interestingly, with enough use, some of the memory networks will no longer need input from the hippocampus. The cortical networks themselves will become self-sustaining. The more that memory is retrieved, the larger and more distributed that network will become.

Memories that were recently formed and have not had time to develop extensive cross-cortical networks are much more likely to be lost following a head injury than are older memories. Indeed, many people who have experienced a brain injury—including concussions—report that they cannot recall some of the events leading up to their accident. This type of memory deficit is known as **retrograde amnesia**, *a condition in which memory for the events preceding trauma or injury is lost* (see Figure 7.12).

Figure 7.12 Retrograde and Anterograde Amnesia

The term *amnesia* can apply to memory problems in both directions. It can wipe out old memories, and it can prevent consolidation of new memories.

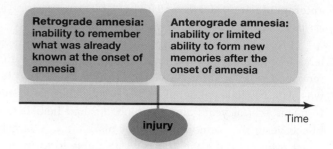

Despite what you might see on soap operas, the "lost time" is generally limited to the seconds or minutes leading up to the injury. The loss of extensive periods of time, as seen in K.C., is quite rare.

The fact that memories can be lost after even minor brain damage shows us that our memory systems are quite delicate. Each of the boxes and arrows in the Atkinson-Shiffrin model (Figure 7.1) can be disrupted in some way; but, the formation and storage of long-term memories seems to be particularly sensitive to injuries. K.C.'s devastating injury shows us that when we lose our memories, we lose an important part of ourselves. So be careful.

Module 7.1d Quiz:

The Cognitive Neuroscience of Memory

Know . . .

1. _____ is a process that all memories must undergo to become long-term memories.
   A. Consolidation
   B. Retrieval
   C. Amnesia
   D. Chunking

Understand . . .

2. Long-term potentiation can be described as
   A. a decrease in a neuron's electrical signalling.
   B. neurons generating stronger signals than before, which then persist.

   C. decreased neural networking.
   D. an example of working memory.

Apply . . .

3. Damage to the hippocampus is most likely to produce _____.
   A. retrograde amnesia
   B. consolidation
   C. anterograde amnesia
   D. seizures

Module 7.1 Summary

7.1a   Know ... the key terminology of memory systems:

amnesia
anterograde amnesia
attention
central executive
chunking
consolidation
control process
declarative (explicit) memory
echoic memory
encoding
episodic buffer
episodic memory
iconic memory
long-term memory (LTM)
long-term potentiation (LTP)
nondeclarative (implicit) memory
phonological loop
proactive interference
procedural memory
rehearsal
retrieval
retroactive interference
retrograde amnesia
semantic memory
sensory memory
serial position effect
short-term memory (STM)
storage
stores
tip-of-the-tongue (TOT) phenomenon
visuospatial sketchpad
working memory

7.1b   Understand ... which structures of the brain are associated with specific memory tasks and how the brain changes as new memories form.

The hippocampus is critical to the formation of new declarative memories. Long-term potentiation at the level of individual synapses between nerve cells is the basic mechanism underlying this process. Long-term memory stores are distributed across the cortex. Working memory likely utilizes the parts of the brain associated with visual and auditory perception, as well as the frontal lobes (for functioning of the central executive).

7.1c   Apply ... your knowledge of the brain basis of memory to predict what types of damage or disease would result in which types of memory loss.

Apply Activity

Try responding to these questions for practice:

1. Dr. Richard trains a rat to navigate a maze and then administers a drug that blocks the biochemical activity involved in long-term potentiation. What will happen to the rat's memory? Will it become stronger? Weaker? Or is it likely the rat will not remember the maze at all?
2. In another study, Dr. Richard removes a portion of the rat's hippocampus one week after it learns to navigate a maze. What will happen to the rat's memory? Will it become stronger? Weaker? Or will it be unaffected by the procedure?

7.1d   Analyze ... the claim that humans have multiple memory systems.

Consider all the evidence from biological and behavioural research, not to mention the evidence from amnesia. Data related to the serial position effect indicate that information at the beginning and end of a list is remembered differently, and even processed and stored differently in the brain. Also, evidence from amnesia studies suggests that LTM and STM can be affected separately by brain damage or disease. Most psychologists agree that these investigations provide evidence supporting the existence of multiple storage systems and control processes.

Module 7.2 Encoding and Retrieving Memories

Tkreykes/Fotolia

 ## Learning Objectives

7.2a Know . . . the key terminology related to forgetting, encoding, and retrieval.

7.2b Understand . . . how the type of cognitive processing employed can affect the chances of remembering what you encounter.

7.2c Apply . . . what you have learned to improve your ability to memorize information.

7.2d Analyze . . . whether emotional memories are more accurate than non-emotional ones.

According to legend, the first person to develop methods of improving memory was the Greek poet Simonides of Ceos (556–468 BCE). After presenting one of his lyric poems at a dinner party in northern Greece, the host, Scopas, told him that he was only going to pay half of the cost of the poem (he clearly wasn't impressed by the work). Soon after this exchange, a grumpy Simonides was told that two men on horses wanted to talk to him outside. While talking to the horsemen, the roof of Scopas' house collapsed, killing everyone inside (Greek legends are not happy places...). When relatives wanted to bury the family, they were unable to figure out who the remains belonged to; no one could recall where the family members had been sitting. Simonides had encoded the information differently than the rest of the guests; he was able to assist the family by creating a visual image of the dinner party and listing who was sitting in each chair. His story demonstrates one of the key points to be discussed in this module—that how you *encode information affects the likelihood of you remembering that information later.*

Focus Questions

1. What causes some memories to be strong while others are weak?

2. How can we improve our memory abilities?

>> Why are some memories easier to recall than others? Why do we forget things? How can you use memory research to improve your performance at school and at work? These questions are addressed in this module, where we focus on factors that influence the encoding and retrieval of memories.

Encoding and Retrieval

In its simplest form, memory consists of encoding new information, storing that information, and then retrieving that stored information at a later time. As discussed in Module 7.1, *encoding* is the process of transforming sensory and perceptual information into memory traces, and *retrieval* is the process of accessing memorized information in order to make use of it in the present moment. In between these two processes is the concept of *storage*, the time and manner in which information is retained between encoding and retrieval. Over the past fifty years, researchers have uncovered a number of factors that influence how our memory systems work, and also how we can improve our chances of remembering information. The most important of these factors appears to be how the information was encoded in the first place.

REHEARSAL: THE BASICS OF ENCODING What would you do if someone gave you the address for a house party but you didn't have a pen or your phone around? How would you keep the address in mind until you had a chance to write it down? If you're like most people, you will recite the address over and over again until you can write it down. This type of memorization is known as rehearsal to psychologists (although your teachers may have called it *learning by rote*), and it is something probably all of us have tried. Indeed, students often try to learn vocabulary terms by reading flashcards with key terms and definitions over and over. But is this strategy effective?

Certainly this approach works some of the time, but is it really the *most* effective way to remember? Unfortunately for all the cue-card-memorizing students out there, the answer is a resounding "no" (Craik & Watkins, 1973). The limitations of this form of rehearsal were shown in a sneaky experiment performed in the 1970s (see Figure 7.13); in this study, participants were asked to remember a four-digit number. After seeing the number, they were asked to repeat a single word until being prompted to report the number. The delay between the presentation of the number and the participants' responses varied from 2 to 18 seconds; this meant that the amount of time each word was repeated also varied. Because participants were trying to remember the digits, they barely paid attention to the word they repeated. Later, when the researchers surprised the participants by asking them to recall the distracting word they had repeated, they found virtually no relationship between the duration of rehearsal (between 2 and 18 seconds) and the proportion of individuals who could recall the word (Glenberg et al., 1977). In other words, longer rehearsal did not lead to better recall. This is not to say that repeating the word had no effect at all; rather, this study demonstrated that repeating information only had a small benefit, and that this benefit was not increased with longer rehearsal times.

It turns out that it is not *how long* we rehearse information, but rather *how* we rehearse it that determines the effectiveness of memory. Individuals in the study just described were engaged in **maintenance rehearsal**—*prolonging*

Figure 7.13 Rote Rehearsal Has Limited Effects on Long-Term Memory

After participants completed the procedure depicted in this figure, they were given a surprise test of their memory for the words that they had recited. There was no difference in the recall of words rehearsed for 2 or 18 seconds. This result suggests that simply repeating the word—maintenance rehearsal—has a limited effect on our memory.

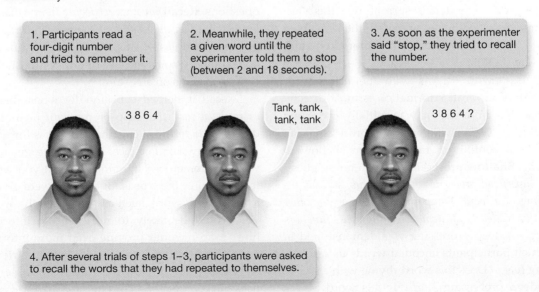

1. Participants read a four-digit number and tried to remember it.

2. Meanwhile, they repeated a given word until the experimenter told them to stop (between 2 and 18 seconds).

3. As soon as the experimenter said "stop," they tried to recall the number.

3 8 6 4

Tank, tank, tank, tank

3 8 6 4 ?

4. After several trials of steps 1–3, participants were asked to recall the words that they had repeated to themselves.

exposure to information by repeating it—which does relatively little to help the formation of long-term memories (although it is better than nothing). By comparison, **elaborative rehearsal**—*prolonging exposure to information by thinking about its meaning*—significantly improves the process of encoding (Craik & Tulving, 1975). For example, repeating the word *bottle,* and then imagining what a bottle looks like and how it is used, is an elaborative technique. In the story that began this module, Simonides used a form of elaborative rehearsal by not only memorizing a list of people at a table (Scopus, Constantine, Helena, etc.), but actively imagining the dinner table and thinking about where people were relative to each other.

Although maintenance rehearsal helps us remember for a very short time, elaborative rehearsal improves long-term learning and remembering. It is worth paying attention to this research and thinking about how it applies to your success as a student (a form of elaborative rehearsal of this information). Obviously, being a student involves encoding a large amount of information into your memory in a relatively small amount of time. Imagine how the two types of rehearsal may come into play in meeting the challenge of university-level learning. Students who simply memorize key terms and repeat the definitions largely fail to employ elaborative rehearsal, and are less likely to do well on an exam. The wise strategy is to try to elaborate on the material.

LEVELS OF PROCESSING Although we often find ourselves using maintenance rehearsal "in a pinch," we rarely use that strategy for information that we intend to remember much later. Instead, we focus on elaborative encoding, where additional sensory or semantic (meaning) information is associated with the to-be-remembered item. But, not all elaborative encoding is created equal. Instead, different types of elaborative encoding can produce markedly different levels of recall. The details surrounding this variability were first described by researchers at the University of Toronto, and led to a framework for memory known as *levels of processing* (LOP).

The LOP framework begins with the understanding that our ability to recall information is most directly related to how that information was initially processed (Craik & Lockhart, 1972). Differences in processing can be described as a continuum ranging from shallow to deep processing. **Shallow processing**, as you might guess, *involves more superficial properties of a stimulus, such as the sound or spelling of a word.* **Deep processing**, *on the other hand, is generally related to an item's meaning or its function.* The superiority of deep processing was demonstrated in a study in which participants encoded words using shallow processing (e.g., "Does this word rhyme with *dust?. . . TRUST*") or deep processing (e.g., "Is this word a synonym for *locomotive?. . .TRAIN*"). When given a surprise

memory test for the words, the differences ranged from recalling as few as 14% of the shallow words to 96% of the deeply processed words (Craik & Tulving, 1975). In essence, they were almost seven times more likely to recall a deeply processed word than one that was processed at only a shallow level. Importantly, such effects are limited to LTM; STM memory rates are unaffected by shallow or deep processing (Rose et al., 2010; Figure 7.14).

Similar effects have been found for another form of deep processing. The **self-reference effect** *occurs when you think about information in terms of how it relates to you or how it is useful to you; this type of encoding will lead to you remembering that information better than you otherwise would have* (Symons & Johnson, 1997). This outcome is not terribly surprising, but it is still helpful to think about when learning new material. The self-reference effect is one of the reasons why your psychology professor (and this textbook) tries to show you how psychological concepts relate to your life—linking a concept to "you" will help you remember it later.

Although encoding strategies clearly influence our ability to remember information later, they only tell part of the story. The conditions in which we attempt to retrieve information from memory can also affect whether or not that information will be recalled.

RETRIEVAL Once information is encoded—be it in a deep or shallow fashion—and stored in memory, the challenge is then to be able to retrieve that information when it is needed. There are two forms of intentional memory retrieval, both of which are familiar to long-suffering students like the readers of this textbook. **Recognition** *involves identifying a stimulus or piece of information when it is presented to you.* Examples of recognition memory would be identifying someone you know on the bus (or in a police lineup), or answering standard multiple-choice test questions. **Recall** *involves retrieving information when asked, but without that information being present during the retrieval process.* Examples of this would be describing a friend's appearance to someone else or answering short-answer or essay questions on an exam.

Recall is helped substantially when there are hints, or *retrieval cues*, that help prompt our memory. The more detailed the retrieval cue, the easier it is for us to produce the memory. For instance, if you were given a list of 30 words to remember, it is unlikely that you would be able to recall all of the words. But, if you were given a hint for a "forgotten" word, such as "gr—" for the word "grape," you would be likely to retrieve that information. The hint "grap-" would provide even more information than "gr—" and would lead to even better retrieval (Tulving & Watkins, 1975). However, life is not a series of word lists. Instead, retrieval cues in the real world often involve places, people, sights, and sounds—in other words, the

Figure 7.14 Levels of Processing Affect Long-Term Memory, but Not Working Memory

When tested immediately after studying words, levels of processing do not seem to affect memory. In contrast, when there is a gap between studying words and being tested, levels of processing are important. When words are encoded based on their meaning (semantics), they are better retained in long-term memory.

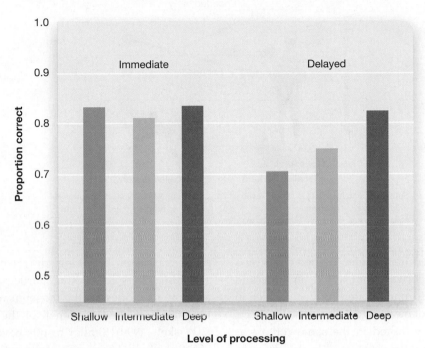

Source: Similarities and diferences between working memory and longterm memory: Evidence from the levels-of-processing span task. *Journal of Experimental Psychology: Learning, Memory, and Cognition*, 36 (2), 471–483.

environment or context in which you are trying to retrieve a memory. Researchers have found that *retrieval is most effective when it occurs in the same context as encoding,* a tendency known as the **encoding specificity principle** (Tulving & Thompson, 1973).

The encoding specificity principle can take many forms. It can include internal contexts such as mood and even whether a person is intoxicated or not. As you'll see in the next section, encoding specificity can also include external contexts such as the physical setting.

Working the Scientific Literacy Model

Context-Dependent Memory

One of the most intuitive forms of encoding specificity is **context-dependent memory**, *the idea that retrieval is more effective when it takes place in the same physical setting (context) as encoding.* But, what elements of the environment make up "context"? Is one sense (e.g., smell) enough to produce this effect? And, does context specificity affect all types of memory equally?

What do we know about context-dependent memory?

The initial demonstrations of context-dependent learning and memory used very simple cues: words. In such studies, participants learned pairs of words; some of the words might be associated with each other (e.g., *bark – dog*) and others might rhyme with each other (e.g., *worse – nurse*). A recall test for the second words in each pair (e.g., *dog* or *nurse*) generally led to respectable memory performance. However, performance improved when the original context (the first word of the word pair) was reinstated and could serve as a retrieval cue; the more information from the original context that was included, the better the level of retrieval (Tulving & Watkins, 1975).

Subsequent studies have focused on the role of environmental contexts on memory. In a classic study, members of a scuba club volunteered to memorize word lists—half of the test participants did so while diving 20 feet (6.7 m) underwater, and half did so while on land (Godden & Baddeley, 1975). After a short delay, the divers were tested again; however, some of the experimental participants had switched locations. This led to four test

Figure 7.15 Context-Dependent Learning

Divers who encoded information on land had better recall on land than underwater. Divers who encoded information underwater had the reverse experience, demonstrating better recall underwater than when on land.

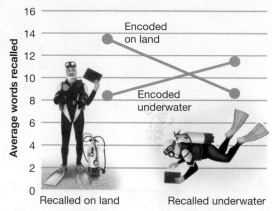

Source: Lilienfeld, Scott O.; Lynn, Steven J; Namy, Laura L.; Woolf, Nancy J., *Psychology: From Inquiry To Understanding*, 2nd Ed., © 2011. Reprinted and Electronically reproduced by permission of Pearson Education, Inc., New York, NY.

groups: trained and tested underwater, trained and tested on dry land, trained underwater but tested on land, and trained on land but tested underwater. As you can see in Figure 7.15, the results demonstrated that context affects memory. Those who were tested in the same context as where encoding took place (i.e., land–land or underwater–underwater) remembered approximately 40% more items than those who switched locations (i.e., land–underwater or underwater–land). Thus, both controlled laboratory studies and studies involving dramatic environmental manipulations have shown that matching the encoding and retrieval contexts leads to better recall of studied material.

How can science explain context-dependent memory?

Context-dependent memory clearly demonstrates that the characteristics of the environment can serve as retrieval cues for memory. In the Godden and Baddeley (1975) study above, the primary cue was likely the feeling of being underwater; however, diving also involves a change of lighting as well as the sounds of the breathing apparatus. In other words, when we encode information, we are also encoding information from a number of different senses (vision, hearing, touch, etc.). Presumably, each of these senses can help trigger memories. For instance, most of you have had the experience where an odour (e.g., cookies) instantly brings back memories (e.g., your grandmother's kitchen). This common phenomenon was tested in a clever experiment by researchers in the U.K. In this study, researchers tested whether memory for a Viking museum in York, U.K., could be enhanced if the memory test occurred in a room with a similar distinctive set of smells as the museum (burned wood, apples, garbage, beef, fish, rope/tar, and

earth . . . perhaps the Viking equivalent of Axe body spray). The researchers found that participants produced more accurate memories for the museum when the smell of the test room matched the smell of the museum (Aggleton & Waskett, 1999). Similar results have been found for the effect of smells on memory for word lists (Stafford et al., 2009). Context-dependent memory has also been found for the flavour of gum being chewed during encoding and retrieval (Baker et al., 2004) as well as for the amount of background noise when students are studying and taking a test (Grant et al., 1998). These results suggest that matching the physical and sensory characteristics of the encoding and retrieval environments affect memory, likely due to the retrieval cues provided by these attributes.

Brain-imaging studies have also provided evidence in favour of context-dependent memory. Studies using fMRI have found increased activity in the hippocampus and parts of the prefrontal cortex (part of the frontal lobes) when the retrieval conditions match the context in which the memory was encoded (Kalisch et al., 2006; Wagner et al., 1998). Activity in the right frontal lobes is particularly sensitive to context, likely because this region is known to be critical for the retrieval process (Tulving et al., 1994).

Can we critically evaluate this evidence?

Although there is evidence that context-dependent memory exists, there are some important limitations to these effects. First, not all types of memory are equally enhanced by returning a person to the context in which he or she encoded the to-be-remembered information. Recognition memory (e.g., multiple-choice questions) is not significantly helped by context; this is likely due to the fact that the presence of the item (e.g., a photograph or one of the options on a test question) serves as a very strong retrieval cue. Context does not add much above and beyond this cue (Fernández & Alonso, 2001). Recall, on the other hand, requires you to generate the to-be-remembered information without any external cues. In this case, returning to the encoding context could help prompt a memory. A second, and related, limitation of context-dependent memory is that not all types of information are equally affected. Information that is central to a memory episode (e.g., a person's face in a photograph or in a conversation) is generally unaffected by context. Peripheral information (e.g., the faces of people who were nearby when you were having a conversation) does seem to be enhanced when a person returns to the original context (Brown, 2003; Sutherland & Hayne, 2001). As a rule, when memory for information is quite good, context will have little effect on accuracy; however, when memory is relatively poor, then returning to the encoding context can improve recall.

There is one additional issue related to context-dependent memory. Researchers at Simon Fraser University have noted that returning a person to the context in which he encoded information can improve recall *and* increase the number of false positives (i.e., saying "I remember" to stimuli that were never seen). Wong and Read (2011) showed participants a video of a staged crime; viewing took place in either a large testing room or a small study room. Participants returned one week later for a follow-up test in which they were asked to identify the culprit from a photo lineup. This test took place either in the same room as the initial viewing of the video or in the opposite room. The catch was that for half of the participants, the photo lineup did not include the person from the original video (the "target absent condition"). The results of the test demonstrated the effect of context: Performance was much higher when the testing took place in the same room as the initial encoding. However, participants who took the test in the same context as they saw the video were also more likely to claim that a photo looked familiar *even in the target-absent condition* (see Figure 7.16). Returning to the encoding context may therefore alter a person's threshold for saying "I remember." This trend is likely due to the retrieval cues associated with the environment leading to a feeling of familiarity that is mistakenly attributed to the to-be-remembered information (Leboe & Whittlesea, 2002), in this case the face of a criminal. This study has clear implications for police procedures, as many police departments encourage returning witnesses to the scene of a crime in order to improve their memories (Hershkowitz et al., 1998; Kebbel et al., 1999).

Figure 7.16 False Familiarity and Context-Dependent Memory

In a study involving the identification of a thief in a staged robbery, participants viewed a robbery and then later selected the thief from a lineup of photographs. If both stages of the study were performed in the same room (i.e., the context had been reinstated), identification of the thief increased. However, we should also keep in mind that participants were also more likely to rate an incorrect face as being familiar; this is shown by the *lower* accuracy score for the Same than for the Different contexts in the Target Absent condition on the right.

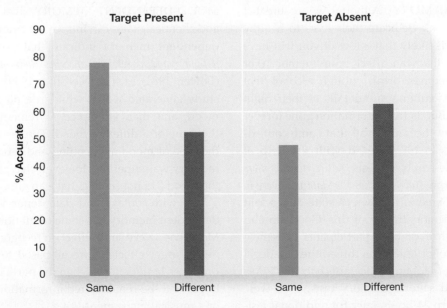

Source: From Positive and negative effects of physical context reinstatement on eyewitness recall and identification. *Applied Cognitive Psychology*, 25, 2-11. Figure 2 (p. 7), 2009 by Carol K. Wong, J. Don Read. Copyright © 2009 by John Wiley & Sons, Inc. Reproduced by permission of John Wiley & Sons, Inc.

Why is this relevant?

One of the most interesting implications of context-dependent memory research is that it implies that some forgotten information is not gone forever, but is instead simply inaccessible because the proper cues have not been provided (Tulving, 1974). This is the assumption made by police investigators who return witnesses to the scene of the crime. It's also similar to some memory-improvement strategies such as the mental imagery technique used by Simonides in the story at the beginning of this module. However, the results of the Wong and Read (2011) photo lineup story do suggest that we need to be cautious in our interpretation of context-dependent memory, as the retrieval cues associated with the context could actually lead to false feelings of familiarity that could have devastating effects on people's lives.

It is usually not difficult to spot these context effects while they are occurring. Almost everyone has had the experience of walking into a room to retrieve something—maybe a specific piece of mail or a roll of tape—only to find that they have no idea what they intended to pick up. We might call this phenomenon *context-dependent forgetting*, if we believe the change in the environment influenced the forgetting. It is certainly frustrating, but can be reversed by the *context reinstatement effect*, which occurs when you return to the original location and the memory suddenly comes back; in the above example, this happens when you walk back into the original room you were in, and suddenly remember, "Oh yeah! Tape!" But, research also shows that these effects are not isolated to external contexts; your *internal* environment can serve as a retrieval cue for your memory as well.

STATE-DEPENDENT MEMORY   Although we are sure that most readers of this book dedicate their lives to healthy eating and exercise, it is likely that a few of you will have consumed substances that can affect your memory. For example, people sometimes drink enough alcohol that they are unable to remember some details of their night out with their friends. But, is that information gone forever or can it be accessed in the same way that some context-dependent memories can be retrieved with the help of environmental cues? Research suggests that *retrieval is more effective when your internal state matches the state you were in during encoding*, a phenomenon known as **state-dependent memory**. In the first demonstration of this, Goodwin and colleagues (1969) got half of their participants extremely drunk (their blood-alcohol level was three times the legal limit); the other half were sober. Participants encoded information and completed several memory tests; they were then instructed to return 24 hours later for additional testing (and a new liver). On Day 2 of testing, half of the participants were again put into a state of severe intoxication;

half of these participants had also been drunk on Day 1, and the other half had been sober. Thus, there were four groups: drunk–drunk (drunk on Day 1 and Day 2), drunk–sober, sober–drunk, and sober–sober. Not surprisingly, the sober–sober group outperformed all of the others. However, tests of recall showed that the drunk–drunk group outperformed the groups in which participants were intoxicated during only one of the two test sessions. The state of intoxication served as a retrieval cue for the participants' memory. As with context-dependent memory, this effect appears to be strongest for declarative memory (e.g., recall), the form of memory that requires the participant to generate the response on her own (Duka et al., 2001).

Similar effects have been found for other substances. For instance, marijuana researchers have found that "experienced smokers" who learned (encoded) information while under the effects of marijuana performed better if they received marijuana before subsequent tests than if they were sober (Hill et al., 1973; Stillman et al., 1974). This group also outperformed participants who encoded information while sober, but were given marijuana before the testing on Day 2. However, the experimenters, in a beautiful example of understatement, did note that "marihuana did produce some overall impairment in performance" (Stillman et al., 1974, p. 81). State-dependent memory has also been observed for caffeine (Kelemen & Creeley, 2003), a finding that might influence how some of you study and take exams. However, it is important to remember that, like context-dependent memory, the effects of state-dependent memory are fairly small and research is generally limited to artificial stimuli such as word lists. There is therefore no guarantee that drinking yourself silly will fill in the memory gaps of a previous wild night.

MOOD-DEPENDENT MEMORY   Just as similar contexts and chemical states can improve memory, studies of **mood-dependent memory** indicate that *people remember better if their mood at retrieval matches their mood during encoding* (Bower, 1981; Eich & Metcalfe, 1989). Volunteers in one study generated words while in a pleasant or unpleasant mood, and then attempted to remember them in either the same or a different mood. The results indicated that if the type of mood at encoding and retrieval matched, then memory was superior. However, changes in the intensity of the mood did not seem to have an effect (Balch et al., 1999).

As with context- and state-dependent memory, mood-dependent memory has some limitations (Eich et al., 1994). Mood has a very small effect on recognition memory; it has much larger effects on recall-based tests. Additionally, it produces larger effects when the participant must generate both the to-be-remembered information (e.g., "an example of a musical instrument is a g_____") than if the stimuli are externally generated (e.g., "remember this word: guitar"). In the first example, the participant must put more of his own cognition into the encoding process; therefore, those cognitive processes become important retrieval cues during a later recall-based test.

Although its effects are limited, mood-dependent memory does show that a person's emotional state can have an effect on encoding and retrieval. As we shall see, the influence of emotion can be even more dramatic when the stimuli themselves are emotional in nature.

Module 7.2a Quiz:

Encoding and Retrieval

Know . . .

1. The time and manner in which information is retained between encoding and retrieval is known as _____.
   A. maintenance rehearsal
   B. storage
   C. elaborative rehearsal
   D. recall

2. Prolonging exposure to information by repeating it to oneself is referred to as _____.
   A. maintenance rehearsal
   B. storage
   C. elaborative rehearsal
   D. recall

Understand . . .

3. According to the levels of processing approach to memory, thinking about synonyms for a word is one method of _____ processing that should _____ memory for that term.
   A. deep; decrease
   B. deep; increase
   C. shallow; increase
   D. shallow; decrease

Apply . . .

4. If you are learning vocabulary for a psychology exam, you are better off using a(n) _____ technique.
   A. maintenance rehearsal
   B. elaborative rehearsal
   C. serial processing
   D. consolidation

5. When taking a math exam, the concept of _____ would indicate that you would do best if you took the exam in the same physical setting as the setting where you learned the material.
   A. context-dependent memory
   B. state-dependent memory
   C. environmental dependency process
   D. sensory-dependent memory

Emotional Memories

Do you remember what you ate for lunch last Tuesday? Is that event imprinted on your memory forever? Unless your lunch was spectacularly good or bad, it's unlikely that the memory of your sandwich will be very vivid. But what if you saw police arrest people who were fighting in the cafeteria? Or, what if you got food poisoning from your tuna sandwich? Suddenly, that lunch would become much more memorable. Indeed, when you think back to different times in your life, the events that first come to mind are often emotional in nature, such as a wonderful birthday party or the fear of starting at a new school. Emotion seems to act as a highlighter for memories, making them easier to retrieve than neutral memories. This is because emotional stimuli and events are generally self-relevant and are associated with arousal responses such as increased heart rate and sweating. In linking emotion and memory back to topics discussed earlier in this module, it seems reasonable to assume that emotion leads to deep processing of information and involves powerful stimuli that can serve as retrieval cues.

The tendency for emotion to enhance our memory for events has been demonstrated in a number of studies (LaBar & Cabeza, 2006; Levine & Pizarro, 2004). For instance, in one experiment, participants viewed a series of images that were emotionally negative (e.g., a snarling dog), emotionally positive (e.g., a puppy), or neutral. The participants rated the images in terms of their emotion (positive vs. negative), arousal (high vs. low), and visual complexity. Two weeks later, the participants were given a memory test for the images that they had rated. Recollection was enhanced for negative and, to a lesser extent, positive images (Ochsner, 2000). Similar results have been found with emotional words (e.g., Kensinger & Corkin, 2003) and images depicting someone's daily activities (Laney et al., 2003). It seems that the emotion-related aspects of stimuli do indeed improve memory, particularly for stimuli that trigger negative emotions.

However, although it is intuitive to think that emotion will boost all forms of memory, psychology researchers have found that emotion has fairly specific effects. For example, people often focus their attention on the emotional content of a scene (e.g., a snake). This information—which typically forms the centre of one's field of vision—is more likely to be remembered than peripheral information (e.g., the flowers near the snake). This phenomenon can take a more sinister turn in the courtroom. Many eyewitnesses to crimes have shown reductions in memory accuracy due to *weapon focus*—the tendency to focus on a weapon at the expense of peripheral information including the identity of the person holding the weapon (Kramer et al., 1990; Loftus et al., 1987).

Research has shown that the memory enhancing effect of emotion is strongest after long (one hour or more) rather than short delays (LaBar & Phelps, 1998; Sharot & Phelps, 2004). This suggests that emotion's largest influence is on the process of consolidation, when information that has recently been transferred from short-term memory (STM) into long-term memory (LTM) is strengthened and made somewhat permanent. Emotion has less of an effect on STM and on recognition memory; these types of memory have much less variability than LTM, thus leaving less room for emotion to influence accuracy levels.

The above studies suggest that emotional material received deeper (rather than shallow) processing. However, level of processing is not the only factor influencing memory and emotions. Emotion can influence memory consolidation even if the stimuli themselves are not emotional in nature. For example, in one study, participants studied a list of words and were then randomly assigned to view a video of oral surgery (the emotional condition) or the way to brush your teeth effectively (presumably *not* the emotional condition). Afterwards, the group members who viewed the surgery video remembered more of the words (see Figure 7.17) (Nielson et al., 2005). The researchers suggested that this effect was due to the emotional arousal associated with seeing the oral surgery video; this arousal could influence the process of consolidation. Other, more invasive, studies support this conclusion. In one experiment, stimulating the vagus nerve (which brings sensory information from the body and internal organs to the brain) led to enhanced memory for neutral words (Clark et al., 1999). Thus, the physiological responses associated with

emotions can lead to stronger memory formation, even if the to-be-remembered information is not directly related to the emotional event.

Researchers have identified many of the biological mechanisms that allow emotion to influence memory (Phelps, 2004). Much of this relationship involves structures in the temporal lobe of the brain: the hippocampus (the structure associated with the encoding of long-term memories) and the amygdala (a structure involved in emotional processing and responding). Brain imaging shows that emotional memories often activate the amygdala, whereas non-emotional memories generated at the same time do not (Sharot et al., 2007). These studies have shown that the amygdala can also alter the activity of several temporal-lobe areas that send input to the hippocampus (Dolcos et al., 2004). As a result, the cells in these brain regions fire together more than they normally would, which may lead to more vivid memories (Kilpatrick & Cahill, 2003; Paz & Paré, 2013; see Figure 7.18). However, this coordinated neural activity still does not guarantee that all of the details of an experience will be remembered with complete accuracy.

FLASHBULB MEMORIES Can you remember where you were when Sidney Crosby scored "the golden goal" against Team USA in the 2010 Olympic hockey final? For non-hockey fans, that afternoon might simply have been a fun time with friends and family, or perhaps was entirely forgettable if they weren't watching the game. But for others, the memory of that event might take on a vivid, almost photographic, quality. This phenomenon led researchers to label such an intense and unique memory as being a **flashbulb memory**—*an extremely vivid and detailed memory about an event and the conditions surrounding how one learned about the event* (Brown & Kulik, 1977). (The term *flashbulb* refers to the flash of an old-fashioned camera.) These highly charged emotional memories typically

---

Figure 7.17 Does Emotion Improve Memory?

In the study by Nielson and colleagues (2005), both groups remembered approximately the same percentage of words at pretest, and then watched dentistry videos unrelated to the word lists. The group whose members watched the more emotional video recalled more of the words in the end, suggesting that the emotional arousal associated with the video helped consolidate memory for the words.

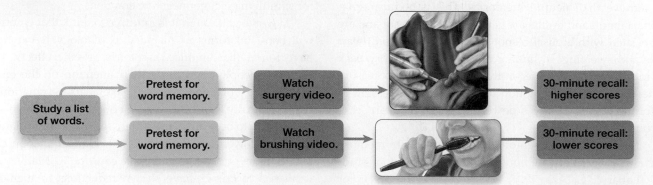

Myths in Mind

The Accuracy of Flashbulb Memories

Although flashbulb memories are very detailed and individuals reciting the details are very confident of their accuracy, it might surprise you to learn that they are not necessarily more accurate than many other memories. For example, researchers examined how university students remembered the September 11, 2001, attacks in comparison to an emotional but more mundane event (Talarico & Rubin, 2003). On September 12, 2001, they asked students to describe the events surrounding the moment they heard about the attacks. For a comparison event, they asked students to describe something memorable from the preceding weekend, just two or three days before the attacks. Over several months, the students were asked to recall details of both events, and the researchers compared the accuracy of the two memories. Although their memory for both events was fading at the same rate and they were equal in accuracy, the students acknowledged the decline in memory only for the mundane events. They continued to feel highly confident in their memories surrounding the September 11 attacks, when, in fact, those memories were not any more accurate. The same pattern has been found for other major flashbulb events, such as the 1986 space shuttle *Challenger* explosion and the verdict in the infamous 1995 murder trial of former NFL star and actor O. J. Simpson (Neisser & Harsch, 1992; Schmolk et al., 2000).

Figure 7.18 Emotion, Memory, and the Brain

Activity in the amygdala influences the activity of nearby regions in the temporal lobes, increasing the degree to which they fire together. This alters the type of input received by the hippocampus from regions of the cortex (the outer part of the temporal lobes).

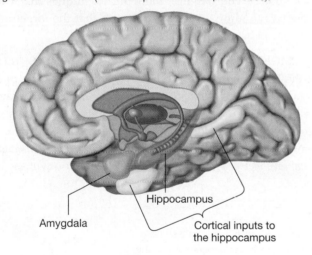

Amygdala

Hippocampus

Cortical inputs to the hippocampus

involve recollections of location, what was happening around oneself at the time of the event, and the emotional reactions of self and others (Brown & Kulik, 1977). Some may be personal memories, such as the memory of an automobile accident. Other events are so widely felt that they seem to form flashbulb memories for an entire society, such as the assassination of U.S. President Kennedy in 1963 (Brown & Kulik, 1977), the explosion of the space shuttles *Challenger* or *Columbia* (Kershaw et al., 2009; Neisser & Harsch, 1992), and the terrorist attacks of September 11, 2001 (Hirst et al., 2009; Paradis et al., 2004). One defining feature of flashbulb memories is that people are highly confident that their recollections are accurate. But is this confidence warranted? Several studies (described in the Myths in Mind section above) suggest that we should give flashbulb memories a second look.

Module 7.2b Quiz:

Emotional Memories

Know . . .

1. _____ are extremely vivid and detailed memories about an event.
   A. Flashbulb memories
   B. Deep memories
   C. Rehearsal memories
   D. Semantic memories

Understand . . .

2. One study had participants view tapes of dental surgery after studying a word list. This study concluded that
   A. emotional videos have no effect on memory.
   B. emotional videos can enhance memory, but only for material related to the video itself.
   C. emotional videos can enhance memory even for unrelated material.
   D. emotional videos can enhance memory for related material, while reducing memory for unrelated material.

Analyze . . .

3. Which statement best sums up the status of flashbulb memories?
   A. Due to the emotional strain of the event, flashbulb memories are largely inaccurate.
   B. Recall for only physical details is highly accurate.
   C. Both emotion and physical details are remembered very accurately.
   D. Over time, memory for details decays, similar to what happens with non-flashbulb memories.

Forgetting and Remembering

Have you ever had the experience of studying intensely for an exam, writing it, and then forgetting almost everything as soon as you walked out of the exam room? This phenomenon is quite common, particularly if you did all of your studying the night before (or morning of) the exam. Forgetting information is probably a good thing, at least if it occurs in moderation. We don't need to remember every detail about every day of our lives. Instead, we want to have some control over what we do remember, thus allowing us to keep the useful information (e.g., terms for an exam) and deleting the less useful information (e.g., the details of a conversation you overheard on the bus). Of course, if we had that type of control, there would be no need to study the intricacies of why we remember and forget things. As you will see, this issue has been researched extensively.

THE FORGETTING CURVE: HOW SOON WE FORGET . . .

It might seem odd that the first research on remembering was actually a documentation of how quickly people forget. However, this approach does make sense: Without knowledge of forgetting, it is difficult to ascertain how well we can remember. This early work was conducted by Hermann Ebbinghaus, whom many psychologists consider the founder of memory research. Ebbinghaus (1885) was his own research participant in his studies; these experiments involved him studying hundreds of nonsense syllables for later memory tests. His rationale was that because none of the syllables had any meaning, none of them should have been easier to remember based on past experiences. Ebbinghaus studied lists of these syllables until he could repeat them twice. He then tested himself repeatedly—this is where his persistence really shows—day after day.

How soon do we forget? The data indicated that Ebbinghaus forgot about half of a list within an hour. If Ebbinghaus had continued to forget at that rate, the rest of the list should be lost after two hours, but that was not the case. After a day, he could generally remember one-third of the material, and he could still recall between 20–25% of the words after a week. The graph in Figure 7.19 shows the basic pattern in his test results, which has come to be known as a *forgetting curve*. It clearly shows that most forgetting occurs right away, and that the rate of forgetting eventually slows to the point where one does not seem to forget at all. These results have stood the test of time. In the century after Ebbinghaus conducted his research, more than 200 articles were published in psychological journals that fit Ebbinghaus's forgetting curve (Rubin & Wenzel, 1996). In fact, one study demonstrated that this forgetting curve applies to information learned over 50 years before (see Figure 7.20; Bahrick, 1984).

Given that the forgetting curve has been documented in hundreds of experiments, it seems inevitable that we will forget most of the information that we attempt to encode. However, as you have undoubtedly learned over the course of your studies, there are techniques that will allow you to improve your memory so that the forgetting curve is not as steep.

MNEMONICS: IMPROVING YOUR MEMORY SKILLS

At the beginning of this module, you read about the poet Simonides and his ability to use mental imagery to improve his memory, thus allowing him to identify the remains of people crushed under a collapsed roof. Simonides was using a primitive type of **mnemonic**—*a technique intended to improve memory for specific information.* As you will see in

---

Figure 7.19 Ebbinghaus's Forgetting Curve

This graph reveals Ebbinghaus's results showing the rate at which he forgot a series of nonsense syllables. You can see that there is a steep decline in performance within the first day and that the rate of forgetting levels off over time.

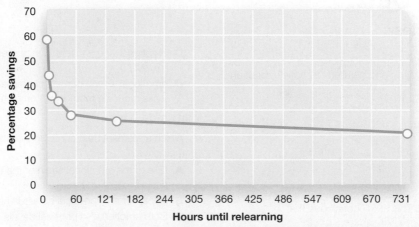

Source: Memory: A Contribution to Experimental Psychology, Hermann Ebbinghaus (1885). Translated by Henry A. Ruger & Clara E. Bussenius (1913). Originally published in New York by Teachers College, Columbia University.

Figure 7.20 Bahrick's Long-Term Forgetting Curve

This forgetting curve depicts the rate at which adults forgot the foreign language they took in high school. Compared to new graduates, those tested three years later forgot much of what they learned. After that, however, test scores stabilized, just as Ebbinghaus's did a century earlier.

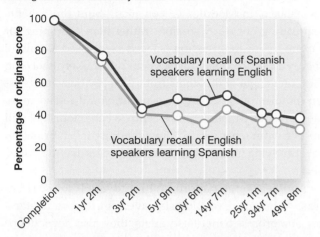

Source: From Bahrick, H. P. (1984). Semantic memory content in permastore: Fifty years of memory for Spanish learned in school. *Journal of Experimental Psychology: General, 113* (1), 1–29. American Psychological Association.

The method of loci relies on mental imagery of a familiar location or path, like this path that students take to class three times a week.

this section, there are a number of different mnemonics that could be used to improve memory, something that might be of interest to overwhelmed students.

The technique that Simonides was using is known as the **method of loci** (pronounced "LOW-sigh"), *a mnemonic that connects words to be remembered to locations along a familiar path.* To use the method of loci, one must first imagine a route that has landmarks or easily identifiable spaces—for example, the things you pass on your way from your home to a friend's house or the seats around a dinner table. Once the path is identified, the learner takes a moment to visually relate the first word on the list to the first location encountered. For example, if you need to remember to pick up noodles, milk, and soap from the store and the first thing you pass on the way to your friend's house is an intersection with a stop sign, you might picture the intersection littered with noodles, and so on down the list. The image doesn't need to be realistic—it just needs to be distinct enough to be memorable. When it is time to recall the items, the learner simply imagines the familiar drive, identifying the items to be purchased as they relate to each location along the path.

However, the method of loci can become a bit cumbersome when a person has to remember hundreds of different facts, as occurs for university exams. A more practical mnemonic is the use of **acronyms**, *pronounceable words whose letters represent the initials of an important phrase or set of items.* For example, the word "scuba" came into being with the invention of the <u>s</u>elf-<u>c</u>ontained <u>u</u>nderwater <u>b</u>reathing <u>a</u>pparatus. "Roy G. Biv" gives you the colours

of the rainbow: red, orange, yellow, green, blue, indigo, and violet. A related mnemonic, the **first-letter technique**, *uses the first letters of a set of items to spell out words that form a sentence.* It is like an acronym, but it tends to be used when the first letters do not spell a pronounceable word (see Figure 7.21). One well-known example is "Every Good Boy Does Fine" for the five lines on the treble clef in musical notation. Another is "My Very Excited Mother Just Served Us Nine Pies" for the nine planets in the solar system (Pluto is now a "dwarf planet"). These types of mnemonic techniques work by organizing the information into a pattern that is easier to remember than the original information. Acronyms have a meaning of their own, so the learner gets the benefit of both elaborative rehearsal and deeper processing.

A number of mnemonic devices are based on the premise of dual coding. **Dual coding** *occurs when information is stored in more than one form*—such as a verbal description

Figure 7.21 The First-Letter Technique

Students of biology often use mnemonics, such as this example of the first letter technique, which helps students remember the taxonomic system.

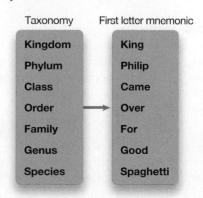

Taxonomy	First letter mnemonic
Kingdom	King
Phylum	Philip
Class	Came
Order	Over
Family	For
Genus	Good
Species	Spaghetti

and a visual image, or a description and a sound—and it regularly produces stronger memories than the use of one form alone (Clark & Paivio, 1991). Dual coding leads to the information receiving deeper, as opposed to shallow, processing; this is because the additional sensory representations create a larger number of memory associations. This leads to a greater number of potential retrieval cues that can be accessed later. For example, most children growing up in North America learned the alphabet with the help of a song. In fact, even adults find themselves humming portions of that song when alphabetizing documents (you'll probably do it too if asked which letter comes after "k"). Both the visual "A-B-C-D" and the musical "eh-bee-see-dee" are encoded together, making memory easier than if you were simply given visual information to remember (e.g., "☞☜☞☜", which is ABCD in the meaningless "wingdings2" font). The simplest explanation for the dual-coding advantage is that twice as much information is stored.

The application of mnemonic strategies can be found in restaurants where servers are not allowed to write out orders. These servers use a variety of the techniques discussed in this chapter. Some use chunking strategies, such as remembering soft drinks for a group of three customers, and cocktails for the other four. They also use the method of loci to link faces with positions at the table. In one study, a waiter was able to recall as many as 20 dinner orders (Ericsson & Polson, 1988). He used the method of loci by linking food type (starch, beef, or fish) with a table location, and he used acronyms to help with encoding salad dressing choices. Thus RaVoSe for a party of three would be ranch, vinegar and oil, and sesame. Servers, as well as memory researchers, will tell you that the worst thing restaurant patrons can do is switch seats, as it completely disrupts the mnemonic devices being used to remember the order (Bekinschtein et al., 2008).

While these mnemonic devices can help with rote memorization, they may not necessarily improve your understanding of material. Researchers have begun to examine other memory boosters that may offer more benefits understanding and retaining information. For example, some research has shown that *desirable difficulties* can aid learning. These techniques make studying slower and more effortful, but result in better overall remembering. For instance, in Module 1.1 you read about the benefits of spreading out study sessions rather than cramming for an exam in one long session (spaced vs. massed learning). When you space out your sessions, it is likely that you will forget some of the items from the previous study session (Smolen et al., 2016). As a result, you'll reread those notes and study them in more depth, a behaviour that will improve your chances of remembering the information later. Studying material in varying orders has a similar effect.

Another popular approach to studying is to use flashcards. Although psychologists have begun to understand how this process benefits students, they also have identified a few pitfalls that can hinder its effects. First is the spacing effect. When studying with flashcards, it is better to use one big stack rather than several smaller stacks; using the entire deck helps take advantage of the effect of spacing the cards. A second potential problem is the fact that students become overconfident and drop flashcards as soon as they believe they have learned the material. In reality, doing so seems to reduce the benefits of overlearning the material (making it more difficult to forget) and spacing out cards in the deck (Kornell, 2009; Kornell & Bjork, 2007). No matter how you study, you should take advantage of the **testing effect**, *the finding that taking practice tests can improve exam performance, even without additional studying*. In fact, researchers have directly compared testing to additional studying and have found that, in some cases, testing actually improves memory more (Roediger et al., 2010). That's why psychology textbooks such as this one include quizzes and online tests.

Module 7.2c Quiz:

Forgetting and Remembering

Know . . .

1. Dual coding seems to help memory by
   A. allowing for maintenance rehearsal.
   B. ensuring that the information is encoded in multiple ways.
   C. ensuring that the information is encoded on two separate occasions.
   D. duplicating the rehearsal effect.

Apply . . .

2. If you are preparing for an exam by using flashcards, you will probably find that you are more confident about some of the items than others. To improve your exam performance, you should

   A. drop the cards you already know.
   B. keep the cards in the deck even if you feel like you know them.
   C. use maintenance rehearsal.
   D. use the method of loci.

3. If you wanted to remember a grocery list using the method of loci, you should

   A. imagine the items on the list on your path through the grocery store.
   B. match rhyming words to each item on your list.
   C. repeat the list to yourself over and over again.
   D. tell a story using the items from the list.

Module 7.2 Summary

7.2a   Know . . . the key terminology related to forgetting, encoding, and retrieval.

acronym
context-dependent memory
deep processing
dual coding
elaborative rehearsal
encoding specificity principle
first-letter technique
flashbulb memory
maintenance rehearsal
method of loci
mnemonic
mood-dependent memory
recall
recognition
self-reference effect
state-dependent memory
shallow processing
testing effect

7.2b   Understand . . . how the type of cognitive processing employed can affect the chances of remembering what you encounter.

Generally speaking, deeper processing makes things more likely to be remembered. Greater depth of processing may be achieved by elaborating on the meaning of the information, through increased emotional content, and through coding in images and sounds simultaneously.

7.2c   Apply . . . what you have learned to improve your ability to memorize information.

Try putting some tools from the chapter into practice. One mnemonic device that might be helpful is the method of loci.

Apply Activity

Have someone create a shopping list for you while you prepare yourself by imagining a familiar path (perhaps the route you take to class or work). When you are ready to learn the list, read a single item on the list and imagine it at some point on the path. Feel free to exaggerate the images in your memory—each item could become the size of a stop sign or might take on the appearance of a particular building or tree that you pass by. Continue this pattern for each individual item until you have learned the list. Then try what Ebbinghaus did: Test your memory over the course of a few days. How do you think you will do?

7.2d   Analyze . . . whether emotional memories are more accurate than non-emotional ones.

Both personal experiences and controlled laboratory studies demonstrate that emotion enhances memory. However, as we learned in the case of flashbulb memories, even memories for details of significant events decline over time, although confidence in memory accuracy typically remains very high.

Module 7.3 Constructing and Reconstructing Memories

RiceWithSugar/Shutterstock.com

 ## Learning Objectives

7.3a Know . . . the key terminology used in discussing how memories are organized and constructed.

7.3b Understand . . . how schemas serve as frameworks for encoding and constructing memories.

7.3c Understand . . . how psychologists can produce false memories in the laboratory.

7.3d Apply . . . what you have learned to judge the reliability of eyewitness testimony.

7.3e Analyze . . . the arguments in the "recovered memory" debate.

In 1992, the Saskatchewan town of Martensville was rocked by a sex abuse scandal. A complaint about a suspicious diaper rash from a parent of a toddler attending a local daycare led to a police investigation. After repeated and extensive interviewing, the children claimed to remember astonishing things including extensive sexual abuse, human sacrifice, a "Devil Church," and a Satanic cult known as The Brotherhood of the Ram. The owners of the daycare along with several other individuals—including five police officers—were eventually arrested. However, a closer examination of the police investigation identified some serious problems. Expert witnesses noted that the questions used in the interviews were leading and suggestive. Upon further examination, many charges were dropped. In fact, only one of the accused was convicted of a crime (molestation). The Saskatchewan government has since paid out millions of dollars to the other accused individuals whose lives were affected by these investigations.

While certainly well-meaning, the investigators—who were not trained to interview child witnesses—forgot a

critical piece of information: Memories are not like photographs perfectly depicting an event from our past. Instead, they are reconstructed each time we retrieve them, and can therefore be altered by a number of different factors.

Focus Questions

1. How is it possible to remember events that never happened?

2. Do these false memories represent memory problems, or are they just a normal part of remembering?

» The true story that opened this module demonstrates that our memories are not perfect. In a less disturbing example, cognitive psychologist and renowned memory researcher Ulric Neisser once recounted what he was doing on December 7, 1941, the day Japan attacked Pearl Harbor. Neisser was sitting in the living room listening to a baseball game on the radio when the program was interrupted with the news (Neisser, 2000). Or was he? He had certainly constructed a very distinct memory for this emotional event, but something must have gone wrong. Baseball season does not last through December. As this example demonstrates, even memory researchers are prone to misremembering. In this module we will examine how such misremembering occurs and what it says about how memories are constructed . . . and reconstructed.

How Memories Are Organized and Constructed

Think about the last time you read a novel or watched a film. What do you recall about the story? If you have a typical memory, you will forget the proper names of locations and characters quickly, but you will be able to remember the basic plot for a very long time (Squire, 1989; Stanhope et al., 1993). The plot may be referred to as the *gist* of the story and it impacts us much more than characters' names, which are often just details. As it turns out, much of the way we store memories depends on our tendency to remember the gist of things.

THE SCHEMA: AN ACTIVE ORGANIZATION PROCESS
The gist of a story gives us "the big picture," or a general structure for the memory; details can be added around that structure. Gist is often influenced by **schemas**, *organized clusters of memories that constitute one's knowledge or beliefs about events, objects, and ideas.* Whenever we encounter familiar events or objects, these schemas become active and affect what we expect, what we pay attention to, and what we remember. Because we use these patterns automatically, it may be difficult to understand what they are, even though we use them throughout our lives. Here is an example; read the following passage through one time:

> The procedure is quite simple. First, you arrange things into different groups. Of course, one pile may be sufficient, depending on how much there is to do. If you have to go somewhere else due to lack of facilities, that is the next step; otherwise, you are pretty well set. It is important not to overdo things. That is, it is better to do too few things at once than too many. At first the whole procedure will seem complicated. Soon, however, it will become just another facet of life. After the procedure is completed, one arranges the materials into different groups again. Then they can be put into their appropriate places. Eventually they will be used once more, and the whole cycle will have to be repeated (Bransford & Johnson, 1973).

At this point, if you were to write down the details of the paragraph solely from memory, how well do you think you would do? Most people do not have high expectations for themselves, but they would blame it on how vague the paragraph seems. Now, what if we tell you the passage is about doing laundry? If you read the paragraph a second time, you should see that it is easier to understand, as well as to remember.

How Schemas Influence Memory

Although schemas are used to explain memory, they can be used to explain many other phenomena as well, such as the way we perceive, remember, and think about people and situations. In each case, schemas provide a ready-made structure that allows us to process new information more quickly than we could without this mental shortcut. This makes schemas extremely useful. But, are they accurate?

What do we know about schemas?

The laundry demonstration tells us quite a bit about schemas and memory. First, most of us have our own personal schema about the process of doing laundry. Refer to the definition of schema—a cluster of memories that constitutes your knowledge about an event (gathering clothes, going to the laundromat), object (what clothes are, what detergent is), or idea (why clean clothes are desirable). When you read the paragraph the first time, you probably did not know what the objects and events were. However, when you were told it was about doing laundry, it *activated* your laundry schema—your personal collection of concepts and memories. Once your schema was activated, you were prepared to make sense of the story and could likely fill in the gaps of your memory for the passage with stored knowledge from your schema in long-term memory (LTM). Second, we should point out that schemas are involved in all three stages of memory: They guide what we attend to during encoding, organize stored memories, and serve as cues when it comes time to retrieve information.

How can science explain schemas?

Research indicates that we remember events using **constructive memory**, *a process by which we first recall a generalized schema and then add in specific details* (Scoboria et al., 2006; Silva et al., 2006). Where do these schemas come from? They appear to be products of culture and experience (e.g., Ross & Wang, 2010). For example, individuals within a culture tend to have schemas related to gender roles—men and women are each assumed to engage in certain jobs and to behave in certain ways. Even if an individual realizes that these schemas are not 100% accurate (in fact, they can be far from accurate in some cases), he or she is likely to engage in schematic processing when having difficulty remembering something specific.

Figure 7.22 Schemas Affect How We Encode and Remember

In this study, memory was accurate when tested immediately, as shown by the small proportion of errors on the "immediate" side of the graph. After two days, however, participants misremembered seeing the schema-inconsistent tasks in line with stereotypes. For example, they misremembered the stay-at-home mother stirring cake batter even if they had actually seen the handyman doing it.

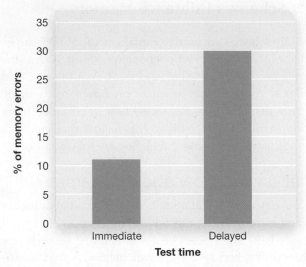

Source: Data from Kleider, H., Pezdek, K., Goldinger, S., & Kirk, A. (2008). Schema–driven source misattribution errors: Remembering the expected from a witnessed event. *Applied Cognitive Psychology*, 22 (1), 1–20.

Figure 7.23 A Brain Network Related to Processing Schemas

Brain-imaging data suggest that encoding information consistent with a schema activates a network involving structures in the medial temporal lobe (including our friend, the hippocampus) and parts of the frontal lobes.

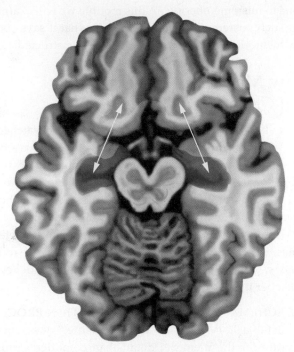

Source: Figure 5 from van Kesteren et al., (2013), Trends in Neuroscience, p. 2358.

A study by Heather Kleider and her associates (2008) demonstrates how schemas influence memory quite well. These investigators had research participants view photographs of a handyman engaged in schema-consistent behaviour (e.g., working on plumbing) as well as a schema-inconsistent tasks (e.g., folding a baby's clothing). Participants also viewed images of a stay-at-home mother performing schema-consistent (e.g., feeding a baby) and schema-inconsistent tasks (e.g., hammering a nail). Immediately after viewing the photographs, participants were quite successful at remembering correctly who had performed what actions. However, after two days, what types of memory mistakes do you think the researchers found? As you can see from Figure 7.22, individuals began making mistakes, and these mistakes were consistent with gender schemas.

Can we critically evaluate the concept of a schema?

The concept of a schema is certainly useful in describing our methods of mental organization, but some psychologists remain skeptical of its validity. After all, you cannot record brain activity and expect to see a *particular* schema,

and individuals generally are not aware that they are using schematic processing. It may even be the case that what we assume are schemas about laundry, gender, or ourselves are different every time we think about these topics. If that is the case, then describing this tendency as a schema might even be misleading.

However, recent brain-imaging studies suggest that schemas do exist and likely help with the process of memory consolidation (Wang & Morris, 2010). Both encoding and retrieving information that was consistent with a schema learned during an experiment led to greater activity in a network involving parts of the medial temporal lobes (including the hippocampus) and the frontal lobes (van Kesteren, Fernandez, et al., 2010; van Kesteren, Rijpkema, et al., 2010; see Figure 7.23). Additionally, adding new information to an existing schema actually changes the expression of genes in the frontal lobes in order to strengthen connections between this region and the hippocampus (Tse et al., 2011). Thus, while we cannot identify the neural correlates for a *specific* schema like that for doing laundry, it *is* possible to see how schemas influence brain activity while new information is encoded and entered into the structure of our LTM.

BIOPSYCHOSOCIAL PERSPECTIVES

Your Earliest Memories

Think back to the earliest memory you can recall: How old were you? It is likely that you do not have any personal or autobiographical memories from before your third birthday. Psychologists have been trying to explain this phenomenon—sometimes called *infantile amnesia*.

Research indicates that self-schemas begin to develop around the ages of 18 to 24 months (Howe, 2003). Without these schemas, it is difficult and maybe even impossible to organize and encode memories about the self. This is not a universal phenomenon, however. Other researchers taking a cross-cultural perspective have found that a sense of self emerges earlier among European Americans than among people living in eastern Asia, which correlates with earlier ages of first memories among European Americans (Fivush & Nelson, 2004; Ross & Wang, 2010). Why might this difference arise? The European

American emphasis on developing a sense of self encourages thinking about personal experiences, which increases the likelihood that personal events—such as your third birthday party with that scary drunken clown, or getting chased by a dog—will be remembered. In contrast, Asian cultures tend to emphasize social harmony and collectiveness over individualism, resulting in a schema that is more socially integrated than in Westerners. This may explain the slightly later onset of autobiographical memory in Asian children. It will be interesting to see if this cultural difference changes as Asian cultures become more "Westernized."

Do these findings mean that we could get infants to remember early life events by teaching them to talk about themselves at an early age? This is not likely. The brains of young children are still developing, so the neural architecture necessary to form stable schemas is not yet in place (Newcombe et al., 2000).

Why is this relevant?

An important aspect of schema-driven processing has to do with how we process information about ourselves. Clinical psychology researchers have become particularly concerned with the ways in which these *self-schemas* may contribute to psychological problems. Consider a person with clinical depression—a condition that involves negative emotion, lack of energy, self-doubt, and self-blame. An individual with depression is likely to have a very negative self-schema, which means that he will pay attention to things that are consistent with the depressive symptoms, and will be more likely to recall events and feelings that are consistent with this schema. Thus the schema contributes to a pattern of thinking and focusing on negative thoughts. Fortunately, researchers have been able to target these schemas in psychotherapy. The evidence shows that by changing their self-schema, individuals are better able to recover from even very serious bouts of depression (Dozois et al., 2009).

Schemas about the self are based on past experiences and are used to organize the encoding of self-relevant information in a way that can influence our responses (Markus, 1977). But self-schemas may serve an additional role during development. Some evidence suggests that the ability to form schemas, particularly self-schemas, plays a critical role in our ability to form memories about our lives.

Module 7.3a Quiz:

How Memories Are Organized and Constructed

Know . . .

1. Schemas appear to affect which of the following stages of memory?
   A. Encoding
   B. Storage
   C. Retrieval
   D. All of these stages

2. The act of remembering through recalling a framework and then adding specific details is known as _____.
   A. constructive memory
   B. confabulation

C. schematic interpretation
D. distinctiveness

Understand . . .

3. Information that does not fit our expectations for a specific context is likely to be forgotten if
   A. it is extremely unusual.
   B. it only fits our expectations for another completely different context.
   C. it is unexpected, but really not that unusual.
   D. it is schema consistent.

Memory Reconstruction

You've all heard the cliché, "You are what you eat." But, it's also becoming increasingly clear to psychologists that "You are what you remember" (Wilson & Ross, 2003). As you read earlier in this module, our memories are organized to a large degree by our schemas, including self-schemas. There is no guarantee, however, that these schemas are 100% accurate. In fact, different motivations can influence which schemas are accessible to us in a given moment, thereby biasing our memory reconstruction. As a result of these motivational influences, the past that we remember is actually influenced by our mental state and by our view of ourselves in the present (Albert, 1977).

This type of biasing effect was nicely demonstrated in a study conducted by researchers at Concordia University and the University of Waterloo (Conway & Ross, 1984). The researchers had one group of participants complete a study skills course while another group remained on a waiting list. The course itself proved completely ineffective, at least in terms of improving study skills. The course did have an interesting effect on memory, however. Participants who completed the study course rated their previous study skills lower than they had rated them prior to taking the course; participants on the waiting list rated their study skills as being unchanged. Therefore, the study course participants revised their memories of their past abilities in a way that allowed them to feel as though they benefited from the course. This memory bias allowed them to feel as though they were improving over time, a bias that almost all of us have about ourselves (Ross & Wilson, 2000).

The results of such studies demonstrate that our memories are not stable, but instead change over time. Indeed, we have all experienced a **false memory**, *remembering events that did not occur, or incorrectly recalling details of an event*. It is important to remember that these incorrect memories do not necessarily indicate a dysfunction of memory, but rather reflect normal memory processes—which are inherently imperfect. As you read in the discussion of schemas, the elements that comprise a memory must be reconstructed each time that memory is retrieved. This reconstruction is influenced by the demands of the current situation. Psychologists have identified several ways in which our memories can be biased, and have explored how these biases can have many real-world implications, such as in the legal system.

THE PERILS OF EYEWITNESS TESTIMONY Have you ever witnessed a crime or even a minor traffic accident? When asked later about what you witnessed, how accurate were your reports? Most of us feel quite confident in our ability to retrieve this type of information. However, psychologists have shown that a number of minor factors can dramatically influence the details of our "memories."

In one classic study, Elizabeth Loftus and John Palmer (1974) showed undergraduate research participants film clips of traffic accidents. Participants were asked to write down a description of what they had seen, and were then asked a specific question: "About how fast were the cars going when they smashed into each other?" However, the exact wording of this question varied across experimental conditions. For some participants, the word "smashed" was

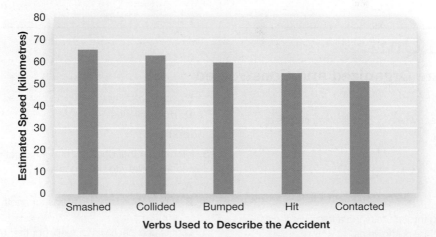

Figure 7.24 The Power of a Word

Simply changing the wording of a question altered participants' recollections of a filmed traffic accident. All participants viewed the same filmed traffic accidents and all participants received the identical question with the exception of one key verb: smashed, collided, bumped, hit, or contacted.

Source: Based on data from Loftus, E. F., & Palmer, J. C. (1974). Reconstruction of automobile destruction: An example of the interaction between language and memory. *Journal of Verbal Learning and Verbal Behavior*, 13, 585–589 (p. 586.).

replaced by "collided," "bumped," "contacted," or "hit." The results of the study were stunning—simply changing one verb in the sentence produced large differences in the estimated speed of the vehicles (see Figure 7.24). At one extreme, the word "smashed" led to an estimate of 65.2 km/h. At the low end of the spectrum, the word "contacted" led to estimates of 51.2 km/h. So, changing the verb altered the remembered speed of the vehicles by 14 km/h. In a follow-up study, Loftus and Palmer also found that participants in the "smashed" condition were more likely to insert false details such as the presence of broken glass into their accident reports. This study was a powerful demonstration of the effect of question wording on memory retrieval and provided police with important information about the need for caution when questioning witnesses.

Another factor that can alter memories of an event—and that has implications for the legal system—is the information that is encoded after the event has occurred, such as rumours, news reports, or hearing about other people's perceptions of the event. If such information was accurate, it could improve people's memories; however, this type of information is not always accurate, which explains why jury members are asked to avoid reading about or watching TV reports related to the case with which they are involved. Psychologists have shown that this legal procedure is a wise one, as a number of studies have demonstrated the **misinformation effect**, *when information occurring after an event becomes part of the memory for that event.* In the original studies of this topic (Loftus, 1975), researchers attempted to use the misinformation effect to change the details of people's memories. For example, in one study, students viewed a videotape of a staged car crash. In the experimental conditions, participants were asked about an object that was not in the video, such as a yield sign (when in fact the scene had contained a stop sign). Later, when asked if they had seen a yield sign, participants in the experimental group were likely to say yes. As this experiment demonstrates, one can change the details of a memory by asking a leading question.

Children are particularly susceptible to misinformation effects and to the effects of a question's wording (Bruck & Ceci, 1999). In one study, five- and six-year-old children watched a janitor (really an actor named Chester as he cleaned some dolls and other toys in a playroom. For half of the children, his behaviour was innocent and simply involved him cleaning the toys. For the other children, Chester's behaviour seemed abusive and involved him treating the toys roughly. The children were later questioned by two interviewers who were (1) accusatory (implying that Chester had been playing with the dolls when he should have been working), (2) innocent (implying that Chester was simply cleaning the dolls), or (3) neutral (not implying anything about Chester's behaviour). When the interviewer's tone matched what the children

Dr. Elizabeth Loftus

Participants in one study viewed the top photo and later were asked about the "yield sign," even though they saw a stop sign. This small bit of misinformation was enough to get many participants to falsely remember seeing a yield sign. Similarly, participants who first viewed the bottom photo could be led to misremember seeing a stop sign with a single misleading question.

saw, such as innocent questioning about Chester when he treated the toys nicely or accusatory questioning when Chester was rough with the toys, the children's reports of the behaviour were quite accurate. However, when the interview technique did not match the observed behaviour (e.g., accusatory questioning when Chester had simply cleaned the toys), the children's responses matched the interviewer's tone. In other words, the tone of the interviewer altered the details of the information that the children retrieved and reported (Thompson et al., 1997).

Similar to adults, children are also dependent on schemas. In one study, researchers told children at school about their clumsy friend Sam Stone. On numerous occasions, they told funny stories about Sam's life, including the times he broke a Barbie doll and tore a sweater. Later, the children met "Sam Stone." During his time in the classroom, he did not perform a single clumsy act. The following day, the teacher showed the children a torn book and a dirty teddy bear, but did not link Sam to these damaged items. When questioned a few weeks later, however, many of the three- and four-year-old children reported that Sam Stone had ruined these objects. Some even claimed to have witnessed these acts themselves (Leichtman & Ceci, 1995). These findings should not lead us to ignore the eyewitness

PSYCH@

Court: Is Eyewitness Testimony Reliable?

While trying to identify the individual responsible for a crime, investigators often present a lineup of a series of individuals (either in person or in photographs) and ask the eyewitness to identify the suspect. Given the constructive nature of memory, it should come as no surprise to hear that an eyewitness gets it wrong from time to time. The consequences of this kind of wrongful conviction are dire—an innocent person may go to jail while a potentially dangerous person stays free.

How can the science of memory improve this process? Here are the six main suggestions for reforming eyewitness identification procedures:

1. *Employ double-blind procedures.* Elsewhere in this book, we discussed how double-blind procedures help reduce experimenter bias. Similarly, a double-blind lineup (i.e., the investigator in the room with the eyewitness has no knowledge of which person is the actual suspect) can prevent an investigator from biasing an eyewitness, either intentionally or accidentally.

2. *Use appropriate instructions.* For example, the investigator should include the statement, "The suspect might not be present in the lineup." Eyewitnesses often assume the guilty person is in the lineup, so they are likely to choose a close match. This risk can be greatly reduced by instructing the eyewitness that the correct answer may be "none of the above."

3. *Compose the lineup carefully.* The lineup should include individuals who match the eyewitness's description of the perpetrator, not the investigator's beliefs about the suspect.

4. *Use sequential lineups.* When an entire lineup is shown simultaneously, this may encourage the witness to assume one of the people is guilty, so they choose the best candidate. If the people in the lineup are presented one at a time, witnesses are less likely to pick out an incorrect suspect because they are willing to consider the next person in the sequence.

5. *Require confidence statements.* Eyewitness confidence can change as a result of an investigator's response, or simply by seeing the same suspect in multiple lineups, neither of which make the testimony any more accurate. Therefore, confidence statements should be taken in the witness's own words after an identification is made.

6. *Record the procedures.* Eyewitness researchers have identified at least a dozen specific things that can go wrong during identification procedures. By recording these procedures, expert witnesses can evaluate the reliability of testimony during hearings.

Recently, Canadian legal experts produced the *2011 Report of the Federal/Provincial/Territorial Heads of Prosecutions Subcommittee on the Prevention of Wrongful Convictions.* This 233-page document presents recommendations to the legal community for the use of eyewitness testimony, among other investigative practices, and highlights the need for testimony from experts, including psychologists.

---

testimony of children; but, they should also remind us (and investigators) that memories—particularly those of children—are not stable and unchanging like a photograph. This research highlights how extremely important it is for legal professionals, such as the police, to practise investigative techniques that avoid biasing witnesses to crimes. Failure to do so could easily result in innocent people being convicted of crimes they did not commit, or conversely, guilty people being set free due to "reasonable doubt" because of questionable eyewitness testimony.

IMAGINATION AND FALSE MEMORIES Because our memories are not always as accurate as we would like them to be, people use a number of techniques to try to help themselves retrieve information. One of these techniques is to imagine the situation that you are trying, but failing, to remember. However, although this strategy seems logical at first, the results of several studies suggest that the retrieved memories may not be very accurate. Research indicates that repeatedly imagining an action

such as breaking a toothpick makes it very difficult for people to remember whether or not they performed that action (Goff & Roediger, 1998). In fact, imagining events can often lead to **imagination inflation**, *the increased confidence in a false memory of an event following repeated imagination of the event.* The more readily and clearly we can imagine events, the more certain we are that the memories are accurate.

To study this effect, researchers created a list of events that may or may not have happened to the individuals in their study (e.g., got in trouble for calling 911, found a $10 bill in a parking lot). The volunteers were first asked to rate their confidence that the event happened. In sessions held over a period of days, participants were asked to imagine these events, until finally they were asked to rate their confidence again. For each item they were asked to imagine, repeated imagination *inflated* their confidence in the memory of the event even if they initially reported that the event had not occurred (Garry et al., 1996; Garry & Polaschek, 2000).

Importantly, imagination inflation is very similar to *guided imagery*, a technique used by some clinicians (and some police investigators) to help people recover details of events that they are unable to remember. It involves a guide giving instructions to participants to imagine certain events. Like the misinformation effect, guided imagery can be used to alter memories for actual events, but it can also create entirely false memories. For example, in one experiment, volunteers were asked to imagine a procedure in which a nurse removed a sample of skin from a finger. Despite the fact that this is not a medical procedure and that it almost certainly never occurred, individuals in the experimental group were more likely than those in the control group to report that this event had actually happened to them (Mazzoni & Memon, 2003). In other words, attempting to imagine an event can implant new—and false—events into a person's memory.

CREATING FALSE MEMORIES IN THE LABORATORY

Given that several research studies have shown that false memories are fairly easy to create, and given that such memories can have dramatic and tragic consequences when they appear in clinical or legal settings, it became important for researchers to develop techniques that would allow them to study false memories in more detail. The first of these techniques to be used was the Deese-Roediger-McDermott (DRM) paradigm (see Figure 7.25). In the **DRM procedure**, *participants study a list of highly related words called semantic associates* (which means they are associated by meaning). The word that would be the

most obvious member of the list just happens to be missing. This missing word is called the *critical lure*. What happens when the participants are given a memory test? A significant proportion of participants remember the critical lure, even though it never appeared on the list (Deese, 1959; Roediger & McDermott, 1995). When individuals recall the critical lure, it is called an *intrusion*, because a false memory is sneaking into an existing memory.

The fact that people make intrusion errors is not particularly surprising. However, the strength of the effect is astonishing. In routine studies, the DRM lures as many as 70% of the participants. The most obvious way to reduce this effect would be to simply explain the DRM procedure and warn participants that intrusions may occur. Although this approach has proved effective in reducing intrusions, false memories still occur (Gallo et al., 1997). Obviously, intrusions are very difficult to prevent, but not because memory is prone to mistakes. In fact, memory is generally accurate and extremely efficient, given the millions of bits of information we encounter every day. Instead, the DRM effect reflects the fact that normal memory processes are constructive.

A second method of creating false memories in the laboratory comes from doctored photographs. For instance, researchers at the University of Victoria and their colleagues exposed undergraduate research participants to altered photographs showing the participant and his or her parent taking a ride on a hot-air balloon, an event that did not actually occur (Wade et al., 2002). For this type of experiment to work, the volunteers in the study had to recruit the help of their family. Their parents provided pictures of the participant from early childhood, along with an explanation of the event, the location, and the people and objects in the photo. The researchers took one of the pictures and digitally cut and pasted it into a balloon ride. On three occasions the participants went through the set of pictures, the true originals plus the doctored photo, in a structured interview process (the kind designed to help police get more details from eyewitnesses). By the end of the third session, half the participants had some memory for the balloon ride event, even though it never occurred (Wade et al., 2002).

Photographic images such as the ones used in the hot-air balloon study leave it to the participant to fill in the gaps as to what "happened" on their balloon ride. Other researchers have gone so far as to create false videotaped evidence of an event (R. Nash et al., 2009). For this method, a volunteer was videotaped watching a graduate student perform an action. The researchers also videotaped the graduate student performing an additional action that the volunteer did not witness. The videos were then spliced together to show the volunteer watching an event that she, in reality, did not actually see. Now imagine you were shown a video of yourself watching an action you had not

Figure 7.25 A Sample Word List and Its Critical Lure for the DRM Procedure

The words on the left side are all closely related to the word "bread"—but "bread" does not actually appear on the list. People who study this list of words are very likely to misremember that "bread" was present.

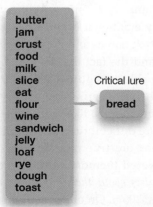

Source: From Roediger, H., & McDermott, K. (1995). Creating false memories: Remembering words not presented in lists. *Journal of Experimental Psychology: Learning, Memory, and Cognition, 21*, 803–814. American Psychological Association.

In one study of false memory, true photos were obtained from volunteers' families (top), and were edited to look like a balloon ride (bottom). About half of the volunteers in this study came to recall some details of an event that never happened to them.

seen before—would you believe it? In fact, a significant portion of the individuals did form memories of the events they had never witnessed. This type of false memory retrieval mirrors that created in the guided imagery exercises used in some clinical settings, a trend that sparked a very contentious debate in both the scientific and legal communities.

THE DANGER OF FALSE REMEMBERING In the early 1990s, Beth Rutherford sought the help of her church counsellor to deal with personal issues. During their sessions, the counsellor managed to convince her that her father, a minister, had raped her. The memory was further elaborated so that she remembered becoming pregnant and that her father had forced her to undergo an abortion using a coat hanger. You can imagine what kind of effects this had on the family. Her father had little choice but to resign from his position, and his reputation was left in

shambles. Although it can be difficult to prove some false memories, this incident is particularly disturbing because it *could* have been supported by medical evidence. When a medical investigation was finally conducted, absolutely no evidence was found that Beth had ever been raped or that she had ever been pregnant (Loftus, 1997).

In this example, Beth's therapist believed that Beth had experienced a **recovered memory**, *a memory of a traumatic event that is suddenly recovered after blocking the memory of that event for a long period of time*, often many years. However, the topic of recovered memories is a contentious one. In the past three decades, psychologists have performed a great deal of research investigating whether it is possible to suppress a memory and whether there are research tools available to help us distinguish between memories that are accurate and those that are not.

This idea that we suppress traumatic memories is popularly known as *repression* from Freudian psychoanalysis (see Module 12.3). According to this idea, a repressed memory could still affect other psychological processes, leading people to suffer in other ways such as experiencing depression. This school of thought suggests that if a repressed memory can be recovered, then a patient can find ways to cope with the trauma. Some therapists espouse this view and use techniques such as hypnosis and guided imagery to try to unearth repressed memories. However, given the research we have discussed about how false memories can be implanted through these types of techniques, there is an obvious danger in the use of these methods.

Can we suppress our memories of traumatic life events? As it turns out, it is *possible,* although it is difficult to determine how common it is. In one survey study, researchers examined the testimony of people who had been imprisoned in Camp Erika, a Nazi concentration camp in The Netherlands, in the early 1940s (Wagenaar & Groeneweg, 1990). Most of the prisoners were able to provide detailed information about their time in the concentration camp, but a minority of prisoners did not remember many emotional events during their imprisonment including the names and appearances of people who tortured them and the fact that they had witnessed murders! But, being able to suppress a horrific memory is very different from then recovering that memory years later.

Recovered memories, like many other types of long-term memory, are difficult to study because one can rarely determine if they are true or false. This uncertainty has led to the **recovered memory controversy**, *a heated debate among psychologists about the validity of recovered memories* (Davis & Loftus, 2009). On one side of the controversy are some clinical mental health workers (although certainly not the majority) who regularly attempt to recover memories they suspect have been repressed. On the opposing side are the many psychologists who point out that the techniques that might help "recover" a memory bear a striking resemblance to those that are used to create false memories in laboratory research; they often involve instructions to remember, attempts to form images, and social reinforcement for reporting memories (Spanos et al., 1994). How can this disagreement be resolved?

One method is to use brain imaging to differentiate true and false memories. Psychologists have found that when people recount information that is true, the visual and other sensory areas of the brain become more active. When revealing falsely remembered information, these same individuals have much less activity in the sensory regions—the brain is not drawing on mental imagery because it was not there in the first place (Dennis et al., 2012; Stark et al., 2010). Interestingly, these brain results do not always map onto the participants' conscious memories of what they had seen. So, this method might be able to distinguish between true and false memories better than the participant himself (M. K. Johnson et al., 2012). However, although these neuroimaging results are promising, these studies did not use stimuli that were as emotional as the recovered memories patients report. Therefore, as with most areas of psychology, much more research is needed in this controversial area.

Although this module provides some frightening examples of how malleable our memories are, there is actually something inspirational about these results. We construct our own memories and, as a result, our own reality. Therefore, we have the power to focus our memories on the positive experiences of our lives, or on the negative ones. It's up to you—remember that.

Module 7.3b Quiz:

Memory Reconstruction

Know . . .

1. If you are presented with a list of 15 words, all of which have something in common, you are most likely participating in a study focusing on _____.
   A. misinformation effects
   B. the DRM procedure
   C. imagination inflation
   D. repression

2. Which of the following effects demonstrates that one can change the details of a memory just by phrasing a question a certain way?
   A. Misinformation effects
   B. The DRM procedure
   C. Imagination inflation
   D. Repression

Apply . . .

3. Jonathan witnessed a robbery. The police asked him to identify the perpetrator from a lineup. You can be most confident in his selection if
   A. the authorities smiled after Jonathan's response so that he would feel comfortable during the lineup procedure.
   B. the authorities had the lineup presented all at the same time so Jonathan could compare the individuals.
   C. the lineup included individuals of different races and ethnicities.
   D. Jonathan was given the option to not choose any of the people from the lineup if no one fit his memory.

Analyze . . .

4. Psychologists who study false memories have engaged in a debate over the validity of recovered memories. Why are they skeptical about claims of recovered memories?
   A. They have never experienced recovered memories themselves.
   B. Many of the techniques used to recover memories in therapy bear a striking similarity to the techniques used to create false memories in research.
   C. Brain scans can easily distinguish between true and false memories.
   D. Scientists have proven that it is impossible to remember something that you have once forgotten.

Module 7.3 Summary

7.3a   Know . . . the key terminology used in discussing how memories are organized and constructed.

constructive memory
DRM procedure
false memory
imagination inflation
misinformation effect
recovered memory
recovered memory controversy
schema

7.3b   Understand . . . how schemas serve as frameworks for encoding and constructing memories.

Schemas guide our attention, telling us what to expect in certain circumstances. They organize long-term memories and provide us with cues when it comes time to retrieve those memories.

7.3c   Understand . . . how psychologists can produce false memories in the laboratory.

Psychologists have found that a number of factors contribute to the construction of false memories, including misinformation, imagination inflation, and the semantic similarities used in the DRM procedure.

7.3d   Apply . . . what you have learned to judge the reliability of eyewitness testimony.

Eyewitness testimony is absolutely crucial to the operation of most legal systems, but how reliable is it? Since 1989,

225 U.S.-based cases of exonerations (convictions that have been overturned due to new evidence after the trial) have been made possible thanks to the help of The Innocence Project. In these cases, the original convictions were based on the following information (some cases included multiple sources):

- Eyewitness misidentification (173 cases)
- Improper or unvalidated forensics (116 cases)
- False confessions (51 cases)
- Questionable information from informants (36 cases)

Apply Activity

What percentage of the exonerations mentioned above involved eyewitness mistakes? What do these data suggest about research on eyewitness testimony?

7.3e   Analyze . . . the arguments in the "recovered memory" debate.

You should first understand the premise behind the idea of recovered memories: Some people believe that if a memory is too painful, it might be blocked from conscious recollection, only to be recovered later through therapeutic techniques. Others argue that it is difficult to prove that a "recovered" memory is actually real, as opposed to falsely constructed. Given how easy it is to create false memories, they argue, any memory believed to be recovered should be viewed with skepticism.

Chapter 8
Thought and Language

8.1 The Organization of Knowledge

- Concepts and Categories 315
  Working the Scientific Literacy Model: Priming and Semantic Networks 318
- Module 8.1a Quiz 319
- Memory, Culture, and Categories 319
- Module 8.1b Quiz 323
- Module 8.1 Summary 323

8.2 Problem Solving, Judgment, and Decision Making

- Defining and Solving Problems 325
- Module 8.2a Quiz 328
- Judgment and Decision Making 328
  Working the Scientific Literacy Model: Maximizing and Satisficing in Complex Decisions 332
- Module 8.2b Quiz 334
- Module 8.2 Summary 335

8.3 Language and Communication

- What Is Language? 337
- Module 8.3a Quiz 341
- The Development of Language 341
- Module 8.3b Quiz 344
- Genes, Evolution, and Language 344
  Working the Scientific Literacy Model: Genes and Language 344
- Module 8.3c Quiz 348
- Module 8.3 Summary 348

Module 8.1 The Organization of Knowledge

Dmitry Vereshchagin/Fotolia

 Learning Objectives

8.1a Know . . . the key terminology associated with concepts and categories.

8.1b Understand . . . theories of how people organize their knowledge about the world.

8.1c Understand . . . how experience and culture can shape the way we organize our knowledge.

8.1d Apply . . . your knowledge to identify prototypical examples.

8.1e Analyze . . . the claim that the language we speak determines how we think.

When Edward regained consciousness in the hospital, his family immediately noticed that something was wrong. The most obvious problem was that he had difficulty recognizing faces, a relatively common disorder known as prosopagosia. *As the doctors performed more testing, it became apparent that Edward had other cognitive problems as well. Edward had difficulty recognizing objects—but not* all *objects. Instead, he couldn't distinguish between different vegetables even though he could use language to describe their appearance. His ability to recognize most other types of objects seemed normal.*

Neurological patients like Edward may seem unrelated to your own life. However, for specific categories of visual information to be lost, they must have been stored in similar areas of the brain before brain damage occurred. Therefore, these cases give us some insight into how the brain stores and organizes the information that we have encoded into memory.

Focus Questions

1. How do people form easily recognizable categories from complex information?

2. How does culture influence the ways in which we categorize information?

>> Each of us has amassed a tremendous amount of knowledge in the course of our lifetime. Indeed, it is impossible to put a number on just how many facts each of us knows. Imagine trying to record everything you ever learned about the world—how many books could you fill? Instead of asking how much we know, psychologists are interested in how we keep track of it all. In this module, we will explore what those processes are like and how

they work. We will start by learning about the key terminology before presenting theories about how knowledge is stored over the long term.

Concepts and Categories

A **concept** *is the mental representation of an object, event, or idea.* Although it seems as though different concepts should be distinct from each other, there are actually very few independent concepts. You do not have just one concept for *chair*, one for *table*, and one for *sofa*. Instead, each of these concepts can be divided into smaller groups with more precise labels, such as *arm chair* or *coffee table*. Similarly, all of these items can be lumped together under the single label, *furniture*. Psychologists use the term **categories** to refer to these *clusters of interrelated concepts*. We form these groups using a process called *categorization*.

CLASSICAL CATEGORIES: DEFINITIONS AND RULES

Categorization is difficult to define in that it involves elements of perception (Chapter 4), memory (Chapter 7), and "higher-order" processes like decision making (Module 8.2) and language (Module 8.3). The earliest approach to the study of categories is referred to as **classical categorization**; *this theory claims that objects or events are categorized according to a certain set of rules or by a specific set of features*—something similar to a dictionary definition (Lakoff & Johnson, 1999; Rouder & Ratcliffe, 2006). Definitions do a fine job of explaining how people categorize items, at least in certain situations. For example, a triangle can be defined as "a figure (usually, a plane rectilinear figure) having three angles and three sides" (*Oxford English Dictionary*, 2011). Using this definition, you should find it easy to categorize the triangles in Figure 8.1.

Classical categorization does not tell the full story of how categorization works, however. We use a variety of cognitive processes in determining which objects fit which category. One of the major problems we confront in this process is **graded membership**—*the observation that some concepts appear to make better category members than others.* For example, see if the definition in Table 8.1 fits your definition of *bird* and then categorize the items in the table.

Ideally, you said yes to the sparrow and penguin, and no to the apple. But did you notice any difference in how you responded to the sparrow and penguin? Psychologists have researched classical categorization using a behavioural measure known as the *sentence-verification technique*, in which volunteers wait for a sentence to appear in front of them on a computer screen and respond as quickly as they can with a yes or no answer to statements such as "A sparrow is a bird," or, "A penguin is a bird." The choice the participant makes, as well as her reaction time to respond, is measured by the researcher. Sentence-verification shows us that some members of a category are recognized faster than others (Olson et al., 2004; Rosch & Mervis, 1975). In other words, subjects almost always answer "yes" faster to sparrow than to penguin. This seems to go against a classical, rule-based categorization system because both sparrows and penguins are equally good fits for the definition, but sparrows are somehow perceived as being more bird-like than penguins. Thus, a modern approach to categorization must explain how "best examples" influence how we categorize items.

PROTOTYPES: CATEGORIZATION BY COMPARISON

When you hear the word *bird*, what mental image comes to mind? Does it resemble an ostrich? Or is your image closer

---

Figure 8.1 Using the Definition of a Triangle to Categorize Shapes

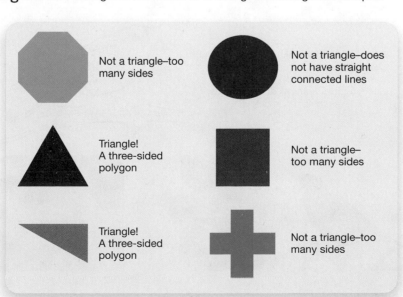

Table 8.1 Categorizing Objects According to the Definition of *Bird*

Definition: "Any of the class Aves of warm-blooded, egg-laying, feathered vertebrates with forelimbs modified to form wings." (American Heritage Dictionary, 2016)

Now categorize a set of items by answering *yes* or *no* regarding the truth of the following sentences.

1. A sparrow is a bird.

2. An apple is a bird.

3. A penguin is a bird.

to a robin, sparrow, or blue jay? The likely image that comes to mind when you imagine a bird is what psychologists call a prototype (see Figure 8.2). **Prototypes** *are mental representations of an average category member* (Rosch, 1973). If you took an average of the three most familiar birds, you would get a prototypical bird.

Prototypes allow for classification by resemblance. When you encounter a little creature you have never seen before, its basic shape—maybe just its silhouette—can be compared to your prototype of a bird. A match will then be made and you can classify the creature as a bird. Notice how different this process is from classical categorization: No rules or definitions are involved, just a set of similarities in overall shape and function.

The main advantage of prototypes is that they help explain why some category members make better examples than others. Ostriches are birds just as much as blue jays are, but they do not resemble the rest of the family very well. In other words, blue jays are closer to the prototypical bird.

Now that you have read about categories based on a set of rules or characteristics (classical categories) and as a general comparison based on resemblances (prototypes), you might wonder which approach is correct. Research says that we can follow either approach—the choice really depends on how complicated a category or a specific example might be. If there are a few major distinctions between items, we use resemblance; if there are complications, we switch to rules (Feldman, 2003; Rouder & Ratcliff, 2004, 2006). For example, in the case of seeing a bat dart by, your first impression might be "bird" because it resembles a bird. But if you investigated further, you will see that a bat fits the classical description of a mammal, not a bird. In other words, it has hair, gives live birth rather than laying eggs, and so on.

NETWORKS AND HIERARCHIES Classical categorization and prototypes only explain part of how we organize information. Each concept that we learn about has similarities to other concepts. A sparrow has physical similarities

Figure 8.2 A Prototypical Bird

A prototypical bird might look something like this one on the right.

It combines features of actual birds, such as those below.

Left: chatursunil/Shutterstock; centre: Al Mueller/Shutterstock; right: Leo/Shutterstock

---

Figure 8.3 A Semantic Network Diagram for the Category "Animal"

The nodes include the basic-level categories, *Bird* and *Fish*. Another node represents the broader category of *Animal*, while the lowest three nodes represent the more specific categories of *Robin*, *Emu*, and *Trout*.

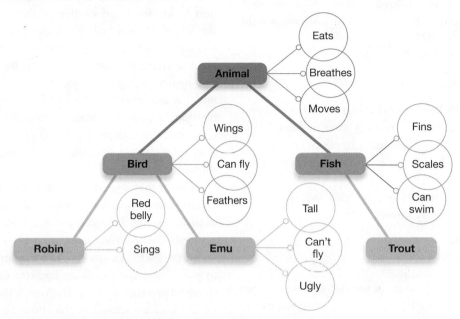

Source: Based on Collins, A. M., & Quillian, M. R. (1969). Retrieval time from semantic memory. *Journal of Verbal Learning and Verbal Behavior, 8,* 240–248.

to a bat (e.g., size and shape); a sparrow will have even more in common with a robin because they are both birds (e.g., size, shape, laying eggs, etc.). These connections among ideas can be represented in a network diagram known as a **semantic network**, *an interconnected set of nodes (or concepts) and the links that join them to form a category* (see Figure 8.3). *Nodes* are circles that represent concepts, and *links* connect them together to represent the structure of a category as well as the relationships among different categories (Collins & Loftus, 1975). In these networks, similar items have more, and stronger, connections than unrelated items.

Something you may notice about Figure 8.3 is that it is arranged in a *hierarchy*—that is, it consists of a structure moving from general to very specific. This organization is important because different levels of the category are useful in different situations. The most frequently used level, in both thought and language, is the *basic-level category*, which is located in the middle row of the diagram (where birds and fish are) (Johnson & Mervis, 1997; Rosch et al., 1976). A number of qualities make the basic-level category unique:

- Basic-level categories are the terms used most often in conversation.
- They are the easiest to pronounce.
- They are the level at which prototypes exist.
- They are the level at which most thinking occurs.

To get a sense for how different category levels influence our thinking, we can compare sentences referring to an object at different levels. Consider what would happen if someone approached you and made any one of the following statements:

- There's an *animal* in your yard.
- There's a *bird* in your yard.
- There's a *robin* in your yard.

The second sentence—"There's a bird in your yard"—is probably the one you are most likely to hear, and it makes reference to a basic level of a category (birds). Many people would respond that the choice of *animal* as a label indicates confusion, claiming that if the speaker knew it was a *bird*, he should have said so; otherwise, it sounds like he is trying to figure out which kind of animal he is looking at. Indeed, *superordinate categories* like "animal" are generally used when someone is uncertain about an object or when he or she wishes to group together a number of different examples from the basic-level category (e.g., birds, cats, dogs). In contrast, when the speaker identifies a *subordinate-level category* like *robin*, it suggests that there is something special about this particular type of bird. It may also indicate that the speaker has expert-level knowledge of the basic category and that using the more specific level is necessary to get her point across in the intended way.

In order to demonstrate the usefulness of semantic networks in our attempt to explain how we organize knowledge, complete this easy test based on the animal network in Figure 8.3. If you were asked to react to dozens of sentences, and the following two sentences were included among them, which do you think you would mark as "true" the fastest?

- *A robin is a bird.*
- *A robin is an animal.*

As you can see in the network diagram, *robin* and *bird* are closer together; in fact, to connect *robin* to *animal*, you must first go through *bird*. Sure enough, people regard the sentence "A robin is a bird" as a true statement faster than "A robin is an animal."

Now consider another set of examples. Which trait do you think you would verify faster?

- *A robin has wings.*
- *A robin eats.*

Using the connecting lines as we did before, we can predict that it would be the first statement about wings. As research shows, our guess would be correct. These results demonstrate that how concepts are arranged in semantic networks can influence how quickly we can access information about them.

Working the Scientific Literacy Model

Priming and Semantic Networks

The thousands of concepts and categories in long-term memory are not isolated, but connected in a number of ways. What are the consequences of forming all the connections in semantic networks?

What do we know about semantic networks?

In your daily life, you notice the connections within semantic networks anytime you encounter one aspect of a category and other related concepts seem to come to mind. Hearing the word "fruit," for example, might lead you to think of an apple, and the apple may lead you to think of a computer, which may lead you to think of a paper that is due tomorrow. These associations illustrate the concept of **priming**—*the activation of individual concepts in long-term memory.* Interestingly, research has shown that priming can also occur without your awareness; "fruit" may not have brought the image of a watermelon to mind, but the concept of a watermelon may have been primed nonetheless.

How can science explain priming effects?

Psychologists can test for priming through reaction time measurements, such as those in the sentence verification tasks discussed earlier or through a method called the *lexical decision task*. With the lexical decision method, a volunteer sits at a computer and stares at a focal point. Next, a string of letters flashes on the screen. The volunteer responds yes or no as quickly as possible to indicate whether the letters spell a word (see Figure 8.4). Using this method, a volunteer should respond faster that "apple" is a word if it follows the word "fruit" (which *is* semantically related) than if it follows the word "bus" (which is *not* semantically related).

Given that lexical decision tasks are highly controlled experiments, we might wonder if they have any impact outside of the laboratory. One test by Jennifer Coane suggests that priming does occur in everyday life (Coane & Balota, 2009). Coane's research team invited volunteers to participate in lexical decision tasks about holidays at different times of the year. The words they chose were based on the holiday season at that time. Sure enough, without any laboratory priming, words such as "nutcracker" and "reindeer" showed priming effects at times when they were *congruent* (or "in season") in December, relative to other times of the year (see Figure 8.5). Similarly, words like "leprechaun" and "shamrock" showed a priming effect during the month of March. Because the researchers did not instigate the priming, it must have been the holiday spirit at work: Decorations and advertisements may serve as constant primes.

Can we critically evaluate this information?

Priming influences thought and behaviour, but is certainly not all-powerful. In fact, it can be very weak at times. Because the strength of priming can vary a great deal, some published experiments have been very difficult to

---

Figure 8.4 A Lexical Decision Task

In a lexical decision task, an individual watches a computer screen as strings of letters are presented. The participant must respond as quickly as possible to indicate whether the letters spell a word (e.g., "desk") or are a non-word (e.g., "sekd").

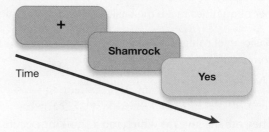

Figure 8.5 Priming Affects the Speed of Responses on a Lexical Decision Task

Average response times were faster when the holiday-themed words were *congruent* (in season), as represented by the blue bars. This finding is consistent for both the first half and the second half of the list of words.

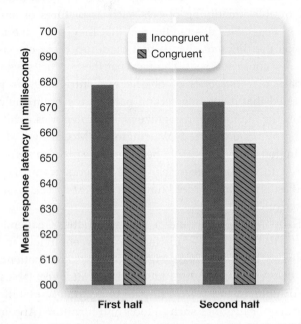

Source: Republished with permission of Springer, from Priming the Holiday Spirit: Persistent Activation due to Extraexperimental Experiences Fig. 1, Pg.1126, *Psychonomic Bulletin & Review*, 16 (6), 1124–1128, 2009. Permission conveyed through Copyright Clearance Center, Inc.

replicate—an important criterion of quality research. So, while most psychologists agree that priming is an important area of research, there have been very open debates at academic conferences and in peer-reviewed journals about the best way to conduct the research and how to interpret the results (Cesario, 2014; Klatzky & Creswell, 2014).

Why is this relevant?

Advertisers know all too well that priming is more than just a curiosity; it can be used in a controlled way to promote specific behaviours. For example, cigarette advertising is not allowed on television stations, but large tobacco companies can sponsor anti-smoking ads. Why would a company advertise against its own product? Researchers brought a group of smokers into the lab to complete a study on television programming and subtly included a specific type of advertisement between segments (they did not reveal the true purpose of the study until after it was completed). Their participants were four times as likely to light up after watching a tobacco-company anti-smoking ad than if they saw the control group ad about supporting a youth sports league (Harris et al., 2013). It would appear that while the verbal message is "don't smoke," the images actually prime the behaviour. Fortunately, more healthful behaviours have been promoted through priming; for example, carefully designed primes have been shown to reduce mindless snacking (Papies & Hamstra, 2010) and binge-drinking in university students (Goode et al., 2014).

Module 8.1a Quiz:

Concepts and Categories

Know . . .

1. A _____ is a mental representation of an average member of a category.
   A. subordinate-level category
   B. prototype
   C. similarity principle
   D. network

2. _____ refer to mental representations of objects, events, or ideas.
   A. Categories
   B. Concepts

C. Primings
D. Networks

Understand . . .

3. Classical categorization approaches do not account for _____, a type of categorization that notes some items make better category members than others.
   A. basic-level categorization
   B. prototyping
   C. priming
   D. graded membership

Memory, Culture, and Categories

In the first part of this module, we examined how we group together concepts to form categories. However, it is important to remember that these processes are based, at least in part, on our experiences. In this section of the module, we examine the role of experience—both in terms of memory processes and cultural influences—on our ability to organize our vast stores of information.

CATEGORIZATION AND EXPERIENCE People integrate new stimuli into categories based on what they have experienced before (Jacoby & Brooks, 1984). When we encounter a new item, we select its category by retrieving the item(s) that are most similar to it from memory (Brooks, 1978). Normally, these procedures lead to fast and accurate categorization. If you see an animal with wings and a beak, you can easily retrieve from memory a bird that you previously saw; doing so will lead you to infer that this new object is a bird, even if it is a type of bird that you might not have encountered before.

However, there are also times when our reliance on previously experienced items can lead us astray. In a series of studies with medical students and practising physicians, Geoffrey Norman and colleagues at McMaster University found that recent exposure to an example from one category can bias how people diagnose new cases (Leblanc et al., 2001; Norman, Brooks, et al., 1989; Norman, Rosenthal, et a., 1989). In one experiment, medical students were taught to diagnose different skin conditions using written rules as well as photographs of these diseases. Some of the photographs were typical examples of that disorder whereas other photographs were unusual cases that resembled other disorders. When tested later, the participants were more likely to rely on the previously viewed photographs than they were on the rules (a fact that would surprise most medical schools); in fact, the unusual photographs viewed during training even led to wrong diagnoses for test items that were textbook examples of that disorder (Allen et al., 1992)! This shows the power that our memory can have on how we take in and organize new information. As an aside, expert physicians were accurate over 90% of the time in most studies, so you can still trust your doctor.

CATEGORIES, MEMORY, AND THE BRAIN The fact that our ability to make categorical decisions is influenced by previous experiences tells us that this process involves memory. Studies of neurological patients like the man discussed at the beginning of this module provide a unique perspective on how these memories are organized in the brain. Some patients with damage to the temporal lobes have trouble identifying objects such as pictures of animals or vegetables despite the fact that they were able to describe the different shapes that made up those objects (i.e., they could still see). The fact that these deficits were for particular *categories* of objects was intriguing, as it suggested that damaging certain parts of the brain could impair the ability to recognize some categories while leaving others unaffected (Warrington & McCarthy, 1983; Warrington & Shallice, 1979). Because these problems were isolated to certain categories, these patients were diagnosed as having a disorder known as *category specific visual agnosia* (or *CSVA*).

Early attempts to find a pattern in these patients' deficits focused on the distinction between living and non-living categories (see Figure 8.6). Several patients with CSVA had difficulties identifying fruits, vegetables, and/or animals but were still able to accurately identify members of categories such as tools and furniture (Arguin et al., 1996; Bunn et al., 1998). However, although CSVA has been observed in a number of patients, researchers also noted that it would be physically impossible for our brains to have specialized regions for *every* category we have encountered. There simply isn't enough space for

---

Figure 8.6 Naming Errors for a CSVA Patient

Patients with CSVA have problems identifying members of specific categories. When asked to identify the object depicted by different line drawings, patient E. W. showed a marked impairment for the recognition of animals. Her ability to name items from other categories demonstrated that her overall perceptual abilities were preserved.

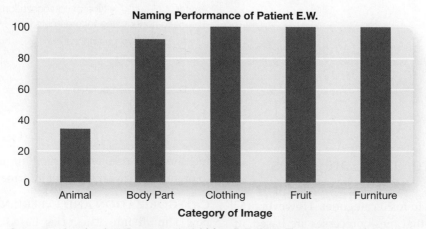

Source: Based on data from Caramazza, A., & Mahon, B. Z. (2003). The organization of conceptual knowledge: the evidence from category-specific semantic deficits. *Trends in Cognitive Sciences, 7* (8), 354–361.

BIOPSYCHOSOCIAL PERSPECTIVES

Culture and Categorical Thinking

Animals, relatives, household appliances, colours, and other entities all fall into categories. However, people from different cultures might differ in how they categorize such objects. In North America, cows are sometimes referred to as "livestock" or "food animals," whereas in India, where cows are regarded as sacred, neither category would apply.

In addition, how objects are *related* to each other differs considerably across cultures. Which of the two photos in Figure 8.7a do you think someone from North America took? Researchers asked both American and Japanese university students to take a picture of someone, from whatever angle or degree of focus they chose. American students were more likely to take close-up pictures, whereas Japanese students typically included surrounding objects (Nisbett & Masuda, 2003). When asked which two objects go together in Figure 8.7b, American college students tend to group cows with chickens—because both are animals. In contrast, Japanese students coupled cows with grass, because grass is what cows eat (Gutchess et al., 2010; Nisbett & Masuda, 2003). These examples demonstrate cross-cultural differences in perceiving how objects are related to their environments. People raised in North America tend to focus on a single characteristic, whereas Japanese people tend to view objects in relation to their environment.

Researchers have even found differences in brain function when people of different cultural backgrounds view and categorize objects (Park & Huang, 2010). Figure 8.8 reveals differences in brain activity when Westerners and East Asians view photos of objects, such as an animal, against a background of grass and trees. Areas of the brain devoted to processing both objects (lateral parts of the occipital lobes) and background (the parahippocampal gyrus, an area underneath the hippocampus) become activated when Westerners view these photos, whereas only areas devoted to background processes become activated in East Asians (Goh et al., 2007). These findings demonstrate that a complete understanding of how humans categorize objects requires application of the biopsychosocial model.

Figure 8.7 Your Culture and Your Point of View

(a) Which of these two pictures do you think a North American would be more likely to take? (b) Which two go together?

(a)

(b)

Top photos: Blend Images/Shutterstock

Source, bottom: Adapted from Nisbett, R. E., & Masuda, T. (2003). Culture and point of view. *Proceedings of the National Academy of Sciences, 100* (19), 11163–11170. Copyright © 2003. Reprinted by permission of National Academy of Sciences.

Figure 8.8 Brain Activity Varies by Culture

Brain regions that are involved in object recognition and processing are activated differently in people from Western and Eastern cultures. Brain regions that are involved in processing individual objects are more highly activated when Westerners view focal objects against background scenery, whereas people from East Asian countries appear to attend to background scenery more closely than focal objects.

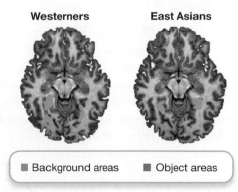

Westerners   East Asians

■ Background areas   ■ Object areas

Source: Park, D. C. & Huang, C.-M. (2010). Culture wires the brain: A cognitive neuroscience perspective. *Perspectives on Psychological Science, 5* (4), 391–400. Reprinted by permission of SAGE Publications.

Myths in Mind
How Many Words for Snow?

Cultural differences in how people think and categorize items have led to the idea of **linguistic relativity** (or the **Whorfian hypothesis**)—*the theory that the language we use determines how we understand (and categorize) the world.* One often-cited example is about the Inuit in Canada's Arctic regions, who are thought to have many words for snow, each with a different meaning. For example, *aput* means snow that is on the ground, and *gana* means falling snow. This observation, which was made in the early 19th century by anthropologist Franz Boas, was often repeated and exaggerated, with claims that Inuit people had dozens of words for different types of snow. With so many words for snow, it was thought that perhaps the Inuit people perceive snow differently than someone who does not live near

it almost year-round. Scholars used the example to argue that language determines how people categorize the world.

Research tells us that we must be careful in over-generalizing the influence of language on categorization. The reality is that the Inuit seem to categorize snow the same way a person from the rest of Canada does. Someone from balmy Winnipeg can tell the difference between falling snow, blowing snow, sticky snow, drifting snow, and "oh-sweet-God-it's-snowing-in-May-snow," just as well as an Inuit who lives with snow for most of the year (Martin, 1986). Therefore, we see that the linguistic relativity hypothesis is incorrect in this case: The difference in vocabulary for snow does not lead to differences in perception.

this to occur. Instead, they proposed that evolutionary pressures led to the development of specialized circuits in the brain for a *small group of categories* that were important for our survival. These categories included animals, fruits and vegetables, members of our own species, and possibly tools (Caramazza & Mahon, 2003). Few, if any, other categories involve such specialized memory storage. This theory can explain most, but not all, of the problems observed in the patients tested thus far. It is also in agreement with brain-imaging studies showing that different parts of the temporal lobes are active when people view items from different categories including animals, tools, and people (Martin et al., 1996). Thus, although different people will vary in terms of the exact location that these categories are stored, it does appear that some categories are stored separately from others.

CATEGORIES AND CULTURE The human brain is wired to perceive similarities and differences and, as we learned from prototypes, the end result of this tendency is to categorize items based on these comparisons as well as on our previous experiences with members of different categories. However, our natural inclination to do so interacts with our cultural experiences; how we categorize objects depends to a great extent on what we have learned about those objects from others in our culture.

Various researchers have explored the relationships between culture and categorization by studying basic-level categories among people from different cultural backgrounds. For example, researchers have asked individuals from traditional villages in Central America to identify a variety of plants and animals that are extremely relevant to their diet, medicine, safety, and other aspects of their lives. Not surprisingly, these individuals referred to plants and animals at a more specific level than North American university students would (Bailenson et al., 2002; Berlin, 1974). Thus, categorization is based—at least to some extent—on cultural learning. Psychologists have also discovered that cultural factors influence not just how we categorize individual objects, but also how objects in our world relate to one another.

Although culture and memory both clearly affect how we describe and categorize our world, we do need to remember to critically analyze the results of these studies. Specifically, as our world becomes more Westernized, it is possible—even likely—that these cultural differences will decrease. These results, then, tell us about cultural differences *at a given time.* As you saw in the Myths in Mind feature above, we should also exercise caution when reading about another form of cultural influences on categorization—linguistic relativity.

Module 8.1b Quiz:

Memory, Culture, and Categories

Know . . .

1. The idea that our language influences how we understand the world is referred to as _____.
   - **A.** the context specificity hypothesis
   - **B.** sentence verification
   - **C.** the Whorfian hypothesis
   - **D.** priming

Understand . . .

2. A neurologist noticed that a patient with temporal-lobe damage seemed to have problems naming specific categories of objects. Based upon what you read in this module, which classes of objects are most likely to be affected by this damage?
   - **A.** Animals and tools
   - **B.** Household objects that he would use quite frequently
   - **C.** Fruits and vegetables
   - **D.** Related items such as animals and hunting weapons

Apply . . .

3. Janice, a medical school student, looked at her grandmother's hospital chart. Although her grandmother appeared to have problems with her intestines, Janice thought the pattern of the lab results resembled those of a patient with lupus she had seen in the clinic earlier that week. Janice is showing an example of
   - **A.** how memory for a previous example can influence categorization decisions.
   - **B.** how people rely on prototypes to categorize objects and events.
   - **C.** how we rely on a set of rules to categorize objects.
   - **D.** how we are able to quickly categorize examples from specific categories.

Analyze . . .

4. Research on linguistic relativity suggests that
   - **A.** language has a complete control over how people categorize the world.
   - **B.** language can have some effects on categorization, but the effects are limited.
   - **C.** language has no effect on categorization.
   - **D.** researchers have not addressed this question.

Module 8.1 Summary

8.1a   Know . . . the key terminology associated with concepts and categories.

categories
classical categorization
concept
graded membership
linguistic relativity
   (Whorfian hypothesis)
priming
prototypes
semantic network

8.1b   Understand . . . theories of how people organize their knowledge about the world.

Certain objects and events are more likely to be associated in clusters. The priming effect demonstrates this phenomenon; for example, hearing the word "fruit" makes it more likely that you will think of "apple" than, say, "table." More specifically, we organize our knowledge about the world through semantic networks, which arrange categories from general to specific levels. Usually we think in terms of basic-level categories, but under some circumstances we can be either more or less specific. Studies of people with brain damage suggest that the neural representations of members of evolutionarily important categories are stored together in the brain. These studies also show us that our previous experience with a category can influence how we categorize and store new stimuli in the brain.

8.1c   Understand . . . how experience and culture can shape the way we organize our knowledge.

One of many possible examples of this influence was discussed. Specifically, ideas of how objects relate to one another differ between people from North America and people from Eastern Asia. People from North America (and Westerners in general) tend to focus on individual, focal objects in a scene, whereas people from Japan tend to focus on how objects are interrelated.

8.1d   Apply . . . your knowledge to identify prototypical examples.

Apply Activity

Try the following questions for practice.

1. What is the best example for the category of fish: a hammerhead shark, a trout, or an eel?
2. What do you consider to be a prototypical sport? Why?
3. Some categories are created spontaneously, yet still have prototypes. For example, what might be a prototypical object for the category "what to save if your house is on fire"?

8.1e   Analyze . . . the claim that the language we speak determines how we think.

Researchers have shown that language can influence the way we think, but it cannot entirely shape how we perceive the world. For example, people can perceive visual and tactile differences between different types of snow even if they don't have unique words for each type.

Module 8.2 Problem Solving, Judgment, and Decision Making

Polaris/Newscom

Learning Objectives

8.2a Know . . . the key terminology of problem solving and decision making.

8.2b Understand . . . the characteristics that problems have in common.

8.2c Understand . . . how obstacles to problem solving are often self-imposed.

8.2d Apply . . . your knowledge to determine if you tend to be a maximizer or a satisficer.

8.2e Analyze . . . whether human thought is primarily logical or intuitive.

Ki-Suck Han was about to die. He had just been shoved onto the subway's tracks and was desperately scrambling to climb back onto the station's platform as the subway train rushed toward him. If you were a few metres away from Mr. Han, what would you have done? What factors would have influenced your actions?

In this case, the person on the platform was R. Umar Abbasi, a freelance photographer working for The New York Post. Mr. Abbasi did not put down his camera and run to help Mr. Han. Instead, he took a well-framed photograph that captured the terrifying scene. The photograph was published on the front page of the Post and was immediately condemned by people who were upset that the photographer didn't try to save Mr. Han's life (and that the Post *used the photograph to make money). In a statement released to other media outlets, the* Post *claimed that Mr. Abbasi felt that he wasn't strong enough to lift the man and instead tried to use his camera's flash to signal the driver. According to this explanation, Mr. Abbasi analyzed the situation and selected a course of action that he felt would be most helpful. Regardless of whether you believe this account, it does illustrate an important point: Reasoning and decision making can be performed in a number of ways and can be influenced by a number of factors. That is why we don't all respond the same way to the same situation.*

Focus Questions

1. How do people make decisions and solve problems?

2. How can having multiple options lead people to be dissatisfied with their decisions?

» In other modules of this text, you have read about how we learn and remember new information (Modules 7.1 and 7.2) and how we organize our knowledge of different concepts (Module 8.1). This module will focus on how we *use* this information to help us solve problems and make decisions. Although it may seem like such "higher-order cognitive abilities" are distinct from memory and categorization, they are actually a wonderful example of how the different topics within the field of psychology relate to each other. When we try to solve a problem or decide between alternatives, we are actually drawing on our knowledge of different concepts and using that information to try to imagine different possible outcomes (Green et al., 2006). How well we perform these tasks depends on a number of factors including our problem-solving strategies and the type of information available to us.

Defining and Solving Problems

You are certainly familiar with the general concept of a problem, but in psychological terminology, **problem solving** means *accomplishing a goal when the solution or the path to the solution is not clear* (Leighton & Sternberg, 2003; Robertson, 2001). Indeed, many of the problems that we face in life contain *obstacles* that interfere with our ability to reach our goals. The challenge, then, is to find a technique or strategy that will allow us to overcome these obstacles. As you will see, there are a number of options that people use for this purpose—although none of them are perfect.

PROBLEM-SOLVING STRATEGIES AND TECHNIQUES
Each of us will face an incredible number of problems in our lives. Some of these problems will be straightforward and easy to solve; however, others will be quite complex and will require us to come up with a novel solution. How do we remember the strategies we can use for routine problems? And, how do we develop new strategies for nonroutine problems? Although these questions *appear* as if they could have an infinite number of answers, there seem to be two common techniques that we use time and again.

One type of strategy is more objective, logical, and slower, whereas the other is more subjective, intuitive, and quicker (Gilovich & Griffin, 2002; Holyoak & Morrison, 2005). The difference between them can be illustrated with an example. Suppose you are trying to figure out where you have left your phone. You've tried the trick of calling yourself using a landline phone, but you couldn't hear it ringing. So, it's not in your house. A *logical* approach might involve making of list of the places you've been in the last 24 hours and then retracing your steps until you (hopefully) find your phone. An *intuitive* approach might involve thinking about previous times you've lost your phone or wallet and using these experiences to guide your search (e.g., "I'm always forgetting my phone at Dan's place, so I should look there first").

When we think logically, we rely on **algorithms**, *problem-solving strategies based on a series of rules*. As such, they are very logical and follow a set of steps, usually in a preset order. Computers are very good at using algorithms because they can follow a preprogrammed set of steps and perform thousands of operations every second. People, however, are not always so rule-bound. We tend to rely on intuition to find strategies and solutions that seem like a good fit for the problem. These are called **heuristics**, *problem-solving strategies that stem from prior experiences and provide an educated guess as to what is the most likely solution*. Heuristics are often quite efficient; these "rules of thumb" are usually accurate and allow us to find solutions and to make decisions quickly. In the example of trying to figure out where you left your phone, you are more likely to put your phone down at a friend's house than on the bus, so that increases the likelihood that your phone is still sitting on his coffee table. Calling your friend to ask about your phone is much simpler than retracing your steps from class to the gym to the grocery store, and so on.

The overall goal of both algorithms and heuristics is to find an accurate solution as efficiently as possible. In many situations, heuristics allow us to solve problems quite rapidly. However, the trade-off is that these shortcuts can occasionally lead to incorrect solutions, a topic we will return to later in this module.

Of course, different problems call for different approaches. In fact, in some cases, it might be useful to start off with one type of problem-solving and then switch to another. Think about how you might play the children's word-game known as hangman, shown in Figure 8.9. Here, the goal state is to spell a word. In the initial state, you have none of the letters or other clues to guide you. So, your obstacles are to overcome (i.e., fill in) blanks without guessing the wrong letters. How would you go about achieving this goal?

Figure 8.9 Problem Solving in Hangman

In a game of hangman, your job is to guess the letters in the word represented by the four blanks to the left. If you get a letter right, your opponent will put it in the correct blank. If you guess an incorrect letter, your opponent will draw a body part on the stick figure. The goal is to guess the word before the entire body is drawn.

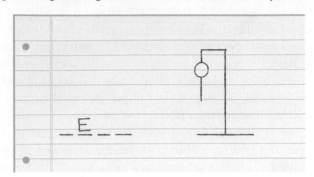

Figure 8.10 The Nine-Dot Problem

Connect all nine dots using only four straight lines and without lifting your pen or pencil (Maier, 1930). The solution to the problem can be seen in Figure 8.11.

Source: Maier, N. F. (1930). Reasoning in humans. I. On direction. *Journal of Comparative Psychology*, 10 (2), 115–143. American Psychological Association.

On one hand, an algorithm might go like this: Guess the letter *A*, then *B*, then *C*, and so on through the alphabet until you lose or until the word is spelled. However, this would not be a very successful approach. An alternative algorithm would be to find out how frequently each letter occurs in the alphabet and then guess the letters in that order until the game ends with you winning or losing. So, you would start out by selecting *E*, then *A*, and so on. On the other hand, a heuristic might be useful. For example, if you discover the last letter is *G*, you might guess that the next-to-last letter is *N*, because you know that many words end with *-ing*. Using a heuristic here would save you time and usually lead to an accurate solution.

As you can see, some problems (such as the hangman game) can be approached with either algorithms or heuristics. In other words, most people start out a game like hangman with an algorithm: Guess the most frequent letters until a recognizable pattern emerges, such as *-ing*, or the letters *-oug* (which are often followed by *h*, as in *tough* or *cough*) appear. At that point, you might switch to heuristics and guess which letters would be most likely to fit in the spaces.

COGNITIVE OBSTACLES Using algorithms or heuristics will often allow you to eventually solve a problem; however, there are times when the problem-solving rules and strategies that you have established might actually get in the way of problem solving. The nine-dot problem (Figure 8.10; Maier, 1930) is a good example of such a *cognitive obstacle*. The goal of this problem is to connect all nine dots using only four straight lines and without lifting your pen or pencil off the paper. Try solving the nine-dot problem before you read further.

Here is something to think about when solving this problem: Most people impose limitations on where the lines can go, even though those limits are not a part of the

rules. Specifically, people often assume that a line cannot extend beyond the dots. As you can see in Figure 8.11, breaking these rules is necessary in order to find a solution to the problem.

Having a routine solution available for a problem generally allows us to solve that problem with less effort than we would use if we encountered it for the first time. This efficiency saves us time and effort. Sometimes, however, routines may impose cognitive barriers that impede solving a problem if circumstances change so that the routine solution no longer works. A **mental set** *is a cognitive obstacle that occurs when an individual attempts to apply a routine solution to what is actually a new type of problem.* Figure 8.12 presents a problem that often elicits a mental set. The answer appears at the bottom of the figure, but make your guess before you check it. Did you get it right? If not, then you probably succumbed to a mental set.

Figure 8.11 One Solution to the Nine-Dot Problem

In this case, the tendency is to see the outer edge of dots as a boundary, and to assume that one cannot go past that boundary. However, if you are willing to extend some of the lines beyond the dots, it is actually quite a simple puzzle to complete.

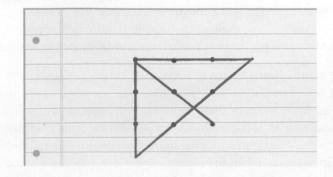

Figure 8.12 The Five-Daughter Problem

Maria's father has five daughters: Lala, Lela, Lila, and Lola. What is the fifth daughter's name?

The fifth daughter's name is Maria.

Figure 8.13 The Two-String Problem

Imagine you are standing between two strings and need to tie them together. The only problem is that you cannot reach both strings at the same time (Maier, 1931). In the room with you is a table, a piece of paper, a pair of pliers, and a ball of cotton. What do you do? For a solution, see Figure 8.16.

Mental sets can occur in many different situations. For instance, a person may experience **functional fixedness**, *which occurs when an individual identifies an object or technique that could potentially solve a problem, but can think of only its most obvious function.* Functional fixedness can be illustrated with a classic thought problem: Figure 8.13 shows two strings hanging from a ceiling. Imagine you are asked to tie the strings together. However, once you grab a string, you cannot let go of it until both are tied together. The problem is, unless you have extraordinarily long arms, you cannot reach the second string while you are holding on to the first one (Maier, 1931). So how would you solve the problem? Figure 8.16 offers one possible answer and an explanation of what makes this problem challenging.

Problem solving occurs in every aspect of life, but as you can see, there are basic cognitive processes that appear no matter what the context. We identify the goal we want to achieve, try to determine the best strategy to do so, and hope that we do not get caught by unexpected obstacles—especially those we create in our own minds.

Of course, not all problems are negative obstacles that must be overcome. Problem solving can also be part of some positive events as well.

PSYCH@

Problem Solving and Humour

Question: Why can't university students take exams at the zoo? *Answer: There are too many cheetahs.*

Jokes often involve a problem that needs to be solved. Solving the problem typically requires at least two steps. The initial step requires the audience to detect that some part of the joke's set-up is not what is expected. Theories of humour sometimes refer to this as *incongruity detection.* Incongruities create an initial tension. In the example we're using, the key word in this joke is "cheetahs." Why would the presence of cheetahs affect exam taking? The trick is to understand that "cheetahs" sounds a lot like "cheaters." So, a zoo would have "cheetahs," but an exam could have "cheaters." Once we understand the incongruity, we no longer feel any tension. *Incongruity resolution* has occurred (Suls, 1972).

At this point, the audience has solved the problem. But, is it funny? Wyer and Collins (1992) suggested that for an incongruity resolution to be funny, the audience or reader would need to elaborate on the joke, possibly thinking about how it relates to them or forming humourous mental images (see Figure 8.14). This process of elaboration should, ideally, lead to an emotional response of amusement, although this might differ across cultures.

Recent neuroimaging studies have manipulated the characteristics of verbal stimuli to allow the researchers to identify brain areas related to nonsense stimuli (incongruities that did not undergo cognitive elaboration) and stimuli that *were* perceived as humourous (incongruities that did undergo elaboration). Incongruity detection and resolution activated areas in the temporal lobes and the medial frontal lobes (close to the middle of the brain). Elaboration activated a network involving the left frontal and parietal lobes (Chan et al., 2013). The purpose of this section wasn't to take the joy out of humour. Instead, it was to show that humour, like most of our behaviours, involves the biopsychosocial model. If we suggested otherwise, we'd be lion.

Figure 8.14 The Comprehension-Elaboration Theory of Humour

Humour is a form of problem solving. With most jokes, we identify the incongruity or "twist" involved in the wording of the joke and then attempt to resolve it. Once we have found the solution, we think about (elaborate on) the joke, oftentimes relating it to ourselves or to mental imagery. These processes lead to a feeling of amusement or, in the case of the cheetah joke, a rolling of the eyes.

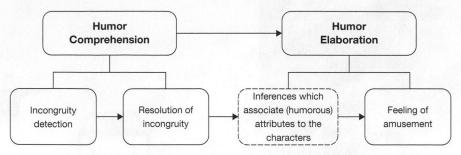

Source: Republished with permission of Elsevier, Inc. from Towards a neural circuit model of verbal humor processing: An fMRI study of the neural substrates of incongruity detection and resolution, *NeuroImage 66* (2013) 169–176. Copyright © 2012. Permission conveyed through Copyright Clearance Center, Inc.

Module 8.2a Quiz:

Defining and Solving Problems

Know . . .

1. _____ are problem-solving strategies that provide a reasonable guess for the solution.
  A. Algorithms
  B. Heuristics
  C. Operators
  D. Subgoals

Understand . . .

2. Javier was attempting to teach his daughter how to tie her shoes. The strategy that would prove most effective in this situation would be a(n) _____.
  A. heuristic
  B. algorithm

  C. obstacle
  D. mental set

3. Jennifer was trying to put together her new bookshelf in her bedroom. Unfortunately, she didn't have a hammer. Frustrated, she went outside and sat down beside some bricks that were left over from a gardening project. Her inability to see that the bricks could be used to hammer in nails is an example of _____.
  A. a mental set
  B. an algorithm
  C. functional fixedness
  D. a heuristic

Judgment and Decision Making

Like problem solving, judgments and decisions can be based on logical algorithms, intuitive heuristics, or a combination of the two types of thought (Gilovich & Griffin, 2002; Holyoak & Morrison, 2005). We tend to use heuristics more often than we realize, even those of us who consider ourselves to be logical thinkers. This isn't necessary a bad thing—heuristics allow us to make efficient judgments and decisions all the time. In this section of the module, we will examine specific types of heuristics, how they positively influence our decision making, and how they can *sometimes* lead us to incorrect conclusions.

CONJUNCTION FALLACIES AND REPRESENTATIVENESS

Linda is 31 years old, single, outspoken, and very bright. She majored in philosophy. As a student, she was deeply concerned with issues of discrimination and social justice, and also participated in antinuclear demonstrations. Which is more likely?

(A) *Linda is a bank teller.*
(B) *Linda is a bank teller and is active in the feminist movement.*

Which answer did you choose? In a study that presented this problem to participants, the researchers reported that (B) was chosen more than 80% of the time. Most respondents stated that option (B) seemed more correct even though option (A) is actually much more likely and would be the correct choice based on the question asked (Tversky & Kahneman, 1982).

So how is the correct answer (A)? Individuals who approach this problem from the stance of probability theory would apply some simple logical steps. The world has a certain number of (A) bank tellers; this number would be considered the *base rate*, or the rate at which you

Figure 8.15 The Conjunction Fallacy

There are more bank tellers in the world than there are bank tellers who are feminists, so there is a greater chance that Linda comes from either (A) or (B) than just (B) alone.

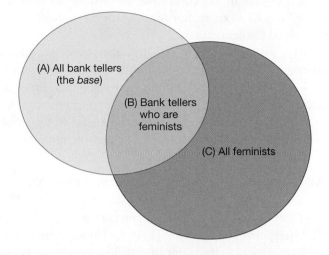

the bank teller example, we cannot identify any traits that seem like a typical bank teller. At the same time, the traits of social activism really do seem to represent a feminist. Thus, the judgment was biased by the fact that Linda seemed representative of a feminist, even though a feminist bank teller will always be rarer than bank tellers in general (i.e., the representativeness heuristic influenced the decision more than logic or mathematical probabilities).

Seeing this type of problem has led many people to question what is wrong with people's ability to use logic: Why is it so easy to get 80% of the people in a study to give the wrong answer? In fact, there is nothing inherently *wrong* with using heuristics; they simply allow individuals to obtain quick answers based on readily available information. In fact, heuristics often lead to correct assumptions about a situation.

Consider this scenario:

You are in a department store trying to find a product that is apparently sold out. At the end of the aisle, you see a young man in tan pants with a red polo shirt—the typical employee's uniform of this chain of stores. Should you stop and consider the probabilities yielding an answer that was technically most correct?

(A) *A young male of this age would wear tan pants and a red polo shirt.*

(B) *A young male of this age would wear tan pants and a red polo shirt and work at this store.*

Or does it make sense to just assume (B) is correct, and to simply ask the young man for help (Shepperd & Koch, 2005)? In this case, it would make perfect sense to assume (B) is correct and not spend time wondering about the best logical way to approach the situation. In other words, heuristics often work and, in the process, save us time and effort. However, there are many situations in which these mental shortcuts can lead to biased or incorrect conclusions.

THE AVAILABILITY HEURISTIC The **availability heuristic** *entails estimating the frequency of an event based on how easily examples of it come to mind.* In other words, we assume that if examples are readily *available,* then they must be very frequent. For example, researchers asked volunteers which was more frequent in the English language:

(A) Words that begin with the letter *K*
(B) Words that have *K* as the third letter

Most subjects chose (A) even though it is not the correct choice. The same thing happened with the consonants *L, N, R,* and *V,* all of which appear as the third letter in a word more often than they appear as the first letter (Tversky & Kahneman, 1973). This outcome reflects the application of the availability heuristic: People base judgments on the information most readily available.

would find a bank teller in the world's population just by asking random people on the street if they are a bank teller. Among the base group, there will be a certain number of (B) bank tellers who are feminists, as shown in Figure 8.15. In other words, the number of bank tellers who are feminists will always be a fraction of (i.e., less than) the total number of bank tellers. But, because many of Linda's qualities could relate to a "feminist," the idea that Linda is a bank teller *and* a feminist feels correct. This type of error, known as the **conjunction fallacy,** *reflects the mistaken belief that finding a specific member in two overlapping categories (i.e., a member of the conjunction of two categories) is more likely than finding any member of one of the larger, general categories.*

The conjunction fallacy demonstrates the use of the **representativeness heuristic:** *making judgments of likelihood based on how well an example represents a specific category.* In

Figure 8.16 A Solution to the Two-String Problem

One solution to the two-string problem from Figure 8.13 is to take the pliers off the table and tie them to one string. This provides enough weight to swing one string back and forth while you grab the other. Many people demonstrate functional fixedness when they approach this problem—they do not think of using the pliers as a weight because its normal function is as a grasping tool.

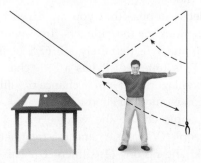

Of course, heuristics often do produce correct answers. Subjects in the same study were asked which was more common in English:

(A) Words that begin with the letter *K*
(B) Words that begin with the letter *T*

In this case, more subjects found that words beginning with *T* were readily available to memory, and they were correct. The heuristic helped provide a quick, intuitive answer.

There are numerous real-world examples of the availability heuristic. In the year following the September 11, 2001 terrorist attacks, people were much more likely to overestimate the likelihood that planes could crash and/or be hijacked. As a result, fewer people flew that year than in the year prior to the attacks, opting instead to travel by car when possible. The availability of the image of planes crashing into the World Trade Center was so vivid and easily retrieved from memory that it influenced decision making. Ironically, this shift proved to be dangerous, particularly given that driving is statistically *much* more dangerous than flying. Gerd Gigerenzer, a German psychologist at the Max Planck Institute in Berlin, examined traffic fatalities on U.S. roads in the years before and after 2001. He found that in the calendar year following these terrorist attacks, there were more than 1500 additional deaths on American roads (when compared to the average of the previous years). Within a year of the attacks, the number of people using planes returned to approximately pre-9/11 levels; so did the number of road fatalities (Gigerenzer, 2004). In other words, for almost a year, people overestimated the risks of flying because it was easier to think of examples of 9/11 than to think of all of the times hijackings and plane crashes did *not* occur; and, they underestimated the risks associated with driving because these images were less available to many people. This example shows us that heuristics, although often useful, can cause us to incorrectly judge the risks associated with many elements of our lives (Gardner, 2008).

ANCHORING AND FRAMING EFFECTS   While the representativeness and availability heuristics involve our ability to remember examples that are similar to the current situation, other heuristics influence our responses based on the way that information is presented. Issues such as the wording of a problem and the problem's frames of reference can have a profound impact on judgments. One such effect, known as the **anchoring effect**, *occurs when an individual attempts to solve a problem involving numbers and uses previous knowledge to keep (i.e., anchor) the response within a limited range.* Sometimes this previous knowledge consists of facts that we can retrieve from memory. For example, imagine that you are asked to name the year that

British Columbia became part of Canada. Although most of you would, of course, excitedly jump from your chair and shout, "1871!" the rest might assume that if Canada became a country in 1867, then B.C. likely joined a few years after that. In this latter case, the birth of our country in 1867 served as an anchor for the judgment about when B.C. joined Confederation.

The anchoring heuristic has also been produced experimentally. In these cases, questions worded in different ways can produce vastly different responses (Epley & Gilovich, 2006; Kahneman & Miller, 1986). For example, consider what might happen if researchers asked the same question to two different groups, using a different anchor each time:

(A) What percentage of countries in the United Nations are from Africa? Is it greater than or less than 10%? What do you think the exact percentage is?
(B) What percentage of countries in the United Nations are from Africa? Is it greater than or less than 65%? What do you think the exact percentage is?

Researchers conducted a study using similar methods and found that individuals in group (A), who received the 10% anchor, estimated the number to be approximately 25%. Individuals in group (B), who received the 65% anchor, estimated the percentage at approximately 45%. In this case, the anchor obviously had a significant effect on the estimates.

The anchoring heuristic can have a large effect on your life. For example, have you ever had to bargain with someone while travelling? Or have you ever negotiated the price of a car? If you are able to establish a low anchor during bargaining, the final price is likely to be much lower than if you let the salesperson dictate the terms. So don't be passive—use what you learn in this course to save yourself some money.

Decision making can also be influenced by how a problem is worded or *framed*. Consider the following dilemma: Imagine that you are a selfless doctor volunteering in a village in a disease-plagued part of Africa. You have two treatment options. Vaccine A has been used before; you know that it will save 200 of the 600 villagers. Vaccine B is untested; it has a 33% chance of saving all 600 people and a 67% chance of saving no one. Which option would you choose?

Now let's suppose that you are given two different treatment options for the villagers. Treatment C has been used before and will definitely kill 67% of the villagers. Treatment D is untested; it has a 33% chance of killing none of the villagers and a 67% chance of killing them all. Which option would you choose?

Most people choose the vaccine that will definitely save 200 people (Vaccine A) and the treatment that has a chance of killing no one (Treatment D). This tendency is

---

Figure 8.17 Framing Effects

When people are asked which vaccine or treatment they would use to help a hypothetical group of villagers, the option they select is influenced by how the question is worded or framed. If the question is worded in terms of saving villagers, most people choose Vaccine A. If the question is worded in terms of killing villagers, most people choose Treatment D.

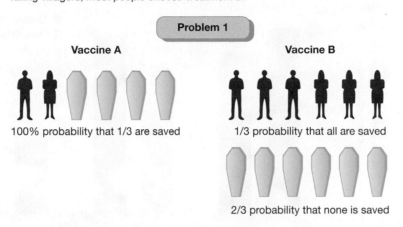

Problem 1

Vaccine A

100% probability that 1/3 are saved

Vaccine B

1/3 probability that all are saved

2/3 probability that none is saved

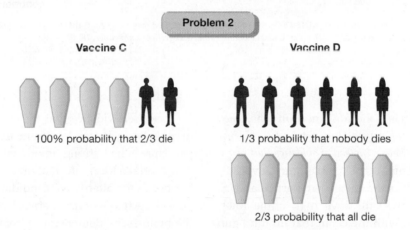

Problem 2

Vaccine C

100% probability that 2/3 die

Vaccine D

1/3 probability that nobody dies

2/3 probability that all die

Source: Wade Carole; Tavris, Carol, *Invitation to Psychology*, 2nd Ed., ©2002, p.121. Adapted and Electronically reproduced by permissin of Pearson Eduation, Inc., Upper Saddle River, New Jersey.

interesting because options A and C are identical as are options B and D. As you can see by looking at Figure 8.17, the only difference between them is that one is framed in terms of saving people and the other is framed in terms of killing people. Yet, people become much more risk-averse when the question is framed in terms of potential losses (or deaths).

BELIEF PERSEVERANCE AND CONFIRMATION BIAS Whenever we solve a problem or make a decision, we have an opportunity to evaluate the outcome to make sure we got it right and to judge how satisfied we are with the decision. However, feeling satisfied does not necessarily mean we are correct.

Let's use an example to make this discussion more concrete. Each time there is a mass shooting in the U.S.,

thousands of gun owners will post messages on social media stating that Americans need to be able to easily purchase more guns in order to protect themselves. Many people (including many Americans), might think this idea is a bit illogical given that easy access to lethal weapons is what makes mass shootings so prevalent in that country. However, gun lovers often engage in (at least) two cognitive biases in order to maintain their beliefs.

One cognitive bias is **belief perseverance**, *when an individual believes he or she has the solution to the problem or the correct answer for a question and will hold onto that belief even in the face of evidence against it.* So, gun advocates will oppose any form of gun control even when presented with evidence from other countries (e.g., Australia) showing that preventing the public from owning assault rifles reduces or even eliminates mass shootings.

Figure 8.18 Ratings of Perceived Contradictions in Political Statements

Democrats and Republicans reached very different conclusions about candidates' contradictory statements. Democrats readily identified the opponent's contradictions but were less likely to do so for their own candidate; the same was true for Republican responders.

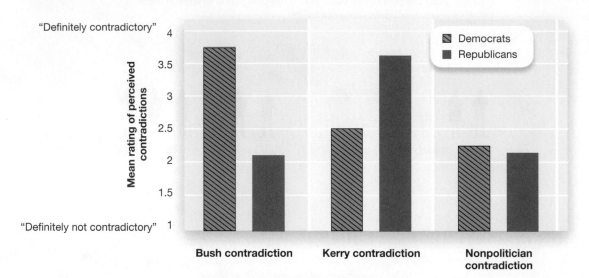

Source: Westen, D., Blagov, P. S., & Harenski, K. (2006). Neural bases for motivated reasoning: An fMRI study of emotional constraints on partisan political judgment in the 2004 U.S. presidential election. *Journal of Cognitive Neuroscience, 18,* 1974–1958. Reprinted with permission of MIT Press.

A second cognitive bias is the **confirmation bias**, *when an individual searches for (or pays attention to) only evidence that will confirm his or her beliefs instead of evidence that might disconfirm them.* To continue our example, gun advocates will often present statistics showing that particular U.S. states with strict gun laws still have high crime rates. These data are consistent with the claim that limiting gun access does not reduce crime. Of course, it ignores a great deal of evidence suggesting that limiting gun access also makes it more difficult for ordinary citizens to commit gun-related violence. In other words, it is a selective representation of the data. The goal of these paragraphs isn't to pick on gun enthusiasts or Americans! But, as mass shootings become more and more common, it is worth looking at some of the biases that are influencing the discussions around these issues.

Brain-imaging research provides an interesting perspective on belief perseverance and confirmation bias. This research shows that people treat evidence in ways that minimize negative or uncomfortable feelings while maximizing positive feelings (Westen et al., 2006). For example, one American study examined the brain regions and self-reported feelings involved in interpreting information about presidential candidates during the 2004 campaign. The participants were all deeply committed to either the Republican (George "Dubya" Bush) or Democratic (John Kerry) candidate, and they all encountered information that was politically threatening toward each candidate

(in this case, evidence that the candidate had contradicted himself). As you can see from the results in Figure 8.18, participants had strong emotional reactions to threatening (self-contradictory) information about their own candidate, but not to the alternative candidate, or a relatively neutral person, such as a retired network news anchor. Analyses of the brain scans demonstrated that participants from both political parties engaged in motivated reasoning. When the threat was directed at the participant's own candidate, brain areas associated with ignoring or suppressing information were more active, whereas few of the regions associated with logical thinking were activated (Westen et al., 2006).

These data demonstrate that a person's beliefs can influence their observable behavioural responses to information as well as the brain activity underlying these behaviours. As we shall see, decision making—and our happiness with those decisions—can also be influenced by a person's personality.

Working the Scientific Literacy Model

Maximizing and Satisficing in Complex Decisions

One privilege of living in a technologically advanced, democratic society is that we get to make many decisions for ourselves. However, for each decision there can be more choices than we can possibly consider. As a result, two types of consumers have emerged in our society. *Satisficers* are individuals who seek to make decisions that are, simply put, "good enough." In contrast, *maximizers* are individuals who attempt to evaluate every option for every choice until they find the perfect fit. Most people exhibit some of both behaviours, satisficing at times and maximizing at other times. However, if you consider all the people you know, you can probably identify at least one person who is an extreme maximizer—he or she will always be comparing products, jobs, classes, and so on, to find out who has made the best decisions. At the same time, you can probably identify an extreme satisficer—the person who will be satisfied with his or her choices as long as they are "good enough."

What do we know about maximizing and satisficing?

If one person settles for the good-enough option while another searches until he finds the best possible option, which individual do you think will be happier with the decision in the end? Most people believe the maximizer will be happier, but this is not always the case. In fact, researchers such as Barry Schwartz of Swarthmore College and his colleagues have no shortage of data about the *paradox of choice*, the observation that more choices can lead to less satisfaction. In one study, the researchers asked participants to recollect both large (more than $100) and small (less than $10) purchases and report the number of options they considered, the time spent shopping and making the decision, and the overall satisfaction with the purchase. Sure enough, those who ranked high on a test of maximization invested more time and effort, but were actually less pleased with the outcome (Schwartz et al., 2002).

In another study, researchers questioned recent university graduates about their job search process. Believe it or not, maximizers averaged 20% higher salaries, but were less happy about their jobs than satisficers (Iyengar et al., 2006). This outcome occurred even though we would assume that maximizers would be more careful when selecting a job—*if* humans were perfectly logical decision makers.

So, now we know that just the presence of alternative choices can drive down satisfaction—but how can that be?

How can science explain maximizing and satisficing?

To answer this question, researchers asked participants to read vignettes that included a trade-off between number of choices and effort (Dar-Nimrod et al., 2009). Try this example for yourself:

> *Your cleaning supplies (e.g., laundry detergent, rags, carpet cleaner, dish soap, toilet paper, glass cleaner) are running low. You have the option of going to the nearest grocery store (5 minutes away), which offers 4 alternatives for each of the items you need, or you can drive to the grand cleaning superstore (25 minutes away), which offers 25 different alternatives for each of the items (for approximately the same price). Which store would you go to?*

In the actual study, maximizers were much more likely to spend the extra time and effort to have more choices. Thus, if you decided to go to the store with more options, you are probably a maximizer. What this scenario does not tell us is whether having more or fewer choices was pleasurable for either maximizers or satisficers.

See how well you understand the nature of maximizers and satisficers by predicting the results of the next study: Participants at the University of British Columbia completed a taste test of *one* piece of chocolate, but they could choose this piece of chocolate from an array of 6 pieces or an array of 30 pieces. When there were 6 pieces, who was happier—maximizers or satisficers? What happened when there were 30 pieces to choose from? As you can see in Table 8.2, the maximizers were happier when there were fewer options. On a satisfaction scale indicating how much they enjoyed the piece of chocolate that they selected, the maximizers scored higher in the 6-piece condition (5.64 out of 7) than in the 30-piece condition (4.73 out of 7; Dar-Nimrod et al., 2009). In contrast, satisficers did not show a statistical difference between the conditions (5.44 and 6.00 for the 6-piece and 30-piece conditions, respectively).

Can we critically evaluate this information?

One hypothesis that seeks to explain the dissatisfaction of maximizers suggests that they invest more in the decision, so they expect more from the outcome. Imagine that a

Table 8.2 Satisfaction of Maximizers and Satisficers

	6 Alternatives	30 Alternatives	Difference
Maximizers	5.64	4.73	−0.91
Satisticers	5.44	6.00	+0.46

Source: Adapted from Dar-Nimrod et al. (2009). The Maximization Paradox: The costs of seeking alternatives. *Personality and Individual Differences, 46,* 631–635, Figure 1 and Table 1.

satisficer and a maximizer purchase the same digital camera for $175. The maximizer may have invested significantly more time and effort into the decision so, in effect, she *feels like* she paid considerably more for the camera.

Regardless of the explanation, we should keep in mind that maximizers and satisficers are preexisting categories. People cannot be randomly assigned to be in one category or another, so these findings represent the outcomes of quasi-experimental research (see Module 2.2). We cannot be sure that the act of maximizing leads to dissatisfaction based on these data. Perhaps maximizers are the people who are generally less satisfied, which in turn leads to maximizing behaviour.

Why is this relevant?

Although we described maximizing and satisficing in terms of purchasing decisions, you might also notice that these styles of decision making can be applied to other situations, such as multiple-choice exams. Do you select the first response that sounds reasonable (satisficing), or do you carefully review each of the responses and compare them to one another before marking your choice (maximizing)? Once you make your choice, do you stick with it, believing it is good enough

(satisficing), or are you willing to change your answer to make the best possible choice (maximizing)? Despite the popular wisdom that you should never change your first response, there may be an advantage to maximizing on exams. Research focusing on more than 1500 individual examinations showed that when people changed their answers, they changed them from incorrect to correct 51% of the time, from correct to incorrect 25% of the time, and from incorrect to another incorrect option 23% of the time (Kruger et al., 2005).

The research discussed above suggests that there are some aspects of our consumer-based society that might actually be making us less happy. This seems counterintuitive given that the overwhelming number of product options available to us almost guarantees that we will get exactly what we want (or *think* we want). It's worth thinking about how the different biases discussed in this module relate to your own life. By examining how *your* thinking is affected by different heuristics and biases, you will gain some interesting insights into why you behave the way you do. You will also be able to increase the amount of control you have over your own life.

Module 8.2b Quiz:

Judgment and Decision Making

Know . . .

1. When an individual makes judgments based on how easily things come to mind, he or she is employing the _____ heuristic.
   A. confirmation
   B. representativeness
   C. availability
   D. belief perseverance

Understand . . .

2. Belief perseverance seems to function by
   A. maximizing positive feelings.
   B. minimizing negative feelings.
   C. maximizing negative feelings while minimizing positive feelings.
   D. minimizing negative feelings while maximizing positive feelings.

Analyze . . .

3. Why do psychologists assert that heuristics are beneficial for problem solving?
   A. Heuristics increase the amount of time we spend arriving at good solutions to problems.
   B. Heuristics decrease our chances of errors dramatically.
   C. Heuristics help us make decisions efficiently.
   D. Heuristics are considered the most logical thought pattern for problem solving.

4. The fact that humans so often rely on heuristics is evidence that
   A. humans are not always rational thinkers.
   B. it is impossible for humans to think logically.
   C. it is impossible for humans to use algorithms.
   D. humans will always succumb to the confirmation bias.

Module 8.2 Summary

8.2a   Know . . . the key terminology of problem solving and decision making.

algorithms
anchoring effect
availability heuristic
belief perseverance
confirmation bias
conjunction fallacy
functional fixedness
heuristics
mental set
problem solving
representativeness heuristic

8.2b   Understand . . . the characteristics that problems have in common.

All problems involve people attempting to reach some sort of goal; this goal can be an observable behaviour like learning to serve a tennis ball or a cognitive behaviour like learning Canada's ten provincial capitals. This process involves forming strategies that will allow the person to reach the goal. It may also require a person to overcome one or more obstacles along the way.

8.2c   Understand . . . how obstacles to problem solving are often self-imposed.

Many obstacles arise from the individual's mental set, which occurs when a person focuses on only one potential solution and does not consider alternatives. Similarly, functional fixedness can arise when an individual does not consider alternative uses for familiar objects.

8.2d   Apply . . . your knowledge to determine if you tend to be a maximizer or a satisficer.

Apply Activity

Rate the following items on a scale from 1 (completely disagree) to 7 (completely agree), with 4 being a neutral response.

1. Whenever I'm faced with a choice, I try to imagine what all the other possibilities are, even ones that aren't present at the moment.
2. No matter how satisfied I am with my job, it's only right for me to be on the lookout for better opportunities.
3. When I am in the car listening to the radio, I often check other stations to see whether something better is playing, even if I am relatively satisfied with what I'm listening to.
4. When I watch TV, I channel surf, often scanning through the available options even while attempting to watch one program.
5. I treat relationships like clothing: I expect to try a lot on before finding the perfect fit.
6. I often find it difficult to shop for a gift for a friend.
7. When shopping, I have a difficult time finding clothing that I really love.
8. No matter what I do, I have the highest standards for myself.
9. I find that writing is very difficult, even if it's just writing to a friend, because it's so difficult to word things just right. I often do several drafts of even simple things.
10. I never settle for second best.

When you are finished, average your ratings together to find your overall score. Scores greater than 4 indicate maximizers; scores less than 4 indicate satisficers. Approximately one-third of the population scores below 3.25 and approximately one-third scores above 4.75. Where does your score place you?

8.2e   Analyze . . . whether human thought is primarily logical or intuitive.

This module provides ample evidence that humans are not always logical. Heuristics are helpful decision-making and problem-solving tools, but they do not always follow logical principles. Even so, the abundance of heuristics does not mean that humans are never logical; instead, they simply point to the limits of our rationality.

Module 8.3 Language and Communication

Manuela Hartling/Reuters

Learning Objectives

8.3a Know . . . the key terminology from the study of language.

8.3b Understand . . . how language is structured.

8.3c Understand . . . how genes and the brain are involved in language use.

8.3d Apply . . . your knowledge to distinguish between units of language such as phonemes and morphemes.

8.3e Analyze . . . whether species other than humans are able to use language.

Dog owners are known for attributing a lot of intelligence, emotion, and "humanness" to their canine pals. Sometimes they may appear to go overboard—such as Rico's owners, who claimed their border collie understood 200 words, most of which referred to different toys and objects he liked to play with. His owners claimed that they could show Rico a toy, repeat its name a few times, and toss the toy into a pile of other objects; Rico would then retrieve the object upon verbal command. Rico's ability appeared to go well beyond the usual "sit," "stay," "heel," and perhaps a few other words that dog owners expect their companions to understand.

Claims about Rico's language talents soon drew the attention of scientists, who skeptically questioned whether the dog was just responding to cues by the owners, such as their possible looks or gestures toward the object they asked their pet to retrieve. The scientists set up a carefully controlled experiment in which no one present in the room knew the location of the object that was requested. Rico correctly retrieved 37 out of 40 objects. The experimenters then tested the owners' claim that Rico could learn object names in just one trial. Rico again confirmed his owners' claims,

and the researchers concluded that his ability to understand new words was comparable to that of a three-year-old child (Kaminski et al., 2004).

However, as you will see in this module, Rico's abilities, while impressive, are dwarfed by those of humans. Our ability to reorganize words into complex thoughts is unique in the animal kingdom and may even have aided our survival as a species.

Focus Questions

1. What is the difference between language and other forms of communication?

2. Might other species, such as chimpanzees, also be capable of learning human language?

>> Communication happens just about anywhere you can find life. Dogs bark, cats meow, monkeys chatter, and mice can emit sounds undetectable to the human ear when communicating. Honeybees perform an elaborate dance to communicate the direction, distance, and quality of food

sources (von Frisch, 1967). Animals even communicate by marking their territories with their distinct scent, much to the chagrin of the world's fire hydrants. Language is among the ways that humans communicate. It is quite unlike the examples of animal communication mentioned previously. So what differentiates language from these other forms of communication? And, what is it about our brains that enables us to turn different sounds and lines into the sophisticated languages found across different human cultures?

What Is Language?

Language is one of the most intensively studied areas in all of psychology. Thousands of experiments have been performed to identify different characteristics of language as well as the brain regions associated with them. But, all fields of study have a birthplace. In the case of the scientific study of language, it began with an interesting case study of a patient in Paris in the early 1860s.

EARLY STUDIES OF LANGUAGE   In 1861, Paul Broca, a physician and founder of the Society of Anthropology of Paris, heard of an interesting medical case. The patient appeared to show a very specific impairment resulting from a stroke suffered 21 years earlier. He could understand speech and had fairly normal mental abilities; however, he had great difficulty *producing* speech and often found himself uttering single words separated by pauses (uh, er . . .). In fact, this patient acquired the nickname "Tan" because it was one of the only sounds that he could reliably produce. Tan had what is known as **aphasia**, *a language disorder caused by damage to the brain structures that support using and understanding language.*

Tan died a few days after being examined by Broca. During the autopsy, Broca noted that the brain damage appeared primarily near the back of the frontal lobes in the left hemisphere. Over the next couple of years, Broca found 12 other patients with similar symptoms and similar brain damage, indicating that Tan was not a unique case. This *region of the left frontal lobe that controls our ability to articulate speech sounds that compose words* is now known as **Broca's area** (see Figure 8.19). The symptoms associated with damage to this region, as seen in Tan, are known as *Broca's aphasia*.

The fact that a brain injury could affect one part of language while leaving others preserved suggested that the ability to use language involves a number of different processes using different areas of the brain. In the years following the publication of Broca's research, other isolated language impairments were discovered. In 1874, a young Prussian (German) physician named Carl Wernicke published a short book detailing his study of different types of aphasia. Wernicke noted that some of his patients

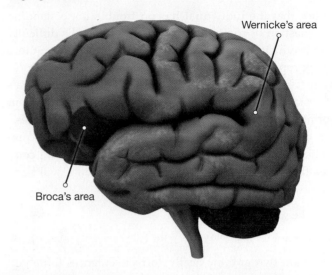

Figure 8.19 Two Language Centres of the Brain
Broca's and Wernicke's areas of the cerebral cortex are critical to language function.

Wernicke's area

Broca's area

had trouble with language *comprehension* rather than language *production*. These patients typically had damage to the posterior superior temporal gyrus (the back and top part of the temporal lobe). This region, now known as **Wernicke's area**, *is the area of the brain most associated with finding the meaning of words* (see Figure 8.19). Damage to this area results in *Wernicke's aphasia*, a language disorder in which a person has difficulty understanding the words he or she hears. These patients are also unable to produce speech that other people can understand—the words are spoken fluently and with a normal intonation and accent, but these words seem randomly thrown together (i.e., what is being said does not make sense). Consider the following example:

> *Examiner:* I'd like to have you tell me something about your problem.
>
> *Person with Wernicke's aphasia:* Yes, I, ugh, cannot hill all of my way. I cannot talk all of the things I do, and part of the part I can go alright, but I cannot tell from the other people. I usually most of my things. I know what can I talk and know what they are, but I cannot always come back even though I know they should be in, and I know should something eely I should know what I'm doing . . .

The important thing to look for in this sample of speech is how the wrong words appear in an otherwise fluent stream of utterances. Contrast this with an example of Broca's aphasia:

> *Examiner:* Tell me, what did you do before you retired?
>
> *Person with Broca's aphasia:* Uh, uh, uh, pub, par, partender, no.

Examiner: Carpenter?

Person with Broca's aphasia: (Nodding to signal yes) Carpenter, tuh, tuh, twenty year.

Notice that the individual has no trouble understanding the question or coming up with the answer. His difficulty is in producing the word *carpenter* and then putting it into an appropriate phrase. Did you also notice the missing "s" from *twenty year*? This is another characteristic of Broca's aphasia: The individual words are often produced without normal grammatical flair: no articles, suffixes, or prefixes.

Broca's aphasia can include some difficulties in comprehending language as well. In general, the more complex the sentence structure, the more difficult it will be to understand. Compare these two sentences:

The girl played the piano.

The piano was played by the girl.

These are two grammatically correct sentences (although the second is somewhat awkward) that have the same meaning but are structured differently. Patients with damage to Broca's area would find it much more difficult to understand the second sentence than the first. This impairment suggests that the distinction between speech production and comprehension is not as simple as was first thought. Indeed, as language became a central topic of research in psychology, researchers quickly realized that this ability—or set of abilities—is among the most complex processes humans perform.

PROPERTIES OF LANGUAGE Language, like many other cognitive abilities, flows so automatically that we often overlook how complicated it really is. However, cases like those described above show us that language is indeed a complex set of skills. Researchers define **language** as *a form of communication that involves the use of spoken, written, or gestural symbols that are combined in a rule-based form.* With this definition in mind, we can distinguish which features of language make it a unique form of communication.

- Language can involve communication about objects and events that are not in the present time and place. We can use language to talk about events happening on another planet or that are happening within atoms. We can also use different tenses to indicate that the topic of the sentence occurred or will occur at a different time. For instance, you can say to your roommate, "I'm going to order pizza tonight," without her thinking the pizza is already there.

- Languages can produce entirely new meanings. It is possible to produce a sentence that has never been uttered before in the history of humankind, simply by reorganizing words in different ways. As long as you select English words and use correct grammar,

others who know the language should be able to understand it. You can also use words in novel ways. Imagine the tabloid newspaper headline: *Bat Boy Found in Cave!* In North American culture, "bat boys" are regular kids who keep track of the baseball bats for baseball players. In this particular tabloid, the story concerned a completely novel creature that was part bat and part boy. Both meanings could be correct, depending upon the context in which the term *bat boy* is used.

- Language is passed down from parents to children. As we will discuss later in this module, children learn to pay attention to the particular sounds of their native language(s) at the expense of other sounds (Werker, 2003). Children also learn words and grammatical rules from parents, teachers, and peers. In other words, even if we have a natural inclination to learn *a* language, experience dictates *which* language(s) we will speak.

Language requires us to link different sounds (or gestures) with different meanings in order to understand and communicate with other people. Therefore, understanding more about these seemingly simple elements of language is essential for understanding language as a whole.

Words can be arranged or combined in novel ways to produce ideas that have never been expressed before.

PHONEMES AND MORPHEMES: THE BASIC INGREDIENTS OF LANGUAGE Languages contain discrete units that exist at differing levels of complexity. When people speak, they assemble these units into larger and more complex units. Some psychologists have used a cooking analogy to explain this phenomenon: We all start with the same basic language ingredients, but they can be mixed together in an unlimited number of ways (Pinker, 1999).

Phonemes *are the most basic of units of speech sounds.* You can identify phonemes rather easily; the phoneme associated with the letter *t* (which is written as /t/, where the two forward slashes indicate a phoneme) is found at the end of the word *pot* or near the beginning of the word *stop*. If you pay close attention to the way you use your tongue, lips, and vocal cords, you will see that phonemes have slight variations depending on the other letters around them. Pay attention to how you pronounce the /t/ phoneme in *stop, stash, stink,* and *stoke.* Your mouth will move in slightly different ways each time, and there will be very slight variations in sound, but they are still the same basic phoneme. Individual phonemes typically do not have any meaning by themselves; if you want someone to stop doing something, asking him to /t/ will not suffice.

Morphemes *are the smallest meaningful units of a language.* Some morphemes are simple words, whereas others may be suffixes or prefixes. For example, the word *pig* is a morpheme—it cannot be broken down into smaller units of meaning. You can combine morphemes, however, if you follow the rules of the language. If you want to pluralize *pig*, you can add the morpheme /-s/, which will give you *pigs*. If you want to describe a person as a pig, you can add the morpheme /-ish/ to get *piggish*. In fact, you can add all kinds of morphemes to a word as long as you follow the rules. You could even say *piggable* (able to be pigged) or *piggify* (to turn into a pig). These words do not make much literal sense, but they combine morphemes according to the rules; thus we can make a reasonable guess as to the speaker's intended meaning. Our ability to combine morphemes into words is one distinguishing feature of language that sets it apart from other forms of communication (e.g., we don't produce a lengthy series of facial expressions to communicate a new idea). In essence, language gives us *productivity*—the ability to combine units of sound into an infinite number of meanings.

Finally, there are the words that make up a language. **Semantics** *is the study of how people come to understand meaning from words.* Humans have a knack for this kind of interpretation, and each of us has an extensive mental dictionary to prove it. Not only do normal speakers know tens of thousands of words, but they can often understand new words they have never heard before based on their understanding of morphemes.

Although phonemes, morphemes, and semantics have an obvious role in spoken language, they also play a role in our ability to read. When you recognize a word, you effortlessly translate the word's visual form (known as its *orthography*) into the sounds that make up that word (known as its *phonology* or *phonological code*). These sounds are combined into a word, at which point you can access its meaning or semantics. However, not all people are able to translate orthography into sounds. Individuals with *dyslexia* have difficulties translating words into speech sounds. Indeed, children with dyslexia show less activity in the left fusiform cortex (at the bottom of the brain where the temporal and occipital lobes meet), a brain area involved with word recognition and with linking word and sound representations (Desroches et al., 2010). This difficulty linking letters with phonemes leads to unusually slow reading in both children and adults despite the fact that these people have normal hearing and are cognitively and neurologically healthy (Desroches & Joanisse, 2009; Shaywitz, 1998).

This research into the specific impairments associated with dyslexia allows scientists and educators to develop treatment programs to help children improve their reading and language abilities. One of the most successful programs has been developed by Maureen Lovett and her colleagues at Sick Kids Hospital in Toronto and Brock University. Their Phonological and Strategy Training (PHAST) program (now marketed as Empower™ Reading to earn research money for the hospital) has been used to assist over 6000 students with reading disabilities. Rather than focusing on only one aspect of language, this program teaches children new word-identification and reading-comprehension strategies while also educating them about how words and phrases are structured (so that they know what to expect when they see new words or groups of words). Children who completed these programs showed improvements on a number of measures of reading and passage comprehension (Frijters et al., 2013; Lovett et al., 2012). Given that 5–15% of the population has some form of reading impairment, treatment programs like PHAST could have a dramatic effect on our educational system.

As you can see, languages derive their complexity from several elements, including phonemes, morphemes, and semantics. And, when these systems are not functioning properly, language abilities suffer. But phonemes, morphemes, and semantics are just the list of the ingredients of language—we still need to figure out how to mix these ingredients together.

SYNTAX: THE LANGUAGE RECIPE Perhaps the most remarkable aspect of language is **syntax**, *the rules for combining words and morphemes into meaningful phrases and sentences*—the recipe for language. Children master the syntax of their native language before they leave elementary school. They can string together morphemes and words when they

Figure 8.20 Syntax Allows Us to Understand Language by the Organization of the Words

The rules of syntax help us divide a sentence into noun phrases, verb phrases, and other parts of speech.

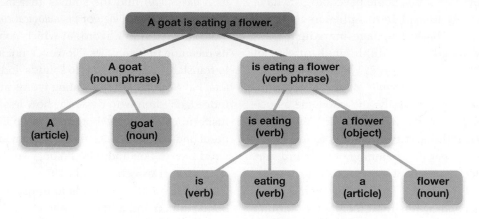

Source: Adapted from S. Pinker. (1994). *The Language Instinct.* New York: HarperCollins.

speak, and they can easily distinguish between well-formed *and* ill-formed sentences. But despite mastering those rules, most speakers cannot tell you what the rules are; syntax just seems to come naturally. It might seem odd that people can do so much with language without a full understanding of its inner workings. Of course, people can also learn how to walk without any understanding of the biochemistry that allows their leg muscles to contract and relax.

The most basic units of syntax are nouns and verbs. They are all that is required to construct a well-formed sentence, such as *Goats eat.* Noun–verb sentences are perfectly adequate, if a bit limited, so we build phrases out of nouns and verbs, as the diagram in Figure 8.20 demonstrates.

Syntax also helps explain why the order of words in a sentence has such a strong effect on what the sentence means. For example, how would you make a question out of this statement?

(A) *A goat is in the garden.*
(B) IS *a goat* _____ *in the garden?*

This example demonstrates that a statement (A) can be turned into a well-formed question (B) just by moving the verb *is* to the beginning of the sentence. Perhaps that is one of the hidden rules of syntax. Try it again:

(A) *A goat that is eating a flower is in the garden.*
(B) IS *a goat that* _____ *eating a flower is in the garden?*

As you can see, the rule "move *is* to the beginning of the sentence" does not apply in this case. Do you know why? It is because we moved the wrong *is*. The phrase *that is eating a flower* is a part of the noun phrase because it describes the goat. We should have moved the *is* from the verb phrase. Try it again:

(A) *A goat that is eating a flower is in the garden.*
(B) IS *a goat that is eating a flower* _____ *in the garden?*

This is a well-formed sentence. It may be grammatically awkward, but the syntax is understandable (Pinker, 1994).

As you can see from these examples, the order of words in a sentence helps determine what the sentence means, and syntax is the set of rules we use to determine that order.

PRAGMATICS: THE FINISHING TOUCHES If syntax is the recipe for language, pragmatics is the icing on the cake. **Pragmatics** *is the study of nonlinguistic elements of language use.* It places heavy emphasis on the speaker's behaviours and the social situation (Carston, 2002).

Pragmatics reminds us that sometimes *what* is said is not as important as *how* it is said. For example, a student who says, "I ate a 50-pound cheeseburger," is most likely stretching the truth, but you probably would not call him a liar. Pragmatics helps us understand what he implied. The voracious student was actually *flouting*—or blatantly disobeying—a rule of language in a way that is obvious (Grice, 1975; Horn & Ward, 2004). There are all sorts of ways in which flouting the rules can lead to implied, rather than literal, meanings; a sample of these are shown in Table 8.3.

Importantly, pragmatics depends upon both the speaker (or writer) and listener (or reader) understanding that rules are being flouted in order to produce a desired meaning. If you speak with visitors from a different country, you may find that they don't understand what you mean when you flout the rules of Canadian English or use slang (shortened language). When we say "The goalie stood on his head," most hockey-mad Canadians understand that we are commenting on a goaltender's amazing game; however, someone new to hockey would be baffled by this expression. This is another example of how experience—in this case with a culture—influences how we use and interpret language.

Table 8.3 Pragmatic Rules Guiding Language Use

The Rule	Flouting the Rule	The Implication
Say what you believe is true.	My roommate is a *giraffe*.	He does not *really* live with a giraffe. Maybe his roommate is very tall?
Say only what is relevant.	Is my blind date good-looking? *He's got a great personality.*	She didn't answer my question. He's probably not good-looking.
Say only as much as you need to.	I like my lab partner, but he's no *Einstein*.	Of course he's not Einstein. Why is she bothering to tell me this? She probably means that her partner is not very smart.

Module 8.3a Quiz:

What Is Language?

Know . . .

1. What are the rules that govern how words are strung together into meaningful sentences?
   - **A.** Semantics
   - **B.** Pragmatics
   - **C.** Morphemics
   - **D.** Syntax

2. The study of how people extract meaning from words is called _____.
   - **A.** syntax
   - **B.** pragmatics
   - **C.** semantics
   - **D.** flouting

Understand . . .

3. Besides being based in a different region of the brain, a major distinction between Broca's aphasia and Wernicke's aphasia is that
   - **A.** words from people with Broca's aphasia are strung together fluently, but often make little sense.

   - **B.** Broca's aphasia is due to a FOXP2 mutation.
   - **C.** Wernicke's aphasia results in extreme stuttering.
   - **D.** words from people with Wernicke's aphasia are strung together fluently, but often make little sense.

Apply . . .

4. _____ is an example of a morpheme, while _____ is a phoneme.
   - **A.** /dis/; /ta/
   - **B.** /a/; /like/
   - **C.** /da/; /ah/
   - **D.** /non/; /able/

The Development of Language

Human vocal tracts are capable of producing approximately 200 different phonemes. However, no language uses all of these sounds. Jul'hoan, one of the "clicking languages" of Botswana, contains almost 100 sounds (including over 80 different consonant sounds). In contrast, English contains about 40 sounds. But, if Canadians are genetically identical to people in southern Africa, why are our languages different? And, why can't we produce and distinguish between some of the sounds of these other languages? It turns out that experience plays a major role in your ability to speak the language, or languages, that you do.

INFANTS, SOUND PERCEPTION, AND LANGUAGE ACQUISITION Say the following phrase out loud: "Your doll." Now, say this phrase: "This doll." Did you notice a difference in how you pronounced *doll* in these two situations? If English is your first language, it is quite likely that you didn't notice the slight change in how the letter "d" was expressed. But, Hindi speakers would have no problem making this distinction. To them, the two instances of the word *doll* would be pronounced differently and would mean *lentils* and *branch,* respectively.

Janet Werker of the University of British Columbia and her colleagues found that very young English-learning infants are able to distinguish between these two "d" sounds. But, by 10 months of age, the infants begin hearing sounds in a way that is consistent with their native language; because English has only one "d" sound, English-learning infants stop detecting the difference between these two sounds (Werker & Tees, 1984; Werker et al., 2012). This change is not a weakness on the part of English-learning infants. Rather, it is evidence that they are learning the statistical principles of their language. Infants who hear only English words will group different pronunciations of the letter "d" into one category because that is how this sound is used in English. Hindi-learning children will learn to separate different types of "d" sounds because this distinction is important. A related study using two "k" sounds from an Interior Salish (First Nations) language from British Columbia produced similar results—English-learning infants showed a significant drop-off in hearing sounds for the non-English language after 8–10 months (Werker & Tees, 1984).

In addition to becoming experts at identifying the sounds of their own language, infants also learn how to separate a string of sounds into meaningful groups (i.e., into words). Infants as young as two months old show a preference for speech sounds over perceptually similar non-speech sounds (Vouloumanos & Werker, 2004). And, when presented with pronounceable non-words (e.g., *strak*), infants prefer to hear words that follow the rules of their language. An English-learning baby would prefer non-words beginning in "str" to those beginning in "rst" because there are a large number of English words that begin with "str" (Jusczyk et al., 1993). Additionally, newborn infants can distinguish between function words (e.g., prepositions) and content words (e.g., nouns and verbs) based on their sound properties (Shi et al., 1999). By six months of age, infants prefer the content words (Shi & Werker, 2001), thus showing that they are learning which sounds are most useful for understanding the meaning of a statement.

By the age of 20 months, the children are able to use the perceptual categories that they developed in order to rapidly learn new words. In some cases, children can perform **fast mapping**—*the ability to map words onto concepts or objects after only a single exposure*. Human children seem to have a fast-mapping capacity that is superior to any other organism on the planet. This skill is one potential explanation for the *naming explosion*, a rapid increase in vocabulary size that occurs at this stage of development.

The naming explosion has two biological explanations as well. First, at this stage of development, the brain begins to perform language-related functions in the left hemisphere, similar to the highly efficient adult brain; prior to this stage, this information was stored and analyzed by both hemispheres (Mills et al., 1997). Second, the naming explosion has also been linked to an increase in the amount of myelin on the brain's axons, a change that would increase the speed of communication between neurons (Pujol et al., 2006). These changes would influence not only the understanding of language, but also how a child uses language to convey increasingly complex thoughts such as "How does Spiderman stick to walls?" and "Why did Dad's hair fall out?"

PRODUCING SPOKEN LANGUAGE Learning to identify and organize speech sounds is obviously an important part of language development. An equally critical skill is producing speech that other people will be able to understand. Early psychologists focused only on behavioural approaches to language learning. They believed that language was learned through imitating sounds and being reinforced for pronouncing and using words correctly (Skinner, 1985). Although it is certainly true that imitation and reinforcement are involved in language acquisition, they are only one part of this complex process (Messer, 2000). Here are a few examples that illustrate how learning through imitation and reinforcement is just one component of language development:

- Children often produce phrases that include incorrect grammar or word forms. Because adults do not (often) use these phrases, it is highly unlikely that such phrases are imitations.

- Children learn irregular verbs and pluralizations on a word-by-word basis. At first, they will use *ran* and *geese* correctly. However, when children begin to use grammar on their own, they over-generalize the rules. A child who learns the /-ed/ morpheme for past tense will start saying *runned* instead of *ran*. When she learns that /-s/ means more than one, she will begin to say *gooses* instead of *geese*. It is also unlikely that children would produce these forms by imitating.

- When children use poor grammar, or when they over-generalize their rules, parents may try to correct them. Although children will acknowledge their parents' attempts at instruction, this method does not seem to work. Instead, children go right back to over-generalizing.

In light of these and many other examples, it seems clear that an exclusively behaviourist approach falls short in explaining how language is learned. After all, there are profound differences in the success of children and adults in learning a new language: Whereas adults typically struggle, children seem to learn the language effortlessly. If reinforcement and imitation were the primary means by which language was acquired, then adults should be able to learn just as well as children.

The fact that children seem to learn language differently than adults has led psychologists to use the term *language acquisition* when referring to children instead of *language learning*. The study of language acquisition has revealed remarkable similarities among children from all over the world. Regardless of the language, children seem to develop this capability in stages, as shown in Table 8.4.

SENSITIVE PERIODS FOR LANGUAGE The phases of language development described above suggest that younger brains are particularly well-suited to acquiring languages; this is not the case for older brains. Imagine a family with two young children who immigrated to Canada from a remote Russian village where no one spoke

Table 8.4 Milestones in Language Acquisition and Speech

Average Time of Onset (Months)	Milestone	Example
1–2	Cooing	Ahhh, ai-ai-ai
4–10	Babbling (consonants start)	Ab-ah-da-ba
8–16	Single-word stage	Up, mama, papa
24	Two-word stage	Go potty
24+	Complete, meaningful phrases strung together	I want to talk to Grandpa.

English. The parents would struggle with English courses, while the children would attend English-speaking schools. Within a few years, the parents would have accumulated some vocabulary but they would likely still have difficulty with pronunciation and grammar (Russian-speaking people often omit articles such as *the*). Meanwhile, their children would likely pick up English without much effort and have language skills equivalent to those of their classmates; they would have roughly the same vocabulary, the same accents, and even the same slang.

Why can children pick up a language so much more easily than adults? Most psychologists agree that there is a *sensitive period* for language—a time during childhood in which children's brains are primed to develop language skills (see also Module 10.1). Children can absorb language almost effortlessly, but this ability seems to fade away starting around age seven. Thus, when families immigrate to a country that uses a different language, young children are able to pick up this language much more quickly than their parents (Hakuta et al., 2003; Hernandez & Li, 2007).

A stunning example of critical periods comes from Nicaragua. Until 1979, there was no sign language in this Central American country. Because there were no schools for people with hearing impairments, there was no (perceived) need for a common sign language. When the first schools for the deaf were established, adults and teenaged students attempted to learn to read lips. While few mastered this skill, these students did do something even more astonishing: They developed their own primitive sign language. This language, *Lenguaje de Signos Nicaragüese (LSN)*, involves a number of elaborate gestures similar to a game of charades and did not have a consistent set of grammatical rules. But, it was a start. Children who attended these schools at an early age (i.e., during the sensitive period for language acquisition) used this language as the basis for a more fluent version of sign language: *Idioma de Signos Nicaragüese (ISN)*. ISN has grammatical rules and can be used to express a number of complicated, abstract ideas (Pinker, 1994). It is now the standard sign language in Nicaragua. The difference between LSN and ISN is similar to the difference between adults and children learning a new language. If you acquire the new language during

childhood, you will be much more fluent than if you try to acquire it during adulthood (Senghas, 2003; Senghas et al., 2004).

THE BILINGUAL BRAIN Let's go back to the example of the Russian-speaking family who immigrated to balmy Canada. The young children learning English would also be speaking Russian at home with their parents. As a result, they would be learning two languages essentially at the same time. What effect would this situation have on their ability to learn each language?

Although bilingualism leads to many benefits (see below), there are some costs to learning more than one language. Bilingual children tend to have a smaller vocabulary in each language than unilingual children (Mahon & Crutchley, 2006). In adulthood, this difference is shown not by vocabulary size, but by how easily bilinguals can access words. Compared to unilingual adults, bilingual adults are slower at naming pictures (Roberts et al., 2002), have more difficulty on tests that ask them to list words starting with a particular letter (Rosselli et al., 2000), have more tip-of-the-tongue experiences in which they can't quite retrieve a word (Gollan & Acenas, 2004), and are slower and less accurate when making word/non-word judgments (Ransdell & Fischler, 1987). These problems with accessing words may be due to the fact that they use each language less than a unilingual person would use their single language (Michael & Gollan, 2005).

The benefits of bilingualism, however, appear to far outweigh the costs. One difference that has been repeatedly observed is that bilingual individuals are much better than their unilingual counterparts on tests that require them to control their attention or their thoughts. These abilities, known as *executive functions* (or *executive control*), enable people who speak more than one language to inhibit one language while speaking and listening to another (or to limit the interference across languages). If they didn't, they would produce confusing sentences like *The chien is tres sick*. Although most of you can figure out that this person is talking about a sick dog, you can see how such sentences would make communication challenging. Researchers have found that bilinguals score better than unilinguals on tests of executive control throughout the lifespan, beginning in infancy (Kovacs & Mehler, 2009) and the toddler years (Poulin-Dubois et al., 2011) and continuing throughout adulthood (Costa et al., 2008) and into old age (Bialystok et al., 2004). Bilingualism has also recently been shown to have important health benefits. Because the executive control involved with bilingualism uses areas in the frontal lobes, these regions may form more connections in bilinguals than unilinguals (Bialystok, 2009, 2011a, 2011b). As a result, these brains likely have more back-up systems if damage occurs. Indeed, Ellen Bialystok at York University and her colleagues have shown that being bilingual helps protect against the onset of dementia and Alzheimer's disease (Bialystok et al., 2007; Schweizer et al., 2012), a finding that leaves many at a loss for words.

Module 8.3b Quiz:

The Development of Language

Know . . .

1. What is fast mapping?
   A. The rapid rate at which chimpanzees learn sign language
   B. The ability of children to map concepts to words with only a single example
   C. The very short period of time that language input can be useful for language development
   D. A major difficulty that people face when affected by Broca's aphasia

Understand . . .

2. The term "sensitive period" is relevant to language acquisition because
   A. exposure to language is needed during this time for language abilities to develop normally.
   B. Broca's area is active only during this period.
   C. it is what distinguishes humans from the apes.
   D. it indicates that language is an instinct.

Analyze . . .

3. What is the most accurate conclusion from studies of bilingualism and the brain?
   A. Being bilingual causes the brain to form a larger number of connections than it normally would.
   B. Being bilingual reduces the firing rate of the frontal lobes.
   C. Only knowing one language allows people to improve their executive functioning.
   D. Being bilingual makes it more likely that a person will have language problems if they suffer brain damage.

Genes, Evolution, and Language

This module began with a discussion of two brain areas that are critical for language production and comprehension: Broca's area and Wernicke's area, respectively. But, these brain areas didn't appear out of nowhere. Rather, genetics and evolutionary pressures led to the development of our language-friendly brains. Given recent advances in our understanding of the human genome (see Module 3.1), it should come as no surprise that researchers are actively searching for the genes involved with language abilities.

Working the Scientific Literacy Model

Genes and Language

Given that language is a universal trait of the human species, it likely involves a number of different genes. These genes would, of course, also interact with the environment. In this section we examine whether it is possible that specific genes are related to language.

What do we know about genes and language?

Many scientists believe that the evidence is overwhelming that language is a unique feature of the human species, and that language evolved to solve problems related to survival and reproductive fitness. Language adds greater efficiency to thought, allows us to transmit information without requiring us to have direct experience with potentially dangerous situations, and, ultimately, facilitates communicating social needs and desires. Claims that language promotes survival and reproductive success are difficult to test directly with scientific experimentation, but there is a soundness to the logic of the speculation. We can also move beyond speculation and actually examine how genes play a role in human language. As with all complex psychological traits, there are likely many genes associated with language. Nevertheless, amid all of these myriad possibilities, one gene has been identified that is of particular importance.

How can science explain a genetic basis of language?

Studies of this gene have primarily focused on the KE family (their name is abbreviated to maintain their

Figure 8.21 Inheritance Pattern for the Mutated FOXP2 Gene in the KE Family

Family members who are "affected" have inherited a mutated form of the FOXP2 gene, which results in difficulty with articulating words. As you can see from the centre of the figure, the mutated gene is traced to a female family member and has been passed on to the individuals of the next two generations.

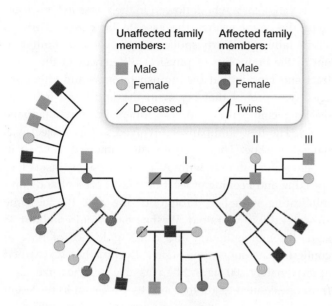

Source: Republished with permission of Nature Publishing Group, from FOXP2 and the neuroanatomy of speech and language, Fig. 1, *Nature Reviews Neuroscience*, 6, 131–138 by Faraneh Vargha-Khadem, David G. Gadian, Andrew Copp; Mortimer Mishkin. Copyright 2005; permission conveyed through Copyright Clearance Center, Inc.

confidentiality). Many members of this family have inherited a mutated version of a gene on chromosome 7 (see Figure 8.21; Vargha-Khadem et al., 2005). Each gene has a name—and this one is called FOXP2. All humans carry a copy of the FOXP2 gene, but the KE family passes down a mutated copy. Those who inherit the mutated copy have great difficulty putting thoughts into words (Tomblin et al.,

2009). Thus, it appears that the physical and chemical processes that FOXP2 codes for are related to language function.

What evidence indicates that this gene is specifically involved in language? If you were to ask the members of the family who inherited the mutant form of the gene to speak about how to change the batteries in a flashlight, they would be at a loss. A rather jumbled mixture of sounds and words might come out, but nothing that could be easily understood. However, these same individuals have no problem actually performing the task. Their challenges with using language are primarily restricted to the use of words, not with their ability to *think*.

Scientists have used brain-imaging methods to further test whether the FOXP2 mutation affects language. One group of researchers compared brain activity of family members who inherited the mutation of FOXP2 with those who did not (Liégeois et al., 2003). During the brain scans, the participants were asked to generate words themselves, and also to repeat words back to the experimenters. As you can see from Figure 8.22, the members of the family who were unaffected by the mutation showed normal brain activity: Broca's area of the left hemisphere became activated, just as expected. In contrast, Broca's area in the affected family members was silent, and the brain activity that did occur was unusual for this type of task.

Can we critically evaluate this evidence?

As you have now read, language has multiple components. Being able to articulate words is just one of many aspects of using and understanding language. The research on FOXP2 is very important, but reveals only how a single gene relates to one aspect of language use. There are almost certainly a large number of different genes working together to produce *each* component of language. To their credit, FOXP2 researchers are quick to point out that many

Figure 8.22 Brain Scans Taken While Members of the KE Family Completed a Speech Task

The unaffected group shows a normal pattern of activity in Broca's area, while the affected group shows an unusual pattern.

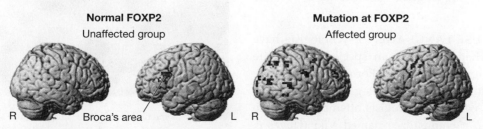

Source: Republished with permission of Nature Publishing Group, from Source: Language fMRI abnormalities associated with FOXP2 gene mutation, Figure 1, *Nature Neuroscience*, 6, 1230–1237, Copyright © 2003. permission conveyed through Copyright Clearance Center, Inc.

other genes will need to be identified before we can claim to understand the genetic basis of language; FOXP2 is just the beginning.

It is also worth noting that although the FOXP2 gene affects human speech production, it does occur in other species that do not produce sophisticated language. This gene is found in both mice and birds as well as in humans, and the human version shares a very similar molecular structure to the versions observed in these other species. Interestingly, the molecular structure and activity of the FOXP2 gene in songbirds (unlike non-songbirds) is similar to that in humans, again highlighting its possible role in producing meaningful sounds (Vargha-Khadem et al., 2005).

Why is this relevant?

This work illuminates at least part of the complex relationship between genes and language. Other individual genes that have direct links to language function will likely be discovered as research continues. It is possible that this information could be used to help us further understand the genetic basis of language disorders. The fact that the FOXP2 gene is found in many other species suggests that it may play a role in one of the components of language rather than being *the* gene for language. Thus, scientists will have to perform additional research in order to understand why and how human language became so much more complex than that of any other species.

The fact that animals such as songbirds have some of the same language-related genes as humans suggests that other species may have *some* language abilities. As it turns out, many monkey species have areas in their brains that are similar to Broca's and Wernicke's area. As in humans, these regions are connected by white-matter pathways, thus allowing them to communicate with each other (Galaburda & Pandya, 1982). These areas appear to be involved with the control of facial and throat muscles and with identifying when other monkeys have made a vocalization. This is, of course, a far cry from human language. But, the fact that some monkey species have similar "neural hardware" to humans does lead to some interesting speculations about language abilities in the animal kingdom.

CAN ANIMALS USE LANGUAGE? Psychologists have been studying whether nonhuman species can acquire human language for many decades. Formal studies of language learning in nonhuman species gained momentum in the mid-1950s when psychologists attempted to teach spoken English to a chimpanzee named Viki (Hayes & Hayes, 1951). Viki was **cross-fostered**, *meaning that she was raised as a member of a family that was not of the same species.*

Like humans, chimps come into the world dependent on adults for care, so the humans who raised Viki were basically foster parents. Although the psychologists learned a lot about how smart chimpanzees can be, they did not learn that Viki was capable of language—she managed to whisper only about four words after several years of trying.

Psychologists who followed in these researchers' footsteps did not consider the case to be closed. Perhaps Viki's failure to learn spoken English was a limitation not of the brain, but of physical differences in the vocal tract and tongue that distinguish humans and chimpanzees. One project that began in the mid-1960s involved teaching chimpanzees to use American Sign Language (ASL). The first chimpanzee involved in this project was named Washoe. The psychologists immersed Washoe in an environment rich with ASL, using signs instead of speaking and keeping at least one adult present and communicating with her throughout the day. By the time she turned two years old, Washoe had acquired about 35 signs through imitation and direct guidance of how to configure and move her hands. Eventually, she learned approximately 200 signs. She was able to generalize signs from one context to another and to use a sign to represent

Washoe was the first chimpanzee taught to use some of the signs of American Sign Language. Washoe died in 2007 at age 42 and throughout her life challenged many to examine their beliefs about human uniqueness.

Photo permission granted by Friends of Washoe

entire categories of objects, not just specific examples. For example, while Washoe learned the sign for the word "open" on a limited number of doors and cupboards, she subsequently signed "open" to many different doors, cupboards, and even her pop bottles. The findings with Washoe were later replicated with other chimps (Gardner et al., 1989).

Instead of using sign language, some researchers have developed a completely artificial language to teach to apes. This language consists of symbols called *lexigrams*—small keys on a computerized board that represent words and, therefore, can be combined to form complex ideas and phrases. One subject of the research using this language is a bonobo named Kanzi (bonobos are another species of chimpanzee). Kanzi has learned approximately 350 symbols through training, but he learned his first symbols simply by watching as researchers attempted to teach his mother how to use the language. In addition to the lexigrams he produces, Kanzi seems to recognize about 3000 spoken words. His trainers claim that Kanzi's skills constitute language (Savage-Rumbaugh & Lewin, 1994). They argue that he can understand symbols and at least some syntax; that he acquired symbols simply by being around others who used them; and that he produced symbols without specific training or reinforcement. Those who work with Kanzi conclude that his communication skills are quite similar to those of a young human in terms of both the elements of language (semantics and syntax) and the acquisition of language (natural and without effortful training).

Despite their ability to communicate in complex ways, debate continues to swirl about whether these animals are using language. Many language researchers point out that chimpanzees' signing and artificial language use is very different from how humans use language. Is the vastness of the difference important? Is using 200 signs different in some critical way from being able to use 4000 signs, roughly the number found in the ASL dictionary (Stokoe et al., 1976)? If our only criterion for whether a communication system constitutes language is the number of words used, then we can say that nonhuman species acquire some language skills after extensive training. But as you have learned in this module, human language involves more than just using words. In particular, our manipulation of phonemes, morphemes, and syntax allow us to utter an infinite number of words and sentences, thereby conveying an infinite number of thoughts.

Some researchers who have worked closely with language-trained apes observed too many critical differences between humans and chimps to conclude that language extends beyond our species (Seidenberg & Pettito, 1979). For example:

- One major argument is that apes are communicating only with symbols, not with the phrase-based syntax used by humans. Although some evidence of syntax has been reported, the majority of their "utterances" consist of single signs, a couple of signs strung together, or apparently random sequences.

- There is little reputable experimental evidence showing that apes pass their language skills to other apes.

- Productivity—creating new words (gestures) and using existing gestures to name new objects or events—is rare, if it occurs at all.

- Some of the researchers become very engaged in the lives of these animals and talk about them as friends and family members (Fouts, 1997; Savage-Rumbaugh & Lewin, 1994). This tendency has left critics to wonder the extent to which personal attachments to the animals might interfere with the objectivity of the data.

It must be pointed out that the communication systems of different animals have their own adaptive functions. It is possible that some species simply didn't have a need to develop a complex form of language. However, in the case of chimpanzees, this point doesn't hold true. Both humans and chimpanzees evolved in small groups in (for the most part) similar parts of the world; thus, chimpanzees would have faced many of the same social and environmental pressures as humans. However, their brains, although quite sophisticated, are not as large or well-developed as those of humans. It seems, therefore, that a major factor in humanity's unique language abilities is the wonderful complexity and plasticity of the human brain.

MICHAEL NICHOLS/National Geographic Creative

Kanzi is a bonobo chimpanzee that has learned to use an artificial language consisting of graphical symbols that correspond to words. Kanzi can type out responses by pushing buttons with these symbols, shown in this photo. Researchers are also interested in Kanzi's ability to understand spoken English (which is transmitted to the headphones by an experimenter who is not in the room).

Module 8.3c Quiz:

Genes, Evolution, and Language

Know . . .

1. Which nonhuman species has had the greatest success at learning a human language?
   A. Border collies
   B. Bonobo chimpanzees
   C. Dolphins
   D. Rhesus monkeys

Understand . . .

2. Studies of the KE family and the FOXP2 gene indicate that
   A. language is controlled entirely by a single gene found on chromosome 7.
   B. language is still fluent despite a mutation to this gene.
   C. this particular gene is related to one specific aspect of language.
   D. mutations affecting this gene lead to highly expressive language skills.

Analyze . . .

3. What is the most accurate conclusion from research conducted on primate language abilities?
   A. Primates can learn some aspects of human language, though many differences remain.
   B. Primates can learn human language in full.
   C. Primates cannot learn human language in any way.
   D. Primates can respond to verbal commands, but there is no evidence they can respond to visual cues such as images or hand signals.

Module 8.3 Summary

8.3a   Know . . . the key terminology from the study of language.

aphasia
Broca's area
cross-foster
fast mapping
language
morpheme
phoneme
pragmatics
semantics
syntax
Wernicke's area

8.3b   Understand . . . how language is structured.

Sentences are broken down into words that are arranged according to grammatical rules (syntax). The relationship between words and their meaning is referred to as semantics. Words can be broken down into morphemes, the smallest meaningful units of speech, and phonemes, the smallest sound units that make up speech.

8.3c   Understand . . . how genes and the brain are involved in language use.

Studies of the KE family show that the FOXP2 gene is involved in our ability to speak. However, mutation to this gene does not necessarily impair people's ability to think.

Thus, the FOXP2 gene seems to be important for just one of many aspects of human language. Multiple brain areas are involved in language—two particularly important ones are Broca's and Wernicke's areas.

8.3d   Apply . . . your knowledge to distinguish between units of language such as phonemes and morphemes.

Apply Activity

Which of these represent a single phoneme and which represent a morpheme? Do any of them represent both?

1. /dis/
2. /s/
3. /k/

8.3e   Analyze . . . whether species other than humans are able to use language.

Nonhuman species certainly seem capable of acquiring certain aspects of human language. Studies with apes have shown that they can learn and use some sign language or, in the case of Kanzi, an artificial language system involving arbitrary symbols. However, critics have pointed out that many differences between human and nonhuman language use remain.

Chapter 9
Intelligence Testing

9.1 Measuring Intelligence

- Different Approaches to Intelligence Testing   351
- Module 9.1a Quiz   355
- The Checkered Past of Intelligence Testing   356
  Working the Scientific Literacy Model: Beliefs about Intelligence   358
- Module 9.1b Quiz   360
- Module 9.1 Summary   361

9.2 Understanding Intelligence

- Intelligence as a Single, General Ability   363
- Module 9.2a Quiz   365
- Intelligence as Multiple, Specific Abilities   365
  Working the Scientific Literacy Model: Testing for Fluid and Crystallized Intelligence   366
- Module 9.2b Quiz   371
- The Battle of the Sexes   371
- Module 9.2c Quiz   372
- Module 9.2 Summary   373

9.3 Biological, Environmental, and Behavioural Influences on Intelligence

- Biological Influences on Intelligence   375
  Working the Scientific Literacy Model: Brain Size and Intelligence   377
- Module 9.3a Quiz   379
- Environmental Influences on Intelligence   379
- Module 9.3b Quiz   382
- Behavioural Influences on Intelligence   382
- Module 9.3c Quiz   384
- Module 9.3 Summary   384

Module 9.1 Measuring Intelligence

The Canadian Press / Edmonton Journal

Leilani Muir, who passed away in Alberta in 2016.

⌄ Learning Objectives

9.1a Know . . . the key terminology associated with intelligence and intelligence testing.

9.1b Understand . . . the reasoning behind the eugenics movements and its use of intelligence tests.

9.1c Apply . . . the concepts of entity theory and incremental theory to help kids succeed in school.

9.1d Analyze . . . why it is difficult to remove all cultural bias from intelligence testing.

Leilani Muir kept trying to get pregnant, but to no avail. Finally, frustrated, she went to her doctor to see if there was a medical explanation. It turned out that there was, but not one that she expected; the doctors found that her fallopian tubes had been surgically destroyed, permanently sterilizing her.

How could someone's fallopian tubes be destroyed without them knowing? Tragically, forced sterilization was a not uncommon practice in the United States and parts of Canada for almost half of the 20th century. In 1928, Alberta passed the Sexual Sterilization Act, *giving doctors the power to sterilize people deemed to be "genetically unfit," without their*

consent. One of the criteria that could qualify a person for being genetically unfit was getting a low score on an IQ test, which was the reason for Leilani's own sterilization.

Leilani Muir is one of the tens of thousands of victims of the misguided application of intelligence tests. Born into a poor farming family near Calgary, Alberta, Leilani was entered by her parents into the Provincial Training School for Mental Defectives when she was 11. A few years later, when given an intelligence test, she scored 64, which was below the 70 point cut-off required by law for forced sterilization. When she was 14, she was told by doctors she needed to have her appendix removed. Trusting the good doctors, she went under the knife, never knowing the full extent of the surgery she was about to undergo. After the surgery, she was never informed that her fallopian tubes had been destroyed, and had to find out on her own after her many attempts to get pregnant. Later in her life, Leilani had her IQ re-tested. She scored 89, which is close to average.

In 1996, Leilani received some measure of justice. She sued the government of Alberta and won her case, becoming the first person to receive compensation for injustices committed under the Sexual Sterilization Act. *For her lifetime of not being able to have children, she received almost $750 000 in damages.*

Focus Questions

1. How have intelligence tests been misused in modern society?

2. Why do we have the types of intelligence tests that we have?

>> What happened to Leilani Muir was terrible and should never have happened. But this story also serves to drive home an extremely important truth about psychology, and science in general—*it is important to measure things properly.* This may sound trite, but Leilani's story underscores the importance of ensuring that the research carried out in psychology and other disciplines is as rigorous as possible. Research isn't just about writing complicated articles that only scientists and academics read; its real-world implications may ripple through society and affect people's lives in countless ways. In Leilani's case, her misfortune was the result of both inhumane policies passed by government and the failure to accurately measure her intelligence. Intelligence is not something like the length or mass of a physical object; there is no "objective" standard to which we can compare our measures to see if they are accurate. Instead, we have to rely upon rigorous testing of our methodologies.

So, how *can* we measure intelligence accurately? What does science say? As you will see in this module, this question is not easy to answer. Intelligence measures have a very checkered past, making the whole notion of intelligence one of the most hotly contested areas in all of psychology.

Different Approaches to Intelligence Testing

Intelligence is a surprisingly difficult concept to define. You undoubtedly know people who earn similar grades even though one may seem to be "smarter" than the other. You likely also know people who do very well in school and have "book smarts," but have difficulty in

Mary Evans Picture Library / Alamy Stock Photo

Francis Galton believed that intelligence was something people inherit. Thus, he believed that an individual's relatives were a better predictor of intelligence than practice and effort.

many other aspects of life, perhaps lacking "street smarts." Furthermore, you may perceive a person to be intelligent or unintelligent, but how do you know your perceptions are not biased by their confidence, social skills, or other qualities? The history of psychology has seen many different attempts to define and measure intelligence. In this module, we will examine some of the more influential of these attempts, and then explore some of the important social implications of intelligence testing.

INTELLIGENCE AND PERCEPTION: GALTON'S ANTHROPOMETRIC APPROACH The systematic attempt to measure intelligence in the modern era began with Francis Galton (1822–1911) (who is often given the appellation "Sir," because he was knighted in 1909). Galton believed that because people learn about the world through their senses, those with superior sensory abilities would be able to learn more about it. Thus, he argued, sensory abilities should be an indicator of a person's intelligence. In 1884, Galton created a set of 17 sensory tests, such as the highest and lowest sounds people could hear or their ability to tell the difference between objects of slightly different weights, and began testing people's abilities in his *anthropometric* laboratory. **Anthropometrics** (literally, "the measurement of people") referred to *methods of measuring physical and mental variation in humans.* Galton's lab attracted many visitors, allowing him to measure the sensory abilities of thousands of people in England (Gillham, 2001).

One of Galton's colleagues, James McKeen Cattell, took his tests to the United States and began measuring the abilities of university students. This research revealed, however, that people's abilities on different sensory tests were not correlated with each other, or only very weakly. For example, having exceptional eyesight seemed to signify little about whether one would have exceptional hearing. Clearly, this was a problem, because if two measures don't correlate well with each other, then they can't both be indicators of the same thing, in this case, intelligence. Cattell also found that students' scores on the sensory tests did not predict their grades, which one would expect would also be an indicator of intelligence. As a result, Galton's approach to measuring intelligence was generally abandoned.

INTELLIGENCE AND THINKING: THE STANFORD–BINET TEST In contrast to Galton, a prominent French psychologist, Alfred Binet, argued that intelligence should be indicated by more complex thinking processes, such as memory, attention, and comprehension. This view has influenced most intelligence researchers up to the present day; they define **intelligence** as *the ability to think, understand, reason, and adapt to or overcome obstacles* (Neisser et al., 1996). From this perspective, intelligence reflects how well people are able to reason and solve problems, plus their accumulated knowledge.

In 1904, Binet and his colleague, Theodore Simon, were hired by the French government to develop a test to measure intelligence. At the end of the 19th century, institutional reforms in France had made primary school education available to all children. As a result, French educators struggled to deliver a curriculum to students ranging from the very bright to those who found school exceptionally challenging. To respond to this problem, the French government wanted an objective way of identifying "retarded" children who would benefit from specialized education (Siegler, 1992).

Binet and Simon experimented with a wide variety of tasks, trying to capture the complex thinking processes that presumably comprised intelligence. They settled on thirty tasks, arranged in order of increasing difficulty. For example, simple tasks included repeating sentences and defining common words like "house." More difficult tasks included constructing sentences using combinations of certain words (e.g., Paris, river, fortune), reproducing drawings from memory, and being able to explain how two things differed from each other. Very difficult tasks included being able to define abstract concepts and to logically reason through a problem (Fancher, 1985).

Binet and Simon gave their test to samples of children from different age groups to establish the average test score for each age. Binet argued that a child's test score measured her **mental age**, *the average intellectual ability score for children of a specific age*. For example, if a 7-year-old's score was the same as the average score for 7-year-olds, she would have a mental age of 7, whereas if it was the same as the average score for 10-year-olds, she would have a mental age of 10, even though her chronological age would be 7 in both cases. A child with a mental age lower than her chronological age would be expected to struggle in school and to require remedial education.

The practicality of Binet and Simon's test was apparent to others, and soon researchers in the United States began to adapt it for their own use. Lewis Terman at Stanford University adapted the test for American children and established average scores for each age level by administering the test to thousands of children. In 1916, he published the first version of his adapted test, and named it the Stanford-Binet Intelligence Scale (Siegler, 1992).

Terman and others almost immediately began describing the **Stanford-Binet test** as *a test intended to measure innate levels of intelligence*. This differed substantially from Binet, who had viewed his test as a measure of a child's current abilities, not as a measure of an innate capacity. There is a crucial difference between believing that test scores reflect a changeable ability or believing they reflect an innate capacity that is presumably fixed. The interpretation of intelligence as an innate ability set the stage for the incredibly misguided use of intelligence tests in the decades that followed, as we discuss later in this module.

To better reflect people's presumably innate levels of intelligence, Terman adopted William Stern's concept of the **intelligence quotient**, or **IQ**, a label that has stuck to the present day. *IQ is calculated by taking a person's mental age, dividing it by his chronological age, and then multiplying by 100.* For example, a 10-year-old child with a mental age of 7 would have an IQ of $7/10 \times 100 = 70$. On the other hand, if a child's mental and chronological ages were the same, the IQ score would always be 100, regardless of the age of the child; thus, 100 became the standard IQ for the "average child."

To see the conceptual difference implied by these two ways of reporting intelligence, consider the following two statements. Does one sound more optimistic than the other?

- He has a mental age of 7, so he is 3 years behind.
- He has an IQ of 70, so he is 30 points below average.

To many people, being 3 years behind in mental age seems changeable; with sufficient work and assistance, it feels like such a child should be able to catch up to his peers. On the other hand, having an IQ that's 30 points below average sounds like the diagnosis of a permanent condition; such a person seems doomed to be "unintelligent" forever.

One other odd feature of both Binet's mental age concept and Stern's IQ was that they didn't generalize very well to adult populations. For example, are 80-year olds twice as intelligent as 40-year-olds? After all, an 80-year-old who was as intelligent as an average 40-year-old would

Figure 9.1 The Normal Distribution of Scores for a Standardized Intelligence Test

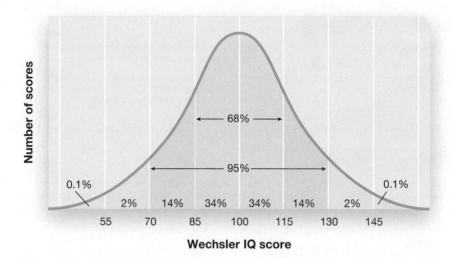

have an IQ of 50 (40/80 × 100 = 50); clearly, this doesn't make sense. Similarly, imagine a 30-year-old with a mental age of 30; her IQ would be 100. But in 10 years, when she was 40, if her mental age stayed at 30, she would have an IQ of only 75 (30/40 × 100 = 75). Given that IQ scores remain constant after about age 16 (Eysenck, 1994), this would mean that adults get progressively less smart with every year that they age. Although children may sometimes think exactly this about their parents, their parents would clearly have a different opinion.

To adjust for this problem, psychologists began to use a different measure, *deviation IQ,* for calculating the IQ of adults (Wechsler, 1939). The **deviation IQ** *is calculated by comparing the person's test score with the average score for people of the same age.* In order to calculate deviation IQs, one must first establish the norm, or average, for a population. To do so, psychologists administer tests to huge numbers of people and use these scores to estimate the average for people of different ages. These averages are then used as baselines against which to compare a person.

Because "average" is defined to be 100, a deviation IQ of 100 means that the person is average, whereas an IQ of 115 would mean that the person's IQ is above average (see Figure 9.1). One advantage of using deviation IQ scores is that it avoids the problem of IQ scores that consistently decline with age because scores are calculated relative to others of the same age.

THE WECHSLER ADULT INTELLIGENCE SCALE In an ironic twist, the **Wechsler Adult Intelligence Scale (WAIS),** *the most common intelligence test in use today for adolescents and adults,* was developed by a man who himself had been labelled as "feeble minded" by intelligence tests after immigrating to the United States from Romania at the age of nine. David Wechsler originally developed the scale in 1955 and it is now in its fourth edition.

The WAIS provides a single IQ score for each test taker—the *Full Scale IQ*—but also breaks intelligence into a *General Ability Index* (GAI) and a *Cognitive Proficiency Index* (CPI), as shown in Figure 9.2. The GAI is computed

Figure 9.2 Subscales of the Wechsler Adult Intelligence Scale

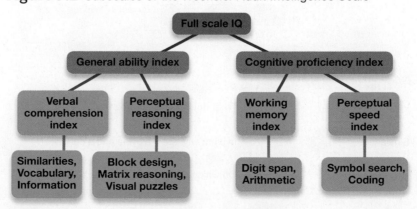

Figure 9.3 Types of Problems Used to Measure Intelligence

These hypothetical problems are consistent with the types seen on the Wechsler Adult Intelligence Scale.

Processing Speed Index

| Symbol search | View groupings of symbols for specific numbers of each symbol, and fill in a blank with a missing symbol. |
| Coding | Match different symbols with specific numbers, and fill in a blank with a correct symbol given a certain number. |

Working Memory Index

| Arithmetic | Jack has $16 and owes $8 to Hank and $4 to Frank. What percentage of the original $16 will Jack still have after he pays Hank and Frank? |
| Digit span | Recall the order of number strings in both forward and reverse directions. |

Perceptual Reasoning Index

| Matrix reasoning | View the pattern in the top two rows and fill in the blank of the third row. |

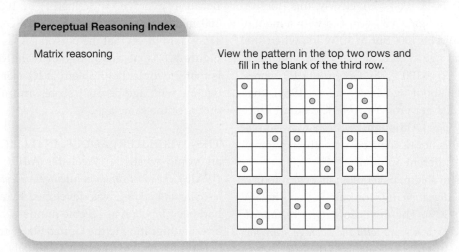

Block Design

Which three pieces are needed to make this puzzle?

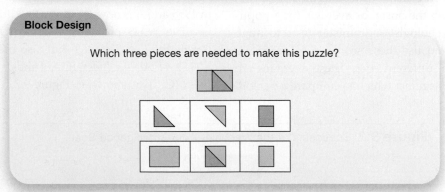

Verbal Comprehension Index

Vocabulary	What does *profligate* mean?
Similarities	In what way are a bicycle and a car alike?
Information	On which continent is Japan located?

from scores on the Verbal Comprehension and Perceptual Reasoning indices. These measures tap into an individual's intellectual abilities, but without placing much emphasis on how fast he can solve problems and make decisions. The CPI, in contrast, is based on the Working Memory and Processing Speed subtests. It is included in the Full Scale IQ category because greater working memory capacity and processing speed allow more cognitive resources to be devoted to reasoning and solving problems. Figure 9.3 shows some sample test items from the WAIS.

RAVEN'S PROGRESSIVE MATRICES Although the Stanford-Binet test and the WAIS have been widely used across North America, they have also been criticized by a number of researchers. One of the key problems with many intelligence tests, such as these, is that questions often are biased to favour people from the test developer's culture or who primarily speak the test developer's language. This cultural bias puts people from different cultures, social classes, educational levels, and primary languages, at an immediate disadvantage. Clearly, this is a problem, because a person's "intelligence" should not be affected by whether they are fluent in English or familiar with Western culture. In response to this problem, psychologists have tried to develop "culture-free" tests.

In the 1930s, John Raven developed **Raven's Progressive Matrices**, *an intelligence test that is based on pictures, not words, thus making it relatively unaffected by language or cultural background.* The main set of tasks found in Raven's Progressive Matrices measure the extent to which test takers can see patterns in the shapes and colours within a matrix and then determine which shape or colour would complete the pattern (see Figure 9.4).

Figure 9.4 Sample Problem from Raven's Progressive Matrices

Which possible pattern (1–8) should go in the blank space? Check your answer at the bottom of the page.

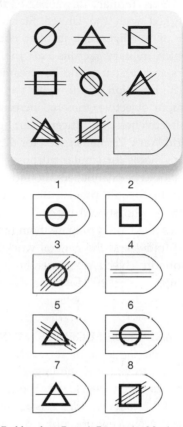

Source: "Sample Problem from Raven's Progressive Matrices," NCS Pearson, 1998.

Answer to Figure 9.4: Pattern 6.

Module 9.1a Quiz:

Different Approaches to Intelligence Testing

Know . . .

1. Galton developed anthropometrics as a means to measure intelligence based on _____.
   A. creativity
   B. perceptual abilities
   C. physical size and body type
   D. brain convolution

Understand . . .

2. The deviation IQ is calculated by comparing an individual's test score
   A. at one point in time to that same person's test score at a different point in time.
   B. to that same person's test score from a different IQ test; the "deviation" between the tests is a measure of whether either test is inaccurate.

C. to that same individual's school grades.
D. to the average score for other people who are the same age.

3. In an attempt to be culturally unbiased, Raven's Progressive Matrices relies upon what types of questions?
   A. Verbal analogies
   B. Spatial calculations
   C. Visual patterns
   D. Practical problems that are encountered in every culture

Apply . . .

4. If someone's mental age is double her chronological age, what would her IQ be?
   A. 100
   B. 50
   C. 200
   D. Cannot be determined with this information

The Checkered Past of Intelligence Testing

IQ testing in North America got a significant boost during World War I. Lewis Terman, developer of the Stanford-Binet test, worked with the United States military to develop a set of intelligence tests that could be used to identify which military recruits had the potential to become officers and which should be streamed into non-officer roles. The intention was to make the officer selection process more objective, thereby increasing the efficiency and effectiveness of officer training programs. Following World War I, Terman argued for the use of intelligence tests in schools for similar purposes—identifying students who should be channelled into more "advanced" academic topics that would prepare them for higher education, and others who should be channelled into more skill-based topics that would prepare them for direct entry into the skilled trades and the general workforce. Armed with his purportedly objective IQ tests, he was a man on a mission to improve society. However, the way he went about doing so was rife with problems.

IQ TESTING AND THE EUGENICS MOVEMENT In order to understand the logic of Terman and his followers, it is important to examine the larger societal context in which his theories were developed. The end of the 19th and beginning of the 20th centuries was a remarkable time in human history. A few centuries of European colonialism had spread Western influence through much of the world. The Industrial Revolution, which was concentrated in the West, compounded this, making Western nations more powerful militarily, technologically, and economically. And in the sciences, Darwin's paradigm-shattering work on the origin of species firmly established the idea of evolution by natural selection (see Module 3.1), permanently transforming our scientific understanding of the living world.

Although an exciting time for the advancement of human knowledge, this confluence of events also had some very negative consequences, especially in terms of how colonialism affected non-Western cultures and people of non-White ethnicities. However, the stage was set for social "visionaries" to apply Darwin's ideas to human culture, and to explain the military–economic–technological dominance of Western cultures by assuming that Westerners (and especially White people) were genetically superior. This explanation served as a handy justification for the colonial powers' imposition of Western-European values on other cultures; in fact, it was often viewed that the colonizers were actually doing other cultures a favour, helping to "civilize" them by assimilating them into a "superior" cultural system.

The *social Darwinism* that emerged gave rise to one of the uglier social movements of recent times—*eugenics*,

Many people viewed eugenics as a way to "improve" the human gene pool. Their definition of "improve" is certainly up for debate.

which means "good genes" (Gillham, 2001). The history of eugenics is intimately intertwined with the history of intelligence testing. In fact, Francis Galton himself, a cousin of Charles Darwin, coined the term *eugenics*, gaining credibility for his ideas after making an extensive study of the heritability of intelligence.

Galton noticed that many members of his own family were successful businessmen and some, like Charles Darwin, eminent scientists. He studied other families and concluded that eminence ran in families, which he believed was due to "good breeding." Although families share more than genes, such as wealth, privilege, and social status, Galton believed that genes were the basis of the family patterns he observed (Fancher, 2009).

Galton's views influenced Lewis Terman, who promoted an explicitly eugenic philosophy; he argued for the superiority of his own "race," and in the interest of

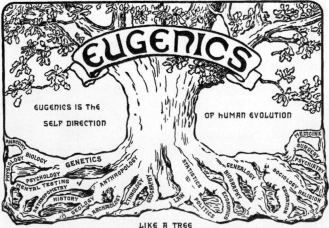

Supporters of eugenics often noted that its logic was based on research and philosophy from many different fields. Doing so put the focus on the abstract intellectual characteristics of eugenics rather than on some of its disturbing, real-world implications.

"improving" society, believed that his IQ tests provided a strong empirical justification for eugenic practices. One such practice was the forced sterilization of people like Leilani Muir, whom we discussed at the beginning of this module.

As Terman administered his tests to more people, it seemed like his race-based beliefs were verified by his data. Simply put, people from other cultures and other apparent ethnic backgrounds, didn't score as highly on his tests as did White people from the West (i.e., the U.S., Canada, and Western Europe, for the most part). For example, 40% of new immigrants to Canada and the United States scored so low they were classified as "feebleminded" (Kevles, 1985). As a result, Terman concluded that people from non-Western cultures and non-White ethnicities generally had lower IQs, and he therefore argued that it was appropriate (even desirable) to stream them into less challenging academic pursuits and jobs of lower status. For example, he wrote, "High-grade or border-line deficiency . . . is very, very common among Spanish-Indian and Mexican families of the Southwest and also among negroes. Their dullness seems to be racial, or at least inherent in the family stocks from which they come. . . . Children of this group should be segregated into separate classes. . . . They cannot master abstractions but they can often be made into efficient workers . . . from a eugenic point of view they constitute a grave problem because of their unusually prolific breeding" (Terman, 1916, pp. 91–92).

Such ideas gained enough popularity that forced sterilization was carried out in at least 30 states and two Canadian provinces, lasting for almost half a century. In Alberta, the *Sexual Sterilization Act* remained in force until 1972, by which time more than 2800 people had undergone sterilization procedures in that province alone. And as you might have guessed, new immigrants, the poor, Native people, and Black people were sterilized far more often than middle and upper class White people.

THE RACE AND IQ CONTROVERSY   One of the reasons intelligence tests played so well into the agendas of eugenicists is that, from Terman onwards, researchers over the last century have consistently found differences in the IQ scores of people from different ethnic groups. Before we go any further, we want to acknowledge that this is a difficult, and potentially upsetting, set of research findings. However, it's important to take a close look at this research, and to understand the controversy that surrounds it, because these findings are well known in the world of intelligence testing and could be easily misused by those who are motivated by prejudiced views. As you will see, when you take a close look at the science, the story is not nearly as clear as it may appear at first glance.

The root of this issue about "race and IQ" is that there is a clear and reliable hierarchy of IQ scores across different ethnic groups. This was first discovered in the early 1900s,

and by the 1920s, the United States passed legislation making it standard to administer intelligence tests to new immigrants arriving at Ellis Island for entry into the country. The result was that overwhelming numbers of immigrants were officially classified as "morons" or "feebleminded." Some psychologists suspected that these tests were unfair, and that the low scores of these minority groups might be due to language barriers and a lack of knowledge of American culture. Nevertheless, as intelligence tests were developed that were increasingly culturally sensitive—such as Raven's Progressive Matrices—these differences persisted. Specifically, Asian people tended to score the highest, followed by Whites, followed by Latinos and Blacks; this has been found in samples in several parts of the world, including Canada (Rushton & Jensen, 2005). Other researchers have found that Native people in Canada score lower as a group than Canadians with European ancestry (e.g., Beiser & Gotowiec, 2000).

The race–IQ research hit the general public in 1994 with the publication of *The Bell Curve* (Herrnstein & Murray, 1994), which became a bestseller. This book focused on over two decades of research that replicated the race differences in IQ that we mentioned earlier. Herrnstein and Murray also argued that human intelligence is a strong predictor of many different personal and social outcomes, such as workplace performance, income, and the likelihood of being involved in criminal activities. Additionally, *The Bell Curve* argued that those of high intelligence were reproducing less than those of low intelligence, leading to a dangerous population trend in the United States. They believed that America was becoming an increasingly divided society, populated by a small class of "cognitive elite," and a large underclass with lower intelligence. They argued that a healthy society would be a *meritocracy*, in which people who had the most ability and worked the hardest would receive the most wealth, power, and status. Those who didn't have what it took to rise to the top, such as those with low IQs, should be allowed to live out their fates, and should not therefore be helped by programs such as Head Start, affirmative action programs, or scholarships for members of visible minorities. Instead, the system should simply allow people with the most demonstrable merit to rise to the top, regardless of their cultural or ethnic backgrounds. Although many people agree with the idea of a meritocracy in principle, a huge problem arises in implementing a meritocracy when the system is set up to systematically give certain groups advantages over other groups; in this situation, assessing true "merit" is far from straightforward.

As you can imagine, research on the race–IQ gap sparked bitter controversy. Within the academic world, some researchers have claimed that these findings are valid (e.g., Gottfredson, 2005), whereas others have argued that these results are based on flawed methodologies and poor measurements (e.g., Lieberman, 2001; Nisbett, 2005). Others have sought to discredit Herrnstein and Murray's conclusions, in particular their argument that the differences in IQ scores between ethnic groups means that there are inherent, genetic differences in intelligence between the groups. Within the general public, reaction was similarly mixed; however, this research does get used by some people to justify policies such as limiting immigration, discontinuing affirmative action programs, and otherwise working to overturn decades of progress made in the fight for civil rights and equality.

PROBLEMS WITH THE RACIAL SUPERIORITY INTERPRETATION In many ways, the simplest critique of the racial superiority interpretation of these test score differences is that the tests themselves are culturally biased. This critique was lodged against intelligence tests from the time of Terman and, as we discussed earlier, a considerable amount of research focused on creating tests that were not biased due to language and culture. But in spite of all this work, the test score differences between ethnic groups remained.

A more subtle critique was that it wasn't necessarily the tests that were biased, but the very process of testing itself. If people in minority groups are less familiar with standardized tests, if they are less motivated to do well on the tests, or if they are less able to focus on performing well during the testing sessions, they will be more likely to produce lower test scores. This indeed seems to be the case; researchers have found that cultural background affects many aspects of the testing process including how comfortable people are in a formal testing environment, how motivated they are to perform well on such tests, and their ability to establish rapport with the test administrators (Anastasi & Urbina, 1996).

Research has also indicated that the IQ differences may be due to a process known as **stereotype threat**, which *occurs when negative stereotypes about a group cause group members to underperform on ability tests* (Steele, 1997). In other words, if a Black person is reminded of the stereotype that Black people perform more poorly than White people on intelligence tests, she may end up scoring lower on that test as a result. Researchers have identified at least three reasons why this may happen. First, stereotype threat increases arousal due to the fact that individuals are aware of the negative stereotype about their group, and are concerned that a poor performance may reflect poorly on their group; this arousal then undermines their test performance. Second, stereotype threat causes people to become more self-focused, paying more attention to how well they are performing; this leaves fewer cognitive resources for them to focus on the test itself. Third, stereotype threat increases the tendency for people to actively try to inhibit negative thoughts they may have, which also reduces the cognitive resources that could otherwise be used to focus on the test

(Schmader et al., 2008). There have now been more than 200 studies on stereotype threat (Nisbett et al., 2012), establishing it as a reliable phenomenon that regularly suppresses the test scores of members of stereotyped groups.

These concerns cast doubt on the *validity* of IQ scores for members of non-White ethnic and cultural groups, suggesting that differences in test scores do not necessarily reflect differences in the underlying ability being tested (i.e., intelligence), but instead may reflect other factors, such as such as linguistic or cultural bias in the testing situation.

Another important critique has been lodged against the race–IQ research, arguing that even if one believes that the tests are valid and that there are intelligence differences between groups in society, these may not be the result of innate, genetic differences between the groups. For example, consider the circumstances that poor people and ethnic minorities face in countries like Canada or the United States. People from such groups tend to experience a host of factors that contribute to poorer cognitive and neurological development, such as poorer nutrition, greater stress, lower-quality schools, higher rates of illness (Acevedo-Garcia et al., 2008) with reduced access to medical treatment, and greater exposure to toxins such as lead (Dilworth-Bart & Moore, 2006).

One additional, subtle factor that may interfere with the test performances of people from disadvantaged groups is that the life experiences of people in those groups may encourage them to adopt certain beliefs about themselves, which then interfere with their motivations to perform their best. For example, if early experiences in educational settings lead people to believe that they are not intelligent, and that this is a fixed quality, they will tend to believe that there is little they can do to change their own intelligence, and as a result, they won't try very hard to do so. However, recent research suggests that it *is* possible to improve one's intelligence—but one has to believe this in order to take the necessary steps to make it happen.

Working the Scientific Literacy Model

Beliefs about Intelligence

Think of something you're not very good at (or maybe have never even tried), like juggling knives, solving Sudoku puzzles, or speaking Gaelic. Most likely, you would expect that even if your initial attempts didn't go well, with practice you could get better.

Now think about how smart you are. Do you think you could make yourself smarter? Do you ever say things like "I'm no good at math," or "I just can't do multiple choice tests?" Do you think about these abilities the same way that you think about knife-juggling?

Many people hold implicit beliefs that their intelligence level is relatively fixed and find it surprising that intelligence is, in fact, highly changeable. Ironically, this mistaken belief itself will tend to limit people's potential to change their own intelligence. This is an especially important issue for students, as children's self-perceptions of their mental abilities have a very strong influence on their academic performance (Greven et al., 2009).

What do we know about the kinds of beliefs that may affect test scores?

Research into this phenomenon has helped to shed light on the frustrating mystery of why some people seem to consistently fall short of reaching their potential. Carol Dweck (2002) has found that people seem to hold one of two theories about the nature of intelligence. They may hold an **entity theory**: *the belief that intelligence is a fixed characteristic and relatively difficult (or impossible) to change;* or they may hold an **incremental theory**: *the belief that intelligence can be shaped by experiences, practice, and effort.* Whether one holds to an entity theory or incremental theory has powerful effects on one's academic performance.

How can science test whether beliefs affect performance?

In experiments by Dweck and her colleagues, students were identified as holding either entity theory or incremental theory beliefs. The students had the chance to answer 476 general knowledge questions dealing with topics such as history, literature, math, and geography. They received immediate feedback on whether their answers were correct or incorrect. Those who held entity beliefs were more likely to give up in the face of highly challenging problems, and they were likely to withdraw from situations that resulted in failure. These individuals seemed to believe that intelligence was something you either had, or you didn't; thus, when encountering difficult problems or feelings of failure, they seemed to conclude "Well, I guess I don't have it," and as a result, gave up trying (Mangels et al., 2006). As Homer Simpson has said, "Kids, you tried your best and you failed miserably. The lesson is, never try" (Richdale & Kirkland, 1994). To the entity theorist, difficulty is a sign of inadequacy.

In comparison, people with incremental views of intelligence were more resilient (Mangels et al., 2006), continuing to work hard even when faced with challenges and failures. After all, if intelligence and ability can change, then rather than getting discouraged by difficulties, one should keep working hard, improving one's abilities.

Because resilience is such a desirable trait, Dweck and her colleagues tested a group of junior high students to see whether incremental views could be taught (Blackwell et al., 2007). In a randomized, controlled experiment, they taught one group of Grade 7 students incremental theory— that they could control and change their abilities. This group's grades increased over the school year, whereas the control group's grades actually declined (Figure 9.5).

Figure 9.5 Personal Beliefs Influence Grades

Students who held incremental views of intelligence (i.e., the belief that intelligence can change with effort) show improved grades in math compared to students who believed that intelligence was an unchanging entity (Blackwell et al., 2007).

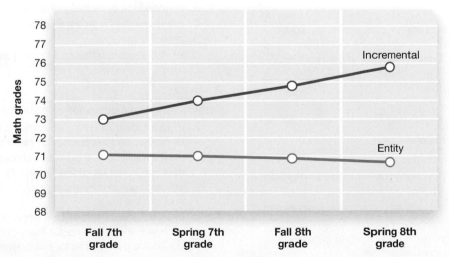

Source: From Implicit theories of intelligence predict achievement across an Adult Transition: A Longitudinal Study and an intervention." *Child Development*, Vol 78, No 1, Pg 246-263 byLisa S. Blackwell, Kali H. Trzesniewski, Carol Sorich Dweck. Copyright © 2007 by John Wiley & Sons, Inc. Reproduced by permission of John Wiley & Sons, Inc.

The moral of the story? If you think you can, you might; but if you think you can't, you won't.

Can we critically evaluate this research?

These findings suggest that it is desirable to help people adopt incremental beliefs about their abilities. However, is this always for the best? What if, in some situations, it is true that no matter how hard a person tries, he or she is unlikely to succeed, and continuing to try at all costs may be detrimental to the person's well-being, or may close the door on other opportunities that may have turned out better? At what point do we encourage people to be more "realistic" and to accept their limitations? So far, these remain unanswered questions in this literature.

An additional difficulty surrounding these studies is that it is not fully clear what mechanisms might be causing the improvements. Does the incremental view of intelligence lead to increased attention, effort, and time invested in studying? Does it lead to less-critical self-judgments following failure experiences? Or, does it have a positive effect on mood, which has been shown to improve performance on tests of perception and creativity (Isen et al., 1987)? In order to better understand why these mindsets work the way they do, and perhaps, how to apply them more effectively, a great deal of research is needed to determine which mechanisms are operating in which circumstances. However, regardless of the mechanism(s) involved, the fact that it is possible to help students by changing their view of intelligence could be a powerful force for educational change in the future.

Why is this relevant?

This research has huge potential to be applied in schools and to become a part of standard parenting practice. Teaching people to adopt the view that intelligence and other abilities are trainable skills should give them a greater feeling of control over their lives, strengthen their motivations, enhance their resilience to difficulty, and improve their goal-striving success. Carol Dweck and Lisa Sorich Blackwell have designed a program called Brainology to teach students from elementary through high school that the brain can be trained and strengthened through practice. They hope that programs such as this can counteract the disempowering effects of stereotypes by helping members of stereotyped groups to have greater resilience and to avoid succumbing to negative beliefs about themselves. Not only is intelligence changeable, as this research shows, but perhaps society itself can be changed through the widespread application of this research.

Module 9.1b Quiz:

The Checkered Past of Intelligence Testing

Know . . .

1. People who believe that intelligence is relatively fixed are said to advocate a(n) _____ theory of intelligence.
   A. incremental
   B. entity
   C. sexist
   D. hereditary

2. When people are aware of stereotypes about their social group, and their social group membership is brought to their minds, they may experience a reduction in their performance on a stereotype-relevant task. This is known as _____.
   A. incremental intelligence
   B. hereditary intelligence
   C. stereotype threat
   D. intelligence discrimination

3. Eugenics was a movement that promoted
   A. the use of genetic engineering technologies to improve the human gene pool.
   B. the assimilation of one culture into another, often as part of colonialism.
   C. using measures of physical capabilities (e.g., visual acuity) as estimates of a person's intelligence.
   D. preventing people from reproducing if they were deemed to be genetically inferior, so as to improve the human gene pool.

Apply . . .

4. As a major exam approaches, a teacher who is hoping to reduce stereotype threat and promote an incremental theory of intelligence would most likely
   A. remind test takers that males tend to do poorly on the problems.
   B. remind students that they inherited their IQ from their parents.
   C. cite research of a recent study showing that a particular gene is linked to IQ.
   D. let students know that hard work is the best way to prepare for the exam.

Analyze . . .

5. According to the discussion of the race and IQ controversy
   A. there are clear IQ differences between people of different ethnicities, and these probably have a genetic basis.
   B. the use of Raven's Progressive Matrices has shown that there are in fact no differences in IQ between the "races"; any such group differences must be due to cultural biases built into the tests.
   C. many scholars believe that the ethnic differences in IQ are so large that one could argue that a person's race should be considered a relevant factor in important decisions, such as who to let into medical school or who to hire for a specific job.
   D. even if tests are constructed that are culturally unbiased, the testing process itself may still favour some cultures over others.

Module 9.1 Summary

9.1a   Know . . . the key terminology associated with intelligence and intelligence testing.

anthropometrics
deviation IQ
entity theory
incremental theory
intelligence
intelligence quotient (IQ)
mental age
Raven's Progressive Matrices
Stanford-Binet test
stereotype threat
Wechsler Adult Intelligence Scale (WAIS)

9.1b   Understand . . . the reasoning behind the eugenics movements and its use of intelligence tests.

The eugenicists believed that abilities like intelligence were inborn, and thus, by encouraging reproduction between people with higher IQs, and reducing the birthrate of people with lower IQs, the gene pool of humankind could be improved.

9.1c   Apply . . . the concepts of entity theory and incremental theory to help kids succeed in school.

One of the key reasons that people stop trying to succeed in school, and then eventually drop out, is that they hold a belief that their basic abilities, such as their intelligence, are fixed. Not trying then guarantees that they perform poorly, which reinforces their tendency to not try. However, this downward spiral can be stopped by training young people to think of themselves as changeable. Specifically, learning to think that the brain is like a muscle that can be strengthened through exercise leads people to improve their scores on intelligence tests, helps them become more resilient to negative circumstances, and enables them to respond to life's challenges more effectively.

9.1d   Analyze . . . why it is difficult to remove all cultural bias from intelligence testing.

There are many reasons why the process of intelligence testing may be systematically biased, resulting in inaccuracies when testing people from certain cultural groups: Tests may contain content that is more relevant or familiar to some cultures; the method of testing (e.g., paper-and-pencil multiple-choice questions) may be more familiar to people from some cultures; the environment of testing may make people from some cultures less comfortable; the presence of negative stereotypes about one's group may interfere with test-taking abilities; and the internalization of self-defeating beliefs may affect performance.

Module 9.2 Understanding Intelligence

Lane V. Erickson/Shutterstock

Learning Objectives

9.2a Know . . . the key terminology related to understanding intelligence.

9.2b Understand . . . why intelligence is divided into fluid and crystallized types.

9.2c Understand . . . intelligence differences between males and females.

9.2d Apply . . . your knowledge to identify examples from the triarchic theory of intelligence.

9.2e Analyze . . . whether teachers should spend time tailoring lessons to each individual student's learning style.

Blind Tom was born into a Black slave family in 1849. When his mother was bought in a slave auction by General James Bethune, Tom was included in the sale for nothing because he was blind and believed to be useless. Indeed, Tom was not "smart" in the normal sense of the term. Even as an adult he could speak fewer than 100 words and would never be able to go to school. But he could play more than 7000 pieces on the piano, including a huge classical music repertoire and many of his own compositions. Tom could play, flawlessly, Beethoven, Mendelssohn, Bach, Chopin, Verdi, Rossini, and many others, even after hearing a piece only a single time. As an 11-year-old, he played at the White House, and by 16 went on a world tour. A panel of expert musicians performed a series of musical experiments on him, and universally agreed

he was "among the most wonderful phenomena in musical history." Despite his dramatic linguistic limitations, he could reproduce, perfectly, up to a 15-minute conversation without losing a single syllable, and could do so in English, French, or German, without understanding any part of what he was saying. In the mid-1800s, he was considered to be the "eighth wonder of the world."

*Today, Tom would be considered a **savant**, an individual with low mental capacity in most domains but extraordinary abilities in other specific areas such as music, mathematics, or art. The existence of savants complicates our discussion of intelligence considerably. Normally, the label "intelligent" or "unintelligent" is taken to indicate some sort of overall ability, the amount of raw brainpower* *available to the person, akin to an engine's horsepower. But this doesn't map onto savants at all—they have seemingly unlimited "horsepower" for certain skills and virtually none for many others. The existence of savants, and the more general phenomenon of people being good at some things (e.g., math, science) but not others (e.g., languages, art), challenges our understanding of intelligence and makes us ask more deeply, what is intelligence? Is it one ability? Or is it many?*

Focus Questions

1. Is intelligence one ability or many?

2. How have psychologists attempted to measure intelligence?

》 When we draw conclusions about someone's intelligence (e.g., Sally is really smart!), we intuitively know what we mean. Right? Being intelligent has to do with a person's abilities to think, understand, reason, learn, and find solutions to problems. But this intuitive understanding unravels quickly when you start considering the questions it raises. Are these abilities related to each other? Does the content of a person's intelligence matter? That is, does it mean the same thing if a person is very good at different things, like math, music, history, poetry, and child rearing? Or should intelligence be thought of more as a person's abilities on these specific types of tasks? Perhaps that would mean that there isn't any such thing as "intelligence" per se, but rather a whole host of narrower "intelligences." As you will learn in this module, a full picture of intelligence involves considering a variety of different perspectives.

Intelligence as a Single, General Ability

When we say someone is intelligent, we usually are implying they have a high level of generalized cognitive ability. We expect intelligent people to be "intelligent" in many different ways, about many different topics. We wouldn't normally call someone intelligent if she were good at, say, making up limericks, but nothing else. Intelligence should manifest itself in many different domains.

Scientific evidence for intelligence as a general ability dates back to early 20th-century work by Charles Spearman, who began by developing techniques to calculate correlations among multiple measures of mental abilities (Spearman, 1923). One of these techniques, known as **factor analysis**, *is a statistical technique that examines correlations between variables to find clusters of related variables, or "factors."* For example, imagine that scores on tests of vocabulary, reading comprehension, and verbal reasoning

correlate highly together; these would form a "language ability" factor. Similarly, imagine that scores on algebra, geometry, and calculus questions correlate highly together; these would form a "math ability" factor. However, if the language variables don't correlate very well with the math variables, then you have some confidence that these are separate factors; in this case, it would imply that there are at least two types of independent abilities: math and language abilities. For there to be an overarching general ability called "intelligence," one would expect that tests of different types of abilities would all correlate with each other, forming only one factor.

SPEARMAN'S GENERAL INTELLIGENCE Spearman found that schoolchildren's grades in different school subjects were positively correlated, even though the content of the different topics (e.g., math vs. history) was very different. This led Spearman to hypothesize the existence of a **general intelligence factor** (abbreviated as "*g*"). Spearman believed that *g represented a person's "mental energy," reflecting his belief that some people's brains are simply more "powerful" than others* (Sternberg, 2003). This has greatly influenced psychologists up to the present day, cementing within the field the notion that *intelligence* is a basic cognitive trait comprising the ability to learn, reason, and solve problems, regardless of their nature; common intelligence tests in use today calculate *g* as an "overall" measure of intelligence (Johnson et al., 2008).

But is *g* real? Does it predict anything meaningful? In fact, *g* does predict many important phenomena. For example, *g* correlates quite highly with high school and university grades (Neisser et al., 1996), how many years a person will stay in school, and how much they will earn afterwards (Ceci & Williams, 1997).

General intelligence scores also predict many seemingly unrelated phenomena, such as how long people are likely to live (Gottfredson & Deary, 2004), how quickly they can make snap judgments on perceptual discrimination tasks (i.e., laboratory tasks that test how quickly people form perceptions; Deary & Stough, 1996), and how well people can exert self-control (Shamosh et al., 2008). Some other examples of *g*'s influences are depicted in Figure 9.6.

In the workplace, intelligence test scores not only predict who gets hired, but also how well people perform at a wide variety of jobs. In fact, the correlation is so strong that after almost a century of research (Schmidt & Hunter, 1998), general mental ability has emerged as the single best predictor of job performance (correlation = .53; Hunter & Hunter, 1984). Overall intelligence is a far better predictor than the applicant's level of education (correlation = .10) or how well the applicant does in the

Figure 9.6 General Intelligence Is Related to Many Different Life Outcomes

General intelligence (*g*) predicts not just intellectual ability, but also psychological well-being, income, and successful long-term relationships.

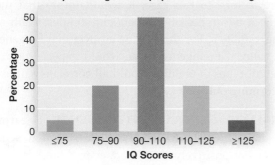

Total percentage of the population in this range:

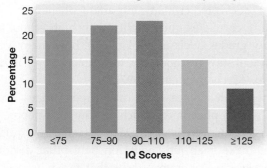

Individuals in this range who divorced within five years:

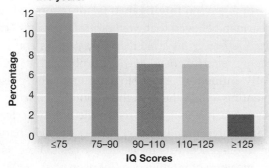

Individuals in this range who live in poverty:

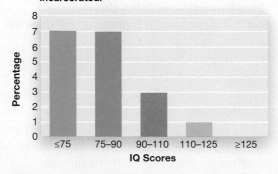

Individuals in this range who have been incarcerated:

Source: Based on "General Intelligence is related to Various Outcomes" Adapted from Herrnstein, R., & Murray, C. (1994). *The bell curve: Intelligence and class structure in American life.* New York: Free Press.; Gottfredson, L. (1997). Why g matters : Complexity of everyday life. Intelligence, 24 , 79–132.

job interview itself (correlation = .14). It is amazing to think that in order to make a good hiring decision, a manager would be better off using a single number given by an IQ test than actually sitting down and interviewing applicants face to face!

The usefulness of *g* is also shown by modern neuroscience research findings that overall intelligence predicts how well our brains work. For example, Tony Vernon at Western University and his colleagues have found that general intelligence test scores predict how efficiently we conduct impulses along nerve fibres and across synapses (Johnson et al., 2005; Reed et al., 2004). This efficiency of nerve conduction allows for more efficient information processing overall. As a result, when working on a task, the brains of highly intelligent people don't have to work as hard as those of less intelligent people; high IQ brains show less overall brain activation than others for the same task (Grabner et al., 2003; Haier et al., 1992).

Thus, overall intelligence, as indicated by *g*, is related to many real-world phenomena, from how well we do at work to how well our brains function.

DOES *g* TELL US THE WHOLE STORY? Clearly, *g* reflects something real. However, we have to remember that correlation does not equal causation. It is possible that the effects of *g* are due to motivation, self-confidence, or other variables. For example, one would expect that being motivated to succeed, as well as being highly self-confident, could lead to better grades, better IQ scores, and better job performance. Therefore, it is important to be cautious when interpreting these results.

We should also ask whether *g* can explain everything about a person's intelligence. For example, how could a single number possibly capture the kinds of genius exhibited by savants like Blind Tom, who are exceptionally talented in some domains but then severely impaired in others? It is easy to find other examples in your own experience; surely, you have known people who were very talented in art or music but terrible in math or science? Or perhaps you have known an incredibly smart person who was socially awkward, or a charismatic and charming person whom you'd never want as your chemistry partner? There may be many ways of being intelligent, and reducing such diversity to a single number seems to overlook the different types of intelligence that people have.

Module 9.2a Quiz:

Intelligence as a Single, General Ability

Know . . .

1. Spearman believed that
   A. people have multiple types of intelligence.
   B. intelligence scores for math and history courses should not be correlated.
   C. statistics cannot help researchers understand how different types of intelligence are related to each other.
   D. some people's brains are more "powerful" than others, thus giving them more "mental energy."

Understand . . .

2. What is factor analysis?
   A. A method of ranking individuals by their intelligence
   B. A statistical procedure that is used to identify which sets of psychological measures are highly correlated with each other

   C. The technique of choice for testing for a single, general intelligence
   D. The technique for testing the difference between two means

3. Researchers who argue that g is a valid way of understanding intelligence would NOT point to research showing
   A. people with high g make perceptual judgments more quickly.
   B. people with high g are more likely to succeed at their jobs.
   C. the brains of people with low g conduct impulses more slowly.
   D. people with low g are better able to do some tasks than people with high g.

Intelligence as Multiple, Specific Abilities

Spearman himself believed that g didn't fully capture intelligence because his own analyses showed that although different items on an intelligence test were correlated with each other, their correlations were never 1.0, and usually far less than that. Thus, g cannot be the whole story; there must, at the very least, be other factors that account for the variability in how well people respond to different questions.

One possible explanation is that in addition to a generalized intelligence, people also possess a number of specific skills. Individual differences on these skills may explain some of the variability on intelligence tests that is not accounted for by g. In a flurry of creativity, Spearman chose the inspired name "s" to represent this specific-level, skill-based intelligence. His two-factor theory of intelligence was therefore comprised of g and s, where g represents one's general, overarching intelligence, and s represents one's skill or ability level for a given task.

Nobody has seriously questioned the s part of Spearman's theory; obviously, each task in life, from opening a coconut, to solving calculus problems, requires abilities that are specific to the task. However, the concept of g has come under heavy fire throughout the intervening decades, leading to several different theories of *multiple* intelligences.

The first influential theory of multiple intelligences was created by Louis Thurstone, who examined scores of general intelligence tests using factor analysis, and found seven different clusters of what he termed *primary mental abilities*. Thurstone's seven factors were word fluency (the person's ability to produce language fluently), verbal comprehension, numeric abilities, spatial visualization, memory, perceptual speed, and reasoning (Thurstone, 1938). He argued that there was no meaningful g, but that intelligence needed to be understood at the level of these primary mental abilities that functioned independently of each other. However, Spearman (1939) fired back, arguing that Thurstone's seven primary mental abilities were in fact correlated with each other, suggesting that there was after all an overarching general intelligence.

A highly technical and statistical debate raged for several more decades between proponents of g and proponents of multiple intelligences, until it was eventually decided that both of them were right.

THE HIERARCHICAL MODEL OF INTELLIGENCE The controversy was largely settled by the widespread adoption of hierarchical models that describe how some types of intelligence are "nested" within others in a similar manner to how, for example, a person is nested within her community, which may be nested within a city. The general hierarchical model describes how our lowest-level abilities (those relevant to a particular task, like Spearman's s) are nested within a middle level that roughly corresponds to Thurstone's primary mental abilities (although not necessarily the specific ones that Thurstone hypothesized), and these are nested within a general intelligence (Spearman's g; Gustaffson, 1988). By the mid-1990s, analyses of prior research on intelligence concluded that almost all intelligence studies were best explained by a three-level hierarchy (Carroll, 1993).

What this means is that we have an overarching general intelligence, which is made up of a small number of sub-abilities, each of which is made up of a large number of specific abilities that apply to individual tasks.

However, even this didn't completely settle the debate about what intelligence really is, because it left open a great deal of room for different theories of the best way to describe the middle-level factors. And as you will see in the next section, even the debate about *g* has been updated in recent years.

Testing for Fluid and Crystallized Intelligence

The concept of *g* implies that performance on all aspects of an intelligence test is influenced by this central ability. But careful analyses of many data sets, and recent neurobiological evidence, have shown that there may be two types of *g* that have come to be called fluid intelligence (Gf) and crystallized intelligence (Gc).

What do we know about fluid and crystallized intelligence?

The distinction between fluid and crystallized intelligence is basically the difference between "figuring things out" and "knowing what to do from past experience." **Fluid intelligence (Gf)** is *a type of intelligence used in learning new information and solving new problems not based on knowledge the person already possesses.* Tests of Gf involve problems such as pattern recognition and solving geometric puzzles, neither of which is heavily dependent on past experience. For example, Raven's Progressive Matrices, in which a person is asked to complete a series of geometric patterns of increasing complexity (see Module 9.1), is the most widely used measure of Gf. In contrast, **crystallized intelligence (Gc)** is *a type of intelligence that draws upon past learning and experience.* Tests of Gc, such as tests of vocabulary and general knowledge, depend heavily on individuals' prior knowledge to come up with the correct answers (Figure 9.7; Cattell, 1971).

Gf and Gc are thought to be largely separate from each other, with two important exceptions. One is that having greater fluid intelligence means that the person is better able to process information and to learn; therefore, greater Gf may, over time, lead to greater Gc, as the person who processes more information will gain more crystallized knowledge (Horn & Cattell, 1967). Note, however, that this compelling hypothesis has received little empirical support thus far (Nisbett et al., 2012). The second is

---

Figure 9.7 Fluid and Crystallized Intelligence

Fluid intelligence is dynamic and changing, and may eventually become crystallized into a more permanent form.

Figure 9.8 Measuring Fluid Intelligence

The Tower of London problem has several versions, each of which requires the test taker to plan and keep track of rules. For example, the task might involve moving the coloured beads from the initial position so that they match any of the various end goal positions.

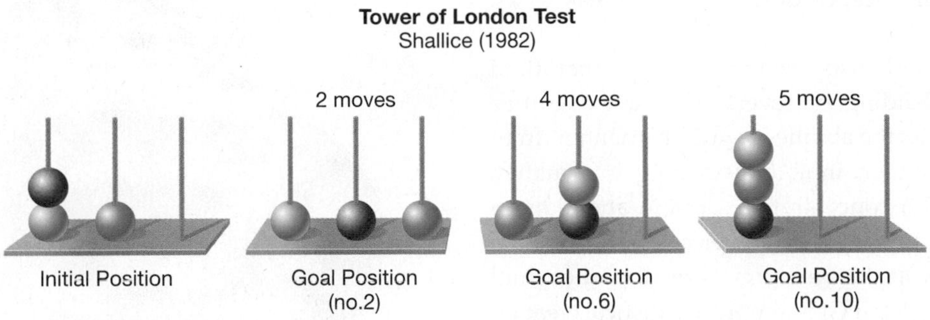

Tower of London Test
Shallice (1982)

| | 2 moves | 4 moves | 5 moves |

Initial Position | Goal Position (no.2) | Goal Position (no.6) | Goal Position (no.10)

Source: Shallice, T. (1982). Specific impairments of planning. *Philosophical Transcripts of the Royal Society of London, B 298*, 199–209. "Measuring Fluid Intelligence." Copyright © 1982 by The Royal Society. Reprinted by permission of The Royal Society.

that it is difficult, perhaps impossible, to measure Gf without tapping into people's pre-existing knowledge and experience, as we discuss below.

How can science help distinguish between fluid and crystallized intelligence?

One interesting line of research that supports the Gf/Gc distinction comes from examining how each type changes over the lifespan (Cattell, 1971; Horn & Cattell, 1967). In one study, people aged 20 to 89 years were given a wide array of tasks, including the Block Design task (see Figure 9.3), the Tower of London puzzle (see Figure 9.8), and tests of reaction time. Researchers have found that performance in Gf-tasks declines after a certain age, which some research estimates as middle adulthood (Bugg et al., 2006), whereas other studies place the beginning of the decline as early as the end of adolescence (Avolio & Waldman, 1994; Baltes & Lindenberger, 1997). Measures of Gc (see Figure 9.9), by comparison, show greater stability as a person ages (Schaie, 1994). Healthy, older adults generally do not show much decline, if any, in their crystallized knowledge, at least until they reach their elderly years (Miller et al., 2009).

Neurobiological evidence further backs this up. The functioning of brain regions associated with Gf tasks declines sooner than the functioning of those regions supporting Gc tasks (Geake & Hansen, 2010). For example, the decline of Gf with age is associated with reduced efficiency in the prefrontal cortex (Braver & Barch, 2002), a key brain region involved in the cognitive abilities that underlie fluid intelligence (as discussed below). In contrast, this brain region does not play a central role

in crystallized intelligence, which is more dependent on long-term memory systems that involve a number of different regions of the cortex.

Figure 9.9 Measuring Crystallized Intelligence

Crystallized intelligence refers to facts, such as names of countries.

- Which South American countries are these?

PACIFIC OCEAN

ATLANTIC OCEAN

- Do *irony* and *coincidence* mean the same thing?
- What does *abstruse* mean?

Can we critically evaluate crystallized and fluid intelligence?

There are certainly questions we can ask about crystallized and fluid intelligence. For one, is there really any such thing as fluid intelligence, or does it merely break down into specific sub-abilities?

Cognitive psychologists generally accept that fluid intelligence is a blending of several different cognitive abilities. For example, the abilities to switch attention from one stimulus to another, inhibit distracting information from interfering with concentration, sustain attention on something at will, and keep multiple pieces of information in working memory at the same time, are all part of fluid intelligence (Blair, 2006). If Gf is simply a statistical creation that reflects the integration of these different processes, perhaps researchers would be better off focusing their attention on these systems, rather than the more abstract construct Gf.

Another critique is that fluid and crystallized intelligence are not, after all, entirely separable. Consider the fact that crystallized intelligence involves not only possessing knowledge, but also being able to access that knowledge when it's needed. Fluid cognitive processes, and the brain areas that support them such as the prefrontal cortex, play important roles in both storing and retrieving crystallized knowledge from long-term memory (Ranganath et al., 2003).

Similarly, tests of fluid intelligence likely also draw upon crystallized knowledge. For example, complete-the-pattern tasks such as Raven's Progressive Matrices may predominantly reflect fluid intelligence, but people who have never seen any type of similar task or had any practice with such an exercise will likely struggle with them more than someone with prior exposure to similar tasks. Imagine learning a new card game—you would have to rely on your fluid intelligence to help you learn the rules, figure out effective strategies, and outsmart your opponents. However, your overall knowledge of cards, games, and strategies will help you, especially if you compare yourself to a person who has played no such games in his life.

Why is this relevant?

Recognizing the distinctiveness of Gf and Gc can help to reduce stereotypes and expectations about intelligence in older persons, reminding people that although certain kinds of intelligence may decline with age, other types that rely on accumulated knowledge and wisdom may even increase as we get older (Kaufman, 2001). Also, research on fluid intelligence has helped psychologists to develop a much more detailed understanding of the full complement of cognitive processes that make up intelligence, and to devise tests that measure these processes more precisely.

Figure 9.10 The Triarchic Theory of Intelligence

According to psychologist Robert Sternberg, intelligence comprises three overlapping yet distinct components.

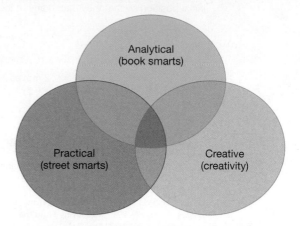

Source: Lilienfeld, Scott O.; Lynn, Steven J; Namy, Laura L.; Woolf, Nancy J., *Psychology: From Inquiry To Understanding*, Books A La Carte Edition, 2nd Ed., ©2011. Reprinted and Electronically reproduced by permission of Pearson Education, Inc., New York, NY.

STERNBERG'S TRIARCHIC THEORY OF INTELLIGENCE
Other influential models of intelligence have been proposed in attempts to move beyond *g*. For example, Robert Sternberg (1983, 1988) developed the **triarchic theory of intelligence**, *a theory that divides intelligence into three distinct types: analytical, practical, and creative* (see Figure 9.10). These components can be described in the following ways:

- *Analytical intelligence* is "book smarts." It's the ability to reason logically through a problem and to find solutions. It also reflects the kinds of abilities that are largely tested on standard intelligence tests that measure *g*. Most intelligence tests predominantly measure analytical intelligence, while generally ignoring the other types.

- *Practical intelligence* is "street smarts." It's the ability to find solutions to real-world problems that are encountered in daily life, especially those that involve other people. Practical intelligence is what helps people adjust to new environments, learn how to get things done, and accomplish their goals. Practical intelligence is believed to have a great deal to do with one's job performance and success.

- *Creative intelligence* is the ability to generate new ideas and novel solutions to problems. Obviously, artists must have some level of creative intelligence, because they are, by definition, trying to create things that are new. It also takes creative intelligence to be a scientist because creative thinking is often required to conceive of good scientific hypotheses and develop ways of testing them (Sternberg et al., 2001).

Myths in Mind

Learning Styles

One of the biggest arenas in which people have applied the idea that there are multiple types of intelligence is the widespread belief in educational settings that different people process information better through specific modalities, such as sight, hearing, and bodily movement. If this is true, then it suggests that people have different learning styles (e.g., people may be visual learners, auditory learners, tactile learners, etc.), and therefore, educators would be more effective if they tailor their lesson plans to the learning styles of their students, or at least ensure that they appeal to a variety of learning styles.

However, finding evidence to support this has proven difficult. In fact, dozens of studies have failed to show any benefit for tailoring information to an individual's apparent learning style (Pasher et al., 2008). This result probably reflects the fact that regardless of how you encounter information—through reading, watching, listening, or moving around—retaining it over the long term largely depends on how deeply you process and store the *meaning* of the information (Willingham, 2004), which in turn is related to how motivated students are to learn. As a result, rather than trying to match the way that information is presented to the presumed learning styles of students, it is likely far more important for teachers to be able to engage students in ways they find interesting, meaningful, fun, personally relevant, and experientially engaging.

Sternberg believed that both practical and creative intelligences are better than analytical intelligence at predicting real-world outcomes, such as job success (Sternberg et al., 1995). However, some psychologists have criticized Sternberg's studies of job performance, arguing that the test items that were supposed to measure practical intelligence were merely measuring job-related knowledge (Schmidt & Hunter, 1993). Other psychologists have questioned whether creative intelligence, one of the key components of Sternberg's theory, actually involves "intelligence" per se, or is instead measuring the tendency to think in ways that challenge norms and conventions (Gottfredson, 2003; Jensen, 1993). These critiques show us how challenging it can be to define intelligence, and to predict how intelligence—or intelligences—will influence real-world behaviours.

GARDNER'S THEORY OF MULTIPLE INTELLIGENCES

Howard Gardner proposed an especially elaborate theory of multiple intelligences. Gardner was inspired by specific cases, such as people who were savants (discussed in the introduction to this module), who had extraordinary abilities in limited domains, very poor abilities in many others, and low *g*. Gardner also was influenced by cases of people with brain damage, which indicated that some specific abilities could be dramatically affected while others remained intact (Gardner, 1983, 1999). He also noted that "normal people" (presumably, those of us who are not savants and also don't have brain damage) differ widely in their abilities and talents, having a knack for some things but hopeless at others, which doesn't fit the notion that intelligence is a single, overarching ability.

Based on his observations, Gardner proposed a theory of **multiple intelligences**, *a model claiming that there are seven (now updated to at least nine) different forms of intelligence, each independent from the others* (see Table 9.1). As intuitively appealing as this is, critics have pointed out that few of Gardner's intelligences can be accurately and reliably measured, making his theory unfalsifiable and difficult to research. For example, how would you

Table 9.1 Gardner's Proposed Forms of Intelligence

Verbal/linguistic intelligence	The ability to read, write, and speak effectively
Logical/mathematical intelligence	The ability to think with numbers and use abstract thought; the ability to use logic or mathematical operations to solve problems
Visuospatial intelligence	The ability to create mental pictures, manipulate them in the imagination, and use them to solve problems
Bodily/kinesthetic intelligence	The ability to control body movements, to balance, and to sense how one's body is situated
Musical/rhythmical intelligence	The ability to produce and comprehend tonal and rhythmic patterns
Interpersonal intelligence	The ability to detect another person's emotional states, motives, and thoughts
Self/intrapersonal intelligence	Self-awareness; the ability to accurately judge one's own abilities, and identify one's own emotions and motives
Naturalist intelligence	The ability to recognize and identify processes in the natural world—plants, animals, and so on
Existential intelligence	The tendency and ability to ask questions about purpose in life and the meaning of human existence

Source: Based on The Nine Types of Intelligence By Howard Gardner

PSYCH @

The NFL Draft

One rather interesting application of IQ has been to try to predict who will succeed in their careers. One test in particular, the Wonderlic Personnel Test, is widely used to predict career success in many different types of jobs (Schmidt & Hunter, 1998; Schmidt et al., 1981). It has even become famous to National Football League (NFL) fans, because Wonderlic scores are one of many factors that influence which college players are drafted by NFL teams. This is no small thing—high draft picks receive multimillion dollar contracts. The logic behind using Wonderlic scores is that football is a highly complex game, involving learning and memorizing many complicated strategies, following all the rules, and being able to update strategies "on the fly." Football is not only about being agile, fast, and strong; it might also involve intelligence.

But does the Wonderlic, a 50-item, 12-minute IQ test, actually predict NFL success, as the NFL has believed since the 1970s? According to research, the answer is "only sometimes," but not the way you might think.

After studying 762 players from the 2002, 2003, and 2004 drafts and measuring their performance in multiple ways, researchers concluded that there was no significant correlation between Wonderlic scores and performance. What's more, the performance of only two football positions, tight end and defensive back, showed any significant correlation with Wonderlic scores, and it was in a negative direction (Lyons et al., 2009)! This means that *lower* intelligence scores predicted greater football success for these positions.

It seems that NFL teams would be well advised to throw out the Wonderlic test entirely, or perhaps only use it to screen for defensive backs and tight ends, and choose the lower-scoring players. No offence is intended whatsoever to football players, who may be extremely intelligent individuals, but in general, being highly intelligent does not seem to be an advantage in professional football. In the now immortalized words of former Washington Redskins quarterback Joe Thiesmann, "Nobody in the game of football should be called a genius. A genius is somebody like Norman Einstein."

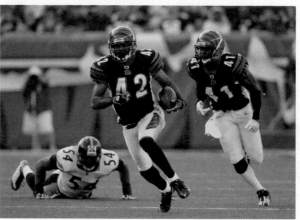

Ed Reinke/AP Images

The Wonderlic Personnel Test is supposed to predict success in professional football, although it is not always very successful. This failure could be because of low validity.

reliably measure "existential intelligence" or "bodily/kinesthetic intelligence"? You cannot simply ask people how existential they are, or how well they are able to attune to their bodies, relative to other people. Creating operational definitions of these concepts has proven to be a difficult challenge, and has held back empirical work on Gardner's theory. This is not a critique against Gardner specifically, but rather, highlights the need for researchers to develop better ways of measuring intelligence (Tirri & Nokelainen, 2008).

Gardner's theory has set off a firestorm of controversy in the more than 30 years since its initial proposal, gaining little traction in the academic literature, but being widely embraced in applied fields, such as education. While critics point to the lack of reliable ways of measuring Gardner's different intelligences, proponents argue that there is more to a good theory than whether you can measure its constructs. From the applied perspective, Gardner's theory is *useful*. It helps teachers to create more diverse and engaging lesson plans to connect with and motivate students with different strengths. It helps

people to see themselves as capable in different ways, rather than feeling limited by their IQ score, especially if it is not very high. And, it helps explain the wide range of human abilities and accomplishments far better than a mere IQ score.

From this perspective, perhaps the "psychometric supremacists" (Kornhaber, 2004), who insist that variables must be reliably quantifiable, might be missing the point. After all, even though IQ scores, for example, predict real-world outcomes like job status and income and offer a reliable means for identifying students who qualify for extra educational attention (such as "gifted" students or students with learning issues), they help very little in understanding people's strengths or weaknesses, and offer little to no guidance in actually helping people to improve their performance in different areas. Besides, IQ tests are almost exclusively based on highly unrealistic and limited testing situations, such as answering questions on paper-and-pencil tests while sitting in a room, whereas Gardner's theory was formed out of real-world observations of the abilities of people with a wide range of accomplishments.

Given that it is essentially impossible to objectively quantify many different types of abilities (e.g., being a good dancer, farmer, actor, comedian), it follows that you cannot judge a theory that purports to explain such abilities on the same grounds as theories about more easily quantifiable constructs.

The debate over Gardner's theory lays bare a fundamental tension in the psychological sciences, which is that sometimes at least, the nuances of human behaviour cannot be easily measured, or perhaps even be measured at all. Should the observations and wisdom of teachers with decades of experience be discounted because scientists cannot develop quantifiable measures of certain constructs? However, if you accept the argument that "human experience" can trump psychometrically rigorous evidence, then where do you draw the line? Does this not throw into question the whole scientific basis of psychology itself?

We can't resolve these questions for you here, but they remain excellent questions. The debate rages on.

Module 9.2b Quiz:

Intelligence as Multiple, Specific Abilities

Know . . .

1. Which of the following is *not* part of the triarchic theory of intelligence?
   A. Practical intelligence
   B. Analytical intelligence
   C. Kinesthetic intelligence
   D. Creative intelligence

2. _____ proposed that there are multiple forms of intelligence, each independent from the others.
   A. Robert Sternberg
   B. Howard Gardner
   C. L. L. Thurstone
   D. Raymond Cattell

3. The ability to adapt to new situations and solve new problems reflects _____ intelligence(s), whereas the ability to draw on one's experiences and knowledge reflects _____ intelligence(s).
   A. fluid; crystallized
   B. crystallized; fluid

   C. general; multiple
   D. multiple; general

Analyze . . .

4. The hierarchical model of intelligence claims that
   A. some types of intelligence are more powerful and desirable than others.
   B. intelligence is broken down into two factors, a higher-level factor called g, and a lower-level factor called s.
   C. scores on intelligence tests are affected by different levels of factors, ranging from lower-level factors such as physical health, to higher-level factors such as a person's motivation for doing well on a test.
   D. intelligence is comprised of three levels of factors, which are roughly similar to Spearman's g, Thurstone's primary mental abilities, and Spearman's s.

The Battle of the Sexes

The distinction between g and multiple intelligences plays an important role in the oft-asked question, "Who is smarter, females or males?" Although earlier studies showed some average intelligence differences between males and females, this has not been upheld by subsequent research and is likely the result of bias in the tests that favoured males over females. One of the most conclusive studies used 42 different tests of mental abilities to compare males and females and found almost no differences in intelligence between the sexes (Johnson & Bouchard, 2007).

Some research has found that although males and females have the same average IQ score, there is much greater variability in male scores, which suggests that there are more men with substantial intellectual challenges, as well as more men who are at the top of the brainpower heap (Deary et al., 2007; Dykiert et al., 2009). However, this may not be as simple as it appears. For example, one type of test that shows this male advantage at the upper levels of ability examines math skills on standardized tests. A few decades ago, about 12 times more males than females scored at the very top (Benbow & Stanley, 1983). This difference has decreased in recent years to 3–4 times as many males scoring at the top end of the spectrum. Not surprisingly, this change has occurred just as the number of math courses being taken by females—and the efforts made to increase female enrollment in such courses—has increased. So, the difference in results between the sexes is still there, but has been vastly reduced by making math education more accessible for females (Wai et al., 2010).

The apparent advantage enjoyed by males may also be the result of an unintentional selection bias. More males than females drop out of secondary school; because these males would have lower IQs, on average, the result is that

Figure 9.11 Mental Rotation and Verbal Fluency Tasks

Some research indicates that, on average, males outperform females on mental rotation tasks (a), while females outperform men on verbal fluency (b).

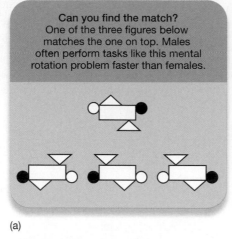

Can you find the match? One of the three figures below matches the one on top. Males often perform tasks like this mental rotation problem faster than females.

(a)

Conversely, women tend to outperform men on verbal fluency tasks like this one.

In 60 seconds, name as many words that start with the letter "G" that you can think of.

OR

In 60 seconds, name as many different kinds of animals you can think of.

(b)

fewer low-IQ men attend university. Therefore, most of the samples of students used in psychology studies are skewed in that they under-represent men with low IQs. This biased sampling of males and females would make it seem like men have higher fluid intelligence, when in reality they may not (Flynn & Rossi-Casé, 2011).

So, who *is* smarter, males or females? Neither. The best data seems to show that they are basically equal in overall intelligence.

DO MALES AND FEMALES HAVE UNIQUE COGNITIVE SKILLS? Although the results discussed above suggest that males and females are equally intelligent, when multiple intelligences are considered, rather than overall IQ, a clear difference between the sexes does emerge. Females are, on average, better at verbal abilities, some memory tasks, and the ability to read people's basic emotions, whereas males have the advantage on visuospatial abilities, such as mentally rotating objects or aiming at objects (see Figure 9.11; Halpern & LaMay, 2000; Johnson & Bouchard, 2007; Tottenham et al., 2005; Weiss et al., 2003).

This finding is frequently offered as an explanation for why males are more represented in fields like engineering, science, and mathematics. However, there are many other factors that could explain the under-representation of women in these disciplines, such as prevalent stereotypes that discourage girls from entering the maths and sciences, parents from supporting them in doing so, and teachers from evaluating females' work without bias.

Overlooking the many other factors that limit females' participation in the maths and sciences is a dangerous thing to do. This was dramatically shown in 2005 when the President of Harvard University, Lawrence Summers, was removed from his position shortly after making a speech in which he argued that innate differences between the sexes may be responsible for under-representation of women in science and engineering. The outrage many expressed at his comments reflected the fact that many people realize that highlighting innate differences while minimizing or ignoring systemic factors only serves to perpetuate problems, not solve them.

Module 9.2c Quiz:

The Battle of the Sexes

Know . . .

1. Men tend to outperform women on tasks requiring _____, whereas women outperform men on tasks requiring _____.
   A. spatial abilities; the ability to read people's emotions
   B. practical intelligence; interpersonal intelligence
   C. memory; creativity
   D. logic; intuition

Analyze . . .

2. Research on gender differences in intelligence leads to the general conclusion that
   A. males are more intelligent than females.
   B. females are more intelligent than males.
   C. males and females are equal in overall intelligence.
   D. it has been impossible, thus far, to tell which gender is more intelligent.

Module 9.2 Summary

9.2a   Know . . . the key terminology related to understanding intelligence.

crystallized intelligence (Gc)
factor analysis
fluid intelligence (Gf)
general intelligence factor (*g*)
multiple intelligences
savant
triarchic theory of intelligence

9.2b   Understand . . . why intelligence is divided into fluid and crystallized types.

Mental abilities encompass both the amount of knowledge accumulated and the ability to solve new problems. This understanding is consistent not only with our common views of intelligence, but also with the results of decades of intelligence testing. Also, the observation that fluid intelligence can decline over the lifespan, even as crystallized intelligence remains constant, lends further support to the contention that they are different abilities.

9.2c   Understand . . . intelligence differences between males and females.

Males and females generally show equal levels of overall intelligence, as measured by standard intelligence tests. However, men do outperform women on some tasks, particularly spatial tasks such as mentally rotating objects, whereas women outperform men on other tasks, such as perceiving emotions. Although there are some male–female differences in specific abilities, such as math, it is not yet clear whether these reflect innate differences between the sexes, or whether other factors are responsible, such as reduced enrollment of women in math classes and the presence of stereotype threat in testing sessions.

9.2d   Apply . . . your knowledge to identify examples from the triarchic theory of intelligence.

This theory proposes the existence of analytical, practical, and creative forms of intelligence.

Apply Activity

Classify whether the individual in the following scenario is low, medium, or high in regard to each of the three aspects of intelligence.

Katrina is an excellent chemist. She has always performed well in school, so it is no surprise that she earned her PhD from a prestigious institution. Despite her many contributions and discoveries related to chemistry, however, she seems to fall short in some domains. For example, Katrina does not know how to cook her own meals and if anything breaks at her house, she has to rely on someone else to fix it.

9.2e   Analyze . . . whether teachers should spend time tailoring lessons to each individual student's learning style.

Certainly, no one would want to discourage teachers from being attentive to the unique characteristics that each student brings to the classroom. However, large-scale reviews of research suggest that there is little basis for individualized teaching based on learning styles (e.g., auditory, visual, kinesthetic).

Module 9.3 Biological, Environmental, and Behavioural Influences on Intelligence

Miguel Medina/AFP/Newscom

Learning Objectives

9.3a Know . . . the key terminology related to heredity, environment, and intelligence.

9.3b Understand . . . different approaches to studying the genetic basis of intelligence.

9.3c Apply . . . your knowledge of environmental and behavioural effects on intelligence

to understand how to enhance your own cognitive abilities.

9.3d Analyze . . . the belief that older children are more intelligent than their younger siblings.

In 1955, the world lost one of the most brilliant scientists in history, Albert Einstein. Although you are probably familiar with his greatest scientific achievements, you may not know about what happened to him after he died—or more specifically, what happened to his brain.

Upon his death, a forward-thinking pathologist, Dr. Thomas Harvey, removed Einstein's brain (his body was later cremated) so that it could be studied in the hope that medical scientists would eventually unlock the secret to his genius. Dr. Harvey took photographs of Einstein's brain, and then it was sliced up into hundreds of tissue samples placed on microscope slides, and 240 larger blocks of brain matter, which were preserved in fluid. Surprisingly, Dr. Harvey concluded that the brain wasn't at all remarkable, except for being smaller than average (1230 grams, compared to the average of 1300–1400 grams).

You might expect that Einstein's brain was intensively studied by leading neurologists. But, instead, the brain mysteriously disappeared. Twenty-two years later, a journalist named Steven Levy tried to find Einstein's brain. The search was fruitless until Levy tracked down Dr. Harvey in Wichita, Kansas, and interviewed him in his office. Dr. Harvey was initially reluctant to tell Levy anything about the brain, but eventually admitted that he still had it. In fact, he kept it right there in his office! Sheepishly, Dr. Harvey opened a box labelled "Costa Cider" and there, inside two large jars, floated the chunks of Einstein's brain. Levy later wrote, "My eyes were fixed upon that jar as I tried to comprehend that these pieces of gunk bobbing up and down had caused a revolution in physics and quite possibly changed the course of civilization. Swirling in formaldehyde was the power of the smashed atom, the mystery of the universe's black holes, the utter miracle of human achievement."

Since that time, several research teams have discovered important abnormalities in Einstein's brain. Einstein had a higher than normal ratio of glial cells to neurons in the left parietal lobe (Diamond et al., 1985) and parts of the temporal lobes (Kigar et al., 1997), and a higher density of neurons in the right frontal lobe (Anderson & Harvey, 1996). Einstein's parietal lobe has been shown to be about 15% larger than average, and to contain an extra fold (Witelson et al., 1999). The frontal lobes contain extra convolutions (folds and creases) as well. These extra folds increase the surface area and neural connectivity in those areas.

How might these unique features have affected Einstein's intelligence? The frontal lobes are heavily involved in abstract thought, and the parietal lobes are involved in spatial processing, which plays a substantial role in mathematics. Thus, these unique brain features may provide a key part of the neuroanatomical explanation for Einstein's remarkable abilities in math and physics. Einstein not only had a unique mind, but a unique brain.

Focus Questions

1. Which biological and environmental factors have been found to be important contributors to intelligence?

2. Is it possible for people to enhance their own intelligence?

» Wouldn't it be wonderful to be as smart as Einstein? Or even just smarter than you already are? Imagine if you could boost your IQ, upgrading your brain like you might upgrade a hard drive. You could learn more easily, think faster, and remember more. What benefits might you enjoy? Greater success? A cure for cancer? A Nobel Prize? At least you might not have to study as much to get good grades. As you will read in this module, there are in fact ways to improve your intelligence (although perhaps not to "Einsteinian" levels). However, to understand how these techniques can benefit us, we must also understand how our biology and our environment—"nature" and "nurture"—interact to influence intelligence.

Biological Influences on Intelligence

The story of Einstein's brain shows us, once again, that our behaviours and abilities are linked to our biology. However, although scientists have been interested in these topics for over 100 years, we are only beginning to understand the complex processes that influence measures like IQ scores. In this section, we discuss the genetic and neural factors that influence intelligence, and how they may interact with our environment.

THE GENETICS OF INTELLIGENCE: TWIN AND ADOPTION STUDIES The belief that intelligence is a capacity that we are born with has been widely held since the early studies of intelligence. However, early researchers lacked today's sophisticated methods for studying genetic influences, so they had to rely upon their observations of whether intelligence ran in families, which it seemed to do (see Module 9.1). Since those early days, many studies have been conducted to see just how large the genetic influence on intelligence may be.

Studies of twins and children who have been adopted have been key tools allowing researchers to begin estimating the genetic contribution to intelligence. Decades of such research have shown that genetic similarity does contribute to intelligence test scores. Several important findings from this line of study are summarized in Figure 9.12 (Plomin & Spinath, 2004). The most obvious trend in the figure shows that as the degree of genetic relatedness increases, similarity in IQ scores also increases. The last two bars on the right of Figure 9.12 present perhaps the strongest evidence for a genetic basis for intelligence. The intelligence scores of identical twins correlate with each other at about .85 when they are raised in the same home, which is much higher than the correlation for fraternal twins. Even when identical twins are adopted and raised apart, their intelligence scores are still correlated at approximately .80—a very strong relationship. In fact, this is about the same correlation that researchers find when individuals take the same intelligence test twice and are compared with themselves!

THE HERITABILITY OF INTELLIGENCE Overall, the heritability of intelligence is estimated to be between 40% and 80% (Nisbett et al., 2012). However, interpreting what this means is extremely tricky. People often think that this means 40% or more of a person's intelligence is determined by genes. But this is a serious misunderstanding of heritability.

A heritability estimate describes how much of the differences *between people in a sample* can be accounted for by differences in their genes (see Module 3.1). This may not sound like a crucial distinction, but in fact it's extremely important! It means that a heritability estimate is not a single, fixed number; instead, it is a number that *depends on the sample of people being studied*. Heritability estimates for different samples can be very different. For example, the heritability of intelligence for wealthy people has been estimated to be about 72%, but for people living in poverty, it's only 10% (Turkheimer et al., 2003). Why might this be?

The key to solving this puzzle is to recognize that heritability estimates depend on other factors, such as how different or similar people's environments are. If people in a sample inhabit highly similar environments, the heritability estimate will be higher, whereas if they inhabit highly diverse environments, the heritability estimate will be lower. Because most wealthy people have access to good nutrition, good schools, plenty of enrichment

Figure 9.12 Intelligence and Genetic Relatedness

Several types of comparisons reveal genetic contributions to intelligence (Plomin & Spinath, 2004). Generally, the closer the biological relationship between people, the more similar their intelligence scores.

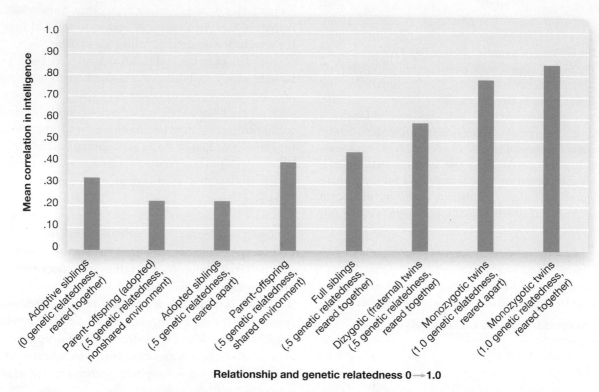

Source: Adapted from Plomin, R., & Spinath, F. M. (2004). Intelligence: Genetics, genes, and genomics. *Journal of Personality & Social Psychology*, 86 (1), 112–129.

opportunities, and strong parental support for education, these factors contribute fairly equally to the intelligence of wealthy people; thus, differences in their intelligence scores are largely explained by genetic differences. But the environments inhabited by people living in poverty differ widely. Some may receive good schooling and others very little. Some may receive proper nutrition (e.g., poor farming families that grow their own food), whereas others may be chronically malnourished (e.g., children in poor inner-city neighbourhoods). For poorer families, these differences in the environment would impact intelligence (as we discuss later in this module), leading to lower heritability estimates.

There are many other problems with interpreting heritability estimates as indications that genes *cause* differences in intelligence. Two of the most important both have to do with an under-appreciation for how genes interact with the environment. First, as discussed in Module 3.1, genes do not operate in isolation from the environment. We know now that the "nature vs. nurture" debate has evolved into a discussion of how "nurture shapes nature." Environmental factors determine how genes express themselves and influence the organism.

Second, genes that influence intelligence may do so indirectly, operating through other factors. For example, imagine genes that promote novelty-seeking. People with these genes would be more likely to expose themselves to new ideas and new ways of doing things. This tendency to explore, rooted in their genes, may lead them to become more intelligent. However, in more dangerous environments, these novelty-seeking genes could expose the person to more danger. Therefore, genes that encourage exploratory behaviour might be related to higher intelligence in relatively safe environments, but in dangerous environments might be related to getting eaten by cavebears more often.

BEHAVIOURAL GENOMICS Twin and adoption studies show that some of the individual differences observed in intelligence scores can be attributed to genetic factors. But these studies do not tell us which genes account for the differences. To answer that question, researchers use *behavioural genomics*, a technique that examines how specific genes interact with the environment to influence behaviours, including those related to intelligence. Thus far, the main focus of the behavioural genomics approach to intelligence is to identify genes that are related to cognitive abilities, such as learning and problem solving (Deary et al., 2010).

Overall, studies scanning the whole human genome show that intelligence levels can be predicted, to some degree, by the collection of genes that individuals inherit (Craig & Plomin, 2006; Plomin & Spinath, 2004). These collections of genes seem to pool together to influence general cognitive ability; although each contributes a small amount, the contributions combine to have a larger effect. However, although almost 300 individual genes have been found to have a large impact on various forms of mental retardation (Inlow & Restifo, 2004), very few genes have been found to explain normal variation in intelligence (Butcher et al., 2008). In one large study that scanned the entire genome of 7000 people, researchers found a mere six genetic markers that predicted cognitive ability. Taken together, these six markers only explained 1% of the variability in cognitive ability (Butcher et al., 2008). Thus, there is still a long way to go before we can say that we understand the genetic contributors to intelligence.

One way of speeding the research up has been to develop ways of experimenting with genes directly, in order to see what they do. **Gene knockout (KO) studies** *involve removing a specific gene and comparing the characteristics of animals with and without that gene.* In one of the first knockout studies of intelligence, researchers discovered that removing one particular gene disrupted the ability of mice to learn spatial layouts (Silva et al., 1992). Since this investigation was completed, numerous studies using gene knockout methods have shown that specific genes are related to performance on tasks that have been adapted to study learning and cognitive abilities in animals (Robinson et al., 2011).

Scientists can also take the opposite approach; instead of knocking genes out, they can insert genetic material into mouse chromosomes to study the changes associated with the new gene. The animal that receives this so-called gene transplant is referred to as a *transgenic* animal. Although this approach may sound like science fiction, it has already yielded important discoveries, such as transgenic mice that are better than average learners (Cao et al., 2007; Tang et al., 1999).

One now-famous example is the creation of "Doogie mice," named after the 1990s TV character Doogie Howser (played by a young Neil Patrick Harris), a genius who became a medical doctor while still a teenager. Doogie mice were created by manipulating a single gene, NR2B (Tang et al., 1999). This gene encodes the NMDA receptor, which plays a crucial role in learning and memory. Having more NMDA receptors should, therefore, allow organisms to retain more information (and possibly to access it more quickly). Consistent with this view, Doogie mice with altered NR2B genes learned significantly faster and had better memories than did other mice. For example, when

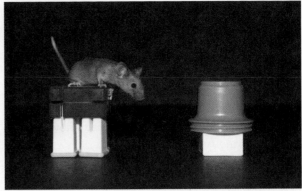

The Princeton University lab mouse, Doogie, is able to learn faster than other mice thanks to a bit of genetic engineering. Researchers inserted a gene known as NR2B that helps create new synapses and leads to quicker learning.

the Doogie mice and normal mice were put into a tank of water in which they had to find a hidden platform in order to escape, the Doogie mice took half as many trials to remember how to get out of the tank.

The different types of studies reviewed in this section show us that genes do have some effect on intelligence. What they don't really show us is *how* these effects occur. What causes individual differences in intelligence? One theory suggests that these differences could be due to varying brain size.

Working the Scientific Literacy Model

Brain Size and Intelligence

Are bigger brains more intelligent? We often assume that to be the case—think of the cartoon characters that are super-geniuses; they almost always have gigantic heads. Or think about what it means to call someone a "pea brain." Psychologists have not been immune to this belief, and many studies have searched for a correlation between brain size and intelligence.

What do we know about brain size and intelligence?

Brain-based approaches to measuring intelligence rest on a common-sense assumption: Thinking occurs in the brain, so a larger brain should be related to greater intelligence. But does scientific evidence support this assumption? In the days before modern brain imaging was possible, researchers typically obtained skulls from deceased subjects, filled them with fine-grained matter such as metal pellets, and then transferred the pellets to a flask to measure the volume. These efforts taught us very little about intelligence and brain or skull size, but a lot about problems with measurement and racial prejudice. In some cases, the studies were highly flawed and inevitably led to conclusions that Caucasian males (including the Caucasian male scientists who conducted these experiments) had the largest brains and, therefore, were the smartest of the human race (Gould, 1981). Modern approaches to studying the brain and intelligence are far more sophisticated, thanks to newer techniques and a more enlightened knowledge of the brain's form and functions.

How can science explain the relationship between brain size and intelligence?

In relatively rare cases, researchers have had the two most important pieces of data needed: brains, and people attached to those brains who had taken intelligence tests when they were alive. In one ambitious study at McMaster University, Sandra Witelson and her colleagues (2006) collected 100 brains of deceased individuals who had previously completed the Wechsler Adult Intelligence Scale (WAIS). Detailed anatomical examinations and size measurements were made on the entire brains and certain regions that support cognitive skills. For women and right-handed men (but not left-handed men), 36% of the variation in verbal intelligence scores was accounted for by the size of the brain; however, brain size did not significantly account for the other component of intelligence that was measured, visuospatial abilities. Thus, it appears that brain size does predict intelligence, but certainly doesn't tell the whole story.

In addition to the size of the brain and its various regions, there are other features of our neuroanatomy that might be important to consider. The most obvious, perhaps, is the convoluted surface of fissures and folds (called gyri; pronounced "ji-rye") that comprise the outer part of the cerebral cortex (see Figure 9.13). Interestingly, the number and size of these cerebral gyri seems strongly related to intelligence across different species; species that have complex cognitive and social lives, such as elephants, dolphins, and primates, have particularly convoluted cortices (Marino, 2002; Rogers et al., 2010). And indeed, even within humans, careful studies using brain imaging technology have shown that having more convolutions on the surface of certain parts of the cortex was also positively correlated with scores on the WAIS intelligence test, accounting for approximately 25% of the variability in WAIS scores (Luders et al., 2008).

Can we critically evaluate this issue?

A common critique of studies examining brain size and IQ is that it is not always clear what processes or abilities are being tested. IQ scores could be measuring a number of things including working memory, processing speed, ability to pay attention, or even motivation to perform well on the test. Therefore, when studies show that brain size can account for 25% of the variability in IQ scores, it is not always clear what ability (or abilities) are underlying these results.

Another potential problem is the *third-variable problem*; even if brain size and performance on intelligence tests are correlated with each other, it might be the case that they are both related to some other factor, like stress, nutrition, physical health, environmental toxins, or the amount of enriching stimulation experienced during childhood (Choi et al., 2008). If these other factors can account for the relationship between brain size and intelligence, then the brain–IQ relationship itself may be overestimated.

A final critique is simply the recognition that there is more to intelligence than just the size of one's brain. After all, if brain size explains 25% of the variability in IQ scores, the other 75% must be due to other things.

Figure 9.13 Does Intelligence Increase with Brain Size?

While the size of the brain may have a modest relationship to intelligence, the convolutions or "gyri" along the surface of the cortex are another important factor: Increased convolutions are associated with higher intelligence test scores.

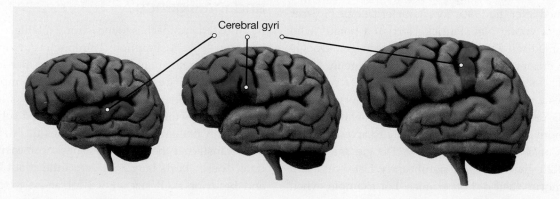

Cerebral gyri

Why is this relevant?

This research is important for reasons that go far beyond the issue of intelligence and IQ tests. More generally, research on the neurology of intelligence has furthered our understanding of the relationship between brain structure and function, which are related to many important phenomena. For example, certain harmful patterns of behaviour, such as anorexia nervosa (a psychological disorder marked by self-starvation) or prolonged periods of alcohol abuse, both have been shown to lead to changes in cognitive abilities and corresponding loss of brain volume (e.g., McCormick et al., 2008; Schottenbauer et al., 2007). Measurements of brain volume have also played a key role in understanding the impaired neurological and cognitive development of children growing up in institutional settings (e.g., orphanages), as well as how these children benefit from adoption, foster care, or increased social contact (Sheridan et al., 2012). Better understanding of how experiences like anorexia, alcoholism, and child neglect affect brain development may provide ways of developing effective interventions that could help people who have suffered from such experiences.

Module 9.3a Quiz:

Biological Influences on Intelligence

Know . . .

1. When scientists insert genetic material into an animal's genome, the result is called a _____.
   A. genomic animal
   B. transgenic animal
   C. knockout animal
   D. fraternal twin

Understand . . .

2. How do gene knockout studies help to identify the contribution of specific genes to intelligence?
   A. After removing or suppressing a portion of genetic material, scientists can look for changes in intelligence.
   B. After inserting genetic material, scientists can see how intelligence has changed.
   C. Scientists can rank animals in terms of intelligence and then see how the most intelligent animals differ genetically from the least intelligent.

   D. They allow scientists to compare identical and fraternal twins.

Analyze . . .

3. Identical twins, whether reared together or apart, tend to score very similarly on standardized measures of intelligence. Which of the following statements does this finding support?
   A. Intelligence levels are based on environmental factors for both twins reared together and twins reared apart.
   B. Environmental factors are stronger influences on twins raised together compared to twins reared apart.
   C. The "intelligence gene" is identical in both twins reared together and reared apart.
   D. Genes are an important source of individual variations in intelligence test scores.

Environmental Influences on Intelligence

As described earlier, research on the *biological* underpinnings of intelligence repeatedly emphasizes the importance of *environmental* factors. For example, environmental conditions determine which genes get expressed ("turned on") for a given individual; thus, without the right circumstances, genes can't appropriately affect the person's development. Also, brain areas involved in intelligence are responsive to a wide variety of environmental factors. The full story of how "nature" influences intelligence is intricately bound up with the story of how "nurture" influences intelligence.

Both animal and human studies have demonstrated how environmental factors influence cognitive abilities. Controlled experiments with animals show that growing up in physically and socially stimulating environments results in faster learning and enhanced brain development compared to growing up in a dull environment (Hebb, 1947; Tashiro et al., 2007). For example, classic studies in the 1960s showed that rats who grew up in enriched environments (i.e., these rats enjoyed toys, ladders, and tunnels) ended up with bigger brains than rats who grew up in impoverished environments (i.e., simple wire cages). Not only were their cerebral cortices approximately 5% larger (Diamond et al., 1964; Rosenzweig et al., 1962), but their cortices contained 25% more synapses (Diamond et al., 1964). With more synapses, the brain can make more associations, potentially enhancing cognitive abilities such as learning and creativity. In this section, we review some of the major environmental factors that influence intelligence.

BIRTH ORDER One of the most hotly debated environmental factors affecting intelligence is simply whether you were the oldest child in your family, or whether you were lower in the pecking order of your siblings. Debate about this issue has raged for many decades within psychology.

John Dominis/Getty Images

Socioeconomic status is related to intelligence. People from low-socioeconomic backgrounds typically have far fewer opportunities to access educational and other important resources that contribute to intellectual growth.

Regardless of the larger debate about why birth order might affect intelligence, the evidence seems to indicate that it does. For example, a 2007 study of more than 240 000 people in Norway found that the IQs of first-born children are, on average, about three points higher than those of second-born children and four points higher than those of third-born children (Kristensen & Bjerkedal, 2007).

Why might this be? The most important factor, researchers believe, is that older siblings, like it or not, end up tutoring and mentoring younger siblings, imparting the wisdom they have gained through experience on to their younger siblings. Although this may help the younger sibling, the act of teaching their knowledge benefits the older sibling more (Zajonc, 1976). The act of teaching requires the older sibling to rehearse previously remembered information and to reorganize it in a way that their younger sibling will understand. Teaching therefore leads to a deeper processing of the information, which, in turn, increases the likelihood that it will be remembered later (see Module 7.2).

Before any first-born children reading this section start building monuments to their greatness, it is important to note that the differences between the IQs of first- and later-born siblings are quite small: three or four points. There will definitely be many individual families in which the later-born kids have higher IQs than their first-born siblings. Nevertheless, this finding is one example of how environments can influence intelligence.

SOCIOECONOMIC STATUS One of the most robust findings in the intelligence literature is that IQ correlates strongly with socioeconomic status (SES). It is perhaps no surprise that children growing up in wealthy homes have, on average, higher IQs than those growing up in poverty (Turkheimer et al., 2003), but there may be many reasons for this that have nothing to do with the "innate" or potential intelligence of the rich or the poor. Think of the many environmental differences and greater access to resources and opportunities enjoyed by the wealthy! For example, consider how much language children are exposed to at home; one U.S. study estimated that by age three, children of professional parents will have heard 30 million words, children of working-class parents will have heard only 20 million words, and children of unemployed African-American mothers will have heard only 10 million words. Furthermore, the *level* of vocabulary is strikingly different for families in the different socioeconomic categories, with professional families using the most sophisticated language (Hart & Risley, 1995).

Other studies have shown that higher SES homes are much more enriching and supportive of children's intellectual development—high SES parents talk to their children more; have more books, magazines, and newspapers in the home; give them more access to computers; take them to more learning experiences outside the home (e.g., visits to museums); and are less punitive toward their children (Bradley et al., 1993; Phillips et al., 1998).

Unfortunately, the effects of SES don't end here. SES interacts with a number of other factors that can influence intelligence, including nutrition, stress, and education. The difference between rich and poor people's exposure to these factors almost certainly affects the IQ gap between the two groups.

NUTRITION It's a cliché we are all familiar with—"you are what you eat." Yet over the past century, the quality of the North American diet has plummeted as we have adopted foods that are highly processed, high in sugar and fat, low in fibre and nutrients, and laden with chemicals (preservatives, colours, and flavourings). Some evidence suggests that poor nutrition could have negative effects on intelligence. For example, research has shown that diets high in saturated fat quickly lead to sharp declines in cognitive functioning in both animal and human subjects. In contrast, diets low in such fats and high in fruits, vegetables, fish, and whole grains are associated with higher cognitive functioning (Greenwood & Winocur, 2005; Parrott & Greenwood, 2007).

A massive longitudinal study on diet is currently underway in the United Kingdom. The Avon Longitudinal Study of Parents and Children is following the development of children born to 14 000 women in the early 1990s. This research has shown that a "poor" diet (high in fat, sugar, and processed foods) early in life leads to reliably lower IQ scores by age 8.5, whereas a "health-conscious" diet (emphasizing salads, rice, pastas, fish, and fruit) leads to higher IQs. Importantly, this was true even when researchers accounted for the effects of other variables, such as socioeconomic status (Northstone et al., 2012).

So what kinds of foods should we eat to maximize our brainpower? Although research on nutrition and intelligence is still relatively new, it would appear that eating foods low in saturated fats and rich in omega-3 fats, whole grains, and fruits and veggies are your smartest bets.

STRESS High levels of stress in economically poor populations is also a major factor in explaining the rich–poor IQ gap. People living in poverty are exposed to high levels of stress through many converging factors, ranging from higher levels of environmental noise and toxins, to more family conflict and community violence, to less economic security and fewer employment opportunities. These and many other stresses increase the amounts of stress hormones such as cortisol in their bodies, which in turn is related to poorer cognitive functioning (Evans & Schamberg, 2009). High levels of stress also interfere with working memory (the ability to hold multiple pieces of information in memory at one time; Evans & Schamberg, 2009), and the ability to persevere when faced with challenging tasks, such as difficult questions on an IQ test (Evans & Stecker, 2004). These deficits interfere with learning in school (Blair & Razza, 2007; Ferrer & McArdle, 2004).

The toxic effects of chronic stress show up in the brain as well, damaging the neural circuitry of the prefrontal cortex and hippocampus, which are critical for working memory and other cognitive abilities (e.g., controlling attention, cognitive flexibility) as well as for the consolidation and storage of long-term memories (McEwen, 2000). In short, too much stress makes us not only less healthy, but can make us less intelligent as well.

EDUCATION One of the great hopes of modern society has been that universal education would level the playing field, allowing all children, rich and poor alike, access to the resources necessary to achieve success. Certainly, attending school has been shown to have a large impact on IQ scores (Ceci, 1991). During school, children accumulate factual knowledge, learn basic language and math skills, and learn skills related to scientific reasoning and problem solving. Children's IQ scores are significantly lower if they do not attend school (Ceci & Williams, 1997; Nisbett,

2009). In fact, for most children, IQ drops even over the months of summer holiday (Ceci, 1991; Jencks et al., 1972), although the wealthiest 20% actually show gains in IQ over the summer, presumably because they enjoy activities that are even more enriching than the kinds of experiences delivered in the classroom (Burkam et al., 2004; Cooper et al., 2000). However, although education has the potential to help erase the rich–poor gap in IQ, its effectiveness at doing so will depend on whether the rich and poor have equal access to the same quality of education and other support and resources that would allow them to make full use of educational opportunities.

Clearly, environmental factors such as nutrition, stress, and education all influence intelligence, which gives us some clues as to how society can contribute to improving the intelligence of the population. Interestingly, exactly such a trend has been widely observed across the last half-century or so; it appears that generation after generation, people are getting smarter!

THE FLYNN EFFECT: IS *EVERYONE* GETTING SMARTER?
The **Flynn effect**, named after researcher James Flynn, *refers to the steady population level increases in intelligence test scores over time* (Figure 9.14). This effect has been found in numerous situations across a number of countries. For example, in the Dutch and French militaries, IQ scores of new recruits rose dramatically between the 1950s and 1980s—21 points for the Dutch and about 30 for the French (Flynn, 1987). From 1932 to 2007, Flynn estimates that, in general, IQ scores rose about one point every three years (Flynn, 2007).

The magnitude of the Flynn effect is striking. In the Dutch study noted above, today's group of 18-year-olds would score 35 points higher than 18-year-olds in 1950. The average person back then had an IQ of 100, but the average person today, taking the same test, would score 135, which is above the cut-off considered "gifted" in most gifted education programs! Or consider this the opposite way—if the average person today scored 100 on today's test, the average person in 1950 would score about 65, enough to qualify as mentally disabled.

How can we explain this increase? Nobody knows for sure, but one of the most likely explanations is that modern society requires certain types of intellectual skills, such as abstract thinking, scientific reasoning, classification, and logical analysis. These have been increasingly emphasized since the Industrial Revolution, and particularly since the information economy and advent of computers have restructured society over the past half-century or so. Each successive generation spends more time manipulating information with their minds; more time with visual media in the form of television, video games, and now the Internet; and more time in school. It seems reasonable to propose that these shifts in information processing led to the increases in IQ scores (Nisbett et al., 2012).

Figure 9.14 The Flynn Effect

For decades, there has been a general trend toward increasing IQ scores. This trend, called the Flynn effect, has been occurring since standardized IQ tests have been administered.

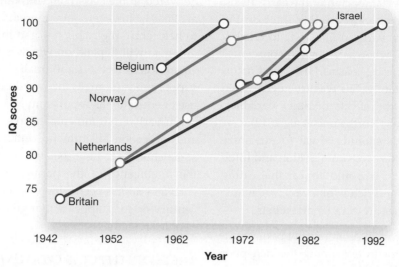

Source: Flynn, J. R. (1999). Searching for justice: The discovery of IQ gains over time. *American Psychologist, 54*, 5–20.

Module 9.3b Quiz:

Environmental Influences on Intelligence

Understand . . .

1. What have controlled experiments with animals found in regard to the effects of the environment on intelligence?

  A. Stimulating environments result in faster learning and enhanced brain development.

  B. Deprived environments result in faster learning and enhanced brain development.

  C. Stimulating environments result in slower learning and poorer brain development.

  D. Deprived environments have no effect on learning and brain development.

2. In which way have psychologists NOT studied the major environmental factors that, through their interaction with genes, influence intelligence?

  A. By measuring stress hormones among poor and affluent children and correlating them with intelligence test scores

  B. By depriving some children of education and comparing them to others who attended school

  C. By measuring children's nutrition and then correlating it with intelligence scores

  D. By correlating children's birth order in their family with intelligence scores

Analyze . . .

3. What effect does birth order have on intelligence scores? Why is this the case?

  A. Older children often have lower IQs than their siblings because their parents spend more time taking care of younger children.

  B. Younger siblings often have higher IQs because their older siblings spent time teaching them new information and skills.

  C. Younger siblings have lower IQs because they have had less time to learn information and skills.

  D. Older children typically have slightly higher IQs, likely because they reinforce their knowledge by teaching younger siblings.

Behavioural Influences on Intelligence

If you want to make yourself more intelligent, we've covered a number of ways to do that—eat a brain-healthy diet, learn how to manage stress better, keep yourself educated (if not in formal schooling, then perhaps by continuing to be an active learner), and expose yourself to diverse and stimulating activities. But is there anything else you can do? For example, if you want bigger muscles, you can go to the gym and exercise. Can you do the same thing for the brain?

BRAIN TRAINING PROGRAMS   One potential technique to improve intelligence is the use of "brain training" programs designed to improve working memory and other cognitive skills. The idea behind such programs is that playing games related to memory and attention will not only improve your performance on these games, but will also help you use those abilities in other, real-world situations.

Research in this area initially appeared quite promising. For instance, in one line of research, a computer task (the "N-back" task) was used as an exercise program for working memory. In this task, people are presented with a stimulus, such as squares that light up on a grid, and are asked to press a key if the position on the grid is the same as the last trial. The task gets progressively more difficult, requiring participants to remember what happened two, three, or more trials ago (although it takes considerable practice for most people to be able to reliably remember what happened even three trials ago). Practising the N-back task was shown to not only improve performance at that task, but also to increase participants' fluid intelligence (Jaeggi et al., 2008). Importantly, the benefits were not merely short term, but lasted for at least three months (Jaeggi et al., 2011).

However, recent reviews of this area of research suggest that we should be cautious when interpreting the results (and media reports). Many studies of brain-training programs involved small sample sizes; other studies included major methodological flaws such as a lack of a control group (Simons et al., 2016). A more careful examination of this research area suggests that the effects of brain-training programs are typically quite limited. Practising games related to working memory will improve working memory, but will rarely have an effect on other types of tasks, particularly on behaviours occurring outside of the laboratory (Melby-Lervåg & Hulme, 2013). Although these results are disappointing—particularly for people who have spent money on expensive brain-training programs—they help remind us of the importance of being critical consumers of scientific information.

NOOTROPIC DRUGS   Another behaviour that many people believe improves their cognitive functioning is the use of certain drugs. **Nootropic substances** (meaning "affecting the mind") *are substances that are believed to beneficially affect intelligence.* Nootropics can work through many different mechanisms, from increasing overall arousal and alertness, to changing the availability of certain neurotransmitters, to stimulating nerve growth in the brain.

Certainly, these drugs can work for many people. For example, two drugs commonly used are methylphenidate (Ritalin) and modafinil (Provigil). Methylphenidate is a drug that inhibits the reuptake of norepinephrine and dopamine, thus leaving more of these neurotransmitters in the synapses between cells. Although generally prescribed to help people with attentional disorders, Ritalin can also boost cognitive functioning in the general population (Elliott et al., 1997). Modafinil, originally developed to treat narcolepsy (a sleep disorder), is known to boost short-term memory and planning abilities by affecting the reuptake of dopamine (Turner et al., 2003).

Boosting the brain, however, does not come without risk. For example, the long-term effects of such drugs are poorly understood and potential side effects can be severe. There can also be dependency issues as people come to rely on such drugs and use them more regularly, and problems with providing unfair advantages to people willing to take such drugs, which puts pressure on others to take them as well in order to stay competitive (Sahakian & Morein-Zamir, 2007). Because of these risks, a September 2013 review in the *Canadian Medical Association Journal* recommended that doctors "should seriously consider refusing to prescribe medications for cognitive enhancement to healthy individuals" (Forlini et al., 2013, p. 1047).

These risks have to be weighed against the potential benefits of developing these drugs, at least for clinical populations. For example, researchers in the United Kingdom have argued that if nootropic drugs could improve the cognitive functioning of Alzheimer's patients by even a small amount, such as a mere 1% change in the severity of the disease each year, this would be enough not only to dramatically improve the lives of people with Alzheimer's and their families, but to completely erase the predicted increases in long-term health care costs for the U.K.'s aging population (Sahakian & Morein-Zamir, 2007).

As with most questions concerning the ethical and optimally desirable uses of technologies, there are no easy answers when it comes to nootropic drugs. But we would caution you—there are much safer ways to increase your performance than ingesting substances that can affect your brain in unknown ways.

In sum, although few people are blessed with brains as abnormally intelligent as Einstein's, there are practical things anyone can do to maximize their potential brainpower. From eating better to providing our brains with challenging exercises, we can use the science of intelligence to make the most out of our genetic inheritance.

Module 9.3c Quiz:

Behavioural Influences on Intelligence

Know . . .

1. A commonly used nootropic drug is _____.
   A. Tylenol
   B. Ecstasy
   C. Ritalin
   D. Lamictal

Understand . . .

2. Which of the following seems to be affected by brain-training tasks like the N-back task?
   A. Crystallized intelligence
   B. Fluid intelligence

C. A person's dominant learning style
D. A person's belief that they are more intelligent

Analyze . . .

3. Research on nootropic drugs shows that
   A. they have a much larger effect on intelligence than do environmental factors such as socioeconomic status.
   B. they show low addiction rates and are therefore quite safe.
   C. they have a larger effect on long-term memory than on working memory.
   D. these drugs can produce increases in intelligence in some individuals.

Module 9.3 Summary

9.3a   Know . . . the key terminology related to heredity, environment, and intelligence.

Flynn effect
gene knockout (KO) studies
nootropic substances
video deficit

9.3b   Understand . . . different approaches to studying the genetic basis of intelligence.

Behavioural genetics typically involves conducting twin or adoption studies. Behavioural genomics involves looking at gene–behaviour relationships at the molecular level. This approach often involves using animal models, including knockout and transgenic models.

9.3c   Apply . . . your knowledge of environmental and behavioural effects on intelligence to understand how to enhance your own cognitive abilities.

Based on the research we reviewed, there are many different strategies that are good bets for enhancing the cognitive abilities that underlie your own intelligence. (Note: some of these strategies are known to be helpful for children, and the effects on adult intelligence are not well researched.)

• Choose challenging activities and environments that are stimulating and enriching.

• Eat diets low in saturated fat and processed foods and high in omega-3 fatty acids, nuts, seeds, fruits, and antioxidant-rich vegetables.
• Reduce sources of stress and increase your ability to handle stress well.
• Remain an active learner by continually adding to your education or learning.
• Don't spend too much time watching TV and other media that are relatively poor at challenging your cognitive abilities.

The use of nootropic drugs remains a potential strategy for enhancing your cognitive faculties; however, given the potential side effects, addictive possibilities, and the uncertainty regarding the long-term consequences of using such drugs, this option may not be the best way to influence intelligence.

9.3d   Analyze . . . the belief that older children are more intelligent than their younger siblings.

Reviews of intelligence tests show that the oldest child in a family tends to have higher IQs than their younger siblings. However, this effect is quite small: 3 IQ points. Importantly, this difference is not due to the genetic superiority of the older siblings; rather, it is likely related to the fact that older children often spend time teaching things to their younger siblings.

Chapter 10
Lifespan Development

10.1 Physical Development from Conception through Infancy

- Methods for Measuring Developmental Trends   387
- Module 10.1a Quiz   388
- Zygotes to Infants: From One Cell to Billions   388
  Working the Scientific Literacy Model: The Long-Term
  Effects of Premature Birth   392
- Module 10.1b Quiz   394
- Sensory and Motor Development in Infancy   394
- Module 10.1c Quiz   399
- Module 10.1 Summary   399

10.2 Infancy and Childhood: Cognitive and Emotional Development

- Cognitive Changes: Piaget's Cognitive Development Theory   401
  Working the Scientific Literacy Model: Evaluating Piaget   404
- Module 10.2a Quiz   406
- Social Development, Attachment, and Self-Awareness   406
- Module 10.2b Quiz   412
- Psychosocial Development   412
- Module 10.2c Quiz   415
- Module 10.2 Summary   415

10.3 Adolescence

- Physical Changes in Adolescence   418
- Module 10.3a Quiz   419
- Emotional Challenges in Adolescence   419
  Working the Scientific Literacy Model: Adolescent Risk
  and Decision Making   420
- Module 10.3b Quiz   422
- Cognitive Development: Moral Reasoning vs. Emotions   422
- Module 10.3c Quiz   425
- Social Development: Identity and Relationships   425
- Module 10.3d Quiz   427
- Module 10.3 Summary   427

10.4 Adulthood and Aging

- From Adolescence through Middle Age   429
- Module 10.4a Quiz   433
- Late Adulthood   433
  Working the Scientific Literacy Model: Aging and Cognitive Change   436
- Module 10.4b Quiz   437
- Module 10.4 Summary   438

Module 10.1 Physical Development from Conception through Infancy

Leungchopan/Fotolia

 ## Learning Objectives

10.1a Know . . . the key terminology related to prenatal and infant physical development.

10.1b Understand . . . the pros and cons to different research designs in developmental psychology.

10.1c Apply . . . your understanding to identify the best ways expectant parents can ensure the health of their developing fetus.

10.1d Analyze . . . the effects of preterm birth.

It is difficult to overstate the sheer miracle and profundity of birth. Consider the following story, told by a new father. "About two days after the birth of my first child, I was driving to the hospital and had one of 'those moments,' an awe moment, when reality seems clear and wondrous. What triggered it was that the person driving down the highway in the car next to mine yawned. Suddenly, I remembered my newborn baby yawning just the day before, and somehow, it hit me—we are all just giant babies, all of us, the power broker in the business suit, the teenager in jeans and a hoodie, the tired soccer parent in the mini-van and the elderly couple holding hands on the sidewalk. Although we have invented these complex inner worlds for ourselves, with all of our cherished opinions, political beliefs, dreams, and aspirations, at our essence, we are giant babies. We have the same basic needs as babies—food, security, love, air, water. Our bodies are basically the

same, only bigger. Our brains are basically the same, only substantially more developed. Our movements are even basically the same, just more coordinated. I like to remember that now and then, when I feel intimidated by someone, or when I feel too self-important. Just giant babies!"

Of course, we don't stay "just babies" over our lives. We develop in many complex ways as we age and learn to function in the world. Understanding how we change, and how we stay the same, over the course of our lives, is what developmental psychology is all about.

Focus Questions

1. How does the brain develop, starting even before birth?

2. What factors can significantly harm or enhance babies' neurological development?

>> **Developmental psychology** *is the study of human physical, cognitive, social, and behavioural characteristics across the lifespan.* Take just about anything you have encountered so far in this text, and you will probably find psychologists approaching it from a developmental perspective. From neuroscientists to cultural psychologists, examining how we function and change across different stages of life raises many central and fascinating questions.

Methods for Measuring Developmental Trends

Studying development requires some special methods for measuring and tracking change over time. A **cross-sectional design** *is used to measure and compare samples of people at different ages at a given point in time.* For example, to study cognition from infancy to adulthood, you could compare people of different age groups—say, groups of 1-, 5-, 10-, and 20-year-olds. In contrast, a **longitudinal design** *follows the development of the same set of individuals through time.* With this type of study, you would select a sample of infants and measure their cognitive development periodically over the course of 20 years (see Figure 10.1)

These different methods have different strengths and weaknesses. Cross-sectional designs are relatively cheap and easy to administer, and they allow a study to be done quickly (because you don't have to wait around while your participants age). On the other hand, they can suffer from **cohort effects**, which are *differences between people that result from being born in different time periods.* For example, if you find differences between people born in the 2000s with those born in the 1970s, this may reflect any number of differences between people from those time periods—such as differences in technological advances, parenting norms, cultural changes, environmental pollutants, nutritional practices, or many other factors. This creates big problems in interpreting the findings of a study—do differences between the age groups reflect normal developmental processes or do they reflect more general differences between people born into these time periods?

A longitudinal study fixes the problem of cohort effects, but these studies are often difficult to carry out and tend to be costly and time consuming to follow, due to the logistic challenges involved in following a group of people for a long period of time. Longitudinal designs often suffer from the problem of *attrition*, which occurs when participants drop out of a study for various reasons, such as losing interest or moving away.

The combination and accumulation of cross-sectional and longitudinal studies has taught us a great deal about the processes of human development. This can help parents and educators who want to have a positive influence on children's development. It can help us understand how to better serve the needs of those who are aging. And it can help all of us, who just want to better understand who we are, and why we turned out the way that we did.

One quite famous example of a longitudinal study is the *Seven-up* series, which is a documentary and extensive longitudinal study of a group of people who started the study at age 7, more than 50 years ago. Watching the series is a fascinating look at how people retain basic features of their personality over pretty much their entire lifespan, whereas they also change as their circumstances take them down different paths in life. If you are interested, you can find this series online; search for "7 up," "14 up," etc., up to "56 up," which was released in 2013.

PATTERNS OF DEVELOPMENT: STAGES AND CONTINUITY One of the challenges that has faced developmental psychologists is that human development does not unfold in a gradual, smooth, linear fashion; instead, periods of seeming stability are interrupted by sudden, often dramatic upheavals and shifts in functioning as a person transitions from one pattern of functioning to a qualitatively different one. This common pattern, relatively stable periods interspersed with periods of rapid reorganization, has been reflected in many different *stage models* of human development. According to these models, specific stages of development can be described, differentiated by qualitatively different patterns of how people function. In between these stages, rapid shifts in thinking and behaving occur, leading to a new set of patterns that manifest as the next stage. Stage models have played an important role in helping psychologists understand both continuity and change over time.

Figure 10.1 Cross-Sectional and Longitudinal Methods

In cross-sectional studies, different groups of people—typically of different ages—are compared at a single point in time. In longitudinal studies, the same group of subjects is tracked over multiple points in time.

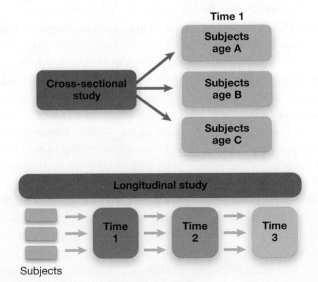

Module 10.1a Quiz:

Methods for Measuring Developmental Trends

Know . . .

1. Studies that examine factors in groups of people of different ages (e.g., a group of 15–20 year-olds; a group of 35–40 year-olds; and a group of 75–80 year-olds), are employing a _____ research design.
   A. cohort
   B. longitudinal
   C. cross-sectional
   D. stage-model

Apply . . .

2. A researcher has only one year to complete a study on a topic that spans the entire range of childhood. To complete the study, she should use a _____ design.
   A. cohort
   B. longitudinal
   C. correlational
   D. cross-sectional

Analyze . . .

3. Which of the following is a factor that would be *least* likely to be a cohort effect for a study on cognitive development in healthy people?
   A. Differences in genes between individuals
   B. Differences in educational practices over time
   C. Changes in the legal drinking age
   D. Changes in prescription drug use

Zygotes to Infants: From One Cell to Billions

The earliest stage of development begins at the moment of conception, when a single sperm (out of approximately 200 million that start the journey into the vagina), is able to find its way into the ovum (egg cell). At this moment, the ovum releases a chemical that bars any other sperm from entering, and *the nuclei of egg and sperm fuse, forming the* **zygote**. Out of the mysterious formation of this single cell, the rest of our lives flow.

FERTILIZATION AND GESTATION The formation of the zygote through the fertilization of the ovum marks the beginning of the **germinal stage**, *the first phase of prenatal development, which spans from conception to two weeks.* Shortly after it forms, the zygote begins dividing, first into two cells, then four, then eight, and so on. The zygote also travels down the fallopian tubes toward the uterus, where it becomes implanted into the lining of the uterus (Table 10.1). The ball of cells, now called a blastocyst, splits into two groups. The inner group of cells develops into the fetus. The outer group of cells forms the placenta, which will pass oxygen, nutrients, and waste to and from the fetus.

The **embryonic stage** *spans weeks two through eight, during which time the embryo begins developing major physical structures such as the heart and nervous system, as well as the beginnings of arms, legs, hands, and feet.*

The **fetal stage** *spans week eight through birth, during which time the skeletal, organ, and nervous systems become more developed and specialized.* Muscles develop and the fetus begins to move. Sleeping and waking cycles start and the senses become fine-tuned—even to the point where the fetus is responsive to external cues (these events are summarized in Table 10.1).

FETAL BRAIN DEVELOPMENT The beginnings of the human brain can be seen during the embryonic stage, between the second and third weeks of gestation, when some cells migrate to the appropriate locations and begin to differentiate into nerve cells. The first major development in the brain is the formation of the neural tube, which occurs only 2 weeks after conception. A layer of specialized cells begins to fold over onto itself, structurally differentiating between itself and the other cells. This tube-shaped structure eventually develops into the brain and spinal cord (Lenroot & Gledd, 2007; O'Rahilly & Mueller, 2008). The first signs of the major divisions of the brain—the forebrain, the midbrain, and the hindbrain—are apparent at only 4 weeks (see Figure 10.2). Around 7 weeks, neurons and synapses develop in the spinal cord, giving rise to a new ability—movement; the fetus's own movements then provide a new source of sensory information, which further stimulates the central nervous system's development of increasingly coordinated movements (Kurjak, Pooh, et al., 2005). By 11 weeks, differentiations between the cerebral hemisphere, the cerebellum, and the brain stem are apparent, and by the end of the second trimester, the outer surface of the cerebral cortex has started to fold into the distinctive gyri and sulci (ridges and folds) that give the outer cortex its wrinkled appearance. It is around the same time period that a fatty tissue called myelin begins to build up around developing nerve cells, a process called *myelination*. Myelin is centrally important; by insulating nerve cells, it enables them to conduct messages more rapidly and efficiently (see Module 3.2; Giedd, 2008), thereby

Table 10.1 Phases of Prenatal Development

A summary of the stages of human prenatal development and some of the major events at each.

GERMINAL: 0 TO 2 WEEKS

Major Events

Migration of the blastocyst from the fallopian tubes and its implantation in the uterus. Cellular divisions take place that eventually lead to multiple organ, nervous system, and skin tissues.

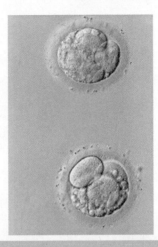

EMBRYONIC: 2 TO 8 WEEKS

Major Events

Stage in which basic cell layers become differentiated. Major structures such as the head, heart, limbs, hands, and feet emerge. The embryo attaches to the placenta, the structure that allows for the exchange of oxygen and nutrients and the removal of wastes.

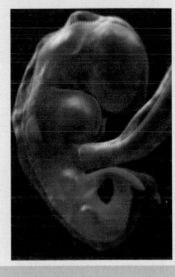

FETAL STAGE: 8 WEEKS TO BIRTH

Major Events

Brain development progresses as distinct regions take form. The circulatory, respiratory, digestive, and other bodily systems develop. Sex organs appear at around the third month of gestation.

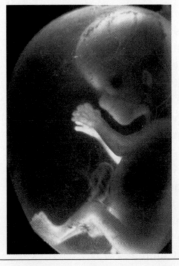

Figure 10.2 Fetal Brain Development

The origins of the major regions of the brain are already detectable at four weeks' gestation. Their differentiation progresses rapidly, with the major forebrain, midbrain, and hindbrain regions becoming increasingly specialized.

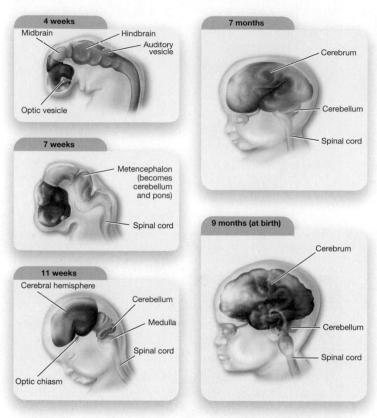

allowing for the large-scale functioning and integration of neural networks.

At birth, the newborn has an estimated 100 billion neurons and a brain that is approximately 25% the size and weight of an adult brain. Astonishingly, this means that at birth, the infant has created virtually all of the neurons that will comprise the adult brain, growing up to 4000 new neurons per *second* in the womb (Brown et al., 2001). However, most of the connections between these neurons have not yet been established in the brain of a newborn (Kolb, 1989, 1995). This gives us a key insight into one of our core human capacities—our ability to adapt to highly diverse environments. Although the basic shape and structure of our brains is guided by the human genome, the strength of the connections between brain regions is dependent upon experience.

The child's brain has a vast number of synapses, far more than it will have as an adult in fact, which is why the child's brain is so responsive to external input. The brain is learning, at a very basic level, what the world is like, and what it needs to be able to do in order to perceive and function effectively in the world. Children's brains have a very high amount of *plasticity*, so that whatever environments

the child endures while growing up, her developing brain will be best able to learn to perceive and adapt to those environments. Our brains generally develop the patterns of biological organization that correspond to the world that we've experienced.

This means that in a deep and personal way, who we are depends on the environments that structure our brains. Ironically, this profound reliance upon the outside world is also the reason why human babies are so helpless (and make such bad Frisbee partners). We humans have relatively little pre-programmed into us and thus, we can do very little at birth relative to so many other animals. However, this seemingly profound weakness is offset by two huge, truly world-altering strengths: the incredible plasticity of our neurobiology, and the social support systems that keep us alive when we are very young. These advantages also give us the luxury of slowly developing over a long period of time. As a result, our increasingly complex neurobiological systems can learn to adapt and function effectively across a vast diversity of specific circumstances. The net result of this flexibility is that humans have been able to flourish in practically every ecosystem on the surface of the planet.

NUTRITION, TERATOGENS, AND FETAL DEVELOPMENT The rapidly developing fetal brain is highly vulnerable to environmental influences; for example, the quality of a pregnant woman's diet can have a long-lasting impact on her child's development. In fact, proper nutrition is the single most important non-genetic factor affecting fetal development (aside from the obvious need to avoid exposure to toxic substances; Phillips, 2006). The nutritional demands of a developing infant are such that women typically require an almost 20% increase in energy intake during pregnancy, including sufficient quantities of protein (which affects neurological development; Morgane et al., 2002) and essential nutrients (especially omega-3 fatty acids, folic acid, zinc, calcium, and magnesium). Given that most people's diets do not provide enough of these critical nutrients, supplements are generally considered to be a good idea (Ramakrishnan et al., 1999).

Fetal malnutrition can have severe consequences, producing low-birth-weight babies who are more likely to suffer from a variety of diseases and illnesses, and are more likely to have cognitive deficits that can persist long after birth. Children who were malnourished in the womb are more likely to experience attention deficit disorders and difficulties controlling their emotions, due to underdeveloped prefrontal cortices and other brain areas involved in self-control (Morgane et al., 2002). A wide variety of effects on mental health have been suggested;

for example, one study showed that babies who were born in Holland during a famine in World War II experienced a variety of physical problems (Stein et al., 1975) and had a much higher risk of developing psychological disorders, such as schizophrenia and antisocial personality disorder (Neugebauer et al., 1999; Susser et al., 1999).

Fetal development can also be disrupted through exposure to **teratogens**, *substances, such as drugs or environmental toxins, that impair the process of development.* One of the most famous and heartbreaking examples of teratogens was the use of thalidomide, a sedative that was hailed as a wonder drug for helping pregnant women deal with morning sickness during pregnancy. Available in Canada from 1959 to 1962, thalidomide was disastrous, causing miscarriages, severe birth defects such as blindness and deafness, plus its most well-known effect, *phocomelia*, in which victims' hands, feet, or both emerged directly from their shoulders or hips, functioning more like flippers than limbs; indeed, *phocomelia* is taken from the Greek words *phoke*, which means "seal," and *melos*, which means "limb" (www.thalidomide.ca/faq-en/#12). It is estimated that up to twenty thousand babies were born with disabilities as a result of being exposed to thalidomide. In most countries, victims were able to secure financial support through class action lawsuits; however, in Canada, the government has steadfastly refused to provide much support to victims, who face ongoing severe challenges in their lives.

More common teratogens are alcohol and tobacco, although their effects differ widely depending on the volume consumed and the exact time when exposure occurs during pregnancy. First described in the 1970s (Jones & Smith, 1973), **fetal alcohol syndrome** *involves abnormalities in mental functioning, growth, and facial development in the offspring of women who use alcohol during pregnancy.* This condition occurs in approximately 1 per 1000 births worldwide, but the specific rates likely vary greatly between regions, and little is known about specific regional variability. It also seems likely that FAS is underreported, and thus the effects of FAS may be far more widespread than is widely recognized (Morleo et al., 2011).

This is particularly worrisome when one considers that research suggests there is no safe limit for alcohol consumption by a pregnant woman; even one drink per day can be enough to cause impaired fetal development (O'Leary et al., 2010; Streissguth & Connor, 2001). Alcohol, like many other substances, readily passes through the placental membranes, leaving the developing fetus vulnerable to its effects, which include reduced mental functioning and impulsivity (Olson et al., 1997; Streissguth et al., 1999). It is concerning, then, to acknowledge that about 1 in 10 pregnancies in Canada involve ingesting alcohol (Walker et al., 2011), and in some communities, such as those in isolated Northern regions, more than 60% of pregnancies have been shown to be alcohol-exposed (Muckle et al., 2011). Given that any amount of reduced drinking during pregnancy helps to reduce the risks of FAS, there is a clear role for public health and awareness campaigns, family and school efforts, and our own personal contributions

Dpa picture alliance/Alamy Stock Photo

Victims of thalidomide; this sedative seemed like a miracle drug in the late 1950s, until its tragic effects on fetal development became apparent.

Betty Udesen/KRT/Newscom

Fetal alcohol syndrome is diagnosed based on facial abnormalities, growth problems, and behavioural and cognitive deficits.

to social norms, to tackle this together, and to eradicate, or at least minimize, alcohol consumption during pregnancy.

Smoking can also expose the developing fetus to teratogens, decreasing blood oxygen and raising concentrations of nicotine and carbon monoxide, as well as increasing the risk of miscarriage or death during infancy. Babies born to mothers who smoke are twice as likely to have low birth weight and have a 30% chance of premature birth—both factors that increase the newborn's risk of illness or death. Evidence also suggests that smoking during pregnancy increases the risk that the child will experience problems with emotional development and impulse control (Brion et al., 2010; Wiebe et al., 2014), as well as attentional and other behavioural problems (Makin et al., 1991). These behavioural outcomes could be the outgrowth of impaired biological function; for example, there is evidence that prenatal exposure to nicotine interferes with the development of the serotonergic system, interfering with neurogenesis, and with the expression of receptors that affect synaptic functioning (Hellström-Lindahl et al., 2001; Falk et al., 2005). Tobacco exposure may also interfere with the development of brain areas related to self-regulation (e.g., the prefrontal cortex), which then leads to poorer self-control and an

increase in emotional and behavioural problems over time (Marroun et al., 2014).

We must note, however, that there is an ongoing debate in the literature as to whether this is a causal relationship, or whether this is a third variable problem; in particular, there are a variety of familial risk factors (e.g., poverty, low parental education, etc.) that are related both to smoking during pregnancy and to the various developmental deficits that have been reported. Recent studies that attempted to statistically account for these third variable factors are somewhat inconclusive; some find very little direct relationship between maternal smoking during pregnancy and children's development, whereas other report specific relationships that cannot be explained as being due to other variables. The jury is still out, but on the whole, researchers tentatively conclude that maternal smoking during pregnancy has a causal influence on various developmental outcomes (Melchior et al., 2015; Palmer et al., 2016).

Smoking is implicated in other risk-factors for infants as well, perhaps most notably being the tragedy of sudden infant death syndrome (SIDS). Babies exposed to smoke are as much as three times more likely to die from SIDS (Centers for Disease Control and Prevention [CDC], 2009a; Rogers, 2009). Even exposure to second-hand smoke during pregnancy carries similar risks (Best, 2009). Thankfully, after major public health campaigns, the rate of SIDS has been declining substantially, dropping in Canada by 71% from 1981 to 2009 (Public Health Agency of Canada, 2014). These campaigns targeted three key behaviours: breast-feeding, putting infants to sleep on their backs (rather than their stomachs), and reducing smoking during pregnancy. To be fair, researchers don't know how much each of these individual behaviours have contributed to the reduction in SIDS. Researchers will continue trying to disentangle exactly what factors are related to reductions in rates of SIDS so that campaigns can even more effectively target the factors that make the biggest difference.

Clearly, teratogens exact a major cost on society, causing deficits that range from very specific (e.g., improperly formed limbs), to more general effects on development (e.g., premature birth causing overall low birth weight).

Working the Scientific Literacy Model

The Long-Term Effects of Premature Birth

The human mother's womb has evolved to be a close-to-ideal environment for a fetus's delicate brain and body to prepare for life outside the womb. Premature birth thrusts the vulnerable baby into a much less congenial environment before she is ready; what effects does this have on development?

What do we know about premature birth?

Typically, humans are born at a gestational age of around 40 weeks. **Preterm infants** *are born earlier than 36 weeks.* Premature babies often have underdeveloped brains and lungs, which present a host of immediate challenges, such as breathing on their own and maintaining an appropriate body temperature. With modern medical care, babies born at 30 weeks have a very good chance of surviving (approximately 95%), although for those born at 25 weeks, survival rates drop to only slightly above 50% (Dani et al., 2009; Jones et al., 2005). Although babies born at less than 25 weeks often survive, they run a very high risk of damage to the brain and other major organs. To try to reduce these risks and improve outcomes as much as possible, medical science is continually seeking better procedures for nurturing preterm infants.

How can science be used to help preterm infants?

Researchers and doctors have compared different methods for improving survival and normal development in preterm infants. One program, called the Newborn Individualized Developmental Care and Assessment Program (NIDCAP), is a behaviourally based intervention in which preterm infants are closely observed and given intensive care during early development. To keep the delicate brain protected against potentially harmful experiences, NIDCAP calls for minimal lights, sound levels, and stress.

Controlled studies suggest that this program works. Researchers randomly assigned 117 infants born at 29 weeks or less gestational age to receive either NIDCAP or standard care in a prenatal intensive care unit. Within 9 months of birth, the infants who received the NIDCAP care showed significantly improved motor skills, attention, and other behavioural skills, as well as superior brain development (McAnulty et al., 2009). A longitudinal study indicates that these initial gains last for a long time. Even at eight years of age, those who were born preterm and given NIDCAP treatment scored higher on measures of thinking and problem solving, and also showed better frontal lobe functioning, than children who were born preterm but did not have NIDCAP treatment (McAnulty et al., 2010).

Can we critically evaluate this research?

The chief limitation of this longitudinal study is its small sample size (only 22 children across the two conditions). Such a small sample size presents problems from a statistical perspective, increasing the likelihood that random chance plays a substantial role in the results. Small samples also make it difficult to test the effects of interacting factors, such as whether the effectiveness of the program

Kangaroo care—skin-to-skin contact between babies and caregivers—is now encouraged for promoting optimal infant development.

may depend on the child's gender, on family socioeconomic status, ethnicity, or other factors. This study also does not identify *why* the program works—what specific mechanisms it affects that in turn improve development. It is not known which brain systems are beneficially affected by the program, or which aspects of the treatment itself are responsible for the effects. These remain questions for future research.

Why is this relevant?

Worldwide, an estimated 9% of infants are born preterm (Villar et al., 2003). For these children, medical advances have increased the likelihood of survival, and behaviourally based interventions such as NIDCAP may reduce the chances of long-term negative effects of preterm birth. This fits with a growing literature on other behavioural interventions that have shown promise in improving outcomes for preterm infants. For example, massaging preterm infants for a mere 15 minutes per day can result in a 50% greater daily weight gain (Field et al., 2006) and reduce stress-related behaviours (Hernandez-Reif et al., 2007). Another method called *kangaroo care* focuses on promoting skin-to-skin contact between infants and caregivers, and encouraging breastfeeding. These practices have been shown to improve the physical and psychological health of preterm infants (Conde-Agudelo et al., 2011), and are becoming widely adopted into mainstream medical practice.

The fact that teratogens can influence the development of the fetal brain—and in some cases lead to premature birth—has made (most) parents quite vigilant about these potential dangers. As you've read in this section, these concerns are well-founded. However, it is also important that parents examine the evidence for each potential threat

Victoria Boland Photography/Flickr/Getty Images

Myths in Mind
Vaccinations and Autism

When you consider all the attention paid to developing better ways to promote healthy infant development, it is ironic and tragic that a surprising number of people actively avoid one of the key ways of preventing some of the most serious childhood illnesses—vaccination. A major controversy erupted in the late 1990s about a widely administered vaccine designed to prevent measles, mumps, and rubella (MMR). Research from one British lab linked the MMR vaccine to the development of autism, and even though the science was later discredited and the key researcher (Andrew Wakefield) lost his license to practise medicine, he continued to promote his views against vaccines through public speaking appearances and rallies, and the anti-vaccine movement remained convinced that vaccines were scarier than the diseases they prevented.

The net result has been a public health tragedy. For example, in Canada, measles was considered to have been eliminated as an endemic disease by 1997; any further cases would have to have been imported from other areas of the world. The United States followed shortly thereafter, eliminating measles by the year 2000, with less than 100 new cases imported into the country each year, which were easily dealt with because of large-scale immunity. However, as the anti-vaccine movement continued to proselytize its conspiracy theories about the medical establishment and pharmaceutical industries, these gains began to reverse. By 2011, more than 30 European countries, plus Canada and the U.S., saw huge spikes in measles cases, with worrying outbreaks occurring in France, Quebec, and California (CDC 2015; Sherrard et al., 2015).

The take-home message? There is no evidence that vaccines cause autism. On the contrary, all the evidence suggests that vaccines prevent far more problems than they may cause.

---

to see if it is credible. In Module 2.3, we briefly discussed Andrew Wakefield, a British researcher who fabricated some of his data showing a link between vaccinations and autism. In that module, we focused on the ethical violations that he committed. The Myths in Mind box illustrates how this researcher's lapse in ethics has had a profound effect on the health and safety of tens of thousands of innocent children.

Module 10.1b Quiz:
Zygotes to Infants: From One Cell to Billions

Know . . .

1. A developing human is called a(n) _____ during the time between weeks 2 and 8 of development.
   A. embryo
   B. zygote
   C. fetus
   D. germinal

2. In which stage do the skeletal, organ, and nervous systems become more developed and specialized?
   A. Embryonic stage
   B. Fetal stage
   C. Germinal stage
   D. Gestational stage

Understand . . .

3. Which of the following would *not* qualify as a teratogen?
   A. Cigarette smoke
   B. Alcohol
   C. Prescription drugs
   D. All of the above are possible teratogens

Analyze . . .

4. Which of the following statements best summarizes the effects of preterm birth?
   A. Preterm births are typically fatal.
   B. The worrisome effects of preterm birth are exaggerated. There is little to worry about.
   C. Preterm birth may cause physical and cognitive problems.
   D. Cohort effects make it impossible to answer this question.

Sensory and Motor Development in Infancy

Compared to the offspring of other species, healthy newborn humans have fairly limited abilities. Horses, snakes, deer, and many other organisms come into the world with a few basic skills, such as walking (or slithering), that enable them to move about the world, get food, and have at least a chance of evading predators. But human infants depend entirely on caregivers to keep them alive as they slowly develop their senses, strength, and coordination. In this section, we shift our focus to newborns to find out how movement and sensation develop in the first year of life.

It's strange to think about what the world of an infant must be like. As adults, we depend heavily on our top-down processes (see Module 4.1) to help us label, categorize, perceive, and make sense of the world, but infants have developed very few top-down patterns when they are born. Their brains are pretty close to being "blank slates," and life must be, as William James so aptly put it, a "blooming, buzzing confusion."

However, babies aren't quite as "blank" as we have historically assumed. In fact, they are even starting to perceive and make sense of their world while still in the womb. By month four of prenatal development, the brain starts receiving signals from the eyes and ears. By seven to eight months, not only can infants hear, they seem to be actually listening. This amazing finding comes from studies in which developing fetuses were exposed to certain stimuli, and then their preference for these stimuli was tested upon birth. In one study, mothers read stories, including *The Cat in the Hat*, twice daily during the final six weeks of pregnancy. At birth, their babies were given a pacifier that controlled a tape recording of their mother's voice reading different stories. Babies sucked the pacifier much more to hear their mothers read *The Cat in the Hat* compared to hearing stories the moms had not read to them in the womb (DeCasper & Spence, 1986). Newborn babies also show a preference for their mother's voice over other women's voices. For example, a study involving researchers at Queen's University showed that babies responded positively when they heard poems read by their mother, but not when the poems were read by a stranger (Kisilevsky et al., 2003). (Unfortunately for fathers, babies up to at least 4 months old don't prefer their dad's voice over other men's [DeCasper & Prescott, 1984; Ward & Cooper, 1999].)

The auditory patterning of babies' brains is so significant that they have already started to internalize the sounds of their own native tongue, even before they are born. Recently, researchers analyzed the crying sounds of 60 babies born to either French or German parents and discovered that babies actually cry with an accent. The cries of French babies rose in intensity toward the end of their cry while German babies started at high intensity and then trailed off. This difference was apparent at only a few days of age and reflects the same sound patterns characteristic of their respective languages (Mampe et al., 2009). So, babies are actively learning about their cultural environment even while in the womb.

The visual system is not as well developed at birth, however. Enthusiastic family members who stand around making goofy faces at a newborn baby are not really interacting with the child; newborns have only about 1/40th of the visual acuity of adults (Sireteanu, 1999), and can only see about as far away as is necessary to see their mother's face while breastfeeding (about 30 cm or less). It takes

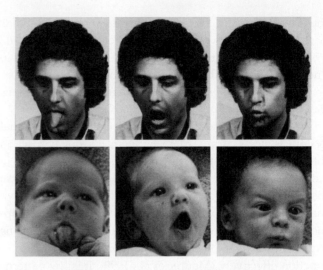

At just a few days of age, infants will imitate the facial expressions of others (Meltzoff & Moore, 1977).
From Meltzoff, A. N., & Moore, M. K. (1977). Imitation of facial and manual gestures by human neonates. *Science, 198*, 75–78.

6 months or more before they reach 20/20 visual acuity. Colour vision, depth perception, and shape discrimination all get a slow start as well. Colour discrimination happens at about 2 months of age, depth perception at 4 months, and it takes a full 8 months before infants can perceive shapes and objects about as well as adults (Csibra et al., 2000; Fantz, 1961). Nevertheless, even newborns are highly responsive to visual cues if they're close enough to see them. They will track moving objects, and will stare intently at objects they haven't seen before, although after a while they habituate to an object and lose interest in looking at it (Slater et al., 1988).

Babies' visual responses to the world illustrate a major theme within psychology, which is that humans are fundamentally social creatures. By a few days of age, newborns will imitate the facial expressions of others (Meltzoff & Moore, 1977). Newborns prefer to look at stimuli that look like faces, compared to stimuli that have all the same features but are scrambled so that they don't look like faces (see Figure 10.3). Infants also take longer to habituate to

Figure 10.3 Experimental Stimuli for Studying Visual Habituation in Infants

Infants were shown three types of stimuli, a face-like stimulus, a neutral stimulus, and a scrambled-face stimulus.

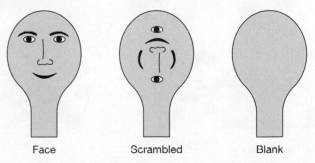

Face   Scrambled   Blank

the face-like stimuli, suggesting that the human face holds particular importance even for newborns (Johnson et al., 1991). This social attuning was dramatically illustrated in one study (Reissland, 1988), which showed that within *one hour* of birth, newborns begin to imitate facial expressions that they see!

Interestingly, the proper development of the visual system is not guaranteed to happen; it's not hardwired into our genes. Instead, the visual system develops in response to the infant experiencing a world of diverse visual input. Research at McMaster University has shown that even though babies possess the necessary "equipment" for proper vision, this equipment needs to be exposed to a diverse visual world in order to learn how to function effectively (Maurer et al., 1999); it is the patterns in the world which develop the appropriate neural pathways in the visual cortex (see Module 4.2).

Although being exposed to a complex world is essential for the development of the human visual system, *interacting* with this world is also necessary for the visual system to properly develop. This was illustrated by research involving an ingenious device—*the visual cliff*. Originally, researchers in 1960 (Gibson & Walk, 1960) found that infants would be reluctant to crawl over the deep side, seeming to understand depth and danger right from birth. However, researchers eventually discovered that only babies who had some experience crawling showed fear of the deep end (Campos et al., 1992).

In contrast to vision, the taste and olfactory systems are relatively well developed at birth. Similar to adults, newborns cringe when they smell something rotten or pungent (such as ammonia), and they show a strong preference for the taste of sweets. Odours are strong memory cues for infants as well. For example, infants can learn that a toy will work in the presence of one odour but not others, and they can retain this memory over several days (Schroers et al., 2007). Newborn infants can also smell the difference between their mother's breastmilk and that of a stranger. Infants even turn their heads toward the scent of breastmilk, which helps to initiate nursing (Porter & Winberg, 1999).

MOTOR DEVELOPMENT IN THE FIRST YEAR

Although the motor system takes many years to develop a high degree of coordination (good luck getting an infant to wield a steak knife), the beginnings of the motor system develop very early. A mere five months after conception, the fetus begins to have control of voluntary motor movements. In the last months of gestation, the muscles and nervous system are developed enough to demonstrate basic **reflexes**—*involuntary muscular reactions to specific types of stimulation*. These reflexes provide newborns and infants with a set of innate responses for feeding and interacting with their caregivers (see Table 10.2 for a partial list of important infant reflexes). We evolved these reflexes because they help the infant survive (e.g., the rooting reflex helps the infant find and latch onto the breast; the grasping reflex helps the infant hold onto the caregiver, which was probably pretty important especially for our tree-dwelling ancestors), and they often begin the motor learning process that leads to the development of more complex motor skills (e.g., there is a stepping reflex that may help the infant learn to better sense and control her legs in order to support eventual walking behaviour).

Interestingly, reflexes also provide important diagnostic information concerning the infant's development. If the infant is developing normally, most of the primary, basic reflexes should disappear by the time the infant is about 6 months old, as the motor processes involved in these reflexes become integrated into the child's developing neurology, in particular, the sensorimotor systems. The outcome of this integration is a pretty big deal—voluntary control over the body. Thus, if these reflexes persist longer than about six months, this may indicate neural issues that may interfere with developing proper motor control (Volpe, 2008).

Over the first 12 to 18 months after birth, infants' motor abilities progress through fairly reliable stages—from crawling, to standing, to walking (see Figure 10.4). Although the majority of infants develop this way, there is still some variability; for example, some infants largely bypass the crawling stage, developing a kind of bum-sliding movement instead, and then proceed directly to standing and walking. The age at which infants can perform each of these movements differs from one individual to the next. In contrast to reflexes, the development of motor skills seems to rely more on practice and deliberate effort, which in turn is related to environmental influences, such as cultural practices. For example, Jamaican mothers typically expect their babies to walk earlier than British or Indian mothers, and sure enough, Jamaican babies do

Mark Richard/PhotoEdit, Inc.

The visual cliff.

Table 10.2 A Few Key Infant Reflexes

THE ROOTING REFLEX

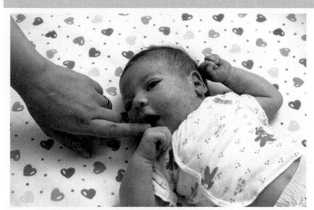

Cathy Melloan Resources/PhotoEdit, Inc.

The *rooting reflex* is elicited by stimulation to the corners of the mouth, which causes infants to orient themselves toward the stimulation and make sucking motions. The rooting reflex helps the infant begin feeding immediately after birth.

THE MORO REFLEX

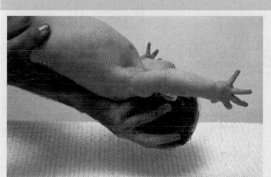

Petit Format/Photo Researchers, Inc./Science Source

The *Moro reflex*, also known as the "startle" reflex, occurs when infants lose support of their head. Infants grimace and reach their arms outward and then inward in a hugging motion. This may be a protective reflex that allows the infant to hold on to the mother when support is suddenly lost.

THE GRASPING REFLEX

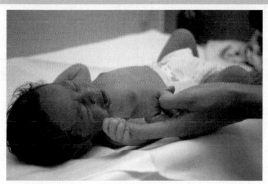

Denise Hager/Catchlight Visual Services/Alamy Stock Photo

The *grasping reflex* is elicited by stimulating the infant's palm. The infant's grasp is remarkably strong and facilitates safely holding on to one's caregiver.

walk earlier, likely because they are given more encouragement and opportunities to learn (Hopkins & Westra, 1989; Zelazo et al., 1993).

One area of the body that undergoes astonishing development during infancy is the brain. Although the major brain structures are all present at birth, they continue developing right into adulthood. One key change is the myelination of axons (see Module 3.2), which begins prenatally, accelerates through infancy and childhood, and then continues gradually for many years. Myelination is centrally important for the proper development of the infant, and occurs in a reliable sequence, starting with tactile and kinesthetic systems (involving sensory and motor pathways), then moving to the vestibular, visual, and auditory systems (Espenschade & Eckert, 1980; Deoni et al., 2011). Myelination of sensorimotor systems allows for the emergence of voluntary motor control (Espenschade & Eckert, 1980). By 12 months of age, the myelination of motoric pathways can be seen in the infant's newfound abilities to stand and balance, begin walking, and gain voluntary control over the pincer grasp (pressing the forefinger and thumb together).

Figure 10.4 Motor Skills Develop in Stages

This series shows infants in different stages of development: (a) raising the head, (b) rolling over, (c) propping up, (d) sitting up, (e) crawling, and (f) walking.

(a)   (b)

(c)   (d)   (e)   (f)

Top, left: bendao/Shutterstock; top, right: Bubbles Photolibrary/Alamy Stock Photo; bottom, left: imageBROKER/Glow Images; bottom, centre left: OLJ Studio/Shutterstock; bottom, centre right: Corbis Bridge/Alamy Stock Photo; bottom, right: Eric Gevaert/Shutterstock

Two other neural processes, synaptogenesis and synaptic pruning, further help to coordinate the functioning of the developing brain. **Synaptogenesis** describes *the forming of new synaptic connections*, which occurs at blinding speed through infancy and childhood and continues through the lifespan. **Synaptic pruning**, *the loss of weak nerve cell connections*, accelerates during brain development through infancy and childhood (Figure 10.5), then tapers off until adolescence (see Module 10.3). Synaptogenesis and synaptic pruning serve to increase neural efficiency by

Figure 10.5 The Processes of Synaptic Pruning

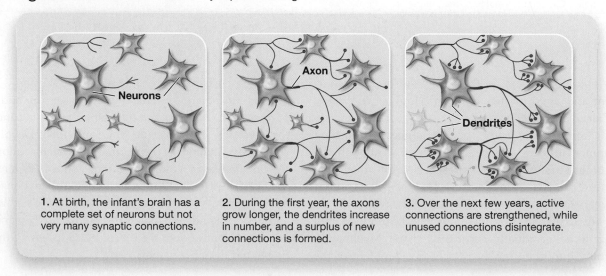

1. At birth, the infant's brain has a complete set of neurons but not very many synaptic connections.

2. During the first year, the axons grow longer, the dendrites increase in number, and a surplus of new connections is formed.

3. Over the next few years, active connections are strengthened, while unused connections disintegrate.

strengthening needed connections between nerve cells and weeding out unnecessary ones.

In summary, the journey from zygote to *you* begins dramatically, with biological pathways being formed at a breakneck pace both prenatally and after birth, giving rise to sensory and motor abilities that allow infants to become competent perceivers and actors in the external world. Most motor abilities require substantial time for infants to learn to coordinate the many different muscles involved, which depends heavily on infants' interactions with the environment. From the very beginnings of our lives, nature and nurture are inextricably intertwined.

Module 10.1c Quiz:
Sensory and Motor Development in Infancy

Know . . .

1. Three processes account for the main ways in which the brain develops after birth. These three processes are
   A. myelination, synaptogenesis, and synaptic pruning.
   B. myelination, synaptic reorganization, and increased neurotransmitter production.
   C. synaptogenesis, synaptic pruning, and increased neurotransmitter production.
   D. cell growth, myelination, and synaptic organization.

Understand . . .

2. The development of infant motor skills is best described as
   A. a genetic process with no environmental influence.
   B. completely due to the effects of encouragement.
   C. a mixture of biological maturation and learning.
   D. progressing in continuous, rather than stage, fashion.

Module 10.1 Summary

10.1a   Know . . . the key terminology related to prenatal and infant physical development.

cohort effect
cross-sectional design
developmental psychology
embryonic stage
fetal alcohol syndrome
fetal stage
germinal stage
longitudinal design
preterm infant
reflexes
synaptic pruning
synaptogenesis
teratogen
zygote

10.1b   Understand . . . the pros and cons to different research designs in developmental psychology.

Cross-sectional designs, in which a researcher studies a sample of people at one time, have the advantage of being faster, and generally cheaper, allowing research to be completed quickly; however, they may suffer from cohort effects because people of different ages in the sample are also from somewhat different historical time periods and, thus, any differences between them could reflect a historical process and not a developmental one. Longitudinal designs, in which a researcher follows a sample of people over a span of time, have the advantage of being able to track changes in the same people, thus giving more direct insight into developmental processes. However, such studies take longer to complete, thus slowing down the research process, and they can suffer from attrition, in which people drop out of the study over time.

10.1c   Apply . . . your understanding to identify the best ways expectant parents can ensure the health of their developing fetus.

The key to healthy fetal development is ensuring a chemically ideal environment. The most important factors are adequate nutrition and avoiding teratogens. Best nutritional practices include approximately a 20% increase in the mother's caloric intake, additional protein, and ensuring sufficient quantities of essential nutrients (which usually involves taking nutritional supplements). Avoiding teratogens involves giving up smoking and drinking alcohol, and getting good medical advice concerning any medications that the expectant mother may be taking.

10.1d   Analyze . . . the effects of preterm birth.

Health risks increase considerably with very premature births (e.g., those occurring at just 25 weeks' gestation). Use of proper caregiving procedures, especially personalized care that emphasizes mother–infant contact, breastfeeding, and minimal sensory stimulation for the underdeveloped brain, increases the chances that preterm infants will remain healthy.

Module 10.2 Infancy and Childhood: Cognitive and Emotional Development

Getty Images

Learning Objectives

10.2a Know . . . the terminology associated with infancy and childhood.

10.2b Understand . . . the cognitive changes that occur during infancy and childhood.

10.2c Understand . . . the importance of attachment and the different styles of attachment.

10.2d Apply . . . the concept of scaffolding and the zone of proximal development to understand how to best promote learning.

10.2e Analyze . . . how to effectively discipline children in order to promote moral behaviour.

Many parents have turned to Disney's Baby Einstein *line of books, toys, and DVDs in hopes of entertaining and enriching their children. These materials certainly are entertaining enough that children watch them. But do they work? Do these products actually increase cognitive skills? The advertising pitch is certainly persuasive, arguing that these products were designed to help babies explore music, art, language, science, poetry, and nature through engaging images, characters, and music. How could that be bad? However, the American Academy of Pediatrics recommends that children younger than two years should not watch television at all, based on research showing that memory and language skills are slower to develop in infants who regularly watch television (Christakis, 2009). Further, research specifically on* Baby Einstein *videos has shown that they have no effect on vocabulary development (Richert et al., 2010; Robb et al., 2009). Instead of watching commercial programs on electronic screens, reading with caregivers turns out to be related to greater vocabulary comprehension and production. Thus, using the "electronic babysitter" might be justifiable in order to give parents a break* *or let them get some things done, but caregivers shouldn't fool themselves into thinking that it's actually promoting their children's development.*

Focus Questions

1. Which types of activities do infants and young children need for their psychological development?

2. Why are social interactions so important for healthy development?

≫ The transition from baby to toddler is perhaps the most biologically and behaviourally dramatic time in people's lives. It is a mere year or two during which we grow from highly incapable, drooling babies, to highly coordinated and capable children. The physical, cognitive, and social transitions that occur between infancy and childhood are remarkably ordered, yet are also influenced by individual genetic and sociocultural factors. In this module, we integrate some important stage perspectives to explain psychological development through childhood.

One key insight to emerge from several lines of research is that for many systems, certain periods of development seem to be exceptionally important for long-term functioning. A **sensitive period** is *a window of time during which exposure to a specific type of environmental stimulation is needed for normal development of a specific ability.* For example, to become fluent in language, infants need to be exposed to speech during their first few years of life. Long-term deficits can emerge if the needed stimulation, such as language, is missing during a sensitive period. Sensitive periods of development are a widespread phenomenon. They have been found in humans and other species for abilities such as depth perception, balance, recognition of parents and, in humans at least, identifying with a particular culture (Cheung et al., 2011). However, although sensitive periods can explain the emergence of many perceptual (and some cognitive) abilities, they are only one of many mechanisms underlying human development.

Over the past century, many psychologists have attempted to explain how children's mental abilities develop and expand. One of the most influential figures in this search was a Swiss psychologist named Jean Piaget (1896–1980).

Cognitive Changes: Piaget's Cognitive Development Theory

Jean Piaget developed many of his theories in an unorthodox manner: he studied his own family. However, this was not done in a casual manner. Piaget actively studied, made copious notes of his observations, and even ran specific tests and measurements on his own children as they were growing up. The theories that resulted from this extensive personal project laid much of the groundwork for the modern science of **cognitive development**—*the study of changes in memory, thought, and reasoning processes that occur throughout the lifespan.* In his own work, Piaget focused on cognitive development from infancy through early adolescence.

Piaget's central interest was in explaining how children learn to think and reason. According to Piaget, learning is all about accumulating and modifying knowledge, which involves two central processes that he called assimilation and accommodation. **Assimilation** is *fitting new information into the belief system one already possesses.* For example, young children may think that all girls have long hair and, as they encounter more examples of this pattern, they will assimilate them into their current understanding. Of course, eventually they will to run into girls with short hair or boys with long hair, and their beliefs will be challenged by this information. They may, at first,

misunderstand, assuming a short-haired girl is actually a boy and a long-haired boy is actually a girl. But over time they will learn that their rigid categories of long-haired girl and short-haired boy need to be altered. This is called **accommodation**, *a creative process whereby people modify their belief structures based on experience.* Our belief systems help us make sense of the world (assimilation), but as we encounter information that challenges our beliefs, we develop a more complex understanding of the world (accommodation). Deeply understanding assimilation and accommodation gets right to the heart of how to help people learn new things, as well as why people so often resist new information and may vigorously hold on to their beliefs.

Based on his observations of his children, Piaget concluded that cognitive development passes through four distinct *stages* from birth through early adolescence: the sensorimotor, preoperational, concrete operational, and formal operational stages. Passing out of one stage and into the next occurs when the child achieves the important developmental milestone of that stage (see Table 10.3).

THE SENSORIMOTOR STAGE: LIVING IN THE MATERIAL WORLD The earliest period of cognitive development is known as the **sensorimotor stage**; *this stage spans from birth to two years, during which infants' thinking about and exploration of the world are based on immediate sensory (e.g., seeing, feeling) and motor (e.g., grabbing, mouthing) experiences.* During this time, infants are completely immersed in the present moment, responding exclusively to direct sensory input. As soon as an object is out of sight and out of reach, it will cease to exist (at least in the minds of young infants): Out of sight, out of mind.

This is obviously not how the world works. Thus, the first major milestone of cognitive development proposed by Piaget is **object permanence**, *the ability to understand that objects exist even when they cannot be directly perceived.*

Table 10.3 Piaget's Stages of Cognitive Development

Stage	Description
Sensorimotor (0–2 years)	Cognitive experience is based on direct sensory experience with the world, as well as motor movements that allow infants to interact with the world. Object permanence is the significant developmental milestone of this stage.
Preoperational (2–7 years)	Thinking moves beyond the immediate appearance of objects. The child understands physical conservation and that symbols, language, and drawings can be used to represent ideas.
Concrete operational (7–11 years)	The ability to perform mental transformations on objects that are physically present emerges. Thinking becomes logical and organized.
Formal operational (11 years–adulthood)	The capacity for abstract and hypothetical thinking develops. Scientific reasoning becomes possible.

Object permanence is tested by examining reactions that infants have to objects when they cannot be seen. Children who have object permanence will attempt to reach around the barrier or will continue looking in the direction of the desired object.

To test for object permanence, Piaget would allow an infant to reach for a toy, and then place a screen or a barrier between the infant and the toy so that the toy was no longer visible to the infant. If the reaching or looking stopped, it would suggest that the infant did not have a mental representation of the object when it was not visible. This would indicate that the infant had not yet developed object permanence.

Notice that this is not a problem for a two-year-old child. He can be *very* aware that his favourite toy awaits him in another room while he has to sit at the dinner table; in fact, he might not be able to get the toy out of his mind, and may take revenge on the evil tyrants who won't get it for him by screaming throughout the meal.

THE PREOPERATIONAL STAGE: QUANTITY AND NUMBERS According to Piaget, once children have mastered sensorimotor tasks, they have progressed to the **preoperational stage** (ages two to seven). This stage is devoted to *language development, the use of symbols, pretend play, and mastering the concept of conservation* (discussed below). During this stage, children can think about physical objects, although they have not quite attained abstract thinking abilities. They may count objects and use numbers, yet they cannot mentally manipulate information or see things from other points of view.

This inability to manipulate abstract information is shown by testing a child's understanding of **conservation**, *the knowledge that the quantity or amount of an object is not the same as the physical arrangement and appearance of that object.* Conservation can be tested in a number of ways (see Figure 10.6). For example, in a *conservation of liquid* task, a child is shown two identical glasses, each containing the same amount of liquid. The researcher then pours the liquid from one glass into a differently shaped container, typically one that is taller and narrower. Although the amount of liquid is still the same, many children believe that the tall, thin glass contains more fluid because it looks

"bigger" (i.e., taller). The *conservation of number* task produces similar effects. In this task, a child is presented with two identical rows of seven pennies each (see the bottom part of Figure 10.6). The experimenter then spreads out one of the rows so that it is longer, but still has the same number of coins. If you ask the child, "Which row has more?" a three-year-old would likely point to the row that

---

Figure 10.6 Testing Conservation

A child views two equal amounts of fluid, one of which is then poured into a taller, narrower container. Children who do not yet understand conservation believe that there is more fluid in the tall container compared to the shorter one. A similar version of this task can be tested using equal arrays of separate objects.

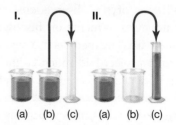

I.   II.

(a) (b) (c)   (a) (b) (c)

Row A
Row B

Which has more, row A or row B, or do they both have the same?

Row A
Row B

Now which has more, row A or row B, or do they both have the same?

Source: Lilienfeld, Scott O.; Lynn, Steven J; Namy, Laura L.; Woolf, Nancy J., *Psychology: From Inquiry To Understanding*, 2nd Ed., ©2011. Reprinted and Electronically reproduced by permission of Pearson Education, Inc., New York, NY.

was spread out because a child in the preoperational stage focuses on the simpler method of answering based on immediate perception, instead of applying more sophisticated mental operations (such as counting the pennies).

Although tests of conservation provide compelling demonstrations of the limits of children's cognitive abilities, Piaget's conclusions were not universally accepted. Some researchers have challenged Piaget's pessimism about the abilities of young children, arguing that their inability to perform certain tasks was a function of the child's interpretation of the task, not their underlying cognitive limitations (see the Working the Scientific Literacy Model feature). For example, when three-year-old children are presented with the pennies conservation task described above, but M&Ms are substituted for the pennies, everything changes. All of a sudden, children exhibit much more sophisticated thinking. If you put more M&Ms tightly packed together so they take up less space than a line of M&Ms that is more spread out, children will pick the more tightly packed but "smaller" row, understanding that it contains more candy—especially if they get to eat the candy from the row they choose (Mehler & Bever, 1967).

In fact, even before children start to use and understand numbers, they acquire a basic understanding of quantity. Very soon after they are born, infants appear to understand what it means to have *less* or *more* of something. This suggests that the infants who chose the longer row of pennies in the example above may simply have misunderstood the question, not the underlying rule of conservation. To them, *more* could simply have meant *longer*.

Although Piaget clearly underestimated the cognitive abilities of young children, researchers *have* identified common errors that very young children make but older children typically do not make. The children in Figure 10.7 are committing *scale* errors in the sense that they appear to interact with a doll-sized slide and a toy car as if they were the real thing, rather than miniatures (DeLoache et al., 2004). By 2 to 2½ years of age, scale errors decline as children begin to understand properties of objects and how they are related. This understanding is one of many advances children make as they progress toward more abstract thinking.

At around 3 years of age children begin to understand symbolic information. For example, 3-year-olds understand that a scale model of a room can symbolize an actual room (Figure 10.7). Children who view an experimenter placing a miniature toy within the scale model will quickly locate the actual toy when allowed to enter the room symbolized by the scale model (DeLoache, 1995). Abilities such as this are precursors to more advanced abilities of mental abstraction.

THE CONCRETE OPERATIONAL STAGE: USING LOGICAL THOUGHT Conservation is one of the main skills marking the transition from the preoperational stage to

Figure 10.7 Scale Errors and Testing for Scale Model Comprehension

The children in photos (a) and (b) are making scale errors. One child is attempting to slide down a toy slide and another is attempting to enter a toy car. Three-year-olds understand that a scale model represents an actual room (c). The adult pictured is using a scale model to indicate the location of a hidden object in an actual room of this type. At around 3 years of age, children understand that the scale model symbolizes an actual room and will go directly to the hidden object after viewing the scale model.

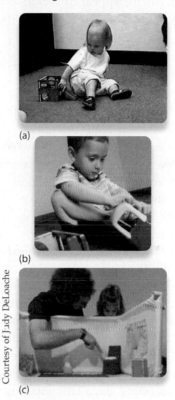

(a)

(b)

Courtesy of Judy DeLoache

(c)

the **concrete operational stage** *(ages 7 to 11 years), when children develop skills in logical thinking and manipulating numbers.* Children in the concrete operational stage are able to classify objects according to properties such as size, value, shape, or some other physical characteristic. Their thinking becomes increasingly logical and organized. For example, a child in the concrete operational stage recognizes that if X is more than Y, and Y is more than Z, then X is more than Z (a property called *transitivity*). This ability to think logically about physical objects sets the stage for them to think logically about abstractions in the fourth and final stage of cognitive development.

THE FORMAL OPERATIONAL STAGE: ABSTRACT AND HYPOTHETICAL THOUGHT The **formal operational stage** *(ages 11 to adulthood) involves the development of advanced cognitive processes such as abstract reasoning and hypothetical thinking.* Scientific thinking, such as gathering evidence and systematically testing possibilities, is characteristic of this stage.

Working the Scientific Literacy Model

Evaluating Piaget

Piaget was immensely successful in opening our eyes to the cognitive development of infants and children. Nevertheless, advances in testing methods have shown that he may have underestimated some aspects of infant cognitive abilities. In fact, infants appear to understand some basic principles of their physical and social worlds very shortly after birth.

What do we know about cognitive abilities in infants?

The **core knowledge hypothesis** proposes that *infants have inborn abilities for understanding some key aspects of their environment* (Spelke & Kinzler, 2007). It is a bold claim to say that babies know something about the world before they have even experienced it, so we should closely examine the evidence for this hypothesis.

How can *we* know what infants know or what they perceive? One frequently used method for answering this question relies on the habituation–dishabituation response. **Habituation** *refers to a decrease in responding with repeated exposure to an event.* For example, if an infant is shown the same stimulus over and over, she will stop looking at it. Conversely, infants are quite responsive to novelty or changes in their environment. Thus, if the stimulus suddenly changes, the infant will display **dishabituation,** *an increase in responsiveness with the presentation of a new stimulus.* In other words, the infant will return her gaze to the location that she previously found boring. Research on habituation and dishabituation in infants led to the

Lawrence Migdale / Photo Researchers, Inc. / Science Source

A popular method for testing infant cognitive abilities is to measure the amount of time infants look at stimuli. Researchers measure habituation and dishabituation to infer what infants understand.

development of measurement techniques based on what infants will look at and for how long. These techniques now allow researchers to test infants even younger than Piaget was able to.

How can science help explain infant cognitive abilities?

Measurement techniques based on what infants look at have been used to measure whether infants understand many different concepts, including abstract numbers—an ability that most people imagine appears much later in development. For example, Elizabeth Spelke and colleagues conducted a study in which 16 infants just *two days old* were shown sets of either 4 or 12 identical small shapes (e.g., yellow triangles, purple circles) on a video screen. The researchers also made a sound 4 or 12 times (e.g., tu-tu-tu-tu or ra-ra-ra-ra-ra-ra-ra-ra-ra-ra-ra-ra) at the same time they showed the shapes (see Figure 10.8). Researchers varied whether the number of shapes the infants saw matched the number of tones they heard (e.g., 4 yellow triangles and

Figure 10.8 Testing Infants' Understanding of Quantity

In this study, infants listened to tones that were repeated either 4 or 12 times while they looked at objects that had either 4 or 12 components. Infants spent more time looking at visual arrays when the number of items they saw matched the number of tones they heard.

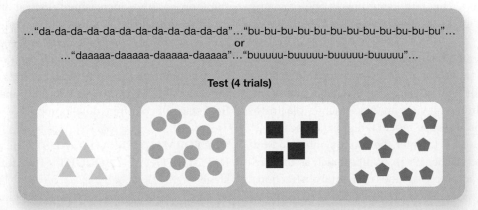

…"da-da-da-da-da-da-da-da-da-da-da-da"…"bu-bu-bu-bu-bu-bu-bu-bu-bu-bu-bu-bu"…
or
…"daaaaa-daaaaa-daaaaa-daaaaa"…"buuuuu-buuuuu-buuuuu-buuuuu"…

Test (4 trials)

Source: Figure 1 from "Newborn Infants Perceive Abstract Numbers" by V. Izard, C. Spann, E. S. Spelke, & A. Streri (2009), *Proceedings of the National Academy of Sciences*, 106, 10382–10385. Copyright © 2009. Reprinted by permission of PNAS.

4 "ra" tones), or not (e.g., 4 purple circles and 12 "ra" tones). The infants were most attentive when what they saw and heard matched. In other words, they looked longer at the shapes when the number of shapes matched the number of sounds, compared to when they did not match; this is taken as evidence that even very young infants have a rudimentary appreciation for abstract numbers (Izard et al., 2009).

Can we critically evaluate this research?

Many of the studies of early cognitive development discussed in this module used the "looking time" procedure, although not all psychologists agree that it is an ideal way of determining what infants understand or perceive (Aslin, 2007; Rivera et al., 1999). We cannot know exactly what infants are thinking, and perhaps they look longer at events and stimuli simply because these are more interesting rather than because they understand anything in particular about them. Inferring mental states that participants cannot themselves validate certainly leaves room for alternative explanations.

Also, the sample sizes in these studies are often fairly small, due to the cost and complexity of researching infants. In the study of shapes and tones just described, only 16 infants managed to complete the study. Forty-five others were too fussy or sleepy to successfully finish the task.

Why is this relevant?

The key insight provided by this research is that cognitive development in young infants is much more sophisticated than psychologists previously assumed. With each study that examines the cognitive capacities of infants, we learn that infants are not just slobbery blobs that need to be fed and diapered—though it certainly can feel that way when you are a new parent. Now we are learning that infants can understand more than we might expect, and can reason in more complex ways than we had believed.

One thing that parents and caregivers can learn from this research is to see their children as complex learners who use sensation and movement to develop their emerging cognitive abilities. Caregivers can encourage this process by talking to them using diverse vocabulary, exploring rhythm and music, allowing them to feel different objects, and exposing them to different textures and sensations.

Piaget's theories have had a lasting impact on modern developmental psychology. In addition to providing insights into the minds of young children, Piaget's work inspired numerous other researchers to study cognitive development. Many of these new discoveries complement, rather than entirely contradict, Piaget's foundational work.

COMPLEMENTARY APPROACHES TO PIAGET In the many decades since Piaget's work, psychologists have explored how children's social contexts affect their cognitive development. For example, in a learning context, other people can support and facilitate children's learning, or can make it more difficult. Children who try to master a skill by themselves may run into obstacles that would be easier to overcome with a little assistance or guidance from another person, or they may give up on a task when a little encouragement could have given them the boost needed to persevere and succeed. At the opposite extreme, children who have everything done for them and who are not allowed to work through problems themselves may become relatively incapable of finding solutions on their own, and may not develop feelings of competence that support striving for goals and overcoming challenges. Therefore, it seems reasonable to expect that optimal development will occur somewhere between the extremes of children doing everything on their own without any support, versus having others over-involved in their activities.

Russian psychologist Lev Vygotsky (1978) proposed that *development is ideal when children attempt skills and activities that are just beyond what they can do alone, but they have guidance from adults who are attentive to their progress;* this concept is termed the **zone of proximal development** (Singer & Goldin-Meadow, 2005). Teaching in order to keep children in the zone of proximal development is called **scaffolding**, *a highly attentive approach to teaching in which the teacher matches guidance to the learner's needs.*

Cross-cultural research on parent–infant interactions shows that scaffolding is exercised in different ways (Rogoff et al., 1993). For example, in one study, 12- to 24-month-old children were offered a toy that required pulling a string to make it move. Parents from Turkey, Guatemala, and the United States were observed interacting with their infants as they attempted to figure out how the toy worked. All parents used scaffolding when they spoke and gestured

Caregivers who are attentive to the learning and abilities of a developing child provide scaffolding for cognitive development.

to their children to encourage them to pull the string, but mother–child pairs from Guatemala were much more communicative with each other, both verbally and through gestures such as touching and using the direction of their gaze to encourage the behaviour. Over time, this kind of sensitive scaffolding should result in children who are more seamlessly integrated into the daily life of the family and community, rather than merely relegated to "play"

activities in specialized "kid-friendly" environments. This means that children who are appropriately scaffolded are able to be useful and self-sufficient at much earlier ages than is normal in contemporary North American society. This kind of scaffolding approach to everyday life tasks is one of the foundational practices in many alternative education systems, such as the Montessori system.

Module 10.2a Quiz:

Cognitive Changes: Piaget's Cognitive Development Theory

Know . . .

1. Recognizing that the quantity of an object does not change despite changes in its physical arrangement or appearance is referred to as _____.
   A. object permanence
   B. scale comprehension
   C. conservation
   D. number sense

2. Parents who attend to their children's psychological abilities and guide them through the learning process are using _____.
   A. scaffolding
   B. tutoring
   C. core knowledge
   D. the zone of proximal development

3. What is the correct order of Piaget's stages of cognitive development?
   A. Preoperational, sensorimotor, concrete operational, formal operational
   B. Sensorimotor, preoperational, formal operational, concrete operational

C. Sensorimotor, preoperational, concrete operational, formal operational
D. Preoperational, concrete operational, sensorimotor, formal operational

Apply . . .

4. A child in the sensorimotor stage may quit looking or reaching for a toy if you move it out of sight. This behaviour reflects the fact that the child has not developed _____.
   A. core knowledge
   B. object permanence
   C. conservation
   D. to the preoperational stage

Analyze . . .

5. Research on newborns indicates that they have a sense of number and quantity. What does this finding suggest about Piaget's theory of cognitive development?
   A. It confirms what Piaget claimed about infants in the sensorimotor phase.
   B. Some infants are born with superior intelligence.
   C. Piaget may have underestimated some cognitive abilities of infants and children.
   D. Culture determines what infants are capable of doing.

Social Development, Attachment, and Self-Awareness

It seems rather obvious to point out that human infants are profoundly dependent on their caregivers for pretty much everything, from food and relief from dirty diapers, to being held and soothed when they are upset. Based on Piaget's insight that the infant's experiential world is largely comprised of physical sensation and movement, one might expect that physical interactions with caregivers make up a huge part of an infant's reality. As a result, the infant's emerging feelings of safety and security, or conversely, fear and distress, may be highly affected by the basic, physical connection with caregivers.

Nowadays, it is perhaps not a stunning insight to realize that being touched and held, seeing facial expressions that are responsive to one's own, and hearing soothing

vocalizations, are important for helping infants to feel secure in what is otherwise a pretty big, unknown and potentially scary world. However, in the mid-20th century, it was a major insight to realize how sensitively attuned infants are to their social world, and how deeply they are affected by how they are treated by those they depend upon. Whether caregivers are loving and responsive, or perhaps neglectful or cruel, in the first months of life, can affect the developing child in ways that last for the rest of their lives.

Understanding the intense social bonding that occurs between humans revolves around the central concept of **attachment**, *the enduring emotional bond formed between individuals, initially between infants and caregivers.* Attachment motivations are deeply rooted in our psychology, compelling us to seek out others for physical and psychological comfort, particularly when we feel stressed or insecure

(Bowlby, 1951). Infants draw upon a remarkable repertoire of behaviours that are geared towards seeking attachment, such as crying, cooing, gurgling, and smiling, and adults are generally responsive to these rudimentary but effective communications.

WHAT *IS* ATTACHMENT?   In the early decades of modern psychology, dominant theories of motivation emphasized biological drives, such as hunger and thirst, that motivated people to satisfy their basic needs. From this perspective, the motivation that drove infants to connect with caregivers, like their mother, was simple; mom fed them, reducing their hunger, and thus, they developed a behavioural interdependence with mom, and through basic conditioning processes (i.e., associating mom with the pleasure and comfort of food), formed an emotional attachment with mom as well. Such a description of love is never going to fill a book of poetry, but it seemed to scientifically and objectively account for the infant–caregiver bond.

However, in the 1950s, a psychologist by the name of Harry Harlow made an extremely interesting observation, although one so seemingly innocuous that most of us likely would have overlooked it. Harlow was conducting research on infant rhesus monkeys, and was raising these monkeys in cages without any contact with their mothers. In the course of this research, he noticed that the baby monkeys seemed to cling passionately to the cloth pads that lined their cages, and they would become very distressed when these pads were removed for cleaning. This simple observation made Harlow start to wonder what function the pads served for the monkeys. The monkeys didn't eat the pads, obviously, so why should they be so attached to them?

Harlow designed an ingenious set of studies, testing whether it was physical comfort or primary drive reduction that drove the formation of attachment. He placed rhesus monkeys in cages, right from birth, and gave them two pseudo-mothers: one was a cylinder of mesh wire wrapped with soft terry-cloth, loosely resembling an adult monkey; the other was an identical cylinder but without the cloth covering. To then test whether reducing the monkeys' hunger was important for the formation of attachment, Harlow simply varied which of the "mothers" was the food source. For some monkeys, the terry-cloth mother had a bottle affixed to it and thus was the infant's food source, whereas for other monkeys, the bottle was affixed to the wire mother. The question was, who would the monkeys bond with? Did their emotional attachment actually depend on which of the "mothers" fed them?

The contest between mothers wasn't even close. No matter who had the bottle, the baby monkeys spent almost all their time with the cloth mother, pretty much ignoring the wire mother except for the small amount of time they spent actually feeding, when she had the bottle (see Figure 10.9). Furthermore, the monkeys seemed emotionally attached to the cloth mother, depending on her to meet their emotional needs. For example, researchers devised experiments in which the baby monkeys would be frightened (e.g., surprising them with a metallic contraption that looked like a vicious monster), and they would watch which mother the infants would run to for comfort and security. Over and over again, they ran to the cloth mother (the videos from this experiment are heartbreaking). The implications were clear—attachment is not about reducing fundamental biological drives; it's about feeling secure, which has a strong basis in feeling physically comforted.

TYPES OF ATTACHMENT   In order to measure attachment bonds in human infants, obviously it is unethical to raise babies in cages with fake mothers and then scare them half to death to see who they crawl to. Instead, psychologists have developed methods of studying infant attachment that are only mildly stressful and mimic natural situations. One method capitalizes on *stranger anxiety*—signs of distress that infants begin to show toward strangers at about eight months of age. Mary Ainsworth developed a measurement system, based on the belief that different characteristic patterns of responding to stranger anxiety indicated different types of emotional security, or attachment style.

Ainsworth (1978) developed a procedure called the **strange situation**, *a way of measuring infant attachment by observing how infants behave when exposed to different experiences that involve anxiety and comfort.* The procedure involves a sequence of scripted experiences that expose children to some mild anxiety (e.g., the presence of a

Nina Leen/The LIFE Picture Collection/Getty Images

A baby monkey clings to a cloth-covered object—Harlow called this object the *cloth mother*—even though in this case the wire "mother" provided food.

Figure 10.9 Harlow's Monkeys: Time Spent on Wire and Cloth Mother Surrogates

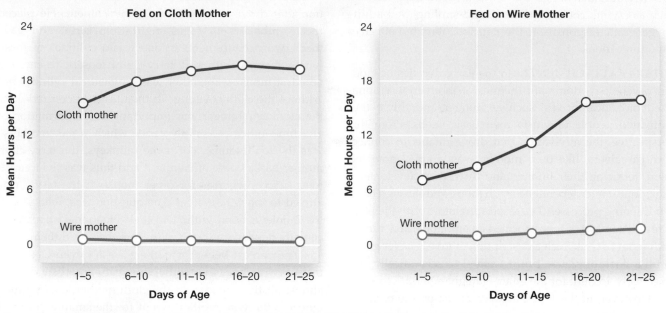

Source: Harlow, H. F. (1958). The nature of love. *American Psychologist*, 13(12), 673–685. From the American Psychological Association.

stranger, being left alone with the stranger), and the potential to receive some comfort from their caregiver. For example, the child and caregiver spend a few minutes in a room with some toys; a stranger enters, the caregiver leaves, and then the caregiver returns. In each segment of the procedure, the child's behaviour is carefully observed. Ainsworth noted three broad patterns of behaviour that she believed reflected three different attachment styles (see Figure 10.10):

1. *Secure attachment.* The caregiver is a secure base that the child turns toward occasionally, "checking in" for reassurance as she explores the room. The child shows some distress when the caregiver leaves, and avoids the stranger. When the caregiver returns, the child seeks comfort and her distress is relieved.

2. *Insecure attachment.* Two subtypes were distinguished:
   - *Anxious/Ambivalent.* The caregiver is a base of security, but the child depends too strongly on the caregiver, exhibiting "clingy" behaviours rather than being comfortable exploring the room on his own. The child is very upset when the caregiver leaves, and is quite fearful toward the stranger. When the caregiver returns, the child seeks comfort, but then also resists it and pushes the caregiver away, not allowing his distress to be easily alleviated.
   - *Avoidant.* The child behaves as though she does not need the caregiver at all, and plays in the room as though she is oblivious to the caregiver. The child is not upset when the caregiver leaves, and is unconcerned about the stranger. When the caregiver returns, the child does not seek contact.

3. Subsequent research identified a fourth attachment style, *disorganized* (Main & Solomon, 1990), which is best characterized by instability; the child has learned (typically through inconsistent and often abusive

Figure 10.10 The Strange Situation

Studies of attachment by Mary Ainsworth involved a mother leaving her infant with a stranger. Ainsworth believed that the infants' attachment styles could be categorized according to their behavioural responses to the mother leaving and returning.

Source: Lilienfeld, Scott O.; Lynn, Steven J; Namy, Laura L.; Woolf, Nancy J., *Psychology: From Inquiry To Understanding*, 2nd Ed., © 2011. Reprinted and Electronically reproduced by permission of Pearson Education, Inc., New York, NY.

experiences) that caregivers are sources of both fear and comfort, leaving the child oscillating between wanting to get away and wanting to be reassured. The child experiences a strong ambivalence, and reinforces this through his own inconsistent behaviour, seeking closeness and then pulling away, or often simply "freezing," paralyzed with indecision.

Attachment is important not only in infancy, but throughout one's life. Even in adult romantic relationships, attachment styles (gained during infancy!) are still at work (Hofer, 2006). The specific patterns of behaviour that characterize different attachment styles can be seen, albeit in somewhat more complex forms, in adult relationships (Hazan & Shaver, 1987; Mikulincer & Shaver, 2007). Attachment styles predict many different relationship behaviours, including how we form and dissolve relationships, specific issues and insecurities that arise in relationships, and likely patterns of communication and conflict. For example, in one large, longitudinal study spanning more than 20 years, people who were securely attached as infants were better able to recover from interpersonal conflict with their romantic partners (Salvatore et al., 2011). It appears that the father described at the beginning of Module 10.1 was correct; we really are similar to "giant babies."

DEVELOPMENT OF ATTACHMENT Given that attachment styles are so important, how do they form in the first place? Research consistently has shown that one's attachment style largely reflects one's early attachment experiences (e.g., whether caregivers tend to be loving, accepting, and responsive, or critical, rejecting, and unresponsive, or simply inconsistent and unpredictable). This makes sense; after all, attachment styles are understood to be learned patterns of behaviour that the developing child adopts in order to adapt to the key relationships in her life. This is a major insight for parents to take seriously, because the consequences of one's own behaviour as a parent can resonate throughout the rest of the child's life. Most important, perhaps, is parental responsiveness. For example, Ainsworth's research (Ainsworth, 1978) showed that maternal sensitivity (i.e., being highly attuned to the infant's signals and communication, and responding appropriately) is key to developing a secure attachment style. More contemporary research has expanded this to included non-maternal caregivers; yes Dads, you're important too.

At this point, especially if you feel you have somewhat of a less-than-secure attachment style, you might be wondering whether you are doomed to remain this way forever. After all, we have been emphasizing the long-term stability of attachment styles that are formed early in life. Nevertheless, it is important to note that attachment styles *can* change. Insecurely attached people can certainly find their attachment style becoming more secure through having supportive relationship experiences, whether they are intimate/romantic relationships or other sorts of supportive relationships such as one may establish with a therapist (Bowlby, 1988). The reason that attachment styles tend to be relatively consistent over time is that they tend to condition the same types of behaviour patterns and relationship outcomes that led to their formation in the first place. Just think about how much more difficult it would be for a highly avoidant or highly insecure and "needy" person to develop the sorts of patterns in relationships that would help them to feel loved and accepted, compared to somebody who is already secure. Nevertheless, if a person is able to establish healthy relationship patterns in adulthood, they can undo the effects of less-than-ideal early attachment experiences.

While it was initially believed that ideal parenting called for parents to be highly sensitive to the child, leading to closely coordinated emotional interactions between them, recent studies have shown that highly sensitive caregivers actually demonstrate *moderate* coordination with their children (Hane et al., 2003). Both under-responsiveness and over-involvement/hypersensitivity to an infant's needs and emotions are correlated with the development of insecure attachment styles (Beebe et al., 2010). The ideal parent does not reflexively respond to all the child's needs, but is sensitive to *how much* responsiveness the child needs. In the next section we will learn how this type of parental sensitivity is connected to the development of self-awareness, as well as to the ability to take other people's perspectives.

SELF AWARENESS Between 18–24 months of age, toddlers begin to gain **self-awareness**, *the ability to recognize one's individuality*. Becoming aware of one's self goes hand-in-hand with becoming aware of others as separate beings, and thus, self-awareness and the development of pro-social and moral motivations are intricately intertwined, as we discuss below.

The presence of self-awareness is typically tested by observing infants' reactions to their reflection in a mirror or on video (Bahrick & Watson, 1985; Bard et al., 2006). Self-awareness becomes increasingly sophisticated over the course of development, progressing from the ability to recognize oneself in a mirror to the ability to reflect on one's own feelings, decisions, and appearance. By the time children reach their fifth birthday, they become self-reflective, show concern for others, and are intensely interested in the causes of other people's behaviour.

Young children are often described as **egocentric**, *meaning that they only consider their own perspective* (Piaget & Inhelder, 1956). This does not imply that children are selfish or inconsiderate, but that they merely lack the cognitive ability to understand the perspective of others. For example, a two-year-old may attempt to hide by simply covering her own eyes. From her perspective, she *is* hidden.

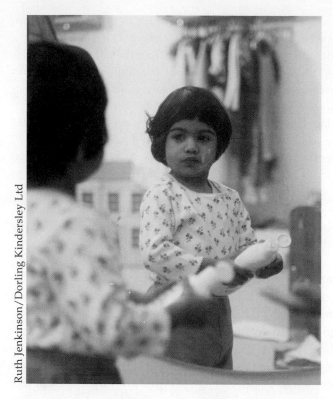

By two years of age, toddlers can recognize themselves in mirrors.

Ruth Jenkinson/Dorling Kindersley Ltd

Figure 10.11 Piaget's Test for Egocentric Perspective in Children

Piaget used the three-mountain task to test whether children can take someone else's perspective. The child would view the object from one perspective while another person viewed it from a different point of view. According to Piaget, children are no longer exclusively egocentric if they understand that the other person sees the object differently.

Source: Lilienfeld, Scott O.; Lynn, Steven J; Namy, Laura L.; Woolf, Nancy J., *Psychology: From Inquiry To Understanding*, 2nd Ed., © 2011. Reprinted and Electronically reproduced by permission of Pearson Education, Inc., New York, NY.

Piaget believed that children were predominantly egocentric until the end of the preoperational phase (ending around age seven). He tested for egocentrism by sitting a child in front of an object, and then presenting pictures of that object from four angles. While sitting opposite the child, Piaget would ask him or her to identify which image represented the object from Piaget's own perspective. Children's egocentricity was demonstrated by selecting the image corresponding to their own perspective, rather than being able to imagine what Piaget would be seeing (Figure 10.11).

Modern research indicates that children take the perspective of others long before the preoperational phase is complete. Perspective taking in young children has been demonstrated in studies of **theory of mind**—*the ability to understand that other people have thoughts, beliefs, and perspectives that may be different from one's own.* Consider the following scenario:

> *An experimenter offers three-year-old Andrea a box of chocolates. Upon opening the box, Andrea discovers not candy, but rather pencils. Joseph enters the room and she watches as Joseph is offered the same box. The researcher asks Andrea, "What does Joseph expect to find in the box?"*

If Andrea answers "pencils," this indicates that she believes Joseph knows the same thing she does. However, if Andrea tells the experimenter that Joseph expects to see chocolates, it demonstrates that she is taking Joseph's mental perspective, understanding that he does not possess her knowledge that the "chocolate box" actually contains

pencils (Lillard, 1998; Wimmer & Perner, 1983). Children typically pass this test at ages four to five, although younger children may pass it if they are told that Joseph is about to be tricked (Figure 10.12). Of course, the shift away from egocentric thought does not occur overnight. Older children may still have difficulty taking the perspective of others; in fact, even adults aren't that great at it much of the time. Maintaining a healthy awareness of the distinction between self and other, and accepting the uniqueness of the other person's perspective is a continual process.

Psychological research now indicates that self-awareness and theory of mind are in constant development right from birth. Early in children's lives, emotions are often experienced as chaotic, overwhelming, and unintegrated combinations of physical sensations, non-verbal representations, and ideas. As caregivers respond to children's emotions, the children learn how to interpret and organize their emotions; this helps them become more aware of their own feelings (Fonagy & Target, 1997). As children gain the ability to understand their internal states with greater clarity, it enhances their ability to represent the mental states of others.

This process helps to explain why it is important that caregivers not over-identify with a child's emotions. If their emotional exchange is completely synchronized (e.g., the child experiences fear and the adult also experiences fear) then the child simply gets her fear reinforced, rather than gaining the ability to *understand* that she is feeling fear.

Figure 10.12 A Theory-of-Mind Task

There are different methods of testing false beliefs. In this example, Andrea is asked what she thinks Joseph expects to find in the "chocolate box." If she has developed theory-of-mind skills, she will be able to differentiate between her knowledge of the box's contents (pencils) and what Joseph would expect to find (chocolates).

In a study of how mothers behave after their infants received an injection, Fonagy et al. (1995) observed that the mothers who most effectively soothed their child reflected their child's emotions, but also included other emotional displays in their mirroring, such as smiling or questioning. The mother's complex representation of the child's experience ensured that the child recognized it as related to, but not identical to his own emotion. This serves to alter the child's negative emotions by helping him to implicitly build coping responses into the experience (Fonagy & Target, 1997). Therefore, in the early stages of life, these face-to-face exchanges of emotional signals help the child's brain learn how to understand and deal with emotions (Beebe et al., 1997).

Module 10.2b Quiz:
Social Development, Attachment, and Self-Awareness

Know . . .

1. The emotional bond that forms between a caregiver and a child is referred to as _____.
   A. a love–hate relationship
   B. dependence
   C. attachment
   D. egocentrism

Understand . . .

2. Infants who are insecurely attached may do which of the following when a parent leaves and then returns during the strange situation procedure?
   A. Show anger when the parent leaves but happiness when they return
   B. Show anger when the parent leaves and show little reaction when they return
   C. Refuse to engage with the stranger in the room
   D. Show happiness when the parent leaves and anger when they return

Apply . . .

3. Oliver and his dad read a book several times. In that book, the main character expects to receive a hockey sweater for his birthday. However, due to a mix-up at the store, the gift box instead contains a pair of shoes. Because Oliver had read the book several times, he remembered that the box contained shoes. If Oliver was seven years old, what do you think he would say if he was asked, "What does the main character *think* is in the box?" What would his two-year-old sister say if asked the same question?
   A. Oliver would say that the character thought the box contained a hockey sweater; his sister would say that the character would expect to find shoes.
   B. Oliver would say that the character thought the box contained a shoes; his sister would say that the character would expect to find a hockey sweater.
   C. Both children would say that the main character would expect to find a hockey sweater in the gift box.
   D. Both children would say that the main character would expect to find a pair of shoes in the gift box.

4. A child who you know seems to behave inconsistently towards his parents; sometimes, he is quite "clingy" and dependent, but other times is very independent and rejects the parents' affection. This is descriptive of a(n) _____ attachment style.
   A. secure
   B. anxious/ambivalent
   C. avoidant
   D. disorganized

Psychosocial Development

In the previous section, we saw the powerful effect that attachment can have on a child's behaviour. Importantly, we also saw that attachment-related behaviours that are observed in infants and young children can sometimes predict how those individuals will behave as adults. This shows us that our development is actually a life-long process rather than a series of isolated stages.

A pioneer in the study of *development across the lifespan* was Erik Erikson, a German-American psychologist (who married a Canadian dancer). He proposed a theory of development consisting of overlapping stages that extend from infancy to old age. In this module, we will examine the stages of development that relate to infancy and childhood. We will return to Erikson's work again in Modules 10.3 (Adolescence) and 10.4 (Adulthood), each time discussing the parts of his theory that apply to those stages of development. Curious readers can look ahead to Table 10.5 in Module 10.4 to see a depiction of Erikson's model in its entirety.

DEVELOPMENT ACROSS THE LIFESPAN Erikson's theory of development across the lifespan included elements of both cognitive and social development. Erikson's theory centred around the notion that at different ages, people face particular developmental *crises*, or *challenges*, based on emotional needs that are most relevant to them at that stage of life. If people are able to successfully rise to the challenge and get their emotional needs met, then they develop in a healthy way. But, if this process is disrupted for some reason and people are not able to successfully navigate a stage, the rest of the person's personality and development could be impacted by certain deficits in their psychosocial functioning. For example, people could struggle with feeling worthless or useless, feeling insecure in relationships, feeling motivated, and so on. Understanding fully how Erikson's insights apply to specific problems people face lies beyond our discussion here, but you can make some reasonable inferences based on a general understanding of his theory.

The first stage, *Infancy*, focuses on the issue of *trust vs. mistrust*. The infant's key challenge in life is developing a basic sense of security, of feeling comfortable (or at least not terrified) in a strange and often indifferent world. Infants just want to know that everything is okay, and this starts with being held—being physically connected through touch and affectionate contact. As the infant develops more complex social relationships, their basic emotional security (or insecurity) grows out of the trust vs. mistrust that develops out of this stage.

The second stage, *Toddlerhood*, focuses on the challenge of *autonomy vs. shame*. The toddler, able to move herself about increasingly independently, is poised to discover a whole new world. The toddler discovers that she is a separate creature from others and from the environment; thus, exploring her feelings of *autonomy*—exercising her will as an individual in the world—becomes very important. (If you've ever hung out with a toddler for extended periods of time, you have probably experienced their stubborn resistance, like emphatically stating "No!" to whatever you have suggested, for no clear reason.)

By the end of the first two stages, the person is, ideally, secure, and they feel a basic sense of themselves as having separate needs from others. On the other hand, if these stages were not successfully navigated, the person may struggle with feelings of inadequacy or low self-worth, and these will play out in their subsequent development.

The third stage, *Early childhood*, is characterized as the challenge of *initiative vs. guilt*. Building on the emotional security and sense of self-assurance that comes from the first two stages, here the growing child learns to take responsibility for herself while feeling like she has the ability to influence parts of her physical and social world. These preschool-years involve children pushing their boundaries and experimenting with what they can do with their rapidly developing bodies, and then experiencing guilt when they are scolded or otherwise encounter the disapproval of others, such as their parents. If this stage is navigated successfully, the child develops increased confidence and a sense of personal control and responsibility.

The fourth stage, *Childhood*, is all about *industry vs. inferiority*. Here the child is focused on the tasks of life, particularly school and the various skill development activities that take place for that big chunk of childhood. This is an important part of the child's increasing feeling of being in control of her actions, leading her to be able to regulate herself to achieve long-term goals, develop productive habits, and gain a sense of herself as actively engaged in her own life.

Taking Erikson's first four stages together, you can see how childhood ties together emotional development with the feeling of being a competent individual. You can also see how the challenges associated with these stages are tied together with the quality of one's key relationships and the many complex ways in which others (e.g., parents) help or hinder the child's ability to meet their emotional needs.

PARENTING AND PROSOCIAL BEHAVIOUR One of the central questions of development that every parent faces when raising their own children is "How can I help this child become 'good'?" The capacity to be a moral person is often considered to begin around the time a child develops theory of mind (the sense of themselves and others as separate beings with separate thoughts). Certainly, being aware of one's emotions, and understanding the emotions of others, are important parts of prosocial motivations and behaviours. However, recent research seems to indicate that the basic capacity for morality is built right into us and manifests long before we develop the cognitive sophistication to recognize *self* and *others*. Children show a natural predisposition toward prosocial behaviour very early in their development (Hamlin et al., 2007; Warneken & Tomasello, 2013). Even one-day-old infants experience distress when they hear other infants cry, exhibiting a basic sense of empathy.

However, it is important to distinguish exactly what is meant by *empathy*. Surely, the one-day-old babies aren't actually lying there, aware of the perspectives of the other infants, recognizing that when an infant cries, he is sad, and then feeling sadness in response to that awareness. One-day-old infants don't have that much cognitive processing going on; there's no way they can engage in very complex perspective taking. Rather, they simply feel what is going on around them; they mirror the world around them in their own actual feelings, virtually without any filter at all.

What this means is that when children are very young, they experience others' distress directly as their own personal distress or discomfort. This makes them motivated primarily to reduce their own distress, not necessarily to help the other person (Eisenberg, 2005). Helping the other person might be one way to alleviate one's distress, but there might be easier ways, like ignoring them, or even shouting at them! For example, watching a parent cry is upsetting to a young child, and sometimes the child may seek to comfort the parent, such as by offering his teddy bear; other times, however, children might just close their eyes and plug their ears, or leave and go to a different room where they don't have to see the parent, thereby alleviating their own distress. Many developmental psychologists believe that in order for explicitly prosocial motives to develop, children must learn to attribute their negative feelings to *the other person's* distress, thereby becoming motivated to reduce the other person's suffering, not just their own reaction to it (Mascolo & Fischer, 2007; Zahn-Waxler & Radke-Yarrow, 1990).

Recently, researchers at the University of British Columbia and other universities demonstrated that the roots of moral motivation go back much further than we once believed, all the way to very early infancy. Studies using puppets engaging in kind and helpful, or nasty and selfish behaviours show that even very young infants (as young as three months old!) seem to know the difference between good and bad, and prefer others who are helpful (Hamlin et al., 2007, 2010). By eight months of age, infants make complex moral discriminations, preferring others who are kind to someone who is prosocial, but reversing this and preferring others who are unkind to someone who is antisocial (Hamlin et al., 2011). Thus, from the first months of our lives, long before we have been "taught right from wrong," we are able to recognize, and prefer, the good.

As children move into the toddler years, prosocial behaviours increase in scope and complexity. Around their first birthday, children demonstrate *instrumental helping*, providing practical assistance such as helping to retrieve an object that is out of reach (Liszkowski et al., 2006; Warneken & Tomasello, 2007). By their second birthday, they begin to exhibit *empathic helping*, providing help in order to make someone feel better (Zahn-Waxler et al., 1992). In one study, children younger than two were observed to be happier when giving to others over receiving treats themselves, even when the giving occurred at a cost to their own resources (Aknin et al., 2012).

PARENTING AND ATTACHMENT In humans, the tension between helping others versus being concerned for oneself reflects a kind of tug-of-war between two psychobiological systems, the **attachment behavioural system**, *which is focused on meeting our own needs for security*, and the **caregiving behavioural system**, *which is focused on meeting the needs of others*. Each system guides our behaviour when it is activated; however, the attachment system is primary, and if it is activated, it tends to shut down the caregiving system. What this means in everyday experience is that if a person feels insecure herself, it will be hard for her to take others' needs into consideration. However, if attachment needs are fulfilled, then the caregiving system responds to others' distress, motivating the person to care for others (Mikulincer & Shaver, 2005). Thus, raising kind, moral children is about helping them feel loved and secure, not just teaching them right from wrong.

This changes the emphasis in parenting, a lot! Consider the classic problems faced by all parents—they need kids to do certain things—get up, eat breakfast, get dressed, brush teeth, brush hair, pack a backpack for school, get lunch, leave the house on time, stop interrupting, be nice

to siblings. . . . It's no wonder many parenting books promise a simple, step-by-step method for getting children to behave the way parents want.

Faced with the constant challenge of managing their kids' behaviour, parents commonly turn to the principles of operant conditioning, using rewards (e.g., Smarties, physical affection, loving words) and punishments (e.g., angry tone of voice, time-outs, criticism) as necessary. Indeed, this is so pervasive that most of us don't think twice about it; how could rewarding good behaviour and punishing bad behaviour be a problem? However, children are not merely stimulus-response machines, and this pervasive use of *conditional approaches* (i.e., rewards and punishments that are conditionally applied based on the child's behaviour) can have significant unintended and even destructive consequences. One oft-overlooked problem is that even if conditional approaches do successfully produce the desired behaviours, these behaviours don't tend to persist over the long term (Deci at al., 1999). When rewards or punishments are not available to guide behaviour, children may find it difficult to motivate themselves to "do the right thing."

Another downside to the conditional parenting approach is the impact it may have on children's self-esteem and emotional security. Because children learn to associate feeling good about themselves with the experience of receiving rewards and avoiding punishment, their self-esteem becomes more dependent upon *external* sources of validation. Instead of helping to nurture a truly secure child, parents may unwittingly be encouraging a sense of conditional self-worth, that is, the feeling that you are a good and valuable person only when you are behaving the "right" way.

Although these conditional approaches may seem fairly normal when it comes to raising children, think about it for a moment in a different context, such as your romantic relationship. Imagine that you and your partner decide to go to a couple's counsellor, and you are told that every time your partner behaves in ways you don't like, you should respond with negativity, such as withdrawing affection, speaking sharply and angrily, physically forcing him to sit in a corner for a certain amount of time, or taking away one of his favourite possessions. You also should use rewards as a way of getting your partner to do things you want—promise him pie, or physical intimacy, or buy him something nice. Our guess is that you would conclude it's time to get a different counsellor. Yet, this is often how we raise children.

A mountain of research has revealed the downside of taking this kind of conditional approach to parenting. Children who experience their parents' regard for them as conditional report more negativity and resentment toward their parents; they also feel greater internal pressure to do well, which is called **introjection**, *the internalization of the conditional regard of significant others* (Assor et al., 2004).

Unfortunately, the more that people motivate themselves through introjection, the more unstable their self-esteem (Kernis et al., 2000), and the worse they tend to cope with failure (Grolnick & Ryan, 1989).

So what works better? Research clearly shows that moral development and healthy attachment is associated with more frequent use of **inductive discipline**, *which involves explaining the consequences of a child's actions on other people, activating empathy for others' feelings* (Hoffman & Saltzsein, 1967). Providing a rationale for a parent's decisions, showing empathy and understanding of the child's emotions, supporting her autonomy, and allowing her choice whenever possible all promote positive outcomes such as greater mastery of skills, increased emotional and behavioural self-control, better ability to persist at difficult tasks, and a deeper internalization of moral values (Deci et al., 1994; Frodi et al., 1985). When it comes to raising moral children, the "golden rule" seems to apply just as well—do unto your children as you would have someone do unto you.

Module 10.2c Quiz:

Psychosocial Development

Know . . .

1. The primary challenge in Eriksen's "Childhood" stage of development is _____.
   A. trust vs. mistrust
   B. industry vs. inferiority
   C. initiative vs. guilt
   D. autonomy vs. shame and doubt

Understand . . .

2. Marcus is very careful to teach his daughter about morality, using stories like Aesop's Fables, because he wants her to be a good person when she grows up. However, you notice that he often seems emotionally unavailable, and frequently criticizes her (presumably in order to improve her behaviour). Marcus seems to underappreciate the role of _____ in moral development.
   A. Piaget's theory of cognitive development
   B. emotional security
   C. behaviourism
   D. theory of mind

3. If parents excessively reward and praise their children, particularly based on the children's performance, they risk their children developing a high degree of
   A. attachment anxiety.
   B. introjection.
   C. inductive discipline.
   D. extrojection.

Analyze . . .

4. One very common behavioural problem is when a person is too upset or emotionally triggered to be open to listening to another person's perspective. This is the same basic dynamic as the
   A. relationship between inductive discipline and introjected motivation.
   B. relationship between the threat object and the terry-cloth mother (for rhesus monkeys).
   C. relationship between the attachment behavioural system and the caregiving behavioural system.
   D. parent–child relationship.

Module 10.2 Summary

10.2a   Know . . . the key terminology associated with infancy and childhood.

accommodation
assimilation
attachment
attachment behavioural system
caregiving behavioural system
cognitive development
concrete operational stage
conservation
core knowledge hypothesis
dishabituation
egocentric
formal operational stage
habituation
inductive discipline
introjection

object permanence
preoperational stage
scaffolding
self-awareness
sensitive period
sensorimotor stage
strange situation
theory of mind
zone of proximal development

10.2b   Understand . . . the cognitive changes that occur during infancy and childhood.

According to Piaget's theory of cognitive development, infants mature through childhood via orderly transitions across the sensorimotor, preoperational, concrete operational, and formal operational stages. This progression reflects a general transition from engaging in the world through purely concrete, sensory experiences, to an increasing ability to hold and manipulate abstract representations in one's mind.

10.2c Understand . . . the importance of attachment and the different styles of attachment.

In developmental psychology, attachment refers to the enduring social bond between child and caregiver. Based on the quality of this bond, which is dependent upon appropriately responsive parenting, individuals develop an attachment style, which is their internalized feeling of security and self-worth. Children are either securely or insecurely attached, and insecure attachments can be further divided into disorganized, anxious/ambivalent, and avoidant styles.

10.2d Apply . . . the concept of scaffolding and the zone of proximal development to understand how to best promote learning.

According to Vygotsky, cognitive development unfolds in a social context. Adults who are attuned to the child's experience can help to scaffold the child's learning, guiding them such that they focus on challenges that lie on the very edge of their capabilities. This keeps a child fully engaged in the zone of proximal development, maximizing their skill development.

10.2e Analyze . . . how to effectively discipline children in order to promote moral behaviour.

Internalizing prosocial motives comes from children developing a secure attachment, experiencing empathy and receiving inductive discipline. Children have an innate sense of morality, but this can be interfered with if their attachment needs are insufficiently met. Therefore, responsive parenting that helps the child feel secure lays the foundation for the child to become less self-focused. As the child cognitively develops and can more explicitly take others' perspectives, inductive reasoning that emphasizes perspective taking and empathy builds the habit of "doing good" because the child genuinely cares, rather than because the child wants to receive approval or to avoid punishment.

Module 10.3 Adolescence

Picture Partners/Alamy Stock Photo

 Learning Objectives

10.3a Know . . . the key terminology concerning adolescent development.

10.3b Understand . . . the process of identity formation during adolescence.

10.3c Understand . . . the importance of relationships in adolescence.

10.3d Understand . . . the functions of moral emotions.

10.3e Apply . . . your understanding of the categories of moral reasoning.

10.3f Analyze . . . the relationship between brain development and adolescent judgment and risk taking.

The Internet can be a healthy part of your social life and a necessary research tool for your education. Indeed, as the Internet has become more of a platform for social networking, at least moderate use of the Internet is associated with greater social involvement (Gross, 2004) and stronger academic motivation (Willoughby, 2008). However, the Internet has its dangers. One is that use may become pathological, with people turning to the Internet as a way of coping with life's difficulties, much the same as people turn to drugs, alcohol, sex, or their career. Even psychologically healthy adolescents can get hooked on the Internet, and such pathological use can lead to depression (Lam & Peng, 2010). The Internet may also carry social dangers, such as bullying and public humiliation, now that

one's indiscretions or mistakes can be posted online to haunt people for years to come. In 2012, 15-year-old Amanda Todd from British Columbia was cruelly ostracized and humiliated by her peers after revealing photos of her were posted online. Although she switched schools, she couldn't escape the online bullying, and she tragically committed suicide.

The Internet has revolutionized society in a single human generation. But we don't know how it will affect human development, particularly in the challenging period of adolescence when people are forming their identities and often committing some of their biggest mistakes. This will undoubtedly be a major focus for research, and will raise major questions for society in the years to come.

Focus Questions

1.   What types of changes occur during adolescence?

2.   Why do adolescents so often seem to make risky decisions?

Amanda Todd: A tragic case of cyber-bullying.

》 "It was the best of times; it was the worst of times." For many people, this pretty much sums up adolescence, a time of confusion, pimples, and existential angst, as well as hanging out with friends, gaining greater independence from parents, and focusing intensely on intimate relationships. This often tumultuous time between childhood and adulthood involves many physical changes, increasing cognitive sophistication, and a great deal of emotional and social volatility.

Physical Changes in Adolescence

The physical transition from childhood to adolescence starts with puberty, culminating in reproductive maturity. Puberty begins at approximately age 11 in girls and age 13 in boys, although there is wide variation. The changes that occur during puberty are primarily caused by hormonal activity. Physical growth is stimulated by the pituitary gland, under the control of the *hypothalamus*, which regulates the release of hormones such as testosterone and estrogen. These hormones also contribute to the development of *primary and secondary sex traits* in boys and girls. **Primary sex traits** are *changes in the body that are part of reproduction* (e.g., enlargement of the genitals, ability to ejaculate, the onset of menstruation). **Secondary sex traits** are *changes in the body that are not part of reproduction*, such as the growth of pubic hair, increased breast size in females, and increased muscle mass in males (Figure 10.13).

Figure 10.13 Physical Changes That Accompany Puberty in Male and Female Adolescents

Hormonal changes accelerate the development of physical traits in males and females. Changes involve maturation of the reproductive system (primary sex traits) as well as secondary sex traits such as enlargement of breasts in women and increased muscle mass in males.

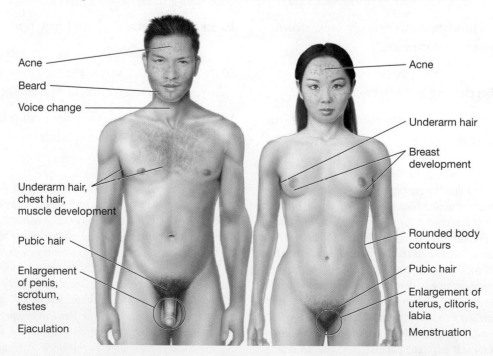

Acne

Beard

Voice change

Underarm hair, chest hair, muscle development

Pubic hair

Enlargement of penis, scrotum, testes

Ejaculation

Acne

Underarm hair

Breast development

Rounded body contours

Pubic hair

Enlargement of uterus, clitoris, labia

Menstruation

Source: Lilienfeld, Scott O.; Lynn, Steven J; Namy, Laura L.; Woolf, Nancy J., *Psychology: From Inquiry To Understanding*, Books A La Carte Edition, 2nd Ed., © 2011. Reprinted and Electronically reproduced by permission of Pearson Education, Inc., New York, NY.

For girls, **menarche**—*the onset of menstruation*—typically occurs around age 12. The timing of menarche is influenced by physiological and environmental factors, such as nutrition, genetics, physical activity levels, illness (Ellis & Garber, 2000), and family structure, such as the absence of a father (Bogaert, 2008). Boys are considered to reach sexual maturity at **spermarche**, *their first ejaculation of sperm,* at around age 14.

Interestingly, puberty happens much earlier now than it did 100 years ago. American teens in the 19th century started puberty at 16–17 on average; nowadays, about one-third of boys show the beginnings of physical maturation at age 9 (Reiter & Lee, 2001), as do almost 40% of European-American girls, and almost 80% of African-American girls (Herman-Giddens et al., 1997). This is probably because of behavioural changes that increase body fat (e.g., poor nutrition, insufficient exercise), and environmental stresses that increase stress hormones in the body. As the environment changes, our biology changes along with it.

Teens' rapidly-developing bodies bring a host of developmental challenges, from feelings of self-consciousness and a heightened desire to be attractive and to fit in, to increasing sexual interest and experimentation,

to the negative moods that accompany hormonal fluctuations (Warren & Brooks-Gunn, 1989). Adolescents who begin to physically develop earlier than their peers can face additional challenges. Early-developing females often have to cope with being teased and having their bodies made into objects of others' attention. Early-developing boys tend to have it easier; their masculine traits are often regarded positively by both themselves and their peers. Nevertheless, early developers of either gender run a greater risk of drug and alcohol abuse and of unwanted pregnancies.

Recent research has shown that adolescence is a time of major brain changes as well. In particular, the frontal lobes undergo a massive increase in myelination, speeding up neural firing by up to 100-fold in those areas (Barnea-Goraly et al., 2005; Sowell et al., 2003). The frontal lobes also undergo a wave of synaptic pruning, during which relatively unused synaptic connections are broken, leaving a more efficiently functioning brain. The net result of these changes is an increase in teens' abilities to exert self-control. However, during adolescence this process is merely under way, not completed, leaving teens often struggling with volatile emotional experiences.

Module 10.3a Quiz:

Physical Changes Challenges in Adolescence

Know . . .

1. One of the changes that occurs in puberty is the beginning of menstruation for females. This event is known as _____.
   - **A.** estradiol
   - **B.** menarche
   - **C.** a primary sex trait
   - **D.** spermarche

2. A brain area that shows large changes during adolescence is the _____.
   - **A.** motor cortex
   - **B.** visual cortex
   - **C.** frontal lobes
   - **D.** brainstem

Understand . . .

3. One of the major differences between primary and secondary sex characteristics is that
   - **A.** primary sex characteristics are directly related to reproductive function.
   - **B.** secondary sex characteristics are directly related to reproductive function.
   - **C.** whether a person is male or female depends on the secondary sex characteristics.
   - **D.** primary sex characteristics are unique to human reproductive anatomy.

Emotional Challenges in Adolescence

The physical and emotional changes associated with puberty are widely believed to be connected to each other. For example, mood swings and experimental high-risk behaviours are attributed to "raging hormones." But is this characterization of adolescence accurate? Are most teens hormonally supercharged animals, constantly desiring to hook up with the first attractive (or even unattractive) person to cross their path?

The belief that adolescence is tumultuous has held sway in popular culture as well as in psychology since at least the early 1900s (Hall, 1904); some theorists even believed that the absence of extreme volatility was an indication of arrested development (Freud, 1958). However, this belief came under fire from cultural anthropologists (Benedict, 1938; Mead, 1928), who discovered that in many non-Western cultures, the transition from childhood to adulthood happened remarkably smoothly; children simply began to take on more and more responsibilities, and then moved into their adult roles without such a dramatic and volatile transition.

In the decades since, research has painted a somewhat mixed picture of adolescence. On the up side, the majority of teens keep their forays into debauchery fairly minimal and do not let their larger lives get unduly harmed by their experimentation. Most teens also grow out of these patterns fairly readily and move into adulthood relatively unscathed by their teenage experiences (Bachman et al., 1997). Navigating adolescence successfully leaves teens feeling they know who they are, having constructed a healthy social identity, and having learned to identify at least some of their own personal values and goals. On the down side, however, the emotional road through adolescence also contains its fair share of bumps. Teens are prone to experiencing particularly intense and volatile emotions (Dahl, 2001; Rosenblum & Lewis, 2003), including heightened feelings of anxiety and depression (Van Oort et al., 2009).

EMOTIONAL REGULATION DURING ADOLESCENCE
Adolescence is a time when teens must learn to control their emotions (McLaughlin et al., 2011). Research at Queen's University has shown that one key to adolescents effectively regulating their emotions is to be able to draw flexibly upon a diverse set of self-control strategies. Adolescents who rely upon a limited number of adaptive strategies (e.g., learning to suppress emotions, or conversely, learning to always reach out and talk to people about their feelings) and narrowly rely upon their chosen strategies are at greater risk for developing symptoms of anxiety and depression (Lougheed & Hollenstein, 2012).

One of the most flexible and powerful strategies for dealing with emotions is cognitive reframing (see Module 16.2), where we learn to look at our experience through a different "frame." For example, failure can be reframed as an opportunity to learn, and a threatening experience as a challenge to be overcome. The ability to effectively choose reframing strategies, especially when under the grip of strong emotions, relies upon a sophisticated cognitive control network involving the frontal and parietal lobes (McClure et al., 2004). These are precisely the brain areas that are undergoing the most development during adolescence. Thus, helping adolescents learn self-control strategies is critically important, not only for developing good habits, but for helping them to develop the cognitive control systems in their brains. Failing to provide this guidance is a lost opportunity for making a major difference in the lives of today's youth.

The ability to reframe is critical to one of the most important skills adolescents need to hone as they move into adulthood—the ability to **delay gratification**, *putting off immediate temptations in order to focus on longer-term goals.*

For example, should you party with your friends, or study for the test next week? Adolescents who master this skill are far more likely to be successful in life. An inability to delay gratification reflects a tendency to discount the future in order to live in the moment, which lies at the heart of a wide range of dysfunctional behaviours ranging from addictions and unsafe sex, to racking up credit card debt and failing to meet deadlines.

Unfortunately, the ability (or inability) to delay gratification tends to be quite stable throughout childhood and adolescence. A brilliant set of studies begun in the 1960s looked at what young children would do if given a difficult temptation—they could have a marshmallow immediately, or they could wait for 15 minutes, at which point they would be given two marshmallows. It's a pretty simple choice right? A mere 15 minutes and the marshmallow feast doubles in size! However, preschool-aged children find it excruciating to resist this temptation. In one study (Mischel & Ebbesen, 1970), when the marshmallow was temptingly placed right in front of the children, they could only wait for, on average, one minute!

The finding that made these studies famous in psychology was that the length of time kids could delay their marshmallowy gratification predicted how well-adjusted they would become in adolescence, many years later. The child who could wait longer for a marshmallow at age 4 was better adjusted both psychologically and socially at age 15, and had higher SAT scores by the end of high school (Shoda et al., 1990)! (SATs are standardized tests written by American students at the end of high school, and are a major part of determining acceptance to college and university.) Clearly, being able to delay gratification is an important skill.

Importantly, this is also a skill that people can learn. In fact, the challenge of delaying gratification is basically the same as the challenge of controlling emotions, and the same strategies are useful, such as cognitive reframing. Even preschool-aged children can use them. In the simplest and most literal reframing study, children were instructed to simply imagine that the marshmallow was a picture, not a real object, and to do this by mentally drawing a picture frame around the object. Incredibly, this simple imagination tactic increased the average wait time to a full 18 minutes (Moore et al., 1976).

Working the Scientific Literacy Model

Adolescent Risk and Decision Making

One of the nightmares of every parent is the smorgasbord of disasters waiting for adolescents as they explore their increasing independence—sexually transmitted diseases, drugs, and the whole host of alluring activities parents wish were never invented (despite their own fond memories of their younger years . . .).

What do we know about adolescence and risky decision making?

Parents do have some reason to fear; research shows that adolescents are particularly prone to behaving impulsively and making risky decisions (Chambers et al., 2003; Steinberg, 2007). As a result, driving recklessly, unsafe sex (Arnett, 1992), drug and alcohol abuse, accidents, and violence are more common during adolescence than during any other stage of life (Chambers & Potenza, 2003; Steinberg, 2008).

Why do adolescents often make such bad judgment calls? Adolescence is a perfect storm of risk-inducing factors, including a teenage culture that glorifies high-risk activities, intense peer pressure, increased freedom from parents, a growing ability to critically question the values and traditions of society, and a brain that is ripe for risk due to still-developing cognitive control systems (especially the prefrontal cortex) and well-developed reward systems located in limbic areas (Casey et al., 2008; Galvan et al., 2006). Indeed, teenage neurophysiology is a battleground of opposing urges; the reward system acts like the proverbial devil on one's shoulder, urging "Do it! Do it!" while the underdeveloped prefrontal areas play the role of the beleaguered angel, pleading "Don't do it! It's not worth it!"

How can science test the link between brain function and decision making in adolescents?

Modern technology has enabled researchers to look at the brain activity of adolescents in the process of making risky decisions. In one study, adolescents had their brains scanned using functional magnetic resonance imaging while they played a betting game. In this experiment, participants had to make a decision between a high-risk, high-reward choice (placing a $6 bet with a 25% chance of winning), and a low-risk, low-reward choice (placing a $1 bet with a 50% chance of winning).

Adolescents who selected the high-risk choice had less brain activity in their prefrontal cortex than those who selected the low-risk choice (Figure 10.14; Shad et al., 2011). It seems that choosing the high-risk gamble was, in a sense, easier; those teens simply focused on how much they wanted the bigger reward, and ignored the higher likelihood that they would lose. On the other hand, making the low-risk choice involved some neurological conflict; those teens wanted the bigger reward, but restrained themselves by taking into account the probabilities. This restraint involved the frontal lobes.

Figure 10.14 Extended Brain Development
The prefrontal cortex (circled in blue) continues to develop through adolescence and into young adulthood.

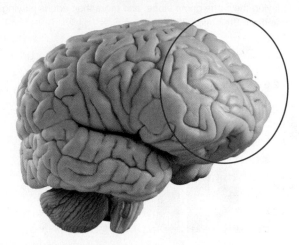

werbefoto-burger.ch/Fotolia

This study helps to shed light on adolescent decision making in general. Compared to adults, adolescents have less-developed frontal lobes, and are therefore more likely to default to their strong reward impulses, rather than restraining their desires as a result of more sober and complex calculations of what would be in their best interest overall.

Can we critically evaluate this explanation for risky decision making?

This brain-based explanation does not fully *explain* adolescents' behaviour, in at least two important ways. First, in this particular study, it's not clear whether the prefrontal activation reflects teens thinking in more complex ways, or whether it shows that they are consciously restraining themselves from following their reward-focused desires. Is the key factor here about complex thought or self-control?

Second, in everyday decisions, other factors likely influence teens' preference for risk, such as the size of rewards and costs, the importance of long-term goals, personality characteristics such as extraversion (which is related to reward sensitivity), and the social context in which the decisions occur. For example, psychologists have found that in some situations, adolescents are no more likely to engage in risky behaviour than adults. But when other teens are around, this propensity changes (see Figure 10.15). In fact, the presence of other teens can weaken the activity in the frontal lobes (Segalowitz et al., 2012). Clearly, realistic strategies for reducing adolescent risk taking should also consider the important role that situational factors play in adolescents' decision making.

Figure 10.15 What Drives Teenagers to Take Risks?

One key factor in risk taking is simply *other teenagers*. When teens play a driving video game with other teens, they crash more than when playing the same game alone, and more than adults playing the game (from Steinberg, 2007).

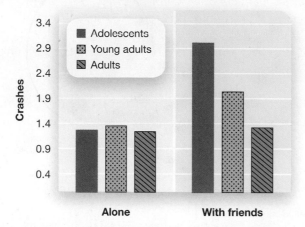

Source: Adapted from figure 2, p. 630 in "Peer Influence on Risk-Taking, Risk Preference, and Risky Decision-Making in Adolescence and Adulthood: An Experimental Study" by M. Gardner & L. Stein-berg (2005). *Developmental Psychology*, 41 (4), 652–635.

Why is this relevant

Research on the developing adolescent brain helps explain problems with risk and impulse control, which could lead to the development of programs that could steer adolescents toward making better decisions. If we could figure out how to enhance prefrontal functioning in teens, or how to get more of them to engage in practices like meditation that would do the same thing, we could potentially reduce their tendency to make unnecessarily risky decisions.

Module 10.3b Quiz:
Emotional Challenges in Adolescence

Understand . . .

1. Adolescent decision making is often problematic or dangerous because teens have
    A. underdeveloped limbic areas responsible for reward, and well-developed prefrontal areas.
    B. well-developed limbic areas responsible for reward, and underdeveloped prefrontal areas.
    C. only partly moved out of the concrete operational stage of cognitive development.
    D. poorly formed sets of goals.

2. The length of time children can wait in the marshmallow task is an indicator of
    A. the age at which they begin to develop secondary sex characteristics.
    B. intelligence.
    C. self-control.
    D. emotional security.

Apply . . .

3. After finishing Grade 10, Naomi got a job giving music lessons at a day camp for kids aged 6–8. She was very excited. However, the first week was a disaster. The kids misbehaved and some instruments were broken. That weekend, she thought about what had happened. Rather than viewing the past week as a failure, she decided to view it as a learning experience that could help her do a better job when she taught a new group of kids the next week. Naomi's thought process is an example of _____.
    A. goal formation
    B. cognitive reframing
    C. autonomy
    D. concrete operations

Cognitive Development: Moral Reasoning vs. Emotions

As we have just seen, making wise decisions depends on the prefrontal cortex. This area is involved in higher cognitive abilities, such as abstract reasoning and logic (what Piaget referred to as *formal operational* thinking; see Module 10.2), which also begin to show substantial improvements starting at about age 12. Since Piaget, psychologists have generally believed that the shift to formal operational thinking laid the foundation for effective moral reasoning.

For adolescents, this increase in complex cognitive ability allows them to consider abstract moral principles, to view problems from multiple perspectives, and to think more flexibly.

KOHLBERG'S MORAL DEVELOPMENT: LEARNING RIGHT FROM WRONG The most influential theory of the development of moral reasoning was created by Lawrence Kohlberg, after studying how people reasoned through complex moral dilemmas. Imagine the following scenario, unlikely as it may be:

A trolley is hurtling down the tracks toward a group of five unsuspecting people. You are standing next to a lever that, if pulled, would direct the trolley onto another track, thereby saving the five individuals. However, on the second track stands a single, unsuspecting person, who would be struck by the diverted trolley.

What would you choose to do? Would you pull the lever, directly causing one person to die, but saving five others? Or would you be unwilling to directly cause someone's death and therefore do nothing? Moral dilemmas provide interesting tests of reasoning because they place values in conflict with each other. Obviously, five lives are more than one, yet most people are also unwilling to take a direct action that would cause a person to be killed.

But even more important than *what* you would choose is *why* you would choose it. Kohlberg (1984) believed that people's reasons evolved as they grew up and became better able to think in complex ways. By analyzing people's reasons for their decisions in these sorts of dilemmas, he developed a stage theory of moral development, here organized into three general stages (see Table 10.4).

At the preconventional level, people reason largely based on self-interest, such as avoiding punishment. This is what parents predominantly appeal to when they threaten children with time-outs, spankings, or taking away toys. At the conventional level, people reason largely based on social conventions (e.g., tradition) and the dictates of authority figures; this is what parents are appealing to with the famously frustrating, "Because I said so!" At the postconventional level, people reason based on abstract principles such as justice and fairness, thus enabling them to critically question and examine social conventions, and to consider complex situations in which different values may conflict.

The shift to postconventional morality is a key development, for without this shift, it is unlikely that the individual will rebel against authority or work against unjust practices if they are accepted by society at large. Indeed, social reformers always encounter resistance from members of society who hold to "traditional" values and think of change as destructive and destabilizing.

Kohlberg regarded the three stages of moral reasoning as universal to all humans; however, because he developed his theory mostly through the study of how *males* reason about moral dilemmas, other researchers argued that he had failed to consider that females may reason about moral issues differently. Carol Gilligan (1982) suggested that females base moral decisions on a standard of *caring for others*, rather than the "masculine" focus on standards of justice and fairness that Kohlberg emphasized. Some support has been found for this; women are more likely to highlight the importance of maintaining harmony in their relationships with others (Lyons, 1983). On the other hand, men and women generally make highly similar judgments about moral dilemmas (Boldizar et al., 1989), and both genders make use of both caring and justice principles (Clopton & Sorell, 1993). This has led other researchers to question the importance of the gender distinction at all (Jaffee & Hyde, 2000).

However, a potentially more devastating critique has been made against the moral reasoning perspective in general, based on research showing that moral reasoning doesn't actually predict behaviour very well (Carpendale, 2000; Haidt, 2001) *Knowing* that something is right or wrong is very different from *feeling* that it is right or wrong. According to Jonathan Haidt's *social intuitionist model* of morality, in our everyday lives our moral decisions are largely based on how we feel, not what we think. Haidt argues that moral judgments are guided by intuitive, emotional reactions, like our "gut feelings," and then afterwards, we construct arguments to support our judgments. For example, imagine the following scenario (adapted from Haidt, 2001):

Julie and Steven are brother and sister. They are travelling together in France on summer vacation from college. One night they are staying alone in a cabin near the beach. They decide that it would be interesting and fun if they shared a "romantic" evening together. At the very least it would be a new experience for each of them. They both enjoy the experience but they decide not to do it again. They keep that night as a special secret, which makes them feel even closer to each other.

Table 10.4 Kohlberg's Stages of Moral Reasoning

Stage of Moral Development	Description	Application to Trolley Dilemma
Preconventional morality	*Characterized by self-interest in seeking reward or avoiding punishment.* Preconventional morality is considered a very basic and egocentric form of moral reasoning.	"I would not flip the trolley track switch because I would get in trouble."
Conventional morality	*Regards social conventions and rules as guides for appropriate moral behaviour.* Directives from parents, teachers, and the law are used as guidelines for moral behaviour.	"I would not flip the switch. It is illegal to kill, and if I willfully intervened I would probably violate the law."
Postconventional morality	*Considers rules and laws as relative.* Right and wrong are determined by more abstract principles of justice and rights.	"I would flip the switch. The value of five lives exceeds that of one, so saving them is the right thing to do even if it means I am killing one person who would otherwise not have died."

Emotion is a major component of moral thinking and decision making.

How do you react to this scenario? Was what took place between the two siblings morally acceptable? If you are like most people, you probably did *not* think carefully through this scenario, consider different perspectives, and examine your reasoning before making a decision. Instead, you probably had a gut reaction, like "Brother and sister!?!? Gross! No way!" and made your decision almost instantly.

It is only after making a decision that most people engage in more thoughtful and reflective reasoning, trying to justify their decision. For some scenarios, it is easy to come up with justifications, such as "Brothers and sisters should not engage in romance because it could lead to sexual intercourse, which could produce genetic problems for the offspring," or "They shouldn't do it because if the family found out, it would be devastating." However, it's not hard to construct a scenario that lies outside of such justifications, such as the brother and sister being infertile and having no other surviving family members. Faced with such a scenario,

people might be hard pressed to find a justification; often, in such situations, people become flustered and confused, and resort to emphatically stating something like "I don't know—it just isn't right!" Or simply, "Ewww . . ." Their intuitive emotional reaction has told them it's wrong, but their more cognitive, effortful reasoning process is having a difficult time explaining *why* it's wrong; interestingly, in such situations, people generally do not change their judgments, instead trusting their intuitive reaction. The feeling of disgust is stronger than their inability to explain themselves, which is another piece of evidence that suggests that it's not moral *reasoning* that is important, but moral *feelings*.

The improvements in emotional regulation that occur during adolescence have an influence on moral behaviour. Without some control over emotional reactions, people can become overwhelmed by the personal distress they experience upon encountering the suffering of others (Eisenberg, 2000), and end up attending to their own needs rather than others'. Self-control, in turn, involves brain areas that are rapidly developing in adolescents, particularly the prefrontal cortex.

It is interesting to consider that the development of key moral emotions, such as empathy, is intimately bound up with the extent to which one's social relationships have been healthy right from birth (see Module 10.2). People who are regularly socially included and treated well by others are more likely to develop trust and security, which results in well-developed areas of the prefrontal cortex necessary for good decision making and well-developed moral emotional systems. This shows us that the early roots of moral behaviour reach all the way back into infancy, when attachment styles are initially formed, and extend into adolescence and beyond, when complex cognitive and self-control abilities are strengthened.

Biopsychosocial Perspectives
Emotion and Disgust

The social intuitionist model describes moral judgments as being driven primarily by emotional reactions. Many psychologists believe that these reactions draw upon evolutionarily ancient systems that evolved for functional reasons. For example, the disgust system evolved to keep us from ingesting substances that were harmful to us, such as feces and toxic plants. As we developed into more complex social beings, our judgments of *good* and *bad* involved neural circuits that were more cognitive and conceptual; however, these higher-level cognitive systems evolved after our more basic physiological responses, and therefore are intertwined with the functioning of the older systems.

In terms of moral reasoning, what this means is that the cognitive systems that reason about right and wrong grew out of emotional systems that in turn grew out of systems of physiological responses of accepting or rejecting a substance

from one's body. From this perspective, *good* and *bad* are not moral judgments, per se, but rather, are elaborations of more simple physiological responses of acceptance or repulsion. One surprising hypothesis one could derive is that the feeling of actual, physical disgust may strongly influence supposedly moral judgments.

This has been tested in several different ways. One creative set of studies first activated physiological symptoms of repulsion, for example, by getting subjects to sit at a disgustingly dirty work station, or to smell fart spray (Schnall et al., 2008). These disgust-inducing experiences led people to make more severe judgments of moral violations. Also, neuroimaging studies show that certain moral dilemmas trigger emotional areas in the brain, and this emotional activation determines the decision that subjects make (Greene & Haidt, 2002; Greene et al., 2001).

Module 10.3c Quiz:
Cognitive Development: Moral Reasoning vs. Emotions

Know . . .

1. A stage of morality that views rules and laws as being related to abstract principles of right and wrong is the _____ stage.
   - **A.** postconventional
   - **B.** preconventional
   - **C.** preoperational
   - **D.** conventional

Understand . . .

2. What is the relationship between physical feelings of disgust and moral judgments?
   - **A.** Both physical and moral disgust activate the same brain areas, but do not directly influence each other.
   - **B.** Physical and moral disgust influence each other, but through unique neural pathways.
   - **C.** Physically disgusting stimuli increase the severity of a person's moral judgments.
   - **D.** It is impossible to ethically test this relationship.

Apply . . .

3. Rachel believes that it is wrong to steal only because doing so could land her in jail. Which level of Kohlberg's moral development scheme is Rachel applying in this scenario?
   - **A.** postconventional
   - **B.** preconventional
   - **C.** preoperational
   - **D.** conventional

Social Development: Identity and Relationships

The final aspect of adolescence to consider is the role of social relationships. To teenagers, friends are everything—the people who will support your story to your parents about why you came home late, who laugh hysterically with you at 3:00 in the morning, and who help you feel that your choice of clothing is actually cool. Friends are central to two of the most important changes that occur during adolescence—the formation of a personal identity, and the shift away from family relationships and toward peer and romantic relationships. These major changes in teens' lives are sources of growth and maturation, but are also often sources of distress and conflict.

WHO AM I? IDENTITY FORMATION DURING ADOLESCENCE A major issue faced by adolescents is forming an **identity**, which is *a clear sense of what kind of person you are, what types of people you belong with, and what roles you should play in society*. It involves coming to appreciate and express one's attitudes and values (Arnett, 2000; Lefkowitz, 2005), which are, in large part, realized through identifying more closely with peers and being accepted into valued social groups.

You may recall Erikson's theory of psychosocial development from Module 10.2 (see Table 10.5, in Module 10.4 for an overview). Erikson described the stage of *adolescence* as involving the struggle of *identity vs. role confusion*. Adolescents are seeking to define who they are, in large part through their attachment to specific social groups; doing this successfully allows them to enter adulthood with a sense of their own authenticity and self-awareness.

In fact, forming an identity is so important in the teenage years that adolescents may actually experience numerous *identity crises* before they reach young adulthood. An identity crisis involves curiosity, questioning, and exploration of different identities. It can also involve attaching oneself to different goals and values, different styles of music and fashion, and different subcultural groups, all the while wondering where one best fits in, and who one really is.

The process of exploring different identities, and experiencing more independence from the family, sets the stage for potential conflict, particularly with parents. Even well-meaning parents may feel somewhat threatened as their teenage son or daughter starts to establish more distance or starts to experiment with identities they feel are unwise. They may feel hurt and want to hold onto their closeness with their child. They may also feel concerned and want to protect their child from making mistakes they will later regret. So, parents may simply be trying to help, but their advice, rules, or insistence that the teen abandon certain goals ("There's no way you're giving up math and science to take drama and music!") may be interpreted as being restrictive or controlling. This, not surprisingly, can lead to conflict. And the more conflict teens perceive at home, the more they may turn to peers.

PEER GROUPS Friendships are a major priority for most adolescents. Friendships generally take place within a broader social context of small groups or *cliques*, and the membership and intensity of friendships within a clique constantly change (Cairns & Cairns, 1994). Adolescent *crowds*—often identified with specific labels, such as "jocks," "geeks," "Goths," or "druggies"—are larger than cliques and are characterized by common social and behavioural conventions.

Adolescents who can't find their place in social networks have a difficult time; social exclusion can be a devastating experience. When rejected by peers, some adolescents turn to virtual social networks for online friendships, or join distinctive sub-groups in order to gain acceptance. This tendency to seek acceptance within specific groups is obviously not limited to teenagers, but adolescence is a time of

For decades, television shows and movies have offered glimpses into life within adolescent cliques and crowds. The portrayals may be exaggerated, but they are often successful because viewers can closely identify with the characters' experiences.

particular social vulnerability because adolescents are, in general, so actively working on their "identity project."

One of the most troubling outcomes of social rejection is the experience of shame, which is a feeling that there is something wrong with you. It can be accompanied by feelings of worthlessness, inferiority, or just a more subtle, gnawing feeling that there is something wrong with you, that you need to prove yourself, and that you aren't quite good enough. Shame-prone individuals have often experienced substantial social rejection; a key source is within the family, such as when a child's attachment needs are consistently unmet.

Many psychologists believe that shame and other negative emotions that are connected to social rejection, bullying, teasing, and being publicly humiliated can lead to tragic outbursts of violence, such as the school shootings that have become disturbingly frequent in the United States in recent years. In almost all cases of school shootings, social rejection is a key factor that precedes the violent outburst (Leary et al., 2003; Tangney & Dearing, 2002). Just as the *security* from having one's need to belong satisfied leads to the development of empathy and moral behaviours (see Module 10.2), the *insecurity* from having one's need to belong go unmet can lead to violence.

ROMANTIC RELATIONSHIPS As children mature into teenagers, their attachment needs shift, not fully but in important ways, into their intimate or romantic relationships. Here, the dramas of their interpersonal systems play out on a new stage. In other words, teenagers are pretty interested in being attracted to each other. This opens up the potential exploration of new worlds of emotional and physical intimacy and intensity.

Many people, for many different reasons, may feel uncomfortable with adolescents exploring and engaging in sexual behaviour. Perhaps unsurprisingly, North American teenagers themselves don't seem to agree. Between 40–50% of Canadian teens aged 15–19 report having had sexual

intercourse (Boyce et al., 2006; Rotermann, 2008), and the proportion who have engaged in other forms of sexual acts such as oral sex is considerably higher. More than 80% of American adolescents report engaging in non-intercourse sex acts before the age of 16 (Bauserman & Davis, 1996), and more than half of Canadian teens in Grade 11 report having experienced oral sex (Boyce et al., 2006). Some teens turn to oral sex because they see it as less risky than intercourse, both for one's health and social reputation (Halpern-Fisher et al., 2005).

Same-sex sexual encounters are also very common and typically occur by early adolescence (Savin-Williams & Cohen, 2004), although contrary to stereotypes, such an experience is not an indication of whether a person identifies themselves as homosexual, or as having any other sexual orientation. In fact, the majority (60%) of people who identify themselves as heterosexual have had at least one same-sex encounter (Remafedi et al., 1992). For many, this is part of the experimentation that comes with figuring out who you are and establishing an identity.

The process by which adolescents come to recognize their sexual orientation depends on many factors, including how they are perceived by their family and peers. Because of some people's still-existing prejudices against non-heterosexual orientations, it is not uncommon for many people who don't identify as heterosexual to experience some difficulty accepting their sexuality, and thus, to struggle with feelings of rejection toward themselves. However, this process is not always difficult or traumatic; it largely depends on how supportive family and other relationships can be. Nevertheless, despite these extra identity challenges, homosexuals have about the same level of psychological well-being as heterosexuals (Rieger & Savin-Williams, 2011).

Although sexual exploration is a normal part of adolescence, it can unfortunately be dangerous for many people. Research at the University of New Brunswick has shown that among Canadian teens in Grade 11, approximately 60% of both males and females reported having experienced psychological aggression against them by their romantic relationship partner. About 40% experienced sexual aggression, generally in the form of being coerced or pressured into having sex (Sears & Byers, 2010). In addition, each year in North America, millions of teens face the life upheaval of an unplanned pregnancy, sexually transmitted diseases, or simply having sex that they will later regret.

Overall, the emotional upheaval of relationships, from the ecstasy of attraction, to the heartbreak of being rejected or cheated on, to the loneliness one may feel in the absence of relationships, consumes a great deal of many teenagers' attention and resources and is a central part of the often tumultuous experience of adolescence.

Module 10.3d Quiz:
Social Development: Identity and Relationships

Know . . .

1. The kind of person you are, the types of people you belong with, and the roles that you feel you should play in society are often referred to as your _____.
   A. crowd
   B. peer group
   C. autonomy
   D. identity

Understand . . .

2. For most teens, the most devastating experience would be
   A. failing at an important competition.
   B. being rejected by their friends.
   C. being rejected on a first date.
   D. having a physical injury.

Module 10.3 Summary

10.3a   Know . . . the key terminology concerning adolescent development.

conventional morality
delay gratification
identity
menarche
postconventional morality
preconventional morality
primary sex traits
secondary sex traits
spermarche

10.3b   Understand . . . the process of identity formation during adolescence.

A major challenge of adolescence is the formation of a personal identity, which involves exploring different values and behaviours, and seeking inclusion in different social groups. The eventual outcome, if navigated successfully, is a relatively stable and personally satisfying sense of self.

10.3c   Understand . . . the importance of relationships in adolescence.

Teenagers undergo a general shift in their social attachments as family becomes less central and friends and intimate relationships take on increased significance. The failure to establish a sense of belonging is an important precursor to dysfunctional behaviours and violence.

10.3d   Understand . . . the functions of moral emotions.

Contrary to theories of moral reasoning, recent research on moral emotions, such as disgust, suggests that these feelings are what lead to moral behaviour, and reasoning generally follows as a way of justifying the behaviour to oneself.

10.3e   Apply . . . your understanding of the categories of moral reasoning.

Apply Activity

Read the following scenarios and identify which category of moral reasoning (preconventional, conventional, or postconventional) applies to each.

1. Jeff discovers that the security camera at his job is disabled. He decides it is okay to steal because there's no way he's going to get caught.
2. Margaret is aware that a classmate has been sending hostile text messages to various people at her school. Although she does not receive these messages, and she does not personally know any of the victims, Margaret reports the offending individual to school officials.

10.3f   Analyze . . . the relationship between brain development and adolescent judgment and risk taking.

Many problems with judgment and decision making involve a kind of tug-of-war between emotional reward systems in the limbic areas of the brain, and the prefrontal cortex, which is involved in planning, reasoning, emotion, and impulse control. Because the prefrontal cortex is still developing during adolescence, particularly through myelination and synaptic pruning, it is often not sufficient to override the allure of immediate temptations, leading to failures to delay gratification.

Module 10.4 Adulthood and Aging

reppans / Alamy Stock Photo

Learning Objectives

10.4a Know . . . the key terminology concerning adulthood and aging.

10.4b Know . . . the key areas of growth experienced by emerging adults.

10.4c Understand . . . age-related disorders such as Alzheimer's disease.

10.4d Understand . . . how cognitive abilities change with age.

10.4e Apply . . . effective communication principles to the challenge of improving your own relationships.

10.4f Analyze . . . the stereotype that old age is a time of unhappiness.

"Use it or lose it." This is one of those sayings that you grow up hearing, and you think, "Yeah, whatever, I'm young and awesome; I'm never going to lose it." But time goes by, and like it or not, the day will come when you may find yourself puffing at the top of a flight of stairs, or standing in the kitchen wondering why you're there. You may wonder, what's happened to me? Why do I feel so old?

We all know that if you stay physically active, your body will stay stronger and healthier as you age, maintaining better cardiovascular fitness, muscle tone, balance, and bone density. Thankfully, recent advances in neuroscience confirm that the same thing is true for the brain. If you use it, you're less likely to lose it. This is important because, unfortunately, brain connections are exactly what people lose as they age, particularly from their 60s onward, resulting in less neural connectivity and reductions in grey and white matter volume. These neurological losses are accompanied by gradual declines in some types of cognitive functioning.

The fact that exercising your brain slows down the neural signs of aging—and even reduces the likelihood of developing age-related disorders such as Alzheimer's disease—is

great news. And even better news is that exercising your brain is actually fun! It's not like spending countless hours on the brain equivalent of a treadmill, memorizing pi to 35 decimal places. Instead, neurological exercisers are those who regularly stay actively involved in things they love—games, sports, social activities, hobbies, and in general remaining life-long learners. This makes getting old sound not so bad after all. . . .

Focus Questions

1. What are the key developmental challenges adults face as they age?

2. How does aging affect cognitive functioning?

>> Becoming an adult does not entail crossing any specific line. It's not as clear-cut as adolescence; after all, puberty is kind of hard to miss. In Canada, you are considered to be an adult from a legal perspective at 18. Still,

it's questionable whether 18-year-olds are fully fledged adults; they have essentially the same lifestyle as 17-year-olds, often at home or in student housing, with relatively few responsibilities beyond brushing their teeth and dragging themselves to work or school. As time goes by, people get increasingly integrated into working society, begin careers, usually establish long-term relationships, pay bills, possibly have children, and in a variety of ways conform to the expectations and responsibilities of adulthood. As they move slowly from adolescence toward retirement and beyond, adults go through a number of changes—physically, socially, emotionally, cognitively, and neurologically. This module will examine these changes across the different stages of adult development.

From Adolescence through Middle Age

When we are children and adolescents, we often feel like we can't wait to grow up. Many of you can likely remember how large and mature 18-year-olds seemed when you were younger. Eighteen-year-olds went to university, had jobs, and seemed so poised. Now that many of you are in this age range, you can see that this view of emerging adults is a bit naïve. That said, people in this age group have their entire adult lives in front of them. The adventure is beginning.

EMERGING ADULTS The time between adolescence and adulthood is a period of great personal challenge and potential growth. *Emerging adults* confront many adaptive challenges; they may leave home for the first time; start college, university, or full-time work; become more financially responsible for themselves; commit to and cohabit with romantic partners; and, of course, deal with the endless crises of their friends.

Adults inhabit a much more complex world than children, and this becomes increasingly clear as the demands of life, and the need to be responsible for yourself, increase. How well individuals navigate these challenges is important for setting the stage of the next phases of life, and affects feelings of self-worth and confidence in handling the challenges of adulthood. On the other hand, adulthood also brings a huge amount of freedom. You make money, you can travel, eat what you want, and (usually) do what you want. You can settle into your identity as a human being, and you can become comfortable in your own skin. Of course, all of this freedom operates within a complex web of social relationships and responsibilities, and adulthood involves balancing these various factors over time.

Researchers at the University of Guelph conducted an in-depth study of the experiences of these emerging adults, identifying three main areas of personal growth: relationships, new possibilities, and personal strengths

(Gottlieb et al., 2007). Interestingly, these correspond perfectly to the domains of relatedness, autonomy, and competence that are widely viewed as key pillars of healthy development throughout the lifespan (these are discussed in depth in Module 11.3).

In the *relationships* domain, most people in this study felt that they had grown in their abilities to trust others, to recruit support from others, and generally to be able to establish strong and intimate connections. This increased intimacy is an outgrowth of people learning to be themselves with others, to know who they are, and to connect in ways that accept and encourage people's authenticity. The domain of *new possibilities* reflects the greater freedom that emerging adults enjoy to choose activities that better fit their goals and interests, to broaden their horizons, and to actively search for what they want to do with their lives. The domain of *personal strength* reflects the confidence young adults gain as they confront more serious life challenges and discover that they can handle them.

The emergence into adulthood is a time, therefore, of immense opportunity. As a person comes into their own, they can engage with the world that much more confidently and effectively. And that seems to be the story of adulthood: greater opportunities, greater challenges.

EARLY AND MIDDLE ADULTHOOD The first few decades of early adulthood are typically the healthiest and most vigorous times of life. People in their 20s to 40s are usually stronger, faster, and healthier than young children or older people. After adolescence, when one has finished growing, one enters a kind of plateau period of physical development in which the body changes quite slowly (aside from obvious exceptions, like pregnancy). For women, this period starts to shift at approximately age 50 with the onset of **menopause**, *the termination of the menstrual cycle and reproductive ability*. The physical changes associated with menopause, particularly the reduction in estrogen, can result in symptoms such as hot flashes, a reduced sex drive, and mood swings. Psychologically, some women experience a period of adjustment, perhaps feeling like they are no longer "young" or as potentially worthwhile; these types of adjustment problems are common to many different major life changes, and as always, the severity of such symptoms varies widely among individuals. Men, on the other hand, don't experience a physical change as substantial as menopause during middle adulthood, although testosterone production and sexual motivation typically decline.

Early and middle adulthood are also an important time for relationships, particularly of the romantic variety. This links back to Erik Erikson's theory of development across the lifespan (see Table 10.5). As mentioned in earlier modules, in each of Erikson's stages, the individual faces a specific developmental challenge, or crisis

Table 10.5 Erikson's Stages of Psychosocial Development

ClickPop/Shutterstock

Infancy: trust vs. mistrust: Developing a sense of trust and security toward caregivers.

Tracy Whiteside/Shutterstock

Adolescence: identity vs. role confusion: Achieving a sense of self and future direction.

Picture Partners/Alamy Stock Photo

Toddlerhood: autonomy vs. shame and doubt: Seeking independence and gaining self-sufficiency.

OLJ Studio/Shutterstock

Young adulthood: intimacy vs. isolation: Developing the ability to initiate and maintain intimate relationships.

Monkey Business Images/Shutterstock

Preschool/early childhood: initiative vs. guilt: Active exploration of the environment and taking personal initiative.

Belinda Pretorius/Shutterstock

Adulthood: generativity vs. stagnation: The focus is on satisfying personal and family needs, as well as contributing to society.

keith morris/Alamy Stock Photo

Childhood: industry vs. inferiority: Striving to master tasks and challenges of childhood, particularly those faced in school. Child begins pursuing unique interests.

Digital Vision/Photodisc/Getty Images

Aging: ego integrity vs. despair: Coping with the prospect of death while looking back on life with a sense of contentment and integrity for accomplishments.

of development. If she successfully resolves this crisis and overcomes this challenge, the person becomes better able to rise to the challenges of subsequent stages and moves on in life, letting go of specific issues that characterized the earlier stages. However, if the stage is not successfully resolved, lingering issues can interfere with the person's subsequent development.

According to Erikson's theory, the first four stages of development are completed during infancy and childhood (see Module 10.2); the fifth stage takes place during adolescence (see Module 10.3). In the sixth stage, *Young adulthood,* the individual must cope with the conflict between *intimacy and isolation.* This stage places emphasis on establishing and maintaining close relationships. The following stage of *Adulthood* involves the tension of *generativity vs. stagnation,* during which the person either becomes productively engaged in the world, playing somehow useful roles in the world, or else the person "stagnates," becoming overly absorbed with their own lives, and failing to give back to the world in a useful way.

Thus, putting these two stages together gives a decent picture of much of the central foci in an adult's life. Adulthood is this challenge of balancing one's own personal needs with one's relationships, while also fulfilling family responsibilities and playing a variety of different roles in society (depending on things like one's career, and the roles one may play in the community). A key part of these stages is marriage (or cohabitation), perhaps the most important relationship(s) of adulthood.

LOVE AND MARRIAGE Although not all long-term committed relationships proceed to marriage, it remains the norm, with 67% of Canadian families involving a married couple (with or without children). However, in recent years the proportion of married-couple families has been dropping from 70.5% in 2001. Common-law and lone-parent families each account for about 16% of families (Statistics Canada, 2012c).

Consistent with Erikson's theorizing, being able to establish a committed, long-term relationship seems to be good for people (although not in all cases, such as abusive relationships). On average, being in such a relationship is associated with greater health, longer life (Coombs, 1991; Koball et al., 2010), and increased happiness (Wayment & Peplau, 1995). Numerous factors are involved in these benefits. For example, married couples encourage each other to stay active and eat healthier diets, are more satisfied with their sex lives (and have sex more frequently than those who stay single, "swinging single" myths notwithstanding), and enjoy greater financial security (Waite & Gallagher, 2000).

But is it really *marriage* that makes people happier? Or is it due to living together in a committed relationship? Many people believe that living together before marriage

is harmful to a relationship, whereas others believe it is a wise thing to do before making the commitment to marry a person. Until a few years ago, research suggested that despite the beliefs of more progressively minded folks, cohabiting before marriage appeared to be associated with weaker relationships in a variety of ways (e.g., Stack & Eshleman, 1998). However, a dramatic reversal of this opinion occurred after a large international study of relationships across 27 different countries (Lee & Ono, 2012) showed that the reason people in common-law relationships seem less happy, on average, is actually because of *cultural intolerance of these types of relationships.* In cultures with more traditional gender roles, cohabiting outside of marriage is frowned upon, and couples who do so suffer a social cost. This negatively affects women in particular, whose happiness depends more heavily on family relationships and interpersonal ties (Aldous & Ganey, 1999). In more egalitarian societies, common-law relationships are not judged as negatively, and consequently, there seems to be no cost to living with a partner before marriage. Indeed, many people would argue that it is a good idea, leading people to make better decisions when choosing a life partner.

Despite the promise of "until death do us part," about 40% of Canadian marriages end in divorce (Statistics Canada, 2004; see Figure 10.16). One of the key factors that determines whether a marriage will end, and the factor that we have the most control over, is how well partners in a relationship are able to communicate with each other, particularly when they are having a conflict. Several decades of behavioural studies by Dr. John Gottman looked at the communication patterns of couples and led to some key insights about what makes relationships break down and how relationship partners can prevent breakdowns from happening.

By observing a couple interacting in his wonderfully named "love lab," Gottman has been able to predict with up to 94% accuracy whether a relationship will end in divorce (e.g., Buehlman et al., 1992; Gottman & Levenson, 2002). Across multiple studies, certain patterns of behaviour are highly predictive of relationship break-up. He calls them, rather dramatically, the *Four Horsemen of the Apocalypse* (Gottman & Levenson, 1992, 2002). They include:

- *Criticism*: picking out flaws, expressing disappointments, correcting each other, and making negative comments about a spouse's friends and family
- *Defensiveness*: responding to perceived attacks with counter-attacks
- *Contempt*: dismissive eye rolls, sarcastic comments, and a cutting tone of voice
- *Stonewalling*: shutting down verbally and emotionally

Figure 10.16 Marriage and Divorce Trends in Canada

Starting in the 1960s, Canadian divorce rates began rising quickly. They have been fairly steady for the past 20 years.

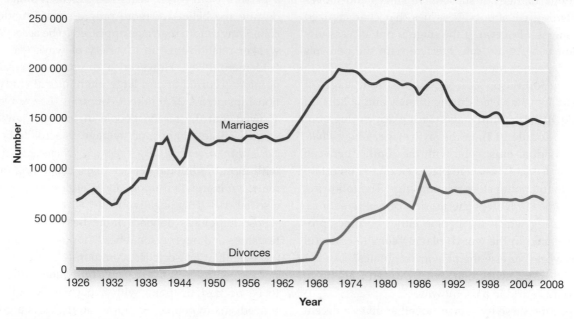

Source: Statistics Canada, Divorce cases in civil court, 2010/2011, Juristat Article, Catalogue no. 85-002-X, 2012. Reproduced and distributed on an "as is" basis with the permission of Statistics Canada.

Studying these four patterns of destructive communication is like studying a trouble-shooting manual for the relationships of early and middle adulthood. Avoid these patterns and nurture their opposing tendencies (such as understanding, empathy, and acceptance), and your relationships will have a much better chance of being positive and fulfilling.

PARENTING One common (although by no means universal) aspect of intimate relationships is the raising of children and having something you identify as "a family" together. This is one of the most powerful routes by which

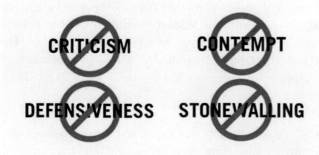

The Gottman Institute

The Four Horsemen of the (Relationship) Apocalypse. Learning to recognize and change these negative communication patterns can make many relationships better.

Source: Recognizing the Four Horsemen of the (Relationship) Apocalypse. Reprinted with permission of the Gottman Institute at www.gottman.com

people experience a deepening in their feelings of being connected to others. Certainly, whether a person is ready for it or not, parenting basically forces you to become less self-centred. All of a sudden, there is another being who is utterly dependent on you for its survival and its healthy development for many years.

The experience of becoming a parent, as with any other huge shift in one's life, causes a person to reorganize their identity to some degree. Life is not just about them anymore. And indeed, you would be miserable and feel terrible about yourself if you ignored your child, tending instead to your own completely independent needs.

Of course, making this transition—with the exhaustion, stress, and massive changes that accompany it—is not easy. As a result, research tends to show a rather sad pattern, but one worth examining nonetheless: within a fairly short period of time (usually around two years) of having children, parents typically report that their marital satisfaction declines (Belsky & Rovine, 1990). Marital satisfaction is usually highest before the birth of the first child, then is reduced until the children enter school (Cowan & Cowan, 1995; Shapiro et al., 2000), and not uncommonly, remains low until the children actually leave home as young adults themselves (Glenn, 1990).

A major upside to this pattern of findings, of course, is that older adults are often poised to enjoy a rekindling of their relationship; their best years are still ahead of them, and they can settle into enjoying their relatively free time together. In fact, the notion of parents suffering in their *empty nest* once their children leave home is largely a myth. Married older adults are just as likely to report being "very satisfied" with marriage as newlyweds (Rollins, 1989). Of course, some parents no doubt take a fresh look at their relationship once it's just the two of them again and discover they no longer have anything in common or don't even like each other that much. But happily, the general trend is actually the opposite—couples find their relationships flourishing again. So, there can be a lot of things to look forward to as one gets older.

Module 10.4a Quiz:
From Adolescence through Middle Age

Know . . .

1. When one person in a relationship tends to withdraw and "shut down" when discussing difficult issues in the relationship, they are _____.
   A. being abusive
   B. stonewalling
   C. guilt-tripping
   D. being contemptuous

2. In Erikson's theory of psychosocial development, what does generativity refer to?
   A. The desire to generate an income
   B. The desire to generate knowledge and learning for oneself
   C. The desire to have offspring
   D. The desire to have a positive impact on the world

3. Research that shows that people are more likely to get divorced if they cohabit before marriage is probably due to
   A. self-reporting biases interfering with people accurately depicting the health of their relationships.
   B. people in some cultures being punished through social and community sanctions if they live in a cohabiting relationship.
   C. biased motivations on the part of the researchers, who asked specific questions that were designed to show what they wanted to find.
   D. journal editors having a conservative bias and thus being more likely to publish studies that show "moral" findings, rather than ones that illustrate unconventional or nontraditional values.

Late Adulthood

The pursuit of happiness is a common theme in contemporary society, and certainly we can all relate to the desire to be happy. But how do we go about achieving "happiness" as we age, and are we generally successful?

HAPPINESS AND RELATIONSHIPS This generally positive story about growing older gets even better when adults begin to transition into the latter decades of life, especially when we consider perhaps the most personal and immediate part of one's happiness— one's own emotions. One of the biggest benefits to growing older is that the emotional turmoil of youth, with its dramatic ups and downs (passions, despair, anger, lust, and all the rest), often gives way to a smoother, more emotionally stable, and generally more positive experience. As a result, late adulthood is often a particularly enjoyable time of life. The Buddhist monk Thich Nnat Hanh has described youth as being like the chaotic mountain stream tumbling down the mountainside, whereas old age is when the stream has broadened into a serene river making the final leg of its journey to the ocean.

Developmental psychologists describe a similar type of personal development through the lens of **socioemotional selectivity theory**, *which describes how older people have learned to select for themselves more positive and nourishing experiences.* Older people seem better able to pay more attention to positive experiences, and to tend to take part in activities that emphasize positive emotions and sharing meaningful connections with others (Carstensen et al., 1999). The net result of this wiser approach to life is that negative emotions often decline with age, while positive emotions actually increase in frequency (Figure 10.17). Simply put, older people are (often)

Figure 10.17 Emotion, Memory, and Aging

Younger people have superior memory for whether they have seen positive, negative, or neutral pictures compared with older people. However, notice that younger people remember positive and negative pictures equally, whereas older people are more likely to remember positive pictures (Charles et al., 2003).

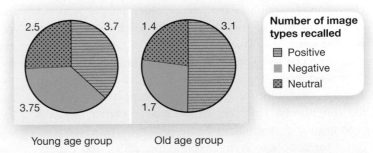

Young age group   Old age group

Source: Data from "At the Intersection of Emotion and Cognition: Aging and the Positivity Effect" by L. L. Carsten-sen & J. A. Mikels, (2005). *Current Directions in Psychological Science*, 14 (3).

happier (Charles & Carstensen, 2009)! This definitely gives us something to look forward to.

Erikson's theory of psychosocial development describes the final stage, spanning approximately 65 years and onward, as *Aging*, the challenge of *ego integrity versus despair*. During this time the older adult contemplates whether she lived a full life and fulfilled major accomplishments, and now can enjoy the support of one's lifetime of relationships and social roles. In contrast, if one only looks back on disappointments and failures, this will be a time of great personal struggle against feelings of despair and regret.

The full story of aging has a downside to it as well; it's not all sunshine and rainbows. Older people experience great challenges: the deaths of their spouse and family members, the loss of close friends and acquaintances, the fading of their physical capabilities, the loss of personal freedoms such as driving or living without assistance, and inevitable health challenges as the body ages. Existentially speaking, older adults also must, sooner or later, face the growing awareness that their time on this earth is drawing to a close. It doesn't take a lot of imagination to understand why younger people often assume that the elderly are unhappy and depressed as they face the imminent "dying of the light." Certainly, depression and even suicide are not unknown to the elderly, although contrary to the stereotype of the unhappy, lonely old person, healthy older adults are no more likely to become depressed than are younger people. The reality is that as long as basic emotional and social needs are met, old age is often a very joyous time, again reflecting the greater wisdom with which older adults approach the challenges of their lives, making the best of things, focusing on what they can be grateful for, and letting things go that are negative, as much as possible (Charles & Carstensen, 2009).

Older adults have had enough experience dealing with the slings and arrows of life that they've learned how to emotionally cope, how to see the glass as half-full rather than half-empty, and how to focus on the positives even as they face the negatives. The active cultivation of positive emotions has been shown to be a key resource that helps people cope with life's challenges (Cohn et al., 2009; Garland et al., 2010). For example, research at Kwantlen University has shown that many older people respond even to the loss of their beloved spouse by focusing on positive emotions (Tweed & Tweed, 2011); this enhanced positive focus leads to better coping overall, such as less depressed mood, the experience of greater social support, and even the ability to provide more support to others in the community. This flies in the face of earlier theorists who argued that grief needed to be "fully processed" in order for people to recover (Bonanno, 2004), and experiencing frequent positive emotions while grieving was actually a sign of pathology (Bowlby, 1980)!

In fact, one of the key lessons that life teaches a person is that many of the challenges one faces carry their own rewards and hidden benefits. As people age, their suffering and loss ends up getting used as fertilizer for their own personal growth. In struggling to deal with the difficulties of life, people often find that they grow in many ways, such as shifting their priorities after realizing what really matters to them, feeling deeply grateful for their close relationships, and feeling deeply motivated to live authentically according to one's own personal values and sense of what is right (Tedeschi & Calhoun, 2004). Older people therefore have ample opportunities for personal growth, and it is important to respect how much of the later years of life can be a supremely rich time for people to invest in their own growth, learning, and practice. Even as death approaches, the benefits to the elderly can be a deep enriching of the gratitude they feel for being alive (Frias et al., 2011).

THE EVENTUAL DECLINE OF AGING Of course, every story has its ending, and as much as we might like to avoid this topic, we also have to acknowledge that the later years of adulthood are accompanied by a certain amount of decline. The body declines and the mind eventually is not as sharp as it once was. Researchers have examined this in great detail and found that the brain, just like other physical systems, shows structural changes and some functional decline with age. These changes include reduced volume of white and grey matter of the cerebral cortex, as well as of the memory-processing hippocampus (Allen et al., 2005). The prefrontal cortex and its connections to subcortical regions are also hit hard by aging (Raz, 2000). The reduced frontal lobe volume may explain why older adults sometimes lose their train of thought and why they sometimes say things that they wouldn't have in the past (e.g., blunt comments, vulgarity). Because it is now common for people to live well into their 80s and beyond, these declines are ever more important to understand because they have many implications for how well older adults will be able to function in their everyday lives.

If one lives well and/or is lucky, one can get pretty much to the end of a natural lifespan with very little cognitive decline. However, there is a lot of variability in how well people will age, neurologically speaking. The negative end of the spectrum is anchored by various *neurodegenerative* conditions. These are medical conditions of aging characterized by the loss of nerve cells and nervous system functioning, which generally worsen over time. Many older adults struggle with attending to the tasks of everyday life, which may indicate the onset of **dementia**, *a mild to severe disruption of mental functioning, memory loss, disorientation, and poor judgment and decision making.* Approximately 14% of people older than 71 years of age have dementia.

PSYCH @

The Driver's Seat

Thanks to technology, the current generation of elderly adults faces issues that previous generations never did. Take driving, for example. Many older adults depend on their cars to shop, maintain a social life, and keep appointments. Research, however, has shown that the cognitive and physical changes in old age may take a toll on driving skill. This decline presents a dilemma for many seniors and their families: How can individuals maintain the independence afforded by driving without endangering themselves and other drivers?

To address this problem, psychologist Karlene Ball developed an intervention called Useful Field of View (UFOV) Speed of Processing training (Ball & Owsley, 1993). UFOV uses computer-based training exercises to increase the portion of the visual field that adults can quickly process and respond to. Laboratory studies show that UFOV actually increases the speed of cognitive processing for older adults (Ball & Owsley, 2000). Records from several U.S. states that have studied the UFOV show that drivers who completed the training were half as likely to have had an accident during the study period.

Nearly 10% of cases of dementia involve the more severe **Alzheimer's disease**—*a degenerative and terminal condition resulting in severe damage to the entire brain.* Alzheimer's disease rarely appears before age 60, and it usually lasts 7 to 10 years from onset to death (although some people with Alzheimer's live much longer). Early symptoms include forgetfulness for recent events, poor judgment, and some mood and personality changes. As the disease progresses, people experience severe confusion and memory loss, eventually struggling to recognize even their closest family members. In the most advanced stages of Alzheimer's disease, affected individuals may fail to recognize themselves and may lose control of basic bodily processes such as bowel and bladder control.

What accounts for such extensive deterioration of cognitive abilities? Alzheimer's disease involves a buildup of proteins that clump together in the spaces between neurons, interrupting their normal activity. These are often referred to as *plaques*. Another type of protein tangles within nerve cells, which severely disrupts their structural integrity and functioning (Figure 10.18). These are often referred to as *neurofibrillary tangles* (or simply as *tangles*). Many different research groups are currently searching for specific genes that are associated with Alzheimer's disease. The genetic risk (i.e., the heritability of the disease) is very high for people who develop an early-onset form (age 30–60) of Alzheimer's disease (Bertram et al., 2010). In those individuals with later-onset (age 60+) disease, the genetic link is not as consistent.

Figure 10.18 How Alzheimer's Disease Affects the Brain

Advanced Alzheimer's disease is marked by significant loss of both grey and white matter throughout the brain. The brain of a person with Alzheimer's disease typically has a large buildup of a protein called beta-amyloid, which kills nerve cells. Also, tau proteins, which maintain the structure of nerve cells, are often found to be defective in the Alzheimer's brain, resulting in neurofibrillary tangles.

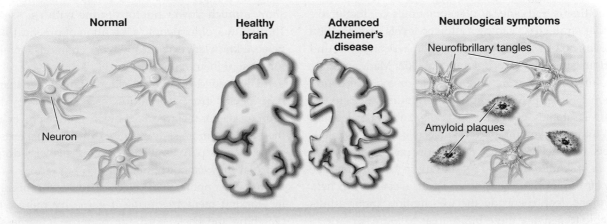

Source: Based on information from National Institute of Aging. (2008). Part 2: What happens to the brain in AD. In *Alzheimer's Disease: Unraveling the mystery*. U.S. Department of Health and Human Services. NIH Publication No. 08-3782. Retrieved from https://www.nia.nih.gov/sites/default/files/alzheimers_disease_unraveling_the_mystery_2.pdf

Alzheimer's disease illustrates a worst-case scenario of the aging brain. However, even in normal brains, structural changes occur which also cause a variety of cognitive challenges that increase as the person gets older.

Aging and Cognitive Change

How does the normal aging process affect cognitive abilities such as intelligence, learning, and memory? People commonly believe that a loss of cognitive abilities is an inevitable part of aging, even for those who do not develop dementia or Alzheimer's disease. However, the reality of aging and cognition is not so simple.

What do we know about different cognitive abilities?

There are many different cognitive abilities, including different memory and attentional abilities. One useful distinction is made between cognitive tasks that involve processes such as problem solving, reasoning, processing speed, and mental flexibility; these tasks are said to involve *fluid intelligence*. Other tasks tap into *crystallized intelligence*, which is based on accumulated knowledge and skills (Module 9.2), such as recognizing famous people like David Suzuki or Justin Bieber. Although fluid intelligence reaches a peak during young adulthood and then slowly declines, crystallized intelligence remains largely intact into old age.

How can science explain age-related differences in cognitive abilities?

Researchers have not yet fully solved the riddle of why some cognitive abilities decline with age. There are many different potential explanations. Neurological studies of brain function suggest two leading possibilities.

The first is that older adults sometimes use ineffective cognitive strategies, leading to lower levels of activation of relevant brain areas. This has been repeatedly found in various studies (e.g., Logan et al., 2002; Madden et al., 1996). Interestingly, it may be possible to enhance neural function in older people simply by reminding them to use effective strategies. For example, Logan and her colleagues (2002) found that, compared to subjects in their 20s, older subjects (in their 70s and 80s) performed worse on a memory task and showed less activity in key frontal lobe areas. However, by giving older adults strategies to help them more deeply encode the information, older adults were able to activate these brain areas to a greater extent, thus improving their memories for the information. This work suggests that a key to helping older adults resist the decline of their cognitive abilities is to help them learn effective strategies for making better use of their cognitive resources.

A second possible explanation for reduced cognitive abilities in older people is that older brains show more general, non-specific brain activation for a given task (Cabeza, 2002). They may do so either because they are compensating for deficits in one area by recruiting other areas, or possibly because they are less capable of limiting activation to the appropriate, specialized neural areas. Involving more widely distributed brain areas in a given task would generally result in slower processing speed, which could help to explain some of the cognitive deficits (e.g., fluid intelligence) seen in older adults.

Can we critically evaluate our assumptions about age-related cognitive changes?

Although older people show declines on laboratory tests of some cognitive functions, we should guard against the stereotypic assumption that the elderly are somehow less intellectually capable than the rest of us. In most cultures and for most of history, older people have been widely respected and honoured as wisdom keepers for their communities; respect for one's elders is, in fact, the historical norm, whereas modern Western society's tendency to disregard the perspectives of the elderly, assuming that they are out of touch and their opinions are no longer relevant, is the aberration.

The wisdom of elderly people is evident in their approach not only to emotional well-being, as we discussed earlier in this module, but also in how they deal with their own cognitive abilities. In everyday life, as opposed to most laboratory tests, the decline in cognitive abilities does not necessarily translate into decline in practical skills, for at least two important reasons. The first is that while the episodic and working memory systems may not work as well, the procedural and semantic memory systems show a much slower rate of decline with age (see Figure 10.19). Thus, older people's retention of practical skills and general knowledge about the world remains largely intact for most of their lives.

The second reason the elderly fare better than might be expected from laboratory tests is that they learn to compensate for their reduced raw cognitive power by using their abilities more skillfully. For example, in a chess game, older players play as well as young players, despite the fact that they cannot remember chess positions as well as their young opponents. They compensate for this reduction in working memory during a game by more efficiently searching the chessboard for patterns (Charness, 1981). Having more experience to draw upon in many domains of life gives older people an advantage because they will be

Figure 10.19 Memory and Aging

Several types of memory systems exist, not all of which are equally affected by age. An older person's ability to remember events, such as words that appeared on a list (episodic memory), is more likely to decline than his or her memory for facts and concepts (semantic memory).

better able to develop strategies that allow them to process information more efficiently (Salthouse, 1987).

Why is this relevant?

In a society that increasingly relegates its elderly to seniors' residences, largely removing them from their families and the larger community, it is important to remember that older people actually retain their faculties much better than might be expected. This is especially true for older adults who practice specific cognition-enhancing behaviours. What keeps the aging brain sharp? It's pretty simple really, as researchers at the University of Alberta and others have shown—staying physically active, practising cognitively challenging activities (and they don't have to be crosswords and brain teaser puzzles; intrinsically enjoyable hobbies work just fine), and remaining socially connected and active (Small et al., 2012; Stine-Morrow, 2007). In addition, diets low in saturated fats and rich in antioxidants, omega-3 fatty acids, and B vitamins help to maintain cognitive functioning and neural plasticity (Mattson, 2000; Molteni et al., 2002). As a society, providing opportunities and resources for seniors to remain active, socially engaged, and well-nourished will allow them to enjoy high-quality lives well into old age.

Module 10.4b Quiz:

Late Adulthood

Understand . . .

1. Socioemotional selectivity theory describes how older adults
    A. are better at socializing in general, because they have a lifetime of practice; thus, they tend to make friends very easily, and this keeps them functioning well.
    B. are better at selecting emotions that are socially acceptable based on the current circumstance. This causes them much less stress and is why they are generally happier.
    C. have usually invested so much of their lives in a few close relationships that now they have a network of support in those friends who were selected based on their tendency to be socially and emotionally supportive.
    D. are better at paying attention to positive things, rather than excessively dwelling on the negatives.

2. Once someone is diagnosed with Alzheimer's disease, they are likely to
    A. experience escalating pain and a reduction of their physical capabilities.
    B. exhibit emotional volatility and a tendency towards irrational, violent behaviour.
    C. exhibit confused, forgetful behaviour and a general decline in cognitive abilities.
    D. experience intense hallucinations, especially involving people who have died.

Apply . . .

3. Which of the following best describes the effects of aging on intelligence?

   A. Fluid intelligence tends to decrease, but working memory tends to increase.

   B. Fluid intelligence tends to decrease, but crystallized intelligence tends to increase.

   C. Crystallized intelligence tends to increase, but the ability to skillfully use one's abilities decreases.

   D. Aging is unrelated to intelligence, except in the case of brain disorders and diseases such as dementia or Alzheimer's disease.

Module 10.4 Summary

10.4a Know . . . the key terminology concerning adulthood and aging.

Alzheimer's disease
dementia
menopause
socioemotional selectivity theory

10.4b Know . . . the key areas of growth experienced by emerging adults.

People making the transition from adolescence to adulthood face substantial life challenges that contribute to personal growth in three main areas: relationships (i.e., cultivating true intimacy and trust); new possibilities (i.e., exploring what they really want to do with their lives and choosing a compatible path that reflects their interests); and personal strengths (i.e., the skills and competencies that come from successfully facing challenges).

10.4c Understand . . . age-related disorders such as Alzheimer's disease.

Alzheimer's disease is a form of dementia that is characterized by significant decline in memory, cognition, and, eventually, basic bodily functioning. It seems to be caused by two different brain abnormalities—the buildup of proteins that clump together in the spaces between neurons, plus degeneration of a structural protein that forms tangles within nerve cells.

10.4d Understand . . . how cognitive abilities change with age.

Aging adults typically experience a general decline in cognitive abilities, especially those related to fluid intelligence, such as working memory. However, older adults also develop compensatory strategies that enable them to remain highly functional in their daily lives, despite their slow decline in processing capability.

10.4e Apply . . . effective communication principles to the challenge of improving your own relationships.

Apply Activity

In this module, you read about John Gottman's research into the Four Horsemen of the (Relationship) Apocalypse. Identify which of the four relationship-harming behaviours are most apparent in each of the three descriptions below.

1. Molly and David are arguing—David feels that Molly spends too much of her time talking on the phone with her friends rather than spending time with him. Molly rolls her eyes and says "I didn't realize you needed to be entertained 24 hours a day."

2. Nicole is upset that her husband Greg isn't putting in enough hours at his job to make a good income. When she talks to Greg about this, he becomes distant and ends the discussion.

3. Juan and Maria are having marital problems. When frustrated, Juan often complains about Maria's mother and about how Maria's friends are immature. This upsets Maria.

10.4f Analyze . . . the stereotype that old age is a time of unhappiness.

Research shows that older adults do face issues that might lead to unhappiness—for example, health problems, loss of loved ones, and reductions in personal freedom. However, such challenges often lead to growth and a deepened appreciation for life and other people. The result is that many older people become skilled at focusing on the positives of life and pay less attention to the negatives, leading to an *increase* in life satisfaction, rather than a decrease.

Chapter 11
Motivation and Emotion

11.1 Hunger and Eating

- Physiological Aspects of Hunger **442**
- Module 11.1a Quiz **445**
- Psychological Aspects of Hunger **445**
- Module 11.1b Quiz **447**
- Disorders of Eating **448**

  Working the Scientific Literacy Model: The Effect of Media Depictions of Beauty on Body Image **450**
- Module 11.1c Quiz **451**
- Module 11.1 Summary **451**

11.2 Sex

- Human Sexual Behaviour: Psychological Influences **453**
- Module 11.2a Quiz **455**
- Human Sexual Behaviour: Physiological Influences **455**
- Module 11.2b Quiz **460**
- Human Sexual Behaviour: Cultural Influences **460**

  Working the Scientific Literacy Model: Does Sex Sell? **462**
- Module 11.2c Quiz **463**
- Module 11.2 Summary **464**

11.3 Social and Achievement Motivation

- Belonging and Love Needs **466**

  Working the Scientific Literacy Model: Terror Management Theory and the Need to Belong **468**
- Module 11.3a Quiz **470**
- Achievement Motivation **470**
- Module 11.3b Quiz **474**
- Module 11.3 Summary **475**

11.4 Emotion

- Physiology of Emotion **477**
- Module 11.4a Quiz **479**
- Experiencing Emotions **479**

  Working the Scientific Literacy Model: The Two-Factor Theory of Emotion **481**
- Module 11.4b Quiz **484**
- Expressing Emotions **484**
- Module 11.4c Quiz **488**
- Module 11.4 Summary **489**

Module 11.1 Hunger and Eating

Satchan/Corbis/Bridge/Glow Images

 ## Learning Objectives

11.1a Know . . . the key terminology of motivation and hunger.

11.1b Understand . . . the biological, cognitive, and social processes that shape eating patterns.

11.1c Understand . . . the causes of common eating disorders.

11.1d Apply . . . your knowledge of hunger regulation to better understand and evaluate your own eating patterns.

11.1e Analyze . . . the role of the media on people's body image.

It was Janice's first year of university. She'd made it through the first three months of the semester with impressive grades, but was now dealing with her first ever set of final exams. After a long afternoon of studying History, Janice felt like she was starving. She walked over to the cafeteria and was overwhelmed by the number of options. She saw a friend eating a greasy pizza and immediately ordered one for herself (but with a salad, which of course made the meal healthy). She finished the enormous plate of food and felt like she couldn't eat another bite. She crawled back to the library and began studying for her Chemistry exam that was scheduled for the next morning. But, despite having just eaten a large meal, Janice found herself munching on candy that she'd snuck into the library (a guilty habit that was now as much a part of studying as her textbooks). The more anxious she got about this exam, the more she mindlessly moved the sugary snacks from their bag into her mouth. Janice's experience shows us that eating isn't just a simple behaviour we use for survival. Hunger is a biological drive that influences what we pay attention

to and interacts with our past experiences and current mental states such as excitement and anxiety. Hunger is a psychological behaviour.

Focus Questions

1. What are some ways that our physical and social environments affect eating?

2. What makes us feel hungry or full?

≫ Although this module focuses on behaviours related to eating and hunger, it also serves as an introduction to the concept of motivation. **Motivation** *concerns the physiological and psychological processes underlying the initiation of behaviours that direct organisms toward specific goals.* These initiating factors, or *motives*, can take many forms. They can involve satisfying bodily needs such as drinking when

Figure 11.1 Maintaining Balance

Homeostasis is the process of maintaining relatively stable internal states. For example, this diagram illustrates how homeostasis regulates thirst and the body's fluid levels. The body detects that fluid levels are low and sends signals to the brain that motivate us to drink; once fluid levels are normal, this motivation decreases. A pack of psychology professors are, of course, just out of view in this photo, battling a group of Kenyans for third place.

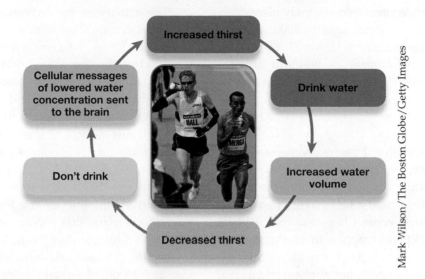

Mark Wilson/The Boston Globe/Getty Images

you are thirsty, but they can also include social behaviours such as seeking out other people when you are lonely. The fact that you are reading Chapter 11 of a university textbook shows you the breadth of this concept—you are likely motivated to achieve academic success. In all of these cases, a behaviour is being initiated in order to complete some sort of goal-directed behaviour.

At its most basic level, motivation is essential to an individual's survival because it contributes to **homeostasis**, *the body's physiological processes that allow it to maintain consistent internal states in response to the outer environment* (see Figure 11.1). For example, when the body's water levels fall below normal, cells release chemical compounds that maintain the structure and fluid levels

of cells. Receptors in the body respond to the increased concentrations of these compounds, as well as to the lower water volume, and send messages to the brain. The result is the sudden awareness that you are thirsty, which motivates you to drink water. This process is known as a **drive**, *a biological trigger that tells us we may be deprived of something and causes us to seek out what is needed, such as food or water* (Figure 11.2). The *stimuli we seek out in order to reduce drives* are known as **incentives**. In this example, the incentive would be water; however, in other modules, incentives will range from sex (see Module 11.2) to feeling like you belong, or even to a more abstract feeling of reaching your potential as a human (see Module 11.3).

Figure 11.2 Drives and Incentives

Our motivation to reduce a drive, or in response to an incentive, can lead to the same behaviour.

There are times, however, when our behaviours cannot be explained by a desire to reach a state of homeostasis. Instead, our motivations are influenced by an internal or external source of stress. Stress often leads us to use more resources than we normally would. Stress is particularly challenging to our homeostasis because it is difficult predict how long you will be in that energy-consuming state—you don't schedule stress into your day planner. As a result, our motivational systems have to make a prediction about the resources that our bodies will require, and then initiate motivational behaviours that will drive us to acquire those resources. This process is known as **allostasis**, *motivation that is not only influenced by current needs, but also by the anticipation of future needs caused by stress* (Sterling, 2011).

To make the relationship between homeostasis and allostasis more concrete, let's think back to the example of Janice eating candy while stressing out about her exams. The experience of anxiety used a lot of Janice's energy, as did the effort required to control her emotions. If Janice didn't increase her food consumption to meet these new energy demands, her energy level would quickly dip below optimal levels. As a result, her physical and mental well-being would then suffer. So, if Janice were not stressed out, homeostasis would drive her toward consuming a particular number of calories; however, allostasis—which involves the influence of stress on homeostasis—would drive her to consume a greater number of calories (and would be *one* reason why she was snacking). Of course, our ability to predict our future needs is not perfect, which explains why psychological variables (e.g., stress, desire to appear attractive, the need to feel "in control") can have such a strong influence on behaviours like eating and drinking, which don't seem "psychological" at all.

In this module, we will examine how these physical and psychological factors influence our motivation to eat. We will also examine how social factors can alter our eating habits in negative and self-destructive ways.

Physiological Aspects of Hunger

Hunger is not simply a homeostatic mechanism. The need to consume enough nutrients so that you have enough energy to function involves physiological responses *as well as* more complex cognitive and emotional factors (Dagher, 2012). The brain areas involved with these factors interact with the brain areas that control our appetites.

The "on" and "off" switches involved in hunger can be found in a few regions of the **hypothalamus**, *a set of nuclei found on the bottom surface of the brain*. Researchers have found that electrically stimulating the lateral hypothalamus causes rats to begin to eat; thus, this structure may serve as an "on" switch (Delgado & Anand, 1952). In contrast, stimulating the ventromedial region of the hypothalamus causes rats to stop eating. Damaging the ventromedial region removes the "off switch" in the brain; in lab animals, this damage leads to obesity because the animals don't stop eating (Figure 11.3). A related area, the *paraventricular* nucleus of the hypothalamus, also signals that it is time to stop eating by inhibiting the lateral hypothalamus.

The activity of the hypothalamus is influenced by hormones that are released in response to the energy needs of your body. So, your brain influences your body *and* your body influences your brain! A key function of the hypothalamus is to monitor blood chemistry for indicators of the levels of sugars and hormones necessary for you to have enough energy to function. For example, the hypothalamus detects changes in the level of **glucose**, *a sugar that serves as a primary energy source for the brain and the rest of the body*. Highly specialized neurons called glucostats can detect glucose levels in the fluid outside of the cell. If these levels are too low, glucostats signal the hypothalamus that energy supplies are low, leading to increased hunger (Langhans, 1996a, 1996b). After food reaches the stomach and intestines, sugars are absorbed into the bloodstream and transported throughout the body. Insulin, a hormone secreted by the pancreas, helps

Voisin/Phanie/Photo Researchers, Inc./Science Source

The rat on the left has swollen to enormous proportions after researchers created lesions to its ventromedial hypothalamus. Compare it to the more typical rat on the right.

Figure 11.3 The Hypothalamus and Hunger

The hypothalamus acts as an on/off switch for hunger. The lateral region of the hypothalamus signals when it is time to eat, while the ventromedial and paraventricular regions signal when it is time to stop eating.

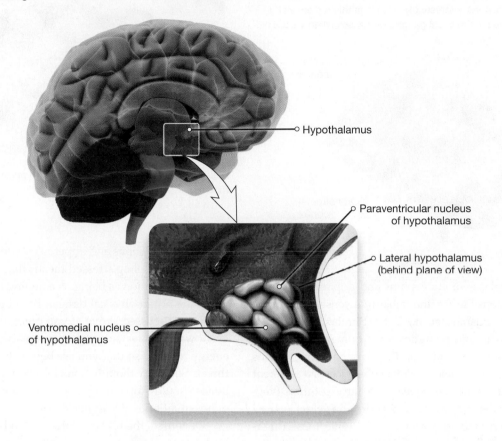

Hypothalamus

Paraventricular nucleus of hypothalamus

Lateral hypothalamus (behind plane of view)

Ventromedial nucleus of hypothalamus

Source: From Weiten. Psychology, 9E. © 2013 South-Western, a part of Cengage Learning, Inc. Reproduced by permission. www.cengage.com/permissions.

cells store this circulating glucose for future use. As insulin levels rise in response to consumption of a meal, hunger decreases—but so do glucose levels, which, after a few hours, leads to hunger again.

Of course, if our motivation to eat was based entirely on the relationship between glucose and the hypothalamus, then our eating behaviours would be quite simple: we'd consume whatever food was available until our need for glucose was satisfied. We all know that is not the case. Eating is influenced by a number of other factors including the characteristics of the available food and how much of it we have already eaten.

FOOD AND REWARD In the example that started this module, poor stressed-out Janice ate pizza, salad, and candy. But, humans evolved in environments in which food was not this plentiful or rich in variety. Sometimes, after a successful hunting expedition, food was abundant; however, at other times, food was quite scarce. Humans quickly learned that the best strategy was to "eat while

you can" because there was no guarantee that another meal would be forthcoming any time soon. And, given that we need a great deal of energy to keep our bodies functioning properly, it would make sense to consume fatty foods, a very rich source of energy. Over the course of evolution, our bodies responded to this need with a number of systems that made the consumption of high-energy foods pleasurable. In other words, we developed bodies that were hard-wired to *like* some foods more than others.

Imagine eating poutine, Québec's cardiovascular equivalent of Russian roulette. It's clearly bad for you (there is no diet poutine), yet people still enthusiastically eat it. Indeed, some of the most popular foods in Canada are loaded with fats, including red meat, cheese, ice cream, and anything deep-fried. Psychologists and neuroscientists are discovering why people can be so driven to consume these and other fattening foods. Scientists suggest that we crave fats because we have specialized receptors on the tongue that are sensitive to the fat content of food. Research with animals shows that these receptors send messages to the brain that

Figure 11.4 The Pleasure of Taste

When fat receptors of the tongue are stimulated, the cingulate cortex—a region of the brain involved in emotional processing—is activated. The orbitofrontal cortex is involved in linking food taste and texture with reward. Interestingly, activity in this region, along with reward centres in the basal ganglia, decreases when we are no longer motivated to eat.

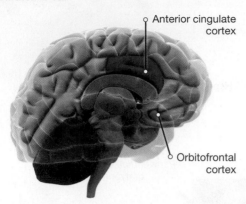

Anterior cingulate cortex

Orbitofrontal cortex

Cells in the orbitofrontal cortex respond to perceptual qualities of food texture, such as the difference between a runny spaghetti sauce and a thick one.

stimulate the release of endorphins and dopamine, both of which are responsible for the subjective sense of pleasure and reward (Mizushige et al., 2007). Similar results were found in brain imaging studies with human participants (Rolls, 2010). In one study, participants had their brains scanned while they tasted various substances. At different times, the participants tasted either a fatty solution (vegetable oil), sucrose (a sweet taste), or a tasteless control substance. Brain activity was recorded while these different taste stimuli were delivered in liquefied form into the mouths of the participants through a small plastic tube. The participants were also asked to rate the pleasantness of each stimulus. Overall, the participants rated the fatty substance favourably, and the brain scans showed activity in regions of the brain associated with pleasure sensations when they tasted fat (de Araujo & Rolls, 2004; see Figure 11.4).

In some situations, high-energy food can be a more powerful reinforcer than highly addictive drugs (Christensen et al., 2008). Some people even report cravings for a *sugar fix*—a term that seems to imply that addiction to candy and chocolate bars is comparable to an addiction to a drug like heroin. The phrase "sugar fix" may seem an exaggeration, but is it possible that sugar actually does act like a drug? Sugar and some addictive drugs share an interesting similarity. Ordinary sucrose—plain white granulated sugar—can stimulate release of the neurotransmitter dopamine in the nucleus accumbens, a brain region associated with the reinforcing effects of substances such as amphetamines and cocaine (Rada et al., 2005; see Module 5.3).

These studies may help to explain why Janice, our long-suffering student, craved fatty and sugary foods while cramming for exams. Her motivation to eat was also influenced by her stress level. Stress affects a person's level of *ghrelin*, a hormone secreted in the stomach that stimulates

stomach contractions and appetite (Kristensson et al., 2006). Additionally, feeling stressed means that you are viewing a particular situation as being threatening in some way, even if you are not in physical danger. Based on the principle of allostasis discussed above, if you predict that an upcoming event will be threatening, you will react by stocking up on energy reserves so that you are better able to deal with this threat. So, even though homeostasis would indicate that Janice should stop eating, her psychological interpretation of her situation will lead her to continue munching away.

Of course, the reward value of food is also influenced by how much of it we have consumed—even the most stressed-out student will stop eating eventually. Indeed, we have all experienced the feeling of being "full." A full stomach is one cue for **satiation**—*the point in a meal when we are no longer motivated to eat.* That feeling is caused, in part, by cholecystokinin (mercifully abbreviated to CCK) (Badman & Flier, 2005). Neurons release CCK when the intestines expand. The ventromedial hypothalamus receives this information and decreases appetite. Scientists at the Montreal Neurological Institute used neuroimaging to investigate how satiation and the reward value of food might be linked. These researchers scanned people's brains while feeding them pieces of chocolate. At first, the participants rated the chocolate as being quite tasty and pleasurable; this led to activity in reward centres in the orbitofrontal cortex (the part of the frontal lobes just above your eyes) and basal ganglia (Small et al., 2001). Activity was also found in the insula, which receives information about taste. But, after participants had consumed several pieces of chocolate, this formerly pleasurable food became less appealing (i.e., they became "sick of it"). Interestingly, as participants' ratings of the chocolate became more negative, the activity in reward centres decreased. This study shows us that our physiological and psychological motivations to eat influence each other.

Module 11.1a Quiz:

Physiological Aspects of Hunger

Know . . .

1. The _____ region of the hypothalamus is associated with the onset of eating, while the _____ region is associated with the offset.
   A. lateral; ventromedial
   B. ventromedial; lateral
   C. anterior; posterior
   D. anterior; ventromedial

2. _____ is a sugar that serves as a vital energy source for the human body; its levels are monitored by the nervous system.
   A. Ghrelin
   B. CCK
   C. Glucose
   D. Insulin

Understand . . .

3. Why do psychologists believe the lateral hypothalamus generates hunger signals that contribute to people's motivation to eat?

A. This brain structure responds to glucose levels.
B. When the lateral hypothalamus is stimulated, laboratory animals eat more.
C. Skinny people have smaller nuclei in this area.
D. The lateral hypothalamus releases CCK, which reduces hunger.

Analyze . . .

4. How do evolutionary psychologists explain our desire to eat particular foods?
   A. We eat fatty foods because they are most accessible.
   B. The foods we now find pleasurable are often high-energy foods that would have enhanced our chances for survival in the past.
   C. People who consume sugar-free food have less energy and are less likely to reproduce, thus making them less evolutionarily fit.
   D. People have adapted our food intake to match our current North American lifestyle.

Psychological Aspects of Hunger

The previous section of this module described a number of biological influences on our motivation to eat. In this section of the module, we highlight cognitive and social factors that affect this important behaviour.

ATTENTION AND EATING The quantity of food that we eat is not entirely controlled by the brain or by evolutionary mechanisms. Instead, something as simple as attention can have a huge effect on how much we consume. Imagine sitting down to your favourite meal. Many of us would eat a lot, but then watching each helping disappear would probably serve as a reminder that it is approaching time to stop. But what if someone (or some drug) interfered with your ability to keep track of how much you had eaten? This scenario is not what we would expect in normal situations, but it would allow for an ideal test of how food availability affects how much you will eat.

Psychologists have created such a situation in the laboratory through a technique known as the bottomless bowl of soup. Volunteers were asked to eat soup until they had had enough. In the experimental condition, a tube continued to fill the soup bowl from the bottom so that it could not be detected by the volunteers. These individuals stopped eating after consuming, on average, over 70% more than those participants who knowingly refilled their bowls. Even more interesting is what happened—or did not happen—in terms of feelings and thoughts: The individuals eating from bottomless bowls did not feel any more satiated, nor did they believe they had eaten any

more than the individuals in the control group. It turns out we are not so good at putting on the brakes when we cannot keep track of how much we have consumed (Wansink et al., 2005).

The results of the bottomless soup bowl study can be explained by **unit bias**, *the tendency to assume that the unit of sale or portioning is an appropriate amount to consume*. In some cases, this assumption works well. A single banana comes individually wrapped and makes for a healthy portion; it is an ideal unit (Geier et al., 2006). In contrast, packaged foods often come in sizes that are too large to be healthy. A bottle of pop today is likely to be 600 mL, but a few decades ago the same brand of soda came in a 177 mL bottle. Despite the huge difference in volume, each is seen as constituting one unit of pop. As a consequence, you are now likely to consume more than three times as much pop in one sitting as your grandparents would have. Surprisingly, the unit bias affects our consumption almost as much as the taste of the food! In one study, participants were given fresh or stale (14-day-old) popcorn in either a small (120 g) or large (240 g) container. When the container was large, participants ate more popcorn . . . even if it was incredibly stale and tasted like styrofoam (Wansink & Kim, 2005). A similar effect was found for people at a Super Bowl party. The larger bowls implied that it was "normal" for people to eat more (Wansink & Cheney, 2005). Researchers have concluded that increasing the size of the dishes increases consumption by 18–25% for meals and 30–45% for snack foods (Wansink, 1996).

Compare a modern soft drink serving (top) to the historical serving size (bottom). Despite the massive increase in volume, modern consumers still consider the unit of packaging as a normal-sized serving.

This expansion of portion sizes—and waistlines—is being felt worldwide. As North-American-style fast-food chains expand into Asia, the prevalence of diabetes has increased (Pan et al., 2012). This is likely why some countries limit portion sizes and others, such as France, require all fast-food chains and snack products to have warning labels. But, before we beat ourselves up about how greedy our culture is, we should get some perspective: This upward trend in the size of our meals has been going on for a long time. This was demonstrated in a clever study examining the portion sizes of food in paintings depicting the same scene from the Bible (the last supper of Jesus). The study examined portion sizes in paintings over the last millennium (1000–2000 C.E.). Sure enough, the plate sizes and portion sizes increased over the years (Wansink & Wansink, 2010).

Given this information about the role of attention, container sizes, and culture, what changes do you think should be made in the food industry to make Canada a healthier place?

EATING AND SEMANTIC NETWORKS   Although attention and the unit bias play powerful roles in our motivation to eat, they are not the only cognitive factors that influence this behaviour. Imagine you are in a university cafeteria. As you push your tray along the counter, you have the option of selecting a number of different foods. What motivates you to select healthy options such as carrots as opposed to unhealthy options such as cookies?

It turns out that our food selections can be influenced by the presence of certain other foods. These items, known as **trigger foods**, *affect the selection of healthy and unhealthy foods simply by being present among possible food alternatives.* In fact, trigger foods don't need to be selected to affect eating behaviour. In a study of high school cafeterias, researchers found that the presence of containers of applesauce or fruit cocktail increased the likelihood that students would take cookies, ice cream bars, and other unhealthy snacks. In contrast, the presence of green beans or bananas decreased the likelihood that students would take unhealthy snacks (Hanks et al., 2012). What could be causing these effects?

One factor that could explain these results is *priming*, a concept discussed in earlier modules of this book (see Modules 4.1 and 8.1). In priming, previous exposure to a stimulus will affect later responses, either to that stimulus or to something related to it. The related items are typically part of that stimulus' *semantic network*, a group of interconnected concepts (see Module 8.1). When you see a banana, you often think of its colour and shape, of the fact that it is a fruit, and possibly of animals that eat them. But, when you think of fruit cocktail, your semantic network likely includes characteristics such as syrup and sweet-tasting (see Figure 11.5). Researchers suggest that activating the concepts of sweet or sugary in your mind makes other foods that are also sweet or sugary more appealing, thus leading to an unhealthy food selection (Hanks et al., 2012). In other words, how we link together concepts in our minds can also affect the food we put in our bodies.

EATING AND THE SOCIAL CONTEXT   In addition to physical and cognitive influences, food intake is affected by social motives as well. Have you ever gone to a party feeling not a hint of hunger, yet spent the first hour sampling each of the snacks laid out on the dining room table because you were nervous and didn't know what else to do with yourself? Whether the presence of other people increases or decreases our motivation to eat is influenced

Figure 11.5 Trigger Foods and Semantic Networks

Unhealthy foods are often part of semantic networks that include terms such as "sweet" and "sugar." Activation of these nodes in a network increases the likelihood that we will select other foods that are also related to "sweet" and "sugary."

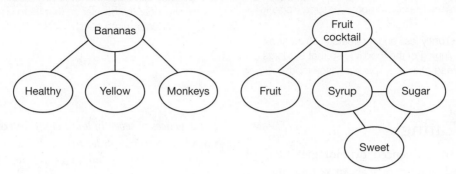

by the social situation (Herman et al., 2003). Here are a few examples:

- *Social facilitation: Eating more.* Dinner hosts (and grandmothers) may encourage guests to take second and even third helpings, and individuals with a reputation for big appetites will be prodded to eat the most. Perhaps the strongest element of social facilitation is just the time spent at the table: The longer a person sits socializing, the more likely he or she is to continue nibbling (Berry et al., 1985).

- *Impression management: Eating less.* Sometimes people self-consciously control their behaviour so that others will see them in a certain way—a phenomenon known as *impression management*. For example, you probably know that it is polite to chew with your mouth closed. Similarly, the *minimal eating norm* suggests that another aspect of good manners—at least in some social and cultural settings—is to eat small amounts to avoid seeming rude (Herman et al., 2003).

- *Modelling: Eating whatever they eat.* At first exposure to a situation, such as a business dinner, a new employee may notice that no one eats much and everyone takes their time. The newcomer will see the others as models, and so he too will restrain his eating. Later, he may drop by his friend's family reunion where everyone is having a second or third helping and undoing their belts so their stomachs can expand more. In this case, he will be likely to eat more, even if he is already feeling full (Herman et al., 2003).

Clearly, eating is not just a matter of maintaining homeostasis. It is best described as a behaviour motivated by biological, social, and individual psychological factors.

Module 11.1b Quiz:

Psychological Aspects of Hunger

Know . . .

1. The minimal eating social norm is the observation that people tend to
   A. eat as little as possible in just about every social situation imaginable.
   B. view eating reasonably sized portions as the polite thing to do.
   C. encourage one another to eat too much.
   D. eat as much as possible to flatter the cook.

Understand . . .

2. Being around others
   A. can lead you to eat more than you normally would.
   B. can lead you to eat less than you normally would.
   C. can lead you to eat more or less than normal, depending on what others are doing.
   D. does not influence our eating.

Apply . . .

3. In Europe, the typical container of fruit and yogurt is roughly 177 mL. In North America, the same food item is usually packaged in 237 mL containers. The unit bias suggests that
   A. a German person visiting Canada would be likely to eat the entire container, even though it contains 25% more than the typical German serving.
   B. a Canadian visiting Germany would almost certainly miss the extra 50 mL of yogurt.
   C. a German person visiting Canada would carefully evaluate the differences in packaging to ensure that he or she does not consume more than usual.
   D. all people would be unsatisfied with the 177 mL serving in Germany.

4. Teachers at a Fredericton high school have become concerned about the eating habits of their students. Unfortunately, their school has a contract with a snack food company stating that a number of sugary treats must be available for students to potentially purchase. How can these teachers use psychological research to decrease the consumption of sugary snack foods?

   A. They can place slightly less sugary treats such as applesauce at the beginning of the food line so that students select those instead of the company's snack foods.

   B. They can place healthy options like green beans at the beginning of the food line.

   C. They can tell the high school students that sugar is bad for them, as students always listen to wise teachers.

   D. They can place the unhealthy foods at the end of the food line near the cashier so that there is no room left on the students' lunch trays.

Disorders of Eating

Our dietary habits are influenced by biological dispositions, our beliefs and perceptions about eating and our bodies, as well as sociocultural factors. Unfortunately, these motivational systems do not always lead us to good health. The past few decades have seen a dramatic rise in the rates of **obesity**, *a disorder of positive energy balance, in which energy intake exceeds energy expenditure.* Indeed, over the last 15 years, surveys have consistently shown that approximately 60% of males and 45% of females are overweight or obese (extremely overweight; Statistics Canada, 2016). However, in some individuals, hunger-related motivations move in the opposite direction—leading them to under-eat. While skipping dessert at Dairy Queen might not be a bad idea, avoiding or restricting the consumption of healthy food is obviously problematic. In the next section, we discuss some of the motivations underlying disorders affecting the motivation to eat.

ANOREXIA AND BULIMIA The two most common forms of eating disorders are anorexia nervosa and bulimia (see Table 11.1). **Anorexia nervosa** *is an eating disorder that involves (1) self-starvation, (2) intense fear of weight gain and dissatisfaction with one's body, and (3) denial of the serious consequences of severely low weight.* In contrast, **bulimia nervosa** *is an eating disorder that is characterized by periods of food deprivation, binge-eating, and purging.* The periods of binging involve short bursts of intense calorie consumption. These are followed by purging (generally self-induced vomiting), fasting, laxative or diuretic use, and/or intense exercise. Both disorders usually occur during mid-to-late adolescence and have been on the rise during the 20th century (Hudson et al., 2007).

Studies of these disorders have found that bulimia is marked by a tendency to be impulsive, whereas anorexia is not (Matsunaga et al., 2000). Bulimics are also much more likely to enter treatment programs because they find the binge–purge cycle disturbing. Anorexics, on the other hand, often appear indifferent to the negative effects of food deprivation on their health (Polivy & Herman, 2002). Although there are clear differences between anorexia and bulimia, both involve changes in the motivation to eat and both are dangerous. A critical question, then, is: Why do eating disorders develop in some people but not others?

One factor is stress. Patients with eating disorders report greater levels of premorbid (before the disorder began) life stress than do age- and gender-matched individuals without eating disorders (Schmidt et al., 1997).

Table 11.1 Statistical Characteristics of Eating Disorders

The incidence of eating disorders in Canadians is similar to that of other Western nations. To put these numbers into a global perspective, a 2004 study found that the incidence rate of anorexia varied from 0.1% to 5.3% in females in Western countries (no male data were available). Bulimia rates ranged from 0.3% to 7.3% (Norway) in females in Western countries and from 0.46% to 3.2% in non-Western countries (Makino et al., 2004). Thanks to researchers working with government agencies, prevention programs are now in place in all Western and most non-Western countries.

Lifetime prevalence of anorexia	Women: 0.9%	Men: 0.3%
Lifetime prevalence of bulimia	Women: 1.5%	Men: 0.5%
	Women and Men Combined	
Percentage of people with anorexia who are receiving treatment	34%	
Percentage of people with bulimia who are receiving treatment	43%	
Average duration of anorexia	1.7 years	
Average duration of bulimia	8 years	

Source: Data from Hudson, J., Hiripi, E., Pope, H., & Kessler, R. (2007). The prevalence and correlates of eating disorders in the National Comorbidity Survey replication. *Biological Psychiatry, 61*, 348–358.

These life stresses tend to make people feel as though they have no control over their lives. However, stress alone isn't enough to create an eating disorder. Instead, the perceived loss of control interacts with psychological variables such as depression, guilt, anxiety, and perfectionism (Vohs et al., 1999); low self-esteem (Button et al., 1996); and/or suppressed anger (Geller et al., 2000). This *combination* of stress and psychological vulnerability dramatically increases the chances of developing an eating disorder (Ball & Lee, 2002; Raffi et al., 2000).

There are also a number of social factors that can lead to eating disorders. Peer influence is often viewed as the number-one cause of these conditions (Stice, 1998). Adolescents, particularly females, learn attitudes and behaviours from their friends. This learning comes in the form of examples and encouragement, as well as from teasing and nasty remarks when an individual doesn't live up to the idealized (thin) standards depicted in the media (Levine et al., 1994). In fact, numerous pro-anorexia websites have emerged over the past decade, offering "thinspiration" for people engaging in extreme dieting; similar messages now appear on social media sites such as Pinterest. By posting photographs and messages on these sites, individuals with eating disorders create a much larger peer group than before, making dangerous eating disorders seem normal. This is a worrisome trend.

Families are also a major influence on individuals with eating disorders. They often compliment anorexic girls for being slim and praise their self-control. This serves as a source of reinforcement for the eating disorder (Branch & Eurman, 1980). Bulimic patients reported that their families were competitive, prone to jealousy, and tended to intrude in each other's lives (Rorty et al., 2000). Importantly, adolescent girls whose families allow them to have some autonomy (i.e., control over their own lives) tend to have lower rates of eating disorders, suggesting that control is a major factor in these conditions (Polivy & Herman, 2002).

So, how do stress, peer pressure, and family issues lead to eating disorders? Researchers suggest that some people use eating disorders as a coping mechanism to deal with their difficult-to-control lives (Troop, 1998). By making weight and eating the primary focus of one's life, individuals gain some feelings of security (both physical and emotional) as well as a feeling of being in control of some aspect of their life. Indeed, after binging in the laboratory, individuals with bulimia reported feeling less anxiety, tension, and guilt, although feelings of depression remained the same (Kaye et al., 1986). In contrast, when these feelings of control are reduced, studies have shown that individuals with eating disorders become more pessimistic and report feeling fatter than before

TIFFANY BROWN/WPN/Photoshot

People with anorexia experience severely distorted views of their body. Although dangerously underweight, they continue to both feel fat and fear being fat. Both males and females may become anorexic.

(Waller & Hodgson, 1996). Evolutionary psychologists have suggested that this need for control extends to the woman's reproductive system as well. The *reproduction suppression hypothesis* states that females who believe they have low levels of social support from romantic partners and family members are more likely to engage in dieting behaviour (Juda et al., 2004). This change in food intake can influence ovulation (Frisch & Barbieri, 2002) and lead to a loss of menstrual periods (amenorrhea), making it less likely that the woman will become pregnant. Such data again suggest that eating disorders are an attempt to gain control over complex and stressful lives (Wasser & Barash, 1983).

Males, although less prone to these problems than females, also develop eating disorders. Adolescents and young men may starve themselves during periods of high exercise to lose weight and achieve muscle mass (Ricciardelli & McCabe, 2004). Ironically, although they have positive views of their own bodies, these men with "reverse anorexia" are just as obsessive and perfectionistic about their bodies as people with anorexia (Davis & Scott-Robertson, 2000). And, both groups are particularly sensitive to media depictions of "perfect bodies" that, for almost everybody, are unattainable.

Working the Scientific Literacy Model

The Effect of Media Depictions of Beauty on Body Image

One concern regarding eating disorders is the role that culture and the media play in their onset. Specifically, people with regular exposure to Western culture are more likely to develop bulimia than members of cultures without such exposure (Keel & Klump, 2003).

What do we know about the effect of media depictions of beauty on body image?

We often don't critically analyze the effects that media depictions of beauty can have on people, particularly on sensitive teenagers. In the 1950s, Marilyn Monroe—who was busty and had big hips—was considered gorgeous. Today, A-list actresses are pressured to have body shapes that are virtually impossible to achieve: a very thin body and large breasts. Failure to meet this standard will lead to mockery in magazines and on gossip websites. For example, in *People* magazine's "Worst Dressed" section, the writers freely use weight-related words when discussing why an article of clothing is a fashion "fail" (Crumpton, 1997). The result is that people who are not unnaturally thin may view their bodies as being ugly. But, do these media depictions of "perfection" influence how girls and women view themselves?

How can science explain the effect of the media on people's body image?

The average North American woman is 163 cm (5'4") and weighs 64 kg (140 lbs); the average model is 180 cm (5'11") and weighs 53 kg (117 lbs) (National [U.S.] Eating Disorders Association, 2002). Studies have shown that increased exposure to media (TV, magazines, Internet) is related to decreased satisfaction with one's body (Hofschire & Greenberg, 2002), particularly in people whose self-esteem is based on meeting socially defined standards (Williams et al., 2014); it is also related to a greater internalization of the slender ideal for female body shape (Stice & Shaw, 1994). Researchers at Wilfrid Laurier University found that females were more likely to compare themselves to unrealistic popular culture figures than were men when they were describing their own bodies; they did not do so when describing their social skills (Strahan et al., 2006). When the prominence of cultural norms was increased, all participants (female and male) were more likely to compare themselves with a model and felt worse after doing so. These results suggest that women are more consistently exposed to media depictions of "perfect bodies," but that men are also sensitive to these pressures. In a follow-up study, female participants were exposed either to commercials containing attractive and thin women or to neutral stimuli. The results indicated that viewing media depictions of beauty decreased women's satisfaction with their own bodies and made them more concerned with what other people thought of them (Strahan et al., 2008).

Can we critically evaluate this research?

It is easy to say that participants in psychology studies are simply answering the way they think the experimenter wants them to. However, the studies described above are consistent with recent brain-imaging data as well. Individuals with anorexia showed increased activity in the amygdala, a brain area related to fear and emotional arousal, when they were shown negative words related to body image; neutral words did not have this effect (Miyake et al., 2010). Women with bulimia had greater levels of activity in medial frontal lobe regions related to emotional processing during the viewing of overweight as opposed to thin bodies; non-bulimic women did not show this activity. Finally, when women with eating disorders were shown images comparing themselves to idealized (model) bodies, the insula—a brain region related to disgust—fired (Friederich et al., 2010). Together, these studies corroborate the questionnaire-based results that idealized media depictions of beauty have negative emotional consequences on vulnerable individuals.

Why is this relevant?

Understanding the relationship between the media and disorders of body image allows teachers, parents, and health-care practitioners to design programs to help image-conscious individuals. In Canada, several programs are now in place that aim to teach people to deal with social pressures and to have a realistic body image (McVey et al., 2009; Yuile & McVey, 2009). Importantly, knowledge about media influences can reduce its effects. When public school students completed activities that contested the idea that women needed to be thin and beautiful and men needed to be tall and muscular in order to succeed, the influence of media depictions decreased substantially (Strahan et al., 2008). Not everyone needs to keep up with the Kardashians.

Module 11.1c Quiz:

Disorders of Eating

Know . . .

1. What is one difference between anorexia and bulimia?
   A. Anorexia involves periods of self-starvation, whereas bulimia does not.
   B. Bulimia involves purging (such as self-induced vomiting), whereas this is less characteristic in anorexia.
   C. Anorexia occurs in females only, whereas bulimia occurs in both females and males.
   D. Anorexia and bulimia are actually two terms for the same disorder.

Apply . . .

2. Which of the following is the most likely predictor of someone's chances of developing an eating disorder?
   A. Activity of the parietal somatosensory cortex
   B. Decreased sensitivity to the reward value of food
   C. Exposure to idealized versions of body type and thinness
   D. Fat receptors on the tongue

Module 11.1 Summary

11.1a   Know . . . the key terminology of motivation and hunger.

allostasis
anorexia nervosa
bulimia nervosa
drive
glucose
homeostasis
hypothalamus

incentives
motivation
obesity
satiation
trigger foods
unit bias

11.1b   Understand . . . the biological, cognitive, and social processes that shape eating patterns.

Energy is delivered through the bloodstream in the form of glucose found in food; the hormone insulin helps the cells throughout the body store this fuel. CCK signals fullness (satiety). These substances are monitored by the hypothalamus, which signals hunger when not enough glucose is available to the cells. You should also have an understanding of the effects of psychological cues, such as the unit bias, trigger foods, and the variety of available foods; as well as social cues, such as the minimal eating norm.

11.1c   Understand . . . the causes of common eating disorders.

This module discussed issues related to anorexia and bulimia, both of which involve periods of self-starvation and a fear of gaining weight. Bulimia also includes purging, such as through vomiting or the use of laxatives. Stress, peer pressure, and idealized depictions of beauty all influence the prevalence of eating disorders. It is likely that many people with eating disorders are attempting to establish a feeling of control over some aspect(s) of their lives.

11.1d   Apply . . . your knowledge of hunger regulation to better understand and evaluate your own eating patterns.

Do you finish an entire package of a food item, as the minimal eating norm would suggest? Or do you check to ensure you are getting an appropriate serving size? Try this activity to find out exactly how you eat.

Apply Activity

Starting first thing tomorrow, keep a food diary for the next three days. Record everything you eat over this period, including when you ate, what you ate, and what made you feel like eating. It is important to be honest with yourself and to be reflective: Did you eat because your stomach rumbled, because you were craving something, or perhaps because the food was just there? It is okay to list more than one reason for each entry in your food diary. At the end of the three-day period, tally how often each reason for eating appeared in your diary. Make note of what proportion of the time you ate for each reason. Ask yourself: Are the results surprising? Do they make you want to think more about the reasons you eat? (Note: You can also try to work from memory and recreate a food diary from the past three or four days, but the results might not be as accurate.)

11.1e   Analyze . . . the role of the media on people's body image.

A number of studies using different methodologies—questionnaires and brain scanning—have shown that the media's idealized depictions of beauty have a negative influence on people's body image (and happiness). With this knowledge, you should be able to identify these misrepresentations of what a normal body should look like, to recognize that the motivation to eat is important, and to see that beauty is not necessarily Size 2.

Module 11.2 Sex

Somos Images / Alamy Stock Photo

Learning Objectives

11.2a Know . . . the key terminology associated with sexual motivation.

11.2b Understand . . . similarities and differences in sexual responses in men and women.

11.2c Apply . . . research on sex and advertising to the commercials and Internet ads you see each day.

11.2d Analyze . . . different explanations for what determines sexual orientation.

Why do humans have sex? Psychologists Cindy Meston and David Buss have asked just this question in their research on human sexual motivation. Specifically, they asked American college students why they have sex and tabulated the many different responses offered by both males and females (Meston & Buss, 2007). There are so many possible answers to this very open-ended question—how many do you think they came up with? Certainly more than if we asked the same about why birds, bees, or meerkats have sex. Here are some of the reasons the students came up with:

- *"I wanted to get back at my partner for cheating on me."*
- *"Because of a bet."*
- *"I wanted to end the relationship."*
- *"It feels good."*
- *"I wanted to show my affection toward the other person."*
- *"I wanted to feel closer to God."*

Although we will never know for sure, birds, bees, and meerkats likely have sex to reproduce (a reason that was far down the list for college students). The motivation to have sex naturally has its complex, underlying physiology. As we will see in this module, however, human sexual motivation

is expressed and experienced in diverse ways—at least 237 different ways, according to Meston and Buss's research.

Focus Questions

1. How do psychologists explain the diverse sexual motivations of humans?

2. How do psychologists explain variations in sexual orientation?

» Imagine seeing an attractive person walking along the beach, a toned body glistening in the hot summer sun. Then you and the object of your desire make eye contact and it is clear that the interest is mutual. Your initial response might seem like a white-hot biological drive. This is your **libido**—*the motivation for sexual activity and pleasure.* But, whether you immediately act on this motivation is dependent upon a number of factors, not just "hotness." As researchers delve into the complex topic of sexual behaviour, it is becoming increasingly clear that our motivations are shaped by physiological, psychological, and social factors, and that these factors interact with each other differently in different people.

Human Sexual Behaviour: Psychological Influences

Although its main evolutionary purpose is reproduction, sexual motivation is actually expressed in many different ways. Sexual themes are common in television, movies, video games, humour, advertising, and other media, and discussions of sex and sexuality influence social life, school, and the workplace. It is even part of politics, with heated debates occurring about the public school sex education program in Ontario, about whether government officials should attend Pride parades, and, bizarrely, about the size of U.S. presidential nominee Donald Trump's genitals. Obviously, sex is a very important and relevant topic for psychology. But it is also one of the most challenging topics to study. Sex generally happens in private, and many people prefer to keep it that way. Nonetheless, psychologists use a variety of methods to understand the complexities of human sexual behaviour, including interviews, questionnaires, physiological measures, and even direct observations of behaviour. Interviews and questionnaires are (obviously) the least intrusive techniques and, therefore, the most commonly used.

PSYCHOLOGICAL MEASURES OF SEXUAL MOTIVATION One of the first scientists to tackle the topic of human sexual behaviour was zoology professor Alfred Kinsey. Kinsey began his research on human sexuality by interviewing his students about their sexual histories. Between 1938 and 1952, Kinsey and his colleagues at Indiana University interviewed thousands of people and published their results in a pair of books known informally as the Kinsey Reports (1948, 1953). By modern standards, Kinsey's methods were quite flawed and rather controversial. Kinsey tended to make sweeping generalizations about his findings that were based on very limited samples. Despite these practices, Kinsey's work on sexuality continues to influence discussion on sexual behaviour and motivation.

The fact that Kinsey dared to apply science to sexuality was offensive to many people at the time. During an era when the phrase "sexual orientation" did not even exist, Kinsey reported that 37% of the males whom he interviewed had at least one homosexual experience resulting in orgasm; this was absolutely shocking at the time. (The corresponding figure for females in his studies was 13%.) Contrary to the conventional thinking of his time, Kinsey believed that heterosexuality and homosexuality fell on a continuous scale, an idea that remains with us today.

It is important to note that the methods for studying sexual behaviour have changed since Kinsey conducted his groundbreaking investigations. Extensive interviews

Keystone-France/Gamma-Keystone/Getty Images

Alfred Kinsey's research into sexual behaviours paved the way for future generations of scientists to study sexual motivation. Can you think of some modern research tools that weren't available during Kinsey's time?

have been largely replaced with anonymously completed questionnaires that encourage participants to provide more candid responses. Studies also include larger and more representative samples. For example, at the beginning of this module, we introduced a study conducted by psychologists Cindy Meston and David Buss, who asked more than 1500 U.S. college students to identify their reasons for having sex. We listed a few reasons provided by the students—some conventional (to express affection) and others perhaps more surprising (to feel closer to God). We return to this study to discuss some general themes that emerged—notably, the four shown in Figure 11.6.

As you can see in Figure 11.6, physical, personal, and social factors underlie sexual motivation. For the respondents in Meston and Buss's study, physical reasons were related to the pleasure of the sex itself. Many respondents used sex for what might be described as instrumental reasons—sex was a means of accomplishing a goal such as financial or personal gain, or revenge. Students were also motivated by emotional reasons and because of feelings of insecurity (although there is little evidence to suggest that sex leads to any long-term improvements in this regard). Reproduction ranked very far down the list. Sexual motivation is also tied to relationship context. A study conducted at the University of Ottawa found that

Figure 11.6 Why Have Sex?

Self-reported reasons for having sex by undergraduate students (Meston & Buss, 2007).

1. For physical reasons.

"The person's physical appearance turned me on."

"I wanted to achieve an orgasm."

2. To help attain a goal.

"I wanted to get a raise."

"I wanted to hurt an enemy."

3. For emotional reasons.

"I realized I was in love."

"I wanted to intensify my relationship."

4. Because of insecurity.

"I felt obligated to."

"I wanted to be nice."

Anna Khomulo/Fotolia

females are more motivated by physical pleasure when seeking out short-term relationships, but are motivated by emotional factors when seeking out long-term relationships (Armstrong & Reissing, 2015). This pattern occurred for women across the continuum of sexual orientation. You can evaluate your own attitudes about sex and compare them with others by completing the activity in Table 11.2.

Age is also a factor in sexual motivation. Although young people don't typically associate older individuals with sex (Thompson et al., 2014), survey studies show that almost three-fourths of the 57- to 64-year-old respondents reported sexual contact with a partner in the past year, as did half of the 64- to 75-year-olds and one-fourth of the 75- to 85-year-old respondents (Lindau et al., 2007). While these numbers aren't at the level of sexual activity of average university students, they do show that the motivation to have sex continues throughout the lifetime. It is also worth noting that surveys indicate that the sexual motives of middle-aged women are the same as women aged 18 to 22 years: pleasure, love, and commitment (Meston et al., 2009).

The survey and interview methods discussed to this point have provided a rich set of data about human sexuality. Other researchers have approached this topic from a biological standpoint by looking at the physiological and brain basis of sexual motivation (Pfaus et al., 2012), a topic we will consider in the next section of this module.

Table 11.2 Attitudes Toward Sex Survey

How do you feel about sexuality? You can apply what we have learned from research to understand if you take a generally permissive attitude (people have the right to do what they want) or a more conservative one. Respond to each of the items below by assigning a score on a scale from 1 (strongly agree) to 5 (strongly disagree). Note that it is not necessary to be sexually active to complete this scale—simply respond to the general principle of each item.

1. I do not need to be committed to a person to have sex with him or her.

2. Casual sex is acceptable.

3. I would like to have sex with many partners.

4. One-night stands are sometimes enjoyable.

5. It is okay to have ongoing sexual relationships with more than one person at a time.

6. Sex as a simple exchange of favours is okay if both people agree to it.

7. The best sex is with no strings attached.

8. Life would have fewer problems if people could have sex more freely.

9. It is possible to enjoy sex with a person and not like that person very much.

10. It is okay for sex to be just a good physical release.

Once you have assigned a number to each item, average your responses to get your overall score. In one study of more than 200 college students, men averaged a score of 3.63 and women averaged a score of 4.47 on this scale (Hendrick et al., 2006). How do you compare? Given what you have learned about the biological and cultural factors that influence sexuality, are you surprised by the gender difference? Which other factors might influence the norms?

Module 11.2a Quiz:

Human Sexual Behaviour: Psychological Influences

Know . . .

1. _____ refers to one's motivation for sexual behaviour and pleasure.
   - **A.** Libido
   - **B.** Excitement
   - **C.** Orgasm
   - **D.** Cybersex

2. According to research on sexual motivation in college students, which of the following is *not* a primary reason students offer for having sex?
   - **A.** Emotional reasons
   - **B.** Physical reasons
   - **C.** Social reasons
   - **D.** Reproduction

Human Sexual Behaviour: Physiological Influences

PHYSIOLOGICAL MEASURES OF SEX Our physiological and psychological motives for having sex are not separate. Sexual arousal (a biological state) can influence what we pay attention to and how we respond to it; in other words, it can influence our feelings of desire (Pfaus & Scepkowski, 2005). Although several decades of research have helped identify many of the biological processes associated with sexual motivation, it is important to remember that all of these biological processes are influenced by a person's psychological state.

William Masters and Virginia Johnson performed some of the earliest studies of sexual behaviour in the 1950s. These researchers described the human sexual response cycle based on their observations of 27 male and 118 female prostitutes who agreed to masturbate or to have intercourse while under observation (Masters & Johnson, 1966). Participants were monitored with heart rate and blood pressure equipment, as well as with more peculiar devices such as the penile plethysmograph or vaginal photoplethysmograph, which are designed to measure blood flow to the genitalia in men and women, respectively. Masters and Johnson's initial study allowed them to develop their methods and work with participants who, according to the researchers, were less likely to be sexually inhibited than non-prostitutes. Masters and Johnson followed up this study with observations of hundreds of men and women to characterize the physiological changes that occur during sex.

Figure 11.7 summarizes Masters and Johnson's (1966) observations of human sexual responding in males and females. The **sexual response cycle** *describes the phases*

Figure 11.7 Sexual Response Cycles

(a) Masters and Johnson's studies showed that males typically experience a single orgasm followed by a refractory period—a time during which orgasm cannot be physically achieved again. Then they experience resolution, unless they continue sexual activity. (b) Women typically have a more varied sexual response profile than men. Here are a few examples. Line A indicates a woman who has multiple orgasms, Line B a woman who does not experience orgasm, and Line C a woman who has a single orgasm.

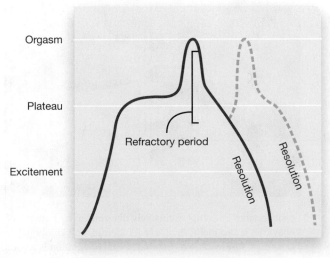

(a) The male sexual response cycle

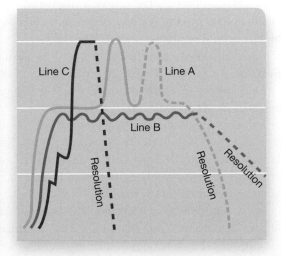

(b) The female sexual response cycle

of physiological change during sexual activity, which comprises four primary stages: excitement, plateau, orgasm, and resolution. Dividing the sexual response cycle into phases allowed the researchers to describe the cascade of physiological changes that occur during sexual behaviour. The cycle applies to both male and female sexual responses, although there are differences between sexes in how these stages are experienced and their duration. The work of Masters and Johnson and those who have followed in their footsteps reveals a complex picture of male and female sexual responses.

One topic of particular interest is how males and females differ in their patterns of orgasm. In one study, 21% to 32% of women reported that they did not experience orgasm during masturbation or sexual intercourse (Dunn et al., 2005), whereas only 2% of men did not experience orgasm. Men usually experience a single orgasm followed by a **refractory period**, *a time period during which erection and orgasm are not physically possible.* In contrast, some women experience multiple orgasms without a refractory period.

Recent brain-imaging studies have shown that much of the sexual response cycle is influenced by the hypothalamus. In one stimulating study, researchers examined the brain activity of women when they experienced an orgasm while being monitored by functional MRIs (Komisaruk, 2005). Physical stimulation led to activity in the hypothalamus which, in turn, stimulated the pituitary gland to release a hormone called *oxytocin*. Oxytocin plays a role in orgasms as well as in the feeling of trust (Zak, 2008). Blood levels of oxytocin surge just after orgasm and may remain elevated for at least five minutes in both females and males (Carmichael et al., 1994; Murphy et al., 1990). This hormonal response may promote bonding between sexual partners, as one of our fundamental motivations as humans is to feel connected to others (see Module 11.3).

SEXUAL ORIENTATION: BIOLOGY AND ENVIRONMENT Although the research discussed thus far has shed light on many aspects of sexual behaviour, there are still questions that have not been answered. A topic that has garnered considerable interest is **sexual orientation**, *the consistent preference for sexual relations with members of the opposite sex (heterosexuality), same sex (homosexuality), or either sex (bisexuality).* Current definitions of sexual orientation focus on the psychological aspects of sexuality (e.g., desire, emotion, identification) rather than strictly behavioural criteria (Bailey et al., 2000). For example, a person can have a sexual orientation but never have sexual contact throughout his or her life.

There is a popular misconception that homosexual behaviour is "unnatural" and that it is only a human behaviour. However, as you will see in this section, there is a great deal of evidence showing that homosexuality is common in a number of species (Roselli et al., 2004), and, like most behaviours, is influenced by biological, cognitive, and social factors.

Homosexuality has not always been as widely accepted as it is today, however. Indeed, psychologists have long struggled to find a satisfactory explanation for variations in sexual orientation. Sigmund Freud (1905) advanced the theory that male homosexuality could be traced to the presence of a domineering mother and a weak father figure. As recently as 1987, Ellis and Ames argued that homosexuality could be caused by experiencing seduction from an older sibling or playmate. Both theories lack scientific evidence to confirm their validity. Modern researchers have begun to examine the degree to which sexual orientation is based on choices people make and on biologically related factors such as genetics or differences in brain anatomy.

In the early 1990s, neuroscientist Simon LeVay compared the brains of deceased gay and heterosexual males. In his work, he found that an area of the hypothalamus was, on average, smaller in gay men compared to heterosexual men (Figure 11.8; LeVay, 1991). LeVay's results created a storm of controversy among both scientists and the public. Many people incorrectly interpreted his findings as proof that homosexuality was biologically, and therefore genetically, determined. In fact, the differences in the hypothalamus could have been due to environmental

BananaStock/Getty Images

Sexual orientation is not exclusively determined by patterns of sexual behaviour. It also includes aspects of identity and emotional connection. Scientists are discovering that sexual orientation is an outcome of complex gene and environmental interactions.

Figure 11.8 Sexual Orientation and the Brain

An early study of the brain basis of sexual orientation found that homosexual males had a smaller subregion (INAH3) of the hypothalamus within the medial pre-optic area (LeVay, 1991).

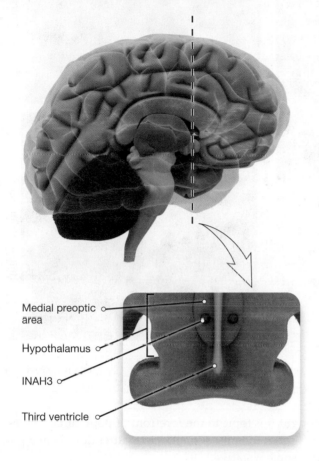

Medial preoptic area

Hypothalamus

INAH3

Third ventricle

orientation. Brain-imaging studies have shown that sexual stimuli elicit different patterns of activity in heterosexual and homosexual individuals. In one study, homosexual men and heterosexual women showed greater activation in the medial preoptic area of the hypothalamus while smelling a male derivative of testosterone found in sweat. This brain region, which is involved in sexual behaviour in many different species, including humans, did not become activated when heterosexual men smelled male sweat (Savic et al., 2005). Homosexual males and heterosexual females also showed greater activity in the brain's reward centres when viewing pictures of aroused male genitalia. The same brain regions were active when homosexual women and heterosexual men viewed pictures of female genitalia (Ponseti et al., 2006). These findings might not provide the final answer about the neural basis of sexual orientation, but they do indicate that differences in sexual motivation are related to differences in patterns of brain activity.

Other research suggests that sexual orientation may be influenced by a combination of genes. Evidence for this comes from twin studies that have identified higher genetic correlations between identical twins compared with fraternal twin pairs. Several twin studies examining the genetic basis of sexual orientation have been conducted. Genetic correlations between .30 and .60 for homosexuality have been reported for both men and women, suggesting that approximately half of the individual differences found in sexual orientation are due to genetic factors (Figure 11.9; Bailey & Pillard, 1995; Bailey et al.,

factors—LeVay's study was not designed to test either conclusion.

Scientists have been skeptical of LeVay's results, in part because they have proved difficult to replicate (Lasco et al., 2002). The region of the hypothalamus he identified was only smaller *on average* in gay men versus heterosexual men, and the ranges in size were overlapping, with some gay men having a larger hypothalamic region than some heterosexual men. In addition, the purportedly homosexual men whom LeVay studied died of complications associated with HIV, which could have accounted for the differences in their brains. Although its results are not considered definitive, LeVay's study stimulated considerable scientific curiosity and debate about links between the brain and sexual orientation. Subsequent research has shown that differences in sexual orientation are associated with the size of the amygdalae (structures related to emotional responses; Savic & Lindström, 2008) and also the thickness of several regions of the cortex (Abé et al., 2014).

In addition to differences in brain *structure*, the brain's *functioning* may also differ according to one's sexual

Figure 11.9 Genetics and Sexual Orientation

Twin studies tend to show consistently higher genetic correlations for sexual orientation between male identical twins compared to fraternal twins. This finding indicates that male homosexuality has a genetic basis. Results of studies comparing female identical and fraternal twins are not as consistent.

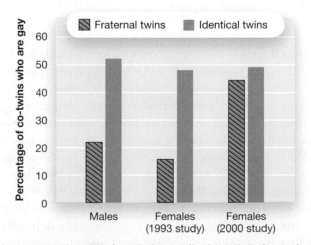

Sources: Based on data from Bailey & Pillard (1995), Bailey et al. (1993), and Bailey et al. (2000).

Homosexual behaviour has been reported in many different nonhuman species such as bonobo chimpanzees, koala bears, bottlenose dolphins, and sheep. In fact, researchers have found that 8% to 10% of rams show preferences for mounting other rams, and the most obvious difference researchers have found between male-preferring and female-preferring rams is a smaller region of the hypothalamus in the former (Roselli et al., 2004).

1993; Kirk et al., 2000). This result tends to hold true for gay men across multiple studies. In contrast, studies have failed to confirm a genetic relationship between genes and homosexuality in women (Bailey et al., 2000; Långström et al., 2010). Thus, genes appear to play at least some role in sexual orientation, particularly for men. However, this statement does not mean that sexual orientation is *determined* by genetics. The brain and endocrine system are remarkably sensitive to the environment, and they interact with a variety of sociocultural factors (Meston & Ahrold, 2010). More research investigating these interactions is clearly necessary.

TRANSGENDER AND TRANSSEXUAL INDIVIDUALS

Most Canadian universities have an office or organization dedicated to supporting Lesbian, Gay, Bisexual, and Transgender (LGBT) individuals, doing their utmost to provide them with emotional, social, and sometimes legal assistance. Thus far, we have discussed many issues related to sexual orientation, the "LGB" in the above acronym. Until recently, relatively little was known about transgender individuals. However, the recent decision of Bruce Jenner, a former Olympic gold medalist and one of the Kardashian clan, to go public with the fact that he identifies as a female (Caitlyn Jenner) has

brought this topic to the forefront of popular culture and has brought Jenner a great deal of attention—some positive, some negative.

The term **transgender** refers to *individuals who experience a mismatch between the gender that they identify with and their biological sex* (Oliven, 1965). It does *not* refer to an individual's sexual orientation. **Transsexual**, on the other hand, *refers to the subset of transgender individuals who wish to permanently transition from their birth sex to the gender with which they identify* (Bevan, 2014). Many transsexual individuals seek medical assistance in the form of sexual reassignment surgery.

In the past ten years, researchers have begun to investigate whether there are brain-based differences between transgender individuals and the rest of the population (Kreukels & Guillamon, 2016). They suggest that sex hormones such as testosterone influence the sex differentiation of the genitals in the first 6–12 weeks of prenatal development; sexual differentiation of brain structures (i.e., the differences that exist between male and female brains) begin to occur in the second half of prenatal development. In transgender individuals, it is possible that sex hormones caused the genitals and body to develop in the direction of one sex (e.g., male), while the brain and gender developed in the opposite direction (e.g.,

PSYCH@

Sex Ed

In 2015, the Government of Ontario introduced a new sexual education curriculum that attracted national attention. In addition to learning the names and functions of different parts of the male and female reproductive systems, students would learn about sexting, consent, contraception, sexual orientation, and gender identity. As noted earlier in this module, some of these topics—particularly gender identity and sexual orientation—have been associated with ill-informed explanations; the goal of the sexual education program was to provide students with scientifically accurate information. Although the majority of parents supported the updating of the curriculum, a very vocal minority opposed the teaching of topics related to homosexuality, abortion, and contraception. This conflict leads to some very important questions about sexual education. What topics should be included? Who should teach them? And, do students benefit from this information?

A 2010 survey of over 1000 Ontario parents found strong support for the teaching of sexual health information in schools (McKay et al., 2014). Parents agreed that students should learn the proper names for body parts, issues related to physical and emotional development, and information about contraception.

Although sexual orientation and media literacy received lower ratings, the average rating was still above three on a 4-point scale. Parents were most comfortable with their children learning sexual health information from their family, their doctor, or their teachers (as opposed to social media or peers).

Of course, not all teachers are equally capable of providing this information. In a different survey study conducted by researchers at the University of New Brunswick, middle-school students (grades 6–8) indicated that it was essential to provide students with accurate information in an interesting, engaging manner. It was also essential that this information be taught by an instructor comfortable discussing sexual issues (Byers et al., 2013). Teachers themselves had similar views—individuals who were younger, had experience and training teaching sexual health information, and felt comfortable talking about these issues were more willing to teach "sex ed" (Cohen et al., 2012). Hopefully, these teachers will be able to effectively deliver Ontario's new curriculum so that students will leave middle school with a decent understanding of sex; this will help teens make informed decisions about the very adult issues they will soon face.

---

female; Swaab & Garcia-Falgueras, 2009). Consistent with this view, researchers have found that volume of some

Caitlyn Jenner's public transition from male to female has put a spotlight on issues related to transgender individuals. Time will tell whether this attention will lead to increased respect and improved healthcare for transgender individuals.

nuclei in the hypothalamus of male-to-female (MtF) transsexuals resembled female rather than male brains (Garcia-Falgueras & Swaab, 2008). Researchers have also found that the brains of females transitioning to males (FtM) and males transitioning to females (MtF) differ from each other, with MtF individuals having more white-matter connections between subcortical areas (lower in the brain) than FtM individuals (Hahn et al., 2015). Of course, as this line of research is still in its early stages, we must be cautious when drawing conclusions.

It is important to note that this research was not making any moral judgments about anyone—it was simply an investigation into differences between groups of people. That said, transgender and transsexual individuals *do* face many struggles in our society, and experience stress and discrimination that can affect healthcare and their general well-being (Dargie et al., 2014; Hughto et al., 2015). In an effort to counter these negative effects, organizations such as the Canadian Psychological Association (CPA) have produced literature aimed at helping transgender individuals deal with their negative emotions (CPA, 2016). This information is also useful for educators, as it will allow them to help adolescents who are experiencing gender uncertainty, and to provide accurate information to other students receiving education about sex ("sex ed").

Frederick M. Brown/Getty Images

Module 11.2b Quiz:

Human Sexual Behaviour: Physiological Influences

Know . . .

1. In what order do the phases of the sexual response cycle occur?

   A. Plateau, orgasm, resolution, excitement

   B. Excitement, plateau, orgasm, resolution

   C. Orgasm, resolution, excitement, plateau

   D. Excitement, orgasm, resolution, plateau

Understand . . .

2. The male sexual response cycle includes a(n) _____ during which erection and orgasm are not physically possible, whereas the female sexual response cycle often does not.

   A. plateau

   B. refractory period

   C. oxytocin release

   D. sensitive period

3. What is one biological explanation for the mismatch between the gender that transgender individuals identify with and their biological sex?

   A. Oxytocin levels are abnormally low in transgender individuals, which influences how the frontal lobes of the brain will develop early in life.

   B. The levels of sex hormones such as testosterone are abnormally high in transgender individuals.

   C. Sex hormones cause sex differences in the genitals at an early stage of prenatal development and sex differences in the brain at a later stage of prenatal development.

   D. Sex hormones cause sex differences in the brain at an early stage of prenatal development and sex differences in the genitals at a later stage of prenatal development.

Analyze . . .

4. Brain differences between homosexual and heterosexual adults should be interpreted as

   A. a result of both genetic and environmental factors.

   B. due solely to inherited, genetic differences.

   C. proof that the brain structure between homosexual men and heterosexual women is identical.

   D. due solely to environmental factors.

Human Sexual Behaviour: Cultural Influences

How is an 18-year-old woman "supposed to" act when she is interesting in having sex? How about an 18-year-old guy? Although we'd all love to say that people should act any way they want, **gender roles**, *the accepted attitudes and behaviours of males and females in a given society*, exist. These gender roles are flexible over time, however. Your great-grandmothers were unlikely to wear revealing clothing or have "hook ups" or "friends with benefits"; this norm changed across generations. Indeed, across generations, there have been significant changes in male and female **sexual scripts**, *the set of rules and assumptions about the sexual behaviours of males and females*. For most of human history, male sexual behaviour was based on competition. Men would value sexual conquests and the physical attractiveness of females. Females, on the other hand, would be taught to be less promiscuous and to focus on developing a stable relationship before engaging in sexual intercourse. There are a number of reasons for this difference. First, females have a limited supply of eggs that can be fertilized. They therefore have to be careful about which male does the fertilizing (Trivers, 1972). Because children require resources (food, clothing, shelter, money, etc.), and females were not traditionally in the workforce, it was important to be certain that a potential mate would be a good provider. Males, on the other hand, have a seemingly unlimited supply of sperm that can be replenished quickly. If their evolutionary goal is to pass on their genetic information to as many people as possible, males are able to do this by impregnating as many women as possible (whereas women would have to give birth a large number of times, which is much more difficult). Although this might not be the stated goal of most men, the sexual motivation to have sex with large numbers of women still exists. Additionally, males have higher levels of **testosterone**, *a hormone that is involved in the development of sex characteristics and the motivation of sexual behaviour*. Thus, there are social, evolutionary, and hormonal reasons for the sexual scripts in our culture.

But, this evolutionary explanation is only part of the explanation for gender roles and sexual scripts. For a large part of human history, societies were set up in a way that gave men greater power than women. Indeed, in many cultures, women were viewed as possessions—first of their fathers and then of their husbands. Limiting the sexual expressiveness of women limited their ability to feel empowered, and allowed the "status quo" of the patriarchy (male-dominated society) to continue.

But, as we noted, these scripts are changing. Why do you think that is? Although there are dozens of potential explanations, there are three that are particularly important. The first is the emergence of the Women's Rights Movement over the last 130 years. This movement challenged the core values of the patriarchal society and put pressure on lawmakers to allow women to have equal economic and political rights such as voting. The result was that women were perceived as people rather than possessions. A second, related, cause was the increasing presence of women in the workforce. This economic independence meant that females could take care of themselves if they became pregnant. Therefore, they didn't need to be as careful about who they had sex with. The third reason for changing sexual scripts was "the pill." The U.S. Federal Drug Administration approved the drug *Enovid* for use as a contraceptive on June 23, 1960 (Marks, 2001); the pill was legalized in Canada in 1969. This allowed women to have control over when they were going to become pregnant, thus giving them much more control over their sexual behaviours. The importance of contraceptives cannot be overstated. Imagine how people's lives would be changed if pregnancy was a strong possibility every time someone had sex.

Of course, it is important to note that not all females or males follow the same sexual scripts. Different ethnicities and religious groups have their own scripts as well. For instance, researchers at the University of British Columbia found that Chinese women (born in China or Taiwan, but living in Canada) reported more conservative sexual attitudes (Woo et al., 2010) and lower levels of sexual desire than Euro-Canadian women (Woo et al., 2012). Why would this occur? Researchers have found that **sex guilt**, *negative emotional feelings for having violated culturally*

The development of birth control pills allowed women greater control over whether they would become pregnant, and dramatically changed our society.

accepted standards of appropriate sexual behaviour, is a major factor in these differences. Interestingly, these differences decrease for individuals who become more involved with mainstream Western culture, suggesting that a number of social and cultural factors influence sexual motivations (Brotto et al., 2005).

Sexual scripts also exist in homosexual relationships. Indeed, researchers in this field have highlighted the butch (traditionally masculine) and femme (traditionally feminine) gender roles of some lesbians (Blair & Hoskin, 2016; Munt, 1998). However, research suggests that these sexual scripts are more flexible than in heterosexual relationships, possibly due to the fact that many homosexual individuals do not follow gender roles to the same degree as do heterosexual individuals (Kurdek, 2005).

SEX AND TECHNOLOGY What type of sexual scripts would develop if people could engage in sexual behaviour anonymously without having to physically interact with another person? Although your grandparents may have considered that question to be science fiction pornography, in the past two decades electronic media such as the Internet, text messaging, instant messaging, and social networking sites have become common outlets for sexual expression. Electronic media are often used for viewing pornography, having online sexual encounters, and meeting others for sex offline (i.e., in the real world). Adolescents, as well as both single and married adults, may engage in cybersex—that is, the use of the Internet and computer equipment for sending sexually explicit images and messages to a partner. An estimated one in three adults today has engaged in cybersex (Daneback et al., 2005). These experiences tend to occur with a person's primary sexual partner, although interactions do occur with known non-partners and with strangers (Shaughnessy et al., 2014).

Unplanned pregnancy and STDs are obviously not an immediate risk of cybersex. However, people tend to communicate with less inhibition via digital media compared to face-to-face encounters. This opens up the possibility for impulsive behaviour such as sending sexually explicit pictures and messages ("sexting"). Many teens have suffered rather harsh legal consequences for sexting. Some U.S. states consider sexting to be a form of underage pornography and those convicted could be required to register as sex offenders. The Supreme Court of Canada has indicated that under-aged teens can possess sexual images of each other assuming it is consensual; however, the distribution of such images is illegal (*R. v. Sharpe*; Supreme Court of Canada, 2001).

Regardless of your opinions of, or experience with, cybersex, it is impossible to ignore the fact that sexual imagery is becoming increasingly common in our society. What is less clear is how this sexuality will affect our day-to-day behaviours.

Does Sex Sell?

The American Apparel advertisement showed a topless model with her back to the camera, her nylon-clad buttocks thrust provocatively toward the viewer. Needless to say, this ad got noticed, as did several other (equally subtle) ads by the same company. But American Apparel isn't alone in using sex to sell its products. H&M has featured giant billboards displaying David Beckham in his underwear. Soft drink companies have young and attractive people drink their products in commercials. And, in a sure sign of the Apocalypse, Paris Hilton wore a skimpy swimsuit, soaped herself up, and writhed on a car in order to sell Carl's Jr. hamburgers. The ad's caption was, "She tells you size doesn't matter. She's lying." Although there is no doubt that such ads attract attention, are they effective in changing consumers' brand preferences? Does sex really sell?

What do we know about sex and advertising?

There are a number of examples of companies being saved by sexual advertising. Woodbury's Facial Soap was near bankruptcy in 1910; however, when a new ad campaign depicted romantic couples and promised that using the product would lead to greater intimacy, sales skyrocketed (Reichert, 2003, 2012). Jovan Musk Oil, a fragrance for men, had advertisements that suggested that it would increase a user's sexual attractiveness; revenue from Jovan's Musk

Gregory Holmgren/Alamy Stock Photo

increased from $1.5 million in 1971 to $77 million in 1978. Based on these, and many more, success stories, the frequency of sexual imagery in ads has increased substantially in the past three decades. A study of 3343 full-page ads that were published in 1983, 1993, and 2003 in popular magazines such as *Esquire, Playboy, Newsweek, Time, Cosmopolitan,* and *Redbook* found that the proportion of sexual ads increased from 15% in 1983 to 27% in 2003 (Reichert et al., 2012). Sexual imagery was most often used to sell health and hygiene products (38%), beauty products (36%), medicine (29%), and clothing (27%). This trend leads to the obvious question: How is sex being used to influence our buying behaviour?

How can scientists explain the effect of sexual imagery on advertising success?

Some advertisements use sexual imagery to attract attention to a product. For example, an attractive model standing next to a car or eating a bowl of cereal will make us pay more attention to that image than we otherwise would. However, such image–product pairings are not always effective. First, researchers at the University of Manitoba found that the blatant use of idealized (i.e., impossibly attractive) models tended to lower people's evaluations of that product (Wan et al., 2013). A second issue relates to memory: Although the consumer might remember the *ad*, they are less likely to remember the *brand* that is being advertised (Reichert & Alvaro, 2001). After Paris Hilton's hamburger ad, Carl's Jr. experienced a 1.7% increase in sales . . . *but archrival Hardees had a similar increase!* However, if sexuality is an integral part of the brand's identity or if the sexuality in the ad is related to the product's function (e.g., condoms), then sexual imagery will enhance our memory for that product (Richmond & Hartman, 1982). This effect is likely due to the sexual imagery being a memory retrieval cue for that product.

Sex has another interesting effect on how we perceive advertisements: It interferes with our ability to think rationally about persuasive material (Reichert et al., 2001). A recent brain-imaging study compared neural responses to advertisements containing sexual or emotional images with responses to advertisements in which an image of the product was presented alongside factual information about the product. The researchers found that sexual ads generated smaller neural responses in several areas of the frontal lobes (Cook et al., 2011). These results suggest that sexual images may lead to less analysis of an ad's contents than a purely fact-based appeal, making us more vulnerable to persuasive material. (This research could certainly make election ads more interesting. . . .)

Can we critically evaluate this evidence?

Although the psychology research investigating whether sex sells is interesting, we do have to be cautious in interpreting it because the stimuli used in the research would be used differently in the real world. Most television or radio ads are seen or heard numerous times; in an experiment, they are often presented only once. Additionally, most ads are targeted at specific demographic groups (e.g., females aged 18–25). Therefore, we, as consumers of research, need to be sure that the experimenters paid attention to the same variables as the marketers. Otherwise, their data don't buy us much.

We also have to remember that not all participants in a study are alike in their sexual views, a fact that was overlooked in many early studies on this topic. Overall, women are less accepting of sexual ads than men, likely due to the fact that most sexual ads are targeted toward heterosexual males (Monk-Turner et al., 2008). Women with more liberal views toward sexuality respond similarly to men—they are much more likely to accept unnecessary sexual imagery than more conservative women (Sengupta & Dahl, 2008). Additionally, women are more likely to accept a sexual advertisement if sex is depicted in a way that is respectful, focusing on devotion rather than on primitive biological urges (Dahl et al., 2009).

Why is this relevant?

The results of numerous studies show that sex *can* sell, *in certain situations*. But, if psychologists and marketers wish to use sex to sell a product, they have to be extremely careful about when and where these ads are displayed, and how sex is depicted. If they fail to do so, their sexy ad campaign might end up being a bust.

Module 11.2c Quiz:

Human Sexual Behaviour: Cultural Influences

Know . . .

1. The accepted attitudes and behaviours of males and females in a given society are known as
   A. sexual orientation.
   B. sex guilt.
   C. gender roles.
   D. sexual scripts.

Understand . . .

2. Sexual content in advertisements can be effective in all of the following cases EXCEPT
   A. when the viewers are liberal-minded males.
   B. when the sexual content is related to the purpose or function of the product being advertised.
   C. when paired with a logical argument for buying the product.
   D. when the viewers are conservative-minded females.

Analyze . . .

3. Future computers will likely include face-recognition software that keeps the computer screen lit up when you're looking at it (this technology is already found in some smart phones). This technology may also make it more difficult for users to remain anonymous in social networking sites or chat rooms. Based on what you've read in this module, what effect will this have?
   A. The loss of anonymity will make people more inhibited because the sexual scripts will become similar to those found in face-to-face encounters.
   B. The loss of anonymity will change the gender roles for males and females, making them more similar.
   C. Social networking sites will become even more popular and sexualized once everyone can see everyone else.
   D. From an evolutionary perspective, the loss of anonymity will influence male sexual behaviour, as it will be possible for them to identify a larger number of potential mates.

Module 11.2 Summary

11.2a Know... the key terminology associated with sexual motivation.

gender roles
libido
refractory period
sex guilt
sexual orientation
sexual response cycle
sexual scripts
testosterone
transgender
transsexual

11.2b Understand... similarities and differences in sexual responses in men and women.

The similarities in sexual response cycles found in men and women can be explained by a common reproductive physiology in both sexes. However, males experience a distinct phase called the refractory period, during which erection or orgasm is not physiologically possible. Both males' and females' sexual behaviours are also influenced by gender scripts and sexual roles, factors that are affected by the culture in which the sexual behaviours are taking place.

11.2c Apply... research on sex and advertising to the commercials and Internet ads you see each day.

The research reviewed in the Working the Scientific Literacy Model section of this module suggests that sexual imagery has a small effect on our consumer behaviour.

In fact, these types of ads are only effective if the use of sexuality is related to the product and is subtle.

Apply Activity

Try to apply this research to the commercials that you are subjected to when you watch television (or to ads that appear on Internet sites, if you don't watch TV). For each ad, ask yourself:

1. How is sexuality being used (blatantly or subtly)?
2. Is the sexuality related to the product?
3. Who is the target audience?
4. Based on what I've read, will this ad be effective increasing sales for this product?

Try this analysis when watching two different types of programs (e.g., one "reality TV" show and one drama or comedy). Do your results differ? Why or why not?

11.2d Analyze... different explanations for what determines sexual orientation.

Several lines of evidence point to biological factors contributing to homosexuality. For example, small differences in brain anatomy—particularly in the hypothalamus—have been observed between homosexual and heterosexual males. Also, twin studies indicate that homosexuality has a significant genetic component, particularly in males. However, biological factors cannot perfectly predict sexual orientation. There is clearly an interaction between biological and environmental factors.

Module 11.3 Social and Achievement Motivation

Inti St Clair/DigitalVision/Getty Images

 ## Learning Objectives

11.3a Know . . . the key terminology of social and achievement motivation.

11.3b Understand . . . how people experience a need to belong.

11.3c Understand . . . the different forms of love.

11.3d Apply . . . theories of motivation to understand your personal motivation to achieve in school or your career.

11.3e Analyze . . . claims that a sense of belonging is something people need versus something they want.

Michelle sat at the end of the gymnasium, watching the varsity girls' basketball team warming up for their game. She was younger than most of the women on the team, but still desperately wanted to be a part of it. She loved playing basketball with her friends, a couple of whom made the team, and decided that if she was going to be a part of it next year, she would have to practise every day. She would also have to work on the skills that were currently weaknesses so that she could become a better player.

This story is very familiar—all of us know someone who vowed to work hard in order to make a team or to improve their position in an organization. The over-arching question of this module is, "Why do we try to achieve these goals?" What is motivating Michelle to work hard to be on the high-profile basketball team with her friends? And,

what factors will make it more or less likely for Michelle to succeed?

Focus Questions

1. How critical are external rewards in motivating us to achieve?

2. How is achievement motivation influenced by the amount of control we have over our actions?

≫ Everyone acknowledges that humans need to satisfy needs for food, water, clothing, and shelter in order to survive. Each of these needs is associated with a motivation, some sort of psychological process that will cause us to perform a particular behaviour. The need for food would lead to the behaviour of eating; the need for water would lead to the behaviour of drinking. But, humans have many different types of needs, some of which are less straightforward than the need to eat. These involve social processes, as well as our need for meaning and a purpose in life. In this module, we discuss some of these social and achievement needs, and try to understand the psychological processes that accompany them.

Belonging and Love Needs

When we think about our different needs, it seems like common sense that some things are more important than others. Eating would obviously be more important than having high self-esteem, for example. In an early attempt to understand the different motivations that drive human behaviour, Abraham Maslow (1943, 1954) described a "hierarchy of needs," with needs associated with our basic physiological survival being more important than social or achievement needs (see Figure 11.10). According to Maslow, once survival needs are met, then we can move to higher-level needs such as belonging or the need for self-esteem. At the highest point of this model lies *self-actualization*, the point at which a person reaches his or her full potential as a creative, deep-thinking, and accepting human being.

Although Maslow's depiction of human needs and motivations seems logical, numerous researchers have criticized this model. First, the idea that we must fulfill one need before moving on to the next (in a way that is similar to levels of a video game) is simplistic (Wahba & Bridwell, 1974). You know from your own life that it is possible to have multiple motivations simultaneously—you can be striving to self-actualize while also experiencing the need to achieve at school. A second criticism was that the hierarchy appeared to be biased toward an individualistic (Western) culture (Hofstede, 1984). Self-actualization, the peak state of Maslow's model, consists of a number of characteristics that put the individual's needs or goals first, sometimes at the expense of humanity as a whole. In collectivistic (primarily Eastern) cultures, such needs would be much less important than acting to ensure that everyone was getting along and that the community, not just the individual, was successful.

However, although the *hierarchy* element of Maslow's model may be inaccurate, his work has highlighted the fact that human motivation extends to a number of different

---

Figure 11.10 Maslow's Hierarchy of Needs

According to Abraham Maslow, human needs are organized as a hierarchy with basic needs at the bottom and personal fulfillment and other uniquely human characteristics at the top.

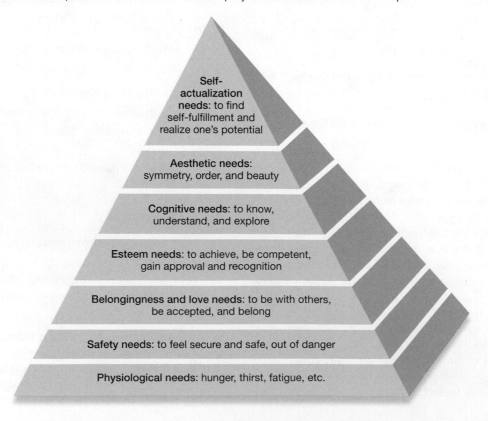

areas rather than being simply a matter of eating, sleeping, and reproducing. Later researchers have noted that we have a number of needs that can, at times, feel as pressing as a grumbling stomach. For example, research suggests that humans have a fundamental need to belong (Baumeister & Leary, 1995), which motivates us to affiliate with other people and to seek meaningful, long-term bonds.

BELONGING IS A NEED, NOT A WANT The **need to belong** (sometimes known as affiliation motivation) *is the motivation to maintain relationships that involve pleasant feelings such as warmth, affection, appreciation, and mutual concern for each person's well-being*. In addition, an individual must have the sense that these feelings are part of a permanent relationship, such as a friendship, kinship, or shared group membership (Baumeister & Leary, 1995). A strong sense of belonging brings more than warmth and happiness; it appears to be fundamental in the same way that food and shelter are needs—these are all things that humans cannot survive without.

Although we all probably want to have pleasant interactions, it is the second part of the definition—a sense of permanence—that is most important for our well-being. Specifically, an individual who has many positive social interactions with a series of different individuals does not enjoy the same satisfaction and other benefits as an individual who interacts with only a few people, but regularly and for a long period of time. For example, an executive who flies all over the continent may have fascinating conversations with fellow passengers every week, yet feel extremely lonely. Meanwhile, imagine a couple living on a rural farm who see only a few neighbours during the week, but see the same people frequently and know them very well. The permanence of their family and community is significant, and they will probably be much more satisfied with their sense of belonging over the long run than will the high-flying executive. Indeed, a substantial number of studies have shown that lonely people like the executive are more likely to feel depressed than are socially connected individuals like the rural farmers (Cacioppo et al., 2006); this leads to significantly lower ratings of happiness and life satisfaction (Cacioppo et al., 2011).

In addition to its effects on mental health, psychologists have found that social connectedness has a dramatic effect on physical health. Research has demonstrated that loneliness is a risk factor for illnesses such as heart disease and cancer (Cacioppo et al., 2003). It also elevates a person's risk for having hypertension, a weaker immune system, and high levels of stress hormones. This relationship holds true even when lonely and non-lonely individuals have the same amount of social interaction—it is the *sense of belonging* that counts (Hawkley et al., 2003). Even very simple indicators such as living alone or an individual's rating of the statement "I feel lonely" predict chances of survival after heart attacks and bypass surgeries (Herlitz et al., 1998; Rozanski et al., 1999). Given that belonging is important for health and happiness, it makes sense that so much of one's life is focused on friends, family, and romantic partners.

LOVE In some cases, the feeling of belonging that accompanies your friendship and family bonds becomes a form of love. You'd be willing to make great sacrifices for these lucky people and you know they would do the same for you. You trust them, look forward to spending time with them, and genuinely cheer for them as they go through life. Of course, this isn't the only type of love that we experience. As you stumble through your teenage years and enter early adulthood, many of you will desire and experience romantic relationships. Some of these will produce an intense feeling that we think of as romantic love.

What *is* romantic love? This is a question that has permeated our culture for thousands of years. Armies of anemic English poets have worked furiously, desperately trying to find the perfect words to describe this wonderful feeling. For most of our history, love has not been seriously discussed in scientific circles. However, this has changed in the last 40 years. In 1974, Berscheid and Walter proposed the first scientific model of love, one that is still widely accepted today (Fehr, 2003). These psychologists suggested that love is composed of two main components: passionate love and companionate love. **Passionate love** *is associated with a physical and emotional longing for the other person*. We feel passionate love at the beginning of a relationship, when we are just getting to know the other person and everything is new. Recent brain-imaging research has shown that feelings of passionate love are associated with activity in areas of the brain related to physical rewards as well as the insula, a region that is sensitive to internal bodily feelings such as having "butterflies in the stomach" (Bartels & Zeki, 2004; Beauregard et al., 2009).

Companionate love, on the other hand, *is related to tenderness, and to the affection we feel when our lives are intertwined with another person* (Hatfield & Rapson, 1993). Although passionate love is certainly more exciting, companionate love appears to have a greater influence on the long-term stability of a relationship. Undergraduate research participants viewed increases in companionate features of love to be more indicative of a loving relationship than passionate features of love. Decreases in companionate love suggested that the relationship was in trouble (Fehr, 1988), and may suggest that the people do not feel as committed to each other as they once did.

Love, therefore, seems to be a very pleasant state. But, what *motivates* people to seek it out? Arthur Aron and his colleagues (2005) have suggested that "love is a mammalian drive to pursue preferred mates" (p. 327). In other words,

Figure 11.11 Love as a Motivational System

(*Left*) Neuroimaging data show that viewing images of your beloved (as opposed to another familiar person) activates the caudate nucleus (the green structures in the brain images), an area in the brain related to experiencing rewards. (*Right*) People who felt greater levels of passionate love showed larger reward responses.

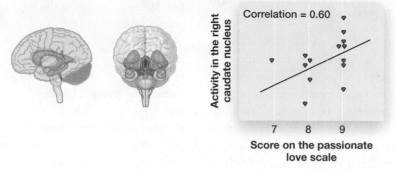

Source: Adapted from Aron, A., Fisher, H., Mashek, D. J., Strong, G., Li, H., & Brown, L. L., "Reward, motivation, and emotion systems associated with early–stage intense romantic love," *Journal of Neurophysiology*, 94, 327–337 (Fig 3).

love may be a goal-oriented state in a way that is similar (but obviously not identical) to hunger and sex drives. To test this hypothesis, these researchers performed fMRI scans on 17 people who were in love. While in the scanner, these participants viewed images of their special someone, as well as photographs of a familiar person. The brain responses to images of the loved one were stronger in dopamine-rich areas that are part of the reward system. Even better, activity in some parts of this system correlated with the participants' responses on a passionate love questionnaire (see Figure 11.11). Activity in other parts of the reward system correlated with the intensity of their reported love and with ratings of facial attractiveness. Importantly, many of these brain areas contain receptors for *oxytocin*, a hormone related to feelings of trust and the desire to be close to someone (Aron et al., 2005).

It's important to note that this motivational view of love is still consistent with the passionate–companionate theory of love. In fact, it adds a mechanism that can explain why we seek out passionate love in the first place: a reward state similar to many other types of motivations.

BELONGING, SELF-ESTEEM, AND OUR WORLDVIEW
Belonging to a group provides us with a number of benefits ranging from physical security (the safety of a group) to the possibility of love (and, in some cases, mating). Belonging also provides an individual with a culture, a group of people who share her view of the world. Feeling as though you are part of a larger, connected group has a number of benefits ranging from improved health (see Module 14.1) to a greater ability to cope with stress (see Module 14.3). It also helps us deal with more philosophical fears, such as our fear of dying.

Working the Scientific Literacy Model

Terror Management Theory and the Need to Belong

As far as scientists can tell, humankind is the only species on earth that is aware of its own mortality. This realization creates some uniquely human problems. How do we cope with the knowledge that we will one day die? And, if we all must die, what makes us think we are more important than other forms of life? For most of us, some combination of our personal identities, family and friends, religious beliefs, and connection with our community distinguish us from other animals. So in some ways, our need to belong may be linked with our fear of dying. Observations such as this led to the development of **terror management theory (TMT)**, *a psychological perspective asserting that the human fear of mortality motivates behaviour, particularly those that preserve self-esteem and our sense of belonging.*

What do we know about terror management theory?

The knowledge of death has the potential to be terrifying; however, very few of us experience this anxiety on a daily basis. Instead, we tend to use *anxiety buffers*—concepts and beliefs that prevent death-related anxiety from entering our conscious mind (Becker, 1971, 1973; Solomon et al., 1991). One anxiety buffer is known as the *cultural worldview*, a belief system about how our world should work. This system provides us with a sense of order and stability in life, feelings that makes it seem as though death were not an immediate possibility. Cultural worldviews can also consist of religious beliefs that influence how we think about the world around us and that provide us with a belief in an afterlife. For people who are not religious, the worldview still provides comfort—the culture that we are a part of will continue even after we are gone (Hayes et al., 2010). An added benefit of a cultural worldview is that it gives people a set of standards that they can live up to. Doing so helps us feel significant and valued, feelings that make up the anxiety buffer that is *self-esteem*. According to TMT, our cultural worldview and self-esteem protect us from the fear of our own mortality. Not surprisingly, most of us are quite protective of them.

How can scientists study terror management theory and the need to belong?

Psychologists typically study TMT by manipulating how aware participants are of death, something they refer to as *mortality salience*. For example, participants might be asked to write a paragraph or two about what happens to our bodies when we die; a control group would write about something that is unpleasant but that does not make mortality more salient (e.g., the discomfort of a root canal). After a brief delay, participants are then presented with stimuli such as a short essay that either criticizes (experimental group) or does not criticize (control group) the participant's cultural worldview; examples might include written passages that were critical of the person's country or university. In most studies, simply writing about death is enough to motivate people to defend their worldview more strongly than participants in the control group, even though individuals were randomly assigned to different conditions.

Importantly, psychologists have also identified ways to reduce the impact of mortality salience. For example, when psychologists followed the mortality-salient stimuli with an exercise in which participants generated positive thoughts about their parents, the effects of mortality salience disappeared (Cox et al., 2008). This and similar experimental procedures suggest that belonging to something more permanent—a family or a community—really does help manage death-related anxiety.

Can we critically evaluate this evidence?

When TMT research began three decades ago, many critics questioned whether it was really thoughts of death that created these experimental effects, or whether the effects simply represented a reaction to the unpleasantness of the study materials. Terror management theorists quickly pointed out that the same effects did not arise among members of control groups who were exposed to unpleasant stimuli ranging from dental pain to the anxiety of public speaking

(Greenberg et al., 2008). Indeed, a recent review of 277 experiments confirmed that responses to mortality salience can be reliably produced in the laboratory (Burke et al., 2010).

Additional support for TMT was provided by Jeff Schimel and his colleagues at the University of Alberta. Rather than showing that worldview protects us from thoughts of mortality, these researchers examined whether death-related thoughts would *increase* if our worldview was somehow compromised (Schimel et al., 2007). In their study, participants read a brief essay criticizing either the Canadian healthcare system or the government of another country. Participants who read the essay that played down the benefits of Canada's healthcare (i.e., an attack on our worldview) were more likely than the control group to complete word fragments with death-related words (e.g., completing COFF- - to make COFFIN rather than COFFEE). These results provide additional evidence that our worldview and our awareness of death and mortality are linked.

Why is this relevant?

TMT has a strong link to politics. Numerous researchers have noted that mortality salience makes people more extreme in their beliefs (Burke et al., 2013), often leading them to become more politically conservative in their statements and attitudes (Jost et al., 2003). This is likely because conservative ideologies and political parties provide unambiguous solutions for death-related problems (e.g., a War on Terror) whereas liberal ideologies and political parties are more likely to promote change, which is by its very definition uncertain. An example of this *conservative shift* came in the 2004 American election. TMT researchers found that when potential voters were exposed to mortality salient information, they became more likely to support Republican (conservative) President George "Dubya" Bush rather than Democratic (somewhat liberal) candidate John Kerry (Cohen et al., 2005; Landau et al., 2004). The anti-Muslim and anti-immigrant statements from multiple Republican presidential candidates in 2016 suggest that this effect did not go unnoticed.

Mortality salience is also used in Canadian elections. Conservative politicians tend to discuss the need for tougher sentences for criminals (mortality salience) more than other parties. And, quite recently, then–Prime Minister Stephen Harper suggested during the 2015 election campaign that Muslims taking the Canadian citizenship oath shouldn't be allowed to wear head coverings; his government was also providing frequent reminders that Canada could suffer a terrorist attack (mortality salience). It is important to note that we are not telling you who to vote for! But, it is also important that you vote for a party based on its ideas, not because of your fear of death and your need to belong.

Psychologists have found that people respond to mortality salience by becoming more protective of their cultural worldview. Politicians sometimes use this tendency to try to influence voting behaviour. Thankfully, the public is becoming more aware of this form of manipulation.

Module 11.3a Quiz:

Belonging and Love Needs

Know . . .

1. Affiliation motivation is
   A. the drive to have as many friends as possible.
   B. the desire to be around other people as often as possible.
   C. the need to have at least a few permanent, meaningful relationships.
   D. the desire to be isolated from others.

2. Which of the following factors increases an individual's risk for illness, heart disease, and even cancer?
   A. Self-actualization
   B. Loneliness
   C. Happiness
   D. Low self-esteem

Understand . . .

3. How is terror management theory related to our need to belong?
   A. Mortality salient thoughts help us prepare for death, thus leading to less anxiety.

B. The fear of death is an anxiety buffer that helps us form groups.
   C. The fear of death makes us more protective of our cultural worldview, including our family, community, and country.
   D. Terror management theory is not related to the need to belong, but is instead related to earlier stages of the hierarchy of needs.

Analyze . . .

4. What point did Maslow intend to communicate when he placed belonging in the middle of his hierarchy of needs?
   A. Individuals generally must take care of physiological needs first, but must satisfy belonging needs before developing healthy self-esteem.
   B. Belonging is not an essential human need.
   C. Individuals generally must first have a healthy self-esteem before one can satisfy the need to belong.
   D. Belonging is more important than physiological needs.

Achievement Motivation

At the beginning of this module, you read about Michelle, a student who desperately wanted to be on the varsity basketball team. Part of that desire was likely related to the need to belong, to be part of a team with her friends. But, that can't explain why she vowed to practise every day so that she would make the team next year. It would be much easier to join a team in a lower-level basketball league,

or to have her friends put together a team in a different sport. But, these solutions weren't part of Michelle's story. Instead, she wanted to improve her basketball skills so that she could be part of the competitive and prestigious league. In other words, she wanted to achieve a specific goal.

Achievement motivation is a very strong force in human behaviour, and refers to *the drive to perform at high* *levels and to accomplish significant goals*. But, this motivation isn't as simple as it sounds. There are a number of reasons *why* Michelle could be motivated to achieve. For example, Michelle might want to make the team in order to receive more respect and attention from her fellow students; she might also really enjoy the game and could have a desire to play it as much as possible. In both cases, Michelle would be attempting to achieve an **approach goal**, *an enjoyable and pleasant incentive that a person is drawn toward, such as praise, financial reward, or a feeling of satisfaction*. But, what if Michelle were motivated to make the team in order to avoid the embarrassment of being "cut" from the team this year? That's a very different mindset than an approach goal. Instead, her behaviour would be motivated by an **avoidance goal**, *an attempt to avoid an unpleasant outcome such as shame, embarrassment, losing money, or feeling emotional pain*.

If achievement motivation were this simple, we could explain most of our behaviour in terms of seeking a reward and/or avoiding suffering. Although both are elements of our behaviour, our motivation to achieve is also influenced by numerous other factors. In the rest of this module, we will discuss how these different factors can influence our motivation to achieve our goals.

SELF-DETERMINATION THEORY When we think about achieving our goals, we can't help but think about making up to-do lists or pro-and-con lists that will help us organize our lives. But, while these techniques provide us with a practical way of examining the choices we face, they don't really tap into the deeper motivation for why we are, or are not, performing a behaviour. Recent psychological research has attempted to fill this void by examining what researchers refer to as universal needs—needs that (almost) all humans experience. Researchers have identified three universal needs (Deci & Vansteenkiste, 2004):

- *Relatedness:* Feeling connected with others, a need satisfied by forming meaningful bonds with other people such as family members, teammates, or colleagues at school and work
- *Autonomy:* The need to feel in control of your own life
- *Competence:* The ability to perform a task at a skill level that is satisfying to the individual

But, our motivation isn't necessarily influenced by how competent we *are*. Instead, it is influenced by how competent we *think* we are. If a very skilled basketball player didn't think she was good enough, she wouldn't practise as hard as she would if she believed in her abilities. (In contrast, watch some of the awful singers making the judges' ears bleed on *American Idol*-type shows; they believe they are good, so they continue to sing . . . sometimes even while security drags them away.) The effect that your perception of your own ability has on motivation

During the mountain stages of competitive cycling races such as the Tour de France, many riders will suddenly lose speed and fall behind the other riders trying to climb the steep mountain roads. This occurs even when the rider is in amazing physical condition. Television commentators say that the cyclist has "popped." Psychologists would say that the rider lost his feeling of self-efficacy.

Rupert Rivett/Alamy Stock Photo

is known as **self-efficacy**, *an individual's confidence that he or she can plan and execute a course of action in order to solve a problem* (Bandura, 1997). When people experience high levels of self-efficacy, their performance improves and they are motivated to choose more challenging tasks to perform (Eccles & Wigfield, 2002). So, if you believe that you can competently do something, you will be more motivated to attempt to do so.

A theme running through all three of our universal human needs—relatedness, autonomy, and competence—is the need to feel in control of your life and your decisions. We want to be able to choose who we associate with and the form those relationships are going to take (relatedness), control the decisions that affect our lives (autonomy), and be in control of the actions necessary to carry out those decisions (competence). These themes are part of **self-determination theory**, *a theory that states that an individual's ability to achieve their goals and attain psychological well-being is influenced by the degree to which he or she is in control of the behaviours necessary to achieve those goals* (Ryan & Deci, 2000). So, if we are able to achieve this control, or at least feel like we have control, then we will be more motivated to perform the actions necessary to achieve that goal. We will also be happier. Self-determination theory has been used to explain a number of behaviours ranging from the likelihood of successfully learning a second language (Noels et al., 2000), the motivation to exercise (P. M. Wilson et al., 2008), the establishment of healthy identities (La Guardia, 2009), and the ability to adapt to life as an international student studying in Canada (Chirkov et al., 2007, 2008). In each case, increasing feelings of competence, autonomy, and relatedness increased motivation.

But, at this point in our discussion, our explanation for why we are motivated to achieve goals only explains very general, deep-seated needs. To more thoroughly explain our behaviours, we need to look more closely at specific factors that could influence motivation.

EXTRINSIC AND INTRINSIC MOTIVATION One way to examine the question of "Why do we try to achieve a goal?" is to determine whether our motivation is externally or internally generated. If you wanted to be on a basketball team in order to be popular, you would be experiencing **extrinsic motivation** (or a **performance motive**), *motivation geared toward gaining rewards or public recognition, or avoiding embarrassment* (Deci, 1971; Vansteenkiste et al., 2006). This form of motivation is not always the most effective, as it requires a person to give up some autonomy. If you play basketball to seem cool, then you must rely on other people's reactions to determine if you succeeded in your goal (i.e., other people control if you are viewed as "cool"). Taken to its most extreme, people can become **amotivational**, *a feeling of having little or no motivation to perform a behaviour*. If your parents forced you to play basketball against your will, you might stop putting forth any effort. In this case, neither the feelings of autonomy nor competence would be met.

Luckily, not all of our motivation is controlled by outside forces; sometimes we do things simply because we enjoy doing them. For example, what if you wanted to become a better basketball player simply for the joy of playing and improving yourself? In this case, the motivation to improve came from within yourself rather than from some external source. This would be an example of **intrinsic motivation** (or **mastery motive**), *the process of being internally motivated to perform behaviours and overcome challenges (e.g., a genuine desire to master a task rather than being motivated by a reward)*.

A study of Grade 5 students showed the profound effect that intrinsic and extrinsic motivation can have on how we respond to challenges and to failures. Children were given sets of puzzle problems and were asked to complete them independently. After successfully solving the first set of puzzles, some of the students were praised for their intelligence (e.g., "You must be smart to do these problems") while others were praised for their work ethic (e.g., "You must have worked hard at these problems"). The psychologists then gave the children another, more difficult, set of problems to complete. This time, the researchers told the children that they had scored lower on these questions. Finally, the children were asked to select the goals that they tended to work toward. This list included performance/extrinsic goals such as choosing easy questions to avoid getting many wrong, as well as mastery/intrinsic goals such as selecting problems that one could learn from.

The results of the experiment were remarkable. The children praised for being smart tended to feel less pleasure during learning and instead tended to worry about how well they were doing. They gave up more easily and performed more poorly. Just under 70% of these students selected performance/extrinsic goals when given a list of options. In contrast, only 10% of the students who were praised for their effort chose performance/extrinsic goals when asked what motivated them. Instead, they focused on working hard, overcoming challenges, and learning from their mistakes. Even more stunning was the fact that the students praised for being smart were three times more likely to lie about their results to other people. Almost 40% of the "smart" students lied about their results, compared with only 13% of the "effort" students. In summary, the students praised for intelligence felt incredible pressure to live up to that label and went to great extents to preserve that image, including selecting easier questions and lying about their results. Based on this study, what parenting techniques do you think would help kids become well-adjusted?

A CONTINUUM OF MOTIVATION It is important to note that intrinsic and extrinsic motivation are not completely separate. Rather, intrinsic motivation, extrinsic motivation, and amotivation can be placed on a continuum that depicts how much self-determination an individual might feel for those behaviours (see Figure 11.12). Critically, where a

---

Figure 11.12 The Continuum of Self-Determination Theory

On this continuum, amotivation would reflect very low levels of self-determination. Intrinsic motivation, on the other hand, would reflect a high degree of self-determination.

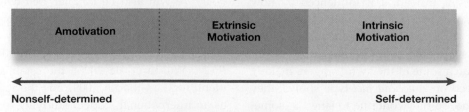

Source: Copyright 2000 From The "What" and "Why" of Goal Pursuits: Human Needs and the Self-Determination of Behavior. *Psychological Inquiry*, 11, 227–268 by Edward L. Deci and Richard M. Ryan. Reproduced by permission of Taylor & Francis LLC, (http://www.tandfonline.com).

given behaviour lies on this continuum can change over time or across situations. For instance, if you give someone a reward (other than verbal praise) for an intrinsically motivated behaviour, the intrinsic motivation decreases, as does the frequency of the behaviour. This change in motivation is known as *the over-justification effect* (Lepper et al., 1973). This decrease in motivation is likely due to the change from being internally motivated (high autonomy) to being dependent upon a reward (low autonomy). So, if you loved basketball, but then started receiving money from your parents for each basket, you would actually feel less motivated to play than you did before! This effect has profound implications for parenting, education, and the business world. For example, if a good student were given rewards for getting good grades, it might reduce how much she identified herself with learning. Businesspeople who work in the hopes of getting a bonus monetary reward will be less likely to identify with the projects or products they are working on. In both cases, the rewards have moved their motivation along the continuum from intrinsic toward extrinsic. This isn't to say that rewards should never be given; sometimes this is the only option to motivate someone. However, as we learn more about the over-justification effect, it is becoming increasingly clear that we need to more carefully consider the effects of rewards on behaviours that were already intrinsically motivated.

A different, but potentially more powerful, change along the continuum can occur for behaviours that were initially extrinsically (externally) motivated. Generally, these behaviours are not associated with much passion, as some outside motivation (e.g., money or another person) is stimulating this behaviour. But, over time, it is possible that some of these behaviours will become *internalized* so that they are part of a person's identity. A basketball player might begin working out because it will increase the odds that she will be recruited to play for a team and will become popular. Over time, however, she might become enthusiastic about exercising for its own sake, and could make that part of her identity long after her basketball career ended. By making exercising part of her identity, the basketball player gains autonomy over this behaviour, because *she* is the one motivating it, not some external source like a coach. Internalized behaviours are more likely to be performed—and performed well—than extrinsically motivated behaviours that are not internalized.

Of course, there is one important limitation to our discussion of intrinsic and extrinsic motivation: most of the studies used data from university students in Western countries. Recently, psychologists have begun examine whether motivational processes differ across cultures.

CULTURAL DIFFERENCES IN MOTIVATION The fact that there are cultural differences in motivation should surprise no one. Western culture tends to promote autonomy and the individual, whereas Eastern cultures put more emphasis on meeting the needs of the community. In other words, the actions of North Americans are often controlled by the individual, whereas the actions of people in Eastern cultures (e.g., East Asians) are often jointly controlled by the individual and her family and community (Markus & Kitayama, 2003). As a result, while intrinsically motivated behaviours should lead to positive performance and emotions across cultures, the responses to extrinsically motivated behaviours might differ. Specifically, people in individualistic cultures like Canada and the U.S. will be less motivated to perform these behaviours than people from "collectivistic" Eastern culture; this latter group will view extrinsically motivated actions as being performed to help their family or community. In fact, if these individuals feel like they are making the decision to act collectively, they will experience an improvement in subjective well-being similar to that found when they engage in intrinsically motivated behaviour (Chirkov et al., 2003).

Cultural differences have also been observed in the motivation to improve one's self. Researchers at the University of British Columbia, in collaboration with colleagues in Kyoto, Japan, examined how Canadian (of European ancestry) and Japanese students responded to failure (Heine et al., 2001). Participants were asked to complete a Remote Associates Task in which they were to identify a word that linked together three other words (e.g., *dust, struck,* and *ship* could be linked by the word *star*). The participants were told that this test measured emotional intelligence and creativity. The researchers found that Japanese participants were more motivated to work on the task after failing than after performing well; European-Canadian participants showed the opposite pattern. Follow-up studies found that these differences were likely due (in part) to cultural differences in the importance of effort in success. Failure decreased motivation to work in Canadian students but increased motivation in Japanese students (Heine et al., 2001).

Culture may play a slightly more complicated role for some Canadians, however. Many people in our country are first- or second-generation immigrants from another culture; they can therefore identify with their family's ancestral culture (e.g., China) or with their current culture (Canada, a "Western" society). How are these *bicultural* individuals influenced by intrinsic and extrinsic motivation? It turns out that the answer depends upon which culture the individual identifies with at any given moment. Using a diary study in which participants were prompted to submit electronic entries at different points in the day for ten days, Elaine Perunovic and her colleagues found that when bicultural Asian Canadians identified with Western culture, extrinsic motivation was linked with negative emotions, likely due to a loss of a feeling of autonomy (see Figure 11.13). In contrast, when these

Figure 11.13 Cultural Differences in Extrinsic Motivation

Extrinsic motivation was linked with negative emotions when Asian Canadians identified with their Western culture. It did not affect negative emotions when participants identified with their Asian heritage. Intrinsic motivation showed no cultural differences.

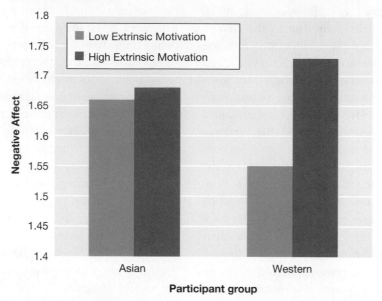

Source: Perunovic, W.Q.E, Heller, D., Ross, M., & Komar, S. (2010). The within-person dynamics of intrinsic and extrinsic motivation, affective states, and cultural identification: A diary study of bicultural individuals. *Social Psychological and Personality Science, 2*(6), 635-641. Figure 1, p. 639.

participants identified with their Asian culture, their levels of negative emotions were unaffected by extrinsic motivation. There were no cultural differences in intrinsic motivation (Perunovic et al., 2011).

Taken together, these results show that motivation can be influenced by culture. It also shows the power of the need to belong—the Eastern focus on the community rather than the individual made extrinsically motivated behaviour seem less like a burden and more like a group decision.

Module 11.3b Quiz:

Achievement Motivation

Know . . .

1. If a student is a pre-med major because he is curious about how the body works and how it recovers from disease, psychologists would say that he has _____ motives. If the student is studying pre-med only because he thinks this major will impress people, then psychologists would say that he has _____ motives.

   A. mastery; performance

   B. performance; mastery

   C. performance; avoidance

   D. avoidance; mastery

2. An individual's belief that he or she will be able to complete a task is known as

   A. implicit motivation.

   B. self-efficacy.

   C. approach motivation.

   D. avoidance motivation.

Apply . . .

3. A recent immigrant from Korea is working on a group project with two Canadian colleagues whose families immigrated to Canada several generations ago. The assignment is quite boring and was assigned by the regional manager of the company they work for. Based on what you've read in this module, how will the Korean-Canadian differ from the "single culture" Canadians?

   A. Both groups will experience a large increase in negative emotions.

   B. The Korean-Canadian's negative emotions will not be affected when he is thinking about his new Western culture.

   C. The Korean-Canadian's negative emotions will not be affected when he is thinking about his Korean culture.

   D. The Korean-Canadian will show a larger emotional response to the situation than his colleagues.

Module 11.3 Summary

11.3a Know . . . the key terminology of social and achievement motivation.

achievement motivation
amotivation
approach goal
avoidance goal
companionate love
extrinsic motivation
intrinsic motivation
mastery motive
need to belong (affiliation motivation)
passionate love
performance motive
self-determination theory
self-efficacy
terror management theory (TMT)

11.3b Understand . . . how people experience a need to belong.

Psychologists have discovered a number of ways in which people are motivated to enter into personal relationships. People seek out friendships, romantic relationships, and group membership to satisfy this need.

11.3c Understand . . . the different forms of love.

Passionate love involves a physical and emotional longing for the other person. It typically occurs at the beginning of a relationship. Companionate love involves the tender-

ness and affection felt when one's life is intertwined with another person's. Companionate love has a greater influence on the long-term stability of relationships.

11.3d Apply . . . theories of motivation to understand your personal motivation to achieve in school or your career.

How would you describe your motivation for school? Are you just trying to earn good grades, or do you find yourself motivated because you are interested in learning?

Apply Activity

Complete the four brief questionnaires included in Table 11.3 to see how your motives stack up relative to other students.

11.3e Analyze . . . claims that a sense of belonging is something people need versus something they want.

Although belonging may not be the most basic type of need on the hierarchy of needs—those positions are usually assigned to food, water, and shelter—it is a significant need nonetheless. Research has shown that living without a feeling of belonging has some drastic consequences. Not only is loneliness related to depression, but it is also associated with a reduced lifespan. The fact that belonging is essential to good health and longevity provides strong support for classifying it as a need, not just something people want.

Table 11.3 Application Activity

Thinking about your Psychology course, respond to each statement by assigning a score on a scale of 1 ("Not at all true of me") to 7 ("Very true of me"). Then find your average response for each set of three questions. Compare your scores to the averages for each score.

	Mastery	**Performance**
APPROACH	1. I want to learn as much as possible from this class.	1. It is important for me to do better than other students.
	2. It is important for me to understand the content of this course as thoroughly as possible.	2. It is important for me to do well compared to others in this class.
	3. I desire to completely master the material presented in this class.	3. My goal in this class is to get a better grade than most of the other students.
	Average score: 5.52	Average score: 4.82
AVOIDANCE	1. I worry that I may not learn all that I possibly could in this class.	1. I just want to avoid doing poorly in this class.
	2. Sometimes I'm afraid that I may not understand the content of this class as thoroughly as possible.	2. My goal in this class is to avoid performing poorly.
	3. I am often concerned that I may not learn all that there is to learn in this class.	3. My fear of performing poorly in this class is often what motivates me.
	Average score: 3.89	Average score: 4.49

Source: Based on Elliot, AJ & McGregor, HA (2001). A 2 × 2 achievement goal framework. Journal of Personality and Social Psychology, 80,501-519. URL: https://selfdeterminationtheory.org/SDT/documents/2001_ElliotMcGregor.pdf.

Module 11.4 Emotion

Matteo photos/Shutterstock

 ## Learning Objectives

11.4a Know . . . the key terminology associated with emotion.

11.4b Understand . . . how the nervous system responds to emotions.

11.4c Understand . . . cultural similarities and differences in emotional expressions.

11.4d Apply . . . your knowledge of theories of emotion to new examples.

11.4e Analyze . . . what purpose(s) do facial expressions serve?

Imagine the following scenario: You are sitting in your bedroom watching television. Suddenly, you notice something moving beside one of your textbooks. Your heart rate increases slightly and your palms begin to sweat as you move closer to the moving object.

At this point—before we know how this story resolves itself—it is important to examine some details about your emotional response. First, the "you" in this story was very quick to locate and pay attention to a potentially threatening stimulus; nothing else in your environment seemed to matter for that instant. The moving object could have been a leaf or clump of dust that was being moved by the air conditioning in your house. Or, it could have been a spider or, worse yet, a spider with a knife in its mouth and death in its heart. What is important to note is that before you were even able to consciously identify what the object was, your body was preparing itself to act. You were afraid, and your body responded with an increase in heart rate, sweating, and muscle tension. Once you determine whether the moving object is dangerous or not, you can either increase or decrease your emotional reaction. If it is just a "dust bunny," you don't need to feel

fear. However, if it is a well-armed spider, then your initial emotional response may be appropriate.

This example illustrates the key parts of an emotional experience: We detect an emotional item, we have an initial emotional reaction preparing us to respond, and then, after we analyze the situation, we increase or decrease that response. In this module, we will take a closer look at these different parts of our emotional responses in an effort to better understand the emotions that we experience every day.

Focus Questions

1. What role does the brain play in our emotional experiences?

2. How do the labels we give our emotions, such as fear, happiness, and sadness, relate to their corresponding physical sensations?

≫ Like most concepts in psychology, the term *emotion* can mean a number of different things. Common

Children who are born both deaf and blind show the same facial expressions and emotions as people who see and hear. This is one of many pieces of evidence that our emotions have a strong biological basis.

convention in psychology is to define an **emotion** as being *a behaviour with the following three components: (a) a subjective thought and/or experience with (b) accompanying patterns of neural activity and physical arousal and (c) an observable behavioural expression (e.g., an emotional facial expression or changes in muscle tension).* Although this definition still includes thoughts and *feelings,* it also shows that our current understanding of emotion encompasses other elements as well. In particular, it shows us that the emotions we experience include a biological response.

Physiology of Emotion

In the example at the beginning of this module, we noted that emotional behaviours are actually quite complex and involve a number of different components. Although we often think of emotional responses occurring in a number of separate stages, recent research suggests that this view might be a bit too simple (Pessoa & Adolphs, 2010). Instead, our neural responses to emotions are best thought of as a series of networks or loops. Each network involves a group of neural structures that work together to produce different parts of your emotional response (e.g., increased heart rate); however, these networks can also provide feedback to each other. These interactions allow you to modify your emotional responses as you learn more about your situation. In this section, we will discuss the different areas of the nervous system that are involved in emotions and will show how different areas work together to produce the emotional behaviours that have allowed our species to survive in a dangerous world.

THE INITIAL RESPONSE The human brain shows emotion-dependent responses within approximately 150 ms of seeing or hearing a potential threat (Pizzagalli et al., 2002). The goal of this early activity isn't to consciously identify an emotional stimulus. Instead, the purpose of this initial brain activity is to tag or highlight that stimulus so that it receives extra processing by brain structures at later stages of perception. For an example of this phenomenon, look at Figure 11.14. There are many different objects in this scene,

Figure 11.14 How Emotional Elements of a Scene Attract Our Attention

Most of us are very quick to notice threatening stimuli such as snakes and spiders (left panel). This ability is due, in part, to interactions between the amygdala and our sensory cortices. Sensory cortices (e.g., the visual cortex) send signals *to* the amygdala that influence its activity. Feedback *from* the amygdala causes an increase in activity in sensory regions such as the visual cortex (right panel), leading to more attention being paid to the parts of our visual world that contain the threatening stimulus. These areas continue to influence each other through these pathways.

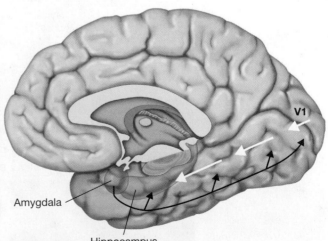

V1

Amygdala

Hippocampus

Source: Republished with permission of Elsevier Science, Inc., from How brains beware: neural mechanisms of emotional attention. *TRENDS in Cognitive Sciences* by Vuilleumier, P. Vol. 9 (12), 585–594. Figure 1a, p. 588. Permission conveyed through Copyright Clearance Center, Inc.

yet you likely paid more attention to the snake than to anything else. Why does this happen? How does your brain make some stimuli more important than others, and what consequences follow from that?

A critical brain area involved in this process is the **amygdala**, *a group of nuclei in the medial portion (near the middle) of the temporal lobes in each hemisphere of the brain.* The amygdala receives sensory input from the cortex, the outer part of your brain, approximately 200 ms after an emotional stimulus appears (Krolak-Salmon et al., 2004). The amygdala fires when we perceive stimuli that are emotionally arousing, and is especially sensitive to fear-relevant images and sounds. However, the firing of the amygdala on its own does very little—it is the amygdala's projections to other brain structures that lead to the observable behaviours that we think of as being emotional responses. When the amygdala receives input about a stimulus that might be emotionally meaningful or threatening, it sends feedback to sensory areas so that they fire more than they would for a non-emotional stimulus. So, when you see a spider or hear a dog growling, your amygdala will help to increase the activity in your visual

and auditory cortices, respectively. The result is that we end up paying more attention to these potentially emotional stimuli. Sensory cortices and the amygdala continue to influence each other through these "feedback loops" throughout the emotional experience (Vuilleumier, 2005).

THE AUTONOMIC RESPONSE: FIGHT OR FLIGHT? An emotional response obviously involves more than simply perceiving a threat—we need to prepare our body to physically respond to the emotional stimulus, if necessary. Importantly, this preparation needs to occur instinctively and as rapidly as possible. The *autonomic nervous system* (ANS) specializes in such responses. As you read in Module 3.3, the ANS consists of two systems: (1) the *sympathetic nervous system*, which helps recruit energy to prepare you for a response (e.g., to fight or flee from a potential threat), and (2) the *parasympathetic nervous system,* which helps preserve energy and calms you down if no response is necessary (Figure 11.15). Think back to the example at the beginning of this module. If the moving object were a large and angry spider, the sympathetic nervous system would mobilize resources so that you had

Figure 11.15 The Autonomic Nervous System and Emotional Responding

The ANS is involved in emotional responding. The sympathetic division prepares the body to respond to stress, and the parasympathetic division restores the body to normal conditions.

Parasympathetic		Sympathetic
Pupils constricted	**Eyes**	Pupils dilated
Salivating	**Mouth**	Dry
No goose bumps	**Skin**	Goose bumps
Dry	**Palms**	Sweaty
Constricted passages	**Lungs**	Dilated passages
Decreased rate	**Heart**	Increased rate
Directed toward internal organs and muscles	**Blood**	Directed to muscles
Decreased activity	**Adrenal glands**	Increased activity
Stimulated	**Digestion**	Inhibited

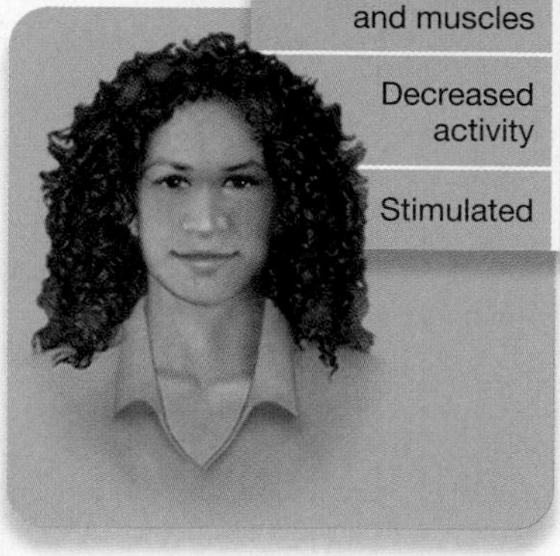

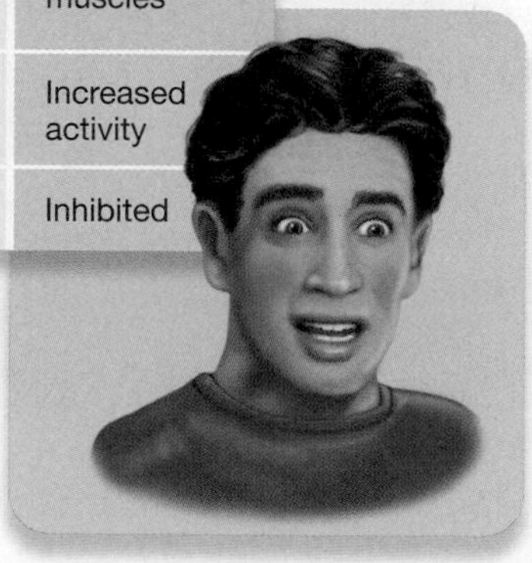

enough energy either to do battle with this threatening creature or to run away from it. If you discovered that you weren't in immediate danger (e.g., a moving object is a leaf, not a spider), the parasympathetic nervous system would become active in an attempt to return you to a normal level of emotional arousal.

THE EMOTIONAL RESPONSE: MOVEMENT If your body is going to mobilize its energy resources during an emotional response, it also needs to plan for what it is going to do with them. In other words, the nervous system needs to prepare your body to make a movement in response to the emotion you are experiencing (e.g., squishing the spider). The problem for us is that even the simplest of movements requires the coordination of a number of different parts of your nervous system so that the muscles move in the appropriate order. Research in the last couple of years has found that emotional stimuli—particularly *threatening* emotional stimuli—trigger an increase in activity in brain areas related to planning movements (Pereira et al., 2010) and in several regions of the spinal cord (Smith & Kornelsen, 2011). This activity suggests that our nervous system is becoming prepared to make a movement if one is necessary—this preparation likely increases the speed and efficiency of our emotional responses.

EMOTIONAL REGULATION As we saw in the example at the beginning of this module, it makes sense from a survival standpoint to have rapid emotional responses and *then* to decide if the responses are correct or not. However,

this evaluative stage of emotional responses is the most complex and involves a number of areas within our frontal lobes. The frontal lobes receive information directly from the amygdala and from sensory areas whose activity is influenced by the amygdala. As a result, the frontal lobes have access to highly detailed information about a stimulus or situation as well as information about the initial responses of other brain networks. The frontal lobes must determine whether the instinctive emotional responses produced by earlier stages of processing are the best ones for that given situation. In some cases, the frontal lobes will analyze the situation and agree that an emotional response is necessary. It will then generate a behaviour that is appropriate for that situation (e.g., you should continue to run away from the spider). In other cases, the frontal lobes will analyze the situation and decide that a stimulus is not emotional (e.g., the moving object was just dust or a leaf, not a spider). In this case, it is necessary to decrease the emotional responses so that the ANS is not depleting the body's resources. So, in the first situation (running away from the spider), the amygdala and ANS influence the frontal lobes; in the second situation, the frontal lobes send feedback that reduces the intensity of the initial emotional response. This constant communication between brain regions is an important characteristic of our emotional system (Mayberg et al., 1999), and explains why we can sometimes feel emotionally out of control and at other times feel "cool, calm, and collected."

Module 11.4a Quiz:

Physiology of Emotion

Know . . .

1. Feedback from the _____ can influence the firing of your visual and auditory cortex.
   A. hippocampus
   B. hindbrain
   C. amygdala
   D. hypothalamus

Understand . . .

2. A few minutes after narrowly avoiding a car accident, your arousal returns to a baseline state because of activity in the _____.
   A. sympathetic nervous system
   B. parasympathetic nervous system
   C. hypothalamus
   D. amygdala

Apply . . .

3. Elizabeth has a form of epilepsy that cannot be controlled by medications. In an effort to stop her seizures, doctors removed the amygdala from both sides of her brain. How will this likely affect her experience of fear?
   A. She will have difficulties with emotional regulation.
   B. Her parasympathetic nervous system will no longer function properly.
   C. She will have a smaller initial reaction to emotional images.
   D. She will be unaffected by this surgical procedure.

Experiencing Emotions

Try this: hold a pencil or straw in your mouth sideways without letting your lips touch it—just your teeth. Wait for a few seconds. How do you feel? Happy? Sad? Afraid? Why do you think you feel this way?

When we think of the term *emotion*, we rarely think about complex interconnected responses in our brains. Instead, we think of the subjective, personalized *feelings* that we experience such as happiness or fear. For example, we've already discussed how seeing an unidentified moving object in your bedroom can trigger activity in a number of physiological systems leading to the firing of millions of neurons in your brain and in the autonomic nervous system throughout your body. But, you would think of that experience as a *feeling of fear*. How are the physiological response and the psychological feeling related? Which comes first and, importantly, how would one test this question?

The earliest scientific theory of emotions was independently developed by William James, one of the founders of psychology in North America, and a Danish researcher named Carl Lange. Now known as the **James-Lange theory of emotion**, *this view suggested that our physiological reactions to stimuli (e.g., a racing heart)* precede *the emotional experience (e.g., the fear)*. In other words, your subjective feelings such as happiness or fear follow your physiological responses. But, the James-Lange theory goes one step further, claiming that your feeling of fear is *determined* by how your body responds. According to this theory, emotion would be experienced in the following way: (1) based on your initial perception of a stimulus, your heart starts to race, (2) your brain receives feedback about that response, and then (3) the brain decides that based on the feedback it has received, you should feel fear. This sequence of events may contradict your own common-sense experience of emotion. If so, you are not alone. Some prominent researchers from the same era disagreed with James and Lange.

Walter Cannon and Philip Bard developed an alternative to the James-Lange theory (see Figure 11.16). They noted that some of the internal organs involved in emotional feelings could not respond quickly enough to be the first step in an emotional response. They also suggested that the feedback from the body was not specific enough to create the different emotions that we experience. Instead, the **Cannon-Bard theory of emotion** *suggested that the brain interprets a situation and generates subjective emotional feelings, and that these representations in the brain trigger responses in the body*. This theory suggests that these emotional processes occur very quickly, so that the steps occur almost simultaneously.

For several decades, the Cannon-Bard theory was the most widely accepted view of our emotional behaviours. However, as clever researchers examined emotions in more detail, this "common-sense" theory began to show its limitations (another example of scientific knowledge evolving). In fact, there is more empirical support for the James-Lange theory than for the Cannon-Bard theory. This is likely due to the fact that some of the bodily feedback involved in emotional responses is caused by facial responses that have direct connections to the brain rather than by slow responses from internal organs. Indeed, the **facial feedback hypothesis** is a key feature in modern interpretations of the James-Lange theory (see Figure 11.17). This hypothesis *suggests that our emotional expressions can influence our subjective emotional states*. So, if your lips are smiling, you will feel happier. Did you feel happier when you held your pencil or straw in your teeth a few minutes ago? Research participants who performed this action were essentially smiling whether they meant to or not. As the facial feedback hypothesis predicted, the participants reported elevated levels of happiness (Strack et al., 1988).

Figure 11.16 Competing Theories of Emotion

What is the correct order of events when it comes to emotional experiences? The James-Lange and Cannon-Bard theories differ in their predictions.

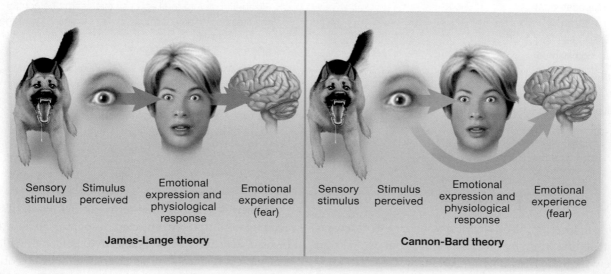

Source: Adapted from Dr. Silvia Helena Cardosa, http://www.cerebromente.org.br/m05/mente/tub6.gif.

Figure 11.17 The Facial Feedback Hypothesis

Psychologists have found that inducing a facial expression, such as a frown or a smile, can have mild effects on how people feel. This lends support to the facial feedback hypothesis.

(a)

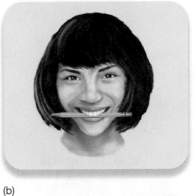
(b)

What is a potential alternative explanation for this result? If you tried this example in front of other people, the answer would become readily apparent: You look and feel silly. In order to rule out the possibility that making *any* artificial face would improve your mood, researchers had participants make a different facial expression. Hold the pencil sideways in your mouth using only your lips—don't let your teeth come into contact with the pencil. The result is a slight pout. This is an experimental method of producing a sad face and, sure enough, it leads to a less positive mood (Larsen et al., 1992).

Research support for the facial feedback hypothesis has been mixed. In support of this hypothesis is a study by researchers who tested the effect of Botox injections on emotions (Havas et al., 2010). Botox interferes with the movement of muscles by inhibiting the release of the neurotransmitter acetylcholine, which is found at the junctions between muscles and nerves. Less movement of the skin leads to fewer wrinkles. Although Botox injections can make some people look younger, they also reduce the person's ability to move his or her face. Research has shown that this impairment in facial movement can slightly dampen emotional experiences. However, the facial feedback hypothesis is not supported by all studies. Researchers have shown that surprise is not as affected by facial feedback as other emotions (Reisenzen & Studtman, 2007). Therefore, we need to be cautious about over-generalizing this hypothesis to all emotions and all situations.

Working the Scientific Literacy Model

The Two-Factor Theory of Emotion

To this point, our discussion of emotions has focused on physical reactions. However, our emotional feelings also involve thoughts, memories, beliefs, and interpretations of different stimuli and situations. How do these different factors interact to produce our emotional experiences? In the 1960s, two researchers developed a theory of emotion that addressed this question.

What do we know about the two-factor theory of emotions?

Researchers Stanley Schachter and Jerome Singer (1962) agreed with James and Lange that our physical reactions give rise to our emotional experiences. However, they also pointed out that many different emotions can elicit physiological arousal. How do we choose which emotion goes with this arousal? Schachter and Singer suggested that it is our interpretation of *why* we are aroused that creates the emotional experience. Their theory, the **two-factor theory**, *holds that patterns of physical arousal and the cognitive labels we attach to them form the basis of our emotional experiences.* Physical arousal is the first factor to come into play (as James and Lange predicted) and along with this comes a cognitive label for the experience, such as "I am sad." Combining the two factors, the physical and cognitive, gives rise to the emotional experience of sadness (see Figure 11.18).

How can science explain the two-factor theory?

To test this theory, Schachter and Singer performed a study in which participants were given different cognitive labels for the same physical feeling. These researchers injected three groups of volunteers with adrenaline (epinephrine), a stimulant that increases a person's heart rate, causes sweating, and makes a person's face feel warm and flushed. So, all participants experienced the same physical symptoms. However, the cognitive explanation for those symptoms was manipulated by the experimenters. One group of

Figure 11.18 Two-Factor Theory of Emotion

According to Schachter and Singer, emotions are experiences composed of physiological responses and the cognitive labels we give them.

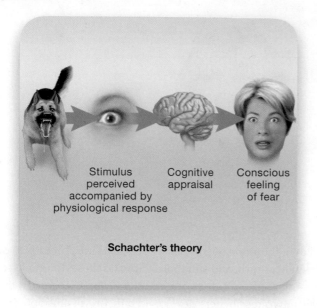

Stimulus perceived accompanied by physiological response

Cognitive appraisal

Conscious feeling of fear

Schachter's theory

Figure 11.19 Results from Schachter and Singer's Study

If participants knew that their racing heart was due to a drug injected by the experimenter, their emotional responses to the actor in the study were smaller. This graph depicts the number of angry statements and acts performed by participants in the angry condition of the experiment.

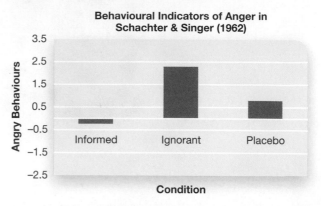

Source: Graph based on Schachter, S., & Singer, J. (1962). Cognitive, social, and physiological determinants of emotional state. *Psychological Review, 69*, 379–399. Table 5, p. 392.

participants was correctly informed about the symptoms (the Informed Group). Another group was provided no information at all; they were (politely) called the Ignorant Group. The third group of participants was given incorrect information about the injection; these people were told that adrenaline leads to numbing, itchiness, and a slight headache (the Misinformed Group). Thus, only the Informed Group had a correct cognitive explanation for their physical feelings. A final group of participants was injected with a saline solution; this was the control condition. The experimenters then had each participant sit in a room with another participant who, in reality, was an actor paid to create an emotional scene. In one version of the study, the experimenters told the participants that they would have to wait for 20 minutes before receiving a vision test, and that they could doodle on the papers left in the room. After the experimenter left the room, the actor began to behave in an excited fashion, playing basketball with crumpled up paper and playing with props that had been left in the room (e.g., hula-hoops). In other words, the actor was behaving euphorically (extremely happily). In another version of the study, participants were asked to fill out questionnaires during the 20-minute delay period. The questions were quite personal in nature, and oftentimes mildly offensive (e.g., "With how many men [other than your father] has your mother had extramarital relationships? 4 and under _____, 5–9 _____, 10 and over _____"). After reading these questions, the

actor became quite angry and tore up the sheet of paper while swearing.

The question the experimenters wanted to answer was whether the participant's response to the actor was affected by the cognitive explanation they had been given for the effects of adrenaline. Presumably, if you knew that you were going to have your heart rate increase due to a drug, then you would attribute any changes in your heart rate to the drug, not to the actor. In contrast, if you didn't know about the effects of adrenaline, then you would assume that your heart was racing because you were having an emotional response to the actor. As predicted, in both the euphoria and the anger conditions, the participants' emotional responses were influenced by their ability to explain their physical symptoms. When people understood the adrenaline was going to make their heart race, they reported smaller emotional reactions to the actor than when they were ignorant of the drug's effects (see Figure 11.19). This classic study provided the first evidence that our cognitive interpretation of an emotional event can have a dramatic effect on how we experience that situation. In the process, it showed a limitation of the James-Lange theory. That theory would assume that the emotional experience (anger or euphoria) would be due to different physiological causes. Instead, the same physiological stimulus—adrenaline—led to different emotional responses in the two experimental conditions.

Bill Aron/PhotoEdit, Inc.

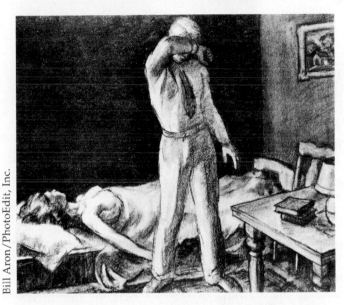

Bill Aron/PhotoEdit, Inc.

An example of the Thematic Apperception Test stimuli used in the Capilano bridge experiment. Males in the high-arousal condition produced stories that included more sexual imagery than did participants in the control condition.

Can we critically evaluate these findings?

One criticism of Schachter and Sutton's experiment is that it might not apply to the real world. Very few of us are given injections of adrenaline and made to watch someone acting in an emotionally extreme manner. In order to test the generalizability of these results, Donald Dutton and Arthur Aron (1974) from the University of British Columbia performed an innovative experiment that provided strong support for the two-factor theory. In this study, a female experimenter told male participants that she was investigating the effects of scenic attractions on creative expression. Participants were asked to cross a bridge before completing the Thematic Apperception Test, an open-ended test in which participants create stories to go along with a set of pictures. The independent variable of this study was the bridge the participants crossed. In the control condition, individuals crossed a solid wooden bridge that was approximately 3 metres above a small, shallow stream. In the experimental condition, individuals crossed the Capilano Canyon Suspension Bridge, which, as the name would suggest, crosses the Capilano Canyon near Vancouver. This bridge is 120 metres long, hangs 75 metres above rocks and rapids, and has a tendency to sway, which can create the impression that one is about to fall over the edge. Needless to say, the experimental condition would produce greater levels of emotional arousal. Interestingly, participants who were in the experimental condition included significantly more sexual imagery in their stories than did participants in the control condition. The explanation for this result is that the participants experienced stronger emotions when crossing the suspension bridge, but misattributed the arousal to the pictures. Stronger support for this explanation came from an interesting addition to the study. After the participants had completed the Thematic Apperception Test, the female experimenter tore off a sheet of paper and wrote down "her number" (a fake phone number set up by the experimenters). Only 12.5% of the control participants phoned the woman's number; 50% of the experimental participants phoned the same woman. When participants experienced emotional arousal, they interpreted it as attraction to the experimenter. Keep this result in mind the next time someone wants to take you to a scary movie for a first date.

Why is this relevant?

Studies of the two-factor theory of emotions show us that although we do have rapid physiological responses to emotional situations, it is our *interpretation* of those events that leads to our emotional experiences. This obviously doesn't mean that you will never be upset. But, knowing that you *can* control how you interpret some of the emotional (or even the aggravating day-to-day) events of your life means that you can try to reduce the negative effects that emotional situations can have on you. So, ironically, a study involving an injection of adrenaline and the induction of angry emotions may teach you how to become happier. It's up to you.

Module 11.4b Quiz:

Experiencing Emotions

Understand . . .

1. Which of the following is a weakness of the James-Lange theory of emotion?

A. Cognitive appraisal is not a component.

B. The theory does not address the subjective feeling of emotion.

C. The theory ignores the role of physiological reactions.

D. Awareness always precedes physiological reactions during emotions.

Apply . . .

2. Raj's mother tells him to smile more if he wants to feel better. Her statement is consistent with the

A. emotional transfer hypothesis.

B. two-factor theory of emotion.

C. facial feedback hypothesis.

D. cortical theory of emotion.

3. Nguyen is paralyzed from the neck down and does not experience the autonomic responses that usually accompany fear. Despite this injury, he continues to experience fear. Which theory of emotion is contradicted by this observation?

A. Cannon-Bard

B. Two-factor theory

C. James-Lange theory

D. Physiological theory

Expressing Emotions

Are you a good liar? Can you tell when someone else is lying to you? How confident are you in your lie detection abilities? Although most of us believe we are quite good at spotting someone else's deception, the truth is that our accuracy is quite poor. In order to fix this problem, researchers attempted to create a lie detector test that measured the responses of our autonomic nervous system. This machine, a *polygraph,* measures whether heart rate and sweating increase when a person responds to different events or questions. Sudden changes in these levels suggest that the person is experiencing stress and may be hiding something. However, after extensive testing, the polygraph was shown to be an inaccurate measure of lie detection; evidence gathered using this technique is not admissible in Canadian courts.

Fortunately, psychologist Paul Ekman and his colleagues (Ekman et al., 1999) have developed a new technique for lie detection. Using videotapes of several research participants, Ekman and colleagues found that our faces give us away when we try to lie. Although we can fake an emotional expression within a fraction of a second, our real emotional response can be seen on our faces before this mask is in place. Ekman called these brief expressions of our true feelings *microexpressions,* and is training police officers to detect them in order to catch criminals. But, use your critical thinking skills for a moment: What do microexpressions really tell you? Yes, the face is expressing someone's inner state, and yes, it appears that a person is concealing how they are feeling. But, microexpressions cannot tell you *why* they are doing so. Instead, police officers have to make assumptions about the person's motives based on the microexpressions on his or her face.

This all sounds very dramatic, but we make assumptions about other people's feelings and motives all the time.

It is quite rare for someone to tell you exactly how he or she feels. Instead, you observe other people's faces and body movements in order to make an educated guess about what thoughts and feelings are going on inside their heads. They, in turn, do the same with you. In this section of the module, we will examine these processes, as well as how culture can influence how emotions are expressed and interpreted.

EMOTIONAL FACES AND BODIES Our primary method of communicating our emotional feelings is through our facial expressions. Each of these expressions has its own unique combination of muscle movements, such as the crinkling of muscles near the eye (*orbicularis oculi*) and the movement of the mouth (*zygomatic major*) during smiling. But why are certain combinations of muscle movements associated with particular feelings? Although researchers are still trying to solve parts of this puzzle, researchers at the University of Toronto have highlighted some important characteristics of expressions of fear and disgust. Imagine changing a really stinky diaper—something even dung beetles would walk away from. The powerful odour feels like it's crawling up your nostrils. Your natural reaction is to make a disgusted face, which involves scrunching up your nose. This expression isn't just for show, however. It also reduces airflow into your nostrils, thus limiting the amount of the disgusting substance(s) that can enter your body (Chapman et al., 2009; Susskind & Anderson, 2008). This makes evolutionary sense, as some disgusting substances could threaten a person's health. In contrast, when we experience fear, our eyes open wide and we tend to inhale deeply (see Figure 11.20). This is likely due to the fact that when we're afraid, we are being threatened and therefore need to be able to take in as much information as possible in order to develop the best plan of action to keep ourselves safe.

Figure 11.20 Nostril Airflow Associated with Disgust and Fear

The images depict the opening of nasal passageways during the experience of disgust (left), a neutral emotion (centre), and fear (right). Note that the passageways are constricted during disgust, but opened wider during fear. This difference is reflected in the volume of airflow breathed in during each facial expression.

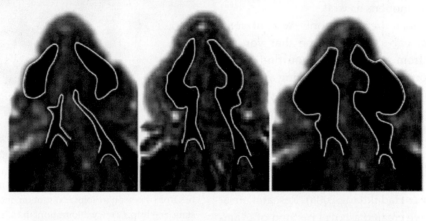

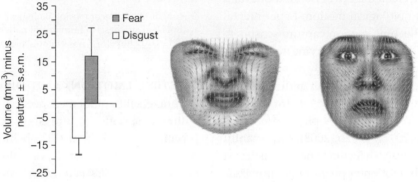

Source: Susskind, J. M., Lee, D. H., Cusi, A., Feiman, R., Grabski, W., & Anderson, A. K. (2008). Expressing fear enhances sensory acquisition. *Nature Neuroscience, 11*(7), 843–850. Top image is Figure 6c, p. 846; bottom-left image is Figure 5b, p. 846; bottom-right image is Figure 2a-b, p. 844.

These results show that the strange facial geometry that makes up our emotional expressions is not random—our expressions have a purpose that will enhance our ability to survive (Shariff & Tracy, 2011).

Importantly, these expressions appear all over the world, suggesting that they are an innate part of being human. Charles Darwin (1872) was the first person to recognize that facial expressions of emotion were universal. During his extensive travels, he noted that people from different cultures formed similar facial expressions and were able to understand the emotions of others. In the late 1960s, Paul Ekman performed cross-cultural studies that supported Darwin's hypothesis. Ekman and his colleagues photographed North Americans expressing six basic emotions—fear, happiness, disgust, anger, surprise, and sadness. They then travelled to an isolated region of Papua New Guinea (an island country north of Australia) to see if individuals who were unfamiliar with Caucasian faces could still recognize the emotions they displayed. Sure

Paul Ekman, Ph.D./Paul Ekman Group, LLC

The meaning behind facial expressions changes with subtle modifications. For example, one version of smiling is genuine, while another is reserved for social graces. Genuine smiles, known as *Duchenne's smiles*, involve a crinkling of muscles at the corner of the eye. Fake smiles tend not to have this crinkling (unless you practise, which is mildly creepy). However, even if you learn to fake your emotions, your face can give you away. Psychologist Paul Ekman (pictured above) has shown that our real emotional responses appear on our faces for a fraction of a second before being covered up with our social mask.

enough, tribesmen from the Fore ethnic group were able to accurately identify the emotions of the actors (Ekman & Friesen, 1969). The researchers then asked the tribesmen to make their own facial expressions for each emotion. As would be expected, research participants in the U.S. were able to recognize these emotions as well.

But, facial expressions aren't our only way of communicating our emotional states. Imagine that you are sitting across a table from someone that you find attractive. Or, what if you found the person annoying and really wished your friend would return from the washroom so that you could leave? Even if you didn't express any emotion with your face, your body would likely give away what you were feeling in both situations. *Body language* provides almost as much emotional information as facial expressions; it also activates a number of similar brain areas (de Gelder & Hadjikhani, 2006). Researchers at Queen's University have created a novel method of examining body language and biological motion. Experimental stimuli are created by attaching motion capture sensors to different parts of people's bodies and having them make different movements such as walking. By averaging the types of movements across a number of individuals, it is possible to see the different body movement patterns of men and women, happy and sad people, and nervous or relaxed people (Troje 2002a, 2002b, 2008). Importantly, like the recognition of faces, detecting characteristics of body language and body motion appears to be universal, as many of the effects were observed in Mundurucu indigenous people in Amazonian regions of Brazil (Pica et al., 2011).

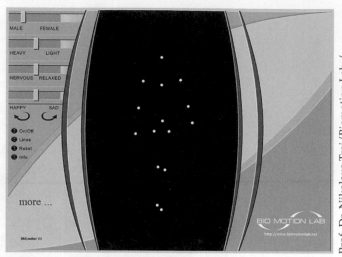

Prof. Dr. Nikolaus Troj/Biomotion Lab / Queen's University

Point-of-light technology can be used to infer a number of characteristics from a person's biological motion, including his or her emotional state. See http://www.biomotionlab.ca/Demos/BMLwalker.html.

Troje, N. F. (2002) Decomposing biological motion: A framework for analysis and synthesis of human gait patterns. *Journal of Vision*, 2, 371-387. URL: https://www.biomotionlab.ca/Demos/BMLwalker.html.

CULTURE, EMOTION, AND DISPLAY RULES Despite the universality of many aspects of emotion, people raised within a specific culture show characteristics that are specific to their region (Elfenbein & Ambady, 2003). Put simply, cultural groups have unique **emotional dialects**, or *variations across cultures in how common emotions are expressed*. For example, people from North America and from Gabon (a country in West Africa) both experience contempt. However, North Americans are more likely to lower their brow, and Gabonese people are more likely to raise their upper lip when expressing this emotion.

The situation or context is a major factor in determining when members of different cultures express specific emotions. **Display rules** *refer to the unwritten expectations we have regarding when it is appropriate to show a certain emotion*. Think about embarrassing situations. In North America, we tend to blush and look away when embarrassed. In Japan, on the other hand, people tend to smile. They aren't happy, but do their best not to show embarrassment. Indeed, numerous studies have documented differences in display rules between North American and Japanese individuals, often highlighting interesting and subtle differences. For instance, imagine seeing someone displaying a highly intense emotion such as a very happy face. You would probably assume that their internal state was just as joyous as their face. Now, imagine that you see someone expressing a low-intensity expression (e.g., a smile that is only 50% as powerful as normal). How do you think that person is feeling? David Matsumoto and his colleagues (2002) noticed that while American and Japanese participants agreed about the person's emotional state when viewing high-intensity emotions, they differed

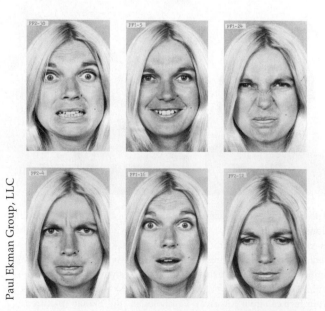

Paul Ekman Group, LLC

Individuals in isolated areas of the world were able to identify the emotions expressed by these faces, suggesting that these expressions are universal.

when the emotions were less intense. American participants assumed that the person was feeling the emotion less strongly. Japanese participants, on the other hand, assumed that the person felt the emotion strongly, but wasn't in a position to outwardly express that intensity. In other words, the Japanese participants were assuming that the person being photographed was obeying particular display rules that limited his or her expressiveness (Matsumoto et al., 2002).

Culture-specific display rules such as these can be found the world over and show us that we need to be cautious about over-generalizing the meaning of different displays of emotions (Elfenbein et al., 2007). It remains to be seen whether the worldwide use of programs like Facebook, Snapchat, and Instagram will reduce cultural differences in display rules.

Although it may seem like cultural display rules are fairly stable, they can vary over time. A recent examination of American high school yearbook photos shows how cultural expectations can influence how we express ourselves (Ginosar et al., 2015). Researchers collected over 37 000 high school photographs and used computers to create "average photos" for males and females in each decade since 1900. As you can see in Figure 11.21, students at the turn of the twentieth century were expected to remain quite serious, whereas students from the current decade (i.e., most of the readers of this book) were encouraged to smile happily (or to fake it convincingly). In fact, if you take a trip to the

portrait gallery of any art museum, you'll see that smiling when being photographed or painted has only become commonplace in the last 50 years. This shows us that our point in history, as well as our location on a map, can have a large effect on our emotional display rules.

CULTURE, CONTEXT, AND EMOTION Understanding another person's emotional state can also be influenced by the context in which that emotion is being displayed. Importantly, the role that context plays in the interpretation of others' emotions varies across cultures. Some cultures (e.g., Western countries) focus on the person expressing the emotion; people in other cultures (e.g., Asian countries) tend to also pay attention to those *around* the person expressing that emotion. So, do these different ways of looking at a situation translate into differences in how people of various cultures interpret emotions? To answer this question, psychologists asked students from both Western and Asian universities to judge the emotion of the central figure in the scenes depicted in Figure 11.22. Western students tended to focus on the facial expression of the central figure. Thus, if the individual was smiling, they would report he was happy, and they did not interpret his happiness with respect to how the surrounding people appeared to feel. In contrast, Asian students interpreted the central figure's emotion in reference to what people in the background might be feeling (Masuda et al., 2008). So, in the right panel of Figure 11.22, a Westerner

Figure 11.21 Averaged Photographs of Male and Female High School Students from 1900 to the Present Decade

Why do you think people are more emotionally expressive now than they were 100 years ago? There are a number of possibilities ranging from world events, to financial stability, to how familiar (and comfortable) people were with being photographed.

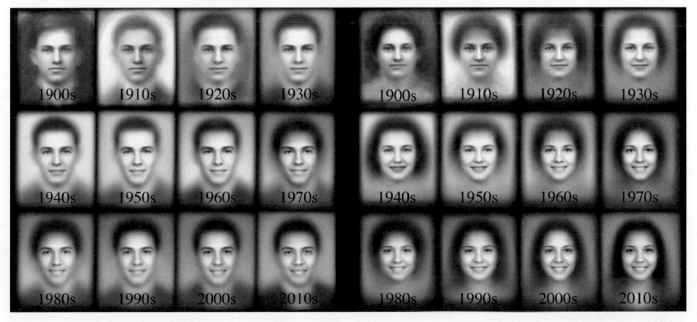

Source: Ginosar, S., Rakelly, K., Sachs, S., Yin, B., & Efros, A.A. (2015). *A century of portraits: A visual historical record of American high school yearbooks*. Figure 1 from Extreme Imaging Workshop, International Conference on Computer Vision, ICCV.

Figure 11.22 How is the Man in the Middle of These Pictures Feeling?

Source: Based on Masuda, T., Ellsworth, P. C., Mesquita, B., Leu, J., Tanida, S., & van de Veerdonk, E. (2008). "Placing the face in context: Cultural differences in the perception of facial emotion." *Journal of Personality and Social Psychology*, 94, 365–381. URL: https://sites.ualberta.ca/~tmasuda/index.files/MasudaEllsworthMesquitaLeuTanidavandeVeerdonk2008.pdf.

might report that the central figure was happy, while an Asian person might assume that the central figure was happy at the expense of the other people.

The tendency for Asian students to focus on people in the background was further confirmed in two different ways. First, Asian students were more accurate than Western students in remembering whether they saw specific individuals in the background. Also, using a device that tracks the eye movements of the participants, the researchers discovered that Asian students spent more time actually looking at the entire picture, rather than just the central character (Figure 11.23; Masuda et al., 2008). Interestingly, a subsequent study found that Canadian-born students with Asian ancestry acted more like North American participants than Japanese participants (Masuda et al., 2012). Together, these experiments show us that although the perception of emotional expressions is universal, the interpretation of why those expressions are being displayed is very culture-dependent.

Figure 11.23 East–West Differences in Interpreting Emotion

In comparison to Asian people, Westerners spend more time looking at the focal individual in a scene and interpret his or her emotions without reference to surrounding individuals (Masuda et al., 2008).

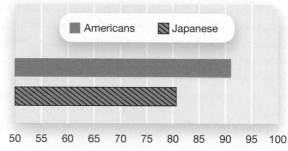

Ratio of the attention to the centre figure

Source: Based on Masuda, T., Ellsworth, P. C., Mesquita, B., Leu, J., Tanida, S., & van de Veerdonk, E. (2008). "Placing the face in context: Cultural differences in the perception of facial emotion." *Journal of Personality and Social Psychology*, 94, 365–381. URL: https://sites.ualberta.ca/~tmasuda/index.files/MasudaEllsworthMesquitaLeuTanidavandeVeerdonk2008.pdf.

Module 11.4c Quiz:

Expressing Emotions

Know . . .

1. A(n) _____ refers to when it is appropriate to show a specific emotion.

    A. emotional dialect

    B. display rule

    C. context rule

    D. display dialect

Understand . . .

2. Which of the following is an example of an emotional dialect?

    A. Experiencing anger

    B. Avoiding laughter in church

    C. Raising one's chin in contempt

    D. Smiling as a sign of happiness

3. Which of the following is an example of a display rule?

    A. Biting one's lip in embarrassment

    B. Dropping one's jaw in surprise

    C. Suppressing anger during a debate

    D. Expressing happiness to a loved one

Module 11.4 Summary

11.4a Know . . . the key terminology associated with emotion.

amygdala
Cannon-Bard theory of emotion
display rules
emotion
emotional dialects
facial feedback hypothesis
James-Lange theory of emotion
two-factor theory

11.4b Understand . . . how the nervous system responds to emotions.

Our biological responses to emotions occur in many different parts of our nervous system. Our brain has a rapid-response system involving the amygdala, which can fire within a few hundred milliseconds. This system triggers activity in other brain areas and influences how much attention a stimulus will receive. Our sympathetic nervous system also responds quickly. Soon after, brain and spinal cord areas related to movement become active in order to prepare us for a response. Finally, frontal lobe regions examine the situation to determine whether we should continue the emotional response or change our behaviour to conserve energy.

11.4c Understand . . . cultural similarities and differences in emotional expressions.

Emotions such as fear, anger, happiness, sadness, surprise, and disgust appear to be human universals—all people experience them regardless of culture. At the same time, we cannot completely explain human emotions without references to cultural variation in the form of dialects and display rules.

11.4d Apply . . . your knowledge of theories of emotion to new examples.

Apply Activity

Try this exercise. Spend 10 seconds looking at the Sanskrit figure on the left in Figure 11.24 while slowly nodding your head. Now, spend about 10 seconds looking at the figure on the right while slowly moving your head from side to side.

Now, imagine that you had to choose one image to display on the wall of your home. Which one would you choose—the one on the left or the one on the right?

What is important about this exercise is not which figure you chose; rather, it is the application of emotion theories to the problem. Consider the facial feedback study, and try to explain how the head movements could potentially influence one's preference for a symbol. This module provided examples of what researchers have found using similar techniques.

11.4e Analyze . . . what purpose(s) do facial expressions serve?

Facial expressions allow us to show the outside world what we are feeling. But, they serve other functions as well. For instance, facial expressions of disgust actually restrict the amount of air entering the body, possibly to protect us from contaminants. Expressions of fear serve to increase the amount of sensory information available to us, thus helping us to select the more appropriate response to that stimulus or situation.

Figure 11.24 Application Activity

Chapter 12
Personality

12.1 Contemporary Approaches to Personality

- The Trait Perspective 492
- Module 12.1a Quiz 496
- Beyond the Big Five: The Personality of Evil? 496
  Working the Scientific Literacy Model: Right-Wing
  Authoritarianism at the Group Level 497
- Module 12.1b Quiz 498
- Personality Traits over the Lifespan 499
- Module 12.1c Quiz 501
- Behaviourist and Social-Cognitive Perspectives 501
- Module 12.1d Quiz 503
- Module 12.1 Summary 503

12.2 Cultural and Biological Approaches to Personality

- Culture and Personality 506
- Module 12.2a Quiz 508
- How Genes Affect Personality 508
  Working the Scientific Literacy Model: From Molecules to Personality 510
- Module 12.2b Quiz 511
- The Role of Evolution in Personality 511
- Module 12.2c Quiz 513
- The Brain and Personality 514
- Module 12.2d Quiz 516
- Module 12.2 Summary 516

12.3 Psychodynamic and Humanistic Approaches to Personality

- The Psychodynamic Perspective 519
  Working the Scientific Literacy Model: Perceiving Others
  as a Projective Test 526
- Module 12.3a Quiz 527
- Alternatives to the Psychodynamic Approach 527
- Module 12.3b Quiz 529
- Module 12.3 Summary 529

Module 12.1 Contemporary Approaches to Personality

Pearson Education

Learning Objectives

12.1a Know . . . the key terminology associated with contemporary approaches to personality.

12.1b Understand . . . the behaviourist and social-cognitive views of personality.

12.1c Apply . . . the Big Five personality traits to understand your own personality.

12.1d Analyze . . . the personality roots of violence and prejudice.

12.1e Analyze . . . the relative roles of personality traits and psychological and physical states in determining behaviour.

What does your living space say about you? That alphabetized bookshelf and bathroom full of grooming products suggest conscientiousness. The photos of Mount Everest and major European cities reveal an openness to experiencing new and exciting things. The three pet cats and extensive DVD collection? Possibly signs of an introverted homebody.

It might sound like we are just making assumptions here, but scientific research backs up the notion that personality can be measured by examining the details of our dwellings. Psychologist Sam Gosling and his students have, with permission, closely scrutinized people's offices and bedrooms for clues about their personality (Gosling, 2008; Gosling et al., 2002). Teams of seven or eight observers entered people's

bedrooms and offices and rated the personality types of the occupants with a standardized personality test. Not only did the observers reach close consensus on many measures of personality, but their ratings also matched up with how the occupants rated their own personality.

If you look around your own room, some parts of it may symbolize the "core" of who you are, whereas others reflect less "deep," more superficial details about yourself. For example, your book collection and most treasured belongings may be very revealing, but what about the clothing strewn all over the floor? Does it mean that you are a lazy slob? Or that you are ambitious and live a busy life? Or simply that you are enjoying the freedom of not living with your parents? Which is more appropriate as an explanation: the dispositional (i.e., rooted in the kind of person you are) or the situational (i.e., external, circumstantial factors)? A key challenge for personality psychologists is figuring out how our personalities and circumstances work together in shaping our behaviour. This raises many important questions, to be addressed later in this module.

Focus Questions

1.   What are the basic traits that make up human personality?

2.   To what extent are our preferences, thoughts, and behaviours determined by situational factors in-the-moment, versus more stable personality traits?

» When you say to your friend, "Yeah, our date was pretty good. They were okay, but you know, they weren't my kind of person," we understand that "my kind of person" means something. We accept that the person being described is some "kind of person"—that they have regular patterns and ways of being. This is the person's **personality**; their *characteristic pattern of thinking, feeling, and behaving that is unique to each individual, and remains relatively consistent over time and situations.* Psychologists have long searched for a theory of personality that can describe and explain how people develop these patterns, because we all want to find out what "kind of person" we are.

The Trait Perspective

If there are semi-stable patterns that differ from person to person, how can we measure those patterns? This quest, to shine the light of science on the very nature of our own selves, has resulted in two broad approaches to personality measurement: the *idiographic approach* and the *nomothetic approach.*

When you try to figure out the people you know very well, you probably intuitively adopt an **idiographic approach**, focusing on *creating detailed descriptions of a specific person's unique personality characteristics.* So, when you are trying to figure out just what IS the problem with one of your friends or family members, you build a theory of the way that they are, the way your friendship or family history has affected them, and the weird idiosyncrasies that make them do the things they do. In doing so, you are taking an idiographic approach.

Idiographic approaches are helpful not only for understanding yourself and your social world, but also for examining the full range of human experience, from the most disturbed to the healthiest and most highly functioning individuals. For example, criminal profilers may focus on a detailed study of a serial killer in order to help police in their investigation. At the other extreme, Abraham Maslow

wanted to understand the people who had lived up to their fullest potential, who were in Maslow's terms, "self-actualized." Accordingly, Maslow performed detailed analyses of the biographies of famous people who were widely regarded as being wise and fully functioning (Maslow, 1970). Maslow's findings launched decades of work trying to uncover what makes human beings thrive and develop to their maximum potential.

In contrast, psychologists who take a **nomothetic approach** *examine personality in large groups of people, with the aim of making generalizations about personality structure.* Rather than trying to understand a specific person, psychologists taking a nomothetic approach may want to understand what personality factors, or traits, are relevant to understanding people. For example, wanting to know whether a certain "type" of person is more likely to exhibit a certain behaviour pattern (e.g., are people who are extraverted more likely to develop attentional disorders?), is a nomothetic question. Answering a question like this requires measuring some specific variable (e.g., extraversion) and examining whether it correlates with specific outcomes (e.g., attentional disorders). The key to nomothetic research is to identify the important personality traits that are related to whatever it is that you are interested in understanding.

There are many examples of nomothetic research in Canadian universities. Dr. Gordon Flett at York University has examined personality predictors of alcohol, drug use, and depression in university students (e.g., Flett et al., 2009; Goldstein et al., 2009; Goldstein & Flett, 2009). Dr. Lawrence Walker at the University of British Columbia has sought to identify the "moral personality," seeking the personality factors that predict courage and heroism (Walker & Frimer, 2007; Walker et al., 2010). Dr. Jacob Hirsh at the Rotman School of Management in Toronto has examined the personality predictors of pro-environmental motivations (Hirsh, 2010; Hirsh & Dolderman, 2007). Taking a nomothetic approach allows psychologists to examine what types of people are more or less likely to engage in certain behaviours, which is an important step toward being able to reduce undesired behaviours or more effectively promote desired ones.

EARLY TRAIT RESEARCH   So, who are you anyway? What kind of person are you? Try to answer these questions. Seriously—stop reading right now, take out a piece of paper, and try to describe the kind of person you are. Write down "I am . . ." and complete the sentence 10 times.

Now take a look at your list. If you're like most people, your list probably has quite a few personality traits—words like extraverted or introverted, funny, ambitious, lazy, anxious, or easy-going. A **personality trait** describes *a specific psychological characteristic that makes up part of a person's personality; how that person is "most of the time."*

Trait descriptors are useful as shortcuts to understanding people. Traits summarize a great deal of information about a person and help to predict how that person will behave across a range of situations. For example, an "extraverted" person is more likely to be comfortable in social situations, go to parties, and have a large number of friends than someone who is "introverted."

As you can imagine, many different traits could be used to describe people, such as "shy," "cheerful," "outgoing," and "adventurous." The first systematic attempt to identify all possible traits (in the English language) was made in the 1930s by Gordon Allport, who tallied nearly 18 000 English words that could be used to describe an individual's physical and psychological attributes (Allport & Odbert, 1936). (Perhaps Allport himself would be described as "patient," "methodical," and "weird to talk to at a party.") Allport then developed a theory of personality structure by organizing these words into traits, launching a strong trend in personality psychology that continues to this day—attempting to identify and measure the key personality traits.

To accomplish this, trait researchers have devised many different types of personality "scales." Some, like the ones used in psychology research and described later in this chapter, are rigorously evaluated. Others, like the ones you find in popular magazines, are of questionable value. For example, *Cosmopolitan* regularly includes personality scales in which you can discover all sorts of things about yourself; while it is possible that *Cosmo* has a team of highly qualified psychologists rigorously designing these scales, we do not recommend that you base your life decisions on your results to the "Are You Enough of a Bad Girl?" quiz.

It is clear that people love to know what "kind" of person they are. However, it is often easier to make people *believe* that you are measuring their personality than it is to actually measure it. In fact, it is remarkably easy for people to be convinced that a personality profile describes them well. This can occur even when the profile is patently false and was not generated to describe them at all. This is popularly known as "the Barnum effect," after the circus showman P. T. Barnum, due to his apparent statement "there's a sucker born every minute." (Ironically, P. T. Barnum never actually said this quote, which is widely attributed to him [Saxon, 1989].) The Barnum effect hearkens back to the late 1940s, when psychologist Bertram Forer gave research participants a personality test and then generated a personality description that subjects believed was based on their test responses. Even though all participants were given exactly the same personality description, they found the profile to be highly convincing and descriptive of them as an individual. When asked to rate how well the profile described them, on a scale ranging from 0 (very poor) to 5 (excellent), the average rating was an impressive 4.26 (Forer, 1949)!

Table 12.1 Bertram Forer's Personality Profile

Forer provided the following profile to all of the participants in his study, regardless of their answers on a personality test.

> You have a great need for other people to like and admire you. You have a tendency to be critical of yourself. You have a great deal of unused capacity that you have not turned to your advantage. While you have some personality weaknesses, you are generally able to compensate for them. Your sexual adjustment has presented problems for you. Disciplined and self-controlled outside, you tend to be worried and insecure inside. At times you have serious doubts as to whether you have made the right decision or done the right thing. You prefer a certain amount of change and variety and become dissatisfied when hemmed in by restrictions and limitations. You pride yourself as an independent thinker and do not accept others' statements without satisfactory proof. You have found it unwise to be too frank in revealing yourself to others. At times you are extraverted, affable, sociable, while at other times you are introverted, wary, and reserved. Some of your aspirations tend to be pretty unrealistic. Security is one of your major goals in life.

Source: Forer, B. R. (1949). The fallacy of personal validation: A classroom demonstration of gullibility. *Journal of Abnormal and Social Psychology, 44*, 118–123.

As you can see from the profile Forer used (see Table 12.1), the statements were fairly general and most of them could apply to most people, at least some of the time. It is easy for people to see themselves in statements such as "While you have some personality weaknesses, you are generally able to compensate for them," and of course, just about everybody tends to be extraverted *sometimes* and introverted other times, or to have unrealistic goals. The Barnum effect may be a key reason why personality tests of questionable validity (as well as horoscopes, astrologers, psychics, and the like) are so widely believed.

In contrast, rigorous empirical research over the past several decades has narrowed the many potential personality traits into a small number of factors. The statistical technique called **factor analysis** is *used to group items that people respond to similarly*; for instance, the terms *friendly*, *warm*, and *kind* have similar meanings, and can be grouped in a cluster, referred to as a *factor*.

THE FIVE FACTOR MODEL Using factor analysis, psychologist Raymond Cattell (1946) narrowed the list of key personality traits to 16, thereby simplifying and standardizing the number of dimensions psychologists needed to describe the composition of personality. Forty years later, McCrae and Costa (1987) created the **Five Factor Model (FFM)**, *a trait-based theory of personality based on the finding that personality can be described using five major dimensions*; this model has become the most popular trait-based approach for academic personality researchers, and has been cited in hundreds of research articles.

To understand the Big Five traits, consider what characteristics are associated with people high and low on that trait. These are the "kinds of people" described by each trait (see Figure 12.1).

Figure 12.1 The Big Five Personality Dimensions

A widely used measure of personality is the NEO-PI-R. Individuals rate themselves on multiple questions that reflect the traits of openness, conscientiousness, extraversion, agreeableness, and neuroticism. (To help you remember the Big Five, note that the first letters of the traits spell out OCEAN.)

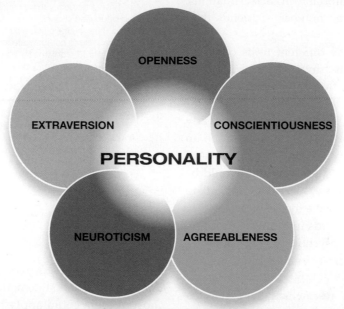

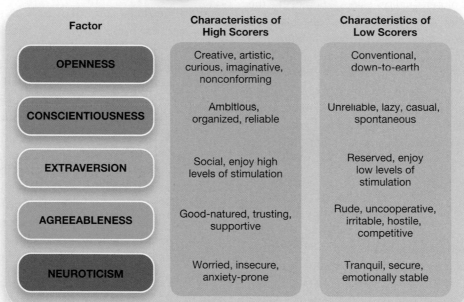

Factor	Characteristics of High Scorers	Characteristics of Low Scorers
OPENNESS	Creative, artistic, curious, imaginative, nonconforming	Conventional, down-to-earth
CONSCIENTIOUSNESS	Ambitious, organized, reliable	Unreliable, lazy, casual, spontaneous
EXTRAVERSION	Social, enjoy high levels of stimulation	Reserved, enjoy low levels of stimulation
AGREEABLENESS	Good-natured, trusting, supportive	Rude, uncooperative, irritable, hostile, competitive
NEUROTICISM	Worried, insecure, anxiety-prone	Tranquil, secure, emotionally stable

Source: Based on McCrae, R. R., & Costa, P. (1987). Validation of the Five-Factor Model of personality across instruments and observers. *Journal of Personality and Social Psychology, 52* (1), 81–90.

OPENNESS Individuals high in openness (high Os) are the dreamers and creative types; they tend to be more "open" to new things—ideas, opinions, and perspectives that differ from theirs, and new ways of seeing a problem that they had not considered. They are more open to new experiences, tending to be curious and appreciative of art and unusual ideas. As a result, they often hold beliefs that would be considered "unconventional." High Os are also likely to think more abstractly and to be more sensitively aware of their emotions.

Individuals low in openness (low Os) are the defenders of the system, preferring the conventional, the tried and true. They avoid the unknown and find security in the known. They prefer things that are tangible rather than symbolic, priding themselves on being "practical." Low Os prefer things to be straightforward and generally dislike subtlety and complexity. They approach new information somewhat defensively—preferring to learn about things they already believe in, and paying less attention to information that challenges their perspective. Low Os tend to be resistant to change and suspicious of their emotions, placing more emphasis on the attempt to be rational and logical.

CONSCIENTIOUSNESS Highly conscientious people (high Cs) are the organizers—efficient, self-disciplined, and dependable. They are the ones who meet deadlines, plan ahead to achieve their goals, and are comfortable with schedules and lists, although at the expense of being flexible and spontaneous at times. High Cs are great employees and students, tending to achieve more in their careers due to their achievement orientation and tendency to get things done on time. They also live longer, perhaps because they are more likely to engage in the positive health behaviours (e.g., eating well and exercising regularly) that the less conscientious among us never quite get around to doing. . . .

Low Cs are the easy-going ones, fun to hang out with, but not so great as collaborators on a project. Low Cs tend to be disorganized, careless with details, and have difficulty meeting deadlines. Although they may want to perform well at a task, they have difficulty disciplining themselves enough to actually get things done. Low Cs feel uncomfortable with schedules and detailed plans, preferring to "be in the moment." Although low Cs suffer somewhat in life due to their lack of self-discipline, they benefit by not being as stressed about details and being able to still enjoy themselves when things don't go according to plan.

EXTRAVERSION Extraverts (high Es) are the socializers and sensation seekers. They are comfortable in more stimulating environments, and thus love the company of others, being seen as outgoing and energetic. Extraverts tend to be more assertive, talkative, and enthusiastic, preferring high levels of stimulation and excitement much of the time. They are fun to be around, but sometimes take things too far, as their love of stimulation puts them at higher risk for dangerous activities such as substance abuse.

Introverts (low Es) are the quiet ones. Although they like social contact, introverts also need time for solitary activities and "recharging their batteries." They can be overwhelmed by the high levels of stimulation preferred by extraverts, so while the extraverts party it up and compete for all the attention, the introverts sit on the couch in the corner having great conversations with a friend or two. Introverts tend to be more cautious and reserved, and they are great when you need someone to really talk to.

AGREEABLENESS Highly agreeable people (high As) are warm and friendly people who are easy to like, easy to be friends with, and easy to have as part of your group. They are kind, compassionate, and empathetic, and tend to be helpful and altruistic. They place strong value on getting along with people and are generally willing to put their own interests aside in order to please others or avoid conflict. Agreeable people are the ones who make it really hard to choose what movie to watch, because they always want to know what movie *you* want to watch. . . . As you might expect, they make great team members, but their leadership skills often suffer because they are unwilling to assert their opinion.

Low As are the type who "put themselves first." They value being authentic more than pandering to other people's needs, making them more likely to assert their opinions and engage in conflict if necessary. Low As suffer socially somewhat, as they tend to be seen as cold, unfriendly, uncooperative, and unkind. They are often skeptical of other people's motives, and tend to be less trusting of human nature in general. As you might expect, low As don't experience much empathy, and tend to be self-interested rather than altruistic.

NEUROTICISM To be called "neurotic" is not generally considered a compliment. Indeed, people high in neuroticism (high Ns) are often difficult to deal with, as their emotional volatility and general tendency to experience negative emotions makes them not much fun to be around. High Ns tend to be quite sensitive and experience strong reactions to stressful situations; as a result, they often interpret situations as overly threatening and magnify small frustrations into major problems. When they experience negative emotions, they have difficulty relaxing and "letting go" of their negative feelings, which makes these feelings persist, and persist, and persist. As a result of their difficulties regulating negative emotions, high Ns are the most vulnerable to anxiety and depressive disorders.

Low Ns, on the other hand, are the prototypical mentally healthy people. They tend to be secure and confident, and let go of negative emotions easily. Rather than blowing things out of proportion, the low Ns take the good with the bad, and deal with problems as they arise, but feel no need to create problems where there aren't any, or to obsessively look for problems until they find them. Low Ns are excellent at managing their emotions, and are regarded by others as "stable."

Taken together, the Big Five factors are extremely useful for understanding people's behaviours, thoughts, and emotions, and predicting why people do the things that they do. Nevertheless, despite the usefulness of the Big Five, psychologists often find that there are other personality traits, outside of the Big Five, that are useful for understanding certain things, such as why people do things that are "evil."

Module 12.1a Quiz:

The Trait Perspective

Know . . .

1. Which of the following statements best describes the difference between the nomothetic and idiographic approaches to personality?

   A. The nomothetic approach focuses on traits found across large groups, whereas the idiographic approach focuses on individuals.

   B. The idiographic approach focuses on traits found across large groups, whereas the nomothetic approach focuses on individuals.

   C. The idiographic approach relies on measures such as the Big Five, whereas the Big Five is of no use to a nomothetic approach.

   D. The idiographic approach allows psychologists to ask questions about the genetic and cultural basis of personality traits.

Understand . . .

2. _____ is the Big Five factor that will likely have the greatest influence on whether you get along with the people you work with.

   A. Agreeableness

   B. Extraversion

   C. Openness

   D. Neuroticism

Apply . . .

3. You are the type of person who tends to go to the same restaurant and order the same thing, sticking to your daily routine. You have even turned down opportunities to travel to new destinations. Which of the Big Five factors best relates to this description of your personality?

   A. Agreeableness

   B. Conscientiousness

   C. Openness

   D. Neuroticism

Beyond the Big Five: The Personality of Evil?

Most people struggle when they think about truly destructive human behaviours: child abuse, wartime atrocities, the Holocaust, 9/11. The more horror we allow ourselves to contemplate, the more we must ask *why?* Why do people do such terrible things?

Following World War II, such questions were a major focus in personality psychology, as the world wanted to understand the rise of fascism and Hitler's ability to mobilize millions of people to carry out his plans of destruction. Early research by Theodore Adorno suggested that a key personality type, the *authoritarian personality*, was a big piece of the puzzle. Authoritarians were theorized to be rigid and dogmatic in their thinking, to separate their social world into strict categories of *Us* and *Them*, and then to believe strongly in the superiority of *Us* and the inferiority of *Them*. As a result, authoritarians were more likely to endorse and engage in prejudice and violence, particularly toward people in the "them" category (Adorno et al., 1950). Although there is some overlap between this construct and other, related personality factors (e.g., openness to experience), over the past several decades, personality researchers have discovered important personality traits that extend the Five Factor Model and help to shed light on the problem of human "evil." Three lines of research are particularly important.

HONESTY–HUMILITY First, Michael Ashton at Brock University and his colleagues have developed the

HEXACO model of personality, *a six-factor theory that generally replicates the five factors of the FFM and adds one additional factor: Honesty–Humility.* Individuals scoring highly on this factor (high HHs) tend to be sincere, honest, and modest, whereas those with low scores (low HHs) are deceitful, greedy, and pompous (Ashton & Lee, 2007). Whereas high HHs are more likely to perform altruistic, pro-social behaviours, low HHs harbour more selfish, anti-social, and violent tendencies (Ashton & Lee, 2008; de Vries & van Kampen, 2010), being more likely to "do whatever it takes" to get what they want, to manipulate others, and to break the rules (Bourdage et al., 2007). Interestingly, low HHs feel a strong sense of self-importance and a feeling of entitlement, like they deserve to have their desires fulfilled. Thus, the HEXACO model seems to describe "evil" as heavily involving an excessive importance placed on the self, and none placed on the other (except in terms of how the other can be used to further the goals of the self).

THE DARK TRIAD A different set of research studies conducted at the University of British Columbia has uncovered three traits that are believed to be central to understanding the personality roots of evil. This **Dark Triad**—*Machiavellianism, psychopathy, and narcissism—describe a person who is socially destructive, aggressive, dishonest, and likely to commit harm in general* (Paulhus & Williams, 2002). Taken together, these traits also describe a person who gives excessive importance to the self, and little to no importance to others.

Machiavellianism is a tendency to use people and to be manipulative and deceitful, lacking respect for others and focusing predominantly on one's own self-interest.

Relationships are approached strategically, using other people for how they might be able to provide some sort of benefit to the self.

Psychopathy is a general tendency toward having shallow emotional responses. Individuals scoring high in psychopathy veer toward highly stimulating activities and tend to feel little empathy for others. They often get a thrill out of conflict, exerting control, or even harming others, and feel little remorse for their actions.

Narcissism reflects an egotistical preoccupation with self-image and an excessive sense of self-importance. The extreme narcissist is "full of himself" (or herself). In Greek legend, the hunter Narcissus was filled with excessive pride and adoration toward himself. This was his fatal flaw, however, as he was so transfixed by his own gaze reflecting in a pool of water that he died by the poolside, still staring at his reflection. Narcissists can often be charming, but are difficult to have as relationship partners because they tend to always put themselves first rather than considering their partner's needs.

Considering these traits separately yields some important insights; for example, people high on different traits may become aggressive for different reasons (Jones & Paulhus, 2010). But their real power comes when you consider them all together. The convergence of these three factors, the Dark Triad, strongly predicts anti-social tendencies. People who score highly on all three of the Dark Triad traits are substantially more likely to commit harm to others, having little empathy or other constraints to prevent them from doing so.

RIGHT-WING AUTHORITARIANISM In a third line of research, Bob Altemeyer at the University of Manitoba has identified **Right-Wing Authoritarianism (RWA)** *as a problematic set of personality characteristics that also predisposes people to certain types of violent or anti-social tendencies. RWA involves three key tendencies:*

1. *obeying orders and deferring to the established authorities in a society;*
2. *supporting aggression against those who dissent or differ from the established social order; and*
3. *believing strongly in maintaining the existing social order* (Altemeyer, 1996).

At the centre of the RWA personality is a strong tendency to think in dogmatic terms, where, metaphorically speaking, everything is either black or white, with no shades of grey. RWAs tend to hold strong beliefs and are highly resistant to changing them (Altemeyer, 1996). They are generally more prejudiced, tending to negatively judge people who hold different perspectives from them (see Module 13.2). As a result, RWAs are likely to advocate a harsh stance toward people who deviate from the established social order, such as political activists, feminists, atheists,

and members of ethnic minorities (Goodman & Moradi, 2008; Haddock et al., 1993; Narby et al., 1993). Given their unquestioning acceptance of authority figures, high RWAs are more likely to agree with unethical decisions made by leaders (Son Hing et al., 2007), and to have positive attitudes toward corrupt governments (Altemeyer, 1996).

As a result of these tendencies, high RWA individuals were likely instrumental in the rise of fascism that led to World War II, and will likely play important roles in the repressive dictatorships, destructive business practices, and unhealthy family structures of the future.

The theory of Right-Wing Authoritarianism also shares with the previous two theories an emphasis on people placing excessive emphasis on their own self-importance. In the case of RWA, this manifests as excessive certainty and unwavering conviction in one's personal opinions, coupled with strong in-group favouritism and beliefs that are prejudiced and derogatory towards members of other "out-groups."

Working the Scientific Literacy Model

Right-Wing Authoritarianism at the Group Level

What do we know about RWA?

As we discussed above, personality researchers have identified RWA as a cluster of characteristics that make society a less warm and friendly place, being related to generally harmful tendencies such as holding prejudiced views against other groups and an excessive and closed-minded allegiance to societal conventions. It's relatively easy to imagine how people who are high in RWA might end up behaving in social situations. But it's another thing entirely to consider what could happen in situations involving lots of people high in RWA. When a group of closed-minded, prejudiced, violence-prone individuals get together, what could possibly go wrong?

How can science determine how RWA affects groups?

In one fascinating and highly disturbing study, Altemeyer (1996) selected high- and low-RWA participants to play a complex role-playing simulation of the Earth's future, called the Global Change Game. This game is generally played by 50–70 people who are organized into groups that represent different regions of the world; these groups then make decisions about how their region behaves on the international stage. For example, participants decide how their region will deal with problems such as environmental degradation, poverty, overpopulation, and military threats. The simulated conditions of the Earth change depending on the actions of the players, thus providing a fairly realistic simulation of the challenges of governance in the international community.

In order to test how RWAs play the game, Altemeyer ran through the game two times, once with 67 individuals who scored very low on the RWA scale, and once with 68 people who scored very high. Each simulation covered 40 years of time into Earth's future. The results were, frankly, astonishing.

In the low-RWA group, there were no wars or military build-up over the 40-year time period. Instead, regions steadily downsized their militaries and diverted the money into humanitarian and environmental projects. They also collectively resolved challenges through international meetings and cooperation. At one point, a global crisis occurred due to a threat to the Earth's ozone layer; players responded by holding a group meeting, and agreeing to make large investments in technology development so that they could collectively solve the problem. By the end of the game, food, health services, and jobs were provided for almost all people on Earth, resulting in a peaceful, stable world.

In the high-RWA group, players tended to interpret the actions of others as aggressive and responded in kind. Militaries quickly grew and war ensued, leading to a global nuclear war that wiped out every human being on the planet. At this point, the players were given a second chance to play, starting at a point prior to the nuclear war. Despite having the chance to learn from their earlier mistakes, the players nevertheless were incapable of getting along with each other. When the ozone crisis occurred, no international summit was called and only one region took action to avert the crisis. Instead of cooperation, players remained suspicious of each other and rapidly developed their militaries. One major military conflict killed 400 million people, and players poured so much money into military expenses that devastating social and environmental problems were never dealt with. At the end of the 40-year period, the world was again divided into armed camps on the brink of all-out war.

At the very least, this simulation suggests that we have to consider not only how factors like RWA operate in isolation, but how they operate in interaction with other people in real situations. Studying how personality characteristics operate on more collective scales is a major new frontier for the personality field that needs further exploration. It also suggests that we need to think carefully, as a society, about the personality characteristics of the people we allow into positions of power. Because these simulations suggest quite strongly that if several highly authoritarian leaders ended up in some sort of conflict, they may be highly prone to escalating conflicts to acts of extreme violence.

Can we critically evaluate this research?

There are several methodological limitations to this study that should be taken into consideration when evaluating the findings. First, there are external validity concerns; for example, playing a game with no real consequences does not necessarily indicate how people would respond in a real-life situation. It is possible that in a real situation, people would be more sensitive to the consequences of their actions and would not be so willing to risk human lives. Furthermore, the simulations were only performed on one night with each group; therefore, results could have been due to chance factors, such as particular individuals having a strong impact on the outcomes. Also, because only university students participated in the study, the results may not generalize to the rest of the population. Obviously, this was not a highly controlled set of studies, and the findings must therefore be interpreted very cautiously. However, as a case study of this particular type of competitive circumstance involving high- and low-RWAs, the results remain quite alarming and suggestive.

Why is this relevant?

This research illustrates the highly destructive impact that authoritarian personalities may have in group settings, and it sounds a clear bell of warning in the 21st century. We are living in a time in which our world faces unprecedented challenges that require international cooperation, yet intolerance and intergroup hostilities are rampant and ideological fundamentalism and fanaticism heavily influence politics in many countries. Greater understanding of the potential roots of intergroup hostility in individuals' personalities is urgently needed at this time.

Module 12.1b Quiz:

Beyond the Big Five: The Personality of Evil?

Know . . .

1. How does the HEXACO model of personality differ from the Big Five factors?
   A. HEXACO is a nomothetic model whereas the Big Five is an idiographic model.
   B. The Big Five model includes five traits whereas the HEXACO model explains personality using three traits.
   C. HEXACO is the only personality theory to include psychopathy.
   D. HEXACO includes a sixth personality trait: honesty–humility.

Understand . . .

2. One reason for going beyond the Big Five, such as the three lines of research on Honesty–Humility, the Dark Triad, and Right-Wing Authoritarianism, is

   A. they predict anti-social tendencies, such as violence and prejudice, better than the Big Five traits.

   B. they are idiographic approaches, which supplement the nomothetic approach taken in the Five Factor Model.

   C. these three theories account for states and situational factors, whereas the Big Five does not.

   D. these three theories can be used to diagnose personality disorders that could justify preventative action, such as incarcerating "dangerous" personalities before they are able to commit any crimes and cause harm to others.

Apply . . .

3. Lisa and Elaine work at the same place and were both being considered for a promotion. In order secure the promotion for herself, Lisa told her bosses lies about Elaine being selfish and difficult to work with. As a result, Elaine did not receive the promotion. Lisa's behaviour is an example of which personality trait?

   A. Machiavellianism

   B. Psychopathy

   C. Neuroticism

   D. Humility

Personality Traits over the Lifespan

Have you ever looked back on something you wrote several years ago, perhaps in a diary or journal, and wondered, "Who was that person who wrote these things?" Or maybe you have looked back at someone you once dated and wondered, "Who was I when I chose to date that person? It certainly wasn't 'me'!" One of the most fascinating issues in personality psychology is whether we stay basically the same, or whether our fundamental personalities change as we age.

TEMPERAMENTS A mountain of research from different areas within psychology has revealed considerable stability in our personalities. In fact, given the large genetic contribution to personality factors, our personalities start even before we are born, so could be expected to remain largely stable over time (Plomin & Caspi, 1999; Yamagata et al., 2006).

In child development studies, researchers have found that infants possess different *temperaments* right from birth, which also supports the view that the seeds of our personalities are present right from the start. Infants display their temperamental differences along dimensions such as activity level, mood, attention span, and distractibility (Rothbart & Bates, 2006; Thomas & Chess, 1977). As most parents with multiple children can attest, kids come "hardwired" to be a certain way. Some infants are generally active and happy, whereas others are more tranquil, and still others are easily upset. So, if you're a parent pulling your hair out with your chronically distressed child who seems impossible to deal with, don't judge yourself too harshly. Remind yourself that infants have different temperaments and your power as a parent is small compared to the power of their genes.

Thus, temperament seems to represent an innate, biological foundation upon which personality is built. This, combined with the genetic research, suggests that personality traits should be stable over time. To some extent, research confirms that this is the case: Infant temperament predicts the adult personality traits of neuroticism, extraversion, and conscientiousness (Evans & Rothbart, 2007).

One amazing study that followed the same children from age 3 until adulthood showed that temperament at 3 years of age was strongly predictive of behavioural tendencies, personality, and life outcomes many years later (Caspi, 2000). Three main temperaments were identified: *well-adjusted* (capable of self-control, confident, not overly upset by new people or situations); *under controlled* (impulsive, restless, distractible, emotionally volatile); and *inhibited* (socially uncomfortable, fearful, easily upset by strangers). Just over 10 years later, children of different temperaments had developed quite different behaviour patterns. The *under-controlled* children (relative to the other groups) had become the most likely to engage in *externalizing behaviours* (fighting, lying, disobeying), whereas the *inhibited* children developed mainly *internalizing* behaviour patterns (e.g., worrying, crying easily). By age 18, their emerging adult personalities were reflections of their temperaments at age 3.

IS PERSONALITY STABLE OVER TIME? There are a number of factors—both behavioural and biological—that make personality stable over time. Personality processes tend to become self-perpetuating; personality traits that lead to behaviours that receive positive reinforcement are more likely to become stable characteristics of that individual (Heatherton & Weinberger, 1994). As an example, take the personality factor of conscientiousness. As we discussed earlier, highly conscientious people will tend to be organized, punctual, and dependable; they are therefore more likely to succeed, be respected by others, and create professional opportunities for themselves. As they experience success, this feeds back to reinforce those qualities.

You can also understand how "personality is destiny" by considering the basic insight of neuroscience: neurons that fire together wire together. Thus, we know that the more that people practise a certain skill, the more they train their brains to be good at that skill. Similarly, the more that people practise being extraverted, open-minded, conscientious, agreeable, or neurotic, the more they train their brains to function in that manner. This can also be

---

Figure 12.2 Personality Stability and Change over the Lifespan

Average scores of Big Five traits change over the lifespan. Generally, most traits become more positive through adulthood, although there are anomalies. Social dominance (an aspect of extraversion) remains stable after age 40. Conscientiousness does not begin rising until after the college years. Openness to experience only rises up to the college years, then remains largely stable until old age, when it declines (Roberts et al., 2006).

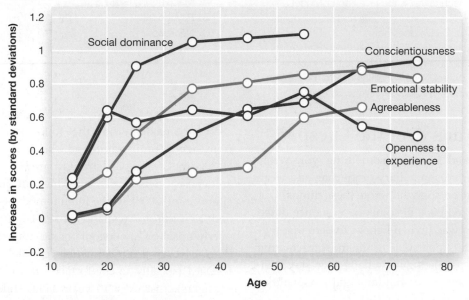

Source: Based on Roberts, B., Walton, K., & Viechtbauer, W. (2006). Patterns of mean-level change in personality traits across the life-course: A meta-analysis of longitudinal studies. *Psychological Bulletin, 132* (1), 1–25.

---

seen as a positive feedback system; personality structures influence patterns in the person's life and build networks in the person's brain in ways that reinforce themselves, leading personality to be quite stable over time. Consistent with this view, researchers analyzing the results of over 150 studies involving almost 50 000 participants found that personality stability is lowest for young children and highest for people over 50 (Roberts & DelVecchio, 2000).

However, research has also shown that personality *can* change, particularly in late adolescence and early adulthood. For example, young adults tend to experience fewer negative emotions than do adolescents, reflecting decreases in neuroticism. Also, conscientiousness, agreeableness, and social dominance (an aspect of extraversion) all increase in early adulthood (Roberts et al., 2006; see Figure 12.2). Take a moment and consider why personalities change in these systematic ways over time. One likely explanation is that, over time, our environments change and so do the roles we play in those environments. For example, adults have to be more conscientious than children because they have so many more responsibilities—like taking care of their unconscientious children! Over time there are many such changes—in our environments, our social roles, the amount of choice and power we have, the sophistication of our thinking processes, the development of our bodies and brains, and many other things—so there may be many reasons why personalities change over time.

Nevertheless, even these data describe a kind of personality stability, in that although people's personality traits may fluctuate over time, their rank ordering in the population remains very stable. That is, people who are more extraverted than others at time one also tend to be more extraverted than others at time two, even though the overall level of extraversion may change over that time period (McCrae & Costa, 1990).

PERSONALITY TRAITS AND STATES Trait labels may go a long way toward describing what people are like. However, many psychologists are quick to point out that no matter how useful traits may seem, people's behaviour is also determined by situational factors and context. You may know someone whom you would describe as very calm and tranquil, yet one day he curses and screams at other drivers on the road. In contrast to a personality trait, a **state** *is a temporary physical or psychological engagement that influences behaviour.* Perhaps your normally calm friend lashed out at other drivers on the road because he was criticized earlier that day or made a mistake that made him feel foolish, and so he was defensively displacing his bad feelings onto other people. Even people who seem highly consistent in how they express their neuroticism, agreeableness, or extraversion will not behave in the same way across all situations, and this observation has led to some strong criticisms of trait theories of personality (Mischel, 1968; Mischel &

Shoda, 1998). However, we generally understand now that states and traits work together; traits describe a person's general personality tendencies, whereas states describe what that person is like in specific sets of circumstances.

The specific ways in which states and situational factors interact to influence us is a challenging topic that research has only begun to scratch the surface of. Try to think of the number of different situations or states you find yourself in across any average day. For example, you can be awake, asleep, or half-asleep; happy; sad; excited; skeptical; embarrassed; confident; or unsure of yourself. You could be having a crisis or you could be completely relaxed. The list could go on forever—and as you might have guessed, psychologists have tried to see just how long it goes. In one study, 77 college students were asked to describe as many situations as they could that they

might encounter. Their total reached more than 7000. Perhaps you can now see why many psychologists would rather focus on five personality dimensions. Fortunately, Saucier and colleagues (2007) took these 7000 situations and reduced them to four general aspects of situations that are most likely to influence our behaviour:

1. Locations (e.g., being at work, school, or home)
2. Associations (e.g., being with friends, alone, or with family)
3. Activities (e.g., awake, rushed, studying)
4. Subjective states (e.g., mad, sick, drunk, happy)

These situations influence how and when our personality traits are expressed. Identifying these situations is important because they interact with personality traits to determine our behaviour.

Module 12.1c Quiz:
Personality Traits over the Lifespan

Know . . .

1. Which of the following is *not* a situational factor that is likely to influence your behaviour?
   A. The location in which a behaviour is being performed
   B. The degree to which you are an extravert
   C. Whether you are drunk or sober
   D. The people that you are with at the time

Understand . . .

2. In studies of children's temperament, which label would most likely be applied to children who tended to be impulsive, restless, and distractible?
   A. internalized
   B. well-adjusted

C. inhibited
D. under-controlled

Analyze . . .

3. Your friend, who is normally introverted, is outraged at the taxi driver who is trying to overcharge you. He is cursing at the driver in a verbal altercation. This event is most likely due to his _____.
   A. temperament
   B. subjective state
   C. idealized self
   D. Big Five personality traits

Behaviourist and Social-Cognitive Perspectives

You probably didn't have much trouble understanding the trait perspective to personality; indeed, using traits to describe people is something we do regularly, particularly in Western cultures. However, the trait approach does tend to reinforce certain assumptions that other psychologists have called into question. Most importantly, the trait approach reinforces the assumption that we carry our personality characteristics around inside us; we treat traits like they are "things" that we "have," which then influence our thoughts, feelings, and behaviours. This approach does not examine how personalities are influenced by our experiences.

THE BEHAVIOURIST PERSPECTIVE The behaviourist would note any identifiable patterns of behaviour and

seek to understand how that behaviour was elicited by specific environmental conditions. Notable psychologist B. F. Skinner, for example, believed that "personality" is simply a description of the response tendencies that occur in different situations. For example, when with a group of people, your behavioural responses to that situation might include dominating the conversation, asking a lot of questions, laughing along at other people's jokes, or generally remaining silent. Presumably, the behaviours you engage in are based on your past experiences; if you tend to dominate the conversation and laugh at people's jokes, then you were likely reinforced for those behaviours in the past. A behaviourist might note that using the personality dimension of "extraversion" is an unnecessary addition—it is just a label that does not help us understand the simple relationship between stimulus and response (Figure 12.3).

Figure 12.3 Behavioural and Social-Cognitive Approaches to Personality

(a) Behaviourist Account of Personality. Behaviourists thought that what psychologists call personality was an expression of relationships between behaviour, rewards, and punishment. Behaviourists avoided referring to personality traits and dispositions, instead focusing on how past experiences predict future behaviours. For example, whether someone tends to be pessimistic might be based on past experiences of feeling a lost sense of control. **(b) Reciprocal Determinism and the Social-Cognitive Approach.** According to Albert Bandura and colleagues, personality is a product of dynamic interactions between behaviour and reinforcement, and, importantly, the beliefs, expectancies, and dispositions of the individual.

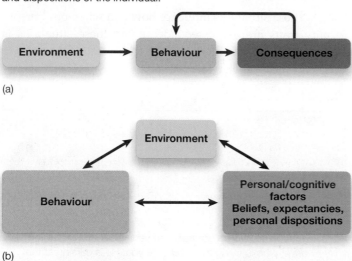

(a)

(b)

Source: Ciccarelli, Saundra K.; White, J. Noland, *Psychology: An Exploration* (Subscription) 2nd Ed., ©2012. Reprinted and Electronically reproduced by permission of Pearson Education, Inc., New York, NY.

THE SOCIAL-COGNITIVE PERSPECTIVE In the mid-20th century, behaviourism gave way to the emerging social-cognitive perspective; this had a major impact on our understanding of personality. Specifically, the social-cognitive theorists, like Albert Bandura, placed central importance on the role of cognition and the person's inner subjective interpretation of their circumstances. No longer was the individual simply an object, affected by environmental circumstances; now the person became an agent, actively constructing meaning out of her circumstances, and then making choices to behave in ways that affect those circumstances. From a social-cognitive perspective, what became clear was the *relationship* between the person and the environment, plus how this relationship is bound up with the person's thoughts and interpretations.

According to Bandura's social-cognitive theory, personality develops out of the person's interaction with the environment, but where this differs from behaviourism is that the person ends up forming *beliefs* about their relationship to the environment, especially beliefs about their own actions and the likely consequences that will follow from their choices. For example, Bandura was keenly

interested in the concept of *self-efficacy*, the belief that ones' attempts to accomplish a specific task will be successful. People with a higher degree of self-efficacy are far more likely to take action, especially difficult actions where the rewards are not immediately obvious, whereas people with little self-efficacy for a task will be unlikely to try, and will give up more easily. Thus, Bandura emphasized how beliefs, such as self-efficacy beliefs, form out of our interactions with the environment. These beliefs then become their own causal force, exerting influence over our behaviours and how we interact with the environment.

If you put all this together, you can see how Bandura saw personality as a kind of integrated web of many different processes. His central idea was called **reciprocal determinism**, based on the idea that the person and the environment co-create each other; thus personality is what emerges from the *interactions between behaviour, internal (personal) factors, and external (situational) factors, all of which mutually influence each other* (see Figure 12.3). The ultimate goal of a social-cognitive perspective is to achieve a fully holistic understanding of the person as a system of interdependent processes.

Researchers like Bandura appreciated the added insight that was encouraged by taking a social-cognitive approach to understanding people. Focusing on thoughts and beliefs opened up whole layers of beliefs, interpretations, expectations, and biases for consideration. For example, examining a person's beliefs may reveal that they think they are worthless, that other people generally won't like them, that they tend to mess things up, or have other self-defeating convictions. These beliefs may be the most important force keeping their "personality" (i.e., their pattern of interaction with the environment) from changing. The hope, therefore, is that by learning to change some aspects of the social-cognitive system, such as self-defeating beliefs, the whole system can change.

For example, imagine a person who is highly neurotic (from a trait perspective). Knowing this may make the person want to improve and become less neurotic and unpleasant to be around. But, this doesn't really give much guidance as to how to actually DO this. What is one supposed to change, in order to "be a different person?"

A social-cognitive theorist like Bandura would take a look at the processes through which the person seemed to express and reinforce their neuroticism. Perhaps the person holds certain expectations, like fear-based beliefs that things will generally turn out poorly, or that other people can't be trusted to do the right thing. As a result, the person feels a lot of anxiety and tries to deal with this by controlling things around them, thus developing a pattern of being controlling, critical, and unwilling to trust or rely on others. As you start to "unpack" this whole system of self-reinforcing beliefs and behaviours, you find the specific factors that could help that person change. For example, perhaps this specific person could examine the beliefs they hold about trusting other people and identify how these are connected to other beliefs (e.g., "I will do a better job if I do it myself"), which in turn are connected to other beliefs (e.g., "If I mess things up, people will be angry with me"). Through this kind of "analysis" of related beliefs, the person uncovers specific leverage points—processes that they can change that will then change their belief system.

Module 12.1d Quiz:

Behaviourist and Social-Cognitive Perspectives

Know . . .

1. Which of the following concepts developed by Bandura refers to interactions that occur among behaviour, internal factors, and external factors as an explanation for personality?

   A. Reciprocal determinism

   B. Positive psychology

   C. Intersubjectivity

   D. Egocentrism

Understand . . .

2. Kaitlin describes herself as unmotivated. She has not felt rewarded by her attempts to succeed at school or work and, therefore, has given up trying. How might a psychologist who adopts a strict behaviourist approach account for Kaitlin's behaviour?

   A. Kaitlin believes that she cannot succeed and, therefore, avoids putting herself in situations where she might fail.

   B. Kaitlin has a history of not being reinforced for trying to succeed and, therefore, has stopped trying.

   C. Kaitlin focuses too much on negatives and does not have a positive outlook on life.

   D. Kaitlin has low levels of the trait known as extraversion.

Analyze . . .

3. Alternative approaches to personality such as the behaviourist and cognitive approaches complement trait theories of personality because

   A. these alternative approaches help to account for how traits interact with behaviour and personal experience.

   B. trait theories focus on the negatives of personality.

   C. it is easier to observe behaviour than to ask someone to fill out a personality inventory.

   D. trait theories focus only on the positive aspects of personality.

Module 12.1 Summary

12.1a Know . . . the key terminology associated with contemporary approaches to personality.

the Dark Triad
factor analysis
Five Factor Model (FFM)
HEXACO model of personality
idiographic approach
nomothetic approach
personality
personality trait
reciprocal determinism
Right-Wing Authoritarianism (RWA)
state

12.1b Understand . . . the behaviourist and social-cognitive views of personality.

A strict behavioural account of personality identifies the stimuli that control a person's responses. From a behaviourist perspective, there is little need for trait terminology, such as neuroticism or conscientiousness, and no reference to cognitive factors such as beliefs or thoughts. The social-cognitive approach to personality instead emphasizes that situations, behaviours, and thoughts reciprocally determine each other.

12.1c Apply . . . the Big Five personality traits to understand your own personality.

Psychologists usually describe individuals based on their scores on personality tests involving the Big Five traits, such that someone might rate high, medium, or low on each trait.

Apply Activity

Use Table 12.2 on page 504 to describe your own personality in terms of the Big Five, and cite examples of specific behaviours and habits that correspond to each trait. Before you begin this exercise, review Figure 12.1, which outlines some of the major characteristics of high and low scores on each of the five factors.

12.1d Analyze . . . the personality roots of violence and prejudice.

Canadian researchers have identified three sets of factors that predict violence and prejudice that are not fully captured by the Five Factor Model. The first is the Honesty–Humility dimension of the HEXACO model of personality. The second is the Dark Triad of psychopathy, Machiavellianism, and narcissism. The third is Right-Wing

Table 12.2 Applying the Five Factor Model

For each trait, try to determine if you would score low, medium, or high if you were to complete a test based on the Five Factor Model. Cite specific examples of behaviours and preferences that support your ranking.

Factor	Low / Medium / High	Specific Examples
Openness		
Conscientiousness		
Extraversion		
Agreeableness		
Neuroticism		

Authoritarianism. Research has found that these traits predict many dysfunctional patterns of thoughts, emotions, and behaviours. Understanding the causal underpinnings of these traits and developing strategies to help individuals with such personality traits would be a key advance in promoting a healthier and more peaceful society.

12.1e Analyze . . . the relative roles of personality traits and psychological and physical states in determining behaviour.

The debate over whether personality traits influence behaviour or whether situational factors play a bigger role in behaviour is ongoing in the field of personality psychology. In reality, both sets of factors are important. Personality traits can be remarkably consistent, yet the situations we find ourselves in can lead to unexpected behaviour.

Module 12.2 Cultural and Biological Approaches to Personality

Christopher Futcher/E+/Getty Images

⌄ Learning Objectives

12.2a Know . . . the key terminology associated with cultural and biological approaches to personality.

12.2b Understand . . . how evolutionary theories explain personality.

12.2c Apply . . . your knowledge to understand how arousal is related to extraversion.

12.2d Analyze . . . claims that males and females have fundamentally different personalities.

12.2e Analyze . . . the genetic basis of personality.

Apparently, if you're travelling abroad, it is a good idea to sew a Canadian flag somewhere onto your backpack. The reason is that people in most parts of the world, people believe that Canadians are generally nice, polite, and friendly. So, wearing the maple leaf should elicit positive responses from other people.

Are these beliefs about Canadians true? Obviously, there are all sorts of different people living in a country. Nevertheless, there does often seem to be a kind of "national character," doesn't there? Just try this—imagine the prototypical Swedish person. Now notice what came to your mind. The manic Swedish chef? Icy blond supermodels drinking vodka in a snowbank and looking at you with cool disdain? Now imagine a British person. Japanese? Australian? Iraqi? Jamaican? Did you find that specific types of people popped into your head for

each example? Whether we endorse specific stereotypes or not, we certainly have absorbed basic sets of beliefs about people from different cultures, and they tend to come to our minds. But are these ideas accurate? Is there such a thing as "national character" that applies to entire populations?

These questions are extremely interesting but unfortunately, we don't yet have all the answers. Personality psychologists are extensively studying cultural differences and similarities in personality and are working to understand how broad cultural forces interact with other factors to give rise to our personalities. In this module, we will explore the convergence of cross-cultural, evolutionary, and biological perspectives. By the end, we will have a better understanding of how these factors interact.

Focus Questions

1.   Does culture influence the types of personality traits we find across human societies?

2.   How do evolutionary and biological approaches add to our understanding of personality?

Culture and Personality

Would you say Americans are WEIRD? It's okay, don't feel uncomfortable; this is a bit of a trick question. In this particular case, "WEIRD" stands for "Western, Educated, Industrialized, Rich, and Democratic." So yes, it would be fair to say that, on average, people from several different cultures are WEIRD—Canadians, Western Europeans, Australians, and definitely Americans (Henrich et al., 2010).

So, why does this matter? Consider this: Do you think there are any major differences between people who are WEIRD and people who are not? Of course there are. An "average" Torontonian likely would have very little in common with an "average" rural Mongolian farmer, for example.

Now consider that *almost everything you know* about psychology is based on studying people from WEIRD cultures. One study conducted at the University of British Columbia showed that 96% of psychology studies are conducted on a mere 12% of the population—the WEIRD ones (Henrich et al., 2010). This means our whole "scientific" understanding of the human animal is based on studying one specific, small, subgroup. Doesn't that seem a little. . .weird?

At the very least, this reminds us to be cautious in applying findings from psychology studies to the human species at large. It also means that we need to better understand the similarities and differences between people in different cultures. For example, in terms of personality, one starting place would be to examine whether there are any important differences between the WEIRD and everyone else.

UNIVERSALS AND DIFFERENCES ACROSS CULTURES: THE BIG FIVE The Five Factor Model of personality centres around five personality dimensions: neuroticism, extraversion, openness to experience, agreeableness, and conscientiousness. However, because these factors were discovered by researchers working in WEIRD places—the United States, Canada, and Europe—it is possible that the Five Factor Model only accounts for personality in WEIRD populations and may not apply to the rest of the world.

To find out whether the Big Five traits are truly universal, an enormous team of psychologists (there were 127 authors on this single article) measured the Big Five dimensions in more than 17 000 people speaking 28 different languages and inhabiting 56 countries on 6 continents (they did not visit Antarctica). In all cultures that were studied, the Big Five factors were reliably found. Despite the many differences that may exist between cultures, the people in those cultures do appear to share the same basic personality structures (McCrae et al., 2005; Schmitt et al., 2007). This is an incredible finding, suggesting that the basic systems in the human personality are, in a sense, deeper than culture. Although individual personalities differ enormously, the basic machinery of the human personality system seems universal.

PERSONALITY STRUCTURES IN DIFFERENT CULTURES The study described above is groundbreaking in its global scope, but a key methodological challenge remains. Because the Five Factor Model was originally created by performing a factor analysis of the personality adjectives in the English language, the kinds of questions that are asked on Big Five questionnaires are designed to measure the Big Five factors, and no others. Thus, when the scale is given to people from other cultures, the scale itself brings the biases of Western culture and the English language right along with it. What if other languages used different types of adjectives to describe personality? What if other cultures had different personality traits than the ones that emerge in the West? Re-analyzing personality from different linguistic starting points might reveal new personality factors that lie outside of the Big Five.

Researchers have begun to address this limitation, analyzing personality structure using personality descriptors in other languages; this work has already revealed unique personality factors not captured in the Big Five (Heine & Buchtel, 2009). For example, Cheung and colleagues (1996) examined indigenous Chinese personality traits, looking for patterns among the personality descriptors used in Chinese, rather than English. They found 26 new personality traits in total, and when they performed a factor-analysis on all the traits including these 26 new ones, they found a quite different structure from the Big Five.

Instead of five traits, these researchers found four: dependability, social potency, individualism, and interpersonal relatedness. The first three traits were very similar to three of the Big Five traits (neuroticism, extraversion, and agreeableness, respectively), but the fourth, interpersonal relatedness, was unique. Interpersonal relatedness is a combination of characteristics concerning social harmony, tradition, and an emphasis on one's social relationships. This may reflect a distinct personality dimension in the Chinese psyche, emphasizing the more socially interdependent nature of the self in this culture.

Other researchers have added to our multicultural understanding of personality, analyzing the personality traits found in Filipino, Spanish, and Greek languages, and seeking a more integrated cross-cultural theory of personality (Benet-Martinez & John, 1998; Church, 2001; Saucier et al., 2005). Each analysis has revealed new factors that seem to be independent of the Big Five.

Cross-cultural work on personality is still in its infancy, and clearly, many questions remain. At this point, most psychologists would agree that the Five Factor Model captures important and perhaps universal dimensions of personality, but also might miss important cultural-specific qualities that can only be understood by analyzing personality from that culture's own perspective.

COMPARING PERSONALITY TRAITS BETWEEN NATIONS Despite the difficulties noted above, one important advantage of personality scales that have been translated into different languages is that psychologists can test for personality differences across cultures. Many such differences have been found. For example, consider the countries with the highest and lowest averages on each of the Big Five traits in Table 12.3 (Schmitt et al., 2007). (Interestingly, Canada falls roughly in the middle in each case.)

Table 12.3 Cultural Differences in the Big Five Personality Traits

	Highest	Lowest
Extraversion	Serbia, Croatia	Bangladesh, France
Openness	Chile, Belgium	Hong Kong, Japan
Agreeableness	Jordan, Democratic Republic of the Congo	Japan, Lithuania
Conscientiousness	Ethiopia, Democratic Republic of the Congo	Japan, South Korea
Neuroticism	Japan, Argentina	Democratic Republic of the Congo, Slovenia

Source: Based on data from Schmitt, D. P., Allik, J., McCrae, R. R., Benet-Martinez, V., et al. (2007). The geographic distribution of Big Five personality traits: Patterns and profiles of human self-descriptions across 56 nations. *Journal of Cross-Cultural Psychology, 38,* 173–212.

Biopsychosocial Perspectives
How Culture Shapes Our Development: Cultural Differences in the Self

During the 2000 Olympics in Sydney, Australia, two gold-medal–winning athletes were interviewed about their success. In explaining her success during the race, Misty Hyman, who won the 200-metre butterfly for the United States, said, "I think I just stayed focused. It was time to show the world what I could do. I am just glad I was able to do it. I knew I could beat Suzy O'Neil, deep down in my heart I believed it, and I know this whole week the doubts kept creeping in, they were with me on the blocks, but I just said, 'No, this is my night.'"

In contrast, Naoko Takahashi, after winning the marathon for Japan, said, "Here is the best coach in the world, the best manager in the world, and all of the people who support me—all of these things were getting together and became a gold medal. So I think I didn't get it alone, not only by myself" (Markus et al., 2006).

This striking example illustrates how people's behaviour can be shaped by broad cultural factors. Misty Hyman, from the individualistic United States, seems to be more self-promoting, explaining her success as being due to her own characteristics, her willpower, and belief in herself. Naoko Takahashi, from collectivistic Japan, takes her moment of Olympic glory as an opportunity to highlight the ways in which she was assisted by so many people in her life, de-emphasizing her own contribution in favour of honouring others.

Whether a culture predominantly emphasizes individualism or collectivism has many effects on personality, affecting how people see themselves and how they behave in many situations. Researchers have found that when describing themselves, predominantly individualistic people use more personal adjectives (e.g., "I am extraverted"; "I have a good sense of humour"). Predominantly collectivistic people tend to describe themselves more relationally, in terms of their connections to other people ("I am a son"; "I am a sister"), and their affiliations with specific social groups ("I am Canadian"; "I am a Trekkie").

This difference in self-definition results in differences in the stability of personality across different situations. The individualistic person is the same across most situations, whereas the more collectivistic person feels that who you are depends on who you're with; the self that you are emerges within a social context and is attuned to that context.

Perhaps because they define their self-concepts more rigidly, individualistic people are more likely to be defensive in specific ways. To the collectivistic person, the self is fluid and changeable from situation to situation; thus there is not the same need to defend a single specific self-concept. But to the individualist, the self is supposed to exist as a separate "thing," one that persists from situation to situation, and as a result, individualists have a stronger need to maintain a positive view of their self-concepts. Individualists are likely to emphasize their positive qualities. And, as with Misty Hyman, when things turn out well for them, they take most of the credit themselves. On the other hand, if the individualist fails, they are pretty good at finding other circumstantial factors to blame (Heine, 2003; Markus & Kitayama, 1991).

The influence of culture can even be seen in the brain. In one study (Chiao et al., 2009), participants were put into fMRI scanners to monitor their brain activity while they made judgments about different sentences. In order to manipulate whether subjects were thinking of themselves in a more individualistic or collectivistic manner, researchers asked subjects to make different types of judgments about the sentences. For some sentences, they judged the degree to which it described them in general (individualistic-self task), whereas for others they judged how well it described them when they were with their mothers (collectivistic-self task). Amazingly, their brain scans were able to tell the difference between individualists and collectivists. In the brain, part of the medial prefrontal cortex is involved when processing information related to the self. This area was most active for individualistic participants when they were making judgments about themselves in general, whereas collectivists showed the greatest amount of activation in this area when making judgments about themselves in relation to their mothers. Thus, to individualists, the individualistic task was processed by their brains as most self-relevant, whereas for collectivists, it was the collectivistic task that was most self-relevant.

What do these differences really mean? Do they reflect actual personality differences between the people in those countries? Or could other things account for the findings? Many of the personality differences do seem puzzling. For example, why are Argentinians so neurotic, compared to people from the Democratic Republic of the Congo? Why are the Japanese so much less conscientious than Ethiopians? In fact, many of the findings in these large-scale cross-cultural studies defy cultural stereotypes (Terracciano et al., 2005), and it is a huge challenge for researchers to understand whether or not these differences are real.

One striking cultural difference that researchers have struggled to understand is also illustrated in Table 12.3. Isn't it interesting that a single country, Japan, ranked lowest of all countries on three out of the five traits (openness, agreeableness, and conscientiousness)? Given the general desirability of these traits, that is a fairly critical evaluation of the Japanese personality! (The fact that they are among the most neurotic countries makes it seem even worse.) In fact, people from the entire South Asian part of the world rated their own personalities relatively negatively. Are these differences real? Is such a vast swath of humanity really so different from the rest of the world? It turns out that there may be a different explanation for at least some of the cultural differences found in personality studies. It is possible that people from different cultures have different **response styles**—*characteristic ways of responding to questions*; these response styles can be strongly influenced by cultural norms. For example, in one culture it may be more

socially acceptable to say highly positive things about yourself, whereas in another culture the same behaviour may be considered rude or boastful. Indeed, researchers at the University of British Columbia have shown that there are such norms in South Asian cultures, discouraging people from emphasizing their strengths and successes, and instead encouraging people to be modest, humble, even self-critical (Heine, 2003; Markus & Kitayama, 1991; Mezulis et al., 2004).

An important critique of cross-cultural research is that it may lead to an emphasis on how cultures differ from each other, and obscure the fact that there is so much individual diversity *within* a culture that the average differences *between* cultures may not be that important after all. Therefore, it is important not to over-emphasize small average differences between groups and unduly reinforce group-based stereotypes.

Consistent with this point, the authors of the huge study discussed earlier finally concluded that the differences found in average trait ratings in different cultures are not sufficiently strong to justify beliefs in national character. "No convincing evidence has demonstrated that beliefs about national character" have any basis in fact, "despite their wide adoption and resistance to change" (Schmitt et al., 2007). Thus, the very researchers who are looking for cross-cultural differences in personality ended up concluding that these differences are so small that it is misleading to think that people in different cultures are "different types of people."

Module 12.2a Quiz:

Culture and Personality

Know . . .

1. What does the WEIRD acronym refer to?
   A. Psychologists' preoccupation with abnormal personalities
   B. A single, specific group on which major perspectives and theories of personality are based
   C. A database that compiles personality profiles from people of all walks of life
   D. The application of personality to the various cultures from East Asia

2. Psychologists have primarily relied on _____ to measure personality traits in other cultures.
   A. behavioural observations
   B. interviews

   C. the Cannon-Bard theory
   D. the Big Five trait theory

Analyze . . .

3. Results from applying the Big Five personality traits in other countries reveal that
   A. people all over the world are identical in the patterns of their personality traits.
   B. people all over the world are radically different in the patterns of their personality traits.
   C. there are some cross-cultural differences as well as many similarities in the patterns of people's personality traits.
   D. the Big Five was not understood in other parts of the world because of language translation problems.

How Genes Affect Personality

In the first part of this module, we discussed cultural influences on personality. This topic would clearly fall on the "nurture" side of the nature–nurture continuum. In this section of the module, we will examine personality from

a different perspective: genetics. We all know that we can inherit physical traits from our parents. But, can you be born with your mother's sense of humour or your father's agreeableness? And, is it possible to separate the contribution of your genes from that of your upbringing?

TWIN STUDIES Researchers attempting to tease apart the contributions made by our genes and our environments faced a key challenge, which was that families share not only genes, but also many environmental factors. For example, if you were to observe a behaviour pattern that runs in families, such as alcoholism or anxiety, you might be tempted to conclude that because of the strong family inclination toward this pattern, there must be genetic roots. But family members also often live in the same home, share many experiences together, and are exposed to many of the same stresses and other circumstances. How then do you know if the pattern you observe is due to the shared genes or the shared environments?

The use of twins as research subjects was a brilliant way of overcoming this challenge (see Module 3.1). Comparing twins who were identical (monozygotic) to twins who were fraternal (dizygotic) allowed researchers to estimate the influence of genetic factors on personality. Research on the Big Five personality traits of twins has shown that identical twins show a stronger correlation for each personality trait than do fraternal twins. The correlations for identical twin pairs are approximately .50 for all five factors, significantly higher than the correlations for fraternal twin pairs (who average approximately .20). This implies that the increased similarity in the personalities of identical twins is due to their shared genes.

But you might ask, how do researchers know that it's the increased genetic similarity of identical twins that is responsible for their similar personalities? Maybe identical twins also tend to share more similar environments than fraternal twins, and this is the reason for their personality similarity. Identical twins are often treated in very similar ways, especially during their younger and formative years. If this is true, then the strong correlations between identical twin pairs might be environmentally based.

An impressive line of research directly examines this question. The Minnesota Study of Twins Reared Apart located over 100 sets of twins and triplets who were raised in separate households, and compared them to those raised in the same household. Amazingly, identical twins raised *in different households* are about as similar to each other as identical twins raised in the same household! In fact, fraternal twins who are raised in the same home are actually more different from each other than identical twins who are raised in completely different families (Bouchard et al., 1990; Tellegen et al., 1998).

Other studies of adopted children support these findings. On average, the personalities of adoptive parents have no influence on the personality characteristics of their adopted children. Although it may be hard to believe, siblings who are adopted (i.e., not genetically related) and raised in the same household are *no more similar in personality than two people picked randomly off the street* (Plomin & Caspi, 1999). The genetic influences on personality are

Paula Bernstein and Elyse Schein are identical twins who were separated at birth, and upon uniting at age 35 discovered they shared some uncanny similarities. They were editors for their high-school newspapers, chose to study film in university, sucked their fingers but not their thumbs as toddlers, have an odd habit of typing into the air, and share very similar tastes in books, among other similarities.

strong indeed (see Module 3.1 for further discussion of the genetic contributions to behaviour).

It is important to note that this does not mean that parents are incapable of influencing their children's personality development. Obviously, parents who abuse their children, or on the positive side, parents who put extraordinary efforts into cultivating positive personality traits in their children, are likely to have an impact on their children's personalities. Knowing that a trait is statistically associated with genetic factors tells you virtually nothing about the extent to which a specific person could be affected by a specific set of environmental conditions. Parents can, of course, have positive or negative influences on their children's development, and it is important not to deemphasize this when examining biological and genetic studies.

One further challenge of this research is to move beyond estimating the overall heritability of traits, and

Gerald Levey and Mark Newman are identical twins who were reared apart. When they eventually met they had many similarities—for example, both chose the same profession, loved John Wayne movies and *The Three Stooges,* and had a fondness for professional wrestling.

begin to uncover which specific genes are linked to personality outcomes. New advances in gene sequencing techniques and molecular genetics methods are allowing scientists to do just that.

Working the Scientific Literacy Model

From Molecules to Personality

It's pretty mind-blowing to know that who you are was determined to a fair degree before you were even born, by whatever genes you happened to inherit from your parents. Researchers are just beginning to piece together which specific genes influence which traits.

What do we know about specific genes and personality?

Although scientists have not identified a specific gene or genes involved in the expression of specific personality factors, such as neuroticism or agreeableness, they have discovered genes that code for specific brain chemicals that, in turn, are related to personality. For example, one of the genes that codes for serotonin activity has been found on human chromosome 17. Specifically, this gene codes for proteins that transport serotonin molecules within the tiny spaces (synapses) between nerve cells. Many of our genes are polymorphic (*poly* = "multiple"; *morph* = "form"), meaning that there are different versions of the same gene that lead to different physical or behavioural characteristics. Two possible variations of the "serotonin transporter gene" have been identified: a short copy and a long copy.

How do scientists study genes and personality?

To study genes and personality, one method is to compare responses on self-report questionnaires of people who have inherited different copies of a specific gene. People who inherit short copies of the serotonin transporter gene from one or both parents seem predisposed to anxiety, shyness, and experiencing negative emotional reactions in interpersonal situations (Battaglia et al., 2005; Lesch et al., 1996). However, other researchers have suggested that these differences may depend on which of the many different varieties of self-report questionnaires are used (Schinka et al., 2004).

Another method for studying genes and personality is to conduct experiments and compare the responses of people with different copies of a gene. In one study, participants provided a hair sample so researchers could extract DNA to determine which combination of serotonin transporter genes they had inherited. The participants completed a task that monitored their attentional focus to pictures of positive (e.g., a smiling infant), negative (a black

Figure 12.4 Genes, Serotonin, and Personality

People who inherit two copies of the long version of the serotonin transporter gene fixate on positive images and avoid looking at negative images. People who inherit the short version of this gene are not biased toward attending to positive imagery.

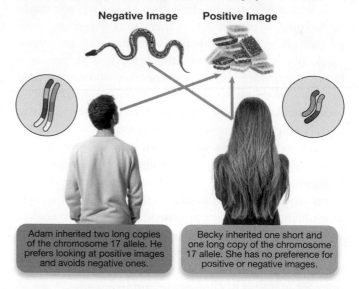

Negative Image   Positive Image

Adam inherited two long copies of the chromosome 17 allele. He prefers looking at positive images and avoids negative ones.

Becky inherited one short and one long copy of the chromosome 17 allele. She has no preference for positive or negative images.

widow spider), or neutral (a kitchen table) stimuli. Previous research has shown that people who have problems with anxiety focus their attention on threatening stimuli more than non-anxious people (Bar-Haim et al., 2007). Researchers found that participants who had inherited two long copies of the gene were biased toward looking at positive images more frequently and for longer periods of time. On the other hand, people who inherited one or two short versions of the gene spent more time looking at negative images (Figure 12.4; Fox et al., 2009). It seems that inheriting short copies of this gene increases anxiety levels in general, and seems to steer people toward giving excessive attention to negative and threatening information.

Can we critically evaluate this evidence?

It is important to keep in mind that, in most cases, there is no single gene causing a single outcome in a person. Most phenomena are understood to be caused by multiple genes interacting with the environment. At this point the general consensus is that a vast number of genes, each of which has only a very small effect, account for individual differences in personality (Terracciano et al., 2010). It is also important to note that these are correlational studies, and inferring causality from such data is highly problematic.

Why is this relevant?

Knowledge about how genes and personality are related can help psychologists identify risk factors for developing mental disorders. As we will see in other parts of this text, genetic studies of personality help us better understand the biological basis of psychological disorders such as anxiety and depression. This work raises some interesting possibilities, such as the potential to screen individuals to assess their risk of developing a disorder. In turn, at-risk individuals might be better helped with early detection and treatment. Also, knowing about the genetic underpinnings of personality is highly informative to theorists seeking to understand how our personality traits, and the variability of traits across cultures, evolved in the first place.

Module 12.2b Quiz:
How Genes Affect Personality

Know . . .

1. Researchers have found that short copies of the _____ transporter genes make people predisposed to anxiety, shyness, and experiencing negative emotional reactions in interpersonal situations.
   - **A.** serotonin
   - **B.** dopamine
   - **C.** norepinephrine
   - **D.** glutamate

Understand . . .

2. Even when identical twins are reared apart, they still tend to be very similar in personality. How is this strong evidence that genes contribute to personality?
   - **A.** Identical twins who were reared apart were most likely treated in very similar ways.
   - **B.** The similarities remain, even though there were probably significant differences in how the siblings were raised.
   - **C.** There are fewer similarities when twins are reared together.
   - **D.** Actually, identical twins who are raised apart show very little similarity.

3. Which of the following statements best describes what psychologists now know about the genetic basis of personality?
   - **A.** Hundreds of genes have been identified that are directly linked to specific personality traits.
   - **B.** Technology is not sophisticated enough to link genes and personality characteristics.
   - **C.** Some genes have been identified that are related to certain aspects of personality function.
   - **D.** Genes do not contribute to personality characteristics.

The Role of Evolution in Personality

Evolutionary psychologists emphasize that our personality structures are built right into our species because they conferred selective advantages to humans possessing certain traits. But the human species is related to other species as well, and so one would expect that we may share at least some aspects of our personalities with other species.

ANIMAL BEHAVIOUR: THE EVOLUTIONARY ROOTS OF PERSONALITY One compelling argument for the usefulness of the evolutionary perspective on personality is the presence of personality traits in numerous nonhuman species. For example, scientists have studied one particular species of bird (*Parus major*) that lives in Europe and Asia. These birds display two different patterns of behaviour when they encounter new environments, corresponding to a "fast-exploring" or "slow-exploring" personality type. The fast-exploring types are aggressive and bold in their exploration of new environments, and tend to rely more on routine ways of responding to the environment rather than being responsive to external cues. The slow-exploring types are passive, shy when confronted with new environments, and more responsive to the external environment, changing their behaviour more readily to suit changes in the environment. These two personality types are known to have a strong genetic basis. Which of the two personality types is adaptive depends on what kind of year the birds are having. If there are limited resources, aggressive, fast-exploring females, and timid, slow-exploring males have greater reproductive success. In years where resources are plentiful, it is the opposite—slow-exploring females and fast-exploring males have greater success. There are complex reasons why males and females have personality factors that are oppositely adaptive to the environment, but the important point is that the basic personality dimension of aggressiveness vs. passivity is represented in these birds and has been clearly tied to the birds' adaptive advantage in different environments (Dingemanse et al., 2004).

The suggestion that animals have personalities may not strike you as all that surprising. Many people who have had close and extended experience with animals, from farmers to pet owners, would say that animals have personalities. For example, dog lovers don't feel that their pet is a totally incomprehensible beast; instead, they attribute qualities, emotions, and personality quirks that are very "human" to the beloved animal. This may merely illustrate our tendency to anthropomorphize the living world, seeing other species through our own egocentric lens, but it may also reflect our shared genetic heritage with other species.

Researchers who wish to study animal personalities face a daunting task, particularly considering that nonhuman animals are usually not very adept at filling out personality scales. To overcome this problem, one approach for measuring the Big Five factors in animals was

Psychologists are finding that measures of human personality are applicable to diverse species such as hyenas, octopuses, and chimpanzees, among many others.

for individuals who are familiar with the animals to rate their behaviours according to the five factors. Typically, observers strongly agree on their ratings of extraversion and neuroticism in animals (Gosling, 2001). In fact, several of the Big Five personality traits have been found in a rich diversity of species—such as rhinos, primates, hedgehogs, and even ants (Gosling, 2001)! In one study of chimpanzees, our closest primate relatives, a list of adjectives was taken from the Big Five test and people who were familiar with the chimpanzee subjects rated how well the adjectives applied to each chimp on a scale of 1 to 7. Of the Big Five traits, extraversion, conscientiousness, and agreeableness were reliably found in the chimps (Weiss et al., 2007).

The presence of basic personality dimensions may be extremely widespread in the living world; some researchers even argue you do not need a backbone to have a personality. Researchers at the University of Lethbridge, Alberta, have shown that octopuses show stable individual differences in measures of activity, reactivity, and avoidance (Mather & Anderson, 1993).

WHY THERE ARE SO MANY DIFFERENT PERSONALITIES: THE EVOLUTIONARY EXPLANATION David Zuroff of McGill University argues that evolutionary perspectives can make a major contribution to our understanding of personality, helping us to understand why we acquired the specific traits that we did (Zuroff et al., 2010). This question is left largely unaddressed by most personality theories, which focus on content (e.g., What personality traits are there?), rather than on process (e.g., Why do we have these traits in the first place? What functions do they serve?).

Evolutionary perspectives can help us to understand *why* humans have evolved the particular personality traits that we have. To the extent that the Big Five traits are built right into our biology, these traits must have been selected for by being adaptive in past evolutionary epochs, helping to promote our survival and reproductive success.

For example, individuals high in extraversion would be more likely to rise in social hierarchies, playing leadership and social networking roles in a community; on the other hand, extraverts tend to be risk takers and sensation seekers, and it would therefore be desirable to offset these qualities with a healthy proportion of introverts in a group.

People high in conscientiousness would be reliable and dependable, and others would learn to count on them to get things done, clearly desirable qualities in a mate. However, the person low in conscientiousness may be an attractive partner to mate with for other reasons, such as their spontaneity and willingness to not always take life too seriously.

People low in neuroticism would be the emotional stalwarts of the community, the people who didn't crack under pressure but kept a level head and could be counted on in crises. However, being high in neuroticism could pay off at times; for example, groups may benefit from having some highly neurotic people around, because they would be more attuned to danger and act as a voice of caution to keep others from making dangerous decisions.

People high in agreeableness would be the friends who are there for you when you need them, and they would generally help to promote harmony and solidarity as groups work together on larger projects; whereas those low in agreeableness may be useful for providing a critical perspective and ensuring that the group doesn't make rash decisions.

People high in openness would be imaginative and creative, helping to build bridges between members of different subgroups in the community, and challenging ideas so that the community doesn't rigidify into dogma and closed-mindedness. On the other hand, those low in openness may be useful for preserving traditions and helping to identify a coherent sense of identity within the community.

As you can see, being either high or low in each Big Five trait could be desirable, depending on the situation.

Myths in Mind

Men Are from Mars, Women Are from Venus

Much is often made about apparent differences in how men and women think and behave. This comparison can sometimes get stretched pretty far, such as the implication inherent in the title of the 1992 self-help book *Men Are from Mars, Women Are from Venus* (Gray, 1992). The notion that men and women may as well be from different planets is strongly reinforced by the popular media.

To what extent does science back up this hypothesis when it comes to personality? On the one hand, there is strong evidence that men and women differ on their Big Five personality ratings. Women generally report higher levels of extraversion, conscientiousness, agreeableness, and neuroticism than men. This finding has been noted in comparisons made across dozens of cultures (Schmitt et al., 2008). On the other hand, these gender differences are quite small, and are vastly overwhelmed by the variability *within* each gender. In other words, there are a lot of men who seem like they're from Venus, and a lot of women who seem like they're from Mars. So, even though there is a gender difference in personality, it is so small as to hardly allow the characterization that men and women are fundamentally different from each other.

In an interesting twist, however, this research also found that the gender differences are related to economic factors. Specifically, the countries showing the *largest* gender differences in personality also have greater access to resources such as health care, education, and wealth. Men and women in countries with fewer social and economic resources tend to be more similar in their self-reported personality scores. This phenomenon may occur because a lack of resources tends to constrain the behaviours and social roles of individuals, thus making people more similar to each other at the expense of their personal individuation. On the other hand, abundant prosperity opens up more opportunities for personal expression and allows individual differences to flourish (Schmitt et al., 2008).

The conclusion seems to be that men and women do have different personalities, on average. Nevertheless, the differences are so small that Mars and Venus must be pretty similar places, so to speak. A good title might sell a lot of books, but does little to inform the general public about what scientific studies truly reveal about human behaviour.

Thus, the complex blends of personality types across society evolved because different traits were desirable in different circumstances. Just as there are different niches to which animal species adapt in an ecosystem, there are different social niches to which people can adapt in society. The extravert and the introvert, the neurotic and the secure, the conscientious and the careless gravitate toward the respective niches they best fill.

Given that specific traits have certain strengths and weaknesses, it seems likely that the different traits evolved because a mixture of traits with complementary strengths and weaknesses would be advantageous at the group level, if not necessarily at the individual level. In other words, to understand why we evolved the traits that we did, we have to consider traits not operating in isolation but, instead, operating at a more communal level.

Module 12.2c Quiz:

The Role of Evolution in Personality

Apply . . .

1. What is an important piece of evidence supporting an evolutionary basis of personality?
   A. Changes in personality can be seen over generations.
   B. Personality traits are stable in the sense that they are common among humans and can be found in nonhuman species.
   C. Personality traits are not stable and cannot be found in nonhuman species.
   D. No valid evidence supports an evolutionary approach to personality.

Analyze . . .

2. According to evolutionary psychologists, there is great diversity in human personality because
   A. only five personality traits could be useful for our species' survival.

   B. different traits are most adaptive in different situations.
   C. a person with a diverse personality is best able to adapt to different situations.
   D. some personality traits are most adaptive for mating, whereas others are more adaptive for survival.

3. Which of the following statements best summarizes personality differences between men and women?
   A. Averages of some traits such as extraversion and neuroticism tend to differ between men and women, but these differences are very small.
   B. Males and females inherit separate sets of genes that cause their differences in personality.
   C. Research shows that men and women really do not differ in personality.
   D. Males are generally agreeable, whereas women are generally conscientious.

In the final section of this module, we examine biological explanations for our personality traits. Can differences in the volume of brain structures or the activity of brain regions explain, at least in part, why personalities vary?

The Brain and Personality

Modern biological approaches for investigating the brain and behaviour build on many ancient traditions of medicine that connected the mind to the body and sought to understand the person in terms of bodily processes. For much of the past 2000 years, Western medicine was guided by the theory of **humourism**, *which explained both physical illnesses and disorders of personality as resulting from imbalances in key fluids in the body*—the four "humours." In the late 1700s and into the 1800s, early psychologists promoted **phrenology**—*the theory that personality characteristics could be assessed by carefully measuring the shape of the skull.* However, these early biological approaches have long since fallen out of fashion, and the field has made major strides in understanding actual biological systems that are involved in personality processes.

EXTRAVERSION AND AROUSAL A big step forward occurred in the mid-20th century, when researchers began convincingly linking personality characteristics with specific brain systems. One of the most influential pioneers in this field, Hans Eysenck (1967), proposed an **arousal theory of extraversion**, *arguing that extraversion is determined by people's threshold for arousal*; according to this theory, people high in extraversion (i.e., extraverts) have a higher threshold for arousal than people low in extraversion (i.e., introverts). As a result, extraverts generally seek greater amounts of stimulation, whereas introverts seek to limit the amount of stimulation they experience so as to not become overwhelmed with excessive arousal. One brain system, the **ascending reticular activating system (ARAS)**, *plays a central role in controlling this arousal response.* Research on Eysenck's ideas has demonstrated that extraverts do have less reactive ARASs compared to introverts. Put simply, for a given "kick," introverts have a stronger response, which is why introverts tend to avoid excessive stimulation, whereas extraverts tend to seek it out.

Another influential model of the brain–personality relationship was proposed by Jeffrey Gray, whose approach/inhibition model of motivation (Gray, 1991) describes two major brain systems for processing rewards and punishments: the behavioural activation system and the behavioural inhibition system.

The **behavioural activation system (BAS)** *is a "GO" system, arousing the person to action in the pursuit of desired goals.* This system is responsive to rewards and fairly unresponsive to possible negative consequences; greater BAS activation therefore is associated with greater positive emotional responses and approach motivation. The

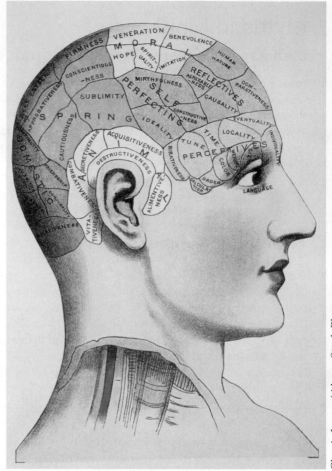

Phrenologists believed that different personality traits were housed in different regions of the brain.

other system, the **behavioural inhibition system (BIS)**, *is more of a "danger" system, motivating the person to action in order to avoid punishments or other negative outcomes.* The BIS is therefore associated with greater negative emotional responses and avoidance motivation.

As you might expect, several of the Big Five factors are correlated with activation of the BIS/BAS systems. The most consistent finding is that extraversion is especially related to BAS activation, whereas neuroticism is related to BIS activation (e.g., Gomez et al., 2000). This evidence is beginning to build at different levels of analysis, but it takes a long time for such complex studies to accumulate. However, just considering the link between extraversion and BAS activation, we can see data focused on at least three different levels of analysis: behavioural, neurochemical, and emotional. For example, extraverts tend to act impulsively when presented with the possibility of rewards, even ignoring the risk of punishment (Patterson & Newman, 1993). Extraverts show a stronger dopamine response to rewarding stimuli (Depue & Collins, 1999). And, extraverts tend to experience more positive emotions in a range of situations (Ashby et al., 1999; Lucas et al., 2000). Thus, a trait measure of extraversion reflects the functioning of many different systems, providing a great example of the integration of science across many different areas of study.

CONTEMPORARY RESEARCH: IMAGES OF PERSONALITY IN THE BRAIN Modern-day researchers use brain-imaging technology to test for relationships between personality and the brain. Neuroscientists have tested whether each of the Big Five personality traits is associated with a different brain region, and whether these regions correspond to the behaviours associated with these traits. The general conclusion has been that indeed, there are many relationships between personality traits and the functioning of specific brain areas, although this research is in its infancy and we have a long way to go before we can confidently discuss "personality in the brain." However, we can discuss some preliminary findings of this line of inquiry.

Extraversion: Extraverts have a larger medial orbitofrontal cortex (part of the prefrontal cortex; DeYoung et al., 2010), and generally show less activation in the amygdala (Canli et al., 2002). The medial orbitofrontal cortex is involved in processing reward, which is consistent with extraverts' greater reward sensitivity (i.e., strong BAS). The amygdala, on the other hand, is involved in processing novelty, danger, and fear, which extraverts tend to pay less attention to (i.e., weak BIS), hence their *under*-active amygdalae (see Figure 12.5).

Neuroticism: Neuroticism is associated with the size of various brain areas, such as a smaller dorsomedial prefrontal cortex, a smaller hippocampus, and a larger mid-cingulate gyrus (an area right above the corpus callosum; DeYoung et al., 2010). Each of these areas is involved in abilities that are central to neuroticism. The dorsomedial

prefrontal cortex is involved in controlling emotions (Ochsner & Gross, 2005), the hippocampus in controlling obsessive negative thinking (Gray & McNaughton, 2000), and the mid-cingulate gyrus in detecting errors and perceiving pain—whether physical or emotional pain (Carter et al., 1998; Eisenberger & Lieberman, 2004). These are the kinds of processes that define highly neurotic people. They have difficulty controlling their emotions, often fall prey to obsessive negative thinking, and are highly sensitive when they make mistakes or feel pain.

Agreeableness: People high in agreeableness show less brain volume in an area called the left superior temporal sulcus (DeYoung et al., 2010), which is activated when one is interpreting another person's actions or intentions (Pelphrey & Morris, 2006). They also show greater volume in an area called the posterior cingulate cortex, which is involved in empathy and perspective-taking (DeYoung et al., 2010). These brain areas match the tendency for people high in agreeableness to be more socially attuned and to have more empathy for others.

Conscientiousness: People high in this trait have larger brain volume in the middle frontal gyrus in the left prefrontal cortex (DeYoung et al., 2010), which is involved in working memory processes and in carrying out actions that you have planned. These functions are implicated in effective self-control, which is a key strength of the highly conscientious person.

Openness to Experience: Individuals high in openness to experience have been shown to have greater activation in the dorsolateral prefrontal cortex, which is involved in creativity and intelligence, as well as other brain systems involved in the integration of the self and the environment

---

Figure 12.5 Measuring Personality and Brain Anatomy

People's self-ratings of the Big Five traits correspond to their brain volume in specific regions. Here we see two (among several) regions of the brain where size is positively correlated with ratings of conscientiousness and extraversion (DeYoung et al., 2010).

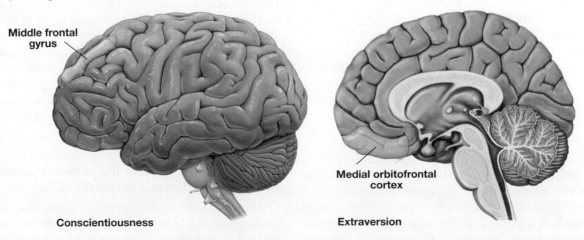

Middle frontal gyrus

Medial orbitofrontal cortex

Conscientiousness

Extraversion

Source: Based loosely on DeYoung, C. G., Hirsh, J. B., Shane, M. S., Papademetris, X., Rajeevan, N., & Gray, J. R. (2010). Testing predictions from personality neuroscience: Brain structure and the big five. *Psychological Science, 21* (6), 820–828.

(Adelstein et al., 2011). These systems reflect the tendencies for people high in openness to be creative, integrative thinkers.

Although the ability to link brain regions to personality processes at such a refined level has only become possible recently, neuroscientists are beginning to find brain regions that differ reliably between people with different personality traits. This does not mean that these brain differences *cause* the personality differences, but it does suggest that these brain regions are involved in serving neurological functions that are related to personality processes at some level. The causal connections might be indirect and highly varied, challenging us with incredible complexity, both of personality itself but also complexity of the neurological architecture of the brain.

This complexity reminds us that in most cases, there will be no specific brain area involved uniquely in a personality trait; for example, there is no "centre of extraversion" in the brain. Any trait plays itself out through many different thoughts, feelings, and behaviours, each of which involves many different brain systems. What ends up manifesting as a stable pattern that we identify as a personality trait therefore represents patterns of activation across many different brain systems.

So we may never be able to point at a single region (or even a few regions) and declare it to be the centre of any single personality trait. That said, we have come a long way from the days when personality was described in terms of the four humours of blood, phlegm, and black and yellow bile.

Module 12.2d Quiz:

The Brain and Personality

Know . . .

1. An outdated approach claiming that behaviour and personality were based on the sizes of various regions of the skull surface was called
   A. magnetic resonance imaging.
   B. alchemy.
   C. phrenology.
   D. humourism.

2. Hans Eysenck believed that extraversion was tied most closely to the functioning of the
   A. limbic system.
   B. parasympathetic nervous system.

   C. ascending reticular activating system.
   D. amygdala.

Apply . . .

3. You are looking at an fMRI brain scan of a subject in a research study. The scan shows that the person generally has greater activation in the dorsolateral prefrontal cortex and less activation in the amygdala. Based on this information, what guess would you make about the person's personality profile?
   A. Low on extraversion, high on conscientiousness
   B. High on openness to experience, high on extraversion
   C. Low in neuroticism, high on extraversion
   D. Low in neuroticism, high on conscientiousness

Module 12.2 Summary

12.2a Know . . . the key terminology associated with cultural and biological approaches to personality.

arousal theory of extraversion
ascending reticular activating system (ARAS)
behavioural activation system (BAS)
behavioural inhibition system (BIS)
humourism
phrenology
response styles

12.2b Understand . . . how evolutionary theories explain personality.

Evolutionary psychologists theorize that personality traits evolved because they solved environmental and social problems encountered by our distant ancestors. Although this hypothesis is difficult to test directly, different sources of evidence lend support to it. The widespread occurrence of these personality traits among different species indicates that they are adaptive.

12.2c Apply . . . your knowledge to understand how arousal is related to extraversion.

Although extraversion is commonly interpreted to indicate how sociable and friendly people are, it is more fundamentally related to how reactive people are to stimulation. Highly extraverted people have less reactive ascending reticular activating systems (ARAS), which means that they don't get as big of a "kick" out of a given level of stimulation; this causes them to prefer more stimulating environments, relative to introverts, who have more reactive ARASs, and therefore prefer lower levels of stimulation so that they do not feel overwhelmed.

12.2d Analyze . . . claims that males and females have fundamentally different personalities.

Claims of major sex differences in personality are sometimes made to support popular-book sales. In reality, the general consensus in psychological science is that males and females are more alike than different when it comes to personality. Both, of course, share common personality dimensions. Although females tend to be, on average, more conscientious, agreeable, extraverted, and neurotic than males, these differences are very small, and there is no evidence to support claims that men and women are fundamentally different in personality.

12.2e   Analyze . . . the genetic basis of personality.

Heritability studies show that personality traits are substantially predicted by genetic variation. Studies of twins and adopted children also back this up, showing that identical twins are far more similar in personality than fraternal twins, and that the home in which people grow up has much less influence over their personalities than the genes they inherited from their biological parents. However, despite this evidence for genetic influences on personality, one cannot conclude that personality is "hard wired" and therefore unchangeable. Personality emerges through the interaction of genes and the environment; thus, a given genetic make-up can express itself differently in different environments.

Module 12.3 Psychodynamic and Humanistic Approaches to Personality

blas/Fotolia

 ## Learning Objectives

12.3a Know . . . the key terminology related to the psychodynamic and humanistic approaches to personality.

12.3b Understand . . . how people use defence mechanisms to cope with conflicting thoughts and feelings.

12.3c Understand . . . the developmental stages Freud used to explain the origins of personality.

12.3d Apply . . . both psychodynamic and humanistic perspectives to explain personality.

12.3e Analyze . . . whether projective tests are valid measures of personality.

12.3f Analyze . . . the strengths and weaknesses of psychodynamic perspectives.

Abraham Maslow, who was introduced in Module 11.3, was fascinated by people who actually live up to their potential. Many of us want to follow today's pop-culture slogans to "live for the moment," "be all that you can be," and "do one thing every day that scares you"—but somehow, most of us never quite get around to it. Perhaps you've experienced that nagging feeling that life is passing you by and the epic adventure you thought your life was going to be is somehow more mundane than you'd hoped? Apparently, this doesn't happen to everybody; some people really do seem to live inspiring and fulfilling lives, and these were the personalities that Maslow wanted to understand.

In striking contrast to much of the cynicism of the 20th century, Maslow believed that although we have the capacity for great evil, at the very foundation of our being we are inherently good. He argued that the more we open ourselves to our

inherent goodness, the more we will see reality clearly, rather than through our biases; the more we will be empowered and able to confront life courageously, rather than shrinking from challenges because of our insecurities; and the more we can focus on helping others rather than tending to our own needs and wants. The end result of pursuing personal growth is to become fully, vibrantly alive.

"Laboring under the effects of deficiency motivation is like looking at the world through a clouded lens, and removing those effects is like replacing the clouded lens with a clear one. Self-actualizing persons' contact with reality is simply more direct. And along with this unfiltered, unmediated directness of their contact with reality comes also a vastly heightened ability to appreciate again and again, freshly and naively, the basic goods of life, with awe, pleasure, wonder, and even ecstasy, however stale those experiences may have become for others." (Maslow, 1968)

Is it possible to live such a life? Maslow thought so, and personality researchers are still following his call and trying to decipher the magic ingredients that allow some people to truly thrive in life.

Focus Questions

1. How do the psychodynamic and humanistic approaches give you insight into your own personality?

2. How do people use psychological defences to protect themselves from emotionally troubling events?

» Maslow hoped that his work would help people learn how to cultivate these qualities within themselves. His optimistic vision of human nature was a major break from the personality psychology of the day, which largely grew out of a Freudian psychodynamic perspective. As we discuss below, to the Freudians, personality was a battleground between opposing forces in the psyche, as people struggled to defend themselves against the negativity that loomed in their unconscious. In contrast, Maslow and the humanists explored a positive, growth-oriented side to personality that we need to fully appreciate in order to have a more complete picture of the human personality.

Although neither Freudian psychoanalysis nor Maslow's humanistic theories have retained their once-prominent positions in psychology, they remain highly influential approaches in society at large, and have inspired and guided generations of people to live their lives more fully.

The Psychodynamic Perspective

As one of the best known and most influential psychologists of all time, Sigmund Freud often does not get the respect you might think he would deserve. Many of his theories have not stood the test of time and are now largely ignored. Many of his theories are difficult or impossible to integrate with more modern approaches, such as social-cognitive and neuroscience perspectives. Indeed, some of his theories are even regarded as ridiculous by many people (e.g., the Oedipus complex, discussed later in this module). Freud was definitely a colourful character. He was a passionate user and advocate of cocaine before its addictive and destructive properties were known. He was rumoured to have been a tyrant towards his followers, allowing people to express little dissent from his views. Freud has been critiqued as having an obsession with sex, as having created unfalsifiable and therefore unscientific theories, and as using only a limited cross-section of humanity (mostly women seeking counselling in Victorian-era Europe) upon which to base rather grand and sweeping theories about human nature.

However, despite the criticisms, Freud was a pioneer in the study of personality and the treatment of psychological disorders. He laid much of the foundation for our basic understanding of consciousness, which is still with us today, as are many of his key insights. When a drug addict admits to being "in denial" of his addiction, an abuse survivor talks about how she "repressed" her memories and feelings for many years, or someone accuses you of "projecting" your anger onto other people, they are displaying Freud's ideas.

Interestingly, Freud was not trained in psychology, but was instead a neurologist. The launch of his scientific career was anything but glamorous; he spent many hours peering through microscopes at tissue samples, searching for the elusive testicles of the male eel, which had not yet been discovered. Freud's extraordinary attention to detail, along with the unwitting cooperation of many hundreds of eels, led him to eventually make the discovery. Which might make you ask, what kind of person exhaustively searches for eel testicles? No doubt, Freudian theorists would have an interesting answer to that question.

After leaving his scientific career to be trained as a physician, Freud began to accept clients who sought his help for psychological difficulties. Initially, Freud believed that their issues could be resolved through investigating their physiology and isolating the biological factors that contributed to their problems. However, after examining some of his patients, he realized that their emotional struggles often could not be understood at the physiological level; instead, he had to delve into the mysterious depths of the mind. This led him to begin trying to understand the personalities of his patients and the psychological dynamics that led to the problems they were experiencing.

Over time, his observations and ideas coalesced into his *psychodynamic theory*, which isn't really a "theory" at all, but rather an evolving family of different theories and ideas that share many key features, which we discuss in this module (also, see Westen, 1998).

ASSUMPTIONS OF PSYCHODYNAMIC THEORIES A universal assumption of psychodynamic theories is that personality and behaviour are shaped by powerful forces in consciousness, a great deal of which is hidden from our awareness in the mysterious unconscious. By emphasizing the unconscious, Freud threw into doubt many of our common feelings and beliefs. For example, we like to feel like we are in control of ourselves and our behaviour reflects conscious choices that we make. We believe that we know why we do the things we do—that our behaviour makes sense to us. We also like to believe that when we do something embarrassing, immoral, or just plain stupid, that we were somehow "out of control" or that it was a mistake.

From a psychodynamic perspective, however, there are no mistakes, and we have very little control over ourselves and remarkably little insight into the reasons for our own behaviours. Everything we think, feel, and do results from psychological dynamics that are so deeply buried in our unconscious that we have no direct access to them; our mind is a "black box," even to ourselves.

To understand the implications of Freud's psychodynamic theory, we will explore its key concepts and how they apply to personality psychology.

UNCONSCIOUS PROCESSES AND PSYCHODYNAMICS Freud grounded his theories on a model of consciousness that distinguished between different levels of mental life, most importantly between the conscious mind and the unconscious. The **conscious mind** *is your current awareness, containing everything you are aware of right now.* The **unconscious mind** *is a much more vast and powerful but inaccessible part of your consciousness, operating without your conscious endorsement or will to influence and guide your behaviours.* The unconscious mind houses your full lifetime of memories and experiences, including those that you can no longer bring into conscious awareness, such as emotional patterns that were created in early childhood or even infancy. It also contains your preferences and desires, which can influence you in ways that may be obvious, or in ways so subtle that you are not even aware of them. The relationship between these two levels of consciousness is often described using an iceberg metaphor of consciousness (Figure 12.6). With icebergs, the part you can see

above the surface is a small fraction of the entire iceberg, while most of its bulk lurks beneath the surface. Similarly, the conscious mind is a small fraction of the entire psyche, most of which lurks beneath the surface of our awareness in the depths of the unconscious.

The mysterious, vast, inaccessible unconscious is viewed as the primary driver of our behaviours, controlling us in countless ways. Even seemingly trivial behaviours, such as slips of the tongue, were argued to reflect the workings of the unconscious. In fact, these slips, famously called "Freudian slips," are very useful to the observant person, because they offer a glimpse into the unconscious. When people make a Freudian slip, their conscious mind intends to say something appropriate to the circumstances, but their unconscious mind leads them to say what they were "really thinking." As the classic psychologist joke goes, "The definition of a Freudian slip: when you mean to say one thing but you end up saying a-mother."

Freud believed fervently in the value of these "psychopathologies of everyday life" and developed several techniques that psychoanalysts could employ to use such small clues to gain access into the netherworld of the unconscious. (We revisit this later in this module.) Freud and other psychoanalysts argued that much of what manifests as personality reflects patterns that emerge as people attempt to resolve conflicts between their conscious and unconscious minds.

Figure 12.6 The Freudian Structure of Personality

A popular depiction of how Freud viewed personality features an iceberg, with the unconscious mind residing below the surface and conscious awareness at only the tip of the iceberg. The id is completely submerged, whereas the ego and the superego operate at both unconscious and conscious levels.

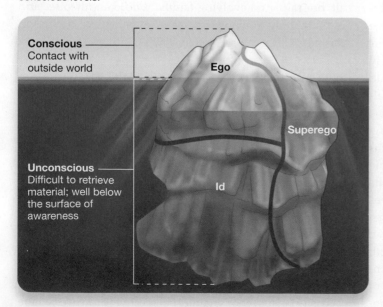

Conscious
Contact with
outside world

Ego

Superego

Unconscious
Difficult to retrieve
material; well below
the surface of
awareness

Id

Source: Lilienfeld, Scott O.; Lynn, Steven J; Namy, Laura L.; Woolf, Nancy J., *Psychology: From Inquiry to Understanding*, 2nd Ed., ©2011, pp.546. Reprinted and Electronically reproduced by permission of Pearson Education, Inc., New York, NY.

THE STRUCTURE OF PERSONALITY Have you ever done something you knew at the time was wrong? Like eating that brownie when you knew you shouldn't? Losing your temper? Hooking up with that attractive person even though they have a boyfriend or girlfriend (or you do)? To explain this type of all-too-common conflict, Freud hypothesized that the human psyche consists of three basic structures, which are often in conflict with each other: the *id*, the *ego*, and the *superego* (Figure 12.6).

The **id** *represents a collection of basic biological drives, including those directed toward sex and aggression.* Freud believed the id was fuelled by an energy called *libido*. Although this term is more commonly used in reference to sexual energy, the libido also controls other biological urges such as hunger. The id operates according to the *pleasure principle*, motivating people to seek out experiences that bring pleasure, with little regard for the appropriateness or consequences of their realization. Because the id represents our basic animal desires, it is present right from birth and is the predominant force controlling our actions in the earliest stages of our lives. The id gets us into trouble though, and increasingly so as we get older and society frowns on some of the unrestrained urges of our lusty animal selves. Because society imposes constraints on our behaviour, the id must be restrained from its animal nature; and that is where the ego and superego come into play.

The **superego** *is comprised of our values and moral standards.* Our superego tells us what we *ought* to do, whereas the id tells us what our animal body *wants* to do. Freud believed that the superego forms over time as we become socialized into our family and larger community and we are taught the values and norms of our society. The superego represents a process of internalization, through which we adopt the values and standards of others and make them our own, and consequently, we feel good or bad about ourselves based on whether we think we are being "good" or "bad." When we behave immorally, the superego chastises us, similarly to how our parents may have done, thereby encouraging us to "do the right thing."

In between the devilish, indulgent id and the angelic, puritanical superego sits the beleaguered **ego**, *the decision maker, frequently under tension, trying to reconcile the opposing urges of the id and superego.* The ego has to be plugged into reality; if it listened to the id all the time, we would be social deviants, instantly gratifying ourselves at every turn, but if it listened to the superego all the time, we would cut ourselves off from much of our raw passion and zest for life. The ego seeks to balance the two forces, operating according to what Freud called the *reality principle.* The id, ego, and superego are in constant tension, and it is this tension that gives rise to personality in two key ways.

First, different people's personalities may reflect differences in the relative strengths of their id, ego, and superego. You can easily imagine a person guided by an extremely strong superego versus a person guided by an extremely strong id. Indeed, these would likely be two completely different types of people. In this deep, structural sense, individuals' personalities are patterned by their own particular blend of ego, id, and superego. Each person's unique combination of biology (id), upbringing and sociocultural circumstances (superego), and their uniquely personal awareness and will (ego), ends up developing into their personality.

The second key dynamic that generates much of personality is how one reacts to anxiety. Anxiety plays a huge role in psychodynamic thought, because anxiety is the experiential (what we feel) result of the tension between the id, ego, and superego. When these systems are out of balance, we experience the deprivation of one system as a kind of basic anxiety. This drives negative thoughts and feelings, which ideally would serve as messages to us—signals that "something is wrong; this system is not in harmony."

Anxiety can be about something huge and overwhelming (e.g., having abuse occur in one's family) or about something mundane and seemingly trivial (e.g., wearing the wrong thing to a party), but it's important to note that in either case, the anxiety itself has a kind of life of its own; for example, we can experience truly crushing and debilitating anxiety about something that others would think was silly (e.g., wearing the wrong thing to a party), whereas people can, through psychological defences (as we discuss shortly), defend themselves against even profound anxiety (such as being unwilling to face the reality of abuse occurring in one's family).

According to Freud, the ego engages in anxiety-defence throughout the day. From worrying about failing, to how we look, to whether someone likes us, to how something we did will be perceived by other people, we feel anxiety. We could wonder whether we made a good decision, feel guilty, wonder if we are losing our looks or our charm as we age, or deal with basically an infinite variety of potential things to worry about and feel badly about. Dealing with this constant drama is the job of the ego. And of course, there is its classic job, which is to figure out what to do when part of us wants to do the bad thing (whatever that may be), and part of us is scared or feels ashamed or otherwise knows we "shouldn't" do the bad thing.

It's easy to feel a bit sorry for the ego. Sure, it gets to be in control a lot of the time, but it also never really gets a break, always having to be on the job to keep us from becoming overwhelmed by anxiety. From Freud's perspective, consciousness is a constant battleground for the ego, negotiating between the id and superego, while also protecting itself from countless sources of anxiety.

DEFENCE MECHANISMS Oftentimes, the ego is unable to resolve the anxieties that plague it. Instead, it focuses merely on protecting itself from excessive anxiety, seeking some way of minimizing or avoiding the negativity it is experiencing. Imagine a young child caught between Mom and Dad screaming at each other. Having no way to resolve their conflict, he plugs his ears and hides in the closet. The child can't resolve the negativity, so he tries to escape it. This is what the ego does when it employs its **defence mechanisms**, *unconscious strategies the ego uses to reduce or avoid anxiety* (Freud, 1936; see Table 12.4). In fact, the literal acts of plugging one's ears and running into the closet are examples of *denial*, which is a very common defence mechanism.

Defence mechanisms play key roles in many important social phenomena, such as prejudice and discrimination. For example, imagine a CEO of a company choosing not to hire a member of an ethnic minority; the CEO may protect herself from admitting the possibility that the choice was racially motivated by engaging in *rationalization*, reasoning that the applicant didn't seem as impressive, professional, or "like she will fit into our team." You can imagine the thought, "It had nothing to do with race, of course! I just want to hire the best person for the job, and I felt that she wasn't the right fit. After all, I have a lot of experience in this company, and I trust my sense of who is going to work

Table 12.4 Examples of Some Major Defence Mechanisms

Defence Mechanism	Definition	Example
Denial	Refusing to acknowledge unpleasant information, particularly about oneself.	People deny all sorts of things—ways in which they are to blame for their relationship problems; bad things that other members of their family may be doing; dangerous behaviours, such as drinking while pregnant, that they may be engaged in; and truly, just about anything. Simply blocking distressing things from one's mind can be a remarkably effective strategy (until it eventually comes back to haunt you).
Displacement	Transforming an unacceptable impulse into a less unacceptable or neutral behaviour.	After getting criticized by your boss at work, you go home and yell at your spouse or criticize your roommate for not doing more housework. One way or another, you "take out your anger" on a less dangerous target than your boss.
Identification	Unconsciously assuming the characteristics of a more powerful person in order to reduce feelings of anxiety or negative feelings about the self.	A child acts like their favourite hero-figure or an adult copies a trend-setting celebrity. By associating with a powerful, successful figure, one feels more powerful and successful too.
Projection	Perceiving in other people the qualities that you don't want to admit to possessing yourself.	The classic insecure, tyrannical parent, who sees hostility and "attitude" in other people, like his kids or his wife, thinking that other people are always seeing themselves as superior and are looking down their noses others. Projection also allows us to see "evil" and aggression in our enemies while we invade and bomb them.
Rationalization	Attempting to hide one's true motives (even from oneself!) by providing what seems like a reasonable explanation for unacceptable feelings or behaviours.	People who are prejudiced against certain types or groups of other people may not see themselves as racist, but may instead believe that the group they are prejudiced against actually does possess certain negative qualities. By believing that people from the disliked group are violent, or lazy, or unintelligent, the person never has to confront their own prejudice.
Reaction Formation	Altering an impulse that one finds personally unacceptable into its opposite.	People who are judgmental and condemning of homosexuality, yet have homosexual impulses themselves. For example, homophobic men tend to have greater penile arousal, compared to non-homophobic men, when looking at male-on-male pornography (Adams et al., 1996).
Repression	Keeping distressing information out of conscious awareness by burying it in the unconscious.	Many people believe that victims of abuse or violence are sometimes able to *repress* their traumatic memories, essentially "forgetting" that the trauma occurred. Nevertheless, the trauma remains in their unconscious, causing them to react in ways that are driven by this unconscious material.
Sublimation	Transforming unacceptable impulses into socially acceptable or even pro-social alternatives.	Someone with a great deal of aggression may become a football player or a boxer. Freud believed that sublimation was one of the cornerstones of civilization, the mechanism by which base human desires were harnessed to give rise to great works of art, invention, and scientific advance. Sublimation operates to make you feel better by finding socially acceptable outlets for unconscious drives and urges.

out and who isn't." You can see how easily a person's own reasoning process can be hijacked by the ego in order to protect itself, and the line between what is true and what merely appears to be true can so easily be blurred.

Unfortunately, although defence mechanisms may keep us from feeling anxiety in the moment, they are ultimately dysfunctional for a variety of reasons. One is simply that undesirable tendencies are not confronted and problems are not dealt with; instead, immense energy is devoted to maintaining the defence mechanisms and trying to feel okay. For example, alcoholics (and often their families) sometimes go to great lengths to avoid having to admit that they have a problem, which only worsens the impact of alcohol on their lives. Freud's (and others') work on defence mechanisms remains influential to this day, particularly in the mental health field, where defence mechanisms often play important roles in therapy for psychological disorders.

PERSONALITY DEVELOPMENT: THE PSYCHOSEXUAL STAGES Freud's theory of personality also involved a sophisticated understanding of development. Freud believed that the personality developed as the person learned to channel the energy of the libido into appropriate forms of self-expression. Thus, to Freud, development of the infant and child is ruled by the id, involving the young child struggling to contain and channel sexual urges and feelings. The child is a bundle of animal impulses, and development is therefore based on the ego and superego developing properly through appropriate socialization experiences as the child grows up. Freud highlighted specific developmental challenges that children faced at different points of their lives, developing a stage theory of psycho-sexual development that tracked the progression children went through as they matured through the various stages (see Table 12.5).

Interestingly, most of Freud's stages happened in the first five years of life, reflecting the central importance of the developmental milestones that occur in the first five years. At each stage, the libido manifests in particular areas of the body, depending on what areas of the body are most salient and important at that particular time of life. For example, as babies, sucking for food and comfort is a central activity,

Table 12.5 Freud's Stages of Psychosexual Development

Stage	Pleasure Focus	Key Dynamics
Oral (0–18 months)	Actions of the mouth—sucking, chewing, swallowing	This stage is about the foundation of the ego. Fixation at this stage represents a basic lack of self-confidence and "ego strength," leaving the person more dependent on, and therefore vulnerable to, external sources of support.
Anal (18–36 months)	Bowel elimination, control	This stage is about the development of a sense of control and competence. Fixation at this stage leads to an "anal retentive" or "anal expulsive" personality, manifesting either as an obsession with cleanliness, order, and control, or as a disorganized person.
Phallic (3–6 years)	Genitals	The key personality challenge is the Oedipus complex, through which a person further develops the superego due to the internalization of values from the parents. Fixation at this stage leads to problems with jealousy and obsessions with power and sex.
Latency (6 years until puberty)	External activities	Ideally, this stage is fairly conflict-free. People focus on developing themselves, discovering their interests through sports, arts, and general activities. Fixation at this stage was not considered to be a big concern.
Genital (puberty to adulthood)	Sexual activities with others	Ideally, this stage is also fairly conflict-free. People focus on fully and authentically engaging in the world, provided they are not fixated at earlier stages.

whereas for toddlers, learning to control the bowels and become toilet-trained is a pretty major focus; these physical challenges were reflected by Freud as specific stages (in this case the oral and anal stages). When these bodily areas are relevant to the person, they become a focus for the id, which attempts to derive as much pleasure as possible from gaining gratification in those areas. Thus, each of these important regions becomes a battleground pitting the child's id against the restrictions of the external world.

If the child was able to release their libidinal energy appropriately through the part of the body that was relevant at that time, this would help them have a healthy relationship with themselves and they would be free to focus on the next stages of development. However, if their need satisfaction was thwarted or interfered with, they would become fixated at that stage. **Fixation** *involves becoming preoccupied with obtaining the pleasure associated with a particular stage as a result of not being able to adequately regulate themselves and satisfy their needs at that stage.* Fixation can occur either because of conflict and excessive parental interference (e.g., criticizing the child for making mistakes during toilet training), or because the child is allowed to overindulge in that form of pleasure-seeking behaviour (e.g., the *Simpsons* character Maggie is in serious danger of developing an oral fixation).

THE ORAL STAGE (0–18 MONTHS) For babies, the mouth is where it's at; all the action that really matters happens through their mouths: feeding, comfort, teething, and even the early experiences of aggression. As a result, the mouth is a major focus for both pleasure and frustration, and the ego has to learn to satisfy the id's desire for biting and sucking with the superego's admonishments about what is appropriate in a situation. If this goes well, the infant develops a basic sense of security and empowerment; this is the initial foundation for the ego.

However, if the infant either can't satisfy its need for security, comfort, or food, or conversely, if it is overindulged so that it develops an emotional attachment to using its mouth, then it will develop an *oral fixation*. Instead of having a healthy ability to self-assert, the infant may develop to be dependent, have an addictive personality, and seek to "consume" the world for its own emotional needs. Fixating at the oral stage means that the person never fully develops their ego, and is therefore more vulnerable to anxiety and less capable at adjusting to social reality.

THE ANAL STAGE (18 MONTHS–3 YEARS) Toddlers begin to become aware of themselves as separate individuals at the same time that they are gaining control over the bowels. Toilet training thus becomes the focal activity at this stage. Freud believed that if bathroom skills were learned successfully and positively with support and encouragement from caregivers, the result was a sense of competence and confidence that would lead the toddler to develop into a well-adjusted and productive adult. But if parents were too strict and critical of toddlers, making them feel bad about "having accidents" and putting too much pressure on them, they could become fixated at this stage, struggling with issues like shame and control. Eventually, they could become "anal retentive" adults, a rather rigid personality excessively concerned with cleanliness and order with a high need for control and little emotional openness. Or, if parents were too lenient and provided too little support for toilet training, this would produce an "anal expulsive" adult who exhibits opposite qualities of carelessness, disorganization, and general irresponsibility.

THE PHALLIC STAGE (3–6 YEARS) This early childhood stage is a crucially important stage in Freud's view, although this is where people often find Freud's theories hard to swallow and many reject his ideas altogether. We believe it is worth considering what insights there may be in Freud's thinking, even if some of the specific details seem questionable. Also, keep in mind that the full development of Freud's theories is far more brilliant and detailed than what we are able to capture in a brief overview.

From ages 3 to 6 years, bodily attention shifts to the genitals as children become aware of the differences between boys and girls and start to heavily identify with one gender. Boys go through the now-infamous *Oedipus complex*. Freud theorized that in boys, the attachment to the mother that was achieved during infancy (through oral means) now gets expressed in the phallus. He claimed that a boy in this stage become sexually attracted to his mother. The boy also realizes that he is in competition with his father for his mother's affections; this creates resentment toward the father and, in the wonderful logic of young children, makes the boy want to kill his father. During this stage, boys struggle with highly conflicted feelings toward their fathers, feeling both attached to and hostile toward them. This is a very difficult time emotionally, as boys are torn between such strong feelings and desires. Freud represents this anguish with the Greek tragedy of *Oedipus Rex* (by Sophocles); in this story, the main character, Oedipus, kills his father without knowing he has done so, and ends up marrying his mother. When he eventually learns what he has done, he is so overcome with horror that he stabs his own eyes, blinding himself. (The ancient Greeks were fairly intense.)

Freud used highly sexual language to describe the phallic stage, although it is important to remember that the literal descriptions can also be understood to provide metaphoric insights into personality. According to Freud, little boys are quite distressed to learn that their mothers do not have penises; they reason that something must have happened to cut them off. And if that happened to their mothers, it might happen to them! Furthermore, it stands to reason that it was the powerful father figure who did the nasty deed, thus causing a great deal of *castration anxiety*, the fear of castration by one's father. (Metaphorically, castration anxiety is the fear of emasculation.) Boys resolve this fear, and thus the Oedipus complex, by learning to identify with the father, developing a close bond with him, while repressing sexual feelings for the mother.

For girls, the logic was considerably more complicated and Freud revised his theories somewhat over time. Freud believed that girls also want to sexually possess their mothers and feel competition with their fathers. When girls discover that they themselves lack a penis, they experience *penis envy*, which is pretty much exactly what it sounds like. As a result, girls redirect their sexual interest to their fathers, and subsequently men in general, because that's the way to get a penis. Having a child someday, particularly a boy, is also likely to be highly desired, because having a boy is (according to Freud) another way of obtaining a penis.

As mentioned earlier, Freud's theories are considered to be very deep and often profound, although it requires a lot of "unpacking" to get to those insights. For example, with regards to penis envy, you can take the penis as more of a symbol of power and masculinity, rather than as a literal penis. You can therefore take the envy of the penis to represent the female child's desire for empowerment, which she would gain through association with masculine traits and pursuits. When you think about it this way, you can see some potential merit to Freud's ideas. But for the most part, this part of Freud's theory has had little influence on the rest of the field. Also, we assume that the critiques of Freud's ideas about women are painfully obvious at this point; indeed, these critiques of the phallic stage, as well as its general inaccuracy as a description of the psychological experiences of most people, have been devastating to this part of Freud's theories.

The importance of the phallic stage is that, at its resolution, the child has formed a healthy relationship with the parents, resulting in the internalization of parental values, which completes the formation of the superego. Successfully transitioning out of this stage leaves the child well prepared as a moral being. On the other hand, becoming fixated at this stage has striking negative consequences. People become plagued with jealousy and preoccupied with sex, seduction, competitiveness, and power.

Freud believed that girls never entirely resolve their Oedipus complexes (the term *Electra complex* was coined by Carl Jung but rejected by Freud), leaving women with somewhat less well-developed superegos and thus, a less reliable morality. He theorized that to the extent that Oedipal issues remain, women will seek to control and dominate men through their sexuality or submissiveness because, of course, men have the penises that women envy.

THE LATENCY STAGE (6–13 YEARS)   After the lurid sexuality and emotional drama of the phallic stage, the *latency stage* is downright boring. Between ages 5 and 13, the ego and superego have achieved a degree of general calm. The sexual nature of the libido is deemphasized, and it is instead directed into more productive activities than trying to mate with and murder one's parents, such as education, hobbies, and hanging out with friends. This is a period of rich personal development for children, during which they gain many of their intellectual, social, artistic, and physical skills. Interestingly, people don't get fixated at this stage, because personality is largely formed by the end of the phallic stage, and if people are not fixated at an earlier stage, they become relatively free to pursue their interests.

THE GENITAL STAGE   The onset of puberty marks the beginning of this stage, which continues throughout adulthood. This is the time during which the person emerges into a mature adult personality, with a fully developed capacity for productive work and satisfying and loving relationships. However, those who remain fixated at previous stages will suffer from underdeveloped personalities, which cause any number of problems in their subsequent adulthoods.

Modern psychodynamic psychologists generally agree that Freud's stages of psychosexual development are not an accurate view of personality development. However, even this is not entirely clear; clinical psychologists often report observing patterns that are consistent with Freud's observations of each stage of psychosexual development (Westen, 1998). For example, one study reported that young children are more likely to show affection to the same-sexed parent and aggression toward the opposite-sexed parent (Watson & Getz, 1990). This is reminiscent of the Oedipus complex, although the underlying mechanisms are not necessarily the same (i.e., notice there is no reference to sexual attraction or murderous intent).

A huge challenge faced (and never surmounted) by Freudian thinkers was how to empirically measure many of the concepts and processes described in Freud's theories. For example, how exactly does one measure the contents of the unconscious? How can we measure something that, by definition, people are unaware of?

EXPLORING THE UNCONSCIOUS WITH PROJECTIVE TESTS

As discussed earlier in this module, Freud devised a number of techniques for peering into the inner workings of the unconscious, such as analyzing the "psychopathologies of everyday life" for evidence of defence mechanisms and hidden motivations. Freud also refined methods, such as dream analysis and free association, which were believed to reveal unconscious material by side-stepping the conscious mind. For example, dream analysis was based on the belief that the material in the unconscious, although not accessible to the conscious mind, nevertheless was depicted in our dreams. However, because much of the unconscious operates without language, dreams would not be literal, but symbolic representations of the contents of the unconscious. Thus, the dream analyst had to learn to properly interpret the symbolic meaning of dreams in order to understand what could be learned from the unconscious.

Since Freud's time, psychodynamic psychologists have attempted to develop more standardized techniques for probing the unconscious. One popular approach is to use **projective tests**, *personality tests in which ambiguous images are presented to an individual to elicit responses that reflect unconscious desires or conflicts.* They are called "projective" because the image can be interpreted in different ways, and the particular interpretation a person chooses is thought to be a projection of her unconscious.

One of the most familiar projective tests is the **Rorschach inkblot test**, *in which people are asked to describe what they see in an inkblot, and psychologists interpret this*

Figure 12.7 The Rorschach Inkblot Test

Some psychologists attempt to measure personality characteristics by analyzing the verbal responses clients use to describe what they see in an inkblot such as this.

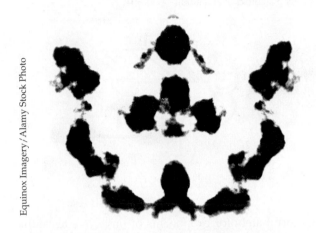

Equinox Imagery / Alamy Stock Photo

description using a standardized scoring and interpretation method (Exner, 1991; see Figure 12.7). Another projective test is the **Thematic Apperception Test (TAT)**, *which asks respondents to tell stories about ambiguous pictures involving various interpersonal situations* (Figure 12.8). For example, a picture might show a man and woman looking at each other with blank expressions. Subjects are asked to tell a story about the picture. Who are these people? What emotions are they feeling? Why are they looking at each other that way? The details in the story that a person makes up are thought to be a projection of their personality functioning, and thus, a way of illuminating their unconscious.

Figure 12.8 The Thematic Apperception Test

In this projective test, the individual is asked to tell a story about what is happening in the image. The responses to this task are believed by some to give important insights into an individual's personality.

Ken Karp / Pearson Education

Figure 12.9 Figure Drawing as a Projective Test

Figure drawing is another projective technique used by many psychologists. The content of the drawings is analyzed and interpreted by the therapist. It turns out that these drawings are somewhat related to artistic ability and intelligence, but not personality (Lilienfeld et al., 2000).

Unfortunately for proponents of projective tests, they have not fared well in empirical research, receiving criticism for low reliability and validity. Low reliability indicates that the test will not give the same measurement on subsequent assessments of the same person. Low validity indicates that the test does not actually measure what it purports to measure. For example, although projective tests are supposed to measure personality functioning, in some cases, such as the figure-drawing test shown in Figure 12.9, they actually measure a combination of artistic ability and intelligence (see Lilienfeld et al., 2000). Time and again, research has indicated serious limitations regarding the reliability and validity of projective tests (Garb et al., 2005; Lilienfeld et al., 2000).

Despite criticisms from some researchers, many therapists claim that they have experienced significant breakthroughs by using projective tests. A survey in the mid-1990s estimated that 43% of clinical psychologists and psychiatrists made frequent use of projective tests (Watkins et al., 1995). More recently, a survey of school psychologists showed that the TAT and Rorschach were used by 30% and 14% of these professionals, respectively, although their popularity appears to be declining (Hojnoski et al., 2006).

Working the Scientific Literacy Model

Perceiving Others as a Projective Test

There are clearly problems with the reliability and validity of some projective tests, but the basic idea of projection remains compelling to many psychologists. Could there be some way to measure projection with greater accuracy? One promising direction is to look at how people make judgments about what other people are like.

What do we know about the way people perceive others?

People have a seemingly natural inclination to make assumptions about what others are like, even if only very limited information is available. We may judge people we hardly know as friendly, aggressive, selfish, or trustworthy, for example. But with virtually no information to guide us, how do we make these judgments? One possibility is that we make guesses as to what other people are like by using our own self-concepts as a guide. With no other information to go on, we tend to assume that most people are kind of like us. The trait of Machiavellianism (see Module 12.1) provides a great example. People who exhibit this trait are generally willing and able to manipulate and deceive others to get what they want. Interestingly, they are more likely than the general population to see others as being cynical and selfish (Christie & Geis, 1970). Thus, psychologists suggest that the degree to which an individual sees people as selfish and cynical is, to an extent, a projection of his own Machiavellianism (Wood et al., 2010).

How can scientists study how projection relates to personality?

Although projection was initially a psychodynamic idea, contemporary researchers have begun to apply it to other approaches, such as the trait approach. In one study, participants rated both themselves and others in terms of personality traits such as the Big Five, narcissism (i.e., excessive self-importance), and symptoms of depression. Researchers found that the way that participants viewed themselves was related to how they viewed others. For example, people who viewed themselves positively (as agreeable, intelligent, and satisfied with life) were likely to view others the same way (Wood et al., 2010). This provided evidence that how people perceive others appears to be a projection of how they perceive themselves.

Can we critically evaluate this research?

The results of this study indicate that self-ratings and ratings of others are correlated. However, the correlations themselves are not very large, meaning that psychologists cannot make *precise* predictions about a rater's personality based on that individual's ratings of others, but rather can make only *general* statements. Furthermore, this study does not provide evidence that projection is actually occurring (i.e., that people are actually using their own self-concepts to guide their impressions of others). It could be the case that people are simply positive or negative in general, such as being optimistic or pessimistic. The positive, optimistic person would tend to see herself and others positively, and the negative, pessimistic person would do the opposite.

Thus, the correlation between ratings of self and other simply reflects a general disposition, not a specific process of projection.

Why is this relevant?

Standard projective tests such as the Rorschach inkblot test and the Thematic Apperception Test are fraught with problems and controversy. It would be unheard of for modern medical doctors to diagnose disorders using procedures that are as unreliable and of as questionable validity as these tests. Thus it is important to search for new and better methods that might reveal meaningful information about the individuals taking them. Psychology need not necessarily abandon projective tests altogether, as the benefits of adding rigour and scrutiny to them has shown that they can be of value (e.g., Schultheiss & Brunstein, 2001).

Module 12.3a Quiz:

The Psychodynamic Perspective

Know . . .

1. According to Freud, the _____ is the personality component that is responsible for seeking to immediately satisfy basic biological needs.
   A. id
   B. ego
   C. superego
   D. libido

2. According to Freud, in which order do the stages of psychosexual development occur?
   A. Oral, anal, phallic, latency, genital
   B. Oral, anal, genital, phallic, latency
   C. Anal, oral, phallic, latency, genital
   D. Latency, oral, anal, genital, phallic

Understand . . .

3. A defence mechanism would be employed
   A. by the id to create anxiety.
   B. by the superego to reduce or avoid anxiety.
   C. by the ego to reduce or avoid anxiety.
   D. by the superego to create anxiety.

Apply . . .

4. Dan lied to avoid getting in trouble with his parents, but now he is experiencing anxiety caused by extreme guilt. According to Freud, these negative feelings would arise due to the activity of the _____.
   A. Oedipus complex
   B. ego
   C. superego
   D. libido

Analyze . . .

5. Why have some psychologists questioned the reliability of projective tests?
   A. Judges very often agree on how to interpret an individual test.
   B. Individuals often score quite differently if tested at two different times.
   C. The tests may not measure what they claim to measure.
   D. These tests often provide disturbing details about a person's unconscious.

Alternatives to the Psychodynamic Approach

Freud attracted many followers, but some of his contemporaries took psychodynamic psychology in different directions. They recognized that sex and aggression are not the only motives driving personality development; indeed, other motivational forces, such as the need for belonging, the need for achievement, and the need for integrity or wholeness, are important aspects of personality.

ANALYTICAL PSYCHOLOGY Carl Jung (1875–1961) made a dramatic break from Freud over disagreements about a number of issues, founding the analytical psychology movement. **Analytical psychology** *focuses on the role of unconscious archetypes in personality development.* The archetypes were believed to be housed in a region of the unconscious unique to Jung's theories. In contrast to the Freudian unconscious, Jung believed that there were two main types of the unconscious, a **personal unconscious**, which was basically the same as the Freudian unconscious, *a vast repository of experiences and patterns absorbed during the person's life*, and a collective unconscious, which is not held within the individual person. The **collective unconscious** is *a separate, non-personal realm of the unconscious that holds the collective memories and mythologies of humankind, stretching deep into our ancestral past.* Jung thought of the personal and collective unconscious as entirely different "levels" of consciousness, although they are so different from one another as to be basically completely different things. The personal unconscious is still housed within the person, but the collective unconscious is more like a larger field of forces, which shape the individual personality in certain characteristic ways.

Within analytical psychology, archetypes played a central role; **archetypes** *are images and symbols that reflect common patterns of experience across all cultures.* There are many different archetypes and several particularly important ones, including the Mother, the Child, the Trickster, the Wise Old Man, the Hero, and the Shadow, among others. The Shadow archetype represents unwanted aspects of the self that the person is unwilling to acknowledge; this archetype has been particularly influential among psychologists who emphasize personal growth, individual empowerment, and healing from trauma (e.g., Ford, 2002). These archetypes were thought to represent major narrative patterns in human experience, part of the universal tapestry of human life. Thus, when archetypal symbols appeared (for example, in a person's dreams), it was believed that they could be interpreted and would give important insights into the person's personal growth and well-being. Archetypes are a very popular aspect of Jungian psychology, but they have not had much of an impact on the rest of the field, again due to their unscientific nature.

THE POWER OF SOCIAL FACTORS Alfred Adler (1870–1937) initially differentiated himself from Freud by arguing for the importance of social dynamics and conscious thoughts (as opposed to sexual and aggressive drives in the unconscious) as determinants of behaviour. He rejected the centrality of the pleasure principle, instead emphasizing the **inferiority complex**, *the struggle many people have with feelings of inferiority, which stem from experiences of helplessness and powerlessness during childhood*. Adler described how people strive to compensate for their feelings of inferiority by trying to appear competent and, in many cases, overcompensate for inferior feelings by trying to be or appear superior to others. Adler's theories of the importance of the need for power have had a profound influence on the field of psychology and continue to inspire contemporary research (e.g., Watts, 2000).

Karen Horney (1885–1952) also disagreed with Freud's heavy emphasis on sex, and especially infantile sexuality. Instead, Horney (disappointingly pronounced "HORN-eye") focused on the importance of social and cultural factors, arguing that to understand personality one should focus on the functioning of a person's present self, rather than overwhelmingly focusing on the unconscious, which was largely formed in early childhood. Horney highlighted the role of interpersonal conflict between children and their parents as important to personality development. She also strongly advocated against Freud's "phallocentrism" (i.e., emphasis on the penis). To counter his theory of the Oedipus complex, Horney argued instead that men suffer from "womb envy," because men can never experience the miracle of birth and of carrying another human life as part of oneself, or the experiences of breastfeeding and other biological acts of motherhood. She said that men attempted to compensate for their perceived deficiencies by focusing on work and by devaluing and subjugating women. While Freud believed that women suffered from penis envy, Horney argued that any "envy" Freud observed in the female psyche was envy of the patriarchal power enjoyed by men, not of men's sexual equipment (Paris, 1994).

As you can see, psychodynamic theorists have separated themselves in a number of important ways. Contemporary psychodynamic psychologists work mostly in the field of clinical and counselling psychology. And, despite some differences, modern psychodynamic psychologists do share many of the core attributes of psychoanalytic thought: an emphasis on the unconscious, internal conflicts between opposing forces within personality, and the influence of early experiences on adult personality (Westen, 1998).

HUMANISTIC PERSPECTIVES Reacting against the pessimism and disempowerment inherent in Freudian approaches, the humanistic psychologists wanted to explore the potential for humans to become truly free and deeply fulfilled. Thinking outside the boxes of behaviourism and psychodynamic theories, the humanistic psychologists emphasized the individual's free will to make choices, highlighted positive motivations for personal growth and development, and explored the upper ranges of human experience, such as feelings of transcendence, love, and fulfillment. Proponents of the humanistic approach believed it would become the "third force" in psychology, after psychoanalysis and behaviourism.

Among the many influential humanistic psychologists, Carl Rogers was perhaps uniquely responsible for helping to launch the movement and for cementing certain ideas in the field that remain to this day. Rather than the Freudian depiction of people plagued by complexes and defences, Rogers championed a **person-centred perspective**, founded on the assumption that *people are basically good, and given the right environment their personality will develop fully and normally*. Rogers believed that people possess immense inner resources for growth and resilience, and a desire for **self-actualization**, which is *the drive to grow and fulfill one's potential*.

According to Rogers, fully functioning, self-actualized people deeply accept themselves and are highly self-aware; having moved beyond the need to erect defences to ward off negative feelings, they become aware of their inherent goodness. Rogers believed that the more self-actualized a person becomes, the more his inherently good nature will dominate his personality. Other leading humanistic psychologists, such as Abraham Maslow, also sought to identify the characteristics of fully functioning, self-actualizing people. Research on human strengths and virtues continues to this day, gaining new life in recent years through the positive psychology movement, with renewed interest in topics like personal growth, gratitude, authenticity, and meaning.

Module 12.3b Quiz:

Alternatives to the Psychodynamic Approach

Know . . .

1. The aspect of consciousness proposed by Carl Jung that is a store of archetypes representing symbols and experiences common to all cultures is called the _____.
   - A. preconscious
   - B. subconscious
   - C. analytical conscious
   - D. collective unconscious

2. In contrast to psychodynamic theories, humanistic theories emphasize
   - A. free will.
   - B. how personalities are determined by biology.
   - C. how personality is determined by the environment.
   - D. how defence mechanisms affect behaviour.

Apply . . .

3. Alexandra's older sister is praised for being good at math, but Alexandra struggles with the subject. What would the resulting feelings of being "not good enough" be called?
   - A. Negative reinforcement
   - B. Negative archetype
   - C. Inferiority complex
   - D. Oedipus complex

Analyze . . .

4. Which of the following is *not* a critique of Freud's psychodynamic approach to personality?
   - A. It focuses on situations we cannot control.
   - B. It does not yield many scientifically testable hypotheses.
   - C. It was based on a very limited sample of subjects.
   - D. It has not been found useful or applicable to clinical psychology.

Module 12.3 Summary

12.3a   Know . . . the key terminology related to the psychodynamic and humanistic approaches to personality.

analytical psychology
archetypes
collective unconscious
conscious mind
defence mechanisms
ego
fixation
id
inferiority complex
person-centred perspective
personal unconscious
projective tests
Rorschach inkblot test
self-actualization
superego
Thematic Apperception Test (TAT)
unconscious mind

12.3b   Understand . . . how people use defence mechanisms to cope with conflicting thoughts and feelings.

According to the psychodynamic perspective, defence mechanisms activate whenever we are threatened by feelings of anxiety due to conflicts between different systems within consciousness. These mechanisms include denying and repressing urges, displacing them, or finding more acceptable ways of expressing them.

12.3c   Understand . . . the developmental stages Freud used to explain the origins of personality.

To explain personality development, Freud began with the concept of libido—the id's energy source for the drives that originate at different focal points of the body from infancy to adolescence. Each of the stages of psychosexual development—oral, anal, phallic, latent, and genital—is associated with a unique form of conflict as the ego and superego develop. Failure to resolve the corresponding conflict can result in a fixation, in which the person is stuck at a certain phase of development, and this can cause problems later in life.

12.3d   Apply . . . both psychodynamic and humanistic perspectives to explain personality.

Apply Activity

To apply the psychodynamic approach to understand someone's personality, you would consider the role that unconscious processes play in determining behaviour, as well as the conflicts that exist between a person's impulses and his need to regulate them. Review Freud's structure of the mind (illustrated in Figure 12.6) and the psychosexual stages of development. What might each of the following situations mean from Freud's perspective?

1. A student cannot concentrate on her homework until every little item on her desk is in its appropriate place.

2. An individual commits violent acts against others without feeling any remorse.

To apply the humanistic perspective to understand personality, you would look at the person's motivations for personal growth and fulfillment and consider whether they embody the set of traits described by Maslow as characterizing self-actualized people. In each of the following scenarios, which personality characteristic could the person work on changing in order to move toward becoming self-actualized?

1. Dave is a pragmatic guy, preferring the hard, cold facts of reality to fantasies about how life could be different. He is not afraid to express what he really thinks, and is not very concerned about whether other people accept or reject him. Because he is so comfortable with himself, he has little anxiety and can behave spontaneously and freely in most situations. He feels strongly patriotic toward his country, and thinks that government should focus on issues like taxes and the economy, rather than trying to help people who are disadvantaged due to poverty.

2. Zoe is enthusiastic about life and has a strong spiritual practice, using meditation and prayer to feel closer to the divine. She feels profound empathy for people in all parts of the world and is described by her family as a "bleeding heart," someone who cares strongly for people who are worse off than her. She regrets some of the choices she made earlier in life, and although she tries to learn from them, finds herself often nostalgically thinking about the past. She has many friends and is very socially active, in part because she is such a people-pleaser that she is good at presenting herself in such a way that she makes other people comfortable.

12.3e   Analyze . . . whether projective tests are valid measures of personality.

In this module you learned about projective tests such as the Rorschach inkblot test and the Thematic Apperception Test, which some psychologists believe are useful tools that give them insight into unconscious processes. However, projective tests do not appear to be valid ways of assessing characteristics of a person's personality.

12.3f   Analyze . . . the strengths and weaknesses of psychodynamic perspectives.

Psychodynamic theories can provide some compelling explanations for human motivation. For example, it is easy to understand how social and moral conflicts arise when couched in terms of a struggle between the id and the ego. At the same time, this approach does not have a lot of scientific support. Its key concepts, such as the id, ego, and superego, are theoretical constructs that cannot be empirically measured. Also, the psychosexual stages of development are no longer believed to be accurate descriptions of stages that children go through while growing up.

Chapter 13
Social Psychology

13.1 The Power of the Situation: Social Influences on Behaviour

- The Person and the Situation 533
- Module 13.1a Quiz 537
- The Asch Experiments: Conformity 537

  Working the Scientific Literacy Model: Examining Why People Conform: Seeing Is Believing 538
- Module 13.1b Quiz 540
- The Bystander Effect: Situational Influences on Helping Behaviour 541
- Module 13.1c Quiz 544
- Social Roles and Obedience 544
- Module 13.1d Quiz 549
- Module 13.1 Summary 549

13.2 Social Cognition

- Person Perception 552
- Module 13.2a Quiz 554
- The Self in the Social World 554
- Module 13.2b Quiz 557
- Stereotypes, Prejudice, and Discrimination 557

  Working the Scientific Literacy Model: Explicit versus Implicit Measures of Prejudice 559
- Module 13.2c Quiz 562
- Module 13.2 Summary 563

13.3 Attitudes, Behaviour, and Effective Communication

- Changing People's Behaviour 565
- Module 13.3a Quiz 566
- Using the Central Route Effectively 566

  Working the Scientific Literacy Model: The Identifiable Victim Effect 568
- Module 13.3b Quiz 571
- Using the Peripheral Route Effectively 572
- Module 13.3c Quiz 574
- The Attitude–Behaviour Feedback Loop 574
- Module 13.3d Quiz 576
- Module 13.3 Summary 576

Module 13.1 The Power of the Situation: Social Influences on Behaviour

Ted Pink / Alamy Stock Photo

 Learning Objectives

13.1a Know . . . the key terminology associated with social influence.

13.1b Understand . . . why individuals conform to others' behaviours.

13.1c Understand . . . how individuals and groups can influence behaviours.

13.1d Apply . . . your knowledge of the bystander effect to ensure that you will be helped if you are in an emergency.

13.1e Analyze . . . whether guards who participate in abuse are inherently bad people, or whether their behaviour is the product of social influences.

In an interview for the British Broadcasting Corporation (BBC), Joe Darby described what it felt like when he started looking at the pictures. They'd been given to him on a CD by a colleague, Charles Graner. They seemed innocent at first, scenes of soldiers at different locations around Baghdad, Iraq. Then he saw a pyramid of naked men, climbing on top of each other. It made him laugh. However, he soon realized these were not people joking around; these were pictures of Iraqi prisoners being tortured and degraded, in the very prison he was working in.

He saw images of his fellow soldier, Charles Graner, physically assaulting a group of handcuffed prisoners. He saw a photo of naked male prisoners with bags over their heads positioned in sexually suggestive poses. And he saw many images of another fellow soldier, Lynndie England, leading prisoners around on a leash, standing behind a pile of naked prisoners while giving a thumbs-up sign, and posing with an Iraqi prisoner who had died.

Then, Joe Darby made the critical decision: He decided to turn the pictures over to the Army's criminal investigation

unit, blowing the whistle on an appalling situation of torture and corruption that implicated the US military and some high-ranking government officials. You may have seen some of these photos yourself, as they were splashed across newspapers and websites around the world. They are chilling, to the extreme, depicting tortures committed by U.S. soldiers against Iraqi citizens in, of all places, Abu Ghraib. Ironically, this prison was renowned for its use of brutal torture under the dictatorship of Saddam Hussein, who was the leader that the U.S. soldiers were "liberating" the Iraqi people from.

When he decided to hand over the pictures, Darby feared that he would be putting himself at serious risk for retaliation from his fellow soldiers. It would be all too easy for any of his fellow soldiers to quietly kill him in his sleep. However, because he had made his reports anonymously, none of the other soldiers knew that he was the whistle-blower. Astonishingly, it was none other than Donald Rumsfeld, the Secretary of Defense at the time, who blew Darby's cover. Rumsfeld appeared on TV and personally thanked Joe Darby, by name, for turning in the photos; this unbelievable mistake left Darby unprotected and completely vulnerable to any who would seek revenge.

When his fellow soldiers found out, he was widely congratulated, but back in his home town, Darby was regarded as a traitor. In his words, "You have some people who don't view it as right and wrong. They view it as: I put American soldiers in prison over Iraqis." For their own security, Darby, his wife, and children were placed in protective custody. Today, they remain in an undisclosed location, accompanied by a military escort whenever they go out—even for something as simple as a trip to the grocery store.

When we learn about atrocities like Abu Ghraib, we want to understand how people could ever do such things. The hope is that by understanding the social and psychological dynamics that lead to these tragedies, we may be able to prevent more of them in the future, and make it easier for heroes such as Joe Darby to come forward and do the right thing. One thing is certain, people can *resist social pressures in any circumstance. And when they do, it pays off in a deep sense of inner conviction and a clear conscience. Joe Darby says that after all he and his family have been through, "I've never regretted for one second what I did when I was in Iraq, to turn those pictures in."*

Focus Questions

1. What leads people to engage in horrific acts against others?

2. How much are our behaviours influenced by others?

The Person and the Situation

Most of us grew up with a clear distinction between right and wrong and the belief that the world is comprised of good guys and bad guys. Then we assume that we're the good guys, and so are people who are "like us." After all, we don't go around murdering, torturing, or committing crimes, right? So when terrible things happen, we assume that it's "other" people who do these things: fundamentally different types of people—bad guys. Although this may be a comforting way to experience the world, it has at least one big downside. When terrible things do occur, we generally look for which bad people to blame, and as a result, we fail to question or challenge the larger system.

Dr. Philip Zimbardo, a highly influential social psychologist of the last half century, is a champion of this alternative view. He says it's not the bad apples, but the bad barrels. After carefully studying over a thousand pictures of abusive acts occurring in Abu Ghraib, Zimbardo concluded that the tragedy should be seen as an outgrowth of the whole system, and that the blame likely goes very high up the chain of military/political leadership, because a situation was intentionally created that systematically promoted or endorsed the use of violence against Iraqi prison detainees.

REUTERS/Alamy Stock Photo

For example, there was a general lack of supervision over guards' treatment of detainees, a pervasive and constant fear of terrorism, the presence of many non-military personnel hired from private security companies who didn't have the same public accountability as military officers, the general danger and stress of living in the area, physical and mental exhaustion, language and cultural barriers that would make it easier to fall into *Us* vs. *Them* ways of thinking (see Module 13.2), frequent changes made to the official rules on what were considered acceptable methods for interrogation, the prevalence of social norms condoning prejudice towards outgroups (e.g., Iraqis, Muslims, prisoners) and favouritism towards ingroup members (e.g., Americans, soldiers, prison guards).

Courtesy Wikipedia/ZUMA Press/Newscom

Finally, there were contributing factors high up the chain of military and political command. For example, at the prison itself the soldiers who interrogated detainees experienced immense pressure from higher up the chain of command to "get results" when interrogating detainees; they were also frequently, and conveniently, left unsupervised when with detainees, so that when they "worked them over" their superiors would be officially unaware. At the highest level of government, President Bush changed the U.S.'s official policy on torture, even stepping outside of the Geneva Convention prohibiting torture, all in the name of "fighting terrorism." One could argue that this created powerful cultural pressures towards, and provided legitimacy to the use of, torture and violence. Zimbardo believes that all of these situational factors worked together, not strictly to *cause* a specific act to occur, but to make it more likely that soldiers in those conditions would commit violent acts (Zimbardo, 2004, 2007).

It's disturbing to fully consider the situational explanation for "evil." Most of us would rather believe in the dispositional, bad apples explanation. Otherwise we have to face the possibility that we also have the capacity to do terrible things if we fall into the wrong circumstances. On the other hand, if we fail to appreciate the power of the situation, how can we prevent history from repeating itself? How can we learn the lessons taught by Abu Ghraib, or by the Holocaust, if we assume that these things occurred as aberrations, rather than recognizing that certain predictable, situational factors make these types of tragedies more likely to occur?

We must also remember that the situational analysis is never enough to fully explain a behaviour pattern. Individuals retain free will (or so we assume). People are still, in the final analysis, responsible for their behaviour. For example, in Abu Ghraib, most of the soldiers did not behave abusively; they seemed to be able to resist the power of the situation. Joe Darby even had the courage to step forward and report the abuses so that the rest of the world found out what was going on.

To try to fully understand social reality, social psychologists study the *interaction between the person and the situation*. Kurt Lewin (1936), a key founder (often regarded as the grandfather) of social psychology, expressed this insight as $B = f(P,E)$: *Behaviour* is a function of the *Person* and the *Environment*. This insight challenged the Freudian theories of the early 20th century, which explained a person's behaviour as being guided by unconscious forces that were rooted in that person's distant personal past. It also challenged behaviourism, with its emphasis on the person's history of conditioning. Social psychologists, in contrast, emphasized the role of the individual in choosing how to interpret a situation, and ultimately, how to respond. They also focused on the person's experience in the present moment. Lewin brought a metaphor from physics into psychology, arguing that a person's behaviour was the consequence of sets of forces operating on the person, and once an analyst sufficiently understood the forces, then the person's behaviour could be predicted, just as one could analyze the trajectory of an object by understanding the physical forces (gravity, friction, etc.) operating on the object. This general approach was extremely influential in social psychology and has been widely applied in the business world. Theories of how to create change in organizations often incorporate Lewin's logic, analyzing the forces operating in the situation and determining which forces to change.

The past 80 years or so of research in social psychology that has flowed from this insight has pieced together a deep understanding of the situational forces and individual characteristics that determine human behaviour.

MIMICRY AND SOCIAL NORMS Our analysis begins by considering the powerful, and often overlooked, ways in which we are influenced by the people who are immediately around us. For example, although we are often unaware of it, we tend to engage in **mimicry**, *taking on for ourselves the behaviours, emotional displays, and facial expressions of others.*

For example, the **chameleon effect** (Chartrand & Bargh, 1999) describes how *people mimic others non-consciously, automatically copying others' behaviours even without realizing it*. You tend to laugh and smile when others are laughing and smiling. More generally, you make the same emotional expressions on your face as those you see on the faces around you, and then pick up their moods as well. And if someone else is whispering, you will likely whisper, even if it is to ask, "Why are we whispering?" The examples are literally endless; practically every moment of social interaction between people involves mimicry.

This kind of subtly attuned mimicry is highly functional (Lakin et al., 2003), much of the time serving as a "social glue," helping to coordinate behaviours in social settings, helping people to feel reassured and validated by each other, sending the unconsciously processed message to others that you are kind of like them, and more so, that you are paying attention to them in that moment.

Humans are a social species, and coordinating our behaviour with others is a key part of learning to function in the social world. It is often a good idea to see what other people are doing and "go with the flow." Learning through observation is one of our key activities in life (see Module 6.3), and probably has been for a long part of our evolutionary past. It's what we humans do.

The vast bulk of this social processing occurs through implicit, unconscious processes that we can examine at multiple levels of analysis. For example, there are implicit processes of attention, perception, emotions, and behaviour that are described in social psychology (see also Module 13.2). There is emotional synchrony and influence that flows between people and through groups and social networks, and there is even physiological synchrony that ties people together, such as how people's hormone levels synchronize when they live with each other. The point is, a lot goes on that links us together with other people and we are consciously aware of very little of it.

The social benefits of mimicry can be seen by how they affect social interactions. For example, people mimic others more when they are trying to make a good impression (Lakin & Chartrand, 2003). It does seem to work: when someone adopts similar bodily movements and gestures to your own (even quite subtly), you tend to like them more (Chartrand & Bargh, 1999). However, it's a different story if you try to *intentionally* mimic people's behaviour in order to manipulate them. Consciously trying to "steer" this process could lead you into trouble, just like focusing too much on a well-practised movement can cause you to mess it up. Indeed, if someone notices that a person is mimicking them, they like that person less as a result (Maddux et al., 2008); so, if you are using this power for your own nefarious purposes, at the very least, be subtle about it!

Given that mimicry is so implicit and deeply ingrained, it would make sense to expect that we humans would find it awfully difficult to resist being influenced by each other. In many different situations, we tend to conform to the **social norms** that are evident. Social norms are *the (usually unwritten) guidelines for how to behave in social contexts.* Norms influence everything from our manners (e.g., you probably make different jokes when out with your friends than when you meet your boy/girlfriend's parents for the first time), to the amount of alcohol we drink, food we eat, clothes we wear, and even the beliefs and attitudes we express. Social norms govern much of our behaviour, even though people often fail to realize this and instead believe that their behaviour is freely chosen (Nolan et al., 2008). Much social psychological research has shown that people have relatively poor insight into the actual causal factors that influence their behaviour much of the time; we aren't in control of ourselves as much as we would like to believe (Nisbett & Wilson, 1977).

Mimicry and social norms reflect the fact that much of our lives are spent in groups; whether it's hanging out with friends, doing a work or school project, performing artistically, and so on, small groups are hard to avoid. A key question in social psychology is whether people behave differently in groups than they do as individuals, and how behaviour changes as a result of being in a group.

GROUP DYNAMICS: SOCIAL LOAFING AND SOCIAL FACILITATION Let's start with a question about your own experiences in groups—how do you feel about group assignments? Do you like them because they're an opportunity to get to know people, or maybe because the group

can accomplish something more impressive together than they could alone? Or do you hate group projects because other people waste so much time, or because people don't have very good ideas, or because some people are slackers whose work doesn't meet your standards and you end up having to do everything? You probably have some kind of opinion on group projects. But here's the thing—regardless of your feelings, you are almost certainly going to be working in groups in your future. Whether it's your job, family and community groups, or the group project your charming professor assigns to your class, it's pretty tough to avoid working with other people.

Often one of the main purposes of a group is to produce better work than an individual could by working alone. But does this really happen? Do groups produce better work, making the most out of individuals' ideas and encouraging their best efforts? Or do they produce poorer outcomes, limiting people's creativity and enabling them to slack off? Oddly enough, the answer to both questions is "yes, sometimes."

Groups sometimes produce poorer outcomes due to **social loafing**, *which occurs when an individual puts less effort into working on a task with others.* There are various phrases for describing this—coasting, slacking, free-riding. Social loafing can occur in all sorts of tasks, including physical activities (e.g., swimming, rope-pulling), cognitive activities (e.g., problem solving, perceptual tests), and creativity (e.g., song writing), and across all types of groups, regardless of age, gender, or nationality (Karau & Williams, 2001; Latané et al., 2006). One reason why people loaf is because they think others in the group are also not doing their best, setting up an apparent social norm that "people in this group don't work very hard." There are two likely outcomes of social loafing. Either the group performs quite poorly (i.e., crashes and burns), or a small number of people end up saving the group by doing everything themselves.

Given the importance and inescapability of group work, it is important to understand what factors encourage loafing, so we can avoid them.

- **Low efficacy beliefs.** This occurs if tasks are too difficult or complex, so people don't know where to start. Structure tasks so people know exactly what to do, provide clear deadlines, and give people feedback so they know how well they are doing and how they can improve.

- **Believing that one's contributions are not important to the group.** This occurs if people can't see how their own input matters to the group. Overcome this by helping people understand how group members rely on and affect each other, and assigning tasks to people that they feel are significant or they've had some say in choosing (if possible).

- **Not caring about the group's outcome.** This occurs when a person is not personally identified with the group, perhaps feeling socially rejected from the group or perceiving the group as unsuccessful or unimportant. Overcome this by making the group's goals and values clear and explicit, encouraging friendships to form and group activities to be fun and socially rewarding.

- **Feeling like others are not trying very hard**. As discussed earlier, people loaf if they feel others are loafing (Karau & Williams, 2001). Overcome this by providing feedback about the progress of group members on their individual tasks; strong groups often have regular meetings where people's progress is discussed and, ideally, celebrated!

In contrast to social loafing, **social facilitation** *occurs when one's performance is affected by the presence of others.* For example, in probably the first social psychology experiment ever published, Norman Triplett (1898) found that cyclists ride faster when racing against each other than when trying to beat the clock. Many other researchers have found similar effects, even in animals. For example, ants are able to dig more when other ants are working alongside them (Chen, 1937) and even cockroaches run down a runway more quickly when other cockroaches are around (Zajonc et al., 1969).

The presence of others doesn't always improve performance, however. We're all familiar with the athlete who "choked" at the big moment. The presence of others is likely to interfere with our performance when our skills are poor or the task is difficult. Even the cockroaches mentioned earlier did more poorly when other cockroaches watched them try to navigate a more complex maze (Zajonc et al., 1969).

There are many different mechanisms that explain the social facilitation effect (Uziel, 2007). One of the most important is that the presence of others is (emotionally) arousing, and arousal tends to strengthen our dominant responses. When the task is simple (e.g., run in a straight line), our dominant responses are the right ones, but when the task is very complex (e.g., juggle three axes), we need to be able to control our responses more carefully, and then arousal decreases performance. Thus, the effects of arousal due to social facilitation depend on one's skills and the difficulty of the task; the greater the skills and the simpler the tasks, the more likely the presence of others will enhance performance. For true masters of a skill, audiences and competitors generally enhance performance, but novices tend to perform best in practice sessions when nobody's watching (Bell & Yee, 1989; MacCracken & Stadulis, 1985).

GROUPTHINK In the same way that feeling evaluated tends to limit one's full abilities, the pressures that build within groups also often limit creativity, leading people to hold back their ideas. **Groupthink** refers to this *stifling of diversity that occurs when individuals are not able to express their true perspectives, instead having to focus more on maintaining harmony in the group and on not being evaluated negatively.*

In contrast with our optimistic visions of group "brainstorming" sessions that are wildly creative and inventive, the reality of group performance is quite a bit less impressive. Group members can feel evaluative or competitive pressures within the group, and as a result, the group norm is not as safe or supportive; this makes it feel more risky to put yourself out there and say something really radical and crazy. So, instead of a frenzy of creativity in which group members gleefully pile idea upon idea, group brainstorming often ends up being a kind of polite and restrained process, where a few ideas are aired and then the group quickly moves towards implementing something. In short, group brainstorming often fails.

When group members are more concerned with avoiding disagreements than with generating ideas, three main problems occur. First, group members may minimize or ignore potential problems and risks in the ideas they are considering. The lack of ability to critically question or disagree with ideas means that people will emphasize potential rewards and successes and overlook potentially disastrous things that might go wrong. Second, groups will likely settle too quickly on ideas, because social pressures will make people uncomfortable with prolonging a decision-making process. Instead, they will simply agree with one of the existing ideas. As a result, many potential ideas are never brought to the table for consideration. Third, groups often become overconfident and therefore less likely to carefully examine the consequences of their decisions, leading them to be less likely to learn from their mistakes (Ahlfinger & Esser, 2001; Janis, 1972). All things considered, groupthink seems like a pretty bad outcome! (Interestingly, the main thing that groupthink is good for is implementing ideas—getting things done. It's choosing the right things to do that groupthink interferes with.)

Historically, groupthink has been identified in some truly terrible decisions, including the 1986 decision to go ahead with the launch of the space shuttle *Challenger* despite safety concerns (the shuttle broke apart 73 seconds into its flight, killing seven astronauts); the escalation of the Vietnam War; and the 1961 Bay of Pigs invasion, when a U.S.-sponsored military invasion attempted to orchestrate an overthrow of Cuban leader Fidel Castro and was soundly defeated, to the immense embarrassment of the U.S. In each case, leaders committed themselves to a course of action without taking into consideration all the different perspectives and opinions that were available. An example of groupthink in your lifetime was the U.S. war in Iraq. The original official justification for the invasion was that former Iraqi leader Saddam Hussein was manufacturing weapons of massive destruction (WMDs). However, the Bush administration was widely criticized for not giving equal consideration to different types of information before making its decisions. Specifically, information that supported the assertion that Saddam Hussein was manufacturing WMDs was considered valid and given serious weight, whereas information that countered this assertion tended to be rejected as invalid or based on uninformed testimony. In the end, the military action that resulted from this decision involved the deaths of hundreds of thousands of Iraqi citizens and thousands of U.S. soldiers. Now, more than a decade later, no WMDs have been found, and that region remains in turmoil.

Some groups are more susceptible to groupthink than others. Laboratory research revealed that when groupthink occurs, there is often a strong or "directive" leader—specifically, an individual who suppresses dissenters and encourages the group to consider fewer alternative ideas (Ahlfinger & Esser, 2001). Also, groups in which members are more similar to each other, especially in terms of shared sociopolitical perspectives, are more likely to fall into groupthink (e.g., Schulz-Hardt et al., 2000).

Module 13.1a Quiz:

The Person and the Situation

Know . . .

1. According to Kurt Lewin, human behaviour is governed by the formula $B = f(P, E)$. In this formula, E refers to
   A. environment.
   B. education.
   C. ego.
   D. extraversion.

Understand . . .

2. The chameleon effect occurs when
   A. individuals withdraw from social interactions.
   B. individuals try to use subtle means of persuasion.
   C. individuals turn their backs on a group member.
   D. individuals unintentionally mimic another's behaviour.

3. Groupthink is *least* likely to occur when
   A. group members have very different sociopolitical values.
   B. group members become excited about their progress.
   C. a leader emerges who suppresses dissent.
   D. the group refuses to consider alternatives.

Analyze . . .

4. Which of the following does *not* explain why social loafing may occur?
   A. The individual believes that even if the group succeeds, there will be very little reward in it for each individual group member.
   B. The individual believes that the group will fail no matter what his or her contribution is.
   C. The individual believes that he or she has little to contribute to a group.
   D. The group is engaged in a particularly complicated project.

The Asch Experiments: Conformity

Groupthink can occur easily without a strong leader simply because of conformity pressures that arise spontaneously in groups. Classic experiments on conformity were performed in the 1950s by Solomon Asch. In his now-famous studies, participants were seated at a table along with several other people who *seemed* like other participants but who were, in fact, "confederates," people who were secretly working with the experimenter. Participants and confederates were asked to look at an image of three lines, and choose which line was the same length as a "standard line." The task was designed to be so easy (see Figure 13.1) that when people were allowed to give their answers privately, they were correct almost 100% of the time. However, things changed when answers were spoken aloud in front of a group. For the first couple of trials, everybody gave the correct answer, making the participant's job easy. But then, something weird happened; each of the confederates started giving the same wrong answer,

Figure 13.1 Perceptual Judgment Task in Asch's Conformity Studies

Which of the comparison lines is the same length as the standard line? In Asch's experiments, many people conformed to the confederates and gave the wrong answer.

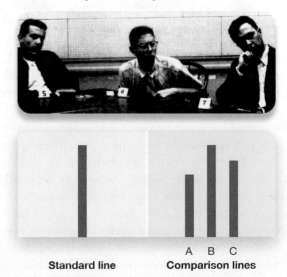

Standard line   Comparison lines
A B C

Table 13.1 Personal and Situational Factors Contribute to Conformity

People Tend to Be Less Likely to Conform When . . .	People Tend to Be More Likely to Conform When . . .
Only one other person is in the vicinity	There is a larger group in the vicinity
There are only male group members	There is a high proportion of female group members
There are only strangers in the room	There are friends, family, or acquaintances in the vicinity
There are extremely clear and simple tasks	The task is unclear or ambiguous
There is one other nonconformist in the room	Others conform first
Responses are made anonymously	Responses are made publicly

one after another. Then it was the participant's turn. What would he do? Would he go along with the rest of the group and give the clearly wrong answer? Or would he say what he knew to be the right answer?

This is a situation in which unconscious mimicking doesn't apply, because the behaviour is very consciously chosen. And, it is not an ambiguous situation at all. However, conformity pressures were strong enough that 75% of people gave the wrong answer on at least one of the 12 trials in which the confederates gave the wrong answer. Each time confederates gave the wrong answer, about one third of the participants conformed (Asch, 1951, 1955, 1956).

Why would people choose an answer they knew to be wrong? There are two main types of social influence. **Normative influence** *is the result of social pressure to adopt a group's perspective in order to be accepted, rather than rejected, by the group.* In contrast, **informational influence** *occurs when people feel the group is giving them useful information.* Although both types of influence can certainly affect behaviour, there is a big difference between them: informational influence tends to lead to actual belief change (i.e., the person comes to adopt the beliefs of the group), whereas normative influence does not necessarily lead people to privately accept the information that they may, publicly, be demonstrating their agreement with.

In the Asch study, both types of influence seemed to be occurring. For example, some of the conforming participants said afterwards that they thought they had misunderstood something, or that there was some sort of "trick" the others picked up on that they didn't, because surely the others couldn't all be wrong if they were all saying the same thing. Other people reported that they didn't want to stand out or make a scene by being the disagreeable person, so they just went along with the group. In everyday contexts, both types of influence are often at work, making us easily swayed by other people. We will be especially vulnerable to social influence when we are uncertain about the situation, although as Asch showed us, social influence is powerful enough to make us doubt ourselves even when the situation is pretty clear and unambiguous. Many factors work together to determine, in a given situation, the strength of social influence pressures and whether or not a person ends up conforming (see Table 13.1).

Working the Scientific Literacy Model

Examining Why People Conform: Seeing Is Believing

For more than half a century, social psychologists have wondered why subjects in the Asch experiment conformed to the group. Did they consciously choose to conform solely because they didn't want to incur a social cost by seeming different from everyone else (normative influence), or did the group's collective opinion actually change the subjects' own perceptions of the lines (informational influence)? More generally, is it possible that if enough people insist that reality is different from how it appears, then you will actually perceive a different reality?

What do we know about measuring choosing vs. perceiving?

The simplest way of assessing why people conform is, of course, to ask them, which Asch did in some of his original studies. However, other research has shown that people often don't have accurate insight into their own reasons for doing things (Nisbett & Wilson, 1977). Relying on self-reports only gives insight into the *theories* people have about their own behaviour, not necessarily the actual reasons why they did what they did.

Recent advances in neuroscience have given researchers the ability to see which areas of the brain are associated with perceptual processes, such as seeing, and processes that more directly involve the self, such as making a choice. If one is consciously making a choice that one knows to be wrong, this should activate parts of the prefrontal cortex that involve executive function abilities, whereas the act of perceiving visual stimuli has its own patterns of activation spread through the frontal, occipital, and parietal cortices. So, in the Asch study, a neurological measurement technique like this might help us to see directly which types of social influence are occurring. One hypothesis could be that informational influence might involve greater activation of visual perception areas of the brain, because subjects are "seeing" the stimulus differently and therefore may be paying special attention to the act of seeing. Conversely, if normative influence is occurring, subjects may activate the executive function areas of the prefrontal cortex, reflecting that they are making intentional choices to override their own knowledge of the right answer, in order to give the socially desirable response. Thus, different patterns of brain activation might shed light on people's reasons for conforming.

How can science study people's reasons for conforming, when they may be unaware of the reasons themselves?

In an ingenious study, subjects went through an Asch-like procedure while their brains were being scanned in an fMRI machine (Berns et al., 2005). Subjects were asked to make judgments about a perceptual task, while also being given information about the perceptions of other people in the experiment, many of which were wrong. The task required subjects to mentally rotate figures in order to determine whether a shape was the same or different from a comparison shape (i.e., like the Asch study, but with shapes instead of lines). Researchers then compared subjects' brain activation when they conformed to the incorrect judgments of the group vs. when they did not conform but instead stuck to their own independent perceptions.

When subjects conformed, reporting the same judgment as the group, activation occurred in regions of the brain associated with visual perception (i.e., parts of the visual cortex and parietal lobes). This was interpreted to mean that when conforming, these subjects were, in fact, perceiving these stimuli in a different way—that the difference was in their *perceptions*. On the other hand, when subjects refused to conform to the group's incorrect judgments, they activated areas of the amygdala that are associated with negative emotion (LeDoux, 2000) and with processing social information (Amaral et al., 2003; Singer et al., 2004). This suggests that going against the group's judgments was an emotionally taxing thing for people to do, involving negative emotion and a heightened social awareness. This may be the brain indicator of the heavy emotional load of standing up for what you believe in.

Can we critically evaluate this evidence?

This fascinating study may give us insight into what can happen when people conform to groups, but it leaves wide open the question of what happens in different situations, including the Asch study. In this study, people were mentally rotating shapes, which is a more challenging task than the line judgments in Asch's study. Although people's perceptions on the mental rotation task could be swayed by the group's judgment, this does not necessarily imply that people's perceptions on Asch's much simpler task could

also be swayed in the same way. It is important to keep in mind that the different operational details of the experiments, indeed of any experiment, have important implications for how the results should be interpreted.

There are also multiple ways of interpreting the brain-imaging data. For example, in general, people pay more attention to stimuli that are related to emotional responses; so, some of the activity might be related to attention rather than to the emotions associated with conformity (or refusing to conform). In short, it's not clear from a single study exactly what the activation of specific brain areas means; as with all research, it's necessary for studies to accumulate and the evidence to converge.

Why is this relevant?

This study suggests that when people conform to a group, it can potentially change their basic perceptions about the world at a deep level. This suggests that if enough people say something is true, not only may we go along with the group, we may start to experience the world in the same way. This study also suggests that going against the group, standing up for what you believe, can be a threatening experience, requiring us to experience difficult emotions like fear.

Empowering people to resist the influence of destructive groups or authority figures is a huge puzzle science is still trying to solve. Many forces operate together, some seemingly positive and some seemingly negative, all influencing how empowered a person feels to go against a group. For example, resisting social influence is likely related to one's own confidence and self-esteem, expertise, social status, authority, moral conviction, prejudice against the group, the status or desirability of the group, and undoubtedly many other factors that influence how the person feels in that particular moment. Although social psychologists now have a pretty good understanding of how these factors operate, we obviously have a long way to go in our society before we can apply this knowledge fully and effectively.

Follow-up experiments to the Asch study illuminated two additional, very important aspects of conformity situations. First, there is a fascinating relationship between conformity rates and the size of the group. Asch found very low conformity if only one or two people gave a wrong answer. But once there are three or more people, conformity rates shoot up to their maximum level (Asch, 1951); it only takes a few people to exert "group pressure."

This finding has deep implications for our understanding of how group norms operate in our everyday lives. Group norms are not just abstract, overarching cultural forces that affect all of us in every situation. Instead, group norms are created spontaneously in each situation. Whenever a few people get together, they establish implicit norms that govern the behaviour of the people in the group. For example, think of the norms that are transmitted as people laugh at a demeaning joke; as co-workers pass along malicious gossip; as a boy is cheered on for eating his seventh slice of pizza while a girl is looked at askance when she loads up her plate a buffet; as kids turn away from a child in the schoolyard who is being bullied or laughed at; as friends laugh at someone's story about how much alcohol they drank before "somehow" managing to drive home.

Now, think about how these situations can be different when people speak up and say they are offended by racist jokes; when co-workers create cultures of support instead of gossip; when both boys and girls are encouraged to eat healthily and love their bodies; when people stand up together against a bully; and when people make sure their friends are sober before they let them get behind the wheel. The norms that operate in our everyday lives can make such a big difference.

The second important finding to come out of the Asch studies was that even though groups are powerful, individuals can also be very powerful. In some variations of Asch's studies, one of the confederates would also give the right answer, going against the rest of the group. This single dissenting voice was enough to shatter the group's power, reducing the rate of conformity to one quarter of its original level (Asch, 1955). This shows that groups are most powerful when they are unanimous, but a single person's courage can burst that bubble and liberate the voices of others who may privately disagree with the group. This is a key reason why it is so important to speak out about what you believe in.

It's important for people to realize how much power they wield as individuals, because when you are caught in a situation of group pressure, the pressures can indeed feel enormously powerful. For example, with regards to the Abu Ghraib abuses discussed earlier, it is important to understand the normative pressures that were in operation. For example, there is a strong culture in the military of not questioning orders and maintaining solidarity in the ranks; these sorts of pressures create a culture of conformity, maximizing the likelihood of outcomes like groupthink. In such an environment, it can seem awfully hard to go against the group, and as we discussed, Joe Darby was afraid of what would happen if others knew he was the whistleblower. However, once his identity was revealed, his fellow soldiers expressed widespread support and appreciation for his courage. They had also been harbouring their own private disapproval of what was happening, but they were unwilling to be "the only one" to come forward.

Module 13.1b Quiz:

The Asch Experiments: Conformity

Know . . .

1. Social pressure to adopt a group's perspective in order to be accepted, rather than rejected, by the group is known as _____.
   A. normative influence
   B. social cognitive influence
   C. informational influence
   D. sociocultural influence

Apply . . .

2. Which of the following is a reasonable conclusion to draw from the Asch studies?
   A. Conformity pressures are so powerful that it is almost impossible to help people stand up against a group's majority opinion.
   B. Conformity always happens because people simply choose to agree with the group just to fit in; conformity can never, however, lead people to privately accept a group's perspective.
   C. People will conform in most situations that involve a great deal of uncertainty; but when people are certain of what is "right," most will disagree with the group if the group holds a different opinion from them.

D. Even a single individual has a great deal of power in group settings, because by being willing to publicly disagree with the group, conformity pressures are significantly reduced for others.

3. Diane was a member of her university's student union. The members of the union were debating whether to continue funding the university's daycare, which was losing money. Diane wanted to continue providing money to the daycare, yet found that other members of the council wanted to close it. If Diane behaved similarly to the participants in Asch's conformity experiments, which response will she most likely make?
   A. Diane will vote to continue funding the daycare, even if she is the only person voting that way.
   B. Diane will lose her motivation to be a part of the students' union.
   C. If another member of the students' council also objects to closing the daycare, Diane will vote to keep it open.
   D. Diane will side with the President of the student union in order to ensure that she is on the same side as the most powerful member of the group.

The Bystander Effect: Situational Influences on Helping Behaviour

One of the most powerful examinations of the ways that social situations influence us has been the study of helping behaviour. Although all of us would like to live in a society in which people will help us when we need it, the truth is often, sadly, quite different.

One tragic example of this, which has become famous in our culture, unfolded in the middle of a cold night, on March 13, 1964. A young woman, Kitty Genovese, was physically assaulted outside an apartment complex in New York City. She screamed and made enough noise that many people (38, it was later revealed) came to their windows to try to see what was going on. One person shouted through his window, which scared the attacker off, and Kitty stumbled around the corner of the building, out of sight of most of the residents. The attacker then returned and attacked her again, stabbing and sexually assaulting her. In total, her ordeal lasted more than half an hour. When the police were finally called, it was too late to save Kitty's life.

A couple of weeks later, *The New York Times* published a front-page article, with the headline, "37 Who Saw Murder Didn't Call the Police. Apathy at Stabbing of Queens Woman Shocks Inspector." People were shocked and outraged that so many could have allowed a young woman to be assaulted without lifting a finger to help her. How is it possible that not one person intervened? Have we become so selfish and disconnected from each other that we don't get involved even when someone's life is on the line?

Before continuing, we should mention that several decades later, it has been revealed that the murder did not really occur the way it was reported, and the way that most psychology textbooks have repeated ever since. It seemed that only a few of the residents had been able to see anything in the parking lot, and only for a few moments. It was not clear to the residents exactly what was going on, so their inability to act could have, in many cases, been due to simple uncertainty, not realizing for sure that a crime was occurring. After all, when you live in a highly populated urban area, it is not uncommon to hear noises, including shouting, in the middle of the night, and you can't be calling the police every time someone shouts and yells on the street for a minute. So, some of the apparent apathy could have been due to confusion and uncertainty, rather than a lack of caring. Also, it was reported later that some of the residents apparently did try to phone the police, so it may have been a mistake to conclude that "nobody" tried to help (Manning et al., 2007).

Nevertheless, the horrifying belief that so many people could have stood by doing nothing while a woman was murdered launched an important line of research that found similar effects in many different situations. The **bystander effect** describes the counterintuitive finding that *the presence of other people actually reduces the likelihood of helping behaviour.* This is counterintuitive because, usually, one would assume that if there is a certain chance of one person doing something, like helping, then the more people that are around, the greater the cumulative chance should be that *someone* will help. However, it seems in many cases that as the number of people in a situation increases, helping rates actually decrease!

There are different explanations for the bystander effect in different situations. The first was offered by social psychologists Bibb Latané and John Darley (1968) after the Genovese murder. They suggested a rather surprising theory that ran counter to common intuitions. What if the thing that everybody found so surprising was actually the explanation? Instead of being surprised that nobody intervened despite the large number of people at their windows, what if nobody intervened in the situation *because* there were so many people involved?

Consider the perspective of each person, standing by their window that night in New York in 1964, looking out at a dark parking lot where they heard shouting. They likely wondered, "What's going on? Is it serious? Is it two people having a relationship argument? Is it a drunken

Kitty Genovese: Her tragic murder in 1964 led to groundbreaking studies on the bystander effect.

New York Daily News/Getty Images

Figure 13.2 Diffusion of Responsibility

If one person witnesses an emergency, it is as if 100% of the responsibility for helping falls on that person. If 10 people witness an emergency, that responsibility is diffused, so it is as if each person feels only 10% of the responsibility—which may not be enough to motivate a person to act.

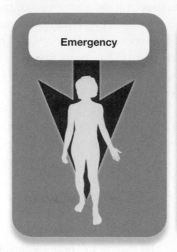
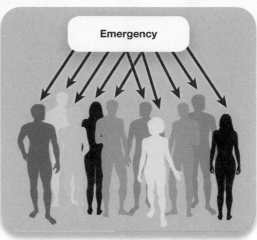

argument between friends? Or merely people having fun and yelling as some sort of prank? Should I do something, like call the police? Is that maybe a bit excessive? Or does the situation warrant it? I'm not *exactly* sure what's happening . . . maybe I'll wait a minute and see if I get a better sense of what's happening. . . . Hey, look at all the other people standing at their windows." And then, the critical moment happens—they conclude, "Someone else has probably called the police," or "Someone else probably has a better sense of what's happening," or they may even (somewhat selfishly) think, "I don't really want to get involved . . . but look, someone else will do it."

The problem is, of course, that if everybody thinks someone else will take on the responsibility of helping, nobody will do anything. Latané and Darley called this **diffusion of responsibility**, *the reduced personal responsibility that a person feels when more people are present in a situation* (Figure 13.2).

Other studies have explored this effect by simulating emergencies. For example, in one study, subjects believed they were interacting with other people who were in different rooms in the experiment, talking over an intercom system. One of the other voices on the intercom started to clearly have a seizure and require some help (this was, of course, not real, but subjects didn't know that). In one condition of the experiment, participants interacted with the other person alone and nobody else was available to help. In other conditions, participants believed there were other participants sitting at other intercom terminals, who were all available to help. Consistent with diffusion of responsibility, people took longer to react to the calls for help, the more people they believed were available to respond (Latané & Darley, 1968). The take-home message is that the

more people there are in a situation, the more likely it is that any one person will assume "someone else will do it."

The second explanation offered for the bystander effect is that there is often a mismatch between the public behaviour that people display and the private beliefs or thoughts the people may be having. As a result, the *social norms operating in the situation (i.e., the expressions of people's public behaviour), may be quite different from the actual beliefs held by the people themselves*; this is called **pluralistic ignorance**.

Pluralistic ignorance is one of the most powerful factors invisibly shaping our lives, and indeed our society. It operates in many different situations: racist jokes and comments that people don't react to; political decisions or corporate policies that others don't express their disapproval of; a child being bullied and taunted on the playground that nobody stands up for; unjust social practices that the general public passively accepts and allows to continue.

In fact, pluralistic ignorance could potentially be so powerful that it becomes a group norm, which then governs the behaviour of individual people within the group, even though nobody in the group actually agrees with the group norm. Think of how messed up that is! A group could pressure people to do things that each group member, privately, disagrees with. Of course, what likely happens in most real-world situations is that pluralistic ignorance and social influence (e.g., power, authority, etc.) work together so that a few people in a group can impose their values or perspectives onto the group, and then pluralistic ignorance works to keep everyone else from expressing their true thoughts and feelings. As a result, it only takes a few people to "steer" the behaviour of most others, and once those few people have power, it can be hard for the other group members to make change happen.

The bystander effect, diffusion of responsibility, and pluralistic ignorance can often work together to ensure that people who need help don't get it.

A key reason why pluralistic ignorance happens is simply that when we are out in the public sphere, the normative adult behaviour is to "play it cool." Most adults adopt expressions of general neutrality, most of the time, and you only have to walk down the street for two minutes to test this out. Obviously, there are many exceptions, but few adults are as constantly goofy, emotionally volatile, and expressive as, say, your average 3-year-old (which, to be honest, is probably a good thing). As a result, the immediate impression that people give, most of the time, is "I'm cool, and everything is fine," or as the common meme goes, keep calm and carry on.

One classic study of pluralistic ignorance demonstrated the power of this tendency for people to remain expressively restrained, even to the point that they would put their lives in potential peril. Imagine being a subject in this study: You are sitting in a room, filling out questionnaires; suddenly you notice a little bit of smoke, wafting into the room from a vent. What do you do?

Your intuition probably tells you that you would get up and check it out, especially if the smoke didn't stop. You would go over and smell it, perhaps look outside the room, or maybe find the experimenter to report it. Especially if the smoke continued to build, minute after minute, you would take some action. We all learned when we were kids how to get out of burning buildings, right?

If you are sitting in this room all by yourself, then your intuition is probably right. But what if you are sitting in the room with other people? This changes things, doesn't it? You might not want to embarrass yourself by jumping up right away. After all, maybe the smoke is just mist from a broken air conditioner or something equally benign.

So, in this situation, you pause, considering what to do, looking out of the corner of your eyes at the others in the room. But everyone else isn't responding either; they are just filling out their questionnaires, perhaps occasionally looking around as well, but "playing it cool." It's possible that every single person is privately thinking, "There might be a fire!" but publicly, each person is displaying no evidence of their private concerns, so they all sit there while smoke continues to fill up the room.

Exactly this pattern of behaviour was observed in the rather incredible "smoke-filled room study" (Latané & Darley, 1968), which had subjects go through the experience just described. Most subjects (75%) who sat in the smoky room by themselves got up to investigate within six minutes, but if the subjects were in a room with two other people who gave no indication of being concerned about the smoke, only 10% of the subjects took action to investigate. In a specific crisis situation in which people would normally help or take action, the mere presence of other people sets up various social forces that can prevent people from doing so, including embarrassment (Karakashian et al., 2006), pluralistic ignorance (Prentice & Miller, 1993), and diffusion of responsibility (Darley & Latané, 1968).

So if YOU are ever in an emergency situation and need someone's help, it is important to cut through any confusion, pluralistic ignorance, or diffusion of responsibility (Schroeder et al., 1995). If possible, clearly ask for help, from a specific person, with a specific command: "Hey you! In the red shirt! I need help! Call 911!" (Or whatever specific behaviour you need.)

Module 13.1c Quiz:

The Bystander Effect

Know . . .

1. The reduced personal responsibility that a person feels in a situation when more people are present is known as _____.
   A. diffusion of responsibility
   B. conformity
   C. the bystander effect
   D. pluralistic ignorance

Understand . . .

2. Which of the following is the most plausible explanation for the bystander effect?
   A. There are more people who simply do not care enough to help others than originally thought.
   B. People fear embarrassment that could come from helping another person.

C. The person in need is likely to be unrelated, and nonrelatives are not worth helping.
   D. Bystanders refuse to help because of their own experiences; when they were in need, nobody helped them.

Apply . . .

3. Darcey made a racist joke to a group of people at a party. Although Megan was a member of an anti-racism committee at her school, she didn't raise any objection to the joke. This is an example of _____.
   A. bystander apathy
   B. pluralistic ignorance
   C. the chameleon effect
   D. groupthink

Social Roles and Obedience

In contrast to social norms, which are general rules that apply to members of a group, **social roles** *are more specific sets of expectations for how someone in a specific position should behave.* The key word here is "specific." Roles emerge within a specific position in society—such as professor, student, parent, and prison guard—because the rest of society expects the person to behave in accordance with the role. In a sense, the person's individuality gets subsumed by the role, and what they might freely choose to do takes a back seat to what society expects of someone in that role. Roles can be incredibly powerful, leading people to do things they would never believe themselves capable of.

World War II had a major influence on the field of social psychology, particularly in bringing the concept of social roles to the forefront of study. The Holocaust was extremely troubling; how could seemingly ordinary people condone, and in many cases take part in, the state-sanctioned killing of millions of Jewish people, gypsies, homosexuals, and political dissidents? It seemed like only truly disturbed individuals would be willing to engage in such atrocities. The work of two psychologists changed this view, however, and showed us that social roles can have a powerful effect on our behaviour.

THE STANFORD PRISON STUDY In 1971, Philip Zimbardo, a social psychologist at Stanford University, wanted to study the impact that situations could have on people. Would otherwise "good" people do "bad" things if placed in a bad situation? He placed an ad in the paper asking for volunteers for a prison simulation experiment. After giving the respondents a battery of psychological tests, Zimbardo selected the most psychologically stable people to be participants. He then randomly assigned nine

to take on the role of prison guards, and nine to become prisoners.

The study began dramatically, as the police arrested the new "prisoners" outside of their homes, in full view of their neighbours. (Zimbardo enlisted the help of the local police department to help maximize the realism of this part of his study.) These newly arrested men were taken to the police station, where they were fingerprinted and held in a cell, then blindfolded and transferred to the basement of Stanford University's Psychology Department. Zimbardo had transformed the basement into a simulated prison, complete with cells with barred doors and cots for sleeping. The prisoners were strip-searched and sprayed with de-lousing spray, then given a smock to wear (with no underwear), a nylon stocking for their heads, a chain around their ankles, and an ID number, which was to be their only personal identification while in the study (i.e., they couldn't use their names anymore). The guards were given uniforms, and were given authority to oversee the daily lives of the prisoners. And thus the study began.

What happened next took everybody by surprise. By the morning of the second day, the situation had started to deteriorate to the point that the prisoners staged a rebellion and refused to cooperate with the guards. The guards responded with force, blasting the prisoners with spray from a fire extinguisher, and physically subduing them. The stress was so intense that within the first 36 hours of the experiment, one of the prisoners completely broke down, exhibiting such severe signs of emotional distress that he was taken out of the study.

The prisoners quickly became absorbed into their roles, following the guards' orders, trying to avoid punishment, referring to themselves only with ID numbers instead of their names, and generally trying to adapt as

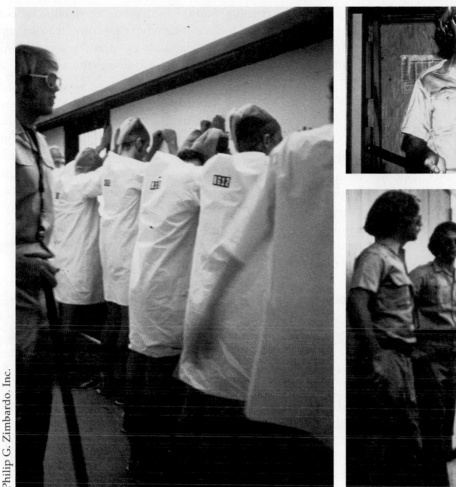

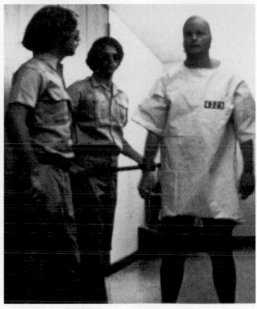

Philip G. Zimbardo. Inc.

Volunteers were randomly assigned to play guards or prisoners in the Stanford Prison Study in 1971. Each group took their roles so seriously, and their behaviours degraded so quickly, that the researchers called off the experiment before it was even halfway completed.

well as they could to their situation. The guards also fell into their roles, quickly starting to treat the prisoners with disrespect, engaging in ever-escalating tactics of control and humiliation. Prisoners were made to do push-ups and their sleep was interrupted for "counts" during which they had to line up and say their ID numbers, for up to a few hours at a time. Guards mocked and verbally harassed the prisoners, forced them to clean toilets with their bare hands, controlled when the prisoners were allowed to use the toilet, and even played humiliating, sexually degrading games. For prisoners who were rebellious or difficult, the guards set up a solitary confinement cell in what had previously been a broom closet.

Zimbardo himself, who had assumed the title of Prison Superintendent, also fell into his role. As he freely admits, he quickly lost his more objective perspective as a psychologist running a study, and instead started to view it as "his prison" containing "prisoners and guards," not young men from the community who were research participants.

The situation took a serious toll on the prisoners; many exhibited stress-related symptoms including screaming, crying, even becoming ill. Amazingly, although at least

50 outside observers were allowed to see what was going on, nobody questioned the ethics or expressed significant concern for the prisoners, until one graduate student, upon seeing the prisoners being marched down the hall on a "toilet run" with sacks over their heads, confronted Zimbardo with the unethical nature of the study. At that point, Zimbardo realized things had gotten out of hand and called off the study, a mere six days into the planned two-week simulation of prison life.

The Stanford Prison Study could not be repeated today due to the ethical standards that have since come into force. Nevertheless, it remains a stunning example of the power of social roles and how they play out in specific situations. A social role, even one that is randomly assigned, can make otherwise bright, well-adjusted people do things that they would never dream possible for themselves. You can likely see the connection between the Stanford experiment and the tragedies of Abu Ghraib. In both cases, a host of situational factors encouraged brutal behaviour. This is the power of the situation. However, as we discussed earlier, situational forces don't deserve all the blame; in both Abu Ghraib and Zimbardo's prison study, not all people were affected equally. In Abu Ghraib, only relatively few soldiers appear to have committed the majority of the documented abuses. In Zimbardo's study, some people took on their role as guards with far more sadism than others, whereas other guards treated the prisoners more kindly. Understanding precisely what personal factors lead people to be better able to resist destructive situations is a key focus in the field today.

OBEDIENCE TO AUTHORITY: THE MILGRAM EXPERIMENT   One additional factor in Abu Ghraib was the military command structure. Prison guards were often given orders to "soften up" the detainees for questioning; softening up implied a variety of tactics, including general harassment and rough treatment, humiliating prisoners by forcing them to be naked and put in compromising positions, terrorizing prisoners with attack dogs and electrical cables, and committing outright physical torture, including brutal water-boarding and other practices too awful to describe here. The fact that such horrendous things happened is a grim reminder of just how powerful social influence factors can be.

Most of us, however, believe that *we* would never do such things, no matter how powerful the situation. If we were asked to harm somebody against their will, and we disagreed with it, we would say no. Right? The Milgram obedience experiments (1963, 1974) thoroughly shattered our ability to legitimately hold this belief. In his now-famous studies, Stanley Milgram showed the world just how powerful authority could be, and how easily otherwise good, normal people could be made to do something horrific, something that probably none of us would believe ourselves willing to do.

Consider what happened in Milgram's study:

- Participants are told the study is about the effects of punishment on memory. They, and the other supposed participant (who is actually a confederate), a friendly middle-aged man, draw slips of paper in order to determine who will be the "teacher" and who will be the "learner." The draw is secretly rigged so that the participants are always the teacher.

- The teacher's job is to read a series of word pairs to the learner, and then to test him on his memory of the word pairs. The learner will be in a separate room hooked up to an electric shock machine. Each time the learner gets an answer wrong, the teacher is to administer a shock by flipping a switch on a panel in front of him, and increasing the voltage after each wrong answer. The switches go up by 15 volts until reaching a maximum of 450 volts, which is labelled "xxx." This process is watched by "the experimenter," a man wearing a lab coat.

- As the experiment progresses, the learner starts to make sounds of discomfort in the other room, grunting audibly as he is shocked. By 150 volts he is protesting loudly and saying that he no longer wants to continue in the study. If the subjects continue reading the word pairs and increasing the shock level, the learner gets to the point of screaming in pain, demanding and pleading, over and over again, to be let out, pleading that he can't take it anymore, even that his heart condition is bothering him and his heart is acting up. And then, at 330 volts, the learner falls silent and gives no further responses. At this point, subjects are informed by the experimenter that a non-response is to be considered "wrong," and the punishing shock is to be administered.

- If, at any point, subjects express concern for the learner, or say that they don't want to continue, the experimenter simply says a few stock responses, such as "Please continue" or, "The experiment requires that you continue."

The "shock generator" that the teacher operated, purportedly to punish the learner.

From the film *Obedience* © 1968 by Stanley Milgram, © renewed 1993 by Alexandra Milgram, and distributed by Penn State Media Sales.

The "learner" gets set up to participate in the experiment. He is being hooked up to the device that the teacher believes will deliver a shock.

From the film *Obedience* © 1968 by Stanley Milgram, © renewed 1993 by Alexandra Milgram, and distributed by Penn State Media Sales.

The experimenter explains to the "teacher" what the experimental procedure entails and how to use the shock generator.

From the film *Obedience* © 1968 by Stanley Milgram. © renewed 1993 by Alexandra Milgram, distributed by Penn State Media Sales.

Although most subjects were highly obedient, some, such as this person, refused to continue complying with the experimenter's orders.

From the film *Obedience* © 1968 by Stanley Milgram. © renewed 1993 by Alexandra Milgram, distributed by Penn State Media Sales.

Now, let's step back for a moment and put the situation in perspective. As part of a psychology experiment, people are asked to shock a person in another room and ignore this person as he expresses increasing discomfort, screams repeatedly, begs and pleads to be let out of the experiment, angrily refuses to continue, indicates that he might be having a heart attack, and eventually falls completely silent. And there is no compelling reason for people to continue, except a man in a lab coat telling them to do so. This seems absurd, when you stop and think about it. Surely almost nobody would actually do such a thing!

What would you do? If you are like most people, you probably feel that you would refuse to continue whenever the "learner" said that he didn't want to continue (which happened quite early, 150 volts). The moment the other person withdraws consent, you would stop, right?

Careful analyses across many replications of the Milgram study concluded that this moment of decision making is, in fact, the critical point (Packer, 2008). This is the moment when more subjects disobey the experimenter than any other moment. This is the point at which the true moral conflict becomes clear, between the rights and safety of the learner versus the authority of the experimenter. It is heartening that this is a choice point at which many people choose to follow their morals and disobey the experimenter.

But overall, the story is actually pretty grim. Even though *some* people rebelled at this point, the large majority of subjects actually continued, despite the protestations of the learner, who would have been, quite literally, a victim of abuse if this were a real situation. It is worth really stopping and thinking about this for a moment, because this finding is truly astonishing—most of the subjects, across all the replications of these experiments, chose to harm another person who had withdrawn consent, simply because an "authority figure" told them to.

It's important to point out that subjects were not sadistic torturers, gleefully putting the learner through misery. Subjects were deeply distressed themselves, and most of them, many times, over and over, tried to stop the experiment, telling the experimenter they didn't want to continue, arguing with him, and so on. But the experimenter was implacable, refusing to take no for an answer and just insisting that they continue. The experimenter forced subjects into a situation where "just saying no" wasn't enough; they had to *insist*, even beyond the point of being polite. It is quite telling that many of the participants in Milgram's study found it difficult to resist the experimenter because they didn't want to seem rude, and were simply uncomfortable disagreeing with someone so emphatically and taking action. This embarrassment held people back, astonishingly having more power than the man in the other room, literally screaming and begging to be let out of the experiment.

But, surely *you* wouldn't go all the way to the end, shocking that poor man, potentially to death . . . would you? This is one of the most unbelievable findings in the history of psychology. Milgram found that two out of every three people (65% to be exact) would do just that—slowly electrocute an innocent, desperately protesting man into oblivion, simply because a psychology experimenter insisted that they do so.

Most people would never expect this outcome, believing "the average person" to be far more ethical and able to do the right thing, when it came to a life or death situation. Indeed, a group of psychiatrists at Yale University were asked to predict ahead of time how many people would obey all the way to the end of the experiment, and they estimated it would be about 1 in 1000—the base rate of sadistic or psychopathic individuals in the population (Milgram, 1974). Also, the experimental sessions were observed by numerous people through one-way mirrors, who were unequivocally surprised and appalled at the subjects' failure to effectively rebel.

Subjects in this experiment were clearly distressed by what they were doing to the learner. They became very tense and frequently turned to the experimenter, saying that they didn't want to continue, expressing concern for the learner, even worrying that they might be killing him. But time and time again, they ended up following the experimenter's commands, turned back to the shock machine, and increased the voltage.

Milgram wrote,

> In a large number of cases, the degree of tension reached extremes that are rarely seen in sociopsychological laboratory studies. Subjects were observed to sweat, tremble, stutter, bite their lips, groan, and dig their fingernails into their flesh. These were characteristic rather than exceptional responses. . . . At one point he (one of the participants) pushed his fist into his forehead and muttered, "Oh God, let's stop it." And yet he continued to respond to every word of the experimenter, and obeyed to the end. . . . I observed a mature and initially poised businessman enter the laboratory smiling and confident. Within 20 minutes he was reduced to a twitching, shuddering wreck, who was rapidly approaching nervous collapse. . . . (1963, p. 371–378)

Clearly, it was not easy for the subjects to commit harm to another person, but it was even more difficult to break out of the power of the situation and refuse to obey.

Interestingly, Milgram ran other variants of this experiment, trying to see what might change obedience rates. Milgram tried to reduce the situational pressure in several ways, such as having the experimenter deliver his orders from a different location using the telephone, or reducing the stature and reputation of the authority figure by holding the experiment in a private company's downtown commercial space rather than at prestigious Yale University.

Milgram also tried to increase the personal directness with which subjects would experience the learner's distress, such as by having subjects and learners in the same room so that subjects had to watch the learner shout and writhe in pain. In one condition, subjects even had to physically force the learner's hand onto a shock plate while the learner struggled. Astonishingly, although the rates of obedience are somewhat lower, they remain disturbingly high. The fact that 30% of us would physically force a struggling person to receive pain against his will is disturbing, to say the least.

There were two especially interesting and powerful variations. One experiment looked at whether it is easier for a group to resist the experimenter, pitting the power of the group against the power of authority. In this experiment, there were three teachers making decisions collectively. Two of the teachers were confederates, pretending to be real subjects; the other teacher was the actual subject. When the two confederate teachers would make the decision to not continue with the experiment, 90% of subjects also refused. (We would note that it seems surprising that only 90% of them refused, leaving a full 10% of people still obeying the experimenter to the bitter end. Still, 10% obedience is a far cry from the 65% of the original study.) This particular variation is important because it illustrates again the power of dissent. As in the Asch study, if even a couple of people are courageous enough to fight for what is "right," they make it much easier for others to do the same.

Then there is one final condition, examining a crucial explanation that has been given for the Holocaust, known as the Eichmann factor. Adolf Eichmann was one of the central administrators of the Holocaust of WWII, in charge of overseeing the transportation of Jewish people who were deported to the concentration camps to be executed. In his famous trial for war crimes in 1962, Eichmann's defence was, essentially, that he was a mere bureaucrat. He didn't have any real power, but just performed menial tasks, not understanding or being responsible for the larger enterprise. In other words, he was a paper pusher, not a war criminal. He didn't actually cause harm to people. He merely organized train schedules and such things; he was "just doing his job." This led sociologist Hannah Arendt to coin the term "the banality of evil," describing the theory that oftentimes, much of the individual behaviour that allows for great harm to be perpetrated, often is not carried out by evil monsters out of malice and hatred, but instead, by rather ordinary people, doing jobs far removed from their ultimate consequence, who are merely caught up in a much larger system.

This final Milgram experiment quite chillingly examines one part of the "banality of evil," the removal of the individual's actions from the ultimate consequences (e.g., Eichmann organizing train schedules, not actually marching people into gas chambers). To simulate this, subjects only had to read the word pairs to the learner; it was another person who actually threw the switches to deliver the electric shocks. This allowed subjects to feel even less responsible. By splitting the process into multiple components, with multiple people involved in different ways, it was easy for each individual to feel not responsible, and not powerful enough to do anything about it. The result was that 92.5% (37/40) of subjects obeyed the experimenter right to the end. Here's the power of authority combining with "diffusion of responsibility," and the results are, frankly, horrific.

Milgram himself believed that these studies provided insight into the horrors of the Holocaust, particularly how so many millions of people could be "evil" enough to willingly participate in the Nazi death machine, or to stand passively by while such a brutal genocide took place.

The simple, yet profound, insight from the Milgram study is that it's not a question of people being good or evil; it's a question of the power of social situations. It is, in fact, not difficult to construct situations that are powerful enough to overwhelm even the deep moral convictions and courage of most people. As Milgram noted, "This is, perhaps, the most fundamental lesson of our study: Ordinary people, simply doing their jobs, and without any particular hostility on their part, can become agents in a terrible destructive process. Moreover, even when the destructive effects of their work become patently clear, and they are asked to carry out actions incompatible with fundamental standards of morality, relatively few people have the resources needed to resist authority" (2009).

In sum, situational forces can exert immense pressure on individuals, making an analysis of personal responsibility very tricky. However, social psychologists would generally agree that, in the final analysis, people are responsible for their behaviours. No matter how powerful the situational forces may be, individuals can always resist them and make a free choice, and history is full of examples of such courageous behaviour. In fact, one of Dr. Zimbardo's most recent projects, the Heroic Imagination Project (heroicimagination.org), is focused on understanding the factors that lead people to behave heroically. It is hoped that by unlocking the secrets of heroism, courage, and compassion, we can help society evolve in a healthier direction, and potentially avoid future atrocities.

Module 13.1d Quiz:

Social Roles and Obedience

Know . . .

1. _____ is complying with instructions from an individual who has authority.

   A. Obedience

   B. Groupthink

   C. Conformity

   D. Mimicry

Understand . . .

2. How did the Stanford Prison Study researchers come to the conclusion that roles, and not individual personalities, were the main influence on the volunteers' behaviour?

   A. The volunteer "prison guards" were specifically instructed to respond brutally.

   B. The "prisoners" were actually actors hired by the researchers.

   C. The prisoners and prison guards were psychologically similar prior to the start of the experience.

   D. The researchers actually believed that personality is more important than social roles.

Apply . . .

3. According to variations of the Milgram experiment,

   A. women are much more obedient to authority figures than men are.

   B. most of the power of the situation was the general reputation of Yale as an institution; people assumed that the consequences of the shocks couldn't be too terrible, because it was, after all, happening at Yale.

   C. people are much less obedient now than they were shortly after World War II; so, Milgram's findings are historically important, but are not relevant to modern generations.

   D. one of the most effective ways to get people to disobey an authority figure is to make sure they have some companions who will do it too.

Module 13.1 Summary

13.1a   Know . . . the key terminology associated with social influence.

bystander effect
chameleon effect
diffusion of responsibility
groupthink
informational influence
mimicry
normative influence
pluralistic ignorance
social facilitation
social loafing
social norms
social roles

13.1b   Understand . . . why individuals conform to others' behaviours.

At its most basic level, conforming begins with mimicry, in which people simply imitate others' behaviours. Mimicry seems to help form social bonds and encourages prosocial, helping behaviour. Conformity usually describes the way an individual's more complex behaviours evolve to become like the behaviours of the group. People may conform because they want to be accepted by the group, or they may conform because the group's way of perceiving reality actually influences the person's own perceptions.

13.1c   Understand . . . how individuals and groups can influence behaviours.

In many different situations, other people can change how we behave. In helping situations, the presence of others tends to decrease the likelihood that someone will help another in distress. In other situations, the presence of even a few more people can set up conformity pressures that influence us to behave like the others in the group. Interestingly, these conformity pressures can be largely eliminated in at least some situations if even a single individual is willing to go against the group and break its unanimity. In many situations we are placed into social roles and feel like we have to live up to the responsibilities of that role, even if we would normally behave differently. When authority figures are involved, these social pressures can become even more powerful—so powerful that many people cannot resist complying.

13.1d   Apply . . . your knowledge of the bystander effect to ensure that you will be helped if you are in an emergency.

People are least likely to help if they don't feel personally responsible for taking action, if they are unsure what to do to help, or if they are unsure whether the situation is a genuine emergency. Thus, you can best ensure that others will help you if you make very clear that it's an emergency and you need help, if you make a specific person responsible for helping, and if you tell that person exactly what he or she needs to do.

13.1e Analyze . . . whether guards who participate in abuse are inherently bad people, or if their behaviour is the product of social influences.

Behaviour is a function of the person and the situation. Therefore it is impossible to say in general the extent to which guards who participate in abuse are driven by their own character traits or by situational forces. A full analysis must take both sets of factors into consideration. Clearly though, in situations in which people are pressured to abuse prisoners, peer pressure is exerted through the expectations and behaviours of others, and the authorities in charge condone the abuse, it becomes far more likely that some guards will become abusive. Nevertheless, even the strictest social psychological analysis would never remove the final responsibility from the person; no matter the situation, we can always choose how to respond.

Module 13.2 Social Cognition

w85/ZUMA Press/Newscom

⌄ Learning Objectives

13.2a Know . . . the key terminology associated with social cognition.

13.2b Understand . . . how we form first impressions and how these impressions influence us.

13.2c Apply . . . your understanding of social cognition to the problem of overcoming prejudice and discrimination.

13.2d Analyze . . . whether people who commit discriminatory acts are necessarily prejudiced.

One February night in 1999, four New York City plainclothes police officers were patrolling a Bronx neighbourhood when they saw a lone man on the street. The officers thought he was behaving suspiciously, so they decided to question him. Upon orders from the police to stop, the man ducked into the vestibule of an apartment building, reaching for the door with one hand and putting the other into his pocket. Officers feared he was reaching for a gun. One officer opened fire on the man, and the other three followed, firing a total of 41 shots, 19 of which hit the man and killed him on the spot.

Tragically, the victim of the shooting was a peaceful and unarmed 24-year-old man named Amadou Diallo. By all accounts, Diallo was a friendly, industrious, and law-abiding man from Guinea, West Africa, who had come to New York in hopes of attaining a college education. He had turned away from the police presumably because he didn't know they were police (they were not in uniform and were driving an unmarked car); besides, whenever four guys jump out of a car in the middle of the night in the Bronx and start yelling and running toward you, running into the safety of your home is a sensible thing to do. His hand went into his pocket because he was reaching for his wallet.

Much of New York was in an uproar over the shooting, and the turmoil was only heightened after the four police officers were found not guilty of any criminal wrongdoing in court. Half of all New Yorkers disagreed with the verdict, and that figure reached almost 80% among Africans and African Americans (Connelly, 2000). People of all backgrounds attributed the shooting to hostile prejudice. On the other hand, many other people and most police officers defended the actions of the four officers, blaming the stressful environment in which they work and the need for them to make a snap decision in a potentially life-threatening situation.

Was prejudice an issue in Diallo's death? If he had been a White man, would the same thing have happened? In recent years, these same questions have played a major role in North American society, with notable movements Idle No More and #BlackLivesMatter creating not only robust and healthy communities, but also a massive increase in public awareness, boots-on-the-streets activism, and meaningful political dialogue and change.

Central to issues of race, class, gender, sexual orientation, and all other forms of discrimination, is understanding how human beings actually do process information about the social world, and how stereotypes, prejudice and other social processes influence people's perceptions and behaviours. These are the questions we explore in this module.

Focus Questions

1. How do we make judgments and form impressions about other people?

2. Can stereotypes affect our behaviour in ways that we are unaware of? Could such processes have played a role in the killing of Amadou Diallo?

》 The field of social-cognitive psychology is a fusion of social psychology's emphasis on social situations and cognitive psychology's emphasis on cognitions (perceptions, thoughts, and beliefs). Social-cognitive researchers study the cognitions that people have about social situations, and how situations influence cognitive processes. It is an exciting area to study because it deals directly with the everyday social experiences we encounter in our lives.

One of the central ideas in this field is that there are two major types of processes in our consciousness: explicit processes and implicit processes. **Explicit processes**, *which correspond roughly to "conscious" thought, are deliberative, effortful, relatively slow, and generally under our intentional control.* This explicit level of consciousness is our subjective inner awareness, our "mind" as we know it. **Implicit processes** *comprise our "unconscious" thought; they are intuitive, automatic, effortless, very fast, and operate largely outside of our intentional control.* The implicit level of consciousness is the larger set of patterns that govern how our mind generally functions—all the "lower-level" processes that comprise the vast bulk of what our brains actually do (Chaiken & Trope, 1999; Kahneman, 2003; Todorov et al., 2005).

These two sets of processes work together to regulate our bodies, continually update our perceptions, infuse emotional evaluations and layers of personal meaning to our experiences, and affect how we think, make decisions, and self-reflect. But not only do these two sets of processes carry out their independent functions, they also can influence each other. For example, explicit processes influence implicit processes when our beliefs (e.g., my friend Bob is a kind person!) influence how we process information (e.g., how much attention we pay to Bob's positive and negative behaviours). On the other hand, implicit processes can influence explicit processes, such as when our automatic tendency to categorize a person into a stereotyped group influences the judgments we make about that person. Explicit and implicit processes are intertwined, each influencing the other as we navigate the social world. In social-cognitive psychology, *models of behaviour that account for both implicit and explicit processes are called* **dual-process models** (Chaiken & Trope, 1999).

One of the major contributions that this understanding has given us is how our conscious acts are conditioned or influenced by a huge amount of unconscious processing. For example, when a person makes a specific choice to do something, that decision occurs *after* a whole slew of processes have already occurred—the person paying attention in the first place (choosing some parts of reality to focus on and ignoring many others), interpreting information into an overall understanding, evaluating different pieces of information and forming judgments and beliefs. So, who really made this decision then? And how can you say that it was a conscious act, if the vast bulk of the processing was actually unconscious? The critical insight is that because implicit processes happen so quickly and subtly, our presumably conscious and intentional acts are constantly being influenced and guided by our implicit processes, and we are not generally aware of this at all.

Consider the police officers in the Amadou Diallo shooting. As soon as they saw a Black man on the street late at night in the Bronx, a "Black male stereotype" may have become implicitly activated (Bargh, 1999); this stereotype then would have guided their explicit thinking, resulting in disaster. Indeed, the Black stereotype may have influenced their very first moment of interpretation, which was that Diallo was "acting suspiciously." It would have continued to influence the officers' interpretations of the rest of Amadou's behaviours, until the critical moment, forming the perception that he was reaching for a gun.

That's the double-edged sword of implicit processes; they help us process information efficiently, but they do so through creating biases. And when these biases lead to bad judgments or decisions, it is very difficult to recognize this or fix it, because we are not consciously aware of these implicit processes at work.

Person Perception

The effects of implicit processes are dramatically illustrated by research on **person perception**, *the processes by which individuals categorize and form judgments about other people* (Kenny, 2004). Person perception begins the instant we encounter another person, guided by our past experiences with people and the interpersonal knowledge we have absorbed from our culture. When we make a first impression of someone, we rely heavily on implicit processes, using whatever schemas we may have available. Schemas are organized clusters of knowledge, beliefs, and expectations about individuals and groups, which influence our attention and perceptual processes in many ways (see Module 7.3). For example, a person's visible characteristics (e.g., gender, race, age, style of dress) all activate schemas, and these schemas can bring certain traits to mind automatically.

THIN SLICES OF BEHAVIOUR   One amazing aspect of these implicit processes is just how accurate and practically instantaneous they can be. For example, within the first minute of seeing your professor at the front of the room, you have already evaluated her and made some basic judgments; if you were to fill out your course evaluations after, say, one minute of the first class (which would seem highly unfair!), your ratings would likely be very similar to your course evaluations after an entire semester's worth of exposure to that person (Ambady & Rosenthal, 1993; Tom et al., 2010). What happens in these situations is that we make very rapid, implicit judgments based on **thin slices of behaviour**, *very small samples of a person's behaviour*. In even a few seconds, our implicit processes, guiding our perceptions holistically and using well-practised heuristics, are able to perceive very small cues and subtle patterns. This gives us instantaneous, intuitive accuracy, at least in part.

Surprisingly, many of our social judgments are made in this way—instantaneously, based on very little information. Whether it's judging people based on tiny snippets of conversations we happen to overhear (Holleran et al., 2009; Mehl et al., 2006), or catching a mere glimpse of their face (e.g., we judge trustworthiness, competence, likability, and aggressiveness after seeing a photograph for less than one second; Willis & Todorov, 2006). Research by Nicholas Rule from the University of Toronto has shown that we can tell surprising things about people given incredibly little information. For example, people can guess a male's sexual orientation at rates greater than chance after viewing his photograph for a mere 1/20th of a second (Rule & Ambady, 2008), and Americans can accurately guess whether other people tend to vote Republican or Democrat merely by looking at a photograph of their face (Rule & Ambady, 2010).

Republicans are viewed as having more powerful faces, but Democrats' are seen as warmer.

Thin-slice research demonstrates just how quickly impressions are formed, and how surprisingly accurate they often can be. Of course, they are not perfectly accurate, and therein lies the problem.

SELF-FULFILLING PROPHECIES AND OTHER CONSEQUENCES OF FIRST IMPRESSIONS   First impressions have a big impact on many of our social behaviours. Even very simple cues, such as facial appearance, guide a wide range of behaviours, from how a jury treats a defendant to how people vote. For example, one study asked participants to act as jurors and evaluate evidence against a defendant. If shown a photograph of a defendant who simply "looked more trustworthy," participants were less likely to come to a guilty verdict (Porter et al., 2010). In another study, the outcome of U.S. elections of congressional candidates could be predicted 70% of the time simply using participants' judgments of how competent the candidates appeared in photographs (Todorov et al., 2005).

The fact that our implicit judgments can influence our perceptions and behaviours has countless implications for our social lives, particularly in terms of **self-fulfilling prophecies**, *which occur when a first impression (or an expectation) affects one's behaviour, and then that affects other people's behaviour, leading one to "confirm" the initial impression or expectation.* For example, if you expect someone you meet to be warm and friendly, you will probably be more at ease with them and will treat them in a warm and friendly manner yourself. This friendly behaviour will make them comfortable and will lead them to behave warm and friendly in return, leaving you with the conclusion that they are—surprise!—warm and friendly. You can

Thin slices of behaviour research shows that, in mere seconds, people form impressions that are surprisingly accurate. For example, you could get students to fill out course evaluations in university, evaluating the teaching capability of their professor, in the first minute of the first class, and they would be about the same as ratings taken after an entire semester of being taught by that professor.

easily imagine the opposite process, if your initial expectation is that the person will be cold and unfriendly.

Self-fulfilling prophecies affect our lives in many different ways. For example, if a person is confident, they are going to behave different than if they assume they are going to fail, nobody is going to like them, and they will continue to be a loser. You already know this; you've seen it countless times. It's the difference between the socially confident person who goes to a party where he doesn't know anybody and ends up having the best time and talking to all sorts of great people; versus the person who goes to the party and expects that it will be awkward and nobody will like him, so he hangs back, keeps to himself, doesn't initiate many conversations, and is stiff and uncomfortable, so that

he ends up not having a very good time after all. "See, I knew it all along . . . I shouldn't have gone in the first place. . ." is a self-fulfilling prophecy.

This idea has truly caught fire in North America society because it fits in so well with the "positive thinking" paradigm that so many people believe. And indeed, there is some sense to this. Every coach, athlete, parent, teacher, and anyone who has been a child at some point knows that, in the moment, if a person has no confidence and assumes, "I can't do it", then they're right; they can't. This is one of the basic lessons of growing up that we all learn at some point; you have to believe in yourself. Because if you don't, your lack of belief becomes a self-fulfilling prophecy. This is one way that our implicit processes shape our social realities.

Module 13.2a Quiz:

Person Perception

Know . . .

1. _____ are very quick, effortless, and automatic, whereas _____ are slower, more careful, and effortful.
   - **A.** Explicit processes; implicit processes
   - **B.** Implicit processes; explicit processes
   - **C.** Internal attributions; external attributions
   - **D.** External attributions; internal attributions

Understand . . .

2. Which of the following statements about thin slices of behaviour is most accurate?
   - **A.** Thin slices of behaviour lead to inaccurate impressions of others.
   - **B.** In many instances, lasting and often accurate impressions of others form in just a few moments.
   - **C.** Thin-slice impressions are 100% accurate.
   - **D.** Thin slices work only when rating the attractiveness of others.

Apply . . .

3. Shania feels sure that her boss doesn't like her. As a result, every time her boss is around, Shania acts more restrained and less warm and friendly. This causes her boss to, in fact, find her unfriendly and start to not like her. This is an illustration of
   - **A.** a self-fulfilling prophecy.
   - **B.** thin slices of behaviour.
   - **C.** implicit processes being stronger than explicit processes.
   - **D.** explicit processes being stronger than implicit processes.

The Self in the Social World

How do we decide what information to use when we're trying to understand other people or form impressions of them? What schemas do we activate to guide our judgments? As discussed above, we may use subtle cues in people's faces or non-verbal behaviours, but what else guides our judgments? Certainly, if the person falls into a group about which there are specific stereotypes, such as categories based on race, class, and gender, then these stereotypes often are automatically activated and can colour our judgments (Bargh, 1999). But one additional schema that is highly accessible, contains a vast amount of information, and is therefore often used in guiding our social judgments—is ourselves! Much of the time, we look out at the social world through the lens of our own self-concepts.

This has two very important consequences. The first is that we tend to think that the way we are is the way

people *should* be, and therefore, people who are substantially different from us have something wrong with them. The second is that we have a strong tendency to split the world into *Us* and *Them*, and we are motivated to see *Us* more positively than how we see *Them*. Understanding these dynamics gets right to the heart of why there is so much intergroup hostility in the world. It also reveals a tragic irony, which is that in the quest to feel good about ourselves and be happy, we sow the seeds that will grow into distrust, prejudice, and discrimination, thereby causing much suffering and unhappiness. Let's examine these arguments carefully, because they have major implications for understanding why the world is the way it is.

PROJECTING THE SELF ONTO OTHERS: FALSE CONSENSUS AND NAIVE REALISM One way in which our self-concept affects our social perceptions is that we tend to *project* our self-concepts onto the social world; this means that the qualities we see in ourselves and the attitudes and opinions that we hold, we tend to assume are similar for society at large. If we are sports fans, we assume that sports is generally important for other people as well. Even qualities we have that we know are not popular are still projected onto society; so, for example, if we are believers in Scientology, we will tend to assume that a larger proportion of the population believes in Scientology than is likely the case, and we will assume there are more Scientology believers out there than a non-believer would assume. *This tendency to project the self-concept onto the social world is known as the* **false consensus effect** (Marks & Miller, 1987). It's important to understand that this is a pretty sensible way to be, much of the time. After all, if we have to make guesses about people, why not base these guesses on ourselves?

We also generally assume that *our perceptions of reality are accurate, that we see things the way they are;* this is called **naive realism** (Ross & Ward, 1996). And it makes sense that we would make this assumption. After all, who wants to assume that they are walking around deluded and wrong all the time? Imagine being beset by doubts constantly, your life uncertain and stressful because you are never able to trust your own judgments. So instead, we operate under a basic framework of "I make sense," and then, by extension, "the people that I agree with, who are kind of like me, also make sense." And then, of course, by one more extension, "the people who I disagree with are deluded, wrong, and quite fundamentally different from me." You can see the problem here. At the personal level, we just want to feel good about ourselves and function effectively in the world. But at the group level, we create intergroup biases and an *Us* vs. *Them* way of thinking.

SELF-SERVING BIASES AND ATTRIBUTIONS   This tendency toward naive realism reflects a larger, more general need to want to feel positively about ourselves, to have a positive sense of self-evaluation or self-esteem (Allport, 1955; Maslow, 1968; Sedikides & Strube, 1995). Undergraduate students clearly enjoy boosts to their self-esteem, reporting preferring to receive such a boost even over eating a favourite food, getting paid, having sex, or seeing a best friend (Bushman et al., 2011). We strive to maintain our positive self-feelings through a host of **self-serving biases**, *which are biased ways of processing self-relevant information to enhance our positive self-evaluation* (Miller & Ross, 1975). For example, we tend to take credit for our successes but blame our failures on other people, circumstances, or bad luck.

One of the sneaky outgrowths of these self-serving biases and motivations is that for many of the qualities and skills that are important to us, we assume that we are "better" than average. This rather appropriately named *better than average effect* has been shown in many different domains. We even tend to prefer the letters in our name, especially our initials, over the other letters of the alphabet (Nuttin, 1985; Pelham et al., 2005); our letters are "better than average." An extreme example of the better than average effect was shown in one study of almost one million American students; a whopping 85% viewed themselves as "above average" in their ability to get along with other people, and a full 25% believed they were in the top 1% of this ability (Alicke & Olesya, 2005). If only the laws of math would allow this to be true. . . .

These same self-serving processes also influence the way we explain or interpret people's behaviour. Much in the same way that first impressions are formed implicitly (which we discussed earlier), our explanations for behaviours tend to start out as automatic and seemingly intuitive. Imagine that you're driving down the highway and all of a sudden some other driver swerves in front of you, honking; you slam on the brakes and turn the wheel sharply, narrowly avoiding a collision. Quick—what is the first thing that comes to mind about the other driver? Probably, your first thought is not the kindest or gentlest; you assume the other driver is an aggressive jerk, or maybe a bad driver. You yell, "You idiot!" and shake your fist. This type of explanation is called an **internal attribution** (also known as a *dispositional* attribution), *whereby the observer (yourself, in the above example) explains the behaviour of the actor (the driver who cut in front of you) in terms of some innate quality of that person (being an aggressive jerk, bad driver, or all-around "idiot")* (see Figure 13.3).

But of course, there may be other reasons for the driver's behaviour. Perhaps he is swerving out of the way of a piece of debris on the road, or just blew a tire, or just received a phone call that his partner is in the hospital and so is distracted, or he's tired after a long day and didn't look in his blind spot that one crucial moment before swerving in front of you. These are **external attributions** (also known as *situational* attributions), *whereby the observer explains the actor's behaviour as the result of the situation* (Heider, 1958). Generally, these external attributions are not what first come to mind; rather, we come to them after thinking about it for a bit, and realizing that maybe there were other factors causing the person's behaviour that we didn't initially consider.

This *tendency to over-emphasize internal (dispositional) attributions and under-emphasize external (situational) factors when explaining other people's behaviour* is known as the **fundamental attribution error (FAE)** (Ross, 1977). On the other hand, when we explain *our own* behaviours, we tend to emphasize whichever kind of explanation paints us in the best light. For our negative behaviours, the mistakes we make and embarrassing things we do, our attributions are much more generous. We emphasize the situational factors that cause us to do undesirable things (e.g., we had a headache, we were under a lot of stress, a family member

Figure 13.3 Internal and External Attributions

Internal attributions are based on qualities or actions of the individual, whereas external attributions focus on the context in which the individual is situated.

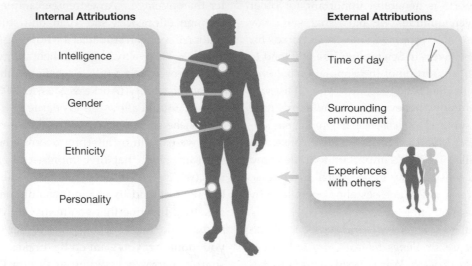

was sick, and so on). This obviously protects us from having to feel incompetent or foolish. However, it also might prevent us from taking responsibility for negative behaviours sometimes.

On the other hand, when our behaviours are desirable, self-serving biases work in the opposite direction; we take as much credit as we can for our successes (e.g., we worked really hard to deserve that promotion, we faced a lot of setbacks but we persevered and didn't give up).

One rather ironic wrinkle in the story of the FAE is that it doesn't seem to be quite as "fundamental" as was originally thought. Research on cross-cultural differences has shown that people make the FAE the most in predominantly individualistic cultures such as Canada or the United States, and the least in more collectivistic cultures such as China or Japan. This different approach to explaining others' behaviour can be seen in how people interpret social events such as news stories. For example, after reading about recent mass murderers in the newspaper, subjects from China are more likely to emphasize situational explanations for the murders (such as recent stressful events in the person's life), whereas North American subjects are much more likely to emphasize dispositional explanations (such as the murderer being an evil person; Morris & Peng, 1994). This greater emphasis on situational factors in collectivistic societies reflects stronger values toward maintaining harmony in interpersonal relationships and fulfilling one's social roles in the larger community, values which lead people to be more aware of situational information (Choi et al., 1999; Nisbett, 2003).

INGROUPS AND OUTGROUPS   Although this desire to feel good about ourselves seems functional and healthy, it often has negative side effects. As we discussed earlier,

our self-serving processes also reinforce a tendency to be biased against others. We are motivated to be biased against others because one of the key ways we maintain positive feelings about ourselves is through our identification with larger social groups (Fein & Spencer, 1997), and we can therefore make ourselves feel good by feeling positively towards these groups. In turn, one way to feel positively about our own group is to focus on how much better we are than other groups we compare ourselves to. *Groups we feel positively toward and identify with* are our **ingroups**, including our family, home team, and co-workers. In contrast, **outgroups** *are those "other" groups that we don't identify with*. In fact, we actively *dis*-identify with outgroups.

This where our self-serving biases can be so destructive. *As positive biases toward the self get extended to include one's ingroups, people become motivated to see their ingroups as superior to their outgroups*—engaging in **ingroup bias** and potentially, outgroup derogation. All in the service of maintaining our self-esteem, we carve the world into categories of *Us* and *Them* and then we automatically show a preference for *Us*.

An extremely clever set of studies that began in the 1970s added a crucial insight to the discussion of how we process information about groups. In real-world social interactions between people, there is already a lot of relevant group information available simply based on the physical characteristics of the individuals. Rather than creating groups based on established characteristics such as ethnicity or gender, researchers using the *minimal group paradigm* divided participants into new groups based on essentially meaningless criteria. In different studies, people were divided into groups based on whether they preferred one painting over another (Tajfel, 1970; Tajfel et al., 1971), or whether they flipped heads or tails on a coin toss

(Locksley et al., 1980). These newly formed groups had no history, no actual affiliation with each other, and no future together after the experiment was over.

Amazingly, even these completely meaningless ways of forming groups are enough to drive prejudice and discrimination; for example, if people are asked to distribute money between the two groups, they consistently give more to their new ingroup members. These results suggest that the process of categorizing the world into *Us* and *Them* is a fundamental and practically unavoidable part of how we process the social world. It also has some sobering implications. If the people in the group who flipped heads in a coin toss prefer their fellow Heads over those nasty Tails, even though they have no history of animosity, no competition over resources, or any other grounds whatsoever on which to base their preferences, imagine how much more powerful people's biases will be when faced with real-world distinctions and long histories of conflict and violence. Appreciating the deeply biasing influences of making ingroup–outgroup distinctions in the first place adds an important layer to our understanding of these larger conflicts.

In closing this section, we have to reiterate how important it is to understand that, like them or not, we cannot simply dispense with these psychological processes, despite all the trouble they cause us. All of these processes serve important functions for us. Without the false consensus effect and our tendency to project our self-concept onto others, we would be in a great deal of uncertainty about what other people are like; it would be like living on a planet of mysterious and unpredictable aliens. Without naive realism, we would be plagued by doubts and would constantly second-guess our perceptions of the world. Without a positive sense of self-evaluation, it would be easy to feel useless, helpless, and generally miserable. Without the ability to attach ourselves to desired ingroups and distance ourselves from undesired outgroups it would be hard to feel a sense of belonging, which is indispensable to our well-being and healthy identity (Cacioppo et al., 2003; Myers & Diener, 1995; Tajfel & Turner, 1986). What we need to do then, is to learn to find a balance between our need to feel good about ourselves and our ingroups, and our more enlightened awareness of our fundamental equality with all people.

Module 13.2b Quiz:
The Self in the Social World

Know . . .

1. The tendency to see your ingroup as superior to outgroups is known as _____.
   A. fundamental attribution error
   B. outgroup bias
   C. minimal group bias
   D. ingroup bias

Apply . . .

2. Which of the following would be an example of the fundamental attribution error?
   A. Assuming that your low grade on a math exam is due to how busy you've been, whereas another student's low grade is due to him being a poor student
   B. Assuming that you crashed your car because you're a poor driver, whereas your brother's car crash was likely because of the icy roads
   C. Assuming that your excellent performance in a 10-km run is due to hard work and consistent training, and that the same explanation fits for all of the other fast runners
   D. Assuming that genetics can fundamentally explain all human behaviour

3. Jeanette loves reading—she reads at least one book each week despite having a busy work schedule. When she finds out that none of her coworkers enjoy reading novels, she is absolutely shocked, as she assumed everyone liked to read. Jeanette's beliefs are an example of _____.
   A. naive realism
   B. self-serving bias
   C. the false consensus effect
   D. thin slices

4. Donald, once poor, inherited $5 million and decided to donate $1000 to a local charity. Donald believes he took this step because he is a kind and generous man. Donald might be demonstrating _____.
   A. the fundamental attribution error
   B. hindsight bias
   C. self-serving bias
   D. concepts of cognitive dissonance

Stereotypes, Prejudice, and Discrimination

Obviously, the roots of prejudice are planted very deeply in our psyches, stemming ultimately from our deep-rooted attachment to our own selves and our automatic social categorization tendencies. Thus, while at the explicit level we may strive to be egalitarian and not discriminate based on dimensions such as race, class, and gender, our normally functioning implicit processes continually split the world into *Us* and *Them*. In fact, using ERP technology to measure brain activation, research has shown that the perceptual system starts to react differently to people based on race and gender within a mere 200 milliseconds

Myths in Mind

Are Only Negative Aspects of Stereotypes Problematic?

The first examples that come to mind when stereotyping a group are usually based on negative characteristics. However, it is certainly not the case that all stereotypic associations are negative; men and women are stereotypically associated with different strengths, for example.

What might be counterintuitive to many people is that even the positive aspects of a stereotype carry a kind of hidden danger, leading to a tendency for people to believe it is okay to emphasize the positive aspects of a stereotype in a "benevolent or well-intentioned way." This has been examined a great deal with regard to sexism. Researchers have distinguished between *hostile sexism*, or stereotypes that have negative views of one or both sexes, and *benevolent sexism*, which includes positive views of one or both sexes (Glick & Fiske, 1996, 2001). For example, consider the somewhat dated saying that women are "the fairer sex." A person using this phrase may mean it as a compliment, implying that women are virtuous, nurturing, and empathetic.

However, even stereotypes that a person may defend as being "well-intentioned" can place restrictions on an individual's behaviour. If we consider women to be "virtuous," they may be held to different sexual standards than men and, as a result, may be judged more harshly when they violate those standards. Similarly, considering women to be nurturing and empathetic reinforces the notion that women are the primary hubs of family life, and therefore less inclined toward career advancement in our competitive world. The belief in women's nurturance may feed the belief that their career is never the primary one in a two-gender household, and that when it comes time to raise a family, they will step back from their careers while the man will be the primary breadwinner, thus setting discriminatory practices in motion in the workplace and contributing to making women more dependent on men for financial security. Even when women go toe-to-toe with men in the workplace, they may be hindered in careers that call for assertive or aggressive behaviours (such as being successful in the business world) because the "fairer sex" stereotype is pervasive in the organization (Glick & Fiske, 1996, 2001). Thus, even seemingly positive aspects of a stereotype can result in negative, unforeseen consequences.

(Ito & Urland, 2003). When we try to change these implicit tendencies, we are battling our vast and speedy implicit system with our weak and ponderously slow explicit system. Much of the time, our explicit, consciously controlled self is going to lose, and we will fall prey to our implicit biases. These implicit biases lay the foundation for stereotyping, prejudice, and intergroup discrimination.

From a social-cognitive perspective, a **stereotype** *is a cognitive structure, a set of beliefs about the characteristics that are held by members of a specific social group; these beliefs function as schemas, serving to guide how we process information about our social world.* Based on stereotypic beliefs, **prejudice** *is an affective, emotionally laden response to members of outgroups, including holding negative attitudes and making critical judgments of other groups.* Stereotyping and prejudice lead to **discrimination**, *behaviour that disfavours or disadvantages members of a certain social group.* Taken together, stereotyping, prejudice, and discrimination underlie many of the destructive "isms" in society—racism, sexism, and classism, among others. One of the central goals of social-cognitive psychology has been to understand how these processes work.

PREJUDICE IN A POLITICALLY CORRECT WORLD   In recent decades, norms have changed greatly in terms of what is appropriate to say about other people. This increased sensitivity to social diversity and equality, such as society's greater acceptance of LGBTQ expressions of sexuality, or belief in gender and ethnic equality, is sometimes disparagingly referred to as "political correctness." The label carries the suggestion that the battles for equality are basically over, and now if people in disadvantaged groups raise concerns about how they are treated in our society, they are just looking for excuses, such as when people say someone is "playing the race card" as though they are using their ethnicity merely as a tool to try to take advantage of society. The truth is quite different. Outgroup stereotypes and prejudices are by no means a thing of the past, and neither are the discriminatory practices that go along with them. Just ask Muslims in the post-9/11 world how stigmatized they feel every time there is a "terrorist" attack somewhere in the world. Or, ask a young Black person whether they feel they are treated exactly the same as Whites by their teachers, or the police, or potential employers. Or, look at the outcry after a young girl in Steubenville, Ohio, was sexually assaulted while unconscious at a party and two prominent high school football players in the community were found criminally responsible; many people felt that *she* had ruined *their* lives, and not the other way around. Or, look at the disturbingly common and unabashed expression of negative views against Canada's Native people in the wake of the Idle No More protests of recent years. Clearly, the full story of stereotypes and prejudice plays out in the lives of millions of people who are placed into the category of "other" by one group or another.

In the United States, despite the victories of the civil rights movement in shifting the racial attitudes of the general North American population, there is still prejudice toward non-White cultural groups. For example, it still seems as though Black men in particular experience the legal system differently from others. Black men in the U.S. are incarcerated far more often than any other groups, and experience substantially more physical and aggressive treatment from police (Smith, 2004). Records of police encounters over the past 30 years confirm what many minority groups have long claimed—that the police use more aggressive techniques on minority suspects than White suspects (Inn, Wheeler, & Sparling, 1977; Smith, 2004; Weitzer & Tuch, 2004). This is not a new phenomenon; historically, Black suspects have also been five times more likely to die in police confrontations than White suspects (U.S. Department of Justice, 2001).

This prejudice has seeped into the basic social-psychological functioning of many people. For example, even though the general public denounces prejudice and discrimination and holds values of universal equality, studies of implicit processes tell a different story. When people (generally, White people) first are exposed to Black faces, this automatically influences a variety of physiological responses, including the activation of facial muscles, cardiovascular responses, and brain activity related to fear and negative emotions (Cunningham et al., 2004; Eberhardt, 2005).

In fact, measures of brain activity reveal the battle between implicit and explicit processes. Over very short amounts of time, exposure to White or Black faces activates implicit processes such as those described above, indicating a racially biased pattern of processing. However, over longer periods of time, such as 30 seconds, brain activity shifts, showing heightened activity in the prefrontal cortex. This area relates to the control of emotions and abstract thinking, consistent with a neurological effort to bring values into one's mind in order to control emotional reactions. This teaches us a powerful lesson: Even if people abhor prejudice at the explicit level of their awareness, they may *implicitly* hold negative stereotypes and experience prejudiced emotional reactions.

Clearly, there can be important discrepancies between stereotyping, prejudice, and discrimination at the explicit and implicit levels. This has created huge challenges for researchers attempting to study these processes, because of course simply asking subjects how they feel is only going to reveal their explicit processes, which rarely include overt racism and sexism. This has led to the invention of measurement techniques to try to reveal implicit processes.

Working the Scientific Literacy Model

Explicit versus Implicit Measures of Prejudice

If a great deal of modern prejudice has "gone underground" in the sense that people hide it and give politically correct responses at the explicit level, how can researchers accurately measure prejudice in today's society?

What do we know about measuring prejudice?

Psychologists have developed clever ways of measuring the forms of stereotyping and prejudice that are kept silent, either intentionally or because individuals are unaware of their own prejudices (Greenwald & Banaji, 1995; Nosek, 2007). In order to do so, researchers needed to come up with measurement devices that would reveal people's implicit processes. This is no easy challenge, because implicit processes can operate so quickly (in less than a second), and so subtly that we are typically not consciously aware of them.

How can science study implicit prejudice?

A major research breakthrough occurred in the 1990s with the invention of the **Implicit Associations Test (IAT;** Greenwald et al., 1998). The IAT *measures how fast people can respond to images or words flashed on a computer screen.* To complete the test, a person uses two fingers and two computer buttons, and responds to stimuli, as directed (see Figure 13.4). In round 1, subjects are supposed to press one button if they see a White face or a positive word (such as "peace"), and a different button if they see a Black face or a negative word (such as "war"). Thus, in this round, the buttons are associating stereotype-consistent stimuli. With these particular pairings, it takes people around 800 milliseconds (four-fifths of a second) to press the correct button.

Round 2 rearranges the associations. This time subjects press one button if they see a White face or a negative word, and a different button if they see a Black face or a positive word. Thus, in this round, the buttons are associating the stimuli in stereotype-inconsistent ways. In this situation, people take an average of 1015 milliseconds to press the correct button, more than one-fifth of a second longer than in round 1. (To control for any possible effects of going first vs. going second, the order in which a person goes through these tasks is usually counterbalanced across subjects, with some going in the order presented here, and others in the reverse order.)

Why does it take longer to respond when there is a Black/positive button than when there is a Black/negative button? The researchers reasoned that racial schemas associate more negativity with Blacks than with Whites. Because schemas guide information processing, they facilitate the processing of information that is schema-consistent; thus, it is easier for a person to make snap judgments to always press one button for either Black or negative stimuli. But schema-inconsistent information is more difficult to process; thus, having two different buttons for Black and for negative means that a person has to override their automatic, implicit association between Black and negative, in order to choose the correct response. The size of the reaction time discrepancy between these two rounds is

Figure 13.4 The IAT Procedure

To complete one condition in the IAT (a), participants must use one button to identify Black faces and negative words and another button to identify White faces and positive words. In the other condition (b), the positive and negative words are switched to be paired with the other race (Black/positive and White/negative). Average response times are faster when Black is paired with negative words and White is paired with positive words (c). Is this a sign of hidden prejudice?

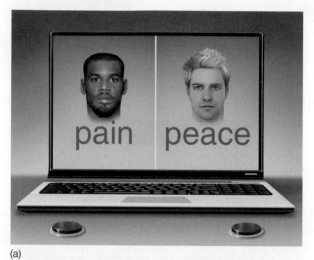

(a)

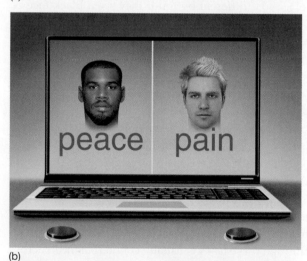

(b)

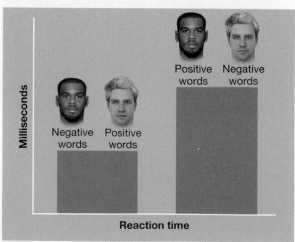

(c)

believed to be a direct measure of the strength of people's implicitly held negative beliefs or stereotypic associations with Blacks.

The IAT was a major breakthrough, suddenly allowing us to directly measure a person's implicit biases. Researchers quickly started to develop ways of measuring all sorts of implicit things—implicit attitudes, self-esteem, feelings of connection to nature, and prejudice towards many different groups.

Can we critically evaluate this evidence?

Although the data gathered with this instrument show reliable results, some psychologists have questioned the test's validity: Is the IAT really a measure of prejudice? Or is it possible that the IAT is merely measuring the extent to which people have been exposed to negative stereotypes, but have not necessarily developed prejudices? After all, simply knowing about a stereotype does not mean an individual believes it, uses it to judge people, or engages in discriminatory behaviour.

Studies by Elizabeth Phelps and her colleagues (2000) suggest that the IAT reflects a person's emotional reactions to outgroup members. In her studies, White participants were shown pictures of Black and White faces while having their brains scanned using fMRI. The amount of activity detected in the amygdala (a brain area related to fear responses) when looking at Black faces was positively correlated with participants' IAT measures of implicit prejudice (see Figure 13.5). This suggests that the IAT is measuring something real enough to be reflected in neural activity in areas related to fear and emotional processing.

Why is this relevant?

The development of the IAT has fostered a great deal of research and has been applied to at least a dozen forms of stereotyping, including stereotypes of social classes (Rudman et al., 2002), sexual orientation (Banse et al., 2001), and even fraternity and sorority members (Wells & Corts, 2008). The results of all these tests illustrate that implicit prejudice seems to be more prevalent than people are willing to express in explicit tests (Nosek et al., 2002). The IAT is also being applied to clinical settings. For example, one research group developed an IAT that measures attitudes about alcohol use. This instrument can successfully predict how much alcohol someone is likely to consume, even when explicit measures fail to do so (Ostafin et al., 2008). To the extent that this methodology is valid, it is extremely valuable, giving us a window into people's private minds.

Figure 13.5 Implicit Associations and the Brain

Researchers displayed photographs of Black and White faces. In White participants, Black faces elicited more activity than White faces in the amygdala, an emotion centre of the brain. This activity was positively correlated with participants' responses on the IAT.

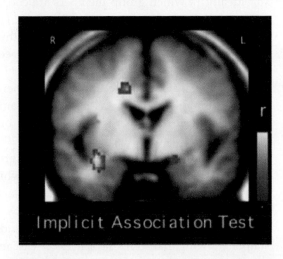

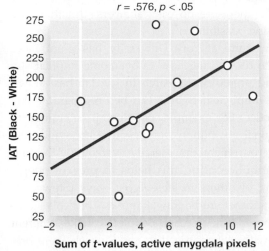

Source: Elizabeth A. Phelps, Kevin J. O'Connor, William A. Cunningham, E. Sumie Funayama, J. Christopher Gatenby, John C. Gore and Mahzarin R. Banaji, 'Performance on Indirect Measures of Race Evaluation Predicts Amygdala Activation', *Journal of Cognitive Neuroscience*, 12:5 (September, 2000), pp. 729-738. © 2000 by the Massachusetts Institute of Technology.

PSYCH@

The Law Enforcement Academy

Imagine that instead of linking positive or negative terms with Black faces in the IAT, you were asked to make a snap decision whether or not to shoot a potential criminal. A number of researchers have used video-game-like tasks to put participants in these situations. In these video simulations, a figure will suddenly appear, either holding a weapon or a non-weapon (e.g., a wallet or a cell phone). It turns out that when making these split-second decisions, people are a little bit slower to decide whether or not to shoot a Black man holding a non-weapon, and they make the wrong decision more often. When a Black man is holding a gun, however, they make the "shoot" decision more quickly than if the gun is held by a White man (Correll et al., 2007; Correll et al., 2006). The logic is similar to the IAT discussed above. Because Black and "gun" are stereotypically consistent with each other, people have an easier time processing these stimuli together than when Black and "wallet" are paired with each other. Just like the situation in the Amadou Diallo case then, people are more likely to mistakenly shoot a Black man holding a wallet, believing that he might be holding a gun; at least, they're more likely to do this in a video game.

Certainly a video game pales in comparison to the adrenaline-fuelled confrontation that occurred that fateful night in the Bronx. It is easy to imagine that the stress of a real confrontation, combined with the complexity of a real-world situation, would lead to an even higher chance of a mistaken shooting occurring (Saus et al., 2006). To combat any implicit influence of race on an officer's decision to shoot, most law enforcement agencies in North America have developed extensive training programs, part of which focuses on making shoot–don't-shoot decisions (Cordner & Shain, 2011). Programs may simulate a variety of firearms combat situations using a combination of walk-through sets with cardboard figures, and realistic mock-combat against other people armed with foam pellet guns. Research suggests that this training is helpful; even student volunteers in the lab can be trained to reduce shooting errors through such means (Correll et al., 2007; Plant & Peruche, 2005).

ZUMA Press/Newscom

The split-second differences in the IAT may be related to officers' increased use of deadly force with Black suspects, including cases where the suspect is unarmed. Here, a police officer undergoes virtual reality training designed to reduce shooting errors.

IMPROVING INTERGROUP RELATIONS We are left with an immense practical challenge: How can we overcome the implicit processes we have examined in this module and work toward eliminating harmful stereotypes, prejudices, and discrimination from our society? Unfortunately, there are no easy answers. But there are some promising possibilities.

Keri Kawakami at York University has spent more than a decade researching how to overcome implicit stereotyping and prejudice. Research in her lab has shown that people's implicit networks can be "reprogrammed" through practice. For example, people can be trained to make situational attributions for negative behaviours by stereotyped group members, thereby overcoming the fundamental attribution error; this helps to prevent people from thinking of others in stereotypic ways (Stewart et al., 2010). In another study, Kawakami and her colleagues used a computer task to teach people to make different associations with a stereotyped group. Subjects were presented with photographs of Blacks and Whites, coupled with either stereotypic or non-stereotypic traits, and were instructed to respond "NO" to stereotypic pairings, and "YES" to non-stereotypic pairings. After extensive training involving many such trials, subjects no longer activated negative racial stereotypes, even at the implicit level (Kawakami et al., 2000). This suggests that, over time, as our society continues to evolve in an increasingly egalitarian, non-prejudiced direction, it may be possible for people to *un*learn the stereotypes that history has provided us with. However, there is a huge gap between the kind of intensive training that Kawakami's participants experienced in the lab and the real-world experience of individuals who are bombarded with both stereotypic and non-stereotypic messages on a daily basis. Nevertheless, these results suggest that it is at least possible for people to "reprogram" themselves.

One of the most well-supported ideas in all of social psychology is the **contact hypothesis**, *which predicts that social contact between members of different groups is extremely important to overcoming prejudice* (Allport, 1954; Pettigrew & Tropp, 2006), especially if that contact occurs in settings in which the groups have equal status and power, and ideally, in which group members are cooperating on tasks or pursuing common goals (Sherif, 1961). Negative stereotypes and the attendant prejudices thrive under conditions of ignorance, whereas allowing people to get to know members of outgroups, to work together to pursue common goals, to come to appreciate their membership in common groups or as part of the same ingroup (e.g., we're both Blue Jays fans, Canadians, or members of the human species; Gaertner & Dovidio, 2000), and to develop friendships with members of outgroups (Pettigrew, 1997, 1998) are all different ways in which contact helps to overcome prejudice. In fact, contact between members of different groups not only helps to combat their own prejudices, but that of their friends as well; simply knowing that someone is friends with an outgroup member serves to decrease the prejudice of that person's friends (Wright et al., 1997).

Coming to see our fellow human beings as all part of the same human family is an opportunity that recent advances in technology (the Internet, space exploration), economics (globalization), and ironically, global problems (climate change, nuclear proliferation) have made available to all of us. This global perspective shift may, one hopes, help us to overcome our age-old group prejudices. Astronauts who travel into space and look back on this one little planet that we inhabit often report that the experience profoundly affects them.

> "The first day or so we all pointed to our countries. The third or fourth day we were pointing to our continents. By the fifth day, we were aware of only one Earth."
> —I Congress of the Association of Space Explorers Cernay, France October 2-6, 1985. Quote of Sultan bin Salman Al-Saud, © 1985 Association of Space Explorers. Used by permission.

Module 13.2c Quiz:
Stereotypes, Prejudice, and Discrimination

Know . . .

1. _____ prejudice refers to situations in which a person stereotypes a group of people based on hidden, unacknowledged feelings.
   - **A.** Explicit
   - **B.** Discriminative
   - **C.** Associative
   - **D.** Implicit

Understand . . .

2. Unconscious forms of prejudice are believed to be measured with the implicit associations test. This test is based on
   - **A.** people creating lists of words that come to mind when they see a person of a specific race.
   - **B.** how long it takes people to respond to positive or negative words along with Black or White faces.
   - **C.** changes in heart rate that accompany photos of people from different racial backgrounds.
   - **D.** increased activity in the emotional centres of the brain that are associated with specific races.

Apply . . .

3. Jacques believed that everyone from Alberta was a racist "redneck." He was therefore quite nervous when he found out that he'd have to work with two Albertans who were visiting from his company's Edmonton office. After spending some time with the two men, however, he realized that his views about Albertans were incorrect. This is an example of _____.

A. the Notley effect

B. conformity

C. the contact hypothesis

D. pluralistic ignorance

Analyze . . .

4. Which of the following statements about stereotypes and prejudice is *false*?

A. Stereotypes can be expressed outwardly and very explicitly.

B. All stereotypes are of negative characteristics.

C. Stereotypes are often experienced implicitly.

D. Prejudice has become increasingly unpopular in both Canada and the United States.

Module 13.2 Summary

13.2a   Know . . . the key terminology associated with social cognition.

contact hypothesis
discrimination
dual-process models
explicit processes
external (situational) attribution
false consensus effect
fundamental attribution error (FAE)
Implicit Associations Test (IAT)
implicit processes
ingroup bias
ingroups
internal (dispositional) attribution
naive realism
outgroups
person perception
prejudice
self-fulfilling prophecy
self-serving bias
stereotype
thin slices of behaviour

13.2b   Understand . . . how we form first impressions and how these impressions influence us.

We quickly form impressions, even when only thin slices of behaviour are available to us. These impressions can be surprisingly accurate, but they can also affect our behaviour in ways that tend to confirm our initial impressions; this is the phenomenon of self-fulfilling prophecies.

13.2c   Apply . . . your understanding of social cognition to the problem of overcoming prejudice and discrimination.

The key to overcoming prejudice and discrimination seems to be to help people create different schemas in their mind for members of outgroups. This can be done by retraining people to make different automatic associations with outgroup members, such as training them to consciously reject pairing of the outgroup with negative or stereotyped traits. Different schemas can also be created through realizing a common identity between oneself and the other person, which can occur from extended contact, cooperation on mutual goals, or adopting more inclusive and abstract categories (e.g., human family) for thinking about people.

13.2d   Analyze . . . whether people who commit discriminatory acts are necessarily prejudiced.

It is certainly possible for people to commit discriminatory acts without being prejudiced. Regardless of prejudice, stereotypes are absorbed from the larger culture, and these can function as interpersonal schemas that can guide how we see things and how we implicitly process information. This can cause us to behave in a discriminatory fashion without us intending to, such as being more likely to assume an ambiguous object is a gun if held by a Black man, compared to when it is held by a White man.

Module 13.3 Attitudes, Behaviour, and Effective Communication

ZUMA Press, Inc./Alamy Stock Photo

 ## Learning Objectives

13.3a Know . . . the key terminology in research on attitudes, behaviour, and effective communication.

13.3b Understand . . . how behaviours influence attitudes in terms of cognitive dissonance theory.

13.3c Apply . . . your understanding of the central route to describe how a message should be designed.

13.3d Analyze . . . the difficulties communicators face in trying to convince the public to take action on climate change.

Bill McKibben is a man on a mission. He wants to save the planet. Actually, to be more accurate, he wants to save the kind of planet that humans can live on. But unlike many people with such ambitious dreams, Bill has a few very important factors on his side.

First, he knows what he is talking about when it comes to saving the planet, having published many books and articles on the topic over the past few decades. Second, he has the full weight of the scientific community behind his cause, which agrees that the human species is heading rapidly for catastrophe as we push global warming higher and higher. And third, he has a global organization, 350.org, spanning almost every country on Earth, with hundreds of thousands of members. He also has some significant victories under his belt, from organizing the most widespread days of political activism in history to raising unprecedented opposition to key government decisions, such as whether or not to pass the Keystone XL pipeline that would take oil from Alberta's oilsands and transport it across the United States.

For Bill McKibben, and for the human species more generally, to succeed in the fight against climate change, there are some big barriers to overcome. Psychology provides a great

deal of insight into how to rise to such a societal challenge. Any social problem is, at some level, a problem of human behaviour, and finding solutions therefore inevitably involves changing human behaviour.

Focus Questions

1. What is the relationship between attitudes and behaviour?

2. How should communications be structured so as to be as persuasive as possible?

 According to the American Psychological Association's official task force on climate change, "Addressing climate change is arguably one of the most pressing tasks facing this planet and its inhabitants" (American Psychological Association, 2010, p. 6). The task force was comprised of a carefully chosen group of highly regarded senior scientists, including the University of Victoria's Robert Gifford. Their overall assessment agrees with the perspective of the

United Nations, whose Secretary General Ban Ki-Moon said in 2009 that climate change was the greatest issue of the 21st century. Using the insights of psychology to find solutions to climate change is increasingly becoming a focus for applied psychologists who specialize in communication and behaviour change. Although this module will use climate change as a running example, the principles being discussed can apply to almost any social issue that affects our society. Hopefully this module will help motivate you to change our world for the better.

Changing People's Behaviour

Four of the most common approaches taken to attempt to change the public's behaviour on a large scale are technological, legal, economic, and social. The technological approach focuses on making desired behaviours easier and undesired behaviours more difficult; for example, public transit systems make it easier to get to work without driving; having alternative energy technologies (like solar panels) widely available make it easier for people to reduce their carbon footprint; having a public recycling system with separate bins makes it easier for people to recycle, and so on. The idea is to get the technology right so that people will behave in the desired way. The legal approach focuses on policy change, using laws to encourage positive behaviours and discourage negative behaviours. The economic approach focuses on financial incentives and penalties, generally through taxes and pricing. Generally, if the "right" thing to do is cheaper, and the "wrong" thing to do is more expensive, people will choose the "right" behaviour. The social approach focuses on using information and communication to raise awareness, educate people, and create positive community organizations to encourage the desired behaviours.

Although each of these approaches obviously can have an impact on public behaviour, each one by itself is insufficient for solving or adapting to major global problems like climate change. The biggest problem with the technological, legal, and economic perspectives (aside from the problem that they can't, realistically, be applied to every behaviour that is relevant to climate change) is that developing and implementing the technological solutions, or passing the laws and setting the price incentives that would be required to sufficiently change behaviour, can only happen if the public at large will support such changes. Any politician who tries to, for example, increase gas taxes in order to encourage the shift to a sustainable energy economy is going to have to overcome some stiff public resistance. Clearly, finding solutions to our environmental challenges requires that the public supports the solutions.

Inevitably, as you consider how to achieve the technological, legal, or economic changes that might change public behaviour, you often end up at the problem of how to get the support of the general public. This takes us to the fourth approach: social. There are a vast number of social mechanisms for changing human behaviour; however, for the purpose of illustrating the application of social psychology to problems like climate change, we focus on one of the most commonly employed social tactics: raising awareness.

The basic assumption behind the raising awareness approach is that people will generally do the right thing if they have the right information. People's behaviours reflect their attitudes and beliefs (what they think is important, right vs. wrong, etc.), which in turn, reflect the information that they have available. So to change behaviour, you have to give people information that will help change their beliefs and attitudes. Therein lies the logic behind public service announcements, pamphlets, billboards, education campaigns, and the vast majority of the behaviour change attempts occurring in society (McKenzie-Mohr, 2000). Learning how to communicate effectively in order to influence attitudes and behaviour has been a major focus of psychology for most of its history, and we have learned a great deal about how to do so.

PERSUASION: CHANGING ATTITUDES THROUGH COMMUNICATION Social psychologists have discovered many important principles underlying effective communication, giving us a set of tools for influencing all sorts of behaviours, from wearing condoms to eating chocolate bars. These tools are employed for a wide variety of behaviour change purposes, from standard marketing goals like getting us to buy more stuff, to pro-social causes such as getting us to donate blood or to volunteer for a charitable organization.

If you are preparing a persuasive message, understanding what is likely to connect with and have an impact on your audience is extremely important. These factors are explored by the **elaboration likelihood model (ELM)** of persuasive communication. The ELM predicts that *when audiences are sufficiently motivated to pay attention to a message (i.e., they care about the issue) and they have the opportunity for careful processing (i.e., they have the cognitive resources available to understand the message), they will be persuaded by the facts of the argument, the substance; when either of these two factors (motivation and opportunity) are missing, people will tend to be persuaded by other factors.* According to this model of persuasion, information can appeal to people through two general routes: *the central route* and *the peripheral route* (Cacioppo et al., 1986).

The **central route to persuasion** is all about substance. It *occurs when people pay close attention to the content of a message, evaluate the evidence presented, and examine the logic of the arguments.* If the message is sufficiently compelling, they will be convinced, internalizing the message as something they believe in (see Figure 13.6). As a result, attitude or belief change that occurs through the central route tends to be strong and long-lasting.

Figure 13.6 Central and Peripheral Routes to Persuasion

There are two ways that communications can persuade people. In the central route people are persuaded by the content of a message, while in the peripheral route they are influenced by the way the content is presented, the *style* over the *substance*.

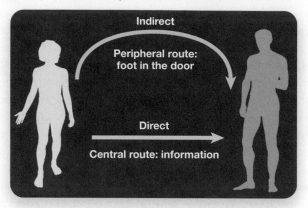

However, much of the time, people are not going to pay sufficient attention to the content of a message, and instead, *persuasion will depend upon other features that are not directly related to the message itself,* such as the attractiveness of the person delivering the information, or the number of arguments made (regardless of the quality of those arguments). When taking the **peripheral route to persuasion** it's all about style, not substance. Although persuasion is typically not as powerful through the peripheral route, it is nevertheless often a superior route through which to reach people, in part because it's so much easier. Even though people may not be paying much attention or may not really care about your issue, they can be persuaded if you can skillfully wield peripheral tools. Peripheral tools are quite dangerous, as a result, because they can make even relatively weak arguments potentially have an impact on people, whereas relatively strong and important arguments, if they are packaged in a more boring, less peripherally appealing way, can be overlooked. Anyone who has spent time on the Internet has encountered some form of propaganda, advertising, or scam that puts information together in a way that sounds extremely appealing, even if it is based on no actual truth at all. But peripheral tools are powerful enough that even the most unlikely of theories or perspectives can gain traction in society if it's packaged the right way.

Module 13.3a Quiz:

Changing People's Behaviour

Understand . . .

1. Which of the following is *not* a common approach used to change the public's behaviour?
   A. technological
   B. social
   C. economic
   D. conformity

Apply . . .

2. Which of the following is an example of using the central route to persuasion?
   A. An organization having a visually interesting webpage.
   B. An organization providing factually correct scientific data.
   C. An organization using a funny and attractive spokesperson.
   D. An organization having a cool theme song as part of their commercials.

3. Ahmed's grandparents immigrated to Canada from Egypt in the 1970s. He wants to raise awareness about the positive effects immigration can have on a society. To do so, he prints out a list of the benefits of immigration and puts copies in people's mailboxes. How successful will Ahmed's attempts at persuasion be—and why?
   A. Ahmed will have great success because he used the peripheral route to persuasion successfully.
   B. Ahmed will be successful because he is using both the central and peripheral routes to persuasion.
   C. Ahmed will not be successful because although he used the central route to persuasion well, he did a poor job using the peripheral route.
   D. Ahmed will not be successful because he used both the central and peripheral routes to persuasion poorly.

Using the Central Route Effectively

In order to use the central route effectively, you need to be confident that you have the facts on your side. If you feel your perspective makes logical, rational sense, then it makes sense to appeal to the central route. This means getting your audience to pay close attention to your arguments. In order to do that, you have two key factors to work with: motivation and opportunity. People will be more likely to process information through the central route when they are highly motivated and when they have the knowledge or expertise to understand the information. Thus, the central route is most reliable when people are highly motivated about the topic, when they have sufficient time and freedom from distraction, and when the information is not overwhelmingly complex relative to their knowledge (i.e., if the audience is not very knowledgeable, the information has to be simple, but if the audience has more expertise, then obviously the information can be more nuanced and complex). With these factors in mind, this section of the module will examine some key strategies for maximizing the central route.

MAKE IT PERSONAL   Imagine for a moment that your friend has some juicy, scandalous gossip to tell you. There would be a big difference in your desire to hear it if it were about (1) one of her friends whom you do not know; (2) one of your friends; (3) you! Clearly, your desire to get this information is directly related to how personally relevant it is. Making a message self-relevant is crucially important to motivating people to care and pay attention.

It can be surprisingly easy to make information self-relevant. The simple perspective-shift of going from a third-person to a first-person type of description makes a huge difference in how personally relevant something feels. For a moment, look back to the previous paragraph. In that paragraph, our opening sentence could have been, "Making a message self-relevant is very important, blah blah. . . ." Instead, we said "Imagine for a moment that your friend has some juicy, scandalous gossip . . ." Even subtle nuances, such as appealing to "you," the reader, can make a message more personally engaging.

Consider one striking study from the early 1980s (Gregory et al., 1982), a time when cable television (CATV) was still making its way into the North American viewing market. Researchers compared two very similar persuasive appeals, which were presented to two samples of homeowners to try to convince them to subscribe to CATV.

> In the information-only condition, homeowners were presented with this appeal: *CATV will provide a broader entertainment and information service to its subscribers. Used properly, a person can plan in advance to enjoy events offered. Instead of spending money on the babysitter and gas, and putting up with the hassles of going out, more time can be spent at home with family, alone, or with friends.*
>
> In the imagination condition, homeowners received this appeal: *Take a moment and imagine how CATV will provide you with a broader entertainment and information service. When you use it properly, you will be able to plan in advance which of the events offered you wish to enjoy. Take a moment and think of how, instead of spending money on the babysitter and gas, and then having to put up with the hassles of going out, you will be able to spend your time at home, with your family, alone, or with your friends.*

As you can see, the two appeals are almost identical, providing the exact same arguments; from a purely logical perspective, they should have exactly the same impact. However, their impact differed dramatically: Only 19.5% of the people who received the information-only appeal signed up for CATV, whereas a whopping 47% subscribed

when they were simply told to imagine themselves in the scenario! Imagine the profit difference between selling your product to 1 in 5 people or 1 in 2 people. This is the power of making things personal.

This power has been explained by **construal-level theory** (Trope & Liberman, 2010), *which describes how information affects us differently depending on our psychological distance from the information*. Information that is specific, personal, and described in terms of concrete details feels more personal, or closer to us; whereas information that is more general, impersonal, and described in more abstract terms feels less personal, or more distant. Importantly, psychological distance depends not only on geography (people or places that are farther away are less personal), but temporal factors (distant future or past times feel less personal), social factors (people or groups that are further removed from one's identity are less personal), how abstract the information is (abstractions are less personal than things that are specific), and even the level of certainty one feels about an outcome (outcomes that are less certain are less personal).

Communicators should be able to make their messages feel more personally relevant to the audience by working with these factors, bringing the message close to home in time and space, showing how it affects the audience themselves or their social groups, and making consequences or outcomes as certain as possible.

Climate change communicators, unfortunately, have struggled with this. As a result, their communications have often felt "distant" to many people. If the goal is to create psychological closeness and relevance, climate change communications typically involve exactly the wrong types of information. The term "climate change" itself implies something global and abstract; when people do think of specific others who may suffer due to climate change, they tend to think of others in the distant future or in distant parts of the world (Leiserowitz et al., 2010; Lorenzoni & Pidgeon, 2006). Also, scientists have been honest about communicating the inherent uncertainty of scientific predictions, leading people to emphasize the uncertainty in the science. And finally, communicating about "the climate" inherently involves abstractions, because the climate is an abstraction, as is "global temperature," "rates of greenhouse gas emissions," and much of the important information that climate scientists are trying to communicate. As a result, people often experience climate change as psychologically distant, rather than personally relevant (Liberman & Trope, 2008; Milfont, 2010). Bringing the consequences of climate change home for a given audience, bringing them close in time and space, and changing the focus of the discussion to the certainty of what scientists do know rather than the uncertainty of what they don't, should make the message much more powerful (Spence et al., 2012).

Working the Scientific Literacy Model

The Identifiable Victim Effect

An additional challenge for people worried about climate change is that it is difficult to show *how* people will be affected by this issue. Issues seem less real when there is no story to accompany them. Contrast climate change with some other very important social issues facing people in North America. The issue of gun control in the United States is influenced by stories such as the horrendous shooting death of 20 children and six adults in Sandy Hook Elementary School in 2012. The crisis facing refugees fleeing war-torn Syria gained international attention when heartbreaking photographs showed the body of three-year-old Alan Kurdi. Racial tensions in the United States, which led to the Black Lives Matter movement, are all-too-often linked with violence, such as the police killing of Michael Brown in Ferguson, Missouri in 2014. These are all upsetting social issues filled with real human tragedy.

Although it is by no means a competition, approximately 400 000 people die every year due to climate-change–related disasters (DARA, 2012). And this is just at the very beginning of the climate changes that scientists have been warning us about! Researchers at Stanford University concluded that human civilization itself is headed rapidly toward global collapse due to an escalating mix of environmental problems such as climate change and the acidification of the oceans (Ehrlich & Ehrlich, 2013); this collapse will likely occur in the next few generations, possibly affecting *your* children and grandchildren. Given this terrifying possibility, why have climate scientists (and environmental psychologists) been so unsuccessful in persuading people to change their behaviour? The answer might lie in how they tell their story.

What do we know about communicating about tragedy?

Many experiments have shown that information about tragedies has much more impact if it focuses on specific details and concrete events than if it relies upon more abstract, statistical information. For example, the **identifiable victim effect** *describes how people are more powerfully moved to action by the story of a single suffering person than by information about a whole group of people.*

In one study (Small et al., 2007), researchers gave subjects a chance to donate up to $5 of their earnings from participating in the study to an organization, Save the Children, based on information provided in one of three different conditions. In the *identifiable victim condition*, participants read about Rokia, a 7-year-old girl from Mali, Africa, who was desperately poor and facing severe hunger and possibly starvation. In the *statistical victims*

Figure 13.7 The Identifiable Victim Effect

Participants were willing to donate more money after reading about a specific victim of starvation than they were after reading statistics about widespread starvation. Surprisingly, combining the story of a specific victim *and* general statistics led to levels of donations similar to the statistics-only condition.

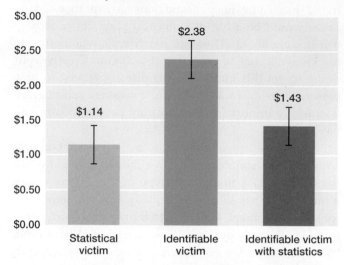

Source: Republished with permission of Elsevier Science, Inc., from Sympathy and callousness: The impact of deliberative thought on donations to identifiable and statistical victims, *Organizational Behavior and Human Decision Processes*, 102, 143–153. Fig 3, p.149. Deborah A. Small, George Loewenstein and Paul Slovic. March 2007. Permission conveyed through Copyright Clearance Center, Inc.

condition, participants read about food shortages and rainfall deficits affecting more than 20 million people in four countries in Africa. In the third, *combined condition*, both types of information were provided; participants read about Rokia and then were also given statistical information about mass suffering in African countries.

The identifiable victim effect was clearly demonstrated; people who read about Rokia gave significantly more ($2.38) than people who read general statistical information ($1.14). Clearly, Rokia tugs on the heart-strings more than abstract numbers do (see Figure 13.7). It is worth pointing out how strictly illogical this is; if we were rational processors of information, we would respond more strongly to statistics, which is essentially many, many Rokia-like stories combined with each other, than to one single story of Rokia which is, after all, "just an anecdote."

One interesting twist in this study was that participants who were given information about Rokia combined with the statistics donated only $1.43, which was statistically no different than what participants gave after being presented with the statistics alone, and was certainly much less than participants gave after only hearing Rokia's story. This study suggests that trying to simultaneously appeal to the head *and* the heart might not always work! This has enormous implications for anyone who wants to communicate to others; you have to very carefully consider the balance of your factual information and technical details with your stories, jokes, images and metaphors. Clearly, it's not as simple as "have solid facts and tell a good story," because sometimes, combining the two approaches doesn't work.

How can science explain the identifiable victim effect?

Earlier in the module, we mentioned that abstract information is experienced as more *psychologically distant* than concrete, specific information. But this doesn't go far enough to help us understand the findings in this Rokia study. There are two key results to explain. First, why is Rokia's individual story more impactful than millions of Rokia stories presented in the form of statistical information? Second, why does combining Rokia's story with statistics actually make it *less* likely for people to act?

To understand these findings, psychologists rely upon dual-process models (see Module 13.2) of information processing (Stanovich & West, 2000). The **experiential system** (Epstein, 1994), *operates more implicitly, quickly, and intuitively and is predominantly emotional*; this system responds strongly to personal experiences, images, stories, and other people's emotions. In contrast, the **analytic system** *operates more at the explicit level of consciousness, is slower and more methodical, and uses logic and discursive thinking (i.e., reasoning using language) to try to understand reality*. The analytic system specializes in *understanding*, whereas the experiential system specializes in *intuition and feeling*. With these systems in mind, you can begin to see why Rokia's story would be so powerful; Rokia's story speaks to the experiential system, thereby triggering emotional responses, such as empathy, that would motivate people to give to charity. The abstract statistics, however, speak to the analytic system, the head rather than the heart. Less emotional impact leads to less motivational strength (Barrett & Salovey, 2002; Forgas, 2000). Without emotions, information about the suffering of millions of people becomes "just a number," an abstraction that is difficult to *feel*.

Although one might expect that the most effective approach would simply be to appeal to both systems, it seems that in some situations at least, involving the analytic system at all can backfire. It is as though the analytic system inhibits or shuts down the experiential system, putting people in more of a cold, analytic frame of mind, so that they have little access to their emotional responses. This may be why the condition that included both Rokia and the statistics was no more motivating than the statistics alone. The cold, analytic way of thinking that was activated by the statistics made Rokia's emotional story have less impact than it had on its own (Loewenstein et al., 2001; Slovic et al., 2002). Nobel prize–winning biochemist Albert Szent Gyorgi sums this idea up nicely when he talks about the difficulties trying to wrap your head around the consequences of nuclear war. "I am deeply moved if I see one man suffering and would risk my life for him. Then I talk impersonally about the possible pulverization of our big cities, with a hundred million dead. I am unable to multiply one man's suffering by a hundred million" (Slovic, 2007).

Can we critically evaluate this evidence?

Taken by itself, this single study cannot tell us whether individual stories are more motivating than statistics; it merely tells us that *this* particular story is more motivating than *these* particular statistics. Specific stories and specific statistics will have different impacts in specific situations with specific people. Obviously, every particular convergence of circumstances is different. Sometimes, a certain story will be particularly powerful; other times a certain statistic will be. Importantly, we don't know how the impact of statistical information vs. emotional stories changes over the long term or with repeated exposure. You have surely encountered news stories before that have made you feel very strong emotions in the moment, but within even a few days you largely forgot about them, and you never actually made a contribution to the cause or took any sort of action. This happens all the time. Things "go viral" and then, not too long afterwards, everybody gets over it and moves on to something else.

Obviously, we cannot dispense with talking about statistical, abstract information if we are to communicate with each other about what is happening in the world. It therefore becomes extremely important to understand how the experiential and analytic systems can work together, and how to make the best use of them in crafting effective communication strategies.

Why is this relevant?

This research is highly relevant to the challenge of motivating people to take action on major societal issues such as climate change (e.g., Slovic, 2007). The basic principle for communicating in a way that motivates behaviour change is to personally engage the person to reduce the psychological distance of the information. There are many ways to do this, including framing information in a personal way (see the TEDxUofT talk, "Everything You Love"), describing abstract information as personal experiences, focusing on the near future rather than the distant future, emphasizing specific actions that will make a difference, and using social media strategies so that information comes from friends rather than from strangers.

Nevertheless, despite all the tools that we have to communicate and influence behaviour more effectively, countless questions remain concerning how to make the best use of these tools. These questions will have to be answered over and over again, as we seek (and hopefully find!) solutions to the challenges we face, from our personal lives to issues of global scale like climate change. One of the biggest challenges that must be overcome when communicating about any issue is to understand how to connect the issue to the *values* of the people receiving the message.

VALUE APPEALS   As any good marketer knows, audiences are much more likely to listen to a message that is framed in such a way that it seems relevant to their values. Interestingly, pro-environmental behaviours have often been framed in ways that go *against* people's self-interest, involving trade-offs between the economy *or* the environment, jobs *or* trees, comfort and convenience *or* personal sacrifice (Schultz & Zelezny, 2003). And as noble as it might be to sit in the dark, shivering through the winter and eating only locally grown root vegetables while having two-minute showers once a week, these are unlikely to be the next hot behaviour trends.

Researchers have uncovered three major value frames that are relevant in environmental discussions. *Biospheric* values emphasize the perspectives and value of other species, ecosystems, and nature itself (e.g., save the polar bears, save the rainforests, save the Earth!). *Social-altruistic* values emphasize the perspectives and consequences experienced by other people (e.g., climate change will substantially affect the poor, and will take away the rights and freedoms of future generations; Stern & Dietz, 1994). However, a major problem that environmentally concerned people run into is that biospheric and social-altruistic value frames are often not compatible with our *egoistic* values, which focus on self-enhancement, personal success, material wealth, and independence (Schultz & Zelezny, 2003; Schwartz, 1994). Unfortunately, because modern capitalism has so deeply wed material success with personal success and "happiness," people often find that our individualistic strivings for success and happiness are often at odds with our concern for collective issues like the environment.

It's possible that environmental messages would be more motivating if they were framed in egoistic terms. For example, messages concerning pro-environmental behaviours could emphasize financial savings (e.g., saving energy = saving money), personal empowerment (e.g., feel like you're making a difference!), the importance of community (e.g. gardening will bring your community together), economic opportunities (e.g., renewable energy is the fastest-growing sector of the energy economy), and even fun and friendship (e.g., attending environmental protests is actually really fun—you meet the coolest people).

From a strategic point of view, appealing to your audience's values generally enhances the impact of messages; however, as we'll discuss at the end of this module, appealing to your audience's existing values may, in some cases, be detrimental to your cause.

PREACHING OR FLIP-FLOPPING? ONE-SIDED VS. TWO-SIDED MESSAGES   One potential downside to taking a straightforward values approach is that you might sound "preachy." People may feel like you are shoving your values onto them, and therefore reject your arguments. On the other hand, if you don't make your own position clear and advocate clearly for your values, people may think you are a "flip flopper" who doesn't stand for anything in particular, or they may just get confused while you describe all aspects of an argument, and stop paying attention.

In short, is it better to give a one-sided message, arguing for a specific position, or a two-sided appeal that acknowledges different perspectives? You might think that the one-sided message is strongest, because it's least likely to raise doubts in the audience's mind, but research suggests otherwise (O'Keefe, 1999). It is actually more persuasive if you acknowledge opposing arguments than if you just preach from your own soap-box, unless your audience is unlikely to ever hear information that counters your message.

By giving a two-sided message, you make it more likely that your audience will see you as trustworthy and honest. But you gain in another, sneakier way as well. By bringing up, and shooting down, opposing arguments, you help your audience resist those arguments in the future. This is called **attitude inoculation**, *a strategy for strengthening attitudes and making them more resistant to change by first exposing people to a weak counter-argument and then refuting that argument* (Compton & Pfau, 2005; McGuire, 1961). This strategy operates in a similar way to how the flu shot protects you from the flu. When you get injected with a weakened version of the flu virus, your immune system has a chance to respond, building up the antibodies it will need when the real flu comes along. So, by exposing your audience to counter-arguments and then showing why those counter-arguments are not correct, you give your audience the necessary information they will need to resist those counter-arguments when they hear them later.

EMOTIONS IN THE CENTRAL ROUTE   Taking the central route has been the chief strategy of climate change communicators, and unfortunately, they've had a pretty tough go of it. The well-funded "climate change denial" movement has been able to spread enough misinformation through the media that many people have been left confused about what to believe. Negative emotions such as confusion are much more damaging than you might expect, influencing people to process information in a different way. Even very subtle manipulations of confusion can have this effect.

For example, research by Norbert Schwarz and his colleagues has shown that even the font or the colour of the text used in a message can change how skeptical people are of the information. If the font is a little bit more difficult to read (e.g., **font like this**, compared to *font like this*), or if the text doesn't contrast as starkly from the background and thus is also more difficult to read, people tend to be more skeptical of the message (Winkielman et al., 2002).

What seems to happen is that the person experiences a subtle amount of negative emotion, which biases their information processing in a negative manner. As a result, they pay more attention to weaknesses in the information and claims that they disagree with, the net result being that they are less easily persuaded. Schwarz explains that **processing fluency**, *which is the ease with which information is processed*, biases the person's processing of the information; thus, even insignificant aspects of a communication can, through triggering negative affect, influence the communication's persuasive impact. Political strategists attempt to influence the public's emotions for similar reasons through the use of negative political advertising (attack ads; see Module 6.1).

Another key factor that can easily derail communication is the message's complexity. If your arguments are overly technical, complex, or convoluted, or use specialized language, this can also activate negative emotion for people and bias them against your message. Also, people will simply lose interest in a message they don't understand and stop paying attention. This is a big challenge for communicating about technical topics like climate change. Strangely, experts are often terrible at communicating their knowledge, tending to forget that their audience may not understand the technical language they use and the subtleties of what they are saying. Chip and Dan Heath (2007) call this the "curse of knowledge." Anybody who has ever

listened to an expert being interviewed on the news has likely experienced this phenomenon. The expert may find the conversation fascinating and rife with meaning, but to the audience it may sound like a monotonous drone.

The curse of knowledge was shown in an innovative experiment (Newton, 1991) in which subjects were assigned to be "tappers" or "listeners." The tappers were asked to tap the rhythm to a selection of extremely well-known songs, like "Happy Birthday," while the listeners tried to guess the songs. To the tappers, the songs were totally obvious; when they tapped out "Happy Birthday," they would hear the words and the tune in their heads and it seemed pretty likely that the listeners would be able to guess the song; in fact, they estimated that listeners would guess about 50% of the songs. To the listeners, however, the vague "tap-tap-TAP-tap TAP TAP" didn't amount to much; they guessed the correct songs a mere 2.5% of the time!

This study illustrates how people with knowledge tend to overestimate the amount of knowledge their audience will have. When you are communicating, remember to keep your audience's perspective in mind and fight the urge to use impressively long words, acronyms, and technical lingo. Saying less, and saying it in less complex ways, is often saying more.

Module 13.3b Quiz:
Using the Central Route Effectively

Know . . .

1. A strategy for strengthening attitudes and making them more resistant to change by first exposing people to a weak counter-argument and then refuting that argument is known as _____.
   - **A.** attitude inoculation
   - **B.** social-altruistic processing
   - **C.** analytic processing
   - **D.** value framing

Understand . . .

2. One of the challenges that people have when trying to persuade other people is that
   - **A.** social-altruistic values have a much larger effect on behaviour than other value frames.
   - **B.** social-altruistic and biospheric value frames are often inconsistent with egoistic value frames.
   - **C.** biospheric and egoistic value frames are often in conflict with social-altruistic value frames.
   - **D.** value frames have a very small effect on human behaviour.

Apply . . .

3. Which of the following statements about a (fictitious) anti-anxiety medication—Leafobarbital—should be most persuasive?
   - **A.** "Many individuals have found that Leafobarbital reduces their anxiety."
   - **B.** "Think of how Leafobarbital could have changed your anxiety-filled high-school years."
   - **C.** "Over 80% of people in a test group in Thailand found Leafobarbital to effectively reduce their anxiety."
   - **D.** "Imagine what your life would be like if you were anxiety free. Leafobarbital will change the way you feel."

Analyze . . .

4. Which is the best explanation for the identifiable victim effect?
   - **A.** Our experiential and analytic systems of processing information work together to produce a logical response.
   - **B.** The analytic system inhibits the experiential systems responses, thus providing a greater identification with the victim.
   - **C.** The analytic system responds to the logical content of the identifiable victim's story.
   - **D.** The experiential system responds to the emotional content of the identifiable victim's story.

Using the Peripheral Route Effectively

To be an effective communicator, you can't ignore the peripheral route. Half a century of social psychology research has identified several powerful factors of influence. There are more than can be represented here, but we will discuss several of the most important ones. You may recognize many of these, because they have undoubtedly been used against you many times, from corporations trying to sell you products to people trying to get you to do them a favour.

AUTHORITY   The use of experts and authority figures to deliver a message can often enhance the impact of the message (Cialdini, 2001). Even people who look like experts but have no real authority on a subject can be used effectively. For example, an extremely successful ad campaign in the 1970s for decaffeinated coffee used a man who had absolutely no expert knowledge of coffee or its health effects; however, as an actor, he played Marcus Welby, M.D., who was a very popular TV doctor at the time. Dressing the part is important as well; a man wearing a suit who jaywalks across a red light will be followed by 3.5 times as many people as the same man wearing casual clothes (Lefkowitz et al., 1955).

LIKING   We believe people we like. Communicators who connect with their audience get their message across more effectively (Cialdini, 2001). Liking can be influenced by numerous factors, including attractiveness. For example, in a study performed for the American Heart Association, attractive fundraisers generated almost twice as many donations (42% versus 23%) as their less-attractive counterparts (Reingen & Kernan, 1993). In the 1972 Canadian federal election, candidates who were rated as physically attractive got three times as many votes as unattractive ones (Efrain & Patterson, 1974); in fact, politically unpopular parties had substantially less attractive candidates, which may have been a big part of their party's lack of success at the polls! It is interesting to note that voters themselves insisted that their choices were not influenced by something as superficial as appearance. (In an interesting coincidence, the Prime Minister at that time was Pierre Elliott Trudeau—his son, Justin, has also received some attention for his appearance.)

Thus, there are good reasons to be pleasant and appealing, and to look your best, at least from a persuasion perspective. Highlighting any similarities you may share with your audience, loosening up a little and speaking informally, appropriate use of humour, and even complimenting the audience, can all enhance your likability and increase the effectiveness of your communication.

SOCIAL VALIDATION   Because humans are such a social species, we use the behaviour of others as a guide to inform us of what we should do (e.g., conformity and social norms; Module 13.2). As an influence tactic, social validation can be incredibly powerful. Social validation is at work whenever you hear that a novel is a bestseller, a piece of music has topped the charts, there's a long line-up outside a night-club, or "polls indicate" that a political candidate is popular.

One such example of social validation used in climate change communication occurred in the spring of 2013 when Bill McKibben's organization, 350.org, and several other organizations submitted a petition with one million signatures, urging President Obama to not allow the Keystone XL pipeline to transport oil from Canada's oilsands to the United States. Afterward, the fact that a million signatures were gathered became a major part of their organization's marketing messages. You can see how social validation becomes a major tool for communicators; obviously, proponents of the pipeline would want to downplay these facts, whereas opponents of the pipeline would want to highlight them.

Somewhat ironically, social validation is also often misused by communicators. For example, people may try to highlight the urgency of a behaviour change or the seriousness of an issue by pointing out how *few* people are currently doing something desirable (such as wearing condoms during casual sex or reducing one's carbon footprint), or how many people are currently doing something *un*desirable (eating a high sugar diet or leaving the lights on all the time). Although the information may be true and the intentions are good, these communications can easily backfire. In one study, a suicide intervention program in New Jersey told people about the high rates of teenage suicides; as a result, people who went through the program became *more* likely to think of suicide as a way out of their problems (Cialdini, 2001).

RECIPROCITY   You scratch my back, I'll scratch yours. All cultures have a strong social norm that obligates people to repay to others what they have received. This strong social norm is used by influence specialists all the time, and it can be so sneaky we often don't realize it. Just think of the "free samples" offered by vendors, the "free trial workout" offered by health clubs, and even the "free personality assessments" offered by the Church of Scientology. Each makes you feel a debt or obligation. The principle of reciprocity is one reason why corporations donate to politicians' campaigns, and why pharmaceutical companies spend millions of dollars funding research, organizing conferences, and providing gifts, stationery, calendars, and even pens to doctors and family health clinics (Cialdini, 2001).

Reciprocity is often used in a two-step manner called the **door-in-the-face technique**, *which involves asking for something relatively big, then following with a request for* *something relatively small.* The logic is that once someone has scaled back their request, you are obligated to meet them part way. Professional negotiators will always start with a proposal they don't really expect to get; but they know that once they "give up" some of the things they want, the opposing side is obligated to do the same. The door-in-the-face technique can be used to surprising effectiveness.

In one well-known study by Bob Cialdini (Cialdini et al., 1975), people were approached on the street and asked whether they would be willing to volunteer to chaperone inmates from a juvenile detention centre for a day trip to the zoo. When simply asked, 17% said yes. A second set of people were approached and submitted to a door-in-the-face manipulation; they were first asked if they would be willing to volunteer for two hours per week as a counsellor at the juvenile detention centre, and make a commitment for two years. Everybody said no. But when they were subsequently asked whether they would merely agree to volunteer to chaperone inmates from the detention centre on a trip to the zoo for the day, an astonishing 50% said yes. This one-two punch is very effective, both because it makes the person feel obligated to say yes after you have "backed down," and because the second request doesn't *seem* as onerous when presented after the first, bigger request.

CONSISTENCY One of the most powerful influence techniques, especially for long-term behaviour change, is an old salesperson's trick called the **foot-in-the-door technique**, *which involves making a simple request followed by a more substantial request.* To the travelling salesmen of days gone by, literally getting one's foot in the door meant that a homeowner could not shut you out. In social psychology, the idea is that once you get the person to agree to even a small request, it's harder for them to say no to a subsequent request (Burger, 1999; Cialdini, 2000).

The foot-in-the-door technique is also a sneaky strategy, because the initial request can be so small that virtually everyone would say yes to it; nevertheless, it's powerful, because it makes use of a very strong motivation held by many people—the need for psychological consistency. We'll describe this in more detail, but just think of how people usually react to being called a hypocrite and you'll get a sense of the power of the need for consistency. So, the foot-in-the-door technique packs another powerful one-two punch—an initial request that's hard to refuse locks you in, and then you get cornered into agreeing to a much larger request (see Figure 13.8).

For example, if you are at the beach and you want to go swimming, how can you be sure nobody is going to steal your stuff? Just ask someone to watch your things for you! Simple as that. Although this may seem intuitive, you may be surprised by just how powerful this simple request can be. In one experiment, an experimenter posed

Figure 13.8 Two-Step Persuasion Techniques to Encourage Community Service

The foot-in-the-door technique (top) starts with a small request and then moves on to a larger request. The door-in-the-face technique (bottom) does the reverse. It begins with a highly demanding request and then appears to settle for a much smaller one.

"Would you you sign a petition for this cause?" "Sure!" "Could you also give an hour of your time to volunteer for the cause?"

"Would you be willing to volunteer four days each week to help our cause?" "Well, how about just spending an hour with us this Saturday afternoon?"

as a person sunbathing on the beach, who at one point got up and asked whoever was close them to watch his things; everybody said yes. Then he left, and shortly afterwards, as you might expect, a mock-thief came along and attempted to steal the experimenter's radio. An astonishing 95% of the people who agreed to watch his things attempted to interfere with the would-be thief, even to the point of chasing the thief down the beach! But in the control condition, when no one was asked, only 20% of people tried to stop the thief (Cialdini, 2001). Imagine that—an additional 75% of us will become heroic vigilantes just because some stranger casually asks us on a beach to watch his stuff.

Commitments can be extremely subtle, another reason they are sneaky. For example, one restaurant owner was able to reduce the rate of no-shows (people who reserve a table but then don't show up) from 30% all the way down to 10% by changing two words in the script that his employees used when scheduling reservations over the phone. In the old script, the receptionist would say, "Please call if you have to change your plans." In the revised script, she said "Would you please call if you have to change your plans?" Then she would wait for a couple of seconds until the person responded and said yes (Cialdini, 2001). Saying "yes" is an active commitment, and that tiny act was enough to get two-thirds of the no-shows to call first and cancel. Other studies have shown that written commitments ("sign here . . .") are even more effective than verbal commitments, and commitments that can be made public are the most effective of all.

Module 13.3c Quiz:
Using the Peripheral Route Effectively

Understand . . .

1. Harinder asked Doug to help him carry some boxes from his car into his backyard. Once that small task was done, Harinder then asked Doug to help him assemble a shed that he had bought. This technique of making a simple request followed by a more substantial request is known as _____.
   A. the door-in-the-face technique
   B. the foot-in-the-door technique
   C. social validation
   D. the nuisance effect

Apply . . .

2. Which attempt at persuasion would be *least* effective?
   A. A bearded man in a leather jacket telling you which type of motorcycle you should buy
   B. A well-dressed politician asking you to support her political party
   C. Someone asking you to be the first person to sign a petition about an important social issue
   D. Someone asking you to sign an online petition that had already been signed by over 100 000 Canadian students

3. Kendra wanted to go to Ottawa for the weekend with her friends, but was afraid that her parents would object. In order to persuade (or manipulate) them, she first asked them if she could travel to Amsterdam with her friends. Her parents said, "No." The next day she asked if she could at least go to Ottawa. Her parents eventually agreed to this request. This is an example of _____.
   A. the door-in-the-face technique
   B. the foot-in-the-door technique
   C. social validation
   D. the capital effect

The Attitude–Behaviour Feedback Loop

As we mentioned earlier, the reason the foot-in-the-door approach works so well is because people have a general need to be psychologically consistent—for their attitudes, beliefs, and behaviours to match up with each other. Much of the time, we maintain a feeling of consistency by letting our beliefs and attitudes guide our behaviours. We act in the way we think and feel is right. But, the relationship between our actions and beliefs is not always this straightforward.

COGNITIVE DISSONANCE Groundbreaking work by Leon Festinger (1957) showed that we can also maintain a feeling of consistency by simply changing our beliefs to be consistent with our behaviour. Festinger (1957) proposed **cognitive dissonance theory**, describing that *when we hold inconsistent beliefs, this creates a kind of aversive inner tension, or "dissonance"; we are then motivated to reduce this tension in whatever way we can*, often by simply changing the beliefs that created the dissonance in the first place.

This sort of belief change was observed in a dramatic way by Festinger and two of his colleagues when they infiltrated a doomsday cult in the 1950s. December 21, 1954, was the date the world was supposed to end, according to the cult's leader, Marian Keech (not her real name). Keech told her followers that she was receiving messages from aliens who lived on the planet Clarion. The aliens had warned of an impending flood that would destroy life on Earth, but they promised to come in a spaceship and rescue Keech and her followers before the final cataclysm. If the members kept their faith, the aliens were supposed to contact them at midnight. The cult members were so convinced of impending doom that they gave away their possessions, quit their jobs, and prepared for the end.

Festinger and his colleagues, not being big believers in alien messages about the end of the world, wondered what would happen when the prophecy failed to come true. So, on December 20th, the cult members, including Festinger and his colleagues, gathered together and waited for the spaceship to arrive. Midnight came . . . and went. A few minutes after midnight the group decided the clocks were fast and any minute now, the aliens would be contacting them. Then an hour passed. And another. The group waited all night, increasingly confused, wondering what was going on.

Finally, at 4:45 a.m., it was apparent the Clarions weren't coming to whisk them away. Keech had been wrong. The cult members had made fools out of themselves and ruined their lives. You might think that they would slink back to their normal lives, beg for their jobs back, and try to recover from the embarrassment. But no, the opposite happened. Keech suddenly got another message from the Clarions! They told her that because her little group had been so faithful, waiting all night for them to come, God had decided not to destroy the Earth after all. They weren't fools; they were heroes! Convinced that they had saved the world, Keech and most of her followers (some decided this was ridiculous and ditched them at this point) became even more evangelical, contacting newspapers and media outlets, spreading the good word that the world had been saved (Festinger et al., 1956).

Festinger and Carlsmith (1959) tested cognitive dissonance theory by having subjects come to their lab and spend an hour engaged in a mind-numbing study that required them to perform menial, repetitive tasks.

Afterward, the subjects were told that in a different condition of the study, a research assistant meets subjects beforehand and gives them positive expectations of the study, telling them that it's a fun and interesting study. Unfortunately, the person called in sick that day, and so the subjects were asked if they would play the part of the research assistant for the next, incoming subject. All they had to do was sit in the waiting room, and when the next subject came in, chat with them and tell them the study was fun and interesting. Little did the unsuspecting participants know that this was what the real study was about, getting them to tell a "little white lie" and then seeing how it affected their attitudes.

The subjects were also offered one of two amounts of payment if they agreed to go along with the deception. Some subjects were paid $1, and others were paid $20. After agreeing to play along and deceiving the person in the waiting room, subjects then filled out a few measures of their perceptions of the study. Lo and behold, after lying about the study, the subjects actually felt more positively toward it! But not all the subjects felt this way, only those who were paid $1. Why might this be?

The subjects who were paid $20 had more than enough justification for telling a little white lie—"I did it for the money." But getting paid $1 seems hardly worth it; these subjects were left in a state of uncomfortable dissonance, caught between the beliefs "deceiving people is wrong" and "I just lied to somebody for a measly $1." However, by changing their attitudes—"I didn't really lie; this study was actually pretty interesting!"—subjects were able to resolve their dissonance and feel good again.

Cognitive dissonance theory can help to explain many puzzling phenomena of everyday life. For example, why would perfectly sane young people crawl through ice water in their underwear while others stood around shouting at them, throwing snowballs, and even spanking them? In the winter of 2013, exactly such an event happened at Ryerson University, when aspiring frosh leaders went through a "hazing ritual." When it came to light, university administrators and even Ontario's premier were shocked and appalled, although no official action was taken except to express disapproval.

Students at Dalhousie University, in the same year, were not so lucky; Dalhousie suspended its entire women's hockey team in January, except for the rookies, who also lost their season as a result of not having a team to play with. The previous September, the team had held a party at which the rookies were subjected to hazing, and when it came to light, the university administration reacted based on a "zero tolerance" policy.

But why does hazing occur? People have traditionally believed that submitting new group members to rituals that are embarrassing, humiliating, even painful and dangerous helps to bond new members to the organization, deepening their commitment and their feelings of belonging. Cognitive dissonance theory suggests they are right. Being humiliated and embarrassed would be generally dissonant with the belief "I am a reasonable, self-respecting person." But after you have just publicly degraded yourself, it's not easy to feel that way. One way to reduce the dissonance (or discomfort) and reconcile your belief about what you just did with your belief that you are a reasonable, self-respecting person is to change one of your beliefs a little bit. For example, if you suffered in order to join a really exclusive, super-cool, awesome group, then this makes sense; of course you would suffer in order to join *that* group! And this is exactly what people seem to do; after initiation rituals, they enhance their perceptions that *this* is a group worth belonging to.

Interestingly, because cognitive dissonance is based on the need for self-consistency, it does not appear to work in quite the same way across cultures. In more collectivistic societies, for example, the need for self-consistency is not as strong, because it is more widely recognized that one's "self" is more fluid, manifesting differently in different social situations. This is reflected in collectivists experiencing less dissonance after making choices. However, research conducted at the University of Waterloo has shown that people from collectivist cultures do experience dissonance after making difficult choices for their friends (Hoshino-Browne et al., 2005). It appears that the need for self-consistency still exists; it's just that the "self" is more interpersonal than personal.

ATTITUDES AND ACTIONS If attitudes influence behaviours, and behaviours influence attitudes, then you can see that the two are connected to each other in a circular fashion, with each affecting the other in a self-reinforcing cycle. Because each process affects the other, what happens in these causal loops is that initially small changes can grow into very large changes over time. For example, an initially small behaviour change can feed back to strengthen the person's attitude toward that behaviour, which leads to greater behaviour changes in the future.

Clearly, sometimes this works, as we saw earlier with the cognitive dissonance examples, the power of commitments, and the foot-in-the-door technique. With regard to climate change and the environmental movement, the hope for many decades has been that this foot-in-the-door approach would build increasingly pro-environmental attitudes in the general public in order to move society toward sustainability. By getting the public to adopt relatively easy behaviours, like recycling or using compact fluorescent light bulbs, the hope has been that this would strengthen pro-environmental attitudes and spill over, or generalize, to other behaviours and greater support for environmental laws and policies. This *spillover effect* has been the basic rationale for the general marketing approach to environmental behaviour change: appeal to whatever values people hold (e.g., the money they'll save), and encourage the adoption of whatever behaviours seem most likely. For example, you may recall a TV commercial of recent years by the David Suzuki Foundation, in which a man was informed of how much beer money he would save if he got rid of his extra fridge in the basement. Unplugging your fridge today, protesting in the streets tomorrow!

Unfortunately for anybody hoping to use the foot-in-the-door technique to change society in major ways, the strategy seems most effective for encouraging the adoption of similar behaviours (e.g., signing a petition for a cause today will make it more likely that you'll volunteer for that cause in the future), but it does not reliably spill over to a wider range of behaviours. Spillover is even less likely if there are clear, extrinsically motivating reasons for engaging in the behaviour, such as saving beer money. Just like Festinger's subjects didn't need to change their attitudes when they were paid $20 for lying, people whose primary reason for conserving energy is to save money are not likely to strengthen their pro-environmental attitudes more generally. After all, they just did it for the money.

Nevertheless, as we have reviewed, psychologists have provided many insights and tools for communicating more effectively to change people's behaviour. Hopefully some of the readers of this book will use these tools to make the world a better—and more environmentally sustainable—place. It's up to *you*.

Module 13.3d Quiz:

The Attitude–Behaviour Feedback Loop

Understand . . .

1. Some of the participants in Festinger's classic study of cognitive dissonance were only paid $1 to lie to another group of participants. Members of this $1 group ended up viewing the boring experiment as being more important and interesting than another group of participants who were paid $20 to lie. What is the explanation for this group difference?

    A. The members of the $20 group were so happy about receiving that much money that they were unable to generate any emotional response about the experiment itself.

    B. The people in the $20 group were already a bunch of liars, so they were unaffected by the study.

    C. The members of the $20 group felt guilty about accepting so much money; this made them feel less positive toward the experiment than people who only received $1.

    D. The members of the $1 group didn't want to feel like they lied for only $1, so they altered their beliefs about the experiment so that their beliefs matched their actions.

Apply . . .

2. Athletes at many universities in North America undergo humiliating hazing rituals when they join a team. How are these rituals related to cognitive dissonance?

    A. The intense emotions associated with hazing tap into the experiential processing system and increase the athletes' approval of the team.

    B. Athletes who undergo hazing will increase their positive beliefs about the team in order to justify having suffered through the humiliating rituals.

    C. Athletes who view the team more positively are more likely to be willing to undergo hazing rituals.

    D. There is no relationship between hazing and cognitive dissonance.

Module 13.3 Summary

13.3a   Know . . . the key terminology in research on attitudes, behaviour, and effective communication.

analytic system
attitude inoculation
central route to persuasion
cognitive dissonance theory
construal-level theory
door-in-the-face technique
elaboration likelihood model (ELM)
experiential system
foot-in-the-door technique
identifiable victim effect

peripheral route to persuasion
processing fluency

13.3b   Understand . . . how behaviours influence attitudes in terms of cognitive dissonance theory.

When people hold cognitions that conflict with each other, such as when they are aware that they have behaved in a way that runs counter to their beliefs or attitudes, they experience an uncomfortable state of arousal known as cognitive dissonance. In order to reduce this dissonance, they need to change one of their conflicting cognitions, which often results in changing their attitudes in order to reflect the behaviour they just performed. In this way, behaviours and attitudes influence each other.

13.3c Apply . . . your understanding of the central route to describe how a message should be designed.

In order to design an effective message using the central route to persuasion, you must start with solid, convincing facts. Then personalize the message, making it self-relevant for your audience, such as by directly engaging them in a scenario you describe, by describing how the message is relevant to them personally, or by framing the message in terms of values that your audience members hold. Also, keep your message from being unnecessarily complex, so as to maintain the interest of your audience. If your audience is likely to hear opposing viewpoints, be sure to construct a two-sided message that includes those opposing arguments, and then provide solid reasons for why the opposing arguments are not valid. It also makes sense to use peripheral cues to further strengthen your message, such as appealing to authority, mentioning similarities between yourself and the audience, using humour appropriately, and relying predominantly on specific stories rather than on abstract data and statistics.

13.3d Analyze . . . the difficulties communicators face in trying to convince the public to take action on climate change.

Climate change communicators face some key challenges. Traditionally, the environmental movement has framed its messages in ways that run counter to predominant North American values, making many people wary of environmental messages or at least likely to see them as not relevant to themselves. Furthermore, climate change is experienced as psychologically distant from the public, with consequences that people feel are generally going to be experienced by people in other parts of the world and by future generations. Climate change information is also highly technical and complex, and is abstract and statistical in nature, given that climate change is a global phenomenon that doesn't easily boil down to specific stories about specific people. There is also inherent uncertainty in scientific research, which has made it difficult to express climate change information in a way that would seem "certain" to the public.

Chapter 14
Health, Stress, and Coping

14.1 Behaviour and Health

- Smoking 580

  Working the Scientific Literacy Model: Media Exposure and Smoking 580
- Module 14.1a Quiz 582
- Obesity 582
- Module 14.1b Quiz 586
- Psychosocial Influences on Health 586
- Module 14.1c Quiz 588
- Module 14.1 Summary 588

14.2 Stress and Illness

- What Causes Stress? 591
- Module 14.2a Quiz 593
- Physiology of Stress 593

  Working the Scientific Literacy Model: Hormones, Relationships, and Health 596
- Module 14.2b Quiz 597
- Stress, Immunity, and Illness 597
- Module 14.2c Quiz 600
- Module 14.2 Summary 601

14.3 Coping and Well-Being

- Coping 603
- Module 14.3a Quiz 608
- Perceived Control 609

  Working the Scientific Literacy Model: Compensatory Control and Health 610
- Module 14.3b Quiz 612
- Module 14.3 Summary 612

Module 14.1 Behaviour and Health

Stock_wales/Alamy Stock Photo

Learning Objectives

14.1a Know . . . the key terminology related to health psychology.

14.1b Understand . . . how genetic and environmental factors influence obesity.

14.1c Apply . . . your knowledge of persuasion and health to examine the effectiveness of different types of cigarette warnings.

14.1d Analyze . . . whether media depictions of smoking affect smoking in adolescents.

Should we have to pay more for unhealthy or nonessential food items that contribute to obesity and other expensive health conditions? In fact, taxes on these items are becoming increasingly common. In March 2015, the city of Berkeley, California instituted a "sugar tax" on sugary drinks such as colas in an effort to curb the increasing rates of diabetes and obesity. Sugary soft drinks contribute hundreds of calories to our daily diet without providing any nutrition, and do little to leave a person feeling full and satisfied. City officials assumed that taxing these beverages would reduce sugar intake and improve people's health. Preliminary data suggest that they were correct. Residents surveyed after the tax went into effect reported consuming 21% fewer sugar-sweetened beverages and 26% less cola (Falbe et al., 2016). Based on this initial success, it should come as no surprise that similar taxes were included in political campaigns in a number of municipalities during the November 2016 U.S. election. It seems a foregone conclusion that these taxes will soon appear in Canada as well. On the one hand, these fees may sound like the government interfering with our individual freedom to eat and drink what we like. On the other hand, there is a parallel precedent for sugar tax plans—namely, the massive taxes on cigarettes that serve to discourage smoking and help cover the costs of *treating smoking-related illnesses. Plans such as sugar taxes tell us that issues related to health and behaviour are becoming common topics of conversation in many areas of society.*

Focus Questions

1. Which factors contribute to weight problems, and how much control over them can people expect to have?

2. To what extent is physical health based on psychological processes such as choice and decision?

≫ To what degree do you believe your behaviour affects your health? Each day we make choices that shape our physical and mental health. We decide what to eat and what to avoid eating, whether to exercise or to relax on the couch. Some people choose to light up a cigarette whenever the chance arises. Others make a point of avoiding places where people are likely to smoke. The choices people make about their career paths similarly influence their health. Workplace stress levels for air traffic controllers are quite different from those experienced by small-town librarians. The numerous and complex connections between behaviour and health certainly have created an important niche for *health psychologists*. These researchers study both the positive and negative effects that humans' behaviour and decisions have on their health, survival, and well-being.

The need for health psychologists has increased considerably over the last century, as most premature deaths today are attributable to lifestyle factors. In the early 1900s, people in Canada were likely to die from influenza, pneumonia, tuberculosis, measles, and other contagious diseases. Advances in medicine have served to keep these conditions under much better control. Instead, people are now much more likely to die from tobacco use, alcohol use, obesity, and inactivity. In fact, more than half of all deaths in Canada in 2009 were caused by heart disease, cancer, stroke, and diabetes. Although genetics plays a role in these diseases, they have also been linked to unhealthy behaviours such as a poor diet and smoking (Statistics Canada, 2012a). Clearly, then, our physical and mental well-being are connected to the health decisions that we make.

Smoking

One of the most widely studied health behaviours is tobacco use. Smoking cigarettes causes life-shortening health problems including lung, mouth, and throat cancer; heart disease; and pulmonary diseases such as emphysema. Recent reports indicate that 21% of all deaths in Canada over the past decade were due to smoking-related illnesses (Jones et al., 2010). The life expectancy of the average smoker is between 7 and 14 years shorter than that of a nonsmoker (Centers for Disease Control and Prevention [CDC], 2002; Streppel et al., 2007). This number depends upon how much, and for how long, a person smoked. Quitting by the age of 30 greatly reduces the likelihood that a person will die of smoking-related cancers, a statistic that is quite relevant to university students (Statistics Canada, 2012b)! The costs in lives and money attributable to smoking are massive, as shown in Table 14.1. Despite these starkly ominous figures, 19.9% of Canadian adults—22.3% of males and 17.5% of females—smoke cigarettes (Statistics Canada, 2012b). In other words, 5.8 million Canadians perform a behaviour that is quite likely to harm or even

Table 14.1 Health Costs of Tobacco Use

- Tobacco use causes an estimated 5 million deaths worldwide each year.
- Cigarette smoking is the leading preventable cause of death in North America.
- One in five Canadian deaths is due to cigarette smoking.
- Close to 1000 Canadians die each year as a result of second-hand smoke.

Sources: Based on CDC, 2009b; Rehm et al., 2006; Statistics Canada, 2012b.

kill them. It should come as no surprise that such a statistic would interest psychologists.

Working the Scientific Literacy Model

Media Exposure and Smoking

If smoking is so dangerous, why do people do it? Why don't they do something safer, like juggle scorpions? This is a perplexing question not only for psychologists, but also for many smokers. One reason may be the exposure young people have to other people who smoke: parents, friends, and even characters on television and in the movies.

What do we know about media influences on smoking?

Each day approximately 250 adolescents in Canada try their first cigarette, and many will go on to become full-time smokers (Health Canada, 2008). There are many possible reasons why adolescents try smoking, including whether family members smoke, whether smoking is common in their culture, personality characteristics, and socioeconomic status. Adolescents may also begin smoking because they associate it with particular traits such as attractiveness, rebelliousness, and individualism. One factor that has received an increasing amount of attention from psychologists and health-care providers is the role of the media. Specifically, does exposure to smoking in movies and entertainment lead teens to begin smoking? Actors in many popular television shows and movies smoke. Additionally, photographs in fashion and entertainment magazines show stars such as Johnny Depp and Kristen Stewart looking cool and smoking cigarettes. Indeed, smokers are often portrayed as sophisticated and self-assured, traits that many adolescents hope to possess. In contrast, very few movies and magazines show someone with emphysema or lung cancer.

How can science help us analyze the effects of smoking in the movies?

To what extent do positive images of smoking in movies (and TV and magazines) contribute to adolescent smoking? This question has been addressed using a variety of methods. In one study, researchers conducted a random-digit-dialing survey of 6522 U.S. adolescents from all major geographic regions and socioeconomic groups (Sargent, 2005). The adolescents reported their age and indicated whether they smoked, and were asked to identify whether they had seen specific popular movies that featured smoking. The more exposure the adolescents had to movies that featured smoking, the more likely they were to have

Figure 14.1 Number of Smoking Images in Popular Movies from 2002 to 2015

This graph depicts the number times tobacco appears in movies from 2002 to 2015. Note that although the overall trend is downward, there are some years in which tobacco incidents are quite prevalent, even in youth-rated movies.

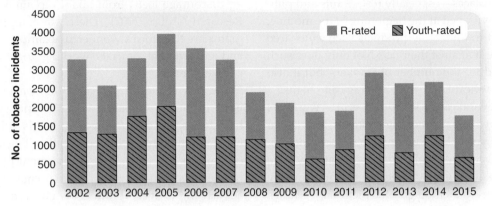

Source: 2015 Numbers: After rebound, film smoking falls to near-lows, Centre for Tobacco Control Research and Education, 2015. Copyright © 2015 by Center for Tobacco Control Research and Education. Used by permission.

tried smoking. This relationship persisted even after the researchers controlled for important variables such as socioeconomic status, personality, and parental and peer influences on smoking (Heatherton & Sargent, 2009).

The effect of smoking scenes on behaviour has also been tested in the laboratory. In one study, 100 cigarette smokers between the ages of 18 and 25 watched either a 10-minute video with smoking scenes or a video that did not reference smoking. In the break that followed the video presentation, participants who saw smoking scenes were significantly more likely to light up a cigarette (Shmueli et al., 2010). This result is likely due to the fact that smoking cues such as images of smokers or of smoking paraphernalia (packages, lighters, etc.) elicit cravings in smokers (Balter et al., 2015).

It appears that how people identify with smokers may also influence their decision to smoke. An experimental study showed that adolescents who had positive responses to a protagonist in a movie clip who smoked were much more likely to associate smoking with their own identities. This correlation was observed in both adolescents who already smoked and even those who did not smoke (Dal Cin et al., 2007).

Can we critically evaluate this evidence?

It is very difficult to establish that watching movie stars smoke cigarettes causes adolescents to take up smoking, even though the correlations might suggest that it does. When researchers tracked the amount of smoking featured in popular movies from 1990 to 2007, they found that as the incidence of smoking in movies rose, smoking among adolescents increased after a short period of time. Likewise, when smoking in movies decreased, a decline in adolescent smoking followed (Heatherton & Sargent, 2009). However,

the problem with these correlations is that multiple explanations could be put forth for why they exist. Although the researchers would like to demonstrate that smoking in movies influences audience members, perhaps the truth is the other way around: People who are already willing to smoke might be more attracted to movies that feature smoking.

Why is this relevant?

Smoking by young people raises serious concerns about the health and well-being of those individuals who start smoking at such an early age. In addition, cigarette-related illness imposes a major societal burden in terms of lost work productivity and rising health-care costs. As the research shows, cigarette smoking in movies is just one of many influences on smoking behaviour. Of course, it may be one influence that could be easier to control than, say, peer pressure. With scientific research in hand, advocacy groups such as Smoke Free Movies, the (U.S.) National Association of Attorneys General, and Physicians for a Smoke-Free Canada have a sound basis for arguing against smoking in movies—especially those that adolescents are likely to watch.

It appears that the work of these advocacy groups is paying off. After peaking in the middle of the last decade, the number of films including smoking is on the decline (Polansky, 2016). However, as you can see in Figure 14.1, this decline is not a steady one. For example, the number of "tobacco incidents" in PG-13 movies specifically targeted to teens increased from 565 in 2010 to 1155 in 2012; therefore, the curtain hasn't fallen on this issue.

EFFORTS TO PREVENT SMOKING Given the health problems (to the smokers *and* to the people around them) and enormous healthcare costs associated with smoking, both healthcare workers and government officials recognize that more work has to be done to reduce smoking levels. Provincial and municipal laws are reducing the risks posed by second-hand smoke exposure by banning smoking in many public places—especially restaurants and public buildings. As mentioned at the beginning of the module, steep taxes applied to unhealthy products such as tobacco also act as a deterrent against their use. Not only does such a policy tend to reduce the number of smokers, but it also raises funds for healthcare and anti-smoking campaigns.

In the 1990s, several countries added written warnings to cigarette packages (e.g., "Smoking seriously harms you and others around you") in an attempt to reduce smoking rates. Unfortunately, these labels have had relatively little effect. However, in 2001, Canada became the first country to require companies to include graphic pictorial warnings on cigarette packages. These images included rotting teeth, black lungs, diseased hearts, and sick children; they were also paired with a verbal message. Researchers found that the image-based warnings were much more likely to be noticed by both smokers and non-smokers than were text-only messages (Fong et al., 2009; Hammond et al., 2003). They were also more useful than text-only messages in educating people about the risks associated with smoking (Environics Research Group, 2007; Li & Yong, 2009).

Image-based warnings on cigarette packages are now used in over 30 countries (Hammond, 2011). Numerous studies have shown that these warnings are quite memorable and are having the desired effect. Over 40% of Canadian smokers indicated that the graphic warnings

motivated them to quit (Hammond et al., 2007). And, although it is impossible to accurately state how many people avoided smoking because of the ads, surveys of Canadian adolescents suggest that these warning labels do discourage teens from taking up smoking (Environics Research Group, 2007). These smoking-prevention programs are therefore a wonderful example of psychologists and government officials working together to improve people's health.

A new challenge that health officials must face is the issue of e-cigarettes or "vaping." Vaping is not quite as harmful as traditional smoking, but is still not a healthy habit. Although it is technically illegal to advertise e-cigarettes in Canada, the enforcement of these laws has not been as stringent as for regular cigarettes. In the U.S., advertising of these products *is* allowed. A recent study found that most of the exposure that adolescents had to e-cigarettes occurred on cable television networks (Duke et al., 2014). It remains to be seen whether this form of smoking will lead to an increase in adolescent smoking rates.

Despite this potential challenge, there is some good news related to smoking rates. The prevalence of smoking in Canada declined steadily over the 1990s and early 2000s (Statistics Canada, 2012b); in 2001, 28.1% of men and 23.8% of women smoked, 5.8% and 6.3% higher than the current rates. The decrease is even more dramatic among young adults. In 2001, 33.2% of Canadians aged 18–19 smoked; in 2011, this number dropped to 19.8%. These data tell us that anti-smoking efforts are working—but that there is still work to be done.

Module 14.1a Quiz:

Smoking

Know . . .

1. What does a health psychologist study?
   A. The positive impacts that our behaviour has on our health
   B. The negative impacts that our behaviour has on our health
   C. The chance that we will survive based on our decisions
   D. Both the positive and the negative impacts that our behaviour and decisions have on our health and survival

2. In modern times, the leading causes of death in industrialized nations such as Canada are _____.
   A. viral infections
   B. bacterial infections
   C. lifestyle factors
   D. an equal combination of the above factors

Analyze . . .

3. Which of the following statements is the best evidence that viewing smoking in movies plays a causal (rather than correlational) role in influencing people's perception of smoking and willingness to try smoking?
   A. Long-term trends show that increased or decreased incidence of smoking by adolescents follows increases or decreases in rates of smoking in movies.
   B. The more adolescents smoke, the more smoking occurs in movies.
   C. Advertisements for smoking occur more frequently when smoking rates decrease.
   D. Adolescent smoking occurs at roughly the same rate regardless of how smoking is depicted in films.

Obesity

Most college and university students are familiar with the term "freshman 15"—the supposed number of pounds students can expect to gain during their first year of school

(15 pounds equals 6.8 kg). This term has stuck because weight gain during the first year of university (at least in North America) has become common, if not expected. It is unclear exactly how the term originated, and research has shown that the 15-pound estimate is actually inflated.

In reality, male and female students who gain weight during their early university career put on an average of 6 pounds, or 2.7 kg (Gropper et al., 2009).

What accounts for this phenomenon? Several factors that are probably all too familiar to many readers: increased food intake, decreased physical activity, and, for many students, increased levels of alcohol consumption. The lifestyle changes that students face during university affect physical health. In addition, university in general (and the first year in particular) presents new challenges that bring on a great deal of both positive and negative stress, especially if students move away from home. The freshman 15 (or 6) and other health-related issues are based on lifestyle decisions we make. Six pounds (2.7 kg) is not a lot of weight—but habits formed during any period of time, freshman year or otherwise, can be difficult to break. In this section, we will examine factors that lead us to put on weight as well as ways to use our knowledge of psychology to help us lose it.

DEFINING HEALTHY WEIGHTS AND OBESITY It is important to define your terms when discussing a concept. Doing so ensures that all researchers are talking about the same thing when they use terms like *overweight* or *obese*. When discussing weight, psychologists and health-care workers must also factor in a person's height; being 200 pounds (91 kg) is healthy for someone who is 6'4" (193 cm), but would be quite unhealthy for someone who is 5'2" (157 cm). To account for height differences, people use the **body mass index (BMI)**, *a statistic commonly used for estimating a healthy body weight given an individual's height.* The BMI is calculated by dividing the person's weight (kg) by the square of the person's height (in metres). So, if a person were 180 cm tall and weighed 100 kg, their BMI would be $100 / 1.8^2$; the outcome of this equation, 30.9, would be found on a table of BMI scores. In everyday usage, the BMI is used to screen people for weight categories that indicate whether they are considered normal weight, underweight, overweight, or obese. Someone in the healthy weight range would have a BMI between 18.5 and 24.9. People with a BMI that is less than 18.5 are considered to be underweight and may be at risk of having an eating disorder (see Module 11.1). A BMI of 25–29.9 is considered overweight, and a BMI over 30 is considered obese.

Obesity is becoming a growing concern across Canada. It is associated with numerous detrimental health consequences, such as cardiovascular disease, diabetes, osteoarthritis (degeneration of bone and cartilage material), and some forms of cancer. According to Statistics Canada (2011), 24% of Canadian adults are obese, with almost identical percentages for males and females, although these rates differ across provinces (see Figure 14.2). Although this number is significantly lower than the 34.4% obesity rate in the U.S. (Shields et al., 2011), we cannot afford to

Figure 14.2 Obesity Rates in Canada

The rates of obesity differ from province to province. More information about Canadian obesity rates is available in the *2011–2012 Canadian Community Health Survey*.

Obesity Trends among Canadian Adults CCHS, 2011–2012

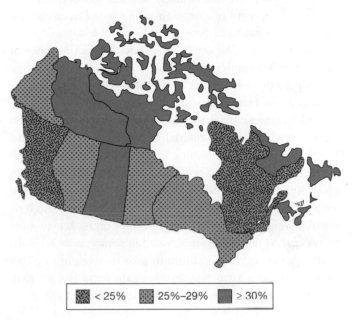

| ▨ < 25% | ▦ 25%–29% | ■ ≥ 30% |

Source: Based on data from Navaneelan, T., & Janz, T. (2014). Adjusting the scales: Obesity in the Canadian population after correcting for respondent bias. *Health at a Glance*. Statistics Canada Catalogue no. 82-624-X. Retrieved from http://www.statcan.gc.ca/pub/82-624-x/2014001/article/11922-eng.htm.

become arrogant. With a quarter of our population being obese and another quarter reporting a body-mass index that is overweight, it is clear that body weight is a major health issue in our society. Even more alarming is that obesity rates are on the rise. When examining obesity rates from the mid-1970s until 2004, researchers found that these rates remained constant until the mid-1990s, at which point they spiked upward to the current levels (Shields & Tjepkema, 2006). This report also noted that Canadians—particularly males—are becoming obese earlier in life, which means that weight-related health problems could occur at an earlier age than they have for previous generations. In fact, some researchers are concerned that these health problems could lead to shorter life expectancies than were enjoyed by previous generations (Olshansky et al., 2005).

Given that obesity is common *and* has a number of negative health consequences, researchers are actively trying to understand its causes. As discussed in Module 11.1, weight is gained because of a positive energy balance, meaning that too many calories come in and not enough are expended. Obviously, overeating can lead to obesity. But, several other factors are involved as well, including genetic, lifestyle, and social variables.

GENETICS AND BODY WEIGHT Twin, family, and adoption studies all suggest that genes account for between 50% and 90% of the variation in body weight (Maes et al., 1997). Genetic factors influence body type, metabolism, and other physiological processes that contribute to body weight and size.

Some researchers have suggested that genes contribute to the development of a **set point**, *a hypothesized mechanism that serves to maintain body weight around a physiologically programmed level*. The set point is not an exact number of pounds or kilograms, but rather a relatively small range encompassing 10% to 20% of one's weight (Garrow & Stalley, 1975; Harris, 1990). Your initial set point is controlled by genetic mechanisms, but your actual weight can be modified by environmental factors—namely, what and how much you eat. According to set point theory, if an individual gains 10% of his body weight (e.g., increasing from 150 to 165 pounds, or 68 to 75 kg) his set point would make a corresponding shift upward—the body acts as though its normal weight is now the larger 165 pounds. Metabolism slows correspondingly, such that this person now requires additional energy expenditure to take the weight off. This process explains why people who gain extra weight may shed a few pounds with relative ease, but find it overwhelmingly difficult to continue losing or even maintaining their weight once they reach an initial goal. Their bodies naturally pull their weight back to the set point.

Set point theory has a long tradition in the field of nutrition, but its validity is challenged by research suggesting that weight gain and difficulty with weight loss are unrelated to a physiological set point. Rather, individual differences in physical activity may be a stronger determinant of who succeeds at losing weight and keeping it off.

Specifically, people who gain weight expend less energy in their normal day-to-day activities (Weinsier et al., 2002). Thus, the difficulty with losing the weight may be related to lower activity levels, rather than to an increase or decrease in a person's set point.

THE SEDENTARY LIFESTYLE How do you spend your time when you're not at school or at work? Do you watch television? Or do you work out, or curl up with a good book? Research shows us that how you spend your time can have a large effect on your waistline.

Although there are number of activities that could increase the likelihood of someone being obese, data from the 2007 Canadian Community Health Survey (CCHS) suggest that television is the biggest culprit (see Figure 14.3). This survey showed that as the number of hours of television viewing increased, so did obesity rates. Only 13.7% of men who watch five or fewer hours of television per week were obese; compare this to the 25.0% obesity rate for men who watched 21 or more hours of television. Similar patterns were observed for females.

In contrast, the number of hours spent in front of a computer did not affect obesity rates, at least in males; females who spent more than 11 hours/week in front of a computer had a *slightly* higher rate of obesity than those who spent little time using a computer (18.2% vs. 15.3%, respectively). Why was there a strong relationship between television viewing and obesity and a weak relationship between computer use and obesity? Both involve sitting in front of glowing rectangles. One possibility is that computer use—be it video games, social media like Instagram or Twitter, or even typing up an essay for history class—involves a greater degree of engagement than

Figure 14.3 Obesity Rates and Television Viewing in Canadian Adults Aged 20–64

For both males and females, obesity rates were positively correlated with the number of hours spent watching television each week.

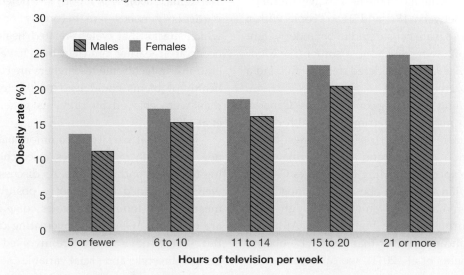

sitting on the couch and passively watching television. It is therefore more likely that people will snack while watching television.

Studies of children's obesity rates are less ambiguous. In addition to the strong relationship between television viewing and weight, researchers also have found that the amount of time that children spend playing video games is positively correlated with levels of obesity (Stettler et al., 2004). Although some video game systems such as the Wii involve physical activity, these options claim only a small portion of the overall market. Instead, many games involve sitting in front of a computer or television screen rather than engaging in exercise; this sedentary lifestyle can lead to poor dietary and exercise habits (which may continue into adulthood), and helps to explain the high childhood obesity rates found in many industrialized countries, including Canada.

SOCIAL FACTORS In addition to genetics and activity levels, obesity rates are also affected by social factors, including influences from one's family. Similarities in body weight among family members are naturally influenced by what and how much they are eating. What children eat is largely based on what their parents provide and allow them to eat, and eating patterns developed in childhood are generally carried into adulthood.

Sociocultural influences on eating certainly extend beyond the family. Food advertisements trigger eating—after watching a commercial for buttery microwave popcorn, you may have found yourself rummaging around in the kitchen in search of that last bag you hope is still there. Researchers have found that children who see food commercials while watching a 30-minute cartoon program consume 45% more snack food than do children who view nonfood commercials. The researchers estimated that this difference could lead to an additional 10 pounds (4.5 kg) of extra weight gained each year (Harris et al., 2009). Of course, corporations selling unhealthy food are aware of the power of advertising and use clever marketing techniques to promote unhealthy foods, often targeting children by linking their food with positive emotions (and toys). Luckily, in some regions of North America, lawmakers are attempting to prevent the corporations from directly targeting children by limiting when commercials can air (e.g., not during Saturday morning cartoons) and preventing them from including toys in kids' meals. The hope is that these restrictions will reduce unhealthy eating behaviours in children, thus helping them avoid the dangers of obesity.

PSYCHOLOGY AND WEIGHT LOSS Given that obesity is quite common and needs to be dealt with, how can people use psychological research to help them lose weight? The first step is to think critically about the weight-loss options that are out there. Some advertisements tell people that they can lose weight without exercising, just by taking a pill. Such options are often gimmicks. Instead, we

---

BIOPSYCHOSOCIAL PERSPECTIVES
Ethnicity, Economics, and Obesity

Genetics, social influences, and lifestyle factors all play roles in obesity. But what about broader influences, such as socioeconomic status and ethnicity? To address this question, start by classifying the following statements about obesity as either true or false:

1. In Canada, obesity rates are unrelated to ethnicity.
2. Obesity has no effect on a person's wages.
3. Obesity is related to socioeconomic factors in Canadian adults.
4. Obesity can have a negative, long-term impact on the brain.

Nutritious, nonprocessed foods tend to be more expensive, which may have led you to predict that obesity would be more prevalent in people in lower socioeconomic brackets (e.g., low income or poverty). Also, diet seems to be influenced by sociocultural factors, including the types of foods people grow up eating. What do the data say about these issues?

1. False. Statistics Canada reports that First Nations people who did not live on reserves, Métis, and Inuit people have, on average, a greater prevalence of obesity than other Canadians (Statistics Canada, 2013a).

2. False. Research on employment statistics indicates that workers who are overweight or obese are paid less than thin colleagues with similar qualifications—a finding that has led economists to suggest that the disparity in wage earnings is about equal to the size of the difference in medical costs incurred by thin versus overweight and obese people (Bhattacharya & Bundorf, 2005).

3. True. Data from the 2011–2012 *Canadian Community Health Survey* show that obesity is more common in people with lower income levels, both for males and females. One factor (of many) influencing this effect is the availability of healthy food options. Fast-food outlets are more numerous in low-income neighbourhoods than in richer areas (Hemphill et al., 2008).

4. True. Obesity can have a negative, long-term impact on the brain. Researchers have found that people who are obese have, on average, 8% less brain tissue than people who are lean. The average brain of an individual with obesity in his 70s looks approximately 16 years older than a lean person of the same age (Raji et al., 2010).

need to find a way to effectively motivate people to change their behaviours (i.e., to eat healthy foods and exercise). A study from the University of Waterloo suggests that thinking positively about oneself can promote healthy weight loss. In the first part of the study, participants wrote about either self-defining values that made them feel positively about themselves (e.g., friendships, religious beliefs, relationships) or about other values. At a follow-up session two-and-a-half months later, the self-defined value group weighed less, had lower body-mass indices, and had smaller waistlines (Logel & Cohen, 2012). It is likely that the positive emotion manipulation reduced the participants' stress regarding dieting. Given that stress leads to an increase in the number of calories consumed (see Module 11.1), reducing stress could lead to a reduction in the amount of food consumed.

Of course, losing weight is only half the battle; we also have to maintain that weight loss. There are a number of challenges involved with this. First, obese individuals pay more attention to food cues (Polivy et al., 2008) and find them more rewarding than non-obese people (Stice et al., 2008). Additionally, the drive to eat and the perceived value of food increase as more time passes since the last meal (Raynor & Epstein, 2003); this makes it difficult to remove snacks from one's routine. Several studies have shown that girls and adolescents who attempt to diet are heavier later in life (Field et al., 2003; Stice et al., 2005). The restraint involved in dieting—especially avoiding certain highly reinforcing foods—may actually make the foods even more reinforcing in the long run. All of these factors help explain why obesity is such a difficult condition to overcome—it's not simply a matter of losing a few pounds.

Module 14.1b Quiz:

Obesity

Know . . .

1. _____ is a hypothesized mechanism that serves to maintain body weight around a physiologically programmed level.
   A. BMI
   B. A set point
   C. Obesity
   D. A sedentary lifestyle

2. In Canada, researchers have found that obesity rates are related to ethnicity in what way?
   A. Obesity rates are not related to ethnicity.
   B. Caucasian adults have a greater prevalence of obesity.
   C. First Nations adults have a greater prevalence of obesity.
   D. Asian adults have a greater prevalence of obesity.

Understand. . . .

3. Which of the following factors is not related to a person's weight?
   A. Exposure to food advertisements
   B. Sedentary lifestyle
   C. Ethnicity
   D. All of the above are related to weight.

Apply. . . .

4. To avoid gaining weight during the first year of university, a person should do all of the following except
   A. increase physical activity.
   B. decrease caloric intake.
   C. be aware of the new stressors the individual will face.
   D. increase alcohol intake.

Psychosocial Influences on Health

The environments where we work, live, and play and the people with whom we interact influence both our physical and mental health. This fact seems fairly obvious, but its importance is sometimes overlooked. Think about the different neighbourhoods in your city. Some are wealthy; others are economically disadvantaged. Some are safe; others have higher crime rates. Consider the experiences that kids would have growing up in each of these neighbourhoods. How would their lives differ? And, how would these experiences affect their well-being?

POVERTY AND DISCRIMINATION Health and wealth increase together, and it appears that socioeconomic factors have numerous positive and negative effects. People who live in affluent communities not only enjoy better access to healthcare, but also have a greater sense of control over their environments and have the resources needed to maintain a lifestyle of their choosing. Individuals who lack this sense of control live in circumstances that can compromise their health. People who experience poverty, discrimination, and other social stressors have higher incidences of depression, anxiety, and other mental health problems (Tracy et al., 2008).

Furthermore, health problems are magnified by stress. Heart disease is prevalent in socioeconomically disadvantaged populations, and children who experience adverse socioeconomic circumstances (e.g., less than 12 years of education or living in a low-income household) are at greater risk for developing heart disease in adulthood (Fiscella et al., 2009; Galobardes et al., 2006). This relationship likely reflects the compound effects of stress, as well as the poorer diet that is often found among individuals residing in communities of low socioeconomic status.

People who are of low socioeconomic status are at increased risk for poor health. Numerous factors, including limited access to healthcare, stress, poor nutrition, and discrimination, collectively place children growing up in these communities at greater risk for developing health problems. Importantly, this photo is *not* from a poor developing nation. It is from one of the richest nations in the world: Canada.

Discrimination is another stressor that can compromise both physical and mental health. This kind of stressor is particularly problematic because it is often uncontrollable and unpredictable. Being a target of prejudice and discrimination is linked to increased blood pressure, heart rate, and secretions of stress hormones, which when experienced over long periods of time compromise physical health. For example, when people perceive that they are the targets of racism, their blood pressure remains elevated throughout the day and it recovers poorly during sleep (Brondolo et al., 2008a, 2008b; Steffen et al., 2003). Discrimination also puts people at greater risk for engaging in unhealthy behaviours such as smoking and substance abuse (Bennett et al., 2005; Landrine & Klonoff, 1996). Finally, discrimination, or even the perception of discrimination, can put the body on sustained alert against threats. The stress response that this state elicits can have negative, long-term effects on physical health, as you will read in Module 14.2.

FAMILY AND SOCIAL ENVIRONMENT   Our close, interpersonal relationships have a major impact on health and life satisfaction (Elgar et al., 2011). In fact, chronic social isolation is as great a mortality risk as smoking, obesity, and high blood pressure (Cacioppo & Cacioppo, 2014). **Social resilience**, *the ability to keep positive relationships and to endure and recover from social isolation and life stressors,* can protect individuals from negative health consequences of loneliness and social isolation (Cacioppo et al., 2011).

Marriage is typically the primary social relationship that people establish and has been shown to have long-term health benefits. Married people tend to live longer and have better mental and physical health than do non-married adults. Married couples enjoy the benefits of social support and combined resources, and they tend to have better health habits.

This is good news for married couples, but are both members of a heterosexual marriage benefiting equally from their union? It turns out that men enjoy greater health benefits from marriage. Unmarried women are 50% more likely to die from heart disease, several forms of cancer, cirrhosis of the liver, and other preventable diseases than are married women; this effect of marriage is even higher in men, with unmarried men being 250% more likely to die from these causes (Berkman & Breslow, 1983; Ross et al., 1990). Several possible reasons for this disparity in the health benefits gained from marriage have been suggested. One likely contributor is the greater role that women take in recognizing and supporting healthy behaviours in others.

It should be noted that heterosexual marriages are not the only form of relationship. Currently, there are relatively little data about the health benefits of homosexual marriages. The studies that do exist indicate that legally recognized marriages (like we have in Canada) provide the same benefits as are found for heterosexual couples (Riggle et al., 2010; Wight et al., 2013). As more countries and U.S. states legalize these marriages, it will be possible to investigate whether both partners benefit equally or if, like heterosexual marriages, one partner appears to gain more health benefits than the other.

Of course, marriage can also be a considerable source of stress. Marital problems are among the most stressful experiences that people can have. Married couples who are experiencing ongoing problems with their relationship tend to experience more depression and greater incidences of physical illness than happily married couples (Kiecolt-Glaser & Newton, 2001). Marital problems and divorce also affect the emotional and physical health of children, particularly if they are younger during problematic periods of a marriage or during the parents' actual divorce. Adolescents of divorced parents are at a slightly higher risk of engaging in delinquent behaviours (Amato, 2001). While divorce can negatively affect the health of children, parents who continue engaging in high-quality parenting during marital discord protect children from many of the negative effects on health attributable to divorce (Hetherington et al., 1998).

SOCIAL CONTAGION   Families are not the only interpersonal influence on how we think and act. The social group(s) that we belong to can also have a large effect on our health-related behaviours. Social scientists have found that unhealthy behaviours such as smoking or having a poor diet spread throughout one's social group. You have likely observed this phenomenon in action—if one or two people in a group of friends start to eat a lot of junk food, it is easy for the others in the group to pick

Social contagion in the dorms. Your roommate may influence your GPA more than you know—for better or for worse. At Dartmouth College in the U.S., students are randomly assigned to their dorm rooms rather than matched on various characteristics, as is customary at many schools. This practice makes Dartmouth's roommate pairs a diverse mixture. Professor Bruce Sacerdote (2001) found that GPA levels are influenced by one's roommate. Students with high GPAs elevate the GPAs of their lower-scoring roommates, and vice versa.

up this habit as well. These changes can work in either direction, positive or negative. Just as social-group influence can lead to smoking, it can also lead to training for a half-marathon.

These phenomena are examples of **social contagion**, *the often subtle, unintentional spreading of a behaviour as a result of social interactions*. Social contagion of body weight, smoking, and other health-related behaviours has been documented in the Framingham Heart Study. The U.S. National Heart Institute began this ongoing study in 1948 to track 15 000 residents of Framingham, Massachusetts. Participants made regular visits to their doctors, who recorded important health statistics such as heart rate, body weight, and other standard physical measures. Scientists working with the Framingham data noticed that over time, clusters of people from this study group became increasingly similar in certain characteristics—such as body weight increases or decreases, starting or quitting smoking, and even levels of happiness (Christakis & Fowler, 2007, 2008; Fowler & Christakis, 2008). It turns out that the groups who showed similar patterns in their health statistics were also friends with one another. This work demonstrates just how powerful social factors can be. Of course, this research doesn't only mean that you should be wary of your friends and their unhealthy behaviours. It also shows that through social contagion, you can be a positive force in the lives of the people around you.

Module 14.1c Quiz:

Psychosocial Influences on Health

Know . . .

1. Which psychological term refers to the often subtle, unintentional spreading of a behaviour as a result of social interactions?
   A. Health psychology
   B. Social contagion
   C. Discrimination
   D. Observational learning

2. Based on the research discussed in this module, which of the following is the *lowest* risk factor for health problems?
   A. Being an unmarried adult
   B. Experiencing discrimination

   C. Having an identical twin who is overweight
   D. Being a married adult

Understand. . . .

3. Which of the following statements about how discrimination influences health is most accurate?
   A. Experiencing discrimination stimulates the stress response, which can bring about long-term health problems.
   B. People who experience discrimination are likely to compensate for it by making positive health-related choices.
   C. An immediate increase in heart rate is the biggest problem associated with experiencing discrimination.
   D. Discrimination is unrelated to poor health.

Module 14.1 Summary

14.1a   Know . . . the key terminology related to health psychology.

body mass index (BMI)
set point
social contagion
social resilience

14.1b   Understand . . . how genetic and environmental factors influence obesity.

Some research suggests that genetics influences our set point, a weight (or range of weights) that our body tends to maintain; however, weight is influenced by several other factors as well. Environmental influences on weight gain are abundant. Cultural, family, and socioeconomic factors

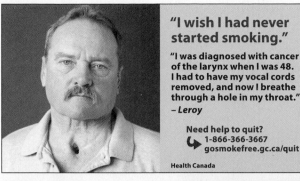

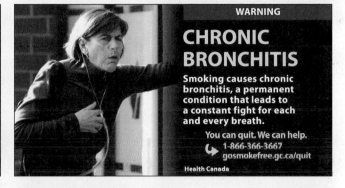

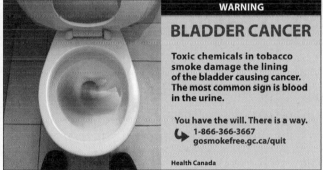

influence activity levels and diet, even in very subtle ways, such as through social contagion.

14.1c Apply . . . your knowledge of persuasion and health to examine the effectiveness of different types of cigarette warnings.

In this module, you read about efforts by different countries to reduce smoking rates. In Canada, cigarette packages contain different types of emotional images depicting the dangers of smoking. But, the audience for these packages is diverse—some people viewing the images are life-long smokers who *should* quit whereas others are teenagers who are considering smoking.

Apply Activity

Consider the images shown here. Which images target young people and which images target long-time smokers?

What differences do you see between the two types of images? What types of imagery do you think would be most effective in influencing the behaviour of the two groups?

Now try using a search engine like Google Images to look at cigarette packages from different countries. How does the packaging differ from Canadian cigarette packages? Why do you think these cultural differences exist?

14.1d Analyze . . . whether media depictions of smoking affect smoking in adolescents.

Correlational trends certainly show that smoking in popular movies is positively correlated with smoking among adolescents (e.g., increased exposure is related to increased incidence of smoking). Controlled laboratory studies suggest a cause-and-effect relationship exists between identification with story protagonists who smoke and smoking behaviour by young viewers.

Module 14.2 Stress and Illness

Imagesource/Glow Images

 ## Learning Objectives

14.2a Know . . . the key terminology associated with stress and illness.

14.2b Understand . . . the physiological reactions that occur under stress.

14.2c Understand . . . how the immune system is connected to stress responses.

14.2d Apply . . . a measure of stressful events to your own experiences.

14.2e Analyze . . . the claim that ulcers are caused by stress.

The frustration and embarrassment of choking under pressure is undeniable. Whether the stakes are a championship title or admission to an elite university, a sudden, inexplicable shift to subpar performance can be devastating. According to psychologist Sian Beilock, the culprit in such a case may be the negative effects that stress has on working memory—the short-term capacity to hold and manipulate information. Calculating a 15% tip for a bill of $43.84 at a restaurant, or while the pizza delivery person waits, requires working memory processes. The pressure of your date watching you or the pizza delivery person looking on impatiently may result in your appearing either foolishly generous or just plain cheap.

Beilock has conducted experiments on how stress affects the cognitive resources needed for problem solving. For example, in one study, research volunteers were asked to solve math problems. Some were told that if they solved the problems correctly, they would earn money for themselves as well as for a partner they were paired with; if they did not perform well, both the volunteer and the partner would lose money. Beilock and her colleagues have found that this type of pressure draws resources away from the working memory processes needed for success (Beilock, 2008, 2010). Stressful thoughts readily

occupy working memory space and cause the unfortunate experience of choking under pressure. The fact that the physiological response of stress can be caused by a social situation and can then affect a cognitive ability like working memory demonstrates, once again, the importance of the biopsychosocial model in understanding human behaviour.

Focus Questions

1. How does stress affect the brain and body?

2. How do individuals differ in how they handle stress?

》 Imagine a student near the end of the semester with several papers due and final exams looming. Now imagine someone who has worked at the same job for 25 years being told that he needs to learn a new computer system or he will be laid off. Or, think about a soccer player in a championship game that will be decided by penalty kicks; she walks up to place the ball on the penalty spot, knowing that if she misses her team will lose. If you were asked to

out—*or not stressed out enough*—she will not perform at an optimal level. Critically, many elite athletes are able to compare their current emotional state with the level of stress they had experienced prior to good performances; they can then attempt to adjust their current state to more closely match their optimal one (Jokela & Hanin, 1999).

The data described in this section leads to an obvious question: *How* does a physiological response—stress—affect our mental life and cognitive abilities? In the next section of this module, we will examine how your brain and body can produce the *feelings* and *sensations* associated with the experience of stress.

Module 14.2a Quiz:

What Causes Stress?

Understand. . . .

1. Some people are at their best when they are under a lot of pressure; other people reach their best level of performance when they are under relatively little stress. This difference best reflects the concept of

- **A.** primary appraisal of stress.
- **B.** secondary appraisal of stress.
- **C.** an individual zone of optimal functioning.
- **D.** the emotional arousal effect.

Apply. . . .

2. Shea had to move to Montreal as part of his job. He did not speak much French and didn't know many people in the city. He was quite concerned. However, he realized that he would quickly meet people through his job and that this social network would help him get settled. According to the cognitive appraisal theory of stress, what would you call Shea's initial thoughts on moving to Montreal?

- **A.** Primary appraisal of stress
- **B.** Secondary appraisal of stress

- **C.** Individual zone of optimal functioning
- **D.** Emotional arousal effect

3. Claire was usually a little bit nervous before writing exams. However, prior to writing her first Canadian History exam, Claire noticed that she didn't really feel any stress at all. She ended up getting a C+ on the exam, well below her normal performance. What is the best explanation for her poor mark?

- **A.** Claire's stress consumed her cognitive resources, thus leading to a poor grade.
- **B.** Claire's stress level during the exam did not provide her with enough emotional arousal to perform at her best.
- **C.** The test was so difficult that Claire's stress levels were not important.
- **D.** The test was too complex for Claire, so her stress impaired her performance.

Physiology of Stress

Think about the last time you experienced stress. How did you *feel*? Although stress depends upon our mental appraisal of a situation or event, the physiological response to stress occurs throughout most of the body. Indeed, you can literally feel yourself react to acute stressors, such as giving a presentation in class, as well as chronic stressors, such as the cumulative effect of a challenging school year. Walter Cannon, an early researcher into the phenomenon of stress, noted that the physical responses to stressors were somewhat general, despite the fact that stress can come from a variety of sources that may be biological, cognitive, or social in nature. Cannon described this general reaction as a **fight-or-flight response**, *a set of physiological changes that occur in response to psychological or physical threats*. This discovery laid the foundation for the modern study of stress, with several researchers building upon Cannon's pioneering work.

Hans Selye (1950, 1956) of the Université de Montréal looked beyond the immediate fight-or-flight response and saw the unfolding of a larger pattern during responses to stress. He named this pattern the **general adaptation**

syndrome (GAS), *a theory of stress responses involving stages of alarm, resistance, and exhaustion* (see Figure 14.6). As GAS illustrates, a stressful event, such as a mild shock if you are a rat or a pop quiz (or a mild shock) if you are a university student, first elicits an *alarm* reaction. Alarm consists of your recognition of the threat and the physiological reactions that accompany it, including increases in blood pressure, muscle tension, heart rate, and adrenaline release. As the stressful event continues, the individual enters the second part of this adaptive response, known as *resistance*. Resistance is characterized by an individual using his or her physical and mental resources to respond to the stressor in an appropriate way (e.g., furiously studying for a quiz or running away from predators). However, an animal (or student) can't maintain this level of energy use forever. The third and final stage of the GAS is often referred to as *exhaustion*; this occurs when the stressful experience depletes your physical resources and your physiological stress response, and thus your ability to cope, declines.

Since the work of Cannon and Selye, psychologists have further uncovered the highly complex physiological interactions that occur during and after stress. Modern

Figure 14.6 The General Adaptation Syndrome

This graph depicts the body's resistance to stress. After the initial shock associated with the stressor (see the dip in resistance early in the Alarm phase), the body recruits resources to allow it to deal with the stressful situation or event. This ability to cope with the stressor peaks in the Resistance phase of the GAS. However, if the individual doesn't overcome the stressor, eventually he or she will be unable to resist the stress; this final phase is known as the Exhaustion phase.

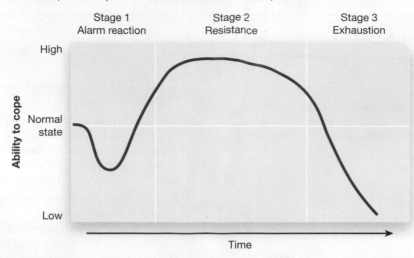

Source: Source: Based on "Stress and the General Adaptation Syndrome" by Hans Selye, *British Medical Journal*, June 17, 1950.

descriptions of the physiology of stress involve both the autonomic nervous system (ANS) and endocrine (hormone) responses.

THE STRESS PATHWAYS Sweaty palms, an increased heart rate, and gastrointestinal sensations (i.e., "butterflies in the stomach") are part of stress responses to both positive and negative events. Many of these bodily responses are the result of activity in the autonomic pathway, which originates in the brain and extends to the body where you *feel* stress the most. Recall from Module 3.3 that the nervous system consists of the central nervous system (brain and spinal cord) and the peripheral nervous system, which includes the ANS. In response to stress, the hypothalamus stimulates part of the ANS known as the sympathetic nervous system, which then causes the inner part of the adrenal glands known as the *adrenal medulla* (found on top of the kidneys) to release epinephrine and norepinephrine (also known as adrenaline and noradenaline). These chemicals then trigger the bodily changes associated with the fight-or-flight response (see Figure 14.7).

Another physiological system involved in the stress response is the **hypothalamic–pituitary–adrenal (HPA) axis**, *a neural and endocrine circuit that provides communication between the nervous system (the hypothalamus) and the endocrine system (pituitary and adrenal glands)*. When you perceive that you are in a stressful situation, the hypothalamus and pituitary gland work together to stimulate the release of **cortisol**, *a hormone secreted by the adrenal cortex (the outer part of the adrenal gland) that prepares the body*

to respond to stressful circumstances. Cortisol may stimulate increased access to energy stores or lead to decreased inflammation. In summary, both the sympathetic nervous system (through the release of epinephrine and norepinephrine) and the HPA axis (through the release of cortisol) function to prepare us to respond to stress.

With rare medical exceptions, humans mount both autonomic and HPA axis responses to stress. These responses are highly adaptive and promote behaviours that help our survival (e.g., being more vigilant or running extra fast). However, as you will see, not everyone responds to these stress responses in the same way.

OXYTOCIN: TO TEND AND BEFRIEND One observation you have likely made is that males and females often respond to stress and threat in different ways. Although many of these differences are a product of societal expectations (e.g., men are typically expected to hide their stress), there are in fact some differences in the HPA axis of males and females. Numerous experiments have found that males have a larger cortisol response to stress than females. This difference occurs for both real-world stressors such as exams and laboratory-based stressors such as having to give a speech (Kudielka & Kirschbaum, 2005). As a result, males tend to respond to threats with a rapid expenditure of energy (fight or flight).

Shelley Taylor and her colleagues at UCLA have suggested that whereas men are more likely to react to stress or threats with a fight-or-flight response, women are more likely to have a more social *tend-and-befriend* response

Figure 14.7 Stress Pathways of the Body

The stress pathways of the body include the autonomic nervous system and the HPA axis. Both systems converge on the adrenal glands. The autonomic response involves stimulation of the adrenal medulla by the sympathetic nervous system, resulting in the release of epinephrine and norepinephrine—chemicals that stimulate the fight-or-flight response. Activity of the HPA axis results in stimulation of the adrenal cortex, which releases cortisol into the bloodstream.

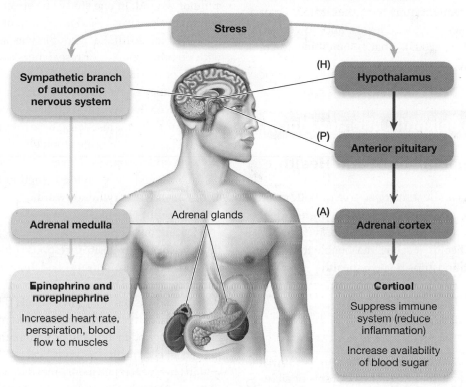

(Taylor et al., 2000; Taylor, 2006). This view makes sense if you think about the history of our species. Over the course of our species' evolution, females have had to care for dependent and vulnerable children. Running away from a stressful situation would have required abandoning

According to the tend-and-befriend theory, females often respond to stress by seeking out social support networks. Although there are physiological explanations for sex differences in stress responses, we should also remember that cognitive and social factors also influence these behaviours.

offspring; getting into a fight risked the possibility of death or injury. Both of these responses would have reduced the likelihood that their offspring would have survived. Instead, it made more sense to seek out stable friendship networks for support during times of stress. Doing so provided comfort, but also the potential for additional resources to help with offspring. This is not to say that women don't have any instinctive fight-or-flight response or that men have no need to tend and befriend; rather, these researchers are suggesting that there are sex differences in which response is *more likely* to occur.

The tend-and-befriend reaction may be promoted by the release of **oxytocin**, *a stress-sensitive hormone that is typically associated with maternal bonding and social relationships*. Oxytocin influences a number of behaviours including the contraction of the uterus when a woman is in labour, romantic attachment, social bonding, trust, wound healing, and orgasm (although not all at the same time; Caldwell & Young III, 2006; Lee et al., 2009). Although oxytocin is clearly involved in a number of behaviours, its role in stress is particularly important. Animal studies have shown that stimulating the release of oxytocin reduces activity in the sympathetic nervous system (one of the parts of the stress network) and blood pressure

(Carter, 1998). In humans, women who are breastfeeding and thus have high levels of oxytocin show lower stress responses to physical and psychological stress (Light et al., 2000); similar findings were reported in men who were given doses of oxytocin (Heinrichs et al., 2003). And, most relevant to the tend-and-befriend hypothesis, women who receive more frequent hugs from their romantic partners also had higher oxytocin levels and lower stress responses (Light et al., 2005). That's something to think about when studying for exams.

Working the Scientific Literacy Model

Hormones, Relationships, and Health

Social relationships can be a major source of both positive and negative stress, and they can provide a great deal of support during our most stressful times. Given the links between stress and health, it seems reasonable to ask: How do our personal relationships relate to health?

What do we know about hormones, relationships, and health?

Many family events and relationships can be stressful. Almost everyone has argued with their parents or siblings. Holidays and weddings can be fun, but they also involve a lot of planning and, at times, "intense discussion." Sometimes relationships—particularly with close friends or romantic partners—become very difficult and tense, and may even lead to chronic stress responses that adversely affect a person's health. However, other relationships can be quite fulfilling, and can lead to strong social bonds that last a lifetime. These positive relationships have been linked to specific hormonal responses in the body.

Two hormones, oxytocin and vasopressin, are involved in social behaviour and bonding. We previously discussed the role of oxytocin in moderating stress responses, particularly in females. Oxytocin has been shown to inhibit activity in the amygdala, a brain region involved with fear and threat responses (Kirsch et al., 2005). It may also prevent the release of cortisol (Heinrichs et al., 2003). Vasopressin also has stress-reducing functions. Like oxytocin, the release of vasopressin is controlled by the hypothalamus and pituitary gland, and affects the levels of stress hormones released by the adrenal gland (Goland et al., 1991). People with high vasopressin levels tend to report better relationship quality with their spouses (Walum et al., 2008). However, oxytocin and vasopressin have health functions that go beyond improving social bonds. Both of these hormones interact with the immune system, specifically to reduce inflammation.

How can science explain connections between hormones, relationships, and health?

A common, if not surprising, method for measuring immunity and health is to see how quickly people recover from a minor wound. In one study, the effect of marital stress on wound healing was tested in a group of 37 married couples (Gouin et al., 2010). Each couple was asked to sit together with no other couples or researchers present and complete a series of marital interaction tasks, including a discussion of the history of their marriage and a task in which both spouses were instructed to discuss something they wished to change about themselves. These interactions were videotaped. The researchers also took blood samples to measure oxytocin and vasopressin levels. Additionally, each participant consented to receiving a suction blister on the forearm, which is a very minor wound created with a medical vacuum pump. It's like a hickey—but a hickey *for science*.

During the marital interaction tasks, those who engaged their partner with positive responses including acceptance, support, and self-disclosure had higher levels of oxytocin and vasopressin. Those who responded with hostility, withdrawal, and distress had lower levels (Figure 14.8). In addition, the suction blister wounds healed more quickly over an eight-day period in individuals with high oxytocin and vasopressin levels. (Suction wounds heal to 100% within 12 days.)

In another experiment, married couples were given either an intranasal solution of oxytocin or a placebo. They then engaged in discussion about conflict within their marriage. Those who received a boost of oxytocin showed more positive, constructive behaviour during their discussion compared to couples in the placebo group. The researchers also measured cortisol levels from saliva samples obtained from each individual. Those in the oxytocin group had lower levels of this stress hormone compared to couples in the placebo group (Ditzen et al., 2009).

Can we critically evaluate this evidence?

It might be tempting to conclude that a boost of oxytocin or vasopressin could be the key to marital happiness, stress reduction, and physical health. Although the studies you just read about are related to these important qualities, it is important to avoid oversimplifying what their results mean. Claims that homeopathic oxytocin remedies can make anyone happier and better at love, marriage, sex, and even "mind reading" should be looked at with skepticism. Advertisements for such products are not hard to find. However, scientists are still in the relatively early stages of learning just how oxytocin and vasopressin affect social behaviour in humans, and how they are related to immune system function (Gouin et al., 2010; Macdonald & Macdonald, 2010).

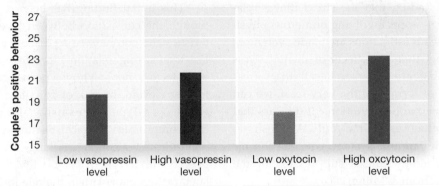

Figure 14.8 Relationship Quality Is Related to Physiological Responses

Higher oxytocin and vasopressin levels are associated with positive social interactions between married couples.

Source: Republished with permission of Elsevier Science, Inc., from Marital behavior, oxytocin, vasopressin, and wound healing by Jean-Philippe Gouin et. al., *Psychoneuroendocrinology*, 35(7):1082-90, 2010; permission conveyed through Copyright Clearance Center, Inc.

Why is this relevant?

Although these studies were conducted with married couples, the physiological and physical healing benefits of close, positive social relationships extend to romantic relationships, friendships, and family. Procedures for healing physical injury currently focus on repair to damaged areas and preventing infection from setting in. In addition to these critical steps, it appears that managing psychological stress is also important for facilitating recovery from wounds (Gouin & Kiecolt-Glaser, 2011). As we shall see in the next section of this module, stress can also affect a number of other aspects of our physical health.

Module 14.2b Quiz:

Physiology of Stress

Know . . .

1. Which of the following is *not* a component of Selye's general adaptation syndrome?
   A. Resistance
   B. Alarm
   C. Flight
   D. Exhaustion

2. Which of the following is a major player in the chemical response comprising the autonomic fight-or-flight stress response system?
   A. Cortisol
   B. Epinephrine
   C. Dopamine
   D. Oxytocin

Understand. . . .

3. A major difference between the tend-and-befriend stress response and the responses mediated by the autonomic pathway and the HPA axis is that
   A. the tend-and-befriend response involves cortisol activity.
   B. men are more likely to express the tend-and-befriend response.
   C. the tend-and-befriend response facilitates care for offspring and others in a social group.
   D. the tend-and-befriend response is a negative stress reaction, whereas the autonomic pathway and HPA axis responses are positive reactions.

4. High ____ levels and low ____ levels are associated with elevated stress.
   A. vasopressin; cortisol
   B. oxytocin; vasopressin
   C. cortisol; oxytocin
   D. vasopressin; epinephrine

Stress, Immunity, and Illness

You have likely had the experience of getting sick in the midst of a period of high stress. You are not alone; dozens of experimental and correlational studies have shown, for example, that stress increases the likelihood that people will succumb to the cold virus (Cohen et al., 1998). In fact, one study suggests that final exams—an obvious stressor for students—may be bad for you. In this investigation, medical students provided blood samples during the term and again during the final exam period. Analysis of these blood samples showed reduced immune responses during the high-stress period at the end of the term (Kiecolt-Glaser, 1984). There is a reason this happens: the immune system, which is responsible for protecting the body against infectious disease, has numerous connections with the nervous system, including the stress response systems just discussed (Maier & Watkins, 1998; Selye, 1955). **Psychoneuro-immunology** *is the study of this relationship between immune system and nervous system functioning.*

Psychologists are finding that the stress–illness relationship is a very complex one, involving numerous physiological systems. These investigations are made even more challenging by the fact that the effects of mental stress on physical functioning are diverse. Recall that stress can come in a variety of forms—at the very least, we can divide it into acute and chronic variations. It appears that stress also has dual influences on immunity. Acute stressors tend to activate the immune system, whereas chronic exposure to stress generally causes suppression of the immune system (Segerstrom & Miller, 2004).

STRESS, PERSONALITY, AND HEART DISEASE In addition to making people more prone to catching viruses, high stress levels appear to put people at greater risk for developing **coronary heart disease**—*a condition in which plaques form in the blood vessels that supply the heart with blood and oxygen, resulting in restricted blood flow.* For example, one study followed 12 000 healthy males for a nine-year period and found that men who experienced ongoing stress with their families or at work were 30% more likely to die from coronary heart disease than were men who were not chronically stressed (Matthews & Gump, 2002). Coronary heart disease begins when injury and infection damage the arteries of the heart. This damage triggers the inflammatory response by the immune system—white blood cells travel to affected areas in an attempt to repair the damaged tissue. These cells gather cholesterol and form dangerous plaques, which can rupture, break off, and block blood flow. So how does stress fit into this picture? Stress causes an increased release of those molecules that cause the inflammation that leads to heart complications (Segerstrom & Miller, 2004).

It seems like the link between stress and heart disease should have a simple solution: reduce your stress levels. However, this isn't as straightforward as one might think. The reason is that our stress responses are affected by our personalities. Interestingly, this relationship wasn't discovered by psychologists. Rather, it was noticed by two cardiologists—Meyer Friedman and Ray Rosenman—who were conducting an eight-and-a-half year study of cardiovascular health. As you might expect, they found that people who were prone to stress had poorer physical health (Friedman & Rosenman, 1959). Importantly, a subset of these patients also had a particular group of personality traits that the researchers labelled as Type A. The **Type A personality** *describes people who tend to be impatient and worry about time, and are easily angered, competitive, and highly motivated.* In contrast, the **Type B personality** *describes people who are more laid back and characterized by*

a patient, easygoing, and relaxed disposition (Friedman & Rosenman, 1974). These studies revealed that people who fall in the Type A category are far more likely to have heart attacks than are Type B people.

This initial finding has been replicated many times, though the correlation between levels of Type A characteristics and coronary heart disease is only moderate. This less-than-strong relationship likely reflects the fact that other factors, not just how a person copes with stress, may further elevate the risk of coronary heart disease. People who have a Type A personality also engage in behaviours that compromise physical health, such as drinking large quantities of alcohol, smoking, and sleeping less than people with a Type B personality. Thus, numerous correlated factors may explain the relationship between Type A personality and risk of coronary heart disease. People with Type A personalities are often successful. However, they are also much more likely to experience heart attacks and strokes than are more relaxed, less hostile individuals.

The distinction between Type A and B personalities has not satisfied all behavioural scientists and physicians. Being quick to anger is a characteristic of Type A individuals, but so is being hyper-motivated to succeed at work. Perhaps there is something more specific about personality that increases one's risk for developing heart disease. More recent research has shown that people who are prone to hostility and anger are at greater risk for developing coronary heart disease (Razzini et al., 2008). Other personality characteristics linked to coronary heart disease include anxiety and depression (Barger & Sydeman, 2005; Lett et al., 2004).

Christopher Futcher/E+/Getty Images

Imagine you have a one-hour break between classes, during which you need to get lunch and also visit one of your professors across campus. When you arrive at your professor's office, you see a line of other students awaiting their turn, and the current occupant is blathering on and on about something completely unrelated to schoolwork. How would you tend to react in this situation? Would you become agitated, angry, resentful, and fidgety? Or would you be more inclined to strike up a conversation with others in line to help pass the time? Your answer will likely depend on various factors—but each of us tends to have a common style of responding to stressful events.

Myths in Mind

Stress and Ulcers

Many of the presumed links between stress and health are oversimplified or misunderstood. People typically associate ulcers—open sores in the lining of the esophagus, stomach, and small intestine—with people working in high-stress jobs, such as police officers or air traffic controllers. The belief that stress causes people to develop ulcers is widespread. In actuality, most ulcers are caused by a bacterium, *Helicobacter pylori*, which can cause inflammation of the lining of various regions of the digestive tract. This bacterium is surprisingly common, and approximately 10% to 15% of people who are exposed to it will develop an ulcer resulting from inflammation. Thus, stress does not cause ulcers, although it can worsen their symptoms. Also, smoking, alcohol, pain relievers, and a poor diet—anything that can irritate the digestive system—increases problems associated with ulcers.

Contrary to popular belief, chronic stress, like that experienced by air traffic controllers, will not cause a stomach ulcer.

STRESS, FOOD, AND DRUGS Stress influences heart functioning in other, indirect, ways as well. Survey research has consistently shown that people are drawn toward sweet and fatty foods when they are stressed (Oliver & Wardle, 1999; Steptoe et al., 1998). Laboratory-based studies have shown similar trends. In one experiment, female participants were given stress-inducing tasks to complete including solving a visuospatial puzzle, performing math calculations, and giving a speech in front of what they thought was an audience seated behind a one-way mirror. The women who had the highest levels of the stress hormone cortisol ate more sweet, high-fat snacks than did the less-stressed women (Epel et al., 2001). The relationship between stress and unhealthy food extends to other species as well. Low-status females in a colony of monkeys are often bullied and harassed by high-status females; researchers have noted that the low-status females ate more banana-flavoured pellets than their social superiors (Wilson et al., 2008). Interestingly, similar results were found when monkeys had the opportunity to self-administer cocaine; the subordinate monkeys pressed a lever much more often than the dominant monkeys who presumably had less stress (Morgan et al., 2002).

Obviously, overeating unhealthy food (or doing cocaine) is not a good long-term solution to stress. So, why do some people (and monkeys) use food and drugs to deal with stress? Although it is possible that these substances directly affect the hormones and brain areas associated with stress, most scientists agree that food (and drugs) influence the brain's dopamine reward system (see Modules 5.3 and 6.2). Some research suggests that chronic stress suppresses the reward system (so stressed people would find less joy in things). It is possible that eating rewarding foods increases the activity in this system so that it is closer to normal levels (Adam & Epel, 2007; Dallman et al., 2003). Additionally, as discussed in Module 11.1, people who are stressed are mobilizing the body's resources in case action is required; eating fatty and sugary foods provides the body with extra calories *in anticipation* of the person having to use additional energy to deal with a stressor.

STRESS, THE BRAIN, AND DISEASE Although stress is often linked to cardiovascular problems like heart attacks and strokes, its negative effect on the immune system makes stress a factor in other conditions as well. Acquired immune deficiency syndrome (AIDS) is a disease caused by infection with the human immunodeficiency virus (HIV). This disease saps the immune system's ability to fight off infections to such an extent that even conditions that are relatively harmless to most of the population can be devastating to an individual with AIDS. Patients in industrialized countries with more medical options have a better prognosis than those living in impoverished areas. Retroviral therapies have greatly increased the longevity, health, and overall quality of life of patients. However, people who are HIV-positive need regular vaccination treatments. Unfortunately, stress impedes the body's ability to respond to vaccinations. In turn, studies have shown that those who experience serious emotional distress are less responsive to HIV treatments. Stress-induced elevation of the neurotransmitter norepinephrine—which is involved in emotional arousal and stress responses—can also worsen the condition of the various illnesses associated with AIDS. Patients who have elevated activity of the autonomic nervous system are slower to respond to antiretroviral therapies, which increases their risks of developing certain types of cancer such as B-cell lymphoma (Cole et al., 1998).

Researchers are also finding numerous links between psychosocial factors and cancer progression (Antoni & Lutgendorf, 2007). Several factors, such as the type of cancer and an individual's age, account for why some people rapidly succumb to cancer while others are able to overcome this disease. But, stress levels also affect the progression of cancer. Why is this? It appears that norepinephrine supports cancer cell growth, and that cortisol magnifies this effect. Hormones from the autonomic nervous system stimulate cells that reside in tumours, which ultimately results in growth and proliferation of these masses (Antoni et al., 2006). Thus, when someone experiences stress, the autonomic nervous system and HPA axis naturally respond, but their reactions compromise how well the individual can fight the disease.

For many people, stress levels can be changed and the course of a disease such as cancer can be slowed. For example, individuals who have undergone assertiveness training and learn anger management techniques show reduced autonomic activity and hormonal activity associated with the HPA axis (Antoni et al., 2007). Also, those who are optimistic, cope by using humour, and have a positive outlook on the disease (and thus less stress) show physiological benefits such as greater immune responses (Lutgendorf et al., 2007). These studies show us that how we mentally react to the stressors in our lives can dramatically influence how our body responds to serious illness. In the next module, we will discuss how you can draw from psychology research to improve your ability to cope with stress. Doing so will make you happier—and healthier.

Module 14.2c Quiz:

Stress, Immunity, and Illness

Know . . .

1. What is psychoneuroimmunology?
   A. A condition in which plaques form in the blood vessels that supply the heart with blood and oxygen, resulting in restricted blood flow.
   B. The study of both the positive and negative effects that our behaviour and decisions have on health, survival, and well-being.
   C. The study of the relationship between immune system and nervous system functioning.
   D. A hormone secreted by the adrenal gland.

2. People with _____ personality are patient and easygoing, and have a relaxed disposition, whereas _____ personality individuals tend to be impatient and are easily angered, competitive, and highly motivated.
   A. Type A; Type B
   B. Type H; relaxed
   C. Type B; Type A
   D. relaxed; Type H

Understand. . . .

3. A *direct* effect of stress on coronary health would be
   A. a stress-related increase in inflammation that results in buildup of cholesterol in the arteries.
   B. eating more fattening foods in response to stress.
   C. engaging in increased risky behaviour due to stress.
   D. increased moodiness during periods of stress.

4. How does stress affect cancer?
   A. Stress decreases the number of white blood cells in the body, which results in cancer progression.
   B. Hormones from the autonomic nervous system stimulate cells that reside in tumours, which can in turn stimulate growth and proliferation of the tumours.
   C. Stress decreases the growth of cancer cells.
   D. Stress does not affect cancer.

Analyze . . .

5. Researchers have concluded that the actual cause of ulcers is usually _____.
   A. stress
   B. bacterial infection
   C. genetics
   D. poor diet

Module 14.2 Summary

14.2a   Know . . . the key terminology associated with stress and illness.

coronary heart disease
cortisol
fight-or-flight response
general adaptation syndrome (GAS)
hypothalamic–pituitary–adrenal (HPA) axis
individual zone of optimal functioning (IZOF)
oxytocin
psychoneuroimmunology
stress
Type A personality
Type B personality

14.2b   Understand . . . the physiological reactions that occur under stress.

When a person encounters a stressor, the hypothalamus stimulates the sympathetic nervous system to act, triggering the release of epinephrine and norepinephrine from the adrenal medulla. This reaction is often referred to as the fight-or-flight response. Another part of the stress response system is the HPA axis, in which the hypothalamus stimulates the pituitary gland to release hormones that in turn stimulate the adrenal cortex to release cortisol, which prepares the body to deal with stressful situations.

14.2c   Understand . . . how the immune system is connected to stress responses.

Cortisol suppresses the immune system, leaving people more vulnerable to illness and slowing recovery time from illness and injury.

14.2d   Apply . . . a measure of stressful events to your own experiences.

Apply Activity

To complete this activity, look at Table 14.2. Using the values next to each stressful event listed, add up the numbers that apply to your experiences and compute your total stress score. Holmes and Rahe (1967) found that a score of 300 or more puts people at significant risk for illness, while a score of 150–299 puts people at a moderate risk.

Years later, Renner and Mackin (1998) developed a similar scale for college and university students based on data gathered from a sample of 257 undergraduate students (range: 17–45 years; mean: 19.75 years). Do an Internet search for Renner and Mackin's College Undergraduate Stress Scale and calculate your own stress score. They reported an average stress score of 1247 (standard deviation: 441), with scores ranging from 182 to 2571. How do you compare with their sample?

14.2e   Analyze . . . the claim that ulcers are caused by stress.

Ulcers are damaged areas of the digestive tract often caused by infection with the bacterium *Helicobacter pylori*. Stress and other factors, such as diet and alcohol consumption, can worsen the condition of ulcers, but stress alone does not cause them.

Module 14.3 Coping and Well-Being

John Lund/Stephanie Roeser/Glow Images

 ## Learning Objectives

14.3a Know . . . the key terminology associated with coping and well-being.

14.3b Understand . . . how control over the environment influences coping and outlook.

14.3c Understand . . . positive and negative styles of coping.

14.3d Apply . . . your knowledge of the beneficial effects of optimism to help you reframe stressful situations as positive opportunities.

14.3e Analyze . . . whether activities such as relaxation techniques, meditation, and biofeedback actually help people cope with stress and problems.

What is the best way to cope with a personal disaster, such as losing your job? Writing about how the event makes you feel may not seem like a priority, but according to psychologist James Pennebaker, it may be one of the best strategies for coping and regaining the emotional resources needed to move on. Pennebaker, a leading researcher on the psychological benefits of writing, decided to intervene when a local computing and electronics firm laid off 60 professional workers. All he asked the workers to do was to write, but their instructions on how to write were different: Half the volunteers were randomly assigned to write about their "deepest thoughts and feelings surrounding the job loss, and how their lives, both personal and professional, had been affected" (Spera et al., 1994, p. 725). In contrast, the control group members were told to write about their plans for the day and how they planned to find another job, which is much less personal and emotional. After a month of weekly 20-minute writing sessions, the group members who were writing about their emotions were getting hired much more frequently than the control group members. The participants were randomly assigned to the two groups, *so the differences between the groups can be traced to the writing rather than to pre-existing personality differences. Similar methods have been used in Pennebaker's studies of first-year university students, people grieving the loss of a loved one, and other groups experiencing stressful transitions. The result was the same each time—group members who wrote meaningful narratives of their emotions and thoughts came out ahead, not just in terms of mental health, but physically and in terms of their performance at work or school.*

Focus Questions

1. What are the different ways people cope with stress?

2. Which factors make coping especially challenging?

>> This module is designed to help you. In it, you will read about some widely used solutions for coping with stress and behavioural methods that may potentially help in improving health. We will also discuss some topics that

might be less familiar, but may prove useful in how you cope with stress and negative events. Finally, we will discuss how stress and successful coping are closely related to your sense of control.

Coping

Although understanding how stress works—both physically and mentally—is important, it is the ability to cope with that stress that will dictate whether or not you are happy. **Coping** *refers to the processes used to manage demands, stress, and conflict.* Coping strategies can include *problem-focused coping* and *emotion-focused coping.* Some of us approach a problem or stressor, such as large monetary debt or a setback at work, by taking a problem-solving approach. In other words, we cope by defining the problem and working toward a solution. If you are stressed out by school demands, you could address the problem by setting up a study schedule, dropping a course, or finding a tutor, among many other possible solutions. However, there are times when it is more important to focus on the emotional effects of a stressor than on attempting to find an immediate solution to a problem—in fact, not all stressors are brought about by problems that have identifiable solutions. For example, imagine that your beloved family pet has passed away. In such a situation, you obviously cannot make a list to deal with your grief; however, you *can* find ways to reduce the negative effects your emotions are having, both on yourself and on others. Neither of these styles of coping is necessarily superior to the other—their suitability depends on the nature of the problem (Folkman & Lazarus, 1980). In many instances, both problem-focused coping and emotion-focused coping are used to deal with a stressor.

Of course, not all coping techniques actually help; some may simply replace one problem with another. For example, some people turn to alcohol or drugs to temporarily avoid feelings of stress, and some turn to food. Unfortunately, sitting in front of the television and eating a litre of Häagen-Dazs ice cream from the container is not a healthy method of coping. In this section, we will examine both the positive and negative methods of coping, and then describe several techniques that can be used to improve one's well-being.

POSITIVE COPING STRATEGIES Psychology may have a reputation for focusing on the negative, including how damaging stress can be. In reality, psychologists also study what makes people thrive, even in the face of extreme stress. This area of study, **positive psychology**, *uses scientific methods to study human strengths and potential.* Research in this area has identified numerous adaptive and constructive ways in which people cope with problems. These researchers have found that one of the most powerful tools for coping is also one of the simplest: focusing on positive emotions.

Although it may seem difficult to imagine experiencing positive emotions during times of stress, doing something simple like watching a funny movie can actually help you cope with stress and negative life experiences. Barbara Fredrickson and her colleagues at the University of North Carolina (Chapel Hill) have shown that positive emotions can affect how we perceive and think about the world. For example, these researchers have shown that a negative mood narrows your focus of attention so that you attend to a small part of your environment, whereas positive moods cause the focus of your attention to expand (Fredrickson & Branigan, 2005). Other scientists have demonstrated that positive moods can also increase a person's creativity. In one experiment, participants were shown groups of three words (e.g., *falling, actor, dust*) and were asked to find a word that related all three items (e.g., *star*). Individuals in the positive mood condition scored higher than other participants (Isen et al., 1987). This increase in flexible thinking is crucial during coping, as it would help people experiencing negative emotions reframe their stressors into something less upsetting.

Although the effects of positive emotion on our ability to perceive and think are interesting, the most stunning effect of positive emotions is their effect on our autonomic nervous system. When most of us watch a scary movie, our heart rates increase as we experience fear. Then, after a little while, our heart rates return to normal. But, the speed at which this recovery occurs can be influenced by positive emotions. Researchers have found that when participants watched positive films after seeing a scary movie clip, their heart rate returned to normal faster than when participants viewed a sad or neutral film (see Figure 14.9). The positive emotions seemed to defuse the effects of the negative emotions, thus decreasing the amount of damage that stress and negative emotions can have on the body (Fredrickson & Levenson, 1998). Because positive emotions allow people to broaden their thought processes and to build new intellectual, social, and physical resources, these results are now described as the *broaden-and-build theory* of positive emotions (Fredrickson, 2001, 2003).

OPTIMISM AND PESSIMISM Closely linked to positive emotions is the concept of **optimism**, *the tendency to have a favourable, constructive view on situations and to expect positive outcomes.* People who are optimistic tend to initially perceive situations in a positive way and are also more likely to find positive elements in situations. In contrast, **pessimism** *is the tendency to have a negative perception of life and expect negative outcomes.* These individuals often have what is known as **pessimistic explanatory style**, *which is the tendency to interpret and explain negative events as internally based (i.e., as being due to that person rather than to an external situation) and as a constant, stable quality* (Burns & Seligman, 1989). For example, a laid-off employee who

Figure 14.9 Positive Moods and Recovery from Negative Emotional Events

Research shows that positive moods speed up a person's recovery from negative events. In this study, viewing a video depicting positive emotions (amusement or contentment) caused heart rates to return to normal levels faster than a neutral or sad video (Fredrickson & Levenson, 1998).

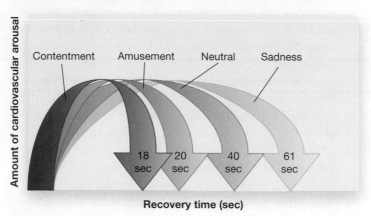

Source: Data from Fredrickson, B. L., & Levenson, R. W. (1998). Positive emotions speed recovery from the cardiovascular sequelae of negative emotions. *Cognition & Emotion, 12*, 191–220. Figure 3, p. 205.

struggles to find a job may attribute the problem to his perceived inability to network properly rather than to the fact that it is tough to find jobs in his field. Pessimism is also often linked with **negative affectivity**, *the tendency to respond to problems with a pattern of anxiety, hostility, anger, guilt, or nervousness.* These negative emotions make it difficult for these individuals to choose an appropriate coping strategy for a given problem (DeLongis & Holtzman, 2005; O'Brien & DeLongis, 1996). For instance, someone with high levels of negativity may deal with a difficult breakup by socially withdrawing from others and by becoming angry and resentful. Such responses also make it more difficult for others to provide social support.

As you might expect after reading the previous section, optimism is correlated with better physical health than pessimism. For example, scientists have shown that women who tend toward pessimism and test positive for the HPV virus (a papilloma virus known to cause cervical cancer) have lower counts of white blood cells that fight disease than do optimistic women with the HPV virus. Long-term studies show similar effects of optimism. In the U.S. Veterans Affairs Normative Aging Study involving a large cohort of male participants, optimists had a lower incidence of coronary heart disease than did pessimists (Kubzansky et al., 2001). Similarly, researchers at the Mayo Clinic administered personality tests assessing optimism and pessimism to patients who came into the clinic for general medical issues during the 1960s. Thirty years later, the data on optimism and pessimism were compared to patient survival. The researchers found a 19% increase in mortality risk in people who were consistently pessimistic (Maruta et al., 2000). Perhaps a good attitude does more

than help individuals cope emotionally with illness; perhaps it actually helps them overcome it.

Although these studies present a convincing case for optimism, there is an alternative explanation for the results: Optimists and pessimists may simply have had different lifestyles. One of these other lifestyle variables (e.g., diet) could potentially explain the health differences between optimists and pessimists. In order to control for this possibility, a group of U.S. researchers conducted longitudinal (long-term) studies of a group of females with nearly identical lifestyles: nuns. The Nun Study, as it is now known, was exceptional in that it allowed researchers to examine how personality factors such as optimism and pessimism affected people over the course of their lifetime while controlling for variables such as diet, work demands, and stress. As part of this study (which is part of a longitudinal study about factors leading to Alzheimer's disease), the researchers examined the handwritten autobiographies of 180 nuns; these documents were written by the nuns when they were entering the order in their early-to-mid twenties. The emotional content of the autobiographies was coded by the researchers to see if positive emotions predicted how long the nuns lived. Here are two excerpts from the study:

> *Sister 1 (low positive emotion): I was born on September 26, 1909, the eldest of seven children, five girls and two boys. . . . My candidate year was spent in the Motherhouse, teaching Chemistry and Second Year Latin at Notre Dame Institute. With God's grace, I intend to do my best for our Order, for the spread of religion and for my personal sanctification.*
>
> *Sister 2 (high positive emotion): God started my life off well by bestowing upon me a grace of inestimable value. . . . The past year which I have spent as a candidate studying at Notre Dame College has been a very happy one. Now I look forward with eager joy to receiving the Holy Habit of Our Lady and to a life of union with Love Divine. (Danner et al., 2001, p. 806)*

The researchers found a strong correlation between positive emotions during young adulthood and the longevity of the nuns—people who were more positive during their twenties lived longer than less positive people (Danner et al., 2001). Similar results have been found with less-controlled populations (Maruta et al., 2000; Peterson et al., 1998), suggesting that the results of the Nun Study are due to optimism and positivity, not to an act of divine intervention.

RESILIENCE Thus far, we have discussed a number of factors that can reduce the effects of stress and promote well-being. However, there are times when negative life events are unavoidable. As you have likely noticed in your own life, individuals differ in their ability to bounce back from events such as disaster, disease, or major loss. This trait is known as **resilience**, *the ability to effectively recover* *from illness or adversity*. Resilient people tend to have one or more factors stacked in their favour. Financial and social resources, opportunities for rest and relaxation, and other positive life circumstances contribute to resiliency. Even so, amazing stories of resiliency can be found among individuals living with unimaginable stress. Thus, the personality and emotional characteristics discussed earlier are also important contributors to resiliency in the face of adversity.

One amazing example is that of Viktor Frankl, an early- and mid-20th-century Austrian psychiatrist. Frankl was already an influential physician and therapist when he, his wife, and family were forced into concentration camps during World War II. Frankl found himself in the role of helping people adjust to life in the concentration camp, even while he himself struggled to survive each day. He encouraged others to tap into whatever psychological resources they had left to cope with very bleak circumstances. Frankl found that one of the most critical parts of surviving in these camps was finding some sort of meaning in life. For some, this could be the desire to reunite with their family when the war eventually ended. For others, it was a love of poetry (astoundingly, some prisoners were able to write poetry in the concentration camps). But, if a prisoner seemed to lose this sense of meaningfulness in his life, Frankl could tell that this prisoner would soon die. As Frankl later noted, "Despair equals Suffering minus Meaning" (Gelman et al., 2000, p. 625). A key challenge, then, was to maintain this sense of meaningfulness so that people had a purpose in their lives. Doing so allowed them to cope and remain resilient while witnessing terrifying events. Eventually Frankl's wife and parents were deported to different concentration camps, where they were murdered. Despite his own enormous losses, Frankl continued helping others to cope and find solace under the worst of circumstances (Frankl, 1959).

Psychologists have long focused on the negative outcomes of stress, but stories such as Frankl's demonstrate that stress and trauma can also lead people to recognize how strong they really are. In fact, psychologists describe the phenomenon of **post-traumatic growth**, *the capacity to grow and experience long-term positive effects in response to negative events* (Tedeschi & Calhoun, 2004). It happens in response to events such as automobile accidents, sexual and physical assault, combat, and severe and chronic illnesses. Individuals who experience post-traumatic growth often report feeling a greater sense of vulnerability, yet over time develop an increased inner strength. They also report finding greater meaning and depth in their relationships, a greater sense of appreciation for what they have, and an increased sense of spirituality (Tedeschi & Calhoun, 2004).

Post-traumatic growth is not an alternative reaction to post-traumatic stress. Rather, the two conditions occur together. Clinicians recognize that the growth occurs during the process of coping, not because of the event itself. Often a clinical psychologist trained in working with trauma victims helps facilitate the growth process and assists the individual in finding the interpersonal and social resources needed for healing. Some of these resources include medications and some form of counselling. It is also becoming increasingly common for people to use other techniques to reduce responses to stress and negative events, including meditation and yoga.

BIOFEEDBACK As you have been reading this chapter, your circulatory system has been pumping blood and maintaining blood pressure, your lungs have been breathing in air, and your digestive system may have been working on a recent meal, all without the tiniest bit of conscious effort. Certainly you can intentionally hold your breath for a moment, but can you hold your heartbeat or change your blood pressure? If you are like most of us, you cannot control all of these autonomic functions, but that does not mean it is impossible.

Biofeedback *is a therapeutic technique involving the use of physiological recording instruments to provide feedback that increases awareness of bodily responses.* The psychologists who developed this technique believed that by seeing or hearing a machine's representation of bodily processes, people could gain awareness of stress responses and bring them under voluntary control. For example, a patient with chronic stress could use feedback on his blood pressure, heart rate, and tension of his facial muscles to monitor and, possibly, control his stress responses. As you can imagine, this ability would have very useful applications to clinical psychology. However, after some very promising findings, the excitement over biofeedback faded, in part because it was found that simple relaxation techniques were just as useful.

MEDITATION AND RELAXATION Many people report significant benefits by using relaxation and meditation

Cindy Charles/PhotoEdit, Inc.

Biofeedback involves the use of physiological monitoring, which allows the patient to see and sometimes hear the output of his or her physiological reactions.

techniques to cope with stress and life's difficult periods. Both techniques are designed to calm emotional responses as well as physiological reactions to stress. **Meditation** *is any procedure that involves a shift in consciousness to a state in which an individual is highly focused, aware, and in control of mental processes*. However, to say "meditation" is a bit simplistic, as meditation has many different techniques and is practised, in some form, in almost every known culture.

In some types of meditation, the individual focuses his or her attention on a chosen object, such as a point on the wall or a physical sensation like the feeling related to breathing. This technique is known as *focused attention (FA) meditation*. When distracting or negative thoughts enter into one's awareness and interfere with meditation, people are taught to accept these thoughts in a nonjudgmental manner, and to then nudge their attention back to its original focus (Lutz et al., 2008). Although this technique is initially quite difficult, over time people become quite good at maintaining their attention on their chosen object.

A second type of meditation is *open monitoring (OM) meditation*. This technique also uses focused attention to train the mind and to reduce the influence of distractions. After initial training with FA, people can transition into the use of OM styles of meditating. Here, meditators pay attention to moment-by-moment sensations without focusing on any particular object (Cahn & Polich, 2006). A key feature of OM is to attempt to experience each sensation intensely, examining its rich sensory properties and emotional characteristics in great depth; however, these sensations should not become the sole focus of attention, preventing the meditator from responding to other sensations.

The idea that the feelings of happiness and relaxation associated with meditation are due, in part, to us becoming more attentive to the present moment and less attentive to our own "stories" has found some support in research performed at the University of Toronto. Norm Farb and colleagues (2007) used fMRI to examine brain activity in trained meditators and a control group of nonmeditators. Participants were asked to take one of two perspectives while reading lists of positive (e.g., *charming*) and negative (e.g., *greedy*) words. During half of the experiment, participants were asked to use a Narrative Focus, which required them to think about what each word meant and how it related to him or her. During the other half of the experiment, participants were asked to use an Experiential Focus, which required them to pay attention to their thoughts and bodily reactions to the words as they happened, but without any judgment or elaboration. If they found themselves distracted by any memories or thoughts inspired by a word, they were to calmly return their attention to the present moment. The results were intriguing: During the Experiential Focus condition (which is quite similar to a meditative state), trained meditators showed a larger decrease in activity in areas of the frontal lobes related to "the self" (the medial prefrontal cortex) than did novices. They also showed increased activity in areas related to the perception of one's bodily states. These results suggest that meditation does in fact help us separate ourselves from our own narratives and live in the present moment.

Given that numerous other studies have shown that meditation leads to decreased levels of anxiety (Chen et al., 2012; Hoffman et al., 2011), it is possible that redirecting attention away from our own self-focused thoughts might improve our ability to be happy. Additionally, meditation has been shown to be very effective in reducing blood pressure, which decreases the likelihood of experiencing long-term problems with hypertension and cardiovascular disease (Rainforth et al., 2007). Taken together, this research suggests that meditation can be used as a method of coping with stress and negative emotions.

Mindfulness-based stress reduction (MBSR) *is a structured relaxation program based on elements of mindfulness meditation*. The primary goal of MBSR is to help people to cope and to relax by increasing the link between one's body and one's mind. A common meditative technique used in MBSR is a body scan in which participants pay attention to the sensation of their toes, then their feet, ankles, calves, and so on. By attempting to focus on bodily sensations for 15–20 minutes, the participants engage in a great deal of attentional control; if someone's mind wanders, she is simply asked to bring it back to the body scan without judging herself for the slip-up. During these relaxation exercises, participants are instructed to recognize and become aware of any emotions they may experience, but to then let it go so that the emotion is not part of their identity. Studies using MBSR have found that it reduces stress (Baer et al., 2012) and increases a sense of meaningfulness in life (Dobkin, 2008). Not surprisingly, MBSR also leads to increased brain activity in the insula, a brain area related to perceiving bodily sensations; this area is involved with a person's ability to focus on the present moment (Farb et al., 2013).

Altered brain activity has also been found after people learned a complex form of meditation called *integrated mind–body training (IMBT)*. This technique, developed from traditional Chinese medicine, involves a combination of relaxation and posture correction, as well as instructions for heightening one's awareness of one's body (Tang, 2011). Similar to MBSR, this technique has been shown to enhance the control of attention (Tang et al., 2007). IMBT has also been linked to an increased ability to control bodily physiology. In one study, researchers compared participants who had completed either five days of IMBT or five days of a simpler relaxation training program. The IMBT group showed lower heart rates, breathing rates, and skin conductance responses (a measure of stress) than

Tyler Olson/Shutterstock

Meditation is practised in many cultures, typically to serve the function of promoting health and stress reduction.

did the relaxation training group. These differences appear to be due to activity in a region of the medial (middle) prefrontal cortex called the anterior cingulate gyrus; this area is involved in controlling attention as well as in some emotional responses. In this study, activity within the anterior cingulate was associated with the participants' increased control over parasympathetic nervous system responses. The increased parasympathetic activity accounted for the heightened sense of relaxation experienced while meditating (Tang et al., 2009). Interestingly, later studies showed a strengthening of the white-matter connections between

the anterior cingulate and emotional structures in the base of the brain (Tang et al., 2010), suggesting that IMBT can change how different neural regions interact.

Although meditation does appear to have a number of health benefits, training procedures like MBSR and IMBT might not be for everyone. However, there is a relaxation technique that many people in your class likely already perform: yoga. According to various organizations, approximately 1.5 million Canadians regularly practise yoga (in one of its many forms). Yoga involves directed breathing while participants move their bodies into specific poses. This voluntary breathing can influence activity in the parasympathetic nervous system, leading to a decrease in emotional arousal (Sovik, 2000). Consistent with this view, U.S. college students who performed directed breathing had lower levels of physical and mental stress than did control participants (Cappo & Holmes, 1984). Yoga may also help your immune system; when compared to people in a simple relaxation condition (nature walks and soft music), people who performed yoga had greater changes in gene expression in the immune cells circulating in the bloodstream (Qu et al., 2013).

Thus, scientific studies of meditation and relaxation training in all their forms appear to confirm their health benefits, and are also bringing us closer to understanding precisely *how* these changes to the brain and body help us cope with stress and negativity.

PSYCH@

Church

Stress-reduction techniques like mindfulness are sometimes associated with spiritualism, as many arose as part of different Buddhist traditions; however, a belief in a higher power is not a requirement of these techniques. In contrast, many people use religion as their primary coping mechanism during stressful situations, both large and small. They may use any combination of religious practices, depending on the specific nature of the faith: prayer, meditation, religious counselling, and social support from family and congregations. All of these efforts can provide strength and comfort during difficult times, and they may also be associated with greater overall happiness. Many psychologists have become increasingly curious about the possible health benefits associated with religion and spirituality. Numerous studies have found that people who are very religious and are actively engaged with religious practices do, in fact, live a bit longer than do people who are less religious or nonreligious (McCullough et al., 2000).

A hasty interpretation of these results might lead one to conclude that religion causes people to live longer—that the experiences of prayer and of attending church lead to the greater longevity. However, the studies in this area actually produce correlational, not experimental, data—psychologists cannot

randomly assign people to be religious or not. Consequently, we must consider alternative explanations. For example, lifestyle factors are also at play. Younger and older people of Muslim, Jewish, or Christian faith are more likely to engage in healthy behaviours, including wearing seatbelts, visiting the dentist, and avoiding both the consumption of alcohol and cigarette smoking (reviewed in McCullough & Willoughby, 2009). Religions also tend to have negative views of criminal activity, drug abuse, and risky sexual activity. Thus, the increased longevity is probably related to the greater self-control and self-regulation that are characteristic of many religious belief systems.

Generally, people who are religious show greater well-being and lower levels of depression (Smith et al., 2003). The determination of whether religion protects people from depression depends on the point of view taken, however. People who cope with problems using positive aspects of religion (e.g., treating other people with compassion and kindness, as well as collaborating with others in solving problems) are less prone to depression than religious people who adopt negative appraisals of their problems and concerns, such as viewing problems as a result of a wrathful God's punishment (Ano & Vasconcelles, 2005; McCullough & Willoughby, 2009).

EXERCISE Relaxation training and religious study both require discipline; individuals must follow instructions or teachings in a fairly consistent manner. Staying in good physical condition requires similar devotion, and also produces considerable physical and psychological benefits. However, even short bursts of exercise can be useful. For example, researchers in Germany asked university student participants either to do all-out sprints, to jog, or to do nothing. The students who sprinted were able to learn 20% more items on a vocabulary list than the students who jogged or were inactive (Winter et al., 2007). Why did this occur? Perhaps the sprinters were more motivated than the others. This explanation sounds plausible, but the researchers randomly assigned healthy participants to the three groups—so there should not be anything inherent to the sprinter group that would lead them to learn more words. It appears that the type of exercise they engaged in led to increased cognitive performance. Which physiological processes might account for the cognitive edge the sprinters gained from their intense physical activity? The researchers discovered that the students who engaged in intense exercise had increased levels of dopamine, epinephrine, and **brain-derived neurotrophic factor (BDNF)**—*a protein in the nervous system that promotes survival, growth, and the formation of new synapses.* Cardiovascular exercise also provides immediate benefits in cognitive processing speed, again as measured in university-aged students (Hillman et al., 2003). But, these immediate benefits of exercise are not limited to younger people. When sedentary adults between 60 and 85 years of age take up weekly exercise, they show improved brain functioning and cognitive performance (Hillman et al., 2008; Kramer et al., 1999).

Rigorous exercise has positive effects on the brain and on our cognitive abilities, making it well worth the time and effort.

One important issue to address is whether these short-term effects translate into lifelong cognitive benefits from exercise. Results from long-term studies indicate that a lifestyle that includes regular exercise helps preserve cognitive function and the brain systems that support it (van Praag, 2009). Researchers have found that older people who are at genetic risk for developing Alzheimer's disease and who show cognitive impairments can slow the rate of memory decline by exercising (Lautenschlager et al., 2008). It appears that levels of brain chemicals such as BDNF are boosted by exercise, which helps explain the changes in the brain that account for the cognitive benefits. Furthermore, exercise supports the development of new nerve cells in the hippocampus, a critical area for memory and cognitive activity (van Praag, 2008). Together, these studies tell us that the benefits of exercise go far beyond helping you look good.

Module 14.3a Quiz:

Coping

Know . . .

1. _____ is the tendency to respond to problems with a pattern of anxiety, hostility, anger, guilt, or nervousness.
   A. A coping style
   B. Negative affectivity
   C. Pessimism
   D. An aggression complex

2. What is brain-derived neurotrophic factor (BDNF)?
   A. A protein in the nervous system that promotes survival, growth, and formation of new synapses
   B. A calorie-restricted diet that may involve eating approximately 60% of the normal amount of calories, while continuing to take in the needed nutrients
   C. A neurotransmitter that reduces stress and increases overall well-being
   D. A hormone that is released in those individuals with a healthy diet

Understand. . . .

3. _____ is a positive coping strategy, while _____ is a negative style of coping.
   A. Meditation; resilience
   B. Pessimistic explanatory style; negative affectivity
   C. Meditation; alcohol
   D. Post-traumatic growth; resilience

Apply. . . .

4. Your partner suddenly broke up with you and did not offer an explanation. If you attribute the breakup to your not being a very outgoing person, you are demonstrating _____.
   A. negative affectivity
   B. a pessimistic explanatory style
   C. resilience
   D. a coping style

Analyze . . .

5. What is the most accurate conclusion regarding the effects of meditation on stress and well-being?

   A. Meditation is the absolute best way to combat stress and protect your body from disease.

   B. Advanced training in meditation will decrease stress in a manner similar to simple relaxation techniques.

   C. Meditation helps the practitioner control his or her physiological responses, thereby decreasing stress and preventing health problems such as cardiovascular disease.

   D. Meditation is not a commonly used way of managing stress.

Perceived Control

As Dr. Pennebaker's story from the beginning of this module illustrates, the most stressful of circumstances are the ones that people have little or no control over. For example, children who reside in abusive homes have no control over their circumstances, nor do the victims of natural disasters. Each situation can result in people acquiring a sense that their behaviour has little effect on external events.

Laboratory experiments have demonstrated the negative impact that a lack of control has on health and behaviour. A classic example comes from work on avoidance learning in dogs conducted in the 1960s by Martin Seligman and his colleagues (Seligman & Maier, 1967). In this study, dogs received electrical shocks while strapped into a harness. Half of the dogs learned to press a panel in order to escape the shock, thus providing them some control over their stressor. The other half of the dogs received the same number of shocks as the first group, but had no control over when the shocks would occur. After a delay, each dog was placed in a device known as a shuttle box consisting of two small areas separated by a low divider that the animal could easily jump across (see Figure 14.10). On each experimental trial, a light in the shuttle box was dimmed before the section of the box that the animal was standing on became electrified, thus providing a shock similar to the one experienced in the earlier part of the study. Through trial and error, animals that were in the controllable stress condition learned that they could jump over the divider to the other side of the shuttle box to get away from the shock; after a few trials, this behaviour occurred immediately after the warning tone was presented, which allowed them to avoid the shock altogether. In contrast, the dogs that had experienced the uncontrollable shocks had difficulties learning to escape. Instead, they would lie down, whine, and appear resigned to receive the shock. This finding was described as **learned helplessness**—*an acquired suppression of avoidance or escape behaviour in response to unpleasant, uncontrollable circumstances.*

Later studies provided some interesting insights into learned helplessness, with some potentially important implications for how humans respond to stress. Researchers found that stress responses involve nuclei in the brainstem as well as the ventral (lower) regions of the frontal lobes. When a stressful event is controllable (e.g., being shocked, but having a way to escape), the brainstem produces a stress response such as increased heart rate and blood pressure; however, this response is then inhibited by the frontal lobes (Amat et al., 2005). When a stressful event is not controllable, the brainstem provides a stress response without being inhibited. This finding suggests that the degree to which a person *perceives* a stressor to be controllable will influence whether the stress response will be inhibited, and whether the person will experience an event as being stressful.

The important point about learned helplessness is that the animal, or person, *learns* that their actions cannot remove the stress in one situation (e.g., the harness) and then *generalizes* that helplessness to other situations (e.g., the shuttle box). This is similar to the thought processes of some people with depression. People with depression are prone to hold beliefs that their actions have no influence on external events, and that their environment and circumstances dictate outcomes. Learned helplessness also has similarities to anxiety disorders; namely, increased nervousness and a feeling of being unable to escape a stressor (Maier & Watkins, 2005). Clearly, both aspects of learned helplessness can negatively affect mental and physical well-being. This phenomenon shows that the perception of control can have a dramatic effect on our ability to cope.

Figure 14.10 The Learned Helplessness Procedure

In Seligman and Maier's study, dogs that could avoid a painful shock would quickly learn to do so. Conversely, dogs that initially learned they could not avoid a shock remained passive when the opportunity to do so was given. The acquired failure to avoid or escape unpleasant circumstances that are perceived as uncontrollable is referred to as learned helplessness.

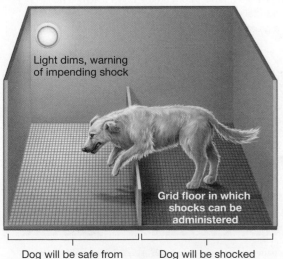

Light dims, warning of impending shock

Grid floor in which shocks can be administered

Dog will be safe from shock on this side

Dog will be shocked on this side

Without it, many humans and some nonhuman species will endure pain and stress rather than initiating ways to avoid or escape it.

Compensatory Control and Health

The idea of a random world in which people lack personal control over events can be discomforting. For example, hurricanes and tornados are often referred to as "acts of God," rather than the result of an unfortunate confluence of meteorological events and human-populated areas. But does having a sense of control lead to better health?

What do we know about how people cope with seemingly random events?

Some people feel as if they are the victims of random events, while others believe themselves to be the beneficiaries of the whims of life. However, the idea that randomness dictates worldly events can create anxiety in people. Even if a person believes randomness is the rule, he or she can become highly motivated to find meaning in the world and, through this search, a sense that the course of events is determined by the will of individuals or God (Kay et al., 2009). In this way, many people cope with stressful life events through **compensatory control**—*psychological strategies people use to preserve a sense of nonrandom order when personal control is compromised* (Kay et al., 2009). For example, people who are skeptical of any divine purpose in the world may change their view in the wake of personal or societal tragedy. These observations are primarily correlational, but researchers have conducted experiments to determine causal relationships between sense of control and beliefs about randomness versus orderliness.

How can science explain compensatory control?

To study compensatory control, researchers have developed a laboratory task that manipulates people's sense of personal control over a situation (Whitson & Galinsky, 2008). In one study, participants completed a concept identification task in which two symbols were presented on a computer screen and the participant had to guess which symbol correctly represented the concept that the computer had chosen (e.g., the colour of the symbol, its shape). The computer provided feedback on whether the participants chose the correct or incorrect symbol after each trial. Half of the participants received accurate feedback, while the other half received completely random feedback—sometimes their correct answers were recorded as incorrect, and vice versa. Participants receiving random feedback reported feeling a lower sense of control on a self-report measure.

Following the concept identification task, the participants then viewed multiple pictures, such as those shown in Figure 14.11. If you look closely, you will see that one of the pictures has a horse-like figure in it, whereas the other image has no discernible pattern. Participants in both conditions reported seeing faintly drawn figures, such as the horse. However, participants who had a diminished sense of control induced by the random feedback they received on the computer task were more likely to report seeing patterns within completely random images (Whitson & Galinsky, 2008).

It appears that when people feel their sense of control is undermined, they compensate by heightening their

Figure 14.11 Seeing Images Where There Are None

Do you see a figure in the image on the left? You may see a figure resembling a horse. What about on the right? There is no discernible image intended for this image. Psychologists have found that individuals who feel as though they lack control are more likely to detect patterns in the image at right than are people who feel a greater sense of control (Whitson & Galinsky, 2008).

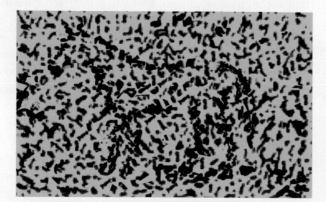 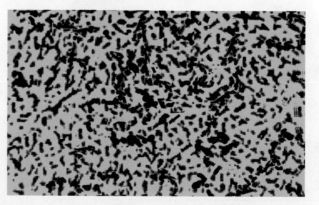

Figure 14.12 Exercising Compensatory Control

When people feel as though they lack control over the world, their need for structure, perceptual order, and beliefs in superstition and conspiracies increases. Participants who perceived that they were in control of events were *unlikely* to see images in snowy pictures (see Figure 14.11) and did *not* hold superstitious beliefs or endorse conspiracy theories. When people perceived that they had lost a sense of control during the experimental procedure, they reported a greater need for structure, perceived images in random arrays, became more superstitious, and endorsed conspiracy theories (Whitson & Galinsky, 2008).

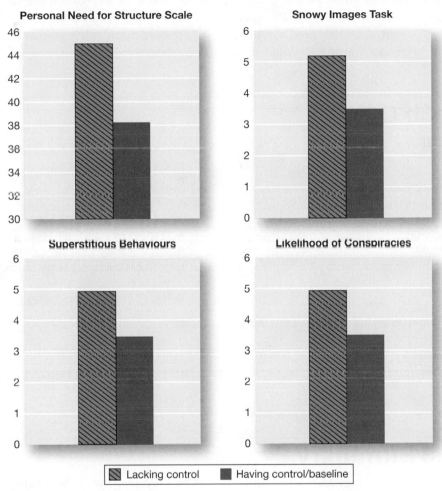

Source: Based on data from Whitson, J. A., & Galinsky, A. D. (2008). Lacking control increases illusory pattern perception. *Science, 322*, 115–117.

search for structure in the world, to the point of calling upon their imagination. This is evident in other domains as well, not just detecting patterns in random, snowy images. People also gain a greater need for structure and become increasingly willing to believe in superstitious rituals and conspiracy theories when their sense of control is diminished (Figure 14.12; Kay et al., 2009; Whitson & Galinsky, 2008).

Can we critically evaluate this evidence?

A major advantage of the study described here is that the researchers were able to experimentally induce a perceived lack of control in the participants who received random

feedback on their performance on the computerized task. The observation that these participants then perceived images within randomness and showed a heightened belief in superstition and conspiracies may help to explain how people respond to lost control outside of the laboratory. Of course, one limitation is that a real-world lack of control, such as that which occurs in the face of a natural disaster or the loss of a job, has far greater consequences. Thus, as with any laboratory experiment, there is a limit to the degree to which the results generalize.

Why is this relevant?

Having a sense of control greatly affects how we think about and interpret the world. In addition, it affects our health.

Individuals who believe they can predict and influence present and future events tend to have improved physical and mental well-being compared to people who believe the opposite. For example, patients who are scheduled to undergo medical procedures, such as a colonoscopy, have reduced anxiety for the procedure if they are given clear, informative tutorials about the procedure before it occurs (Luck et al., 1999).

Researchers have found that when people perceive that they have lost a sense of control during an experimental procedure, they report a greater need for structure, perceive images in random arrays, become more superstitious, and endorse conspiracy theories (Kay et al., 2009). These researchers have also suggested that religion is sometimes used as a form of compensatory control (Kay et al., 2010). What do you think?

People may also compensate for their lack of control by performing superstitious rituals, which can provide a sense of at least partial control over outcomes. This can be seen in everyday examples, such as among athletes who follow the same steps when preparing for a game, as well as in extreme, maladaptive forms, such as in obsessive–compulsive disorder (covered in Module 15.3).

Module 14.3b Quiz:

Perceived Control

Know . . .

1. _____is an acquired suppression of avoidance or escape behaviour in response to unpleasant, uncontrollable circumstances.
   A. Compensatory control
   B. Learned helplessness
   C. Coping
   D. Resilience

Understand . . .

2. People often turn to religion to explain natural disasters. This behaviour demonstrates the concept of _____.
   A. compensatory control
   B. learned helplessness
   C. coping
   D. resilience

3. A mentally healthy person who is prone to claiming that patterns exist where there are none
   A. is showing negative affectivity.
   B. is showing signs of post-traumatic growth.
   C. probably feels a lost sense of control over a problem or situation.
   D. has a pessimistic explanatory style.

Module 14.3 Summary

14.3a   Know . . . the key terminology associated with coping and well-being:

biofeedback
brain-derived neurotrophic factor (BDNF)
compensatory control
coping
learned helplessness
meditation
mindfulness-based stress reduction (MBSR)
negative affectivity
optimism
pessimism
pessimistic explanatory style
post-traumatic growth
resilience

14.3b   Understand . . . how control over the environment influences coping and outlook.

Psychologists have discovered that people (and dogs) become more willing to allow unpleasant events to occur if they learn (or believe) that their behaviour brings no change. Having at least some degree of control helps people (and dogs) cope with these events. When control is threatened, people use compensatory responses, such as detecting order within random images.

14.3c   Understand . . . positive and negative styles of coping.

Whether someone copes using a positive or negative style is related to personality (e.g., optimism versus pessimism).

Positive coping includes the concept of resilience—the ability to recover from adversity, and even benefit from the experience, as is the case with post-traumatic growth. Coping via negative affectivity and pessimism can have both psychological and physiological disadvantages.

14.3d   Apply . . . your knowledge of the beneficial effects of optimism to help you reframe stressful situations as positive opportunities.

Apply Activity

For each of the following four situations, try to think of both a pessimistic and an optimistic way of interpreting the event.

1. You find out that you are one of four people to be scheduled for an interview for a job you really want.
2. Your flight home from Europe is overbooked, so your return home is delayed by a day.
3. Your car has a flat tire and you have to bike 10 km to get to school in time for your 10 a.m. class.
4. Your friend decides to stop attending the kickboxing class that you really enjoy.

How did you feel after each optimistic and pessimistic interpretation? Did you feel better after putting a positive spin on things?

14.3e   Analyze . . . whether activities such as relaxation techniques, meditation, and biofeedback actually help people cope with stress and problems.

Meditation and other relaxation methods have been found to be quite effective in reducing stress. While some training and practice may be necessary, these techniques are by no means inaccessible to those who are motivated to pursue them.

Chapter 15
Psychological Disorders

15.1 Defining and Classifying Psychological Disorders

- Defining Abnormal Behaviour **616**

  Working the Scientific Literacy Model: Labelling and Mental Disorders **619**
- Module 15.1a Quiz **621**
- Applications of Psychological Diagnoses **622**
- Module 15.1b Quiz **623**
- Module 15.1 Summary **623**

15.2 Personality and Dissociative Disorders

- Defining and Classifying Personality Disorders **625**

  Working the Scientific Literacy Model: Antisocial Personality Disorder **626**
- Module 15.2a Quiz **628**
- The Biopsychosocial Approach to Personality Disorders **629**
- Module 15.2b Quiz **629**
- Dissociative Identity Disorder **630**
- Module 15.2c Quiz **631**
- Module 15.2 Summary **631**

15.3 Anxiety, Obsessive-Compulsive, and Depressive Disorders

- Anxiety Disorders **634**

  Working the Scientific Literacy Model: Specific Phobias **635**
- Module 15.3a Quiz **638**
- Mood Disorders **639**
- Module 15.3b Quiz **643**
- Module 15.3 Summary **643**

15.4 Schizophrenia

- Symptoms and Types of Schizophrenia **645**
- Module 15.4a Quiz **647**
- Explaining Schizophrenia **648**

  Working the Scientific Literacy Model: The Neurodevelopmental Hypothesis **649**
- Module 15.4b Quiz **651**
- Module 15.4 Summary **652**

Module 15.1 Defining and Classifying Psychological Disorders

MPI / Archive Photos / Getty Images

Learning Objectives

15.1a Know . . . the key terminology associated with defining and classifying psychological disorders.

15.1b Understand . . . advantages and criticisms associated with the Diagnostic and Statistical Manual of Mental Disorders (DSM-5).

15.1c Apply . . . your knowledge of the mental disorders defence to decide if defendants are criminally responsible for their actions.

15.1d Analyze . . . whether the benefits of labelling psychological disorders outweigh the disadvantages.

Over the centuries, our understanding of psychological disorders has come a very, very long way. In the Middle Ages, people who we would now consider "mentally ill" may have experienced a wide range of reactions from society. They may have been viewed as possessed and requiring religious exorcism or even torture. The reason for these extreme responses was that many people in this era believed that that individuals who exhibited unusual behaviours (such as responding to voices that no one else heard or having hallucinations) were under the sway of evil spirits inhabiting their bodies (Hunter & Macalpine, 1963).

By the 16th century, this belief was part of the witch scares, which for at least two centuries created mass paranoia as the public sought protection from witches, who were believed to gain their power through an allegiance with the devil. Armed with the Malleus Maleficarum *(Hammer of*

the Witches), a 1486 German text filled with detailed instructions for identifying witches, countless people were subjected to "tests," such as looking for the "Devil's mark" on the body, a visible spot such as a mole or birthmark that could be interpreted as a sign of allegiance with the Devil.

"Treatments" for mental illness were directly based on this model of illness (i.e., possession by evil). Brutal imprisonment, torture, and demon exorcism were not designed with human psychology in mind. Their goal was not to rehabilitate dysfunctional thoughts, emotions, and behaviours. Rather, the focus was on driving the demon out of the person's body, or simply executing them, as in the witch-hunting craze that saw the execution of tens of thousands of innocent people (almost all of whom were women).

Thankfully, times have changed.

Focus Questions

1. Are psychological disorders fundamentally different from physical illnesses, or should we view them the same way?

2. Which guidelines or criteria allow psychologists to diagnose a mental disorder such as post-traumatic stress disorder (PTSD)?

» One of the defining characteristics of these early responses to psychological disorders was the desire to identify people who were different. In some cases, these differences really were a cause for concern, with some individuals being a danger to themselves or to others. However, as you just read, many of the people identified as being mentally ill were simply different in some, often minor, way. Although these witch hunts tell us more about the psychological state of the "hunters" than the "witches," they also highlights an issue that still influences psychological care today: What makes a behaviour or characteristic "abnormal?"

Defining Abnormal Behaviour

As the ascension of scientific thought began to displace the religious domination of the Middle Ages, explanations for mental illness shifted from demon possession to physical illnesses. **Asylums**, *residential facilities for the mentally ill*, were set up across Europe, with the general goal of curing the patients' bodily afflictions that gave rise to their symptoms. Their treatments would certainly not meet modern standards of medical care and were generally ineffective, such as draining up to 40% of a person's total blood volume! There were even treatments such as throwing the person into a pit of snakes. As unbelievable as that seems (not to mention how difficult it would be for doctors to make house calls. . .), the hope was to shock the person out of their diseased state (Szasz, 2006).

A fortunate change in society's approach to treating mental illness came with the courageous activism of two heroic figures, Philippe Pinel, a physician in France, and Dorothea Dix, a schoolteacher in the United States (see Module 16.1). Their tireless advocacy for the mentally ill led to widespread reforms that ushered in a new approach, called *moral treatment*, which led to patients being treated with kindness and decency, able to roam the hospital halls and get outside for fresh air. However, there were still virtually no effective treatments, and many people afflicted with mental illness were permanently incarcerated.

By the 1950s, approximately 66 000 people were in psychiatric hospitals in Canada (Greenland et al., 2001). Things began to change in 1955 when the drug chlorpromazine (also known as Thorazine) was introduced. Suddenly, people with schizophrenia and other disorders involving being "out of touch" with reality were able to function independently, even holding down jobs and living at home with their families. The success of chlorpromazine and other medications led to widespread **deinstitutionalization**, *the movement of large numbers of psychiatric in-patients from their care facilities back into regular society*, which led to a drop in the number of psychiatric inpatients by over 80% over the next three decades (Torrey, 1997).

The return of hundreds of thousands of people to regular life had its down sides, however. Many former in-patients quit their medications, slipped back into their disorders, and became homeless. Also, although the treatments at this time were effective in improving many people's symptoms, they were not *cures*. Many challenges remained in reintegrating people with schizophrenia and similar disorders into their families and communities.

Unfortunately, helping people reintegrate into regular life was not a central part of the psychiatric approach to treating mental illnesses. Instead, the guiding paradigm for mental health and mental illness is the medical model, which has held sway since the end of the Middle Ages. The **medical model** *sees psychological conditions through the same lens as Western medicine tends to see physical conditions—as sets of symptoms, causes, and outcomes, with treatments aimed at changing physiological processes in order to alleviate symptoms*. Through this lens, psychological disorders such as depression, anxiety disorders, or autism can be approached in the same manner as conventional medicine would approach diabetes or cancer. What the medical model is generally missing is an appreciation for the whole system of factors that affects the person's overall functioning.

In recent decades, the medical model has begun to give way to the biopsychosocial model, which includes physiological processes within a holistic view of the person as a set of multiple interacting systems (Table 15.1).

Table 15.1 Biological, Psychological, and Sociocultural Factors Influence Both Physical and Mental Disorders

	Diabetes	**Major Depression**
Biological	Genetic influences on pancreatic function; excessive refined sugars	Genetic influences on neurotransmitter production and function; sleep disruption; lack of positive emotional arousal
Psychological	Poor food choices; sedentary lifestyle; alcohol abuse	Negative self-concept; pessimism; negative life experiences
Sociocultural	Familial and cultural foods and traditions; limited budget for groceries; lack of physical and nutritional education in schools; lack of role models	Lack of social support; social withdrawal; lack of psychological services; stigma regarding psychological treatments

For example, depression involves biological factors (e.g., serotonin transmission in the brain), psychological factors (e.g., negative beliefs about the self), and social factors (e.g., relationship rejection and social isolation). Understanding the multiple systems that underlie disorders such as depression gives us greater insight into how to develop more effective treatments; in particular, it becomes easier to see how important it is to use convergent treatment approaches, treating more than one system at a time so as to affect the person's overall functioning (see Modules 16.2 and 16.3).

WHAT IS "NORMAL" BEHAVIOUR?   One of the thorniest problems in the mental health field has always been how to reliably identify who has a mental disorder in the first place (if a disorder is even a *thing* that you can *have*). Given the immense range of apparently normal human behaviour and experience, how can we determine what is abnormal?

You might expect that it would be simple to decide whether or not someone has a disorder—you just have to figure out whether or not they are "normal." However, one of the main insights we have gained as a global society is just how different "normal" can be from different perspectives. "Normal" can be owning slaves, or it can be speaking in tongues during a religious ceremony; it can be living in fear of being shot by an opposing gang or army, or it can be taking part in village dances where everyone links arms and dances together while mostly naked. Or, it can be sitting quietly in a coffee shop reading a psychology textbook.

It is amazing to pause for a moment and think about this diversity, and how, from the perspective of the people living in a particular culture, their practices seem perfectly normal and even *right* (the way things *should* be); but from outside that cultural framework the same practices may seem strange or even absurd. The same applies to individuals—what makes sense from *your* perspective may not make sense to others. "Normal" proves to be very elusive indeed.

This creates a real challenge for the clinical psychologist, who tries to determine whether a person's behaviour and experience are abnormal enough to warrant treatment, and furthermore, what specifically has gone wrong to make them this way, and how it can be fixed. The clinician has to use some sort of perspective as a framework; she has to judge the person's behaviour against some sort of standard. But what should that be? How can this be done without injecting too much bias from the clinician's own perspective?

The key criterion used by psychologists in deciding whether a person has a disorder is whether the person's thoughts, feelings, or behaviours are **maladaptive**, meaning that they *causes distress to oneself or others, impairs day-to-day functioning, or increases the risk of injury or harm to oneself or others* (American Psychiatric Association, 2013). However, there are many exceptions to this guideline. Some behaviours fulfill these criteria but do not necessarily indicate mental illness. Consider the following:

- Heavy drug users and people with psychopathic tendencies may not think they have a problem.
- Family members may be concerned about a person's involvement in a new relationship, or may disapprove of body modifications such as tattoos or piercings.
- Mourning the loss of a loved one or having a religious conversion may interfere with one's day-to-day activities.
- Activists may get arrested for protesting government actions and extreme sports enthusiasts may risk death or injury out of passion for their sport.

Obviously, the criteria for determining whether a given behaviour should be viewed as a disorder are not perfect and cannot account for all circumstances. But, generally speaking, when a person's behaviour and experience start to become significantly dysfunctional, there may be cause for concern. In order to make more specific diagnoses and determine exactly what type of disorder a person may have, mental health professionals rely on a carefully designed system.

PSYCHOLOGY'S PUZZLE: HOW TO DIAGNOSE PSYCHOLOGICAL DISORDERS   The attempt to develop a rigorous system for diagnosing mental illness goes back to at least 1840, when the U.S. government wanted to collect data on mental illness in the country and included in the official census a single category to denote mental illness: "idiocy/insanity." (Apparently, sensitivity had not yet been invented.) By 1917, this had evolved into a guide for mental hospitals, called the "Statistical Manual for the Use of Institutions for the Insane." In World War II, American psychiatrists were hired in large numbers by the U.S. military to aid in the selection of soldiers and to treat mental disturbances resulting from military duty.

Building on the military's diagnostic system, as well as the sixth edition of the World Health Organization's *International Statistical Classification of Disease* (which included mental disorders), the American Psychiatric Association created the **Diagnostic and Statistical Manual of Mental Disorders (DSM)**, *a standardized manual to aid in the diagnosis of disorders*; this edition described the symptoms of 106 different mental disorders. The purpose for developing the DSM was to provide mental health workers with a reliable method for diagnosing mental illness and to ensure consistency across different institutions and hospitals.

It is worth noting that from the very beginning, the DSM was rooted in a psychobiological view, which argued that mental disorders represented an individual's specific reactions to psychological, social, and biological processes. However, other emphases changed over the years, from an initial focus on psychodynamic views to a later focus on cognitive and biological perspectives. By the mid-1990s, the DSM had gone through several revisions and was expanded to include over 350 different disorders.

Why are there now almost four times as many disorders than there were half a century ago? The answer to this question may depend on your perspective. Some would argue that improvements in clinical science have enabled us to better diagnose people, and the new disorders are entirely valid categorizations of symptoms. Another more disturbing possibility is that the creation of ever-more categories of disorders has been engineered in part by pharmaceutical companies as a way of increasing the number of disorders people will need to be treated for. This topic has become a battlefield between those who believe science continually improves our understanding of mental illness, and those who believe that more aspects of human experience are being described as medical "conditions" in order to feed the profits of pharmaceutical companies.

Whatever the ultimate reason, the DSM remains the standard reference manual in the mental health field, particularly in North America. The latest edition, the DSM-5, was published in May 2013. In order to aid in the process of diagnosis, the DSM-5 describes three important pieces of information for each disorder: a set of symptoms and the number of symptoms that must be met in order to have the disorder; the **etiology** (*origins or causes*) of symptoms; and a prognosis or prediction of how these symptoms will persist or change over time.

CRITIQUING THE DSM   The DSM has received its share of criticism over the years. The central issue is, essentially, that there are no perfect ways of measuring psychological disorders. Psychologists and psychiatrists don't have precise tools, like litmus tests in chemistry that can tell you precisely whether something is an acid or a base. Instead, the diagnostic process is highly subjective, involving human subjects and human clinicians trying to make sense of a messy, ever-changing, set of subjective impressions. In order to try to help clinicians cut through some of this confusion, the DSM offers lists of specific symptoms that are indicative of specific disorders. This is an attempt to make the diagnostic process more objective, which should decrease the likelihood that diagnoses are based on individual clinicians' biases.

Unfortunately, this doesn't entirely solve the problem for many reasons. For one, a clinician still has to subjectively decide whether a client displays each symptom and whether it is severe enough to be considered a *symptom* or just *normal experience*. For example, at what precise point does "depressed mood" pass out of the range of normal

experiences (we're all sad sometimes and go through difficult periods in life), and into the pathological range? Another problem is that different disorders often share many common symptoms; as a result, different mental health professionals might make different diagnoses. The DSM was created, in large part, to help making the process of diagnosing a disorder more objective and reliable, but the very nature of human experience is often subjective, vague, and unreliable.

An additional weakness of the DSM is that there is a fine, and essentially arbitrary, line between whether a person is considered to have a disorder or not. For each disorder, the DSM provides a list of possible symptoms and guidelines as to how many of the symptoms the person must have before being given the diagnosis. If a person seems to have the necessary number (e.g., five out of nine possible symptoms), then he has the disorder, but with one symptom less, he doesn't. In practice, what this means is that the diagnosis a person receives, and even whether a person receives any diagnosis at all, can depend on a single symptom. This obviously creates a major accuracy problem.

The DSM, by its very existence, also implies that disorders can be objectively defined; the DSM has a lot of authority, and if a set of symptoms is given a diagnostic label, people conclude that there is a real disorder, like a sickness or a disease, that people can "get." This way of thinking has contributed to the stigmatization of mental illness, and has added to the discomfort and resistance people feel towards the mental health field. It has also led to serious problems when the biases and norms operating in a particular time and place get expressed as scientific fact. For example, in some early versions of the DSM, homosexuality was considered a disorder. Psychologists feel differently now about the diversity of normal sexual experience, and this is reflected in the DSM-5. However, this example does lead one to wonder whether some patterns of behaviour that are currently considered pathological are defined that way because of biases that we hold.

Critics also express concern that giving mental health workers more labels with which to diagnose clients is not necessarily a good thing and may lead to over-diagnosis. For example, consider attention deficit/hyperactivity disorder (ADHD), which is commonly applied to children who have problems adjusting to elementary school (especially boys, who are at least three times more likely to be diagnosed with ADHD than girls; Barkley, 1998). Since being included in the DSM, ADHD diagnoses have skyrocketed, although only in North America (in Europe, ADHD only seems to occur 10% as often). Estimates of the prevalence of ADHD range from the most common rate of 3–5% up to about 20% (Shaywitz & Shaywitz, 1991).

Critics charge that the handy availability of the ADHD diagnosis makes it too easy to label children as having a "condition" and then medicate them. Studies have shown that between 20% to 70% of children diagnosed with ADHD no longer met the criteria once they reached adulthood (Weiss & Hechtman, 1993); this raises the possibility that many children are being medicated for what is, essentially, normal development.

Perhaps one solution for improving the diagnostic accuracy of the DSM—both in general and for ADHD specifically—is to develop more objective, biological indicators such as genetic markers, indicators of neurotransmitter dysfunction, or brain abnormalities, that are involved in the symptoms and functional deficits experienced by the individual. These efforts are underway, although the field has a long way to go before such biological markers can be substantially incorporated into diagnostic criteria (Hyman, 2007).

THE POWER OF A DIAGNOSIS The long-term effects of receiving a specific diagnosis can be substantial. To continue the example of ADHD, for most children, by the time they get assessed for this condition, they will have experienced an accumulation of problematic behaviours—getting in trouble for being restless or misbehaving in class, forgetting to do homework, interrupting frequently during conversations, not paying attention, and falling behind in school. Imagine how welcome such a diagnosis would be, especially perhaps to the parents or teachers who would appreciate having something (like medication), that can help the child function more effectively, or at the very least, become easier to manage.

However, as you have seen, diagnosing disorders is not always a simple task. Imagine, for example, a person with a considerable amount of anxiety, odd behaviour patterns, and a strong need to control the environment, who is evaluated by a clinician in early adulthood when these patterns are just starting to develop. Depending on exactly what had been happening in that person's life and recent experiences, coupled with that clinician's particular biases and ways of interpreting things, several different diagnoses might be possible ranging from personality disorders (Module 15.2) to anxiety disorders or obsessive-compulsive disorder (Module 15.3). Or, the person could be deemed to not have a disorder or to be *sub-clinical*, meaning that his symptoms do not quite meet the criteria for diagnosis. What happens after this point may differ dramatically, depending on the diagnosis. The person may enter treatment programs or take medications for quite different disorders, or the person may not have sufficiently met the criteria for a disorder and may not get the help she needs. Small differences in initial diagnosis can lead to big differences in long-term treatment and outcomes.

An additional concern is that once a person has been labelled as having a disorder, the label itself may change how that person is viewed by others, and how subsequent behaviours are interpreted.

Working the Scientific Literacy Model

Labelling and Mental Disorders

What are the outcomes of diagnosing a person as having a particular disorder? On the positive side, it is hoped that receiving a diagnosis should make people more likely to seek and receive effective treatment. Also, a diagnosis should facilitate communication among mental health professionals: A label indicates a set of symptoms, probable causes, and potential treatments, thus summarizing and highlighting the important pieces of information that will be useful for treating the person. However, these diagnostic labels can also have their drawbacks, such as biasing how people will subsequently interpret the person's actions or experiences, or changing how people feel about themselves.

What do we know about how labels affect people?

It is important to put the following information in the proper context, which is the recognition that diagnostic labels can be very helpful; they can help people understand their experiences and communicate in a standardized way with whoever they may need to as they manage their symptoms and navigate the mental healthcare system. However, it is also, unfortunately, the case that being labelled with a mental illness can potentially damage a person's material, social, and psychological well-being in a variety of ways (Link et al., 1989; Rosenfield, 1997).

For example, seeing oneself as mentally ill can be associated with low self-esteem or feelings of helplessness. In some cases, a diagnosis may lead a person to indulge in even more extreme or destructive behaviour patterns. Because of stigma and negative attitudes towards the mentally ill, people may expect that other people will reject and devalue them. This may lead them to withdraw from social contact and fail to seek the support that could help them (Kroska & Harkness, 2006; Link, 1987). People may also become demoralized about their capabilities and themselves in general, which then interferes with their motivations and goal-related striving. Sadly, in a classic self-fulfilling prophecy, the long-term effects can be that people end up experiencing the social rejection and stigmatization they initially feared (Kroska & Harkness, 2006). In short, diagnostic labels are supposed to help; but they have the potential to cause harm as well. This doesn't necessarily mean we should stop using diagnostic labels; but it does mean that we should be especially concerned about using them accurately.

How can science explain how labels may affect perceptions of another person's behaviour?

One of the most surprising and daring studies ever conducted in psychology occurred in the early 1970s, when eight people, volunteering with David Rosenhan, decided to get themselves committed to psychiatric hospitals. None of the eight were experiencing any symptoms of mental illness, but when they went to their doctors and complained that they were hearing voices, they received diagnoses for schizophrenia or bipolar disorder (a mood disorder discussed in Module 15.3), and were admitted to a psychiatric hospital for observation and treatment. Once they were in the hospital, the challenge was to convince the doctors that there was, in fact, nothing wrong with them and they could be released back to their regular lives.

Once admitted, the volunteers exhibited no further symptoms and simply tried to behave "normally." Nevertheless, their behaviours were often interpreted as abnormal in some way by their doctors, so that even normal behaviours such as asking a question to a doctor, or talking about one's relatively normal childhood, would be interpreted as abnormal by doctors or hospital staff. Despite the volunteers' best efforts to be released, it took from seven to 59 days for their doctors to be convinced their symptoms were in remission; interestingly, in that time period, they were also given a total of 2100 pills to take (which they merely pretended to take but were able to dispose of when nobody was looking) (Rosenhan, 1973).

Can we critically evaluate this information?

It is tempting to ask whether the labels applied to psychological disorders are beneficial or harmful, but this question may actually oversimplify the situation. For one, the advantages of this system are clear for professionals: Labels are a necessary means of identifying and describing the problems they encounter. There is also evidence to suggest that labels help individuals understand their own situation and offer hope for successful treatment. Some psychologists who are in favour of labels have argued that Rosenhan's study failed to address the larger issue of labels because the symptoms he used were so marked and severe. Auditory hallucinations are such a hallmark

of disorders such as schizophrenia that it would be virtually impossible, perhaps even irresponsible, for a doctor to fail to diagnose an appropriate disorder and to use this diagnosis in judging the person's subsequent behaviours. Thus, it seems that labels can be both helpful and harmful in certain instances. In an ideal world, we would be able to keep the labels and get rid of the stigma. This may not be entirely possible, but it is a goal for psychologists and the community to work toward.

Why is this relevant?

Many of the potential costs or risks associated with being diagnosed with a psychological disorder stem from the more general problem of stigma toward mental illness. Researchers from a number of academic areas have identified some techniques that work in reducing stigmatization. For example, research shows that personal contact and knowledge of biopsychosocial explanations of mental illness are associated with a more accepting attitude toward people with psychological disorders (Boyd et al., 2010).

Education seems to matter, too: When individuals are instructed about the first-person experience of mental illness, they show greater acceptance than groups that simply learn the facts about mental illness (Mann & Himelien, 2008). A student organization known as Active Minds operates on university and college campuses in several countries including Canada and the United States and has had success in reducing the stigma associated with mental illness (McKinney, 2009). Keep these findings in mind as you read the rest of this chapter. As an informed student, you will be less likely to judge others and more likely to seek help yourself, or to recommend it to others, if it is ever needed.

The idea of examining behaviour from a biological, psychological (cognitive), and social perspective is a pervading theme in psychology and in this text. This biopsychosocial model is particularly important in clinical psychology. Some disorders are more common in some cultures than in others. The specific symptoms of these disorders can also vary. Whether these differences are due to genetic differences, cultural biases, or a combination of many factors is an important area of research in psychology.

BIOPSYCHOSOCIAL PERSPECTIVES
Symptoms, Treatments, and Culture

Psychological disorders may not present the same across different cultures, and a lack of appreciation for these cultural differences can potentially lead to misdiagnoses. For example, **post-traumatic stress disorder (PTSD)** *is a common psychological illness involving recurring thoughts, images, and nightmares associated with a traumatic event; it induces symptoms of tension and anxiety and can seriously interfere with many aspects of a person's life.* PTSD affects almost 10% of the Canadian population at some point in their lives (Van Ameringen et al., 2008). Given that it seems unlikely that the world will stop having disasters, wars, and violence, PTSD will likely be an unfortunate companion for many on the road of life.

Despite the seemingly universal physiological symptoms of PTSD, researchers have found interesting differences in the cognitive and emotional symptoms between different groups. For example, people who experienced trauma in the U.S.-led war in Afghanistan and the 2004 tsunami in the Indian Ocean showed somewhat different symptoms, depending on whether they were Americans or natives to the region (i.e., Afghans during the war, or Sri Lankans during the tsunami). Americans tended to report difficult internal experiences such as flashbacks, whereas Afghans and Sri Lankans were more likely to experience worries about the welfare of their families and communities. Thus, recurring personal flashbacks seem to be more of an individualistic phenomenon, whereas recurring worries about others seem to be more of a collectivistic phenomenon (Fernando, 2008; Miller et al., 2006). Factoring such cultural differences into diagnostic research and practice is an ongoing challenge.

Cultural differences play a role in treatments as well. For example, one of the more controversial possible breakthroughs in the treatment of PTSD involves psychological therapy combined with carefully prescribed doses of MDMA (the psychoactive component in the street drug ecstasy). Thus far, MDMA, in combination with psychological therapy, has proven to be an effective treatment for cases of PTSD that resist other forms of treatment (Mithoefer et al., 2013; Oehen et al., 2013). The effectiveness seems due to multiple mechanisms. For example, the oxytocin release induced by MDMA helps with the emotional bonding and trust that is essential to the therapeutic alliance between therapist and client (see Module 16.1), and the effects on serotonin seem beneficial for helping to reduce the anxiety that is key to PTSD. In short, MDMA helps people attain an open and secure state of mind so that they can more effectively face the trauma and begin to address, through therapy, the reactions it provokes.

Of course, there are large cultural and sub-cultural differences in the acceptance of drugs such as MDMA, which is illegal in North America. Therefore, it is unclear whether this treatment option will become available to patients with PTSD.

Survivors of major disasters are at risk for developing PTSD. Cultural factors influence the nature of the anxiety that people experience in the wake of such disasters.

Hou Yu/ZUMAPRESS/Newscom

Module 15.1a Quiz:
Defining Abnormal Behaviour

Know . . .

1. Rosenhan's classic study "On Being Sane in Insane Places" showed that
A. psychiatric institutions actually make disorders more likely, because they reinforce odd behaviour and they offer ready-made labels that people use to "pathologize" themselves.
B. therapists who come from a Freudian, psychoanalytic background can easily be tricked into believing people have a disorder that they do not in fact have, whereas therapists who are trained in modern cognitive-behavioural therapy do not make this same mistake.
C. once people have been labelled with a specific disorder, this will change how other people interpret their behaviour and behave toward them.
D. the presence of a mentally healthy person in a group of mentally ill patients can dramatically improve the functional scores of the patients.

Understand . . .

2. Which of the following is a problem with the DSM?
A. There is no objectively definable line separating normal from abnormal; thus, determining whether a person has a disorder or not relies upon criteria for distinguishing normal from abnormal, and those criteria are essentially arbitrary.

B. The construction of the DSM may reflect the influence of the pharmaceutical industry.

C. It may lead to over-diagnosis, because it provides diagnostic labels that can be appealing to people for a variety of reasons (such as offering hope that treatment is possible or making a child's behaviour more manageable).

D. All of the above are potential issues with the DSM.

3. Which of the following is *not* a psychiatric criterion for mental illness?

    A. Expression of behaviour that causes distress to self or others

    B. The condition must be categorical

    C. Impairment of functioning

    D. Increased high-risk behaviour (e.g., drug use, speeding)

Apply . . .

4. Which of the following statements about PTSD is *true*?

    A. People of all cultures experience the exact same concerns after trauma.

    B. Some cultures are immune to stress reactions.

    C. Physiological symptoms of PTSD may be common among people of different cultures, but the specific concerns people have can vary.

    D. PTSD occurs only in cultures that use a medical model.

Applications of Psychological Diagnoses

Perhaps one of the most important things to appreciate about psychological disorders is that there is no perfect test for identifying them. Being able to reliably diagnose particular disorders is a central and ongoing challenge to the mental health fields, and has an impact on problems that range from getting individuals the treatment they need to assessing criminal responsibility in the legal system. The fact that our measurements of psychological disorders are not nearly as accurate as we would like makes these issues even more difficult to deal with. In many cases, we cannot even say with confidence whether someone is mentally ill and what psychological illness or disorder they have.

THE MENTAL DISORDER DEFENCE (AKA THE INSANITY DEFENCE) This lack of diagnostic accuracy plays a big role in the criminal justice system. You have no doubt heard that in some trials a defendant will plead "not guilty by reason of insanity." The legal reasoning behind a person being defined as legally sane (i.e., criminally responsible) or not, is based on the *M'Naghten rule*, which goes all the way back to 1843 in Great Britain. Daniel M'Naghten assassinated the Prime Minister's secretary, but the jury was convinced that he was not guilty. They believed that he had been incapable of knowing that what he did was wrong, so M'Naghten was committed to a mental institution, and the plea "not guilty by reason of insanity" entered the legal profession.

In Canada, the insanity defence is now referred to as the **mental disorder defence**. This defence does not deny that the person committed the offence, but *claims that the defendant was in such an extreme, abnormal state of mind when committing the crime that he or she could not discern that the actions were legally or morally wrong.* For example, a person could cause a car accident or commit murder when in a severely dissociated state, such as could occur due to schizophrenia. Applying the mental disorder defence is extremely tricky, and indeed, it is rarely used. One study showed that this defence is used in less than 1% of cases in

Canadian courts and it has a success rate of less than 25% (Maxwell, 2015).

Whether or not we can objectively and accurately measure "sanity" is extremely important, as it could be the deciding factor in whether a person becomes a convicted felon or receives psychiatric treatment. However, determining whether or not a person was "sane" when they committed a crime is not an easy thing to do.

Consider two well-known Canadian examples of the mental disorder defence. In 2006, in Barrie, Ontario, Elaine Campione drowned both of her daughters (aged 3 years and 19 months) in a bathtub. At the time, she was involved in a custody battle with her ex-husband. Elaine had been diagnosed with a variety of psychological disorders and suffered delusions including that others were trying to steal her children. Her lawyer argued that she was not criminally responsible for her actions, but the Crown countered that even though she was mentally ill, her particular disorders did not prevent her from knowing right from wrong. She was convicted of first-degree murder (Supreme Court of Canada, 2011).

In Edmonton, Alberta in 2013, Nerlin Sarmiento drowned her 7-year-old son in a bathtub. Her lawyer argued that she was so deeply overwhelmed by a major depressive episode that was part of her bipolar disorder that she had become convinced that she was actually rescuing her son from a life of poverty and suffering, and believed that killing him was an act of mercy and kindness. In this case, the courts decided that Nerlin was not criminally responsible for her son's death, and required her to receive psychiatric treatment rather than going to jail (CBC News, 2013).

The critical issue, legally speaking, is whether the person was, at the time of committing the crime, capable of knowing that what they were doing was wrong. The Courts decided that Elaine Campione knew what she was doing was wrong, whereas Nerlin Sarmiento did not. Cases such as these show both the importance of psychology to the legal system and the difficulties associated with understanding a defendant's mental state. They also highlight the importance of accurately diagnosing a patient's condition.

Module 15.1b Quiz:

Applications of Psychological Diagnoses

Know . . .

1. The standard used to judge whether a defendant was capable to knowing that what he or she did was wrong is known as the
   A. McLaughlin rule.
   B. M'Naghten rule.
   C. Criminal Responsibility law.
   D. Law of Effect.

Understand . . .

2. As described in this section, in the legal system the term "insanity"
   A. is itself a psychological disorder.
   B. describes a person with any psychological disorder.
   C. is not recognized.
   D. means that an individual could not distinguish between right and wrong when he or she broke a law.

Module 15.1 Summary

15.1a Know . . . the key terminology associated with defining and classifying psychological disorders.

asylums
deinstitutionalization
Diagnostic and Statistical Manual of Mental Disorders (DSM)
etiology
maladaptive
medical model
mental disorder defence
post-traumatic stress disorder (PTSD)

15.1b Understand . . . the advantages and criticisms associated with the Diagnostic and Statistical Manual of Mental Disorders (DSM-5).

Using the DSM-5 ensures that all psychologists and psychiatrists are using the same criteria to define different psychological disorders; this improves the reliability and consistency of psychological diagnoses. However, the DSM-5 has faced many criticisms. First, psychologists need to decide if a symptom is severe enough to warrant treatment. Second, the number of symptoms that must be present before a disorder is diagnosed seems somewhat arbitrary (e.g., five out of nine possible symptoms). Third, although the large number of possible disorders may make it easier for mental health workers to make a diagnosis, it may also lead to unnecessary diagnoses. Finally, there is currently a need for more biological or genetic markers to be added to the diagnostic criteria for many disorders.

15.1c Apply . . . your knowledge of the mental disorders defence to decide if defendants are criminally responsible for their actions.

The legal consideration of "sanity" hinges on whether a person who commits a crime understands that their actions are wrong in a legal or a moral sense.

Apply Activity

Based on what you read about criminal responsibility and the mental disorders defence, how would you judge the following two cases: guilty or not guilty? (Note: we have "toned down" elements from real-world cases to make them much less graphic. However, anyone who is sensitive to descriptions of violence should feel free to skip this section.)

- *Case 1:* Tyson was diagnosed with schizophrenia two years ago. Although his symptoms have generally been under control, he has heard voices and seen things that weren't really present (hallucinations) on some occasions. During one of these episodes, he thought that someone waiting at the bus stop was a demon walking towards him. Tyson attacked the man, sending him to the hospital overnight.

- *Case 2:* Rick received treatment for depression for several years. Although his symptoms were generally under control, he still had some problems controlling his emotions. While working on a group project at work, Rick became involved in an intense argument with his coworkers who he felt were not working hard enough. Rick attacked one co-worker, sending him to the hospital overnight.

15.1d Analyze . . . whether the benefits of labelling psychological disorders outweigh the disadvantages.

To evaluate the importance of the DSM-5's labels, it would be helpful to consider their functions. They organize large amounts of information about symptoms, causes, and outcomes into terminology that mental health professionals can work with. From a practical point of view, this system meets the requirements of the insurance companies that pay for psychological services. One downside to this process is that once the label is applied, people have a tendency to misinterpret behaviours that are perfectly normal. Another downside is that if insurance and pharmaceutical companies have influence over how the guidelines are decided, then the whole system could be biased in favour of over-diagnosing and over-medicating people.

Module 15.2 Personality and Dissociative Disorders

AileenWuornos / AP Images

Learning Objectives

15.2a Know . . . the key terminology associated with personality and dissociative disorders.

15.2b Understand . . . the phenomenon of dissociation and how a dissociative disorder might occur.

15.2c Apply . . . your knowledge of antisocial personality disorder to explain how it could help people succeed in certain professions.

15.2d Analyze . . . the status of dissociative identity disorder as a legitimate diagnosis.

Warning: this story is potentially triggering or upsetting, particularly to people who have experienced abuse. Aileen Wuornos's life is an unbelievably sad story, so relentlessly tragic that it became the inspiration for the 2003 movie Monster, *for which Charlize Theron won an Oscar for her portrayal of Aileen.*

Aileen grew up in a complete chaos of abuse and mental illness. Her father was incarcerated and mentally ill, and was thus absent from her life. Her mother abandoned her at age 4, and she was adopted by her grandparents. Wuornos later described a childhood of being sexually abused and beaten by her grandfather, of prostituting herself for money and cigarettes to others, and being raped and impregnated at age 13 by a friend of her grandfather's. The baby was given up for adoption and by age 15, Aileen had been thrown out of the house and was supporting herself through prostitution.

With no stable home or healthy family relationships, she had very little capacity to trust or emotionally connect with others. When she was 20, she was, suddenly and surprisingly, wed to a wealthy yacht club owner; this might have been her ticket to a better life, but within weeks it devolved into violence

and conflict, and the marriage was eventually annulled. Over the next decade, Aileen struggled to keep her life together but was arrested numerous times for offences ranging from forging cheques to armed robbery and car theft, leading her to spend some time in prison.

When she was 33 years old, Aileen Wuornos's life of pain and trauma came spilling back out of her in a murderous frenzy. Over a one-year period spanning 1989 and 1990, she murdered seven men across the state of Florida. She initially claimed to have killed them in self-defence, in response to each of them attempting to rape her. Although diagnosed with borderline personality disorder and antisocial personality disorder, Wuornos was determined to be sane at the time of her killings and fit to stand trial. She was convicted and sentenced to death in the state of Florida (Wuornos v. State of Florida, 1994). In 2002, she was executed by lethal injection.

Focus Questions

1.   What are personality disorders and how do they differ from normal personality traits?

2. What are the key characteristics of dissociative disorders? Why does a person develop a dissociative disorder?

》 Chapter 12 described the psychological approaches to personality—the relatively stable patterns of thinking, behaving, and relating to others that make each person unique and that are bound up with that person's identity. In certain unusual cases, personality patterns can become deeply entrenched and maladaptive or destructive, which is described as developing a personality disorder (PD).

Defining and Classifying Personality Disorders

Mental health professionals identify **personality disorders** as *particularly unusual patterns of behaviour (relative to one's cultural context) that are maladaptive, distressing to oneself or others, and resistant to change.* For example, some people feel no empathy toward others, even those in great distress. Others have intense needs and high expectations for receiving the attention and admiration of others, and tend to feel severely rejected if their expectations are not met. Other people may become rapidly and obsessively attached to another person, only to reject that individual at a future time. Obviously, many people experience these basic patterns of behaviour in varying degrees; it is important to remember that personality disorders represent extreme cases. Importantly, personality disorders often persist throughout a person's life.

The DSM-5 identifies 10 distinct personality disorders, which are categorized into three different clusters based on shared features (see Table 15.2). Cluster A disorders are characterized by odd or eccentric behaviour; Cluster B disorders are indicated by dramatic, emotional, and erratic behaviour; Cluster C disorders are characterized by anxious, fearful, and inhibited behaviour. In addition to these 10 disorders, the DSM-5 also identifies Personality Disorder Not Otherwise Specified, which is a diagnosis given to individuals who exhibit patterns of behaviour consistent with that of a personality disorder, but which does not fit into any of the personality disorder categories described above.

Although each personality disorder deserves to be expanded upon, we will explore the four disorders in Cluster B to get a sense of the overarching commonalities shared by disorders in a given cluster, as well as the specific factors that differentiate them.

BORDERLINE PERSONALITY One of the clearest examples of the emotional dysfunction that lies at the core of personality disorders is found in **borderline personality disorder (BPD)** *which is characterized by intense extremes between positive and negative emotions, an unstable sense of self, impulsivity, and difficult social relationships.* People with BPD experience a wide range of emotions including extremely positive states such as joy, excitement, and love, but also very powerful destructive emotions such as anger, despair, and shame.

Their relationships are characterized by instability and intensity. A person with BPD may fall in love quickly and passionately, but also be highly fearful of abandonment and thus react intensely to any sign of rejection or criticism, quickly becoming disgusted with and rejecting their partner. They are often highly manipulative in relationships, attempting to keep the person under their control. In fact, their emotional reactions and ability to be emotionally manipulative in relationships are so strong that therapists typically limit themselves to a very small number of clients with BPD.

Table 15.2 Types of Personality Disorders

When listed in a table, the symptoms of personality disorders seem like characteristics that we all have. In a personality disorder, these symptoms are quite extreme and tend to be stable (if not permanent) traits.

Cluster	Description
Cluster A: odd; eccentric	• **Paranoid Personality Disorder:** See threats where others do not; difficulty trusting others • **Schizoid Personality Disorder:** Difficulty forming close relationships with other people; desire to be left alone, if possible • **Schizotypal Personality Disorder:** Odd or eccentric way of thinking and expressing oneself; difficulty forming close relationships
Cluster B: dramatic; emotional; erratic	• **Borderline Personality Disorder:** Impulsive, manipulative, and an unstable sense of self; volatile relationships • **Narcissistic Personality Disorder:** Intense need for attention and admiration; self-doubt and a fear of abandonment • **Histrionic Personality Disorder:** Excessive attention seeking; flamboyant, dramatic behaviour • **Antisocial Personality Disorder:** Impulsive and prone to risk-taking; reduced concern for the needs of others
Cluster C: anxious; fearful; inhibited	• **Avoidant Personality Disorder:** Tendency to avoid social interactions when possible; fear of rejection and embarrassment • **Dependent Personality Disorder:** Difficulty functioning or making decisions without the help of others; very low self-confidence • **Obsessive–Compulsive Personality Disorder:** A need for order and high expectations for oneself and for others; very upset if these needs aren't met
	• **Personality Disorder Not Otherwise Specified:** Symptoms do not clearly fit into one of the above diagnoses

It is believed that borderline personality disorder arises out of the person's attempts to deal with deeply rooted insecurity and severe emotional disturbances that are ultimately rooted in emotionally difficult experiences, such as inconsistent, abusive, or neglectful parenting. To cope with or escape from negative emotions, the person often engages in impulsive, risky, or self-destructive behaviour, including substance abuse, indiscriminate sex, self-injury such as cutting or burning oneself, and even suicide (American Psychiatric Association, 2013; Linehan, 1993).

NARCISSISTIC PERSONALITY **Narcissistic personality disorder (NPD)** *is characterized by an inflated sense of self-importance and an excessive need for attention and admiration, as well as intense self-doubt and fear of abandonment.* The central focus on the narcissistic person's own feelings and self-importance leaves little room for empathy for others. Instead, they tend to be manipulative and put themselves first, ensuring their own needs are met in their relationships regardless of the toll it takes on others. In many public situations, such as school, people with NPD have a strong sense of entitlement, believing that people should satisfy their demands, and being likely to do whatever it takes, including cheating, in order to ensure their own success (Brunell et al., 2011).

HISTRIONIC PERSONALITY Emotional dysfunction can also be seen in **histrionic personality disorder (HPD)**, *which is characterized by excessive attention seeking*

Narcissus, c.1597-99 (oil on canvas), Caravaggio, Michelangelo Merisi da (1571-1610)/Palazzo Barberini, Rome, Italy/Bridgeman Images

According to Greek mythology, Narcissus discovered his image reflecting on the surface of a pool of water. Unable to tear himself away from the beauty of his own face, Narcissus wasted away and died at the water's edge. In modern times, narcissism describes a person who has an inflated sense of self-importance.

and dramatic behaviour. "Histrionic" comes from a Latin word meaning "like an actor or like a theatrical performance"—an apt label for this disorder. People who have HPD are typically high-functioning because their dramatic nature makes them seem vibrant and attractive in social situations, and they readily use flirtatiousness, sexuality, and flattery to garner the social attention they crave. Similar to the other personality disorders discussed in this section, the histrionic person often engages in indulgent and risky behaviours, and tends to be highly sensitive to criticism and generally manipulative in relationships. The key difference between HPD and the other personality disorders in this cluster is the flamboyance and exhibitionistic tendencies in histrionic behaviour.

Working the Scientific Literacy Model

Antisocial Personality Disorder

In contrast to histrionic personality disorder, which is associated with dramatic behaviour, the diagnosis of **antisocial personality disorder (APD)** is given to individuals who have a *profound lack of empathy or emotional connection with others, a disregard for others' rights or preferences, and a tendency toward imposing their own desires, often violently, onto others regardless of the consequences for other people or, often when younger, other animals.* APD (often referred to as *psychopathy*) tends to be highly resistant to treatment, in part because individuals with APD are not alarmed or distressed by their actions (although others frequently are), and they are thus rarely, if ever, motivated to change.

What do we know about antisocial personality disorder?

People with APD tend to be physically and verbally abusive, and destructive, and frequently find themselves in trouble with the law. Symptoms of the disorder typically appear during childhood and adolescence, including harming or torturing people or animals, destroying property, stealing, and being deceitful (Lynam & Gudonis, 2005). The general public might use the term *psychopath* to describe a person who exhibits these types of behaviour, and indeed, the cold-blooded, remorseless murderer often fits the category of APD.

For some people with severe APD, the antisocial acts they commit are severe, and their lack of guilt or remorse is truly disturbing. This tendency was clearly evident in the words of Aileen Wuornos when she refused to appeal her death sentence:

I killed those men, robbed them as cold as ice. And I'd do it again, too. . . . There's no chance in keeping me alive or anything, because I'd kill again. I have hate crawling through my system. (CNN, 2002)

Keep in mind that serial killers represent only a very small subset of people with antisocial tendencies. In fact, people with APD are sometimes very successful, especially in business, which often rewards the kind of calculating, aggressive disposition of the person with APD; this is particularly true when coupled with the charm and social skills that many people with APD also possess. In fact, business managers often score highly on measures of antisocial personality tendencies, rivalling the scores of people with APD who are in jail. It is interesting to speculate for a moment on the implications for society if we construct our business and economic systems to reward those who are manipulative and lack of empathy.

How can science explain antisocial personality disorder?

You may have heard stories of people who have snapped under stress and committed horrific acts—however, this type of extreme stress response does not at all characterize APD. In fact, researchers have discovered that people with antisocial personality disorder are *under*-reactive to stress. For example, a flash of light, a loud sound, or the sudden appearance of an angry face will startle most people. In contrast, people with APD show very weak startle responses when exposed to unpleasant stimuli. In one study, researchers recorded the electrical signals of the eyeblink muscles while presenting disturbing images to a group of people with APD and a control group without APD. Figure 15.1 illustrates the results—the strength of the startle response is indicated by the height of the bars. The group of people with APD (the bars on the right side) had much weaker responses than the group without APD (on the left; Levenston et al., 2000).

This reduced reactivity to stress is due, in part, to abnormalities in the amygdala (Blair, 2010; Pemment, 2013). In most people, the amygdala fires in response to aversive stimuli; it is also involved with aversive conditioning, a form of emotional learning (see Module 6.1). However individuals with APD show very little amygdala activity in these situations. Additional impairments occur as a result of problems associated with the frontal lobes. The frontal lobes have connections that allow them to reduce the activity of the amygdala and other emotion-related brain regions (see Module 11.4). Individuals with APD, however, have less grey matter in many frontal lobe regions (Yang et al., 2010). They also have less efficient white-matter pathways connecting the frontal lobes and amygdala (Craig et al., 2009). As a result, they have trouble regulating their emotional responses (see Figure 15.2). Additionally, recent research suggests that these brain abnormalities impair this groups' ability to integrate emotional information with logical reasoning centres; thus, people with APD are emotionally cut off from the consequences of their actions, even though they rationally understand them (Baskin-Sommers, 2016).

Figure 15.1 Emotional Responses of Individuals with Antisocial Personality Disorder

This graph shows the strength of autonomic response to three types of pictures: mutilations, assault, and threat. Responses are much greater among control subjects (those who do not have APD; the three bars on the left) than among the individuals with antisocial personality disorder (the three bars on the right).

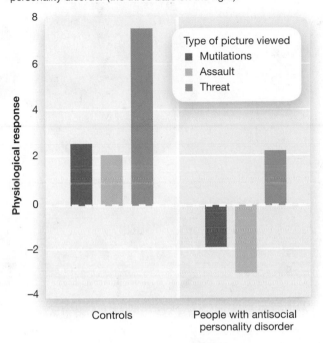

Source: Adapted from Levenston, G. K., Patrick, C. J., Bradley, M. M., & Lang, P. J. (2000). The psychopath as observer: Emotion and attention in picture processing. *Journal of Abnormal Psychology, 109* (3), 373–385.

Can we critically evaluate this information?

One cautionary note to keep in mind when reading about antisocial personality disorder is that we must be careful not to assume that all people with APD are violent criminals, indiscriminately harming others. Ironically, many of the characteristics of APD may themselves be highly desirable, or at least useful, in some professions (Dutton, 2012). The ability to emotionally detach from people, to be manipulative and able to deceive or lie without any moral reservations, to be charming and charismatic so as to appear to connect with people even though you can easily see people as tools to be used to satisfy your own desires, may well be rewarded in the worlds of CEOs, lawyers, salespeople, and undoubtedly many other social environments. These personality traits can give people with APD great power over others, because they are able to use others for their own personal gain without being held back by moral constraints (Lykken, 1995). Thus, the abusive boyfriend, the charming corporate ladder-climber, the intensely focused surgeon, the serial killer, or the socially inhibited hermit may all be outcomes of antisocial personality disorder.

Figure 15.2 Emotion Regulation in the Brain

In healthy brains, regions of the frontal lobes (highlighted in parts A, B, and D) are able to inhibit the activity emotion-related structures such as the amygdala (C). In APD, less inhibition occurs, thus resulting in problems with the regulation of emotions.

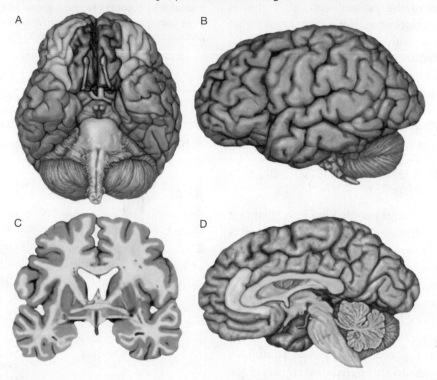

Why is this relevant?

Identifying how physiology and brain function differ in people with APD is certainly helpful for psychologists who are trying to understand the underlying mechanisms of these disturbing behavioural patterns. People with APD tend to be highly resistant to psychological therapies, making it even more critical to understand the underlying biological processes. Also, antisocial patterns are often detectable during childhood and adolescence, which are critical periods of brain development. If a system of early diagnosis and treatment could be instituted, it might be possible to more effectively intervene before the person develops the full manifestation of the disorder, and before they commit any harm.

Module 15.2a Quiz:

Defining and Classifying Personality Disorders

Know . . .

1. Which of the following is *not* a characteristic of personality disorders?
   A. Traits that are inflexible and maladaptive
   B. Significant functional impairment or subjective distress
   C. Marked deviation from cultural expectations
   D. Typically diagnosed with medical tests

Understand . . .

2. _____ refers to a condition marked by a habitual pattern of willingly violating others' personal rights, with very little sign of empathy or remorse.
   A. Borderline personality disorder
   B. Narcissistic personality disorder
   C. Histrionic personality disorder
   D. Antisocial personality disorder

3. _____ involves intense extremes between positive and negative emotions, an unstable sense of self, impulsivity, and difficult social relationships.
   A. Borderline personality disorder
   B. Narcissistic personality disorder
   C. Histrionic personality disorder
   D. Antisocial personality disorder

The Biopsychosocial Approach to Personality Disorders

It is often difficult to identify the causes of personality disorders because they seem to arise from multiple contributing factors over a long period of time. Rather than pinpointing the exact moment a disorder began, psychologists speak in general terms about the types of events that contribute to personality disorders. Adding to the difficulty is the fact that multiple causes are likely at play, and it may be possible for two people to develop the same symptomatic thoughts and behaviours through entirely different routes. The biopsychosocial model provides a comprehensive view, examining personality disorders from three different perspectives.

PSYCHOLOGICAL FACTORS Do people with personality disorders think differently than the rest of the population? Persistent beliefs about the self are a major part of the human personality, and the attempt to compensate for and cope with negative beliefs about oneself is a key part of APD. People with narcissistic (NPD) or histrionic (HPD) personality disorder also tend to have deeply rooted negative beliefs about the self, how they are regarded, and whether they are loved by others. Much of their dysfunctional behaviour patterns stem from attempts to compensate for these negative self-beliefs. For example, the person with NPD may continually seek attention, adoration, and reassurance from others, avoiding negative information about the self at all costs. A similar pattern may be apparent in someone who has a histrionic personality. Attention seeking through engaging in flattery and wearing provocative clothing may help individuals with HPD avoid the negative feelings they associate with being unnoticed.

Adults with APD and children with *conduct disorders* (often a precursor to APD) have difficulty learning tasks that require decision making and following complex rules. Brain-imaging studies show that children with conduct disorders perform worse at these tasks and have reduced activity in the frontal lobes compared with healthy controls and even children with ADHD (Finger et al., 2008). Thus, it appears that cognitive factors and their underlying brain systems are involved in personality disorders.

SOCIOCULTURAL FACTORS Children begin to develop social skills and emotional attachments at home and in their local neighbourhood and community. Not surprisingly, then, troubled homes and communities can contribute to the development of antisocial personality disorder (Meier et al., 2008). People with APD have often themselves experienced trauma or abuse. A history of being treated as an object rather than as a sensitive human being has consequences. The need to defend the self against intensely negative emotions and experiences may effectively shut down (or impair the development of) the emotional circuitry for empathy. This often results in aggression and cruelty toward others, including animals.

In general, personality disorders often involve extensive emotional damage from childhood experiences, ranging from physical violence and sexual abuse to the profound invalidation and insecurity of being repeatedly abandoned or neglected as a child. For example, even less severe cases of borderline personality disorder may arise from a child having his emotions treated as if they were unreal or unimportant (Crowell et al., 2009). The resulting deep insecurity and emotional volatility leave adults with BPD unable to control their emotions, and therefore more vulnerable to everyday life stressors (Glaser et al., 2008).

BIOLOGICAL FACTORS Not everyone who experiences extreme stress and abuse develops a personality disorder, of course. So why do some adapt successfully while others do not? The answer may lie in how stress interacts with biological predispositions for personality disorders. A number of specific genes seem to contribute to emotional instability by affecting serotonin systems in the brain (Crowell et al., 2009). Research also points to unique activity in the limbic system and frontal lobes—brain regions that are associated with emotional responses and impulse control, respectively (Brendel et al., 2005).

Thus, the biopsychosocial model of behaviour can help us understand the different characteristics of personality disorders, which are among the most complex and difficult to treat disorders in the DSM-5. As you will see in the next section of this module, this model can also be useful when attempting to understand one of psychology's most mysterious and controversial conditions: multiple personality disorder.

Module 15.2b Quiz:
The Biopsychosocial Approach to Personality Disorders

Know . . .

1. Some children show a set of symptoms that include difficulty learning tasks that require decision making and following complex rules. This group of symptoms is sometimes referred to as
   A. psychopathy.
   B. borderline personality disorder.
   C. disorder of social attachment.
   D. a conduct disorder.

Apply . . .

2. Which of the following biopsychosocial factors is *least* likely to be related to personality disorders?
   A. Stress reactivity
   B. History of abuse
   C. Decreased activity of the frontal lobes
   D. Enjoyment of pain

Dissociative Identity Disorder

Have you ever been so engaged in driving, reading a book, or playing a game that you were totally unaware of what was going on around you? Have you ever had difficulty determining whether an event, perhaps some long-ago story, really happened the way you now remember it, or whether it was a story that happened to someone else, or even a dream? These types of experiences can be thought of as dissociative experiences, because they are characterized by a sense of separation (dissociation) between the person and her surroundings. Dissociative experiences may arise while you are intensely focused on one activity, or when you drift off while not doing anything in particular, such as daydreaming during a long lecture. People differ in their tendencies to dissociate, but such experiences seem completely normal. In contrast, dissociative states caused by brain injury or psychological trauma are far from harmless.

TYPES OF DISSOCIATIVE DISORDERS In a few cases, some people have such extreme dissociative experiences that they may be diagnosed with a **dissociative disorder**, *a category of mental disorders characterized by a split between a person's conscious awareness and their feelings, cognitions, memory, and identity* (Kihlstrom, 2005). Dissociative disorders include the following conditions:

- *Dissociative fugue:* A period of profound autobiographical memory loss. People in fugue states may go so far as to develop a new identity in a new location with no recollection of their past.

- *Depersonalization disorder:* A strong sense of the surreal, the feeling that one is not connected to one's body, the feeling of disconnection from one's regular identity and awareness.

- *Dissociative amnesia:* A severe loss of memory, usually for a specific stressful event, when no biological cause for amnesia is present.

Probably the most familiar member of this category is **dissociative identity disorder (DID)**, *in which a person experiences a split in identity such that they feel different aspects of themselves as though they were separated from each other. This can be severe enough that the person constructs entirely separate personalities, only one of which will generally be in control at a time.* This is also sometimes referred to as **multiple personality disorder**.

These distinct personalities, or *alters*, may be so different from one another as to have different genders, sexual orientations, memories, personalities, and autobiographical senses of self and who they are. The dissociation of alter identities can be so strong that one alter may have no memory of events experienced by other alters. From Dr. Jekyll and Mr. Hyde to Tyler Durden in *Fight Club*, we have been both fascinated and frightened by the possibility that a single individual can house radically different personalities within his consciousness.

In most cases, dissociative disorders such as DID are thought to be brought on by extreme stress. Some psychologists have hypothesized that during a traumatic event such as being a victim of violence, individuals may cope with the experience by shifting their consciousness to a different perspective. They may go to another place in their mind, or feel as though they are separate from their physical bodies and are watching events happen to them as though their body was a different person. With repeated experiences, this type of dissociation could become an individual's habitual way of coping with trauma, as well as other stressful situations (van der Kolk, 1994). Consistent with this, most cases of DID do include reports of a stressful event or series of events that precipitated the onset of the condition (Putnam, 1989).

IS DISSOCIATIVE IDENTITY DISORDER "REAL?" DID is a very rare condition, affecting only about 1% of psychiatric patients, and therefore only a very small fraction of 1% of the general population (Rifkin et al., 1998). There has been longstanding controversy surrounding whether DID is real. Many of the characteristics of different alters could be faked by people who explicitly (i.e., on purpose) adopt different personas, undergo hypnosis, or are simply influenced by the expectations of psychologists. Importantly, in many of these cases, the different alters begin to *feel* real to the patient (even if they began as inventions). This makes it quite challenging for researchers attempting to test whether DID really exists. A key problem in this debate is that a condition like DID is very difficult to test for in a rigorous fashion, given how personal and subjective the experience of identity is.

One approach to testing for DID is to check for memory dissociations between alter identities. For example, in one study, patients viewed words and pictures and were tested for recall of the stimuli either when they were experiencing the same alter as when they learned them, or when they were experiencing a different alter. The results suggested that some types of learning do not transfer between alter identities (Eich et al., 1997). This finding would suggest that the alters are truly separate identities.

Another approach to examining DID is to record patterns of brain activity. One study using positron emission tomography (PET) actually found differing frontal lobe activity for people with DID while they were experiencing each of their alters (Reinders et al., 2003). (In case you wondered, the researchers obtained consent to participate in the study from both alters.) Although the results of both of these studies are thought-provoking, they do not provide solid evidence for a biological basis of DID. After all, any different state of mind or emotional experience will involve different patterns of brain activity. The fact that the two alters produced different patterns of brain activation may simply reflect that the person was thinking about and experiencing things differently in the two states of mind, not that the alters were actually distinct personalities.

Another questionable aspect of DID is the huge change in the number of cases reported over time. By 1970, there were only 79 documented cases of DID (then referred to as multiple personality disorder). In 1986, there were around 6000; by 1998, the number had risen to more than 40 000 (Lilienfeld & Lynn, 2003). Also, 80% of patients diagnosed with DID were unaware of having the disorder before starting therapy (Putnam, 1989). These observations suggest that DID may have its origins in the context of therapy, rather than being a response to trauma. Also of note, the number of alters changed dramatically; in the early decades up to the 1970s, a person would typically have only one alter; but by the 1980s, people were identified as having many different alters, even dozens or hundreds!

Why did the rate of DID skyrocket from 79 cases to more than 40 000 cases in fewer than three decades? This increased prevalence could simply be a product of awareness. After professionals learned how to identify the disorder, they could begin to diagnose it more effectively.

Or, it may be that a small subset of psychologists find the disorder compelling and are more willing to diagnose it, so they interpret symptoms through that framework, and may (even unintentionally) provoke dissociative symptoms in the context of therapy (Frankel, 1993). The use of highly suggestive techniques such as hypnosis increases the likelihood that this is the case.

Researchers have examined social and therapist effects on DID by observing what happens when the disorder is introduced to other parts of the world. In these cases it appears that DID—whether a disorder or not—has a strong sociocultural component. For example, the disorder was nonexistent in Japan in 1990 (Takahashi, 1990), but Japanese psychologists began diagnosing patients with DID when the disorder was described by North Americans (An et al., 1998). In India, the disorder is recognized, but how the disorder manifests itself is different from in America: Americans with DID switch from alters upon suggestion, whereas people in India who have DID switch alters only upon awakening (North et al., 1993). These observations point to a predominantly sociocultural disorder in which cultural beliefs and therapists determine how the symptoms are manifested (Lilienfeld et al., 1999).

Module 15.2c Quiz:

Dissociative Identity Disorder

Know . . .

1. Dissociative identity disorder is best described as
   A. a lost grasp on reality.
   B. a lack of regard for the feelings of others.
   C. a splitting of identity.
   D. a problem with memory, attention, and the ability to form coherent thoughts.

Understand . . .

2. Fugue is a form of dissociative disorder most commonly associated with
   A. a belief that you no longer exist or are real.
   B. loss of sensation in an appendage with no physical or neurological evidence.

   C. housing multiple personalities in one body
   D. loss of identity and memories of the self.

3. Which of the following is believed to typically bring on dissociative identity disorder?
   A. A physical injury to the head
   B. Extreme stress or trauma
   C. Old age
   D. Genetics

Module 15.2 Summary

15.2a   Know . . . the key terminology associated with personality and dissociative disorders

antisocial personality disorder (APD)
borderline personality disorder (BPD)
dissociative disorder
dissociative identity disorder (DID)
histrionic personality disorder (HPD)
multiple personality disorder

narcissistic personality disorder (NPD)
personality disorders

15.2b   Understand . . . the phenomenon of dissociation and how a dissociative disorder might occur.

Dissociation occurs in everyday phenomena such as daydreaming. However, a dissociative disorder may occur when perceptions of mind, body, and surroundings are severely and chronically separated, such that the person loses his or her previously stable sense of self and identity.

15.2c Apply . . . your knowledge of antisocial personality disorder to explain how it could help people succeed in certain professions.

Some writers have noted that *some* people with antisocial personality disorder do well in certain competitive professions such as working in a corporate finance office.

Apply Activity

1. List three characteristics associated with APD.
2. For each characteristic listed above, write down how that trait or behaviour could be useful in the corporate world.

15.2d Analyze . . . the status of dissociative identity disorder as a legitimate diagnosis.

The lack of a physical basis for the disorder and its unusual rate and patterns of diagnosis bring about skepticism as to whether DID is real or is manufactured, perhaps unwittingly, by the person. It is important to find evidence for differences between alternate personalities that cannot be faked by people or created artificially. Recent research in brain imaging is beginning to look for different patterns of neurological activity that could denote distinct personalities, but this work is in its infancy.

Module 15.3 Anxiety, Obsessive–Compulsive, and Depressive Disorders

Matsunaka Takeya/Aflo/Glow Images

 ## Learning Objectives

15.3a Know . . . the key terminology related to anxiety, obsessive–compulsive, and depressive disorders.

15.3b Understand . . . the different types of anxiety disorders.

15.3c Understand . . . how anxiety or depressive disorders can be self-perpetuating.

15.3d Apply . . . your knowledge of anxiety, obsessive–compulsive, and depressive disorders, so as to be alert to people who may benefit from some help.

15.3e Analyze . . . whether maladaptive aspects of specific phobias might arise from perfectly normal, healthy behaviours.

Of all the things to be afraid of in life, surely one of them is not the possibility that you can catch a mental illness, waking up one morning mentally ill because of some bacteria or germ that you were exposed to. This is generally true; we are pretty safe. In most cases, psychological disorders develop over a period of time. There may be some initial signs that everything is "not quite right" with a person, and then there is a gradual unfolding of more noticeable personality, behavioural, or emotional problems.

Unfortunately, there are documented cases of sudden onset obsessive–compulsive disorder (OCD), in which young children suddenly and without prior warning developed symptoms of OCD, including repetitive behaviours and irrational fears and obsessions. Surprisingly, this sudden surge of OCD-like tendencies came after these children were exposed to bacterial streptococcal infections (Snider & Swedo, 2004). How is it possible that this particular infection seems capable of triggering a sudden-onset psychological disorder in some children?

The answer seems to be that when the immune system mounts its reaction to the bacterial infection, it also damages cells in the caudate, a part of the brain near its centre. As we will see in this module, one theory about OCD is that compulsive, repetitive behaviours (such as hand washing) are ways of dealing with a lost sense of impulse control, the sort of loss that occurs when the caudate is damaged (Huyser et al., 2009). If this theory is correct, a psychological disorder could be acquired virtually overnight . . . at least in this case.

Focus Questions

1. The experience of anxiety drives many different disorders. What are some of the ways that problems with anxiety can manifest?

2. Depression is another very common disorder. Why do people seem to develop depression?

》 Anxiety and mood disorders are extremely common. In fact, a recent survey of over 10 000 Ontario students in Grades 7 through 12 found that 46% of females and 23% of males reported suffering from depression and/or an anxiety disorder (Boak et al., 2015). These staggering statistics show how prevalent these disorders are. Importantly, they also show those suffering from anxiety or depression that they are not alone—other people truly *can* understand how they feel.

Anxiety Disorders

Anxiety disorders are *a category of disorders involving fear or nervousness that is excessive, irrational, and maladaptive.* They also are among the most frequently diagnosed disorders, affecting approximately one in every eight Canadians (Public Health Agency of Canada, 2002), and often occurring with other disorders, such as depression or obsessive–compulsive disorders, substance abuse, or problematic behaviour patterns such as an excessive need to be in control of situations.

Although occasional experiences of anxiety are normal, even functional responses to life circumstances, when anxiety becomes debilitating and interferes with the person's daily life, it clearly becomes a problem. People often attempt to cope with anxiety by limiting themselves to environments, activities, and people that make them feel safe and secure, and by developing rigid habits and ways of doing things that keep life predictable and under control. These patterns evolve in order to help the anxious person manage his or her fear, but they also can limit people's freedom to live their lives as they would like.

In most people's experience, anxiety occurs as a natural part of the fight-or-flight response (Nesse & Ellsworth, 2009). We experience this response as a racing, pounding heartbeat with increased respiration, as our autonomic systems prepare our bodies for quick action. Some people may notice a knot in the stomach and sweaty or clammy hands. These physical changes reflect a shift in energy away from non-emergency tasks like digestion and toward fighting or fleeing. This basic fight-or-flight response seems to be common to all mammals, implying that it has long been evolutionarily adaptive to have an easily triggered system that can quickly arouse the body for action. However, living in our modern, stressed-out society, we activate this stress response system repeatedly throughout our days, to the point where it can become harmful to us (see Module 14.2).

VARIETIES OF ANXIETY DISORDERS What separates anxiety *disorders* from normal experiences of anxiety is the intensity and long duration of the response. Anxiety disorders are also distinct in that the response may not be directly connected to one's current circumstances; instead, the anxiety can be free-floating. Either way,

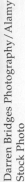

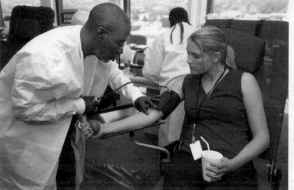

Fight or flight . . . or freeze or faint? In addition to fight-or-flight responses, mammals can also react by freezing—as in the "deer in the headlights" response—or by fainting, as some will do at the sight of blood (Bracha et al., 2004).

anxiety disorders cause a great deal of emotional distress and interfere with people's daily lives. Of course, not all anxiety disorders are the same. Psychologists have identified distinct patterns of experience that have given rise to several major types of anxiety disorders.

Generalized anxiety disorder (GAD) *involves frequently elevated levels of anxiety, generally from the normal challenges and stresses of everyday life.* A person with GAD fears disaster lurking around every corner, and may experience symptoms ranging from difficulty sleeping or breathing to difficulty concentrating because of intrusive thoughts. However, because the anxiety arises out of the ongoing situations and circumstances of life, people often have difficulty understanding their experience and cannot identify specific reasons for which they are anxious (Turk et al., 2005). It is also difficult to resolve the anxiety, despite trying to control situations and trying to attend to every detail so that nothing goes wrong. Instead, as one detail is dealt with, the anxiety shifts to another source, and the control-oriented person is locked into a never-ending scramble to manage life perfectly so as to keep anxiety at bay.

Not surprisingly, people with GAD often have unstable, irritable moods, experience difficulty concentrating, and have sleep problems. Although there are many different types of factors that increase the probability of developing

GAD, ranging from innate, genetic components to current habitual thinking patterns, a convergence of stresses, such as occurs during major life changes, commonly precede the onset of the disorder (Newman & Llera, 2011).

Panic disorder is *an anxiety disorder marked by occasional episodes of sudden, very intense fear.* This condition is distinct from GAD because the anxiety occurs in short segments, but can be much more severe. The key feature of this disorder is **panic attacks**—*brief moments of extreme anxiety that include a rush of physical activity paired with frightening thoughts.* A panic attack escalates when the fear causes increased physical arousal, and the increased physical symptoms feed the frightening thoughts. The escalation rarely goes on for more than ten minutes, after which the individual will eventually return to a more relaxed state.

A substantial subset of people with panic disorder develop a recurring fear that the panic will strike again, particularly in an environment in which they would be exposed and unable to escape from people, such as a shopping mall or other public space. This fear can result in **agoraphobia** (which is often associated with panic disorder), *an intense fear of having a panic attack in public; as a result of this fear, the individual may begin to avoid public settings and increasingly isolate him- or herself.* In its most extreme forms, agoraphobia leads an individual to stay inside his home almost all the time.

Working the Scientific Literacy Model

Specific Phobias

In contrast to GAD, where an individual's anxiety can be applied to just about any situation, a **phobia** is *a severe, irrational fear of a very specific object or situation.* Some of the most common phobias are listed in Table 15.3. Phobias are sometimes divided into two broad categories: specific phobias and social phobias. A **specific phobia** involves *an intense fear of a specific object, activity, or organism.* For example, the person may be afraid of specific animals, heights, thunder, blood, or injections or other medical procedures.

Social phobias, which are also very common, are related to interpersonal situations and relationships and are discussed later.

What do we know about phobias?

Phobias often develop as a result of unpleasant or frightening experiences; there's nothing like getting bitten by a dog to make a person afraid of dogs. That said, the overwhelming majority of the triggers for phobias are objects or situations that we may *need* to fear, or at least be cautious about. For example, people readily develop phobias of spiders, snakes, heights, and drowning—dangers that would have been important over the course of our species' evolution (Öhman & Mineka, 2001; see also Module 6.1). This tendency suggests that there may be a genetic component to some of our specific phobias. Of course, this does not mean that other phobias will be impossible to develop, but rather that people are more biologically predisposed to fear evolutionarily relevant objects or situations.

Interestingly, phobias can also develop without direct, personal experience. Why would a person develop an extreme fear about something that they had no personal experience with, especially if it was something that they, realistically, were unlikely to ever have personal experience with? It doesn't seem rational, or functional. In some cases, these links form through observational learning, such as seeing vicious sharks in movies. In many of these cases, an initial mental link between an object or situation and an emotion can be retrieved from memory and thought about multiple times. We think about the object and become afraid; this fear can, in turn, become a retrieval cue for the object. The result of these feedback loops is that our brains can create powerful experiences, even though they are not real in the sense that they are not being triggered by anything actually happening in the external world at that moment; this tendency is known as *parasitic processing* (Vervaeke & Ferraro, 2012). Indeed, this is essentially how anxiety disorders, including phobias, work! The self-reinforcing nature of anxiety reactions leads them to grow and become more extreme over time (Merckelbach et al., 1996).

Table 15.3 What Are We So Afraid Of?

	Currently Experiencing the Phobia	Have Experienced the Phobia at One Time
Animals (snakes, birds, or other animals)	4.7%	50.3%
Natural environment (e.g., heights, storms, water)	5.9%	62.7%
Blood or bodily injury (including injections)	4.0%	42.5%
Situations (e.g., dentists, hospitals, crowded places)	5.2%	55.6%
Other specific objects	1.0%	10.6%

Source: Stinson, F. S. et al., (2007). "The epidemiology of DSM-IV specific phobia in the USA: Results from the National Epidemiologic Survey on Alcohol and Related Conditions," *Psychological Medicine, 37,* 7, pp. 1047–1059. Table 3, p. 1053. Copyright © 2007 Cambridge University Press. Reprinted with the permission of Cambridge University Press.

How can science explain why some people are more likely than others to develop specific phobias?

For any given individual, there are many factors that determine whether or not a phobia develops. For example, some of the risk factors for phobias include personality characteristics, like shyness and temperamental inhibition, both of which are, interestingly enough, partly genetically determined (Biederman et al., 1990; DiLalla et al., 1994).

Scientists have been piecing together the genetic factors that biologically predispose some people to experience more fear than others. One of the first questions to answer is simply whether or not the tendency to learn fear associations can be transmitted genetically. One group of researchers attempted to answer this using selective breeding techniques with mice. The researchers tested a strain of mice for how easily they could learn a fear association (an auditory tone coupled with an electrical shock). The fear response was measured by the length of time the mice held still—mice typically show fear by freezing in place (Ponder et al., 2007).

By selectively breeding the most fearful mice with each other, and the least fearful mice with each other, researchers could see whether the fear-association response would differ across the generations of these mice families. As Figure 15.3 shows, across four generations, fear responses became more and more distinct, with the third and fourth generations being very different from each other. These patterns of behaviour diverging so substantially in different genetic pools suggests that the fear-based learning system is, at least in part, genetically determined.

Can we critically evaluate this information?

We may question the value of this research because, on the face of it, we don't seem to have learned much about phobias from studying genetic heritability of fear-responses in mice. However, understanding that genes can influence fear responses in another mammalian species suggests that genes likely underlie our own reactions to threatening stimuli and situations. Therefore, behavioural genomics investigations of phobias could provide us with important information.

A second potential criticism of this research is that it only examines fear responses from one perspective: genetics. The authors of those research papers would be the first to admit that the full manifestation of a phobia involves many processes and, therefore, would only be partially explained by a genetic understanding. For instance, observational learning likely plays a large role in the development and maintenance of phobias. Seeing another mouse (or human) react with fear to specific objects or animals would teach a young mouse (or human) that *that* object or animal is to be feared. The fact that multiple factors are involved in the development of phobias provides further support for the use of the biopsychosocial model when explaining behaviour.

Why is this relevant?

In general, understanding causal factors better, targeting causal mechanisms more effectively, and directly manipulating biological systems related to fear and anxiety responses sound like pretty good ideas. A challenge for the future is to understand the interaction between the genetic and other levels of analysis in order to fully develop these tools. Doing so may lead to new treatment for a number of disorders.

Figure 15.3 Anxiety Levels Are Inherited in an Animal Model

Over the course of just a few generations, mice from the highly fearful genetic strain show increasingly strong fear responses as indicated by the height of the red bars.

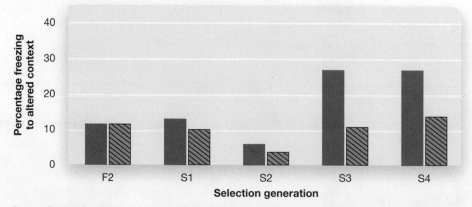

Source: From Selection for contextual fear conditioning affects anxiety-like behaviors and gene expression, *Genes, Brain and Behavior, 6*: 736–749 by C. A. Ponder, C. L. Kliethermes, M. R. Drew, J. Muller, K. Das, V. B. Risbrough, J. C. Crabbe, T. Conrad Gilliam, A. A. Palmer. Copyright © 2007 by John Wiley & Sons, Inc. Reproduced by permission of John Wiley & Sons, Inc.

Thus far, our discussion of phobias has focused on fearful responses to specific stimuli such as snakes (or snakes with knives in their mouths). **Social anxiety disorder**, on the other hand, is *a very strong fear of being judged by others or being embarrassed or humiliated in public.* People who experience social anxiety deal with going out in public by developing familiar routines and retaining control over their ability to exit circumstances if their anxiety becomes too strong. Social anxiety generally leads people to limit their social activities in favour of not exposing themselves to anxiety, thus making it difficult to succeed and live a normal life in many different ways.

Consider the day of a university student who has social anxiety:

- This student always shows up to class just as it begins so he does not have to risk awkward conversation with classmates he does not know, or potentially worse, sitting conspicuously alone and being unable to connect to anyone around him.

- Despite being hungry, the student will not go into the cafeteria because his roommate is not around. He cannot face the prospect of sitting with strangers, especially without his roommate. He finds a quiet spot near the library and gets lunch from a vending machine.

- Walking across a quiet part of campus, he sees his professor approaching. Not knowing if the professor would recognize him, he wonders if he should say hello. Thinking about this issue makes him so tense, he pretends to stop and read a text message to avoid eye contact.

As you can see, the day is a series of unpleasant, tense moments in situations that most people would find completely ordinary. It is also a series of sacrificed opportunities as the person fails over and over again to take advantage of chances for connection and social contact. The distress the student feels and the degree to which he shapes his life around his social phobia suggest that he has social anxiety disorder. Of course, to make a formal diagnosis of this disorder, a psychologist would need to evaluate the student's full set of symptoms and their duration.

THE VICIOUS CYCLE OF ANXIETY DISORDERS As discussed earlier, anxiety disorders tend to be self-perpetuating (Figure 15.4), with anxiety leading to circumstances that provoke further anxiety (Hofmann, 2007). For example, people who are anxious about interacting with others may avoid many social situations because they feel awkward and insecure and don't want to embarrass themselves. As a result, they become even less confident about their ability to interact with people, making them even more likely to avoid social contact in the future; or, if it is unavoidable, to be so anxious and incapable of functioning effectively that the social opportunity turns into a negative experience, further reinforcing the anxiety.

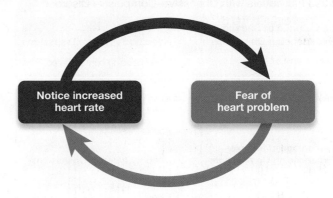

Figure 15.4 The Vicious Cycle of Panic Attacks

Avoiding or interrupting this vicious cycle is central to the treatment of anxiety disorders. Instead of trying to minimize contact with feared situations, which only serves to reinforce the fear, the person must begin to practise confronting the fear. Only through exposing themselves to fear can people learn how to manage their responses or learn how to effectively manage the feared situation. For example, imagine a young girl who gets scratched by the neighbour's cat while trying to pet it. The girl may avoid cats in the future and, years later, still feel nervous and unsure of herself around cats. Only by learning to tolerate and eventually interact with cats will the girl be able to reduce her anxiety. The most important part of psychological therapy for anxiety disorders is **exposure**, in which the person is *repeatedly and in stages exposed to the object of her fear so that she can work past her emotional reactions.* For exposure to be most effective, it should be coupled with helping the person to calm themselves down and to learn to tolerate the aversive feelings they are experiencing (see Module 16.2).

OBSESSIVE–COMPULSIVE DISORDER (OCD) Until 2013, **obsessive–compulsive disorder (OCD)** was categorized as an anxiety disorder. In the DSM-5, OCD was placed into its own category. Individuals with OCD tend to be *plagued by unwanted, inappropriate, and persistent thoughts (obsessions), and to engage in repetitive, often quite ritualistic behaviours (compulsions).* Generally, obsessions and compulsions are linked together, with the compulsive behaviour serving as a means of coping with the anxiety produced by the obsession (see Table 15.4). For example, a common manifestation of OCD is a person who is extremely concerned about germs and cleanliness; he may wash his hands many times each day, insist on only touching other objects through gloves, or become extremely vigilant about the chemicals in food and cleaning products. Alternatively, someone who worries about starting a fire might develop compulsive checking behaviours. Before she can leave her house, she might check that all lamps and appliances are unplugged. She may make the rounds two more times, ensuring that the electrical cords

Table 15.4 Prevalence of Symptoms in a Survey of 293 Individuals with Obsessive–Compulsive Disorder

Percentage of Sample Experiencing Obsession	Specific Types of Obsessions
58%	A fear of being contaminated
56%	Persistent doubting
48%	Need to arrange things in a symmetrical pattern
45%	Aggressive thoughts
Percentage of Sample Experiencing Compulsion	Specific Types of Obsessions
69%	Checking
60%	Cleaning
56%	Repeating actions

Source: Based on Pinto, A., Mancebo, M., Eisen, J., Pagano, M., & Rasmussen, S. (2006). The Brown longitudinal obsessive compulsive study: Clinical features and symptoms of the sample at intake. *Journal of Clinical Psychiatry, 67,* 703–711.

are secured by fasteners at least two feet from the outlet. Finally, she might turn off the light to leave but, to avoid the possibility that the light switch is halfway between on and off, she might count out a series of one to seven in which she turns the light off repeatedly, followed by one last downward swipe to ensure the switch is fully off. Only then can she feel secure in leaving the house.

Although everybody has unwanted thoughts that seem to stick in their heads from time to time, obsessions take root and can last for a very long time, even many years. Obviously, these thoughts tend to be distressing.

As these types of intrusive thinking patterns become more extreme and ever-present, they increasingly interfere with the person's life. Imagine people who obsessively think about cleanliness and germs; everywhere they go in life, they encounter new microbiological terrors, forcing them to adopt elaborate rituals for how to sufficiently clean themselves and how to avoid making contact with germs in many different situations. Many psychologists believe that compulsive behaviours, and the relief they provide, give the person a feeling of control over their anxiety. They just have to perform a very *particular* behaviour in order to feel that control.

We introduced this disorder at the beginning of this module by describing how it can occur suddenly in children. This type of onset is exceedingly rare, and not at all representative of the way that OCD usually develops. OCD generally develops over time, ranging from childhood into early adulthood, by which time most cases of OCD will have manifested themselves.

Although the compulsive behaviour patterns associated with OCD can be quite disruptive to the general activities of everyday life, these patterns also tend to be quite responsive to treatment. In fact, anxiety, depressive, and obsessive–compulsive disorders are all generally amenable to treatment. This provides hope for the millions of Canadians who are affected by these emotionally draining psychological disorders.

Module 15.3a Quiz:

Anxiety Disorders

Know . . .

1. The difference between obsessions and compulsions is that
   A. obsessions are repetitive behaviours, whereas compulsions are fears about specific events.
   B. obsessions are repetitive, unwanted thoughts, whereas compulsions are repetitive behaviours.
   C. obsessions are temporary, whereas compulsions are practically permanent.
   D. obsessions and compulsions are the same thing.

Understand . . .

2. Allison has an intense fear of flying, so much so that she cannot even bear to close her eyes and imagine that she is on a plane. From this brief description, Allison may be experiencing
   A. a specific phobia.
   B. a social phobia.
   C. a generalized phobia.
   D. normal levels of anxiety.

3. Which condition is marked by a strong feeling of tension and worry, no matter what the situation may be?
   A. A specific phobia
   B. A panic attack

   C. Generalized anxiety disorder
   D. Normal feelings of anxiety

4. The idea that anxiety disorders can be self-perpetuating means that
   A. anxiety in one situation always causes anxiety in another situation, regardless of what is happening in those situations.
   B. the emotions associated with anxiety lead to physiological responses, which in turn lead to more anxious emotions, creating a vicious cycle.
   C. you choose when and what to be anxious about.
   D. anxiety is always limited to one situation or place.

Analyze . . .

5. If anxiety leads to the onset of so many different disorders, how can it be a beneficial, adaptive process?
   A. It cannot be an adaptive process.
   B. The physiological response underlying anxiety prepares us to fight or to flee certain stimuli or situations.
   C. Anxiety is a good way to gain sympathy.
   D. The anxiety response evolved to help attract mates.

Mood Disorders

Mood disorders are very common, affecting almost 10% of adults in Canada and the U.S. (Health Canada, 2002; Kessler et al., 2005). Due to a combination of biological, cognitive, and sociocultural differences, rates of depression are twice as high among women as among men, and three times as high among people living in poverty (Hyde et al., 2008). There is also a genetic susceptibility to mood disorders. In this section we discuss the two major types of mood disorders—major depression and bipolar disorder.

TYPES OF MOOD DISORDERS Feelings of sadness and depression are normal aspects of human experience. By comparison, major depression can be very severe and may occur even when there are no events or circumstances we normally associate with a depressed mood. **Major depression** is *a disorder marked by prolonged periods of sadness, feelings of worthlessness and hopelessness, social withdrawal, and cognitive and physical sluggishness.* With this definition, it should be clear that depression involves more than just feeling sad for a long period of time; cognitive activities such as concentrating and making decisions are affected as well, while memories shift toward unpleasant and unhappy events. Physiologically, affected individuals may be lethargic and sleepy, yet also experience insomnia. They may experience changes in appetite and the onset of digestive problems such as constipation or stomach aches.

To fully understand depression requires considering the cumulative, daily impact of life's activities being interfered with by feelings of despair, uselessness, and a lack of energy and motivation. Depression can lead to problems piling up at work and at home, relationships being strained or crumbling, and financial problems starting to interfere with daily life. People deep in depression may find it almost impossible to take care of more than the barest necessities of their lives; their social lives suffer as they stop returning phone calls or emails. Other people may notice and get annoyed or have hurt feelings, which leads

Many people have experienced problems with a mood disorder. Those with depression may experience extended periods of sadness and hopelessness that have no apparent cause.

the depressed person to feel even worse about himself. These examples provide a glimpse of how depression can become such a monster.

In contrast, **bipolar disorder** (formerly referred to as *manic depression*) is *characterized by extreme highs and lows in mood, motivation, and energy.* It shares many symptoms with major depression—some distinguish the two by referring to major depression as *unipolar depression*—but it occurs only about a third as often (NIMH, 2008). Bipolar disorder involves depression at one end and *mania*—an extremely energized, positive mood—at the other end. Mania may take several forms: talking excessively fast, racing thoughts, impulsive and spontaneous decisions, or high-risk behaviours. The experience of a manic episode can be exhilarating and parts of it can be highly enjoyable, but the costs of such excessive, indiscriminate, risky behaviour can be very high. Unfortunately, during a manic state, individuals feel little concern about the potential consequences of their actions. Later, as they come into a more normal frame of mind, they may feel a great deal of remorse and embarrassment for their actions, which contributes to their counter-swing into depression.

Bipolar disorder encompasses both ends of an emotional continuum, and individuals with bipolar disorder can move from one end to the other at different rates. Some people with bipolar disorder experience only a few manic episodes in their lives, whereas others go through several episodes each year. A small number of "rapid cyclers" experience very abrupt mood swings, even within a matter of hours.

COGNITIVE ASPECTS OF DEPRESSION Depression affects cognition as well as emotion. People with depression can become confused and can have difficulty concentrating and making decisions, all of which contribute to growing feelings of helplessness and feeling incapable of doing anything right.

As a depressed person begins to emphasize negative, self-defeating, and self-critical thoughts, they develop a characteristic depressive or *pessimistic explanatory style* (Abramson et al., 1978; Sweeney et al., 1986). A person's explanatory style involves a set of cognitive habits that are important psychological precursors to depression. When faced with the inevitable negative events of life, people with a pessimistic explanatory style tend make the worst of them (instead of making the best of them), so to speak.

For example, when something bad happens, such as the person failing at a task or a project, she tends to make internal, *personal attributions* for the event, blaming herself for what happened ("It's all my fault! I did everything wrong! I messed the whole thing up!"). Depressed individuals also tend to make *stable attributions*, assuming that the situation is going to persist ("It's always going to be like this. There is a fundamental problem, and it's never

Figure 15.5 Three Elements of the Depressive Explanatory Style

The three elements of the depressive explanatory style are internalizing, stabilizing, and globalizing.

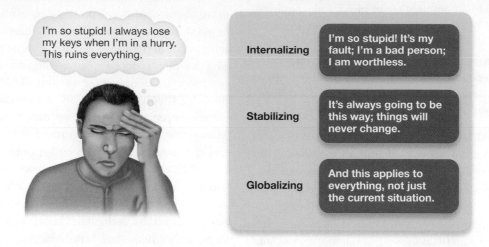

I'm so stupid! I always lose my keys when I'm in a hurry. This ruins everything.

Internalizing — I'm so stupid! It's my fault; I'm a bad person; I am worthless.

Stabilizing — It's always going to be this way; things will never change.

Globalizing — And this applies to everything, not just the current situation.

going to change."). And as they spiral into catastrophic ways of thinking, they make *global attributions*, expanding the impact of the negative event into other domains or into overall life ("I just can't do anything right; I'm going to mess up everything").

The pessimistic explanatory style adds stress and drains energy by constructing a more threatening or hopeless story for the individual. As a result, this explanatory style tends to predict a host of life outcomes from stress and health to success and relationships. To get a sense of how this might work in specific events during a person's day, imagine an individual with depression who does something as minor as losing his keys; refer to Figure 15.5 to see the depressive explanatory style at work. Then extrapolate that same set of patterns across many different events throughout one's life, and you will get a sense of the cumulative burden that this places on the individual.

BIOLOGICAL ASPECTS OF DEPRESSION There is a vast and rapidly growing amount of research on the biological aspects of depression. Brain-imaging research has identified two primary regions of interest related to depression: (1) the limbic system, which is active in emotional responses and processing, and (2) the dorsal (back) of the frontal cortex, which generally plays a role in controlling thoughts and concentrating. As is the case with panic disorder, a vicious cycle appears to occur with depression. The overactive limbic system responds strongly to emotions and sends signals that lead to a decrease in frontal lobe activity, and this decrease in frontal lobe functioning reduces the ability to concentrate and control what one thinks about (Gotlib & Hamilton, 2008).

Various neurotransmitters—especially serotonin, dopamine, and norepinephrine—are involved in depression. Serotonin appears to be particularly important. People with depression typically have lower serotonin levels than non-depressed individuals. Many anti-depressant medications block the reuptake of serotonin, which leaves more serotonin in the synapse, available to stimulate the postsynaptic neurons.

The negative emotions of depression are also linked with stress reactions throughout the body, which tie the neurological aspects of depression (brain regions and neurotransmitters) to physiological systems including the endocrine, digestive, and immune systems. As a result, individuals with depression are at higher risk for a variety of illnesses, as well as for cardiovascular disease. They also have a higher risk of mortality in multiple age ranges; this link to mortality even persists once researchers statistically account for health behaviours and suicide (Penninx et al., 1999; Roblaes et al., 2005). Clearly, depression has implications for a person's health.

Research at the genetic level is also uncovering factors that contribute to the likelihood of being diagnosed with depression. Twin studies suggest an underlying genetic risk for developing major depression (Figure 15.6). Additionally, behavioural genetics researchers have found that people who inherit two copies of the short version of the 5-HTT gene are at greater risk for developing depression, whereas those who inherit two long copies are at a far lower risk (Caspi et al., 2003). But what is critical here is not just which genes are inherited, but also how much stress people experience. Figure 15.7 shows how this relationship works. As the number of major stressful life events increases, those who inherit two copies of the short version of this gene are far more likely to develop depression, whereas those who inherit two long copies are buffered from depression. People who inherit one copy of each gene (are heterozygous)

Figure 15.6 Genetic Relatedness and Major Depression

Identical (monozygotic) twins have a greater chance of both developing major depression compared to fraternal (dizygotic) twins. Notice that the genetic correlation is highest for female monozygotic twins.

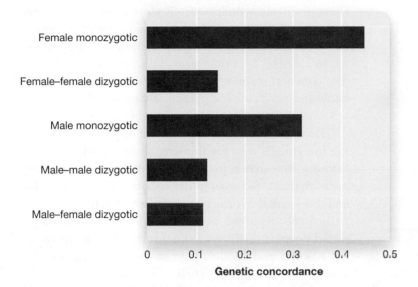

SOCIOCULTURAL AND ENVIRONMENTAL INFLUENCES ON MOOD DISORDERS Biological and cognitive factors influencing depression interact with sociocultural and environmental factors. For example, the quality of one's home neighbourhood can be a risk factor for depression (Cutrona et al., 2006). Poor neighbourhoods are associated with higher daily stress levels due to substandard housing and facilities, increased crime rates, and other difficulties. Also, people living in these neighbourhoods are more vulnerable to economic stressors such as unemployment because they generally lack the social connections and the educational and professional opportunities that are available to people living in high-income areas. In addition, environmental influences, such as poverty, can interact with social factors. For example, poor neighbourhoods often have weaker and less supportive social networks in the community. Lower rates of home ownership and higher rates of turnover make it less likely that people will get to know their neighbours; this makes long-lasting social relationships (i.e., potential sources of support) much less common.

show intermediate responses to stressful events. Notice that the type of serotonin gene inherited has no effect on depression after only one or two major stressful events. The gene–environment interaction becomes apparent after an *accumulation* of events. This *interaction between a genetic predisposition for a disorder and life stress* is known as the **diathesis–stress model** of psychological disorders (*diathesis* is Greek for "disposition" or "vulnerability"). It is just one of many examples of how nature and nurture interact.

SUICIDE It is difficult to imagine a worse outcome for a mood disorder than suicide. For people who have not experienced a mood disorder, it is equally difficult to imagine how anyone could reach such a low point. Nonetheless, suicide remains a serious public health concern. It is the second leading cause of death (behind transportation accidents) among Canadian youth (Public Health Agency of Canada, 2013).

There is significant variation in who is most likely to die by suicide. Suicide is four times more likely among males than among females. Many people believe that adolescents are particularly vulnerable to suicide, but the highest suicide rates are actually observed among the elderly population: The suicide rate for people 65 and older is nearly 60% higher than the rate for teens (CDC, 2010). Fortunately, research, treatment, and public awareness have significantly reduced the suicide rate among youth since the 1980s (Gould et al., 2003). An unfortunate exception to this trend is in Aboriginal communities, where suicide rates remain above the national average.

Suicide often comes as a surprise to the family and friends of the victim, although in some cases clear warning signs are evident (Table 15.5). Among people in their teens and early twenties, the most significant risk factors are mood disorders, recent and extremely stressful life events, a family history of mood disorders (with

Figure 15.7 Gene and Environment Interactions in Depression

Stress interacts with genes and influences whether someone becomes depressed. People who inherit two copies of the short version of a gene that codes for serotonin activity in nerve cells are at an increased risk for becoming depressed in response to major life stressors. Those who inherit two long copies are buffered from becoming depressed as life stressors accumulate.

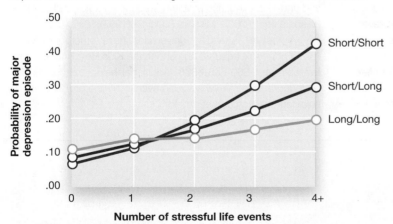

Source: From A Caspi et al., (2003) Influence of Life Stress on Depression: Moderation by a Polymorphism in the 5-HTT Gene, *Science*, Vol. 301, Issue 5631, 386–389. Reprinted with permission from AAAS.

Table 15.5 Warning Signs of Suicide

Learn how to recognize the danger signals. Be concerned if someone you know

- Talks about committing suicide
- Has trouble eating or sleeping
- Exhibits drastic changes in behaviour
- Withdraws from friends or social activities
- Loses interest in school, work, or hobbies
- Prepares for death by writing a will and making final arrangements
- Gives away prized possessions
- Has attempted suicide before
- Takes unnecessary risks
- Has recently experienced serious losses
- Seems preoccupied with death and dying
- Loses interest in his or her personal appearance
- Increases alcohol or drug use

Source: American Psychological Association. (2011). Suicide warning signs. Retrieved from http://www.apa.org/topics/suicide/signs.aspx

or without suicide), easy access to a lethal means of suicide (most significantly, firearms), and the presence of these factors in conjunction with substance abuse (Gould et al., 2003; Moscicki, 2001). For young people, being the victim of bullying and social ostracism is also a risk factor (Klomek et al., 2007).

Certain behavioural signs are often reported by family and friends to have preceded the suicide, giving us behavioural cues to look for in order to identify people at higher risk for committing suicide. For example, an individual may verbally express despair and hopelessness ("I just want to give up; Nothing matters anymore; They'll be better off when I'm gone"), give away personal possessions, suddenly withdraw from work or school, or have crying spells. For a full description of common behavioural symptoms, consult a proper checklist, or even better, be assessed by a professional. But for now, Table 15.5 lists common warning signs of suicide that are useful to know and watch out for, particularly for people you know who may be at higher risk of committing suicide.

Recent research has used a novel method of identifying individuals who are thinking about suicide: machine learning. Researchers in the U.S. created machine-learning codes that allowed a computer to sort through the verbal and non-verbal (voice inflection) characteristics of 379 participants recruited at local hospitals. The algorithm sorted people into three groups—suicidal, mentally ill but not suicidal, and controls (i.e., no psychological disorder present)—with an 85% accuracy rate (Pestian et al., 2017)! Although this is just one study, it does suggest that psychologists and psychiatrists will have additional diagnostic tools at their disposal in the near future.

Of course, the most important factor in saving the lives of individuals who are suicidal is the person's own awareness of his or her condition. There are many options available for those people who make the decision to seek help.

PSYCH@

The Suicide Helpline

Suicide hotlines and helplines perform a vital function in today's society and are used by thousands of people every single day. The first telephone suicide helplines were operated by religious organizations and emphasized empathy and active listening. Although this may certainly be a helpful approach, it may not meet the needs of every caller. Modern suicide helplines are staffed by well-trained volunteers with access to suicide prevention specialists who can aid in effectively helping the distressed person, assess the level of risk, and get the appropriate medical or psychological help. Telephone crisis responders need to flexibly adapt their way of interacting with the caller, based on the caller's needs and where they are at that particular moment. For example, first-time callers tend to benefit more from an active listener, who will be nonjudgmental, compassionate, and reflective (akin to the practice of establishing rapport with a client, which is so central in psychological counselling). People who are repeat callers need an ever-changing combination of many needs met, including compassion and acceptance, empathy and understanding, and problem-solving strategies and activities (Mishara et al., 2007; Mishara & Daigle, 1997).

Almost all Canadian universities have emergency crisis lines. For people aged 20 and under, the Kids Help Phone is also available at 1-800-668-6868. Additional helpful resources can be found at http://www.suicidepreventionlifeline.org/ and http://suicideprevention.ca/need-help/.

Module 15.3b Quiz:

Mood Disorders

Know . . .

1. _____ is characterized by periods of intense depression as well as by periods with elevated mood and energy levels.
   - **A.** Major depression
   - **B.** Unipolar depression
   - **C.** Bipolar disorder
   - **D.** Generalized anxiety disorder

Understand . . .

2. Depression is associated with lower activity in the frontal lobe, which may result in
   - **A.** lack of appetite.
   - **B.** difficulty concentrating and thinking.

   - **C.** periods of elevated mood and energy.
   - **D.** impaired semantic memory.

Apply . . .

3. First-time callers to suicide prevention lines benefit most from
   - **A.** empathy and active listening.
   - **B.** firm, demanding instructions.
   - **C.** extensive problem-solving interventions.
   - **D.** direct referral to the hospital.

Module 15.3 Summary

15.3a   Know . . . the key terminology related to anxiety, obsessive–compulsive, and depressive disorders.

agoraphobia
anxiety disorders
bipolar disorder
diathesis–stress model
exposure
generalized anxiety disorder (GAD)
major depression
obsessive–compulsive disorder (OCD)
panic attacks
panic disorder
parasitic processing
phobia
social anxiety disorder
specific phobia

15.3b   Understand . . . the different types of anxiety disorders.

Although anxiety disorders share many similarities in symptoms, they differ in terms of what brings about the symptoms and the intensity of the responses. The cues that trigger anxiety vary widely. In generalized anxiety disorder, just about anything may cause anxiety, whereas in specific phobias, an individual fears only certain objects. Likewise, the frequency and intensity of anxious feelings can range from near-constant worrying to brief periods of highly intense anxiety in phobias and panic disorder.

15.3c   Understand . . . how anxiety or depressive disorders can be self-perpetuating.

Both depression and anxiety are characterized by a vicious cycle: With anxiety, anxious or fearful thoughts can lead to physiological arousal; physiological arousal can lead to escape and avoidance to get rid of the immediate fear, which in turn reinforces the anxious thoughts. In depression, a similar pattern can occur with depressed thoughts, self-blame, and social withdrawal.

15.3d   Apply . . . your knowledge of anxiety, obsessive–compulsive, and depressive disorders, so as to be alert to people who may benefit from some help.

Apply Activity

Write down at least five warning signs for suicide and identify the number of a locally available suicide helpline.

15.3e   Analyze . . . whether maladaptive aspects of specific phobias might arise from perfectly normal, healthy behaviours.

To analyze this issue, we need to examine the specific symptoms that occur in someone who has a phobia and is showing an adaptive response (fear, anxiety) but to an inappropriate stimulus or situation. It is perfectly reasonable and healthy to be cautious about heights, for example, in the sense that falls can be dangerous, even life-threatening. This reaction is maladaptive only when the fear response is so intense or out of context that it interferes with daily life. Imagine a house painter who cannot climb a ladder or scaffold; unless he overcomes his fear (or finds very short houses to work on), he will have to make major adjustments to accommodate his fear.

Module 15.4 Schizophrenia

Robert P. Matthews/Princeton University/Getty Images

Learning Objectives

15.4a Know . . . the key terminology associated with schizophrenia.

15.4b Understand . . . how different neurotransmitters affect individuals with schizophrenia.

15.4c Understand . . . the genetic and environmental contributions to schizophrenia.

15.4d Apply . . . your knowledge to identify different forms of schizophrenia.

15.4e Analyze . . . claims that schizophrenia is related to genius or violent behaviour.

John Nash is a remarkable story in many ways. He is remarkable for being the inspiration for a movie, A Beautiful Mind. He is remarkable for being a genius, a mathematician, and winner of a Nobel Prize for his work on game theory (Google "Nash equilibrium"), which has become a cornerstone of modern economics and has immense importance in understanding society. He is also remarkable for being an underachiever, you might say, in the sense that Nash undoubtedly did not rise to his full potential, or anything close to it. The world was, at least partially, deprived of one of its most brilliant minds because Nash also had the remarkable characteristic of having schizophrenia.

In 1959, while a professor at MIT, and with his wife expecting their first child, Nash began to experience delusional patterns of thought, developed strange and rigid beliefs, and felt that he was playing some sort of special role as a messenger of some kind, hearing and seeing things that weren't there, even thinking he was being contacted by aliens who were leaving messages for him in newspapers. His ability to function in daily life fluctuated greatly, as he veered between his lucid, brilliant mind and his confused, schizophrenic mind.

His marriage ended shortly thereafter, and Nash eventually spent almost a decade in a psychiatric institution. The voices in his head continued to haunt him for decades. Eventually, he learned how to manage his symptoms and function again in the world. He was able to return to work and even remarried his wife (in 2001). He remained an active mathematician and frequent speaker until his death in 2015, when he and his wife were both killed in a tragic car crash.

John Nash's case raises some central questions about schizophrenia. What are the underlying neurological and cognitive processes that are affected by the disorder and that produce the symptoms of a person's experiences? Are there ways of gaining control over symptoms, possibly by strengthening the underlying systems? What factors contribute to better management of schizophrenic symptoms and to slowing or halting its long-term progression?

Nash's story also challenges some common assumptions about schizophrenia, such as the belief that it is a one-way ticket to insanity and that the person is going to get steadily worse. Or the belief that people with schizophrenia are to be feared, because they are perpetually unstable and likely to do random, unpredictable, even violent or dangerous things. Nash himself managed to live a productive, quiet, peaceful, and generally happy life. Although this isn't always the case with schizophrenia, it is encouraging to know that such happy endings are possible.

Focus Questions

1. Why do some people develop schizophrenia? What are its causal factors?

2. What brain changes are associated with schizophrenia?

» Schizophrenia is often regarded as one of the more devastating psychological illnesses, and indeed, severe cases of schizophrenia involve a shocking loss of basic functioning. Although schizophrenia is not common (affecting only between approximately 4 to 8 out of every 1000 adults worldwide [Bhugra, 2005; Saha et al., 2005]), it seems to be universal, appearing in cultures all over the world and across history. Some of our earliest writings describe people who seem to have lost touch with reality, who "hear voices," and who produce bizarre speech and behaviours. At some earlier times in history, a person experiencing such symptoms may have been suspected of demon possession or some form of witchcraft. At other times and places, such people might be revered as shamans or as having special connections to the spirit world, and may well have played important roles in the community. Now, we would likely diagnose schizophrenia.

Symptoms and Types of Schizophrenia

There are many popular but misguided beliefs regarding schizophrenia. For example, people believe that individuals with schizophrenia have more than one personality; however, this is a completely different disorder known as Dissociative Identity Disorder (DID; see Module 15.2). In reality, **schizophrenia** refers to what many psychologists and psychiatrists believe is *a brain disease that causes the person to experience significant breaks from reality, a lack of integration of thoughts and emotions, and problems with attention and memory.* Symptoms may begin to occur and escalate very gradually, remaining largely unnoticeable for a long time before family members start to perceive a pattern. In other cases, however, symptoms can begin and escalate very rapidly. There is, therefore, a very wide range of possible trajectories that the disease may follow over time.

STAGES OF SCHIZOPHRENIA In most cases of schizophrenia, there are three distinct phases: prodromal, active, and residual. These tend to occur in sequence, although individuals may cycle through all three many times. In the **prodromal phase**, *people may become easily confused and have*

difficulty organizing their thoughts, they may lose interest and begin to withdraw from friends and family, and they may lose their normal motivations, withdraw from life, and spend increasing amounts of time alone, often deeply engrossed in their own thoughts. It is not uncommon for other people to get upset as a result of these behaviours, assuming the person is lazy or otherwise being irresponsible. In the **active phase**, *people typically experience delusional thoughts, hallucinations, or disorganized patterns of thoughts, emotions, and behaviour.* This phase usually transitions into the **residual phase**, *in which people's predominant symptoms have disappeared or lessened considerably, and they may simply be withdrawn, have trouble concentrating, and generally lack motivation.*

There is huge variety in terms of the progression of schizophrenia. Some people cycle through the three stages only a couple of times in their lives, whereas others may cycle repeatedly; typically, the severity of the withdrawal in the residual phase tends to increase with repeated episodes, and their ability to function normally seems to decrease.

The symptoms of schizophrenia are most pronounced in the active phase of the disease, but one must always remember that the transitions between these phases will not be perfectly clean. There may be times when symptoms do not occur during the active phase; there may also be times when they do occur during the residual phase. Additionally, the person with schizophrenia may experience short-term resurgences of symptoms, often triggered by stressful periods or episodes in their lives.

SYMPTOMS OF SCHIZOPHRENIA Schizophrenia is associated with a number of different symptoms. A key distinction is made between positive and negative symptoms (Harvey & Walker, 1987). **Positive symptoms** refer to *the presence of maladaptive behaviours, such as confused and paranoid thinking, and inappropriate emotional reactions.* In contrast, **negative symptoms** involve *the absence of adaptive behaviour, such as absent or flat emotional reactions, lack of interacting with others in a social setting, and lack of motivation.*

One common positive symptom is the presence of **hallucinations**, *alterations in perception, such that a person hears, sees, smells, feels, or tastes something that does not actually exist, except in that person's own mind.* These experiences are often accompanied by **delusions**, *beliefs that are not based on or well integrated with reality.* For example, people may believe that they are someone famous, or that they have a divine purpose; they may believe there is special significance or hidden messages or codes in the media that they encounter; they might believe that everybody despises them, or that they are being constantly followed and that their life is in danger. Or they might believe they can control the wind or communicate telepathically with birds. Many of these symptoms are examples of *delusions of grandeur,* a belief that an individual is more important or talented than he or she really is. For example, consider the following personal account of Kurt Snyder, who wrote a book about his experiences with schizophrenia during college:

> *I thought about fractals and infinity for many years. I always told myself I was on the verge of discovery, but I simply had to think a little bit harder about it. I just wasn't thinking hard enough. The reality is that the problems I was trying to solve were far beyond my mental abilities, but I didn't recognize this fact. Even though I had no evidence to substantiate my self-image, I knew in my heart that I was just like Einstein, and that someday I would get a flash of inspiration. I didn't recognize the truth—that I am not a genius. I kept most of my mathematical ideas to myself and spoke to very few people about them. I was paranoid that someone else would solve the riddle first if I provided the right clues.* (Snyder, 2006, p. 209)

Source: Snyder, K. (2006). Kurt Snyder's personal experience with schizophrenia. *Schizophrenia Bulletin, 32* (2), 209–211. Copyright © 2006 Oxford University Press. Reprinted by permission.

In addition to hallucinations and delusions, individuals with schizophrenia often have **disorganized behaviour**; this term describes *the considerable difficulty people with schizophrenia may have completing the tasks of everyday life—* cooking, taking care of one's hygiene, socializing. They have great difficulty organizing their behaviour enough to complete tasks before getting distracted by other thoughts or things to do. This makes it difficult to follow a project, or even a train of thought, to completion, as their minds may jump from thought to thought uncontrollably.

Provided by Kurt Snyder, author

Kurt Snyder began experiencing schizophrenia in college. *Me, Myself, and Them* is his personal account of living with schizophrenia.

Individuals with schizophrenia experience several additional problems with cognitive functioning. These range from basic, low-level physiological responses, such as excessive eye blinking in response to stimulation (Perry et al., 2002), to more complex cognitive skills, such as those required for standardized achievement tests—test scores tend to drop during adolescence as the disorder begins and progresses (Fuller et al., 2002). Many complex cognitive abilities involve the prefrontal cortex, a brain region that shows significant neurological decline in individuals with schizophrenia (Wright et al., 2000). This may be the reason for deficits in working memory that connect to symptoms associated with schizophrenia, such as the inability to keep track of a train of thought, organize the sequence of a conversation, and handle multiple tasks at once. Working memory deficits may partially explain the disorganized thoughts and speech characteristic of schizophrenia (Park et al., 1999).

Social interaction is often very difficult for people with schizophrenia. These individuals typically have difficulty reasoning about social situations and show relatively poor social adjustment (Done et al., 1994). In addition, their emotional expressions and ability to react to the emotions of others may be impaired (Penn & Combs, 2000). For example, people with schizophrenia may maintain a neutral mask-like expression on their faces, and show little response to smiles or other expressions from people around them. As a result, the person with schizophrenia generally is not as socially competent and strikes others as a little "odd"; this can set social feedback processes in motion (such as others then avoiding eye contact or extended discussions with the schizophrenic person). This, in turn, may cause the person with schizophrenia to become aware of this negative social feedback, to feel self-conscious and uncomfortable, and to be more likely to socially withdraw in the future.

Social withdrawal and isolation is a very common consequence of schizophrenia and may even be related to the long-term outcomes of the disease. Helping people with schizophrenia deal with their own social behaviours and skills is an important factor in the treatment of this disorder.

COMMON SUB-TYPES OF SCHIZOPHRENIA As you can see, numerous symptoms accompany schizophrenia. For some individuals, the symptoms cluster into different patterns, leading mental health professionals in the past to identify subtypes of the disorder. These subtypes were dropped from official practice in 2013, as they are artificial categorizations of complex behaviour patterns, and are often not reliably measurable; but, they are still commonly used and are therefore worth being aware of:

- **Paranoid schizophrenia**: *Symptoms include delusional beliefs that one is being followed, watched, or persecuted, and may also include delusions of grandeur or the belief that one has some secret, insight, power, or some other characteristic that makes one particularly special.*

Myths in Mind

Schizophrenia Is Not a Sign of Violence or of Being a "Mad Genius"

Although schizophrenia is a widely recognized term, it is also widely misunderstood. As was mentioned in the opening story about John Nash, people may believe that schizophrenia makes people violent or dangerous, or causes people to have different personalities. People also commonly believe that the "madness" of schizophrenia is associated with being a genius. It can be difficult to dispel such myths, especially with high-profile cases that fit so well with these common beliefs; cases like John Nash or Ted Kaczynski (aka the "Unabomber"). Similar to Nash, Kaczynski was a very bright mathematician who seemed to slip into schizophrenic delusions. Contrary to Nash, however, Kaczynski's delusions led him to take violent actions against what he perceived to be the evil system of our society. This earned him his Unabomber nickname, because he sent bombs through the mail to prominent researchers at various universities.

The truth is that schizophrenia is not associated with genius but, in fact, with cognitive deficits. In contrast to Ted Kaczynski and John Nash, most people with schizophrenia score slightly below average on IQ tests (Woodberry et al., 2008). Also, people with schizophrenia are only rarely violent. In these cases, other factors such as substance abuse usually play a big role. People with schizophrenia do not have a propensity for violence that is meaningfully different from the rest of the population (Douglas et al., 2009; Fazel et al., 2009). Rather than being violent, people with schizophrenia are likely to isolate themselves and end up in situations in which they are likely to be harmed. In fact, it's the people with schizophrenia who should perhaps fear the rest of society; people with mental illnesses are approximately 10 times more likely to be victims of crime than the rest of the population (Teplin et al., 2005).

- **Disorganized schizophrenia**: *Symptoms include thoughts, speech, behaviours, and emotions that are poorly integrated and incoherent. People with disorganized schizophrenia may also show inappropriate, unpredictable mannerisms.*

- **Catatonic schizophrenia**: *Symptoms include episodes in which a person remains mute and immobile—sometimes in bizarre positions—for extended periods. Individuals may also exhibit repetitive, purposeless movements.*

- **Undifferentiated schizophrenia**: *This category includes individuals who show a combination of symptoms from more than one type of schizophrenia.*

- **Residual schizophrenia**: *This category reflects individuals who show some symptoms of schizophrenia but are either in transition to a full-blown episode or in remission.*

Increasing our knowledge of the complexity—and variability—of schizophrenia has allowed clinicians to improve treatment methods. This will hopefully help reduce stigma surrounding schizophrenia so that people may not behave as negatively toward individuals with this disorder. Unfortunately, a great deal of stigma does remain, in part because of common misunderstandings that many have about schizophrenia.

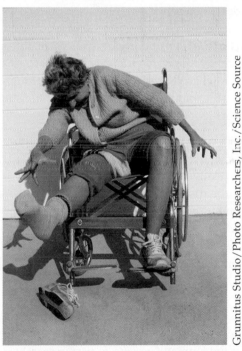

Grunnitus Studio/Photo Researchers, Inc./Science Source

People who experience catatonic schizophrenia will remain immobile, even if in a bizarre position, for extended periods of time.

Module 15.4a Quiz:

Symptoms and Types of Schizophrenia

Know . . .

1. A person with schizophrenia who experiences delusions that she is royalty is experiencing a(n) _____ symptom.

   A. positive

   B. negative

   C. catatonic

   D. undifferentiated

Apply . . .

2. An individual showing poor integration of thinking and emotion visits a psychiatrist claiming that all of her neighbours are watching her. Into which category of schizophrenia might the psychiatrist classify the individual?

 A. Residual

 B. Undifferentiated

 C. Disorganized

 D. Paranoid

Analyze . . .

3. Which of the following statements best summarizes the relationship between schizophrenia and violence?

 A. Generally, people with schizophrenia are no more likely to become violent than non-mentally ill people, and if violence occurs, other factors, such as substance abuse, are likely to contribute to its cause.

 B. People with schizophrenia are twice as likely to be violent as non-mentally ill people.

 C. People with schizophrenia are far more peaceful than non-mentally ill people.

 D. People with schizophrenia cannot differentiate right from wrong, and therefore are prone to violence.

4. There have been several famous cases of people with superior intellectual abilities along with schizophrenia. Does this mean that schizophrenia is the cause or the result of genius?

 A. No; in fact, the average IQ of people with schizophrenia may be slightly lower than average.

 B. Yes; in fact, the average IQ of people with schizophrenia is approximately 15% higher than average.

 C. Yes, because people who are that smart are likely to develop schizophrenia simply because they know too much.

 D. No, because schizophrenia is almost always associated with very low IQs.

Explaining Schizophrenia

So far, we have described schizophrenia based on its psychological and physical characteristics. Researchers are also very curious about the underlying sources of these characteristics and have employed a wide range of techniques to discover what causes schizophrenia. Through the application of the biopsychosocial model, a holistic understanding of schizophrenia is emerging.

GENETICS Studies using twin, adoption, and family history methods have shown that as genetic relatedness increases, the chance that a relative of a person with schizophrenia will also develop the disorder increases (see Figure 15.8). For example, if one identical twin has schizophrenia, the other twin has a 25% to 50% chance of developing it. This rate is significantly higher than the 10% to 17% rate found in dizygotic (fraternal) twin pairs (Gottesman, 1991).

For decades, behavioural genetic scientists have known that genes contribute to schizophrenia, but they have not identified the specific genes that are involved. However, with the benefit of recent technological advances and the data from the Human Genome Project, researchers are beginning to make progress on this question. For example, scientists have discovered a distinct pattern of genetic irregularities that is found in 15% of individuals with schizophrenia, compared with only 5% of healthy controls (Walsh et al., 2008). On the one hand, this relationship suggests a possible genetic contribution to schizophrenia. On the other hand, the genetic abnormality was not found in 85% of the individuals with schizophrenia.

Additional insights were provided by researchers at the University of Alberta. Their first breakthrough came by chance, as is often the case. Researcher Diane Cox was looking at samples of genetic material for research that had nothing to do with schizophrenia, but she noticed samples

from a mother–daughter pair that showed a remarkable similarity; each sample had a break in one of the genes on chromosome 14 (Kamnasaran et al., 2003); as it turned out, both of them had schizophrenia. This important clue led to further breakthroughs about genetic contributions to schizophrenia and the mechanisms through which genes affect the development of the disease (Wong et al., 2013). However, given the complexity of schizophrenia and its symptoms, much more research needs to be performed.

SCHIZOPHRENIA AND THE NERVOUS SYSTEM One important neurological characteristic of people with

---

Figure 15.8 Genetic Influences for Schizophrenia

The more genetic similarity an individual has to a person with schizophrenia, the more likely that he or she will also develop the disorder.

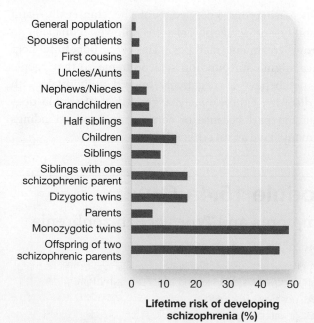

Lifetime risk of developing schizophrenia (%)

Figure 15.9 Brain Volume in One Monozygotic Twin with Schizophrenia and Another without Schizophrenia

The brains of two genetically identical individuals, one affected with schizophrenia and the other unaffected, are shown here. The arrows point to the spaces created by the ventricles of the brain. Note the significant loss of brain matter in the affected individual.

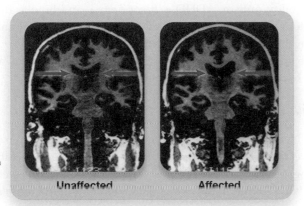

Courtesy of E. Fuller Torrey and Daniel Weinberger

ImageBroker/Alamy Stock Photo

Psychologists have long noted that individuals who are being treated with antipsychotic drugs that block dopamine tend to be heavy smokers. One possible reason is that nicotine helps to stimulate the release of additional dopamine. As a result, heavy nicotine use stimulates the dopamine-rich reward and cognitive centres of the brain (Winterer, 2010).

schizophrenia is the size of the brain's ventricles (the fluid-filled spaces in the core of the brain). People with schizophrenia have ventricles that are 20% to 30% larger than people without schizophrenia (see Figure 15.9; Gottesman & Gould, 2003). The reason for these larger ventricles is a loss of brain matter, which amounts to a reduction of total brain volume by approximately 2% in those individuals with schizophrenia. In particular, the reduced volume can be found in structures such as the amygdala and hippocampus (Wright et al., 2000).

The brains of people with schizophrenia are not just different in size; they also *function* differently. People with schizophrenia show lower levels of activity in their frontal lobes, both in resting states and when engaged in cognitive tasks, suggesting that these brain regions are not functioning at an optimal level (Hill et al., 2004).

Changes in brain *chemistry* are also evident in schizophrenia. People with schizophrenia have an increased rate of firing in dopamine-releasing cells. Some of this overactivity is in a part of the brain known as the basal ganglia, which is involved in a number of functions including reward responses. As a result of this firing, stimuli that should be meaningless are interpreted as being quite noteworthy (Heinz & Schlagenhauf, 2010). Excess firing of these dopaminergic cells can produce the types of positive symptoms associated with schizophrenia, such as hallucinations and delusions; however, dopamine cannot be the whole neurochemical story, as it is unrelated to negative symptoms such as flattened emotion and lack of speech (Andreasen et al., 1995).

Glutamate, another neurotransmitter, appears to be underactive in certain brain regions, including the hippocampus and the frontal cortex. Glutamate is the brain's primary excitatory neurotransmitter, so a reduction of

glutamate in those areas would correspond to a reduction of their functioning. Interestingly, glutamate receptor activity is also inhibited by the drug PCP (angel dust), which in high doses can cause symptoms that mirror those of schizophrenia.

The fact that schizophrenia has been linked with differences in genes, neurotransmitters, and the volume of brain structures suggests that the mechanisms underlying this disorder are not simple. Indeed, as you will read in the next section, one of the best-known hypotheses about the cause of schizophrenia suggests that it involves an interaction between an external agent (possibly a virus) and the brain at some of its earliest stages of development.

Working the Scientific Literacy Model

The Neurodevelopmental Hypothesis

Schizophrenia is obviously a complex disorder, and no single explanation has been able to account for all the variations in its symptoms, severity, and duration. One of the leading perspectives on the causes of schizophrenia is the neurodevelopmental hypothesis, which approaches schizophrenia from a biopsychosocial perspective, emphasizing the interaction between factors at different levels of analysis.

What do we know about the neurodevelopmental hypothesis?

People who develop schizophrenia often exhibit identifiably abnormal patterns of behaviour early on. Indeed, the **neurodevelopmental hypothesis** suggests that *the adult manifestation of what we call "schizophrenia" is the outgrowth of disrupted neurological development early in the person's life*. In fact, schizophrenia may even be set in motion by environmental factors while the person is still in the womb, such as exposure to flu viruses.

One intriguing research finding is that people with schizophrenia are more likely to have been born during winter months (Tochigi et al., 2004). One hypothesis is that winter births carry this higher risk because the onset of the flu season, in the fall, coincides with the second trimester, in which the fetus's brain is developing at an enormous rate. Maternal exposure to the influenza virus at such a critical time of neurological development is argued to be one contributing factor to schizophrenia. More generally, environmental factors that cause stress for the mother while pregnant, such as losing her spouse or experiencing trauma such as war or violence, can impact fetal development; the massive release of stress hormones during such difficult events has a variety of neurological and cognitive effects on the developing fetus, which could increase the risk of developing schizophrenia (Brown & Derkits, 2010; King et al., 2010).

How can science test the neurodevelopmental hypothesis?

The neurodevelopmental hypothesis draws from research on genetic and prenatal factors. However, the developmental emphasis of the hypothesis gains strength from behavioural evidence collected during childhood and adolescence, which shows that people who develop schizophrenia showed warning signs when they were very young. For example, when psychologists viewed home movies of infants and children who subsequently developed schizophrenia, they noted that these children showed some unusual motor (i.e., movement) patterns, primarily on the left side of the body, such as jerky, repeated, and unnecessary arm movements (Walker et al., 1994). These motor patterns were not present in their siblings, who did not have schizophrenia. This evidence suggests that a precursor of schizophrenia is present very early in life, setting in motion the processes and shaping the patterns of brain activity that lead further into the development of the disorder.

In adolescence, psychologists can detect the *schizophrenia prodrome*, a collection of characteristics that resemble mild forms of schizophrenic symptoms. For example, a teenager might become increasingly socially withdrawn and have some difficulty with depression and anxiety. But the most telling problems include experiences that resemble somewhat mild hallucinations and delusions. As one example, a teen might say, "I seem to keep hearing my mother calling my name before I fall asleep, even when I know she isn't home. It is strange . . ." (Walker et al., 2010, p. 206).

Can we critically evaluate this information?

Perhaps the most interesting challenge to this research, and one that has huge implications for our understanding of

developmental disorders, is that the precursors to schizophrenia are not unique to that disorder, but in fact are precursors to a variety of neurodevelopmental disorders. Indeed, the traditional view that the neurodevelopmental disorders are separate and discrete categories is being challenged; instead, the developmental disorders of intellectual disability, autism, ADHD, schizophrenia, and bipolar disorder may in fact be part of a larger syndrome of dysfunction that is rooted in common causes (Owen et al., 2011). The fact that cognitive deficits play such a central role in all these disorders fits with this possibility.

Why is this relevant?

By identifying prenatal risk factors and developmental patterns related to schizophrenia, it may be possible to alter the progression of the disorder. As part of this process, researchers will need to improve our understanding of the types of emotional support pregnant women need in order to reduce the effects of stress hormones on the fetus. A long-term goal of these related research programs would be to prevent schizophrenia from developing, or at least to control its severity (McGlashan et al., 2006; McGorry et al., 2002). To accomplish these goals, researchers will have to rely on all levels of explanation: genetics, prenatal influences, brain structure and function, and psychosocial factors.

It is worth noting that late adolescence and the early twenties is a particularly important time for the proper development of the frontal lobes; this is also the most common time in life for schizophrenia to be diagnosed. Importantly, this is also often one of the more stressful periods in many people's lives, due to the turmoil of adolescence and the trials of early adulthood. The fact that schizophrenia often appears during a particularly stressful stage of development shows us that processes occurring "outside" of the individual (i.e., in the person's social environment) may affect the development of this disorder.

ENVIRONMENTAL AND SOCIAL INFLUENCES ON SCHIZOPHRENIA Long after prenatal development, certain events can increase one's risk of developing schizophrenia. For example, some research suggests that a very small proportion of people who use marijuana develop psychotic symptoms, possibly because the drug interacts with the genes involved in schizophrenia (Caspi et al., 2005). Head injuries occurring prior to age 10 also put people who are genetically vulnerable to schizophrenia at greater risk for developing the disorder (AbdelMalik et al., 2003). Also, being raised in an environment where psychosocial stressors (e.g., interpersonal conflict, social isolation, poverty) are more abundant, such as modern urban environments, puts individuals at greater risk for developing schizophrenia (van Os et al., 2004), because schizophrenic episodes are often triggered by acutely stressful circumstances.

Closely related to the impact of stress on the development of schizophrenia is the role of social support. Research has shown that the progression of schizophrenia is strongly related to the way in which family members support and treat the person with schizophrenia. Families high in *emotional expressiveness* (EE) tend to be overly critical and controlling, whereas families low in EE tend to be more supportive, accepting, and non-judging. As several teams of researchers have found, there are huge differences between people with schizophrenia who live in high-EE versus low-EE families. People with schizophrenia are three to four times more likely to experience a relapse of their symptoms within a nine-month period if they live in high-EE families (Brown et al., 1972; King & Dixon, 1999). This trend has led to the creation of therapeutic interventions designed to help families reduce their negative behaviours and to learn to be more supportive.

However, research by Suzanne King of McGill University indicates that the relationship between EE and schizophrenia may be more complicated than previously thought. People with more severe cases of schizophrenia are more difficult to manage, put more stress on the family, and therefore may end up having more emotionally expressive families (King, 2000). Thus, the full relationship between schizophrenia and emotional expressiveness may involve a two-way causal process, with each factor affecting the other over time.

CULTURE AND SCHIZOPHRENIA In Module 15.1, we introduced the topic of cultural perceptions of mental illness. Differing cultural perspectives are strongly evident when it comes to schizophrenia. For example, ethnicity influences the types of experiences that individuals report having. A U.S.-based study found that Anglo-Americans tend to focus on the mental experiences of the disorder, such as disorganized thinking and emotions. In contrast, Mexican Americans focus more on how schizophrenia affects the body, such as by producing tension or tiredness. They conceive of the disorder as any other form of illness, rather than viewing mental disorders as a separate type of condition (Weisman et al., 2000).

Beliefs about mental illness are linked to varying cultural views of the world (McGruder, 2004). Many people throughout the world, such as the Swahili of Tanzania, believe that what we call schizophrenia is really a sign that spirits have invaded or are communicating with the body. In many cultures, this is actually seen as a good thing, that the person is being gifted with the ability to communicate in some fashion with the spirit world. These individuals are given important status in the community—virtually the opposite to the treatment of schizophrenia in Western culture.

As you think about the different ways that a person with schizophrenia would be treated in these different cultural contexts, and the presumed sophistication of our scientific understanding of what we call schizophrenia, consider one surprising fact—the long-term outcomes for people who have symptoms that would be diagnosed as schizophrenia are actually *better* in developing countries and traditional cultures that have been minimally influenced by the Western medical system. This shows us that regardless of the symptoms of a disorder, people benefit from being treated with kindness and compassion.

Module 15.4b Quiz:

Explaining Schizophrenia

Know . . .

1. The neurodevelopmental hypothesis states that
   A. neural factors are solely responsible for schizophrenia.
   B. social factors are solely responsible for schizophrenia.
   C. irregular biological and environmental factors interact during early development and are responsible for schizophrenia.
   D. prenatal exposure to the influenza virus definitely causes schizophrenia.

Understand . . .

2. Which of the following statements is most accurate concerning the biochemical basis of schizophrenia?
   A. The neurotransmitter dopamine is overly active.
   B. Dopamine is underactive.
   C. Serotonin levels are too low.
   D. There is too much glutamate activity.

3. Evidence for the neurodevelopmental hypothesis includes the fact that young children who eventually develop schizophrenia
   A. report hallucinations as early as four years of age.
   B. show unusual motor patterns such as jerky, repeated movements.
   C. lapse into periods of catatonia.
   D. had the flu during preschool.

Module 15.4 Summary

15.4a Know . . . the key terminology associated with schizophrenia.

active phase
catatonic schizophrenia
delusions
disorganized behaviour
disorganized schizophrenia
hallucinations
negative symptoms
neurodevelopmental hypothesis
paranoid schizophrenia
positive symptoms
prodromal phase
residual phase
residual schizophrenia
schizophrenia
undifferentiated schizophrenia

15.4b Understand . . . how different neurotransmitters affect individuals with schizophrenia.

Part of how we can explain schizophrenia is by identifying the neurotransmitters that are affected by this disorder. Increased dopamine levels are associated with the positive symptoms of schizophrenia, such as having hallucinations or delusions. Reduced levels of glutamate, an excitatory neurotransmitter, have been linked with the negative symptoms of schizophrenia, such as flat emotional reactions and a lack of motivation.

15.4c Understand . . . the genetic and environmental contributions to schizophrenia.

The neurodevelopmental hypothesis claims that at least some neurological abnormalities are present at birth, although it does not state to what degree these abnormalities are genetic or environmental. Nevertheless, some research suggests that prenatal exposure to the flu or to significant amounts of stress hormones are risk factors for this type of mental illness. Genetics seem to play a role, as twin

studies show that if one identical twin has schizophrenia, the other has a 50% chance of developing the disorder—a substantial increase over the 1% occurrence rate in the general population.

15.4d Apply . . . your knowledge to identify different forms of schizophrenia.

Apply Activity

Identify whether the following behaviours are positive or negative symptoms of schizophrenia.

1. Rosalita was helped to a chair and she has sat there, virtually motionless, for about two hours.
2. Eyanna refuses to go to the dentist. "Last time I went," she said, "they put a transmitter in my teeth so that the agents can control my thoughts."
3. Jeff has begun experiencing extreme dissociations. He even has started acting differently and referring to himself as "Dan."
4. Jinhai's language is very difficult to understand. He seems to be talking perfectly well but many of the words he is using are made up and other words are totally out of place.

15.4e Analyze . . . claims that schizophrenia is related to genius or violent behaviour.

As you have read, some high-profile cases highlight people with schizophrenia who are intellectually brilliant. In reality, however, research tells us that the average intelligence of people with schizophrenia is similar to, although slightly lower than, the norm. Similarly, the belief that schizophrenia leads to violence derives from a small group of high-profile examples. In truth, there does not seem to be an increased risk of violence associated with schizophrenia alone.

Chapter 16
Therapies

16.1 Treating Psychological Disorders

- Barriers to Psychological Treatment **655**
- Module 16.1a Quiz **657**
- Mental Health Providers and Settings **657**
- Module 16.1b Quiz **660**
- Evaluating Treatments **660**
  Working the Scientific Literacy Model: Can Self-Help
  Treatments Be Effective? **661**
- Module 16.1c Quiz **662**
- Module 16.1 Summary **663**

16.2 Psychological Therapies

- Insight Therapies **665**
- Module 16.2a Quiz **668**
- Behavioural, Cognitive, and Group Therapies **668**
  Working the Scientific Literacy Model: Virtual Reality Therapies **669**
- Module 16.2b Quiz **674**
- Module 16.2 Summary **674**

16.3 Biomedical Therapies

- Drug Treatments **677**
  Working the Scientific Literacy Model: Is St. John's Wort Effective? **679**
- Module 16.3a Quiz **681**
- Technological and Surgical Methods **682**
- Module 16.3b Quiz **684**
- Module 16.3 Summary **685**

Module 16.1 Treating Psychological Disorders

Ambrophoto / Alamy Stock Photo

Learning Objectives

16.1a Know . . . the key terminology associated with mental health treatment.

16.1b Understand . . . the major barriers to seeking help for psychological disorders.

16.1c Understand . . . the arguments for and against involuntary treatment.

16.1d Apply . . . your knowledge to suggest what approach to therapy is likely most appropriate for a given situation.

16.1e Analyze . . . whether self-help options, such as popular books, are a useful therapy option.

"The Power of Vulnerability" has become one of the most popular TED talks ever given. This simple, from the heart talk involves a brilliant, personable, and completely vulnerable woman, talking about how she went to a therapist because she was having a breakdown (although according to her therapist it was a spiritual awakening). Brené Brown's talk on shame courageously exposed her personal struggle with feelings of shame and "not being good enough" to millions of TED viewers. Her deeply moving story is one that many people can relate to. Brown's crucial message was that it is normal and indeed healthy for a person to go to a therapist to deal with issues like these. By being so open about her experiences, she sets an example for the rest of us that a key step toward overcoming the stigma surrounding mental illness and therapy is to talk about it.

Western culture's strong individualistic emphasis and do-it-yourself mentality fosters the attitude that people need to be independent and "strong." Mental illness is often seen as a sign of weakness, and negative stigma surrounds therapists who are sometimes stereotyped as "quacks" or "shrinks," lost in psycho-babble and out of touch with reality. Indeed, popular culture has often painted an unflattering portrait of

psychologists, from the terrifying Nurse Ratchet in One Flew Over the Cuckoo's Nest, *to the ridiculous Dr. Frasier Crane dispensing psychological wisdom on* Frasier.

Thus, it is worth paying attention when an extremely popular cultural event, like Brown's TED talk, shows the public that therapy is a normal part of many people's lives. Perhaps the stigma associated with mental illness and therapy is finally being overcome.

Focus Questions

1. What are the major barriers that hold people back from seeking psychological help?

2. What are the settings in which psychological therapy typically occurs?

≫ In Chapter 15 we described some of the psychological disorders that affect people. Disorders touch many people's lives, either directly (approximately 20% of people are thought to experience a psychological disorder at some point in their lives; Narrow et al., 2002), or indirectly via friends, family, neighbours, or co-workers who struggle with disorders. Furthermore, if you interpret the term "disorder" more broadly to include experiences like shame, which can markedly reduce or limit a person's overall functioning, then far more than 20% of us would benefit from getting professional help with the issues that hold us back. Clearly, there is a pervasive need for effective psychological treatments. In this module, we provide an overarching view of the approach our society takes to treating psychological disorders, discussing who tends to seek treatment, who provides it, and how treatment approaches are evaluated.

Over the past several decades, attitudes toward therapy have indeed changed. It is now commonplace for celebrities to be open about their traumatic childhoods, relationship problems, drug abuse, and other psychological struggles. Similarly, bookstores have entire sections devoted to psychology, full of advice and insight for people seeking to help themselves or someone they care about. These changes reflect a general normalization of the idea of psychological disorders and a lessening of the stigma surrounding mental illness. This shift is reflected in the high number of people who seek psychological services; each year in Canada, approximately 10% of the population seeks some form of treatment for mental health issues (Lesage et al., 2006).

Nevertheless, not all groups of people are equally likely to seek psychological treatment. In general, women participate in therapy more often than men, and people aged 35 through 55 seek treatment more often than younger adults and the elderly (Addis & Mahalik, 2003; Olfson & Marcus, 2010). People from certain cultural groups are less likely to use psychological services; in Canada, Asian Canadians and people of Native descent are both less likely to seek mental health treatment than White Canadians (Sue & Lam, 2002). Therapy is also a more popular choice for Canadians and Americans in general relative to people from many other countries such as Israel, Hungary, Japan, and Korea (Cohen et al., 1998; Masuda et al., 2005; Yoo & Skovholt, 2001). There are many possible reasons for these differences, ranging from the degree of stigma toward mental illness in different cultures to financial and other barriers that make access to treatment more difficult.

Barriers to Psychological Treatment

Despite the optimism with which we opened this chapter, it is still the case that many people with a disorder do not receive help. For example, in one study of 1600 adults who had been diagnosed with depression or an anxiety disorder, only 30% were receiving some form of therapy (Young et al., 2001). In both Canada and the U.S., surveys show that approximately two-thirds of people with mental health issues do not seek help from the mental health system (Lesage et al., 2006; NIMH, 2011). Furthermore, even when people do seek therapy, about half of them significantly delay doing so after first becoming aware of their mental health issues, often for years (DiClemente & Prochaska, 1985; Prochaska & DiClemente, 1984). Why would people choose not to seek help?

There are many barriers that prevent or delay people from seeking psychological treatment. One problem that almost everyone struggles with is that disorders themselves are inherently ambiguous; there is no objective, easily definable line between "mentally healthy" and "mentally ill" and no litmus test that can tell a person with a high degree of certainty that they need to seek help. Thus, a person may believe he is simply "sad," not depressed, and of course, sadness is a regular part of life, and not everyone who is sad needs to see a therapist. Or, a person may believe she is merely stressed or a bit worried about things, not that she has an anxiety disorder. This inescapable ambiguity makes it unclear exactly when it's desirable for a person to seek treatment.

Also, people very commonly are motivated to not see themselves as mentally ill, so much so that they minimize their symptoms, basically tricking themselves and others to think that they are healthier than they really are. To some, having a mental illness would feel like a sign of weakness or a personal failing, and they may not want to see themselves that way, or may not want to feel like a burden to their families and loved ones. Other people may be unwilling to risk the social stigma and fear they might embarrass themselves or their families, or they may not trust the psychological or psychiatric professions and be skeptical of the efficacy and safety of different treatments (Craske et al., 2005; Mansfield et al., 2005; Vanheusden et al., 2008). Overcoming such skepticism may make a big difference in helping people seek treatment; for example, in one study, 99% of respondents said they would seek mental health treatment if they believed it would be helpful (Fox et al., 2001). There is an important role to be played by educational programs that help people become aware of how different problems can be treated, and help to build confidence in the mental health profession (Fox et al., 2001; Sharp et al., 2006).

The cumulative impact of the different barriers to psychological treatment leaves millions of people delaying or simply never receiving the kind of therapy and support that could seriously improve their lives (P. S. Wang et al., 2005). Understanding these barriers is an important step toward overcoming them.

STIGMA ABOUT MENTAL ILLNESS One common barrier that we alluded to earlier is stigma toward mental illness and toward the process of therapy itself (Corrigan, 2004;

Vogel et al., 2009). You may already understand the effects of stigma—just imagine how different it might be for a business executive to take some time off work to undergo surgery versus taking time off to deal with "emotional issues." Having surgery or some other physical health issue to deal with would likely be far easier for the person to talk to colleagues about, for others in the workplace to offer support and rally around the person, and for the time off to not impact the person's success in the company. Unfortunately, in many professions, mental illness carries a strong stigma that can result in people with psychological disorders experiencing discrimination at the workplace. There may also be social costs, such as being treated differently by friends, family, or potential romantic partners. For example, one out of every two Canadians admits that they would likely not socialize with a friend who had a serious mental illness, and one in four Canadians admits that they are afraid to be around people with serious mental illnesses (Canadian Medical Association, 2008). Obviously, we still have a long way to go before mental illnesses are viewed in the same way as physical ailments.

GENDER ROLES   In many countries with strong gender norms, including Canada and the U.S., there are extra pressures on men to avoid treatment because needing help and going to therapy seem incompatible with the idea of being strong and independent, key aspects of the male gender role. This emphasis on strength and independence leads people to deny that they have any problems, or to believe that they need to "just get over it," as though people can be expected to overcome mental health issues through sheer force of will. This emphasis on individual strength and self-reliance certainly doesn't promote talking about emotions and acknowledging vulnerabilities, steps that would put people on a path toward healing (Berger et al., 2005; Mahalik et al., 2003). In fact, getting men to see therapy differently has presented such a challenge that the National Institute of Mental Health (NIMH) has staged public awareness campaigns in the U.S., such as the "Real Men, Real Depression" campaign. Initial evidence indicates that social marketing messages such as this do succeed in increasing the likelihood people will seek help, perhaps partially overcoming resistance based on traditional gender roles (Bell et al., 2010; Rochlen et al., 2006).

LOGISTICAL BARRIERS: EXPENSE AND AVAILABILITY
Two of the main barriers to mental health treatment are about access—whether people can afford the cost and the time for treatment (Colonna-Pydyn et al., 2007; Craske et al., 2005). Money has a particularly profound influence on the way that the mental health system functions and the kinds of treatments that are available for many people. For example, psychotherapy can be very expensive, generally costing more than $100 per hour, and often much more than that. Therapy is also associated with numerous

indirect costs, such as time away from work, transportation, and possibly childcare.

Unfortunately, government healthcare coverage in Canada generally only includes treatment by psychiatrists, leaving counsellors, psychologists, and many types of therapists less able to reach many people who can't afford their services. The net result of these sorts of funding decisions is to place substantial emphasis on the medical approaches to treating psychological disorders. In practice, this means that most of the money flows to the pharmaceutical industries, hospitals, and psychiatric treatments, leaving many talk-based counsellors and therapists (as well as emerging movements within the field of therapy that are not yet widely recognized) heavily disadvantaged.

This practice may also mean that many people's lives spiral into much greater distress and dysfunction than would be necessary if people were able to get therapeutic help for things like learning to effectively manage emotions, improve relationships in the family, or deal with stress or problematic behaviour patterns. Without easy access to counsellors who could help with issues like these, people often try to cope with life as best they can until problems develop into such major issues that they can no longer avoid seeking help. This often results in the treatment process beginning in a hospital emergency room, which places an extra burden on the public healthcare system (Snowdon, 1999). If an ounce of prevention is worth a pound of cure, as the old saying goes, our current method of funding mental healthcare seems to go in exactly the opposite direction.

To help overcome these barriers, some community organizations provide offices in lower-income areas where private psychotherapists are scarce and needed. Community mental health centres sometimes provide therapy on a sliding scale, which means the cost of a one-hour session varies depending on the patient's income and whether he has additional health benefits from his employer that would cover some of the therapy costs. Drug treatments can also be made more affordable by using generic products as opposed to brand-name ones, although this tends to be resisted by pharmaceutical companies who spend huge sums of money researching and promoting their drugs. In short, efforts are being made to make therapy more accessible to more people, but the cold reality is that unless policy changes are made to open up funding to a wider diversity of mental health treatments, the problem will persist.

INVOLUNTARY TREATMENT   In some cases, people are required (that is, forced) to enter the mental health system against their will. In Canada and the United States, as well as many other countries, people can be compelled through the courts or on the advice of social service agencies or doctors to be treated for mental illness. The majority of these cases arise due to the person engaging in highly erratic or disturbing behaviour, which results in legal trouble and the perception that the person may be a risk to themselves or others. Involuntary treatment can also be required after the person commits harm to others, as in some cases of domestic violence.

This "outpatient commitment" is a highly contentious issue in the field of mental health and in the legal system, because it strips people of some of their basic rights. Proponents of this practice argue that it improves mental health, reduces the costs of mental illness on society, and increases the effectiveness of treatment by ensuring that people with severe disorders receive treatment that they might otherwise avoid; it also may protect society from people who may otherwise commit harm. People who are opposed are concerned that this practice is unethical because it can restrict the freedom and take away the rights of people who have not done anything harmful to themselves or others, force people to receive medications that may alter brain function and have dangerous side effects, and easily be misapplied to certain ethnic groups and lower socioeconomic classes (Kisely et al., 2011).

Research has thus far failed to clear up the controversy. For example, some studies show that a significant number of people benefit from mandated treatment, as indicated by their adherence to treatment and reduced encounters with law enforcement (Hough & O'Brien, 2005; Pollack et al., 2005). On the other hand, many people placed in involuntary treatment programs feel coerced and resentful, and not everyone benefits from the programs. The concern that involuntary treatment decisions can be biased has also been backed up by research. A survey of records in the U.S. indicated that individuals who are lower in socioeconomic status and from African-American or Latino backgrounds are significantly more likely to receive court-ordered treatment (Takeuchi & Cheung, 1998). To be fair, some of this seeming bias may be due to benevolent reasons; for example, if poorer individuals are unable to afford treatment, then a court-ordered treatment may be relied upon to get people the help that they need. But much of this bias may be due to more undesirable reasons, such as prejudice and the general lack of legal power available to people of lower socioeconomic status and marginalized ethnic groups. Thus, supporters of involuntary treatment continue to point to its apparent benefits for some people, whereas opponents point to its apparent costs for others. The debate continues.

Module 16.1a Quiz:

Barriers to Psychological Treatment

Know . . .

1. Which of the following is *not* an argument against the practice of involuntary commitment?
   A. Committing people against their will is wrong because it removes people's basic human rights and freedoms.
   B. Imposing treatments, such as drug treatments, onto people is unethical because the side effects and unintended consequences of the treatment itself may further harm the person.
   C. The decision to commit people to treatment can be biased due to prejudice and stereotypes that exist in society.
   D. Committing people against their will is unnecessary because people can generally get the help they need on their own.

Understand . . .

2. Which of the following is *not* a barrier for people seeking help for a psychological disorder?
   A. The financial costs associated with therapy

   B. The fact that it is more culturally accepted for males to enter therapy
   C. Some people's tendency to minimize their symptoms, making them seem less harmful than they really are
   D. Skepticism toward therapy in general

Apply . . .

3. A person's fear that she may be stigmatized for having a mental illness
   A. is unfounded; our society has advanced too far to still be stigmatizing mental illness.
   B. is based on fear that they may be exposed to severe treatments against their will.
   C. is the sign of delusions, possibly indicating schizophrenia.
   D. is understandable; unfortunately, there may often be professional or social costs when others know someone has had a psychological disorder.

Mental Health Providers and Settings

A wide variety of treatment settings are available for people in need of mental health care. The type of treatment people receive depends on several factors, including their age, the type and severity of the disorder, and the existence of any legal issues and concerns that coincide with the need for treatment. Mental health services include inpatient care, outpatient office visits, the use of prescription drugs, attending therapy sessions, and taking part in support groups. Different types of care tend to be delivered by professionals with different training and skill sets.

MENTAL HEALTH PROVIDERS In popular culture, the terms *psychologist* and *psychiatrist* are often (and

Jerry Cooke/The LIFE Images Collection/Getty Images

Today, some people with severe mental disorders reside in an institution or hospital that specializes in mental health care. These settings are dramatically different than they were just a few decades ago, when they were called "insane asylums" and other unfortunate names.

erroneously) used as if they mean the same thing. In fact, there are some major differences between the two, and even within a category there can be huge differences; certainly not every psychologist nor every psychiatrist takes the same approach as their peers.

Clinical psychologists are perhaps the best-known type of psychologist in the mental health field. **Clinical psychologists** *have obtained PhDs and are able to formally diagnose and treat mental health issues ranging from the everyday and mild to the chronic and severe.* **Counselling psychologists** are *mental health professionals who typically work with people who need help with more common problems such as stress and coping; issues concerning identity, sexuality, and relationships; anxiety and depression; and developmental issues such as childhood trauma.* Counselling psychologists may have either a Master's or PhD degree. Practitioners of clinical and counselling psychology work in many capacities and settings. They may provide individual or group therapy in an office or institution such as a hospital, or they may conduct psychological testing and research. Other people with different levels of training and background also conduct therapy; for example, clinical social workers and psychiatric nurses conduct therapy to help people cope with psychological problems.

Psychiatrists are *medical doctors who specialize in mental health and who are allowed to diagnose and treat mental disorders through prescribing medications.* It is important to note that many psychiatrists also work within an integrative biopsychosocial perspective and perform psychological

counselling and therapy, or work closely with other professionals who provide such services. Historically, in Canada and most U.S. states, clinical psychologists have not been allowed to prescribe medications, so in many settings psychologists and psychiatrists work together, combining medications with psychological therapies. Like clinical psychologists, psychiatrists work in a variety of settings, but they are most frequently found in hospitals and other institutional settings.

INPATIENT TREATMENT AND DEINSTITUTIONALIZATION Throughout much of human history (although certainly not in all cultural settings), people experiencing severe disorders—such as the profound disturbances associated with schizophrenia or Alzheimer's disease—were often separated from society. In the 1800s and 1900s, it was common practice to confine people in an asylum. These actions were generally not considered to be "treatments" because there was no hope that the individuals would get better. Instead, the goals were to protect the public and to provide basic care for individuals whose families could not do so (Wright, 1997).

Sadly, many of the mental institutions of past generations were terrible places for the patients. The creation of large institutions for housing the mentally unwell began in the 14th century due to rapidly growing European populations and mass migration to cities; these trends tended to disrupt the normal family and community traditions that would have provided structure to individuals' lives and the bonds of collective responsibility that people would have had for the mentally ill members of their families. As a result, the number of society's outcasts grew to the point that institutions were built to house them. For the next few centuries, the inmates of these institutions were subjected to brutal confinement, torture, and an almost complete lack of humane conditions. In fact, the modern word *bedlam* derives from this time. In 1403, St. Mary of Bethlehem, a hospital in London, England, began admitting patients with mental issues; the hospital's treatment of these patients was so awful and the hospital was so chaotic that "bedlam" (a mispronunciation of Bethlehem) began to be used to refer to chaos and madness in general (Foucault, 1975).

By the end of the 19th century, psychology was gaining credibility as a science, and asylums were built both to house the mentally ill and to attempt to treat their conditions. Unfortunately, these asylums quickly became overcrowded, and there were not many effective treatments at the time for most disorders. Thus, despite the good intentions, in practical terms the asylums became little more than giant warehouses that separated the mentally ill from the rest of society, only differentiated from the earlier mental institutions in that the most deplorable of conditions had been improved and there was a more explicit emphasis on finding treatments to help manage patients' symptoms.

This pattern continued until the 1960s, when people started to take a dim view toward merely housing those with disorders in dismal asylums. One major contribution to the shift in attitudes was that effective treatments began to be developed for some disorders, largely in the form of medications. As patients' symptoms became more treatable, a society-wide movement toward **deinstitutionalization** occurred, which involved *the movement of large numbers of psychiatric in-patients from their care facilities back into regular society*, generally after having their symptoms alleviated through medication. The next three decades saw about an 85% decrease in the number of psychiatric inpatients (Sealy & Whitehead, 2004), both in Canada and many other countries (Fakhoury & Priebe, 2002). Although a small subset of people remained who required inpatient care, the vast majority of patients who entered the hospital stayed for a relatively short time before they were stabilized, given medication, and sent back (ideally) to the care of their families.

In the decades since this movement began, mental health care providers have amassed many resources and strategies to help people in distress. For example, in as little as three or four days, a patient admitted after a suicide attempt may be fully evaluated, begin medication and therapy, receive education about emergency resources such as suicide hotlines, and then be released. Whereas the goal in the past was to remove the mentally ill from society, now inpatient treatment is geared toward protecting the individual patient from harm while encouraging a quick and successful return to regular society.

Of course, some people still require intensive, long-term care. In place of asylums, many chronic inpatients now live in residential treatment centres. These centres allow inpatients to enjoy much more personal freedom, depending on the severity of the patients' symptoms. Low-level **residential treatment centres** are *housing facilities in which residents receive psychological therapy and life skills training, with the explicit goal of helping residents become re-integrated into society*. Medium- to high-level centres have the same emphasis as low-level centres, but also place restrictions on individuals' freedoms for reasons of safety and stability. These centres function like hospitals inside medium-security prisons, with a high staff-to-resident ratio to ensure that residents' movements and freedom remain under control, with potential escapes prevented by security systems and physical barriers (e.g., locked doors that bar escape). These facilities are intended for individuals with more dangerous histories—such as incidents of physical or sexual assault.

THE IMPORTANCE OF COMMUNITY PSYCHOLOGY
Outpatient therapy and inpatient housing simultaneously grew in popularity through the early 20th century. However, many of the formerly imprisoned patients who were released back into society did not have family or social support structures in place to help them reintegrate successfully. As a result, many mentally ill people faced problems with substance abuse, homelessness, and being victimized or traumatized by people who took advantage of their vulnerable state.

To deal with these issues, some psychologists began to place less emphasis on individual, one-on-one therapy, in favour of working with the community at large. This gave rise to a field known as **community psychology**, *which focuses on identifying how individuals' mental health is influenced by the community in which they live, and emphasizes community-level variables such as social programs, support networks, and community resource centres to help those with mental illness adjust to the challenges of everyday life.*

PSYCH@

The University Mental Health Counselling Centre

In many workplace or education-based communities, mental health services are available to the population through the institution's own services. A good example is university campuses. The stresses of university life can often bring about temporary struggles with mental well-being. Students must deal with the stresses of managing a heavy workload, beginning a career path, and developing an adult identity, and also often juggle work and family obligations along with school. Some students also face lifelong struggles with mental illness. Approximately 15% of university students exhibit symptoms of depression. One study on first-year students at Acadia University found that 7% of male and 14% of female students experienced a major depressive disorder in their first year at school alone (Price et al., 2006)! In general, mental health issues seem to be on the rise in university students; over the past two decades, rates of depression have increased more than 50%, with anxiety disorders and other issues also increasing (American College Health Association, 2007).

University counselling centres typically employ a resident psychologist or psychiatrist, along with a staff of trained counsellors. These centres are in great demand and often have waiting lists. Counsellors are trained to help with the more common student issues, such as stress, anxiety, time management, depression, and relationship issues, but they also often encounter students with more severe disorders than most counselling centres are designed to accommodate (Gallagher, 2007; Voelker, 2003). In these cases, counsellors can help students find appropriate mental health professionals and, potentially, advocate on their behalf.

Through working at a community level rather than narrowly focusing on individuals, community psychologists hope to prevent or minimize the development of disorders, seeking to enhance the factors (such as healthy family relationships) that strengthen people and make them more resilient to the kinds of stresses that can otherwise undermine mental health. For example, to prevent depression, community psychologists may conduct research into the environmental and neighbourhood factors that contribute to stress, anxiety, and depression, and then work with community groups to resolve these problems. In addition, they may develop programs to counter negative cognitive patterns and bolster positive thinking in schools and afterschool programs.

Module 16.1b Quiz:

Mental Health Providers and Settings

Know . . .

1. Which type of provider is generally permitted to prescribe medications?
   A. Psychiatrist
   B. Clinical psychologist
   C. Clinical social worker
   D. Medical psychologist

2. _____ study how individuals' mental health is influenced by their neighbourhood, economics, social groups, and other community-based variables.
   A. Residential treatment centres
   B. Community psychologists

   C. Psychiatrists
   D. Social workers

3. The social movement against keeping the mentally ill in asylums is known as _____.
   A. empirically validated treatments
   B. social work
   C. deinstitutionalization
   D. community psychology

Evaluating Treatments

Given the diversity of treatment approaches and settings that are available, it is important to know which approaches are effective. Aside from the obvious economic logic of society not wasting money on ineffective treatments, it is important for individuals seeking help to get assistance that is effective. In the mid-1990s, the American Psychological Association set up task forces to evaluate different therapy practices and made their findings and recommendations available online to the general public (APA, 2009). This led to a call for more studies to examine the effectiveness of different therapeutic approaches, so that "evidence-based" treatments could be identified and given further financial support, such as being included in insurance companies' health insurance plans.

EMPIRICALLY SUPPORTED TREATMENTS **Empirically supported treatments** (also called evidence-based therapies) are *treatments that have been tested and evaluated* (Chambless & Ollendick, 2001; De Los Reyes & Kazdin, 2008). The most rigorous way of testing whether a certain therapy works is through an experiment. An experiment generally involves randomly assigning volunteers to a treatment group (e.g., a type of therapy) and to a control group. Ideally, experiments are also double-blind, which in this case means that neither the patient nor the individual evaluating the patient is aware of which group the patient is in. However, this level of rigour is often close to impossible to attain when evaluating therapies. One common problem is that it is ethically problematic to place people into a control group that receives no treatment of any kind, because it effectively denies them treatment that they need. It is also generally impossible to use double-blind procedures, given that a therapist, of course, knows which type of treatment she administers, and many clients likely do as well.

Also, it can be very difficult to assess the general effectiveness of a therapeutic approach if therapists themselves differ widely in their own level of relevant skills. Furthermore, each client and therapist is unique, and much of the effectiveness of therapy comes from the **therapeutic alliance**—*the relationship that emerges in therapy*. In fact, the specific type of therapy used is actually less important than the "common factors" of empathy, trust, and the like, which allow the therapist and client to build an appropriately supportive relationship. Establishing a positive relationship therefore depends on various qualities of the therapist and client, as well as the "fit" between the two. Therapists who are more socially skilled (who show warmth, concern, and empathy) tend to be more effective. Similarly, clients who are more open to the process, more willing to trust the therapist, and more willing to recognize and work on their issues are more likely to benefit from therapy (Prochaska & Norcross, 2002).

Therefore, even though many therapists may provide the same therapy, each therapist will have a slightly different personal approach, and each combination of client and therapist will be unique. As a result, it is very difficult to adequately test the effectiveness of many therapeutic approaches to the rigorous extent required for empirical support (DeRubeis & Crits-Cristoph, 1998). This is one rather ironic way in which the understandable desire for "evidence-based treatments" may, in fact, create problematic biases that shift the field towards the types of therapies whose efficacy is robust across different therapists and clients, so is easy to measure. What if there are therapeutic approaches that may be highly successful, but depend on subtle elements of the therapeutic situation? For example, therapies that involve deep work on emotional patterns that stem from childhood trauma or attachment insecurity may depend heavily on difficult-to-measure variables such as the empathic connection between the therapist and the client, or the extent to which the therapist is skilled at being emotionally attuned and empathic, and these approaches may thus not fare as well in attempts to identify evidence-based approaches.

This is, admittedly, a confusing and complex issue. On the one hand, of course we want to have evidence that a particular therapy works, so that clients aren't subjected to (and paying for) the ineffective treatments, the particular biases of therapists, or outdated practices. On the other hand, the very search for "evidence" may bias the field towards particular forms of therapy whose outcomes are reliable and easy to measure, and as a result, discourage people from practising or exposing themselves to forms of therapy that may be profoundly transformative in ways that are more difficult to rigorously evaluate (Westen & Bradley, 2005).

The same challenges have held back research on the effectiveness of self-help treatments. Nevertheless, some research has tried to address this issue, given the explosion of self-help literature in the past few decades.

Working the Scientific Literacy Model

Can Self-Help Treatments Be Effective?

Many people opt to address their psychological problems by using resources that do not involve visiting an actual therapist, such as self-help books, online information, or community workshops. Are these approaches helpful?

What do we know about the availability of self-help treatments?

There is a huge variety of self-help materials available to the public. Just walk down to your local bookstore and check out the psychology section, where you will find books on everything from anxiety and depression to how to raise children, deal with divorce, and optimize your well-being. A quick perusal will reveal that many of these books are written by people with PhDs in the relevant fields (although many are not), but the books also do not always agree with one another on the best approach to whatever issue they are discussing. For example, if you read the popular literature on how to help children deal with emotional struggles, you could catalogue several approaches that were not only different, but actually would work against each other. Which approach is right? How can we know whether self-help literature is effective in general?

How can science test the effectiveness of self-help treatments?

There is some research on this issue, examining whether **bibliotherapy**, *the use of self-help books and other reading materials as a form of therapy*, improves people's symptoms. For example, one study attempted to assess the effectiveness of bibliotherapy over a three-month period in 170 elderly primary-care patients who were experiencing depression. The patients were evenly divided into two groups: both groups received a "standard care" approach, but the self-help group also read a self-help book on depression. After three months, the group who read the self-help book in addition to the standard care showed no signs of reduced depression compared to the control group (Joling et al., 2010). However, as discussed earlier, this is hardly a definitive test of the effectiveness of self-help. It's possible that particular book wasn't effective for this population, but a different one could have been. Or, different books may appeal to different people, so testing a single book on a whole group may show no overall improvement, even though a few individuals may have benefited substantially.

A slightly stronger approach to this question is to perform a meta-analysis, combining numerous studies testing a similar hypothesis. One such analysis combined six separate studies that had tested whether the book *Feeling Good* reduced depressive symptoms. The researchers found that over four weeks, those who read the book had reduced depression compared to those who did not (see Figure 16.1; Anderson et al., 2005). Thus, there *may* be reason to believe that bibliotherapy can be helpful.

Can we critically evaluate this evidence?

The biggest strength of the self-help literature is also its biggest weakness: there are so many books available that it is almost impossible to ensure that they are all credible sources of information. The research presented above used a single book, *Feeling Good,* as the representative of self-help books. Obviously, this is not sufficient evidence in favour of using self-help books to cope with psychological disorders (an issue that the authors of that research were quick to point out). People planning to use self-help books should ensure

Figure 16.1 Results of Six Studies Evaluating the Self-Help Book *Feeling Good*

Research on the book *Feeling Good* shows successful results in reducing symptoms of depression. Comparisons across six studies (identified by author name and publication date) indicate statistically significant improvement in each case (Anderson et al., 2005).

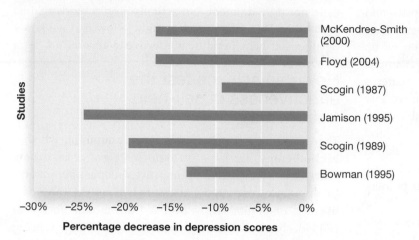

Source: Based on Anderson, L., Lewis, G., Araya, R., Elgie, R., Harrison, G., Proudfoot, J., Schmidt, U., Sharp, D., Weightman, A, & Williams, C. (2005). Self-help books for depression: How can practitioners and patients make the right choice? *British Journal of General Practice, 55*, 387–392.

that the authors have the necessary qualifications to advise people about mental-health issues. If possible, they should also see if the coping strategies promoted in the book have been tested by scientists. Although the dense methods and results sections of academic articles may intimidate some readers, most articles also come with an accessible summary (known as an abstract) that provides readers with the take-home message of the study (i.e., did it work?).

The reason that caution is necessary when using self-help books is that many psychological disorders are both complex and emotionally intense. Exploring the different symptoms of a person's psychological disorder—and examining their causes—can sometimes be a difficult experience. Having a trained therapist aid you in coping with these experiences is often helpful. This is not to say that all self-help books should be avoided. Rather, it is to warn people that these books do not always prepare people for the emotions that can arise as they deal with the symptoms of their psychological disorders.

Why is this relevant?

Self-help options have major advantages over traditional approaches to therapy, which means that if they do work, even in part, this is important to know. For example, self-help options are typically low in cost (e.g., compare $150 for an hour of therapy to $20 for a book), are convenient, and can be accessed anonymously, thereby reducing the barriers of stigma, inconvenience, and cost that often prevent people from accessing therapy. Furthermore, self-help options are extremely easy to find in the self-help section in the bookstore or with a quick online search for self-help programs. Indeed, many people consult online resources to get help for depression, anxiety, substance-abuse problems, and sexual health (Fox, 2005).

That said, research does suggest that self-help approaches, relative to in-person therapy sessions, are less likely to lead people to actually implement changes in their own lives (O'Kearney et al., 2006). If you are experiencing psychological distress, it is probably advisable to speak with a mental health professional at least once—especially if symptoms are severe—to find out whether self-help is appropriate for your situation. A professional may also be able to suggest good resources, which can save you a great deal of wasted energy wading through stacks of self-help literature to find quality information.

Module 16.1c Quiz:

Evaluating Treatments

Know . . .

1. _____ is the relationship that emerges in therapy between the therapist and client, and is an important determinant of the therapy's effectiveness.
   A. Client insight
   B. Bibliotherapy
   C. Therapeutic alliance
   D. Friendship

Understand . . .

2. What does it mean to say that a therapy has "empirical support"?
   A. Insurance companies prefer it.
   B. Therapists prefer to use it.

C. Research studies confirm that it is effective compared to no treatment and possibly compared to other alternatives.
D. Research studies demonstrate that it can do a better job than drugs.

3. Which of the following conclusions best summarizes the effectiveness of bibliotherapy?
   A. It has no benefit whatsoever.
   B. It is more effective than other forms of therapy.
   C. It works, but is addictive.
   D. It may be helpful to many people, but its results are not consistent.

Module 16.1 Summary

16.1a Know . . . the key terminology associated with mental health treatment.

bibliotherapy
clinical psychologist
community psychology
counselling psychologist
deinstitutionalization
empirically supported treatments
psychiatrist
residential treatment centre
therapeutic alliance

16.1b Understand . . . the major barriers to seeking help for psychological disorders.

These barriers include expense, availability, gender, and attitudes toward therapy, which are often influenced by the stigma against therapy that may be held by a particular group (e.g., males in general).

16.1c Understand . . . the arguments for and against involuntary treatment.

Proponents of involuntary treatment argue that it helps to protect innocent people who may otherwise end up being victims of violence at the hands of a psychologically disturbed individual. Proponents also argue that such treatment improves mental health and ensures that people with severe disorders receive appropriate treatment. Opponents argue that there is no good evidence that involuntary treatment benefits the individual, and instead, receiving involuntary treatment may result in the patient feeling coerced or resentful, suggesting that such treatments are not without cost.

16.1d Apply . . . your knowledge to suggest what approach to therapy is likely most appropriate for a given situation.

The appropriate kind of therapeutic setting depends on a host of factors, from what is available and within the person's means to afford, to what sorts of issues the person is experiencing. For common problems such as stress and milder forms of depression and anxiety, seeing a counselling psychologist is likely the best first step; for students, most universities offer counselling services on campus. For more severe and debilitating problems, such as severe anxiety, depression, or schizophrenia, a clinical psychologist or psychiatrist is likely most appropriate. A psychologist will likely engage in a form of psychological therapy, whereas a psychiatrist will likely take a more physiological approach involving prescribing medication.

16.1e Analyze . . . whether self-help options, such as popular books, are a useful therapy option.

Self-help books alone are not likely to be life-changing or good stand-alone treatments for serious problems such as major depression, anxiety, and substance abuse. Even so, research on bibliotherapy indicates that in some cases, when used in conjunction with other methods, reading self-help books can bring about modest improvements. It is, of course, always possible that for a specific individual, any specific self-help book may be profoundly helpful and even life-changing; however, on average, reading self-help books has only a small therapeutic benefit.

Module 16.2 Psychological Therapies

wavebreakmedia/Shutterstock

 ## Learning Objectives

16.2a Know . . . the key terminology related to psychological therapies.

16.2b Understand . . . the general approaches to conducting major types of psychological therapy.

16.2c Apply . . . your knowledge to identify major therapeutic techniques.

16.2d Analyze . . . the pros and cons of the major types of psychological therapy.

Medical doctors are generally required to follow the Hippocratic Oath—a pledge that they will cause no harm to their patients. One way of honouring this oath is to use the safest and most effective treatments. Although we do not generally associate the Hippocratic Oath with psychologists, they also follow the basic tenet, seeking to use techniques that are safe and do not cause harm to their clients. If there is a possibility that a specific type of treatment might worsen a condition, this treatment should therefore be avoided, unless there are no better options.

For example, Scared Straight was a program developed in the 1970s that involved exposing at-risk youth to prisons and prisoners. The interventions were based on the premise that shocking or scaring the youths with the harsh realities of prison life would deter criminal activity. These scare tactics involved blunt descriptions of prison violence, along with verbal aggression directed at adolescents attending the sessions. The program may have succeeded in scaring and shocking adolescents, but the youths who attended these sessions did not necessarily go down a straight path. Many were later

convicted of crimes and incarcerated. In fact, if anything, the program seemed to backfire; according to some analyses, participants in the program showed an increased chance of subsequently committing crimes (Petrosino et al., 2003).

Scared Straight and other methods for helping people can, unintentionally, do more harm than good (Lilienfeld, 2007). Although a rare case, this example reminds us that therapy can be done in many different ways, and we should be cautious in determining which methods are best.

Focus Questions

1. Which options for therapy are available?

2. Are all well-established options equally effective at treating problems?

⟫ In Module 16.1, we introduced psychological therapy as a set of processes for resolving personal, emotional, behavioural, and social problems and improving well-being. Psychological therapy is a broad term, and mental health providers have a veritable smorgasbord of therapeutic approaches to choose from. In this module, we will study several of these approaches. Although the methods are diverse, they are all types of psychological therapy, rather than biological or medical therapy. In psychological approaches, techniques for resolving problems rely heavily upon communication between client and therapist.

Insight Therapies

Psychologists have long believed that self-knowledge and understanding can lead to positive changes in behaviour. This is certainly the case for **insight therapies**, which is *a general term referring to therapy that involves dialogue between client and therapist for the purposes of gaining awareness and understanding of psychological problems and conflicts.* Historically, the formal beginning of insight therapy came with the development of psychoanalysis by Sigmund Freud and its evolution into **psychodynamic therapies**, *forms of insight therapy that emphasize the need to discover and resolve unconscious conflicts.*

PSYCHOANALYSIS: EXPLORING THE UNCONSCIOUS

Psychoanalysis sprang out of Freud's understanding of consciousness. As described in Module 12.3, Freud hypothesized that much of our consciousness occurs at the unconscious level, outside of our awareness. In particular, many fundamental urges, such as sexuality and aggression, were thought to constantly influence how we think and behave, although we are not explicitly aware of these processes. In fact, because these urges are generally socially unacceptable, we actively protect ourselves from becoming aware of them through a variety of psychological defences. As a result, the true causes of our behaviour, and thus of our psychological issues, are hidden in the unconscious. This led Freud to emphasize the importance of "making the unconscious conscious," believing that the process of bringing material from the unconscious into consciousness allowed clients to gain insight into their problems and the past experiences from which they stem. This understanding was believed to liberate clients from the grips of the previously unknown forces that were impacting their lives.

Freud and his followers based their practice on some core ideas summarized in Table 16.1. These core ideas may sound straightforward, except for one crucial point: Accessing the unconscious mind is tricky business. The client cannot tell you much about it because, of course, they are not aware of it. As a result, Freud and his followers invented several methods they believed would help them access the mysterious unconscious realm.

Four of these techniques have been particularly important in the practice of therapy, historically, and are still in use in many different ways today.

Table 16.1 Core Ideas Forming the Basis of Psychoanalysis

- Adults' psychological conflicts have their origins in early experiences.
- These conflicts affect the thoughts and emotions of the individual, and their source often remains outside of conscious awareness.
- The unconscious conflicts and their effects are called neuroses (anxieties).
- By accessing the unconscious mind, the analyst and client can gain a better understanding of the early conflicts that lead to neuroses.
- Once the conflicts are brought to the surface, the analyst and the client can work through them together.

The first technique is **free association**, *during which clients are encouraged to talk or write without censoring their thoughts in any way;* instead, the person allows everything that pops into the mind to come spilling out, no matter how odd or meaningless it may seem. Freud believed that this uncensored thought barrage would reveal clues to the unconscious in ways that clients may not normally have access to.

The second is dream analysis. Freud believed that in the relatively unguarded dreaming mind, the unconscious would be better able to express itself; however, because the unconscious doesn't communicate through the same language-based way of thinking that the conscious mind uses, it expresses itself through symbols that need to be properly interpreted. **Dream analysis** is *a method of examining the details of a dream (the manifest content), in order to gain insight into the true meaning of the dream, the emotional, unconscious material that is being communicated symbolically (the latent content).* Dreams take the form of imagery (sometimes bizarre and nonsensical imagery) and loose storylines, but within this confusing jumble, symbolic truths are believed to be hidden. The psychoanalyst's role was to help clients properly understand these symbolic truths in order to gain insight into their unconscious conflicts.

For example, consider one of Freud's dream analyses: A client dreamed he was riding his bicycle down a street when suddenly a dachshund ran him down and bit his ankle as he attempted to pedal away. Meanwhile, two elderly ladies sat by and laughed at the incident.

The details described are the manifest content, but what might the dream mean—what is the latent content? Freud pointed out that in his waking life the client had repeatedly seen a woman walking a dog and, although he was very attracted to her, he felt great anxiety about approaching her. The man had consciously devised a plan to use the dog as an excuse to strike up a conversation with the woman. Unfortunately, the anxiety caused by fear of rejection manifested itself in an unpleasant dream about being attacked by a dog, accompanied by the humiliation of being laughed at (Freud, 1920, pp. 165–166).

The third strategy is to pay attention to signs of **resistance**. Resistance occurs in therapy when unconscious material surfaces that the client wishes to avoid. Resistance involves *engaging in strategies that keep the information from fully manifesting in conscious awareness.* Resistance may be subtle, such as the client using humour to avoid talking about something painful, or it may be obvious, such as the client skipping sessions, becoming angry at the therapist, or becoming cynical about the whole process. This is actually considered a promising signal for the psychoanalyst because it means that they are beginning to access the unconscious motives of clients' present difficulties. Psychoanalysts then attempt to push through the resistance by making clients aware of how and what they are resisting.

A fourth tool used by psychotherapists involves **transference**, *whereby clients direct certain patterns or emotional experiences toward the therapist, rather than the original person involved in the experiences (e.g., their parents).* For example, if a client is addressing a hidden sexual conflict, then transference may occur through her developing sexual feelings for the analyst. Or as another example, if a client's mother made him feel excessively criticized during childhood, he may tend to see the analyst's behaviours as being critical in a similar way, and respond defensively as though he's being attacked or criticized. Thus, the client's interaction with the analyst becomes a kind of stage on which conflicts with other people are revealed and explored. Transference is a significant milestone in the process of psychotherapy. Once it is reached, the therapist and client can begin to work through specific problems and discuss ways of coping with them.

In sum, there are many different tools that psychotherapists draw upon, including transference, resistance, dream analysis, and free association, that can help to provide direct knowledge of the person's otherwise inaccessible unconscious. Once this material is brought to the light of the client's conscious awareness, then these patterns can begin to be examined and, ideally, changed.

MODERN PSYCHODYNAMIC THERAPIES Today, Freudian-based psychoanalysis is practised by relatively few therapists. Nevertheless, Freud's ideas have remained influential and several newer therapies have evolved from traditional psychoanalysis. In contrast to Freudian methods, these new approaches are more concerned with the client's conscious rather than unconscious experience. They also acknowledge the effect of cultural and interpersonal influences on individual behaviour, and the impact of important needs such as love, power, belonging, and security. Finally, they are more optimistic about people's ability to reach healthy functioning.

One example is **object relations therapy**, *a variation of psychodynamic therapy that focuses on how early childhood experiences and emotional attachments influence later psychological functioning* (see Module 10.2). In contrast to psychoanalysis, object relations therapy does not centre on repressed sexual and aggressive conflicts. Instead, the focus is on "objects," which are the clients' mental representations of themselves and important others. The basic view is that the quality of the early relationship between the child and these "objects" results in the development of mental models for the child. These mental models act to shape the person's perceptions and interpretations in relationships, the general consequence being that the person will tend to form and maintain relationships as an adult that are consistent with the mental models that were formed in childhood. The mental models tell the person what is "normal" and provide an interpretive framework within which to make sense of relationships. The therapist's job is to help the client understand these mental models and the relationship patterns they represent and reinforce. This generally leads to working with relational issues of trust, fear of abandonment, dependence on others, and other relationship factors.

HUMANISTIC–EXISTENTIAL PSYCHOTHERAPY An important new movement in psychotherapy arose during the 1950s, when humanistic psychologists broke from psychoanalytic approaches over several deep differences in their assumptions about people and the theoretical foundation upon which they were building. This humanistic–existential approach can be characterized by at least five key differences from the psychodynamic approaches (listed in Table 16.2). Overall, this new orientation emphasized individual strengths and the potential for growth,

Table 16.2 Contrasting Psychoanalytic and Humanistic Views of Major Psychological Issues and Debates

Issue	Psychoanalysis	Humanistic Therapy
Conscious versus unconscious	Focuses on unconscious drives	Focuses on conscious experience
Determinism versus free will	Behaviour is determined by repressed sexual and aggressive instincts	Behaviour is chosen freely
Weaknesses versus strengths	Everyone has neuroses	Everyone has strengths
Responsibility for change	The analyst interprets and explains to the client what is wrong	The therapist asks the client what is wrong and attempts to help clarify issues
Mechanism of change	Insight into unconscious conflicts allows problems to be worked through	Unconditional positive regard allows a person to heal and become more authentically themselves

and assumed that human nature is fundamentally positive, rather than the essentially negative perspective advanced by psychoanalytic approaches. This shift toward the positive was believed to help individuals access their own sense of personal agency for overcoming their problems.

Humanistic and existential therapies share many similarities: to help people express their authentic selves, to overcome alienation, to become more loving, and to take responsibility for their experiences so that they learn to dwell fully in the present. The major difference between them is that humanistic therapists focus on removing the obstacles that prevent self-actualization from unfolding naturally, whereas existential therapists emphasize the importance of facing painful experiences such as feelings about isolation, death, and meaninglessness, believing that self-actualization involves transforming by facing one's fears and negativity. Even though attaining insight is still an important aspect of these therapies, rather than interpreting the hidden meanings of dreams and free associations, the therapist's role is to listen empathically in order to understand the clients' internal world. This is referred to as a **phenomenological approach**, which means that *the therapist addresses the clients' feelings and thoughts as they unfold in the present moment, rather than looking for unconscious motives or dwelling in the past.*

American psychologist Carl Rogers (1902–1987) developed a version of humanistic therapy called **client-centred therapy** (or **person-centred therapy**), *which focuses on individuals' abilities to solve their own problems and reach their full potential with the encouragement of the therapist.* As a humanist, Rogers believed that all individuals could develop and reach their full potential. However, people experience psychological problems when others impose *conditions of worth*, meaning that they appear to judge or lose affection for a person who does not live up to expectations. Conditions of worth are imposed, for example, by a father who only pays attention or gives praise or encouragement when his child is doing well at something, or who expresses disappointment in the child herself if she does something wrong, focusing more on the child's character failings or lack of will than on the actual behaviour itself and what caused it. If people give the impression that their respect and love for a person are contingent upon the person behaving in certain ways or meeting certain expectations, then they have imposed conditions of worth. Conditions of worth can impact psychological health over the long term, because they increase insecurities within the individual; as a result, the person is likely to change his behaviour in an attempt to regain affection. If this happens frequently, then the individual's behaviour starts to be primarily about gaining affection and approval, living in order to please others rather than being able to express his own authentic self. That, to Carl Rogers, is a key aspect of most psychological dysfunction.

Emotion-focused therapy (EFT) is one promising type of person-centred therapy that has evolved from the humanistic–existential tradition; EFT is based on the well-supported belief that it is better to face and accept difficult emotions and thoughts rather than bottle them inside (Greenberg, 2004; Hayes et al., 2006). Therapists employing this form of therapy aim to help clients overcome their tendency to suppress disturbing thoughts and emotions, so that clients are less defensive overall and have fuller access to their whole range of experiences and emotions.

The most important aspect of all client-centred therapies lies within the dialogue that unfolds between therapist and client. The therapist must show unconditional positive regard through genuine, empathetic, and non-judgmental attention. If the therapist can remove all conditions of worth, clients may begin to express themselves without fear and begin to develop inner strength. Finally, with self-confidence and strength, clients can accept disagreements with others and focus on living their lives to the fullest.

EVALUATING INSIGHT THERAPIES   As discussed in Module 16.1, from an evidence-based perspective, therapies should be used only if there is empirical support that they actually work (although it is worth remembering that an approach may work for some people, even if it doesn't work for most).

Psychodynamic therapies meet some of the criteria for empirically supported therapies, though surprisingly few studies in this area have been conducted with proper research design and control conditions. Ultimately, the effectiveness of insight therapies depends on the condition being treated. The best-designed studies have generally shown that psychodynamic therapy is not effective in treating severe depression or schizophrenia, but it has shown promise for treating panic disorder, dependence on opiate drugs (e.g., heroin), and borderline personality disorder (Gibbons et al., 2008). Psychodynamic therapy may help with major depression, particularly if combined with drug treatment—an approach we will describe in greater detail in Module 16.3.

For less severe conditions, such as mild depression and anxiety, behavioural issues such as dysfunctional habits or motivation and goal-striving difficulties, insight-focused therapies can often make a difference, helping individuals gain understanding and awareness of the nature of their psychological problems. Many people with psychological disorders are able to learn to function effectively without digging deeply into possible "root causes," but instead, by cultivating new, more adaptive behaviours (Weisz et al., 1995).

Research shows that Carl Rogers was accurate in emphasizing the importance of the therapeutic relationship for successful therapy (Horvath & Bedi, 2002;

Wampold, 2001). In fact, a strong alliance is a good predictor of successful therapy *over and above* the specific type of therapy delivered (Bohart et al., 2002), and positive regard (Farber & Lane, 2002) and empathy (Bohart et al., 2002) are both related to therapeutic success (Bohart, 2003).

Research is somewhat inconsistent on the effectiveness of person-centred therapy more generally, although this therapy is reliably more effective than no treatment at all (Greenberg et al., 1994). However, some studies have found it to be no more effective than a placebo treatment (Smith et al., 1980), whereas others have found it to be as effective as cognitive behavioural therapy (Elliott, 2002; Greenberg & Watson, 1998). As discussed earlier, one complicating factor in this research may be the skill of therapists themselves; some therapists may be highly skilled at connecting with clients and establishing good rapport in therapy, whereas others may be less capable in these ways. This difference in therapists' skill could account for these mixed findings, and make it difficult for research studies to then accurately assess the effectiveness of an approach like Rogers's.

Module 16.2a Quiz:

Insight Therapies

Know . . .

1. _____ refers to a phenomenon of psychoanalysis in which the client begins directing emotional responses toward the therapist.
   - A. Resistance
   - B. Befriending
   - C. Objectifying
   - D. Transference

2. In psychoanalysis, resistance occurs when
   - A. a client develops sexual attraction to the analyst.
   - B. a client begins to divert the analysis by joking, becoming cynical, or perhaps refusing to answer questions.
   - C. a therapist begins to have the same feelings as the client.
   - D. the therapist refuses to continue a therapy session.

Understand . . .

3. In psychoanalysis, treatment for psychological problems seems to come from
   - A. the client becoming more conscious of the workings of their unconscious.
   - B. the client receiving unconditional positive regard.
   - C. the therapist understanding and explaining the manifest content of a dream.
   - D. the therapist diagnosing the psychological disorder and providing appropriate drug therapy.

Apply . . .

4. A kindergarten teacher (unintentionally) places conditions of worth on her students. What does this mean?
   - A. She always lets her students know how much she values them.
   - B. She regularly tries to draw compliments out of her students.
   - C. She acts as if a student no longer matters to her or the school if he misbehaves.
   - D. She provides monetary rewards for good behaviour.

Analyze . . .

5. What has research concluded in regard to the effectiveness of insight therapies?
   - A. Insight therapies are always very effective.
   - B. Insight therapies are never effective.
   - C. Insight therapies do not help people gain awareness of the nature of their psychological problems, so they tend to not be effective.
   - D. The effectiveness of insight therapies depends on the conditions that are being treated.

Behavioural, Cognitive, and Group Therapies

Behavioural therapies *attempt to directly address problem behaviours and the environmental factors that trigger them.* At the heart of behavioural therapies is the belief that patterns of behaviour are the result of conditioning and learning that have led to the automatization of maladaptive habits. Thus, behavioural approaches seek to recondition clients, training them to adopt different behavioural responses to situations until they develop new, more functional, habits.

SYSTEMATIC DESENSITIZATION How behavioural therapy works is clearly illustrated by its application to a very common problem: fear of public speaking. Most people experience at least some anxiety about public speaking, but for some, their reaction is so intense that even thinking about making a speech can bring on major anxiety, arousal, and even panic attacks.

To help people learn to handle such an anxiety-inducing situation, therapists will often employ a behavioural technique known as **systematic desensitization**, in which *gradual exposure to a feared stimulus or situation is coupled with relaxation training* (Wolpe, 1990). First, the client is guided towards being able to identify and track their own feelings of anxiety versus relaxation, so that they gain greater awareness "in the moment" of when they are feelings anxious and, critically, what it feels like when those feelings subside. Once the client has this kind of inner awareness, the therapist will expose them to a very mild version of

Table 16.3 Applying Steps of Systematic Desensitization to Fear of Public Speaking

1. Build an anxiety hierarchy. This involves the therapist assisting the client in creating a list of stimuli that arouse fear responses, starting with the stimulus or situation that evokes the least amount of anxiety and ending with the stimulus that elicits the most anxiety.

Think about and visualize:

   1. Thinking about the presentation topic

   2. Writing down ideas for the presentation

   3. Doing library research for a presentation

   4. Preparing slides and note cards

   5. Practising the presentation alone

   6. Practising the presentation with a few friends

   7. Travelling to campus to give the presentation

   8. Sitting in the classroom waiting to be called for your turn

   9. Walking up to the front of the room

   10. Standing up at the podium and looking out at the audience

   11. Beginning to speak; delivering the first couple of lines

2. Relaxation training. During this phase, the client learns to respond to relaxation suggestions from the therapist as they begin to work through the hierarchy. This is typically done using mental imagery while the client is visiting the therapist's office; actual props may be used in some cases (e.g., a podium that the person can stand in front of).

3. Work through the hierarchy. Steps 1 and 2 are combined here as the therapist works through the entire hierarchy, usually over several sessions, until the client is able to manage the anxious feelings while continuing to engage in the relevant behaviours.

the fear-inducing situation, such as imagining walking up to the front of the room where he is going to give the speech. As the client engages in this exercise and feels his anxiety starts to rise, he practises relaxing or engaging in behavioural strategies (e.g., pausing in his imagination, practising a breathing exercise in order to calm down) in order to counteract the anxiety he may feel. With practice, the anxious response to that particular trigger will lessen, and the client then progresses to more realistic and concrete manifestations of the situation, each time practising relaxing until he can learn to tolerate his feelings and counteract them with a relaxation response. This escalation of the intensity of the triggering experience continues slowly, step-by-step, until the client can eventually handle the real thing. This process is described in detail in Table 16.3.

In some cases, clients may undergo a process called *flooding*, in which case the client goes straight to the most challenging part of the hierarchy, exposing himself to the scenario that causes the most anxiety and panic. For example, he may elect to give a long speech in front of 100 strangers. By diving right in and (one hopes) discovering that there are no truly negative consequences, the person may find that they have "gotten over it" and lesser forms of the same activity no longer give them anxiety; it should be noted that this is relatively rarely used, as it can easily overwhelm the person instead and simply reinforce their anxious response.

At the opposite end of the spectrum, clients may find it difficult to even begin to expose themselves to the simplest steps of their anxiety hierarchy. Fortunately, consistent with research showing that fear and anxiety responses can be acquired through observing others

(Olsson & Phelps, 2007), and with research on observational learning or "modelling" (see Module 6.3; Bandura, 1977), even less threatening steps of an anxiety hierarchy can be established using other people instead of oneself in the anxiety-provoking situation. Watching others engage in the anxiety-provoking situation without suffering negative consequences can help people with severe anxiety reactions, such as phobias, learn to tolerate some mild exposure to the feared stimulus.

Recent advances in virtual reality technology are providing new tools for therapists; for example, it is becoming possible to help clients overcome fear reactions in a virtual setting, an advance that holds exciting new possibilities.

Working the Scientific Literacy Model

Virtual Reality Therapies

Systematic desensitization techniques have long been a part of behavioural treatments for fear and anxiety. However, there are some key barriers that can prevent them from being effective. For one, people with fear and anxiety about a specific object or situation usually avoid any contact with it—so even taking the first step toward a therapist's office can be challenging. Also, although mental imagery is typically the method employed with these therapeutic techniques, it may not transfer well to the actual anxiety-provoking situation because mental imagery may not have the same power as the much more vivid, real situation. Virtual reality technology is offering one potential way around these problems.

What do we know about virtual reality exposure?

Virtual reality exposure (VRE) is *a treatment that uses graphical displays to create an experience in which the client seems to be immersed in an actual environment.* This much more vivid environment feels more like the real thing, and shows promise for helping people learn to relax in the face of their fears. Also, virtual reality therapy may help to reduce a person's tendency to use avoidance strategies. Over the past decade, this technology has become increasingly common in helping soldiers returning from military conflicts in Iraq and Afghanistan—many of whom have developed PTSD.

How can scientists study virtual reality exposure?

Psychologists at Emory University in Atlanta have been using a simulator called Virtual Iraq, which was developed to deliver two possible scenarios—being in a Middle Eastern city or driving a Humvee through a desert road in simulated war conditions (Figure 16.2). The weather, time of day, background noise, civilians, aerial craft, and ground vehicles can be programmed by the therapist to change as desired during the exposure sessions. There is also the option to provide simulated gunfire and bomb explosions. Smell cues are available using an air compressor that pumps in odours of burning rubber, garbage, diesel fuel, and gunpowder (Cukor et al., 2009).

Figure 16.2 Virtual Reality Exposure

Combat veterans diagnosed with PTSD have participated in virtual reality therapies involving simulated exposure to traumatic events. Therapists work with clients to help them process and cope with their fears.

Erika Schultz/MCT/Newscom

In one set of trials, 20 soldiers who were diagnosed with PTSD following combat activity underwent VRE therapy. Their PTSD symptoms were measured before and after therapists guided them through VRE treatment in the Virtual Iraq simulator. At the conclusion of their therapy, the soldiers' PTSD symptoms declined by 50%, with 16 of the soldiers no longer meeting the criteria for the disorder (Rizzo et al., 2010). The results included fewer disturbing thoughts about stressful events that occurred during military service; fewer disturbing dreams; reduced physical reactions such as heart pounding, sweating, and trouble breathing; and less avoidance of activities that triggered memories of military service. VRE using the Virtual Iraq simulator appears to work.

Can we critically evaluate this evidence?

From an experimental standpoint, this study should have used a placebo (control) group that received no treatment, or a comparison group that received some other treatment method. In fact, such studies have recently occurred; in one study of U.S. veterans who had served in Iraq or Afghanistan, the effectiveness of VRE sessions was compared to the standard approaches (e.g., prolonged exposure therapy, among other standard treatments), and the VRE approach outperformed the standard approaches (McLay et al., 2011).

It is not clear from this one study whether VRE therapy would be beneficial for disorders other than PTSD. However, other research has shown that virtual reality approaches are useful for helping people in many different types of circumstances, including symptom reduction in people with various phobias (Opriş et al., 2012; Powers & Emmelkamp, 2008), stress management in patients with cancer (Schneider et al., 2011), and body image issues in clients with eating disorders (Riva, 2005).

Why is this relevant?

Virtual reality technologies seem to help overcome key barriers to therapeutic effectiveness. As discussed earlier regarding PTSD, clients typically avoid any stimuli associated with the original trauma, and therefore may be resistant to therapy that will expose them to the trauma. VRE approaches can get around this resistance because the therapist has precise control over the way the client will be exposed to the feared situation and can therefore easily tailor the approach to the client's needs (Hodges et al., 2001).

AVERSIVE CONDITIONING Most people have at least one behaviour they would like to reduce or eliminate, perhaps a nervous habit such as fingernail biting, or an unhealthy behaviour such as smoking. Behavioural principles tell us that these habits are maintained because they bring rewards in some fashion, and thus, changing their rewarding nature can lead to changing the behaviour itself.

Aversive conditioning is *a behavioural technique that involves replacing a positive response to a stimulus with a negative response, typically by using punishment.* One aversive conditioning treatment involves using the drug Antabuse (disulfiram) to reduce problem alcohol consumption. Antabuse causes nausea and vomiting when combined with alcohol, so the drug classically conditions an aversion to alcohol. Antabuse works for some individuals, but there are several reasons why it is not entirely effective (Garbutt, 2009). As you can imagine, the client must have a fairly strong motivation to quit, and must be willing to take the drug knowing that it would make her ill. If she cheats and skips the drug one day, then the treatment will not have much chance of working. Thus, even though aversive conditioning can help people quit, it can require a great deal of willpower to use effectively.

COGNITIVE–BEHAVIOURAL THERAPIES Behavioural therapies, despite their effectiveness at changing problem behaviours, do not directly address problematic thoughts. This is extremely important because some disorders, such as depression, are caused and maintained, in part, by dysfunctional habits of thinking. Two psychodynamically trained psychologists, Albert Ellis (1962) and Aaron Beck (1963), found that people with depression tend to interpret and think about their lives in a negative light. As Ellis, Beck, and others learned more about these thought patterns, it became apparent that therapies should be directed at changing negative cognitions into more realistic and rational thought patterns, as well as helping people learn to control the physiological processes (e.g., arousal) that reinforce negative thinking. Over time, this new approach became known as cognitive–behavioural therapy.

Cognitive–behavioural therapy (CBT) *is a form of therapy that consists of procedures such as cognitive restructuring, stress inoculation training, and exposing people to experiences they may have a tendency to avoid,* as in systematic desensitization (NIMH, 2009). Because avoiding thoughts and stressful situations tends to reinforce the negative feelings that would arise, helping clients to face negativity allows them the opportunity to gain insight into their feelings, to practise a courageous response to negativity, and to learn methods for coping when negativity arises. This type of therapy is far more about the present than about the past. Rather than excavating past traumas or conflicts, CBT therapists help clients become more aware of the thought, emotion, and behaviour patterns that arise in their current

The drug Antabuse is used in aversive conditioning for alcohol consumption. When it is taken and the person subsequently consumes alcohol, Antabuse causes nausea and vomiting. If successful, Antabuse treatment leads to a conditioned aversion to alcohol.

Monika Olszewska/Shutterstock

lives; through this heightened self-awareness, clients learn to identify their habitual dysfunctional tendencies, and then work on building more functional cognitive and behavioural habits.

At the behavioural end of CBT, clients are given exercises and guidance in gaining skills they may be lacking. For example, as with systematic desensitization, clients may learn relaxation techniques, enabling them to better tolerate negative feelings when they arise. A person with social anxiety who has difficulty integrating into social situations may learn and practise certain social skills, such as making "small talk" with people at parties or learning to be more responsive to people's non-verbal cues.

At the cognitive end of CBT, clients are given exercises and strategies to build more functional cognitive habits. Cognitive restructuring involves learning to challenge negative thought patterns, to question self-defeating beliefs, and to view situations in a different light. For example, people with depression or anxiety disorders often hold extreme and irrational beliefs, such as "I can't do anything right," "I have nothing worthwhile to say," "If I fail, it's going to be a total disaster." As they become more aware of these negative beliefs, they can question or dispute them, helping themselves appreciate that these beliefs are far more negative than reality warrants. After all, nobody can do *everything* wrong; nobody has literally

Table 16.4 Applying Cognitive–Behavioural Therapy to the Cognitive Symptoms of Depression

Cognitive Symptoms	Example of CBT Coping Strategy
Internal Attributions: blaming oneself excessively for negative things that happen.	Recognize the role that a person contributed to his problem, but also examine the role of other contextual factors (e.g., the situation, the behaviour of other people).
Stable Attributions: assuming that situations are permanent and irreversible.	In order to highlight the temporary nature of a person's difficulties, provide examples of how things that were true in the past are no longer the case.
Global Attributions: assuming that the results of one negative event will apply to all aspects of a person's life.	Challenge the person to explain exactly how the effects of one negative event will spill over into other parts of his life; provide examples of situations when spillover did *not* occur.

nothing worthwhile to say; and a failure is not "the end of the world," so to speak, but is also an opportunity to learn and improve. An example of applying CBT strategies to the cognitive symptoms of depression is shown in Table 16.4.

Of course, it falls to the client to put the behaviours learned in therapy into practice—noting her automatic thought tendencies as they occur, and then actively practising her cognitive strategies. As the client practises interrupting old thought patterns and actively cultivating new, healthier ones, the healthier patterns should become more easily activated, until eventually they become automatic themselves. In contrast, the depressive thought patterns should fade with disuse, becoming less easily activated over time.

The fact that these exercises change people's functioning has been dramatically demonstrated through neuroimaging studies, which show substantial changes to neurological function after CBT (Frewen et al., 2008). For example, one study at L'Institut Universitaire de Gériatrie de Montréal showed that, before being treated with CBT, people suffering from spider phobia showed activation in certain brain areas when viewing pictures of spiders: part of the prefrontal cortex involved with controlling emotional responses, and part of the hippocampus involved in contextual fear memories. The activation of these two areas likely reflects the automatic reactivation of fear memories that underlie the phobia, plus the person's attempt to override the fear response. After receiving CBT, these areas were no longer active when subjects viewed spider pictures. These neuroimaging results provide us with further evidence that CBT can change a person's thought processes (Paquette et al., 2003).

MINDFULNESS-BASED COGNITIVE THERAPY One of the biggest recent advances in therapeutic practice, spearheaded by researchers at the Centre for Addiction and Mental Health in Toronto, is the integration of meditation-based practices, such as mindfulness, with traditional cognitive–behavioural approaches. In this groundbreaking area of research, East meets West and ancient meets modern, as traditional spiritual practices merge with modern psychological therapies and neuroscientific understanding.

Mindfulness practice and cognitive–behavioural therapy begin in somewhat similar ways—the goal of each is

to get the client better acquainted with her thoughts and feelings, in the present moment of experiencing them. But after this emphasis on increased self-awareness, the two approaches differ significantly. In CBT, there is a basic orientation of "fixing oneself." The purpose of becoming aware of one's patterns of thoughts, feelings, and behaviours is to gain greater control so that the negative patterns get replaced with more positive ones. In contrast, the practice of mindfulness involves consciously adopting an orientation of "accepting" oneself fully. Strictly speaking, from a mindfulness perspective, you don't necessarily have to "do" anything about problematic thoughts and feelings; instead, you make the active choice to accept them as they are, to simply observe them without reacting.

It may sound like "just watching yourself" isn't doing very much. However, it is in fact a highly active and intentional process. In order to be able to watch yourself without reacting to the different thoughts and feelings that arise, you must consciously choose, again and again, to take an attitude of openness and acceptance toward yourself. Dr. Daniel Siegel (2007) describes this attitude as COAL—curious, open, accepting, and loving. COAL is, essentially, the same attitude that parents take toward children in order to help them develop emotional security.

As people develop emotional security by being involved in loving and accepting relationships, this is reflected in the development of certain brain areas that Siegel calls the *social circuitry*. These areas, including parts of the medial prefrontal cortex, are involved in experiencing and managing emotions, feeling empathy and taking the perspective of others, and, generally speaking, reflect an *interpersonal attunement* between oneself and other people. The practice of mindfulness is believed to be a kind of *intrapersonal attunement,* a relationship between oneself and oneself; it seems to involve the same social circuitry, and lead to the same emotional and neurological outcomes as the development of secure attachment. Basically, by practising attending openly and non-reactively to yourself, you become like your own healthy parent. As Siegel describes it, mindfulness is like re-parenting yourself, actually changing your own biological structures that are involved in emotional security. The key insight here is that security comes from having good relationships, and mindfulness offers a specific technique for building a healthier relationship with *yourself*.

A second key way in which mindfulness affects a person is through the experience of **decentring**, *which occurs when a person is able to "step back" from their normal consciousness and examine themselves more objectively, as an observer.* You have no doubt experienced decentring many times, such as when you become aware that you are "talking to yourself" as though there is a private voice in your mind that you can "speak" with, or you may have had the experience of becoming aware of yourself having an experience while you are having the experience. For example, you may be dancing but then you suddenly become acutely *aware* of yourself dancing, as though you are looking at yourself from a third-person perspective.

The ability to decentre is a powerful antidote to difficult thoughts and feelings. By stepping back from your own thoughts and feelings and observing them dispassionately, you detach yourself from the damaging or troubling consequences of your thoughts. This can be similar to watching a young child have a temper tantrum. Because you are not "attached" to the child's thoughts and feelings (let's assume), their anger doesn't affect you in the same way. You have some distance from it, which allows you to think more clearly and decide on the best way to respond to the situation, whereas the child is too caught up in emotion to be able to gain that cognitive control.

Mindfulness-based cognitive therapy (MBCT) *involves combining mindfulness meditation with standard cognitive behavioural therapy tools.* The goals are to reap the benefits of mindfulness practice described above, and then to work on changing dysfunctional patterns using CBT. Many carefully controlled trials have shown that MBCT has powerful effects on people who have experienced a major depressive disorder. After the person emerges from a depressive episode, the practice of MBCT substantially reduces the likelihood of experiencing a relapse, lengthens the amount of time that passes between depressive episodes, and reduces residual depressive symptoms for years after treatment (Bondolfi et al., 2010; Kuyken et al., 2008, 2010).

MBCT seems to have great promise as a therapy for many different conditions. Initial studies suggest it is beneficial for social anxiety disorder and generalized anxiety (Evans et al., 2008; Piet et al., 2010), bipolar disorder (Weber et al., 2010; Williams et al., 2007), depression (Kingston et al., 2007; Williams et al., 2006), hypochondriasis (McManus et al., 2012), and suicidal ideation (Crane & Williams, 2010). Mindfulness exercises are excellent tools for encouraging people to become more growth-oriented, and they are adaptable to both individual therapy and therapy in group settings.

GROUP AND FAMILY THERAPIES In some situations, clients may benefit by participating in group therapy sessions. Group members share their personal stories and experiences, and the bonding and support that occur in this context can be very powerful. To encourage people to open up to each other, therapists may group people together based on the issue that they are dealing with (e.g., alcohol addiction, divorce), or other similarities (e.g., age, ethnicity, gender, sexual orientation, etc.). A final, logistic advantage to group therapy is the cost, which is usually much cheaper than individual therapy. This makes group therapy accessible to a broad range of people across society.

In other situations, psychologists may conduct family therapy. This may occur if a client's difficulties stem from or are reinforced by unhealthy dynamics within the family; for example, people with schizophrenia are far less likely to have their symptoms stay in remission if their families exhibit negative patterns of communication and emotional involvement (Hooley, 2007). Thus, family therapy may be extremely effective for helping people with schizophrenia, generally in conjunction with anti-psychotic drug treatments. Family therapy may also be used to help families deal with specific family members who are highly dysfunctional in some way, such as being addicted or having poor emotional control.

Family therapists generally take a **systems approach**, *an orientation that encourages therapists to see an individual's symptoms as being influenced by many different interacting systems*; one important system is the family system, which can play a big role in the development and maintenance of psychological disorders. For example, imagine a family in which one person is emotionally abusive and controls the other family members by becoming excessively angry. A therapist taking a systems approach would see that behaviour pattern as stemming not only from the individual themselves, but also from the other family members. For example, the other family members may constantly monitor that person and carefully choose their own behaviours so as to avoid making that person angry. Or, the family may stop inviting other people to the house, allowing the angry person to isolate the family within the community. Or, the family members may be too quick to forgive or to apologize themselves and accept the blame whenever the angry person loses his temper, rather than challenging the person and being clear about what the family will and will not tolerate. There are many different ways in which family members contribute to the maintenance of a dysfunctional pattern of behaviour, and a family systems therapist would therefore treat the individual by also working with the other family members to change the larger patterns that reinforce the problematic behaviours.

EVALUATING COGNITIVE–BEHAVIOURAL THERAPIES
Behavioural therapies have been shown to be particularly effective at treating symptoms associated with anxiety disorders, such as obsessive-compulsive disorder and specific

phobias (Chambless & Ollendick, 2001). They have also proved useful for increasing behavioural skills (e.g., social skills) and decreasing problematic behaviours (e.g., social withdrawal).

Cognitive–behavioural therapy has been quite effective in treating depression, which is not too surprising given that this method of therapy was specifically developed for this purpose (Hollon et al., 2002). CBT has also been successful in treating conditions like anxiety, obesity, and eating disorders. In fact, CBT is the most effective treatment currently available for anxiety disorders, particularly over the long term, even outperforming anti-anxiety medications for most adult anxiety disorders (Hofmann & Smits, 2008); furthermore, the effects last much longer than the effects of drugs, which often are effective only so long as the person remains on the medication (Hollon et al., 2006). Neuroimaging research on people with obsessive–compulsive disorder showed that both antidepressant drug (SSRI) and CBT treatments effect

the same changes in neural activity (Schwartz et al., 1996), suggesting that these different approaches target similar neural processes. In many cases, rather than taking an either/or approach, the best outcomes have been found by combining drug treatments with cognitive behavioural therapy; this has been found for several different disorders, including panic disorder with agoraphobia (Starcevic et al., 2004), and depression (McCullough, 2000).

Generally speaking, cognitive and behavioural therapies are the workhorses of psychological treatments; they are quite versatile in their applications and can help to treat a wide variety of disorders. They also take much less time (and are therefore much less expensive) than psychodynamic approaches, and have none of the undesirable side effects of drug treatments. Nevertheless, different treatments work better for different people, and it is worth remembering that for any given person, it is currently impossible to know ahead of time which treatment or combination of treatments may work the best.

Module 16.2b Quiz:

Behavioural, Cognitive, and Group Therapies

Know . . .

1. _____ involves a process in which the client faces feared situations gradually and under controlled conditions.
   A. Client-centred therapy
   B. Family therapy
   C. Insight therapy
   D. Exposure therapy

2. _____ consists of key procedures including exposure, cognitive restructuring, and stress inoculation training.
   A. Cognitive–behavioural therapy
   B. Family therapy
   C. Virtual reality exposure therapy
   D. Exposure therapy

Understand . . .

3. The key difference between mindfulness and cognitive behavioural therapy is that
   A. only CBT involves decentring.
   B. CBT is supported by empirical research, whereas mindfulness is just a practice that comes from Buddhism but has little empirical support.
   C. in CBT, clients practise replacing their dysfunctional thoughts with more functional thoughts; whereas in

mindfulness practice, clients simply watch their thoughts and accept them as they are.
   D. CBT can be combined with drug treatments, but mindfulness cannot.

Apply . . .

4. Neil is facing difficulties with anger and depression. His parents are having trouble managing his behaviours and responding appropriately. To address all of these concerns, the most beneficial treatment in this situation would likely be _____.
   A. cognitive–behavioural therapy
   B. family therapy
   C. virtual reality exposure therapy
   D. exposure therapy

Analyze . . .

5. Cognitive–behavioural therapies seem to be effective because they
   A. help individuals restructure their maladaptive thoughts and beliefs.
   B. teach individuals to brood over problems effectively.
   C. systematically desensitize phobias.
   D. are easier for the therapist to implement.

Module 16.2 Summary

16.2a Know . . . the key terminology related to psychological therapies.

aversive conditioning
behavioural therapy
client-centred therapy (or person-centred therapy)

cognitive-behavioural therapy (CBT)
decentring
dream analysis
free association
insight therapy

mindfulness-based cognitive therapy (MBCT)
object relations therapy
phenomenological approach
psychodynamic therapy
resistance
systematic desensitization
systems approach
transference
virtual reality exposure (VRE)

16.2b Understand . . . the general approaches to conducting major types of psychological therapy.

Psychoanalysis works by uncovering hidden conflicts, whereas humanistic therapy focuses on removing conditions of worth that can hinder a person's growth. Behavioural and cognitive therapies target dysfunctional thought and behaviour patterns, seeking to replace undesirable patterns with more functional ones that clients then practise regularly. Group and family therapies have also been developed and work with social systems that are larger than one individual.

16.2c Apply . . . your knowledge to identify major therapeutic techniques.

Apply Activity

Imagine you are helping someone who has a phobia to find a therapist for treatment. You speak with three professionals about the approach each would take. Match their response with the corresponding school of thought. Note: Not all the schools of therapy will be used.

1. I would ask the individual to describe his train of thought when he encounters the feared object. Then I would ask him to explain why it is irrational to think that way, and we would try to replace his irrational thoughts with more reasonable, less anxiety-provoking beliefs.
2. I would ask the patient to think about his earliest childhood experiences with the object, and then to speak freely about those memories at length. We would try to discover the significance of that object in his early development.
3. We would take an active approach. One important step is to teach the client how to be calm and relaxed while gradually introducing the feared stimulus.

A. Humanistic therapy
B. Cognitive–behavioural therapy
C. Psychodynamic therapy
D. Family therapy
E. Behavioural therapy

16.2d Analyze . . . the pros and cons of the major types of psychological therapy.

Table 16.5 summarizes the pros and cons of the major forms of therapy discussed in this module.

Table 16.5 Pros and Cons of the Major Types of Therapy

	Pros	Cons
Insight therapies	• Can provide deep understanding of the self • Can facilitate substantial personal growth and personal transformation	• Often (but not always) involve long-term therapy, often very expensive • Can have limited application to people with serious disorders
Behavioural and cognitive therapies	• Typically time- and cost-efficient • Address immediate thoughts and behavioural problems • Address both mild and severe problems	• Do not necessarily offer deeper understanding of psychological problems • When used alone, may not be effective for some severe cases and certain disorders (e.g., schizophrenia)
Group/family therapies	• Allows individuals to empathize and relate to others with similar problems • Gives family members insight into how each individual contributes to both positive and negative aspects of family life • Can change the larger social dynamics that reinforce and maintain the disorder	• Does not fully address individual issues (although group and family therapies are often used in combination with individualized therapy)

Module 16.3 Biomedical Therapies

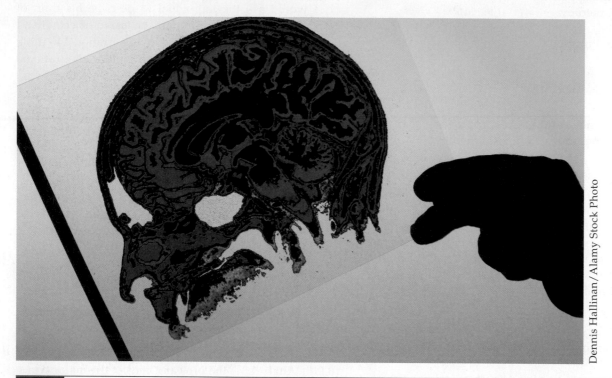

Dennis Hallinan/Alamy Stock Photo

⌄ Learning Objectives

16.3a Know . . . the key terminology associated with biological treatments.

16.3b Understand . . . how the drugs described in this module affect brain functioning.

16.3c Understand . . . the other major medical approaches to therapy.

16.3d Apply . . . your knowledge of drug therapies to different psychological conditions.

16.3e Analyze . . . whether St. John's wort, a popular herbal remedy for depression, works.

The word "depression" used to be taboo; people didn't want to admit to being depressed and have others think they were weak-willed or simply needed "to get it together." Then in 1987 Prozac hit the market, and everything changed. Suddenly there seemed to be a miracle cure for a silent epidemic of depression. Millions of dollars were spent on marketing campaigns that targeted both doctors and the public at large. Rates of depression diagnoses skyrocketed, and sales of Prozac kept pace. Within a decade, Eli Lilly, the company that owned Prozac, was making $2.5 billion per year from Prozac sales alone (Couzin, 2004).

But then people started to voice concerns about this wonder drug and its "sister" drugs, the selective serotonin reuptake inhibitors (SSRIs) known by brand names like Paxil and Zoloft. People alleged that these drugs caused many different side effects, from relatively "mild" problems such as sexual dysfunction, weight gain, and skin rashes, to very serious problems such as seizures, breathing problems, and even thoughts of committing suicide.

The side effect that really got the public's attention (and which Eli Lilly denied), was the increased risk of suicidal thoughts. Dr. David Healy, author of the book Let Them Eat Prozac, *even went so far as to allege that Eli Lilly's own research showed that Prozac led to increased risk for suicidal behaviours, but that they had suppressed the findings. In 2005, documents were leaked to CNN purporting to show that Eli Lilly knew, all the way back in the 1980s, that Prozac users were more than 1200% more likely to attempt suicide than people using several other antidepressants.*

Around the same time, a meta-analysis called into question the usefulness of SSRIs in general. This study concluded that the effects of SSRIs were only slightly better than a placebo (Kirsch et al., 2008). Although later meta-analyses found more positive results (Hieronymus et al., 2016), questions about these medications still exist.

Where does this leave you, as a potential consumer of these drugs? We hope that it leaves you with the awareness that it is important to ask questions and find good research concerning the effectiveness of prescription drugs, as well as their side effects, and to appreciate that there are many different treatment options available for most disorders. The informed "consumer" can, hopefully, make the wisest choice for themselves.

Focus Questions

1. What medical techniques are available for influencing psychological disorders and how do they work?

2. What are the risks and benefits associated with different biomedical approaches?

» The biomedical approach to treating disorders involves using drugs, surgery, or other medical procedures in order to alter the functioning of the central nervous system and correct what is believed to be the underlying biological problem. **Psychopharmacotherapy**—*the use of drugs to manage or reduce clients' symptoms*—is by far the most frequently used biomedical option, and is often employed in conjunction with some form of psychological therapy. Other options, such as surgery or electrically stimulating the brain, are typically used only in situations where no other available treatments have succeeded. In this module, we explore and evaluate each of these biomedical treatment options and examine how they may be used in conjunction with other forms of therapy.

Drug Treatments

Psychotropic drugs are *medications designed to alter psychological functioning.* Drug approaches were first predominantly used in institutional and clinical settings, generally targeting very severe cases. However, in more recent decades, drug treatments have become mainstream

practice for many people experiencing even mild psychological problems and symptoms. This expansion has made certain psychotropic drugs, such as those used to treat depression, among the most prescribed forms of medicine (Olfson & Marcus, 2009).

Psychotropic drugs have been developed to take many different courses of action. First, all psychotropic drugs are designed to cross the **blood–brain barrier**, *a network of tightly packed cells that only allow specific types of substances to move from the bloodstream to the brain in order to protect delicate brain cells against harmful infections and other substances* (see Figure 16.3). After crossing this barrier, psychotropic drugs then affect one or more neurotransmitters. The specific neurotransmitter(s) targeted by a drug will determine which disorders will be responsive to that medication.

ANTIDEPRESSANTS As the name suggests, **antidepressant drugs** are *medications designed to reduce symptoms of depression.* In general, antidepressant drugs target areas of the brain that, when functioning normally, are rich in monoamine neurotransmitters—serotonin, norepinephrine, and dopamine. Since multiple neurotransmitters are involved, antidepressants come in several varieties, each with its own way of altering brain chemistry (Figure 16.4).

Monoamine oxidase inhibitors (MAOIs) were the first type of antidepressant to be developed and widely used. They *work by deactivating monoamine oxidase (MAO), an enzyme that breaks down serotonin, dopamine, and norepinephrine at the synaptic clefts of nerve cells* (see Figure 16.4). When MAO is inhibited, fewer dopamine, serotonin, and norepinephrine neurotransmitters are metabolized, which in turn leaves more of them available for synaptic transmission. Although MAOIs often effectively relieve symptoms of depression, they are used less frequently than other antidepressants, in part because they can cause many

Figure 16.3 How Psychotropic Drugs Reach the Brain

In order to affect the brain in the desired way, psychotropic drugs must cross the blood–brain barrier, a network of densely packed cells that restrict the flow of substances between the capillaries and brain cells.

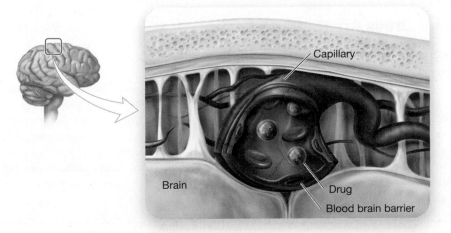

Capillary

Brain

Drug

Blood brain barrier

Figure 16.4 Antidepressant Effects at the Synapse

The major antidepressant drugs have different ways of increasing the transmission of neurotransmitters such as serotonin, dopamine, and norepinephrine at the synapses.

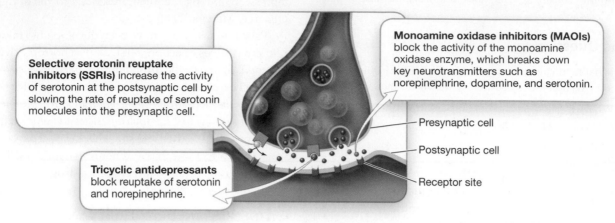

Selective serotonin reuptake inhibitors (SSRIs) increase the activity of serotonin at the postsynaptic cell by slowing the rate of reuptake of serotonin molecules into the presynaptic cell.

Monoamine oxidase inhibitors (MAOIs) block the activity of the monoamine oxidase enzyme, which breaks down key neurotransmitters such as norepinephrine, dopamine, and serotonin.

Presynaptic cell

Postsynaptic cell

Tricyclic antidepressants block reuptake of serotonin and norepinephrine.

Receptor site

side effects, some quite dangerous, especially when they interact with other medications and certain types of foods (e.g., aged cheeses, smoked meats, alcoholic beverages).

Tricyclic antidepressants were among the earliest types of antidepressants on the market and *appear to work by blocking the reuptake of serotonin and norepinephrine* (Figure 16.4). Unfortunately, they also seem to cause many undesirable side effects, including nausea, weight gain, sexual dysfunction, and even seizures.

Given the severity of the side effects associated with MAOIs and tricyclic antidepressants, it should come as no surprise that both patients and physicians were eager for a new form of antidepressant to become available. In 1987, one such drug arrived: fluoxetine (also known as Prozac). Prozac is a **selective serotonin reuptake inhibitor (SSRI)**, *a class of antidepressant drugs that block the reuptake of serotonin*. These antidepressants alleviate some proportion of the symptoms of depression in some clients, although they also come with certain side effects, as discussed in the opening vignette of this module.

Interestingly, it is not yet clear exactly through which mechanisms SSRIs seem to have their effect. The notion that they work by enhancing mood directly is only a hypothesis; there may be other mechanisms involved. For example, serotonin also causes the brain stem to reduce overall arousal, which could be one way of reducing the magnitude of negative emotions in general (Maier & Watkins, 2005). SSRIs also lead to decreased activation of parts of the amygdala, which may reduce the person's negative emotional response to various stimuli (Sheline et al., 2001). SSRIs have also been shown to lead to neurogenesis—the growth of brand-new neurons—in the hippocampus. Reduced hippocampal volume has been connected to depression, so this may be one route through which SSRIs affect depression (Jacobs, 2004). It is important to remember that any drug usually has multiple effects on the brain, and it is difficult to determine exactly which effect may be responsible for the overall impact that the drug has on the person.

At this point, we have discussed both the mechanisms and the limitations of antidepressants. But, this discussion

Myths in Mind
Antidepressant Drugs Are Happiness Pills

A common belief is that antidepressants are happiness in pill form—that their chemical magic can not only cause depression to disappear, but can also bring on optimism and a rush of positive emotion. In reality, antidepressant drugs can alleviate depression (in some individuals), but they do not make people happier than they were before becoming depressed.

The "happiness pill" misconception about antidepressants has led some individuals to believe that taking a high dose of antidepressants will induce a euphoric high, much like cocaine or heroin. This is also a myth. Although some people have

attempted to abuse antidepressants by taking high doses (even crushing and snorting them for quicker delivery to the brain), there is no evidence that an intense rush of happiness results. In fact, SSRIs typically take a couple of weeks to work. Taking a high dose, or snorting crushed-up pills, neither magnifies their effects nor reduces the two-week waiting period before effects become evident.

In short, antidepressants are not "happiness pills" and should not be taken by people who are merely looking to boost their mood.

has been limited to the types of medications that are prescribed by physicians. As you will see in the next section, these are not the only types of remedies available to people trying to cope with depression.

Is St. John's Wort Effective?

People often make the assumption that biomedical therapies are limited to prescription drugs or to procedures provided by a physician. In reality, people often self-prescribe and administer treatments for depression. One popular home remedy is the herbal treatment St. John's wort, found in many health food stores and pharmacies.

What do we know about St. John's wort?

Herbal remedies are often associated with a "hippie" lifestyle or discounted as "unscientific." It is important to remember that any drug—even so-called natural products—will affect the levels of neurotransmitters in your brain. This is how they affect your behaviour. St. John's wort (*Hypericum perforatum*) appears to influence several of the neurotransmitter systems that are altered by traditional antidepressant medications, including serotonin (Butterweck, 2003). However, its most prominent effect appears to be on the levels of epinephrine, a chemical associated with emotional arousal and stress responses. Several studies have shown that St. John's wort causes epinephrine receptors to *down-regulate* (move further away from the synapse; De Marchis et al., 2006; Jakobs et al., 2013). This reduces the impact that epinephrine has on the nervous system. St. John's wort also inhibits the release of glutamate, the brain's primary excitatory neurotransmitter (Chang & Wang, 2010). As you can see, this seemingly simple herbal remedy has fairly complicated effects on the brain.

What have scientific studies found about St. John's wort and depression?

The goal of scientists investigating St. John's wort is to determine if it can be used as an alternative treatment for depression. In order to do this, researchers must demonstrate that St. John's wort reduces depressive symptoms more than a placebo. Several groups of researchers have examined this research question.

Researchers using animal participants have found that St. John's wort reduces a number of different behaviours linked with depression and anxiety (Schmidt & Butterweck, 2015). For example, in the forced swimming test, rodents are placed in an inescapable tank of water.

Researchers can measure how long the rodents actively swim versus how long they remain motionless. The amount of time spent immobile is viewed as a behavioural measure of hopelessness or depression. Researchers have found that antidepressants reduce the amount of time spent motionless; St. John's wort has similar positive effects (Bukhari & Dar, 2013).

Tests involving humans use less-aquatic methods to measure depression; most studies use standardized questionnaires. In order to get the "big picture" of these studies, we can examine *meta-analyses* that combine the results of the different experiments. A recent meta-analysis of 35 experiments involving 6993 patients found that St. John's wort led to reduced levels of depression when compared to placebos. Importantly, it was just as effective as traditional antidepressants, but with fewer side effects (Apaydin et al., 2016).

Can we critically evaluate this evidence?

St. John's wort is not a cure for everyone's depression. Similar to prescription antidepressants, St. John's wort will work for some people while having no effect on others. To date, we have little ability to predict and understand who will benefit from this remedy. There is also uncertainty as to the correct dose of this medication.

Research into St. John's wort is also limited by a lack of human brain-imaging studies. These studies would help identify the specific brain areas affected by this treatment, which would provide researchers with more insight into what cognitive processes are altered when people consume this medication.

Finally, a major limitation of this research is that the quality of the samples of St. John's wort is not standardized or carefully regulated by government agencies. Thus, different samples of the drug might have quite different levels of active ingredients. This adds a lot of uncertainty to the data and makes it more difficult to test the drug's effectiveness (Klaus et al., 2008). Until these uncertainties are controlled for, physicians will likely be hesitant to recommend St. John's wort to patients unless other medications have already been ineffective.

Why is this relevant?

Knowledge about alternative treatments such as St. John's wort can help people with depression make informed choices about what treatment is best for them. The results of studies of St. John's wort appear promising. Indeed, the Canadian Network for Mood and Anxiety Treatments (CANMAT) states that St. John's wort is an effective treatment for mild to moderate depression (Ravindran et al., 2016).

However, individuals should still consult with their doctor. St. John's wort may interact poorly with other medications, particularly other antidepressants (Borrelli & Izzo, 2009). Therefore, it is important for healthcare providers to know all of the substances that a patient is taking. It is also worth noting that although St. John's wort is as effective as many antidepressants, research has not thoroughly tested how it compares to psychological therapies such as cognitive–behavioural therapy.

MOOD STABILIZERS In contrast to antidepressants, which are primarily used to treat depression (unipolar disorder), **mood stabilizers** are *drugs used to prevent or reduce the severity of mood swings experienced by people with bipolar disorder*. **Lithium** was *one of the first mood stabilizers to be prescribed regularly in psychiatry, and from the 1950s to the 1980s was the standard drug treatment for depression and bipolar disorder*. Lithium, a salt compound, can be quite effective, but it can also be toxic to the kidneys and endocrine system. Today, doctors generally prefer to prescribe other drugs because they seem to be more effective and safer than lithium (Thase & Denko, 2008). For example, people with bipolar disorder now often take anticonvulsant medications such as valproate or anti-psychotic medications. Although these medicines can be effective in preventing manic episodes, they are also associated with side effects like weight gain, nausea, and fatigue, and in rare cases, very serious side effects occur including brain damage due to elevated levels of ammonia in the blood (Wadzinski et al., 2007).

ANTIANXIETY DRUGS Sometimes referred to as tranquilizers, **antianxiety drugs** *affect the activity of gamma-aminobutyric acid (GABA), an inhibitory neurotransmitter that reduces neural activity*. These drugs are prescribed to alleviate nervousness and tension, and to prevent and reduce panic attacks. Widely prescribed examples include Xanax (alprazolam), Valium (diazepam), and Ativan (lorazepam). These drugs appear to temporarily alter the structure of GABA receptors, allowing more GABA molecules to inhibit neural activity. The effects of antianxiety drugs are relatively short-lived. They take effect within minutes of ingestion and may last for only a few hours. Given that these drugs facilitate inhibition of the nervous system, it is not surprising that their side effects include drowsiness, tiredness, and impaired attention, especially when they are taken at high doses. More serious side effects include memory impairments, depression, and decreased sex drive. These drugs also have the potential to induce abuse and withdrawal symptoms.

ANTIPSYCHOTIC DRUGS **Antipsychotic drugs** *are generally used to treat symptoms of psychosis, including delusions, hallucinations, and severely disturbed or disorganized thought*. Antipsychotics are the common treatment for schizophrenia and are sometimes prescribed to people with severe mood disorders. There are several classes of antipsychotic drugs.

The first generation of antipsychotic medications (e.g., Thorazine, Halodol) was designed to block dopamine receptors, because symptoms of schizophrenia are related to dopamine activity in the frontal lobes and basal ganglia. However, these drugs had significant side effects, such as seizures, anxiety, nausea, and impotence. One of the more severe and often permanent side effects, **tardive dyskinesia**, is *a movement disorder involving involuntary movements and facial tics*.

Newer antipsychotic medications are referred to as **atypical antipsychotics** or second-generation antipsychotics. *These drugs are less likely to produce side effects including movement disorders (like tardive dyskinesia) that commonly occur with first-generation antipsychotics*. Different atypical antipsychotics vary in their exact effects, but generally speaking they seem to work by affecting dopamine and serotonin transmission. These medications work for approximately half of the people who take them, reducing the severity of symptoms but not necessarily eliminating them altogether (Leucht et al., 2009). Unfortunately, their effects tend to weaken over time, and also come with some risk. For example, Clozapine, a very effective antipsychotic drug, compromises the body's white blood cells. People who take Clozapine must have their blood regularly monitored or the consequences can be extremely severe, potentially even leading to death.

A major challenge for healthcare providers is ensuring that the drugs being provided to patients are safe. Unfortunately, there have been instances in which pharmaceutical companies make some questionable decisions. One of the bigger scandals in the pharmaceutical industry in recent years involved another of the atypical antipsychotic drugs, Zyprexa. Initially, Zyprexa was hailed as a major breakthrough for people with schizophrenia and enjoyed widespread distribution (eventually prescribed to more than 20 million people around the world). Then allegations emerged that Zyprexa caused drastic weight gain and was linked to the onset of diabetes, hyperglycemia, and pancreatitis. Although Eli Lilly officially denied that Zyprexa caused these consequences, as of 2007, the company had paid more than $1.2 billion to settle lawsuits brought against it by almost 30 000 people (Berenson, 2007).

Much of the testing of drugs, and their promotion and marketing to physicians, occurs behind a curtain of secrecy, making it difficult for the public to always know whether drugs are being used appropriately. Again, Zyprexa is a good example. In 2009, Eli Lilly pled guilty to charges involving the "off-label marketing" of Zyprexa (i.e., promoting its use for conditions it wasn't designed to treat). To understand just how much potential harm can occur due to such practices, first consider the possible side effects that were discussed above. Then consider some of the details of this case:

Although Zyprexa was approved in the U.S. by the Food and Drug Administration (FDA) as a treatment for schizophrenia and bipolar disorder, Eli Lilly admitted that they marketed the drug illegally, promoting it to doctors as a treatment for other conditions; this is known as "off-label marketing."

The U.S. Department of Justice concluded that Eli Lilly concentrated these illegal marketing efforts to encourage doctors to prescribe Zyprexa for elderly patients for several conditions, including dementia, Alzheimer's, agitation, aggression, hostility, depression, and generalized sleep disorder, all of which are common symptoms in elderly populations, and none of which were covered under FDA approval. Zyprexa also carries the common side effect of sedation, which was promoted as a therapeutic benefit for the elderly that could help to deal with any "behavioural issues." In fact, using Zyprexa essentially as a sleep aid was captured by the company's sales slogan, "5 at 5," which symbolized how 5 milligrams of Zyprexa given at 5 p.m. would help put elderly patients to sleep for the night. Then Eli Lilly expanded its marketing efforts to recommend that doctors prescribe Zyprexa to adults across the age spectrum for a wide variety of disorders. The company was fined a total of $1.4 billion. It is worth putting this in perspective though: in only one year (2010), Eli Lilly made more than $5 billion from Zyprexa (Stastna, 2013).

EVALUATING DRUG THERAPIES Many people believe that drugs are designed to target the root physical causes of psychological disorders, and that they should therefore be more effective than psychological approaches to therapy. However, these beliefs are not warranted.

In many cases, drugs are not more effective than psychological therapies. For example, with regard to depression, the use of antidepressants has become increasingly accepted among the general public, in part due to well-funded marketing campaigns. However, these drugs are not as effective as they are widely believed to be. Approximately 50% to 60% of people who take antidepressants improve within a few months—compared to 30% of people who improve after taking a placebo (Hollon et al., 2002). Interestingly, about 50% to 60% of people also improve from psychological therapy. Thus, we cannot conclude that drugs are more effective or should replace other approaches to therapy.

In other cases, such as most anxiety disorders, psychological treatments such as cognitive–behavioural therapy (Module 16.2) are generally the most effective treatment (Hofmann & Smits, 2008). A key advantage of CBT is that the effects last long after the treatment is completed (Hollon et al., 2006), whereas antianxiety medications typically are effective only as long as the client maintains the drug regimen (and of course, come with side effects). The superior long-term effect of CBT over drugs has been found for generalized anxiety disorder (Hofmann & Smits, 2008) and panic disorder (Barlow et al., 2000).

In many situations, a combination of treatment approaches may work best; for example, combining psychological therapy with antidepressants has been shown to be more effective in treating major depression than medication alone (Burnand et al., 2002; de Jonghe et al., 2001). A similar pattern is found for some anxiety disorders; combining drugs with CBT is more effective for panic disorder with agoraphobia than either treatment on its own (Starcevic et al., 2004).

Even schizophrenia, which is often viewed to be an organic "brain disease," is more effectively treated by combined approaches. People with schizophrenia tend to have difficulty in self-reflecting, projecting themselves into the past and future (D'Argembeau et al., 2008), engaging in basic self-care, and integrating into regular social life. Although drugs may reduce many symptoms, additional therapy using psychological approaches has been shown to have a huge impact on reducing the likelihood of experiencing further schizophrenic episodes. Some research has shown that the likelihood of experiencing future schizophrenic episodes is affected even more strongly by social factors, such as how much negative emotion and hostility are expressed in the family, than even by whether the person with schizophrenia takes their medication (Hooley & Gotlib, 2000). Clearly, even disorders that are generally viewed as predominantly biological are better understood from a biopsychosocial perspective, because they involve not only straightforward biological mechanisms, but also thoughts, feelings, behaviours, and social relationships.

Module 16.3a Quiz:

Drug Treatments

Know . . .

1. Tardive dyskinesia is
  A. a side effect of antipsychotics that involves motion control problems.
  B. an antidepressant that breaks down enzymes in the synapse.
  C. the growth of new neurons in the adult brain.
  D. a side effect of antidepressant drugs.

Understand . . .

2. _____ affect the nervous system by blocking reuptake of serotonin in neurons.
  A. MAOIs
  B. Antianxiety medications
  C. Mood stabilizers
  D. SSRIs

3. Monoamine oxidase inhibitor drugs work by
   A. boosting the ability of an enzyme to break down serotonin, dopamine, and norepinephrine molecules.
   B. inhibiting the ability of an enzyme to break down serotonin, dopamine, and norepinephrine molecules.
   C. selectively blocking the reuptake of serotonin.
   D. creating new dopamine molecules.

Analyze . . .

4. Generally speaking, which of the following is the most accurate statement about psychotropic drugs?
   A. They are superior to talking therapy.
   B. Their effects are rarely evident until weeks after taking them.
   C. They are usually more effective if combined with some form of psychological treatment.
   D. Although drugs often had bad side effects in the past, modern drugs have largely fixed those problems.

5. Imagine that a friend asks you what you have heard about St. John's wort because he is considering using it to alleviate his depression. What would you say, based on the research?
   A. St. John's wort is as effective as antidepressant drugs for treating depressive symptoms for many people.
   B. St. John's wort is superior to prescription antidepressant medications.
   C. Your friend may as well take a placebo: St. John's wort has never been proven effective at reducing symptoms of depression.
   D. St. John's wort is superior to cognitive–behavioural therapies.

Technological and Surgical Methods

People working in the mental health field have a variety of biomedical approaches available in addition to drugs, ranging from direct surgical interventions to stimulation of brain areas using magnetic pulses. Today, these types of procedures tend to be quite safe and are carefully tested and scrutinized, although this has not always been the case.

You have likely heard of the **frontal lobotomy**, *surgically severing the connections between different regions of the brain;* however you may not know the full, rather chilling, story behind it. Back as far as the 1800s, neurologists experimented with this practice in the hope of "curing" psychological problems. By the 1930s, researchers discovered that by damaging the prefrontal areas of aggressive chimpanzees, the animals would become calmer and more controllable. When Portuguese surgeon Antonio Moniz heard about this at a conference, he thought it might be useful for helping people with severe psychoses and other disorders. He helped to develop the **leucotomy**, *the surgical destruction of brain tissues in the prefrontal cortex.* Drilling small holes into the skull, Moniz would typically insert a small wire loop, a leucotome, through the holes and into the brain matter; a few flips of the wrist later, the surgery is complete and the patient is left to "recover."

Moniz himself had some success with the procedure, reporting a general improvement in the symptoms of several severely depressed, anxious, or otherwise disturbed people, and recommended it as a treatment of last resort when all other methods have failed. But then the technique was popularized and turned into a veritable industry by an enterprising American surgeon, Dr. Walter Freeman. Freeman and his collaborator, Dr. James Watts, further refined the "lobotomy" (as he called the procedure) for about a decade, until he learned of a new method, developed in Italy, for getting into the brain without having to drill holes in the skull. The secret entrance was right through the eye sockets.

Based on this insight, Freeman developed the transorbital lobotomy, which became known as the "icepick lobotomy." Freeman would insert a slender metal shaft, like an icepick, in between the eyeball and eyelid, then with a hammer, would tap it through the bony roof of the eye socket and into the brain. Then he would move it around until the frontal lobes were detached from the rest of the brain (Valenstein, 1973). He was even able to perform this brain-slicing without anesthesia, by first inducing a seizure in the patient through an electroconvulsive shock. Freeman believed the procedure to be miraculously successful. He became a passionate advocate for the lobotomy, and because he was able to perform them so quickly, often more than a dozen in a single day, he travelled around the country in his van, the "lobotomobile," lobotomizing several thousand people in total. His procedure was always controversial, seen as a miraculous cure by some and as a barbaric practice by others, committing unknown amounts of harm and sometimes even ending in the patient's death from cerebral hemorrhaging. Nevertheless, Freeman was a

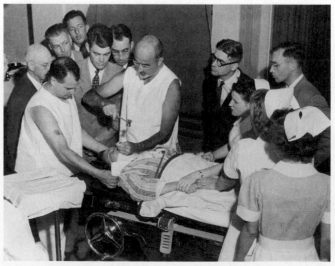

Walter Freeman performing a frontal lobotomy surgery.

Bettmann/Getty Images

medical celebrity for a while, and toured the country teaching his technique to many doctors and psychiatrists. In total, approximately 40 000 lobotomies are believed to have been performed in the United States and thousands more in western Europe. Freeman was eventually barred from practising, although not until 1967. And despite the protestations of many people, the man who started it all, Antonio Moniz, was awarded the Nobel Prize in Medicine in 1949.

By the 1950s, the popularity of the frontal lobotomy was dwindling rapidly. The inconsistent and often very negative results of the procedure, and the effectiveness of new psychotropic medications, convinced most of the field to move away from the lobotomy. Nevertheless, the basic practice of therapeutically destroying brain tissue survives to this day, although the techniques are now vastly more refined and precise.

FOCAL LESIONS One set of techniques involves performing **focal lesions**, *which are small areas of brain tissue that are surgically destroyed.* These brain lesions are only used in some severe cases, when all other treatments have not worked to satisfaction. For example, in some cases of depression and anxiety disorders, lesion surgery has been targeted at a cluster of cells in the anterior cingulate cortex, an area that is overactive in people with these disorders (Cosgrove & Rauch, 2003; Fitzgerald et al., 2005; Steele et al., 2008). This procedure, which is called an anterior cingulotomy, has no more risks or side effects than do many of the drugs used to treat these disorders, and it can reduce symptoms successfully despite other treatments being ineffective. Focal-lesion techniques have only become possible in recent years due to the surgical precision allowed by the use of brain-imaging technology, which allows surgeons to precisely target desired brain areas.

ELECTROCONVULSIVE THERAPY Electroconvulsive therapy (ECT) *involves passing an electrical current through the brain in order to induce a temporary seizure.* This procedure was introduced in the 1930s and has been viewed negatively for much of its history, in part because in its early days it was generally unsafe and easily abused. This procedure was famously, and chillingly, depicted in the book and movie *One Flew Over the Cuckoo's Nest*. Many people believe that ECT causes lasting cognitive impairments, but in fact the majority of research on people who have been treated with it suggests that this is not true (Rose et al., 2003).

Over the years, ECT techniques have improved dramatically. Patients' experiences are much less negative; they are now given sedatives and muscle relaxants to reduce the discomfort they may experience and to prevent injury related to the convulsions. ECT has gone from being viewed as a torturous "shock treatment" to a relatively safe procedure, although it is still reserved for the most severe cases of disorders such as depression and bipolar

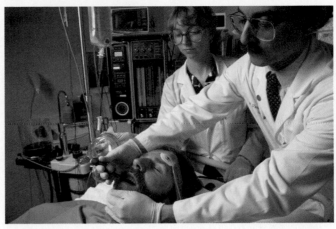

People with depression or bipolar disorder may elect to undergo electroconvulsive therapy if other treatments have not been successful.

disorder. The side effects are relatively mild, typically consisting of some amnesia for events occurring around the time of the treatment.

Why does ECT work? Neuroimaging research suggests that ECT might alter how different brain areas work together as networks. These changes are most pronounced in the frontal lobes (Beall et al., 2012; Perrin et al., 2012), particularly in areas along the midline of the brain (Argyelan et al., 2016). One possible interpretation of this emerging literature is that ECT may alter the patient's tendency to habitually engage in negative thoughts, thereby disrupting the dysfunctional thinking patterns that are characteristic of depression. More research is needed before we will fully understand why ECT works as mysteriously well as it does.

REPETITIVE TRANSCRANIAL MAGNETIC STIMULATION Repetitive transcranial magnetic stimulation (rTMS) is *a therapeutic technique in which a focal area of the brain is exposed to a powerful magnetic field across several different treatment sessions.* The magnetic field can be used to stimulate or inhibit the activity of particular brain areas. Researchers have found that stimulating the left prefrontal cortex, which is typically associated with positive emotional experiences, improves some symptoms of depression. They have also found that reducing the activity of the right prefrontal cortex, which is associated with negative emotional experiences, has the same effect (Berlim et al., 2014). Importantly, rTMS does not have immediate effects. Treatment typically involves between 10 and 25 rTMS sessions, although some accelerated programs are being tested (George et al., 2014). Patients must also return for follow-up appointments every few months.

rTMS has a number of advantages over other treatments. It does not involve anesthesia, induce a seizure, or produce cognitive impairments (Serafini et al., 2015). Additionally, rTMS may hold considerable promise for reducing symptoms of other mental disorders, such as schizophrenia (Slotema et al., 2010; Zaman et al., 2008).

DEEP BRAIN STIMULATION **Deep brain stimulation (DBS)** is *a technique that involves electrically stimulating specific regions of the brain.* The procedure involves inserting thin electrode-tipped wires into the brain and carefully routing them to the targeted brain regions. A small battery connected to the wires is then inserted just beneath the skin surface. Unlike many of the drugs reviewed previously, DBS produces instantaneous results, and seems to work on even severe cases of depression that have been unresponsive to other treatments. As reported by researchers at the Rotman Research Institute in Toronto, who pioneered the application of DBS on depression, the effects seem almost miraculous; patients who are severely depressed report relief from their symptoms instantaneously, as soon as the electricity is applied (Mayberg et al., 2005; McNeely et al., 2008). Other researchers have shown DBS to be effective on symptoms of OCD as well (Aouizerate et al., 2009).

Nevertheless, the technique does come with some risk, most obviously the risk of some internal bleeding and infection from the surgical insertion of the wires. DPS can also cause unintended behavioural effects; most are relatively benign and temporary experiences, such as spontaneous laughter and penile erections, but in some cases it may trigger troublesome states of depression or aggression (Kringelbach et al., 2007).

It is important to note that there are additional therapeutic techniques that are still in development and therefore have not been discussed in this module. Advances in gene therapies, neuroimaging, neurostimulators, and computer science will soon influence how many psychological disorders are treated. These innovations should provide patients with a number of high-quality treatment options. The future of psychology should be exciting.

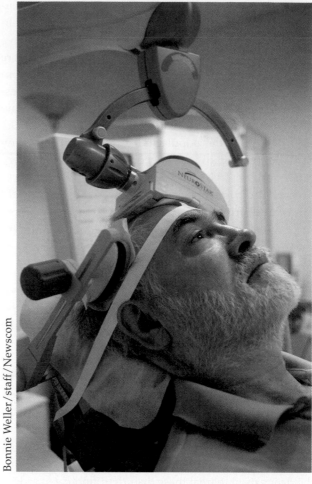

Bonnie Weller/staff/Newscom

Delivering brief pulses of a strong magnetic field to specific regions of the cerebral cortex has been shown to help alleviate symptoms of severe depression and possibly other disorders.

Module 16.3b Quiz:

Technological and Surgical Methods

Understand . . .

1. If a doctor wanted to activate a very specific brain region in the hope of alleviating symptoms of a mental disorder, she would most likely use which of the following procedures?

   A. Focal lesion

   B. Cingulotomy

   C. Electroconvulsive therapy

   D. Deep brain stimulation

2. Which of the following techniques results in intentionally destroying brain cells?

   A. Deep brain stimulation

   B. Electroconvulsive therapy

   C. Focal lesion

   D. Repetitive transcranial magnetic stimulation

Apply . . .

3. Amy has been suffering from depression for many years. She has tried a number of antidepressant medications but suffered so many side effects that her doctor suggested that she stop taking them. Instead, her doctor has recommended that Amy try a new procedure in which a device emitting a magnetic field is placed against Amy's scalp. This device would affect the activity of Amy's frontal lobes. Which technique is Amy's doctor recommending?

   A. Deep brain stimulation

   B. Repetitive transcranial magnetic stimulation

   C. Electroconvulsive therapy

   D. Magnetic resonance imaging

Module 16.3 Summary

16.3a   Know . . . the key terminology associated with biological treatments.

antianxiety drugs
antidepressant drugs
antipsychotic drugs
atypical antipsychotics
blood–brain barrier
deep brain stimulation (DBS)
electroconvulsive therapy (ECT)
focal lesions
frontal lobotomy
leucotomy
lithium
monoamine oxidase inhibitors (MAOIs)
mood stabilizers
psychopharmacotherapy
psychotropic drugs
repetitive transcranial magnetic stimulation (rTMS)
selective serotonin reuptake inhibitor (SSRI)
tardive dyskinesia
tricyclic antidepressants

16.3b   Understand . . . how the drugs described in this module affect brain functioning.

Antidepressant drugs typically target monoamine neurotransmitter activity, with differing mechanisms of action (review Figure 16.4). Many of the antipsychotic drugs on the market reduce dopamine activity in the brain. Antianxiety drugs tend to target GABA receptors and increase activity of this inhibitory neurotransmitter.

16.3c   Understand . . . the other major medical approaches to therapy.

Other procedures available for treating mental illness include electroconvulsive therapy, repetitive transcranial magnetic stimulation, deep brain stimulation, and focal lesions. In some cases, particularly ECT, researchers are still unsure what aspect of the treatment produces the therapeutic results. Stimulation techniques increase the brain activity in targeted areas, whereas lesions prevent brain activity. By targeting the areas responsible for specific behaviours, thoughts, or emotions, treatments can have dramatic effects on the experience of someone with a psychological disorder.

16.3d   Apply . . . your knowledge of drug therapies to different psychological conditions.

Apply Activity

Match the drugs listed in the left column with the condition they are typically prescribed to treat on the right.

Drug	Condition
1. Lithium	a. Anxiety
2. SSRI	b. Depression
3. Xanax	c. Schizophrenia
4. Clozapine	d. Bipolar disorder

16.3e   Analyze . . . whether St. John's wort, a popular herbal remedy for depression, works.

Research into the effects of St. John's wort suggests it may be an effective treatment for many people. The herb works about as well as prescription antidepressants for at least mild to moderate levels of depression, but its efficacy for severe depression is not well established. Using St. John's wort carries the significant advantage of not exposing the person to nearly the same range of potential side effects as prescription drugs, although it is also advisable to consult with a mental health professional rather than self-medicating without any professional support.

Glossary

absolute threshold   the minimum amount of energy or quantity of a stimulus required for it to be reliably detected at least 50% of the time it is presented

accommodation   a creative process whereby people modify their belief structures based on experience

acetylcholine   one of the most widespread neurotransmitters within the body, found at the junctions between nerve cells and skeletal muscles; it is very important for voluntary movement

achievement motivation   the drive to perform at high levels and to accomplish significant goals

acquisition   the initial phase of learning in which a response is established

acronyms   pronounceable words whose letters represent the initials of an important phrase or set of items

action potential   a wave of electrical activity that originates at the beginning of the axon near the cell body and rapidly travels down its length

activation–synthesis hypothesis   suggests that dreams arise from brain activity originating from bursts of excitatory messages from the pons, a part of the brainstem

active phase   phase of schizophrenia during which people typically experience delusional thoughts, hallucinations, or disorganized patterns of thoughts, emotions, and behaviour

adrenal glands   a pair of endocrine glands located adjacent to the kidneys that release stress hormones, such as cortisol and epinephrine

affiliation motivation   see *need to belong*

agonists   drugs that enhance or mimic the effects of a neurotransmitter's action

agoraphobia   often associated with panic disorder, agoraphobia results from an intense fear of having a panic attack in public; as a result of this fear, the individual may begin to avoid public settings and increasingly isolate him- or herself

algorithms   problem-solving strategies based on a series of rules

all-or-none principle   individual nerve cells fire at the same strength every time an action potential occurs

allostasis   motivation is not only influenced by current needs, but also by the anticipation of future needs

Alzheimer's disease   a degenerative and terminal condition resulting in severe damage of the entire brain

amnesia   a profound loss of at least one form of memory

amotivational   a feeling of having little or no motivation to perform a behaviour

amygdala   a group of nuclei in the medial portion (near the middle) of the temporal lobes in each hemisphere of the brain that facilitates memory formation for emotional events, mediates fear responses, and appears to play a role in recognizing and interpreting emotional stimuli, including facial expressions

analytic system   operates at the explicit level of consciousness, is slower and methodical, and uses logic and discursive thinking (i.e., reasoning using language)

analytical psychology   focuses on the role of unconscious archetypes in personality development

anchoring effect   occurs when an individual attempts to solve a problem involving numbers and uses previous knowledge to keep (i.e., anchor) the response within a limited range

anecdotal evidence   an individual's story or testimony about an observation or event that is used to make a claim as evidence

anorexia nervosa   an eating disorder that involves (1) self-starvation, (2) intense fear of weight gain and dissatisfaction with one's body, and (3) denial of the serious consequences of severely low weight

antagonists   inhibit neurotransmitter activity by blocking receptors or preventing synthesis of a neurotransmitter

anterograde amnesia   the inability to form new memories for events occurring after a brain injury

anthropometrics   (literally, "the measurement of people") methods of measuring physical and mental variation in humans

antianxiety drugs   affect the activity of gamma-aminobutyric acid (GABA), an inhibitory neurotransmitter that reduces neural activity

antidepressant drugs   medications designed to reduce symptoms of depression

antipsychotic drugs   generally used to treat symptoms of psychosis, including delusions, hallucinations, and severely disturbed or disorganized thought

antisocial personality disorder (APD)   a profound lack of empathy or emotional connection with others, a disregard for others' rights or preferences, and a tendency toward imposing one's own desires, often violently, onto others regardless of the consequences for other people or, often when younger, other animals

anxiety disorders   a category of disorders involving fear or nervousness that is excessive, irrational, and maladaptive

APD   see *antisocial personality disorder*

aphasia   a language disorder caused by damage to the brain structures that support using and understanding language

appeal to authority   the belief in an "expert's" claim even when no supporting data or scientific evidence is present

appeal to common sense   a claim that appears to be sound, but lacks supporting scientific evidence

appraisal   the cognitive act of assessing and evaluating the potential threat and demands of an event

approach goal   an enjoyable and pleasant incentive that a person is drawn toward, such as praise, financial reward, or a feeling of satisfaction

ARAS   see *ascending reticular activating system*

archetypes   images and symbols that reflect common "truths" held across cultures, such as universal life experiences or types of people

arousal theory of extraversion   extraversion is determined by people's threshold for arousal

ascending reticular activating system (ARAS)   plays a central role in controlling the arousal response

assimilation   a conservative process, whereby people fit new information into the belief systems they already possess

asylums   residential facilities for the mentally ill

attachment   the enduring emotional bond formed between individuals

attachment behavioural system focused on meeting our own needs for security

attention selects which information will be passed on to STM

attitude inoculation a strategy for strengthening attitudes and making them more resistant to change by first exposing people to a weak counter-argument and then refuting that argument

atypical antipsychotics drugs that are less likely to produce side effects including movement disorders (like tardive dyskinesia) that commonly occur with first-generation antipsychotics

autonomic nervous system the portion of the peripheral nervous system responsible for regulating the activity of organs and glands

autonomous sensory meridian response (ASMR) a condition in which specific auditory or visual stimuli trigger tingling sensations in the scalp and neck, sometimes extending across the back and shoulders

availability heuristic entails estimating the frequency of an event based on how easily examples of it come to mind

aversive conditioning a behavioural technique that involves replacing a positive response to a stimulus with a negative response, typically by using punishment

avoidance goal an attempt to avoid an unpleasant outcome such as shame, embarrassment, losing money, or feeling emotional pain

avoidance learning a specific type of negative reinforcement that removes the possibility that a stimulus will occur

axon transports information in the form of electrochemical reactions from the cell body to the end of the neuron

BAS see *behavioural activation system*

basal ganglia a group of three structures that are involved in facilitating planned movements, skill learning, and integrating sensory and movement information with the brain's reward system

BDNF see *brain-derived neurotrophic factor*

behavioural activation system (BAS) a "GO" system, arousing the person to action in the pursuit of desired goals

behavioural genetics the study of how genes and the environment influence behaviour

behavioural genomics the study of how specific genes, in their interactions with the environment, influence behaviour

behavioural inhibition system (BIS) a "danger" system, motivating the person to action in order to avoid punishments or other negative outcomes

behavioural therapies therapies that attempt to directly address problem behaviours and the environmental factors that trigger them

behaviourism an approach that dominated the first half of the 20th century of North American psychology and had a singular focus on studying only observable behaviour, with little to no reference to mental events or instincts as possible influences on behaviour

belief perseverance occurs when an individual believes he or she has the solution to the problem or the correct answer for a question and accepts only evidence that will confirm those beliefs

between-subjects design an experimental design in which we compare the performance of participants who are in different groups

bibliotherapy the use of self-help books and other reading materials as a form of therapy

binocular depth cues distance cues that are based on the differing perspectives of both eyes

biofeedback a therapeutic technique involving the use of physiological recording instruments to provide feedback that increases awareness of bodily responses

biopsychosocial model a means of explaining behaviour as a product of biological, psychological, and sociocultural factors

bipolar disorder characterized by extreme highs and lows in mood, motivation, and energy

BIS see *behavioural inhibition system*

blood–brain barrier a network of tightly packed cells that only allow specific types of substances to move from the bloodstream to the brain in order to protect delicate brain cells against harmful infections and other substances

BMI see *body mass index*

body mass index (BMI) a statistic commonly used for estimating a healthy body weight given an individual's height

borderline personality disorder (BPD) a disorder characterized by intense extremes between positive and negative emotions, an unstable sense of self, impulsivity, and difficult social relationships

bottom-up processing occurs when we perceive individual bits of sensory information (e.g., sounds) and use them to construct a more complex perception (e.g., a message)

BPD see *borderline personality disorder*

brain death a condition in which the brain, specifically including the brainstem, no longer functions

brainstem the "stem" or bottom of the brain and consists of two structures: the medulla and the pons

brain-derived neurotrophic factor (BDNF) a protein in the nervous system that promotes survival, growth, and formation of new synapses

Broca's area a region of the left frontal lobe that controls our ability to articulate speech sounds that compose words

bulimia nervosa an eating disorder that is characterized by periods of food deprivation, binge-eating, and purging

bystander effect the presence of other people actually reduces the likelihood of helping behaviour

Cannon-Bard theory of emotion the brain interprets a situation and generates subjective emotional feelings, and these representations in the brain trigger responses in the body

caregiving behavioural system focused on meeting the needs of others

case study an in-depth report about the details of a specific case

catatonic schizophrenia symptoms include episodes in which a person remains mute and immobile—sometimes in bizarre positions—for extended periods. Individuals may also exhibit repetitive, purposeless movements

categories clusters of interrelated concepts

CBT see *cognitive–behavioural therapy*

cell body the part of a neuron that contains the nucleus that houses the cell's genetic material

central executive the control centre of working memory; it coordinates attention and the exchange of information among the three storage components

central nervous system (CNS) consists of the brain and the spinal cord

central route to persuasion occurs when people pay close attention to the content of a message, evaluate the evidence presented, and examine the logic of the arguments

central tendency a measure of the central point of a distribution

cerebellum (Latin for "little brain") the lobe-like structure at the base of the brain that is involved in the monitoring of movement, maintaining balance, attention, and emotional responses

cerebral cortex   the convoluted, wrinkled outer layer of the brain that is involved in multiple higher functions, such as thought, language, and personality

chameleon effect   people copy others' behaviours even without realizing it

chromosomes   structures in the cellular nucleus that are lined with all of the genes an individual inherits

chunking   organizing smaller units of information into larger, more meaningful units

circadian rhythms   internally driven daily cycles of approximately 24 hours affecting physiological and behavioural processes

classical categorization   a theory that claims that objects or events are categorized according to a certain set of rules or by a specific set of features

classical conditioning   a form of associative learning in which an organism learns to associate a neutral stimulus (e.g., a sound) with a biologically relevant stimulus (e.g., food), which results in a change in the response to the previously neutral stimulus (e.g., salivation)

client-centred therapy   focuses on individuals' abilities to solve their own problems and reach their full potential with the encouragement of the therapist

clinical psychologists   have obtained PhDs and are able to formally diagnose and treat mental health issues ranging from the everyday and mild to the chronic and severe

clinical psychology   the field of psychology that concentrates on the diagnosis and treatment of psychological disorders

cochlea   a fluid-filled membrane that is coiled in a snail-like shape and contains the structures that convert sound into neural impulses

cognitive–behavioural therapy (CBT)   a form of therapy that consists of procedures such as cognitive restructuring, stress inoculation training, and exposing people to experiences they may have a tendency to avoid

cognitive development   the study of changes in memory, thought, and reasoning processes that occur throughout the lifespan

cognitive dissonance theory   when we hold inconsistent beliefs, it creates a kind of aversive inner tension, or "dissonance"; we are then motivated to reduce this tension in whatever way we can

cognitive psychology   a modern psychological perspective that focuses on processes such as memory, thinking, and language

cohort effect   differences between people that result from being born in different time periods

collective unconscious   a separate, non-personal realm of the unconscious that holds the collective memories and mythologies of humankind, stretching deep into our ancestral past

coma   a state marked by a complete loss of consciousness

community psychology   an area of psychology that focuses on identifying how individuals' mental health is influenced by the community in which they live, and emphasizes community-level variables such as social programs, support networks, and community resource centres to help those with mental illness adjust to the challenges of everyday life

companionate love   related to tenderness, and to the affection we feel when our lives are intertwined with another person

compensatory control   psychological strategies people use to preserve a sense of nonrandom order when personal control is compromised

computerized tomography (or CT scans)   a structural neuroimaging technique in which x-rays are sent through the brain by a tube that rotates around the head

concept   the mental representation of an object, event, or idea

concrete operational stage   (ages 7 to 11 years) developmental stage at which children develop skills in logical thinking and manipulating numbers

conditioned emotional responses   consist of emotional and physiological responses that develop to a specific object or situation

conditioned response (CR)   the learned response that occurs to the conditioned stimulus

conditioned stimulus (CS)   a once-neutral stimulus that later elicits a conditioned response because it has a history of being paired with an unconditioned stimulus

conditioned taste aversion   acquired dislike or disgust for a food or drink because it was paired with illness

cones   photoreceptors that are sensitive to the different wavelengths of light that we perceive as colour

confirmation bias   occurs when an individual searches for only evidence that will confirm his or her beliefs instead of evidence that might disconfirm them

confounding variable   a variable outside of the researcher's control that might affect or provide an alternative explanation for the results

conjunction fallacy   reflects the mistaken belief that finding a specific member in two overlapping categories (i.e., a member of the *conjunction* of two categories) is more likely than finding any member of one of the larger, general categories

conscious mind   your current awareness, containing everything you are aware of right now

consciousness   a person's subjective awareness, including thoughts, perceptions, experiences of the world, and self-awareness

conservation   the knowledge that the quantity or amount of an object is not the same as the physical arrangement and appearance of that object

consolidation   the process of converting short-term memories into long-term memories in the brain

construal-level theory   describes how information affects us differently depending on our psychological distance from the information

constructive memory   a process by which we first recall a generalized schema and then add in specific details

contact hypothesis   social contact between members of different groups is extremely important to overcoming prejudice

context-dependent memory   the idea that retrieval is more effective when it takes place in the same physical setting (context) as encoding

continuous reinforcement   every response made results in reinforcement

control group   the group that does not receive the treatment or stimuli targeting a specific behaviour; this group therefore serves as a baseline to which the experimental group is compared

control processes   shift information from one memory store to another

convenience samples   samples of individuals who are the most readily available

conventional morality   regards social conventions and rules as guides for appropriate moral behaviour

convergence   occurs when the eye muscles contract so that both eyes focus on a single object

coping   the processes used to manage demands, stress, and conflict

core knowledge hypothesis   the theory that infants have inborn abilities for understanding some key aspects of their environment

cornea   the clear layer that covers the front portion of the eye and also contributes to the eye's ability to focus

coronary heart disease   a condition in which plaques form in the blood vessels that supply the heart with blood and oxygen, resulting in restricted blood flow

corpus callosum   a collection of neural fibres connecting the two brain hemispheres

correlational research   involves measuring the degree of association between two or more variables

cortisol   a hormone secreted by the adrenal cortex (the outer part of the adrenal gland) that prepares the body to respond to stressful circumstances

counselling psychologists   mental health professionals who typically work with people who need help with more common problems such as stress and coping; issues concerning identity, sexuality, and relationships; anxiety and depression; and developmental issues such as childhood trauma

CR   see *conditioned response*

critical thinking   involves exercising curiosity and skepticism when evaluating the claims of others, and with our own assumptions and beliefs

cross-fostered   being raised as a member of a family that was not of the same species

cross-sectional design   used to measure and compare samples of people at different ages at a given point in time

crystallized intelligence (Gc)   a type of intelligence that draws upon past learning and experience

CS   see *conditioned stimulus*

CT scan   see *computerized tomography*

dark adaptation   the process by which the rods and cones become increasingly sensitive to light under low levels of illumination

Dark Triad   three traits—Machiavellianism, Psychopathy, and Narcissism—that describe a person who is socially destructive, aggressive, dishonest, and likely to commit harm in general

DBS   see *deep brain stimulation*

debriefing   when researchers explain the true nature of the study, and especially the nature of and reason for any deception

decentring   occurs when a person is able to "step back" from their normal consciousness and examine themselves more objectively, as an observer

deception   misleading or only partially informing participants of the true topic or hypothesis under investigation

declarative (explicit) memories   memories that we are consciously aware of and that can be verbalized, including facts about the world and one's own personal experiences

deep brain stimulation (DBS)   a technique that involves electrically stimulating specific regions of the brain

deep processing   memory processing related to an item's meaning or its function

default mode network   a network of brain regions including the medial prefrontal cortex, posterior cingulate gyrus, and medial and lateral regions of the parietal lobe that is most active when an individual is awake but *not* responding to external stimuli

defence mechanisms   unconscious strategies the ego uses to reduce or avoid anxiety

deinstitutionalization   the movement of large numbers of psychiatric in-patients from their care facilities back into regular society

delaying gratification   putting off immediate temptations in order to focus on longer-term goals

delusions   beliefs that are not based on reality (at least from the perspective of the person's general culture)

demand characteristics   inadvertent cues given off by the experimenter or the experimental context that provide information about how participants are expected to behave

dementia   mild to severe disruption of mental functioning, memory loss, disorientation, poor judgment, and decision making

dendrites   small branches radiating from the cell body that receive messages from other cells and transmit those messages toward the rest of the cell

dependent variable   the observation or measurement that is recorded during the experiment and subsequently compared across all groups

descriptive statistics   a set of techniques used to organize, summarize, and interpret data

determinism   the belief that all events are governed by lawful, cause-and-effect relationships

developmental psychology   the study of human physical, cognitive, social, and behavioural characteristics across the lifespan

deviation IQ   calculated by comparing a person's test score with the average score for people of the same age

Diagnostic and Statistical Manual of Mental Disorders (DSM)   a standardized manual to aid in the diagnosis of disorders

diasthesis–stress model   the interaction between a genetic predisposition for a disorder and life stress

DID   see *dissociative identity disorder*

difference threshold   the smallest difference between stimuli that can be reliably detected at least 50% of the time

diffusion of responsibility   the responsibility for taking action is spread across more than one person, thus making no single individual feel personally responsible

diffusion tensor imaging (or DTI)   a form of structural neuroimaging allowing researchers or medical personnel to measure white-matter pathways in the brain

discrimination   (1) occurs when an operant response is made to one stimulus but not to another, even if the stimuli are similar; (2) behaviour that disfavours or disadvantages members of a certain social group in some way

discriminative stimulus   a cue or event that indicates that a response, if made, will be reinforced

dishabituation   the recovery of responsiveness to a habituated stimulus as the result of the presentation of a new stimulus

disorganized behaviour   the considerable difficulty people with schizophrenia may have completing the tasks of everyday life

disorganized schizophrenia   symptoms include thoughts, speech, behaviour, and emotions that are poorly integrated and incoherent; people with disorganized schizophrenia may also show inappropriate, unpredictable mannerisms

display rules   the unwritten expectations we have regarding when it is appropriate to show a certain emotion

dispositional attribution   see *internal attribution*

dissociation theory   explains hypnosis as a unique state in which consciousness is divided into two parts: a lower-level system involved with perception and movement and an "executive" system that evaluates and monitors these behaviours

dissociative disorder   a category of mental disorders characterized by a split between conscious awareness from feeling, cognition, memory, and identity

dissociative identity disorder (DID)   a person experiences a split in identity such that they feel different aspects of themselves as though they were separated from each other; this can be severe enough that the person constructs entirely separate personalities, only one of which will generally be in control at a time

divided attention paying attention to more than one stimulus or task at the same time

dizygotic twins fraternal twins who come from two separate eggs fertilized by two different sperm cells that share the same womb; these twins have approximately 50% of their genetics in common

DNA (deoxyribonucleic acid) a molecule formed in a double-helix shape that contains four amino acids: adenine, cytosine, guanine, and thymine

doctrine of specific nerve energies first proposed in 1826 by the German physiologist Johannes Muller, the doctrine states that the different senses are separated in the brain

door-in-the-face technique involves asking for something relatively big, then following with a request for something relatively small

dopamine a monoamine neurotransmitter involved in such varied functions as mood, control of voluntary movement, and processing of rewarding experiences

double-blind study a study in which neither the participant nor the experimenter knows the exact treatment for any individual

dream analysis a method of examining the details of a dream (the manifest content), in order to gain insight into the true meaning of the dream, the emotional, unconscious material that is being communicated symbolically (the latent content)

drive a biological trigger that tells us we may be deprived of something and causes us to seek out what is needed, such as food or water

DRM procedure participants study a list of highly related words called semantic associates

DSM see *Diagnostic and Statistical Manual of Mental Disorders*

DTI see *diffusion tensor imaging*

dual coding occurs when information is stored in more than one form

dual-process models models of behaviour that account for both implicit and explicit processes

dualism the belief that there are properties of humans that are not material (a mind or soul separate from the body)

echoic memory the auditory form of sensory memory

ecological validity the results of a laboratory study can be applied to or repeated in the natural environment

ecstasy (MDMA) a drug that is typically classified as a stimulant, but also has hallucinogenic effects

ECT see *electroconvulsive therapy*

EEG see *electroencephalogram*

ego the decision maker, frequently under tension, trying to reconcile the opposing urges of the id and superego

egocentric seeing the world only from one's own perspective

elaboration likelihood model (ELM) a model of persuasion that states when audiences are sufficiently motivated to pay attention to a message (i.e., they care about the issue) and they have the opportunity for careful processing (i.e., they have the cognitive resources available to understand the message), they will be persuaded by the facts of the argument, the substance; when either of these two factors (motivation and opportunity) is missing, people will tend to be persuaded by other factors

elaborative rehearsal prolonging exposure to information by thinking about its meaning

electroconvulsive therapy (ECT) involves passing an electrical current through the brain in order to induce a temporary seizure

electroencephalogram (or EEG) measures patterns of brain activity with the use of multiple electrodes attached to the scalp

embryonic stage spans weeks two through eight of the gestational period, during which time the embryo begins developing major physical structures such as the heart and nervous system, as well as the beginnings of arms, legs, hands, and feet

emotion a behaviour with the following three components: (a) a subjective thought and/or experience with (b) accompanying patterns of neural activity and physical arousal and (c) an observable behavioural expression (e.g., an emotional facial expression or changes in muscle tension)

emotional dialects variations across cultures in how common emotions are expressed

empirically supported treatments treatments that have been tested and evaluated

empiricism a philosophical tenet that knowledge comes through experience

encoding specificity principle retrieval is most effective when it occurs in the same context as encoding

encoding the process of storing information in the LTM system

endogenous rhythms biological rhythms that are generated by our body independent of external cues such as light

endorphin a hormone produced by the pituitary gland and the hypothalamus that functions to reduce pain and induce feelings of pleasure

entity theory the belief that intelligence is a fixed characteristic and relatively difficult (or impossible) to change

entrainment when biological rhythms become synchronized to external cues such as light, temperature, or even a clock

epigenetics changes in gene expression that occur as a result of experience and that do not alter the genetic code

episodic buffer a storage component of working memory that combines the images and sounds from the other two components into coherent, story-like episodes

episodic memories declarative memories for personal experiences that seem to be organized around "episodes" and are recalled from a first-person ("I" or "my") perspective

escape learning occurs if a response removes a stimulus that is already present

etiology origins or causes

evidence-based therapies see *empirically supported treatments*

evolution the change in the frequency of genes occurring in an interbreeding population over generations

evolutionary psychology attempts to explain human behaviours based on the beneficial function(s) they may have served in our species' development

experiential system operates implicitly, quickly, and intuitively and is predominantly emotional

experimental group the group in the experiment that receives a treatment or the stimuli targeting a specific behaviour

experimental hypothesis assumes that any differences are due to a variable controlled by the experimenter

explicit memories see *declarative memories*

explicit processes correspond to "conscious" thought: deliberative, effortful, relatively slow, and generally under our intentional control

exposure repeatedly and in stages exposing an individual to the object of his fear so that he can work past his emotional reactions

external (situational) attribution the observer explains the actor's behaviour as the result of the situation

extinction (1) in classical conditioning, the loss or weakening of a conditioned response when a conditioned stimulus and unconditioned stimulus no longer occur together; (2) in operant conditioning, the weakening of an operant response when reinforcement is no longer available

extrinsic motivation motivation geared toward gaining rewards or public recognition, or avoiding embarrassment

facial feedback hypothesis our emotional expressions can influence our subjective emotional states

factor analysis (1) a statistical technique that examines correlations between variables to find clusters of related variables, or "factors"; (2) in personality analysis, grouping items that people respond to similarly; for instance, the terms friendly *and* warm

FAE see *fundamental attribution error*

false consensus effect tendency to project the self-concept onto the social world

false memory remembering events that did not occur, or incorrectly recalling details of an event

falsifiable the hypothesis is precise enough that it could be proven false

fast mapping the ability to map words onto concepts or objects after only a single exposure

fetal alcohol syndrome abnormalities in mental functioning, growth, and facial development in the offspring of women who use alcohol during pregnancy

fetal stage spans week eight through birth of the gestational period, during which time the skeletal, organ, and nervous systems become more developed and specialized

fight-or-flight response a set of physiological changes that occur in response to psychological or physical threats

first-letter technique uses the first letters of a set of items to spell out words that form a sentence

Five Factor Model (FFM) a trait-based theory of personality based on the finding that personality can be described using five major dimensions

fixation becoming preoccupied with obtaining the pleasure associated with a particular Freudian stage as a result of not being able to adequately regulate oneself and satisfy needs at that stage

fixed-interval schedule reinforces the first response occurring after a set amount of time passes

fixed-ratio schedule reinforcement is delivered after a specific number of responses have been completed

flashbulb memory an extremely vivid and detailed memory about an event and the conditions surrounding how one learned about the event

fluid intelligence (Gf) a type of intelligence used in learning new information and solving new problems not based on knowledge the person already possesses

Flynn effect the steady population level increases in intelligence test scores over time

fMRI see *functional magnetic resonance imaging*

focal lesions small areas of brain tissue that are surgically destroyed

foot-in-the-door technique involves making a simple request followed by a more substantial request

forebrain the most visibly obvious region of the brain, consists of all of the neural structures that are located above the midbrain, including all of the folds and grooves on the outer surface of the brain; the multiple interconnected structures in the forebrain are critical to such complex processes as emotion, memory, thinking, and reasoning

formal operational stage (ages 11 to adulthood) the development of advanced cognitive processes such as abstract reasoning and hypothetical thinking

fovea the central region of the retina

free association clients are encouraged to talk or write without censoring their thoughts in any way

frequency the number of observations that fall within a certain category or range of scores

frequency theory the perception of pitch is related to the frequency at which the basilar membrane vibrates

frontal lobes important in numerous higher cognitive functions, such as planning, regulating impulses and emotion, language production, and voluntary movement

frontal lobotomy surgically severing the connections between different regions of the brain

functional fixedness occurs when an individual identifies an object or technique that could potentially solve a problem, but can think of only its most obvious function

functional magnetic resonance imaging (fMRI) measures brain activity by detecting the influx of oxygen-rich blood into neural areas that were just active

functional neuroimaging a type of brain scanning that provides information about which areas of the brain are active when a person performs a particular behaviour

functionalism the study of the purpose and function of behaviour and conscious experience

fundamental attribution error (FAE) the tendency to over-emphasize internal (dispositional) attributions and under-emphasize external (situational) factors when explaining other people's behaviour

g see *general intelligence factor*

GABA (gamma-amino butyric acid) the primary inhibitory neurotransmitter of the nervous system, meaning that it prevents neurons from generating action potentials

GAD see *generalized anxiety disorder*

GAS see *general adaptation syndrome*

gate-control theory explains our experience of pain as an interaction between nerves that transmit pain messages and those that inhibit these messages

Gc see *crystallized intelligence*

gender roles the accepted attitudes and behaviours of males and females in a given society

gene knockout (KO) studies involve removing a specific gene and comparing the characteristics of animals with and without that gene

general adaptation syndrome (GAS) a theory of stress responses involving stages of alarm, resistance, and exhaustion

general intelligence factor (g) a person's "mental energy," reflecting Spearman's belief that some people's brains are simply more "powerful" than others

generalizability the degree to which one set of results can be applied to other situations, individuals, or events

generalization takes place when an operant response occurs in response to a new stimulus that is similar to the stimulus present during original learning

generalized anxiety disorder (GAD) involves frequently elevated levels of anxiety, generally from the normal challenges and stresses of everyday life

genes the basic units of heredity; genes are responsible for guiding the process of creating the proteins that make up our physical structures and regulate development and physiological processes throughout the lifespan

genotype the genetic makeup of an organism—the unique set of genes that comprise that individual's genetic code

germinal stage the first phase of prenatal development, which spans from conception to two weeks

gestalt psychology an approach emphasizing that psychologists need to focus on the whole of perception and experience, rather than its parts

Gf see *fluid intelligence*

glial cells specialized cells of the nervous system that are involved in mounting immune responses in the brain, removing waste, and synchronizing the activity of the billions of neurons that constitute the nervous system

glucose a sugar that serves as a primary energy source for the brain and the rest of the body

glutamate most common excitatory neurotransmitter in the brains of vertebrates

graded membership the observation that some concepts appear to make better category members than others

groupthink the stifling of diversity that occurs when individuals are not able to express their true perspectives, instead having to focus more on maintaining harmony in the group and on not being evaluated negatively

gustatory system functions in the sensation and perception of taste

habituation a decrease in responding with repeated exposure to a stimulus or event

hallucinations alterations in perception, such that a person hears, sees, smells, feels, or tastes something that does not actually exist, except in that person's own mind

hallucinogenic drugs substances that produce perceptual distortions

haptics the active, exploratory aspect of touch sensation and perception

Hawthorne effect behaviour change that occurs as a result of being observed

heritability a statistic, expressed as a number between zero and one, that represents the degree to which genetic differences between individuals contribute to individual differences in a behaviour or trait found in a population

heuristics problem-solving strategies that stem from prior experiences and provide an educated guess as to what is the most likely solution

HEXACO model of personality a six-factor theory that generally replicates the factors of the Five Factor Model and adds one additional factor: Honesty–Humility

hippocampus critical for learning and memory, particularly the formation of new memories

histrionic personality disorder (HPD) characterized by excessive attention seeking and dramatic behaviour

homeostasis the body's physiological processes that allow it to maintain consistent internal states in response to the outer environment

hormones chemicals secreted by the glands of the endocrine system

HPA axis see *hypothalamic–pituitary–adrenal axis*

HPD see *histrionic personality disorder*

humanistic psychology focuses on the unique aspects of each individual human, each person's freedom to act, his or her rational thought, and the belief that humans are fundamentally different from other animals

humourism explained both physical illnesses and disorders of personality as resulting from imbalances in key fluids in the body

hunter-gatherer theory links performance on specific tasks to the different roles performed by males and females over the course of our evolutionary history

hypnosis a procedure of inducing a heightened state of suggestibility

hypothalamic–pituitary–adrenal (HPA) axis a neural and endocrine circuit that provides communication between the nervous system (the hypothalamus) and the endocrine system (pituitary and adrenal glands)

hypothalamus a brain structure that regulates basic biological needs and motivational systems

hypothesis (plural: hypotheses) a testable prediction about processes that can be observed and measured

hypothesis test a statistical method of evaluating whether differences among groups are meaningful, or could have been arrived at by chance alone

IAT see *Implicit Associations Test*

iconic memory the visual form of sensory memory

id a collection of basic biological drives, including those directed toward sex and aggression

identifiable victim effect people are more powerfully moved to action by the story of a single suffering person than by information about a whole group of people

identity a clear sense of what kind of person you are, what types of people you belong with, and what roles you should play in society

idiographic approach creating detailed descriptions of a specific person's unique personality characteristics

illusory correlations relationships that really exist only in the mind, rather than in reality

imagination inflation the increased confidence in a false memory of an event following repeated imagination of the event

imitation recreating someone else's motor behaviour or expression, often to accomplish a specific goal

Implicit Associations Test (IAT) measures how fast people can respond to images or words flashed on a computer screen

implicit memories see *nondeclarative memories*

implicit processes correspond to "unconscious" thought: intuitive, automatic, effortless, very fast, and operate largely outside of our intentional control

inattentional blindness a failure to notice clearly visible events or objects because attention is directed elsewhere

incentives the stimuli we seek out in order to reduce drives

incremental theory the belief that intelligence can be shaped by experiences, practice, and effort

independent variable the variable that the experimenter manipulates to distinguish between two or more groups

individual zone of optimal functioning (IZOF) a range of emotional intensity in which an individual is most likely to perform at his or her best

inductive discipline involves explaining the consequences of a child's actions on other people, activating empathy for others' feelings

inferiority complex the struggle many people have with feelings of inferiority, which stem from experiences of helplessness and powerlessness during childhood

informational influence occurs when people internalize the values and beliefs of the group, coming to believe the same things and feel the same ways themselves

informed consent a potential volunteer must be informed (know the purpose, tasks, and risks involved in the study) and give consent (agree to participate based on the information provided) without pressure

ingroup bias positive biases toward the self get extended to include one's ingroups and people become motivated to see their ingroups as superior to their outgroups

ingroups groups we feel positively toward and identify with

insight therapies a general term referring to therapy that involves dialogue between client and therapist for the purposes of gaining awareness and understanding of psychological problems and conflicts

insomnia a disorder characterized by an extreme lack of sleep

intelligence the ability to think, understand, reason, and adapt to or overcome obstacles

intelligence quotient, or IQ a measure of intelligence computed using a standardized test and calculated by taking a person's mental age, dividing it by his or her chronological age, and then multiplying by 100

intermittent reinforcement see *partial reinforcement*

internal (dispositional) attribution the observer explains the behaviour of the actor in terms of some innate quality of that person

intersexual selection a situation in which members of one sex select a mating partner based on their desirable traits

intrasexual selection a situation in which members of the same sex compete in order to win the opportunity to mate with members of the opposite sex

intrinsic motivation the process of being internally motivated to perform behaviours and overcome challenges (e.g., a genuine desire to master a task rather than being motivated by a reward)

introjection the internalization of the conditional regard of significant others

iris a round muscle that adjusts the size of the pupil; it also gives the eyes their characteristic colour

IZOF see *individual zone of optimal functioning*

James-Lange theory of emotion our physiological reactions to stimuli (e.g., a racing heart) precede the emotional experience (e.g., the fear)

jet lag the discomfort a person feels when sleep cycles are out of synchronization with light and darkness

kinesthesis the sense of bodily motion and position

language a form of communication that involves the use of spoken, written, or gestural symbols that are combined in a rule-based form

latent content the actual symbolic meaning of a dream built on suppressed sexual or aggressive urges

latent learning learning that is not immediately expressed by a response until the organism is reinforced for doing so

law of effect the idea that responses followed by satisfaction will occur again in the same situation whereas those that are not followed by satisfaction become less likely

learned helplessness an acquired suppression of avoidance or escape behaviour in response to unpleasant, uncontrollable circumstances

learning a process by which behaviour or knowledge changes as a result of experience

lens a clear structure that focuses light onto the back of the eye

lesioning a technique in which researchers intentionally damage an area in the brain

leucotomy the surgical destruction of brain tissues in the pre-frontal cortex

libido the motivation for sexual activity and pleasure

limbic system an integrated network involved in emotion and memory

linguistic relativity the theory that the language we use determines how we understand the world

lithium one of the first mood stabilizers to be prescribed regularly in psychiatry, and from the 1950s to the 1980s, was the standard drug treatment for depression and bipolar disorder

locked-in syndrome a disorder in which the patient is aware and awake but, because of an inability to move his or her body, appears unconscious

longitudinal studies studies that follow the same set of individuals for many years, often decades

long-term memory (LTM) holds information for extended periods of time, if not permanently

long-term potentiation (LTP) demonstrated that there is an enduring increase in connectivity and transmission of neural signals between nerve cells that fire together

LTM see *long-term memory*

LTP see *long-term potentiation*

magnetic resonance imaging (MRI) a structural imaging technique in which clear images of the brain are created based on how different neural regions absorb and release energy while in a magnetic field

magnetoencephalography (MEG) a neuroimaging technique that measures the tiny magnetic fields created by the electrical activity of nerve cells in the brain

maintenance rehearsal prolonging exposure to information by repeating it

major depression a disorder marked by prolonged periods of sadness, feelings of worthlessness and hopelessness, social withdrawal, and cognitive and physical sluggishness

maladaptive a behaviour that causes distress to oneself or others, impairs day-to-day functioning, or increases the risk of injury or harm to oneself or others

manifest content the images and storylines that we dream about

MAOIs see *monoamine oxidase inhibitors*

marijuana a drug comprising the leaves and buds of the *Cannabis* plant that produces a combination of hallucinogenic, stimulant, and relaxing (narcotic) effects

mastery motive see *intrinsic motivation*

materialism the belief that humans, and other living beings, are composed exclusively of physical matter

MBCT see *mindfulness-based cognitive therapy*

MBSR see *mindfulness-based stress reduction*

MCS see *minimally conscious state*

MDMA see *ecstasy*

mean the arithmetic average of a set of numbers

median the 50th percentile—the point on the horizontal axis at which 50% of all observations are lower, and 50% of all observations are higher

medical model sees psychological conditions through the same lens as Western medicine tends to see physical conditions—as sets of symptoms, causes, and outcomes, with treatments aimed at changing physiological processes in order to alleviate symptoms

meditation any procedure that involves a shift in consciousness to a state in which an individual is highly focused, aware, and in control of mental processes

MEG see *magnetoencephalography*

menarche the onset of menstruation

menopause the termination of the menstrual cycle and reproductive ability in women

mental age the average intellectual ability score for children of a specific age

mental disorder defence claims that the defendant was in such an extreme, abnormal state of mind when committing the crime that he or she could not discern that the actions were legally or morally wrong

mental set a cognitive obstacle that occurs when an individual attempts to apply a routine solution to what is actually a new type of problem

method of loci a mnemonic that connects words to be remembered to locations along a familiar path

midbrain resides just above the hindbrain, primarily functions as a relay station between sensory and motor areas

mimicry taking on for ourselves the behaviours, emotional displays, and facial expressions of others

mind-wandering an unintentional redirection of attention from one's current task to an unrelated train of thought

mindfulness-based cognitive therapy (MBCT) involves combining mindfulness meditation with standard cognitive–behavioural therapy tools

mindfulness-based stress reduction (MBSR) a structured relaxation program based on elements of mindfulness meditation

minimally conscious state (MCS) a disordered state of consciousness marked by the ability to show some behaviours that suggest at least partial consciousness, even if on an inconsistent basis

misinformation effect when information occurring after an event becomes part of the memory for that event

mnemonic a technique intended to improve memory for specific information

mode the category with the highest frequency (that is, the category with the most observations)

monoamine oxidase inhibitors (MAOIs) work by deactivating monoamine oxidase (MAO), an enzyme that breaks down serotonin, dopamine, and norepinephrine at the synaptic clefts of nerve cells

monocular cues depth cues that we can perceive with only one eye

monozygotic twins twins who come from a single ovum (egg), which makes them genetically identical (almost 100% genetic similarity)

mood-dependent memory people remember better if their mood at retrieval matches their mood during encoding

mood stabilizers drugs used to prevent or reduce the severity of mood swings experienced by people with bipolar disorder

morphemes the smallest meaningful unit of a language

motivation concerns the physiological and psychological processes underlying the initiation of behaviours that direct organisms toward specific goals

MRI see *magnetic resonance imaging*

multimodal integration the ability to combine sensation from different modalities such as vision and hearing into a single integrated perception

multiple intelligences a model claiming that there are eight (now updated to at least nine) different forms of intelligence, each independent from the others

multiple personality disorder see *dissociative identity disorder*

myelin a fatty sheath that insulates axons from one another, resulting in increased speed and efficiency of neural communication

naive realism the assumption that the way we see things is the way that they are

narcissistic personality disorder (NPD) characterized by an inflated sense of self-importance and an excessive need for attention and admiration, as well as intense self-doubt and fear of abandonment

narcolepsy a disorder in which a person experiences extreme daytime sleepiness and even sleep attacks

natural selection the process by which favourable traits become increasingly common in a population of interbreeding individuals, while traits that are unfavourable become less common

naturalistic observations observations that unobtrusively observe and record behaviour as it occurs in the subject's natural environment

nature and nurture relationships the inquiry into how heredity (nature) and environment (nurture) influence behaviour and mental processes

need to belong the motivation to maintain relationships that involve pleasant feelings such as warmth, affection, appreciation, and mutual concern for each person's well-being

negative affectivity the tendency to respond to problems with a pattern of anxiety, hostility, anger, guilt or nervousness

negative punishment occurs when a behaviour decreases because it removes or diminishes a particular stimulus

negative reinforcement involves the strengthening of a behaviour because it removes or diminishes a stimulus

negative symptoms the absence of adaptive behaviour, such as absent or flat emotional reactions, lack of interacting with others in a social setting, and lack of motivation

negatively skewed distribution a distribution in which the curve has an extended tail to the left of the cluster

neurodevelopmental hypothesis the adult manifestation of what we call "schizophrenia" is the outgrowth of disrupted neurological development early in the person's life

neurogenesis the formation of new neurons

neurons one of the major types of cells found in the nervous system, which are responsible for sending and receiving messages throughout the body

neuroplasticity the capacity of the brain to change and rewire itself based on individual experience

neurotransmitters the chemicals that function as messengers allowing neurons to communicate with each other

night terrors intense bouts of panic and arousal that awaken the individual, typically in a heightened emotional state

nightmares particularly vivid and disturbing dreams that occur during REM sleep

nociception the activity of nerve pathways that respond to uncomfortable stimulation

nomothetic approach examines personality in large groups of people, with the aim of making generalizations about personality structure

nondeclarative memories include actions or behaviours that you can remember and perform without awareness

nootropic substances substances that are believed to beneficially affect intelligence

noradrenaline see *norepinephrine*

norepinephrine (also known as noradrenaline) a monoamine synthesized from dopamine molecules that is involved in regulating stress responses, including increasing arousal, attention, and heart rate

normal distribution a symmetrical distribution with values clustered around a central, mean value

normative influence   a social pressure to adopt a group's perspective in order to be accepted, rather than rejected, by a group

null hypothesis   assumes that any differences between groups (or conditions) are due to chance

NPD   see *narcissistic personality disorder*

obesity   a disorder of positive energy balance, in which energy intake exceeds energy expenditure

object permanence   the ability to understand that objects exist even when they cannot be directly perceived

object relations therapy   a variation of psychodynamic therapy that focuses on how early childhood experiences and emotional attachments influence later psychological functioning

objective measurements   the measure of an entity or behaviour that, within an allowed margin of error, is consistent across instruments and observers

observational learning   involves changes in behaviour and knowledge that result from watching others

obsessive–compulsive disorder (OCD)   plagued by unwanted, inappropriate, and persistent thoughts (obsessions), and tending to engage in repetitive, almost ritualistic, behaviours (compulsions)

occipital lobes   located at the rear of the brain and are where visual information is processed

OCD   see *obsessive–compulsive disorder*

olfactory bulb   a structure on the bottom surface of the frontal lobes that serves as the brain's central region for processing smells

olfactory epithelium   a thin layer of cells that are lined by sensory receptors called cilia

olfactory system   involved in smell—the detection of airborne particles with specialized receptors located in the nose

operant conditioning   a type of learning in which behaviour is influenced by consequences

operational definitions   statements that describe the procedures (or operations) and specific measures that are used to record observations

opiates   (also called narcotics) drugs such as heroin and morphine that reduce pain and induce extremely intense feelings of euphoria

opponent-process theory   a theory of colour perception stating that we perceive colour in terms of opposing pairs: red to green, yellow to blue, and white to black

optic nerve   a dense bundle of fibres that connect to the brain

optimism   the tendency to have a favourable, constructive view on situations and to expect positive outcomes

outgroups   those "other" groups that we don't identify with

oxytocin   a stress-sensitive hormone that is typically associated with maternal bonding and social relationships

panic attacks   brief moments of extreme anxiety that include a rush of physical activity paired with frightening thoughts

panic disorder   an anxiety disorder marked by occasional episodes of sudden, very intense fear

paranoid schizophrenia   symptoms include delusional beliefs that one is being followed, watched, or persecuted, and may also include delusions of grandeur or the belief that one has some secret, insight, power, or some other characteristic that makes one particularly special

parasitic processing   mutually reinforcing feedback loops linking different cognitive and neural processes together

parasympathetic nervous system   helps maintain homeostatic balance in the presence of change; following sympathetic arousal, it works to return the body to a baseline, nonemergency state

parietal lobes   involved in our experiences of touch as well our bodily awareness

partial reinforcement effect   a phenomenon in which organisms that have been conditioned under partial reinforcement resist extinction longer than those conditioned under continuous reinforcement

partial reinforcement   only a certain number of responses are rewarded, or a certain amount of time must pass before reinforcement is available

passionate love   associated with a physical and emotional longing for the other person

Pavlovian conditioning   see *classical conditioning*

peer review   a process in which papers submitted for publication in scholarly journals are read and critiqued by experts in the specific field of study

perception   involves attending to, organizing, and interpreting stimuli that we sense

perceptual constancy   the ability to perceive objects as having constant shape, size, and colour despite changes in perspective

performance motive   see *extrinsic motivation*

peripheral nervous system (PNS)   a division of the nervous system that transmits signals between the brain and the rest of the body and is divided into two subcomponents, the somatic system and the autonomic system

peripheral route to persuasion   depends upon features that are not directly related to the message itself, such as the attractiveness of the person delivering the information

persistent vegetative state   state of minimal to no consciousness in which the patient's eyes may be open, and the individual will develop sleep–wake cycles without clear signs of consciousness

person perception   the processes by which individuals categorize and form judgments about other people

personal unconscious   a vast repository of experiences and patterns that are absorbed during the entire experiential unfolding of the person's life

personality   a characteristic pattern of thinking, feeling, and behaving that is unique to each individual, and remains relatively consistent over time and situations

personality disorders   particularly unusual patterns of behaviour (relative to one's cultural context), that are maladaptive, distressing to oneself or others, and resistant to change

personality psychology   the study of how different personality characteristics can influence how we think and act

personality trait   a specific psychological characteristic that makes up part of a person's personality

person-centred perspective   founded on the assumption that people are basically good, and given the right environment their personality will develop fully and normally

person-centred therapy   see *client-centred therapy*

pessimism   the tendency to have a negative perception of life and expect negative outcomes

pessimistic explanatory style   the tendency to interpret and explain negative events as internally based (i.e., as being due to that person rather than to an external situation) and as a constant, stable quality

PET   see *positron emission tomography*

phantom limb sensations   frequently experienced by amputees, who report pain and other sensations coming from the absent limb

phenomenological approach   the therapist addresses the clients' feelings and thoughts as they unfold in the present moment, rather than looking for unconscious motives or dwelling in the past

phenotype   the physical traits and behavioural characteristics that show genetic variation, such as eye colour, the shape and size of facial features, intelligence, and even personality

phobia   a severe, irrational fear of a very specific object or situation

phonemes   the most basic of unit of speech sounds

phonological loop   a storage component of working memory that relies on rehearsal and that stores information as sounds, or an auditory code

phrenology   the theory that personality characteristics could be assessed by carefully measuring the outer skull

physical dependence   the need to take a drug to ward off unpleasant physical withdrawal symptoms

pitch   the perceptual experience of sound wave frequencies

pituitary gland   the master gland of the endocrine system that produces hormones and sends commands about hormone production to the other glands of the endocrine system

place theory of hearing   how we perceive pitch is based on the location (place) along the basilar membrane that sound stimulates

placebo effect   a measurable and experienced improvement in health or behaviour that cannot be attributable to a medication or treatment

pluralistic ignorance   occurs when there is a disjunction between the private beliefs of individuals and the public behaviour they display to others

polysomnography   a set of objective measurements used to examine physiological variables during sleep

population   the group that researchers want to generalize about

positive psychology   uses scientific methods to study human strengths and potential

positive punishment   a process in which a behaviour decreases in frequency because it was followed by a particular, usually unpleasant, stimulus

positive reinforcement   the strengthening of behaviour after potential reinforcers such as praise, money, or nourishment follow that behaviour

positive symptoms   the presence of maladaptive behaviours, such as confused and paranoid thinking, and inappropriate emotional reactions

positively skewed distribution   a distribution in which the long tail is on the right of the cluster

positron emission tomography (or PET)   a type of scan in which a low level of a radioactive isotope is injected into the blood, and its movement to regions of the brain engaged in a particular task is measured

postconventional morality   considers rules and laws as relative

post-traumatic growth   the capacity to grow and experience long-term positive effects in response to negative events

post-traumatic stress disorder (PTSD)   is a common psychological illness involving recurring thoughts, images, and nightmares associated with a traumatic event; it induces symptoms of tension and anxiety and can seriously interfere with many aspects of a person's life

pragmatics   the study of nonlinguistic elements of language use

preconventional morality   characterized by self-interest in seeking reward or avoiding punishment

prejudice   affective, emotionally laden responses to members of outgroups, including holding negative attitudes and making critical judgments of other groups

preoperational stage   (ages two to seven) the stage of development devoted to language development, using symbols, pretend play, and mastering the concept of conservation

preparedness   the biological predisposition to rapidly learn a response to a particular class of stimuli

preserve and protect hypothesis   suggests that two adaptive functions of sleep are preserving energy and protecting the organism from harm

preterm infant   an infant born earlier than 36 weeks of gestation

primary auditory cortex   a major perceptual centre of the brain involved in perceiving what we hear

primary reinforcers   reinforcing stimuli that satisfy basic motivational needs—needs that affect an individual's ability to survive (and, if possible, reproduce)

primary sex traits   changes in the body that are part of reproduction

priming   the activation of individual concepts in long-term memory

principle of parsimony   the simplest of all competing explanations (the most "parsimonious") of a phenomenon should be the one we accept

proactive interference   a process in which the first information learned (e.g., in a list of words) occupies memory, leaving fewer resources to remember the newer information

problem solving   accomplishing a goal when the solution or the path to the solution is not clear

problem-solving theory   the theory that thoughts and concerns are continuous from waking to sleeping, and that dreams may function to facilitate finding solutions to problems encountered while awake

procedural memories   patterns of muscle movements (motor memory)

processing fluency   the ease with which information is processed

prodromal phase   phase of schizophrenia during which people may become easily confused and have difficulty organizing their thoughts, they may lose interest and begin to withdraw from friends and family, and they may lose their normal motivations, withdraw from life, and spend increasing amounts of time alone, often deeply engrossed in their own thoughts

projective tests   personality tests in which ambiguous images are presented to an individual to elicit responses that reflect unconscious desires or conflicts

prototypes   mental representations of an average category member

pseudoscience   an idea that is presented as science but does not actually utilize basic principles of scientific thinking or procedure

psychiatrists   medical doctors who specialize in mental health and who are allowed to diagnose and treat mental disorders primarily through prescribing medications

psychoactive drugs   substances that affect thinking, behaviour, perception, and emotion

psychoanalysis   a psychological approach that attempts to explain how behaviour and personality are influenced by unconscious processes

psychodynamic therapies   forms of insight therapy that emphasize the need to discover and resolve unconscious conflicts

psychological dependence   occurs when emotional need for a drug develops without any underlying physical dependence

psychology   the scientific study of behaviour, thought, and experience, and how they can be affected by physical, mental, social, and environmental factors

psychoneuroimmunology   the study of the relationship between immune system and nervous system functioning

psychopharmacotherapy   the use of drugs to attempt to manage or reduce clients' symptoms

psychophysics   the study of the relationship between the physical world and the mental representation of that world

psychotropic drugs   medications designed to alter psychological functioning

PTSD   see *post-traumatic stress disorder*

punisher   a stimulus that is contingent upon a response, and that results in a decrease in behaviour

punishment   a process that decreases the future probability of a response

pupil   regulates the amount of light that enters the eye by changing its size; it dilates (expands) to allow more light to enter and constricts (shrinks) to allow less light into the eye

qualitative research   examining an issue or behaviour without performing numerical measurements of the variables

quantitative research   examining an issue or behaviour by using numerical measurements and/or statistics

quasi-experimental research   a research technique in which the two or more groups that are compared are selected based on predetermined characteristics, rather than random assignment

random assignment   a technique for dividing samples into two or more groups in which participants are equally likely to be placed in any condition of the experiment

random sample   a sampling technique in which every individual of a population has an equal chance of being included

Raven's Progressive Matrices   an intelligence test that is based on pictures, not words, thus making it relatively unaffected by language or cultural background

recall   retrieving information when asked but without that information being present during the retrieval process

reciprocal determinism   behaviour, internal (personal) factors, and external (situational) factors interact to determine one another, and our personalities are based on interactions among these three aspects

recognition   identifying a stimulus or piece of information when it is presented to you

recovered memory   a memory of a traumatic event that is suddenly recovered after blocking the memory of that event for a long period of time

recovered memory controversy   a heated debate among psychologists about the validity of recovered memories

reflexes   involuntary muscular reactions to specific types of stimulation

refractory period   (1) brief period in which a neuron cannot fire; (2) a time period during which erection and orgasm are not physically possible

rehearsal   repeating information until you do not need to remember it anymore

reinforcement   a process in which an event or reward that follows a response increases the likelihood of that response occurring again

reinforcer   a stimulus that is contingent upon a response, and that increases the probability of that response occurring again

reliability   consistent and stable answers across multiple observations and points in time

REM sleep   a stage of sleep characterized by quickening brain waves, inhibited body movement, and rapid eye movements (REM)

repetitive transcranial magnetic stimulation (rTMS)   a therapeutic technique in which a focal area of the brain is exposed to a powerful magnetic field across several different treatment sessions

replication   the process of repeating a study and finding a similar outcome each time

representativeness heuristic   making judgments of likelihood based on how well an example represents a specific category

research design   a set of methods that allows a hypothesis to be tested

research ethics board (REB)   a committee of researchers and officials at an institution charged with the protection of research participants

residential treatment centres   housing facilities in which residents receive psychological therapy and life skills training with the explicit goal of helping residents become re-integrated into society

residual phase   phase of schizophrenia during which people's predominant symptoms have disappeared or lessened considerably, and they may simply be withdrawn, have trouble concentrating, and generally lack motivation

residual schizophrenia   This category reflects individuals who show some symptoms of schizophrenia but are either in transition to a full-blown episode or in remission

resilience   the ability to effectively recover from illness or adversity

resistance   engaging in strategies that keep information from fully manifesting in conscious awareness

response styles   characteristic ways of responding to questions

resting potential   relatively stable state during which the cell is not transmitting messages

restless legs syndrome   a persistent feeling of discomfort in the legs and the urge to continuously shift them into different positions

restore and repair hypothesis   the idea that the body needs to restore energy levels and repair any wear and tear experienced during the day's activities

retina   lines the inner surface of the eye and consists of specialized receptors that absorb light and send signals related to the properties of light to the brain

retinal disparity   (also called binocular disparity) the difference in relative position of an object as seen by both eyes, which provides information to the brain about depth

retrieval   brings information from LTM back into STM

retroactive interference   the most recently learned information overshadows some older memories that have not yet made it into long-term memory

retrograde amnesia   a condition in which memory for the events preceding trauma or injury is lost

reuptake   a process whereby neurotransmitter molecules that have been released into the synapse are reabsorbed into the axon terminals of the presynaptic neuron

Right-Wing Authoritarianism (RWA)   a problematic set of personality characteristics that also predisposes people to certain types of violent or anti-social tendencies: (1) obeying orders and deferring to the established authorities in a society; (2) supporting aggression against those who dissent or differ from the established social order; and (3) believing strongly in maintaining the existing social order

rods   photoreceptors that occupy peripheral regions of the retina; they are highly sensitive under low light levels

Rorschach inkblot test   a test in which people are asked to describe what they see on an inkblot, and psychologists interpret this description using a standardized scoring and interpretation method

rTMS   see *repetitive transcranial magnetic stimulation*

RWA   see *Right-Wing Authoritarianism*

sample   a select group of population members

satiation   the point in a meal when we are no longer motivated to eat

savant   an individual with low mental capacity in most domains but extraordinary abilities in other specific areas such as music, mathematics, or art

scaffolding a highly attentive approach to teaching in which the teacher matches guidance to the learner's needs

schedules of reinforcement rules that determine when reinforcement is available

schemas organized clusters of memories that constitute one's knowledge about events, objects, and ideas

schizophrenia a brain disease that causes the person to experience significant breaks from reality, a lack of integration of thoughts and emotions, and problems with attention and memory

scientific literacy the ability to understand, analyze, and apply scientific information

scientific method a way of learning about the world through collecting observations, developing theories to explain them, and using the theories to make predictions

sclera is the white, outer surface of the eye

secondary reinforcers stimuli that acquire their reinforcing effects only after we learn that they have value

secondary sex traits changes in the body that are not part of reproduction

sedative drugs sometimes referred to as "downers," depress activity of the central nervous system

selective attention involves focusing on one particular event or task

selective serotonin reuptake inhibitors (SSRIs) a class of antidepressant drugs that block the reuptake of the neurotransmitter serotonin

self-actualization the drive to grow and fulfill one's potential

self-awareness the ability to recognize one's individuality

self-determination theory an individual's ability to achieve their goals and attain psychological well-being is influenced by the degree to which he or she is in control of the behaviours necessary to achieve those goals

self-efficacy an individual's confidence that he or she can plan and execute a course of action in order to solve a problem

self-fulfilling prophecies a first impression (or an expectation) affects one's behaviour, and then that affects other people's behaviour, leading one to "confirm" the initial impression or expectation

self-reference effect occurs when you think about information in terms of how it relates to you or how it is useful to you; this type of encoding will lead to you remembering that information better than you otherwise would have

self-reporting a method in which responses are provided directly by the people who are being studied, typically through face-to-face interviews, phone surveys, paper and pencil tests, and web-based questionnaires

self-serving biases biased ways of processing self-relevant information to enhance our positive self-evaluation

semantic memories declarative memories that include facts about the world

semantic network an interconnected set of nodes (or concepts) and the links that join them to form a category

semantics the study of how people come to understand meaning from words

semicircular canals three fluid-filled canals found in the inner ear that respond when the head moves in different directions (up-down, left-right, forward-backward)

sensation the process of detecting external events with sense organs and turning those stimuli into neural signals

sensitive period a window of time during which exposure to a specific type of environmental stimulation is needed for normal development of a specific ability

sensorimotor stage from birth to two years, a time during which infants' thinking about and exploration of the world are based on immediate sensory (e.g., seeing, feeling) and motor (e.g., grabbing, mouthing) experiences

sensory adaptation the reduction of activity in sensory receptors with repeated exposure to a stimulus

sensory memory a memory store that accurately holds perceptual information for a very brief amount of time

serial position effect in general, most people will recall the first few items from a list and the last few items, but only an item or two from the middle

serotonin a monoamine involved in regulating mood, sleep, aggression, and appetite

set point a hypothesized mechanism that serves to maintain body weight around a physiologically programmed level

sex guilt negative emotional feelings for having violated culturally accepted standards of appropriate sexual behaviour

sexual orientation the consistent preference for sexual relations with members of the opposite sex (heterosexuality), same sex (homosexuality), or either sex (bisexuality)

sexual response cycle the phases of physiological change during sexual activity, which comprises four primary stages: excitement, plateau, orgasm, and resolution

sexual scripts the set of rules and assumptions about the sexual behaviours of males and females

shallow processing encoding more superficial properties of a stimulus, such as the sound or spelling of a word

shaping reinforcing successive approximations of a specific operant response

short-term memory (STM) a memory store with limited capacity and duration (approximately 30 seconds)

signal detection theory whether a stimulus is perceived depends on both sensory experience and judgment made by the subject

single-blind study a study in which participants do not know the true purpose of the study, or else do not know which type of treatment they are receiving (for example, a placebo or a drug)

situational attributions see *external attribution*

sleep apnea a disorder characterized by the temporary inability to breathe during sleep

sleep deprivation occurs when an individual cannot or does not sleep

sleep displacement occurs when an individual is prevented from sleeping at the normal time although she or he may be able to sleep earlier or later in the day than usual

social anxiety disorder a very strong fear of being judged by others or being embarrassed or humiliated in public

social contagion the often subtle, unintentional spreading of a behaviour as a result of social interactions

social desirability (or socially desirable responding) research participants respond in ways that increase the chances that they will be viewed favourably

social facilitation occurs when one's performance is affected by the presence of others

social loafing occurs when an individual puts less effort into working on a task with others

social norms the (usually unwritten) guidelines for how to behave in social contexts

social psychology the study of the influence of other people on our behaviour

social resilience   the ability to keep positive relationships and to endure and recover from social isolation and life stressors

social roles   are more specific sets of expectations for how someone in a specific position should behave

social-cognitive theory   explains hypnosis by emphasizing the degree to which beliefs and expectations contribute to increased suggestibility

socioemotional selectivity theory   describes how older people have learned to select for themselves more positive and nourishing experiences

soma   see *cell body*

somatic nervous system   consists of nerves that control skeletal muscles, which are responsible for voluntary and reflexive movement; it also consists of nerves that receive sensory input from the body

somnambulism   or sleepwalking, a disorder that involves wandering and performing other activities while asleep

sound localization   the process of identifying where sound comes from

specific phobia   an intense fear of a specific object, activity, or organism

spermarche   during puberty, a male's first ejaculation of sperm

spontaneous recovery   the reoccurrence of a previously extinguished conditioned response, typically after some time has passed since extinction

SSRIs   see *selective serotonin reuptake inhibitors*

standard deviation   a measure of variability around the mean

Stanford-Binet test   a test intended to measure innate levels of intelligence

state   a temporary physical or psychological engagement that influences behaviour

state-dependent memory   memory retrieval is more effective when your internal state matches the state you were in during encoding

statistical significance   the means of the groups are farther apart than you would expect them to be by random chance alone

stem cells   a unique type of cell that does not have a predestined function

stereotype   a cognitive structure, a set of beliefs about the characteristics that are held by members of a specific social group; these beliefs function as schemas, serving to guide how we process information about our social world

stereotype threat   occurs when negative stereotypes about a group cause group members to underperform on ability tests

stimulants   a category of drugs that speed up the nervous system, typically enhancing wakefulness and alertness

STM   see *short-term memory*

storage   the time and manner in which information is retained between encoding and retrieval

stores   retain information in memory without using it for any specific purpose

strange situation   a way of measuring infant attachment by observing how infants behave when exposed to different experiences that involve anxiety and comfort

stress   a psychological and physiological reaction that occurs when perceived demands exceed existing resources to meet those demands

structural neuroimaging   a type of brain scanning that produces images of the different structures of the brain

structuralism   an attempt to analyze conscious experience by breaking it down into basic elements, and to understand how these elements work together

superego   comprised of our values and moral standards

sympathetic nervous system   responsible for the fight-or-flight response of an increased heart rate, dilated pupils, and decreased salivary flow—responses that prepare the body for action

synapses   the microscopically small spaces that separate individual nerve cells

synaptic cleft   the minute space between the axon terminal (terminal button) and the dendrite

synaptic pruning   the loss of weak nerve cell connections

synaptogenesis   the forming of new synaptic connections

syntax   the rules for combining words and morphemes into meaningful phrases and sentences

systematic desensitization   gradual exposure to a feared stimulus or situation is coupled with relaxation training

systems approach   an orientation that encourages therapists to see an individual's symptoms as being influenced by many different interacting systems

tardive dyskinesia   a movement disorder involving involuntary movements and facial tics

TAT   see *Thematic Apperception Test*

temporal lobes   located at the sides of the brain near the ears and are involved in hearing, language, and some higher-level aspects of vision such as object and face recognition

teratogens   substances, such as drugs or environmental toxins, that impair the process of fetal development

terror management theory (TMT)   a psychological perspective asserting that the human fear of mortality motivates behaviour, particularly those that preserve self-esteem and our sense of belonging

testing effect   the finding that taking practice tests can improve exam performance, even without additional studying

testosterone   a hormone that is involved in the development of sex characteristics and the motivation of sexual behaviour

thalamus   a set of nuclei involved in relaying sensory information to different regions of the brain

Thematic Apperception Test (TAT)   a test in which respondents are asked to tell stories about ambiguous pictures involving various interpersonal situations

theory   an explanation for a broad range of observations that also generates new hypotheses and integrates numerous findings into a coherent whole

theory of mind   the ability to understand that other people have thoughts, beliefs, and perspectives that may be different from one's own

therapeutic alliance   the relationship between the therapist and the patient that emerges in therapy

thin slices of behaviour   very small samples of a person's behaviour

third variable problem   the possibility that a third, unmeasured variable is actually responsible for a well-established correlation between two variables

tip-of-the-tongue (TOT) phenomenon   when you are able to retrieve similar sounding words or words that start with the same letter but can't quite retrieve the word you actually want

TMT   see *terror management theory*

tolerance   when repeated use of a drug results in a need for a higher dose to get the intended effect

top-down processing when our perceptions are influenced by our expectations or by our prior knowledge

transduction takes place when specialized receptors transform the physical energy of the outside world into neural impulses

transference a psychodynamic process whereby clients direct certain patterns or emotional experiences toward the therapist, rather than the original person involved in the experiences (e.g., their parents)

transgender individuals who experience a mismatch between the gender that they identify with and their biological sex

transsexual the subset of transgender individuals who wish to permanently transition from their birth sex to the gender with which they identify

triarchic theory of intelligence a theory that divides intelligence into three distinct types: analytical, practical, and creative

trichromatic theory maintains that colour vision is determined by three different cone types that are sensitive to short, medium, and long wavelengths of light

tricyclic antidepressants appear to work by blocking the reuptake of serotonin and norepinephrine

trigger foods affect the selection of healthy and unhealthy foods simply by being present among possible food alternatives

two-factor theory patterns of physical arousal and the cognitive labels we attach to them form the basis of our emotional experiences

Type A personality people who tend to be impatient and worry about time, and are easily angered, competitive, and highly motivated

Type B personality people who are more laid back and characterized by a patient, easygoing, and relaxed disposition

unconditioned response (UR) a reflexive, unlearned reaction to an unconditioned stimulus

unconditioned stimulus (US) a stimulus that elicits a reflexive response without learning

unconscious mind a vast and powerful but inaccessible part of your consciousness, operating without your conscious endorsement or will to influence and guide your behaviours

undifferentiated schizophrenia This category includes individuals who show a combination of symptoms from more than one type of schizophrenia

unit bias the tendency to assume that the unit of sale or portioning is an appropriate amount to consume

UR see *unconditioned response*

US see *unconditioned stimulus*

validity the degree to which an instrument or procedure actually measures what it claims to measure

variability the degree to which scores are dispersed in a distribution

variable the object, concept, or event being measured

variable-interval schedule the first response is reinforced following a variable amount of time

variable-ratio schedule the number of responses required to receive reinforcement varies according to an average

vestibular sacs structures that influence your ability to detect when your head is no longer in an upright position

vestibular system a sensory system in the ear that provides information about spatial orientation of the head as well as head motion

video deficit young children do not learn very much from information presented on screens

virtual reality exposure (VRE) a treatment that uses graphical displays to create an experience in which the client seems to be immersed in an actual environment

visuospatial sketchpad a storage component of working memory that maintains visual images and spatial layouts in a visuospatial code

Weber's law states that the just noticeable difference between two stimuli changes as a proportion of those stimuli

Wechsler Adult Intelligence Scale (WAIS) the most common intelligence test in use today for adolescents and adults

Wernicke's area the area of the brain most associated with finding the meaning of words

Whorfian hypothesis see *linguistic relativity*

within-subjects design an experimental design in which the same participants respond to all types of stimuli or experience all experimental conditions

working memory a model of short-term remembering that includes a combination of memory components that can temporarily store small amounts of information for a short period of time

Young-Helmholtz theory see *trichromatic theory*

zeitgeist refers to a general set of beliefs of a particular culture at a specific time in history

zone of proximal development the concept that development is ideal when children attempt skills and activities that are just beyond what they can do alone, but they have guidance from adults who are attentive to their progress

zygote the initial cell formed when the nuclei of egg and sperm fuse

References

AbdelMalik, P., Husted, J., Chow, E. W., & Bassett, A. S. (2003). Childhood head injury and expression of schizophrenia and multiply affected families. *Archives of General Psychiatry, 60,* 231–236.

Abé, C., Johansson, E., Allzén, E., & Savic, I. (2014). Sexual orientation related differences in cortical thickness in male individuals. *PLoS ONE, 9,* e114721.

Abematsu, M., Kagawa, T., Fukuda, S., Inoue, T., Takebayashi, H., Komiya, S., & Taga, T. (2006). Basic fibroblast growth factor endows dorsal telencephalic neural progenitors with the ability to differentiate into oligodendrocytes but not gamma-aminobutyric acidergic neurons. *Journal of Neuroscience Research, 83,* 731–743.

Abouguendia, M., & Noels, K. A. (2001). General and acculturation-related daily hassles and psychological adjustment in first- and second-generation South Asian immigrants to Canada. *International Journal of Psychology, 36,* 163–173.

Abraham, W. (2006). Memory maintenance: The changing nature of neural mechanisms. *Current Directions in Psychological Science, 15,* 5–8.

Abramowitz, E., Barak, Y., Ben-Avi, I., & Knobler, H. (2008). Hypnotherapy in the treatment of chronic combat-related PTSD patients suffering from insomnia: A randomized, zolpidem-controlled clinical trial. *International Journal of Clinical and Experimental Hypnosis, 56,* 270–280.

Abramson, L. Y., Seligman, M. E., & Teasdale, J. D. (1978). Learned helplessness in humans: Critique and reformulation. *Journal of Abnormal Psychology, 87,* 49.

Acevedo-Garcia, D., Osypuk, T. L., McArdle, N., & Williams, D. R. (2008). Towards a policy relevant analysis of geographic and racial/ethnic disparities in child health. *Health Affairs, 27,* 321–333.

Adair, G. (1984). The Hawthorne effect: A reconsideration of the methodological artifact. *Journal of Applied Psychology, 69,* 334–345.

Adam, T. C., & Epel, E. S. (2007). Stress, eating, and the reward system. *Physiology and Behavior, 91,* 449–458.

Adams, H. E., Wright, L. W., & Lohr, B. A. (1996). Is homophobia associated with homosexual arousal? *Journal of Abnormal Psychology, 105,* 440–445.

Addis, M. E., & Mahalik, J. R. (2003). Men, masculinity, and the contexts of help seeking. *American Psychologist, 58,* 5–14.

Adelstein, J. S., Shehzad, Z., Mennes, M., DeYoung, C. G., Zuo, X.-N., et al. (2011). Personality is reflected in the brain's intrinsic functional architecture. *PLoS ONE, 6,* e27633.

Adorno, T. W., Frenkel-Brunswik, E., Levinson, D. J., & Sanford, R. N. (1950). *The authoritarian personality.* New York: Harper and Row.

Aggleton, J. P., & Waskett, L. (1999). The ability of odours to serve as state-dependent cues for real-world memories: Can Viking smells aid the recall of Viking experiences? *British Journal of Psychiatry, 90,* 1–7.

Ahamed, Y., Macdonald, H., Reed, K., Naylor, P.J., Liu-Ambrose, T., & McKay, H. (2007). School-based physical activity does not compromise children's academic performance. *Medicine and Science in Sports and Exercise, 39,* 371–376.

Ahlfinger, N. R., & Esser, J. K. (2001). Testing the groupthink model: Effects of promotional leadership and conformity predisposition. *Social Behavior and Personality, 29,* 31–41.

Ainsworth, M. D. S. (1978). The development of infant–mother attachment. In B. M. Caldwell & H. N. Ricciuti (Eds.), *Review of child development research* (Vol. 3, pp. 1–94). Chicago: University of Chicago Press.

Aknin, L. B., Hamlin, J. K., & Dunn, E. W. (2012). Giving leads to happiness in young children. *PLoS One, 7,* e39211.

Albert, S. (1977). Temporal comparison theory. *Psychological Review, 84,* 485–503.

Aldous, J., & Ganey, R. F. (1999). Family life and the pursuit of happiness: The influence of gender and race. *Journal of Family Issues, 20,* 155–180.

Alicke, M. D., & Olesya, G. (2005). The better-than-average effect. In M. D. Alicke, D. A. Dunning, and J. I. Krueger (Eds). The self in social judgment (pp. 85–106). New York, NY: Psychology Press.

Alladin, A. (2012). Cognitive hypnotherapy for major depressive disorder. *American Journal of Clinical Hypnosis, 54,* 275–293.

Alladin, A., & Alibhai, A. (2007). Cognitive hypnotherapy for depression: An empirical investigation. *International Journal of Clinical and Experimental Hypnosis, 55,* 147–166.

Allen, J. S., Bruss, J., Brown, C. K., & Damasio, H. (2005). Normal neuroanatomical variation due to age: The major lobes and a parcellation of the temporal region. *Neurobiology of Aging, 26*(9), 1245–1260.

Allen, R. (2004). Dopamine and iron in the pathophysiology of restless legs syndrome. *Sleep Medicine, 5,* 385–391.

Allen, S. W., Norman, G. R., & Brooks, L. R. (1992). Experimental studies of learning dermatologic diagnosis: The impact of examples. *Research Basic to Medical Education, 4,* 35–44.

Allport, G. W. (1954). *The nature of prejudice.* Cambridge, MA: Perseus Books.

Allport, G. W. (1955). *Becoming: Basic considerations for a psychology of personality.* New Haven, CT: Yale University Press.

Allport, G., & Odbert, H. W. (1936). Trait names: A psycholexical study. *Psychological Monographs, 47,* 211.

Altemeyer, B. (1996). *The authoritarian specter.* Cambridge, MA: Harvard University Press.

Amaral, D. G., Capitanio, J. P., Jourdain, M., Mason, W. A., Mendoza, S. P., & Prather, M. (2003). The amygdala: Is it an essential component of the neural network for social cognition? *Neuropsychologia, 41,* 235–240.

Amat, J., Baratta, M. V., Paul, E., Bland, S. T., Watkins, L. R., & Maier, S. F. (2005). Medial prefrontal cortex determines how stressor controllability affects behavior and dorsal raphe nucleus. *Nature Neuroscience, 8,* 365–371.

Amato, P. R. (2001). Children of divorce in the 1990s: An update of the Amato and Keith (1991) meta-analysis. *Journal of Family Psychology, 15,* 355–370.

Ambady, N., & Rosenthal, R. (1993). Half a minute: Predicting teacher evaluations from thin slices of nonverbal behavior and physical attractiveness. *Journal of Personality and Social Psychology, 64,* 431–441.

American Academy of Neurology Quality Standards Subcommittee. (1995). Practice parameters for determining brain death in adults. *Neurology, 45,* 1012–1014.

American Academy of Pediatrics. (1999). Media education. *Pediatrics, 104,* 341–342.

American College Health Association. (2007). The American College Health Association National College Health Assessment (ACHA-NCHA) spring 2006 reference group data report (abridged). *Journal of American College Health, 53,* 195–206.

American Heritage Dictionary. (2016). "Bird." Retrieved from https://ahdictionary.com

American Psychiatric Association. (2000). *Diagnostic and statistical manual of mental disorders* (4th ed., text revision). Washington, DC: Author.

American Psychiatric Association. (2013). *Diagnostic and statistical manual of mental disorders* (5th ed.). Arlington, VA: American Psychiatric Publishing.

American Psychological Association. (2004, September). Getting a good night's sleep with the help of psychology. Retrieved June 10, 2011, from http://www.apa.org/research/action/sleep.aspx

American Psychological Association. (2009). Task force on evidence-based practice. Retrieved from http://www.apa.org/practice/ebp.html

American Psychological Association. (2010). Psychology and global climate change: Addressing a multifaceted phenomenon and set of challenges. Retrieved December 31, 2013, from http://www.apa.org/science/about/publications/climate-change.aspx

American Psychological Association. (2011). Suicide warning signs. Retrieved from http://www.apa.org/topics/suicide/signs.aspx

An, K., Kobayashi, S., Tanaka, K., Kaneda, H., Su-gibayashi, M., & Okazaki, J. (1998). Dissociative identity disorder and childhood trauma in Japan. *Psychiatry and Clinical Neurosciences, 52,* 111–114.

Anastasi, A., & Urbina, S. (1996). *Psychological testing.* New York: Prentice Hall.

Anderson, B., & Harvey, T. (1996). Alterations in cortical thickness and neuronal density in the frontal cortex of Albert Einstein. *Neuroscience Letters, 210,* 161–164.

Anderson, C. A., Berkowitz, L., Donnerstein, E., Huesmann, L. R., Johnson, J. D., Linz, D., Malamuth, N. M., & Wartella, E. (2003). The influence of media violence on youth. *Psychological Science in the Public Interest, 4,* 81–110.

Anderson, C. A., Shibuya, A., Ihori, N., Swing, E. L., Bushman, B. J., Sakamoto, A., et al. (2010). Violent video game effects on aggression, empathy, and prosocial behavior in Eastern and Western countries: A meta-analytic review. *Psychological Bulletin, 136,* 151–173.

Anderson, D. R., Huston, A. C., Schmitt, K. L., Linebarger, D. L., & Wright, J. C. (2001). Early childhood television viewing and adolescent behavior. *Monographs of the Society for Research in Child Development, 68* (1, Serial No. 264).

Anderson, L., Lewis, G., Araya, R., Elgie, R., Harrison, G., . . . Williams, C. (2005). Self-help books for depression: How can practitioners and patients make the right choice? *British Journal of General Practice, 55,* 387–392.

Andreasen, N. C., Arndt, S., Alliger, R., Miller, D., & Flaum, M. (1995). Symptoms of schizophrenia: Methods, meaning, and mechanisms. *Archives of General Psychiatry, 52,* 341–351.

Andres, M., Pelgrims, B., Michaux, N., Oliver, E., & Pesenti, M. (2011). Role of distinct parietal areas in arithmetic: An fMRI-guided TMS study. *NeuroImage, 54,* 3048–3056.

Angus Reid Public Opinion. (2012, September 5). Britons and Canadians more likely to endorse evolution than Americans. Retrieved from http://angusreidglobal.com/wp-content/uploads/2012/09/2012.09.05_CreEvo.pdf.

Ano, G. G., & Vasconcelles, E. B. (2005). Religious coping and psychological adjustment to stress: A meta-analysis. *Journal of Clinical Psychology, 61,* 461–480.

Antoni, M., & Lutgendorf, S. (2007). Psychosocial factors and disease progression in cancer. *Current Directions in Psychological Science, 16,* 42–46.

Antoni, M., Lutgendorf, S., Cole, S., Dhabhar, F., Sephton, S., McDonald, P., et al. (2006). The influence of biobehavioral factors on tumor biology, pathways and mechanisms. *Nature Reviews Cancer, 6,* 240–248.

Antoni, M., Schneiderman, N., & Penedo, F. (2007). Behavioral interventions and psychoneuroimmunology. In R. Ader, R. Glaser, N. Cohen, & M. Irwin (Eds.), *Psychoneuroimmunology* (4th ed., pp. 615–703). New York: Academic Press.

Aouizerate, B., Cuny, E., Bardinct, E., Yelnik, J., Martin-Guehl, C., Rotge, J. Y., et al. (2009). Distinct striatal targets in treating obsessive-compulsive disorder and major depression. *Journal of Neurosurgery, 111,* 775–779.

Apaydin, E. A., Maher, A. R., Shanman, R., Booth, M. S., Miles, J. N., Sorbero, M. E., & Hempel, S. (2016). A systematic review of St. John's wort for major depressive disorder. *Systematic Reviews, 5,* 148.

Arendt, J. (2009). Managing jet lag: Some of the problems and possible new solutions. *Sleep Medicine Reviews, 13,* 249–256.

Arguin, M., Bub, D., & Dudek, G. (1996). Shape integration for visual object recognition and its implication in category-specific visual agnosia. *Visual Cognition, 3,* 221–275.

Argyelan, M., Lencz, T., Kaliora, S., Sarpal, D. K. Weissman, N., . . . Petrides, G. (2016). Subgenual cingulate cortical activity predicts the efficacy of electroconvulsive therapy. *Translational Psychiatry, 6,* e789.

Armstrong, H. L., & Reissing, E. D. (2015). Women's motivations to have sex in casual and committed relationships with male and female partners. *Archives of Sexual Behavior, 44,* 921–934.

Arnett, J. (1992). Reckless behavior in adolescence: A developmental perspective. *Developmental Review, 12,* 339–373.

Arnett, J. J. (2000). Emerging adulthood: A theory of development from the late teens through the twenties. *American Psychologist, 55,* 469–480.

Aron, A., Fisher, H., Mashek, D. J., Strong, G., Li, H., & Brown, L. L. (2005). Reward, motivation, and emotion systems associated with early-stage intense romantic love. *Journal of Neurophysiology, 94,* 327–337.

Asch, S. E. (1951). Effects of group pressure upon the modification and distortion of judgments. In H. Guetzkow (Ed.), *Groups, leadership and men: Research in human relations* (pp. 177–190). Oxford, UK: Carnegie Press.

Asch, S. E. (1955). Opinions and social pressure. *Scientific American, 193,* 31–35.

Asch, S. E. (1956). Studies of independence and conformity: A minority of one against a unanimous majority. *Psychological Monographs, 70* (9, No. 416).

Aschoff, J. (1965). Circadian rhythms in man. *Science, 148,* 1427–1432.

Aschoff, J., Gerecke, U., & Wever, R. (1967). Desynchronization of human circadian rhythms. *Japanese Journal of Physiology, 17,* 450–457.

Aschoff, J., & Wever, R. (1962). Spontanperidik des menschen bei ausschluss aller zeitgeber. *Naturwissenschaftern, 49,* 337–342.

Aserinsky, E., & Kleitman, N. (1953). Regularly occurring periods of eye motility, and concomitant phenomena, during sleep. *Science, 118,* 273–274.

Ashby, F. G., Isen, A. M., & Turken, A. U. (1999). A neuropsychological theory of positive affect and its influence on cognition. *Psychological Review, 106,* 529–550.

Ashtari, M., Cervellione, K., Cottone, J., Ardenkani, B. A., & Kumra, S. (2009). Diffusion abnormalities in adolescents and young adults with a history of heavy cannabis use. *Journal of Psychiatry Research, 43,* 189–204.

Ashton, M. C., & Lee, K. (2007). Empirical, theoretical, and practical advantages of the HEXACO model of personality structure. *Personality and Social Psychology Review, 11,* 150–166.

Ashton, M. C., & Lee, K. (2008). The HEXACO Model of Personality Structure and the importance of the H factor. *Social and Personality Psychology Compass, 2,* 1952–1962.

Aslin, R. N. (2007). What's in a look? *Developmental Science, 10,* 48–53.

Assor, A., Roth, G., & Deci, E. L. (2004). The emotional costs of parents' conditional regard: A self-determination theory analysis. *Journal of Personality, 72,* 47–88.

Atkinson, R. C., & Shiffrin, R. M. (1968). Human memory: A proposal system and its control processes. In K.W.S.A.J.T. Spence (Ed.), *The psychology of learning and motivation 8.* London: Academic Press.

Aubrey, J. B., Armstrong, B., Arkin, A., Smith, C. T., & Rose, G. (1999). Total sleep deprivation affects memory for a previously learned route. *Sleep, 22,* S246.

Ausubel, D. P. (1966). Early versus delayed review in meaningful learning. *Psychology in the Schools, 3,* 195–198.

Avena, N. M., Rada, P., & Hoebel, B. G. (2008). Evidence for sugar addiction: Behavioral and neurochemical effects of intermittent, excessive sugar intake. *Neuroscience and Biobehavioral Reviews, 32,* 20–39.

Avolio, B. J., & Waldman, D. A. (1994). Variations in cognitive, perceptual, and psychomotor abilities across the working life span: Examining the effects of race, sex, experience, education, and occupational type. *Psychology and Aging, 9,* 430–442.

Awh, E., Barton, B., & Vogel, E. K. (2007). Visual working memory represents a fixed number of items, regardless of complexity. *Psychological Science, 18,* 622–628.

Aylward, E. H., Park, J. E., Field, K. M., Parsons, A. C., Richards, T. L., . . . & Meltzoff, A. N. (2005). Brain activation during face perception: Evidence of a developmental change. *Journal of Cognitive Neuroscience, 17,* 308–319.

Babyak, M. A., Blumenthal, J. A., Herman, S., Khatri, P., Doraiswamy, P. M., . . . Krishnan, K. R. (2000). Exercise treatment for major depression: Maintenance of therapeutic benefit at 10 months. *Psychosomatic Medicine, 62,* 633–638.

Bachman, J. G., Wadsworth, K. N., O'Malley, P. M., & Johnston, L. D. (1997). *Smoking, drinking, and drug use in young adulthood: The impacts of new freedoms and new responsibilities.* Hillsdale, NJ: Lawrence Erlbaum Associates.

Baddeley, A. (2001). Is working memory still working? *American Psychologist, 56,* 851–864.

Baddeley, A. D., & Hitch, G. (1974). Working memory. In G. H. Bower (Ed.), *The psychology of learning and motivation: Advances in research and theory* (Vol. 8, pp. 47–89). New York: Academic Press.

Baddeley, A. D., Thomson, N., & Buchanan, M. (1975). Word length and the structure of short-term memory. *Journal of Verbal Learning & Verbal Behavior, 14,* 575–589.

Badman, M. K., & Flier, J. S. (2005). The gut and energy balance: Visceral allies in the obesity wars. *Science, 307,* 1909–1914.

Baer, R. A., Carmody, J., & Hunsinger, M. (2012). Weekly change in mindfulness and perceived stress in a mindfulness-based stress reduction program. *Journal of Clinical Psychology, 68,* 755–765.

Bahrick, H. (1984). Semantic memory content in permastore: Fifty years of memory for Spanish learned in school. *Journal of Experimental Psychology: General, 113,* 1–29.

Bahrick, L. E., & Watson, J. S. (1985). Detection of intermodal proprioceptive visual contingency as a potential basis of self-perception in infancy. *Developmental Psychology, 21,* 963–973.

Bailenson, J. N., Shum, M. S., Atran, S., Medin, D., & Coley, J. D. (2002). A bird's eye view: Biological categorization and reasoning within and across cultures. *Cognition, 84,* 1–53.

Bailey, J. M., Dunne, M. P., & Martin, N. G. (2000). Genetic and environmental influences on sexual orientation and its correlates in an Australian twin sample. *Journal of Personality and Social Psychology, 78,* 524–536.

Bailey, J. M., & Pillard, R. C. (1995). Genetics of human sexual orientation. *Annual Review of Sex Research, 6,* 126–150.

Bailey, J. M., Pillard, R. C., Neale, M. C., & Agyei, Y. (1993). Heritable factors influence sexual orientation in women. *Archives of General Psychiatry, 50,* 217–223.

Baird, B., Smallwood, J., & Schooler, J.W. (2011). Back to the future: autobiographical planning and the functionality of mind-wandering. *Consciousness and Cognition, 20,* 1604–1611.

Baker, J. R., Bezance, J. B., Zellaby, E., & Aggleton, J. P. (2004). Chewing gum can produce context-dependent effects upon memory. *Appetite, 43,* 207–210.

Balch, W., Myers, D., & Papotto, C. (1999). Dimensions of mood in mood-dependent memory. *Journal of Experimental Psychology: Learning, Memory, and Cognition, 25,* 70–83.

Ball, K., & Lee, C. (2002). Psychological stress, coping, and symptoms of disordered eating in a community sample of young Australian women. *International Journal of Eating Disorders, 31,* 71–81.

Ball, K., & Owsley, C. (1993). The useful field of view test: a new technique for evaluating age-related declines in visual function. *Journal of the American Optometric Association, 64,* 71–79.

Ball, K., & Owsley, C. (2000). Increasing mobility and reducing accidents of older drivers. In K.W. Schaie and M. Pietrucha (Eds.), *Mobility and transportation in the elderly* (pp. 213–251). New York: Springer.

Baltes, P. B., & Lindenberger, U. (1997). Emergence of a powerful connection between sensory and cognitive functions across the adult life span: A new window to the study of cognitive aging? *Psychology and Aging, 12,* 12–21.

Balter, L. J. T., Good, K. P., & Barrett, S. P. (2015). Smoking cue reactivity in current smokers, former smokers and never smokers. *Addictive Behaviors, 45,* 26–29.

Bandura, A. (1973). *Aggression: A social learning analysis.* Engelwood Cliffs, NJ: Prentice-Hall.

Bandura, A. (1977). *Social learning theory.* Englewood Cliffs, NJ: Prentice Hall.

Bandura, A. (1997). *Self-efficacy: The exercise of control.* New York: W.H. Freeman.

Bandura, A., Ross, D., & Ross, S. A. (1961). Transmission of aggression through imitation of aggressive models. *Journal of Abnormal and Social Psychology, 63,* 575–582.

Bandura, A., Ross, D., & Ross, S. A. (1963). Imitation of film-mediated aggressive models. *Journal of Abnormal and Social Psychology, 66,* 3–11.

Bandura, A., & Walters, R. H. (1963). *Social learning and personality development.* New York: Holt, Rinehart, and Winston.

Banse, R., Seise, J., & Zerbes, N. (2001). Implicit attitudes toward homosexuality: Reliability, validity, and controllability of the IAT. *Zeitschrift fur Experimentelle Psychologie, 48,* 145–160.

Barabasz, M. (2007). Efficacy of hypnotherapy in the treatment of eating disorders. *International Journal of Clinical and Experimental Hypnosis, 55,* 318–335.

Barbanoj, M. J., Riba, J., Clos, S., Giménez, S., Grasa, E., & Romero, S. (2008). Daytime Ayahuasca administration modulates REM and slow-wave sleep in healthy volunteers. *Psychopharmacology (Berl.), 196,* 315–326.

Bard, K. A., Todd, B., Bernier, C., Love, J., & Leavens, D. A. (2006). Self-awareness in human and chimpanzee infants: What is measured and what is meant by the mirror-and-mark test? *Infancy, 9,* 185–213.

Barger, L. K., Cade, B. E., Ayas, N. Y., Cronin, J. W., Rosner, B., Speizer, F. E., & Czeisler, C. A. (2005). Extended work shifts and the risk of motor vehicle crashes among interns. *The New England Journal of Medicine, 352,* 125–134.

Barger, S. D., & Sydeman, S. J. (2005). Does generalized anxiety disorder predict coronary heart disease risk factors independently of major depressive disorder? *Journal of Affective Disorders, 88,* 87–91.

Bargh, J. A. (1999). The cognitive monster. In S. Chaiken & Y. Trope (Eds.), *Dual process theories in social psychology* (pp. 361–382). New York: Guilford Press.

Bar-Haim, Y., Lamy, D., Pergamin, L., Bakermans-Kranenburg, M. J., & van Ijzendoorn, M. H. (2007). Threat-related attentional bias in anxious and nonanxious individuals: A metaanalytic study. *Psychological Bulletin, 133,* 1–24.

Barkley, R. A. (1998). *Attention-deficit/hyperactivity disorder.* Chicago: Guilford Press.

Barlow, D. H., Gorman, J. M., Shear, M. K., & Woods, S. W. (2000). Cognitive-behavioral therapy, imipramine, or their combination for panic disorder: A randomized controlled trial. *Journal of the American Medical Association, 283,* 2529–2536.

Barnea-Goraly, N., Menon, V., Eckert, M., Tamm, L., Bammer, R., Karchemskiy, A., et al. (2005). White matter development during childhood and adolescence: A cross-sectional diffusion tensor imaging study. *Cerebral Cortex, 15,* 1848–1854.

Barnes, C., & Wagner, D. (2009). Changing to Daylight Saving Time cuts into sleep and increases workplace injuries. *Journal of Applied Psychology, 94,* 1305–1317.

Barolo, R., Prado, L., & Merchant, H. (2014). Information processing in the primate basal ganglia during sensory guided and internally driven rhythmic tapping. *Journal of Neuroscience, 34,* 3910–3923.

Baron-Cohen, S., Burt, L., Smith-Laittan, F., Harrison, J., & Bolton, P. (1996). Synaesthesia: Prevalence and familiality. *Perception, 25,* 1073–1079.

Barr, R. (2010). Transfer of learning between 2D and 3D sources during infancy: Informing theory and practice. *Developmental Review, 30,* 128–154.

Barr, R., & Hayne, H. (1999). Developmental changes in imitation from television during infancy. *Child Development, 70,* 1067–1081.

Barratt, E. L., & Davis, N. J. (2015). Autonomous Sensory Meridian Response (ASMR): A flow-like mental state (No. e719v1). *PeerJ PrePrints.*

Barrett, L. F., & Salovey, P. (Eds.). (2002). *The wisdom in feeling: Psychological processes in emotional intelligence.* New York: Guilford Press.

Bartels, S., & Zeki, S. (2004). The neural correlated of maternal and romantic love. *Neuroimage, 21,* 1155–1166.

Barton, J., Castillo, M., & Petrie, R. (2016). Negative campaigning, fundraising, and voter turnout: A field experiment. *Journal of Economic Behavior & Organization, 121,* 99–113.

Bartus, R. T., Dean, R. L., Beer, B., & Lippa, A. S. (1982). The cholinergic hypothesis of geriatric memory dysfunction. *Science, 217,* 408–414.

Baskin-Sommers, A. (2016). Dissecting antisocial behavior: The impact of neural, genetic and environmental factors. *Clinical Psychological Science, 4*, 500–510.

Bassareo, V., & Di Chiara, G. (1999). Differential responsiveness of dopamine transmission to food-stimuli in nucleus accumbens shell/core compartments. *Neuroscience, 89*, 637–641.

Bateman, D. (2001). Neurological assessment of coma. *Journal of Neurology, Neurosurgery & Psychiatry, 71*, i13–i17.

Battaglia, M., Ogliari, A., Zanoni, A., Citterio, A., Pozzoli, U., . . . Marino, C. (2005). Influence of the serotonin transporter promoter gene and shyness on children's cerebral responses to facial expressions. *Archives of General Psychiatry, 62*, 85–94.

Battistella, G., Fornari, E., Annoni, J.-M., Chtioui, H., Dao, K., . . . Giroud, C. (2014). Long-term effects of cannabis on brain structure. *Neuropsychopharmacology, 39*, 2041–2048.

Baumeister, R. F., & Leary, M. R. (1995). The need to belong: Desire for interpersonal attachments as a fundamental human motivation. *Psychological Bulletin, 117*, 497–529.

Bauserman, R., & Davis, C. (1996). Perceptions of early sexual experiences and adult sexual adjustment. *Journal of Psychology and Human Sexuality, 8*, 37–59.

Bavelier, D., Green, C. S., & Dye, M. W. G. (2010). Children, wired: For better and for worse. *Neuron, 67*, 692–701.

Baym, C., Corbett, B., Wright, S., & Bunge, S. (2008). Neural correlates of tic severity and cognitive control in children with Tourette syndrome. *Brain: A Journal of Neurology, 131*(1), 165–179.

Bazarian, J. J., Zhong, J., Blyth, B., Zhu, T., Kavcic, V., & Peterson, D. (2007). Diffusion tensor imaging detects clinically important axonal damage after mild traumatic brain injury: A pilot study. *Journal of Neurotrauma, 24*, 1447–1459.

Beall, E. B., Malone, D. A., Dale, R. M., Muzina, D. J., Koenig, K. A., et al. (2012). Effects of electroconvulsive therapy on brain functional activation and connectivity in depression. *Journal of ECT, 28*, 234–241.

Beauchamp, G. K., & Mennella, J. A. (2009). Early flavor learning and its impact on later feeding behavior. *Journal of Pediatric Gastroenterology and Nutrition, 48*, S25–S30.

Beauregard, M., Courtemanche, J., Paquette, V., & St-Pierre, E. (2009). The neural basis of unconditional love. *Psychiatry Research: Neuroimaging, 172*, 93–98.

Bechara, A., Damasio, A. R., Damasio, H., & Anderson, S. W. (1994). Insensitivity to future consequences following damage to human prefrontal cortex. *Cognition, 50*, 7–15.

Beck, A. T. (1963). Thinking and depression: I. Idiosyncratic content and cognitive distortions. *Archives of General Psychiatry, 9*, 324–333.

Beck, A. T., & Steer, R. A. (1977). *Manual for the Beck Depression Inventory.* San Antonio, TX: Psychology Corporation.

Beck, D. M., & Kastner, S. (2009). Top-down and bottom-up mechanisms in biasing competition in the human brain. *Vision Research, 49*, 1154–1165.

Beck, H. P., Levinson, S., & Irons, G. (2009). Finding little Albert: A journey to John B. Watson's infant laboratory. *American Psychologist, 64*, 605–614.

Becker, E. (1971). *The birth and death of meaning: An interdisciplinary perspective on the problem of man* (2nd ed.). New York, NY: Free Press.

Becker, E. (1973). *The denial of death.* New York, NY: Free Press.

Beebe, B., Jaffe, J., Markese, S., Buck, K., Chen, H., . . . Feldstein, S. (2010). The origins of 12-month attachment: A microanalysis of 4-month mother–infant interaction. *Attachment & Human Development, 12*, 6–141.

Beebe, B., Lachmann, F., & Jaffe, J. (1997). Mother–infant interaction structures and presymbolic self and object representations. *Psychoanalytic Dialogues, 7*, 133–182.

Beeman, E. A. (1947). The relation of the interval between castration and 1st encounter to the aggressive behavior of mind. *Anatomical Record, 99*, 570–571.

Beilock, S. L. (2008). Math performance in stressful situations. *Current Directions in Psychological Science, 17*, 339–343.

Beilock, S. L. (2010). *Choke: What the secrets of the brain reveal about getting it right when you have to.* New York: Free Press.

Beiser, M., & Gotowiec, A. (2000). Accounting for native/non-native differences in IQ scores. *Psychology in the Schools, 37*, 237–252.

Béjot, Y., Jeunet, N., Garrouty, R., Maltaverne, D., Nicolleau, L., Giroud, M., & Didi-Roy, R. (2010). Sexsomnia: An uncommon variety of parasomnia. *Clinical Neurology and Neurosurgery, 112*, 72–75.

Bekinschtein, T. A., Cardozo, J., & Manes, F. F. (2008). Strategies of Buenos Aires waiters to enhance memory capacity in a real-life setting. *Behavioural Neurology, 20*, 65–70.

Bell, P. A., & Yee, L. A. (1989). Skill level and audience effects on performance of a karate drill. *Journal of Social Psychology, 129*, 191–200.

Bell, R. A., Paterniti, D. A., Azari, R., Duberstein, P. R., & Epstein, R. M. (2010). Encouraging patients with depressive symptoms to seek care: A mixed methods approach to message development. *Patient Education and Counseling, 78*, 198–205.

Belsky, J., & Rovine, M. (1990). Patterns of marital change across the transition to parenthood. *Journal of Marriage and the Family, 52*, 109–123.

Bem, S. L. (1981). Gender schema theory: A cognitive account of sex typing. *Psychological Review, 88*, 354–364.

Bem, S. L. (1993). *The lenses of gender: Transforming the debate on sexual inequality.* New Haven, CT: Yale University Press.

Bem, S. L., & Bem, D. J. (1973). Does sex-biased job advertising "aid and abet" sex discrimination? *Journal of Applied Social Psychology, 3*, 6–18.

Benbow, C. P., & Stanley, J. C. (1983). Sex differences in mathematical reasoning ability: More facts. *Science, 222*, 1029–1031.

Benedict, R. (1938). Continuities and discontinuities in cultural conditioning. *Psychiatry: Journal for the Study of Interpersonal Processes, 2*, 161–167.

Benet-Martinez, V., & John, O. P. (1998). Los Cinco Grandes across cultures and ethnic groups: Multitrait method analyses of the Big Five in Spanish and English. *Journal of Personality and Social Psychology, 75*, 729–750.

Bennett, G. G., Wolin, K. Y., Robinson, E. L., Fowler, S., & Edwards, C. L. (2005). Racial/ethnic harassment and tobacco use among African American young adults. *American Journal of Public Health, 95*, 238–240.

Berenson, A. (2007, January 5). Lilly settles with 18,000 over Zyprexa. *New York Times.* Retrieved from http://www.nytimes.com/2007/01/05/business/05drug.html

Berger, J. M., Levant, R., McMillan, K. K., Kelleher, W., & Sellers, A. (2005). Impact of gender role conflict, traditional masculinity ideology, alexithymia, and age on men's attitudes towards psychological help seeking. *Psychology of Men & Masculinity, 6*, 73–78.

Berger, R., & Phillips, N. (1995). Energy conservation and sleep. *Behavioural Brain Research, 69*, 65–73.

Berkman, L. F., & Breslow, L. (1983). *Health and ways of living: The Alameda county study.* New York: Oxford University Press.

Berlim, M. T., van den Eynde, F., Tavor-Perdomo, S., & Daskalakis, Z. J. (2014). Response, remission, and drop-out rates following high-frequency repetitive transcranial magnetic stimulation (rTMS) for treating major depression: A systematic review and meta-analysis of randomized, double-blind and sham-controlled trials. *Psychological Medicine, 44*, 224–239.

Berlin, B. (1974). *Principles of Tzeltal plant classification.* New York: Academic Press.

Berlucchi, G. (2011). Brain plasticity and cognitive neurorehabilitation. *Neuropsychological Rehabilitation, 21*, 560–578.

Berns, G. S., Chappelow, J., Fink, C. F., Pagnoni, G., Martin-Skurski, M. E., & Richards, J. (2005). Neurobiological correlates of social conformity and independence during mental rotation. *Biological Psychiatry, 58*, 245–253.

Berquier, A., & Ashton, R. (1992). Characteristics of the frequent nightmare sufferer. *Journal of Abnormal Psychology, 101*, 246–250.

Berridge, C. W., & Waterhouse, B. D. (2003). The locus coeruleus-noradrenergic system: Modulation of behavioural state and state-dependent cognitive processes. *Brain Research Reviews, 42*, 33–84.

Berridge, K. C., Robinson, T. E., & Aldridge, J. W. (2009). Dissecting components of reward: "liking", "wanting", and learning. *Current Opinion in Pharmacology, 9*(1), 65–73. doi:10.1016/j.coph.2008.12.014

Berry, S. L., Beatty, W. W., & Klesges, R. C. (1985). Sensory and social influences on ice-cream consumption by males and females in a laboratory setting. *Appetite, 6,* 41–45.

Bertram, L., Lill, C. M., & Tanzi, R. E. (2010). The genetics of Alzheimer's disease: Back to the future. *Neuron, 68,* 270–281.

Best, D. (2009). Secondhand and prenatal tobacco smoke exposure. *Pediatrics, 123,* e1017–e1044.

Bestmann, S. (2008). The physiological basis of transcranial magnetic stimulation. *Trends in Cognitive Sciences, 12,* 81–83.

Bevan, T. E. (2014). *The psychobiology of transsexualism and transgenderism.* Santa Barbara: CA: Praeger Publishers.

Bezeau, S., & Graves, R. (2001). Statistical power and effect sizes of clinical neuropsychology research. *Journal of Clinical and Experimental Neuropsychology, 23,* 399–406.

Bhatara, A., Tirovolas, A., Duan, L. M., Levy, B., & Levitin, D. J. (2011). Perception of emotional expression in musical performance. *Journal of Experimental Psychology: Human Perception and Performance, 37,* 921–934.

Bhattacharya, J., & Bundorf, M. K. (2005). The incidence of healthcare costs of obesity. Working Paper #11303. National Bureau of Economic Research.

Bhugra, D. (2005). The global prevalence of schizophrenia. *PloS Medicine, 2,* 372–373.

Bialystok, E. (2009). International symposium on bilingualism lecture. *Bilingualism: Language and Cognition, 12,* 3–11.

Bialystok, E. (2011a). Reshaping the mind: The benefits of bilingualism. *Canadian Journal of Experimental Psychology, 65,* 229–235.

Bialystok, E. (2011b). Coordination of executive functions in monolingual and bilingual children. *Journal of Experimental Child Psychology, 110,* 461–468.

Bialystok, E., Craik, F. I. M., & Freedman, M. (2007). Bilingualism as a protection against the onset of symptoms of dementia. *Neuropsychologia, 45,* 459–464.

Bialystok, E., Craik, F. I. M., Klein, R., & Viswanathan, M. (2004). Bilingualism, aging, cognitive control: Evidence from the Simon task. *Psychology & Aging, 19,* 290–303.

Biederman, J., Rosenbaum, J. F., Hirshfeld, D. R., Faraone, S. V., Bolduc, E. A., Gersten, M., et al. (1990). Psychiatric correlates of behavioral inhibition in young children of parents with and without psychiatric disorders. *Archives of General Psychiatry, 47,* 21.

Bigelow, H. J. (1850). Dr. Harlow's case of recovery from the passage of an iron bar through the head. *American Journal of Medical Sciences, 20,* 13–22.

Birbaumer, N., Veit, R., Lotze, M., Erb, M., Hermann, C., Grodd, W., & Flor, H. (2005). Deficient fear conditioning in psychopathy: A functional magnetic resonance imaging study. *Archives of General Psychiatry, 62,* 799–805.

Bisiach, E., & Luzzatti, C. (1978). Unilateral neglect of representational space. *Cortex, 14,* 129–133.

Bjork, R. A., & Whitten, W. B. (1974). Recency-sensitive retrieval processes in long-term free recall. *Cognitive Psychology, 6,* 173–189.

Blackwell, L., Trzesniewski, K., & Dweck, C. (2007). Implicit theories of intelligence predict achievement across an adolescent transition: A longitudinal study and an intervention. *Child Development, 78,* 246–263.

Blair, C. (2006). How similar are fluid cognition and general intelligence? A developmental neuroscience perspective on fluid cognition as an aspect of human cognitive ability. *Behavioral and Brain Sciences, 29,* 109–160.

Blair, C., & Razza, R. P. (2007). Relating effortful control, executive function, and false belief understanding to emerging math and literacy ability in kindergarten. *Child Development, 78,* 64–663.

Blair, K. L., & Hoskin, R. A. (2016). Contemporary understandings of femme identities and related experiences of discrimination. *Psychology & Sexuality, 7,* 101–115.

Blair, R. J. R. (2010). Psychopathy, frustration, and the role of reactive aggression: The role of the ventromedial prefrontal cortex. *British Journal of Psychology, 101,* 383–399.

Blake, R., Palmeri, T. J., Marois, R., & Kim, C.-Y. (2005). On the perceptual reality of synesthetic color. In L. C. Robertson & N. Sagiv (Eds.), *Synesthesia* (pp. 47–73). Oxford, UK: Oxford University Press.

Blandin, Y., & Proteau, L. (2000). On the cognitive basis of observational learning: Development of mechanisms for the detection and correction of errors. *Quarterly Journal of Experimental Psychology: Human Experimental Psychology, 53,* 846–867.

Blesa, J., Phani, S., Jackson-Lewis, V., & Pzedborski, S. (2012). Classic and new animal models of Parkinson's Disease. *Journal of Biomedicine and Biotechnology, 2012,* 1–10.

Bliss, T., & Collingridge, G. L. (1993). A synaptic model of memory: Long-term potentiation in the hippocampus. *Nature, 361,* 31–39.

Bliss, T., & Lømo, T. (1973). Long-lasting potentiation of synaptic transmission in the dentate area of the anaesthetized rabbit following stimulation of the perforant path. *Journal of Physiology, 232,* 331–356.

Block, R. I., O'Leary, D. S., Hichwa, R. D., Augustinack, J. C., Ponto, L. L. B., Ghoneim, M. M., et al. (2002). Effects of frequent marijuana use on memory-related regional cerebral blood flow. *Pharmacology Biochemistry and Behavior, 72,* 237–250.

Boak, A., Hamilton, H. A., Adlaf, E. M., & Mann, R. E. (2015). *Drug use among Ontario students, 1977–2015: Detailed OSDUHS findings (CAMH Research Document Series No. 41).* Toronto, ON: Centre for Addiction and Mental Health.

Boesch, C. (1991). Teaching among wild chimpanzees. *Animal Behaviour, 41,* 530–532.

Bogaert, A. F. (2008). Menarche and father absence in a national probability sample. *Journal of Biosocial Sciences, 40,* 623–636.

Bogle, K. E., & Smith, B. H. (2009). Illicit methylphenidate use: A review of prevalence, availability, pharmacology, and consequences. *Current Drug Abuse Reviews, 2,* 157–176.

Bohart, A., Elliott, R., Greenberg, L., & Watson, J. (2002). Empathy. In J. C. Norcross (Ed.), *Psychotherapy relationships that work. Therapist contributions and responsiveness to patients* (pp. 89–108). New York: Oxford University Press.

Bohart, A. C. (2003). *Person-centered psychotherapy and related experiential approaches* (pp. 107–148). New York: Guilford Press.

Boldizar, J. P., Wilson, K. L., & Deemer, D. K. (1989). Gender, life experiences, and moral judgment development: A process-oriented approach. *Journal of Personality and Social Psychology, 57,* 229–238.

Bolla, K. I., Brown, K., Eldreth, D., Tate, K., & Cadet, J. L. (2002). Dose-related neurocognitive effects of marijuana use. *Neurology, 59,* 1337–1343.

Boly, M., Faymonville, M. E., Peigneux, P., Lambermont, B., Damas, P., Del Fiore, G., et al. (2004). Auditory processing in severely brain injured patients: Differences between the minimally conscious state and the persistent vegetative state. *Archives of Neurology, 61,* 233–238.

Bonanno, G. A. (2004). Loss, trauma, and human resilience: Have we underestimated the human capacity to thrive after extremely aversive events? *American Psychologist, 58,* 20–28.

Bondolfi, G., Jermann, F., Van der Linden, M., Gex-Fabry, M., Bizzini, L., Rouget, B. W., et al. (2010). Depression relapse prophylaxis with mindfulness-based cognitive therapy: Replication and extension in the Swiss health care system. *Journal of Affective Disorders, 122,* 224–231.

Bonebakker, A. E., Bonke, B., Klein, J., Wolters, G., Stijen, T., Passchier, J., et al. (1996). Information processing during general anesthesia: Evidence for unconscious memory. *Memory & Cognition, 24,* 766–776.

Bonnano, G. A. (2004). Loss, trauma, and human resilience: Have we underestimated the human capacity to thrive after extremely aversive events? *American Psychologist, 59,* 20–28.

Boomsma, D. I., Van Beijsterveldt, C. E. M., & Hudziak, J. J. (2005). Genetic and environmental influences on anxious/depression during childhood: A study from the Netherlands Twin Register. *Genes, Brain, and Behavior, 4,* 466–481.

Booth, A., Shelley, G., Mazur, A., Tharp, G., & Kittok, R. (1989). Testosterone, and winning and losing in human competition. *Hormones & Behavior, 23,* 556–571.

Born, J., Lange, T., Hansen, K., Molle, M., & Fehm, H. L. (1997). Effects of sleep and circadian rhythm on human circulating immune cells. *The Journal of Immunology, 158,* 4454–4464.

Borrelli, F., & Izzo, A. A. (2009). Herb–drug interactions with St. John's wort (Hypericum perforatum): An update on clinical observations. *American Association of Pharmaceutical Scientists' Journal, 11,* 710–727.

Bötzel, K., Schulze, S., & Stodieck, S. R. (1995). Scalp topography and analysis of intracranial sources of face-evoked potentials. *Experimental Brain Research, 104,* 135–143.

Bouchard, T. J., Lykken, D. T., McGue, M., Segal, N. L., & Tellegen, A. (1990). Sources of human psychological differences: The Minnesota study of twins reared apart. *Science, 250,* 223–228.

Bourdage, J. S., Lee, K., Ashton, M. C., & Perry, A. (2007). Big Five and HEXACO model personality correlates of sexuality. *Personality and Individual Differences, 43,* 1506–1516.

Bouton, M. E. (1994). Context, ambiguity, and classical conditioning. *Current Directions in Psychological Science, 3,* 49–53.

Bouton, M. E. (2002). Context, ambiguity, and unlearning: Sources of relapse after behavioral extinction. *Biological Psychiatry, 52,* 976–986.

Boveroux, P., Vanhaudenhuyse, A., Bruno, M. A., Noirhomme, Q., Lauwick, S., . . .& Boly, M. (2010). Breakdown of within- and between-network resting state functional magnetic resonance imaging connectivity during propofol-induced loss of consciousness. *Anesthesiology, 113,* 1038–1053.

Bower, G. H. (1981). Mood and memory. *American Psychologist, 36,* 129–148.

Bowker, A., Boekhoven, B., Nolan, A., Bauhaus, S., Glover, P., Powell, T., & Taylor, S. (2009). Naturalistic observations of spectator behavior at youth hockey games. *The Sport Psychologist, 23,* 301–316.

Bowlby, J. (1951). Maternal care and mental health. *World Health Organization Monograph,* Serial No. 2.

Bowlby, J. (1980). *Attachment and loss, Vol. 3: Loss: Sadness and depression.* New York: Basic Books.

Bowlby, J. (1988). *A secure base: Clinical applications of attachment theory.* London, UK: Routledge.

Boyce, W., Doherty-Poirier, M., MacKinnon, D., Fortin, C., Saab, H., . . . Gallupe, O. (2006). Sexual health of Canadian youth: Findings from the Canadian youth, sexual health and HIV/AIDS study. *Canadian Journal of Human Sexuality, 15,* 59–68.

Boyd, J. E., Katz, E. P., Link, B. G., & Phelan, J. C. (2010). The relationship of multiple aspects of stigma and personal contact with someone hospitalized for mental illness, in a nationally representative sample. *Social Psychiatry and Psychiatric Epidemiology, 45,* 1063–1070.

Bracha, H., Ralston, T., Matsukawa, J., Williams, A., & Bracha, A. (2004). Does "fight or flight" need updating? *Psychosomatics: Journal of Consultation Liaison Psychiatry, 45,* 448–449.

Bradley, R. H., Whiteside, L., Caldwell, B., Casey, P. H., Kelleher, K., et al. (1993). Maternal IQ, the home environment, and child IQ in low birthweight, premature children. *International Journal of Behavioral Development, 16,* 61–74.

Brain Injury Canada. (2016). *About acquired brain injury.* Retrieved from http://braininjurycanada.ca/acquired-brain-injury/

Brain Tumour Foundation of Canada. (2013). *Brain tumour facts.* Retrieved from http://www.braintumour.ca/2494/brain-tumour-facts

Brainard, D. H., & Hurlbert, A. C. (2015). Colour vision: Understanding #TheDress. *Current Biology, 25,* R551–R554.

Branch, C. H., & Eurman, L. J. (1980). Social attitudes towards patients with anorexia nervosa. *The American Journal of Psychiatry, 137,* 631–632.

Bransford, J. D., & Johnson, M. K. (1973). Considerations of some problems of comprehension. In W. Chase (Ed.), *Visual information processing* (pp. 383–438). Oxford, UK: Academic.

Braver, T. S., & Barch, D. M. (2002). A theory of cognitive control, aging cognition, and neuromodulation. *Neuroscience and Biobehavioral Reviews, 26,* 809–817.

Brefczynski-Lewis, J. A., Lutz, A., Schaefer, H. S., Levinson, D. B., & Davidson, R. J. (2007). Neural correlates of attentional expertise in long-term meditation practitioners. *Proceeding of the National Academy of Sciences, 104,* 11483–11488.

Brendel, G. R., Stern, E., & Silbersweig, D. (2005). Defining the neurocircuitry of borderline personality disorder: Functional neuroimaging approaches. *Development and Psychopathology, 17,* 1197–1206.

Brion, M. J., Victora, C., Matijasevich, A., Horta, B., Anselmi, L., . . . Davey Smith, G. (2010). Maternal smoking and child psychological problems: Disentangling causal and noncausal effects. *Pediatrics, 126,* e57–e65.

Broca, P. (1861). Remarques sur le siège de la faculté du langage articule, suivies dune observation daphémie (Perte de la Parole). *Bulletin de la Societé Anatomique de Paris, 6,* 330–357.

Brondolo, E., Brady, N., Thompson, S., Contrada, R. J., Cassells, A., . . . Sweeney, M. (2008a). Perceived racism and negative affect: Analyses of trait and state measures of affect in a community sample. *Journal of Social and Clinical Psychology, 27,* 150–173.

Brondolo, E., Libby, D. J., Denton, E., Thompson, S., Schwartz, J., Sweeney, M., et al. (2008b). Racism and ambulatory blood pressure in a community sample. *Psychosomatic Medicine, 70,* 49–56.

Brook, J. S., Stimmel, M. A., Zhang, C., & Brook, D. W. (2008). The association between earlier marijuana use and subsequent academic achievement and health problems: A longitudinal study. *American Journal of Addiction, 17,* 155–160.

Brooks, D. C., Palmatier, M. I., Garcia, E. O., & Johnson, J. L. (1999). An extinction cue reduced spontaneous recovery of a conditioned taste aversion. *Animal Learning & Behavior, 27,* 77–88.

Brooks, L. R. (1978). Nonanalytic concept formation and memory for instances. In E. Rosch & B. Lloyd (Eds.), *Cognition and categorization* (pp. 169–211). Hillsdale, NJ: Erlbaum.

Brotto, L. A., Chik, H. M., Ryder, A. G., Gorzalka, B. B., & Seal, B. N. (2005). Acculturation and sexual function in Asian women. *Archives of Sexual Behavior, 34,* 613–626.

Brown, A. S., & Derkits, E. J. (2010). Prenatal infection and schizophrenia: A review of epidemiologic and translational studies. *American Journal of Psychiatry, 167,* 261–280.

Brown, A. S., & McNeil, D. (1966). The "tip of the tongue" phenomenon. *Journal of Verbal Learning and Verbal Behavior, 5,* 325–337.

Brown, G. W., Birley, J. L., & Wing, J. K. (1972). Influence of family life on the course of schizophrenic disorders: A replication. *The British Journal of Psychiatry, 121,* 251–258.

Brown, J. (1958). Some tests of decay theory of immediate memory. *Quarterly Journal of Experimental Psychology, 10,* 12–24.

Brown, J. M. (2003). Eyewitness memory for arousing events: Putting things into context. *Applied Cognitive Psychology, 17,* 93–106.

Brown, M., Keyner, R., & Lumsden, A. (2001). *The developing brain.* Oxford, UK: Oxford University Press.

Brown, R., & Kulik, J. (1977). Flashbulb memories. *Cognition, 5,* 73–99.

Brown, R. E., Basheer, R., McKenna, J. T., Strecker, R. E., & McCarley, R. W. (2012). Control of sleep and wakefulness. *Physiology Review, 92,* 1087–1187.

Brown, R. E., & Milner, P. M. (2003). The legacy of Donald O. Hebb: More than the Hebb Synapse. *Nature Reviews Neuroscience, 4,* 1013–1019.

Bruck, M., & Ceci, S. J. (1999). The suggestibility of children's memory. *Annual Review of Psychology, 50,* 419–439.

Brunell, A. B., Staats, S., Barden, J., & Hupp, J. M. (2011). Narcissism and academic dishonesty: The exhibitionism dimension and the lack of guilt. *Personality and Individual Differences, 50,* 323–328.

Buck, L. B., & Axel, R. (1991). A novel multigene family may encode odorant receptors: A molecular basis for odor recognition. *Cell, 65,* 175–187.

Buckholtz, J. W., Treadway, M. T., Cowan, R. L., Woodward, N. D., Li, R., Ansari, M. S., Baldwin, R. M., et al. (2010). Dopaminergic network differences in human impulsivity. *Science, 329,* 532.

Buehlman, K. T., Gottman, J. M., & Katz, L. F. (1992). How a couple views their past predicts their future: Predicting divorce from an oral history interview. *Journal of Family Psychology, 5,* 295–318.

Bugg, J. M., Zook, N. A., DeLosh, E. L., Davalos, D. B., & Davis, H.P. (2006). Age differences in fluid intelligence: Contributions of general slowing and frontal decline. *Brain and Cognition, 62,* 9–16.

Bukhari, I. A., & Dar, A. (2013). Behavioral profile of *hypericum performatum* (St. John's wort) extract. A comparison with standard antidepressants in animal models of depression. *European Review for Medical and Pharmacological Sciences, 17,* 1082–1089.

Bunn, E. M., Tyler, L. K., & Moss, H. E. (1998). Category-specific semantic deficits: The role of familiarity and property type reexamined. *Neuropsychology, 12,* 367–379.

Burger, J. M. (1999). The foot-in-the-door compliance procedure: A multiple-process analysis and review. *Personality and Social Psychology Review, 3*, 303–325.

Burkam, D. T., Ready, D. D., Lee, V. E., & LoGerfo, L. F. (2004). Social-class differences in summer learning between kindergarten and first grade: Model specification and estimation. *Sociology of Education, 77*, 1–31.

Burke, B. L., Kosloff, S., & Landau, M. J. (2013). Death goes to the polls: A meta-analysis of mortality salience effects on political attitudes. *Political Psychology, 34*, 183–199.

Burke, B. L., Martens, A., & Faucher, E. H. (2010). Two decades of terror management theory: A meta-analysis of mortality salience research. *Personality and Social Psychology Review, 14*, 155–195.

Burke, T. M., Markwald, R. R., McHill, A. W., Chinoy, E. D., Snider, J. A., . . .& Wright, Jr., K. P. (2015). Effects of caffeine on the human circadian clock in vivo and in vitro. *Science Translational Medicine, 16*, 305.

Burnand, Y., Andreoli, A., Kolatte, E., Venturini A., & Rosset, N. (2002). Psychodynamic psychotherapy and clomipramine in the treatment of major depression. *Psychiatric Services, 53*, 585–580.

Burns, M., & Seligman, M. (1989). Explanatory style across the life span: Evidence for stability over 52 years. *Journal of Personality and Social Psychology, 56*, 471–477.

Buschkuehl, M., Jaeggi, S. M., Hutchison, S., Perrig-Chiello, P., Däpp, C., Müller, M., et al. (2008). Impact of working memory training on memory performance in old-old adults. *Psychology and Aging, 23*, 743–753.

Bushman, B. J., & Anderson, C. A. (2007). Measuring the strength of the effect of violent media on aggression. *American Psychologist, 62*, 253–254.

Bushman, B. J., Moeller, S. J., & Crocker, J. (2011). Sweets, sex, or self-esteem? Comparing the value of self-esteem boosts with other pleasant rewards. *Journal of Personality, 79*, 993–1012.

Buss, D. M. (1989). Sex differences in human mating preferences: Evolutionary hypotheses tested in 37 different cultures. *Behavioral and Brain Sciences, 12*, 1–49.

Buss, D. M. (2003). *The evolution of desire: Strategies of human mating.* New York: Basic Books.

Buston, P. M., & Emlen, S. T. (2003). Cognitive processes underlying human mate choice: The relationship between self-perception and mate preference in Western society. *Proceedings of the National Academy of Sciences, 100*, 8805–8810.

Butcher, L. M., Davis, O. S. P., Craig, I. W., & Plomin, R. (2008). Genome-wide quantitative trait locus association scan of general cognitive ability using pooled DNA and 500K single nucleotide polymorphism microarrays. *Genes, Brains and Behavior, 7*, 435–446.

Butler, B., & Klein, R. (2009). Inattentional blindness for ignored words: Comparison of explicit and implicit memory tasks. *Consciousness & Cognition, 18*, 811–819.

Butterweck, V. (2003). Mechanisms of action of St. John's wort in depression: What is known? *CNS Drugs, 17*, 539–562.

Button, E. J., Sonuga-Barke, E. J., Davies, J., & Thompson, M. (1996). A prospective study of self-esteem in the reduction of eating problems in adolescent schoolgirls: Questionnaire findings. *British Journal of Clinical Psychology, 35*, 193–203.

Byers, E. S., Sears, H. A., & Foster, L. R. (2013). Factors associated with middle school students' perceptions of the quality of school-based sexual health education. *Sex Education, 13*, 214-227.

Cabeza, R. (2002). Hemispheric asymmetry reduction in older adults: The HAROLD model. *Psychology and Aging, 17*, 85–100.

Caci, H., Deschaux, O., Adan, A., & Natale, V. (2009). Comparing three morningness scales: Age and gender effects, structure and cut-off criteria. *Sleep Medicine, 10*, 240–245.

Cacioppo, J. T., & Cacioppo, S. (2014). Social relationships and health: The toxic effects of perceived social isolation. *Social and Personality Psychology Compass, 8*, 58–72.

Cacioppo, J. T., & Hawkley, L. C. (2003). Social isolation and health, with an emphasis on underlying mechanisms. *Perspectives in Biology and Medicine, 46*, S39–S52.

Cacioppo, J. T., Hawkley, L. C., & Berntson, G. G. (2003). The anatomy of loneliness. *Current Directions in Psychological Science, 12*, 71–74.

Cacioppo, J. T., Hawkley, L. C., Norman, G. J., & Berntson, G. G. (2011). Social isolation. *Annuals of the New York Academy of Sciences, 1231*, 17–22.

Cacioppo, J. T., Hughes, M. E., Waite, L. J., Hawkley, L. C., & Thisted, R. A. (2006). Loneliness as a specific risk factor for depressive symptoms: Cross-sectional and longitudinal analyses. *Psychology and Aging, 21*, 140–151.

Cacioppo, J. T., Petty, R. E., Kao, C., & Rodriguez, R. (1986). Central and peripheral routes to persuasion: An individual difference perspective. *Journal of Personality and Social Psychology, 51*, 1032–1043.

Cacioppo, J. T., Reis, H. T., & Zautra, A. J. (2011). Social resilience. *American Psychologist, 66*, 43–51.

Cahn, B. R., & Polich, J. (2006). Meditation states and traits: EEG, ERP and neuroimaging studies. *Psychological Bulletin, 132*, 180–211.

Cai, D. J., Mednick, S. A., Harrison, E. M., Kanady, J. C., & Mednick, S. C. (2009). REM, not incubation, improves creativity by priming associative networks. *Proceedings of the National Academy of Science USA, 106*, 10130–10134.

Cairns, R., & Cairns, B. (1994). *Lifelines and risks: Pathways of youth in our time.* New York: Cambridge University Press.

Caldwell, H. K., & Young, W. S. (2006). Oxytocin and vasopressin: Genetics and behavioral implications. In A. Lajtha & R. Lim (Eds.), *Handbook of neurochemistry and molecular neurobiology* (pp. 573–607). Berlin: Springer-Verlag.

Campos, J. J., Bertenthal, B. I., & Kermoian, R. (1992). Early experience and emotional development: The emergence of wariness of heights. *Psychological Science, 3*, 61–64.

Canadian Medical Association. (2008). *8th Annual National Report Card on Health Care, August 2008.* Ottawa, ON: Author.

Canadian Psychological Association. (2016). *"Psychology Works" fact sheet: Gender dysphoria in adolescents and adults.* Ottawa, ON: Canadian Psychological Association.

Canli, T., Sivers, H., Whitfield, S. L., Gotlib, I. H., & Gabrieli, J. D. E. (2002). Amygdala response to happy faces as a function of extraversion. *Science, 296*, 2191.

Cao, X., Cui, Z., Feng, R., Tang, Y., Qin, Z., Mei, B., & Tsien, J. (2007). Maintenance of superior learning and memory function in NR2B transgenic mice during ageing. *European Journal of Neuroscience, 25*, 1815–1822.

Capafons, A., Mendoza, M., Espejo, B., Green, J., Lopes-Pires, C., Selma, M., et al. (2008). Attitudes and beliefs about hypnosis: A multicultural study. *Contemporary Hypnosis, 25*, 141–155.

Cappadocia, M. C., Desrocher, M., Pepler, D., & Schroeder, J. H. (2009). Contextualizing the neurobiology of conduct disorder in an emotion dysregulation framework. *Clinical Psychology Review, 29*, 506–518.

Cappo, B. M., & Holmes, D. S. (1984). The utility of prolonged respiratory exhalation for reducing physiological and psychological arousal in non-threatening and threatening situations. *Journal of Psychosomatic Research, 28*, 265–273.

Caramazza, A., & Mahon, B. Z. (2003). The organization of conceptual knowledge: The evidence from category-specific semantic deficits. *Trends in Cognitive Sciences, 7*, 354–361.

Caramazza, A., & Shelton, J. R. (1998). Domain-specific knowledge systems in the brain: The animate-inanimate distinction. *Journal of Cognitive Neuroscience, 10*, 1–34.

Carek, P. J., Laibstain, S. E., & Care, S. M. (2011). Exercise for the treatment of depression and anxiety. *International Journal of Psychiatry in Medicine, 41*, 15–28.

Carhart-Harris, R. L., Muthukumaraswamy, S., Roseman, L., Kaelen, M., Droog, W., Murphy, K., . . . Nutt, D. J. (2016). Neural correlates of the LSD experience revealed by multimodal neuroimaging. *Proceedings of the National Academy of Science USA, 113*, 4853–4858.

Carise, D., Dugosh, K. L., McLellan, A. T., Camilleri, A., Woody, G. E., & Lynch, K. G. (2007). Prescription OxyContin abuse among patients entering addiction treatment. *American Journal of Psychiatry, 164*, 1750–1756.

Carmichael, M. S., Warburton, V. L., Dixen, J. & Davidson, J. M. (1994). Relationships among cardiovascular, muscular, and oxytocin responses during human sexual activity. *Archives of Sexual Behavior, 23*, 59–79.

Carmody, T. P., Duncan, C., Simon, J. A., Solkowitz, S., Huggins, J., Lee, S., & Delucchi, K. (2008). Hypnosis for smoking cessation: A randomized trial. *Nicotine & Tobacco Research, 10,* 811–818.

Carmona, J. E., Holland, A. K., & Harrison, D. W. (2009). Extending the functional cerebral systems theory of emotion to the vestibular modality: A systematic and integrative approach. *Psychological Bulletin, 135,* 286–302.

Carnagey, N. L., Anderson, C. A., & Bushman, B. J. (2007). The effect of video game violence on physiological desensitization to real-life violence. *Journal of Experimental Social Psychology, 43,* 489–496.

Carney, D. R., Cuddy, A. J. C., & Yap, A. J. (2010). Power posing: Brief nonverbal displays affect neuroendocrine levels and risk tolerance. *Psychological Science, 21,* 1363–1368.

Carpendale, J. I. (2000). Kohlberg and Piaget on stages and moral reasoning. *Developmental Review, 20,* 181–205.

Carr, C. E., & Konishi, M. (1990). A circuit for detection of interaural time differences in the brain stem of the barn owl. *Journal of Neuroscience, 10,* 3227–3246.

Carré, J. M., Putnam, S. K., & McCormick, C. M. (2009). Testosterone responses to competition predict future aggressive behaviour at a cost to reward in men. *Psychoneuroendocrinology, 34,* 561–570.

Carroll, J. B. (1993). *Human cognitive abilities: A survey of factor analytic studies.* Cambridge, U.K.: Cambridge University Press.

Carstensen, L. L., Isaacowitz, D., & Charles, S. T. (1999). Taking time seriously: A theory of socioemotional selectivity. *American Psychologist, 54,* 165–181.

Carston, R. (2002). *Thoughts and utterances: The pragmatics of explicit conversation.* New York: Blackwell.

Carter, A. C., Brandon, K., & Goldman, M. S. (2010). The college and noncollege experience: A review of the factors that influence drinking behavior in young adulthood. *Journal of Studies on Alcohol and Drugs, 71,* 742–750.

Carter, C. S. (1998). Neuroendocrine perspectives on social attachment and love. *Psychoneuroendocrinology, 23,* 779–818.

Carter, C. S., Braver, T. S., Barch, D. M., Botvinick, M. M., Noll, D., & Cohen, J. D. (1998). Anterior cingulate cortex, error detection, and the online monitoring of performance. *Science, 280,* 747–749.

Cartwright, R., Agargun, M., Kirkby, J., & Friedman, J. K. (2006). Relation of dreams to waking concerns. *Psychiatry Research, 141,* 261–270.

Caruso, E. M., Waytz, A., & Epley, N. (2010). The intentional mind and the hot hand: Perceiving intentions makes streaks seem likely to continue. *Cognition, 116,* 149–153.

Casey, B. J., Jones, R. M., & Hare, T. A. (2008). The adolescent brain. *Annals of the New York Academy of Sciences, 1124*(1), 111–126.

Caspi, A. (2000). The child is father of the man: Personality continuities from childhood to adulthood. *Journal of Personality and Social Psychology, 78,* 158–172.

Caspi, A., Hariri, A. R., Holmes, A., Uher, R., & Moffitt, T. E. (2010). Genetic sensitivity to the environment: The case of the serotonin transporter gene and its implications for studying complex diseases and traits. *American Journal of Psychiatry, 167,* 509–527.

Caspi, A., Moffitt, T. E., Cannon, M., Taylor, A., Craig, I. W., . . . Poulton, R. (2005). Moderation of the effect of adolescent-onset cannabis use on adult psychosis by a functional polymorphism in the catechol-*O*-methyltransferase gene: Longitudinal evidence of a gene X environment interaction. *Biological Psychiatry, 57,* 1117–1127.

Caspi, A., Sugden, K., Moffitt, T. E., Taylor, A., Craig, I. W., . . . Poulton, R. (2003). Influence of life stress on depression: Moderation by a polymorphism in the 5-HTT gene. *Science, 301,* 386–389.

Cattell, R. B. (1946). *The description and measurement of personality.* New York: Harcourt, Brace & World.

Cattell, R. B. (1971). *Abilities: Their structure, growth, and action.* Boston: Houghton Mifflin.

Cavallera, G., & Giudici, S. (2008). Morningness and eveningness personality: A survey in literature from 1995 up till 2006. *Personality and Individual Differences, 44,* 3–21.

CBC News. (2013, September 13). Edmonton mom found not criminally responsible for drowning son. Retrieved from http://www.cbc.ca/news/canada/edmonton/edmonton-mom-found-not-criminally-responsible-for-drowning-son-1.1829864

Ceci, S. J. (1991). How much does schooling influence general intelligence and its cognitive components? A reassessment of the evidence. *Developmental Psychology, 27,* 703–722.

Ceci, S. J. (1999). The suggestibility of children's memory. *Annual Review of Psychology, 50,* 419–439.

Ceci, S. J., & Williams, W. M. (1997). Schooling, intelligence, and income. *American Psychologist, 52,* 1051–1058.

Centers for Disease Control and Prevention. (2002). Annual smoking-attributable mortality, years of potential life lost, and productivity losses—United States, 1995–1999. *Morbidity and Mortality Weekly Report, 51,* 300–303.

Centers for Disease Control and Prevention. (2009a). Tobacco use and pregnancy. Retrieved August 1, 2010, from http://www.cdc.gov/reproductivehealth/tobaccousepregnancy/index.htm

Centers for Disease Control and Prevention. (2009b, April 17). *National Vital Statistics Reports, 57.*

Centers for Disease Control and Prevention. (2009c). Smoking & tobacco use. Retrieved June 20, 2011, from http://www.cdc.gov/tobacco/data_statistics/fact_sheets/fast_facts/index.htm

Centers for Disease Control and Prevention. (2010).Youth risk behavior surveillance—United States, 2009. *Morbidity and Mortality Weekly Report, 59*(No. SS-5). Retrieved from http://www.cdc.gov/mmwr/pdf/ss/ss5905.pdf

Centers for Disease Control and Prevention. (2015). Measles Cases and Outbreaks. Retrieved October 10, 2016, from http://www.cdc.gov/measles/cases-outbreaks.html

Cepeda, N. N., Pashler, H., Vul, E., et al. (2006). Distributed practice in verbal recall tasks: A review and quantitative synthesis. *Psychological Bulletin, 132,* 354–380.

Certain, L. K., & Kahn, R. S. (2003). Prevalence, correlates, and trajectory of television viewing among infants and toddlers. *Pediatrics,109,* 634–642.

Cesario, J. (2014). Priming, replication, and the hardest science. *Perspectives on Psychological Science, 9,* 40–48.

Chabris, C. F., Weinberger, A., Fontaine, M., & Simons, D. J. (2011). You do not talk about Fight Club if you do not notice Fight Club: Inattentional blindness for a simulated real-world assault. *i-Perception, 2,* 150–153.

Chaiken, S., & Trope, Y. (1999). *Dual-process theories in social psychology.* New York: Guilford Press.

Chambers, R., Chuen Yee Lo, B., & Allen, N. B. (2008). The impact of intensive mindfulness training on attentional control, cognitive style, and affect. *Cognitive Therapy and Research, 32,* 303–322.

Chambers, R. A., & Potenza, M. N. (2003). Neurodevelopment, impulsivity, and adolescent gambling. *Journal of Gambling Studies, 19,* 53–84.

Chambers, R. A., Taylor, J. R., & Potenza, M. N. (2003). Developmental neurocircuitry of motivation in adolescence: A critical period of addiction vulnerability. *The American Journal of Psychiatry, 160,* 1041–1052.

Chambless, D., & Ollendick, T. (2001). Empirically supported psychological interventions: Controversies and evidence. *Annual Review of Psychology, 52,* 685–716.

Champagne, F. A. (2010). Epigenetic influence of social experiences across the lifespan. *Developmental Psychobiology, 52,* 299–311.

Champagne, F. A., Francis, D. D., Mar, A. & Meaney, M. J. (2003). Variations in maternal care in the rat as a mediating influence for the effects of environment on development. *Physiology and Behavior, 79,* 359–371.

Chan, B. L., Witt, R., Charrow, A. P., Magee, A., Howard, R., Pasquina, P. F., & Heilman, K. M. (2007). Mirror therapy and phantom limb pain. *New England Journal of Medicine, 357,* 2206–2207.

Chan, Y.-C., Chou, T.-L., Chen, H.-C., Yeh, Y.-C., & Lavallee, J. P. (2013). Towards a neural circuit model of verbal humor processing: An fMRI study of the neural substrates of incongruity detection and resolution. *NeuroImage, 66,* 169–176.

Chang, Y., & Wang, S. J. (2010). Hypericin, the active component of St. John's wort, inhibits glutamate release in the rat cerbrocortical synaptosomes via a mitogen-activated protein kinase-dependent pathway. *European Journal of Pharmacology, 634,* 53–61.

Changizi, M. (2009). *The vision revolution*. Dallas, TX: Benbella Books.

Chapman, H. A., Kim, D. A., Susskind, J. M., & Anderson, A. K. (2009). In bad taste: Evidence for the oral origins of moral disgust. *Science, 323*, 1222–1226.

Charles, S. T., & Carstensen, L. L. (2009). Social and emotional aging. *Annual Review of Psychology, 61*, 383–409.

Charles, S. T., Mather, M., & Carstensen, L. L. (2003). Focusing on the positive: Age differences in memory for positive, negative, and neutral stimuli. *Journal of Experimental Psychology, 85*, 163–178.

Charness, N. (1981). Search in chess: Age and skill differences. *Journal of Experimental Psychology: Human Perception and Performance, 7*, 467–476.

Chartrand, T. L., & Bargh, J. A. (1999). The chameleon effect: The perception–behavior link and social interaction. *Journal of Personality and Social Psychology, 76*, 893–910.

Chase, P. G., & Dibble, H. L. (1987). Middle Paleolithic symbolism: A review of current evidence and interpretations. *Journal of Anthropological Archaeology, 6*, 263–296.

Chase, W. G., & Simon, H. A. (1973). Perception in chess. *Cognitive Psychology, 4*, 55–81.

Chaudhari, N., Landin, A. M., & Roper, S. D. (2000). A metabotropic glutamate receptor variant functions as a taste receptor. *Nature Neuroscience, 3*, 113–119.

Cheesman, J., & Merikle, P. M. (1986). Distinguishing conscious from unconscious perceptual processes. *Canadian Journal of Psychology, 40*, 343–367.

Chen, I., Vorona, R., Chiu, R., & Ware, J. (2008). A survey of subjective sleepiness and consequences in attending physicians. *Behavioral Sleep Medicine, 6*, 1–15.

Chen, J. L., Penhune, V. B., & Zatorre, R. J. (2008). Listening to musical rhythms recruits motor regions of the brain. *Cerebral Cortex, 18*, 2844–2854.

Chen, K. W., Berger, C. C., Manheimer, E., Forde, D., Magidson, J., . . . Lejuez, C. W. (2012). Meditative therapies for reducing anxiety: A systematic review and meta-analysis of randomized controlled trials. *Depression & Anxiety, 29*, 545–562.

Chen, S. C. (1937). Social modification of the activity of ants in nest-building. *Physiological Zoology, 10*, 420–436.

Chen, Z., & Cowan, N. (2005). Chunk limits and length limits in immediate recall: A reconciliation. *Journal of Experimental Psychology: Learning, Memory, and Cognition, 31*, 1235–1249.

Cheng, H., & Riffe, D. (2008). Attention, perception, and perceived effects: Negative political advertising in a battleground state of the 2004 presidential election. *Mass Communication & Society, 11*, 177–196.

Chentsova-Dutton, Y. E., & Tsai, J. L. (2007). Gender differences in emotional responding among European Americans and Hmong Americans. *Cognition and Emotion, 21*, 162–181.

Cheung, B. Y., Chudek, M., & Heine, S. J. (2011). Evidence for a sensitive period for acculturation: Younger immigrants report acculturating at a faster rate. *Psychological Science, 22*, 147–152.

Cheung, F. M., Leung, K., Fan, R. M., Song, W., Zhang J.-X., & Zhang J.-P. (1996). Development of the Chinese Personality Assessment Inventory. *Journal of Cross-Cultural Psychology, 27*, 181–199.

Chiao, J. Y., Harada, T., Komeda, H., Li, Z., Mano, Y., . . . Iidaka, T. (2009). Neural basis of individualistic and collectivistic views of self. *Human Brain Mapping, 30*, 2813–2820.

Chirkov, V. I., Ryan, R. M., Kim, Y., & Kaplan, U. (2003). Differentiating autonomy from individualism and independence: A self-determination theory perspective on internalization of cultural orientations and well-being. *Journal of Personality and Social Psychology, 84*, 97–110.

Chirkov, V. I., Safdar, S., de Guzman, J., & Playfoird, K. (2008). Further examining the role motivation to study abroad plays in the adaptation of intentional students in Canada. *International Journal of Intercultural Relations, 32*, 427–440.

Chirkov, V. I., Vansteenkiste, M., Tao, R., & Lynch, M. (2007). The role of motivation to study abroad in the adaptation of international students: A self-determination theory approach. *International Journal of Intercultural Relations, 31*, 199–222.

Chistyakov, A.V., Kaplan, B., Rubicheck, O., Kreinin, I., Koren, D., . . . Klein, E. (2005). Antidepressant effects of different schedules of repetitive transcranial magnetic stimulation vs. clomipramine in patients with major depressions: Relationship to changes in cortical excitability. *International Journal of Neuropsychopharmacology, 8*, 223–233.

Choi, I., Nisbett, R. E., & Norenzayan, A. (1999). Causal attribution across cultures: Variation and universality. *Psychological Bulletin, 125*, 47–63.

Choi, Y., Shamosh, N. A., Cho, S., DeYoung, C. G., Lee, M., . . . Lee, K. (2008). Multiple bases of human intelligence revealed by cortical thickness and neural activation. *The Journal of Neuroscience, 28*, 10323–10329.

Chopra, I. C., & Chopra, R.W. (1957). The use of cannabis drugs in India. *Bulletin of Narcotics, 9*, 4–29.

Christakis, D. A. (2009). The effects of media usage: What do we know and what should we learn? *Acta Paediatrica, 98*, 8–16.

Christakis, D. A., Zimmerman, F. J., DiGiuseppe, D. L., & McCarthy, C. A. (2004). Early television exposure and subsequent attentional problems in children. *Pediatrics, 113*, 708–713.

Christakis, N. A., & Fowler, J. H. (2007). The spread of obesity in a large social network over 32 years. *New England Journal of Medicine, 357*, 370–379.

Christakis, N. A., & Fowler, J. H. (2008). The collective dynamics of smoking in a large social network. *New England Journal of Medicine, 358*, 2249–2258.

Christensen, C., Silberberg, A., Hursh, S., Huntsberry, M., & Riley, A. (2008). Essential value of cocaine and food in rats: Tests of the exponential model of demand. *Psychopharmacology, 198*, 221–229.

Christie, R., & Geis, F. L. (1970). *Studies in Machiavellianism*. New York: Academic Press.

Christoff, K., Gordon, A. M., Smallwood, J., Smith, R., & Schooler, J. W. (2009). Experience sampling during fMRI reveals default network and executive systems contributions to mind wandering. *Proceedings of the National Academy of Science USA, 106*, 8719–8724.

Chung, S., & Herrnstein, R. J. (1967). Choice and delay of reinforcement. *Journal of Experimental Analysis of Behavior, 10*, 67–74.

Church, T. A. (2001). Culture and personality: Toward an integrated cultural trait psychology. *Journal of Personality, 68*, 651–703.

Cialdini, R. B. (2000). *Persuasion: Influence and practice* (4th ed.). New York: Allyn & Bacon.

Cialdini, R. B. (2001). Harnessing the science of persuasion. *Harvard Business Review, 79*, 72–81.

Cialdini, R. B., Vincent, J. E., Lewis, S. K., Catalan, J., Wheeler, D., & Darby, B. (1975). Reciprocal concessions procedure for inducing compliance: The door-in-the-face technique. *Journal of Personality and Social Psychology, 31*, 206–215.

Clancy, S. A. (2005). *Abducted: How people come to believe they were kidnapped by aliens*. Cambridge, MA: Harvard University Press.

Claparède, E. (1911/1951). Recognition and me-ness. Translated in D. Repaport (Ed.), *Organization and pathology of thought* (pp. 58–75). New York: Columbia University Press. (Originally published 1911.)

Clark, J. M., & Paivio, A. (1991). Dual coding theory and education. *Educational Psychology Review, 3*, 149–210.

Clark, K. B., Naritoku, D. K., Smith, D. C., Browning, R. A., & Jensen, R. A. (1999). Enhanced recognition memory following vagus nerve stimulation in human subjects. *Nature Neuroscience, 2*, 94–98.

Clark, L. A. (2007). Assessment and diagnosis of personality disorder: Perennial issues and an emerging reconceptualization. *Annual Review of Psychology, 58*, 227–257.

Clarke, D., Pulford, J., Bellringer, M., Abbott, M., & Hodgins, D. C. (2012). An exploratory study of problem gambling on casino versus non-casino electronic gaming machines. *International Journal of Mental Health and Addiction, 10*, 107–121.

Clopton, N. A., & Sorell, G. T. (1993). Gender differences in moral reasoning: Stable or Situational? *Psychology of Women Quarterly, 17*(1), 85–101.

CNN. (2002). Wuornos' last words: "I'll be back." Retrieved December 21, 2010, from http://archives.cnn.com/2002/LAW/10/09/wuornos.execution/index.html

Coane, J. H., & Balota, D. A. (2009). Priming the holiday spirit: Persistent activation due to extraexperimental experiences. *Psychonomic Bulletin & Review, 16,* 1124–1128.

Cohen, B., Guttmann, D., & Lazar, A. (1998). The willingness to seek help: A cross-national comparison. *Cross-Cultural Research: The Journal of Comparative Social Science, 32,* 342–357.

Cohen, F., Ogilvie, D. M., Solomon, S., Greenberg, J., & Pyszczynski, T. (2005). American roulette: The effect of reminders of death on support for George W. Bush in the 2004 presidential election. *Analyses of Social Issues and Public Policy (ASAP), 5,* 177–187.

Cohen, J. (1988). *Statistical power analysis for the behavioral sciences* (2nd ed.). Hillsdale, NJ: Lawrence Erlbaum Associates.

Cohen, J. (1994). The earth is round (p < .05). *American Psychologist, 49,* 997–1003.

Cohen, J. N., Byers, E. S., & Sears, H. A. (2012). Factors affecting Canadian teachers' willingness to teach sexual health education. *Sex Education: Sexuality, Society and Learning, 12,* 299–316.

Cohen, N. J., Eichenbaum, H., Deacedo, B. S., & Corkin, S. (1985). Different memory systems underlying acquisition of procedural and declarative knowledge. In D. S. Olton, E. Gamzu, & S. Corkin (Eds.), *Memory dysfunctions: An integration of animal and human research from preclinical and clinical perspectives* (pp. 54–71). New York: New York Academy of Sciences.

Cohn, M. A., Fredrickson, B. F., Brown, S. L., Mikels, J. A., & Conway, A. M. (2009). Happiness unpacked: Positive emotions increase life satisfaction by building resilience. *Emotion, 9,* 361–368.

Cojan, Y., Piguet, C., & Vuilleumier, P. (2015). What makes your brain suggestible? Hypnotizability is associated with differential brain activity during attention outside of hypnosis. *NeuroImage, 117,* 367–374.

Cole, S., Korin, Y., Fahey, J., & Zack, J. (1998). Norepinephrine accelerates HIV replication via protein kinase A–dependent effects on cytokine production. *Journal of Immunology, 161,* 610–616.

Collins, A. (1988). *In the sleep room: The story of CIA brainwashing experiments in Canada.* Toronto: Key Porter Books.

Collins, A. M., & Loftus, E. F. (1975). A spreading-activation theory of semantic processing. *Psychological Review, 82,* 407–428.

Colonna-Pydyn, C., Gjesfjeld, C., & Greeno, C. (2007). The factor structure of the Barriers to Treatment Participation Scale (BTPS): Implications for future barriers scale development. *Administration and Policy in Mental Health and Mental Health Services Research, 34,* 563–569.

Colwill, R. M., & Rescorla, R. A. (1985). Postconditioning devaluation of a reinforce affects instrumental responding. *Journal of Experimental Psychology: Animal Behavior Processes, 11,* 120–132.

Colwill, R. M., & Rescorla, R. A. (1990). Effect of reinforce devaluation on discriminative control of instrumental behaviour. *Journal of Experimental Psychology, 16,* 40–47.

Comings, D. E., & Blum, K. (2000). Reward deficiency syndrome: Genetic aspects of behavioural disorders. *Progress in Brain Research, 126,* 325–341.

Compton, J. A., & Pfau, M. W. (2005). *Inoculation theory of resistance to influence at maturity: Recent progress in theory development and application and suggestions for future research* (pp. 97–145). Mahwah, NJ: Lawrence Erlbaum Associates.

Conde-Agudelo, A., Belizan, J. M., & Diaz-Rossello, J. (2011). Kangaroo mother care to reduce morbidity and mortality in low birthweight infants. *Cochrane Database of Systematic Reviews, 3.*

Connelly, M. (2000, February 29). Poll finds that half in state disagree with Diallo verdict. *New York Times.* Retrieved from http://www.nytimes.com/2000/02/29/nyregion/poll-finds-that-half-in-state-disagree-with-diallo-verdict.html

Conway, M., & Ross, M. (1984). Getting what you want by revising what you had. *Journal of Personality and Social Psychology, 47,* 738–748.

Cook, E. W., Hodes, R. L., & Lang, P. J. (1986). Preparedness and phobia: Effects of stimulus content on human visceral conditioning. *Journal of Abnormal Psychology, 95,* 195–207.

Cook, I. A., Warren, C., Pajot, S. K., Schairer, D., & Leuchter, A. F. (2011). Regional brain activation with advertising images. *Journal of Neuroscience, Psychology, and Economics, 4,* 147–160.

Coombs, R. H. (1991). Marital status and personal wellbeing: A literature review. *Family Relations, 40,* 97–102.

Cooper, H. M., Charlton, K., Valentine, J. C., & Muhlenbruck, L. (2000). Making the most of summer school: A meta-analytic and narrative review. *Monographs of the Society for Research in Child Development, 65*(1, Serial No. 260).

Cooper, S. J. (2005). Donald O. Hebb's synapse and learning rule: A history and commentary. *Neuroscience and Biobehavioral Reviews, 28,* 851–874.

Corballis, M. C. (1993). *The lopsided ape.* Oxford, UK: Oxford University Press.

Cordner, G., & Shain, C. (2011). The changing landscape of police education and training. *Police Practice and Research, 12,* 281–285.

Coren, S. (1996a). Daylight savings time and traffic accidents. *New England Journal of Medicine, 334,* 924.

Coren, S. (1996b). Accidental death and the shift to daylight savings time. *Perceptual and Motor Skills, 83,* 921–922.

Corkin, S. (2002). What's new with the amnesic patient H.M.? *Nature Reviews Neuroscience, 3,* 153–160.

Corkum, P., Davidson, F. D., Tan-MacNeil, K., & Weiss, S. K. (2014). Sleep in children with neurodevelopmental disorders: A focus on insomnia in children with ADHD and ASD. *Sleep Medical Clinics, 9,* 149–168.

Correll, J., Park, B., Judd, C. M., & Wittenbrink, B. (2007). The influence of stereotypes on decisions to shoot. *European Journal of Social Psychology, 37*(6), 1102–1117.

Correll, J., Urland, G. R., & Ito, T. A. (2006). Event-related potentials and the decision to shoot: The role of threat perception and cognitive control. *Journal of Experimental Social Psychology, 42,* 120–128.

Corrigan, P. (2004). How stigma interferes with mental health care. *American Psychologist, 59,* 614–625.

Corti, M., Patten, C., & Triggs, W. (2012). Repetitive transcranial magnetic stimulation of motor cortex after stroke: A focused review. *American Journal of Physical Medicine and Rehabilitation, 91,* 254–270.

Cosgrove, G. R., & Rauch, S. L. (2003). Stereotactic cingulotomy. *Neurosurgery Clinics of North America, 13,* 225–235.

Costa, A., Hernández, M., & Sebastián-Gallés, N. (2008). Bilingualism aids conflict resolution: Evidence from the ANT task. *Cognition, 106,* 59–86.

Cote, K. A., Milner, C. E., Osip, S. L., Baker, M. L., & Cuthbert, B. P. (2008). Physiological arousal and attention during a week of continuous sleep restriction. *Physiology & Behavior, 95,* 353–364.

Cotman, C. W., & Berchtold, N. C. (2002). Exercise: A behavioral intervention to enhance brain health and plasticity. *Trends in Neuroscience, 26,* 295–301.

Couzin, J. (2004). Volatile chemistry: Children and antidepressants. *Science, 305,* 468–470.

Cowan, C. P., & Cowan, P. A. (1995). Interventions to ease the transition to parenthood: Why they are needed and what they can do. *Family Relations, 44,* 412–423.

Cowan, C. P., & Cowan, P. A. (2000). *When partners become parents: The big life change for couples.* Mahwah, NJ: Lawrence Erlbaum Associates.

Cowan, N. (2008). What are the differences between long-term, short-term, and working memory? *Progress in Brain Research, 169,* 323–338.

Cowan, N., Lichty, W., & Grove, T. R. (1990). Properties of memory for unattended spoken syllables. *Journal of Experimental Psychology: Learning, Memory, and Cognition, 16,* 258–269.

Cowan, R. L., Lyoo, I. K., Sung, S. M., Ahn, K. H., Kim, M. J., Hwang, J., et al. (2003). Reduced cortical gray matter density in human MDMA (Ecstasy) users: A voxel-based morphology study. *Drug and Alcohol Dependence, 72,* 225–235.

Cowan, R. L., Roberts, D. M., & Joers, J. M. (2008). Neuroimaging in humans MDMA (Ecstasy) users: A cortical model. *Annals of the New York Academy of Sciences, 1139,* 291–298.

Cox, C., Arndt, J., Pyszczynksi, T., Greenberg, J., Abdollahi, A., & Solomon, S. (2008). Terror management and adults' attachment to their parents: The safe haven remains. *Journal of Personality and Social Psychology, 94,* 696–717.

Craig, I., & Plomin, R. (2006). Quantitative trait loci for IQ and other complex traits: Single-nucleotide polymorphism genotyping using pooled DNA and microarrays. *Genes, Brain and Behavior, 5*(suppl 1), 32–37.

Craig, L. A., Hong, N. S., & McDonald, R. J. (2011). Revisiting the cholinergic hypothesis in the development of Alzheimer's disease. *Neuroscience and Biobehavioral Reviews, 35*, 1397–1409.

Craig, M. C., Catani, M., Deeley, Q., Latham, R., Daly, E., & Kanaan, R. (2009). Altered connections on the road to psychopathy. *Molecular Psychiatry, 14*, 946–953.

Craik, F., & Lockhart, R. (1972). Levels of processing: A framework for memory research. *Journal of Verbal Learning & Verbal Behavior, 11*, 671–684.

Craik, F., & Tulving, E. (1975). Depth of processing and the retention of words in episodic memory. *Journal of Experimental Psychology: General, 104*, 268–294.

Craik, F., & Watkins, M. (1973).The role of rehearsal in short-term memory. *Journal of Verbal Learning & Verbal Behavior, 12*, 599–607.

Crane, C., & Williams, J. M. G. (2010). Factors associated with attrition from mindfulness based cognitive therapy for suicidal depression. *Mindfulness, 1*, 10–20.

Cranford, R. (2005). Facts, lies, and videotapes: The permanent vegetative state and the sad case of Terri Schiavo. *The Journal of Law, Medicine & Ethics, 33*, 363–371.

Craske, M., Edlund, M., Sullivan, G., Sherbourne, C., Stein, M., & Bystritsky, A. (2005). Perceived unmet need for mental health treatment and barriers to care among patients with panic disorder. *Psychiatric Services, 56*, 988–994.

Crean, R. D., Crane, N. A., & Mason, B. J. (2011). An evidence-based review of acute and long-term effects of cannabis use on executive cognitive functions. *Journal of Addictive Medicine, 5*, 1–8.

Crick, F. (1994). *The astonishing hypothesis*. London: Simon & Schuster Ltd.

Critchley, H., Daly, E., Phillips, M., Brammer, M., Bullmore, E., Williams, S., et al. (2000). Explicit and implicit neural mechanisms for processing of social information from facial expressions: A functional magnetic resonance imaging study. *Human Brain Mapping, 9*, 93–105.

Crompton, S. (2011). What's stressing the stressed? Main sources of stress among workers. *Components of Statistics Canada Catalogue No 11-000-X: Canadian Social Trends*. Ottawa, ON: Statistics Canada.

Crowell, S. E., Beauchaine, T. P., & Linehan, M. M. (2009). A biosocial developmental model of borderline personality: Elaborating and extending Linehan's theory. *Psychological Bulletin, 125*, 495–510.

Crumpton, H. (1997). Persuasive entertainment: Top ten best and worst dressed lists. Paper presented at the Northwest Communication Association Conference, Coeur D'Alene, ID, April 19.

Cruse, D., Chennu, S., Chatelle, C., Bekinschtein, T. A., Fernandez-Espejo, D., Pickard, J. D., et al. (2011). Bedside detection of awareness in the vegetative state: A cohort study. *The Lancet, 378*, 2088–2094.

Cryan, J. F., Markou, A., & Lucki, I. (2002). Assessing antidepressant activity in rodents: Recent developments and future needs. *Trends in Pharmacological Sciences, 23*, 238–245.

Csibra, G., Davis, G., Spratling, M. W., & Johnson, M. H. (2000). Gamma oscillations and object processing in the infant brain. *Science, 290*, 1582–1585.

Cukor, J., Spitalnick, J., Difede, J., Rizzo, A., & Rothbaum, B. O. (2009). Emerging treatments for PTSD. *Clinical Psychology Review, 29*, 715–726.

Cunningham, W. A., Johnson, M. K., Raye, C. L., Gatenby, J. C., Gore, J. C., & Banaji, M. R. (2004). Separable neural components in the processing of Black and White faces. *Psychological Science, 15*, 806–813.

Curran, H. V., & Travill, R. A. (1997). Mood and cognitive effects of ±3,4-methylenedioxymethamphetamine (MDMA, "ecstasy"): weekend "high" followed by mid-week low. *Addiction, 92*, 821–831.

Cutrona, C., Wallace, G., & Wesner, K. (2006). Neighborhood characteristics and depression: An examination of stress processes. *Current Directions in Psychological Science, 15*(4), 188–192.

Cytowic, R. E. (1993). *The man who tasted shapes*. New York: G. P. Putnam's Sons.

D'Argembeau, A., Raffard, S., & Van der Linden, M. (2008). Remembering the past and imaging the future in schizophrenia. *Journal of Abnormal Psychology, 117*, 247–251.

Dabbs, J. M., Carr, T. S., Frady, R. L., & Riad, J. K. (1995). Testosterone, crime, and misbehavior among 692 male prison inmates. *Personality and Individuals Differences, 18*, 627–633.

Dabbs, J. M., & Hargrove, M. F. (1997). Age, testosterone, and behavior among female prison inmates. *Psychosomatic Medicine, 59*, 477–480.

Dagher, A. (2012). Functional brain imaging of appetite. *Trends in Endocrinology and Metabolism, 23*, 250–260.

Dahl, D. W., Sengupta, J., & Vohs, K. D. (2009). Sex in advertising: Gender differences and the role of relationship commitment. *Journal of Consumer Research, 36*, 215–231.

Dahl, R. E. (2001). Affect regulation, brain development, and behavioral/emotional health in adolescence. *CNS Spectrums, 6*, 60–72.

Dal Cin, S., Gibson, B., Zanna, M. P., Shumate, R., & Fong, G. T. (2007). Smoking in the movies, implicit associations of smoking with the self, and intentions to smoke. *Psychological Science, 18*, 559–563.

Dallman, M. F., Pecoraro, N., Akana, S. F., La Fleur, S. E., Gomez, F., Houshyar, H., et al. (2003). Chronic stress and obesity: A new view of "comfort food." *Proceedings of the National Academy of Sciences of the United States of America, 100*, 11696–11701.

Damasio, A. R. (1994). *Descartes' error: Emotion, reason, and the human brain*. New York: Putnam Publishing.

Damisch, L., Stoberock, B., & Mussweiler, T. (2010). Keep your fingers crossed! How superstition improves performance. *Psychological Science, 21*, 1014–1020.

Daneback, K., Cooper, A., & Månsson, S. (2005). An Internet study of cybersex participants. *Archives of Sexual Behavior, 34*, 321–328.

Dani, C., Poggi, C., Romagnoli, C., & Bertini, G. (2009). Survival and major disability rate in infant born at 22–25 weeks of gestation. *Journal of Perinatal Medicine, 37*, 599–608.

Danner, D. D., Snowdon, D. A., & Friesen, W. V. (2001). Positive emotions in early life and longevity: Findings from the nun study. *Journal of Personality and Social Psychology, 80*, 804–813.

DARA. (2012). *Climate vulnerability monitor: A guide to the cold calculus of a hot planet* (2nd ed.). Madrid: Fundacion DARA Internacional.

Dargie, E., Blair, K. L., Pukall, C. F., & Coyle, S. M. (2014). Somewhere under the rainbow: Exploring the identities and experiences of trans persons. *The Canadian Journal of Human Sexuality, 23*, 60–74.

Darley, J. M., & Latané, B. (1968). Bystander intervention in emergencies: Diffusion of responsibility. *Journal of Personality and Social Psychology, 8*, 377–383.

Dar-Nimrod, I., Rawn, C. D., Lehman, D. R., & Schwartz, B. (2009). The maximization paradox: The costs of seeking alternatives. *Personality and Individual Differences, 46*, 631–635.

Darvesh, S., Walsh, R., Kumar, R., Caines, A., Roberts, S., Magee, . . . & Martin E. (2003). Inhibition of human cholinesterases by drugs used to treat Alzheimer disease. *Alzheimer Disease and Associated Disorders, 17*, 117–126.

Darwin, C. (1871). *The descent of man, and selection in relation to sex*. London: John Murray.

Darwin, C. (1872). *The expression of the emotions in man and animals*. London: John Murray.

Dastoor, S. F., Misch, C. E., & Wang, H. L. (2007). Botulinum toxin (Botox) to enhance facial macroesthetics: A literature review. *Journal of Oral Implantology, 33*, 164–171.

Davis, C., & Scott-Robertson, L. (2000). A psychological comparison of females with anorexia nervosa and competitive male bodybuilders: Body-shape ideals in the extreme. *Eating Behaviors, 1*, 33–46.

Davis, C. L., Tomporowski, P. D., McDowell, J. E., Austin, B. P., Miller, P. H., Yanasak, N. E., et al. (2011). Exercise improves executive function and achievement and alters brain activation in overweight children: A randomized, controlled trial. *Health Psychology, 30*, 91–98.

Davis, D., & Loftus, E. F. (2009) Expectancies, emotion and memory reports of visual events. In J. R. Brockmole (Ed.), *The Visual World in Memory* (pp. 178–214). New York: Psychology Press.

Dawson, D., & Reid, K. (1997). Fatigue, alcohol and performance impairment. *Nature, 388,* 235.

de Araujo, I. E., & Rolls, E. T. (2004). Representation in the human brain of food texture and oral fat. *Journal of Neuroscience, 24,* 3086–3093.

De Bruin, E., Beersma, D., & Daan, S. (2002). Sustained mental workload does not affect subsequent sleep intensity. *Journal of Sleep Research, 11,* 113–121.

de Gelder, B., & Hadjikhani, N. (2006). Non-conscious recognition of emotional body language. *Neuro Report, 17,* 583–586.

de Jonghe, F., Kool, S., van Aalst, G., Dekker J., & Peen J. (2001). Combining psychotherapy and antidepressants in the treatment of depression. *Journal of Affective Disorders, 64,* 217–229.

De Los Reyes, A., & Kazdin, A. (2008). When the evidence says, "yes, no, and maybe so": Attending to and interpreting inconsistent findings among evidence-based interventions. *Current Directions in Psychological Science, 17,* 47–51.

De Marchis, G. M., Burgi, S., Kientsch, U., & Honegger, U. E. (2006). Vitamin E reduces antidepressant-related beta-adrenoceptor down-regulation in cultured cells. Comparable effects on St. John's wort and tricyclic antidepressant treatment. *Planta Medica, 72,* 1436–1437.

de Vries, R. E., & van Kampen, D. (2010). The HEXACO and 5DPT models of personality: A comparison and their relationships with psychopathy, egoism, pretentiousness, immorality and Machiavellianism. *Journal of Personality Disorders, 24,* 244–257.

de Waele, C., Baudonniere, P. M., Lepecq, J. C., Tran Ba Huy, P., & Vidal P. P. (2001). Vestibular projections in the human cortex. *Experimental Brain Research, 141,* 541–551.

Deary, I. J., Penke, L., & Johnson, W. (2010). The neuroscience of human intelligence differences. *Nature Reviews Neuroscience, 11,* 201–211.

Deary, I. J., & Stough, C. (1996). Intelligence and inspection time: Achievements, prospects, and problems. *American Psychologist, 51,* 599–608.

Deary, I., Strand, S., Smith, P., & Fernandes, C. (2007). Intelligence and educational achievement. *Intelligence, 35,* 13–21.

DeCasper, A. J., & Prescott, P. A. (1984). Human newborns' perception of male voices: Preference, discrimination, and reinforcing value. *Developmental Psychobiology, 17,* 481–491.

DeCasper, A. J., & Spence, M. J. (1986). Prenatal maternal speech influences newborns' perception of speech sounds. *Infant Behavior and Development, 9,* 133–150.

Deci, E. L. (1971). Effects of externally mediated rewards on intrinsic motivation. *Journal of Personality and Social Psychology, 18,* 105–115.

Deci, E. L., Eghrari, H., Patrick, B. C., & Leone, D. R. (1994). Facilitating internalization: The self-determination theory perspective. *Journal of Personality, 62,* 119–142.

Deci, E. L., Koestner, R., & Ryan, R. M. (1999). A meta-analytic review of experiments examining the effects of extrinsic rewards on intrinsic motivation. *Psychological Bulletin, 125,* 627–668.

Deci, E. L., & Vansteenkiste, M. (2004). Self-determination theory of basic need satisfaction: Understanding human development in positive psychology. *Risershe di Psicologia, 27,* 23–40.

Deese, J. (1959). On the prediction of occurrence of particular verbal intrusions in immediate recall. *Journal of Experimental Psychology, 58,* 17–22.

Deese, J., & Kaufman, R. A. (1957). Serial effects in recall of unorganized and sequentially organized verbal material. *Journal of Experimental Psychology, 54,* 180–187.

Degardin, A., Devos, D., Defebvre, L., Destée, A., Plomhause, L., . . . & Devanne, H. (2012). Effect of intermittent theta-burst stimulation on akinesia and sensorimotor integration in patients with Parkinson's disease. *European Journal of Neuroscience, 36,* 2669–2678.

Delaney, P. F., Verkoeijen, P. J., & Spirgel, A. (2010). Spacing and testing effects: A deeply critical, lengthy, and at times discursive review of the literature. *The Psychology of Learning and Motivation: Advances in Research and Theory, 53,* 63–147.

Delgado, J. M. R., & Anand, B. K. (1952). Increase of food intake induced by electrical stimulation of the lateral hypothalamus. *American Journal of Physiology, 172,* 162–168.

DeLoache, J. S. (1995). Early understanding and use of symbols: The model model. *Current Directions in Psychological Science, 4,* 109–113.

DeLoache, J. S., Uttal, D. H., & Rosengren, K. S. (2004). Scale errors offer evidence for a perception–action dissociation early in life. *Science, 304,* 1027–1029.

DeLongis, A., & Holtzman, S. (2005). Coping in context: The role of stress, social support, and personality in coping. *Journal of Personality, 73,* 1633–1656.

Dempster, F. N. (1988). The spacing effect: A case study of the failure to apply the results of psychological research. *American Psychologist, 43,* 627–634.

Dennis, N. A., Bowman, C. R., & Vandekar, S. N. (2012). True and phantom recollection: An fMRI investigation of similar and distinct neural correlates and connectivity. *NeuroImage, 59,* 2982–2993.

Deoni, S. C. L., Mercure, E., Blasi, A., Gasston, D., Thomson, A., Johnson, M., . . . Murphy, D. G. M. (2011). Mapping infant brain myelination with magnetic resonance imaging. *Journal of Neuroscience, 31,* 784–791.

Depue, R. A., & Collins, P. F. (1999). Neurobiology of the structure of personality: Dopamine, facilitation of incentive motivation, and extraversion. *Behavioral and Brain Sciences, 22,* 491–569.

DeRubeis, R., & Crits-Christoph, P. (1998). Empirically supported individual and group psychological treatments for adult mental disorders. *Journal of Consulting and Clinical Psychology, 66,* 37–52.

Deschner, T., Heistermann, M., Hodges, K., & Boesch, C. (2004). Female sexual swelling size, timing of ovulation, and male behavior in wild West African chimpanzees. *Hormones and Behavior, 46,* 204–215.

Desroches, A. S., Cone, N. E., Bolger, D. J., Bitan, T., Burman, D. D., & Booth, J. R. (2010). Children with reading difficulties show differences in brain regions associated with orthographic processing during spoken language processing. *Brain Research, 1356,* 73–84.

Desroches, A. S., & Joanisse, M. (2009). Dyslexia. In E. Goldstein (Ed.), *Encyclopedia of perception* (pp. 371–373). Thousand Oaks, CA: Sage Publications.

DeYoung, C. G., Hirsh, J. B., Shane, M. S., Papademetris, X., Rajeevan, N., & Gray, J. R. (2010). Testing predictions from personality neuroscience: Brain structure and the Big Five. *Psychological Science, 21,* 820–828.

Di Chiara, G., & Imperato, A. (1988). Drugs abused by humans preferentially increase synaptic dopamine concentrations in the mesolimbic system of freely moving rats. *Proceedings of the National Academy of Science USA, 85,* 5274–5279.

di Pellegrino, G., Fadiga, L., Fogassi, L., Gallese, V., & Rizzolatti, G. (1992). Understanding motor events: A neurophysiological study. *Experimental Brain Research, 91,* 176–180.

Diaz, J. H. (2004). The global epidemiology, syndromic classification, management, and prevention of spider bites. *American Journal of Tropical Medicine and Hygiene, 71,* 239–250.

Diamond, M. C., Krech, D., & Rosenzweig, M. R. (1964). The effects of an enriched environment on the histology of the rat cerebral cortex. *Journal of Comparative Neurology, 123,* 111–120.

Diamond, M. C., Scheibel, A. B., Murphy, G. M. Jr., & Harvey, T. (1985). On the brain of a scientist: Albert Einstein. *Experimental Neurology, 88,* 198–204.

Diana, R. A., Yonelinas, A. P., & Ranganath, C. (2007). Imaging recollection and familiarity in the medial temporal lobe: A three-component model. *Trends in Cognitive Sciences, 11,* 379–386.

Dick, D. M. (2007). Identification of genes influencing a spectrum of externalizing psychopathology. *Current Directions in Psychological Science, 16,* 331–335.

DiClemente, C. C., & J. O. Prochaska (1985). Processes and stages of self-change: Coping and competence in smoking behavior change. In Shiffman & T. A. Wills (Eds.), *Coping and substance use.* New York: Academic Press.

Digdon, N., Powell, R. A., & Harris, B. (2014). Little Albert's alleged neurological impairment: Watson, Rayner and historical revision. *History of Psychology, 17,* 313–324.

DiLalla, L. F., Kagan, J., & Reznick, J. S. (1994). Genetic etiology of behavioral inhibition among 2-year-old children. *Infant Behavior and Development, 17,* 405–412.

Dilworth-Bart, J. E., & Moore, C. F. (2006). Mercy mercy me: Social injustice and the prevention of environmental pollutant exposures among ethnic minority and poor children. *Child Development, 77,* 247–265.

Dingemanse, N. J., Both, C., Drent, P. J., & Tinbergen, J. M. (2004). Fitness consequences in a fluctuating environment. *Proceedings of the Royal Society of London, Series B, 271,* 847–852.

Dinges, D. F. (2006). The state of sleep deprivation: From functional biology to functional consequences. *Sleep Medicine Review, 10,* 303–305.

Dinges, D. F., Maislin, G., Brewster, R. M., Krueger, G. P., & Carroll, R. J. (2005). Pilot test of fatigue management technologies. *Journal of the Transportation Research Board No. 1922, Transportation Research Board of the National Academies, Washington, DC,* 175–182. Retrieved from: http://www.med.upenn.edu/uep/user_documents/Dingesetal.–TRBProceedingspaper05-1234.pdf

Dingledine, R., Borges, K., Bowie, D., & Traynelis, S. F. (1999). The glutamate receptor ion channels. *Pharmacology Review, 51,* 7–61.

DiPaola, S., Riebe, C., & Enns, J. T. (2011). Rembrandt's textural agency: A shared perspective in visual art and science. *Leonardo, 43,* 145–151.

Ditzen, B., Schaer, M., Gabriel, B., Bodenmann, G., Ehlert, U., & Heinrichs, M. (2009). Intranasal oxytocin increases positive communication and reduces cortisol levels during couple conflict. *Biological Psychiatry, 65,* 728–731.

Dixon, M. J., Bub, D. N., & Arguin, M. (1997). The interaction of object form and object meaning in the identification performance of a patient with category specific visual agnosia. *Cognitive Neuropsychology, 14,* 1085–1130.

Dixon, M. J., Desmarais, G., Gomierac, C., Schweizer, T. A., & Bub, D. N. (2002). The role of premorbid expertise on object identification in category-specific visual agnosia. *Cognitive Neuropsychology, 19,* 401–419.

Dixon, M. J., Harrigan, K. A., Sandhu, R., Collins, K., & Fugelsang, J. A. (2010). Losses disguised as wins in modern multi-line video slot machines. *Addiction, 105,* 1819–1824.

Dixon, M.J., Harrigan, K.A., Santesso, D.L., Graydon, C., Fugelsang, J.A., & Collins, K. (2014). The impact of sound in modern multiline video slot machine play. *Journal of Gambling Studies, 30,* 913–929.

Dixon, M. J., Smilek, D., Cudahy, C., & Merikle, P. M. (2000). Five plus two equals yellow. *Nature, 406,* 365.

Dixon, P., & Bortolussi, M. (2013). Construction, integration, and mind wandering in reading. *Canadian Journal of Experimental Psychology, 67,* 1–10.

Dixson, A. F. (1983). Observations on the evolution and behavioural significance of "sexual skin" in female primates. *Advances in the Study of Behavior, 13,* 63–106.

Dixson, B. J., Dixson, A. F., Bishop, P. J., & Parish, A. (2010). Human physique and sexual attractiveness in men and women: a New Zealand-U.S. comparative study. *Archives of Sexual Behavior, 39,* 798–806.

Dobkin, P. L. (2008). Mindfulness-based stress reduction: What processes are at work? *Complementary Therapies in Clinical Practice, 14,* 8–16.

Dolcos, F., LaBar, K. S., & Cabeza, R. (2004). Interaction between the amygdala and the medial temporal lobe memory system predicts better memory for emotional events. *Neuron, 42,* 855–863.

Domjan, M., Cusato, B., & Krause, M. A. (2004). Learning with arbitrary versus ecological conditioned stimuli: Evidence from sexual conditioning. *Psychonomic Bulletin and Review, 11,* 232–246.

Done, D. J., Crow, T. J., Johnstone, E. C., & Sacker, A. (1994). Childhood antecedents of schizophrenia and affective illness: Social adjustment at ages 7 and 11. *British Medical Journal, 309,* 699–703.

Douglas, K. S., Guy, L. S., & Hart, S. D. (2009). Psychosis as a risk factor for violence to others: A meta-analysis. *Psychological Bulletin, 135,* 679–706.

Dovern, A., Fink, G. R., Fromme, A. C., Wohlschläger, A. M., Weiss, P. H., & Riedl, V. (2012). Intrinsic network connectivity reflects consistency of synesthetic experiences. *Journal of Neuroscience, 32,* 7614–7621.

Dow Schull, N. (2012). *Addiction by design: Machine gambling in Las Vegas.* Princeton, NJ: Princeton University Press.

Dozois, D., Bieling, P., Patelis-Siotis, I., Hoar, L., Chudzik, S., McCabe, K., et al. (2009). Changes in self-schema structure in cognitive therapy for major depressive disorder: A randomized clinical trial. *Journal of Consulting and Clinical Psychology, 77,* 1078–1088.

Drachman, D. A. (2007). Do we have a brain to spare? *Neurology, 64,* 2004–2005.

Drachman, D. A., & Leavitt, J. (1974). Human memory and the cholinergic system. *Archives of Neurology, 30,* 113–121.

Duan, Z., Andronescu, M., Schutz, K., McIlwain, S., Kim, Y. J., Lee, C., . . . & Noble, W. S. (2010). A three-dimensional model of the yeast genome. *Nature, 465,* 363–367.

Duka, T., Weissenborn, R., & Dienes, Z. (2001). State-dependant effects of alcohol on recollective experience, familiarity and awareness of memories. *Psychopharmacology, 153,* 295–306.

Duke, J. C., Lee, Y. O., Kim, A. E., Watson, K. A., Arnold, K. Y., . . . Porter, L. (2014). Exposure to electronic cigarette television advertisements among youth and young adults. *Pediatrics, 134,* e29–e36.

Dunn, K. M., Cherkas, L. F., & Spector, T. D. (2005). Genetic influences on variation in female orgasmic function: A twin study. *Biology Letters, 1,* 260–263.

Durante, K. M., Li, N. P., & Haselton, M. G. (2008). Changes in women's choice of dress across the ovulatory cycle: Naturalistic and laboratory task-based evidence. *Personality and Social Psychology Buelletin, 34,* 1451–1460.

During, M. J., & Spencer, D. D. (1993). Extracellular hippocampal glutamate and spontaneous seizure in the conscious human brain. *Lancet, 341,* 1607–1610.

Durmer, J. S., & Dinges, D. F. (2005). Neurocognitive consequences of sleep deprivation. *Seminars in Neurology, 25,* 117–129.

Durrant, J., & Ensom, R. (2012). Physical punishment of children: Lessons from 20 years of research. *Canadian Medical Association Journal, 184,* 1373–1376.

Dutton, D. G., & Aron, A. (1974). Some evidence for heightened sexual attraction under conditions of high anxiety. *Journal of Personality and Social Psychology, 30,* 510–517.

Dutton, K. (2012). *The wisdom of psychopaths: What saints, spies, and serial killers can teach us about success.* Toronto: Doubleday Canada.

Dweck, C. (2002). Beliefs that make smart people dumb. In R. J. Sternberg (Ed.), *Why smart people can be so stupid* (pp. 24–41). New Haven, CT: Yale University Press.

Dykiert, D., Gale, C., & Deary, I. (2009). Are apparent sex differences in mean IQ scores created in part by sample restriction and increased male variance? *Intelligence, 37,* 42–47.

Dzirasa, K., & Covington, H. E. III. (2012). Increasing the validity of experimental models for depression. *Annals of the New York Academy of Sciences, 1265,* 36–45.

Eastwood, J., Snook, B., Luther, K., & Freedman, S. (2016). Engineering comprehensible youth interrogation rights. *New Criminal Law Review, 19,* 42–62.

Ebbinghaus, H. (1885/1913). *Memory: A contribution to experimental psychology.* [Online]. Retrieved from http://psychclassics.yorku.ca/Ebbinghaus/

Eberhardt, J. L. (2005). Imaging race. *American Psychologist, 60,* 181–190.

Eccles, J. S., & Wigfield, A. (2002). Motivational beliefs, values, and goals. *Annual Review of Psychology, 53,* 109–132.

Edwards, A. S. (1917). The distribution of time in learning small amounts of material. In *Studies in psychology: Titchener commemorative volume* (pp. 209–213). Worcester, MA: Wilson.

Edwards, J. G., Gibson, H. E., Jensen, T., Nugent, F., Walther, C., Blickenstaff, J., & Kauer, J. (2012). A novel non-CB1/TRPV1 endocannabinoid-mediated mechanism depresses excitatory synapses on hippocampal CA1 interneurons. *Hippocampus, 22,* 209–221.

Efrain, M. G., & Patterson, E. W. J. (1974). Voters vote beautiful: The effect of physical appearance on a national election. *Canadian Journal of Behavioural Science/Revue canadienne des sciences du comportement, 6,* 352.

Ehrlich, P. R., & Ehrlich, A. H. (2013). Can a collapse of global civilization be avoided? *Proceedings of the Royal Society B: Biological Sciences, 280,* 1754.

Eich, E., Macaulay, D., & Ryan, L. (1994). Mood dependent memory for events of the personal past. *Journal of Experimental Psychology, 123*, 201–215.

Eich, E., Macaulay, D., Lowenstein, R. J., & Dihle, P. H. (1997). Memory, amnesia, and dissociative identity disorder. *Psychological Science, 8*, 417–422.

Eich, E., & Metcalfe, J. (1989). Mood dependent memory for internal versus external events. *Journal of Experimental Psychology, 15*, 443–455.

Eichenbaum, H., Yonelinas, A. P., & Ranganath, C. (2007). The medial temporal lobe and recognition memory. *Annual Review of Neuroscience, 30*, 123–152.

Eisenberg, N. (2000). Emotion, regulation, and moral development. *Annual Review of Psychology, 51*, 665–697.

Eisenberg, N. (2005). The development of empathy-related responding. In G. Carlo & C. P. Edwards (Eds.), *Moral motivation through the life span* (pp. 73–117). Lincoln, NE: University of Nebraska Press.

Eisenberger, N. I., & Lieberman, M. D. (2004). Why rejection hurts: A common neural alarm system for physical and social pain. *Trends in Cognitive Sciences, 8*, 294–300.

Eisenegger, C., Haushofer, J., & Fehr, E. (2011). The role of testosterone in social interaction. *Trends in Cognitive Sciences, 15*, 263–271.

Eiser, A. S. (2005). Physiology and psychology of dreams. *Seminars in Neurology, 25*, 97–105.

Ekman, P., & Friesen, W. V. (1969). The repertoire of nonverbal behavior: Categories, origins, usage, and coding. *Semiotica, 1*, 49–98.

Ekman, P., O'Sullivan, M., & Frank, M. G. (1999). A few can catch a liar. *Psychological Science, 10*, 263–266.

Eldreth, D. A., Matochick, J. A., Cadet, J. L., & Bolla, K. I. (2004). Abnormal brain activity in prefrontal regions in abstinent marijuana users. *NeuroImage, 23*, 914–920.

Elfenbein, H. A., & Ambady, N. (2003). Universals and cultural differences in recognizing emotions. *Current Directions in Psychological Science, 12*, 159–164.

Elfenbein, H. A., Beaupré, M., Lévesque, M., & Hess, U. (2007). Toward a dialect theory: Cultural differences in the expression and recognition of posed facial expressions. *Emotion, 7*, 131–146.

Elgar, F. J., Davis, C. G., Wohl, M. J., Trites, S. J., Zelenski, J. M., & Martin, M. S. (2011). Social capital, health and life satisfaction in 50 countries. *Health & Place, 17*, 1044–1053.

Elkins, G., Marcus, J., Stearns, V., Perfect, M., Rajab, M. H., Ruud, C., et al. (2008). Randomized trial of a hypnosis intervention of hot flashes among breast cancer survivors. *Journal of Clinical Oncology, 26*, 5022–5026.

Elkins, S. R., & Moore, T. M. (2011). A time-series study of the treatment of panic disorder. *Clinical Case Studies, 10*, 3–22.

Elliot, A. J., & Niesta, D. (2008). Romantic red: Red enhances men's attraction to women. *Journal of Personality and Social Psychology, 95*, 1150–1164.

Elliot, A. J., Tracy, J. L., Pazda, A. D., & Beall, A. T. (2013). Red enhances women's attractiveness to men: First evidence suggesting universality. *Journal of Experimental Social Psychology, 49*, 165–168.

Elliott, R. (2002). The effectiveness of humanistic therapies: A meta-analysis. In D. J. Cain (Ed.), *Humanistic psychotherapies: Handbook of research and practice* (pp. 57–81). Washington, DC: American Psychological Association.

Elliott, R., Bohart, A., Watson, J., & Greenberg, L. (2011). Empathy. *Psychotherapy, 48*, 43–49.

Elliott, R., Friston, K. J., & Dolan, R. J. (2000). Dissociable neural responses in human rewards systems. *Journal of Neuroscience, 20*, 6159–6165.

Elliot, R., Newman, J. L., Longe, O. A., & Deakin, J. F. W. (2003). Differential response patterns in the striatum and orbitofrontal cortex to financial reward in humans: a parametric functional magnetic resonance imaging study. *The Journal of Neuroscience, 22*, 303–307.

Elliott, R., Sahakian, B. J., Matthews, K., Bannerjea, A., Rimmer, J., & Robbins, T. W. (1997). Effects of methylphenidate on spatial working memory and planning in healthy young adults. *Psychopharmacology, 131*, 196–206.

Ellis, A. (1962). *Reason and emotion in psychotherapy.* New York: Lyle Stuart.

Ellis, B. J., & Garber, J. (2000). Psychosocial antecedents of variation in girls' pubertal timing: Maternal depression, stepfather presence, and marital and family stress. *Child Development, 71*, 485–501.

Ellis, L., & Ames, M. (1987). Neurohormonal functioning and sexual orientation: A theory of homosexuality–heterosexuality. *Psychological Bulletin, 101*, 233–258.

Environics Research Group. (2007). Testing of mock-ups of health warning messages and warning notices on tobacco product advertisements for smokeless tobacco. Retrieved from http://www.tobaccolabels.ca/health/canada2007w2

Epel, E., Lapidus, R., McEwen, B., & Brownell, K. (2001). Stress may add bite to appetite in women: A laboratory study of stress-induced cortisol and eating behavior. *Psychoneuroendocrinology, 26*, 37–49.

Epley, N., & Gilovich, T. (2006). The anchoring-and-adjustment heuristic: Why the adjustments are insufficient. *Psychological Science, 17*, 311–318.

Epstein, S. (1994). Integration of the cognitive and the psychodynamic unconscious. *American Psychologist, 49*(8), 709–724.

Erickson, K. I., Voss, M. W., Prakash, R. S., Basak, C., Szabo, A., Chaddock, L., et al. (2011). Exercise training increases size of hippocampus and improves memory. *Proceedings of the National Academy of Sciences, 108*, 3017–3022.

Ericsson, K. A., & Polson, P. G. (1988). Memory for restaurant orders. In M. Chi, R. Glaser, & M. Farr (Eds.), *The nature of expertise* (pp. 23–70). Hillsdale, NJ: Erlbaum.

Eriksson, P. S., Perfilieva, E., Björk-Eriksson, T., Alborn, A. M., Nordborg, C., Peterson, D.A., & Gage, F. H. (1998). Neurogenesis in the adult human hippocampus. *Nature Medicine, 4*, 1313–1317.

Espenschade, A., & Eckert, H. (1980). *Motor development.* Columbus, OH: Merrill.

Evans, D., & Rothbart, M. K. (2007). Developing a model for adult temperament. *Journal of Research in Personality, 41*, 868–888.

Evans, G.W. (2003). The built environment and mental health. *Journal of Urban Health, 80*, 536–555.

Evans, G. W., & Schamberg, M. A. (2009). Childhood poverty, chronic stress, and adult working memory. *Proceedings of the National Academy Sciences, 106*(16), 6545–6549.

Evans, G. W., & Stecker, R. (2004). Motivational consequences of environmental stress. *Journal of Environmental Psychology, 24*, 143–165.

Evans, S., Ferrando, S., Findler, M., Stowell, C., Smart, C., & Haglin, D. (2008). Mindfulness-based cognitive therapy for anxiety. *Journal of Anxiety Disorders, 22*, 716–721.

Exner, J. E. (1991). *The Rorschach: A comprehensive system. Vol. 2: Interpretation* (2nd ed.). New York: Wiley.

Eysenck, H. J. (1967). *The biological basis of personality.* Springfield, IL: Charles C. Thomas.

Eysenck, H. J. (1994). Personality: Biological foundations. In P. A. Vernon (Ed.), *The neuropsychology of individual differences.* London: Academic Press.

Fairclough, S. H., & Graham, R. (1999). Impairment of driving performance caused by sleep deprivation or alcohol: A comparative study. *Human Factors, 41*, 118–128.

Fakhoury, W., & Priebe, S. (2002) . The process of de-institutionalisation: An international overview. *Current Opinion in Psychiatry, 15*, 187–192.

Falbe, J., Thompson, H. R., Becker, C. M., Rojas, N. McCulloch, C. E., & Madsen, K. A. (2016). Impact of the Berkeley Excise Tax on sugar-sweetened beverage consumption. *American Journal of Public Health, 106*, 1865–1871.

Falk, L., Nordberg, A., Kjaeldgaard, A., & Hellström-Lindahl, E. (2005). Smoking during early pregnancy affects the expression pattern of both nicotinic and muscarinic acetylcholine receptors in human first trimester brainstem and cerebellum. *Neuroscience, 132*, 389–397.

Fancher, R. E. (1985). *The intelligence men: Makers of the IQ controversy.* New York: W. W. Norton.

Fancher, R. E. (1990). *Pioneers of psychology.* New York: W. W. Norton & Company.

Fancher, R. E. (2009). Scientific cousins: The relationship between Charles Darwin and Francis Galton. *American Psychologist, 64*, 84–92.

Fantz, R. L. (1961). The origin of form perception. *Scientific American, 47*, 627–638.

Farb, N. A., Segal, Z. V., & Anderson, A. K. (2013). Mindfulness meditation training alters cortical representations of interoceptive attention. *Social, Cognitive & Affective Neuroscience, 8*, 15–26.

Farb, N. A. S., Segal, Z. V., Mayberg, H., Bean, J., McKeon, D., . . . Anderson, A. K. (2007). Attending to the present: Mindfulness meditation reveals distinct neural modes of self-reference. *Social Cognitive and Affective Neuroscience, 2*, 313–322.

Farber, B. A., & Lane, J. S. (2002). Positive regard. In J. C. Norcross (Ed.), *Psychotherapy relationships that work* (pp. 175–194). New York: Oxford University Press.

Fay, R. R. (1988). *Hearing in vertebrates: A psychophysics databook.* Winnetka, IL: Hill-Fay Associates.

Fazel, S., Långström, N., Hjern, A., Grann, M., & Lichtenstein, P. (2009). Schizophrenia, substance abuse, and violent crime. *Journal of the American Medical Association, 301*, 2016–2023.

Fecteau, S., Knoch, D., Fregni, F., Sultani, N., Boggio, P., & Pascual-Leone, A. (2007). Diminishing risk-taking behavior by modulating activity in the prefrontal cortex: A direct current stimulation study. *Journal of Neuroscience, 27*, 12500–12505.

Fecteau, S., Pascual-Leone, A., Zald, D. H., Liguori, P., Theoret, H., Boggio, P. S., & Fregni, F. (2007). Activation of prefrontal cortex by transcranial direct current stimulation reduces appetite for risk during ambiguous decision making. *The Journal of Neuroscience, 27*, 6212–6218.

Fehr, B. (1988). Prototype analysis of the concepts of love and commitment. *Journal of Personality and Social Psychology, 55*, 557–579.

Fehr, B. (2003). The status of theory and research on love and commitment. In G. J. O. Fletcher and M. S. Clark (Eds.), *Blackwell handbook of social psychology: Interpersonal processes* (pp. 331–356). Malden, MA: Blackwell Publishers Ltd.

Fein, S., & Spencer, S. J. (1997). Prejudice as self-image maintenance: Affirming the self through derogating others. *Journal of Personality and Social Psychology, 73*, 31–44.

Feinberg, D. R., DeBruine, L. M., Jones, B. C., & Perret, D. I. (2008). The role of femininity and averageness of voice pitch in aesthetic judgements of women's voices. *Perception, 37*, 615–623.

Feinberg, D. R., Jones, B. C., DeBruine, L. M., Moore, F. R., Smith, M. J. L., Cornwell, E. R., et al. (2005). The voice and face of woman: One ornament that signals quality? *Evolution and Human Behavior, 26*, 298–408.

Feldman, J. (2003). The simplicity principle in human concept learning. *Current Directions in Psychological Science, 12*, 227–232.

Fernandes, J. (2013). Effects of negative political advertising and message repetition on candidate evaluation. *Mass Communication and Society, 16*, 268–291.

Fernández, A., & Alonso, M. A. (2001). The relative value of environmental context reinstatement in free recall. *Psicologica, 22*, 253–266.

Fernando, G. A. (2008). Assessing mental health and psychosocial status in communities exposed to traumatic events: Sri Lanka as an example. *American Journal of Orthopsychiatry, 78*, 229–239.

Ferrer, E., & McArdle, J. J. (2004). An experimental analysis of dynamic hypotheses about cognitive abilities and achievement from childhood to early adulthood. *Developmental Psychology, 40*, 935–952.

Ferster, C. B., & Skinner, B. F. (1957). *Schedules of reinforcement.* Englewood Cliffs, NJ: Prentice Hall.

Festinger, L. (1957). *A theory of cognitive dissonance.* Redwood City, CA: Stanford University Press.

Festinger, L., & Carlsmith, J. M. (1959). Cognitive consequences of forced compliance. *Journal of Abnormal and Social Psychology, 58*, 203–210.

Festinger, L., Reicken, H., & Schachter, S. (1956). *When prophecy fails: A social and psychological study of a modern group that predicted the destruction of the world.* New York: Harper-Torchbooks.

Field, A. E., Austin, S. B., Taylor, C. B., Malspeis, S., Rosner, B., Rockett, H. R., et al. (2003). Relation between dieting and weight change among preadolescents and adolescents. *Pediatrics, 112*, 900–906.

Field, T., Diego, M. A., Hernandez-Reif, M., Deeds, O., & Figuereido, B. (2006). Moderate versus light pressure massage therapy leads to greater weight gain in preterm infants. *Infant Behavior and Development, 29*, 574–578.

Filler, A. (2009). Magnetic resonance neurography and diffusion tensor imaging: origins, history, and clinical impact of the first 50,000 cases with an assessment of efficacy and utility in a prospective 5000-patient study group. *Neurosurgery, 65*, A29–43.

Finger, E. C., Marsh, A. A., Mitchell, D. G., Reid, M. E., Sims, C., Budhani, S., et al. (2008). Abnormal ventromedial prefrontal cortex function in children with psychopathic traits during reversal learning. *Archives of General Psychiatry, 65*, 586–594.

Fiorino, D. F., Coury, A., & Phillips, A. G. (1997). Dynamic changes in nucleus accumbens dopamine efflux during the Coolidge effect in male rats. *Journal of Neuroscience, 17*, 4849–4855.

Fiscella, K., Tancredi, D., & Franks, P. (2009). Adding socioeconomic status to Framingham scoring to reduce disparities in coronary risk assessment. *American Heart Journal, 157*, 988–994.

Fischer, P., & Greitemeyer, T. (2006). Music and aggression: The impact of sexual-aggressive song lyrics on aggression-related thoughts, emotions, and behaviour toward the same and the opposite sex. *Personality and Social Psychology Bulletin, 32*, 1165–1176.

Fischer, P., Kastenmüller, A., & Greitmeyer, T. (2010). Media violence and the self: The impact of personalized gaming characters in aggressive video games on aggressive behavior. *Journal of Experimental Social Psychology, 46*, 192–195.

Fitzgerald, K. D., Welsh, R. C., Gehring, W. J., Abelson, J. L., Himle, J. A., . . . Taylor, S. F. (2005). Error-related hyperactivity of the anterior cingulate cortex in obsessive–compulsive disorder. *Biological Psychiatry, 57*, 287–294.

Fitzpatrick, E. M., Johnson, E., & Durieux-Smith, A. (2011). Exploring factors that affect age of cochlear implantation in children. *International Journal of Pediatric Otolaryngology, 75*, 1082–1087.

Fivush, R., & Nelson, K. (2004). Culture and language in the emergence of autobiographical memory. *Psychological Science, 15*, 573–577.

Flett, G. L., Krames, L., & Vredenburg, K. (2009). Personality traits in clinical and remitted depression: An analysis of instrumental-agentic and expressive-communal traits. *Current Psychology, 28*, 240–248.

Floel, A., Poeppel, D., Buffalo, E. A., Braun, A., Wu, C. W., . . . & Cohen, L. G. (2004). Prefrontal cortex asymmetry for memory encoding of words and abstract shapes. *Cerebral Cortex, 14*, 404–409.

Flora, C. (July 2005). The grandmaster experiment. *Psychology Today Magazine.* Retrieved from http://www.psychologytoday.com/articles/200506/the-grandmaster-experiment

Flourens, M. J. P. (1824). *Recherches expe'rimentales sur les proprie'te's et les fonctions du syste'me nerveux dans les animaux verte'bre's.* Paris: Crevot.

Flynn, J. R. (1987). Massive IQ gains in 14 nations: What IQ tests really measure. *Psychological Bulletin, 101*, 171–191.

Flynn, J. R. (2007). *What is intelligence? Beyond the Flynn effect.* New York: Cambridge University Press.

Flynn, J. R., & Rossi-Casé, L. (2011). Modern women match men on Raven's Progressive Matrices. *Personality and Individual Differences, 50*, 799–803.

Foer, J., & Siffre, M. (2008). Caveman: An interview with Michel Siffre. *Cabinet, 30.* Retrieved from http://www.cabinetmagazine.org/issues/30/foer.php

Fogel, S. M., Nader, R., Cote, K. A., & Smith, C. T. (2007). Sleep spindles and learning potential. *Behavioral Neuroscience, 121*, 1–10.

Folkman, S., & Lazarus, R. S. (1980). An analysis of coping in a middle-aged community sample. *Journal of Health and Social Behavior, 21*, 219–239.

Fonagy, P., Steele, M., Steele, H., Leigh, T., Kennedy, R., . . . Target, M. (1995). Attachment, the reflective self, and borderline states: The predictive specificity of the Adult Attachment Interview and pathological emotional development. In *Attachment theory: Social, developmental, and clinical perspectives* (pp. 233–278). Hillsdale, NJ: Analytic Press.

Fonagy, P., & Target, M. (1997). Attachment and reflective function: Their role in self-organization. *Development and Psychopathology, 9*, 679–700.

Fong, G. T., Hammond, D., & Hitchman, S. C. (2009). The impact of pictures on the effectiveness of tobacco warnings. *Bulletin of the World Health Organization, 87*, 640–643.

Fontanilla, D., Johannessen, M., Hajipour, A. R., Cozzi, N. V., Meyer, B. J., & Ruoho, A. E. (2009). The hallucinogen N, N-dimethyl-tryptamine (DMT) is an endogenous sigma-1 receptor regulator. *Science, 323*, 934–937.

Ford, D. (2002). *The dark side of the light chasers*. New York, NY: Riverhead Books.

Forer, B. R. (1949). The fallacy of personal validation: A classroom demonstration of gullibility. *Journal of Abnormal and Social Psychology* (American Psychological Association), *44*, 118–123.

Forgas, J. P. (Ed.). (2000). *Handbook of affect and social cognition*. Mahwah, NJ: Lawrence Erlbaum Associates Publishers.

Forlini, C., Gauthier, S., & Racine, E. (2013). Should physicians prescribe cognitive enhancers to healthy individuals? *Canadian Medical Association Journal, 185*, 1047–1050.

Foroud, T., Edenberg, H. J., & Crabbe, J. C. (2010). Genetic research: Who is at risk for alcoholism? *Alcohol Research & Health, 33*, 64–75.

Foster, E. M., & Watkins, S. (2010). The value of reanalysis: Television viewing and attention problems. *Child Development, 81*, 368–375.

Foucault, M. (1975). *Discipline and punish: The birth of the prison*. New York: Random House.

Fournier, A. K., Ehrhart, I. J., Glindemann, K. E., & Geller, E. (2004). Intervening to decrease alcohol abuse at university parties: Differential reinforcement of intoxication level. *Behavior Modification, 28*, 167–181.

Fouts, R. S. (1997). *Next of kin: What chimpanzees tell us about who we are*. New York: Avon Books.

Fowler, J. H., & Christakis, N. A. (2008). Dynamic spread of happiness in a large social network: Longitudinal analysis over 20 years in the Framingham Heart Study. *British Medical Journal, 337*, a2338.

Fox, E., Ridgewell, A., & Ashwin, C. (2009). Looking on the bright side: Biased attention and the human serotonin transporter gene. *Proceedings of the Royal Society, B., 276*, 1747–1751.

Fox, J., Blank, M., Rovnyak, V., & Barnett, R. (2001). Barriers to help seeking for mental disorders in a rural impoverished population. *Community Mental Health Journal, 37*, 421–436.

Fox, K. C. R., Spreng, R. N., Ellamil, M., Andews-Hanna, J. R., & Christoff, K. (2015). The wandering brain: Meta-analysis of functional neuroimaging studies of mind-wandering and related spontaneous thought processes. *NeuroImage, 111*, 611–621.

Fox, S. (2005). Health information online. Pew Internet and American Life Project. Retrieved from http://www.pewinternet.org

Francis, D., Diorio, J., Liu, D., & Meaney, M. J. (1999). Nongenomic transmission across generations of maternal behavior and stress responses in the rat. *Science, 286*, 1155–1158.

Frankel, F. H. (1993). Adult reconstruction of childhood events in the multiple personality literature. *American Journal of Psychiatry, 150*, 954–958.

Frankl, V. (1959). *Man's search for meaning*. New York: Washington Square Press.

Franks, N., & Richardson, T. (2006). Teaching in tandem-running ants. *Nature, 439*, 153.

Fredrickson, B. L. (2001). The role of positive emotions in positive psychology. *American Psychologist, 56*, 218–226.

Fredrickson, B. L. (2003). The value of positive emotions. *American Scientist, 91*, 330–335.

Fredrickson, B. L., & Branigan, C. (2005). Positive emotions broaden the scope of attention and thought-action repertoires. *Cognition and Emotion, 19*, 313–332.

Fredrickson, B. L., & Levenson, R. W. (1998). Positive emotions speed recovery from the cardiovascular sequelae of negative emotions. *Cognition and Emotion, 12*, 191–220.

French, L., & Pavlidis, P. (2011). Using text mining to link journal articles to neuroanatomical databases. *Journal of Comparative Neurology, 520*, 1772–1783.

Freud, A. (1936). *The ego and the mechanisms of defense*. London: Hogarth Press & Institute of Psycho-Analysis.

Freud, A. (1958). Adolescence. *Psychoanalytic Study of the Child, 13*, 255–278.

Freud, S. (1899/2011). *The interpretation of dreams*. New York: Avon.

Freud, S. (1905/2000). *Three essays on the theory of sexuality*. New York: Basic Books Classics.

Freud, S. (1920). *A general introduction to psychoanalysis*. New York: Liveright Publishing.

Frewen, P. A., Dozois, D. J., & Lanius, R. A. (2008). Neuroimaging studies of psychological interventions for mood and anxiety disorders: Empirical and methodological review. *Clinical Psychology Review, 28*, 228–246.

Frias, A., Watkins, P. C., Webber, A. C., & Froh, J. J. (2011). Death and gratitude: Death reflection enahnces gratitude. *The Journal of Positive Psychology, 6*, 154–162.

Fridlund, A. J., Beck, H. P., Goldie, W. D., & Irons, G. (2012). Little Albert: A neurologically impaired child. *History of Psychology, 15*, 302–327.

Fried, P., Watkinson, B., James, D., & Gray, R. (2002). Current and former marijuana use: Preliminary findings of a longitudinal study of the effects on IQ in young adults. *Canadian Medical Association Journal, 166*, 887–891.

Friederich, H. C., Brooks, S., Uher, R., Campbell, I. C., Giampietro, V., Brammer, M., et al. (2010). Neural correlates of body dissatisfaction in anorexia nervosa. *Neuropsychologia, 48*, 2878–2885.

Friedman, M., & Rosenman, R. (1959). Association of specific overt behaviour pattern with blood and cardiovascular findings. *Journal of the American Medical Association, 169*, 1286–1296.

Friedman, M., & Rosenman, R. H. (1974). *Type A behavior and your heart*. New York: Knopf.

Frijters, J. C., Lovett, M. W., Sevcik, R. A., & Morris, R. D. (2013). Four methods of identifying change in the context of a multiple component reading intervention for struggling middle school readers. *Reading and Writing, 26*, 539–563.

Frisch, R. E., & Barbieri, R. L. (2002). *Female fertility and body fat connection*. Chicago: University of Chicago Press.

Frodi, A., Bridges, L., & Grolnick, W. (1985). Correlates of mastery-related behavior: A short-term longitudinal study of infants in their second year. *Child Development, 56*, 1291–1298.

Fu, C. H., Abel, K. M., Allin, M. P., Gasston, D., Costafreda, S. G., Suckling, J., et al. (2005). Effects of ketamine on prefrontal and striatal regions in an overt verbal fluency task: A functional magnetic resonance imaging study. *Psychopharmacology, 183*, 92–102.

Fujioka, T., Mourad, N., & Trainor, L. J. (2011). Development of auditory-specific brain rhythm in infants. *European Journal of Neuroscience, 33*, 521–529.

Fukushima, H., Terasawa, Y., & Umeda, S. (2011). Association between interoception and empathy: Evidence from heartbeat-evoked brain potential. *International Journal of Psychophysiology, 79*, 259–265.

Fulda, S., & Schulz, H. (2003). Cognitive dysfunction in sleep-related breathing disorders: A meta-analysis. *Sleep Research Online, 5*, 13–43.

Fuller, R., Nopoulos, P., Arndt, S., O'Leary, D., Ho, B. C., & Andreasen, N. C. (2002). Longitudinal assessment of premorbid cognitive functioning in patients with schizophrenia through examination of standardized scholastic test performance. *American Journal of Psychiatry, 159*, 1183–1189.

Furley, P., Memmert, D., & Heller, C. (2010). The dark side of visual awareness in sport—inattentional blindness in a real-world basketball task. *Attention, Perception, & Psychophysics, 72*, 1327–1337.

Gaertner, S. L., & Dovidio, J. F. (2000). *Reducing intergroup bias: The common ingroup identity model*. New York: Psychology Press.

Gais, S., Molle, M., Helms, K., & Born, J. (2002). Learning-dependent increases in sleep spindle density. *Journal of Neuroscience, 22*, 6830–6834.

Galaburda, A. M., & Pandya, D. N. (1982). Role of architectonics and connections in the study of primate brain evolution. In E. Armstrong et al. (Eds.), *Primate brain evolution* (pp. 203–216). New York: Plenum Press.

Galambos, N. L., Vargas Lascano, D. I., Howard, A. L., & Maggs, J. L. (2013). Who sleeps best? Longitudinal patterns and covariates of change in sleep quantity, quality, and timing across four university years. *Behavioral Sleep Medicine, 11*, 8–22.

Galanter, E. (1962). Contemporary psychophysics. In R. Brown, E. Galanter, E. H. Hess, & G. Mandler (Eds.), *New directions in psychology* (p. 231). New York: Holt, Rinehart, & Winston.

Gallagher, R. P. (2007). *National Survey of Counseling Center Directors (2007)*. Washington, DC: International Association of Counseling Services. Retrieved from http://www.iacsinc.org/

Gallo, D., Roberts, M., & Seamon, J. (1997). Remembering words not presented in lists: Can we avoid creating false memories? *Psychonomic Bulletin & Review, 4*, 271–276.

Galobardes, B., Smith, G. D., & Lynch, J. W. (2006). Systematic review of the influence of childhood socioeconomic circumstances on risk for cardiovascular disease in adulthood. *Annals of Epidemiology, 16*, 91–104.

Galton, F. (1869). *Hereditary genius*. London: Macmillan.

Galvan, A., Hare, T. A., Parra, C. E., Penn, J., Voss, H., . . . Casey, B. J. (2006). Earlier development of the accumbens relative to orbitofrontal cortex might underlie risk-taking behavior in adolescents. *The Journal of Neuroscience, 26*, 6885–6892.

Gangestad, S. W., Thornhill, R., & Yeo, R. A. (1994). Facial attractiveness, developmental stability, and fluctuating asymmetry. *Ethology and Sociobiology, 15*, 73–85.

Garb, H. N., Wood, J. M., Lilienfeld, S. O., & Nezworski, M. T. (2005). Roots of the Rorschach controversy. *Clinical Psychology Review, 25*, 97–118.

Garbutt, J. (2009). The state of pharmacotherapy for the treatment of alcohol dependence. *Journal of Substance Abuse Treatment, 36*, S15–S23.

Garcia, J., Ervin, F. R., & Koelling, R. A. (1966). Learning with prolonged delay of reinforcement. *Psychonomic Science, 5*, 121–122.

Garcia-Falgueras, A., & Swaab, D. F. (2008). A sex difference in the hypothalamic uncinate nucleus: relationship to gender identity. *Brain, 131*, 3132–3146.

Gardner, D. (2008). *Risk*. Toronto: McClelland & Stewart.

Gardner, H. (1983). *Frames of mind: The theory of multiple intelligences*. New York: Basic Books.

Gardner, H. (1999). *Intelligence reframed: Multiple intelligences for the 21st century*. New York: Basic Books.

Gardner, R. A., Gardner, B. T., & VanCantfort, T. E. (1989). *Teaching sign language to chimpanzees*. Albany, NY: State University of New York Press.

Garland, E. L., Fredrickson, B. L., Kring, A. M., Johnson, D. P., Meyer, P. S., & Penn, D. L. (2010). Upward spirals of positive emotions counter downward spirals of negativity: Insights from the broaden-and-build theory and affective neuroscience on the treatment of emotion dysfunctions and deficits in psychopathology. *Clinical Psychology Review, 30*, 849–864.

Garrow, J. S., & Stalley, S. (1975). Is there a "set point" for human body weight? *Proceedings of the Nutrition Society, 34*, 84–85.

Garry, M., Manning, C., Loftus, E., & Sherman, S. (1996). Imagination inflation: Imagining a childhood event inflates confidence that it occurred. *Psychonomic Bulletin & Review, 3*, 208–214.

Garry, M., & Polaschek, D. (2000). Imagination and memory. *Current Directions in Psychological Science, 9*, 6–10.

Gaser, C., & Schlaug, G. (2003). Brain structures differ between musicians and non-musicians. *Journal of Neuroscience, 23*, 9240–9245.

Gasser, P., Kirchner, K., & Passie, T. (2015). LSD-assisted psychotherapy for anxiety associated with life-threatening diseases: A qualitative study of acute and sustained subjective effects. *Journal of Pharmacology, 29*, 57–68.

Gaudet, S., Clement, R., & Deuzeman, K. (2005). Daily hassles, ethnic identity and psychological adjustment among Lebanese-Canadians. *International Journal of Psychology, 40*, 157–168.

Gauthier, I., Skudlarski, P., Gore, J. C., & Anderson, A. W. (2000). Expertise for cars and birds recruits brain areas involved in face recognition. *Nature Neuroscience, 3*, 191–197.

Gauthier, I., & Tarr, M. J. (1997). Becoming a "Greeble" expert: Exploring mechanisms for face recognition. *Vision Research, 37*, 1673–1682.

Gauthier, I., Tarr, M. J., Anderson, A. W., Skudlarski, P., & Gore, J. C. (1999). Activation of the middle fusiform "face area" increases with expertise in recognizing novel objects. *Nature Neuroscience, 2*, 568–573.

Gawryluk, J. R., D'arcy, R. C. N., Connolly, J. F., & Weaver, D. F. (2010). Improving the clinical assessment of consciousness with advances in electrophysiological and neuroimaging techniques. *Neurology, 10*, 1–7.

Gazzaniga, M. S. (1967). The split-brain in man. *Scientific American, 217*, 24–29.

Gazzaniga, M. S. (2000). Cerebral specialization and interhemispheric communication. *Brain, 123*, 1293–1326.

Geake, J. G., & Hansen, P. C. (2010). Functional neural correlates of fluid and crystallized intelligence. *Neuroimage, 49*, 3489–3497.

Gegenfurtner, K. R., Bloj, M., & Toscani, M. (2015). The many colours of "the dress." *Current Biology, 25*, R543–R544.

Geier, A., Rozin, P., & Doros, G. (2006). Unit bias: A new heuristic that helps explain the effect of portion size on food intake. *Psychological Science, 17*, 521–525.

Geller, J., Cockell, S. J., Hewitt, P. L., Goldner, E. M., & Flett, G. L. (2000). Inhibited expression of negative emotions and interpersonal orientation in anorexia nervosa. *International Journal of Eating Disorders, 28*, 8–19.

Gelman, M., Kosma, L., Wurm, C. S., & Keks, N. (2000). Viktor Emil Frankl 1905–1997. *American Journal of Psychiatry, 157*, 625.

George, M. S., Raman, R., Benedek, D. M., Pelic, C. G., Grammer, G. G., . . . Stein, M. B. (2014). A two-site pilot randomized 3 day trial of high dose left prefrontal repetitive transcranial magnetic stimulation (rTMS) for suicidal inpatients. *Brain Stimulation, 7*, 421–431.

Gershoff, E. T. (2002). Parental corporal punishment and associated child behaviors and experiences: A meta-analytic and theoretical review. *Psychological Bulletin, 128*, 539–579.

Gershoff, E. T., & Bitensky, S. H. (2007). The case against corporal punishment of children: Converging evidence from social science research and international human rights law and implications for U.S. public policy. *Psychology, Public Policy, and the Law, 13*, 231–272.

Geschwind, N., Peeters, F., Drukker, M., van Os, J., & Wichers, M. (2011). Mindfulness training increases momentary positive emotions and reward experience in adults vulnerable to depression: A randomized controlled trial. *Journal of Consulting and Clinical Psychology, 79*, 618–628.

Gibbons, M., Crits-Christoph, P., & Hearon, B. (2008). The empirical status of psychodynamic therapies. *Annual Review of Clinical Psychology, 4*, 93–108.

Gibson, E. J., & Walk, R. D. (1960). The "visual cliff." *Scientific American, 202*, 67–71.

Giedd, J. N. (2008). The teen brain: Insights from neuroimaging. *Journal of Adolescent Health, 42*, 335–343.

Gigerenzer, G. (2004). Dread risk, September 11, and fatal traffic accidents. *Psychological Science, 15*, 286–287.

Gilbert, D. T., King, G., Pettigrew, S., & Wilson, T. D. (2016). Comment on "Estimating the reproducibility of psychological science." *Science, 351*, 1037a–1037b.

Gillham, N. W. (2001). *A life of Sir Francis Galton: From African exploration to the birth of eugenics*. New York: Oxford University Press.

Gilligan, C. (1982). *In a different voice: Psychological theory and women's development*. Cambridge, MA: Harvard University Press.

Gilovich, T., & Griffin, D. (2002). Introduction: Heuristics and biases: Then and now. In T. Gilovich, D. Griffin, & D. Kahneman (Eds.), *Heuristics and biases: The psychology of intuitive judgment* (pp. 1–18). New York: Cambridge University Press.

Gilovich, T., Vallone, R., & Tversky, A. (1985). The hot hand in basketball: On the misperception of random sequences. *Cognitive Psychology, 17*, 295–314.

Ginosar, S., Rakelly, K., Sachs, S., Yin, B., & Efros, A. A. (2015). *A century of portraits: A visual historical record of American high school yearbooks*. Extreme Imaging Workshop, International Conference on Computer Vision, ICCV.

Glaser, J. P., Os, J. V., Mengelers, R., & Myin-Germeys, I. (2008). A momentary assessment study of the reputed emotional phenotype associated with borderline personality disorder. *Psychological Medicine, 30,* 1–9.

Glenberg, A., Smith, S., & Green, C. (1977). Type I rehearsal: Maintenance and more. *Journal of Verbal Learning & Verbal Behavior, 16,* 339–352.

Glenn, N. D. (1990). Quantitative research on marital quality in the 1980s: A critical review. *Journal of Marriage and the Family, 52,* 818–831.

Glick, P., & Fiske, S. T. (1996). The ambivalent sexism inventory: Differentiating hostile and benevolent sexism. *Journal of Personality and Social Psychology, 70,* 491–512.

Glick, P., & Fiske, S. T. (2001). An ambivalent alliance: Hostile and benevolent sexism as complementary justifications for gender inequality. *American Psychologist, 56,* 109–118.

Glindemann, K. E., Ehrhart, I. J., Drake, E. A., & Geller, E. S. (2007). Reducing excessive alcohol consumption at university fraternity parties: A cost-effective incentive/reward intervention. *Addictive Behaviors, 32,* 39–48.

Gluckman, M., Vlach, H. A., & Sandhofer, C. M. (2014). Spacing simultaneously promotes multiple forms of learning in children's science curriculum. *Applied Cognitive Psychology, 28,* 266–273.

Gobet, F., & Simon, H. A. (1998). Expert chess memory: Revisiting the chunking hypothesis. *Memory, 6,* 225–255.

Godden, D. R., & Baddeley, A. D. (1975). Context-dependent memory in two environments: On land and underwater. *British Journal of Psychology, 66,* 325–331.

Goff, L.M., & Roediger III, H. L. (1998). Imagination inflation for action events: Repeated imaginings lead to illusory recollections. *Memory & Cognition, 26,* 20–33.

Gogtay, N., Giedd, J. N., Lusk, L., Hayashi, K. M., Greenstein, D., Vaituzis, C., et al. (2004). Dynamic mapping of human cortical development during childhood through early adulthood. *Proceedings of the National Academy of Sciences, 101,* 8174–8179.

Goh, J. O., Chee, M. W., Tan, J. C., Venkatraman, V., Hebrank, A., Leshikar, E. D., et al. (2007). Age and culture modulate object processing and object-scene binding in the ventral visual area. *Cognitive, Affective, & Behavioral Neuroscience, 7,* 44–52.

Goland, R. S., Wardlaw, S. L., MacCarter, G., Warren, W. B., & Stark, R. I. (1991). Adrenocorticotropin and cortisol responses to vasopressin during pregnancy. *Journal of Clinical Endocrinology and Metabolism, 73,* 257–261.

Golden, W. L. (2007). Cognitive-behavioral hypnotherapy in the treatment of irritable-bowel–syndrome-induced agoraphobia. *International Journal of Clinical and Experimental Hypnosis, 55,* 131–146.

Goldman-Rakic, P. S. (1996). The prefrontal landscape: Implications of functional architecture for understanding human mentation and the central executive. *Philosophical Transactions of the Royal Society of London (B Biological Sciences), 351*(1346), 1445–1453.

Goldstein, A., & Flett, G. L. (2009). Personality, alcohol use, and drinking motives: A comparison of independent and combined internal drinking motives groups. *Behavior Modification, 33,* 182–198.

Goldstein, A. L., Flett, G. L., Wekerle, C., & Wall, A-M. (2009). Personality, child maltreatment, and substance use: Examining correlates of deliberate self-harm among university students. *Canadian Journal of Behavioural Sciences, 41,* 241–251.

Gollan, T. H., & Acenas, L. R. (2004). What is a TOT? Cognate and translation effects on tip-of-the-tongue states in Spanish-English and Tagalog-English bilinguals. *Journal of Experimental Psychology: Learning, Memory, and Cognition, 30,* 246–269.

Gomez, R., Cooper, A., & Gomez, A. (2000). Susceptibility to positive and negative mood states: Test of Eysenck's, Gray's, and Newman's theories. *Personality and Individual Differences, 29,* 351–365.

Goodale, M. A., Milner, A. D., Jakobson, L. S., & Carey, D. P. (1991). A neurological dissociation between perceiving objects and grasping them. *Nature, 349,* 154–156.

Goodall, J., & Berman, P. (1999). *A reason for hope: A spiritual journey.* New York: Warner Books.

Goode, C., Balzarini, R. H., & Smith, H. J. (2014). Positive peer pressure: Priming member prototypicality can decrease undergraduate drinking. *Journal of Applied Social Psychology, 44,* 567–578.

Goodman, M. B. & Moradi, B. (2008). Attitudes and behaviors toward lesbian and gay persons: Critical correlates and mediated relations. *Journal of Counseling Psychology, 55,* 371–384.

Goodwin, D. W., Powell, B., Bremer, D., Hoine, H., & Stern, J. (1969). Alcohol and recall: State-dependent effects in man. *Science, 163,* 1358–1360.

Gopnik, A. (2010). *The philosophical baby.* New York: Farrar, Straus, & Giroux.

Gosling, S. D. (2001). From mice to men: What can we learn about personality from animal research? *Psychological Bulletin, 127,* 45–86.

Gosling, S. D. (2008). *Snoop: What your stuff says about you.* New York: Basic Books.

Gosling, S. D., Ko, S. J., Mannarelli, T., & Morris, M. E. (2002). A room with a cue: Personality judgments based on offices and bedrooms. *Personality Processes and Individual Differences, 82,* 379–398.

Gosselin, N., Peretz, I., Noulhiane, M., Hasboun, D., Beckett, C., . . . Samson, S. (2005). Impaired recognition of scary music following unilateral temporal lobe excision. *Brain, 128,* 628–640.

Gotlib, I., & Hamilton, J. (2008). Neuroimaging and depression: Current status and unresolved issues. *Current Directions in Psychological Science, 17,* 159–163.

Gottesman, I. (1991). *Schizophrenia genesis.* New York: W. H. Freeman.

Gottesman, I., & Gould, T. D. (2003). The endophenotype concept in psychiatry: Etymology and strategic intentions. *American Journal of Psychiatry, 160,* 636–645.

Gottfredson, L. S. (2003). On Sternberg's "Reply to Gottfredson." *Intelligence, 31,* 415–424.

Gottfredson, L. S. (2005). What if the hereditarian hypothesis is true? *Psychology, Public Policy, and Law, 11,* 311–319.

Gottfredson, L. S., & Deary, I. J. (2004). Intelligence predicts health and longevity, but why? *Current Directions in Psychological Science, 13,* 1–4.

Gottlieb, B. H., Still, E., & Newby-Clark, I. R. (2007). Types and precipitants of growth and decline in emerging adulthood. *Journal of Adolescent Research, 22,* 1–24.

Gottman, J. M., & Levenson, R. W. (1992). Marital processes predictive of later dissolution: Behavior, physiology and health. *Journal of Personality and Social Psychology, 63,* 221–233.

Gottman, J., & Levenson, R. W. (2002). A two-factor model for predicting when a couple will divorce: Exploratory analyses using 14-year longitudinal data. *Family Process, 41,* 83–96.

Gouin, J.-P., Carter, C. S., Pournajafi-Nazarloo, H., Glaser, R., Malarkey, W. B., Loving, T. J., et al. (2010). Marital behavior, oxytocin, vasopressin, and wound healing. *Psychoneuroendocrinology, 35,* 1082–1090.

Gouin, J.-P., & Kiecolt-Glaser, J. K. (2011). The impact of psychological stress on wound healing: Methods and mechanisms. *Immunology and Allergy Clinics of North America, 31,* 81–93.

Gould, M. S., Greenberg, T., Velting, D. M., & Shaffer, D. (2003). Youth suicide risk and preventive interventions: A review of the past 10 years. *Journal of the American Academy of Child and Adolescent Psychiatry, 42,* 386–405.

Gould, S. J. (1981). *The mismeasure of man.* New York: W. W. Norton.

Grabner, R. H., Stern, E., & Neubauer, A. C. (2003). When intelligence loses its impact: Neural efficiency during reasoning in a familiar area. *International Journal of Psychophysiology, 49,* 89–98.

Graf, P., & Schacter, D. L. (1985). Implicit and explicit memory for new associations normal and amnesic subjects. *Journal of Experimental Psychology: Learning, Memory, and Cognition, 11,* 501–518.

Graham, E. R., & Burke, D. M. (2011). Aging increases inattentional blindness to the gorilla in our midst. *Psychology and Aging, 26,* 162–166.

Graham, K., & Wells, S. (2004). Aggression among young adults in the social context of the bar. *Addiction Research and Theory, 9,* 193–219.

Grahn, J. A. (2009). The role of the basal ganglia in beat perception. *The Neurosciences and Music III—Disorders and Plasticity, 1169,* 35–45.

Grahn, J. A., & McAuley, J. D. (2009). Neural bases of individual differences in beat perception. *NeuroImage, 47*, 1894–1903.

Grahn, J. A., & Rowe, J. B. (2009). Feeling the beat: Premotor and striatal interactions in musicians and nonmusicians during beat perception. *Journal of Neuroscience, 29*, 7540–7548.

Grahn, J. A., & Rowe, J. B. (2013). Finding and feeling the musical beat: Striatal dissociations between detection and prediction of regularity. *Cerebral Cortex, 23*, 913–921.

Granpeesheh, D., Tarbox, J., & Dixon, D. R. (2009). Applied behavior analytic interventions for children with autism: A description and review of treatment research. *Annals of Clinical Psychiatry, 21*, 162–173.

Grant, H. M., Bredahl, L. C., Clay, J., Ferrie, J., Groves, J. E., McDorman, T. A., & Dark, V. J. (1998). Context-dependent memory for meaningful material: Information for students. *Applied Cognitive Psychology, 12*, 617–623.

Gray, J. (1992). *Men are from Mars, women are from Venus.* New York: HarperCollins.

Gray, J. A. (1991). Neural systems, emotion and personality. In J. Madden IV (Ed.), *Neurobiology of learning, emotion and affect.* New York: Raven Press.

Gray, J. A., & McNaughton, N. (2000). *The neuropsychology of anxiety: An enquiry into the functions of the septo-hippocampal system.* New York: Oxford University Press.

Green, A. E., Fugelsang, J. A., & Dunbar, K. N. (2006). Automatic activation of categorical and abstract analogical relations in analogical reasoning. *Memory & Cognition, 34*, 1414–1421.

Green, D. M., & Swets, J. A. (1966). *Signal detection theory and psychophysics.* New York: Wiley.

Greenberg, J., Solomon, S., & Arndt, J. (2008). A uniquely human motivation: Terror management. In J. Shah and W. Gardner (Eds.), *Handbook of motivation science* (pp. 113–134). New York, NY: Guilford Press.

Greenberg, L., Elliott, R., & Lietaer, G. (1994). Research on experiential psychotherapies. In A. E. Bergin & S. L. Garfield (Eds.), *Handbook of psychotherapy and behavior change* (4th ed., pp. 509–542). New York: Guilford.

Greenberg, L. S. (2004). Emotion-focused therapy. *Clinical Psychology & Psychotherapy, 11*, 3–16.

Greenberg, L. S., & Watson, J. C. (1998). Experiential therapy of depression: Differential effects of client-centered relationship conditions and process-experiential interventions. *Psychotherapy Research, 8*, 210–224.

Greene, J., & Haidt, J. (2002). How (and where) does moral judgment work? *Trends in Cognitive Sciences, 6*, 517–523.

Greene, J. D., Sommerville, R. B., Nystrom, L. E., Darley, J. M., & Cohen, J. D. (2001). An fMRI investigation of emotional engagement in moral judgment. *Science, 293*, 2105–2108.

Greenland, C., Griffin, J., & Hoffman, B. (2001). Psychiatry in Canada from 1951–2001. In Q. Dae-Grant (Ed.), *Psychiatry in Canada: 50 Years, 1951–2000.* Ottawa: Canadian Psychiatric Association.

Greenwald, A. G., & Banaji, M. R. (1995). Implicit social cognition: Attitudes, self-esteem, and stereotypes. *Psychological Review, 102*, 4–27.

Greenwald, A. G., McGhee, D. E., & Schwartz, J. L. K. (1998). Measuring individual differences in implicit cognition: The implicit association test. *Journal of Personality and Social Psychology, 74*, 1464–1480.

Greenwald, A. G., Spangenberg, E. R., Pratkanis, A. R., & Eskenazi, J. (1991). Double-blind tests of subliminal self-help audiotapes. *Psychological Science, 2*, 119–122.

Greenwood, C. E., & Winocur, G. (2005). High-fat diets, insulin resistance and declining cognitive function. *Neurobiology of Aging, 26*, 42–45.

Gregory, W. L., Cialdini, R. B., & Carpenter, K. M. (1982). Self-relevant scenarios as mediators of likelihood estimates and compliance: Does imagining make it so? *Journal of Personality and Social Psychology, 43*, 89–99.

Greven, C. U., Harlaar, N., Kovas, Y., Chamorro-Premuzic, T., & Plomin, R. (2009). More than just IQ: School achievement is predicted by self-perceived abilities—but for genetic rather than environmental reasons. *Psychological Science, 20*, 753–762.

Grice, P. (1975). Logic and conversation. In P. Cole & J. Morgan (Eds.), *Syntax and semantics* (p. 3). New York: Academic Press.

Griffin, J. A., Umstattd, M. R., & Usdan, S. (2010). Alcohol use and high-risk sexual behaviour among collegiate women: A review of research on alcohol myopia theory. *Journal of American College Health, 58*, 523–532.

Griffiths, R. R., Richards, W. A., Johnson, M. W., McCann, U. D., & Jesse, R. (2008). Mystical-type experiences occasioned by psilocybin mediate the attribution of personal meaning and spiritual significance 14 months later. *Journal of Psychopharmacology, 22*, 621–632.

Grolnick, W. S., & Ryan, R. M. (1989). Parent styles associated with children's self-regulation and competence in school. *Journal of Educational Psychology, 81*, 143–153.

Gropper, S. S., Simmons, K. P., Gaines, A., Drawdy, K., Saunders, D., . . . Connell, L. J. (2009). The freshman 15: A closer look. *Journal of American College Health, 58*, 223–231.

Gross, E. F. (2004). Adolescent Internet use: What we expect, what teens report. *Applied Developmental Psychology, 25*, 633–649.

Gruber, S. A., Dahlgren, M. K., Sagar, K. A., Gönenç, A., & Lukas, S. E. (2014). Worth the wait: Effects of age of onset of marijuana use on white matter and impulsivity. *Psychopharmacology, 231*, 1455–1465.

Gruber, S. A., & Yurgelun-Todd, D. A. (2005). Neuroimaging of marijuana smokers during inhibitory processing: A pilot investigation. *Cognitive Brain Research, 23*, 107–118.

Gruberger, M., Ben-Simon, E., Levkovitz, Y., Zangen, A., & Hendler, T. (2013). Towards a neuroscience of mind-wandering. *Frontiers in Human Neuroscience, 5*, article 56, 1–11.

Guéguen, N. (2012). Color and women attractiveness: When red clothed women are perceived to have more intense sexual intent. *The Journal of Social Psychology, 152*, 261–265.

Guéguen, N., & Jacob, C. (2012a). Clothing color and tipping: Gentlemen patrons give more tips to waitresses with red clothes. *International Journal of Hospital Research, 38*, 275–278.

Guéguen, N., & Jacob, C. (2012b). Lipstick and tipping behaviour: When red lipstick enhance waitresses tips. *International Journal of Hospitality Management, 31*, 1333–1335.

Guldin, W. O., & Grusser, O. J. (1998). Is there a vestibular cortex? *Trends in Neuroscience, 21*, 254–259.

Gustaffson, J. E. (1988). Hierarchical models of individual differences in cognitive abilities. In R. J. Sternberg (Ed.), *Advances in the psychology of human intelligence, Vol. 4* (pp. 35–71). Hillsdale, NJ: Erlbaum.

Gutchess, A. H., Hedden, T., Ketay, S., Aron, A., & Gabrieli, J. D. (2010). Neural differences in the processing of semantic relationships across cultures. *Social, Cognitive and Affective Neuroscience, 5*, 254–263.

Guthrie, E. R. (1952). *The psychology of learning.* New York: Harper & Row.

Haber, J., & Jacob, T. (2007). Alcoholism risk moderation by a socioreligious dimension. *Journal of Studies on Alcohol and Drugs, 68*, 912–922.

Haddock, G., & Zanna, M. P. (1997). Impact of negative advertising on evaluations of political candidates: The 1993 Canadian federal election. *Basic and Applied Social Psychology, 19*, 205–223.

Haddock, G., Zanna, M. P., & Esses, V. M. (1993). Assessing the structure of prejudicial attitudes: The case of attitudes toward homosexuals. *Journal of Personality and Social Psychology, 65*, 1105–1118.

Hahn, A., Kranz, G. S., Küblböck, M., Kaufmann, U., Ganger, S., . . . Lanzenberger, R. (2015). Structural connectivity networks of transgender people. *Cerebral Cortex, 25*, 3527–3534.

Hahn, C., Cowell, J. M., Wiprzycka, U. J., Goldstein, D., Ralph, M., Heasher, L., & Zelazo, P. D. (2012). Circadian rhythms in executive function during the transition to adolescence: The effect of synchrony between chronotype and time of day. *Developmental Science, 15*, 408–416.

Haidt, J. (2001). The emotional dog and its rational tail: A social intuitionist approach to moral judgment. *Psychological Review, 108*, 814–834.

Haier, R. J., Jung, R., Yeo, R. A., Head, K., & Alkire, M. T. (2005). The neuroanatomy of general intelligence: Sex matters. *NeuroImage, 25*, 320–327.

Haier, R. J., Siegel, B. V., Tang, C., Abel, L., & Buchsbaum, M. S. (1992). Intelligence and changes in regional cerebral glucose metabolic rate following learning. *Intelligence 16*, 415–426.

Hakuta, K., Bialystok, E., & Wiley, E. (2003). Critical evidence: A test of the critical-period hypothesis for second-language acquisition. *Psychological Science, 14*, 31–38.

Halberg, F., Peterson, R. E., & Silber, R. H. (1959). Phase relations of 24-hour periodicities in blood corticosterone, mitoses in cortical adrenal parenchyma and total body activity. *Endocrinology, 64*, 222–230.

Halgren, E., Raij, T., Marinkovic, K., Jousmäki, V., & Hari, R. (2000). Cognitive response profile of the human fusiform face area as determined by MEG. *Cerebral Cortex, 10*, 69–81.

Hall, G. S. (1904). *Adolescence* (Vols. 1 & 2). New York: Appleton.

Halpern, D. F. (1996). *Thought and knowledge: An introduction to critical thinking.* Mahwah, NJ: Lawrence Erlbaum.

Halpern, D. F., & Lamay, M. L. (2000). The smarter sex: A critical review of sex differences in intelligence. *Educational Psychology Review, 12*, 229–246.

Halpern, J. H., & Pope, H. G. (2003). Hallucinogen persisting perception disorder: What do we know after 50 years? *Drug and Alcohol Dependence, 69*, 109–119.

Halpern-Fisher, B. L., Cornell, J. L., Kropp, R. Y., & Tschann, J. M. (2005). Oral versus vaginal sex among adolescents: Perceptions, attitudes, and behavior. *Pediatrics, 4*, 845–851.

Hamalainen, M. S., Hari, R., Ilmoniemi, R., Knuutila, J., & Lounasmaa, O. (1993). Magnetoencephalography — Theory, instrumentation, and applications to noninvasive studies of the working human brain. *Reviews of Modern Physics, 65*, 413–497.

Hamlin, J. K., Wynn, K., & Bloom, P. (2007). Social evaluation by preverbal infants. *Nature, 450*, 557–560.

Hamlin, J. K., Wynn, K., & Bloom, P. (2010). Three-month-olds show a negativity bias in their social evaluations. *Developmental Science, 13*, 923–929.

Hamlin, J. K., Wynn, K., Bloom, P., & Mahajan, N. (2011). How infants and toddlers react to antisocial others. *Proceedings of the National Academy of Sciences, 108*, 19931–19936.

Hammond, D. (2011). Health warning messages on tobacco products: A review. *Tobacco Control, 20*, 327–337.

Hammond, D., Ahmed, R., Burkhalter, R., Sae Yang, W., & Leatherdale, S. (2010). Illicit substance use among Canadian youth: Trends between 2002 and 2008. *Canadian Journal of Public Health, 102*, 7–12.

Hammond, D., Fong, G. T., Borland, R., Cummings, K. M., McNeill, A., & Driezen, P (2007). Communicating risk to smokers: The impact of health warnings on cigarette packages. *American Journal of Preventive Medicine, 32*, 202–209.

Hammond, D., Fong, G. T., McDonald, P. W., Cameron, R., & Brown, K. S. (2003). Impact of the graphic Canadian warning labels on adult smoking behavior. *Tobacco Control, 12*, 391–395.

Hane, A. A., Feldstein, S., & Dernetz, V. H. (2003). The relation between coordinated interpersonal timing and maternal sensitivity in four-month-old infants. *Journal of Psycholinguistic Research, 32*, 525–539.

Hanin, Y. L. (2000). *Emotions in sport.* Champaign, IL: Human Kinetics.

Hanks, A. S., Just, D. R., & Wansink, B. (2012). Trigger foods: The influence of "irrelevant" alternatives in school lunchrooms. *Agricultural and Resource Economics Review, 41*, 1–10.

Hardwick, S., & King, L. (2008). *Home Office cannabis potency study 2008.* Sandridge, U.K.: Home Office Scientific Development Branch.

Hare, R. D. (1985). Comparison of procedures for the assessment of psychopathy. *Journal of Consulting and Clinical Psychology, 53*, 7–16.

Harlow, J. M. (1848). Passage of an iron rod through the head. *Boston Medical and Surgical Journal, 39*, 389–393.

Harlow, J. M. (1849). Letter in "medical miscellany." *Boston Medical and Surgical Journal, 39*, 506–507.

Harlow, J. M. (1868). Recovery from the passage of an iron bar through the head. *Publications of the Massachusetts Medical Society, 2*, 327–347.

Harrigan K., MacLaren, V., Brown, D., Dixon, M. J., & Livingstone, C. (2014). Games of chance or masters of illusion: Multiline slots design may promote cognitive distortions. *International Gambling Studies, 14*, 301–317.

Harris, J. L., Bargh, J. A., & Brownell, K. D. (2009). Priming effects of television food advertising on eating behavior. *Health Psychology, 28*, 404–413.

Harris, J. L., Pierce, M., & Bargh, J. A. (2013). Priming effect of antismoking PSAs on smoking behavior: A pilot study. *Tobacco Control, 23*, 285–290.

Harris, R. B. (1990). Role of set-point theory in regulation of body weight. *The Journal of the Federation of American Societies for Experimental Biology, 4*, 3310–3318.

Hart, B., & Risley, T. R. (1995). *Meaningful differences in the everyday experience of young American children.* Baltimore: Paul H. Brookes.

Hartline, D. K., & Colman, D. R. (2007). Rapid conduction and the evolution of giant axons and myelinated fibers. *Current Biology, 17*, R29–35.

Hartman, E., & Brezler, T. (2008). A systematic change in dreams after 9/11/01. *Sleep, 31*, 213–218.

Harvey, P., & Walker, E. (Eds.). (1987). *Positive and negative symptoms of psychosis: Description, research, and future directions.* Hillsdale, NJ: Lawrence Erlbaum Associates.

Haselton, M. G., Mortezaie, M., Pillsworth, E. G., Bleske-Rechek, A., & Frederick, D. A. (2007). Ovulatory shifts in human female ornamentation: Near ovulation, women dress to impress. *Hormones and Behavior, 51*, 40–45.

Hasher, L., Chung, C., May, C. P., & Foong, N. (2002). Age, time of testing, and proactive interference. *Canadian Journal of Experimental Psychology, 56*, 200–207.

Hatfield, E., & Rapson, R. L. (2009). The neuropsychology of passionate love and sexual desire. In E. Cuyler, & M. Ackart (Eds.), *Psychology of social relationships.* Hauppauge, NY: Nova Science.

Havas, D. A., Glenberg, A. M., Gutowski, K. A., Lucarelli, M. J., & Davidson, R. J. (2010). Cosmetic use of Botulinum toxin-A affects processing of emotional language. *Psychological Science, 21*, 895–900.

Hawkins, R. D. (1984). A cellular mechanism of classical conditioning in *aplysia. Journal of Experimental Biology, 112*, 113–128.

Hawkley, L. C., Burleson, M. H., Berntson, G. G., & Cacioppo, J. T. (2003). Loneliness in everyday life: Cardiovascular activity, psychosocial context, and health behaviors. *Journal of Personality & Social Psychology, 85*, 105–120.

Hayes, J., Schimel, J., Arndt, J., & Faucher, E. H. (2010). A theoretical and empirical review of the death-thought accessibility concept in terror management theory. *Psychological Bulletin, 136*, 699–739.

Hayes, K. J., & Hayes, C. (1951). The intellectual development of a home-raised chimpanzee. *Proceedings of the American Philosophical Society, 95*, 105–109.

Hayes, S. C., Luoma, J. B., Bond, F. W., Masuda, A., & Lillis, J. (2006). Acceptance and commitment therapy: Model, processes and outcomes. *Behaviour Research and Therapy, 44*, 1–25.

Hayne, H., Herbert, J., & Simcock, G. (2003). Imitation from television by 24- and 30-month-olds. *Developmental Science, 6*, 254–261.

Hazan, C., & Shaver, P. R. (1987). Romantic love conceptualized as an attachment process. *Journal of Personality and Social Psychology, 52*, 511–524.

Hazell, P. (2007). Drug therapy for attention-deficit/hyperactivity disorder-like symptoms in autistic disorder. *Journal of Paediatrics and Child Health, 43*, 19–24.

He, C., Hotson, L., & Trainor, L. J. (2007). Mismatch responses to pitch changes in early infancy. *Journal of Cognitive Neuroscience, 19*, 878–892.

He, C., Hotson, L., & Trainor, L. J. (2009). Development of infant mismatch responses to auditory pattern changes between 2 and 4 months old. *European Journal of Neuroscience, 29*, 861–867.

Health Canada. (2002). *A report on mental illness in Canada.* Ottawa, ON: Canada.

Health Canada. (2008). Canadian Tobacco Use Monitoring Survey (CTUMS). Retrieved from http://www.hc-sc.gc.ca/hc-ps/tobac-tabac/research-recherche/stat/ctums-esutc_2008-eng.php

Health Canada. (2010). Canadian alcohol and drug use monitoring survey: Summary of results for 2009. Retrieved from http://www.hc-sc.gc.ca/hc-ps/drugs-drogues/stat/_2009/summary-sommaire-eng.php

Healy, J. M. (2004). Early television exposure and subsequent attention problems in children. *American Academy of Pediatrics, 113,* 917–918.

Heart and Stroke Foundation of Canada. (2013). *Statistics.* Retrieved from http://www.heartandstroke.com/site/c.ikIQLcMWJtE/b.3483991/k.34A8/Statistics.htm

Heath, C., & Heath, D. (2007). *Made to stick: Why some ideas survive and others die.* New York: Random House.

Heatherton, T. F., & Sargent, J. D. (2009). Does watching smoking in movies promote teenage smoking? *Current Directions in Psychological Science, 18,* 63–67.

Heatherton, T. F., & Weinberger, J. L. (Eds.). (1994). *Can personality change?* Washington, DC: American Psychological Association.

Hebb, D. O. (1947). The effects of early experience on problem solving at maturity. *American Psychologist, 2,* 306–307.

Hebb, D. O. (1949). *Organization of behavior: A neuropsychological theory.* New York: John Wiley.

Heider, F. (1958). *The psychology of interpersonal relations.* New York: Wiley.

Heilman, K. M., & Valenstein, E. (1979). Mechanisms underlying hemispatial neglect. *Annals of Neurology, 5,* 166–170.

Heine, S. J. (2003). An exploration of cultural variation in self-enhancing and self-improving motivations. In V. Murphy-Berman & J. J. Berman (Eds.), *Nebraska symposium on motivation: Vol. 49. Cross-cultural differences in perspectives on the self* (pp. 101–128). Lincoln: University of Nebraska Press.

Heine, S. J., & Buchtel, E. E. (2009). Personality: The universal and the culturally specific. *Annual Review of Psychology, 60,* 369–394.

Heine, S. J., Lehman, D. R., Ide, E., Leung, C., Kitayama, S., . . . Matsumoto, H. (2001). Divergent consequences of success and failure in Japan and North America: An investigation of self-improving motivations and malleable selves. *Journal of Personality and Social Psychology, 81,* 599–615.

Heinrichs, M., Baumgartner, T., Kirchbaum, C., & Ehlert, U. (2003). Social support and oxytocin interact to suppress cortisol and subjective responses to psychosocial stress. *Biological Psychiatry, 54,* 1389–1398.

Heinz, A., & Schlagenhauf, F. (2010). Dopaminergic dysfunction in schizophrenia: Salience attribution revisited. *Schizophrenia Bulletin, 36,* 472–485.

Hieronymus, F., Emilsson, J. F., Nilsson, S., & Eriksson, E. (2016). Consistent superiority of selective serotonin reuptake inhibitors over placebo in reducing depressed mood in patients with major depression. *Molecular Psychiatry, 21,* 523–530.

Hellström-Lindahl, E., Seiger, A., Kjaeldgaard, A., & Nordberg A. (2001). Nicotine-induced alterations in the expression of nicotinic receptors in primary cultures from human prenatal brain. *Neuroscience, 105,* 527–534.

Hemphill, E., Raine, K., Spence, J. C., & Smoyer-Tomic, K. E. (2008). Exploring obesogenic food environments in Edmonton, Canada: The association between socioeconomic factors and fast-food outlet access. *American Journal of Health Promotion, 22,* 426–432.

Hendrick, C., Hendrick, S. S., & Reich, D. A. (2006). The brief sexual attitudes scale. *Journal of Sex Research, 43,* 76–86.

Hendrickson, A. E., Wagoner, N., & Cowan, M. (1972). An autoradiographic and electron microscopic study of retino-hypothalamic connections. *Zeitschrift für Zellforschung und Mikroskopische Anatomie, 135,* 1–26.

Henrich, J., Heine, S. J., & Norenzayan, A. (2010) The weirdest people in the world? *Behavioral and Brain Sciences, 33,* 61–135.

Herd, D. (2009). Changing images of violence in rap music lyrics: 1979–1997. *Journal of Public Health Policy, 30,* 395–406.

Herlitz, J., Wiklund, I., Caidahl, K., Hartford, M., Haglid, M., & Karlsson, B. W. (1998). The feeling of loneliness prior to coronary artery bypass grafting might be a predictor of short- and long-term postoperative mortality. *European Journal of Vascular and Endovascular Surgery, 16,* 120–125.

Herman, C. P., Roth, D. A., & Polivy, J. (2003). Effects of the presence of others on food intake: A normative interpretation. *Psychological Bulletin, 129,* 873–886.

Herman-Giddens, M. E., Slora, E. J., Wasserman, R. C., Bourdony, C. J., Bhapkar, M. V., . . . Hasemeier, C. M. (1997). Secondary sexual characteristics and menses in young girls seen in office practice: A study from the Pediatric Research in Office Settings network. *Pediatrics, 99,* 505–512.

Hermann, D., Sartorius, A., Welzel, H., Walter, S., Skopp, G., Ende, G., & Mann, K. (2007). Dorsolateral prefrontal cortex N-Acetylaspartate/total creatine (NAA/tCr) loss in male recreational cannabis users. *Biological Psychiatry, 61,* 1281–1289.

Hermans, E. J., Putman, P., Baas, J. M., Koppeschaar, H. P., & van Honk, J. (2006). A single administration of testosterone reduces fear-potentiated startle in humans. *Biological Psychiatry, 59,* 872–874.

Hernandez, A. E., & Li, P. (2007). Age of acquisition: Its neural and computational mechanisms. *Psychological Bulletin, 133,* 638–650.

Hernandez-Reif, M., Diego, M., & Field, T. (2007). Preterm infants show reduced stress behaviors and activity after 5 days of massage therapy. *Infant Behavior and Development, 30,* 557–561.

Herrnstein, R., & Murray, C. (1994). *The bell curve: Intelligence and class structure in American life.* New York: Free Press.

Hershkowitz, I., Orbach, Y., Lamb, M. E., Sternberg, K. J., Horowitz, D., & Hovav, M. (1998). Visiting the scene of the crime: Effects on children's recall of alleged abuse. *Legal and Criminological Psychology, 3,* 195–207.

Hetherington, E. M., Bridges, M., & Insabella, G. M. (1998). What matters? What does not? Five perspectives on the association between marital transitions and children's adjustment. *American Psychologist, 53,* 167–184.

Heyes, C. M., & Galef, B. G. Jr. (Eds.). (1996). *Social learning in animals: The roots of culture.* San Diego: Academic Press.

Higgins, D. M., Peterson, J. B., Lee, A., & Pihl, R. O. (2007). Prefrontal cognitive ability, intelligence, Big Five personality and the prediction of advanced academic and workplace performance. *Journal of Personality and Social Psychology, 93,* 298–319.

Higley, J. D., Mehlman, P. T., Poland, R. E., Taub, D. M., Vickers, J., . . . & Linnoila, M. (1996). CSF testosterone and 5-HIAA correlate with different types of aggressive behaviors. *Biological Psychiatry, 40,* 1067–1082.

Hilgard, E. R. (1986). *Divided consciousness: Multiple controls in human thought and action.* New York: Wiley.

Hill, K. E., Mann, L., Laws, K. R., Stippich, C., & Schröder, J. (2004). Hypofrontality in schizophrenia: A meta-analysis of functional imaging studies. *Acta Psychiatrica Scandinavica, 110,* 243–256.

Hill, S. Y., Schwin, R., Powell, B., & Goodwin, D. W. (1973). State-dependent effects of marihuana on human memory. *Nature, 243,* 241–242.

Hillary, F. G., Schultheis, M.T., Challis, B. H., Millis, S. R., Carnevale, G. J., Galshi, T., & Deluca, J. (2003). Spacing of repetitions improves learning and memory after moderate and severe TBI. *Journal of Clinical Experimental Neuropsychology, 25,* 49–58.

Hillman, C. H., Erickson, K. I., & Kramer, A. F. (2008). Be smart, exercise your heart: Exercise effects on brain and cognition. *Nature Reviews Neuroscience, 9,* 58–65.

Hillman, C. H., Snook, E. M., & Jerome, G. J. (2003). Acute cardiovascular exercise and executive control function. *International Journal of Psychophysiology,48,* 307–314.

Himmelheber, A. M., Sarter, M., & Bruno, J. P. (2000). Increases in cortical acetylcholine release during sustained attention performance in rats. *Cognitive Brain Research, 9,* 313–325.

Hingson, R. W., Zha, W., & Weitzman, E. R. (2009). Magnitude of and trends in alcohol-related mortality and morbidity among U.S. college students ages 18–24, 1998–2005. *Journal of Studies on Alcohol and Drugs, 16* (suppl), 12–20.

Hirsh, J. B. (2010). Personality and environmental concern. *Journal of Environmental Psychology, 30,* 245–248.

Hirsh, J. B., & Dolderman, D. (2007). Personality predictors of consumerism and environmentalism: A preliminary study. *Personality and Individual Differences, 43,* 1583–1593.

Hirst, W., Phelps, E., Buckner, R., Budson, A., Cuc, A., Gabrieli, J., et al. (2009). Long-term memory for the terrorist attack of September 11: Flashbulb memories, event memories, and the factors that influence their retention. *Journal of Experimental Psychology: General, 138,* 161–176.

Hobson, J. A., & McCarley, R. W. (1977). The brain as a dream state generator: An activation-synthesis hypothesis of the dream process. *The American Journal of Psychiatry, 134,* 1335–1348.

Hobson, J., Pace-Schott, E., & Stickgold, R. (2000). Dreaming and the brain: Toward a cognitive neuroscience of conscious states. *Behavioral and Brain Sciences, 23,* 793–842.

Hodges, L. F., Anderson, P., Burdea, G. C., Hoffman, H. G., & Rothbaum, B. O. (2001). VR as a tool in the treatment of psychological and physical disorders. *IEEE Computer Graphics and Applications, 21,* 25–33.

Hodges, N. J., Williams, A. M., Hayes, S. J., & Breslin, G. (2007). What is modelled during observational learning? *Journal of Sport Sciences, 25,* 531–545.

Hodgins, D. C., Stea, J. N., & Grant, J. E. (2011). Gambling disorders. *The Lancet, 378,* 1874–1884.

Hodgkin, A. L. (1937). Evidence for electrical transmission in nerve. *Journal of Physiology, 90,* 183–210.

Hofer, M. A. (2006). Psychobiological roots of early attachment. *Current Directions in Psychological Science, 15,* 84–88.

Hoffman, M. L., & Saltzstein, H. D. (1967). Parent discipline and the child's moral development. *Journal of Personality and Social Psychology, 5,* 45–57.

Hoffman, S. G., Grossman, P., & Hinton, D. E. (2011). Loving-kindness and compassion meditation: Potential for psychological interventions. *Clinical Psychology Review, 31,* 1126–1132.

Hofmann, S. (2007). Cognitive factors that maintain social anxiety disorder: A comprehensive model and its treatment implications. *Cognitive Behaviour Therapy, 36,* 193–209.

Hofmann, S. G., & Smits, J. A. J. (2008). Cognitive-behavioral therapy for adult anxiety disorders: A meta-analysis of randomized placebo-controlled trials. *Journal of Clinical Psychiatry, 69,* 621–632.

Hofschire, L. J., & Greenberg, B. S. (2002). Media's impact on adolescents' body dissatisfaction. In J. D. Brown, J. R. Steele, & K. Walsh-Childers (Eds.), *Sexual teens, sexual media.* Mahwah, NJ: Lawrence Erlbaum Associates.

Hofstede, G. (1984). The cultural relativity of the quality of life concept. *Academy of Management Review, 9,* 389–398.

Hogan, M. J., Kelly, C. A. M., Verrier, D., Newell, J., Hasher, L., & Robertson, I. H. (2009). Optimal time-of-day and consolidation of learning in younger and older adults. *Experimental Aging Research, 35,* 107–128.

Hojnoski, R. L., Morrison, R., Brown, M., & Matthews, W. J. (2006). Projective test use among school psychologists: A survey and critique. *Journal of Psychoeducational Assessment, 24,* 145–159.

Holleran, S. E., Mehl, M. R., & Levitt, S. (2009). Eavesdropping on social life: The accuracy of stranger ratings of daily behavior from thin slices of natural conversations. *Journal of Research in Personality, 43,* 660–672.

Hollerman, J. R., & Schultz, W. (1996). Activity of dopamine neurons during learning in a familiar task context. *Society for Neuroscience Abstracts, 22,* 1388.

Hollon, S. D., Stewart, M. O., & Strunk, D. (2006). Enduring effects for cognitive behavior therapy in the treatment of depression and anxiety. *Annual Review of Psychology, 57,* 285–315.

Hollon, S., Thase, M., & Markowitz, J. (2002). Treatment and prevention of depression. *Psychological Science in the Public Interest, 3,* 39–77.

Holmes, T. H., & Rahe, R. H. (1967). The social readjustment rating scale. *Journal of Psychosomatic Research, 11,* 213–218.

Holyoak, K. J., & Morrison R. G. (2005). Thinking and reasoning: A reader's guide. In K. J. Holyoak & R. G. Morrison (Eds.), *The Cambridge handbook of thinking and reasoning* (pp. 1–9). New York: Cambridge University Press.

Hooker, W. D., & Jones, R.T. (1987). Increased susceptibility to memory intrusions and the Stroop interference effect during acute marijuana intoxication. *Psychopharmacology, 91,* 20–24.

Hooley, J. (2007). Expressed emotion and relapse of psychopathology. *Annual Review of Clinical Psychology, 3,* 329–352.

Hooley, J. M., & Gotlib, I. H. (2000). A diathesis-stress conceptualization of expressed emotion and clinical outcome. *Journal of Applied and Preventive Psychology, 9,* 135–151.

Hooven, C. K., Chabris, C. F., Ellison, P. T., & Kosslyn, S. M. (2004). The relationship of male testosterone to components of mental rotation. *Neuropsychologia, 42,* 782–790.

Hopkins, B., & Westra, T. (1989). Maternal expectations of their infants' development: Some cultural differences. *Developmental Medicine and Child Neurology, 31,* 384–390.

Horn, J. L., & Cattell, R. B. (1967). Age differences in fluid and crystallized intelligence. *Acta Psychologica, 26,* 107–129.

Horn, L. R., & Ward, G. (2004). *The handbook of pragmatics.* Malden, MA: Blackwell.

Horne, J., & Minard, A. (1985). Sleep and sleepiness following a behaviourally "active" day. *Ergonomics, 28,* 567–575.

Horne, P. J., & Erjavec, M. (2007). Do infants show generalized imitation of gestures? *Journal of the Experimental Analysis of Behavior, 87,* 63–87.

Horner, V., & Whiten, A. (2005). Causal knowledge and imitation/emulation switching in chimpanzees (Pan troglodytes) and children (Homo sapiens). *Animal Cognition, 8,* 164–181.

Horvath, A. O., & Bedi, R. P. (2002). The alliance. In J. C. Norcross (Ed.), *Psychotherapy relationships that work: Therapist contributions and responsiveness to patients* (pp. 37–69). New York: Oxford University Press.

Hoshino-Browne, E., Zanna, A. S., Spencer, S. J., Zanna, M. P., Kitayama, S., & Lackenbauer, S. (2005). On the cultural guises of cognitive dissonance: The case of easterners and westerners. *Journal of Personality and Social Psychology, 89,* 294–310.

Hough, W., & O'Brien, K. (2005). The effect of community treatment orders on offending rates. *Psychiatry, Psychology and Law, 12,* 411–423.

Hounsfield, G. N. (1980). Computed medical imaging. *Medical Physics, 7,* 283–291.

Howard, A. L., Patrick, M. E., & Maggs, J. L. (2015). College student affect and heavy drinking: Variable associations across days, semesters, and people. *Psychology and Addictive Behaviors, 29,* 430–443.

Howe, M. L. (2003). Memories from the cradle. *Current Directions in Psychological Science,12,* 62–65.

Hrobjartsson, A., & Gotzsche, P. (2010). Placebo interventions for all clinical conditions. *Cochrane Database of Systematic Reviews, 1,* CD003974.

Huang, C. (2012). Outcome-based observational learning in human infants. *Journal of Comparative Psychology, 126,* 139–149.

Hubel, D. H., & Weisel, T. N. (1959). Receptive fields of single neurons in the cat's striate cortex. *Journal of Physiology, 148,* 574–591.

Hubel, D. H., & Wiesel, T. N. (1962). Receptive fields, binocular interaction and functional architecture in the cat's visual cortex. *Journal of Physiology, 160,* 106–154.

Hudson, J., Hiripi, E., Pope, H., & Kessler, R. (2007). The prevalence and correlates of eating disorders in the National Comorbidity Survey replication. *Biological Psychiatry, 61,* 348–358.

Huesmann, L. R. (2007). The impact of electronic media violence: Scientific theory and research. *Journal of Adolescent Health, 41,* S6–S13.

Huettel, S. A., Song, A. W., & McCarthy, G. (2009). *Functional magnetic resonance imaging* (2nd ed.). Sunderland, MA: Sinauer Associates, Inc.

Huffman, M. A. (1996). Acquisition of innovative cultural behaviors in nonhuman primates: A case study of stone handling, a socially transmitted behavior in Japanese macaques. In C. M. Heyes & B. Galef (Eds.), *Social learning in animals: The roots of culture* (pp. 267–289). San Diego: Academic Press.

Hughes, C. E., & Stevens, A. (2010). What can we learn from the Portuguese decriminalization of illegal drugs? *British Journal of Criminology, 50,* 999–1022.

Hughlings Jackson, J. (1876/1932). Case of large cerebral tumour without optic neuritis and with hemiplegia and imperceptions. In J. Taylor (Ed.), *Selected writings of John Hughlings Jackson* (pp. 146–152). London: Hodder and Stoughton.

Hughto, J. M. W., Reisner, S. L., & Pachankis, J. E. (2015). Transgender stigma and health: A critical review of stigma determinants, mechanisms, and interventions. *Social Science & Medicine, 147,* 222–231.

Hunter, J. E., & Hunter, R. F. (1984). Validity and utility of alternative predictors of job performance. *Psychological Bulletin, 96,* 72–98.

Hunter, R. A., & Macalpine, I. (Eds.). (1963). *Three hundred years of psychiatry, 1535–1860: A history presented in selected English texts.* New York: Oxford University Press.

Hursh, A., Tsukamoto, Y., Smith, R. G., & Sterling, P. (1939). Conduction velocity and diameter of nerve fibers. *American Journal of Physiology, 127*, 131–139.

Huyser, C., Veltman, D. J., de Haan, E., & Boer, F., (2009). Paediatric obsessive–compulsive disorder, a neurodevelopmental disorder? Evidence from neuroimaging. *Neuroscience and Biobehavioral Reviews, 33*, 818–830.

Hyde, J., Mezulis, A., & Abramson, L. (2008). The ABCs of depression: Integrating affective, biological, and cognitive models to explain the emergence of the gender difference in depression. *Psychological Review, 115*, 291–313.

Hyde, K. L., Peretz, I., & Zatorre, R. J. (2008). Evidence for the role of the right auditory cortex in fine pitch resolution. *Neuropsychologia, 46*, 632–639.

Hyman, S. E. (2007). Can neuroscience be integrated into the DSM-V? *Nature Reviews Neuroscience, 8*, 725–732.

Iacoboni, M., Molnar-Szakacs, I., Gallese V., Buccino, G., Mazziotta, F. C., & Rizzolatti, G. (2005). Grasping the intentions of others with one's own mirror neuron system. *PLoS Biology, 3*, e79.

Inlow, J. K., & Restifo, L. L. (2004). Molecular and comparative genetics of mental retardation. *Genetics, 166*, 835–881.

Inn, A., Wheeler, A. C., & Sparling, C. L. (1977). The effects of suspect race and situation hazard on police officer shooting behavior. *Journal of Applied Social Psychology, 7*, 27–37.

Isen, A. M., Daubman, K. A., & Nowicki, G. P. (1987). Positive affect facilitates creative problem solving. *Journal of Personality and Social Psychology, 52*, 112–1131.

Isenberg, D. J. (1986). Group polarization: A critical review and meta-analysis. *Journal of Personality and Social Psychology, 50*, 1141–1151.

Ito, T. A., & Urland, G. R. (2003). Race and gender on the brain. Electrocortical measures of attention to the race and gender of multiply categorizable individuals. *Journal of Personality and Social Psychology, 85*, 616–626.

Iyengar, S. S., Wells, R. E., & Schwartz, B. (2006). Doing better but feeling worse: Looking for the "best" job undermines satisfaction. *Psychological Science, 17*, 143–150.

Izard, V., Sann, C., Spelke, E. S., & Streri, A. (2009). Newborn infants perceive abstract numbers. *Proceedings of the National Academy of Sciences, 106*, 10382–10385.

Jacob, C., Guéguen, N., & Delfosse, C. (2012). She wore something in her hair: The effect of ornamentation on tipping. *Journal of Hospitality Marketing and Management, 21*, 414–420.

Jacobs, B. (2004). Depression: The brain finally gets into the act. *Current Directions in Psychological Science, 13*, 103–106.

Jacoby, L. L., & Brooks, L. R. (1984). Nonanalytic cognition: Memory, perception and concept learning. In G. Bower (Ed.), *The psychology of learning and motivation: Advances in research and theory* (pp. 1–46). San Diego, CA: Academic Press.

Jaeggi, S. M., Buschkuehl, M., Jonides, J., & Perrig, W. J. (2008). Improving fluid intelligence with training on working memory. *Proceedings of the National Academy of Sciences of the United States of America, 105*, 6829–6833.

Jaeggi, S. M., Buschkuehl, M., Jonides, J., & Shah, P. (2011). Short- and long-term benefits of cognitive training. *Proceedings of the National Academy of Sciences of the United States of America, 108*, 10081–10086.

Jaffee, S., & Hyde, J. S. (2000). Gender differences in moral orientation: A meta-analysis. *Psychological Bulletin, 126*, 703–726.

Jager, G., Kahn, R. S., Ven Den Brink, W., Van Ree, J. M., & Ramsey, N. F. (2006). Long-term effects of frequent cannibus use on working memory and attention: An fMRI study. *Psychopharmacology, 185*, 358–368.

Jager, G., Van Kell, H. H., De Win, M. M. L., Kahn, R. S., Van Den brink, W., Van Ree, J. M., & Ramsey, N. F. (2007). Effects of frequent cannabis use on hippocampal activity during an associative memory task. *European Neuropsychopharmacology, 17*, 289–297.

Jakobs, D., Hage-Hulsmann, A., Prenner, L., Kolb, C., Weiser, D., & Haberlein H. (2013). Down-regulation of B1-adrenergic receptors in rat C6 glioblastoma cells by hyperforin and hyperoside from St. John's wort. *Journal of Pharmacy and Pharmacology, 65*, 907–915.

James, T. W., Cullham, J., Humphrey, G. K., Milner, A. D., & Goodale, M. A. (2003). Ventral occipital lesions impair object recognition but not object-directed grasping: An fMRI study. *Brain, 126*, 2463–2475.

James, W. (1890). *The principles of psychology*. New York: Henry Holt and Company.

Jamieson, G. A., & Sheehan, P. W. (2004). An empirical test of Woody and Bower's dissociated-control theory of hypnosis. *The International Journal of Clinical and Experimental Hypnosis, 52*, 232–249.

Janis, I. L. (1972). *Victims of groupthink: A psychological study of foreign policy decisions and fiascoes*. Boston: Houghton Mifflin.

Jencks, C., Smith, M., Acland, H., Bane, M. J., Cohen, D., . . . Michelson, S. (1972). *Inequality: A reassessment of the effect of family and schooling in America*. New York: Harper & Row.

Jensen, A. R. (1993). Test validity: *g* versus "tacit knowledge." *Current Directions in Psychological Science, 2*, 53–56.

Jensen, R. (2006). Behaviorism, latent learning, and cognitive maps: Needed revisions in introductory psychology textbooks. *Behavioral Analysis, 29*, 187–209.

Jewanski, J., Day, S. A., & Ward, J. (2009). A colorful albino: The first documented case of synaesthesia, by Georg Tobias Ludwig Sachs in 1812. *Journal of the History of the Neuroscience: Basic and Clinical Perspectives, 18*, 293–303.

John, E. R., Chesler, P., Bartlett, F., & Victor, I. (1968). Observational learning in cats. *Science, 29*, 1489–1491.

Johns, M. W. (1991). A new method for measuring daytime sleepiness: The Epworth sleepiness scale. *Sleep, 14*, 540–545.

Johnson, W., te Nijenhuis, J., & Bouchard, T. (2008). Still just 1 *g*: Consistent results from five test batteries. *Intelligence, 36*, 81–95.

Johnson, A. M., Reed, T. E., & Vernon, P. A. (2005). Nerve conduction velocity (NCV) is a valid and useful construct for studying human cognitive abilities: A reply to Saint-Amour et al. *Neuropsychologia, 43*, 1845–1846.

Johnson, B. B. (2012). Climate change communication: A provocative inquiry into motives, meanings, and means. *Risk Analysis, 32*, 973–991.

Johnson, J. K., Gross, A. L., Pa, J., McLaren, D. G., Park, L. Q., Manly, J. J., & Alzheimer's Disease Neuroimaging Initiative. (2012). Longitudinal change in neuropsychological performance using latent growth models: a study of mild cognitive impairment. *Brain Imaging and Behavior, 6*, 540–550.

Johnson, K. E., & Mervis, C. B. (1997). Effects of varying levels of expertise on the basic level of categorization. *Journal of Experimental Psychology: General, 126*, 248–277.

Johnson, M. H., Dziurawiec, S., Ellis, H., & Morton, J. (1991). Newborns' preferential tracking of face-like stimuli and its subsequent decline. *Cognition, 40*, 1–19.

Johnson, M. W., Garcia-Romeu, A., Cosimano, M. P., & Griffiths, R. R. (2014). Pilot study of the 5-HT2AR agonist psilocybin in the treatment of tobacco addiction. *Journal of Psychopharmacology, 28*, 983–992.

Johnson, W., & Bouchard, T. J., Jr. (2007). Sex differences in mental abilities: *g* masks the dimensions on which they lie. *Intelligence, 35*, 23–39.

Johnsrude, I. S., Penhune, V. B., & Zatorre, R. J. (2000). Functional specificity in the right human auditory cortex for perceiving pitch direction. *Brain, 123*, 155–163.

Jokela, M., & Hanin, Y. L. (1999). Does the individual zones of optimal functioning model discriminate between successful and less successful athletes?: A meta-analysis. *Journal of Sports Science, 17*, 873–887.

Joling, K. J., van Hout, H. P., Van't Veer-Tazelaar, P. J., van der Horst, H. E., Cuijpers, P., . . . van Marwijk, H. W. (2011). How effective is bibliotherapy for very old adults with subthreshold depression? Randomized controlled trial. *American Journal of Geriatric Psychiatry, 19*, 256–265.

Jones, A., Gublis, A., & Baker, E. H. (2010). Differences in tobacco use between Canada and the United States. *International Journal of Public Health, 55*,167–75.

Jones, D. N., & Paulhus, D. L. (2010). Different provocations trigger aggression in narcissists and psychopaths. *Social and Personality Psychology Science, 1*, 12–18.

Jones, K. L., & Smith, D. W. (1973). Recognition of the fetal alcohol syndrome in early infancy. *Lancet, 2*, 999–1001.

Jones, R. A. K., on behalf of the Collaborative Dexamethasone Trial Follow-up Group (2005). Randomized, controlled trial of Dexamethasone in Neonatal Chronic Lung Disease: 13-to 17-year follow-up study: II. Respiratory status, growth, and blood pressure. *Pediatrics, 116*, 379–384.

Jonides, J., Lacey, S., & Nee, D. (2005). Processes of working memory in mind and brain. *Current Directions in Psychological Science, 14*, 2–5.

Josephson, W. L. (1987). Television violence and children's aggression: Testing the priming, social script, and disinhibition predictions. *Interpersonal Relations and Group Processes, 53*, 882–890.

Jost, J. T., Glaser, J., Kruglanski, A. W., & Sulloway, F. J. (2003). Political conservativism as motivated social cognition. *Psychological Bulletin, 129*, 339–375.

Juda, M. N., Campbell, L., & Crawford, C. B. (2004). Dieting symptomatology in women and perceptions of social support: An evolutionary approach. *Evolution and Human Behavior, 25*, 200–208.

Julius, D., & Basbaum, A. I. (2001). Molecular mechanisms of nociception. *Nature, 413*, 203–210.

Jurcic, J., Pereira, J. A., & Kavanaugh, D. (2007). St. John's wort versus paroxetine for depression. *Canadian Family Physician, 53*, 1511–1513.

Jusczyk, P. W., Friederici, A. D., Wessels, J., Svenkerud, V. Y., & Jusczyk, A. M. (1993). Infants' sensitivity to the sound patterns of native language words. *Journal of Memory and Language, 32*, 402–420.

Kahneman, D. (2003). A perspective on judgment and choice: Mapping bounded rationality. *American Psychologist, 58*, 697–720.

Kahneman, D., & Miller, D. T. (1986). Norm theory: Comparing reality to its alternatives. *Psychological Review, 93*, 136–153.

Kales, A., Soldatos, C. R., Bixler, E. O., Ladda, R. L., Charney, D. S., Weber, G., & Schweitzer, P. K. (1980). Hereditary factors in sleepwalking and night terrors. *The British Journal of Psychiatry, 137*, 111–118.

Kalisch, R., Korenfeld, E., Stephan, K. E., Weiskopf, N., Seymour, B., & Dolan, R. J. (2006). Context-dependent human extinction memory is mediated by a ventromedial prefrontal and hippocampal network. *The Journal of Neuroscience, 26*, 9503–9511.

Kalnin, A. J., Edwards, C. R., Wang, Y., Kato, J., Ide, H., Kabashima, I., et al. (2009). Neural correlates of attitude change following positive and negative advertisements. *Frontiers in Behavioral Neuroscience, 3*, 1–13.

Kam, J. W. Y., & Handy, T. C. (2014). Differential recruitment of executive resources during mind wandering. *Consciousness & Cognition, 26*, 51–63.

Kamata, A., Tenenbaum, G., & Hanin, Y. L. (2002). Individual zones of optimal functioning (IZOF): A probabilistic estimation. *Journal of Sport & Exercise Psychology, 24*, 189–208.

Kaminski, J., Call, J., & Fischer, J. (2004). Word learning in a domestic dog: Evidence for "fast mapping." *Science, 304*, 1682–1683.

Kamnasaran, D., Muir, W. J., Ferguson-Smith, M. A., & Cox, D. W. (2003). Disruption of the neuronal PAS3 gene in a family affected with schizophrenia. *Journal of Medical Genetics, 40*, 325–332.

Kanayama, G., Rogowska, J., Pope, H. G., Gruber, S. A., & Yurgelun-Todd, D. A. (2004). Spatial working memory in heavy cannabis users: A functional magnetic resonance imaging study. *Psychopharmacology, 176*, 239–247.

Kanwisher, N., McDermott, J., & Chun, M. (1997). The fusiform face area: A module in human extrastriate cortex specialized for the perception of faces. *Journal of Neuroscience, 17*, 4302–4311.

Kaplan, S. (2000). New ways to promote proenvironmental behavior: Human nature and environmentally responsible behavior. *Journal of Social Issues, 56*, 491–508.

Kapler, I. V., Weston, T., & Wiseheart, M. (2015). Spacing in a simulated undergraduate classroom: Long-term benefits for factual and higher-level learning. *Learning & Instruction, 36*, 38–45.

Karakashian, L. M., Walter, M. I., & Christopher, A. N. (2006). Fear of negative evaluation affects helping behavior: The bystander effect revisited. *North American Journal of Psychology, 8*, 13–32.

Karau, S. J., & Williams, K. D. (2001). Understanding individual motivation in groups: The collective effort model. In M. E. Turner (Ed.), *Groups at work: Theory and research* (pp. 113–141). Mahwah, NJ: Lawrence Erlbaum Associates.

Kaufman, A. S. (2001). WAIS-III IQs, Horn's theory, and generational changes from young adulthood to old age. *Intelligence, 29*, 131–167.

Kawai, M. (1965). Newly acquired pre-cultural behavior of a natural troop of Japanese monkeys on Koshima Island. *Primates, 6*, 1–30.

Kawakami, K., Dovidio, J. F., Moll, J., Hermsen, S., & Russim, A. (2000). Just say no (to stereotyping): Effects of training in negation of stereotypic associations on stereotype activation. *Journal of Personality and Social Psychology, 78*, 871–888.

Kay, A. C., Gaucher, D., McGregor, I., & Nash, K. (2010). Religious belief as compensatory control. *Personality and Social Psychology Review, 14*, 37–48.

Kay, A. C., Whitson, J. A., Gaucher, D., & Galinsky, A. D. (2009). Compensatory control: Achieving order through the mind, our institutions, and the heavens. *Current Directions in Psychological Science, 18*, 264–268.

Kaye, W. H., Gwirtsman, H. E., George, D. T., Weiss, S. R., & Jimerson, D. C. (1986). Relationship of mood alterations to bingeing behaviour in bulimia. *The British Journal of Psychiatry, 149*, 479–485.

Kebbell, M., Milne, R., & Wagstaff, G. (1999). The cognitive interview: A survey of its forensic effectiveness. *Psychology, Crime, & Law, 5*, 101–115.

Keel, P. K., & Klump, K. L. (2003). Are eating disorders culture-bound syndromes? Implications for conceptualizing their etiology. *Psychological Bulletin, 129*, 747–769.

Kelemen, W. L., & Creeley, C. E. (2003). State-dependent memory effects using caffeine and placebo do not extend to metamemory. *Journal of General Psychology, 13D*, 70–86.

Kennard, M.A. (1942). Cortical reorganization of motor functions: Studies on a series of monkeys of various ages from infancy to maturity. *Archives of Neurology and Psychiatry, 48*, 227–440.

Kenny, D. A. (2004). PERSON: A general model of interpersonal perception. *Personality and Social Psychology Review, 8*, 265–280.

Kensinger, E. A., & Corkin, S. (2003). Memory enhancement for emotional words: Are emotional words more vividly remembered than neutral words? *Memory & Cognition, 31*, 1169–1180.

Kernis, M. H., Paradise, A. W., Whitaker, D. J., Wheatman, S. R., & Goldman, B. N. (2000). Master of one's psychological domain? Not likely if one's self-esteem is unstable. *Personality and Social Psychology Bulletin, 26*, 1297–1305.

Kershaw, T. C., Hemmerich, J. A., & Ahmed, S. (2009). Flashbulb memory for September 11 and the Columbia space shuttle disaster. In M.R. Kelley, *Applied memory* (pp. 129–146). Hauppage, NY: Nova Science Publishers.

Kessler, R. C. (2000). Posttraumatic stress disorder: The burden to the individual and to society. *Journal of Clinical Psychiatry, 61*(suppl. 5), 4–12.

Kessler, R. C., Chiu, W. T., Demler, O., & Walters, E. E. (2005). Prevalence, severity, and comorbidity of twelve-month DSM-IV disorders in the National Comorbidity Survey Replication (NCS-R). *Archives of General Psychiatry, 62*, 617–627.

Kevles, D. J. (1985). *In the name of eugenics: Genetics and the uses of human heredity*. University of California Press.

Kiecolt-Glaser, J. (1984). Psychosocial modifiers of immunocompetence in medical students. *Psychosomatic Medicine, 46*, 7–14.

Kiecolt-Glaser, J. K., & Newton, T. L. (2001). Marriage and health: His and hers. *Psychological Bulletin, 127*, 472–503.

Kigar, D. L., Witelson, S. F., Glezer, I. I., & Harvey, T. (1997). Estimates of cell number in temporal neocortex in the brain of Albert Einstein. *Social Neurosciences Abstracts, 23*, 88–89.

Kihlstrom, J. F. (1997). Hypnosis, memory and amnesia. *Philosophical Transactions of the Royal Society of London B: Biological Sciences, 352*, 1727–1732.

Kihlstrom, J. F. (2005). Dissociative disorders. *Annual Review of Clinical Psychology, 1*, 227–253.

Killingsworth, M. A., & Gilbert, D. T. (2010). A wandering mind is an unhappy mind. *Science, 330*, 932.

Kilpatrick, L., & Cahill, L. (2003). Amygdala modulation of parahippocampal and frontal regions during emotionally influenced memory storage. *NeuroImage, 20*, 2091–2099.

Kim, J. J., & Fanselow, M. S. (1992). Modality-specific retrograde amnesia of fear. *Science, 256*, 675–677.

Kim, P., Leckman, J. F., Mayes, L. C., Feldman, R., Xin, W., & Swain, J. E. (2010). The plasticity of human maternal brain: Longitudinal changes in brain anatomy during the early postpartum period. *Behavioral Neuroscience, 124*, 695–700.

King, D. B., & DeCicco, T. L. (2007). The relationships between dream content and physical health, mood, and self-construal. *Dreaming, 17*, 127–139.

King, S. (2000). Is expressed emotion cause or effect in the mothers of schizophrenic young adults? *Schizophrenia Research, 45*, 65–78.

King, S., & Dixon, M. J. (1999). Expressed emotion and relapse in young schizophrenia outpatients. *Schizophrenia Bulletin, 25*, 377–386.

King, S., St. Hilaire, A., & Heidkamp, D. (2010). Prenatal factors in schizophrenia. *Current Directions in Psychological Science, 19*, 209–213.

Kingston, T., Dooley, B., Bates, A., Lawlor, E., & Malone, K. (2007). Mindfulness-based cognitive therapy for residual depressive symptoms. *Psychology and Psychotherapy: Theory, Research and Practice, 80*, 193–203.

Kinsey, A. C., Pomeroy, W. B., & Martin, C. E. (1948). *Sexual behaviour in the human male*. Philadelphia: W.B. Saunders.

Kinsey, A. C., Pomeroy, W. B., & Matin, C. E. (1953). *Sexual behaviour in the human female*. Philadelphia: W.B. Saunders.

Kirk, K. M., Bailey, J. M., Dunne, M. P., & Martin, N. G. (2000). Measurement models for sexual orientation in a community twin sample. *Behavioral Genetics, 30*, 345–356.

Kirkham, T. C. (2009). Cannabinoids and appetite: Food craving and food pleasure. *International Review of Psychiatry, 21*, 163–171.

Kirsch, I., Deacon, B. J., Huedo-Medina, T., Scoboria, A., Moore, T. J., & Johnson, B. T. (2008). Initial severity and antidepressant benefits: A meta-analysis of data submitted to the food and drug administration. *PLoS Medicine, 5*, 1.

Kirsch, I., & Lynn, S. (1998). Dissociation theories of hypnosis. *Psychological Bulletin, 123*, 100–115.

Kirsch, P., Esslinger, C., Chen, Q., Mier, D., Lis, S., . . . Meyer-Lindenberg, A. (2005). Oxytocin modulates neural circuitry for social cognition and fear in humans. *Journal of Neuroscience, 25*, 11489–11493.

Kirschbaum, C., Pirke, K. M., & Hellhammer, D. K. (1993). The "Trier Social Stress Test"—A tool for investigating psychobiological stress in a laboratory setting. *Neuropsychobiology, 28*, 76–81.

Kirschbaum, C., Wust, S., & Hellhammer, D. (1992). Consistent sex differences in cortisol responses to psychological stress. *Psychosomatic Medicine, 54*, 648–657.

Kisely, S. R., Campbell, L. A., & Preston, N. J. (2011). Compulsory community and involuntary outpatient treatment for people with severe mental disorders. *Cochrane Database of Systematic Reviews, 2*.

Kisilevsky, B. S., Hains, S. M., Lee, K., Xie, X., Huang, H., Ye, H. H., et al. (2003). Effects of experience on fetal voice recognition. *Psychological Science, 14*, 220–224.

Klatzky, R. L., & Creswell, J. D. (2014). An intersensory interaction account of priming effects—and their absence. *Perspectives on Psychological Science, 9*, 49–58.

Klaus, L., Berner, M. M., & Levente, K. (2008). St. John's wort for major depression. In *Cochrane Database of Systematic Reviews: Reviews 2008, 4*. Chichester, UK: John Wiley & Sons.

Kleider, H., Pezdek, K., Goldinger, S., & Kirk, A. (2008). Schema-driven source misattribution errors: Remembering the expected from a witnessed event. *Applied Cognitive Psychology, 22*, 1–20.

Klein, C., & Schlossmacher, M. G. (2006). The genetics of Parkinson disease: Implications for neurological care. *Nauture Clinical Practice, Neurology, 2*, 136–146.

Klein, N. (2007). *The shock doctrine: The rise of disaster capitalism*. New York: Picador.

Klein, R. A., Ratliff, K. A., Vianello, M., Abrams, Jr., R. B., Bahník, S., . . . & Nosek, B. A. (2014). Investigating variation in replicability: A "many labs" replication project. *Social Psychology, 45*, 142–152.

Klerman, G. L., & Weissman, M. M. (1993). *New applications of interpersonal psychotherapy*. Washington DC: American Psychiatric Press.

Klerman, G. L., Weissman, M. M., Rounsaville, B. J., et al. (1984). *Interpersonal psychotherapy of depression*. Northvale, NJ: Jason Aronson Inc.

Klingberg, T., Fernell, E., Olesen, P. J., Johnson, M., Gustafsson, P., . . . Westerberg, H. (2005). Computerized training of working memory in children with ADHD—a randomized, controlled trial. *Journal of the American Academy of Child and Adolescent Psychiatry, 44*, 177–186.

Klomek, A., Marrocco, F., Kleinman, M., Schonfeld, I., & Gould, M. (2007). Bullying, depression, and suicidality in adolescents. *Journal of the American Academy of Child & Adolescent Psychiatry, 46*, 40–49.

Kluger, B. M., & Triggs, W. J. (2007). Use of transcranial magnetic stimulation to influence behavior. *Current Neurology and Neuroscience Reports, 6*, 491–497.

Knaepen, K. Goekint, M., Heyman, E. M., & Meeusen, R. (2010). Neuroplasticity — exercise-induced response of peripheral brain-derived neurotrophic factor: A systematic review of experimental studies in human subjects. *Sports Medicine, 40*, 765–801.

Knutson, B., Fong, G. W., Bennett, S. M., Adams, C. M., & Hommer, D. (2003). A region of mesial prefrontal cortex tracks monetarily rewarding outcomes: Characterization with rapid event-related fMRI. *NeuroImage, 18*, 263–272.

Koball, H. L., Moiduddin, E., Henderson, J., Goesling, B., & Besculides, M. (2010). What do we know about the link between marriage and health? *Journal of Family Issues, 31*, 1019–1040.

Kohlberg, I. (1984). *The psychology of moral development: Essays on moral development* (Vol. II). San Francisco: Harper & Row.

Kolb, B. (1989). Brain development, plasticity, and behavior. *American Psychologist, 44*, 1203–1212.

Kolb, B. (1995). *Brain plasticity and behavior*. Florence, KT: Routledge.

Kolb, B., Teskey, G. C., & Gibb, R. (2010). Factors influencing cerebral plasticity in the normal and injured brain. *Frontiers in Human Neuroscience, 4*, 1–12.

Komisaruk, B. R. (2005). Functional MRI of the brain during orgasm in women. *Annual Review of Sex Research, 16*, 62–86.

Koob, G. F. (1992). Neural mechanisms of drug reinforcement. *Annals of the New York Academy of Sciences, 654*, 171–191.

Koob, G. F., & Volkow, N. D. (2010). Neurocircuitry of addiction. *Neuropsychopharmacology, 35*, 217–238.

Kornell, N. (2009). Optimising learning using flashcards: Spacing is more effective than cramming. *Applied Cognitive Psychology, 23*, 1297–1317.

Kornell, N., & Bjork, R. A. (2007). The promise and perils of self-regulated study. *Psychonomic Bulletin & Review, 14*, 219–224.

Kornelsen, J., Smith, S.D., McIver, T.A., Shoto-Frankenstein, U., Latta, P., & Tomanek, B. (2013). Functional MRI of the thoracic spinal cord during vibration sensation. *Journal of Magnetic Resonance Imaging, 37*, 981–985.

Kornhaber, M. (2004). Multiple intelligences: From the ivory tower to the dusty classroom—but why? *Teachers College Record, 106*, 67–76.

Kotchoubey, B., Kaiser, J., Bostanov, V., Lutzenberger, W., & Birbaumer, N. (2009). Recognition of affective prosody in brain-damaged patients and healthy controls: A neurophysiological study using EEG and whole-head MEG. *Cognitive, Affective, & Behavioral Neuroscience, 9*, 153–167.

Kouprina, N., Pavlicek, A., Mochida, G. H., Solomon, G., Gersch, W., Yoon, Y. H., et al. (2002). Accelerated evolution of the ASPM gene controlling brain size begins prior to human brain expansion. *PloS Biology, 2*, 0653–0663.

Kovacs, A. M., & Mehler, J. (2009). Cognitive gains in 7-month-old bilingual infants. *Current Issue, 106*, 6556–6560.

Kowal, M. A., Hazekamp, A., Colzato, L. S., van Steenbergen, H., van der Wee, N. J., . . . Hommel, B. (2015). Cannabis and creativity: Highly potent cannabis impairs divergent thinking in regular cannabis users. *Psychopharmacology, 232*, 1123–1134.

Kramer, A. F., Hahn, S., Cohen, N. J., Banich, M. T., McAuley, E., Harrison, C. R., et al. (1999). Ageing, fitness and neurocognitive function. *Nature, 400*, 418–419.

Kramer, M., Schoen, L. S., & Kinney, L. (1984). Psychological and behavioral features of disturbed dreamers. *Psychiatric Journal of the University of Ottawa, 9*, 102–106.

Kramer, T. H., Buckhout, R., & Eugenio, P. (1990). Weapon focus, arousal, and eyewitness memory. *Law and Human Behavior, 14*, 167–184.

Kreukels, B. P. C., & Guillamon, A. (2016). Neuroimaging studies in people with gender incongruence. *International Review of Psychiatry, 28*, 120–128.

Krevans, J., & Gibbs, J. C. (1996). Parents' use of inductive discipline: Relations to children's empathy and prosocial behavior. *Child Development, 67,* 3263–3277.

Kringelbach, M. L., Jenkinson, N., Owen, S. L. F., & Aziz, T. Z. (2007). Translational principles of deep brain stimulation. *Nature Reviews Neuroscience, 8,* 623–635.

Kristensen, P., & Bjerkedal, T. (2007). Explaining the relation between birth order and intelligence. *Science, 316,* 1717–1718.

Kristensson, E., Sundqvist, M., Astin, M., Kjerling, M., Mattsson, H., Dornonville de la Cour, C., et al. (2006). Acute psychological stress raises plasma ghrelin in the rat. *Regulatory Peptides, 134,* 114–117.

Krolak-Salmon, P., Hénaff, M.-A., Vighetto, A., Bertrand, O., & Mauguière, F. (2004). Early amygdala reaction to fear spreading in occipital, temporal, and frontal cortex: A depth electrode ERP study in human. *Neuron, 42,* 665–676.

Kroska, A., & Harkness, S. K. (2006). Stigma sentiments and self-meanings: Exploring the modified labeling theory of mental illness. *Social Psychology Quarterly, 69,* 325–348.

Kruger, J., Wirtz, D., & Miller, D. (2005). Counterfactual thinking and the first instinct fallacy. *Journal of Personality and Social Psychology, 88,* 725–735.

Krystal, A. (2009). A compendium of placebo-controlled trials of the risks/benefits of pharmacological treatments for insomnia: The empirical basis for U.S. clinical practice. *Sleep Medicine Reviews, 13,* 265–274.

Kubzansky, L. D., Sparrow, D., Vokonas, P., & Kawachi, I. (2001). Is the glass half empty or half full? A prospective study of optimism and coronary heart disease in the normative aging study. *Psychosomatic Medicine, 63,* 910–916.

Kudielka, B. M., & Kirschbaum, C. (2005). Sex differences in HPA axis responses to stress: A review. *Biological Psychology, 69,* 113–132.

Kurdek, L. A. (2005). Gender and marital satisfaction early in marriage: A growth curve approach. *Journal of Marriage and Family, 67,* 68–84.

Kurjak, A., Pooh, R. K., Merce, L. T., Carrera, J. M., Salihagic-Kadic, A., & Andonotopo, W. (2005). Structural and functional early human development assessed by three-dimensional and four-dimensional sonography. *Fertility and Sterility, 84,* 1285–1299.

Kuyken, W., Byford, S., Taylor, R. S., Watkins, E., Holden, E., White, K., et al. (2008). Mindfulness-based cognitive therapy to prevent relapse in recurrent depression. *Journal of Consulting and Clinical Psychology, 76,* 966–978.

Kuyken, W., Watkins, E., Holden, E., White, K., Taylor, R. S., Byford, S., et al. (2010). How does mindfulness-based cognitive therapy work? *Behaviour Research and Therapy, 48,* 1105–1112.

Kwong, K. K., Belliveau, J. W., Chesler, D. A., Goldberg, I. E., Weisskoff, R. M., Poncelet, B. P., et al. (1992). Dynamic magnetic resonance imaging of human brain activity during primary sensory stimulation. *Proceedings of the National Academy of Sciences of the United States of America, 89,* 5675–5679.

La Guardia, J. G. (2009). Developing who I am: A self-determination theory approach to the establishment of healthy identities. *Educational Psychologist, 44,* 90–104.

LaBar, K. S., & Cabeza, R. (2006). Cognitive neuroscience of emotional memory. *Nature Neuroscience, 7,* 54–64.

LaBar, K. S., & Phelps, E. A. (1998). Arousal-mediated memory consolidation: Role of the medial temporal lobe in humans. *Psychological Science, 9,* 490–493.

Labrie, V., Pai, S., & Petronis, A. (2012). Epigenetics of major psychosis: Progress, problems, and perspectives. *Trends in Genetics, 28,* 427–435.

Lafer-Sousa, R., Hermann, K. L., & Conway, B. R. (2015). Striking individual differences in color perception uncovered by "the dress" photograph. *Current Biology, 25,* R545–R546.

Lakin, J. L., & Chartrand, T. L. (2003). Using nonconscious behavioral mimicry to create affiliation and rapport. *Psychological Science, 14,* 334–339.

Lakin, J. L., Jefferis, V. E., Cheng, C. M., & Chartrand, T. L. (2003). The chameleon effect as social glue: Evidence for the evolutionary significance of nonconscious mimicry. *Journal of Nonverbal Behavior, 27,* 145–162.

Lakoff, G., & Johnson, M. (1999). *Philosophy in the flesh: The embodied mind and its challenge to Western thought.* New York: Basic Books.

Lam, D. H. (1991). Psychosocial family intervention in schizophrenia: A review of empirical studies. *Psychological Medicine, 21,* 423–441.

Lam, L. T., & Peng, Z. (2010). Effect of pathological use of the Internet on adolescent mental health: A prospective study. *Archives of Pediatric and Adolescent Medicine, 164,* 901–906.

Laming, D. (2010). Serial position curves in free recall. *Psychological Review, 117,* 93–133.

Landau, M. J., Solomon, S., Greenberg, J., Cohen, J., Pyszczynski, T., . . . Cook, A. (2004). Deliver us from evil: The effects of mortality salience and reminders of 9/11 on support for President George W. Bush. *Personality and Social Psychology Bulletin, 30,* 1136–1150.

Landrigan, C. P., Rothschild, J. M., Cronin, J. W., Kaushal, R., Burdick, E., Katz, J. T., et al. (2004). Effect of reducing interns' work hours on serious medical errors in intensive care units. *New England Journal of Medicine, 351,* 1838–1848.

Landrine, H., & Klonoff, E. A. (1996). The schedule of racist events: A measure of racial discrimination and a study of its negative physical and mental health consequences. *Journal of Black Psychology, 22,* 144–168.

Landry, M., & Raz, A. (2015). Hypnosis and imaging of the living human brain. *American Journal of Clinical Hypnosis, 57,* 285–313.

Laney, C., Heuer, F., & Reisberg, D. (2003). Thematically-induced arousal in naturally-occurring emotional memories. *Applied Cognitive Psychology, 17,* 995–1004.

Langford, D. J., Crager, S. E., Shehzad, Z., Smith, S. B., Sotocinal, S. G., . . . Mogil, J.S. (2006). Social modulation of pain as evidence for empathy in mice. *Science, 312,* 1967–1970.

Langford, D. J., Tuttle, A. H., Briscoe, C., Harvey-Lewis, C., Baran, I., Gleeson, P., et al. (2011). Varying perceived social threat modulates pain behavior in male mice. *The Journal of Pain, 12,* 125–132.

Langhans, W. (1996a). Metabolic and glucostatic control of feeding. *Proceedings of the Nutritional Society, 55,* 497–515.

Langhans, W. (1996b). Role of the liver in the metabolic control of eating: What we know—and what we do not know. *Neuroscience and Biobehavioral Review, 20,* 145–153.

Langston, J. W., Ballard, P., Tetrud, J. W., & Irwin, I. (1983). Chronic Parkinsonism in humans due to a product of meperidine-analog synthesis. *Science, 219,* 979–980.

Långström, N., Rahman, Q., & Carlstrom, E. (2010). Genetic and environmental effects on same-sex sexual behavior: A population study of twins in Sweden. *Archives of Sexual Behavior, 39,* 75–80.

Large, E. W., & Palmer, C. (2002). Perceiving temporal regularity in music. *Cognitive Science, 26,* 1–37.

Larsen, R. J., Kasimatis, M., & Frey, K. (1992). Facilitating the furrowed brow: An unobtrusive test of the facial feedback hypothesis applied to unpleasant affect. *Cognition & Emotion, 6,* 321–338.

Lasco, M. S., Jordan, T. J., Edgar, M. A., Petito, C. K., & Byne, W. (2002). A lack of dimorphism of sex or sexual orientation in the human anterior commissure. *Brain Research, 936,* 95–98.

Latané, B., & Darley, J. M. (1968). Group inhibition of bystander intervention in emergencies. *Journal of Personality and Social Psychology, 10,* 215–221.

Latané B., Williams, K., & Harkins, S. (2006). Many hands make the light work: The causes and consequences of social loafing. In J. M. Levine & R. L. Moreland (Eds.), *Small groups* (pp. 297–308). New York: Psychology Press.

Lattal, K. A. (2010). Delayed reinforcement of operant behaviour. *Journal of the Experimental Analysis of Behavior, 93,* 129–139.

Laureys, S., Owen, A. M., & Schiff, N. D. (2004). Brain function in coma, vegetative state, and related disorders. *Lancet Neurology, 3,* 537–546.

Lautenschlager, N. T., Cox, K. L., Flicker, L., Foster, J. K., van Bockxmeer, F. M., Xiao, J., et al. (2008). Effect of physical activity on cognitive function in older adults at risk for Alzheimer disease. *The Journal of the American Medical Association, 300,* 1027–1037.

Lavie, P. (2001). Sleep–wake as a biological rhythm. *Annual Review of Psychology, 5,* 277–303.

Laws, K. R., & Kokkalis, J. (2007). Ecstasy (MDMA) and memory function: A meta-analytic update. *Human Psychopharmacology, 22,* 381–388.

Lay, C. H., & Safdar, A. F. (2003). Daily hassles and distress among college students in relation to immigrant and minority status. *Current Psychology, 22*, 3–22.

Lazar, S. W., Kerr, C. E., Wasserman, R. H., Gray, J. R., Greve, D. N., Treadway, M. T., et al. (2005). Meditation experience is associated with increased cortical thickness. *Neuroreport 16*, 1893–1897.

Lazarus, R. S., & Folkman, S. (1984). *Stress, appraisal, and coping.* New York: Springer Publishing Company.

Le Grand, R., Barrie, I., & Tanaka, J. (2005). Testing the face-like versus geometric properties of the NI70 component. *Journal of Cognitive Neuroscience, 12*, 112.

Le Grand, R., Mondloch, C. J., Maurer, D., & Brent, H. P. (2004). Impairment in holistic face processing following early visual deprivation. *Psychological Science, 15*, 762–768.

Leary, M. R., Kowalski, R. M., Smith, L., & Phillips, S. (2003). Teasing, rejection, and violence: Case studies of the school shootings. *Aggressive Behavior, 29*, 202–214.

Lebens, H., Roefs, A., Martijn, C., Houben, K., Nederkoorn, C., & Jansen, A. (2011). Making implicit measures of associations with snack foods more negative through evaluative conditioning. *Eating Behaviors, 12*, 249–253.

Leblanc, V. R., Norman, G. R., & Brooks, L. R. (2001). Effect of a diagnostic suggestion on diagnostic accuracy and identification of clinical features. *Academic Medicine, 76*, S18–S20.

Leboe, J. P., & Whittlesea, B. W. A. (2002). The inferential basis of familiarity and recall. *The Journal of Memory and Language, 46*, 804–829.

Lederman, S. J., Kilgour, A., Kitada, R., Klatzky, R. I., & Hamilton, C. (2007). Haptic face processing. *Canadian Journal of Experimental Psychology, 61*, 230–241.

Lederman, S. J., & Klatzky, R. L. (2004). Haptic identification of common objects: Effects of constraining the manual exploration process. *Perception and Psychophysics, 66*, 618–628.

LeDoux, J. E. (1995). Emotion: Clues from the brain. *Annual Review of Psychology, 46*, 209–235.

LeDoux, J. E. (2000). Emotion circuits in the brain. *Annual Review of Neuroscience, 23*, 155–184.

Lee, G., Byram, A. C., Owen, A. M., Ribary, U., Stoessl, A. J. . . . & Illes, J. (2015). Canadian perspectives on the clinical actionability of neuroimaging in disorders of consciousness. *Canadian Journal of Neurological Sciences, 42*, 96–105.

Lee, H., Xie, L., Yu, M., Kang, H., Feng, T., . . . Benveniste, H. (2015). The effect of body posture on brain glymphatic transport. *Journal of Neuroscience, 35*, 11034–11044.

Lee, H. J., Macbeth, A. H., Pagani, J. H., & Young, W. S. (2009). Oxytocin: The great facilitator of life. *Progress in Neurobiology, 88*, 127–151.

Lee, J. L. C. (2010). Memory reconsolidation mediates the updating of hippocampal memory content. *Frontiers in Behavioural Neuroscience, 11*, 168.

Lee, K., & Ono, H. (2012). Marriage, cohabitation, and happiness: A cross-national analysis of 27 countries. *Journal of Marriage and Family, 74*, 953–972.

Lefkowitz, E. S. (2005). "Things have gotten better": Developmental changes among emerging adults after the transition to university. *Journal of Adolescent Research, 20*, 40–63.

Lefkowitz M., Blake, R. R., & Mouton, J. S. (1955). Status factors in pedestrian violation of traffic signals. *Journal of Abnormal and Social Psychology, 51*, 704–706.

Leichtman, M. D., & Ceci, S. J. (1995). The effects of stereotypes and suggestions on preschoolers' reports. *Developmental Psychology, 31*, 568–578.

Leighton, J. P., & Sternberg, R. J. (2003). Reasoning and problem solving. In A. F. Healy & R. W. Proctor (Eds.), *Handbook of psychology: Experimental psychology* (Vol. 4, pp. 623–648). Hoboken, NJ: John Wiley & Sons.

Leiserowitz, A., Maibach, E., Roser-Renouf, C., & Smith, N. (2010). *Climate change in the American mind: Americans' global warming beliefs and attitudes in January 2010.* Yale University and George Mason University. New Haven, CT: Yale Project on Climate Change Communication.

Lejuez, C. W., Magidson, J. F., Mitchell, S. H., Sinha, R., Stevens, M. C., & de Wit, H. (2010). Behavioral and biological indicators of impulsivity in the development of alcohol use, problems, and disorders. *Alcoholism: Clinical and Experimental Research, 34*, 1334–1345.

Lenroot, R. K., & Giedd, J. N. (2007). The structural development of the human brain as measured longitudinally with magnetic resonance imaging. In Coch, D., Fischer, K. W., & Dawson, G. (Eds.), *Human behavior, learning, and the developing brain: Typical development* (pp. 50–73). New York, NY: Guilford Press.

Lepper, M. P., Greene, D., & Nisbett, R. E. (1973). Undermining children's intrinsic interest with extrinsic reward: A test of the "overjustification" hypothesis. *Journal of Personality and Social Psychology, 28*, 129–137.

Lesage, A., Vasiliadis, H.-M., Gagné, M.-A., Dudgeon, S., Kasman, N., & Hay, C. (2006). *Prevalence of mental illness and related service utilization in Canada: An analysis of the Canadian Community Health Survey.* Mississauga, ON: Canadian Collaborative Mental Health Initiative.

Lesch, K-P., Bengel, D., Heils, A., et al. (1996). Association of anxiety-related traits with a polymorphism in the serotonin transporter gene regulatory region. *Science, 273*, 1527–1531.

Lett, H. S., Blumenthal, J. A., Babyak, M. A., Sherwood, A., Strauman, T., . . . Newman, M.F. (2004). Depression as a risk factor for coronary artery disease: Evidence, mechanisms, and treatment. *Psychosomatic Medicine, 66*, 303–315.

Leucht, S., Arbter, D., Engel, R., Dienel, A., & Kieser, M. (2009). How effective are second-generation antipsychotic drugs? A meta-analysis of placebo-controlled trials. *Molecular Psychiatry, 14*, 429–447.

LeVay, S. (1991). A difference in hypothalamic structure between heterosexual and homosexual men. *Science, 253*, 1034–1037.

Levenston, G. K., Patrick, C. J., Bradley, M. M., & Lang, P. J. (2000). The psychopath as observer: Emotion and attention in picture processing. *Journal of Abnormal Psychology, 109*, 373–385.

Levin, R. (1994). Sleep and dreaming characteristics of frequent nightmare subjects in a university population. *Dreaming, 4*, 127–137.

Levin, R., & Fireman, G. (2002). Nightmare prevalence, nightmare distress, and self-reported psychological disturbance. *Sleep, 25*, 205–212.

Levin, R., & Nielson, T. A. (2007). Disturbed sleeping, posttraumatic disorder, and affect distress: A review and neurocognitive model. *Psychological Bulletin, 133*, 482–528.

Levine, B., Svoboda, E., Hay, J. F., Winocur, G., & Moscovitch, M. (2002). Aging and autobiographical memory: Dissociating episodic from semantic retrieval. *Psychology and Aging, 17*, 677–689.

Levine, L. J., & Pizarro, D. A. (2004). Emotion and memory research: A grumpy overview. *Social Cognition, 22*, 530–554.

Levine, M. P., Smolak, L., & Hayden, H. (1994). The relation of sociocultural factors to eating attitudes and behaviors among middle school girls. *The Journal of Early Adolescence, 14*, 471–490.

Levinson, B. W. (1965). States of awareness during general anaesthesia. *British Journal of Anaethesia, 37*, 544–546.

Levitin, D. (2006). *This is your brain on music: The science of a human obsession.* New York: Dutton Books.

Lewin, K. (1936). *Principles of topological psychology.* New York: McGraw-Hill.

Lewin, T. (2009, October 23). No Einstein in your crib? Get a refund. *The New York Times.*

Lewis, R. G., & Gutmann, L. (2004). Snake venoms and the neuromuscular junction. *Seminars in Neurology, 24*, 175–179.

Li, C. (2010). Primacy effect or recency effect? A long-term memory test of Super Bowl commercials. *Journal of Consumer Behaviour, 9*, 32–44.

Li, L., & Yong, H. H. (2009). Tobacco advertising on the street in Kunming, China. *Tobacco Control, 18*, 63.

Liberman, N., & Trope, Y. (2008). The psychology of transcending the here and now. *Science, 322*, 1201–1205.

Lieberman, L. (2001). How "Caucasoids" got such big crania and why they shrank: From Morton to Rushton. *Current Anthropology, 42*, 69–95.

Lieberman, P. (1984). *The biology and evolution of language.* Cambridge, MA: Harvard University Press.

Liebowitz, M. R. (1983). *The chemistry of love.* Boston: Little, Brown, & Co.

Liégeois, F., Badeweg, T., Connelly, A., Gadian, D. G., Mishkin, M., & Vargha-Khadem, F. (2003). Language fMRI abnormalities associated with FOXP2 gene mutation. *Nature Neuroscience, 6,* 1230–1237.

Light, K. C., Grewen, K. M., & Amico, J. A. (2005). More frequent partner hugs and higher oxytocin levels are linked to lower blood pressure and heart rate for women in premenopausal women. *Biological Psychology, 69,* 5–21.

Light, K. C., Smith, T. E., Johns, J. M., Brownley, K. A., Hofheimer, J. A., & Amico, J. A. (2000). Oxytocin responsivity in mothers of infants: A preliminary study of relationship with BP during laboratory stress and normal ambulatory activity. *Health Psychology, 19,* 560–567.

Lilienfeld, S. (2007). Psychological treatments that cause harm. *Perspectives on Psychological Science, 2,* 53–70.

Lilienfeld, S. O., & Arkowitz, H. (2009, February). Lunacy and the full moon. *Scientific American, 20,* 64–65.

Lilienfeld, S. O., & Lynn, S. J. (2003). Dissociative identity disorder: Multiple personality, multiple controversies. In S. O. Lilienfeld, J. M. Lohr, & S. J. Lynn (Eds.), *Science and pseudoscience in clinical psychology* (pp. 109–142). New York: Guilford Press.

Lilienfeld, S. O., Lynn, S. J., Kirsch, I., Chaves, J. F., Sarbin, T. R., . . . Powell, R. A. (1999). Dissociative identity disorder and the sociocognitive model: Recalling the lessons of the past. *Psychological Bulletin, 125,* 507–523.

Lilienfeld, S. O., Wood, J. M., & Garb, H. N. (2000). The scientific status of projective techniques. *Psychological Science in the Public Interest, 1,* 27–66.

Lillard, A. (1998). Ethnopsychologies: Cultural variations in theories of mind. *Psychological Bulletin, 123,* 3–32.

Lin, C., Davidson, T., & Ancoli-Israel, S. (2008). Gender differences in obstructive sleep apnea and treatment implications. *Sleep Medicine Reviews, 12,* 481–496.

Lindau, S. T., Schumm, L. P., Laumann, E. O., Levinson, W., O'Muircheartaigh, C. A., & Waite, L. J. (2007). A study of sexuality and health among older adults in the United States. *New England Journal of Medicine, 357,* 762–774.

Linde, K., Berner, M. M., & Kriston, L. S. (2008). St. John's wort for major depression. *Cochrane Database of Systemic Reviews, 4,* CD000448.

Lindsay, R. C. L., Semmler, C., Weber, N., Brewer, N. & Lindsay, M. R. (2008). How variations in distance affect eyewitness reports and identification accuracy. *Law & Human Behavior, 32,* 526–535.

Linehan, M. (1993). *Cognitive behavioral treatment of borderline personality disorder.* New York: Guilford Press.

Link, B. G. (1987). Understanding labeling effects in the area of mental disorders: An assessment of the effects of expectations of rejection. *American Sociological Review, 52,* 96–112.

Link, B. G., Cullen, F. T., Struening, E., Shrout, P. E., & Dohrenwend, B. P. (1989). A modified labeling theory approach to mental disorders: An empirical assessment. *American Sociological Review, 54,* 400–423.

Liszkowski, U., Carpenter, M., Striano, T., & Tomasello, M. (2006). 12-and 18-month-olds point to provide information for others. *Journal of Cognition and Development, 7,* 173–187.

Liu, J., Li, J., Li, L., Tian, J., & Lee, K. (2014). See Jesus in toast: Neural and behavioral correlates of face pareidolia. *Cortex, 53,* 60–77.

Liu, X., Lauer, K. K., Ward, B. D., Roa, S. M., Li, S. J., & Hudetz, A. G. (2012). Propofol disrupts functional interactions between sensory and high-order processing of auditory verbal memory. *Human Brain Mapping, 33,* 2487–2498.

Livingstone, M. S., & Conway, B. R. (2004). Was Rembrandt stereoblind? *The New England Journal of Medicine, 351,* 1264–1265.

LoBue, V., Rakison, D. H., & DeLoache, J. S. (2010). Threat perception across the life span: Evidence for multiple converging pathways. *Current Directions in Psychological Science, 19,* 375–379.

Locksley, A., Ortiz, V., & Hepburn, C. (1980). Social categorization and discriminatory behavior: Extinguishing the minimal intergroup discrimination effect. *Journal of Personality and Social Psychology, 39,* 773–783.

Loewenstein, G. F., Weber, E. U., Hsee, C. K., & Welch, N. (2001). Risk as feelings. *Psychological Bulletin, 127,* 267–286.

Loftus, E. F. (1975). Leading questions and the eyewitness report. *Cognitive Psychology, 7,* 560–572.

Loftus, E. F. (1997). Creating false memories. *Scientific America, 277,* 70–75.

Loftus, E. F., & Davis, D. (2006). Recovered memories. *Annual Review of Clinical Psychology, 2,* 469–498.

Loftus, E. F., Loftus, G. R., & Lesso, J. (1987). Some facts about "weapon focus." *Law and Human Behavior, 11,* 55–62.

Loftus, E. F., & Palmer, J. C. (1974). Reconstruction of automobile destruction: An example of the interaction between language and memory. *Journal of Verbal Learning and Verbal Behavior, 13,* 585–589.

Logan, J. M., Sanders, A. L., Snyder, A. Z., Morris, J. C., & Buckner, R. L. (2002). Under-recruitment and nonselective recruitment: Dissociable neural mechanisms associated with aging. *Neuron, 33,* 827–840.

Logel, C., & Cohen, G. L. (2012). The role of the self in physical health: testing the effect of a cause-affirmation intervention on weight loss. *Psychological Science, 23,* 53-55.

Loggia, M. L., Mogil, J. S., & Bushnell, M. C. (2008a). Empathy hurts: Compassion for another increases both sensory and affective components of pain perception. *Pain, 136,* 168–176.

Loggia, M. L., Mogil, J. S., & Bushnell, M. C. (2008b). Experimentally induced mood changes preferentially affect pain unpleasantness. *The Journal of Pain, 9,* 784–791.

Logothetis, N. K., Pauls, J., Augath, M., Trinath, T., & Oeltermann, A. (2001). Neurophysiological investigation of the basis of the fMRI signal. *Nature, 412,* 150–157.

Lømo, T. (1966). Frequency potentiation of excitatory synaptic activity in the dentate area of the hippocampal formation. *Acta Physiological Scandinavica, 68,* 128.

Lorenzoni, I., & Pidgeon, N. F. (2006). Public views on climate change: European and USA perspectives. *Climatic Change, 77,* 73–95.

Losin, E. A. R., Dapretto, M., & Iacoboni, M. (2010). Culture and neuroscience: Additive or synergistic? *Social, Cognitive, and Affective Neuroscience, 5,* 148–158.

Lougheed, J. P., & Hollenstein, T. (2012). A limited repertoire of emotion regulation strategies is associated with internalizing problems in adolescence. *Social Development, 21,* 704–721.

Lovett, M. W., Lacerenza, L., De Palma, M., & Frijters, J. C. (2012). Evaluating the efficacy of remediation for struggling readers in high school. *Journal of Learning Disabilities, 45,* 151–169.

Low, B. S. (1979). Sexual selection and human ornamentation. In N. Chagnon, & W. Irons (Eds.), *Evolutionary biology and human social behaviour* (pp. 462–487). North Slituate, MA: Duxbury Press.

Lubman, D. I., Cheetham, A., & Yücel, M. (2015). Cannabis and adolescent brain development. *Pharmacology & Therapeutics, 148,* 1–16.

Lubow, R. E., & Moore, A. U. (1959). Latent inhibition: The effect of non-reinforced preexposure to the conditioned stimulus. *Journal of Comparative and Physiological Psychology, 52,* 415–419.

Lucas, R. E., Diener, E., Grob. A., Suh, E. M., & Shao, L. (2000). Cross-cultural evidence for the fundamental features of extraversion. *Journal of Personality and Social Psychology, 79,* 452–468.

Luck, A., Pearson, S., Maddern, G., & Hewett, P. (1999). Effects of video information on precolonoscopy anxiety and knowledge: A randomised trial. *Lancet, 354,* 2032–2035.

Luders, E., Narr, K., Bilder, R., Szeszko, P., Gurbani, . . . Gaser, C. (2008). Mapping the relationship between cortical convolution and intelligence: Effects of gender. *Cerebral Cortex, 18,* 2019–2026.

Luo, L., & Craik, F. I. (2008). Aging and memory: A cognitive approach. *Canadian Journal of Psychiatry, 53,* 346–353.

Lutgendorf, S. K., Costanzo, E., & Siegel, S. (2007). Psychosocial influences in oncology: An expanded model of biobehavioral mechanisms. In R. Ader, R. Glaser, N. Cohen, & M. Irwin (Eds.), *Psychoneuroimmunology* (4th ed., pp. 869–895). New York: Academic Press.

Lutz, A., Slagter, H. A., Dunne, J. D., & Davidson, R. J. (2008). Attention regulation and monitoring in meditation. *Trends in Cognitive Sciences, 12,* 163–169.

Lykken, D. T. (1995). *The antisocial personalities.* Mahwah, NJ: Lawrence Erlbaum Associates.

Lynam, D. R., & Gudonis, L. (2005). The development of psychopathology. *Annual Review of Clinical Psychology, 1,* 381–407.

Lynn, S. J., & Kirsch, I. (1996). False memories, hypnosis, and fantasy-proneness. *Psychological Inquiry, 7,* 151–155.

Lynn, S., Nash, M., Rhue, J., Frauman, D., & Sweeney, C. (1984). Non-volition, expectancies, and hypnotic rapport. *Journal of Abnormal Psychology, 93,* 295–303.

Lyons, B. D., Hoffman, B. J., & Michel, J. W. (2009). Not much more than *g*? An examination of the impact of intelligence on NFL performance. *Human Performance, 22,* 225–245.

Lyons, N. P. (1983). Two perspectives: On self, relationships, and morality. *Harvard Educational Review, 53,* 125–145.

Lyznicki, J. M., Doege, T. C., Davis, R. M., & Williams, M. A. (1998). Sleepiness, driving, and motor vehicle crashes. *Journal of the American Medical Association, 279,* 1908–1913.

MacCracken, M. J., & Stadulis, R. E. (1985). Social facilitation of young children's dynamic balance performance. *Journal of Sport Psychology, 7,* 150–165.

MacDonald, A. A., Naci, L., MacDonald, P. A., & Owen, A. M. (2015). Anesthesia and neuroimaging: Investigating the neural correlates of unconsciousness. *Trends in Cognitive Science, 19,* 100–107.

Macdonald, K., & Macdonald, T. M. (2010). The peptide that binds: A systematic review of oxytocin and its prosocial effects in humans. *Harvard Review of Psychiatry, 18,* 1–21.

MacDonald, T. K., & Martineau, A. M. (2002). Self-esteem, mood, and intentions to use condoms: When does low self-esteem lead to risky health behaviors? *Journal of Experimental Social Psychology, 38,* 299–306.

Machado Rocha, F. C., Stéfano, S. C., De Cássia Haiek, R., Rosa Oliveira, L. M., & Da Silveira, D. X. (2008). Therapeutic use of Cannabis sativa on chemotherapy-induced nausea and vomiting among cancer patients: Systematic review and meta-analysis. *European Journal of Cancer Care, 17,* 431–443.

Mack, A., & Rock, I. (1998). *Inattentional blindness.* Cambridge, MA: MIT Press.

MacLean, K. A., Johnson, M. W., & Griffiths, R. R. (2011). Mystical experiences occasioned by the hallucinogenic psilocybin lead to increases in the personality domain of openness. *Journal of Psychopharmacology, 25,* 1453–1461.

Maclean, P. D. (1952). Some psychiatric implications of physiological studies on frontotemporal portion of limbic system (visceral brain). *Electroencephalography and Clinical Neurophysiology, 4,* 407–418.

Macmillan, M. (2008). Phineas Gage: Unravelling the myth. *The Psychologist, 21,* 828–839.

Madden, D.J., Turkington, T. G., Coleman, R. E., Provenzale, J. M., DeGrado, T. R., & Hoffman, J. M. (1996). Adult age differences in regional cerebral blood flow during visual world identification: Evidence from $H_2^{15}O$ PET. *NeuroImage, 3,* 127–142.

Maddux, W. W., Mullen, E., & Galinsky, A. D. (2008). Chameleons bake bigger pies and take bigger pieces: Strategic behavioral mimicry facilitates negotiation outcomes. *Journal of Experimental Social Psychology, 44,* 461–468.

Madill, A., & Gough, B. (2008). Qualitative research and its place in psychological science. *Psychological Methods, 13,* 254–271.

Maes, H. H., Neale, M. C., & Eaves, L. J. (1997). Genetic and environmental factors in relative body weight and human adiposity. *Behavioral Genetics, 27,* 325–351.

Magri, C., Schridde, U., Murayama, Y., Panxeri, S., Logothetis, N. K. (2012). The amplitude and timing of the BOLD signal reflects the relationship between local field potential power at different frequencies. *Journal of Neuroscience, 32,* 1395–1407.

Maguire, E. A., Gadian, D. G., Johnsrude, I. S., Good, C. D., Ashburner, J., Frackowiak, R. S., & Frith, C. D. (2000). Navigation-related structural changes in the hippocampus of taxi drivers. *Proceedings of the National Academy of Sciences, 97,* 4398–4403.

Mahalik, J., Good, G., & Englar-Carlson, M. (2003). Masculinity scripts, presenting concerns, and help seeking: Implications for practice and training. *Professional Psychology: Research and Practice, 34,* 123–131.

Mahon, M., & Crutchley, A. (2006). Performance of typically-developing school-age children with English as an additional language on the British Picture Vocabulary Scales II. *Child Language Teaching and Therapy, 22,* 333–351.

Maier, N. F. (1931). Reasoning in humans. II. The solution of a problem and its appearance in consciousness. *Journal of Comparative Psychology, 12,* 181–194.

Maier, N. R. F. (1930). Reasoning in humans: On direction. *Journal of Comparative Psychology, 10,* 115–143.

Maier, S. F., & Watkins, L. R. (1998). Cytokines for psychologists: Implications of bidirectional immune-to-brain communication for understanding behavior, mood, and cognition. *Psychological Review, 105,* 83–107.

Maier, S. F., & Watkins, L. R. (2005). Stressor controllability and learned helplessness: The roles of the dorsal raphe nucleus, serotonin, and corticotrophin-releasing factor. *Neuroscience and Behavioral Reviews, 29,* 829–841.

Main, M., & Solomon, J. (1990). Procedures for identifying disorganized/disoriented infants during the Ainsworth Strange Situation. In M. Greenberg, D. Cicchetti, & M. Cummings (Eds.), *Attachment in the preschool years,* (pp. 121–160). Chicago: University of Chicago Press.

Makin, J., Fried, P. A., & Watkinson, B. (1991). A comparison of active and passive smoking during pregnancy: Long-term effects. *Neurotoxicology and Teratology, 13,* 5–12.

Makino, M., Tsuboi, K., & Dennerstein, L. (2004). Prevalence of eating disorders: A comparison of Western and non-Western countries. *Medscape General Medicine, 6,* 49.

Mampe, B., Friederici, A. D., Christophe, A., & Wermke, K. (2009). Newborns' cry melody is shaped by their native language. *Current Biology, 19,* 1994–1997.

Mandai, O., Guerrien, A., Sockeel, P., Dujardin, K., & Leconte, P. (1989). REM sleep modifications following a Morse code learning session in humans. *Physiology & Behavior, 46,* 639–642.

Mangels, J. A., Butterfield, B., Lamb, J., Good, C., & Dweck, C. S. (2006). Why do beliefs about intelligence influence learning success? A social cognitive neuroscience model. *Social Cognitive and Affective Neuroscience, 1,* 75–86.

Mangun, G. R., Hillyard, S. A., & Luck, S. J. (1993). Electrocortical substrates of visual selective attention. In D. Meyer & S. Kornblum (Eds.). *Attention and performance 14: Synergiesin experimental psychology, artificial intelligence, and cognitive neuroscience* (pp. 219–243). MIT Press.

Mann, C. E., & Himelein, M. J. (2008). Putting the person back into psychopathology: An intervention to reduce mental illness stigma in the classroom. *Social Psychiatry and Psychiatric Epidemiology, 43,* 545–551.

Manning, R., Levine, M., & Collins, A. (2007). The Kitty Genovese murder and the social psychology of helping: The parable of the 38 witnesses. *American Psychologist, 62,* 555–562.

Mansfield, A. K., Addis, M. E., & Courtenay, W. (2005). Measurement of men's help seeking: Development and evaluation of the barriers to help seeking scale. *Psychology of Men & Masculinity, 6,* 95–108.

Marek, R., Strobel, C., Bredy, T. W., & Sah, P. (2013). The amygdala and medial prefrontal cortex: Partners in the fear circuit. *Journal of Physiology, 591,* 2381–2391.

Maren, S. (2001). Neurobiology of Pavlovian fear conditioning. *Annual Review of Neuroscience, 24,* 897–931.

Marino, L. (2002). Convergence of complex cognitive abilities in cetaceans and primates. *Brain, Behavior, and Evolution, 59,* 21–32.

Mark, V. W., Woods, A. J., Mennemeier, M., Abbas, S., & Taub, E. (2006). Cognitive assessment for CI therapy in the outpatient clinic. *NeuroRehabilitation, 21,* 139–146.

Marks, G., & Miller, N. (1987). Ten years of research on the false-consensus effect: An empirical and theoretical review. *Psychological Bulletin, 102,* 72–90.

Marks, L. V. (2001). *Sexual chemistry: A history of the contraceptive pill.* New Haven: Yale University Press.

Markus, H. (1977). Self-schema and processing information about the self. *Personality and Social Psychology Bulletin, 35,* 63–78.

Markus, H., Uchida, Y., Omoregie, H., Townsend, S., & Kitayama, S. (2006). Going for the gold: Models of agency in Japanese and American contexts. *Psychological Science, 17,* 103–112.

Markus, H. R., & Kitayama, S. (1991). Culture and the self: Implications for cognition, emotion, and motivation. *Psychological Review, 98,* 224–253.

Markus, H. R., & Kitayama, S. (2003). Models of agency: Sociocultural diversity in the construction of action. In V.M. Berman & J.J. Berman (Eds.), *Nebraska symposium on motivation: Cross-cultural differences in perspectives on the self* (Vol. 49, pp. 1–58). Lincoln: University of Nebraska Press.

Marner, L., Nyengaard, J. R., Tang, Y., & Pakkenberg, B. (2003). Marked loss of myelinated nerve fibers in the human brain with age. *Journal of Comparative Neurology, 462,* 144–152.

Marois, R., & Ivanoff, J. (2005). Capacity limits of information processing in the brain. *Trends in Cognitive Sciences, 46,* 774–785.

Marotta, J. J., Genovese, C. R., & Behrmann, M. (2001). A functional MRI study of face recognition in patients with prosopagnosia. *Neuroreport, 12,* 1581–1587.

Marroun, H. E., Schmidt, M. N., Franken, I. H. A., Jaddoe, V. W. V., Hofman, A., . . . White, T. (2014). Prenatal tobacco exposure and brain morphology: A prospective study in young children. *Neuropsychopharmacology, 39,* 792–800.

Martin, A., Wiggs, C. L., Ungerleider, L. G., & Haxby, J. V. (1996). Neural correlates of category-specific knowledge. *Nature, 379,* 649–652.

Martin, L. (1986). "Eskimo words for snow": A case study in the genesis and decay of an anthropological example. *American Anthropologist, 88,* 418–423.

Martin, R. A. (2002). Is laughter the best medicine? Humor, laughter and physical health. *Current Directions in Psychological Science, 11,* 216–220.

Martin, R. A. (2007). *The psychology of humor: An integrative approach.* Burlington, MA: Elsevier Academic Press.

Martinez, D., & Narendran, R. (2010). Imaging neurotransmitter release by drugs of abuse. *Current Topics in Behavioral Neuroscience, 3,* 219–245.

Martin-Santos, R., Fagundo, A. B., Crippa, J. A., Atakan, Z., Bhattacharyya, S., Allen, P., et al. (2010). Neuroimaging in cannabis use: A systematic review of the literature. *Psychological Medicine, 40,* 383–398.

Maruff, P., Falleti, M. G., Collie, A., Darby, D., & McStephen, M. (2005). Fatigue-related impairment in the speed, accuracy and variability of psychomotor performance: Comparison with blood alcohol levels. *Journal of Sleep Research, 14,* 21–27.

Maruta, T., Colligan, R. C., Malinchoc, M., & Offord, K. P. (2000). Optimists vs pessimists: Survival rate among medical patients over a 30-year period. *Mayo Clinic Proceedings, 75,* 140–143.

Mascolo, M. E., & Fischer, K. W. (2007). The codevelopment of self and sociomoral emotions during the toddler years. In C. A. Brownell, & C. B. Kopp (Eds.), *Socioemotional development in the toddler years: Transitions and transformations* (pp. 66–99). New York: Guilford Press.

Mashhoon, Y., Sava, S., Sneider, J. T., Nickerson, L. D., & Silveri, M. M. (2015). Cortical thinness and volume differences associated with marijuana abuse in emerging adults. *Drug and Alcohol Dependence, 155,* 275–83.

Maslow, A. (1943). A theory of human motivation. *Psychological Review, 50,* 370–396.

Maslow, A. (1954). *Motivation and personality.* New York: Harper and Row.

Maslow, A. (1968). *Toward a psychology of being* (2nd ed.). New York: Van Nostrand.

Maslow, A. (1970). *Motivation and personality,.* New York: Harper & Row.

Mashhoon, Y., Sava, S., Sneider, J. T., Nickerson, L. D., & Silveri, M. M. (2015). Cortical thinness and volume differences associated with marijuana abuse in emerging adults. *Drug and Alcohol Dependence, 155,* 275–283.

Masters, W., & Johnson, V. (1966). *Human sexual response.* Oxford, UK: Little, Brown.

Masuda, A., Suzumura, K., Beauchamp, K., Howells, G., & Clay, C. (2005). United States and Japanese college students' attitudes toward seeking professional psychological help. *International Journal of Psychology, 40,* 303–313.

Masuda, T., Ellsworth, P. C., Mesquita, B., Leu, J., Tanida, S., & van de Veerdonk, E. (2008). Placing the face in context: Cultural differences in the perception of facial emotion. *Journal of Personality and Social Psychology, 94,* 365–381.

Masuda, T., Wang, H., Ishii, K., & Ito, K. (2012). Do surrounding figures' emotions affect judgment of the target figure's emotion? Comparing the eye-movement patterns of European Canadians, Asian Canadians, Asian international students, and Japanese. *Frontiers in Integrative Neuroscience, 6,* article 72.

Mather, J. A., & Anderson, R. C. (1993). Personalities of octopuses (*Octopus rubescens*). *Journal of Comparative Psychology, 107,* 336–340.

Matsumoto, D., Consolacion, T., Yamada, H., Suzuki, R., Franklin, B., . . . Uchida, H. (2002). American–Japanese cultural differences in judgements of emotional expressions of different intensities. *Cognition & Emotion, 16,* 721–747.

Matsunaga, H., Kaye, W. H., McConaha, C., Plotnicov, K., Pollice, C., & Rao, R. (2000). Personality disorders among subjects recovered from eating disorders. *International Journal of Eating Disorders, 27,* 353–357.

Matthews, K., & Gump, B. B. (2002). Chronic work stress and marital dissolution increase risk of posttrial mortality in men from the Multiple Risk Factor Intervention Trial. *Archives of Internal Medicine, 162,* 309–315.

Mattson, M. P. (2000). Neuroprotective signaling and the aging brain: Take away my food and let me run. *Brain Research, 886,* 47–53.

Maurer, D., Lewis, T. L., Brent, H. P., & Levin, A. V. (1999). Rapid improvement in the acuity of infants after visual input. *Science, 286* (5437), 108–110.

Maurer, D., & Maurer, C. (1988). *The world of the newborn.* New York: Basic Books.

Maxwell, A. (2015). Adult criminal court statistics in Canada, 2013/2014. *Statistics Canada Catalogue no. 85-002-X.* Ottawa: Statistics Canada.

Mayberg, H. S., Liotti, M., Brannan, S. K., McGinnis, S., Mahurin, R. K., . . . Fox, P. T. (1999). Reciprocal limbic-cortical function and negative mood: Converging PET findings in depression and normal sadness. *The American Journal of Psychiatry, 156,* 675–682.

Mayberg, H. S., Lozano, A. M., Voon, V., McNeely, H. E., Seminowicz, D., Hamani, C., et al. (2005). Deep brain stimulation for treatment-resistant depression. *Neuron, 45,* 651–660.

Mayberg, H. S., Silva, J. A., Brannan, S. K., Tekell, J. L., Mahurin, R. K., McGinnis, S., & Jerabek, P. A. (2002). The functional neuroanatomy of the placebo effect. *American Journal of Psychiatry, 159,* 728–737.

Mayer, G. (2012). The use of sodium oxybate to treat narcolepsy. *Expert Review of Neurotherapeutics, 12,* 519–529.

Mazur, A., & Booth, A. (1998). Testosterone and dominance in men. *Behavioral and Brain Sciences, 21,* 353–363.

Mazur, A., Booth, A., & Dabbs, Jr., J. M. (1992). Testosterone and chess competition. *Social Psychology Quarterly, 55,* 70–77.

Mazzoni, G., & Memon, A. (2003). Imagination can create false autobiographical memories. *Psychological Science, 14,* 186–188.

McAnulty, G., Duffy, F. H., Butler, S., Bernstein, J. H., Zurakowski, D., & Als, H. (2010). Effects of newborn individualized developmental care and assessment program (NIDCAP) at age 8 years: Preliminary data. *Clinical Pediatrics (Philadelphia), 49,* 258–270.

McAnulty, G., Duffy, F. H., Butler, S., Parad, R., Ringer, S., . . . Als, H. (2009). Individualized developmental care for a large sample of very preterm infants: Health, neurobehaviour and neurophysiology. *Acta Paediatrica, 98,* 1920–1926.

McClure, S. M., Laibson, D. I., Loewenstein, G., & Cohen, J. D. (2004). Separate neural systems value immediate and delayed monetary rewards. *Science, 306,* 503–507.

McCormick, L. M., Keel, P. K., Brumm, M. C., Bowers, W., Swayze, V., . . . Andreasen, N. (2008). Implications of starvation-induced change in right dorsal anterior cingulate volume in anorexia nervosa. *International Journal of Eating Disorders, 41,* 602–610.

McCoy, A. (2006). *A question of torture: CIA interrogation from the Cold War to the War on Terror.* New York: Metropolitan Books.

McCrae, R. R. (2001). Trait psychology and culture. *Journal of Personality, 69,* 819–846.

McCrae, R. R., & Costa, P. (1987). Validation of the Five-Factor Model of personality across instruments and observers. *Journal of Personality and Social Psychology, 52,* 81–90.

McCrae, R. R., & Costa, P. T. (1990). *Personality in adulthood.* New York: The Guildford Press.

McCrae, R. R., Terracciano, A., et al. (2005). Personality profiles of cultures: Aggregate personality traits. *Journal of Personality and Social Psychology, 89,* 407–425.

McCulloch, J., Bullock, R. & Teasdale, G. M. (1991). Excitatory amino acid antagonists: Opportunities for the treatment of ischaemic brain damage in man. In B.S. Meldrum (Ed), *Excitatory amino acid antagonists* (pp. 287–325). Oxford: Blackwell.

McCullough, J. P. (2000). *Treatment for chronic depression: Cognitive behavioral analysis system of psychotherapy (CBASP).* New York: Guilford Press.

McCullough, M. E., Hoyt, W. T., Larson, D. B., Koenig, H. G., & Thoresen, C. E. (2000). Religious involvement and mortality: A meta-analytic review. *Health Psychology, 19,* 211–222.

McCullough, M. E., & Willoughby, B. L. (2009). Religion, self-regulation, and self-control: Associations, explanations, and implications. *Psychological Bulletin, 135,* 69–93.

McDaid, C., Duree, K. H., Griffin, S. C., Weatherly, H. L. A., Stradling, J. R., Davies, J. O., et al. (2009). A systematic review of continuous positive airway pressure for obstructive sleep apnoea–hypopnoea syndrome. *Sleep Science Review, 13,* 127–136.

McEwen, B. S. (2000). The neurobiology of stress: From serendipity to clinical relevance. *Brain Research, 886,* 172–189.

McGeown, W. J., Mazzoni, G., Venneri, A., Kirsch, I. (2009). Hypnotic induction decreases anterior default mode activity. *Consciousness and Cognition, 18,* 848–855.

McGlashan, T. H., Zipursky, R. B., Perkins, D., Addington, J., Miller, T., & Woods, S. W. (2006). Randomized double-blind clinical trial of olanzapine versus placebo in patients prodromally symptomatic for psychosis. *American Journal of Psychiatry, 163,* 790–799.

McGorry, P. D., Yung, A. R., Phillips, L. J., Yuen, H. P., Francey, S., & Cosgrave, E. M. (2002). Randomized controlled trial of interventions designed to reduce the risk of progression to first-episode psychosis in a clinical sample with subthreshold symptoms. *Archives of General Psychiatry, 59,* 921–928.

McGruder, J. (2004). Disease models of mental illness and aftercare patient education: Critical observations from meta-analyses, cross-cultural practice and anthropological study. *British Journal of Occupational Therapy, 67,* 310–318.

McGuire, W. J. (1961). The effectiveness of supportive and refutational defenses in immunizing defenses. *Sociometry, 24,* 184–197.

McGurk, H, & MacDonald, J. (1976). Hearing lips and seeing voices. *Nature, 264,* 746–748.

McKay, A., Byers, E. S., Voyer, S. D., Humphreys, T. P., & Markham, C. (2014). Ontario parents' opinions and attitudes towards sexual health education in the schools. *The Canadian Journal of Human Sexuality, 23,* 159–166.

McKenzie-Mohr, D. (2000). Promoting sustainable behavior: An introduction to community-based social marketing. *Journal of Social Issues, 56,* 543–554.

McKinney, K. G. (2009). Initial evaluation of Active Minds: A student organization dedicated to reducing the stigma of mental illness. *Journal of College Student Psychotherapy, 23,* 281–301.

McLaughlin, K. A., Hatzenbuehler, M. L., Mennin, D. S., & Nolen-Hoeksema, S. (2011). Emotion dysregulation and adolescent psychopathology: A prospective study. *Behaviour Research and Therapy, 49,* 544–554.

McLay, R. N., Wood, D. P., Webb-Murphy, J. A., Spira, J. L., Wiederhold, M. D., . . . Wiederhold, B. K. (2011). A randomized, controlled trial of virtual reality exposure therapy for post-traumatic stress disorder in active duty service members with combat-related post-traumatic stress disorder. *Cyberpsychology, Behavior, and Social Networking, 14,* 223–229.

McManus, F., Surawy, C., Muse, K., Vazquez-Montes, M., & Williams, J. M. G. (2012). A randomized clinical trial of mindfulness-based cognitive therapy versus unrestricted services for health anxiety (hypochondriasis). *Journal of Consulting and Clinical Psychology, 80,* 817–828.

McNally, R. J., Lasko, N. B., Clancy, S. A., Macklin, M. L., Pitman, R. K., & Orr, S. P. (2004). Psychophysiological responding during script-driven imagery in people reporting abduction by space aliens. *Psychological Science, 15,* 493–497.

McNeely, H. E., Mayberg, H. S., Lozano, A. M., & Kennedy, S. H. (2008). Neuropsychological impact of Cg25 deep brain stimulation for treatment-resistant depression: Preliminary results over 12 months. *Journal of Nervous and Mental Disease, 196,* 405–410.

McVey, G. L., Gusella, J., Tweed, S., & Ferrari, M. (2009). A controlled evaluation of web-based training for teachers and public health practitioners on the prevention of eating disorders. *Eating Disorders: Journal of Treatment and Prevention, 17,* 1–26.

Mead, M. (1928). *Coming of age in Samoa: A psychological study of primitive youth for Western civilization.* Oxford, UK: William Morrow.

Meehl, P. E. (1967). Theory-testing in psychology and physics: A methodological paradox. *Philosophy of Science, 34,* 103–115.

Mehl, M. R., Gosling, S. D., & Pennebaker, J. W. (2006). Personality in its natural habitat: Manifestations and implicit folk theories of personality in daily life. *Journal of Personality and Social Psychology, 90,* 862–877.

Mehler, J., & Bever, T. G. (1967). Cognitive capacity of very young children. *Science, 158,* 141–142.

Meier, M. H., Slutske, W. S., Arndt, S., & Cadoret, R. J. (2008). Impulsive and callous traits are more strongly associated with delinquent behavior in higher risk neighborhoods among boys and girls. *Journal of Abnormal Psychology, 117,* 377–385.

Melby-Lervåg, M., & Hulme, C. (2013). Is working memory training effective? A meta-analytic review. *Developmental Psychology, 19,* 270–291.

Melchior, M., Hersi, R., van der Waerden, J., Larroque, B., Saurel-Cubizolles, M. J., et al. (2015). Maternal tobacco smoking in pregnancy and children's socio-emotional development at age 5: The EDEN mother-child birth cohort study. *European Psychiatry, 30,* 562–568.

Meldrum, B. S. (2000). Glutamate as a neurotransmitter in the brain: Review of physiology and pathology. *Journal of Nutrition, 130,* 1007S–1015S.

Meltzoff, A. N. (1988). Infant imitation and memory: Nine-month-olds in immediate and deferred tests. *Child Development, 59,* 217–225.

Meltzoff, A. N., & Moore, M. K. (1977). Imitation of facial and manual gestures by human neonates. *Science, 198,* 75–78.

Melzack, R., & Katz, J. (2013). Pain. *Wiley Interdisciplinary Reviews: Cognitive Science, 4,* 1–15.

Melzack, R., & Wall, P. D. (1965). Pain mechanisms: A new theory. *Science, 150,* 971–979.

Melzack, R., & Wall, P. D. (1982). *The challenge of pain.* New York: Basic Books.

Memmert D., & Furley, P. (2007). "I spy with my little eye!": Breadth of attention, inattentional blindness, and tactical decision making in team sports. *Journal of Sport and Exercise Psychology, 29,* 365–347.

Merchant, H., Grahn, J., Trainor, L., Rohrmeier, M., & Fitch, W. T. (2015). Finding the beat: A neural perspective across humans and non-human primates. *Philosophical Transactions of the Royal Society of London B, 370,* 1–16.

Merckelbach, H., de Jong, P. J., Muris, P., & van den Hout, M. A. (1996). The etiology of specific phobias. *Clinical Psychology Review, 16,* 337–361.

Merikle, P. M., & Daneman, M. (1996). Memory for unconsciously perceived events: Evidence from anesthetized patients. *Consciousness and Cognition, 5,* 525–541.

Merikle, P. M., & Skanes, H. E. (1992). Subliminal self-help audiotapes: A search for placebo effects. *Journal of Applied Psychology, 77,* 772–776.

Messer, D. (2000). State of the art: Language acquisition. *The Psychologist, 13,* 138–143.

Meston, C. M., & Ahrold, T. (2010). Ethnic, gender, and acculturation influences on sexual behaviors. *Archives of Sexual Behavior, 39,* 179–189.

Meston, C. M., & Buss, D. M. (2007). Why humans have sex. *Archives of Sexual Behavior, 36,* 477–507.

Meston, C. M., Hamilton, L. D., & Harte, C. B. (2009). Sexual motivation in women as a function of age. *International Society for Sexual Medicine, 6,* 3305–3319.

Meston, C. M., Levin, R. J., Sipski, M. L., Hull, E. M., & Heiman, J. R. (2004). Women's orgasm. *Annual Review of Sex Research, 15,* 173–257.

Meyer, J. S. (2013). 3,4-methylenedioxymethamphetamine (MDMA): Current perspectives. *Substance Abuse and Rehabilitation, 4,* 83–99.

Mezulis, A. H., Abramson, L. Y., Hyde, J. S., & Hankin, B. L. (2004). Is there a universal positivity bias in attributions? A meta-analytic review of individual, developmental, and culture differences in the self-serving attributional bias. *Psychological Bulletin, 130,* 711–747.

Michael, E. B., & Gollan, T. H. (2005). Being and becoming bilingual: Individual differences and consequences for language production. In J.F. Kroll & A. M. B. de Groot (Eds.), *Handbook of bilingualism: Psycholinguistic approach* (pp. 389–407). New York: Oxford University Press.

Mikulincer, M., & Shaver, P. R. (2005). Attachment security, compassion, and altruism. *Current Directions in Psychological Science, 14,* 34–38.

Mikulincer, M., & Shaver, P. R. (2007). *Attachment in adulthood : Structure, dynamics, and change.* New York, NY: Guilford Press.

Milfont, T. L. (2010). Global warming, climate change, and human psychology. In V. Corral-Verdugo, C. Garcia-Cadana, & M. Frjas-Arment (Eds.), *Psychological approaches to sustainability: Current trends in theory, research and practice.* New York: Nova Science.

Milgram, S. (1963). Behavioral study of obedience. *Journal of Abnormal and Social Psychology, 67,* 371–378.

Milgram, S. (1974). *Obedience to authority: An experimental view.* New York: Harpercollins.

Milgram, S. (2009). *Obedience to Authority: An Experimental View.* New York: Harper Collins.

Miller, B. L., & Cummings, J. L. (2007). *The human frontal lobes.* New York: Guilford Press.

Miller, D. T., & Ross, M. (1975). Self-serving biases in the attribution of causality: Fact or fiction? *Psychological Bulletin, 82,* 213–225.

Miller, G. (1956). The magical number seven, plus or minus two: Some limits on our capacity for processing information. *Psychological Review, 63,* 81–97.

Miller, I. J., Jr., & Reedy, F. E. (1990). Variations in human taste bud density and intensity perception. *Physiology and Behavior, 47,* 1213–1219.

Miller, K. E., Omidian, P., Quraishy, A., Quraishy, N., Nasiry, M., . . . Yaqubi, A. (2006). The Afghan Symptom Checklist: A culturally grounded approach to mental health assessment in a conflict zone. *American Journal of Orthopsychiatry, 76,* 423–433.

Miller, L. J., Myers, A., Prinzi, L., & Mittenberg, W. (2009). Changes in intellectual functioning associated with normal aging. *Archives of Clinical Neuropsychology, 24,* 681–688.

Miller, L. L., McFarland, D., Cornett, T. L., & Brightwell, D. (1977). Marijuana and memory impairment: Effect on free recall and recognition memory. *Pharmacology Biochemistry and Behavior, 7,* 99–103.

Milling, L. (2009). Response expectancies: A psychological mechanism of suggested and placebo analgesia. *Contemporary Hypnosis, 26,* 93–110.

Mills, D., Coffey-Corina, S., & Neville, H. (1997). Language comprehension and cerebral specialization from 13 to 20 months. *Developmental Neuropsychology, 13,* 397–445.

Mills, J. N. (1964). Circadian rhythms during and after three months in solitude underground. *Journal of Physiology, 174,* 217–231.

Milner, B. (1962). Les troubles de la mémoire accompagnant des lésions hippocampiques bilatérales. In P. Passouant (Ed.), *Physiologie de l'Hippocampe* (pp. 257–272). Paris: Centre Nationale de la Recherche Scientifique.

Milner, B. (1963). Effects of different brain lesions on card sorting. *Archives of Neurology, 9,* 90–100.

Milner, B., Corkin, S., & Teuber, H. L. (1968). Further analysis of the hippocampal amnesic syndrome: 14-year follow-up study of H.M. *Neuropsychologia 6,* 215–234.

Milner, D., & Goodale, M. A. (2006). *The visual brain in action* (2nd ed). Oxford, UK: Oxford University Press.

Mischel, W. (1968). *Personality and assessment.* New York: Wiley.

Mischel, W. (1981). *Introduction to personality.* New York: Holt, Rinehart and Winston.

Mischel, W., & Ebbesen, E. B. (1970). Attention in delay of gratification. *Journal of Personality and Social Psychology, 16,* 329–337.

Mischel, W., & Shoda, Y. (1998). Reconciling processing dynamics and personality dispositions. *Annual Review of Psychology, 49,* 229–258.

Mishara, B. L., Chagnon, F., Daigle, M., Balan, B., Raymond, S., . . . Berman, A. (2007). Which helper behaviors and intervention styles are related to better short-term outcomes in telephone crisis intervention? Results from a silent monitoring study of calls to the U.S. 1-800-SUICIDE Network. *Suicide and Life Threatening Behavior, 37,* 308–321.

Mishara, B. L., & Daigle, M. S. (1997). Effects of different telephone intervention styles with suicidal callers at two suicide prevention centers: An empirical investigation. *American Journal of Community Psychology, 5,* 861–885.

Mistry, K. B., Minkovitz, C. S., Strobino, D. M., & Borzekowski, D. (2007). Children's television exposure and behavioral and social outcomes at 5.5 years: Does timing of exposure matter? *Pediatrics, 120,* 762–769.

Mitchell, R. W. (1987). A comparative-developmental approach to understanding imitation. In P. P. G. Bateson & P. H. Klopfer (Eds.), *Perspectives in Ethology* (pp. 183–215). New York: Springer.

Mithoefer, M. C., Wagner, M. T., Mithoefer, A. T., Jerome, L., & Doblin, R. (2011). The safety and efficacy of 3,4-methylenedioxymethamphetamine-assisted psychotherapy in subjects with chronic, treatment-resistant posttraumatic stress disorder: The first randomized controlled pilot study. *Journal of Psychopharmacology, 25,* 439–452.

Mithoefer, M. C., Wagner, M. T., Mithoefer, A. T., Jerome, L., Martin, S. F., . . . & Doblin, R. (2013). Durability of improvement in post-traumatic stress disorder symptoms and absence of harmful effects or drug dependency after 3, 4-methylenedioxymethamphetamine-assisted psychotherapy: A prospective long-term follow-up study. *Journal of Psychopharmacology, 27,* 28–39.

Miyake, Y., Okamoto, Y., Onoda, K., Shirao, N., Okamoto, Y., . . . Yamawaki, S. (2010). Neural processing of negative word stimuli concerning body image in patients with eating disorders: An fMRI study. *Neuroimage, 15,* 1333–1339.

Mizushige, T., Inoue, K., & Fushiki, T. (2007). Why is fat so tasty? Chemical reception of fatty acid on the tongue. *Journal of Nutritional Science and Vitaminology, 53,* 1–4.

Molina, J., & Mendoza, M. (2006). Change of attitudes towards hypnosis after a training course. *Australian Journal of Clinical & Experimental Hypnosis, 34,* 146–161.

Molteni, R., Barnard, R. J., Ying, Z., Roberts, C. K., & Gómez-Pinilla, F. (2002). A high-fat, refined sugar diet reduces hippocampal brain-derived neurotrophic factor, neuronal plasticity and learning. *Neuroscience, 112,* 803–814.

Mondloch, C. J., Maurer, D., & Ahola, S. (2006). Becoming a face expert. *Psychological Science, 17,* 930–934.

Monk-Turner, E., Wren, K., McGill, L., Matthiae, C., Brown, S., & Brooks, D. (2008). Who is gazing at whom? A look at how sex is used in magazine advertisements. *Journal of Gender Studies, 17,* 201–209.

Montgomery, G. H., DuHamel, K. N., & Redd, W. H. (2000). A metaanalysis of hypnotically induced analgesia: How effective is hypnosis? *International Journal of Clinical and Experimental Hypnosis, 48,* 138–153.

Montgomery, I., Trinder, J., Fraser, G., & Paxton, S. (1987). Aerobic fitness and exercise: Effect on the sleep of younger and older adults. *Australian Journal of Psychology, 39,* 259–271.

Monti, M. M., Vanhaudenhuyse, A., Coleman, M. R., Boly, M., Pickard, J. D., Tshibanda, L., et al. (2010). Willful modulation of brain activity in disorders of consciousness. *The New England Journal of Medicine, 362,* 579–589.

Mooneyham, B. W., & Schooler, J. W. (2013). The costs and benefits of mind-wandering: A review. *Canadian Journal of Experimental Psychology, 67,* 11–18.

Moore, B., Mischel, W., & Zeiss, A. (1976). Comparative effects of the reward stimulus and its cognitive representation in voluntary delay. *Journal of Personality and Social Psychology, 34,* 419–424.

Moore, L. P., Moore, J. W., & Hauck, W. E. (1982). Conditioning children's attitudes toward alcohol, smoking, and drugs. *Journal of Experimental Education, 50,* 154–158.

Morgan, C. J., Muetzelfeldt, L., & Curran, H. V. (2010). Consequences of chronic ketamine self-administration upon neurocognitive function and psychological wellbeing: A 1-year longitudinal study. *Addiction, 105,* 12–33.

Morgan, D., Grant, K. A., Gage, H. D., Mach, R. H., Kaplan, J. R., Prioleau, O., et al. (2002). Social dominance in monkeys: Dopamine D2 receptors and cocaine self-administration. *Nature Neuroscience, 5,* 169–174.

Morgane, P. J., Mokler, D. J., & Galler, J. R. (2002). Effects of prenatal protein malnutrition on the hippocampal formation. *Neuroscience and Biobehavioral Reviews, 26,* 471–483.

Morin, C., Bootzin, R., Buysse, D., Edinger, J., Espie, C., & Lichstein, K. (2006). Psychological and behavioral treatment of insomnia: Update of the recent evidence (1998–2004). *Sleep: Journal of Sleep and Sleep Disorders Research, 29,* 1398–1414.

Morin, L. P. (2013). Neuroanatomy of the extended circadian rhythm system. *Experimental Neurology, 243,* 4–20.

Morleo, M., Woolfall, K., Dedman, D., Mukherjee, R., Bellis, M. A., & Cook, P. A. (2011). Under-reporting of foetal alcohol spectrum disorders: An analysis of hospital episode statistics. *BMC Pediatrics, 11,* 14.

Morris, C., Novot, A., Arkadir, D., Vaadia, E., & Borgman, H. (2006). Midbrain dopamine neurons encode decisions for future action. *Nature Neuroscience, 9,* 1057–1063.

Morris, M. W., & Peng, K. (1994). Culture and cause: American and Chinese attributions for social and physical events. *Journal of Personality and Social Psychology, 67,* 949–971.

Morris, R. G. M. (1981). Spatial localization does not require the presence of local cues. *Learning and Motivation, 2,* 239–260.

Morris, R. G. M., Garrud, P., Rawlins, J. N., & O'Keefe, J. (1982). Place navigation impaired in rats with hippocampal lesions. *Nature, 297,* 681–683.

Moscicki, E. K. (2001). Epidemiology of completed and attempted suicide: Toward a framework for prevention. *Clinical Neuroscience Research, 1,* 310–323.

Motet, A. (1897). Accès de somnambulisme spontané et provoqué. *Annales d'Hygiene et de Médecine Légale,* 3e série, *37,* 502–525. Cited in L. Thoinot (1911), *Medicolegal aspects of moral offenders.* Philadelphia, PA. Weysse A. David and Company.

Mott, F. W. (1907). Bilateral lesion of the auditory cortical centre: Complete deafness and aphasia. *British Medical Journal, 2,* 310–315.

Mrazek, M. D, Smallwood, J., Franklin, M. S., Chin, J. M., Baird, B., & Schooler, J. W. (2012). The role of mind-wandering in measurements of general aptitude. *Journal of Experimental Psychology: General, 141,* 788–798.

Muckle, G., Laflamme, D., Gagnon, J., Boucher, O., Jacobson, J. L., Jacobson, S. W. (2011). Alcohol, smoking, and drug use among Inuit women of childbearing age during pregnancy and the risk to children. *Alcoholism: Clinical and Experimental Research, 35,* 1081–1091.

Müller, N. G., & Knight, R. T. (2006). The functional neuroanatomy of working memory: Contributions of human brain lesion studies. *Neuroscience, 139,* 51–58.

Munt, S. (1998). *Heroic desire: Lesbian identity and cultural space.* New York: New York University Press.

Murdock, B. B. (1962). The serial position effect of free recall. *Journal of Experimental Psychology, 64,* 482–488.

Murphy, C., Cain, W. S., & Bartoshuk, L. M. (1977). Mutual action of taste and olfaction. *Sensory Processes, 1,* 204–211.

Murphy, G. G., & Glanzman, D. L. (1997). Mediation of classical conditioning in *Aplysia californica* by LTP of sensorimotor synapses. *Science, 278,* 467–471.

Murphy, M. R., Checkley, S. A., Seckl, J. R., & Lightman, S. L. (1990). Naloxone inhibits oxytocin release at orgasm in man. *Journal of Clinical Endocrinology and Metabolism, 71,* 1056–1058.

Murphy, S. T., & Zajonc, R. B. (1993). Affect, cognition, and awareness: Affective priming with optimal and suboptimal stimulus exposures. *Journal of Personality and Social Psychology, 64,* 723–739.

Murtagh, D. R., & Greenwood, K. M. (1995). Identifying effective psychological treatments for insomnia: A meta-analysis. *Journal of Consulting and Clinical Psychology, 63,* 79–89.

Myers, C. E., McGlinchey-Berroth, R., Warren, S., Monti, L., Brawn, C. M., & Gluck, M. A. (2000). Latent learning in medial temporal amnesia: Evidence for disrupted representational but preserved attentional processes. *Neuropsychology, 14,* 3–15.

Myers, D. G., & Diener, E. (1995). Who is happy? *Psychological Science, 6,* 10–19.

Nairne, J. S. (1996). Short-term/working memory. In E. Bjork & R. A. Bjork (Eds.), *Memory* (pp. 101–126). San Diego, CA: Academic Press.

Nakamura, M., Kanbayashi, T., Sugiura, T., & Inoue, Y. (2011). Relationship between clinical characteristics of narcolepsy and CSF orexin-A levels. *Journal of Sleep Research, 20,* 45–49.

Naegele, B., Thouvard, V., Pepin, J. L., Levy, P., Bonnet, C., Perret, J. E., Pellat, J., & Feuerstein, (1995). Deficits of cognitive executive functions in patients with sleep apnea syndrome. *Sleep, 18,* 43–52.

Narby, D. J., Cutler, B. L., & Moran, G. (1993). A meta-analysis of the association between authoritarianism and jurors' perceptions of defendant culpability. *Journal of Applied Psychology, 78,* 34–42.

Narrow, W. E., Rae, D. S., Robins, L. N., & Regier, D. A. (2002). Revised prevalence based estimates of mental disorders in the United States: Using a clinical signficance criterion to reconcile 2 surveys' estimates. *Archives of General Psychiatry, 59,* 115–123.

Nash, M. R., Perez, N., Tasso, A., & Levy, J. L. (2009). Clinical research on the utility of hypnosis in the prevention, diagnosis, and treatment of medical and psychiatric disorders. *International Journal of Clinical and Experimental Hypnosis, 57,* 443–450.

Nash, R., Wade, K., & Lindsay, D. (2009). Digitally manipulating memory: Effects of doctored videos and imagination in distorting beliefs and memories. *Memory & Cognition, 37,* 414–424.

National Eating Disorders Association. (2002). *National eating disorders association statistics: Eating disorders and their precursors.* Retrieved from http://www.nationaleatingdisorders.org/nedaDir/files/documents/handouts/Stats.pdf

National Institute of Mental Health (NIMH). (2008). The numbers count: Mental disorders in America. Retrieved from http://www.nimh.nih.gov/health/publications/the-numbers-count-mental-disorders-in-america/index.shtml

National Institute of Mental Health (NIMH). (2009). Post-traumatic stress disorder (PTSD). Retrieved from http://www.nimh.nih.gov/health/publications/post-traumatic-stress-disorder-ptsd/psychotherapy.shtml

National Institute of Mental Health (NIMH). (2011). Use of mental health services and treatment among adults. Retrieved from http://www.nimh.nih.gov/statistics/3USE_MT_ADULT.shtml

Navaneelan, T., & Janz, T. (2014). Adjusting the scales: Obesity in the Canadian population after correcting for respondent bias. *Health at a Glance.* Statistics Canada Catalogue no. 82-624-X. Retrieved from http://www.statcan.gc.ca/pub/82-624-x/2014001/article/11922-eng.htm

Neisser, U. (2000). Snapshots or benchmarks? In U. Neisser & I. Hyman (Eds.), *Memory observed: Remembering in natural contexts* (2nd ed., pp. 68–74). New York: Worth Publishing.

Neisser, U., Boodoo, G., Bouchard, T. J., Boykin, A. W., Brody, N., . . . Urbina, S. (1996). Intelligence: Knowns and unknowns. *American Psychologist, 51,* 77–101.

Neisser, U., & Harsch, N. (1992). Phantom flashbulbs: False recollections of hearing the news about Challenger. In E. Winograd & U. Neisser (Eds.), *Affect and accuracy in recall: Studies in flashbulb memories* (pp. 9–31). Cambridge, UK: Cambridge University Press.

Nesse, R., & Ellsworth, P. (2009). Evolution, emotions, and emotional disorders. *American Psychologist, 64,* 129–139.

Nestler, E. J., & Hyman, S. E. (2010). Animal models of neuropsychiatric disorders. *Nature Neuroscience, 13,* 1161–1169.

Neugebauer, R., Hoek, H. W., & Susser, E. (1999). Prenatal exposure to wartime famine and development of antisocial personality disorder in early adulthood. *The Journal of the American Medical Association, 282,* 455–462.

Neville, H. J. (1995). Developmental specificity in neurocognitive development in humans. In M. Gazzaniga (Ed.), *The cognitive neurosciences* (pp. 219–231). Cambridge, MA: MIT Press.

New, J., Krasnow, M. M., Truxaw, D., & Gaulin, S. J. C. (2007). Spatial adaptations for plant foraging: Women excel and calories count. *Proceedings of the Royal Society, 274,* 2679–2684.

Newcombe, N. S., Drummey, A., Fox, N. A., et al. (2000). Remembering early childhood: How much, how, and why (or why not). *Current Directions in Psychological Science, 9,* 55–58.

Newman, M. G., & Llera, S. J. (2011). A novel theory of experiential avoidance in generalized anxiety disorder: A review and synthesis of research supporting a contrast avoidance model of worry. *Clinical Psychology Review, 31,* 371–382.

Newton, E. L. (1991). The rocky road from actions to intentions. Dissertation. Available from ProQuest Information and Learning.

Nicki, R. M., Gallagher, T. M., & Cormier, A. E. (2007). Attractiveness of video lottery terminal (VLT) games for problem and non-problem gamblers. *Gambling Research: Journal of the National Association for Gambling Studies (Australia), 19,* 21–35.

Nielsen, T. A., Laberge, L., Paquet, J., Tremblay, R. E., Vitaro, F., & Montplaisir, J. (2000). Development of disturbing dreams during adolescence and their relation to anxiety symptoms. *Sleep, 23,* 1–10.

Nielsen, T. A., Stenstrom, P., & Levin, R. (2006). Nightmare frequency as a function of age, gender, and September 11, 2001: Findings from an Internet questionnaire. *Dreaming, 16,* 145–158.

Nielsen, T. A., Zadra, A. L., Simard, V., Saucier, S., Stentrom, P., Smith, C., & Kuiken, D. (2003). The typical dreams of Canadian university students. *Dreaming, 13,* 211–235.

Nielsen Research. (2010, April 28). U.S. homes add even more TV sets in 2010. Retrieved from http://www.nielsen.com/us/en/newswire/2010/u-s-homes-add-even-more-tv-sets-in-2010.html

Neilsen Research. (2008, October 2). Obama and McCain's ads: Equally "negative." *Neilsenwire.* Retrieved from http://blog.nielsen.com/nielsenwire/media_entertainment/obama-and-mccains-ads-equallynegative/

Nielson, K., Yee, D., & Erickson, K. (2005). Memory enhancement by a semantically unrelated emotional arousal source induced after learning. *Neurobiology of Learning and Memory, 84,* 49–56.

Niogi, S. N., & Mukherjee, P. (2010). Diffusion tensor imaging of mild traumatic brain injury. *Journal of Head Trauma Rehabilitation, 25,* 241–255.

Nisbet, E. K., & Gick, M. L. (2008). Can health psychology help the planet? Applying theory and models of health behaviour to environmental actions. *Canadian Psychology, 49,* 296–303.

Nisbett, R. E. (2003). *The geography of thought: How Asians and Westerners think differently . . . and why.* New York: Free Press.

Nisbett, R. E. (2005). Heredity, environment, and race differences in IQ: A commentary on Rushton and Jensen (2005). *Psychology, Public Policy, and Law, 11,* 302–310.

Nisbett, R. E. (2009). *Intelligence and how to get it: Why schools and cultures count.* New York: Norton.

Nisbett, R. E., Aronson, J., Blair, C., Dickens, W., Flynn, J., Halpern, D. F., & Turkheimer, E. (2012). Intelligence: New findings and theoretical developments. *American Psychologist, 67,* 130–159.

Nisbett, R. E., & Masuda, T. (2003). Culture and point of view. *Proceedings of the National Academy of Sciences, 100,* 11163–11170.

Nisbett, R. E., & Wilson, T. D. (1977). Telling more than we can know: Verbal reports on mental processes. *Psychological Review, 84,* 231.

Noels, K. A., Pelletier, L. G., Clement, R., & Vallerand, R. J. (2000). Why are you learning a second language? Motivational orientations and self-determination theory. *Language Learning, 50,* 57–85.

Nolan, J. M., Schultz, P. W., Cialdini, R. B., Goldstein, N. J., & Griskevicius, V. (2008). Normative social influence is underdetected. *Personality and Social Psychology Bulletin, 34,* 913–923.

Nolte, J. (1999). *The human brain* (4th ed.). St Louis: Mosby.

Norman, D., & Shallice, T. (1986). Attention to action. In R. J. Davidson, G. E. Schwartz, & D. Shapiro (Eds.), *Consciousness and self-regulation* (pp. 1–18). New York: Plenum Press.

Norman, G. R., Brooks, L. R., & Allen, S. W. (1989). Recall by expert medical practitioners and novices as a record of processing. *Journal of Experimental Psychology: Learning, Memory, and Cognition, 15,* 1166–1174.

Norman, G. R., Rosenthal, D., Brooks, L. R., Allen, S. W., & Muzzin, L. J. (1989). The development of expertise in dermatology. *Archives of Dermatology, 125,* 1063–1068.

North, C. S., Ryall, J. E. M., Ricci, D. A., & Wetzel, R. D. (1993). *Multiple personalities, multiple disorders.* New York: Oxford University Press.

Northstone, K., Joinson, C., Emmett, P., Ness, A., & Paus, T. (2012). Are dietary patterns in childhood associated with IQ at 8 years of age? A population-based cohort study. *Journal of Epidemiology and Community Health, 66,* 624–628.

Norton, A., Zipse, L., Marchina, S., & Schlaug, G. (2009). Melodic intonation therapy: Shared insights on how it is done and why it might help. *Annals of the New York Academy of Sciences, 1169,* 431–436.

Nosek, B. A. (2007). Implicit–explicit relations. *Current Directions in Psychological Science, 16,* 65–69.

Nosek, B. A., Banjai, M., & Greenwald, A. G. (2002). Harvesting implicit group attitudes and beliefs from a demonstration web site. *Group Dynamics: Theory, Research, and Practice, 6,* 101–115.

Nosyk, B., Marshall, B. D. L., Fischer, B., Montaner, J. S. G., Wood, E., & Kerr, T. (2012). Increases in the availability of prescribed opioids in a Canadian setting. *Drug and Alcohol Dependence, 126,* 7–12.

Nunn, J. A., Gregory, L. J., Brammer, M., Williams, S. C., Parslow, D. M., Morgan, M. J., et al. (2002). Functional magnetic resonance imaging of synesthesia: Activation of V4/V8 by spoken words. *Nature Neuroscience, 5,* 371–375.

Nuttin, J. M. (1985). Narcissism beyond Gestalt and awareness: The name–letter effect. *European Journal of Social Psychology, 15,* 353–361.

Nyi, P. P., Lai, E. P., Lee, D. Y., Biglete, S. A., Torrecer, G. I., & Anderson, I. B. (2010). Influence of age on Salvia divinorum use: Results of an Internet survey. *Journal of Psychoactive Drugs, 42,* 385–392.

O'Brien, T. B., & DeLongis, A. (1996). The interactional context of problem-, emotion-, and relationship-focused coping: The role of the Big Five personality factors. *Journal of Personality, 64,* 775–813.

O'Kearney, R., Gibson, M., Christensen, H., & Griffiths, K. M. (2006). Effects of a cognitive-behavioural Internet program on depression, vulnerability to depression and stigma in adolescent males: A school-based controlled trial. *Cognitive Behavior Therapy, 35,* 43–54.

O'Leary, C. M., Nassar, N., Kurinczuk, J. J., de Klerk, N., Geelhoed, E., . . . Bower, C. (2010). Prenatal alcohol exposure and risk of birth defects. *Pediatrics, 126,* e843–e850.

O'Rahilly, R., & Mueller, F. (2008). Significant features in the early prenatal development of the human brain. *Annals of Anatomy, 190,* 105–118.

Ochsner, K.N. (2000). Are affective events richly "remembered" or simply familiar? The experience and process of recognizing feelings past. *Journal of Experimental Psychology: General, 129,* 242–261.

Ochsner, K. N., & Gross, J. J. (2005). The cognitive control of emotion. *Trends in Cognitive Sciences, 9,* 242–249.

Oehen, P., Traber, R., Widmer, V., & Schnyder, U. (2013). A randomized, controlled pilot study of MDMA (±3, 4-Methylenedioxymethamphetamine)-assisted psychotherapy for treatment of resistant, chronic post-traumatic stress disorder (PTSD). *Journal of Psychopharmacology, 27*(1), 40–52.

Ogawa, S., Tank, D. W., Menon, R., Ellermann, J. M., Kim, S. G., . . . Ugurbil, K. (1992). Intrinsic signal changes accompanying sensory stimulation: Functional brain mapping with magnetic resonance imaging. *Proceedings of the National Academy of Sciences of the United States of America, 89,* 5951–5955.

Öhman, A., & Mineka, S. (2001). Fears, phobias, and preparedness: Toward an evolved module of fear and fear learning. *Psychological Review, 108,* 483–522.

O'Keefe, D. J. (1999). Variability of persuasive message effects: Meta-analytic evidence and implications. *Document Design, 1,* 87–97.

Olds, J. (1958). Self-stimulation of the brain. *Science, 127,* 315–324.

Olfson, M., & Marcus, S. C. (2010). National trends in outpatient psychotherapy. *American Journal of Psychiatry, 167,* 1456–1463.

Olfson, M., & Marcus, S. C. (2009). National patterns in antidepressant medication treatment. *Archives of General Psychiatry, 66,* 848–856.

Oliveira, T., Gouveia, M. J., & Oliveira, R. F. (2009). Testosterone responsiveness to winning and losing experiences in female soccer players. *Psychoneuroendocrinology, 34,* 1056–1064.

Oliven, J. F. (1965). *Sexual hygiene and pathology*. Philadelphia: J. B. Lippincott Company.

Oliver, G., & Wardle, J. (1999). Perceived effects of stress on food choice. *Physiology and Behavior, 66*, 511–515.

Oliveri, M., & Calvo, G. (2003). Increased visual cortical excitability in ecstasy users: A transcranial magnetic stimulation study. *Journal of Neurology, Neurosurgery, and Psychiatry, 74*, 1136–1138.

Olshansky, S. J., Passaro, D. J., Hershow, R. C., Layden, J., Carnes, B. A., Brody, J., et al. (2005). A potential decline in life expectancy in the United States in the 21st century. *New England Journal of Medicine, 352*, 1138–1145.

Olson, H. C., Streissguth, A. P., Sampson, P. D., Barr, H. M., Bookstein, F. L., & Thiede, K. (1997). Association of prenatal alcohol exposure with behavioral and learning problems in early adolescence. *Journal of the American Academy of Child & Adolescent Psychiatry, 36*, 1187–1194.

Olson, K. R., Lambert, A. J., & Zacks, J. M. (2004). Graded structure and the speed of category verification: On the moderating effects of anticipatory control for social vs. non-social categories. *Journal of Experimental Social Psychology, 40*, 239–246.

Olson, M. A., & Fazio, R. H. (2001). Implicit attitude formation through classical conditioning. *Psychological Science, 12*, 413–417.

Olsson, A., & Phelps, E. (2007). Social learning of fear. *Nature Neuroscience, 10*, 1095–1102.

Open Science Collaboration (2015). Estimating the reproducibility of psychological science. *Science, 349*, 943.

Opriş, D., Pintea, S., García-Palacios, A., Botella, C., Szamosköz, S,., & David, D. (2011). Virtual reality exposure therapy in anxiety disorders: A quantitative meta-analysis. *Depression and Anxiety, 29*, 85–93.

Orne, M. T. (1962). On the social psychology of the pyschological experiment: With particular reference to demand characteristics and their implications. *American Psychologist, 17*, 776–783.

Ostafin, B. D., Marlatt, G., & Greenwald, A. G. (2008). Drinking without thinking: An implicit measure of alcohol motivation predicts failure to control alcohol use. *Behaviour Research and Therapy, 46*, 1210–1219.

Overgaard, M., & Overgaard, R. (2011). Measurements of consciousness in the vegetative state. *The Lancet, 378*, 2052–2054.

Owen, A. (2013). Detecting consciousness: A unique role for neuroimaging. *Annual Review of Psychology, 64*, 109–133.

Owen, A. M., & Coleman, M. R. (2008). Functional neuroimaging of the vegetative state. *Nature Reviews Neuroscience, 9*, 235–243.

Owen, A. M., Coleman, M. R., Boly, M., et al. (2006). Detecting awareness in the vegetative state. *Science, 313*, 1402.

Owen, M. J., O'Donovan, M. C., Thapar, A., & Craddock, N. (2011). Neurodevelopmental hypothesis of schizophrenia. *The British Journal of Psychiatry, 198*, 173–175.

Oxford English Dictionary. (2011). Retrieved June 16, 2011, from http://dictionary.oed.com/entrance.dtl

Packer, D. J. (2008). Identifying systematic disobedience in Milgram's obedience experiments: A meta-analytic review. *Perspectives on Psychological Science, 3*, 301–304.

Paller, K. (2004). Electrical signals of memory and of the awareness of remembering. *Current Directions in Psychological Science, 13*, 49–55.

Pallesen, S., Hilde, I., Havik, O., & Nielsen, G. (2001). Clinical assessment and treatment of insomnia. *Professional Psychology: Research and Practice, 32*, 115–124.

Palmer, R. H. C., Bidwell, L. C., Heath, A. C., Brick, L. A., Madden, P. A. F., & Knopik, V. S. (2016). Effects of maternal smoking during pregnancy on offspring externalizing problems: Contextual effects in a sample of twins. *Behavioral Genetics, 46*, 403–415.

Pan, A., Malik, V. S., & Hu, F. B. (2012). Exporting diabetes mellitus to Asia: The impact of Western-style fast food. *Circulation, 126*, 163–165.

Paparrigopoulos, T. J. (2005). REM sleep behaviour disorder: Clinical profiles and pathophysiology. *International Review of Psychiatry, 17*, 293–300.

Papies, E. K., & Hamstra, P. (2010). Goal priming and eating behavior: Enhancing self-regulation by environmental cues. *Health Psychology, 29*, 384–388.

Paquette, V., Levesque, J., Mensour, B., Leroux, J. M., Beaudoin, G., . . . Beauregard, M. (2003). "Change the mind and you change the brain": Effects of cognitive-behavioral therapy on the neural correlates of spider phobia. *Neuroimage, 18*, 401–409.

Paradis, C., Solomon, L. Z., Florer, F., & Thompson, T. (2004). Flashbulb memories of personal events of 9/11 and the day after for a sample of New York City residents. *Psychological Reports, 95*, 304–310.

Paris, B. J. (1994). *Karen Horney: A psychoanalyst's search for self-understanding*. New Haven, CT: Yale University Press.

Park, D. C., & Huang, C-M. (2010). Culture wires the brain: A cognitive neuroscience perspective. *Perspectives on Psychological Science, 5*, 391–400.

Park, S., Püschel, J., Sauter, B. H., Rentsch, M., & Hell, D. (1999). Spatial working memory deficits and clinical symptoms of schizophrenia: A 4-month follow-up study. *Biological Psychiatry, 46*, 392–400.

Parrott, M. D., & Greenwood, C. E. (2007). Dietary influences on cognitive function with aging. *Annals of the New York Academy of Sciences, 1114*, 389–397.

Parsons, H. M. (1974). What happened at Hawthorne?: New evidence suggests the Hawthorne effect resulted from reinforcement contingencies. *Science, 183*, 922–932.

Pascual-Leone, A., Amedi, A., Fregni, F., & Merabet, L. B. (2005). The plastic human brain cortex. *Annual Review of Neuroscience, 29*, 377–401.

Pascual-Leone, A., & Hamilton, R. (2001). The metamodal organization of the brain. *Progress in Brain Research, 134*, 427–445.

Pasher, H., McDaniel, M., Rohrer, D., & Bjork, R. (2008). Learning styles: Concepts and evidence. *Psychological Science in the Public Interest, 9*, 105–119.

Pashler, H. (1998). *The psychology of attention*. Cambridge, MA: MIT Press.

Patrick, G. T. W., & Gilbert, J. A. (1896). Studies from the psychological laboratory of the University of Iowa: On the effects of loss of sleep. *Psychological Review, 3*, 469–483.

Patterson, C. M., & Newman, J. P. (1993). Reflectivity and learning from aversive events: Toward a psychological mechanism for the syndromes of disinhibition. *Psychological Review, 100*, 716–736.

Patterson, D., & Jensen, M. (2003). Hypnosis and clinical pain. *Psychological Bulletin, 129*, 495–521.

Paul, D. B., & Blumenthal, A. L. (1989). On the trail of little Albert. *Psychological Record, 39*, 547–553.

Paulesu, E., Frith, C., & Frackowiak, R. (1993). The neural correlates of the verbal component of working memory. *Nature, 362*, 342–345.

Paulhus, D. L., & Williams, K. (2002). The dark triad of personality: Narcissism, Machiavellianism, and psychopathy. *Journal of Research in Personality, 36*, 556–568.

Paz, R., & Paré, D. (2013). Physiological basis for emotional modulation of memory circuits by the amygdala. *Current Opinion in Neurobiology, 23*, 381–386.

Peciña, M., Mickey, B. J., Wang, H., Langenecker, S. A., Hodgkinson, C., Shen, P. H., . . . Zubieta, J. K. (2013). DRD2 polymorphisms module reward and emotion processing, dopamine neurotransmission and openness to experience. *Cortex, 49*, 877–890.

Peeters, M., & Giuliano, F. (2007). Central neurophysiology and dopaminergic control of ejaculation. *Neuroscience and Biobehavioral Reviews, 32*, 438–453.

Pelham, B. W., Carvallo, M., & Jones, J. T. (2005). Implicit egoism. *Current Directions in Psychological Science, 14*, 106–110.

Pelphrey, K. A., & Morris, J. P. (2006). Brain mechanisms for interpreting the actions of others from biological-motion cues. *Current Directions in Psychological Science, 15*, 136–140.

Pemment, J. (2013). The neurobiology of antisocial personality disorder: The quest for rehabilitation and treatment. *Aggression and Violent Behavior, 18*, 79–82.

Penfield, W., & Jasper, H. H. (1951). *Epilepsy and the functional anatomy of the human brain*. New York: Little, Brown, and Company.

Peng, S., Zhang, Y., Zhang, J., Wang, H., & Ren, B. (2011). Glutamate receptors and signal transduction in learning and memory. *Molecular Biology Reports, 38*, 453–460.

Penn, D. L., & Combs, D. (2000). Modification of affect perception deficits in schizophrenia. *Schizophrenia Research, 46,* 217–229.

Penninx, B., Geerlings, S., Deeg, D., van Eijk, J., van Tilburg, W., & Beekman, A. (1999). Minor and major depression and the risk of death in older persons. *Archives of General Psychiatry, 56,* 889–895.

Pereira, E. A. C., Lu, G., Wang, S., Schweder, P. M., Hyam, J. A., Stein, J. F., Paterson, D. J., Aziz, T. Z., & Green, A. L. (2010). Ventral periaqueductal grey stimulation alters heart rate variability in humans with chronic pain. *Experimental Neurology, 223,* 574–581.

Perini, F., Cattaneo, L., Carrasco, M., & Schwarzbach, J. V. (2012). Occipital transcranial magnetic stimulation has an activity-dependent suppressive effect. *Journal of Neuroscience, 32,* 12361–12365.

Perloff, R. M. (2002). The third-person effect. In J. Bryant & D. Zillmann (Eds.), *Media effects: Advances in theory and research* (2nd ed., pp. 489–506). Mahwah, NJ: Erlbaum.

Perrin, J. S., Merz, S., Bennett, D. M., Currie, J., Steele, D. J., et al. (2012). Electroconvulsive therapy reduces frontal cortical connectivity in severe depressive disorder. *Proceedings of the National Academy of Sciences, USA, 109,* 5464–5468.

Perry, J. L., & Carroll, M. E. (2008). The role of impulsive behavior in drug abuse. *Psychopharmacology, 200,* 1–26.

Perry, W., Feifel, D., Minassian, A., Bhattacharjie, B. S., & Braff, D. L. (2002). Information processing deficits in acutely psychotic schizophrenia patients medicated and unmedicated at the time of admission. *American Journal of Psychiatry, 159,* 1375–1381.

Pertwee, R. G., & Ross, R. A. (2002). Cannabinoid receptors and their ligands. *Prostaglandins, Leukotrienes and Essential Fatty Acids, 66,* 101–121.

Perunovic, W. Q. E., Heller, D., Ross, M., & Komar, S. (2011). The within-person dynamics of intrinsic and extrinsic motivation, affective states, and cultural identification: A diary study of bicultural individuals. *Social Psychology and Personality Science, 2,* 635–641.

Pessoa, L., & Adolphs, R. (2010). Emotion processing and the amygdala: From a "low road" to "many roads" of evaluating biological significance. *Nature Reviews, Neuroscience, 11,* 773–783.

Pestian, J. P., Sorter, M., Connolly, B., McCullumsmith, C., Gee, T. J., . . . & Rohlfs, L. (2017). A machine learning approach to identifying the thought markers of suicidal subjects: A prospective multicenter trial. *Suicide and Life-Threatening Behavior.* E-pub ahead of print.

Peters, K. R., Ray, L., Smith, V., & Smith, C. (2008). Changes in the density of stage 2 sleep spindles following motor learning in young and older adults. *Journal of Sleep Research, 17,* 23–33.

Peters, R. M., Hackeman, E., & Goldreich, D. (2009). Diminutive digits discern delicate details: Fingertip size and the sex difference in tactile spatial acuity. *The Journal of Neuroscience, 29,* 15756–15761.

Peterson, C., Seligman, M. E. P., Yurko, K. H., Martin, L. R., & Friedman, H. S. (1998). Catastrophizing and untimely death. *Psychological Science, 9,* 49–52.

Peterson, L., & Peterson, M. (1959). Short-term retention of individual verbal items. *Journal of Experimental Psychology, 58,* 193–198.

Peterson, N. R., Pisoni, D. B., & Miyamoto, R. T. (2010). Cochlear implants and spoken language processing abilities: Review and assessment of the literature. *Restorative Neurology and Neuroscience, 28,* 237–250.

Petrosino, A., Turpin-Petrosino, C., & Buehler, J. (2003). Scared Straight and other juvenile awareness programs for preventing juvenile delinquency: A systematic review of the randomized experimental evidence. *Annals of the American Academy of Political and Social Science, 589,* 41–62.

Petrovich, G. D., & Swanson, L. W. (1997). Projections from the lateral part of the central amygdalar nucleus to the postulated fear conditioning circuit. *Brain Research, 763,* 247–254.

Pettigrew, T. F. (1997). Generalised intergroup contact effects on prejudice. *Personality and Social Psychology Bulletin, 23,* 173–185.

Pettigrew, T. F. (1998). Intergroup contact theory. *Annual Review of Psychology, 49,* 65–85.

Pettigrew, T. F., & Tropp, L. R. (2006). A meta-analytic test of intergroup contact theory. *Journal of Personality and Social Psychology, 90,* 751.

Pfaus, J. G., & Scepkowski, L. A. (2005). The biologic basis for libido. *Current Sexual Health Reports, 2,* 95–100.

Pfaus, J. G., Kippin, T. E., Coria-Avila, G. A., Gelez, H., Afonso, . . . Parade, M. (2012). Who, what, where, when (and maybe even why)? How the experience of sexual reward connects sexual desire, preference, and performance. *Archives of Sexual Behavior, 41,* 31–62.

Pfefferbaum, A., Darley, C. F., Tinklenberg, J. R., Walton, R. T., & Kopell, B. S. (1977). Marijuana and memory intrusions. *Journal of Nervous & Mental Disease, 165,* 165–172.

Phelps, E. A. (2004). Human emotion and memory: Interactions of the amygdala and hippocampal complex. *Current Opinion in Neurobiology, 14,* 198–202.

Phelps, E. A., O'Connor, K. J., Cunningham, W. A., Funayama, S., Gatenby, J. C., . . . Banaji, M. R. (2000). Performance on indirect measures of race evaluation predicts amygdala activation. *Journal of Cognitive Neuroscience 12,* 729–738.

Phillips, D. I. W. (2006). External influences on the fetus and their long-term consequences. *Lupus, 15,* 794–800.

Phillips, M., Brooks-Gunn, J., Duncan, G. J., Klebanov, P. K., & Crane, J. (1998). Family background, parenting practices, and the Black–White test score gap. In C. Jencks & M. Phillips (Eds.), *The Black–White test score gap* (pp. 102–145). Washington, DC: Brookings Institution Press.

Phillips, M. L., Bullmore, E. T., Howard, R., Woodruff, P. W., Wright, I. C., . . . David, A. S. (1998). Investigation of facial recognition memory and happy and sad facial expression perception: An fMRI study. *Psychiatry Research, 83,* 127–138.

Phillips, R. G., & LeDoux, J. E. (1992). Differential contribution of amygdala and hippocampus to cued and contextual fear conditioning. *Behavioral Neuroscience, 106,* 274–285.

Phillips-Silver, J. & Trainor, L. J. (2005). Feeling the beat in music: Movement influences rhythm perception in infants. *Science, 308,* 1430.

Piaget, J., & Inhelder, B. (1956). *The child's conception of space.* Boston: Routledge & Kegan Paul.

Pianezza, M. L., Sellers, E. M., & Tyndale, R. F. (1998). Nicotine metabolism defect reduces smoking. *Nature, 393,* 750.

Pica, P., Jackson, S., Blake, R., & Troje, N. F. (2011). Comparing biological motion perception in two distinct human societies. *PLoS One, 6,* e28391.

Piet, J., Hougaard, E., Hecksher, M. S., & Rosenberg, N. K. (2010). A randomized pilot study of mindfulness-based cognitive therapy and group cognitive-behavioral therapy for young adults with social phobia. *Scandinavian Journal of Psychology, 51,* 403–410.

Pinker, S. (1994). *The language instinct.* New York: William Morrow.

Pinker, S. (1999). *Words and rules: The ingredients of language.* New York: Basic Books.

Pinsker, H., Kupfermann, I., Castellucci, V., & Kandel, E. (1970). Habituation and dishabituation of the gill-withdrawal reflex in *Aplysia. Science, 167,* 1740–1742.

Pizzagalli, D. A., Lehmann, D., Hendrick, A. M., Regard, M., Pascual-Marqui, R. D., & Davidson, R. J. (2002). Affective judgments of faces modulate early activity (~160 ms) within the fusiform gyri. *NeuroImage, 16,* 663–677.

Plant, E. A., & Peruche, B. (2005). The consequences of race for police officers' responses to criminal suspects. *Psychological Science, 16,* 180–183.

Plomin, R., & Caspi, A. (1999). Behavioral genetics and personality. In L. A. Pervin & O. P. John (Eds.), *Handbook of personality: Theory and research* (2nd ed., pp. 251–276). New York, NY: Guilford Press.

Plomin, R., Corley, R., DeFries, J. C., & Fulker, D. W. (1997). Nature, nurture, and cognitive development from 1 to 16 years: A parent–offspring adoption study. *Psychological Science, 8,* 442–447.

Plomin, R., & Crabbe, J. (2000). DNA. *Psychological Bulletin, 126,* 806–828.

Plomin, R., & Spinath, F. M. (2004). Intelligence: Genetics, genes, and genomics. *Journal of Personality and Social Psychology, 86,* 112–129.

Polansky, J. (2016). 2015 numbers: After rebound, film smoking falls to near lows. *Smoke Free Movies.* Retrieved from http://smokefreemovies.ucsf.edu/blog/2015-numbers-after-rebound-film-smoking-falls-near-lows

Polansky, J. R., Titus, K., Lanning, N., & Glantz, S. A. (2013). *Smoking in top-grossing US movies, 2012.* San Francisco: Center for Tobacco Control Research and Education.

Polivy, J., & Herman, C. P. (2002). Causes of eating disorders. *Annual Review of Psychology, 53,* 187–213.

Polivy, J., Herman, C. P., & Coelho, J. S. (2008). Caloric restriction in the presence of attractive food cues: External cues, eating, and weight. *Physiology & Behavior, 94,* 729–733.

Pollack, D., McFarland, B., Mahler, J., & Kovas, A. (2005). Outcomes of patients in a low-intensity, short-duration involuntary outpatient commitment program. *Psychiatric Services, 56,* 863–866.

Polymeropoulos, M. H., Lavedan, C., Leroy, E., Ide, S. E., Dehejia, A., Dutra, A., . . . & Nussbaum, R. L. (1997). Mutation in the alpha-synuclein gene identified in families with Parkinson's disease. *Science, 276,* 2045–2047.

Ponder, C. A., Kliethermes, C. L., Drew, M. R., Muller, J. J., Das, K. K, . . . Palmer, A. A. (2007). Selection for contextual fear conditioning affects anxiety-like behaviors and gene expression. *Genes, Brain & Behavior, 6,* 736–749.

Ponseti, J. Bosinski, H. A., Wolff, S., Peller, M., Jansen, O., . . . Siebner, H. R. (2006). A functional endophenotype for sexual orientiation in humans. *NeuroImage, 33,* 825–833.

Pope, H. G., Gruber, A. J., Hudson, J. I., Cohane, G., Huetis, M. A., & Yurgelun-Todd, D. (2003). Early-onset cannabis use and cognitive deficits: What is the nature of the association? *Drug and Alcohol Dependence, 69,* 303–310.

Porter, R. H., & Winberg, J. (1999). Unique salience of maternal breast odors for newborn infants. *Neuroscience and Biobehavioral Reviews, 23,* 439–449.

Porter, S., ten Brinke, L., & Gustaw, C. (2010). Dangerous decisions: The impact of first impressions of trustworthiness on the evaluation of legal evidence and defendant culpability. *Psychology, Crime & Law, 16,* 1–15.

Poulin-Dubois, D., Blaye, A., Coutya, J., & Bialystok, E. (2011). The effects of bilingualism on toddlers' executive functioning. *Journal of Experimental Child Psychology, 108,* 567–579.

Powell, J. L. (2012). Why climate deniers have no scientific credibility—in one pie chart. *Desmog.* Retrieved from http://www.desmogblog.com/2012/11/15/why-climate-deniers-have-no-credibility-science-one-pie-chart

Powers, M. B., & Emmelkamp, P. M. G. (2008). Virtual reality exposure therapy for anxiety disorders: A meta-analysis. *Journal of Anxiety Disorders 39,* 250–261.

Prentice, D. A., & Miller, D. T. (1993). Pluralistic ignorance and alcohol use on campus: Some consequences of misperceiving the social norm. *Journal of Personality and Social Psychology, 64,* 243.

Price, E. L., McLeod, P. J., Gleich, S. S., & Hand, D. (2006). One-year prevalence rates of major depressive disorder in first-year university students. *Canadian Journal of Counselling, 40,* 68–81.

Price, J. S., McQueeny, T., Shollenbarger, S., Browning, E. L., Wieser, J., & Lisdahl, K. M. (2015). Effects of marijuana use on prefrontal and parietal volumes and cognition in emerging adults. *Psychopharmacology, 232,* 2929–2950.

Prochaska, J. O., & DiClemente, C. C. (1984). Self change processes, self efficacy and decisional balance across five stages of smoking cessation. *Advances in cancer control–1983* (pp. 131–140). New York: Alan R. Liss, Inc.

Prochaska, J. O., & DiClemente, C. C. (1985). Common processes of self-change in smoking, weight control, and psychological distress. In S. Shiffman & T. Wills. (Eds.), *Coping and substance abuse: A conceptual framework* (pp. 345–363). New York: Academic Press.

Prochaska, J. O., & Norcross, J. C. (2002). Stage of change. In J. C. Norcross (Ed.), *Psychotherapy relationships that work* (pp. 303–313). New York: Oxford.

Propper R. E., Stickgold, R., Keeley, R., & Christman, S. D. (2007). Is television traumatic? Dreams, stress, and media exposure in the aftermath of September 11, 2001. *Psychological Science, 18,* 334–340.

Public Health Agency of Canada. (2002). *A report on mental illnesses in Canada.* Retrieved from http://www.phac-aspc.gc.ca/publicat/miic-mmac/chap_4-eng.php

Public Health Agency of Canada. (2013). *Leading causes of death, Canada, 2008.* Retrieved from: http://www.phac-aspc.gc.ca/publicat/lcd-pcd97/pdf/lcd-pcd-t1-eng.pdf

Public Health Agency of Canada. (2014). *Sudden Infant Death Syndrome (SIDS) in Canada.* Retrieved from: http://publications.gc.ca/collections/collection_2015/aspc-phac/HP35-51-2014-eng.pdf

Pujol, J., Soriano-Mas, C., Ortiz, H., Sebastian-Galles, N., Losilla, J. M., & Deus, J. (2006). Myelination of language-related areas in the developing brain. *Neurology, 66,* 339–343.

Pulvermüller, F., & Berthier, M. L. (2008). Aphasia therapy on a neuroscience basis. *Aphasiology, 22,* 563–599.

Putnam, F. W. (1989). *Diagnosis and treatment of multiple personality disorder.* New York: Guilford Press.

Qu, S., Olafsrud, S. M., Meza-Zepeda, L. A., & Saatcioglu, F. (2013). Rapid gene expression changes in peripheral blood lymphocytes upon practice of a comprehensive yoga program. *Public Library of Science One, 8,* 1–8.

Quirk, G. J., & Beer, J. S. (2006). Prefrontal involvement in the regulation of emotion: Convergence of rat and human studies. *Current Opinion in Neurobiology, 16,* 723–727.

Rada, P., Avena, N. M., & Hoebel, B. G. (2005). Daily bingeing on sugar repeatedly releases dopamine in the accumbens shell. *Neuroscience, 134,* 737–744.

Raffi, A. R., Rondini, M., Grandi, S., & Fava, G. A. (2000). Life events and prodromal symptoms in bulimia nervosa. *Psychological Medicine, 30,* 727–731.

Raichle, M. E. (2015). The brain's default mode network. *Annual Review of Neuroscience, 38,* 433–447.

Raichle, M. E., MacLeod, A. M., Snyder, A. Z., Powers, W. J., Gusnard, D. A., & Shulman, G. L. (2001). A default mode of brain function. *Proceedings of the National Academy of Sciences USA, 98,* 676–682.

Rainforth, M. V., Schneider, R. H., Nidich, S. I., Gaylord-King, C., Salerno, J. W., & Anderson, J. W. (2007). Stress reduction programs in patients with elevated blood pressure: A systematic review and meta-analysis. *Current Hypertension Reports, 9,* 520–528.

Raji, C. A., Ho, A. J., Parikshak, N. N., Becker, J. T., Lopez, O. L., . . . Thompson, P. M. (2010). Brain structure and obesity. *Human Brain Mapping, 31,* 353–364.

Ramachandran, V. S., & Altschuler, E. L. (2009). The use of visual feedback, in particular mirrorvisual feedback, in restoring brain function. *Brain, 132,* 1693–1710.

Ramachandran, V. S., & Gregory, R. L. (1991). Perceptual filling in of artificially induced scotomas in human vision. *Nature, 350,* 699–702.

Ramachandran, V. S., & Hubbard, E. M. (2003). The phenomenology of synaesthesia. *Journal of Consciousness Studies, 10,* 49–57.

Ramakrishnan, U., Manjrekar, R., Rivera, J., Gonzáles-Cossío, T., & Martorell, R. (1999). Micronutrients and pregnancy outcome: A review of the literature. *Nutrition Research, 19,* 103–159.

Ranganath, C., Johnson, M. K., & D'Esposito, M. (2003). Prefrontal activity associated with working memory and episodic long-term memory. *Neuropsychologia, 41,* 378–389.

Ranganathan, M., & D'Souza, D. C. (2006). The acute effects of cannabinoids on memory in humans: A review. *Psychopharmacology, 188,* 425–444.

Ransdell, S. E., & Fischler, I. (1987). Memory in a monolingual mode: When are bilinguals at a disadvantage. *Journal of Memory and Language, 26,* 392–405.

Rasmussen, E. B., & Newland, M. C. (2008). Asymmetry of reinforcement and punishment in human choice. *Journal of the Experimental Analysis of Behavior, 89,* 157–167.

Rauscher, F. H., Shaw, G. L., & Ky, K. N. (1993). Music and spatial task performance. *Nature, 365,* 611.

Ravindran, A. V., Balneaves, L. G., Faulkner, G., Ortiz, A., McIntosh, D., . . . & the CANMAT Depression Work Group (2016). Canadian Network for Mood and Anxiety Treatments (CANMAT) 2016 clinical guidelines for the management of adults with major depressive disorder: Section 5. Complementary and alternative treatments. *Canadian Journal of Psychiatry, 61,* 576–587.

Raynor, H. A., & Epstein, L. (2003). The relative-reinforcing value of food under differing levels of food deprivation and restriction. *Appetite, 40*, 15–24.

Raz, A., Fan, J., & Posner, M. I. (2005). Hypnotic suggestion reduces conflict in the human brain. *Proceedings of the National Academy of Sciences, 102*, 9978–9983.

Raz, N. (2000). Aging of the brain and its impact on cognitive performance: Integration of structural and functional findings. In F. I. M. Craik & T. A. Salthouse (Eds.), *Handbook of aging and cognition—II.* (pp. 1–90). Mahwah, NJ: Lawrence Erlbaum Associates.

Razzini, C., Bianchi, F., Leo, R., Fortuna, E., Siracusano, A., & Romeo, F. (2008). Correlations between personality factors and coronary artery disease: From type A behaviour pattern to type D personality. *Journal of Cardiovascular Medicine, 9*, 761–768.

Rechtschaffen, A. (1998). Current perspectives on the function of sleep. *Perspectives in Biological Medicine, 41*, 359–390.

Reed, T. E., Vernon, P. A., & Johnson, A. M. (2004). Confirmation of correlation between brain nerve conduction velocity and intelligence level in normal adults. *Intelligence, 32*, 563–572.

Regan, B. C., Julliot, C., Simmen, B., Vienot, F., Charles-Dominique, P., & Mollon, J. D. (2001). Frutis, foliage and the evolution of primate colour vision. *Philosophical Transactions of the Royal Society B: Biological Sciences, 356*, 229–283.

Rehm, J., Baliunas, D., Brochu, S., Fischer, B., Gnam, W., Patra, J., et al. (2006). *The costs of substance abuse in Canada 2002.* Ottawa: Canadian Centre on Substance Abuse.

Reichert, T. (2003). *The erotic history of advertising.* Amherst, NY: Prometheus.

Reichert, T. (2012). Sex in advertising research: A review of content, effects, and functions of sexual information in consumer advertising. *Annual Review of Sex Research, 13*, 241–273.

Reichert, T., & Alvaro, E. (2001). The effects of sexual information on ad and brand processing and recall. *Southwestern Mass Communication Journal, 17*, 9–17.

Reichert, T., Childers, C. C., & Reid, L. N. (2012). How sex in advertising varies by product category: An analysis of three decades of visual sexual imagery in magazine advertising. *Journal of Current Issues & Research in Advertising, 33*, 1–19.

Reichert, T., Heckler, S. E., & Jackson, S. (2001). The effects of sexual social marketing appeals on cognitive processing and persuasion. *Journal of Advertising, 30*, 13–27.

Reilly, S., & Bornovalova, M. A. (2005). Conditioned taste aversion and amygdala lesions in the rat: A critical review. *Neuroscience & Biobehavioral Reviews, 29*, 1067–1088.

Reinders, A. T. S., Nijenhuis, E. R. S., Paans, A. M. J., Korf, J., Willemsen, A. T. M., & den Boer, J. A. (2003). One brain, two selves. *NeuroImage, 20*, 2119–2125.

Reingen, P. H., & Kernan, J. B. (1993). Social perception and interpersonal influence: Some consequences of the physical attractiveness stereotype in a personal selling setting. *Journal of Consumer Psychology, 2*, 25–38.

Reisenzen, R., & Studtman, M. (2007). On the expression and experience of surprise: No evidence for facial feedback, but evidence for a reverse self-inference effect. *Emotion, 7*, 612–627.

Reissland, N. (1988). Neonatal imitation in the first hour of life: Observations in rural Nepal. *Developmental Psychology, 24*, 464–469.

Reiter, E. O., & Lee, P. A. (2001). Have the onset and tempo of puberty changed? *Archives of Pediatrics & Adolescent Medicine, 155*, 988–989.

Remafedi, G., Resnick, M., Blum, R., & Harris, L. (1992). Demography of sexual orientation in adolescents. *Pediatrics, 89*, 714–721.

Rendell, L., & Whitehead, H. (2001). Culture in whales and dolphins. *Behavioral and Brain Sciences, 24*, 309–382.

Renner, M., & Mackin, R. (1998). A life stress instrument for classroom use. *Teaching of Psychology, 25*, 46–48.

Rensink, R. A., O'Regan, J. K., & Clark, J. J. (1997). To see or not to see: The need for attention to perceive changes in scenes. *Psychological Science, 8*, 368–373.

Rensink, R. A., O'Regan, J. K., & Clark J. J. (2000). On the failure to detect changes in scenes across brief interruptions. *Visual Cognition, 7*, 127–145.

Rhodes, G. (2006). The evolutionary psychology of facial beauty. *Annual Review of Psychology, 57*, 199–226.

Ricciardelli, L. A., & McCabe, M. P. (2004). A biopsychosocial model of disordered eating and the pursuit of muscularity in adolescent boys. *Psychological Bulletin, 130*, 179–205.

Richardson, P. J., & Boyd, R. (2005). *Not by genes alone: How culture transformed human evolution.* Chicago: University of Chicago Press.

Richdale, J. (Writer), & Kirland, M. (Director). (1994). Burns' Heir [Television series episode]. In J. L. Brooks & M. Groening (Producers), *The Simpsons.* Los Angeles, CA: 20th Century Fox Television.

Richert, R. A., Robb, M. B., Fender, J. G., & Wartella, E. (2010). Word learning from baby videos. *Archives of Pediatrics & Adolescent Medicine, 164*, 432–437.

Richmond, D., & Hartman, P. T. (1982). Sex appeal in advertising. *Journal of Advertising Research, 22*, 53–61.

Rideout, V., & Hamel, E. (2006). *The media family: Electronic media in the lives of infants, toddlers, preschoolers, and their parents.* Menlo Park, CA: Henry J. Kaiser Foundation.

Rieber, R., & Robinson, D. (Eds.). (1980). *Wilhelm Wundt and the making of a scientific psychology.* New York: Kluwer Academic/Plenum Publishers.

Rieger, G., & Savin-Williams, R. C. (2012). Gender nonconformity, sexual orientation, and psychological well-being. *Archives of Sexual Behavior, 41*, 611–621.

Rifkin, A., Ghisalbert, D., Dimatou, S., Jin, C., & Sethi, M. (1998). Dissociative identity disorder in psychiatric inpatients. *American Journal of Psychiatry, 155*, 844–845.

Riggle, E. D. B., Rostosky, S. S., & Horne, S. G. (2010). Psychological distress, well-being, and legal recognition in same-sex couple relationships. *Journal of Family Psychology, 24*, 82–86.

Risko, E. F., Anderson, N., Sarwal, A., Engelhardt, M., & Kingstone, A. (2012). Everyday attention: Variation in mind wandering and memory in a lecture. *Applied Cognitive Psychology, 26*, 234–242.

Ritterband, L., Thorndike, F., Gonder-Frederick, L., Magee, J., Bailey, E., Saylor, D., et al. (2009). Efficacy of an Internet-based behavioral intervention for adults with insomnia. *Archives of General Psychiatry, 66*, 692–698.

Riva, G. (2005). Virtual reality in psychotherapy: Review. *CyberPsychology & Behavior, 8*, 220–240.

Rivera, S. M., Wakeley, A., & Langer, J. (1999). The drawbridge phenomenon: Representational reasoning or perceptual preference. *Developmental Psychology, 35*, 427–435.

Rizzo, A. S., Difede, J., Rothbaum, B. O., Reger, G., Spitalnick, J., Cukor, J., & McLay, R. (2010). Development and early evaluation of the Virtual Iraq/Afghanistan exposure therapy system for combat-related PTSD. *Annals of the New York Academie of Sciences, 1208*, 114–125.

Rizzolatti, G., & Craighero, L. (2004). The mirror-neuron system. *Annual Review of Neuroscience, 27*, 169–192.

Rizzolatti, G., Fadiga, L., Fogassi, L., & Gallese, V. (1996). Premotor cortex and the recognition of motor actions. *Cognitive Brain Research, 3*, 131–141.

Robb, M. B., Richert, R. A., & Wartella, E. A. (2009). Just a talking book? Word learning from watching baby videos. *British Journal of Developmental Psychology, 27*, 27–45.

Robbins, T. W. (2000). Chemical neuromodulation of frontal-executive functions in humans and other animals. *Experimental Brain Research, 133*, 130–138.

Robbins, T. W., Jones, G. H., & Wilkinson, L. S. (1996). Behavioural and neurochemical effects of early social deprivation in the rat. *Journal of Psychopharmacology, 10*, 39–47.

Roberts, B. W., & DelVecchio, W. F. (2000). The rank-order consistency of personality from childhood to old age: A quantitative review of longitudinal studies. *Psychological Bulletin, 126*, 3–25.

Roberts, B., Walton, K., & Viechtbauer, W. (2006). Patterns of mean-level change in personality traits across the life course: A meta-analysis of longitudinal studies. *Psychological Bulletin, 132*, 1–25.

Roberts, P. M., Garcia, L. J., Desrochers, A., & Hernandez, D. (2002). English performance of proficient bilingual adults on the Boston Naming Test. *Aphasiology, 16*, 635–645.

Roberts, R., Roberts, C., & Duong, H. (2009). Sleepless in adolescence: Prospective data on sleep deprivation, health and functioning. *Journal of Adolescence, 32*, 1045–1057.

Robertson, S. I. (2001). *Problem solving.* New York: Psychology Press.

Robinson, P. N., Krawitz, P., & Mundlos, S. (2011). Strategies for exome and genome sequence data analysis in disease-gene discovery projects. *Clinical Genetics, 80*, 127–132.

Roblaes, T., Glaser, R., & Kiecolt-Glaser, J. (2005). Out of balance: A new look at chronic stress, depression, and immunity.*Current Directions in Psychological Science, 14*, 111–115.

Robleto, K., Poulos, A. M, & Thompson, R. F. (2004). Brain mechanisms of extinction of the classically conditioned eyeblink response. *Learning & Memory, 11*, 517–524.

Rocca, M. A., Valsasina, P., Absinta, M., Riccitelli, G., Rodegher, M. E., . . . Filippi, M. (2010). Default-mode network dysfunction and cognitive impairment in progressive MS. *Neurology, 74*, 1252–1259.

Rocca, M. A., Valsasina, P., Martinelli, V., Misci, P., Falini, A., . . . Filippi, M. (2012). Large-scale neuronal network dysfunction in relapsing-remitting multiple sclerosis. *Neurology, 79*, 1449–1457.

Rochlen, A., McKelley, R., & Pituch, K. (2006). A preliminary examination of the "Real Men. Real Depression" campaign. *Psychology of Men & Masculinity, 7*, 1–13.

Roe, D., & Finger, S. (1996). Gustave Dax and his fight for recognition: An overlooked chapter in the early history of cerebral dominance. *Journal of the History of the Neurosciences, 5*, 228–240.

Roediger, H., Agarwal, P. K., Kang, S. K., & Marsh, E. J. (2010). Benefits of testing memory: Best practices and boundary conditions. In G. M. Davies & D. B. Wright (Eds.), *Current issues in applied memory research* (pp. 13–49). New York: Psychology Press.

Roediger, H. L., & McDermott, K. B. (1995). Creating false memories: Remembering words not presented in lists. *Journal of Experimental Psychology: Learning, Memory, and Cognition, 21*, 803–814.

Rogers, J. M. (2009). Tobacco and pregnancy. *Reproductive Toxicology, 28*, 152–160.

Rogers, J., Kochunov, P., Zilles, K., et al. (2010). On the genetic architecture of cortical folding and brain volume in primates. *Neuroimage, 53*, 1103–1108.

Rogoff, B., Mistry, J., Goncu, A., & Mosier, C. (1993). Guided participation in cultural activity by toddles and caregivers. *Monographs for the Society of Research in Child Development, 58* (serial no. 236).

Rollins, B. C. (1989). Marital quality at midlife. In S. Hunter & M. Sundel (Eds.), *Midlife myths* (pp. 184–194). Newbury Park, CA: Sage.

Rolls, E. T. (2010). Neural representation of fat texture in the mouth. In J-P. Montmayeur & J. le Coutre (Eds.), *Fat detection: Taste, texture, and post ingestive effects* (pp. 197–223). Boca Raton, FL: CRC Press.

Rorty, M., Yager, J., Rossotto, E., & Buckwalter, G. (2000). Parental intrusiveness in adolescence recalled by women with a history of bulimia nervosa and comparison women. *International Journal of Eating Disorders, 28*, 202–208.

Rosch, E. H. (1973). Natural categories. *Cognitive Psychology, 4*, 328–350.

Rosch, E., & Mervis, C. B. (1975). Family resemblances: Studies in the internal structure of categories. *Cognitive Psychology, 7*, 573–605.

Rosch, E., Mervis, C. B., Gray, W., Johnson, D., & Boyes-Braem, P. (1976). Basic objects in natural categories. *Cognitive Psychology, 8*, 382–439.

Rose, D., Wykes, T., Leese, M., Bindman, J., & Fleischmann, P. (2003). Patients' perspectives on electroconvulsive therapy: Systematic review. *British Medical Journal, 326*, 1363–1368.

Rose, N., Myerson, J., Roediger, H., & Hale, S. (2010). Similarities and differences between working memory and long-term memory: Evidence from the levels-of-processing span task. *Journal of Experimental Psychology: Learning, Memory, and Cognition, 36*, 471–483.

Roselli, C. E., Larkin, K., Schrunk, J. M., & Stormshak, F. (2004). Sexual partner preference, hypothalamic morphology and aromatase in rams. *Physiology and Behavior, 83*, 233–245.

Rosenbaum, R. S., Kohler, S., Schacter, D. L., Moscovitch, M., Westmacott, R., Black, S. E., et al. (2005). The case of K.C.: Contributions of a memory-impaired person to memory theory. *Neuropsychologia, 43*, 989–1021.

Rosenblum, G. D., & Lewis, M. (2003). Emotional development in adolescence. In G. D. Rosenblum & M. Lewis (Eds.), *Blackwell Handbook of Adolescence* (pp. 269–289). Malden: Blackwell Publishing.

Rosenfield, S. (1997). Labeling mental illness: The effects of received services and perceived stigma on life satisfaction. *American Sociological Review, 62*, 660–672.

Rosenhan, D. L. (1973). On being sane in insane places. *Science, 179*, 250–258.

Rosenthal, R. (1974). *On the social psychology of the self-fulfilling prophecy: Further evidence for Pygmalion effects and their mediating mechanisms.* New York: MSS Modular Publications.

Rosenthal, R., & Fode, K. L. (1963). The effect of experimenter bias on the performance of the albino rat. *Behavioral Science, 8*, 183–189.

Rosenthal, R., & Jacobson, L. (1966). Teachers' expectancies: Determinates of pupils' IQ gains. *Psychological Reports, 19*, 115–118.

Rosenthal, R., & Jacobson, L. (1968). *Pygmalion in the classroom: Teacher expectation and pupils' intellectual development.* New York: Holt, Rinehart & Winston.

Rosenzweig, M. R., Krech, D., Bennett, E. L., & Diamond, M. C. (1962). Effects of environmental complexity and training on brain chemistry and anatomy: A replication and extension. *Journal of Comparative and Physiological Psychology, 55*, 429–437.

Ross, C. E., Mirowsky, J., & Goldsteen, K. (1990). The impact of the family on health: The decade in review. *Journal of Marriage and the Family, 52*, 1059–1078.

Ross, L. (1977). The intuitive psychologist and his shortcomings. Distortions in the attribution process. In L. Berkowitz (Ed.), *Advances in experimental social psychology* (Vol. 10). New York: Academic Press.

Ross, L., & Ward, A. (1996). Naive realism in everyday life: Implications for social conflict and misunderstanding. In T. Brown, E. S. Reed, & E. Turiel (Eds.), *Values and knowledge* (pp. 103–135). Hillsdale, NJ: Erlbaum.

Ross, M., & Wang, Q. (2010). Why we remember and what we remember: Culture and autobiographical memory. *Perspectives on Psychological Science, 5*, 401–409.

Ross, M., & Wilson, A. E. (2000). Constructing and appraising past selves. In D. L. Schacter & E. Scarry (Eds.), *Memory, brain and belief* (pp. 231–258). Cambridge, MA: Harvard University Press.

Rosselli, M., Ardila, A., Araujo, K., Weekes, V. A., Caracciolo, V., Padilla, M., et al. (2000). Verbal fluency and repetition skills in healthy older Spanish–English bilinguals. *Applied Neuropsychology, 7*, 17–24.

Rossini, P. M., Altamura, C., Ferretti, A., Vernieri, F., Zappasodi, F., Caulo, M., et al. (2004). Does cerebrovascular disease affect the coupling between neuronal activity and local haemodynamics? *Brain, 127*, 99–110.

Rotermann, M. (2008). Trends in teen sexual behaviour and condom use. *Health Reports, 19*, 53–57.

Roth, S. H., Fleischmann, R. M., Burch, F. X., Dietz, F., Bockow, B., Rapoport, R. J., et al. (2000). Around-the-clock, controlled-release oxycodone therapy for osteoarthritis-related pain: Placebo-controlled trial and long-term evaluation. *Archives of Internal Medicine, 160*, 853–860.

Rothbart, M. K., & Bates, J. E. (2006). Temperament. In W. Damon, R. Lerner, & N. Eisenberg (Eds.), *Handbook of child psychology: Vol. 3. Social, emotional, and personality development* (6th ed., pp. 99–166). New York: Wiley.

Rouder, J. N., & Ratcliff, R. (2004). Comparing categorization models. *Journal of Experimental Psychology: General, 133*, 63–82.

Rouder, J. N., & Ratcliff, R. (2006). Comparing exemplar- and rule-based theories of categorization. *Current Directions in Psychological Science, 15*, 9–13.

Rowe, R., Maughan, B., Worthman, C. M., Costello, E. J., & Angold, A. (2004). Testosterone, antisocial behavior, and social dominance in boys: Pubertal development and biosocial interaction. *Biological Psychiatry, 55*, 546–552.

Rozanski, A., Blumenthal, J. A., & Kaplan, J. (1999). Impact of psychological factors on the pathogenesis of cardiovascular disease and implications for therapy. *Circulation, 99*, 2192–2217.

Rubin, D., & Wenzel, A. (1996). One hundred years of forgetting: A quantitative description of retention. *Psychological Review, 103*, 734–760.

Rudman, L. A., Feinburg, J., & Fairchild, K. (2002). Minority members' implicit attitudes: Automatic ingroup bias as a function of group status. *Social Cognition, 20*, 294–320.

Rule, N. O., & Ambady, N. (2008). Brief exposures: Male sexual orientation is accurately perceived at 50 ms. *Journal of Experimental Social Psychology, 44*, 1100–1105.

Rule, N. O., & Ambady, N. (2010). Democrats and Republicans can be differentiated from their faces. *PLoS ONE, 5*, e8733.

Rule, N. O., Macrae, C. N., & Ambady, N. (2009). Ambiguous group membership is extracted automatically from faces. *Psychological Science, 20*, 441–443.

Rusak, B. (1979). Neural mechanisms for entrainment and generation of mammalian circadian rhythms. *Federation Proceedings, 38*, 2589–2595.

Ruseckaite, R., Maddess, T., Danta, G., Lueck, C. J., & James, A.C. (2005). Sparse multifocal stimuli for the detection of multiple sclerosis. *Annals of Neurology, 57*, 904–913.

Rushton, J. P., & Jensen, A. R. (2005). Thirty years of research on race differences in cognitive ability. *Psychology, Public Policy, and Law, 11*, 235–294.

Ryan, R. M., & Deci, E. L. (2000). Self-determination theory and the facilitation of intrinsic motivation, social development, and well-being. *American Psychologist, 55*, 68–78.

Sacerdote, B. (2001). Peer effects with random assignment: Results for Dartmouth roommates. *Quarterly Journal of Economics, 116*, 681–704.

Sachs, G. T. L. (1812). *Historiae naturalis duorum leucaetiopum: Auctoris ipsius et sororis eius*. Erlangen. [Online]. Retrieved from http://mdz10.bib-bvb.de/~db/0001/bsb00012567/images/

Sack, K. (1998, January 15). Georgia's governor seeks musical start for babies. *The New York Times*, p. A12.

Safdar, S. F., & Lay, C. H. (2003). The relations of immigrant-specific and immigrant-nonspecific daily hassles to distress controlling for psychological adjustment and cultural competence. *Journal of Applied Social Psychology, 33*, 299–320.

Sagberg, F. (1999). Road accidents caused by drivers falling asleep. *Accident Analysis & Prevention, 31*, 639–649.

Saha, S., Chant, D., Welham, J., & McGrath, J. (2005). A systematic review of the prevalence of schizophrenia. *PLoS Medicine, 2*(5), e141.

Sahakian, B., & Morein-Zamir, S. (2007). Professor's little helper. *Nature, 450*, 1157–1159.

Sahdra, B. K., MacLean, K. A., Ferrer, E., Shaver, P. R., Rosenberg, E. L., Jabocs, T. L., et al. (2011). Enhanced response inhibition during intensive meditation training predicts improvements in self-reported adaptive socioemotional functioning. *Emotion, 11*, 299–312.

Salo, R., Ursu, S., Buonocore, M. H., Leamon, M. H., & Carter, C. (2010). Impaired prefrontal cortical functioning disrupted adaptive cognitive control in methamphetamine abusers: An fMRI study. *Biological Psychiatry, 65*, 706–709.

Salthouse, T. A. (1987). The role of representations in age differences in analogical reasoning. *Psychology and Aging, 2*, 357–362.

Salvatore, J. E., I-Chun Kuo, S., Steele, R. D., Simpson, J. A., & Collins, W. A. (2011). Recovering from conflict in romantic relationships: A developmental perspective. *Psychological Science, 22*, 376–383.

Sargent, J. D. (2005). Smoking in the movies: Impact on adolescent smoking. *Adolescent Medicine, 16*, 345–370.

Satel, S. & Lilienfeld, S. O. (2013). Addiction and the brain-disease fallacy. *Frontiers in Psychiatry, 3*, 141.

Saucier, G., Bel-Bahar, T., & Fernandez, C. (2007). What modifies the expression of personality tendencies? Defining basic domains of situation variables. *Journal of Personality, 75*, 479–504.

Saucier, G., Georgiades, S., Tsaousis, I., & Goldberg, L. R. (2005). The factor structure of Greek personality adjectives. *Journal of Personality and Social Psychology, 88*, 856–875.

Saus, E., Johnsen, B., Eid, J., Riisem, P., Andersen, R., & Thayer, J. (2006). The effect of brief situational awareness training in a police shooting simulator: An experimental study. *Military Psychology, 18*, s3–s21.

Savage-Rumbaugh, S., & Lewin, R. (1994). *Kanzi: The ape at the brink of the human mind*. New York: Wiley.

Savic, I., Berglund, H., Lindström, P., & Gustafsson, J. (2005). Brain response to putative pheromones in homosexual men. *Proceedings of the National Academy of Sciences of the United States of America, 102*, 7356–7361.

Savic, I., & Lindström, P. (2008). PET and MRI show differences in cerebral asymmetry and functional connectivity between homo- and heterosexual subjects. *Proceedings of the National Academy of Sciences of the United States of America, 105*, 9403–9408.

Savin-Williams, R. C., & Cohen, K. M. (2004). Homoerotic development during childhood and adolescence. *Child Adolescent Psychiatric Clinics of North America, 13*, 529–549.

Saxon, A. H. (1989). *P. T. Barnum: The legend and the man*. New York: Columbia University Press.

Schachter, S., & Singer, J. (1962). Cognitive, social, and physiological determinants of emotional state. *Psychological Review, 69*, 379–399.

Schacter, D. L. (1985). Priming of old and new knowledge in amnesic patients and normal subjects. *Annals of the New York Academy of Sciences, 444*, 41–53.

Schaie, K. W. (1994). The course of adult intellectual development. *American Psychologist, 49*, 304–313.

Scheier, M. F., & Carver, C. S. (1985). Optimism, coping, and health: Assessment and implications of generalized outcome expectancies. *Health Psychology, 4*, 219–247.

Schenck, C. H., Arnulf, I., & Mahowald, M. W. (2007). Sleep and sex: what can go wrong? A review of the literature on sleep-related disorders and abnormal sexual behaviours and experiences. *Sleep, 30*, 683–702.

Schenck, C. H., Lee, S. A., Bornemann, M. A., & Mahowald, M. W. (2009). Potentially lethal behaviors associated with rapid eye movement sleep behavior disorder: Review of the literature and forensic implications. *Journal of Forensic Science, 54*, 1475–1484.

Schenck, C. H., & Mahowald, M. (2002). REM sleep behavior disorder: Clinical, developmental, and neuroscience perspectives 16 years after its formal identification. *Sleep, 25*, 120–138.

Schierenbeck, T., Riemann, D., Berger, M., & Hornyak, M. (2008). Effect of illicit recreational drugs upon sleep: Cocaine, ecstasy and marijuana. *Sleep Medicine Reviews, 12*, 381–389.

Schimel, J., Hayes, J., Williams, T., & Jahrig, J. (2007). Is death really the worm at the core? Converging evidence that worldview threat increases death-thought accessibility. *Journal of Personality and Social Psychology, 92*, 789–803.

Schinka, J. A., Busch, R. M., & Robichaux-Keene, N. (2004). A meta-analysis of the association between the serotonin transporter gene polymorphism (5HTTLPR) and trait anxiety. *Molecular Psychiatry, 9*, 197–202.

Schlaug, G., Marchina, S., & Norton, A. (2009). Evidence for plasticity in white matter tracts of chronic aphasic patients undergoing intense intonation-based speech therapy. *Annals of the New York Academy of Sciences, 1169*, 385–394.

Schlaug, G., Renga, V., & Nair, D. (2008). Transcranial direct current stimulation in stroke recovery. *Archives of Neurology, 65*, 1571–1576.

Schmader, T., Johns, M., & Forbes, C. (2008). An integrated process model of stereotype threat effects on performance. *Psychological Review, 115*, 336–356.

Schmahmann, J. D. (2004). Disorders of the cerebellum: Ataxia, dysmetria of thought, and the cerebellar cognitive affective syndrome. *Journal of Neuropsychiatry and Clinical Neuroscience, 16*, 367–378.

Schmahmann, J. D., & Sherman, J. C. (1998). The cerebellar cognitive affective syndrome. *Brain, 121*, 561–579.

Schmidt, F. L., & Hunter, J. E. (1993). Tacit knowledge, practical intelligence, general mental ability and job knowledge. *Current Directions in Psychological Science, 2*, 8–9.

Schmidt, F. L., & Hunter, J. E. (1998). The validity and utility of selection methods in personnel psychology: Practical and theoretical implications of 85 years of research findings. *Psychological Bulletin, 124*, 262–274.

Schmidt, M., & Butterweck, V. (2015). The mechanisms of action of St. John's wort: An update. *Wiener Medizinische Wochenschrift, 165*, 229–235.

Schmidt, M. E., Pempek, T. A., Kirkorian, H. L., Lund, A. F., & Anderson, D. R. (2008). The effect of background television on the toy play behavior of very young children. *Child Development, 79*, 1137–1151.

Schmidt, M. E., Rich, M., Rifas-Shiman, S. L., Oken, E., & Traveras, E. M. (2009). Viewing television in infancy and child cognition at 3 years of age in a US cohort. *Pediatrics, 123,* e370–e375.

Schmidt, U., Humfress, H., & Treasure, J. (1997). The role of general family environment and sexual and physical abuse in the origins of eating disorders. *European Eating Disorders Review, 5,* 184–207.

Schmitt, D. P., Allik, J., McCrae, R. R., Benet-Martinez, V., et al. (2007). The geographic distribution of Big Five personality traits: Patterns and profiles of human self-descriptions across 56 nations. *Journal of Cross-Cultural Psychology, 38,* 173–212.

Schmitt, D. P., Realo, A., Voracek, M., & Allik, J. (2008). Why can't a man be more like a woman? Sex differences in Big Five personality traits across 55 cultures. *Journal of Personality and Social Psychology, 94,* 168–182.

Schmolk, H., Buffalo, E. A., & Squire, L. R. (2000). Memory distortions develop over time: Recollections of the O. J. Simpson trial verdict after 15 and 32 months. *Psychological Science, 11,* 39–45.

Schnakers, C., Vanhaudenhuyse, A., Giacino, J., Ventura, M., Boly, M., Majerus, S., et al. (2009). Diagnostic accuracy of the vegetative and minimally conscious state: Clinical consensus versus standardized neurobehavioral assessment. *BMC Neurology, 9,* 35.

Schnall, S., Haidt, J., Clore, G. L., & Jordan, A. H. (2008). Disgust as embodied moral judgment. *Personality and Social Psychology Bulletin, 34,* 1096–1109.

Schneider, S. M., Kisby, C. K., & Flint, E. P. (2011). Effect of virtual reality on time perception in patients receiving chemotherapy. *Support Care Cancer, 19,* 555–564.

Schoenberger, N. E., Kirsch, I., Gearan, P., Montgomery, G., Pastyrnak, S., et al. (1997). Hypnotic enhancement of a cognitive behavioral treatment for public speaking anxiety. *Behavior Therapy, 28,* 127–140.

Scholz, J., Klein, M.C., Behrens, T.E.J., & Johansen-Berg, H. (2009). Training induces in white-matter architecture. *Nature Neuroscience, 12,* 1370–1371.

Schottenbauer, M. A., Momenan, R., Kerick, M., & Hommer, D. W. (2007). Relationships among aging, IQ, and intracranial volume in alcoholics and control subjects. *Neuropsychology, 21,* 337–345.

Schredl, M. (2001). Night terrors in children: Prevalence and influencing factors. *Sleep and Hypnosis, 3,* 68–72.

Schredl, M. (2003). Effects of state and trait factors on nightmare frequency. *European Archives of Psychiatry and Clinical Neuroscience, 253,* 241–247.

Schreurs, B. G. (1993). Long-term memory and extinction of the classically conditioned rabbit nictitating membrane response. *Learning and Motivation, 24,* 293–302.

Schreurs, B. G., Gusev, P. A., Tomsic, D., Alkon, D. L., & Shi, T. (1998). Intracellular correlates of acquisition and long-term memory of classical conditioning in Purkinje cell dendrites in slices of rabbit cerebellar lobule HVI. *Journal of Neuroscience, 18,* 5498–5507.

Schroeder, D. A., Penner, L. A., Dovidio, J. F., & Piliavin, J. A. (1995). *The psychology of helping and altruism: Problems and puzzles.* New York: McGraw-Hill.

Schroers, M., Prigot, J., & Fagen, J. (2007). The effect of a salient odor context on memory retrieval in young infants. *Infant Behavior and Development, 30,* 685–689.

Schultheiss, O. C., & Brunstein, J. C. (2001). Assessing implicit motives with a research version of the TAT: Picture profiles, gender differences, and relations to other personality measures. *Journal of Personality Assessment, 77,* 71–86.

Schultheiss, O. C., Wirth, M. M., Torges, C. M., Pang, J. S., Villacorta, M. A., & Welsh, K. M. (2005). Effects of implicit power motivation on men's and women's implicit learning and testosterone changes after social victory or defeat. *Journal of Personality and Social Psychology, 88,* 174–188.

Schultz, P. W., & Zelezny, L. (2003). Reframing environmental messages to be congruent with American values. *Human Ecology Review, 10,* 126–136.

Schultz, W. (1998). Predictive reward signal of dopamine neurons. *Journal of Neurophysiology, 80,* 1–27.

Schultz, W. (2000). Multiple reward signals in the brain. *Nature Reviews Neuroscience, 1,* 199–207.

Schultz, W., & Dickinson, A. (2000). Neuronal coding of prediction errors. *Annual Review of Neuroscience, 23,* 473–500.

Schultz, W., Tremblay, L., & Hollerman, J. R. (2000). Reward processing in primate orbitofrontal cortex and basal ganglia. *Cerebral Cortex, 10,* 272–283.

Schulz-Hardt, S., Frey, D., Luthgens, C., & Moscovici, S. (2000). Biased information search in group decision making. *Journal of Personality and Social Psychology, 78,* 655–669.

Schutter, D. J. L. G., Hofman, D., & Van Honk, J. (2008). Fearful faces selectively increase corticospinal motor tract excitability: A transcranial magnetic stimulation study. *Psychophysiology, 45,* 345–348.

Schwartz, B., Ward, A., Monterosso, J., Lyubomirsky, S., White, K., & Lehman, D. R. (2002). Maximizing versus satisficing: Happiness is a matter of choice. *Journal of Personality and Social Psychology, 83,* 1178–1197.

Schwartz, J. M., Stoessel, P. W., Baxter, L. R., Martin, K. M., & Phelps, M. E. (1996). Systematic changes in cerebral glucose metabolic rate after successful behavior modificiation treatment of obsessive-compulsive disorder. *Archives of General Psychiatry, 53,* 109–113.

Schwartz, S. H. (1994). Are there universal aspects in the structure and contents of human values? *Journal of Social Issues, 50,* 19–45.

Schwartz, T. A., Ware, J., Fischer, C. E., Craik, F. I. M., & Bialystok, E. (2012). Bilingualism as a contributor to cognitive reserve: Evidence from brain atrophy in Alzheimer's disease. *Cortex, 48,* 991–996.

Schweizer, T. A., Alexander, M. P., Cusimano, M., & Stuss, D. T. (2007). Fast and efficient visuotemporal attention requires the cerebellum. *Neuropsychologia, 45,* 3068–3074.

Schweizer, T. A., Oriet, C., Meiran, N., Alexander, M. P., Cusimano, M., & Stuss, D.T. (2007). The cerebellum mediates conflict resolution. *Journal of Cognitive Neuroscience, 19,* 1974–1982.

Schweizer, T. A., Ware, J., Fischer, C. E., Craik, F. I., Bialystok, E. (2012). Bilingualism as a contributor to cognitive reserve: evidence from brain atrophy in Alzheimer's disease. *Cortex, 48,* 991–996.

Scoboria, A., Mazzoni, G., Kirsch, I., & Jimenez, S. (2006). The effects of prevalence and script information on plausibility belief and memory of autobiographical events. *Applied Cognitive Psychology, 20,* 1049–1064.

Scoville, W. B., & Milner, B. (1957). Loss of recent memory after bilateral hippocampal lesions. *Journal of Neurology, Neurosurgery, and Psychiatry, 20,* 11–21.

Seale, J. P., Shellenberger, S., Rodriguez, C., Seale, J. D., & Alvarado, M. (2002). Alcohol use and cultural change in and indigenous population: A case study from Venezuela. *Alcohol and Alcoholism, 37,* 603–608.

Sealy, P., & Whitehead, P. C. (2006). The impact of deinstitutionalization of psychiatric hospitals on psychological distress of the community in Canada. *Journal of Health & Social Policy, 21,* 73–94.

Sears, H. A., & Byers, E. S. (2010). Adolescent girls' and boys' experiences of psychologically, physically, and sexually aggressive behaviors in their dating relationships: Co-occurrence and emotional reaction. *Journal of Aggression, Maltreatment & Trauma, 19,* 517–539.

Sedikides, C., & Strube, M. J. (1995). The multiply motivated self. *Personality and Social Psychology Bulletin, 21,* 1330–1335.

Segal Z. V., Williams J. M. G., & Teasdale J. D. (2002). *Mindfulness-based cognitive therapy for depression: A new approach to preventing relapse.* New York: Guilford.

Segalowitz, S. J., Santesso, D. L., Willoughby, T., Reker, D. L., Campbell, K., . . . Rose-Krasnor, L. (2012). Adolescent peer interaction and trait surgency weaken medial prefrontal cortex responses to failure. *Social, Cognitive, and Affective Neuroscience, 7,* 115–124.

Segerstrom, S. C., & Miller, G. E. (2004). Psychological stress and the immune system: A meta-analytic study of 30 years of inquiry. *Psychological Bulletin, 130,* 601–630.

Seidenberg, M. S., & Pettito, L. A. (1979). Signing behavior in apes: A critical review. *Cognition, 7,* 177–215.

Seligman, M. E. P. (1971). Phobias and preparedness. *Behavior Therapy, 2,* 307–320.

Seligman, M. E. P., Abramson, L. Y., Semmel, A., & von Baeyer, C. (1979). Depressive attributional style. *Journal of Abnormal Psychology, 88*, 242–247.

Seligman, M. E. P., & Csikszentmihalyi, M. (2000). Positive psychology: An introduction. *American Psychologist, 55*, 5–14.

Seligman, M. E., & Maier, S. F. (1967). Failure to escape traumatic shock. *Journal of Experimental Psychology, 74*, 1–9.

Serafini, G., Pompili, M., Belvederi Murri, M., Respino, M., Ghio, L., . . . Amore, M. (2015). The effects of repetitive transcranial magnetic stimulation on cognitive performance in treatment-resistant depression: A systematic review. *Neuropsychobiology, 71*, 125–139.

Selye, H. (1950). Stress and the general adaptation syndrome. *British Medical Journal*, 1385–1392.

Selye, H. (1955). Stress and disease. *Science, 122*, 625–631.

Selye, H. (1956). *The stress of life*. New York: McGraw-Hill.

Senghas, A. (2003). Intergenerational influence and ontogenetic development in the emergence of spatial grammar in Nicaraguan Sign Language. *Cognitive Development, 18*, 511–531.

Senghas, A., Kita, S., & Ozyurek, A. (2004). Children creating core properties of language: Evidence from an emerging sign language in Nicaragua. *Science, 305*, 1779–1782.

Sengupta, J., & Dahl, D. W. (2008). Gender-related reactions to gratuitous sex appeals in advertising. *Journal of Consumer Psychology, 18*, 62–78.

Sergent, J., Ohta, S., & MacDonald, B. (1992). Functional neuroanatomy of face and object processing. A positron emission tomography study. *Brain, 115*, 15–36.

Setchell, J. M., & Wickings, E. J. (2004). Social and seasonal influences on the reproductive cycle in female mandrills (Mandrillus sphinx). *American Journal of Physical Anthropology, 125*, 73–84.

Shad, M. U., Bidesi, A. S., Chen, L-A., Thomas, B. P., Ernst, M., & Rao, U. (2011). Neurobiology of decision-making in adolescents. *Behavioural Brain Research, 217*, 67–76.

Shamosh, N. A., DeYoung, C. G., Green, A. E., Reis, D. L., Johnson, M. R., Conway, A. R. A., et al. (2008). Individual differences in delay discounting: Relation to intelligence, working memory, and anterior prefrontal cortex. *Psychological Science, 19*, 904–911.

Shapiro, A. F., Gottman, J. M., & Carrère, S. (2000). The baby and the marriage: Identifying factors that buffer against decline in marital satisfaction after the first baby arrives. *Journal of Family Psychology, 14*, 59–70.

Shapiro, C. M., Tranjanovic, N. N., & Fedoroff, J. P. (2003). Sexsomnia—a new parasomnia? *Canadian Journal of Psychiatry, 48*, 311–317.

Shariff, A. F., & Tracy, J. L. (2011). What are emotion expressions for? *Current Directions in Psychological Science, 20*, 395–399.

Sharot, T., Martorella, E. A., Delgado, M. R., & Phelps, E. A. (2007). How personal experience modulates the neural circuitry of memories of September 11. *Proceedings of the National Academy of Sciences of the United States of America, 104*, 389–394.

Sharot, T., & Phelps, E. A. (2004). How emotional arousal modulates memory: Disentangling the effects of attention and retention. *Cognitive Affective Behavioural Neuroscience, 4*, 294–306.

Sharp, W., Hargrove, D., Johnson, L., & Deal, W. (2006). Mental health education: An evaluation of a classroom based strategy to modify help seeking for mental health problems. *Journal of College Student Development, 47*, 419–438.

Shaughnessy, K., Byers, E. S., Clowater, S. L., & Kalinowski, A. (2014). Self-appraisals of arousal-oriented online sexual activities in university and community samples. *Archives of Sexual Behavior, 43*, 1187–1197.

Shaywitz, S. E. (1998). Dyslexia. *Current Concepts, 338*, 307–312.

Shaywitz, S. E., & Shaywitz, B. A. (1991). Introduction to the special series on attention deficit disorder. *Journal of Learning Disabilities, 24*, 68–71.

Sheline, Y. I., Barch, D. M., Donnelly, J. M., Ollinger, J. M. Snyder, A. Z., & Mintun, M. A. (2001). Increased amygdala response to masked emotional faces in depressed subjects resolves with antidepressant treatment: An fMRI study. *Biological Psychiatry, 50*, 651–658.

Shenton, M. E., Hamoda, H. M., Schneiderman, J. S., Bouix, S., Pasternak, O., . . . Zafonte, R. (2012). A review of magnetic resonance imaging and diffusion tensor imaging findings in mild traumatic brain injury. *Brain Imaging and Behavior, 6*, 137–192.

Shepperd, J. A., & Koch, E. (2005). Pitfalls in teaching judgment heuristics. *Teaching of Psychology, 32*, 43–46.

Sheridan, M A., Fox, N. A., Zeanah, C. H., McLaughlin, K. A., & Nelson, C. A. (2012). Variation in neural development as a result of exposure to institutionalization early in childhood. *Proceedings of the National Academy of Sciences of the United States of America, 109*, 12927–12932.

Sherif, M. (1961). *The robbers cave experiment: Intergroup conflict and cooperation*. Middletown, CT: Wesleyan University Press.

Sherman, S. M. (2007). The thalamus is more than just a relay. *Current Opinion in Neurobiology, 17*, 417–422.

Sherman, S. M., & Guillery, R. W. (1996). Functional organization of thalamocortical relays. *Journal of Neurophysiology, 76*, 1367–1395.

Sherrard, L., Hiebert, J., & Squires, S. (2015). *Canada communicable disease report: Measles elimination*. CCDR Volume 41-7. Public Health Agency of Canada. Retrieved from http://www.phac-aspc.gc.ca/publicat/ccdr-rmtc/15vol41/dr-rm41-07/ar-01-eng.php

Shi, R., & Werker, J. F. (2001). Six-month-old infants' preferences for lexical words. *Psychological Science, 12*, 70–75.

Shi, R., Werker, J. F., & Morgan, J. L. (1999). Newborn infants' sensitivity to perceptual cues to lexical and grammatical words. *Cognition, 72*, B11–B21.

Shields, M., Carroll, M. D., & Ogden, C. L. (2011). Adult obesity prevalence in Canada and the United States. *Advances in Nutrition, 2*, 368–369.

Shields, M., & Tjekema, M. (2006). Regional differences in obesity. *Health Reports, 17*, 61–67.

Shmueli, D., Prochaska, J. J., & Glantz, S. A. (2010). Effect of smoking scenes in films on immediate smoking: A randomized controlled study. *American Journal of Preventative Medicine, 38*, 351–358.

Shoda, Y., Mischel, W., & Peake, P. K. (1990). Predicting adolescent cognitive and self-regulatory competencies from preschool delay of gratification: Identifying diagnostic conditions. *Developmental Psychology, 26*, 978–986.

Shu, N., Liu, Y., Li, K., Duan, Y., Wang, J., . . . He, Y. (2011). Diffusion tensor tractography reveals disrupted topological efficiency in white matter structural networks in multiple sclerosis. *Cerebral Cortex, 11*, 2565–2577.

Shulgin, A. T., & Nichols, D. E. (1978). Characterization of three new psychotomimetics. In R. C. Stillman and R. E. Willette (Eds.), *The psychopharmacology of hallucinogens* (pp. 74–83). New York: Pergamon Press.

Sibley, C. G., & Duckitt, J. (2008). Personality and prejudice: A metaanalysis and theoretical review. *Personality and Social Psychology Review, 12*, 248–279.

Siegel, D. (2007). *The mindful brain: Reflection and attunement in the cultivation of well-being*. New York: W. W. Norton & Company.

Siegel, J. (1995). Phylogeny and the function of REM sleep. *Behavioural Brain Research, 69*, 29–34.

Siegel, J. (2005). Clues to the functions of mammalian sleep. *Nature, 437*, 1264–1271.

Siegel, S. (1984). Pavlovian conditioning and heroin overdose: Reports by overdose victims. *Bulletin of the Psychonomic Society, 22*, 428–430.

Siegel, S., Baptista, M. A. S., Kim, J. A., McDonald, R. V., & Weise-Kelly, L. (2000). Pavlovian psychopharmacology: The associative basis of tolerance. *Experimental and Clinical Psychopharmacology, 8*, 276–293.

Siegel, S., Hinson, R. E., Krank, M. D., & McCully, J. (1982). Heroin "overdose" death: Contribution of drug-associated environmental cues. *Science, 216*, 436–437.

Siegler, R. S. (1992). The other Alfred Binet. *Developmental Psychology, 28*, 179–190.

Silva, A. J., Paylor, R., Wehner, J. M., & Tonegawa, S. (1992). Impaired spatial learning in alpha-calcium-calmodulin kinase II mutant mice. *Science, 257*, 206–211.

Silva, M., Groeger, J., & Bradshaw, M. (2006). Attention–memory interactions in scene perception. *Spatial Vision, 19*, 9–19.

Silverman, I., Choi, J., & Peters, M. (2007). The hunter-gatherer theory of sex differences in spatial abilities: Data from 40 countries. *Archives of Sexual Behavior, 36*, 261–268.

Silverman, I., & Eals, M. (1992). Sex differences in spatial abilities: Evolutionary theory and data. In J. Barkow, L. Cosmides, & J. Tooby (Eds.), *The adapted mind: Evolutionary psychology and the generation of culture* (533–549). Oxford, UK: Oxford University Press.

Simons, D. J., Boot, W. R., Charness, N., Gathercole, S. E., Chabris, C. F., . . . Stine-Morrow, E. A. L. (2016). Do "brain training" programs work? *Psychological Science in the Public Interest, 17,* 103–186.

Simons, D. J., & Chabris, C. F. (1999). Gorillas in our midst: Sustained inattentional blindness for dynamic events. *Perception, 28,* 1059–1074.

Simons, D. J., & Levin, D. T. (1997). Change blindness. *Trends in Cognitive Sciences, 1,* 261–267.

Singer T., Kiebel, S. J., Winston, J. S., Dolan, R. J., & Frith, C. D. (2004). Brain responses to the acquired moral status of faces. *Neuron, 41,* 653–662.

Singer, M. A., & Goldin-Meadow, S. (2005). Children learn when their teacher's gestures and speech differ. *Psychological Science, 16,* 85–89.

Singh, A., Uijtdewilligen, L., Twisk, J. W., van Mechelen, W., & Chinapaw, M. J. (2012). Physical activity and performance at school: A systematic review of the literature including a methodological quality assessment. *Archives of Pediatrics and Adolescent Medicine, 166,* 49–55.

Sinha, R. (2009). Modeling stress and drug craving in the laboratory: Implications for addiction treatment development. *Addiction Biology, 14,* 84–98.

Sireteanu, R. (1999). Switching on the infant brain. *Science, 286,* 59–61.

Skinner, B. F. (1948). Superstition in the pigeon. *Journal of Experimental Psychology, 38,* 168–172.

Skinner, B. F. (1985). Cognitive science and behaviorism. *British Journal of Psychology, 76,* 291–301.

Skinner, M. K., Anway, M. D., Savenkova, M. I., Gore, A. C., & Crews, D. (2008). Transgenerational epigenetic programming of the brain transcriptome and anxiety behavior. *PLOS One,* e3745.

Slater, A., Morison, V., & Somers, M. (1988). Orientation discrimination and cortical function in the human newborn. *Perception, 17,* 597–602.

Slotema, C. W., Blom, J. D., Hoek, H. W., & Sommer, I. E. (2010). Should we expand the toolbox of psychiatric treatment methods to include repetitive transcranial magnetic stimulation (rTMS)? A meta-analysis of the efficacy of rTMS in psychiatric disorders. *Journal of Clinical Psychiatry, 71,* 873–884.

Slovic, P. (2007). If I look at the mass I will never act: Psychic numbing and genocide. *Judgment and Decision Making, 2,* 79–95.

Slovic, P., Finucane, M., Peters, E., & MacGregor, D. G. (2002). Rational actors or rational fools: Implications of the affect heuristic for behavioral economics. *Journal of Socio-economics, 31,* 329–342.

Small, D. A., Loewenstein, G., & Slovic, P. (2007). Sympathy and callousness: The impact of deliberative thought on donations to identifiable and statistical victims. *Organizational Behavior and Human Decision Processes, 102,* 143–153.

Small, D. M., Jones-Gotman, M., & Dagher, A. (2003). Feeding-induced dopamine release in dorsal striatum correlated with meal pleasantness ratings in healthy human volunteers. *NeuroImage, 19,* 1709–1715.

Small, D. M., Jones-Gotman, M., Zatorre, R. J., Petrides, M., Evans, A. C. (1997). Flavor processing: More than the sum of its parts. *Neuroreport, 8,* 3913–3917.

Small, D. M., Zatorre, R. J., Dagher, A., Evans, A. C., & Jones-Gotman, M. (2001). Changes in brain activity related to eating chocolate. *Brain, 124,* 1720–1733.

Smallwood, J., McSpadden, M., & Schooler, J. (2008). When attention matters: The curious incident of the wandering mind. *Memory & Cognition, 36,* 1144–1150.

Smallwood, J., Schooler, J. W., Turk, D. J., Cunningham, S. J., Burns, P., & Macrae, C. N. (2011). Self-reflection and the temporal focus on the wandering mind. *Consciousness and Cognition, 20,* 1120–1126.

Smilek, D., Moffatt, B. A., Pasternak, J., White, B. N., Dixon, M. J., & Merikle, P. M. (2002). Synaesthesia: A case study of discordant monozygotic twins. *Neurocase, 8,* 338–342.

Smith, B. W. (2004). Structural and organizational predictors of homicide by police. *Policing: An International Journal of Police Strategies and Management, 27,* 539–557.

Smith, C. (1993). Sleep and learning: Some recent findings. In A. Moffit, M. Kramer, & R. Hoffmann (Eds.), *The functions of dreaming.* Albany: SUNY.

Smith, C. (2001). Sleep states and memory processes in humans: Procedural versus declarative memory systems. *Sleep Medicine Reviews, 5,* 491–506.

Smith, C., & Lapp, L. (1991). Increases in number of REMs and REM density in humans following an intensive learning period. *Journal of Sleep Research & Sleep Medicine, 14,* 325–330.

Smith, C., & MacNeil, C. (1994). Impaired motor memory for a pursuit rotor task following Stage 2 sleep loss in college students. *Journal of Sleep Research, 3,* 206–213.

Smith, C. T., Nixon, M. R., & Nadar, R. S. (2004). Posttraining increases in REM sleep intensity implicate REM sleep in memory processing and provide a biological marker of learning potential. *Learning & Memory, 11,* 714–719.

Smith, E., & Delargy, M. (2005). Locked-in syndrome. *British Medical Journal, 330,* 406–409.

Smith, J. E., & Tolson, J. M. (2008). Recognition, diagnosis, and treatment of restless legs syndrome. *Journal of the American Academy of Nurse Practitioners, 20,* 396–401.

Smith, M. L., Glass, G. V., & Miller, T. I. (1980). *The benefits of psychotherapy.* Baltimore: John Hopkins University Press.

Smith, S. D., Fredborg, B. K., & Kornelsen, J. (2016). An examination of the default mode network in individuals with Autonomous Sensory Meridian Response (ASMR). *Social Neuroscience.*

Smith, S. D., & Kornelsen, J. (2011). Emotion-dependent responses in spinal cord neurons: A spinal fMRI study. *Neuroimage, 58,* 269–274.

Smith, S. D., Kornelsen, J., & McIver, T. A. (2013). Putting the body back in embodied emotion. fMRI evidence for the modulation of spinal cord neurons by facial expressions. Poster presented at the 20th Annual meeting of the Cognitive Neuroscience Society, San Francisco, CA, April 13–16.

Smith, T. B., McCullough, M. E., & Poll, J. (2003). Religiousness and depression: Evidence for a main effect and the moderating influence of stressful life events. *Psychological Bulletin, 129,* 614–636.

Smolen, P., Zhang, Y., & Byrne, J. H. (2016). The right time to learn: Mechanisms and optimization of spaced learning. *Nature Reviews Neuroscience, 17,* 77–88.

Snider, L. A., & Swedo, S. E. (2004). PANDAS: Current status and directions for research. *Molecular Psychiatry, 9,* 900–907.

Snook, B., Eastwood, J., & Barron. T. (2014). The next stage in the evolution of interrogations: The PEACE model. *Canadian Criminal Law Review, 18,* 219–239.

Snowdon, L. R. (1999). African American service use for mental health problems. *Journal of Community Psychology, 27,* 303–313.

Snyder, K. (2006). Kurt Snyder's personal experience with schizophrenia. *Schizophrenia Bulletin, 32,* 209–211. Permission conveyed through Copyright Clearance Center, Inc.

Sobel, H. S., Cepeda, N. J., & Kapler, I. V. (2011). Spacing effects in real-world classroom vocabulary learning. *Applied Cognitive Psychology, 25,* 763–767.

Söderlund, H., Moscovitch, M., Kumar, N., Mandic, M., & Levine, B. (2012). As time goes by: Hippocampal connectivity changes with remoteness of autobiographical memory retrieval. *Hippocampus, 22,* 670–679.

Solomon, K. D., Fernández de Castro, L. E., Sandoval, H. P., Biber, J. M., Groat, B., Neff, K. D., et al. (2009). LASIK world literature review: Quality of life and patient satisfaction. *Ophthalmology, 116,* 691–701.

Solomon, S., Greenberg, J., & Pyszczynski, T. (1991). A terror management theory of social behavior: The functions of self-esteem and cultural worldviews. In M. Zanna (Ed.), *Advances in experimental social psychology* (Vol. 24, pp. 93–159). San Diego, CA: Academic Press.

Son Hing, L. S., Bobocel, D. R., Zanna, M. P., & McBride, M. V. (2007). Authoritarian dynamics and unethical decision making: High SDO leaders and high RWA followers. *Journal of Personality and Social Psychology, 92,* 67–81.

Sovik, R. (2000). The science of breathing—The yoga view. *Progress in Brain Research, 122,* 491–505.

Sowell, E. R., Peterson, B. S., Thompson, P. M., Welcome, S. E., Henkenius, A. L., & Toga, A. W. (2003). Mapping cortical change across the human life span. *Nature Neuroscience, 6,* 309–315.

Spanos, N. P., Burgess, C. A., & Burgess, M. F. (1994). Past-life identities, UFO abductions, and satanic ritual abuse: The social construction of memories. *International Journal of Clinical and Experimental Hypnosis, 42,* 433–446.

Spanos, N., Cobb, P., & Gorassini, D. (1985). Failing to resist hypnotic test suggestions: A strategy for self-presenting as deeply hypnotized. *Psychiatry: Journal for the Study of Interpersonal Processes, 48,* 282–292.

Spearman, C. (1923). *The nature of intelligence and the principles of cognition.* London: Macmillan.

Spearman, C. (1939). Thurstone's work re-worked. *The Journal of Educational Psychology, 30,* 1–16.

Spector, F., & Maurer, D. (2009). Synesthesia: A new approach to understanding the development of perception. *Developmental Psychology, 45,* 175–189.

Spelke, E. S., & Kinzler, K. D. (2007). Core knowledge. *Developmental Science, 10,* 89–96.

Spence, A., Poortinga, W., & Pidgeon, N. (2012). The psychological distance of climate change. *Risk Analysis, 32,* 957–972.

Spera, S. P., Buhrfeind, E. D., & Pennebaker, J. W. (1994). Expressive writing and coping with job loss. *Academy of Management Journal, 37,* 722–733.

Sperling, G. (1960). The information available in brief visual presentations. *Psychological Monographs, 74,* 1–29.

Sperry, R. W. (1951). Regulative factors in the orderly growth of neural circuits. *Growth, Suppl. 10,* 63–87.

Sperry, R. W. (1956). Experiments on perceptual integration in animals. *Psychiatric Research Reports, 6,* 151–160.

Sperry, R. W. (1963). Chemoaffinity in the orderly growth of nerve fiber patterns and connections. *Proceedings of the National Academy of Sciences of the United States of America, 50,* 703–710.

Sperry, R. W. (1968). Hemisphere deconnection and unity in conscious awareness. *American Psychologist, 23,* 723–733.

Sperry, R. W. (1974). Lateral specialization in the surgically separated hemispheres. In F. O. Schmitt & F. G. Worden (Eds.), *The neurosciences third study program* (pp. 5–19). Cambridge, MA: MIT Press.

Sperry, R. W. (1982). Some effects of disconnecting the cerebral hemispheres. *Science, 217,* 1223–1226, 1250.

Spires-Jones, T., & Knafo, S. (2012). Spines, plasticity, and cognition in Alzheimer's model mice. *Neural Plasticity, 2012,* 1–10.

Springer, S. P., & Deutsch, G. (1998). *Left brain right brain: Perspective from cognitive neuroscience.* New York: Freeman.

Sproule, B., Brands, B., Li, S., & Catz-Biro, L. (2009). Changing patterns in opioid addiction. *Canadian Family Physician, 55,* 68–69, e1–5.

Squeglia, L. M., Jacobus, J., & Tapert, S. F. (2009). The influence of substance use on adolescent brain development. *Clinical EEG and Neuroscience, 40,* 31–38.

Squire, L. R. (1986). Mechanisms of memory. *Science, 232,* 1612–1619.

Squire, L. R. (1989). On the course of forgetting in very long-term memory. *Journal of Experimental Psychology: Learning, Memory, and Cognition, 15,* 241–245.

Squire, L. R., Wixted, J. T., & Clark, R. E. (2007). Recognition memory and the medial temporal lobe: A new perspective. *Nature Reviews Neuroscience, 8,* 872–83.

Stack, S. & Eshleman, J. R. (1998). Marital status and happiness: A 17-nation study. *Journal of Marriage and Family, 60,* 527–536.

Staffen, W., Kronbichler, M., Aichhorn, M., Mair, A., & Ladurner, G. (2006). Selective brain activity in response to one's own name in the persistent vegetative state. *Journal of Neurology, Neurosurgery, and Psychiatry, 77,* 1383–1384.

Stafford, L. D., Salchi, S., & Waller, B. M. (2009). Odors cue memory for odor-associated words. *Chemosensory Perception, 2,* 59–69.

Stanhope, N., Cohen, G., & Conway, M. (1993).Very long-term retention of a novel. *Applied Cognitive Psychology, 7,* 239–256.

Stanovich, K. E., & West, R. F. (2000). Individual differences in reasoning: Implications for the rationality debate? *Behavioral and Brain Sciences, 23,* 645–665.

Starcevic, V., Linden, M., Uhlenhuth, E. H., Kolar, D., & Latas, M. (2004). Treatment of panic disorder with agoraphobia in an anxiety disorders clinic: Factors influencing psychiatrists' treatment choices. *Psychiatry Research, 125,* 41–52.

Stark, C. E., Okado, Y., & Loftus, E. F. (2010). Imaging the reconstruction of true and false memories using sensory reactivation and the misinformation paradigms. *Learning and Memory, 17,* 485–488

Stastna, K. (2013). Eli Lilly files $500M NAFTA suit against Canada over drug patents. *CBC News.* Retrieved from: http://www.cbc.ca/news/business/eli-lilly-files-500m-nafta-suit-against-canada-over-drug-patents-1.1829854

Statistics Canada. (2003). Canadian community health survey: Mental health and well-being 2002. Retrieved from http://www.statcan.gc.ca/pub/82-617-x/index-eng.htm

Statistics Canada. (2004). Table 101-6511 30 and 50 year total divorce rates per 1,000 marriages, Canada, provinces and territories, annual (rate per 1,000 marriages), CANSIM (database). (Accessed 2013-11-05).

Statistics Canada. (2011). Adult obesity prevalence in Canada and the United States. Health facts sheet. Retrieved from http://www.statcan.gc.ca/pub/82-625-x/2012001/article/11664-eng.htm

Statistics Canada. (2012a). Leading causes of death, by sex. Retrieved from http://www.statcan.gc.ca/tables-tableaux/sum-som/l01/cst01/hlth36a-eng.htm

Statistics Canada. (2012b). Current smoking trends. Retrieved from http://www.statcan.gc.ca/pub/82-624-x/2012001/article/11676-eng.pdf

Statistics Canada. (2012c). *Portrait of families and living arrangements in Canada.* http://www12.statcan.gc.ca/census-recensement/2011/as-sa/98-312-x/98-312-x2011001-eng.pdf

Statistics Canada. (2013a). Select health indicators of First Nations people living off reserve, Metis and Inuit. Retrieved from http://www.statcan.gc.ca/pub/82-624-x/2013001/article/11763-eng.htm

Statistics Canada. (2013b). Summary of results for 2013: Canadian Tobacco, Alcohol and Drugs Survey (CTADS). Retrieved from http://healthycanadians.gc.ca/science-research-sciences-recherches/data-donnees/ctads-ectad/summary-sommaire-2013-eng.php

Statistics Canada. (2016). *Health Indicators.* Catalogue No. 82-221-X. Retrieved from http://www5.statcan.gc.ca/olc-cel/olc.action?objId=82-221-X&objType=2&lang=en&limit=0

Steele, C. (1997). A threat in the air: How stereotypes shape intellectual identity and performance. *American Psychologist, 52,* 613–629.

Steele, C. M., & Josephs, R. A. (1990). Alcohol myopia: Its prized and dangerous effects. *American Psychologist, 45,* 921–933.

Steele, J. D., Christmas, D., Eliamel, M. S., & Matthews, K. (2008). Anterior cingulotomy for major depression: Clinical outcome and relationship to lesion characteristics. *Biological Psychiatry, 63,* 670–677.

Steele, K. M., Ball, T. N., & Runk, R. (1997). Listening to Mozart does not enhance backwards digit span performance. *Perceptual and Motor Skills, 84,* 1179–1184.

Steffen, P. R., McNeilly, M., Anderson, N., & Sherwood, A. (2003). Effects of perceived racism and anger inhibition on ambulatory blood pressure in African Americans. *Psychosomatic Medicine, 65,* 746–750.

Stein, Z., Susser, M., Saenger, G., & Marolla, F. (1975). Famine and human development: The Dutch hunger winter of 1944–1945. New York: Oxford University Press. *Annals of Internal Medicine, 83,* 290.

Steinberg, L. (2004). Risk taking in adolescence: What changes, and why? *Annals of the New York Academy of Sciences, 1021,* 51–58.

Steinberg, L. (2007). Risk taking in adolescence: New perspectives from brain and behavioral science. *Current Directions in Psychological Science, 16,* 55–59.

Steinberg, L. (2008). A social neuroscience perspective on adolescent risk-taking. *Developmental Review, 28,* 78–106.

Steptoe, A., Lipsey, Z., & Wardle, J. (1998). Stress, hassles and variations in alcohol consumption, food choice and physical exercise: A dairy study. *British Journal of Health Psychology, 3,* 51–63.

Sterling, P. (2011). Allostasis: A model of predictive regulation. *Physiology & Behavior, 106,* 5–15.

Stern, P. C., & Dietz, T. (1994). The value basis of environmental concern. *Journal of Social Issues 50*, 65–84.

Sternberg, R. J. (1983). Components of human intelligence. *Cognition, 15*, 1–48.

Sternberg, R. J. (1988). *The triarchic mind: A new theory of human intelligence.* New York: Penguin Books.

Sternberg, R. J. (2003). Intelligence. In I. B. Weiner & D. K. Freedheim (Eds.), *Comprehensive handbook of psychology, Vol. 1.* New York: Wiley.

Sternberg, R. J., Castejón, J. L., Prieto, M. D., Hautamäki, J., & Grigorenko, E. L. (2001). Confirmatory factor analysis of the Sternberg Triarchic Abilities Test in three international samples: An empirical test of the triarchic theory of intelligence. *European Journal of Psychological Assessment, 17*, 1–16.

Sternberg, R. J., Wagner, R. K., Williams, W. M., & Horvath, J. A. (1995). Testing common sense. *American Psychologist, 60*, 46–59.

Stettler, N., Signer, T., & Paolo, S. (2004). Electronic games and childhood obesity. *Nutrition Research Newsletter, 23*, 7–8.

Stevenson, R. A., Schlesinger, J. J., & Wallace, M. T. (2013). Effects of divided attention and operating room noise on perception of pulse oximeter pitch changes: A laboratory study. *Anesthesiology, 118*, 376–381.

Stevenson, R. J., Oaten, M. J., Caste, T. I., Repacholi, B. M., & Wagland, P. (2010). Children's response to adult disgust elicitors: Development and acquisition. *Developmental Psychology, 46*, 165–177.

Stewart, T. L., Latu, I. M., Kawakami, K., & Myers, A. C. (2010). Consider the situation: Reducing automatic stereotyping through Situational Attribution Training. *Journal of Experimental Social Psychology, 46*, 221–225.

Stice, E. (1998). Relations of restraint and negative affect to bulimic pathology: A longitudinal test of three competing models. *International Journal of Eating Disorders, 23*, 243–260.

Stice, E., Presnell, K., Shaw, H., & Rohde, P. (2005). Psychological and behavioral risk factors for obesity onset in adolescent girls: A prospective study. *Journal of Consulting and Clinical Psychology, 73*, 195–202.

Stice, E., & Shaw, H. E. (1994). Adverse effects of the media portrayed thin-ideal on women and linkages to bulimic symptomatology. *Journal of Social and Clinical Psychology, 13*, 288–308.

Stice, E., Spoor, S., Bohon, C., Veldhuizen, M. G., & Small, D. M. (2008). Relation of reward from food intake and anticipated food intake to obesity: A functional magnetic resonance imaging study. *Journal of Abnormal Psychology, 117*, 924–935.

Stickgold, R., LaTanya, J., & Hobson, A. (2000). Visual discrimination learning requires sleep after training. *Nature Neuroscience, 3*, 1237–1238.

Stickgold, R., Scott, L., Rittenhouse, C., & Hobson, J. A. (1999). Sleep-induced changes in associative memory. *Journal of Cognitive Neuroscience, 11*, 182–193.

Stigler, S. (2008). Fisher and the 5% level. *Chance, 21*, 12.

Stillman, R. C., Weingartner, H., Wyatt, R. J., Gillin, J. C., & Eich, J. (1974). State-dependent (dissociative) effects of marihuana on human memory. *Arch Gen Psychiatry, 31*, 81–85.

Stine-Morrow, E. A. L. (2007). The Dumbledore Hypothesis of cognitive aging. *Current Directions in Psychological Science, 16*, 289–293.

Stokoe, W. C., Casterline, D. C., & Croneberg, C. G. (1976). *A dictionary of American Sign Language on linguistic principles* (2nd ed.). Linstok Press: Silver Spring, MD.

Stoodley, C. J., & Schmahmann, J. D. (2010). Evidence for topographic organization in the cerebellum of motor control versus cognitive and affective processing. *Cortex, 46*, 831–844.

Strack, F., Martin, L. L., & Stepper, S. (1988). Inhibiting and facilitating conditions of the human smile: A nonobtrusive test of the facial feedback hypothesis. *Journal of Personality and Social Psychology, 54*, 768–777.

Strahan, E. J., Lafrance, A., Wilson, A. E., Ethier, N., Spencer, S. J., & Zanna, M. J. (2008). Victoria's dirty secret: How sociocultural norms influence adolescent girls and women. *Personality and Social Psychology Bulletin, 34*, 288–301.

Strahan, E. J., Spencer, S. J., & Zanna, M. P. (2002). Subliminal priming and persuasion: Striking while the iron is hot. *Journal of Experimental Social Psychology, 38*, 556–568.

Strahan, E. J., Wilson, A. E., Cressman, K. E., & Bruote, V. M. (2006). Comparing to perfection: How cultural norms for appearance affect social comparisons and self-image. *Body Image, 3*, 211–227.

Strassman, R. (2001). *DMT: Spirit molecule.* Rochester, VT: Park Street Press.

Streissguth, A. P., Barr, H. M., Bookstein, F. L., Sampson, P. D., & Olson, H. C. (1999). The long-term neurocognitive consequences of prenatal alcohol exposure: A 14-year study. *Psychological Science, 10*, 186–190.

Streissguth, A. P., & Connor, P. D. (2001). Fetal alcohol syndrome and other effects of prenatal alcohol: Developmental cognitive neuroscience implications. In C. A. Nelson & M. Luciana (Eds.), *Handbook of developmental cognitive neuroscience* (pp. 505–518). Cambridge, MA: MIT Press.

Strenziok, M., Krueger, F., Deshpande, G., Lenroot, R.K., van der Meer, E., & Grafman, J. (2011). Fronto-parietal regulation of media violence exposure in adolescents: A multi-method study. *Social, Cognitive, and Affective Neuroscience, 6*, 537–547.

Streppel, M. T., Boshuizen, H. C., Ocke, M. C., Kok, F. J., & Kromhout, D. (2007). Mortality and life expectancy in relation to long-term cigarette, cigar, and pipe smoking: The Zutphen study. *Tobacco Control, 16*, 107–113.

Stroman, P. W. (2005). Magnetic resonance imaging of neuronal function in the spinal cord: Spinal FMRI. *Clinical Medicine & Resesarch, 3*, 141–156.

Stuart, E. W., Shimp, T. A., & Engle, R. W. 1990. Classical conditioning of negative attitudes. *Advances in Consumer Research, 17*, 536–540.

Stuss, D. T. (2011). Functions of the frontal lobes: Relation to executive functions. *Journal of the International Neuropsychological Society, 17*, 759–765.

Stuss, D. T., & Knight, R. T. (2002). *Principles of frontal lobe function.* New York: Oxford University Press.

Sue, S., & Lam, A. G. (2002). Cultural and demographic diversity. In J. C. Norcross (Ed.), *Psychotherapy relationships that work: Therapist contributions and responsiveness to patients* (pp. 401–422). New York: Oxford University Press.

Suls, J. (1972). A two-stage model for the appreciation of jokes and cartoons: an information processing analysis. In P. McGhee (Ed.), *The psychology of humor: Theoretical perspectives and empirical issues* (pp. 81–100). New York: Academic Press.

Sumnall, H. R., Measham, F., Brandt, S. D., & Cole, J. C. (2011). Salvia divinorum use and phenomenology: Results from an online survey. *Journal of Psychopharmacology, 25*, 1496–1507.

Supreme Court of Canada. (2001). *R. v. Sharpe*, [2001] 1 S.C.R. 45, 2001 SCC 2.

Supreme Court of Canada. (2004). *Canadian Foundation for Children, Youth and the Law v. Canada (Attorney General)*, [2004] 1 S.C.R. 76, 2004 SCC 4.

Supreme Court of Canada. (2007). *R. v. Trochym*, [2007] 1 S.C.R., 2007 SCC 239.

Supreme Court of Canada. (2015). *R. v. Campione*, 2015 O.N.C.A. 67 (CanLII).

Susser, E. B., Brown, A., & Matte, T. D. (1999). Prenatal factors and adult mental and physical health. *Canadian Journal of Psychiatry, 44*, 326–334.

Susskind, J. M., & Anderson, A. K. (2008). Facial expression form and function. *Nature Neuroscience, 11*, 843–850.

Sutherland, R., & Hayne, H. (2001). The effect of postevent information on adults' eyewitness reports. *Applied Cognitive Psychology, 15*, 249–263.

Suzuki, H., Uchiyama, M., Tagaya, H., Ozaki, A., Kuriyama, K., . . . & Kuga, R. (2004). Dreaming during non-rapid eye movement sleep in the absence of prior rapid eye movement sleep. *Sleep, 27*, 1486–1490.

Swaab, D. F., & Garcia-Falgueras, A. (2009). Sexual differentiation of the human brain in relation to gender identity and sexual orientation. *Functional Neurology, 24*, 17–28.

Sweeney, P. D., Anderson, K., & Bailey, S. (1986). Attributional style in depression: A meta-analytic review. *Journal of Personality and Social Psychology, 50*, 974.

Symons, C. S., & Johnson, B. T. (1997). The self-reference effect in memory: A meta-analysis. *Psychological Bulletin, 121,* 371–394.

Szasz, T. (2006). Mental illness as brain disease: A brief history lesson. *Freeman, 56,* 24.

Szelenberger, W., Niemcewicz, S., & Dabrowska, A. J. (2005). Sleepwalking and night terrors: Psychopathological correlates. *International Review of Psychology, 17,* 263–270.

Tajfel, H. (1970). Experiments in intergroup discrimination. *Scientific American, 223,* 96–102.

Tajfel, H., Billig, M. G., Bundy, R. P., & Flament, C. (1971). Social categorization and intergroup behaviour. *European Journal of Social Psychology, 1,* 149–178.

Tajfel, H., & Turner, J. C. (1986). The social identity theory of intergroup behaviour. In S. Worchel & W. G. Austin (Eds.), *Psychology of intergroup relations* (2nd ed., pp. 7–24). Chicago: Nelson-Hall.

Takahashi, Y. (1990). Is multiple personality really rare in Japan? *Dissociation, 3,* 57–59.

Takeuchi, D., & Cheung, M. (1998). Coercive and voluntary referrals: How ethnic minority adults get into mental health treatment. *Ethnicity & Health, 3,* 149–158.

Talarico, J., & Rubin, D. (2003). Confidence, not consistency, characterizes flashbulb memories. *Psychological Science, 14,* 455–461.

Talmi, D., Grady, C., Goshen-Gottstein, Y., & Moscovitch, M. (2005). Neuroimaging the serial position curve: A test of single-store versus dual-store models. *Psychological Science, 16,* 716–723.

Tanaka, J. W., & Farah, M. J. (1993). Parts and wholes in face recognition. *The Quarterly Journal of Experimental Psychology, 46A,* 225–245.

Tang, Y. (2011). Mechanisms of integrative body-mind training. *Neuroscience Bulletin, 27,* 383–388.

Tang, Y., Lu, Q., Geng, X., Stein, E. A., Yang, Y., & Posner, M. I. (2010). Short-term meditation induces white matter changes in the anterior cingulate. *Proceedings of the National Academy of Sciences of the USA, 107,* 15649–15652.

Tang, Y., Ma, Y., Fan, Y., Feng, H., Wang, J., Feng, S., et al. (2009). Central and autonomic nervous system interaction is altered by short-term meditation. *Proceedings of the National Academy of Sciences, 106,* 8864–8870.

Tang, Y., Ma., Y., Wang, J., Fan, Y., Feng, S., Lu, Q., et al. (2007). Short-term meditation training improves attention and self-regulation. *Proceedings of the National Academy of Science of the United States of America, 104,* 17152–17156.

Tang, Y., Shimizu, E., Dube, G. R., Rampon, C., Kerchner, . . . Tsien, J. Z. (1999). Genetic enhancement of learning and memory in mice. *Nature, 401,* 63–69.

Tangney, J. P., & Dearing, R. L. (2002). *Shame and guilt.* New York: Guilford Publications.

Tascioglu, A. B. (2005) Brief review of vestibular system anatomy and its higher order projections. *Neuroanatomy, 4,* 24–27.

Tashiro, A., Hiroshi, M., & Gage, F. H. (2007). Experience-specific functional modification of the dentate gyrus through adult neurogenesis: A critical period during an immature stage. *The Journal of Neuroscience, 27,* 3252–3259.

Taylor, A. J., & Hort, J. (2004). Measuring proximal stimuli involved in flavour perception. In A. J. Taylor & D. R. Roberts (Eds.), *Flavor perception* (pp. 1–38). Oxford, UK: Blackwell.

Taylor, S. E. (2006). Tend and befriend: Biobehavioral bases of affiliation under stress. *Current Directions in Psychological Science, 15,* 273–277.

Taylor, S. E., Klein, L. C., Lewis, B. P., Gruenewald, T. L., Gurung, R. A. R., & Updegraff, J. A. (2000). Biobehavioral responses to stress in females: Tend-and-befriend, not fight-or-flight. *Psychological Review, 107,* 411–429.

Tedeschi, R. G., & Calhoun, L. G. (2004). Post-traumatic growth: Conceptual foundations and empirical evidence. *Psychological Inquiry, 15,* 1–18.

Tellegen, A., Lykken, D. T., Bouchard, T. J., Wilcox, K. J., Segal, N. L., & Rich, S. (1998). Personality similarity in twins reared apart and together. *Journal of Personality and Social Psychology, 54,* 1031–1039.

Teplin, L. A., McClelland, G. M., Abram, K. M., & Weiner, D. A. (2005). Crime victimization in adults with severe mental illness: Comparison with the National Crime Victimization Survey. *Archives of General Psychiatry, 62,* 911–921.

Terao, Y. & Ugawa, Y. (2002). Basic mechanisms of TMS. *Journal of Clinical Neurophysiology, 19,* 322–343.

Terman, L. M. (1916). *The uses of intelligence tests.* Boston: Houghton Mifflin.

Terracciano, A., Abdel-Khalek, A. M., Adám, N., et al. (2005). National character does not reflect mean personality trait levels in 49 cultures. *Science, 310,* 96–100.

Terracciano, A., Sanna, S, Uda, M., et al. (2010). Genome-wide association scan for five major dimensions of personality. *Molecular Psychiatry, 15,* 647–656.

Thase, M. E., & Denko, T. (2008). Pharmacotherapy of mood disorders. *Annual Review of Clinical Psychology, 4,* 53–91.

Thibedeau, H. (2015). How the Liberals hit a home run with their Blue Jays election ad buy. *CBC News.* Retrieved from http://www.cbc.ca/news/politics/blue-jays-liberal-advertising-1.3314617

Thoinot, L. (1913). *Medicolegal aspects of moral offenses.* A. W. Weysse (translator). Philadelphia: F. A. Davis and Company Publishers.

Thomas, A., & Chess, S. (1977). *Temperament and development.* New York: Brunder/Mazel.

Thompson, A. E., O'Sullivan, L. F., Byers, E. S., & Shaughnessy, K. (2014). Young adults' implicit and explicit attitudes towards the sexuality of older adults. *Canadian Journal on Aging, 33,* 259–270.

Thompson, W. C., Clarke-Stewart, A., & Lepore, S. J. (1997). What did the janitor do? Suggestive interviewing and the accuracy of children's accounts. *Law and Human Behavior, 21,* 405–426.

Thompson, W. F., Russo, F. A., & Quinto, L. (2008). Audio-visual integration of emotional cues in song. *Cognition and Emotion, 22,* 1457–1470.

Thorndike, E. L. (1905). *The elements of psychology.* New York: Seiler.

Thornton, A., & Raihani, N. J. (2010). Identifying teaching in wild animals. *Learning & Behavior, 38,* 297–309.

Thurstone, L. L. (1938). *Primary mental abilities.* Chicago: University of Chicago Press.

Tirri, K., & Nokelainen, P. (2008). Identification of multiple intelligences with the Multiple Intelligence Profiling Questionnaire III. *Psychology Science, 50,* 206–221.

Titchener, E. B. (1898). The postulates of structural psychology. *Philosophical Review, 7,* 449–465.

Tobias, M. C., O'Neill, J., Hudkins, M., Bartzokis, G., Dean, A. C., & London, E. D. (2010). White-matter abnormalities in brain during early abstinence from methamphetamine abuse. *Psychopharmacology, 209,* 13–24.

Tobler, I., Kopp, C., Deboer, T., Rudolph, U. (2001). Diazepam-induced changes in sleep: Role of the $\alpha 1$ GABA$_A$ receptor subtype. *Proceedings of the National Academy of Sciences, 98,* 6464–6469.

Tochigi, M., Okazaki, Y., Kato, N., & Sasaki, T. (2004). What causes seasonality of birth in schizophrenia? *Neuroscience Research, 48,* 1–11.

Todman, D. (2008). Wilder Penfield. *Journal of Neurology, Neurosurgery, & Psychiatry, 255,* 1104–1105.

Todorov, A., Mandisodza, A. N., Goren, A., & Hall, C. (2005). Inferences of competence from faces predict election outcomes. *Science, 308,* 1623–1626.

Tolman, E. C., & Honzik, C. H. (1930). Degrees of hunger, reward and non-reward, and maze learning in rats. *University of California Publications in Psychology,* 4241–4256.

Tom, G., Tong, S. T., & Hesse, C. (2010). Thick slice and thin slice teaching evaluations. *Social Psychology of Education: An International Journal, 13,* 129–136.

Tomblin, J. B., O'Brien, M., Shriberg, L. D., Williams, C., Murray, J., Patil, S., et al. (2009). Language features in a mother and daughter of a chromosome 7;13 translocation involving FOXP2. *Journal of Speech, Language, and Hearing Research, 52,* 1157–1174.

Torrey, E. F. (1997). *Out of the shadows: Confronting America's mental illness crisis.* New York: John Wiley & Sons.

Tottenham, L. S., Saucier, D. M., Elias, L. J., & Gutwin, C. (2005). Men are more accurate than women in aiming at targets in both near space and extrapersonal space. *Perceptual and Motor Skills, 101,* 3–12.

Townsend, J. M., & Levy, G. D. (1990a). Effects of potential partners' costume and physical attractiveness on sexuality and partner selection. *Journal of Psychology, 124,* 371–389.

Townsend, J. M., & Levy, G. D. (1990b). Effects of potential partners' physical attractiveness and socioeconomic status on sexuality and partner selection: Sex differences in reported preferences of university students. *Archives of Sexual Behavior, 19,* 149–164.

Tracy, M., Zimmerman, F. J., Galea, S., et al. (2008). What explains the relation between family poverty and childhood depressive symptoms? *Journal of Psychiatric Research, 42,* 1163–1175.

Trainor, L. J. (2010). Using electroencephalography (EEG) to measure maturation of auditory cortex in infants: Processing pitch, duration and sound location. In R. E. Trembley, R. G. Barr, RDeV. Peters, & M. Bovin (Eds.), *Encyclopedia on early childhood development.* Montreal, QC: Centre of Excellence for Early Childhood Development.

Trainor, L. J., McFadden, M., Hodgson, L., Darragh, L., Barlow, J., Matsos, L., & Sonnadara, R. (2003). Changes in auditory cortex and the development of mismatch negativity between 2 and 6 months of age. *International Journal of Psychophysiology, 51,* 5–15.

Tranel, D., Damasio, H., & Damasio, A. R. (1997). A neural basis for the retrieval of conceptual knowledge. *Neuropsychologia 35,* 1319–1327.

Triplett, N. (1898). The dynamogenic factors in pacemaking and competition. *The American Journal of Psychology, 9,* 507–533.

Trivers, R. L. (1972). Parental investment and sexual selection. In B. Campbell (Ed.), *Sexual selection and the descent of man: 1871–1971* (pp. 136–179). Chicago, IL: Aldine.

Troje, N. F. (2002a). Decomposing biological motion: A framework for analysis and synthesis of human gait patterns. *Journal of Vision, 2,* 371–387.

Troje, N. F. (2002b). The little difference: Fourier based gender classification from biological motion. In R.P. Wurtz & M. Lappe (Eds.), *Dynamic perception.* Berlin: Aka Press.

Troje, N. F. (2008). Retrieving information from human movement patterns. In T. F. Shipley & J. M. Zacks (Eds.), *Understanding events: How humans see, represent, and act on events* (pp. 308–334). New York: Oxford University Press.

Troop, N. A. (1998). Eating disorders as coping strategies: A critique. *European Eating Disorders Review, 6,* 229–237.

Trope, Y., & Liberman, N. (2010). Construal level theory of psychological distance. *Psychological Review, 117,* 440–463.

Tropp, L. R., & Pettigrew, T. F. (2005). Relationships between intergroup contact and prejudice among minority and majority status groups. *Psychological Science, 16,* 951–957.

Troseth, G. L. (2010). Is it life or is it Memorex? Video as a representation of reality. *Developmental Review, 30,* 155–175.

Tse, D., Takeuchi, T., Kakeyama, M., Kajii, Y., Okuno, H., Tohyama, C., et al. (2011). Schema-dependent gene activation and memory encoding in neocortex. *Science, 333,* 891–895.

Tsuchiya, N., Moradi, F., Felsen, C., Yamazaki, M., & Adolphs, R. (2009). Intact rapid detection of fearful faces in the absence of the amygdala. *Nature Neuroscience, 12,* 1224–1225.

Tulving, E. (1972). Episodic and semantic memory. In E. Tulving & W. Donaldson (Eds.), *Organization of memory* (pp. 381–402). New York: Academic Press.

Tulving, E. (1974). Cue-dependent forgetting. *American Scientist, 62,* 74–82.

Tulving, E., Kapur, S., Craik, F. I. M., Moscovitch, M., & Houle, S. (1994). Hemispheric encoding/retrieval asymmetry in episodic memory: Positron emission tomography findings. *Proceedings of the National Academy of Sciences, 91,* 2016–2020.

Tulving, E., & Markowitsch, H. J. (1998). Episodic and declarative memory: Role of the hippocampus. *Hippocampus, 8,* 198–203.

Tulving, E., Schacter, D. L., McLachlan, D. R., & Moscovitch, M. (1988). Priming of semantic autobiographical knowledge: A case study of retrograde amnesia. *Brain and Cognition, 8,* 3–20.

Tulving, E., Schacter, D. L., & Stark, H. A. (1982). Priming effects in word-fragment completion are independent of recognition memory. *Journal of Experimental Psychology, 8,* 336–342.

Tulving, E., & Thompson, D. M. (1973). Encoding specificity and retrieval processes in episodic memory. *Psychological Review, 80,* 352–373.

Tulving E., & Watkins, M. J. (1975). Structure of memory traces. *Psychological Review, 82,* 261–275.

Tupper, K. W., Wood, E., Yensen, R., & Johnson, M. W. (2015). Psychedelic medicine: A re-emerging therapeutic paradigm. *Canadian Medical Association Journal, 187,* 1054–1059.

Turk, C., Heimberg, R., Luterek, J., Mennin, D., & Fresco, D. (2005). Emotion dysregulation in generalized anxiety disorder: A comparison with social anxiety disorder. *Cognitive Therapy and Research, 29,* 89–106.

Turkheimer, E., Haley, A., Waldron, M., D'Onofrio, B., & Gottesman, I. I. (2003). Socioeconomic status modifies heritability of IQ in young children. *Psychological Science, 14,* 623–628.

Turner, D. C., Robbins, L. C., Aron, A. R., Dowson, J., & Sahakian, B. J. (2003). Cognitive enhancing effects of modafinil in healthy volunteers. *Psychopharmacology, 165,* 260–269.

Tversky, A., & Kahneman, D. (1973). Availability: A heuristic for judging frequency and probability. *Cognitive Psychology, 5,* 207–232.

Tversky, A., & Kahneman, D. (1982). The framing of decisions and the psychology of choice. *Science, 211,* 453–458.

Tweed, R. G., & Tweed, C. J. (2011). Positive emotion following spousal bereavement: Desirable or pathological? *Journal of Positive Psychology, 6,* 131–141.

U.S. Department of Justice. (2001). *Policing and homicide, 1976–98: Justifiable homicide by police, police officers murdered by felons* (NCJ180987). Washington, DC: Bureau of Justice Statistics.

Uchimura, N. & North, R. A. (1990). Actions of cocaine on rat nucleus accumbens neurones in vitro. *British Journal of Pharmacology, 99,* 736–740.

Ungerleider, L. G., & Mishkin, M. (1982). Object vision and spatial vision: Two cortical pathways. In D. J. Ingle, M. A. Goodale, & R. J. W. Mansfield (Eds.), *Analysis of visual behaviour* (pp. 296–302). Cambridge, MA: MIT Press.

Upton, N. (1994). Mechanisms of action of new antiepileptic drugs: Rational design and serendipitous finding. *Trends in Pharmacological Science, 15,* 456–463.

Urban, N. B., Girgis, R. R., Talbot, P. S., Kegeles, L. S., Xu, X., . . . & Laruelle, M. (2012). Sustained recreational use of ecstasy is associated with altered pre and postsynaptic markers of serotonin transmission in neocortical areas: A PET study with [11C]DASB and [11C] MDL 100907. *Neuropsychopharmacology, 37,* 1465–1473.

Uziel, L. (2007). Individual differences in the social facilitation effect: A review and meta-analysis. *Journal of Research in Personality, 41,* 579–601.

Valenstein, E. S. (1973). *Brain control: A critical examination of brain stimulation and psychosurgery.* London: Wiley-Interscience.

Valentin, V., & O'Doherty, J. P. (2009). Overlapping prediction errors in dorsal striatum during instrumental learning with juice and money reward in the human brain. *Journal of Neurophysiology, 102,* 3384–3391.

Van Ameringen, M., Mancini, C., Patterson, B., & Boyle, M. H. (2008). Post-traumatic stress disorder in Canada. *CNS Neuroscience and Therapeutics, 14,* 171–181.

Van den Bussche, E., Van den Noortgate, W., & Reynvoet, B. (2009). Mechanisms of masked priming: A meta-analysis. *Psychological Bulletin, 135,* 452–477.

van der Kolk, B. A. (1994). The body keeps score: Memory and the evolving psychobiology of posttraumatic stress. *Harvard Review of Psychiatry, 1,* 253–265.

van Honk, J., Tuiten, A., Hermans, E., Putman, P., Koppeschaar, H., Thijssen, J., . . . & van Doornen, L. (2001). A single administration of testosterone induces cardiac accelerative responses to angry faces in healthy young women. *Behavioral Neuroscience, 115,* 238–242.

van Kesteren, M. T. R., Fernandez, G., Norris, D. G., & Hermans, E. J. (2010). Persistent schema-dependent hippocampal-neocortical connectivity during memory encoding and postencoding rest in humans. *Proceedings of the National Academy of Sciences, 107,* 7550–7555.

van Kesteren, M. T. R., Rijpkema, M., Ruiter, D. J., & Fernandez, G. (2010). Retrieval of associative information congruent with prior knowledge is related to increased medial prefrontal activity and connectivity. *Journal of Neuroscience, 30,* 15888–15894.

Van Oort, F. V. A., Greaves-Lord, K., Verhulst, F. C., Ormel, J., & Huizink, A. C. (2009). The developmental course of anxiety symptoms during adolescence: The TRAILS study. *Journal of Child Psychology and Psychiatry, 50*(10), 1209–1217.

van Os, J., Pedersen, C. B., & Mortensen, P. B. (2004). Confirmation of synergy between urbanicity and familial liability in the causation of psychosis. *American Journal of Psychiatry, 161*, 2312–2314.

van Praag, H. (2008). Neurogenesis and exercise: Past and future directions. *Neuromolecular Medicine, 10*, 128–140.

van Praag, H. (2009). Exercise and the brain: Something to chew on. *Trends in Neuroscience, 32*, 283–290.

van Straten, A., & Cuijpers, P. (2009). Self-help therapy for insomnia: A meta-analysis. *Sleep Medicine Reviews, 13*, 61–71.

Vanheusden, K., Mulder, C. L., van der Ende, J., van Lenthe, F. J., et al. (2008). Young adults face major barriers to seeking help from mental health services. *Patient Education and Counseling 73*, 97–104.

Vansteenkiste, M., Lens, W., & Deci, E. L. (2006). Intrinsic versus extrinsic goal contents in self-determination theory: Another look at the quality of academic motivation. *Educational Psychology, 41*, 19–31.

Vargha-Khadem, F., Gadian, D. G., Copp, A., & Mishkin, M. (2005). FOXP2 and the neuroanatomy of speech and language. *Nature Reviews Neuroscience, 6*, 131–138.

Vervaeke, J., & Ferraro, L. (2012). Relevance, Meaning, and the Cognitive Science of Wisdom. In M. Ferrari and N. Westrate (Eds.), *The scientific study of personal wisdom: From contemplative traditions to neuroscience.* New York, NY: Springer.

Verwey, M., & Amir, S. (2009). Food-entrainable circadian oscillators in the brain. *European Journal of Neuroscience, 30*, 1650–1657.

Villar, J., Merialdi, M., Gülmezoqlu, A. M., Abalos, E., Carroli, G., . . . de Onis, M. (2003). Characteristics of randomized controlled trials included in systematic reviews of nutritional interventions reporting maternal morbidity, mortality, preterm delivery, intrauterine growth restriction and small for gestational age and birth weight outcomes. *Journal of Nutrition, 133*, 1632–1639.

Virdee, K., Cumming, P., Caprioli, D., Jupp, B., Rominger, A., Aigbirhio, F. I., et al. (2012). Applications of positron emissions tomography in animal models of neurological and neuropsychiatric disorders. *Neuroscience and BioBehavioral Reviews, 36*, 1188–1216.

Voelker, R. (2003). Mounting student depression taxing campus mental health services. *Journal of the American Medical Association, 289*, 2055–2056.

Vogel, D. L., Wade, N. G., & Ascheman, P. (2009). Measuring perceptions of stigmatization by others for seeking psychological help: Reliability and validity of a new stigma scale with college students. *Journal of Counseling Psychology, 56*, 301–308.

Vogel, E., Woodman, G., & Luck, S. (2001). Storage of features, conjunctions, and objects in visual working memory. *Journal of Experimental Psychology: Human Perception and Performance, 27*, 92–114.

Vohs, K. D., Bardone, A. M., Joiner, T. E., & Abramson, L. Y. (1999). Perfectionism, perceived weight status, and self-esteem interact to predict bulimic symptoms: A model of bulimic symptoms development. *Journal of Abnormal Psychology, 108*, 695–700.

Vokey, J. R., & Read, J. D. (1985). Subliminal messages. *American Psychologist, 40*, 1231–1239.

Volkow, N. D., Fowler, J. S., Wang, G. J., Baler, R., & Telang, F. (2009). Imaging dopamine's role in drug abuse and addiction. *Neuropharmacology, 56 Supplement 1*, 3–8.

Volpe, J. J. (2008). Neurological examination: Normal and abnormal features. In Volpe, J. J. (Ed.), *Neurology of the Newborn* (5th ed.). Philadelphia, Pa: Saunders Elsevier.

von Frisch, K. (1967). *The dance language and orientation of bees.* Cambridge, MA: Harvard University Press.

Vouloumanos, A., & Werker, J. F. (2004). Tuned to the signal: The privileged status of speech for young infants. *Developmental Science, 3*, 270–276.

Voyer, D., Bowes, A., & Techentin, C. (2008). On the perception of sarcasm in dichotic listening. *Neuropsychology, 22*, 390–399.

Voyer, D., Rodgers, M. A., & McCormick, P. A. (2004). Timing conditions and the magnitude of gender differences on the Mental Rotations Test. *Memory & Cognition, 32*, 72–82.

Vuilleumier, P. (2005). How brains beware: Neural mechanisms of emotional attention. *Trends in Cognitive Sciences, 9*, 585–592.

Vygotsky, L. (1978). *Mind in society: The development of higher psychological processes.* (M. Cole, V. John-Steiner, S. Scribner, & E. Soubermen, Eds.). Cambridge MA: Harvard University Press.

Wade, K. A., Garry, M., Read, J. D., & Lindsay, D. S. (2002). A picture is worth a thousand lies: Using false photographs to create false childhood memories. *Psychonomic Bulletin & Review, 9*, 597–603.

Wadzinski, J., Franks, R., Roane, D., & Bayard, M. (2007). Valproate-associated hyperammonemic encephalopathy. *Journal of the American Board of Family Medicine, 20*, 499–502.

Wagar, B. M., & Thagard, P. (2004). Spiking Phineas Gage: A neurocomputational theory of cognitive-affective integration in decision making. *Psychological Review, 111*, 67–69.

Wagenaar, W. A., & Groeneweg, J. (1990). The memory of concentration camp survivors. *Applied Cognitive Psychology, 4*, 77–87.

Wagner, A. D., Desmond, J. E., Glover, G. H., & Gabrieli, J. D. E. (1998). Prefrontal cortex and recognition memory: Functional-MRI evidence for context-dependent retrieval processes. *Brain, 121*, 1985–2002.

Wagner, G. A., & Morris, E. K. (1987). "Superstitious" behavior in children. *Psychological Record, 37*, 471–488.

Wahba, M. A., & Bridwell, L. G. (1976). Maslow reconsidered: A review of research on the need hierarchy theory. *Organizational Behavior and Human Performance, 15*, 212–240.

Wahlsten, D. (1997). Leilani Muir versus the philosopher king: Eugenics on trial in Alberta. *Genetica, 99*, 185–198.

Wai, J., Cacchio, M., Putallaz, M., & Makel, M. C. (2010). Sex differences in the right tail of cognitive abilities: A 30 year examination. *Intelligence, 38*, 412–423.

Waite, L. J., & Gallagher, M. (2000). *The case for marriage: Why married people are happier, healthier and better off financially.* New York: Doubleday.

Waitt, C., Gerald, M. S., Little, A. C., & Kraiselburd, E. (2006). Selective attention toward female secondary sexual color in male rhesus macaques. *American Journal of Primatology, 68*, 738–744.

Wakefield, A. J., Murch, S. H., Anthony, A., Linnell, J., Casson, D. M., Malik, M., et al. (1998). Retracted: Ileal-lymphoid-nodular hyperplasia, non-specific colitis, and pervasive developmental disorder in children. *Lancet, 351*, 637–641.

Walker, E. G., Savole, T., & Davis, D. (1994). Neuromotor precursors of schizophrenia. *Schizophrenia Bulletin, 20*, 441–451.

Walker, E. G., Shapiro, D., Esterberg, M., & Trotman, H. (2010). Neurodevelopment and schizophrenia: Broadening the focus. *Current Directions in Psychological Science, 19*, 204–208.

Walker, L. J., & Frimer, J. A. (2007). Moral personality of brave and caring exemplars. *Journal of Personality and Social Psychology, 93*, 845–860.

Walker, L. J., Frimer, J. A., & Dunlop, W. L. (2010). Varieties of moral personality: Beyond the banality of heroism. *Journal of Personality, 78*, 907–942.

Walker, M., Al-Sahab, B., Islam, F., & Tamim, H. (2011). The epidemiology of alcohol utilization during pregnancy: An analysis of the Canadian Maternity Experiences Survey (MES). *BMC Pregnancy and Childbirth, 11*, 52.

Walker, M. P., Liston, C., Hobson, J. A., & Stickgold, R. (2002). Cognitive flexibility across the sleep-wake cycle: REM-sleep enhancement of anagram problem solving. *Cognitive Brain Research, 14*, 317–324.

Waller, G. P., & Hodgson, S. (1996). Body image distortion in Anorexia and Bulimia Nervosa: The role of perceived and actual control. *Journal of Nervous & Mental Disease, 184*, 213–219.

Walsh, T., McClellan, J. M., McCarthy, S. E., Addington, A. M., Pierce, S. B., et al. (2008). Rare structural variants disrupt multiple genes in neurodevelopmental pathways in schizophrenia. *Science, 320*, 539–543.

Walther, E., & Grigoriadis, S. (2004). Why sad people like shoes better: The influence of mood on the evaluative conditioning of consumer attitudes. *Psychology and Marketing, 21*, 755–773.

Walum, H., Westberg, L., Henningsson, S., et al. (2008). Genetic variation in vasopressin receptor 1a gene (AVPR1A) associated with pair-bonding behavior in humans. *Proceedings of the National Academy of Sciences, 105*, 14153–14156.

Wampold, B. E. (2001). *The great psychotherapy debate: Model, methods, and findings*. Mahwah, NJ: Lawrence Erlbaum Associates.

Wan, F., Ansons, T. L., Chattopadhyay, A., & Leboe, J. P. (2013). Defensive reactions to slim female images in advertising: The moderating role of mode of exposure. *Organizational Behavior and Human Decision Processes, 120*, 37–46.

Wang, P. S., Berglund, P., Olfson, M., Pincus, H. A., Wells, K. B., & Kessler, R. C. (2005). Failure and delay in initial treatment contact after first onset of mental disorders in the National Comorbidity Survey Replication. *Archives of General Psychiatry, 62*, 603–613.

Wang, S. H., & Morris, R .G. (2010). Hippocampal-neocortical interactions in memory formation, consolidation, and reconsolidation. *Annual Review of Psychology, 61*, 49–79.

Wang, X., Lu, T., Snider, R. K., & Liang, L. (2005). Sustained firing in auditory cortex evoked by preferred stimuli. *Nature, 435*, 341–346.

Wansink, B. (1996). Can package size accelerate usage volume? *Journal of Marketing, 60*, 1–14.

Wansink, B., & Cheney, M. M. (2005). Superbowls: Serving bowl size and food consumption. *Journal of American Medical Association, 293*, 1727–1728.

Wansink, B., & Kim, J. (2005). Bad popcorn in big buckets: Portion size can influence intake as much as taste. *Journal of Nutrition Education and Behavior, 37*, 242–245.

Wansink, B., Painter, J. E., & North, J. (2005). Bottomless bowls: Why visual cues of portion size may influence intake. *Obesity Research, 13*, 93–100.

Wansink, B., & Wansink, C. S. (2010). The largest last supper: Depictions of food portions and plate size increased over the millennium. *International Journal of Obesity, 34*, 943–944.

Ward, C. D., & Cooper, R. P. (1999). A lack of evidence in 4-month-old human infants for paternal voice preference. *Developmental Psychobiology, 35*, 49–59.

Ward, L. M., MacLean, S. E., & Kirschner, A. (2010). Stochastic resonance modulates neural synchronization within and between cortical sources. *PLoS One, 5*, e14371.

Ware, M. A., Wang, T., Shapiro, S., Robinson, A., Dubruet, T., Huynh, T., Gamsa, A., Bennett, G. J., & Collet, J. (2010). Smoked cannabis for chronic neuropathic pain: a randomized controlled trial. *Canadian Medical Association Journal, 182*, E694–E701.

Warfield, D. (1973). The study of hearing in animals. In Gray, W. (Ed.), *Methods of Animal Experimentation* (Vol. IV, pp. 43–143). London: Academic Press.

Warneken F., & Tomasello, M. (2007). Helping and cooperation at 14 months of age. *Infancy, 11*, 271–294.

Warneken, F., & Tomasello, M. (2013). The emergence of contingent reciprocity in young children. *Journal of Experimental Child Psychology, 116*, 338–350.

Warren, M. P., & Brooks-Gunn, J. (1989). Mood and behavior during adolescence: Evidence for hormonal factors. *Journal of Clinical Endocrinology and Metabolism, 69*, 77–83.

Warrington, E. K., & McCarthy, R. (1987). Categories of knowledge: Further fractionations and an attempted integration. *Brain, 110*, 1273–1296.

Warrington, E. K., & Shallice, T. (1979). Semantic access dyslexia. *Brain, 102*, 43–63.

Wasser, S. K., & Barash, D. P. (1983). Reproductive suppression among female mammals: Implication for biomedicine and sexual selection theory. *Quarterly Review of Biology, 58*, 523–538.

Watkins, C. E., Campbell, V. L., Neiberding, R., & Hallmark, R. (1995). Contemporary practice of psychological assessment by clinical psychologists. *Professional Psychology: Research and Practice, 26*, 54–60.

Watkins, K. E., Vargha-Khadem, F., Ashburner, J., Passingham, R. E., Connelly, A., . . . Gadian, D. G. (2002). MRI analysis of an inherited speech and language disorder: Structural brain abnormalities. *Brain, 125*, 465–478.

Watson, J. B. (1913). Psychology as the behaviorist views it. *Psychological Review, 20*, 158–177.

Watson, J. B. (1930). *Behaviorism*. Chicago: University of Chicago Press.

Watson, J. B., & Rayner, R. R. (1920). Conditioned emotional reactions. *Journal of Experimental Psychology, 3*, 1–14.

Watson, J. C., Gordon, L. B., Stermac, L., Kalogerakos, F., & Steckley, P. (2003). Comparing the effectiveness of process-experiential with cognitive-behavioral psychotherapy in the treatment of depression. *Journal of Consulting and Counseling Psychology, 71*, 773–781.

Watson, M. W., & Getz, K. (1990). The relationship between Oedipal behaviors and children's family role concepts. *Merrill-Palmer Quarterly, 36*, 487–505.

Watts, R. E. (2000). Adlerian counseling: A viable approach for contemporary practice. *TCA Journal, 28*, 11–23.

Wayment, H. A., & Peplau, L. A. (1995). Social support and well-being among lesbian and heterosexual women: A structural modeling approach. *Personality and Social Psychology Bulletin, 21*, 1189–1199.

Weaver, A. D., MacKeigan, K. L., & MacDonald, H. A. (2011). Experience and perceptions of young adults in friends with benefits relationships: A qualitative study. *The Canadian Journal of Human Sexuality, 20*, 41–53.

Weaver, I. C., Cervoni, N., Champagne, F. A., D'Alessio, A. C., Sharma, S., Seckl, J. R., . . . & Meaney, M. J. (2004). Epigenetic programming by maternal behavior. *Nature Neuroscience, 7*, 847–854.

Webb, W. B., & Cartwright, R. D. (1978). Sleep and dreams. *Annual Review of Psychology, 29*, 223–252.

Weber, B., Jermann, F., Gex-Fabry, M., Nallet, A., Bondolfi, G., & Aubry, J. M. (2010). Mindfulness-based cognitive therapy for bipolar disorder: A feasibility trial. *European Psychiatry, 25*, 334–337.

Wechsler, D. (1939). *The measurement of adult intelligence*. Baltimore: Williams & Witkins

Wechsler, D. (2009). *Wechsler Memory Scale–Fourth Edition*. San Antonio, TX: Pearson.

Weeks, D. L., & Anderson, L. P. (2000). The interaction of observational learning with overt practice: Effects on motor skill learning. *Acta Psychologica, 104*, 259–271.

Weinsier, R. L., Hunter, G. R., Desmond, R. A., Byrne, N. M., Zuckerman, P. A., & Darnell, B. (2002). Free-living activity expenditure in women successful and unsuccessful at maintaining a normal body weight. *American Journal of Clinical Nutrition, 75*, 499–504.

Weisman, A. G., Lopez, S. R., Ventura, J., Nuechterlein, K. H., Goldstein, M. J., & Hwang, S. (2000). A comparison of psychiatric symptoms between Anglo-Americans and Mexican-Americans with schizophrenia. *Schizophrenia Bulletin, 26*, 817–824.

Weiss, A., King, J. E., & Hopkins, W. D. (2007). A cross-setting study of chimpanzee (*Pan troglodytes*) personality structure and development: Zoological parks and Yerkes National Primate Research Center. *American Journal of Primatology, 69*, 1264.

Weiss, E., Kemmler, G., Deisenhammer, E., Fleischhacker, W., & Delazer, M. (2003). Sex differences in cognitive functions. *Personality and Individual Differences, 35*, 863–875.

Weiss, G., & Hechtman, L. T. (1993). *Hyperactive children grown up: ADHD in children, adolescents, and adults*. New York: Guilford Press.

Weissman, M. M., Markowitz, J. C., Klerman, G. L. (2000). *Comprehensive guide to interpersonal psychotherapy*. New York: Basic Books.

Weisz, J. R., Weiss, B., Han, S. S., Granger, D. A., & Morton, T. (1995). Effects of psychotherapy with children and adolescents revisited: A meta-analysis of treatment outcome studies. *Psychological Bulletin, 117*, 450–468.

Weitzer, R., & Tuch, S. A. (2004). Race and perceptions of police misconduct. *Social Problems, 51*, 305–325.

Wells, B., & Corts, D. P. (2008). Attitudes towards fraternities and sororities: Evidence of implicit, ingroup favoritism. *College Student Journal, 42*, 842-846.

Wenk, G. (2010). *Your brain on food: How chemicals control your thoughts and feelings*. Oxford, UK: Oxford University Press.

Werker, J. F. (2003). Baby steps to learning language. *Journal of Pediatrics (Supplement: Special Issue), 143*, S62–S69.

Werker, J. F., & Lalonde, C. E. (1988). Cross-language speech perception: Initial capabilities and developmental change. *Developmental Psychology, 24*, 672–683.

Werker, J. F., & Tees, R. C. (1984). Phonemic and phonetic factors in adult cross-language speech perception. *Journal of the Acoustical Society of America, 75,* 1866–1878.

Werker, J. F., Yeung, H. H., & Yoshida, K. A. (2012). How do infants become experts at native-speech perception? *Current Directions in Psychological Science, 21,* 221–226.

Wernicke, C. (1874). *Der aphasische symptomencomplex.* Breslau: Kohn and Weigert.

Westen, D. (1998). The scientific legacy of Sigmund Freud: Toward a psychodynamically informed psychological science. *Psychological Bulletin, 124,* 333–371.

Westen, D., Blagov, P. S., & Harenski, K. (2006). Neural bases for motivated reasoning: An fMRI study of emotional constraints on partisan political judgment in the 2004 U.S. presidential election. *Journal of Cognitive Neuroscience, 18,* 1974–1958.

Westen, D., & Bradley, R. (2005). Empirically supported complexity: Rethinking evidence-based practice in psychotherapy. *Current Directions in Psychological Science, 14,* 266–271.

Wever, E. G., & Bray, C. W. (1930). The nature of acoustic response: The relation between sound frequency and frequency of impulses in the auditory nerve. *Journal of Experimental Psychology, 13,* 3733–3787.

Wever, R. A., Polasek, J., & Wildgruber, C. M. (1983). Bright light affects human circadian rhythms. *European Journal of Physiology, 396,* 85–87.

Whishaw, I. Q. (1991). Latent learning in a swimming pool place task by rats: Evidence for the use of associative and not cognitive mapping processes. *Quarterly Journal of Experimental Psychology B, 43,* 83–103.

White, C., Brown, J., & Edwards, M. (2013). Altered visual perception in long-term ecstasy (MDMA) users. *Psychopharmacology, 229,* 155–165.

Whiten, A. (2000). Primate culture and social learning. *Cognitive Science, 24,* 477–508.

Whitson, J. A., & Galinsky, A. D. (2008). Lacking control increases illusory pattern perception. *Science, 322,* 115–117.

Whorf, B. L. (1973). *Language, thought, and reality: Selected writings of Benjamin Whorf.* J. B. Carroll (Ed.). Oxford, UK: Technology Press of MIT.

Wiebe, S. A., Fang, H., Johnson, C., James, K. E., & Espy, K. A. (2014). Determining the impact of prenatal tobacco exposure on self-regulation at 6 months. *Developmental Psychology, 50,* 1746–1756.

Wiens, S. (2005). Interoception in emotional experience. *Current Opinion in Neurology, 18,* 442–447.

Wight, R. G., LeBlanc, A. J., & Badgett, M. V. L. (2013). Same-sex legal marriage and psychological well-being: Findings from the California Health Interview Survey. *American Journal of Public Health, 103,* 339–346.

Wijdicks, E. F. (2006). Minimally conscious state vs. persistent vegetative state: The case of Terry (Wallis) vs. the case of Terri (Schiavo). *Mayo Clinic Proceedings, 81,* 1155–1158.

Wijnen, V. J. M., van Boxtel, G. J. M., Eilander, H. J., & de Gelder, B. (2007). Mismatch negativity predicts recovery from the vegetative state. *Clinical Neurophysiology, 118,* 597–605.

Williams, J. M. G., Alatiq, Y., Crane, C., Barnhofer, T., Fennell, M. J. V., Duggan, D. S., et al. (2007). Mindfulness-based cognitive therapy (MBCT) in bipolar disorder: Preliminary evaluation of immediate effects on between-episode functioning. *Journal of Affective Disorders, 107,* 275–279.

Williams, J. M. G., Duggan, D. S., Crane, C., & Fennell, M. J. V. (2006). Mindfulness-based cognitive therapy for prevention of recurrence of suicidal behaviour. *Journal of Clinical Psychology, 62,* 201–210.

Williams, K. M., Nathanson, C., & Paulhus, D. L. (2010). Identifying and profiling scholastic cheaters: Their personality, cognitive ability, and motivation. *Journal of Experimental Psychology: Applied, 16,* 293–307.

Williams, T. J., Schimel, J., Hayes, J., & Usta, M. (2014). Following and resisting body image ideals in advertising: The moderating role of extrinsic contingency focus. *Self and Identity, 13,* 398–418.

Williamson, A. M., & Feyer, A. (2000). Moderate sleep deprivation produces impairments in cognitive and motor performance equivalent to legally prescribed levels of alcohol intoxication. *Occupational & Environmental Medicine, 57,* 649–655.

Willingham, D. T. (2004). Reframing the mind: How Howard Gardner became a hero among educators by simply by redefining talents as "intelligences." *Education Next, 4,* 19–24.

Willis, J., & Todorov, A. (2006). First impressions: Making up your mind after a 100-ms exposure to a face. *Psychological Science, 17,* 592–598.

Willner, P., Towell, A., Sampson, D., Sophokleous, S., & Muscat, R. (1987). Reduction of sucrose preference by chronic unpredictable mild stress, and its restoration by a tricyclic antidepressant. *Psychopharmacology, 93,* 358–364.

Willoughby, T. (2008). A short-term longitudinal study of Internet and computer game use by adolescent boys and girls: Prevalence, frequency of use, and psychosocial predictors. *Developmental Psychology, 44,* 195–204.

Wilson, A. E., & Ross, M. (2003). The identity function of autobiographical memory: Time is on our side. *Memory, 11,* 137–149.

Wilson, M. E., Fisher, J., Fischer, A., Lee, V., Harris, R. B., & Bartness, T. J. (2008). Quantifying food intake in socially housed monkeys: Social status effects on caloric consumption. *Physiology & Behavior, 94,* 586–594.

Wilson, P. M., Mack, D. E., & Grattan, K. P. (2008). Understanding motivation for exercise: A self-determination theory perspective. *Canadian Psychology, 49,* 250–256.

Wimmer, F., Hoffmann, R. F., Bonato, R. A., & Moffitt, A. R. (1992). The effects of sleep deprivation on divergent thinking and attention processes. *Journal of Sleep Research, 1,* 223–230.

Wimmer, H., & Perner, J. (1983). Beliefs about beliefs: Representation and constrained function of wrong beliefs in young children's understanding of deceptions. *Cognition, 13,* 103–128.

Winkielman, P., Schwarz, N., & Nowak, A. (2002). Affect and processing dynamics: Perceptual fluency enhances evaluations. In *Emotional cognition: From brain to behaviour* (pp. 111–135). Amsterdam, Netherlands: John Benjamins Publishing Company.

Winkler, I., Haden, G., Lading, O., Sziller, I., & Honing, H. (2008). Newborn infants detect the beat in music. *Proceedings of the National Academy of Science the United States of America, 106,* 2468–2471.

Winter, B., Breitenstein, C., Mooren, F. C., Voelker, K., Fobker, M., Lechtermann, A., et al. (2007). High impact running improves learning. *Neurobiology of Learning and Memory, 87,* 597–609.

Winterer, G. (2010). Why do patients with schizophrenia smoke? *Current Opinion in Psychiatry, 23,* 112–119.

Witelson, S. F., Beresh, H., & Kigar, D. L. (2006). Intelligence and brain size in 100 postmortem brains: Sex, lateralization and age factors. *Brain: A Journal of Neurology, 129,* 386–398.

Witelson, S. F., Kigar, D. L., & Harvey, T. (1999). The exceptional brain of Albert Einstein. *The Lancet, 353,* 2149–2153.

Wobber, V., Hare, B., Maboto, J., Lipson, S., Wrangham, R., & Ellison, P. T. (2010). Differential changes in steroid hormones before competition in bonobos and chimpanzees. *Proceedings of the National Academy of Sciences USA, 107,* 12457–12462.

Wojtowicz, J.M. (2012). Adult neurogenesis. From circuits to models. *Behavioural Brain Research, 227,* 490–496.

Wolpe, J. (1990). *The practice of behavior therapy.* Elmsford, NY: Pergamon Press.

Wong, C. K., & Read, J. D. (2011). Positive and negative effects of physical context reinstatement on eyewitness recall and identification. *Applied Cognitive Psychology, 25,* 2–11.

Wong, J., Rothmond, D. A., Webster, M. J., & Weickert, C. S. (2013). Increases in two truncated TrkB isoforms in the prefrontal cortex of people with schizophrenia. *Schizophrenia Bulletin, 39*(1), 130–140.

Woo, J. S. T., Brotto, L. A., & Gorcalka, B. (2010). Sex guilt and culture-linked barriers to testicular examinations. *International Journal of Sexual Health, 22,* 144–154.

Woo, J. S. T., Brotto, L. A., & Gorzalka, B. (2012). The relationship between sex guilt and sexual desire in a community sample of

Chinese and Euro-Canadian women. *Journal of Sex Research, 49,* 290–298.

Wood, D., Harms, P., & Vazire, S. (2010). Perceiver effects as projective tests: What your perceptions of others say about you. *Journal of Personality and Social Psychology, 99,* 174–190.

Woodberry, K. A., Giuliano, A. J., & Seidman, L. J. (2008). Premorbid IQ in schizophrenia. *American Journal of Psychiatry, 165,* 579–587.

Woodward, N. D., Zald, D. H., Ding, Z., Riccardi, P., Ansari, M. S., . . . Kessler, R.M. (2009). Cerebral morphology and dopamine D2/D3 receptor distribution in humans: A combined [18F]fallypride and voxel-based morphometry study. *Neuroimage, 46,* 31–38.

Woodworth, R. S. (1929). *Psychology: A study of mental life* (2nd ed.). [Online]. Retrieved from http://www.gutenberg.org/files/31382/31382-h/31382-h.htm

Woody, E. Z., & Bowers, K. (1994). A frontal assault on dissociated control. In S. J. Lynn & J. W. Rhue (Eds.), *Dissociation: Clinical and theoretical perspectives* (pp. 52–79). New York: Guilford Press.

Woody, E. Z., & Farvolden, P. (1998). Dissociation in hypnosis and frontal executive function. *American Journal of Clinical Hypnosis, 40,* 206–216.

Wright, D. (1997). Getting out of the asylum: Understanding the confinement of the insane in the nineteenth century. *Social History of Medicine, 10,* 137–155.

Wright, I. C., Rabe-Hesketh, S., Woodruff, P. W., David, A. S., Murray, R. M., & Bullmore, E. T. (2000). Meta-analysis of regional brain volumes in schizophrenia. *American Journal of Psychiatry, 157,* 16–25.

Wright, J. C., Huston, A. C., Scantlin, R., & Kotler, J. (2001). The Early Window Project: "Sesame Street" prepares children for school. In S. M. Fisch & R. T. Truglio (Eds.), *"G" is for "growing": Thirty years of research on children and* Sesame Street (pp. 97–114). Mahwah, NJ: Lawrence Erlbaum.

Wright, S. C., Aron, A., McLaughlin-Volpe, T., & Ropp, S. A. (1997). The extended contact effect: Knowledge of cross-group friendships and prejudice. *Journal of Personality and Social Psychology, 73,* 73–90.

Wuornos v. State of Florida, 19 Fla. Law W. S 455 (September 22, 1994).

Wyer, Jr., R. S., & Collins, J. E. (1992). A theory of humor elicitation. *Psychological Review, 99,* 663–688.

Yamagata, S., Suzuki, A., Ando, J., Ono, Y., Kijima, N., . . . & Jang, K. L. (2006). Is the genetic structure of human personality universal? A cross-cultural twin study from North America, Europe, and Asia. *Journal of Personality and Social Psychology, 90,* 987–998.

Yamamoto, T. (2007). Brain regions responsible for the expression of conditioned taste aversion in rats. *Chemical Senses, 32,* 105–109.

Yamamoto, T., & Fujimoto, Y. (1991). Brain mechanisms of taste aversion learning in the rat. *Brain Research Bulletin, 27,* 403–306.

Yamamoto, T., Matsuo, R., Kiyomitsu, Y., & Kitamura, R. (1989). Taste responses of cortical neurons in freely ingesting rats. *Journal of Neurophysiology, 61,* 1244–1258.

Yamazaki, T., & Tanaka, S. (2009). Computational models of timing mechanisms in the cerebellar granular layer. *Cerebellum, 8,* 423–432.

Yang, L. J., & Schnaar, R. L. (2008). Axon regeneration inhibitors. *Neurological Research, 30,* 1047–1052.

Yang, Y., Raine, A., Colletti, P., Toga, A., & Narr, K. (2010). Morphological alterations in the prefrontal cortex and the amygdala in unsuccessful psychopaths. *Journal of Abnormal Psychology, 119,* 546–554.

Ybarra, O., Burnstein, E., Winkielman, P., Keller, M., Manis, M., Chan, E., & Rodriguez, J. (2008). Mental exercising through simple socializing: Social interaction promotes general cognitive functioning. *Personality and Social Psychology Bulletin, 34,* 248–259.

Yerkes, R. M., & Dodson, J. D. (1908). The relation of strength of stimulus to rapidity of habit formation. *Journal of Comparative Neurology and Psychology, 18,* 459–482.

Yoo, S. K., & Skovholt, T. M. (2001). Cross-cultural examination of depression expression and help-seeking behavior: A comparative study of American and Korean college students. *Journal of College Counseling, 4,* 10–19.

Young, A. S., Klap, R., Sherbourne, C. D., & Wells, K. B. (2001). The quality of care for depressive and anxiety disorders in the United States. *Archives of General Psychiatry, 58,* 55–61.

Young, S. N., & Leyton, M. (2002). The role of serotonin in human mood and social interaction: Insight from altered tryptophan levels. *Pharmacology Biochemistry and Behavior, 71,* 857–865.

Yuile, A., & McVey, G. L. (2009). The role of social influence in the prevention of disordered eating among young adolescent females. *Journal of School Mental Health, 2,* 47–60.

Zadra, A., & Donderi, D. C. (2000). Nightmares and bad dreams: Their prevalence and relationship to well-being. *Journal of Abnormal Psychology, 109,* 273–281.

Zahn-Waxler, C., & Radke-Yarrow, M. (1990). The origins of empathic concern. *Motivation and Emotion, 14,* 107–130.

Zahn-Waxler, C., Radke-Yarrow, M., Wagner, E., & Chapman, M. (1992). Development of concern for others. *Developmental Psychology, 28,* 126–136.

Zajonc, R. B. (1976). Family configuration and intelligence. *Science, 192,* 227–236.

Zajonc, R. B., Heingartner, A., & Herman, E. M. (1969). Social enhancement and impairment of performance in the cockroach. *Journal of Personality and Social Psychology, 13,* 83–92.

Zak, P. J. (2008). The neurobiology of trust. *Scientific American, 298,* 88–92.

Zald, D. H., Boileau, I., El-Dearedy, W., Gunn, R., McGlone, F., Dichter, G. S., & Dagher, A. (2004). Dopamine transmission in the human striatum during monetary reward tasks. *Journal of Neuroscience, 24,* 4105–4112.

Zalesky, A., Solwij, N., Yücel, M., Lubman, D. I., Takagi, M., . . . Seal, M. (2012). Effect of long-term cannabis use on axonal fibre connectivity. *Brain, 135,* 2245–2255.

Zaman, R., Thind, D., & Kocmur, M. (2008). Transcranial magnetic stimulation in schizophrenia. *Neuroendocrinological Letters, 1,* 147–160.

Zanna, M. P., Kiesler, C. A., & Pikonis, P. A. (1970). Positive and negative attitudinal affect established by classical conditioning. *Journal of Personality and Social Psychology, 14,* 321–328.

Zatorre, R. J., & Zarate, J. M. (2010). Cortical processing of music. In D. Poeppel, T. Overath, A. N. Popper, and R. R. Fay (eds.), *The human auditory cortex.* New York: Springer.

Zelazo, N. A., Zelazo, P. R., Cohen, K. M., & Zelazo, P. D. (1993). Specificity of practice effects on elementary neuromotor patterns. *Developmental Psychology, 29,* 686–691.

Zentall, T. R. (2012). Perspectives on observational learning in animals. *Journal of Comparative Psychology, 126,* 114–128.

Zhu, J., Yung, W., Chow, B. K., Chan, Y., & Wang, J. (2006). The cerebellar-hypothalamic circuits: Potential pathways underlying cerebellar involvement in somatic-visceral integration. *Brain Research Reviews, 52,* 93–106.

Zimbardo, P. G. (2004). *A situationist perspective on the psychology of evil: Understanding how good people are transformed into perpetrators.* New York: Guilford Press.

Zimbardo, P. G. (2007). *The Lucifer effect: Understanding how good people turn evil.* New York: Random House.

Zimmerman, F. J., & Christakis, D. A. (2005). Children's television viewing and cognitive outcomes: A longitudinal analysis of national data. *Archives of Pediatric and Adolescent Medicine, 159,* 619–625.

Zimmerman, F. J., Christakis, D. A., & Meltzoff, A. N. (2007). Association between media viewing and language development in children under 2 years. *Journal of Pediatrics, 151,* 354–368.

Zucker, R. A., Donovan, J. E., Masten, A. S., Mattson, M. E., & Moss, H. B. (2008). Early developmental processes and the continuity of risk for underage drinking and problem drinking. *Pediatrics, 121,* 5252–5272.

Zuroff, D. C., Fournier, M. A., Patall, E. A., & Leybman, M. J. (2010). Steps toward an evolutionary personality psychology: Individual differences in the social rank domain. *Canadian Psychology, 51,* 58–66.

Name Index

A

AbdelMalik, P., 650
Abé, C., 457
Abematsu, M., 90
Abouguendia, M., 25
Abraham, W., 284
Abramowitz, E., 201
Abramson, L. Y., 639
Acenas, L. R., 343
Acevedo-Garcia, D., 358
Adair, G., 34
Adam, T. C., 599
Addis, M. E., 655
Adelstein, J. S., 516
Adolphs, R., 477
Adorno, T., 496
Adreasen, N. C., 649
Aggleton, J. P., 292
Ahamed, Y., 111
Ahlfinger, N. R., 536, 537
Ahmed, R., 223f
Ahrold, T., 458
Ainsworth, M. D. S., 407, 409
Aknin, L. B., 414
Alampay, D. A., 135f
Albert, S., 306
Aldous, J., 431
Alexander, B. K., 214, 214f
Alexander, M. P., 105
Alibhai, A., 201
Alicke, M. D., 555
Alladin, A., 201
Allen, J. S., 434
Allen, R., 194
Allen, S. W., 320
Allik, J., 507t
Allport, G., 493, 555
Alonso, M. A., 293
Altemeyer, B., 497
Altschuler, E. L., 172
Alvaro, E., 462
Amaral, D. G., 539
Amat, J., 609
Amato, P. R., 587
Ambady, N., 486, 553
American Academy of Neurology, 205
American College Health Association, 659
American Heritage Dictionary, 316t
American Psychiatric Association, 617, 626
American Psychological Association (APA), 14f, 196t, 564, 642t, 660
Ames, M., 456
Amir, S., 182

An, K., 631
Anand, B. K., 442
Anastasi, A., 358
Anderson, A. K., 484, 485f
Anderson, B., 375
Anderson, C. A., 265, 266, 267
Anderson, L., 661, 662f
Anderson, L. P., 264
Anderson, R. C., 512
Andres, M., 118
Angus Reid Public Opinion, 4
Ano, G. G., 607
Antoni, M., 600
Aouizerate, B., 684
Apaydin, E. A., 679
Arcimboldo, G., 148f
Arendt, J., 189
Arguin, M., 320
Argyelan, M., 683
Arkowitz, H., 48
Armstrong, H. L., 454
Arnett, J. J., 421, 425
Aron, A., 467, 468, 468f, 483
Asch, S. E., 538, 539, 540
Aschoff, J., 183
Aserinsky, E., 191
Ashby, F. G., 514
Ashtari, M., 221
Ashton, M. C., 496
Ashton, R., 194
Aslin, R. N., 405
Assor, A., 414
Atkinson, R. C., 272
Aubrey, J. B., 193
Ausubel, D. P., 7
Avena, N. M., 107
Avolio, B. J., 367
Awh, E., 280
Axel, R., 175
Aylward, E. H., 149

B

Bachman, J. G., 420
Baddeley, A. D., 279, 280, 281, 291, 292
Badeweg, T., 345f
Badman, M. K., 444
Baer, R. A., 606
Bahrick, H. P., 298, 299f
Bahrick, L. E., 409
Bailenson, J. N., 322
Bailey, J. M., 456, 457, 457f, 458
Baird, B., 204, 204f
Baker, J. R., 292
Balch, W., 294
Ball, K., 435, 449

Balota, D. A., 318, 319f
Balter, L. J. T., 581
Baltes, P. B., 367
Banaji, M. R., 559
Bandura, A., 263, 265, 471, 669
Banse, R., 560
Barash, D. P., 449
Barbanoj, M. J., 218
Barbasz, M., 201
Barbieri, R. L., 449
Barch, D. M., 367
Bard, K. A., 409
Barger, L. K., 188
Barger, S. D., 598
Bargh, J. A., 534, 535, 552, 554
Bar-Haim, Y., 510
Barkley, R. A., 618
Barlow, D. H., 681
Barnea-Goraly, N., 419
Barnes, C., 187
Barolo, R., 163
Baron-Cohen, S., 177
Barratt, E. L., 177, 178f
Barrett, L. F., 569
Bartels, S., 467
Barton, J., 240
Bartus, R. T., 95
Basbaum, A. I., 169
Baskin-Sommers, A., 627
Bassareo, V., 212
Bateman, D., 205
Bates, J. E., 499
Battaglia, M., 510
Battistella, G., 220
Baumeister, R. F., 467
Bauserman, R., 426
Bavelier, D., 129
Baym, C., 106
Bazarian, J. J., 120
Beall, E. B., 683
Beauchamp, G. K., 174
Beauregard, M., 467
Bechara, A., 45
Beck, A. T., 32, 671
Beck, D. M., 135
Beck, H. P., 235
Becker, E., 468
Beckinschtein, T. A., 300
Bedi, R. P., 667
Beebe, B., 409, 411
Beeman, E. A., 98
Beer, J. S., 45
Beilock, S., 590
Beiser, M., 357
Béjot, Y., 195
Bell, P. A., 536

Bell, R. A., 656
Belsky, J., 432
Bem, D. J., 25
Bem, S. L., 25
Benbow, C. P., 371
Benedict, R., 419
Benet-Martinez, V., 506, 507t
Bennett, G. G., 587
Berchtold, N. C., 111
Berenson, A., 680
Berger, J. M., 656
Berger, R., 186
Berkman, L. F., 587
Berlim, M. T., 683
Berlin, B., 322
Berlucchi, G., 113
Berns, G. S., 539
Berquier, A., 194
Berridge, C. W., 95, 107
Berry, S. L., 447
Berthier, M. L., 114
Bertram, L., 435
Bestmann, S., 118
Bevan, T. E., 458
Bever, T. G., 403
Bezeau, S., 68
Bhatara, A., 156
Bhattacharya, J., 585
Bhugra, D., 645
Bialystok, E., 344
Biederman, J., 636
Bigelow, H. J., 43
Birbaumer, N., 236, 237f
Bisiach, E., 109
Bitensky, S. H., 257
Bjerkedal, T., 380
Bjork, R. A., 278, 300
Blackwell, L. S., 359, 359f
Blagov, P. S., 332f
Blair, C., 381
Blair, K. L., 461
Blair, R. J. R., 368, 627
Blake, R., 167
Blandin, Y., 265
Blesa, J., 57
Bliss, T., 284
Block, R. I., 220
Blum, K., 250
Blumenthal, A. L., 235
Boesch, C., 264
Bogaert, A. F., 419
Bogle, K. E., 222
Bohart, A., 668
Boldizar, J. P., 423
Bolla, K. I., 220
Boly, M., 209
Bonanno, G. A., 434
Bondolfi, G., 673
Bonnebakker, A. E., 199
Boomsma, D. I., 76, 77
Booth, A., 97, 98
Born, J., 186
Bornovalova, M. A., 238

Borrelli, F., 680
Bortolussi, M., 203
Bötzel, K., 120
Bouchard, Jr., T. J., 371, 372
Bouchard, T. J., 509
Bourdage, J. S., 496
Bouton, M. E., 234
Boveroux, P., 200
Bower, G. H., 294
Bowers, K., 201
Bowker, A., 46
Bowlby, J., 407, 409, 434
Boyce, W., 426
Boyd, J. E., 620
Boyd, R., 78
Bracha, H., 634
Bradley, M. M., 627f
Bradley, R., 661
Bradley, R. H., 380
Brainard, D. H., 150
Brain Tumour Foundation of
     Canada, 114
Branch, C. H., 449
Branigan, C., 603
Bransford, J. D., 303
Braver, T. S., 367
Bray, C. W., 161
Brendel, G. R., 629
Breslow, L., 587
Bridwell, L. G., 466
Brion, M. J., 392
Brondolo, E., 587
Brook, J. S., 221
Brooks, D. C., 234
Brooks, L. R., 319, 320
Brooks Gunn, J., 419
Brotto, L. A., 461
Brown, A. S., 276, 650
Brown, G. W., 651
Brown, J., 280
Brown, J. M., 293
Brown, L. L., 468f
Brown, M., 390
Brown, R., 127f, 296, 297
Brown, R. E., 21, 192
Bruck, M., 307
Brunell, A. B., 626
Brunstein, J. C., 527
Buccino, G., 266f
Buchtel, E. E., 506
Buck, L. B., 175
Buckholtz, J. W., 250
Buehlman, K. T., 431
Bugelski, B. R., 135f
Bugg, J. M., 367
Bukhari, I. A., 679
Bundorf, M. K., 585
Bunn, E. M., 320
Burger, J. M., 573
Burkam, D. T., 381
Burke, B. L., 469
Burke, D. M., 137
Burke, T. M., 189

Burkhalter, R., 223f
Burnand, Y., 681
Burns, M., 603
Bushman, B. J., 266, 267, 555
Buss, D. M., 84, 85, 452
Buston, P. M., 48
Butcher, L. M., 377
Butler, B., 137
Butterweck, V., 679
Button, E. J., 449
Byers, E. S., 427, 459

C
Cabeza, E. A., 295, 436
Caci, H., 183
Cacioppo, J. T., 467, 557, 565, 587
Cacioppo, S., 587
Cahill, L., 296
Cahn, B. R., 606
Cai, D. J., 192
Cairns, B., 425
Cairns, R., 425
Caldwell, H. K., 595
Calhoun, L. G., 434, 605
Calvo, G., 217
Campos, J. J., 396
Canadian Community Health Survey
     (CCHS), 193
2007 Canadian Community Health
     Survey (CCHS), 584f
2011-2012 Canadian Community
     Health Survey (CCHS), 583f, 585
Canadian Medical Association, 656
Canadian Psychological Association
     (CPA), 459
Cauli, T., 515
Cao, X., 377
Capafons, A., 200
Cappadocia, M. C., 95
Cappo, B. M., 607
Caramazza, A., 148, 320f, 322
Cardosa, S. H., 480f
Carhart-Harris, R. L., 218
Carise, D., 223
Carlsmith, J. M., 574
Carlson, N. R., 106f, 232f
Carmichael, M. S., 456
Carmody, T. P., 201
Carmona, J. E., 165
Carpendale, J. I., 423
Carr, C. E., 160
Carré, J. M., 98
Carroll, J. B., 365
Carroll, M. E., 214
Carston, R., 340
Cartensen, L. L., 433, 433t, 434
Carter, A. C., 224
Carter, C. S., 515, 596
Cartwright, R. D., 191
Caruso, E. M., 48
Casey, B. J., 421
Caspi, A., 75f, 499, 509, 640, 641f, 650
Cattell, R. B., 366, 367, 493

Cavallera, C., 184
CBC News, 622
Ceci, S. J., 307, 363, 381
Centers for Disease Control and
    Prevention (CDC), 392, 394, 580,
    580*t*, 641
Cepeda, N. N., 7
Cesario, J., 319
Chabris, C. F., 136
Chaiken, S., 552
Chambers, R. A., 421
Chambless, D., 660, 674
Champagne, F. A., 78
Chan, B. L., 172, 173*f*
Chan, Y-C., 327, 328*f*
Chang, K-E., 328
Chang, Y., 679
Changizi, M., 84
Chapman, H. A., 484
Charles, S. T., 433*t*, 434
Charness, N., 436
Chartrand, T. L., 534, 535
Chase, P. G., 80
Chase, W. G., 275
Chaudhari, N., 174
Cheesman, J., 132
Chen, H-C., 328*f*
Chen, I., 188
Chen, J. L., 162
Chen, K. W., 606
Chen, S. C., 536
Chen, Z., 280
Cheney, M. M., 445
Cheng, H., 241
Cheng, P. C., 276*f*
Chentsova-Dutton, Y. E., 213
Chess, S., 499
Cheung, B. Y., 401
Cheung, F. M., 506
Cheung, M., 657
Chiao, J. Y., 507
Chirkov, V. I., 471, 473
Choi, I., 556
Choi, J., 83*f*
Choi, Y., 378
Chopra, I. C., 219
Chopra, R. W., 219
Chou, T-L., 328*f*
Christakis, D. A., 400
Christakis, N. A., 588
Christensen, C., 444
Christie, R., 526
Christoff, K., 203
Chung, S., 251
Church, T. A., 506
Cialdini, R. B., 572, 573
Ciccarelli, S., 102*f*, 140*f*, 143*f*, 147*f*,
    161*f*, 170*f*, 502*f*, 592*f*
Clancy, S. A., 9
Claparède, E., 283
Clark, J. J., 274*f*
Clark, J. M., 300
Clark, K. B., 296

Clarke, D., 257
Clopton, N. A., 423
CNN, 626
Coambs, R. B., 214*f*
Coane, J. H., 318, 319*f*
Cohen, B., 597, 655
Cohen, F., 469
Cohen, G. L., 586
Cohen, J., 68, 69
Cohen, J. N., 459
Cohen, K. M., 426
Cohen, N. J., 285
Cohn, M. A., 434
Cojan, Y., 202
Cole, S., 600
Coleman, D. R., 91
Coleman, M. R., 205
Collins, A., 53
Collins, A. M., 275, 317, 317*f*
Collins, J. E., 327
Collins, P. F., 514
Colonna-Pydyn, C., 656
Colwill, R. M., 251, 252
Combs, D., 646
Comings, D. E., 250
Compton, J. A., 570
Conde-Agudelo, A., 393
Connelly, A., 345*f*
Connelly, M., 547
Connolly, J. F., 206*f*
Connor, P. D., 391
Conway, B. R., 153
Conway, M., 306
Cook, E. W., 237
Cook, I. A., 462
Coombs, R. H., 431
Cooper, H. M., 381
Cooper, R. P., 395
Copp, A., 345*f*
Corballis, M. C., 111
Cordner, G., 561
Coren, S., 187, 187*f*
Corkin, S., 285, 295
Corkum, P., 194
Correll, J., 561
Corrigan, P., 655
Corti, M., 118
Corts, D. P., 560
Cosgrove, G. R., 683
Costa, A., 344, 500
Costa, P. T., 493, 494*f*
Cote, K. A., 188
Cotman, C. W., 111
Couzin, J., 676
Covington, H. E. III, 58
Cowan, C. P., 432
Cowan, N., 279, 280
Cowan, P. A., 432
Cowan, R. L., 217
Cox, C., 469
Crabbe, J., 75
Craig, I., 377
Craig, L. A., 95

Craig, M. C., 627
Craighero, L., 265
Craik, F. I., 282, 289, 290
Cramer, R., 87*f*
Crane, C., 673
Cranford, R., 205
Craske, M., 655, 656
Crean, R. D., 219
Creeley, C. E., 294
Creswell, J. D., 319
Crick, F., 200
Critchley, H., 132
Crits-Cristoph, P., 660
Croker, S., 276*f*
Crompton, S., 591
Crowell, S. E., 629
Crumpton, H., 450
Cruse, D., 208
Crutchley, A., 343
Cryan, J. F., 58
Csibra, G., 395
Csikszentmihalyi, M., 26
Cuijpers, P., 196
Cukor, J., 670
Cummings, J. L., 110
Cunningham, W. A.,
    559, 561*f*
Curran, H. V., 217
Cusi, A., 485*f*
Cutrona, C., 641
Cytowic, R. E., 167

D
Dabbs, J. M., 98
Dagher, A., 442
Dahl, D. W., 412, 463
Daigle, M. S., 642
Dal Cin, S., 581
Dallman, M. F., 599
Damasio, A. R., 45
Damisch, L., 256
Daneback, K., 461
Daneman, M., 199
Dani, C., 393
Danner, D. D., 604
Dar, A., 679
DARA, 568
D'Arcy, R. C. N., 206*f*
D'Argembeau, A., 681
Dargie, E., 459
Darley, J. M., 541, 542, 543
Dar-Nimrod, I., 333, 333*t*
Darvesh, S., 95
Darwin, C., 485
Das, K. K., 636*f*
Davis, C., 426, 449
Davis, C. L., 111
Davis, D., 202, 310
Davis, N. J., 177, 178*f*
Dawson, D., 188
de Araujo, I. E., 444
Dearing, R. L., 426
Deary, I., 371

Deary, I. J., 363, 377
De Bruin, E., 186
DeCasper, A. J., 395
Deci, E. L., 414, 415, 471, 472, 472f
DeCicco, T. L., 191
Deese, J., 277, 309
Defazio, J. N., 183f
Degardin, A., 118
de Jonghe, F., 681
Delaney, P. F., 7
Delargy, M., 209
Delgado, J. M. R., 442
DeLoache, J. S., 403
DeLongis, A., 604
De Los Reyes, A., 660
DelVecchio, W. F., 500
De Marchis, G. M., 679
Dement, W. C., 183f, 185f
Dempster, F. N., 7
Denko, T., 680
Dennis, N. A., 311
Deoni, S. C. L., 397
Depue, R. A., 514
Derkits, E. J., 650
DeRubeis, R., 661
Deschner, T., 84
Desrochco, A. S., 339
Deutsch, G., 104, 111
de Vries, R. E., 496
de Waele, C., 165
DeYoung, C. G., 112, 515, 515f
Diamond, M. C., 375, 379
Diana, R. A., 110
Diaz, J. II., 95
Dibble, H. L., 80
Di Chiara, G., 212
Dickinson, A., 250, 251
DiClemente, C. C., 655
Diener, E., 557
Dietz, T., 570
Digdon, N., 235
DiLalla, L. F., 636
Dilworth-Bart, J. E., 358
Dingemanse, N. J., 511
Dinges, D. F., 188
Dingledine, R., 94
DiPaola, S., 153
di Pellegrino, G., 265
Ditzen, B., 596
Dixon, M. J., 148, 167, 255, 651
Dixon, P., 203
Dixson, A. F., 84
Dobkin, P. L., 606
Dodson, J. D., 592
Dolcos, F., 296
Dolderman, D., 27, 492
Domjan, M., 242
Donderi, D. C., 194
Done, D. J., 646
Douglas, K. S., 27, 647
Dovidio, J. F., 562
Dow Schull, N., 255
Dozois, D., 305

Drachman, D. A., 95, 108
Drew, M. R., 636f
D'Souza, D. C., 219, 220
Duka, T., 294
Duke, J. C., 582
Dunn, K. M., 456
Durante, K. M., 72
During, M. J., 94
Durmer, J. S., 188
Durrant, J., 257
Dutton, D., 483
Dutton, K., 627
Dweck, C., 359
Dweck, C. S., 359f
Dykiert, D., 371
Dzirasa, K., 58

E

Eals, M., 81
Eastwood, J., 3, 27
Ebbinghaus, H., 277, 298, 298f
Ebbsen, E. B., 420
Eberhardt, J. L., 559
Eccles, J. S., 471
Eckert, H., 397
Edwards, A. S., 7
Edwards, J. G., 218
Efrain, M. G., 572
Ehrlich, A. H., 568
Ehrlich, P. R., 568
Eich, E., 294, 630
Eichenbaum, H., 110
Eisenberg, N., 413
Eisenberger, N. I., 515
Eisenegger, C., 98, 99f
Eiser, A. S., 190
Ekman, P., 484
Eldreth, D. A., 220
Elfenbein, H. A., 486, 487
Elgar, F. J., 587
Elkins, G., 201
Elkins, S. R., 44
Elliot, A. J., 84, 475t
Elliott, R., 107, 250, 383, 668
Ellis, A., 671
Ellis, B. J., 419
Ellis, L., 456
Ellsworth, P., 634
Emlen, S. T., 48
Emmelkamp, P. M. G., 670
Ensom, R., 257
Environics Research Group, 582
Epel, E., 599
Epel, E. S., 599
Epley, N., 330
Epstein, L., 586
Epstein, S., 569
Erickson, K., 292f
Erickson, K. I., 111
Ericsson, K. A., 300
Eriksson, P. S., 90, 113
Erjavec, M., 265
Eshleman, J. R., 431

Espenschade, A., 397
Esser, J. K., 536, 537
Eurman, L. J., 449
Evans, D., 499
Evans, G. W., 381
Evans, S., 673
Exner, J. E., 525
Eysenck, H. J., 353, 514

F

Fairclough, S. H., 188
Fakhoury, W., 659
Falbe, J., 579
Falk, L., 392
Fancher, R. E., 20, 352, 356
Faneslow, M. S., 236
Fantz, R. L., 395
Farah, M. J., 148
Farb, N. A. S., 606
Farber, B. A., 668
Farvolden, P., 201
Fay, R. R., 158f
Fazel, S., 647
Fazio, R. H., 240
Fecteau, S., 118
Fehr, E., 99f, 467
Feiman, R., 485f
Fein, S., 556
Feldman, J., 316
Fernado, G. A., 621
Fernandes, J., 240
Fernández, A., 293
Ferraro, L., 635
Ferrer, F., 381
Ferster, C. B., 252
Festinger, L., 574
Feyer, A., 188
Field, A. E., 586
Field, T., 393
Filler, A., 119
Finger, E. C., 629
Fiorino, D. F., 212
Fireman, G., 194
Fiscella, K., 586
Fischer, K. W., 414
Fischer, P., 266
Fischler, I., 343
Fisher, H., 468f
Fiske, S. T., 558
Fitzgerald, K. D., 683
Fitzpatrick, E. M., 159
Fivush, R., 305
Flett, G. L., 492
Flier, J. S., 444
Floel, A., 118
Flor, Dr. H., 237f
Flora, C., 275
Flourens, M. J. P., 105
Flynn, J. R., 372, 381, 382f
Fode, K. L., 36
Foer, J., 183
Fogel, S. M., 185, 193
Folkman, S., 591, 603

Fonagy, P., 410, 411
Fong, G. T., 582
Fontanilla, D., 218
Ford, D., 528
Forer, B. R., 493, 493f
Forgas, J. P., 569
Forlini, C., 383
Foroud, T., 213
Foucault, M., 658
Fournier, A. K., 224
Fowler, J. H., 588
Fox, E., 204, 510
Fox, J., 655
Fox, S., 662
Francis, D., 78
Frankel, F. H., 631
Frankl, V., 605
Franks, N., 264
Fredrickson, B. L., 26, 603, 604f
French, L., 78
Freud, S., 419, 456, 665
Frewen, P. A., 672
Frias, A., 434
Fridlund, A. J., 235
Fried, P., 220
Friederich, H. C., 450
Friedman, M., 598
Frijters, J. C., 339
Frisch, R. E., 449
Frodi, A., 415
Fu, C. H., 218
Fujimoto, Y., 238
Fujioka, T., 161
Fulda, S., 196
Fuller, R., 646
Funayama, E. S., 561f
Furley, P., 137
Fuster, J. M., 81f

G
Gadian, D. G., 345f
Gaertner, S. L., 562
Gais, S., 185
Galaburda, A. M., 346
Galambos, N. L., 183
Galanter, E., 127f, 129
Galef, B. G., Jr., 263
Galinsky, A. D., 610, 610f, 611, 611f
Gallagher, M., 431
Gallagher, R. P., 659
Gallese, V., 266f
Gallo, R., 309
Gallup polls, 4
Galobardes, B., 586
Galvan, A., 421
Ganey, R. F., 431
Gangestad, S. W., 84
Garb, H. N., 526
Garber, J., 419
Garbutt, J., 671
Garcia, J., 238
Garcia-Falgueras, A., 459
Gardner, D., 330

Gardner, H., 369
Gardner, M., 422f
Gardner, R. A., 347
Garland, E. L., 434
Garrow, J. S., 584
Garry, M., 308
Gaser, C., 113
Gasser, P., 218
Gatenby, J. C., 561f
Gaudet, S., 25
Gauthier, I., 150, 150f
Gawryluk, J. R., 205, 206f, 208
Gazzaniga, M. S., 111
Geake, J. G., 367
Gegenfurtner, K. R., 150
Geier, A., 445
Geis, L., 526
Geller, E. S., 224
Geller, J., 449
Gelman, M., 605
George, M. S., 683
Gershoff, E. T., 257
Geschwind, N., 78
Getz, K., 525
Gibbons, M., 667
Gibson, E. J., 396
Gick, M. L., 27
Giedd, J. N., 388
Gigerenzer, G., 330
Gilbert, D. T., 38, 203
Gilbert, J. A., 188
Gillham, N. W., 351, 356
Gilligan, C., 423
Gilovich, T., 48, 325, 328, 330
Ginosar, S., 487, 487f
Giudici, S., 184
Giuliano, F., 107
Glanzman, D. L., 231
Glaser, J. P., 629
Gledd, J. N., 388
Glenberg, A., 289
Glenn, N. D., 432
Glick, P., 558
Glindemann, K. E., 224
Gluckman, M., 7, 8f
Gobet, F., 275, 276f
Godden, D. R., 291, 292
Goff, L. M., 308
Gogtay, N., 220
Goh, J. O., 321
Goland, R. S., 596
Golden, W. L., 201
Goldinger, S., 304f
Goldin-Meadow, S., 405
Goldman-Rakic, P. S., 110
Goldstein, A. L., 492
Gollan, T. H., 343, 344
Gomez, R., 514
Goodale, M. A., 108, 151, 152
Goode, C., 319
Goodman, M. B., 497
Goodwin, D. W., 294
Gopnik, A., 62

Gore, J. C., 561f
Gosling, S. D., 491, 512
Gosselin, N., 156
Gotlib, I., 640, 681
Gotowiec, A., 357
Gottesman, I., 648, 649
Gottfredson, L. S., 357, 363, 369
Gottlieb, B. H., 429
Gottman, J. M., 431
Gotzsche, P., 37
Gough, B., 43
Gouin, J.-P., 596, 597
Gould, M. S., 641, 642
Gould, S. J., 378
Gould, T. D., 649
Grabner, R. H., 364
Grabski, W., 485f
Graf, P., 283
Graham, E. R., 136
Graham, K., 46
Graham, R., 188
Grahn, J. A., 162, 163
Granpeesheh, D., 248
Grant, H. M., 292
Graves, R., 68
Gray, J., 513
Gray, J. A., 514, 515
Gray, J. R., 515f
Green, A. E., 325
Green, D. M., 130
Greenberg, B. S., 450
Greenberg, L. S., 667, 668
Greene, J., 424
Greenland, C., 616
Greenwald, A. G., 131, 559
Greenwood, C. E., 381
Greenwood, K. M., 196
Gregory, R. L., 142, 567
Greitmeyer, T., 266
Greven, C. U., 359
Grice, P., 340
Griffin, D., 325, 328
Griffin, J. A., 224
Griffiths, R. R., 211
Grigoriadis, S., 240
Groeneweg, J., 310
Grolnick, W. S., 415
Gropper, S. S., 583
Gross, E. F., 417, 515
Groth, G., 85f
Gruber, S. A., 220, 221
Gruberger, M., 203
Grusser, O. J., 165
Gudonis, L., 626
Guéguen, N., 84
Guillamon, A., 458
Guldin, W. O., 165
Gump, B. B., 598
Gustaffson, J. E., 365
Gutchess, A. H., 321
Gutmann, L., 95

H

Haber, J., 213
Hadaway, P. F., 214f
Haddock, G., 241, 497
Hahn, A., 459
Hahn, C., 184
Haidt, J., 423, 424
Haier, R. J., 364
Hakuta, K., 343
Halberg, F., 182
Hale, S., 291f
Hall, C. S., 419
Halpern, D. F., 8, 372
Halpern, J. H., 218
Halpern-Fisher, B. L., 426
Hamalainen, M. S., 121
Hamilton, J., 640
Hamilton, R., 113
Hamlin, J. K., 413, 414
Hammond, D., 222, 223f, 582
Hamstra, M., 319
Handy, T. C., 203
Hane, A. A., 409
Hanin, Y. L., 592, 593
Hanks, A. S., 446
Hansen, P. C., 367
Hardwick, S., 220
Harenski, K., 332f
Hargrove, M. F., 98
Harkness, S. K., 619
Harlow, H. F., 408f
Harlow, J. M., 43, 44
Harris, J. L., 319, 585
Harris, R. B., 584
Harsch, N., 297
Hart, B., 380
Hartline, D. K., 91
Hartman, T. P., 462
Harvey, P., 645
Harvey, T., 375
Haselton, M. G., 72
Hasher, L., 184
Hatfield, E., 467
Havas, D. A., 481
Hawkins, R. D., 231
Hawkley, L. C., 467
Hayes, C., 346
Hayes, J., 469
Hayes, K. J., 346
Hayes, S. C., 667
Hayne, H., 293
Hazan, C., 409
Hazell, P., 94
He, C., 161
Health Canada, 219, 223, 580, 639
Healy, D., 676
Healy, J. M., 129
Heart and Stroke Foundation of
    Canada, 114
Heath, C., 571
Heath, D., 571
Heatherton, T. F., 499, 581
Hebb, D. O., 21, 283, 379

Hechtman, L. T., 619
Heider, F., 555
Heilman, K. M., 109
Heine, S. J., 473, 506, 507, 508
Heinrichs, M., 596
Heinz, A., 649
Heller, D., 474f
Hellström-Lindahl, E., 392
Hemphill, E., 585
Hendrickson, A. E., 182
Henrich, J., 506
Herd, D., 266
Herlitz, J., 467
Herman, C. P., 447, 448, 449
Herman-Giddens, M. E., 419
Hermann, D., 220
Hermans, E. J., 98
Hernandez, A. E., 343
Hernandez-Reif, M., 393
Hernstein, R. J., 251
Herrnstein, R., 357, 364f
Hershkovitz, I., 293
Hess, E. H., 127f
Hetherington, E. M., 587
Heyes, C. M., 263
Hieronymus, F., 676
Higley, J. D., 98
Hilgard, E. R., 201
Hill, S. Y., 294, 649
Hillary, F. G., 8
Hillman, C. H., 111, 608
Himelien, M. J., 620
Himmelheber, A. M., 95
Hingson, R. W., 224
Hiripi, E., 448t
Hirsh, J. B., 27, 492, 515f
Hirst, W., 297
Hitch, G., 279
Hobson, J. A., 190
Hodges, L. F., 670
Hodges, N. J., 265
Hodgins, D. C., 244
Hodgson, S., 449
Hoehn, K., 109f
Hofer, M. A., 409
Hoffman, M. L., 415
Hoffman, S. G., 606
Hofmann, S., 637
Hofmann, S. G., 674, 681
Hofschire, L. J., 450
Hofstede, G., 466
Hogan, M. J., 184
Hojnoski, R. L., 526
Hollenstein, T., 420
Holleran, S. E., 553
Hollerman, J. R., 251
Hollon, S., 674, 681
Holmes, D. S., 607
Holmes, T. H., 591, 592t
Holtzman, S., 604
Holyoak, K. J., 325, 328
Honzik, C. H., 261, 261f
Hooker, W. D., 219–220

Hooley, J., 673, 681
Hooven, C. K., 82
Hopkins, B., 397
Horn, J. L., 366, 367
Horn, L. R., 340
Horne, J., 186
Horne, P. J., 265
Horner, V., 260
Hort, J., 173
Horvath, A. O., 667
Hoshino-Browne, E., 575
Hoskin, R. A., 461
Hough, W., 657
Hounsfield, G. N., 119
Houska, J., 87f
Howard, A. L., 224
Howe, M. L., 305
Hrobjartsson, A., 37
Huang, C., 264
Huang, C.-M., 321, 321f
Hubbard, E. M., 177, 177f
Hubel, D. H., 146
Hudson, J., 448, 448t
Huesmann, L. R., 265
Huettel, S. A., 120, 122
Huffman, M. A., 264
Hughes, C. F., 225
Hughlings Jackson, J., 109
Hughto, J. M. W., 459
Hulme, C., 383
Hunter, J. E., 363, 369, 370
Hunter, R. A., 615
Hurlbert, A. C., 150
Hursh, A., 91
Husain, M., 110f
Huyser, C., 633
Hyde, J. S., 423, 639
Hyde, K. L., 161, 162
Hyman, S. E., 57, 58, 619

I

Iacoboni, M., 265, 266f
Imperato, A., 212
Inhelder, B., 409
Inlow, J. K., 377
Inn, A., 559
Isen, A. M., 360, 603
Ito, T. A., 558
Ivanoff, J., 274
Izard, V., 404f, 405
Izzo, A. A., 680

J

Jacob, C., 84
Jacob, T., 213
Jacobs, B., 678
Jacobson, L., 36
Jacoby, L. L., 319
Jaeggi, S. M., 383
Jaffee, S., 423
Jager, G., 220
Jakobs, D., 679
James, T. W., 148, 271
Jamieson, G. A., 201

Janis, I. L., 536
Janz, T., 583f
Jasper, H. H., 21
Jencks, C., 381
Jensen, A. R., 357, 369
Jensen, R., 262
Jenson, M., 202
Jewanski, J., 177
Joanisse, M., 339
John, E. R., 263
John, O. P., 506
Johns, M. W., 198t
Johnson, A. M., 364
Johnson, B. T., 290
Johnson, J. K., 120
Johnson, K. E., 317
Johnson, M., 315
Johnson, M. K., 303, 311
Johnson, V., 455
Johnson, W., 363, 371, 372
Johnsrude, I. S., 162
Jokela, M., 593
Joling, K. J., 661
Jones, D. N., 497, 580
Jones, K. L., 391
Jones, R. A. K., 393
Jones, R. T., 219–220
Jonides, J., 279
Josephs, R. A., 224
Josephson, W. L., 266
Juda, M. N., 449
Julius, D., 169
Jusczyk, P. W., 342

K

Kahneman, D., 328, 329, 330, 552
Kales, A., 194
Kalisch, R., 292
Kalnin, A. J., 267
Kam, J. W. Y., 203
Kamata, A., 582
Kaminski, J., 336
Kamnasaran, D., 648
Kanayama, G., 220
Kanwisher, N., 123, 148
Kapler, I. V., 7
Karakashian, L. M., 543
Karau, S. J., 535, 536
Kastner, S., 135
Kaufman, A. S., 368
Kaufman, R. A., 277
Kawai, M., 264
Kawakami, K., 562
Kay, A. C., 610, 611, 612
Kaye, W. H., 449
Kazdin, A., 660
Kebbel, M., 293
Keel, P. K., 450
Kelemen, W. L., 294
Kennard, M. A., 114
Kenny, D. A., 552
Kenrick, D. T., 85f
Kensinger, E. A., 295

Kernan, J. B., 572
Kernis, M. H., 415
Kershaw, T. C., 297
Kessler, R., 448t
Kessler, R. C., 639
Kevles, D. J., 357
Kiecolt-Claser, J., 587, 597
Kigar, D. L., 375
Kihlstrom, J. F., 202, 630
Killingsworth, M. A., 203
Kilpatrick, L., 296
Kim, J., 445
Kim, J. J., 236
Kim, P., 114
King, D. B., 191
King, L., 220
King, S., 650, 651
Kingston, T., 673
Kinsey, A. C., 453
Kinzler, K. D., 404
Kirk, A., 304f, 458
Kirkham, T. C., 218
Kirkland, M., 359
Kirsch, I., 9, 200, 676
Kirsch, P., 596
Kirschbaum, C., 594
Kisely, S. R., 657
Kisilevsky, B. S., 395
Kitayama, S., 473, 507, 508
Klatzky, R. L., 168, 319
Klaus, L., 679
Kleider, H., 304, 304f
Klein, C., 75
Klein, N., 53
Klein, R., 137
Klein, R. A., 38
Kleitman, N., 191
Kliethermes, C. L., 636f
Klomek, A., 642
Klonoff, E. A., 587
Kluger, B. M., 118
Klump, K. L., 450
Knaepen, K., 114
Knafo, S., 57
Knight, R. T., 110, 278
Knutson, B., 250
Koball, H. L., 431
Koch, E., 329
Kohlberg, I., 423
Kokkalis, J., 217
Kolb, B., 113, 390
Komar, S., 474f
Komisaruk, B. R., 456
Konishi, M., 160
Koob, G. F., 95, 212
Kornell, N., 300
Kornelsen, J., 123, 479
Kornhaber, M., 370
Kotchoubey, B., 207
Kouprina, N., 108
Kovacs, A. M., 344
Kowal, M. A., 220
Kramer, A. F., 608

Kramer, T. H., 296
Kreukels, B. P. C., 458
Kringelbach, M. L., 684
Kristensen, P., 380
Kristensson, E., 444
Krolak-Salmon, P., 478
Kroska, A., 619
Kruger, J., 334
Krystal, A., 196
Kubzansky, L. D., 604
Kudielka, B. M., 594
Kulik, J., 296, 297
Kurdek, L. A., 461
Kurjak, A., 388
Kuyken, W., 673
Kwong, K. K., 122

L

LaBar, K. S., 295, 296
Labrie, V., 78
Lafer-Sousa, R., 150
La Guardia, J. G., 471
Lakin, J. L., 534, 535
Lakoff, G., 315
Lalonde, C. E., 161
Lam, A. G., 655
Lam, L. T., 417
LaMay, M. L., 372
Laming, D., 277
Landau, M. J., 469
Landrigan, C. P., 188, 188f
Landrine, H., 587
Landry, M., 201
Lane, J. S., 668
Lane, P. C., 276f
Laney, C., 295
Lang, P. J., 627f
Langford, D. J., 172
Langhans, W., 442
Langston, J. W., 57
Långström, N., 458
Lapp, L., 192
Large, E. W., 162
Larsen, R. J., 481
Lasco, M. S., 457
Latané, B., 535, 541, 542, 543
Laureys, S., 205, 206f, 209f
Lautenschlager, N. T., 608
Lavalee, J. P., 328
Lavie, P., 182, 183, 187, 188
Laws, K. R., 217
Lay, C. H., 591
Lazarus, R. S., 591, 603
Leary, M. R., 426, 467
Leatherdale, S., 223f
Leavitt, J., 95
Lebens, H., 240
Leblanc, V. R., 320
Leboe, J. P., 293
Lederman, S. J., 168
LeDoux, J. E., 236, 539
Lee, C., 449
Lee, D. H., 485f

Lee, G., 205
Lee, H., 186
Lee, H. J., 595
Lee, J. L. C., 286
Lee, K., 431, 496
Lee, P. A., 419
Lefkowitz, E. S., 425, 572
Le Grand, R., 149
Leichtman, M. D., 307
Leighton, J. P., 325
Leiserowitz, A., 567
Lejuez, C. W., 214
Lenroot, R. K., 388
Lepper, M. P., 473
Lesage, A., 655
Lesch, K-P., 510
Lett, H. S., 598
Leucht, S., 680
LeVay, S., 456, 457f
Levenson, R. W., 431, 603, 604f
Levenston, G. K., 627, 627f
Levin, D. T., 274
Levin, R., 194
Levine, B., 282
Levine, L. J., 295
Levine, M. P., 449
Levinson, B. W., 199
Levitin, D., 162, 163
Levy, G. D., 85
Lewin, K., 534
Lewin, R., 347
Lewis, M., 420
Lewis, R. G., 95
Leyton, M., 95
Li, C., 277
Li, H., 468f
Li, L., 582
Li, P., 343
Liang, K-C., 328f
Liberman, N., 567
Lieberman, L., 358
Lieberman, M. D., 515
Liégeois, F., 345, 345f
Light, K. C., 596
Lilienfeld, S. O., 15f, 48, 73f, 82f, 90f,
    91f, 93f, 97f, 103f, 105f, 107f, 108f,
    112f, 114f, 123, 145f, 147f, 151f,
    157f, 160f, 172f, 174f, 175f, 195f,
    246f, 253f, 368f, 402f, 408f, 410f,
    418f, 520f, 526, 526f, 631, 664
Lillard, A., 410
Lin, C., 195
Lindau, S. T., 454
Lindenberger, U., 367
Lindsay, R. C. L., 27
Lindström, P., 457
Linehan, M., 626
Link, B. G., 619
Lipinski, R., 87f
Liszkowski, U., 414
Liu, J., 149
Liu, X., 200
Livingstone, M. S., 153

Llera, S. J., 635
LoBue, V., 263
Lockhart, R., 290
Locksley, A., 557
Loewenstein, C., 568f, 569
Loftus, E. F., 202, 275, 296, 306, 306f,
    307, 310, 317
Logan, J. M., 436
Logel, C., 586
Loggia, M. L., 170, 171
Logothetis, N. K., 123
Lømo, T., 283
Lorenzoni, I., 567
Losin, E. A. R., 25
Lougheed, J. P., 420
Lovett, M. W., 339
Low, B. S., 84
Lu, T., 161
Lubman, D. I., 220
Lubow, R. E., 239
Lucas, R. E., 514
Luck, A., 612
Luders, E., 378
Luo, L., 282
Lutgendorf, S., 600
Lutz, A., 606
Luzatti, C., 109
Lykken, D. T., 627
Lynam, D. R., 626
Lynn, S., 200, 201
Lynn, S. J., 9, 15f, 73f, 82f, 90f, 91f,
    93f, 97f, 103f, 105f, 107f, 108f,
    112f, 114f, 145f147f, 151f, 157f,
    160f, 172f, 174f, 175f, 195f, 246f,
    253f, 368f, 402f, 408f, 410f, 418f,
    520f, 631
Lyons, B. D., 370
Lyons, N. P., 423
Lyznicki, J. M., 188

M
Macalpine, I., 615
MacCracken, M. J., 536
MacDonald, A. A., 199
Macdonald, K., 596
MacDonald, T. K., 224
Macdonald, T. M., 596
Machado Rocha, F. C., 218
Mack, A., 136
MacLean, K. A., 211
Maclean, P. D., 107
Macmillan, M., 44
MacNeil, C., 193
Madden, D. J., 436
Maddux, W. W., 535
Madill, A., 43
Maes, H. H., 584
Magri, C., 122
Maguire, E. A., 285
Mahalik, J. R., 655, 656
Mahon, B. Z., 148, 320f, 322
Mahon, M., 343
Mahowald, M., 196

Maier, N. F., 326, 326f, 327, 327f
Maier, S. F., 598, 609, 609f, 678
Main, M., 408
Makin, J., 392
Makino, M., 448t
Malhotra, P., 110f
Mampe, B., 395
Mandai, O., 192
Mandler, G., 127f
Mangels, J. A., 359
Mangun, G. R., 120
Mann, C. E., 620
Manning, R., 541
Mansfield, A. K., 655
Marcus, S. C., 655, 677
Marek, R., 236
Maren, S., 236
Marieb, E. N., 109f
Marino, L., 378
Mark, V. W., 114
Markowitsch, H. J., 282
Marks, G., 555
Marks, L. V., 461
Markus, H., 305, 507, 508
Markus, H. R., 473
Marner, L., 108
Marois, R., 274
Marroun, H. E., 392
Martibeau, A. M., 224
Martin, A., 322
Martin, L., 322
Martin, R. A., 42
Martinez, D., 95
Martin-Santos, R., 220
Maruff, P., 188
Maruta, T., 604
Mascolo, M. E., 414
Mashek, D. J., 468f
Mashhoon, Y., 221
Maslow, A., 466, 492, 518, 555
Masters, W., 455
Masuda, A., 655
Masuda, T., 321, 321f, 487, 488, 488f
Mather, J. A., 512
Matsumoto, D., 486, 487
Matsunaga, H., 448
Matthews, K., 598
Mattson, M. P., 437
Maurer, C., 128
Maurer, D., 128, 396
Maxwell, A., 622
Mayberg, H. S., 37, 479, 684
Mayer, G., 196
Mazur, A., 97, 98
Mazziotta, J. C., 266f
Mazzoni, G., 309
McAnulty, G., 393
McArdle, J. J., 381
McAuley, J. D., 162
McCabe, M. P., 449
McCarley, R. W., 190
McCarthy, R., 320
McClure, S. M., 420

McCormick, L. M., 379
McCoy, A., 53
McCrae, R. R., 493, 494f, 500, 507t
McCulloch, J., 94
McCullough, J. P., 674
McCullough, M. E., 607
McDaid, C., 195
McDermott, K. B., 309
McEwen, B. S., 381
McGeown, W. J., 201
McGlashan, T. H., 650
McGorry, P. D., 650
McGregor. H. A., 475t
McGruder, J., 651
McGuire, W. J., 570
McKay, A., 459
McKenzie-Mohr, D., 565
McKinney, K. G., 620
McLaughlin, K. A., 420
McLay, R. N., 670
McManus, F., 673
McNally, R. J., 9
McNaughton, N., 515
McNeely, H. E., 684
McNeil, D., 276
McVey, G. L., 450
Mead, M., 419
Meehl, P. E., 68
Mehl, M. R., 553
Mehler, J., 344, 403
Meier, M. H., 629
Melby-Lervåg, M., 383
Melchior, M., 392
Meldrum, B. S., 94
Meltzoff, A. N., 264, 265
Melzack, R., 169, 170, 171f
Memmert, D., 137
Memon, A., 309
Mendoza, M., 200
Mennella, J. A., 174
Merchant, H., 162
Merckelbach, H., 635
Merikle, P. M., 131, 132, 199
Mervis, C. B., 315, 317
Messer, D., 342
Meston, C. M., 107, 452, 454, 458
Metcalfe, J., 294
Meteer, J., 87f
Metzloff, A. N., 395, 395f
Meyer, J. S., 217
Mezulis, A. H., 508
Michael, E. B., 343
Mikels, J. A., 433f
Mikulincer, M., 409, 414
Milan, A., 432f
Milfont, T. L., 567
Milgram, S., 546, 547
Miller, B. L., 110
Miller, D. T., 330, 543
Miller, G. A., 275
Miller, G. E., 598
Miller, K. E., 621
Miller, L. J., 367

Miller, L. J., Jr., 174
Miller, L. L., 219
Miller, N., 555
Milling, L., 201
Mills, D., 342
Mills, J. N., 183
Milner, A. D., 151
Milner, B., 110, 278, 284, 285
Milner, D., 108
Milner, P. M., 21
Minard, A., 186
Mineka, S., 237, 635
Mischel, W., 420, 500
Mishara, B. L., 642
Mishkin, M., 151, 345f
Mitchell, R. W., 265
Mithoefer, M. C., 218, 621
Miyake, Y., 450
Mizushige, T., 444
Molina, J., 200
Molnar-Szakacs, I., 266f
Molteni, R., 437
Mondloch, C. J., 149
Monk-Turner, E., 463
Montgomery, G. H., 202
Montgomery, I., 186
Monti, M. M., 207, 208f
Mooneyham, B. W., 203
Moore, A. U., 239
Moore, B., 420
Moore, C. F., 358
Moore, L. P., 240
Moore, M. K., 265, 395, 395f
Moore, T. M., 44
Moradi, B., 497
Morein-Zamir, S., 383
Morgan, C. J., 218
Morgan, D., 599
Morgane, P. J., 390
Morin, C., 196
Morin, L. P., 182
Morleo, M., 391
Morris, E. K., 256
Morris, G., 250
Morris, J. P., 515
Morris, M. W., 556
Morris, R. G. M., 117, 118
Morris, R. H., 304
Morrison, R. G., 325, 328
Moscicki, E. K., 642
Motet, A., 195
Mott, F. W., 109
Mrazek, M. D., 203
Muckle, G., 391
Mueller, F., 388
Mukherjee, P., 120
Muller, J. J., 636f
Müller, N. G., 278
Munt, S., 461
Murdock, B. B., 278
Murphy, C., 175
Murphy, G. G., 231
Murphy, M. R., 456

Murphy, S. T., 239
Murray, C., 357, 364f
Murtagh, D. R., 196
Myers, D. G., 557
Myerson, J., 291f

N

Naëgelé, B., 195
Nairne, J. S., 275
Nakamura, M., 196
Namy, L. L., 15f, 73f, 82f, 90f, 91f, 93f, 97f, 103f, 105f, 107f, 108f, 112f, 114f, 145f, 147f, 151f, 157f, 160f, 172f, 174f, 175f, 195f, 246f, 253f, 368f, 402f, 408f, 410f, 418f, 520f
Narendren, R., 95
Narrow, N. E., 655
Nash, M. R., 201
Nash, R., 309
National Eating Disorders Association, 450
National Insitute of Mental Health (NIMH), 639, 655, 671
Navaneelan, T., 583f
Neisser, U., 297, 303, 352, 363
Nelson, K., 305
Nesse, R., 634
Nestler, E. J., 57, 58
Neugebauer, R., 391
Neville, H. J., 128
New, J., 82
Newcombe, N. S., 305
Newland, M. C., 256
Newman, J. P., 514
Newman, M. G., 635
Newton, E. L., 571
Newton, T. L., 587
Nichols, D. E., 217
Nicki, R. M., 257
Nielsen, K., 292f
Nielsen, T. A., 190, 194
Nielsen Research, 239
Nielson, K., 296, 296f
Niesta, D., 84
Niogi, S. N., 120
Nisbet, E. K., 27
Nisbett, R. E., 321, 321f, 358, 366, 375, 381, 535, 538, 556
Noels, K. A., 25, 471
Nokelainen, P., 370
Nolan, J. M., 535
Noland, J., 170f
Nolte, J., 104
Norcross, J. C., 660
Norman, D., 201
Norman, G. R., 320
North, C. S., 631
North, R. A., 107
Northstone, K., 381
Norton, A., 113
Nosek, B. A., 559, 560
Nosyk, b., 223
Nunn, J. A., 177

Nuttin, J. M., 555
Nyi, P. P., 219

O

O'Brien, K., 657
O'Brien, T. B., 604
Ochsner, K. N., 295, 515
O'Connor, K. J., 561f
Odbert, H. W., 493
O'Doherty, J. P., 250
Ogawa, S., 122
Öhman, A., 237, 635
O'Kearney, R., 662
O'Keefe, D. J., 570
Olds, J., 107
O'Leary, C. M., 391
Olesya, G., 555
Olfson, M., 655, 677
Oliveira, T., 98
Oliven, J. F., 458
Oliver, G., 599
Oliver, I., 276f
Oliveri, M., 217
Ollendick, T., 660, 674
Olshansky, S. J., 583
Olson, H. C., 391
Olson, K. R., 315
Olson, M. A., 240
Olsson, A., 669
Ono, H., 431
Open Science Collaboration
    (OSC), 38
Opris, D., 670
O'Rahilly, R., 388
O'Regan, J. K., 274f
Oriet, C., 105
Orne, M. T., 35
Ostafin, B. D., 560
Overgaard, M., 208
Overgaard, R., 208
Owen, A., 207
Owen, A. M., 205, 206f, 207, 209f
Owen, M. J., 650
Owsley, C., 435
Oxford English Dictionary, 315

P

Packer, D. J., 547
Pallesen, S., 194, 196
Palmer, A. A., 636f
Palmer, C., 162
Palmer, J. C., 306, 306f
Palmer, R. H. C., 392
Palvio, A., 300
Pandya, D. N., 346
Papademetris, X., 515f
Papies, E. K., 319
Paquette, V., 672
Paradis, C., 297
Paré, D., 296
Paris, B. J., 528
Park, D. C., 321, 321f
Park, S., 646

Parrigopoulos, T. J., 195
Parrott, M. D., 381
Parsons, H. M., 34
Parton, A., 110f
Pascual-Leone, A., 113
Pasher, H., 369
Pashler, H., 136, 274
Patrick, C. J., 627f
Patrick, G. T. W., 188
Patterson, C. M., 514
Patterson, D., 202
Patterson, E. W. J., 572
Paul, D. B., 235
Paulesu, E., 281
Paulhus, D. L., 496, 497
Pavlidis, P., 78
Paz, R., 296
Peciña, M., 213
Peeters, M., 107
Pefretz, I., 162
Pelham, B. W., 555
Pelphrey, K. A., 515
Pemment, J., 627
Penfield, W., 21
Peng, K., 556
Peng, Z., 417
Penn, D. L., 646
Penninx, B., 640
Peplau, L. A., 431
Pereira, M. G., 479
Perini, F., 118
Perloff, R. M., 241
Perner, J., 410
Perrin, J. S., 683
Perry, J. L., 214
Perry, W., 646
Pertwee, R. G., 220
Peruche, B., 561
Perunovic, W. Q. E., 474, 474f
Pessoa, L., 477
Peters, K. R., 193
Peters, M., 83f
Peterson, C., 604
Peterson, L., 280
Peterson, M., 280
Peterson, N. R., 159
Petrosino, A., 664
Petrovich, G. D., 165
Pettigrew, T. F., 562
Pettito, L. A., 347
Pezdek, K., 304f
Pfau, M. W., 570
Pfaus, J. G., 454, 455
Pfefferbaum, A., 220
Phelps, E., 669
Phelps, E. A., 296, 560, 561f
Phillips, D. I. W., 390
Phillips, M., 380
Phillips, M. L., 123
Phillips, N., 186
Phillips, R. G., 236
Phillips-Silver, J., 162
Piaget, J., 401, 409

Pianezza, M. L., 213
Pica, P., 486
Pidgeon, N. F., 567
Piet, J., 673
Pillard, R. C., 457, 457f
Pine, J. M., 276
Pinker, S., 339, 340, 340f, 343
Pinsker, H., 231
Pinto, A., 638t
Pizarro, D. A., 295
Pizzagalli, D. A., 477
Plant, E. A., 561
Plomin, R., 75, 375, 376f, 377, 499, 509
Polansky, J., 581, 581f
Polaschek, D., 308
Polich, J., 606
Polivy, J., 448, 449, 586
Pollack, D., 657
Polson, P. G., 300
Polymeropoulos, M. H., 75
Ponder, C. A., 636, 636f
Ponseti, J., 457
Pooh, R. K., 388
Pope, H., 448t
Pope, H. G., 218, 220, 221
Porter, R. H., 396
Porter, S., 553
Potenza, M. N., 421
Poulin-Dubois, D., 344
Powers, M. B., 670
Prentice, D. A., 543
Prescott, P. A., 395
Price, E. L., 659
Price, J. S., 221
Priebe, S., 659
Prochaska, J. O., 655, 660
Propper, R. E., 191
Proteau, L., 265
Public Health Agency of Canada,
    392, 634, 641
Pujol, J., 342
Pulvermüller, F., 114
Putnam, F. W., 630, 631

Q

Qu, S., 607
Quillian, M. R., 317f
Quirk, G. J., 45

R

R. v. Sharpe; Supreme Court of
    Canada, 461
Rada, P., 444
Radke-Yarrow, M., 414
Raffi, A. R., 449
Rahe, R. H., 591, 592t
Raichle, M. E., 203, 204f
Raihani, N. J., 264
Rainforth, M. V., 606
Rajeevan, N., 515f
Raji, C. A., 585
Ramachandran, V. S., 142, 172,
    177, 177f

Ramakrishnan, U., 390
Ranaji, M. R., 561*f*
Ranganath, C., 368
Ranganathan, M., 219, 220
Ransdell, S. E., 343
Rapson, R. L., 467
Rasmussen, E. B., 256
Ratcliffe, R., 315, 316
Rauch, S. L., 683
Rauscher, F. H., 30
Ravindran, A. V., 679
Rayner, R. R., 235
Raynor, H. A., 586
Raz, A., 201, 434
Razza, R. P., 381
Razzini, C., 598
Read, J. D., 134, 293, 293*f*, 294
Rechtschaffen, A., 186
Reed, T. E., 364
Reedy, F. E., 174
Regan, B. C., 141
Reichert, T., 462
Reid, K., 188
Reilly, S., 238
Reingen, P. H., 572
Reisenzen, R., 481
Reissing, E. D., 454
Reissland, N., 396
Reiter, E. O., 419
Remafedi, G., 426
Rendell, L., 264
Rensink, R. A., 274, 274*f*
Rescoria, R. A., 251, 252
Restifo, L. L., 377
Rhodes, G., 84
Ricciardelli, L. A., 449
Richardson, P. J., 78
Richardson, T., 264
Richdale, J., 359
Richert, R. A., 400
Richmond, D., 462
Rieber, R., 18
Riffe, G., 241
Rifkin, A., 630
Riggle, E. D. B., 587
Rijpkema, M., 304
Risko, E. F., 203, 204
Risley, T. R., 380
Ritterband, L., 196
Riva, G., 670
Rivera, S. M., 405
Rizzolatti, G., 265, 266*f*
Robb, M. B., 400
Robbins, T. W., 95
Roberts, B. W., 500, 500*f*
Roberts, P. M., 343
Roberts, R., 188
Robertson, S. I., 325
Robinson, D., 18
Robinson, P. N., 377
Roblaes, T., 640
Robleto, K., 233
Rocca, M. A., 91

Rochlen, A., 656
Rock, I., 136
Roediger, H., 291*f*, 300
Roediger, H. L., 309
Roediger III, H. L., 308
Roffwarg, H. P., 183*f*
Rogers, J., 378
Rogers, J. M., 392
Rogoff, B., 405
Rollins, B. C., 433
Rolls, E. T., 444
Rorty, M., 449
Rosch, E., 315, 316, 317
Rose, D., 683
Rose, N., 290, 291*f*
Roselli, C. E., 456, 458*f*
Rosenbaum, R. S., 271
Rosenblum, G. D., 420
Rosenfield, S., 619
Rosenhan, D. L., 620
Rosenman, R., 598
Rosenthal, D., 320
Rosenthal, R., 36, 553
Rosenzweig, M. R., 379
Ross, C. E., 587
Ross, L., 555
Ross, M., 303, 305, 306, 474*f*
Ross, R. A., 220
Rosselli, M., 343
Rossi-Casé, L., 372
Rossini, P. M., 208
Rotermann, M., 426
Rothbart, M. K., 499
Rouder, J. N., 315, 316
Rovine, M., 432
Rowe, J. B., 162
Rowe, R., 98
Rozanski, A., 467
Rubin, D., 297, 298
Rudman, L. A., 560
Rule, N. O., 553
Rusak, B., 183
Ruseckaite, R., 121
Rushton, J. P., 357
Ryan, R. M., 415, 471, 472*f*

S
Sacerdote, B., 588
Sachs, G. T. L., 177
Sack, K., 30
Sadalla, E. K., 85*f*
Sae Yang, W., 223*f*
Safdar, S. F., 591
Sagberg, F., 188
Saha, S., 645
Sahakian, B., 383
Salo, R., 217
Salovey, P., 569
Saltzsein, H. G., 415
Salvatore, J. E., 409
Sann, C., 404*f*
Sargent, J. D., 580, 581
Satel, S., 123

Saucier, G., 501, 506
Saus, E., 561
Savage-Rumbaugh, S., 347
Savic, I., 457
Savin-Williams, R. C., 426
Saxon, A. H., 493
Scepkowski, L. A., 455
Schacter, D. L., 283
Schacter, S., 481, 482*f*
Schaie, K. W., 367
Schamberg, M. A., 381
Schenck, C. H., 181, 195
Schierenbeck, T., 194
Schiff, N. D., 206*f*, 209*f*
Schimel, J., 469
Schinka, J. A., 510
Schlagenhauf, F., 649
Schlaug, G., 113, 118
Schlossmacher, M. G., 75
Schmader, T., 358
Schmahmann, J. D., 105
Schmidt, F. L., 363, 369, 370
Schmidt, M., 679
Schmidt, U., 448
Schmitt, D. P., 507, 507*t*, 508, 513
Schmolk, H., 297
Schnaar, R. L., 113
Schnakers, C., 206
Schnall, S., 423
Schneider, S. M., 670
Schoenberger, N. E., 201
Scholz, J., 113
Schooner, J. W., 203
Schottenbauer, M. A., 379
Schredl, M., 194
Schreurs, B. G., 233
Schroeder, D. A., 543
Schroers, M., 396
Schultheiss, O. C., 98, 527
Schultz, P. W., 570
Schultz, W., 212, 250, 251
Schulz, H., 196
Schulz-Hardt, S., 537
Schwartz, B., 333
Schwartz, J. M., 674
Schwartz, S. H., 570
Schweizer, T. A., 105, 344
Scoboria, A., 303
Scott-Robertson, L., 449
Scoville, W. B., 278, 284
Seale, J. P., 224
Sealy, P., 659
Sears, H. A., 427
Sedikides, C., 555
Segalowitz, S. J., 421
Segerstrom, S. C., 598
Seidenberg, M. S., 347
Seligman, M., 603, 609, 609*f*
Seligman, M. E. P., 26, 237
Selye, H., 593, 594*f*, 598
Senghas, A., 343
Sengupta, J., 463
Serafini, N., 683

Sergent, J., 121
Setchell, J. M., 84
Shad, M. U., 421
Shain, C., 561
Shallice, T., 201, 320, 367f
Shamosh, N. A., 363
Shane, M. S., 515f
Shapiro, C. M., 195
Shapiroi, A. F., 432
Shariff, A. F., 485
Sharot, T., 296
Sharp, W., 655
Shaughnessy, K., 461
Shaver, P. R., 409, 414
Shaw, H. E., 450
Shaywitz, B. A., 618
Shaywitz, S. E., 339, 618
Sheehan, P. W., 201
Sheline, Y. I., 678
Shenton, M. E., 120
Shepperd, J. A., 329
Sheridan, M. A., 379
Sherman, J. C., 105
Sherrard, L., 394
Shi, R., 342
Shields, M., 583
Shiffrin, R. M., 272
Shoda, Y., 500–501
Shulgin, A. T., 217
Shumueli, D., 581
Siegel, D., 672
Siegel, J., 186
Siegel, S., 212, 241
Siegler, R. S., 352
Siffre, M., 183
Silva, A. J., 377
Silva, M., 303
Silverman, I., 81, 82, 83f
Simon, H. A., 275
Simons, D. J., 136, 274, 383
Singer, J., 481, 482f
Singer, M. A., 405
Singer, T., 539
Singh, A., 111
Sinha, R., 241
Sireteanu, R., 395
Skanes, H. E., 131
Skinner, B. F., 252, 256, 342
Skinner, M. K., 78
Skovholt, T. M., 655
Slater, A., 395
Slotema, C. W., 683
Slovic, P., 568f, 569
Small, D. A., 568, 568f
Small, D. M., 107, 175,
    437, 444
Smallwood, J., 203
Smilek, D., 177
Smith, B. H., 222
Smith, B. W., 559
Smith, C. T., 192, 193
Smith, D. W., 391
Smith, E., 209

Smith, J. E., 194
Smith, M. L., 668
Smith, S. D., 177, 479
Smith, T. B., 607
Smits, J. A. J., 674, 681
Smolen, P., 300
Snider, L. A., 633
Snook, B., 27
Snowdon, L. R., 656
Snyder, K., 646
Sobel, H. S., 7
Söderlund, H., 286
Solomon, J., 408
Solomon, K. D., 145
Solomon, S., 468
Son Hing, L. S., 497
Sorell, G. T., 423
Sovik, R., 607
Sowell, E. R., 419
Spanos, N. P., 9, 201, 311
Sparling, C. L., 559
Spearman, C., 365
Spector, F., 128
Spelke, E. S., 404, 404f
Spence, A., 567
Spence, M. J., 395
Spencer, D. D., 94
Spencer, S. J., 556
Spera, S. P., 602
Sperling, G., 273
Sperry, R. W., 111, 113, 114
Spinath, F. M., 375, 376f, 377
Spires-Jones, T., 57
Springer, S. P., 104, 111
Sproule, B., 222, 223
Squeglia, L. M., 221
Squire, L. R., 107, 284, 303
Stack, S., 431
Stadulis, R. E., 536
Staffen, W., 207
Stafford, L. D., 292
Stalley, S., 584
Stanhope, N., 303
Stanley, J. C., 371
Stanovich, K. E., 569
Starcevic, V., 674, 681
Stark, C. E., 311
Stastna, K., 681
Statistics Canada, 193, 221, 431, 448,
    580, 582, 583, 585
Stecker, R., 381
Steele, C., 38, 358
Steele, C. M., 224
Steele, J. D., 683
Steer, R. A., 32
Steffen, P. R., 587
Stein, Z., 391
Steinberg, L., 421, 422f
Steptoe, A., 599
Sterling, P., 442
Stern, P. C., 570
Sternberg, R. J., 92f, 325, 363,
    368, 369

Stettler, N., 585
Stevens, A., 225
Stevenson, R. J., 136, 263
Stewart, T. L., 562
Stice, E., 449, 450, 586
Stickgold, R., 192
Stillman, R. C., 294
Stine-Morrow, E. A. L., 437
Stinson, F. S., 635t
Stokoe, W. C., 347
Stoodley, C. J., 105
Stough, C., 363
Strack, F., 480
Strahan, E. J., 132, 450
Strassman, R., 218
Streissguth, A. P., 391
Strenziok, M., 267
Streppel, M. T., 580
Streri, A., 404f
Stroman, P. W., 123
Strong, G., 468f
Strube, M. J., 555
Stuart, E. W., 240
Studtman, M., 481
Stuss, D. T., 80, 110
Sue, S., 655
Suls, J., 327
Sumnall, H. R., 219
Supreme Court of Canada, 257, 622
Susser, E. B., 391
Susskind, J. M., 484, 485f
Sutherland, R., 293
Suzuki, H., 192
Swaab, D. F., 459
Swanson, L. W., 165
Swebo, S. E., 633
Sweeney, P. D., 639
Swets, J. A., 130
Sydeman, S. J., 598
Symons, C. S., 290
Szasz, T., 616
Szelenbeerger, SW., 194

T
Tajfel, H., 556, 557
Takeuchi, D., 657
Talarico, J., 297
Talmi, D., 277
Tanaka, J. W., 148
Tanaka, S., 105
Tang, Y., 26, 377, 606, 607
Tangney, J. P., 426
Target, M., 410, 411
Tarr, M. J., 150f
Tascioglu, A. B., 165
Tashiro, A., 90, 379
Tavris, C., 331f
Taylor, A. J., 173
Taylor, S. E., 25, 595
Tedeschi, R. G., 434, 605
Tees, R. C., 341, 342
Tellegen, A., 509
Teplin, L. A., 647

Terao, Y., 118
Terman, L. M., 357
Terracciano, A., 510
Thagard, P., 45
Thase, M. E., 680
Thibedeau, H., 241
Thoinot, L., 195
Thomas, A., 499
Thompson, A. E., 454
Thompson, D. M., 291
Thompson, W. C., 307
Thorndike, E. L., 20, 246
Thornton, A., 264
Tirri, K., 370
Titchener, E. B., 18
Tjepkema, M., 583
Tobias, M. C., 216
Tobler, I., 95
Tochigi, M., 650
Todman, D., 21
Todorov, A., 552, 553
Tolman, E. C., 261, 261f
Tolson, J. M., 194
Tom, G., 553
Tomasello, M., 413, 414
Tomblin, J B., 345
Torrey, E. F., 616
Tottenham, L. S., 372
Townsend, J. M., 85
Tracy, J. L., 485
Tracy, M., 586
Trainor, L. J., 161, 162
Tranel, D., 148
Travill, R. A., 217
Triggs, W. J., 118
Triplett, N., 536
Trivers, R. L., 85, 460
Troje, N. F., 486, 486f
Troop, N. A., 449
Trope, Y., 552, 567
Trost, M. R., 85f
Trzesniewski, K. H., 359f
Tsai, J. L., 213
Tse, D., 304
Tsuchiya, N., 45
Tuch, S. A., 559
Tulving, E., 220, 271, 282, 290, 291,
    292, 294
Tupper, K. W., 218
Turk, C., 634
Turkheimer, E., 375, 380
Turner, D. C., 383
Turner, J. C., 557
Tversky, A., 328, 329
Tweed, C. J., 434
Tweed, R. G., 434

U

Uchimura, N., 107
Ugawa, Y., 118
Ungerleider, L. G., 151
Urban, N. B., 217
Urbina, S., 358

Urland, G. R., 558
U.S. Department of Justice, 559
Uziel, L., 536

V

Valenstein, E., 109, 682
Valentin, V., 250
Van Ameringen, M., 621
Van den Bussche, E., 132
van der Kolk, B. A., 630
Vanheusden, K., 655
van Honk, J., 98
van Kampen, D., 496
van Kesteren, M. T. R., 304
Van Oort, F. V. A., 420
van Os, J., 650
van Praag, H., 608
Vansteenkiste, M., 471, 472
van Straten, A., 196
Vargha-Khadem, F., 345, 345f, 346
Vasconcelles, E. B., 607
Vervaeke, J., 635
Verwey, M., 182
Villar, J., 393
Virdee, K., 57
Voelker, R., 659
Vogel, D. L., 656
Vogel, E., 280
Vohs, K. D., 449
Vokey, J. R., 134
Volkow, N. D., 95, 212
Volpe, J. J., 396
von Frisch, K., 337
Vorona, R., 188
Vouloumanos, A., 342
Voyer, D., 82, 161
Vuilleumier, P., 477f, 478

W

Wade, C., 331f
Wade, K. A., 309
Wadzinski, J., 680
Wagar, D., 45
Wagenaar, W. A., 310
Wagner, A. D., 292
Wagner, D., 187
Wagner, G. A., 256
Wahba, M. A., 466
Wai, J., 371
Waite, L. J., 431
Waitt, C., 84
Wakefield, A. J., 59
Waldman, D. A., 367
Walk, R. D., 396
Walker, E., 645
Walker, E. G., 650
Walker, L. J., 492, 650
Walker, M., 391
Wall, P. D., 169, 170, 171f
Waller, G. P., 449
Walsh, T., 648
Walters, R. H., 263
Walther, E., 240

Walum, H., 596
Wampold, B. E., 668
Wan, F., 462
Wang, P. S., 655
Wang, Q., 303, 305
Wang, S. H., 304
Wang, S. J., 679
Wang, X., 161
Wansink, B., 445, 446
Wansink, B. S., 446
Ward, A., 555
Ward, C. D., 395
Ward, G., 340
Ward, L. M., 200
Wardle, J., 599
Ware, M. A., 218
Warfield, D., 158f
Warneken, F., 413, 414
Warren, M. J., 419
Warrington, E. K., 320
Waskett, L., 292
Wasser, S. K., 449
Waterhouse, B. D., 95
Watkins, C. E., 526
Watkins, L. R., 598, 609, 678
Watkins, M., 289
Watkins, M. J., 291
Watson, J. B., 20, 21, 235
Watson, J. C., 668
Watson, J. S., 409
Watson, M. W., 525
Watts, R. E., 528
Wayment, H. A., 431
Weaver, A. D., 43
Weaver, D. F., 206f
Weaver, I. C., 78
Webb, W. B., 191
Weber, B., 673
Wechsler, D., 278, 353
Weeks, D. L., 264
Weinberger, J. L., 499
Weinsier, R. L., 584
Weisman, A. G., 651
Weiss, A., 512
Weiss, E., 372
Weiss, G., 619
Weisz, J. R., 667
Weiten, W., 443f
Weitzer, R., 559
Wells, B., 560
Wells, S., 46
Wenk, G., 212
Wenzel, A., 298
Werker, J. F., 161, 338,
    341, 342
Wernicke, C., 109
West, R. F., 569
Westen, D., 332, 332f, 519, 525,
    528, 661
Westra, T., 397
Wever, E. G., 161, 183
Wheeler, A. C., 559
Whishaw, I. Q., 262

White, J. N., 102*f*, 140*f*, 143*f*, 147*f*, 161*f*, 170*f*, 502*f*, 592*f*
Whitehead, H., 264
Whitehead, P. C., 659
Whiten, A., 260, 265
Whitson, J. A., 610, 610*f*, 611, 611*f*
Whitten, W. B., 278
Whittlesea, B. W. A., 293
Wickings, E. J., 84
Wiebe, S. A., 392
Wiens, S., 171
Wiesel, T. N., 146
Wigfield, A., 471
Wight, R. G., 587
Wijdicks, E. F., 206
Wijnen, V. J. M., 208
Williams, J. M. G., 673
Williams, K., 496
Williams, K. D., 535, 536
Williams, W. M., 363, 381
Williamson, A. M., 188
Willingham, D. T., 369
Willis, J., 553
Willner, P., 57
Willoughby, B. L., 607
Willoughby, T., 417
Wilson, A. E., 306
Wilson, M. E., 599
Wilson, P. M., 471
Wilson, T. D., 535, 538
Wimmer, F., 188
Wimmer, H., 410
Winberg, J., 396

Winkielman, P., 570
Winkler, I., 162
Winocur, G., 381
Winter, B., 608
Witelson, S. F., 375, 378
Wobber, V., 98
Wojtowicz, J. M., 90
Wolpe, J., 668
Wong, C. K., 293, 293*f*, 294
Wong, J., 648
Woo, J. S. T., 461
Wood, D., 526
Woodberry, K. A., 647
Woodward, N. D., 121
Woodworth, R. S., 262
Woody, E. Z., 201
Woolf, N. J., 15*f*, 73*f*, 82*f*, 90*f*, 91*f*, 93*f*, 97*f*, 103*f*, 105*f*, 107*f*, 108*f*, 112*f*, 114*f*, 145*f*147*f*, 151*f*, 157*f*, 160*f*, 172*f*, 174*f*, 175*f*, 195*f*, 246*f*, 253*f*, 368*f*, 402*f*, 408*f*, 410*f*, 418*f*, 520*f*
Wright, I. C., 646, 649
Wright, S. C., 562, 658
Wuornos v. State of Florida (1994), 624
Wyer, Jr., R. S., 327

X
Xie, L., 186

Y
Yamagata, S., 499
Yamamoto, T., 238
Yamazaki, T., 105

Yang, L. J., 113
Yang, Y., 627
Yee, D., 292*f*
Yee, L. A., 536
Yeh, Y-C., 328*f*
Yerkes, R. M., 592
Yong, H. H., 582
Yoo, S. K., 655
Young, A. S., 655
Young, S. N., 95
Young, W. S., 595
Yuile, A., 450
Yurgelun-Todd, D. A., 220

Z
Zadra, A., 194
Zahn-Waxler, C., 414
Zajonc, R. B., 239, 380, 536
Zak, P. J., 456
Zald, D. H., 107
Zalesky, A., 220
Zaman, R., 683
Zanna, M. P., 240, 241
Zarate, J. M., 162
Zatorre, R. J., 162
Zeki, S., 467
Zelazo, N. A., 397
Zelezny, L., 570
Zentall, T. R., 265
Zhu, J., 105
Zimbardo, P. G., 534, 544
Zucker, R. A., 214
Zuroff, D. C., 512

Subject Index

A

Abbasi, Umar R., 324, 325
Aboriginal peoples
  suicide rates for, 641
absolute thresholds, 129, 129*f*
  differences in across species, 129
Abu Ghraib prison, 532, 533, 534, 540, 545, 546
academic journals, 37–38
  peer review before publication in, 38
Acadia University, 659
achievement motivation, 470–472
  approach goal in, 471
  avoidance goal in, 471
acquired immune deficiency syndrome (AIDS), 599
acronyms, 299
acuity (sensitivity), 168
Adler, Arthur, 528
adolescence, 417
  effects of the Internet on development in, 417
  brain factors in high-risk decisions, 421, 421*f*
  cigarette smoking in, 580
  cognitive reframng strategy in, 420
  decision making during, 420–421
  delay gratification, 420
  developmental changes in, 419
  development of moral reasoning in, 422–423
  emotional challenges in, 419–420
  emotional regulation during, 420, 423
  emotion and disgust in, 424
  explanations for high-risk decisions, 421–422
  identity formation in, 425
  identity *vs.* role confusion in, 425
  major brain changes in, 419
  menarche for girls in, 419
  parental conflicts in, 425
  peer groups, 425–426
  physical changes in, 418–420, 418*f*
  primary sex traits in, 418
  risk-inducing factors in, 421
  Scared Straight program and, 664
  self-control strategies in, 420
  sexual aggression in, 427
  sexual orientation in, 426
  social networks, 425–426
  social relationships in, 425–426
  spermarche for boys in, 419
  teenage romance in, 426
Adorno, Theodore, 496
adulthood,
  early and middle, 429–430
  menopause for women in, 429
  parenting, 432–433
  physical changes in, 429
  psychosocial development stages in, 430*t*, 431
  relationships in, 431
  starting of, 429
adulthood development, 428–430
adult relationships,
  break up behaviours, 431–432
  common-law, 431
  divorce, 431
  gender and culture factors in, 431
  marriage, 431
adults,
  emerging, 429
advertising,
  sex and, 462
age-related disorders, 428
aggression,
  in music, 266
  relationship to aggressive behaviour, 267
  testosterone and, 97–98
  viewing of leading to increased, 266
aging,
  challenges in, 434
  cognitive decline and, 434, 435
  compensating for loss of cognitive power, 436–437
  crystallized intelligence and, 436
  cultivation of positive emotions during, 434
  decline in, 434
  emotional stability and, 433–434, 433t
  fluid intelligence and, 436
  memory and, 437, 437*f*
  reasons for cognitive decline and, 435–436
  wisdom in, 436
agoraphobia, 635
Ainsworth, Mary, 407, 408, 409
alcohol, 224
  abuse, 379
  binge drinking, 224
  effects on brain, 224
  lowered inhibitions from, 224
  in most cultures, 224
  short-term rewards from drinking, 224
  as teratogen and effects on fetus, 391
alcohol abuse, 224
  linked to health problems, 224
alcoholism,
  combination of genes in those suffering, 76
Alexander, Bruce, 214
algorithms, 325, 326
Allan Memorial Institute, McGill University, 53
allostasis, 442
  compared to homeostasis, 442
Allport, Gordon, 493
Altemeyer, Bob, 497, 498
Alzheimer's disease, 57, 58, 344, 383, 428, 435
  acetylcholine and, 95
  effects on brain of, 435, 435*f*
  gene expression to treat, 78
  neurogenesis and, 90
  no single gene responsible for, 76
  risk factor gene in, 75
American Academy of Pediatrics, 400
American Heart Association, 572
American Psychiatric Association, 617
American Psychological Association (APA), 19, 564, 660
American Sign Language (ASL), 346
amnesia, 283
  anterograde, 285, 286*f*
  memory and brain and, 284–285
  retrograde, 286, 286*f*
amotivational, 472
amphetamines, 216–217
  long-term use as brain altering effect, 216–217
  stimulant effects on brain, 216*f*
anal stage (of psychodynamic theory), 523, 523*t*
analytical psychology, 527
  archetypes in, 527–528
analytic system, 569
anchoring effect, 330
ancient Greece,
  behavioural insights, 12
  classification system for human behaviour, 12
  four temperaments, 12
  influence of four humours, 12
  personality classification, 12
anecdotal evidence, 39
animal models of disease, 57
  characteristics of, 58
  critical evaluations of, 58
  ethics of, 57
  methods used, 57
  relevance for humans, 58
  scientific testing of, 58
  usefulness of, 57
  validity of, 57
anorexia nervosa, 379, 448, 449
  brain imaging studies and, 450
anterograde amnesia, 285, 286*f*
anthropology, 16, 17
anthropometrics, 351
antianxiety drugs, 680
anti-bullying policy, 27

antidepressants, 677
   anticyclics, 678
   effects at synapse, 678*f*
   happiness pill misconception of, 678
   monoamine oxidase inhibitors
      (MAOIs), 677
   selective serotonin reuptake
      inhibitors (SSRIs), 676, 678
antipsychotic drugs, 680
   atypical antipsychotics, 680
   tardive dyskinesia side effect of, 680
antisocial personality disorder (APD),
      236, 391, 625*t*, 626–627
   emotional responses in, 627, 627*f*
   physiology and brain function in,
      627–628, 628*f*
   psychopath term for, 626
   under reaction to stress in, 627
   symptoms of, 626
anxiety,
   medications, 211
   as natural part of fight-or-flight
      response, 634
   personality and reactions to, 521
anxiety buffers, 468
   cultural worldview as, 468–469
anxiety disorders, 619
   characteristics of, 634
   cognitive behavioural therapy
      (CBT) for, 674
   generalized anxiety disorder
      (GAD), 634–635
   interrupting cycle of anxiety as
      central treatment for, 637
   panic disorder, 635
   self-perpetuating, 637, 637*f*
   social anxiety disorder, 637
   statistics, 634
   variety of, 634
aphasia, 337
applied behaviour analysis
      (ABA), 248
applied psychology studies, 7, 27
Archimboldo, Giuseppe, 148
Arendt, Hannah, 548
Aron, Arthur, 467
arousal theory of extraversion, 514
ascending reticular activating system
      (ARAS), 514
Asch, Solomon, 537, 538, 539, 548
Aschoff, Jürgen, 183
Ashton, Michael, 496
associative learning, 228–230, 229*f*
   classical conditioning as part of,
      229–230
astrology, 4
   compared to science, 4
asylums, 616, 658–659
Atkinson, Richard, 272
Atkinson-Shiffrin model, 272, 272*f*
   attention process in, 272–273
   compared to working memory
      model, 279
   control processes in, 272
   delicacy of memory systems, 286
   functional system, 272–273

as introduction to memory
      formation, 278
   long-term memory (LTM), 272,
      275–276
   neat and tidy boxes in, 276
   retrieval process in, 273
   sensory memory store in, 272, 273
   short-term memory (STM), 272,
      274–275
atrocities, 532, 533
attachment, 406–407
   behavioural patterns that
      characterize styles of, 409
   change of styles of, 409
   development, 409
   disorganized type, 408–409
   importance of through life, 409
   infant behaviours, 407
   insecure anxious/ambivalent type,
      408
   insecure avoidant type, 408
   parenting and styles of, 409, 414
   secure type, 408
   styles as learned behaviour
      patterns, 409
   theories of, 407
   types of, 407–408
attachment behaviour system, 414
attention deficit hyperactivity disorder
      (ADHD), 194, 216, 222, 618, 619
attitude-behaviour feedback loop,
      574–575
attitude inoculation, 570
atypical antipsychotics, 680
authoritarian personality, 496
autism, 57
   gene expression and, 78
   vaccinations and, 394
autonomic nervous system (ANS),
      102–104, 103*f*
   effects of positive emotions on, 603
   fight or flight responses, 478–479,
      478*f*
   parasympathetic nervous system
      component of, 103, 103*f*, 478
   preparation for movement by, 479
   stress effects on, 594
   sympathetic nervous system
      component of, 103, 103*f*, 478
autonomous sensory meridian
      response (ASMR), 177, 178*f*
aversive conditioning, 671
avoidance learning, 247
Avon Longitudinal Study of Parents
      and Children, 381

B

Baby Einstein (books, toys, DVDs),
      400
backward messages in music, 134
   scientific explanation for, 134–135
Baddeley, Alan, 279
Ball, Karlene, 435
banality of evil, 548
Bandura, Albert, 263, 502
barbiturate abuse, 222

Bard, Philip, 480
bar graphs, 63
Barnum, P. T., 493
Barnum effect, 493
Bartlett, Frederick, 22
Bauby, Jean-Dominique, 209
Bay of Pigs invasion (1961), 537
Beatles, 134
Beautiful Mind, A (movie), 644
Beck, Aaron, 671
Beck Depression Inventory, 32
Beckham, David, 462
behaviour,
   media violence and, 265
   self-knowledge and positive, 665
   situational analysis for, 533, 534
behavioural activation system (BAS),
      514
behavioural genetics, 75–76
   adopted children study for genetics
      and behaviour, 77
   combinations of genes influence
      traits, 76
   environmental factors in, 75–76
   heritability from twin studies, 76 77
   twin and adoption studies, 75–76
behavioural genomics, 75, 376–377
   as study of DNA and gene-behav-
      iour relationship, 75
behavioural influences,
   on intelligence, 382–383
behavioural inhibition system (BIS),
      514
behavioural therapies, 668–670
   aversive conditioning, 671
   for people with fear and anxiety
      problems, 668–669, 669*t*
   systematic desensitization in,
      668–669
   workings of, 668–669
behaviourism, 19–20
   compared to humanistic
      psychology, 21
   personality and, 501–502, 502*f*
   radical, 20–21
   social psychology as challenge to,
      534
behaviourist psychology. *See*
      behaviourism
behaviours,
   transmission of, 264
Beilock, Sian, 590
belief perseverance, 331
   brain imaging research and, 332
Belknap, Ray, 126
Bell Curve, The (Herrnstein & Murray,
      1994), 357
bell curve (normal distribution), 63
belonging, sense of, 467
   as form of love, 467
   as a need, 467
   sense of permanence of, 467
   terror management theory (TMT)
      and, 468–469
Bem, Sandra, 25
Bethune, James, 362

"Better by You, Better Than Me"
(song), 126
Bialystok, Ellen, 344
biases in scientific research, 34
    anonymity techniques to reduce,
        36, 37
    confidentiality techniques to reduce,
        36–37
    critical evaluation of, 36
    double-blind study to minimize, 37
    experimenter, 36
    object, 34
    observation, 34
    participant anxiety about the
        experiment, 37
    participants' expectations, 37
    researcher, 37
    single-blind study to minimize, 37
    social desirability, 34
    subject, 34
bibliotherapy, 661–662
    caution because of complexities of
        mental disorders, 662
    effectiveness of, 661
    evaluation of research into
        effectiveness of, 661–662, 662f
Bieber, Justin, 436
bilingualism, 343–344
    benefits of, 343–344
    costs of, 343
    health benefits of, 344
Bilodeau, Alexandre, 164, 165
Binet, Alfred, 352
biofeedback, 605
biological perspective of human
        behaviour, 5, 5f
    influence of medicine on, 15–16
biological psychology, 17
biological rhythms, 182
biopsychosocial model, 5–6, 5f
    of behaviour, 73
    of mental illness, 616–617, 616t
bipolar disorder, 622
    characterized by extreme highs and
        lows, 639
Birbiglia, Mike, 181
birth, 386
    premature, 392–393
birth control pills, 461
birth order,
    intelligence and, 380
Black Lives Matter movement, 551,
    568
Blackwell, Lisa Sorich, 360
blank slate, 395
Blind Tom, 362, 364
Boas, Franz, 322
body language, 486
borderline personality disorder (BDP),
    625–626, 625t
bottomless bowl of soup, 445
    unit bias explanation, 445
bottom-up processing, 135
brain, human,
    auditory perception and, 161–163
    Broca's area, 337, 337f

CB1 receptors and drug responses,
    221f
cerebral cortex, 108
cerebral hemispheres, 104
    classical conditioning and, 231–232
corpus callosum, 111
development of during infancy,
    397–399
dorsal compared to ventral stream
    of perception, 151–152
dorsal stream of perception,
    151–152, 152f
emotional regulation in, 628f
endocrine system and, 96–97
exercise and health of, 111, 437
exercising to slow aging process, 428
forebrain area, 104, 105f
frontal lobe, 108f, 110
grey and white matter, 108, 108f
hemispheric specialization, 111
hindbrain area, 104–105, 105f
hippocampus, 284f, 285
hypothalamus, 96, 97, 107
midbrain area, 104, 105–106, 105f
motor cortex, 109f, 110
neuroplasticity of, 112–113
nucleus accumbens, 249, 250, 250f
occipital lobe, 108–109, 108f
olfactory bulb, 175
organization of, 101
organizes sensations into coherent
    perceptions, 127, 128f
parietal lobe, 108f, 109
pituitary gland, 96, 97
reward processing in, 249–250, 250f
secondary gustatory cortex, 174
size of and intelligence, 377–378
somatosensory cortex, 109f, 110, 168
stored memories and, 285–286
suprachiasmatic nucleus (SCN) of
    hypothalamus, 182
temporal lobe, 108f, 109–110
thalamus as sensory relay station,
    146, 174
from thalamus to visual cortex, 146
ventral stream of vision, 148
vestibular system and, 165
visual cortex and feature detection
    cells, 146, 147f
visual functions of ventral and
    dorsal streams, 146, 147f
visual perception and, 146–147
visual system pathways, 145–146,
    147f
Wernicke's area, 337, 337f
brain cells,
    regeneration of, 90
brain damage, 116
    studying patients with, 117
brain death, 205
    positron emission tomography
        (PET) scan of, 206f
brain-derived neurotrophic factor
    (BDNF), 608
brain development,
    fetal, 388, 390, 390f

brain-imaging technology, 17, 45
    functional magnetic resonance
        imaging (fMRI), 25, 26
brain injury,
    neuroplasticity and, 113–114
    numbers of, 114
brain-personality relationship, 514
brainstem, 104
    medulla in, 104, 105f
    pons structure in, 104, 105f
brain training programs, 382
brain tumours, 114
brainwashing, 53
Breaking Bad (TV program), 216
British Broadcasting Corporation
    (BBC), 532
Broca, Paul, 16, 337
Broca's aphasia, 337
Broca's area, 337, 337f, 344, 346
Brock University, 149, 339, 496
Brotherhood of the Ram, The, 302
Brown, Brené, 654
Brown, Michael, 568
Buddhism, 607
bulimia nervosa, 448, 449
    brain imaging studies and, 450
bullying, 417
Bush, George W., 205, 469, 534, 537
Buss, David, 453
bystander effect, 541–543
    diffusion of responsibility as
        explanation for, 541–542, 542f
    explanations for, 541–542
    pluralistic ignorance explanation
        for, 542–543
    smoke-filled room study and, 543

C

cable television (CATV), 567
caffeine, 213, 215
    withdrawal, 215
Caillebottein, Gustave, 153, 153f
Cameron, Donald Ewen, 53, 60
Campbell, Kim, 241
Camp Erika, Netherlands, 310
Campione, Elaine, 622
2002 Canadian Community Health
    Survey, 193
2007 Canadian Community Health
    Survey (GGHS), 584
Canadian Heritage Moment (television
    show), 101
Canadian Medical Association Journal,
    257, 383
Canadian Network for Mood and
    Anxiety Treatments (CANMAT),
    679
Cannon, Walter, 480, 593
Cannon-Baird theory of emotion, 480,
    480f
    compared to James-Lange theory of
        emotion, 480, 480f
caregivers,
    infant's feelings affected by, 405, 406
caregiving behavioural system, 414
Carleton University, Ottawa, 45

Cartwright, Rosalind, 191
case studies, 43–44
  critical evaluations of role of in
      research, 45
  as form of scientific research, 44
  Phineas Gage, 43–44
  science tests for usefulness of, 44–45
  strengths and limitations of, 50–51,
      50*t*
Castro, Fidel, 537
categories, 315
  basic-level, 317
  hierarchy of, 317
  levels of and influence on thinking,
      317
  study of, 315
  subordinate-level, 317
categorization, 315
  based on experiences, 319–320
  brain activity variation by culture,
      321, 321*f*, 322
  brain involvement in memory and,
      320
  classical, 315
  by comparison, 315–316
  comparison of classical and
      prototypes in, 316
  cultural perspective on, 321, 321*f*,
      322
category specific visual agnosia
      (CSVA), 320–321, 320*f*
Cat in the Hat, The, 395
Cattell, James McKeen, 352
Cattell, Raymond, 493
causation,
  not equal to correlation, 364
cellular consolidation, 284
Central Intelligence Agency (CIA), 53
central nervous system (CNS),
  brain and spinal cord make up, 102,
      102*f*
central route to persuasion, 565, 566*f*
  effective use of, 566
  emotional content in messages,
      570–571
  personalizing the message, 567
  processing fluency in, 571
central tendency,
  the mean, 63–64
  the median, 64
  the mode, 64
  in skewed distribution, 65*f*
  in symmetrical distributions, 64*f*
Centre for Addiction and Mental
      Health, Toronto, 672
chaining process, 248
Challenger space shuttle explosion
      (1986), 297, 537
chameleon effect, 534
change blindness, 274, 274*f*
changing people's behaviour, 564–566
  economic approach to, 565
  legal approach to, 565
  social approach to, 565–567
  technological approach to, 565
Chara, Zdeno, 116

charisma, 239
chemical senses, 173
  taste and smell, 173–175
childhood,
  cognitive development in, 404–406
  egocentric in, 409–410
  personality seeds already in, 499
  perspective taking in, 409–410
  transition from infancy to, 400–402
child neglect, 379
Chomsky, Noam, 23
Chrétien, Jean, 240
chromosomes, human, 73, 73*f*, 74, 74*f*
Cialdini, Bob, 573
CIA mind-control research program,
      53, 54, 55
cigarette smoking, 579
  adolescent, 580, 581
  analysis of effects of in movies,
      580–581
  costs of in lives and money, 580,
      580*t*
  decline in rates of, 582
  evaluation of effects of in movies,
      581
  image-based warnings on packages,
      582
  life expectancy of, 580
  life-shortening health problems
      from, 580
  media influences on, 580
  policies to restrict, 581–582
  social-group influences on, 588
Circadian rhythms, 182
  change with age, 183–184, 183*f*
  endogenous rhythms explanation,
      183
  entertainment explanation, 183
  release of melatonin at night in, 182
  strength of, 188
  suprachiasmatic nucleus of
      hypothalamus in, 182
circannual rhythms, 182
civil rights movement (U.S.), 558
Claparède, 283
classical categorization, 315
  graded membership problem with,
      315
classical conditioning, 19, 20
  acquisition in, 233, 233*f*
  advertising application, 235,
      239–240
  as biological process in brain,
      231–235
  compared to operant conditioning,
      245, 245*t*, 251*t*
  conditioned response (CR), 230,
      230*f*, 231
  conditioned stimulus (CS), 230,
      230*f*, 231
  discrimination in, 234, 234*f*
  drug response application, 235,
      241–243
  drug tolerance and, 241–242
  emotional learning application, 235
  evolutionary function of, 231

extinction in, 233–234, 233*f*
flexibility of responses in, 233
food aversion application, 235,
      237–238
as form of associative learning,
      229–230
neutral stimulus (NS) elicits a
      response, 229, 230–231, 230*f*
Pavlov and, 229–230, 229*f*, 230*f*
spontaneous recovery in, 233–234,
      233*f*
stimulus generalization in, 234, 234*f*
unconditioned response (UR), 230
unconditioned stimulus (US), 230
use of to create negative attitudes,
      240
client-centred therapy (person-centred
      therapy), 667
  importance of therapeutic relation-
      ship in, 667
Clifford, Ribert, 564
climate change, 562, 564
  personalize communication for
      effective persuasion against, 567
  value frames in discussions on, 570
clinical psychologists, 658
  medication prescription and, 658
clinical psychology, 15
Coane, Jennifer, 318
cocaine, 215, 216
  stimulant effects on brain, 216*f*
cochlea implants, 158–159, 160*f*, 161*f*
cognitive affective behavioural
      syndrome, 105
cognitive appraisal theory of stress,
      591, 591*f*
  primary step, 591
  secondary step, 591
cognitive-behavioural therapy (CBT),
      201
  for depression, anxiety, obesity and
      eating disorders, 674
  group and family therapies, 673
  revaluation of, 673–674
cognitive behavioural therapy (CBT),
      671–672
  application of for depression
      symptoms, 672, 672*t*
  cognitive restructuring in, 671–672
  neuroimaging studies and, 672
  relaxation techniques for dealing
      with negative feelings in, 671
cognitive bias, 331–332
  belief perseverance, 332
  confirmation bias, 332
cognitive development, science of, 401
  studies of early, 405
cognitive development theory,
      401–402
  accommodation in, 401
  assimilation in, 401
  concrete operational stage of, 401*t*,
      403
  conservation testing in, 402–403,
      402*f*
  evaluation of, 404–405

cognitive development theory, (*Cont.*)
    formal operational stage of, 401*t*, 403–404, 422
        object permanence as first major milestone, 401–402
        preoperational stage of, 401*t*, 402–403
        sensorimotor stage of, 401, 401*t*, 402
cognitive dissonance theory, 574–575
    based on need for self-consistency, 575
    as explanations for puzzling phenomena, 575
cognitive hypnotherapy, 201
cognitive learning, 229
cognitive neuroscience, 25
cognitive obstacles to problem solving, 326
    mental set as, 326
cognitive perspective, 22
    memory study, 22–23
cognitive reframing, 420
    delay gratification from, 420
cognitive skills,
    development of, 400
Cohen, Jacob, 69
cohort effects, 387
    in cross-sectional studies, 387
    in longitudinal studies, 387
colour constancy, 150
Columbia space shuttle explosion (1981), 297
communication,
    about tragedy, 568
    construal-level theory of, 567
    effective, 565
    message complexity can derail, 571
    personalize for effective, 567
    to persuade others to change, 565
    value appeals, 570
community psychology, 659–660
compensatory control, 610
    relevance of, 611–612
    studying, 610–611
computerized tomography (CT scan), 119, 119*f*
computer simulations, 45
concept, 315
conception, 388
Concordia University, 156, 306
concussion, 116
conditioned drug tolerance, 241–242
    possibility of fatal consequences for drug abusers, 241
conditioned emotional responses, 235–236
    brain regions responsible for, 235–236
conditioned response (CR) in classical conditioning, 230*f*, 231
    evolutionary function of, 231
conduct disorders, 629
confirmation bias, 332
    brain imagine research and, 332
conformity, 537–538, 537*f*
    evaluation of research into, 539

individual power and, 540
    mimicry as beginning of, 549
    neuroscience and reasons for, 538
    personal and situational factors in, 538, 538*t*
    reasons for, 538
    research into, 539
    size of group and, 539–540
    social influences, 538
conjunction fallacy, 329, 329*f*
conscientiousness,
    stability of over lifespan, 499–500, 500*f*
conscious mind, 520
consciousness, 181–182
    acts are conditioned or influenced by unconscious processing, 552
    altered states to examine, 200
    brain death as lowest level of, 205
    coma as loss of, 205
    evaluation of studies into in vegetative state, 207
    explanations for in vegetative state, 207
    explicit and implicit processes in, 552
    importance of in medical decisions, 205
    levels of, 205–206, 206*f*
    locked-in syndrome, 209
    minimally conscious state (MCS), 209
    neuroimaging studies of vegetative state, 207–209
    permanent vegetative state, 206, 207
    persistent vegetative state, 205–206, 207
    PET images of brain activity in levels of, 209*f*
    understanding, 200
construal-level theory of communication, 567
contact hypothesis, 562
context-dependent learning, 292*f*
    brain-imaging studies and, 292
    context-dependent forgetting, 294
    context reinstatement effect, 294
    false familiarity and, 293, 293*f*
    implications of, 294
    limitations of effects of, 292–293
context-dependent memory, 291–292
    scientific explanations for, 292
contextual fear conditioning, 236
continuous perception, 273–274
continuous reinforcement, 253
Controlled Drugs and Substances Act, 219
coping, 602, 603
    effects of positive emotions and, 603
    positive strategies, 603
    strategies, 603
core knowledge hypothesis, 404
Coren, Stanley, 187
coronary heart disease, 598
corporal punishment, 257
    side effects of, 257

correlational research, 47–49
    correlation coefficient as measure of association, 47
    direction characteristic of, 47
    illusory correlations, 48
    magnitude characteristic of, 47
    not equal to causation, 364
    scatterplots, 47, 47*f*
    strengths and limitations of, 50*t*, 51
    into testosterone and aggression relationship, 98
    third variable problem, 48
corridor illusion, 153f
Cosmopolitan, 462, 493
counselling psychologists, 658
Cox, Diane, 648
Criminal Code of Canada, 257
critical thinking stage of scientific literacy model, 6, 6*f*
    applying results to real-world situations, 8
    avoidance of emotional thinking in, 8–9
    consideration of alternative viewpoints and interpretations, 9
    core habits and skills for development of, 8–9
    curiosity and, 8
    definition, 8
    examine assumptions and biases in, 8
    examine nature and source of evidence in, 8
    importance of, 8
    principle of parsimony in, 9
    skepticism and, 8
    tolerance of ambiguity in, 9
cross-cultural psychology, 25
cross-fostered, 346
cross-sectional designs (for measuring developmental trends), 387, 387*f*
    strengths and weaknesses of, 387
crystallized intelligence, 366–367, 366*f*
    changes over the lifespan, 367
    as distinguished from fluid intelligence, 367
    measurement of, 367*f*
    neurobiological evidence for lifespan changes, 367–368
    through lifespan, 436
cultural differences, 263
    behaviours shaped by, 507
    brain and, 507
    in display rules, 486–487
    in extrinsic and intrinsic motivations, 473–474, 474*f*
    importance of understanding, 506
    individualism *vs.* collectivism, 507
    in motivation, 473–474
    in normal behaviour, 617
    in personality structures, 506
    in response styles, 508
    in understanding facial expressions, 487–488
cultural learning, 322

cultural norms,
eating disorders and, 450
cultural perspective,
on categorical thinking, 321, 321*f*, 322
curious, open, accepting, and loving (COAL) attitude, 672
cybersex, 461

D

Dalhousie University, 575
Darby, Joe, 532, 533, 534, 540
dark adaptation, 143–144
Dark Ages, 12
Dark Triad, 496–497, 497
Darley, John, 541, 542
Darwin, Charles, 13–14, 17, 18, 79, 80, 83, 356, 485
data,
central tendency, 63–64
distribution of, 63
negatively skewed distribution, 63, 64*f*
normal distribution, 63
positively skewed distribution, 63, 64*f*
testing, 66–67
David Suzuki Foundation, 576
Daylight Savings Time, 187
car accidents and, 187, 187*f*
decision making,
conjunction fallacy errors in, 329
heuristics in, 328
judgment and, 328
maximizers invest more in, 333–334
maximizing, 333–334
multiple-choice tests and, 334
paradox of choice, 333
probability theory and, 328–329
satisfying, 333–334
declarative (explicit) memories, 282, 282*f*
episodic memories, 223*f*, 282
semantic memories, 282, 282*f*
deep brain stimulation (DBS), 684
Deese-Roediger-McDermott (DRM) paradigm, 309, 309*f*
semantic associates in, 309
default mode network, 203–204, 204*f*
defence mechanisms, 521–522, 522*t*
defensive responses, 231
fleeing, 231
freezing, 231
deinstitutionalization, 616, 658–659
delayed reinforcement, 251
demand characteristics, 35–36
problem of when studying clinical populations, 36
testing effects of on behaviour, 36
dementia, 344, 434
deoxyribonucleic acid (DNA), 73
ribosomal, 78
Depp, Johnny, 580
depression, 57, 434
anhedonia as symptom of, 58
biological aspects of, 640

cognitive aspects of, 639–640
cognitive-behavioural therapy (CBT) for, 672, 672*t*, 674
dorsal of frontal cortex and, 640
genetic factors in, 640–641, 641*f*
limbic system and, 640
medications, 211
multiple systems underlying, 617
selective serotonin reuptake inhibitors (SSRIs) for, 676
serotonin levels ad, 640
St. John's wort and, 676–678
depressive explanatory style, 639–640, 640*f*
depth perception, 152, 154
binocular depth cues, 152
monocular cues, 152, 154, 154*f*
pictorial depth cues, 153
retinal disparity in, 152
stereoscopic vision, 152
descriptive statistics,
central tendency type, 63–64
frequency type, 63
to give big picture of results, 63
variability type, 63, 65–66
desirable difficulties, 300
determinism, 12
cause-and-effect relationships in, 12
development across the lifespan, 412–413
adolescence and identity *vs.* role confusion, 425
autonomy as key pillar in, 429
childhood and issue of industry *vs.* inferiority, 413
competence as key pillar in, 429
early childhood and issue of initiative *vs.* guilt, 413
emotional development and competency, 413
infancy stage and issue of trust *vs.* mistrust, 413
particular developmental challenges at different ages, 412–413
relatedness as key pillar in, 429
toddlerhood stage and issue of autonomy *vs.* shame, 413
developmental psychology, 387
developmental stages,
prenatal stage, 388
sensitive period in, 401
developmental trends,
challenges in measuring, 387
cross-sectional design for measuring, 387
longitudinal study for measuring, 387
stage models in, 387–388
deviation IQ, 353
diagnosis,
effects of labelling on people, 619
changing the label of, 619
difficulties of, 617, 618, 619
long-term effects of receiving, 619
reducing stigmatization from labelling, 620
sub-clinical, 619

Diagnostic and Statistical Manual of Mental Disorders (DSM), 617
criticisms of, 618–619
set and number of symptoms, etiology and prognosis in, 618
Diallo, Amadfou, 551, 552
diathesis-stress model of psychological disorders, 640–641
diets, 580
difference threshold, 129
diffusion of responsibility, 542, 542*f*
diffusion tensor imaging (DTI), 119*f*, 120
discrimination, 250, 551
effects of on health, 587
explicit *vs.* implicit processes, 559
from stereotyping and prejudice, 558
discriminative stimulus, 250
display rules, 486–487
culture-specific, 487
dissociative disorders, 630–631
characterization of, 630
depersonalization disorder condition in, 630
dissociative amnesia condition in, 630
dissociative fugue condition in, 630
dissociative identity disorder (DID), 630–631
stress as cause of, 630
dissociative identity disorder (DID), 630
changes in diagnosis numbers of, 631
controversies over reality of, 630
as distinguished from schizophrenia, 645
testing for, 630–631
divided attention, 136
Diving Bell and the Butterfly, The (movie), 209
divorce, 431
Dix, Dorothea, 616
dizygotic (fraternal) twins, 76
personality and genetics research, 509
doctrine of specific nerve energies, 127–1289, 176
Dodson, John, 592
door-in-the-face technique for reciprocity, 572–573
dopamine release, 216
associated with drug highs, 212
secondary reinforcers and, 250
double-blind study, 37
Down syndrome,
chromosomal abnormality in, 74
dream analysis, 665
dream theory, 190–191
activation-synthesis hypothesis, 190–191, 191*f*
dreams as wish fulfillment, 190
factor analysis in, 190
importance of Freud's work, 190
latent content, 190

dream theory, (Cont.)
  manifest content, 190
  problem-solving theory, 191
  psychoanalytic approach, 190
drives, 441, 441f
drug abuse, 222
  see also alcohol abuse
  prescription drugs, 222–223
  prevention of prescription drug,
    223–224
  recreational drugs, 215, 218
drug addiction, 57
drug-neurotransmitter relationship,
  212–213
drugs,
  biological causes of dependence,
    213–214
  cognitive causes of dependence, 213
  cultural influences on usage, 219
  decriminalization of, 225
  definition, 212
  legality vs. illegality, 224–225
  long-term effects on brain, 213–214
  neurotransmitters and effects of
    different, 212
  personality traits and dependence,
    214
  physical long-term dependence, 213
  physiological long-term effects, 213
  physiological short-term effects,
    212–213
  psychological long-term
    dependence, 213
  psychological long-term effects, 213
  psychological short-term effects,
    212–213
  recreational, 215, 215t
  short-term effects on the brain, 212
  social causes of dependence,
    213–214
  social support for dependence, 214
  tolerance, 213
  withdrawal symptoms, 213
dualism, 13
dual-process models of behaviour, 552
  identifiable victim effect and, 569
Dunn, Robert, 283
Dweck, Carol, 359, 360
dyslexia, 339

E

ear, human,
  auditory canal, 157
  cochlea, 157–158
  detect sound waves and transform
    into neural signals function, 157
  eardrum, 157
  gathers and analyzes frequency and
    amplitude of sound waves, 157
  inner region, 157, 159f
  middle region of, 157, 159f
  ossicles convert sound vibrations to
    neural impulses, 157
  outer region of, 157, 159f
  pinna, 157
  structure, 157–158, 159f

eating,
  attention and, 445–446
  fatty foods, 443–444
  high-energy food as reinforcer, 444
  hypothalamus and, 442–443, 443f
  impression management and, 447
  increase in portion sizes, 446
  modelling and, 447
  physiological factors in, 442–443
  priming as factor in junk food, 446
  rewards for, 443–444
  semantic networks and, 446
  social facilitation and, 447
  social motives for, 446–447
  taste as pleasure in, 443, 444
  trigger foods and, 446
  unit bias and, 445
eating disorders, 448–450, 448t
  anorexia nervosa, 448
  bulimia nervosa, 448
  cognitive-behavioural therapy
    (CBT) for, 674
  family influences on, 449
  male, 449
  obesity, 448
  peer pressure on, 449
  perfect body descriptions in media
    and, 449, 450
  programs for, 450
  reverse anorexia, 449
  role of culture and media in, 450
  social factors in, 449
  statistical characteristics of, 448,
    448t
  stress factor in, 448–449
Ebbinghaus, Hermann, 22, 298
Ebbington, Herman, 7
echoic memory, 273
e-cigarettes (vaping), 582
ecological validity in scientific
  method, 34
economics, 16, 17
ecstasy,
  changes in brain structure in
    chronic users of, 217
  as club drug, 217
  neuroimaging studies of long-term
    users, 217
education,
  effects of on intelligence, 381
Edwin Smith papyrus, 11
Eichmann, Adolf, 548
Einstein, Albert, 374
Einstein's brain, 374–375
Ekman, Paul, 484, 485
elaboration-likelihood model (ELM) of
  persuasive communication, 565
Electra complex, 524
electroconvulsive therapy (ECT), 683
  workings of, 683
electroencephalogram (EEG), 120–121,
  121f, 123t
  to define sleep cycles, 184–185, 184f,
    190, 191
  event-related potentials (ERPs),
    120–121

Ellis, Albert, 671
emerging adults, 429
  new possibilities for, 429
  personal strengths as, 429
  relationships as, 429
Emory University, Atlanta, 670
emotional expressiveness (EE), 651
emotional regulation, 479
emotional synchrony, 534–535
emotion-focused therapy (EFT), 667
emotion(s),
  autonomic nervous system (ANS)
    and, 478, 478f
  biological mechanisms to influence
    memory, 296
  body language, 486
  competing theories of, 480, 480f
  cultural context for understanding
    someone else's, 487–488
  definition of, 477
  display rules and culture, 486–487
  expressing, 484
  faces and bodies to express, 484–486
  influence of on memory
    consolidation, 296
  memory enhancing effect of, 296
  nervous system's initial response,
    477
  physiology of, 477–479
  specific effects of on memory,
    295–296, 296f
  two-factor theory of, 481, 482f
  universal facial expressions of,
    485–486
empathy, 413
  development of during adolescence,
    423
  as influence on pain perception,
    171–172
emphatic helping, 414
empirically supported treatments
  (evidence-based therapies),
  660–661
  problematic biases in, 661
empiricism, 12
  knowledge through experience in, 12
encoding memory, 289
  alcoholic influences and, 294
  elaborative rehearsal, 290
  levels of processing (LOP), 290
  limitations of rehearsal
    memorization, 289
  maintenance rehearsal, 289–290
  marijuana influences and, 294
  mood-dependent memory and, 294
  rehearsal memorization, 289
  state-dependent memory and, 294
encoding specificity principle, 291
  context-dependent memory as
    intuitive form of, 291
endocrine system, 96–97, 97f
  adrenal glands in, 97
  brain and, 96–97
  as contributor towards homeostasis,
    96
  nervous system and, 97

entity theory, 359–360
environmental factors,
    birth order and intelligence, 379–380
    in fetal brain development, 390
    influence of on cognitive abilities,
        379
    intelligence and, 379–381
    nutrition and intelligence, 380–381
    socioeconomic status (SES) and
        intelligence, 380
    stress and intelligence, 381
epigenetics, 78
epilepsy, 21, 57
    seizures, 111
episodic buffer, 279, 281
Epworth sleepiness scale, 198t
Erikson, Erik, 412, 413, 429, 431
Esquire, 462
ethical standards, 235
    punishment application and,
        256–257
    Stanford prison study and, 545
etiology, 618
eugenics, 17, 356–357
European colonialism, 356
evaluative conditioning, 239–240, 241
evidence-based therapies. *See*
    empirically supported treatments
    (evidence-based therapies)
evolutionary psychology, 19, 72, 73,
    80, 81
    colour red and sexual receptivity in
        animals, 84
    different traits for different
        circumstances, 512–513
    gender roles, 460–461
    many different personalities and,
        512
    need for control, 449
    particular personality traits, 512
    personality and, 511–513
    sexual scripts in, 460–461
    sexual selection in, 84–85
    spatial memory and sex differences,
        80
experiential system, 569
experimental research,
    animal welfare in, 56
    between-subjects design, 50
    confounding variable in, 49–50
    control group, 50
    dependent variables in, 50
    elements of experiments, 49f
    experimental group, 50
    experimental method, 49–50
    importance of placebos in, 37
    independent variables in, 50
    quasi-experimental method, 50–51
    random assignment element in, 49
    strengths and limitations of, 50t, 51
    within-subjects design, 50
explicit processes, 552
    stereotyping, prejudice and
        discrimination as, 559
*Expression of the Emotions in Man and
    Animals, The* (Darwin, 1872), 13, 15

external attributions (situational
    attributions), 555, 556f
extinction, 251
eyes, human, 140–142
    blind spot, 142
    cones receptors, 143
    gathering light, 140–141
    importance of wavelength for
        vision, 140–141
    iris, 141
    light as hue and saturation, 141,
        141f
    from light to nerve impulse,
        142–143
    optic nerve, 141–142
    from optic nerve to optic chasm in
        brain, 146
    primary function of, 140
    pupil, 141
    retina, 141
    rods photoreceptors, 141, 143
    sclera, 141
    structure, 141–143, 142f
eyewitness testimony, 27, 306–307,
    306f
    appropriate instructions to improve,
        308
    careful lineups to improve, 308
    confidence statements to improve,
        308
    double-blind procedures to
        improve, 308
    misinformation effect in, 307
    record procedures to improve, 308
    science of memory and, 308
    sequential lineups to improve, 308

F
face pareidolia (illusory perceptions of
    faces), 149
face perception, 148
    experience in, 149
    face inversion effect, 148, 149f
    fusiform face area (FFA) of brain,
        148–149
    importance of specific brain region
        for, 150
    skill increase with age, 149
facial feedback hypothesis, 480–481,
    481f
    mixed research support for, 481
factor analysis, 363
    for personality traits, 493
false consensus effect, 555
false memory, 306
    brain imaging studies to
        differentiate true from, 311
    creation of in the laboratory,
        309–310
    critical lure in, 309, 309f
    dangers of, 310
    Deese-Roediger-McDermott (DRM)
        procedure in, 309, 309f
    doctored photographs and, 309–310
    imagination and, 308–309
family,

effects of on stress, 596
    emotional expressiveness (EE) and
        schizophrenia, 651
    influences on eating disorders, 449
famine, 391
Farb, Norm, 606
fascism, 497
fear conditioning,
    brain and, 236–237, 237f
    comparing fear of snakes to guns,
        236–237
    contextual, 236
    evolutionary role for, 236–237
    preparedness evolutionary
        explanation in, 237
fear instinct, 236
Fechner, William Gustav, 13, 15f, 18,
    129
Feeling Good: The New Mood Therapy
    (Burns, 1980), 661–662, 662f
fentanyl,
    dangers of, 221
fertilization, 388
fetal alcohol syndrome (FAS), 391–392
fetal brain,
    development of, 388, 390
    environmental influences on, 390
    importance of nutrition, 390–391
    teratogens and effects on, 391
Fight Club (movie), 630
first impressions, 553
    self-fulfilling prophecies as conse-
        quence of, 553–554
Fisher, Ronald, 68
Five Factor Model (FFM),
    across nations, 507–508
    agreeableness factor, 494f, 495
    animals and, 511–512
    brain anatomy and personality
        traits, 515–516
    conscientiousness factor, 494f, 495
    extraversion factor, 494f, 495
    gender and, 513
    neuroticism factor, 494f, 495
    openness factor, 494f, 4494
    projection and traits of, 526
    trait based theory of personality,
        493–494, 494f
    twins and, 509
    universality of, 506, 507t
    and WEIRD, 506
flashbulb memories, 296–297
    accuracy of, 297
flashcards, 300
Flett, Dr. Gordon, 492
fluid intelligence, 366–367, 366f
    changes over the lifespan, 367
    as distinguished from crystallized
        intelligence, 367
    measurement of, 367f
    neurobiological evidence for
        lifespan changes, 367–368
    through lifespan, 436
fluoxetine (Prozac), 676, 678
Flynn, James, 381
Flynn effect, 381, 382f

focal lesions (anterior cingulotomy), 683
Folkman, Susan, 591
Food and Drug Administration (FDA) (U.S.), 680
forced sterilization, 350, 357
forebrain, 104, 105*f*, 106
    basal ganglia, 106–107, 106*f*
    emotions, memory and thought processes in, 106
    limbic system, 107–108, 107*f*
    thalamus, 107–108
    ventricles, 106
Forer, Bertram, 493
forgetting curve, 298, 298*f*
    long-term, 299*f*
Four Horsemen of the Apocalypse (Gottman), 431
framing effect, 330–331, 331*f*
Framingham Heart Study, 588
Frankl, Viktor, 605
Frasier (TV series), 654
free association (as strategy in psychoanalysis), 665
Freeman, Dr. Walter, 682, 683
Freud, Anna, 24
Freud, Sigmund, 16, 21, 39, 44, 190, 456, 519, 520, 521, 522, 523, 524, 525, 528, 665
Freudian slip, 520
Friedman, Meyer, 598
frontal lobotomy, 682
    popularity of, 683
functional fixedness, 327
functionalism, 19
functional magnetic resonance imaging (fMRI), 25, 26, 32, 122, 122*f*, 123*t*, 203
    to communicate with a vegetative patient, 208*f*
    critical evaluation of behavioural research, 123
    explanations for behaviour examination by, 122–123
    human behaviour and, 122
    importance of, 123
    to show location of fusiform face area (FFA) of brain, 148, 150
fundamental attribution error (FAE), 555–556
    cross-cultural differences in, 556
fusiform face area (FFA), 148–149
    expertise and, 149–150, 150*f*
    explanations for, 149–150

G

Gage, Phineas, 43, 44, 45
Galen of Pergamon, 12
Gall, Franz, 15
Galton, Sir Francis, 17, 351, 356
gambling addictions, 244
    combination of classical and operant conditioning in, 257
gambling industry, 244
Gardner, Howard, 369
gate-control theory, 169–170
    updates to, 170

Gates, Bill, 65
Gauthier, Isabel, 149
Geller, Scott, 224
gender differences, personality traits and, 513
gender roles, 460
gene expression, 78
    cultural influences on, 78
    environmental influences on, 78
    influence of genetics and environment on, 78
    as lifelong process, 78
gene knockout (KO) studies, 377
general adaptation syndrome (GAS), 593, 594*f*
    stages of, 593, 594*f*
general intelligence factor, 363
    as part of the whole, 364
    as predicator of how well brains work, 364
    related to many life outcomes, 363–364, 364*f*
generalizability in scientific method, 33
    over-generalization, 34
    population-size study, 33
    sample study, 33
generalization, 250
generalized anxiety disorder (GAD), 634–635
    factors in, 634–635
genes,
    as basic units of heredity, 73, 78
    heterozygous, 74
    homozygous, 74
    influence of genetics and environment on expression of, 78
genetic code, 73
    deoxyribonucleic acid (DNA) molecules, 73, 73*f*
    genes as basic units of heredity, 73, 74
    genotypes, 74, 75
    human chromosomes, 73, 73*f*, 74, 74*f*
    nucleotides, 73
genetic inheritance, 74–75, 75*f*
genetics, 17
    influences of on physical traits, 73
Geneva Convention, 534
genital stage (of psychodynamic theory), 523*t*, 524–525
Genovese, Kitty, 541
Geschwind, Dan, 78
Gestalt psychology, 22, 133, 133*f*
    closure principle, 133, 133*f*
    continuity principle, 133, 133*f*
    figure-ground principle, 133
    proximity principle, 133, 133*f*
    similarity principle, 133, 133*f*
gestation, 388
Gigerenzer, Gerd, 330
Gilligan, Carol, 423
Glasgow Coma Scale (GCS), 207
glial cells, 91
Glindemann, Kent, 224

Global Change Game, 497–498
globalization, 562
global warming, 564
glucose, 442, 443
Goodall, Dr. Jane, 149
Gopnik, Dr. Allison, 62
Gottman, Dr. John, 431
Government of Ontario, 459
Graduate Record Exam (GRE), 63, 63*f*
Grahn, Jessica, 162
Graner, Charles, 532
Grant MacEwan University, Edmonton, 235
Gray, Jeffrey, 514
"Great Dress Debate, The" (2015), 150
Greebles, 150, 150*f*
Griffiths, Roland, 211
group dynamics, 535–536
    purposes of group in, 535
    social facilitation in, 536
    social loafing, 535–536
groupthink, 536–537
    changes perceptions of world, 539
    conformity pressures in groups, 537
    definition, 536
    historically poor decisions identified with, 536–537
    problems with, 536–537
    susceptibility of some groups to, 537
guided imagery, 309
gun control (in U.S.), 568
gustatory system,
    function of sensation and perception of taste, 173–174
    gustatory cortex in brain, 174
    papillae receptors on tongue's surface, 174, 174*f*
    taste buds on the tongue, 174, 174*f*
Gyorgi, Albert Szent, 569

H

Haas, Tommy, 139
habituation-dishabituation response, 404
Haidt, Jonathan, 423
Halifax Consciousness Scanner, 208–209
hallucinogenics, 217–218
    dimethyltryptamine (DMT), 218
    ecstasy, 217
    ketamine, 218
    lysergic acid diethylamide (LSD), 218
    psilocybin (magic) mushrooms, 218
    salvia divinorum, 219
    serious negative side-effects of, 218
Han, Ki-Suck, 324, 325
Harlow, Dr. J. M., 44
Harlow, Harry, 407
Harper, Stephen, 469
Harris, Neil Patrick, 377
Harvard University, 372
Harvey, Dr. Thomas, 374
Haselton, Martie, 72, 73
Hawthorne effect, 34, 131

Hawthorne Works, Western Electric Company, 34
health,
    compensatory control and, 610
    discrimination stressor effect on, 587
    family effects on, 587
    group pressures effect on, 587–588
    interpersonal relationships' impact on, 587
    marriage and stress effects on, 587
    psychosocial influences on, 586–588
    social contagion and, 587–588
    social environment and, 587
    socioeconomic factors in, 586
    stressors magnification effect on, 586
Health Canada, 219
health psychology, 580–582
Healy, Dr. David, 676
Hebb, Donald, 21, 232, 283
Hebb Rule, 232, 232f, 234
Hebb's Law, 21
hemispheric specialization of brain, 111–112
    asymmetries, 112t
    left brain for language and mathematics, 111
    right brain for visual and spatial skills, 111
    split brain studies and, 111–112
Hering, Ewald, 144
heritability, 76–77
    affected by amount of genetic variability, 77
    affected by environmental variability, 77
    of anxiety and depression, 77
    intelligence and other factors in, 375–376
    nature and nurture relationships from, 77
heterosexuality, 452
heuristics, 325, 326
    anchoring effect and, 330
    availability, 329–330
    in decision making, 328
    framing effect and, 330–331, 331f
    representativeness, 329
HEXACO model of personality, 496
Hickenlooper, John, 224
hierarchy of needs, 466, 466f
    criticisms of, 466
    self-actualization level in, 466
    self-esteem level in, 466
Hilton, Paris, 462
hindbrain,
    brainstem in, 104
    cerebellum, 105
    life-sustaining processes in, 104
    reticular formation, 104–105
hippocampus, 284f, 285
    damage to, 295f
Hippocrates, 12
Hippocratic Oath, 664
Hirsh, Dr. Jacob, 492

histograms, 63, 63f
    vertical axis shows frequency, 63
History of Pendennis, The (Thackery), 203
histrionic personality disorder (HPD), 625t, 626
    psychological factors in, 629
Hitler, Adolf, 17, 496
HMS Beagle, 79
Holocaust, 23, 496, 534, 544, 548
    Eichmann factor and, 548
homeostasis, 441, 442
    compared to allostasis, 442
    hunger as more than mechanism of, 442–443
homosexuality, 452, 456–457
    genetics and, 456–458, 457f
Honzik, C. H., 261
hormones, 96–97
    endocrine system and, 96
    endorphins, 97
    morphine and, 97
    social behaviour and, 596
    testosterone, 97–98
Horner, Victoria, 260
Horney, Karen, 24, 528
horoscopes, 4
Hubel, David, 146
human behaviour,
    brain and, 21–22
    cultural viewpoints on, 25
    demand characteristics as concern when studying, 35
    sexual theories of, 25
human consciousness, 18
human factors psychologists, 27
human genome, 75, 344
Human Genome Project, 75, 648
human immunodeficiency virus (HIV), 599
    pessimism connections to, 604
humanistic-existential psychotherapy, 666–667, 666t
    compared to psychodynamic approaches, 666–667, 666t
humanistic psychology, 21, 519
    compared to behaviourism, 21
    compared to psychoanalysis, 21
    person-centred perspective, 528
    self-actualization, 528
human knowledge,
    advancement of at end of 19th century, 356
human psyche,
    ego, 520, 520f, 521
    id, 520–521, 520f, 522, 523
    libido, 522
    superego, 520, 520f, 521
humans,
    as social beings, 395
human sensory abilities, 129
humour,
    comprehension-elaboration model of, 327, 328f
    problem solving and, 327
humourism, theory of, 514

hunger,
    as biological drive, 440
    food and reward, 443–444
    hypothalamus and, 442–443, 443f
    physiological aspects of, 442–443
    psychological aspects of, 445
hunter-gatherer theory, 81
    ancestral behaviour effects on modern behaviour, 82–83
    in differing cultures, 82
Huntingdon's disease, 57
    basal ganglia malfunction and movement disorders, 106
Hussein, Saddam, 532, 537
hypnosis, 16
    with cognitive-behavioural therapy (CBT), 201
    compared to sleep, 200
    court testimony based on, 202
    definition, 200
    dissociation theory, 201
    as interaction between unconscious thoughts and a supervisory system, 200–201
    as pain treatment, 201, 202
    to recover lost memories, 202
    social-cognitive theory, 201
    theories, 200–201
    as therapeutic tool, 201
hypnotic suggestions,
    challenge, 200
    cognitive-perceptual, 200
    ideomotor, 200
hypothalamic-pituitary-adrenal (HPA) axis, 594
hypothalamus, 442
    in sexual response cycle, 456
hypotheses, 3, 3f
    falsifiable, 4, 39
hypothesis testing, 66–67, 67f
    variability effects on, 67f

I

icepick lobotomy, 682–683
identifiable victim effect, 568–569
    analytic system and, 569
    evaluation of research into, 569
    experiential system and, 569
    scientific explanations for, 569
identity crises, 425
ideographic approach (to personality), 492
Idioma de Signos Nicaragüese (ISN), 343
Idle No More movement, 551
imagination inflation, 308–309
imitation, 460
    cognitive explanations for, 265
    as form of operant learning, 265
    as a key to learning new skills, 260
    media and behaviour, 265
    mirror neuron system in, 265, 266f
    neuroscientists and functions of, 265
    as primary mechanism in observational learning, 265

immigration, 25
    cultural differences in motivation, 473–474, 474f
    stress from, 591
Implicit Associations Test (IAT), 559–560, 560f
    evaluation of evidence from, 560
    relevance of, 560
implicit processes, 552
    double-edged sword in, 552
    person perception research as illustration of, 552
    stereotyping, prejudice and discrimination as, 559
    thin slices of behaviour and, 553
inattentional blindness, 136–137
    common phenomena explanations, 136–137
incentives, 441, 441f
income taxes, 579
incongruity detection, 327
incremental theory, 359–360
individualistic emphasis of Western culture, 654
individual zone of optimal functioning (IZOF), 592–593
Industrial Revolution, 356
infancy,
    auditory patterns in brains during, 395
    brain development during, 397–399
    caregivers' role in cognitive development, 405, 406
    cognitive development in, 404–405
    moral motivations in, 414
    motor skills development, 396–397, 398f
    sensory and motor development in, 394
    taste and olfactory systems in, 396
    transition to childhood from, 400–402
    visual responses during, 395–396
    visual system development in, 395–396
infantile amnesia, 305
infant reflexes,
    as diagnostic tool, 396
    grasping, 397t
    moro, 397t
    rooting, 397t
inferiority complex, 528
informed consent for research studies, 55, 55f, 56
    equal opportunities element in, 56
    freedom to choose element in, 56
    right to withdraw element in, 56
    right to withhold responses element in, 56
infradian rhythm, 182
ingroups, 556
inpatient treatment, 658–659
insight therapies (for mental illness), 665
    evaluation of, 667–668
insomnia,

defined in terms of rested feelings during day, 193
    extreme lack of sleep characteristic, 193
    maintenance, 193–194
    onset, 193
    rates of, 193
    terminal (early morning), 194
Institutional Review Boards (US), 54
instrumental helping, 414
integrated mind-body training (IMBT), 606–607
    enhancement of attention using, 606–607
intelligence,
    see also multiple intelligences
    accurate measurement of, 351–352
    anthropometrics to test abilities, 351
    behavioural influences on, 382–383
    beliefs about, 359
    birth order and, 379–380
    brain features in, 375–376
    brain size and, 377–378
    classical music and, 30–31
    crystallized, 366–367, 366f
    cultural bias in tests for, 355
    definitions of, 351, 352
    entity theory about nature of, 359–360
    environmental factors in, 379–381
    fluid, 366–367, 366f
    Flynn effect and, 381, 382f
    genetic contributions to, 375–376
    genetic links to traits, 76
    genetic relatedness and, 376, 376f
    heritability of, 375–376
    hierarchical model of, 365–366
    incremental theory about nature of, 359–360
    inherent genetic differences in, 358
    measurements of male and female, 371–372
    as multiple specific abilities, 365
    nootropic substances and effects on, 383
    nutrition and, 380–381
    perception and, 351–352
    problems used to measure, 354f
    as single general ability, 363
    socioeconomic status (SES) and, 380
    Stanford-Binet test, 352
    stress factors on, 381
    triarchic theory of, 368–369
    two-factor theory of, 365
    universal education and, 381
    Wechsler Adult Intelligence Scale (WAIS), 353, 355
intelligence quotient (IQ), 351, 352
    career success application, 370
    compared to mental age, 352–353
    deviation IQ, 353
    racial bias in tests, 356–358
    racial superiority interpretation, 356–358
    during World War I, 356
internal attribution (dispositional attribution), 555, 556f

International Statistical Classification of Disease, 617
Internet, 417
    effects on adolescent development, 417
    dangers, 417
    sexual motivation and, 461
Interpretation of Dreams, The (Freud, 1899), 190
intersexual selection, 83–84
Interview with the Vampire (Rice), 203
intrapersonal attachment, 672
intrasexual selection, 83
introjection, 414
introspection, 18
Inuit peoples,
    words for snow and, 322
involuntary treatment (for mental illness), 656–657
    as contentious issue, 657
    ethics of, 657
    research studies and, 657

J
James, William, 18, 19, 271, 395, 480
James-Lange theory of emotion, 480
    compared to Cannon-Baird theory of emotion, 480, 480f
    facial feedback hypothesis in, 480–481, 481f
Jasper, Herbert, 21
Jaws (movie), 156
Jenner, Bruce (Caitlyn), 458
John Hopkins University, Baltimore, 20
John Hopkins University, Maryland, 211
Johnson, Virginia, 455, 456
Josephson, Wendy, 266
Journal of Cognitive Neuroscience, 38
Judas Priest, 126, 134, 135
Jung, Carl, 524, 527
Jungian psychology, 527–528
    archetypes in, 527–528

K
Kaczynski, Ted ("Unabomber"), 647
kangaroo care, 393
Kawakami, Keri, 562
Kennedy, John, 297
Ki-Moon, Ban, 565
kinesthesis (sense of bodily motion and position), 169, 169f
King, Stephen, 32
King, Suzanne, 651
Kinsey, Alfred, 453
Kinsey Reports, 453
Kleider, Heather, 304
knowledge application stage of scientific literacy model, 6, 6f
    distributed (spaced) learning, 7, 8f
    massed learning, 7, 8f
knowledge gathering stage of scientific literacy model, 6, 6f, 7
    distributed (spaced) learning, 7, 8f
    massed learning, 7, 8f

Kohlberg, Lawrence, 422
Kurdi, Alan, 568
Kwantlen University, 434

L

Lancet, The, 59
Lange, Carl, 480
language,
  acquisition of, 341, 342, 343*t*
  animals and, 346–347
  brain functions for, 337–338, 337*f*
  complexity of genetic relationship
    with, 346
  critical differences between humans
    and animals and, 347
  definition, 338
  development of, 341–343
  development of spoken, 342, 343*t*
  fast mapping, 342
  features that make it unique form of
    communication, 338
  as form of communication, 336–337
  genetics and environment in
    abilities of, 344–345, 345*f*
  imitation and reinforcement
    involved in acquisition of, 342
  learning from infancy, 341–342
  more difficult to acquire for older
    brains, 342–343
  morphemes as basic ingredient of,
    339
  multiple components of, 345–346
  naming explosion, 342
  phonemes as basic ingredient of,
    339
  pragmatics and, 340
  properties of, 338
  semantics as basic ingredient of, 339
  sensitive period for learning, 343
  shared genes with animals, 346–347
  sound perception, 341, 342
  syntax aspect of, 339–340, 340*f*
Latané, Bob, 541, 542
late adulthood,
  achieving happiness in, 433
  emotional stability during, 433–434,
    433*t*
latency stage (of psychodynamic
    theory), 523*t*, 524
latent inhibition, 239
latent learning, 261
  cognitive map controversy and, 261,
    262
  learning happening without
    behavioural evidence of it, 261
  operant learning and, 262
lateral geniculate nucleus (LGN), 146
law of effect, 246, 246*f*
Lazarus, Richard, 591
learned helplessness, 609
  procedure, 609, 609*f*
learning, 228–230
  acquisition as initial phase in
    learning, 233, 233*f*
  associative, 228–229
  cognitive, 229

fear, 236–237
  latent, 261–264
  observational, 262–264
  process of, 229
  stimulus-organism-response
    (S-O-R) theory of, 262
  without reinforcement, 261, 261*f*
learning by rote, 289
learning styles, 369
Led Zeppelin, 134
Lenuaje de Signos Nicaragüese (LSN),
  343
Lesbian, Gay, Bisexual, and
    Transgender (LGFBT), 458, 558
lesioning, 117
Let Them Eat Prozac (Healy), 676
leucotomy, 682
LeVay, Simon, 456
levels of processing (LOP) framework,
  290
  effects on long term not working
    memory, 291*f*
  deep processing, 290
  shallow processing, 290
Levy, Steven, 374
Lewin, Kurt, 24, 534
lexical decision task, 318, 318*f*
lexigrams, 347
Liberal Party, 240, 241
libido, 452
lie detection, 484
light, 140
  amplitude property, 140, 141
  colour perception by retina, 144
  effects on rods and cones in eye, 143
  purity property, 141, 141*f*
  as radiation in narrow band of
    electromagnetic spectrum, 140,
    140*f*
  wavelength property, 140–141, 140*f*
limbic system, 107, 107*f*
  amygdala, 107
  hippocampus, 107
linguistic relativity, 322
L'Institut Universitaire de Gériatrie de
  Montréal, 672
lithium,
  as mood stabilizer, 680
Little Albert study, 235
localization of brain function, 15–16
locked-in syndrome, 209
Loftus, Elizabeth, 306, 307
longitudinal studies (for measuring
  developmental trends), 76, 387,
  387*f*
  Seven-up series study, 387
  strengths and weaknesses of, 387
long-term memory (LTM), 272,
  275–276
  behavioural differences between
    short-term memory (STM) and,
    277
  declarative (explicit) memories, 282,
    282*f*
  levels of processing (LOP) effects
    on, 291*f*

  limitations of rote rehearsal on, 289,
    289*f*
  nondeclarative (implicit) memories,
    282, 282*f*, 283
  organization of information by
    semantic categorization, 275–276
  organization of information word
    sound and looks, 276
long-term potentiation (LTP), 283, 284
love,
  companionate, 467
  compared to hunger and sex drives,
    468
  motivations for, 467–468
  passionate, 467
  romantic, 467
  as sense of belonging, 467
Lovett, Maureen, 339
LTM. *See* long-term memory (LTM)
lysergic acid diethylamide (LSD), 218

M

MacDonald, John, 177
Machiavellianism, 496–497, 526
"Magical Number Seven, Plus or
    Minus Two, The: Some Limits
    on Our Capacity for Processing
    Information" (Miller, 1956),
    275
magnetic resonance imaging (MRI),
  119–120, 119*f*
magnetoencephalography (MEG), 121,
  123*t*
major depression, 639
  definition of, 639
  genetic and environmental
    interactions in, 640–641, 641*f*
  pessimistic explanatory style in,
    639–640, 640*f*
  twin studies show underlying
    genetic risk of, 640
maladaptive behaviours, 617
Malleus Maleficarum (Hammer of the
    Witches), 615
malnutrition,
  fetal, 390–391
mania, 639
Many Labs Project (MLP), 38
Marcus Welby, M.D. (tv show), 572
marijuana, 218–219
  cognitive effects of, 220, 221
  effects on memory and cognition,
    219–220
  evaluation of neuroimaging results
    of users, 220
  hallucinogenic, stimulating and
    narcotic effects, 218
  legalization of, 225
  as most commonly used
    recreational drug, 221
  neuroimaging results of users, 220
  teenage users and brain effects,
    220–221
Martensville, Saskatchewan sex abuse
    scandal (1992), 302
Martin, Rod, 42

Maslow, Abraham, 21, 466, 466*f*, 492, 518, 519, 528
Massachusetts Institute of Technology (MIT), 644
Masters, William, 455, 456
mastery motive, 472
materialism, 13
Max Planck Institute, Berlin, 330
Mayberg, Helen, 37
Mayo Clinic, 604
McCain, John, 239
McCarthy, Jenny, 60
McGill University, 121, 284, 512, 651
McGurk, Harry, 177
McGurk effect, 177
McKibben, Bill, 564, 572
McMaster University, 128, 149, 241, 320, 378, 396
medical model, 16
    of mental illness, 616
meditation, 605–607
    brain activity measurements during, 606
    focused attention (FA), 606
    integrated mind-body training IMBT), 606–607
    open monitoring (OE), 606
Meehl, Paul, 68
Melodic Intonation Therapy (MIT), 113
Memorial University, Newfoundland, 27
memory,
    Atkinson-Shiffrin model, 272, 272*f*
    brain and storage of, 285–286
    at cellular level, 283–284
    chunking, 275, 280
    cognitive neuroscience of, 283–286
    as collection of several systems that store information, 272
    consolidation of, 284
    construction of, 303
    context-dependent, 291–292
    delicacy of systems of, 286
    disruption of consolidation of, 284–285, 285*f*
    echoic, 273
    effects of marijuana on long-term, 219–220
    emotion and, 295–296, 296*f*
    encoding of, 289, 290
    episodic, 271
    false, 306
    flashcards to improve, 300
    forgetting and remembering, 298
    imperfection of, 272, 302
    importance of hippocampus for process, 284*f*
    improving, 288
    information storage, 289
    long-term memory (LTM), 272, 275–276
    mnemonics to help improve skills, 298–299
    multiple memory stores, 278
    organization of, 303

procedural, 283
    retrieval, 289, 290–291
    role of environmental contexts on, 291–292, 292*f*
    sensory, 272, 273–274
    short-term memory (STM), 272, 274–275
    unit of information, 275
    working, 279–281
memory organization, 303
    schemas in, 303
memory reconstruction, 306
memory research, 7, 21, 22
memory storage, 286
    brain and, 286
Men Are from Mars, Women Are from Venus (Gray, 1992), 513
mental age, 352
    compared to intelligence quotient (IQ), 352–353
mental disorder defence (*a.k.a.* insanity defence), 622
    M'Naughten rule in, 622
mental disorders, 510–511
    see also mental illness; psychological disorders
    ambiguity of compared to mentally healthy, 655
    availability as barrier to therapy for, 656
    expense as barrier to therapy for, 656
    forced entry into mental health system for, 656–657
    identification of, 617
    labelling effects on perceptions of others, 620
    labelling of, 619
    seen as sign of weakness or personal failure, 655
    stigma attached to, 619, 620
mental health providers, 657–659
    university, 659
mental illness, 615
    see also mental disorders; psychological disorders
    cultural views of, 651
    explanations for moved from demon possession to physical illnesses, 615–616
    involuntary treatments for, 656–657
    medications for, 616
    moral treatment of, 616
    multiple systems underlying, 616–617, 616*t*
    outpatient commitment as contentious issue in, 657
    as sign of weakness, 654
    social costs of, 656
    stigma associated with, 654, 655–656
    workplace stigma for sufferers of, 656
mental-rotation task, 81, 82, 82*f*
Mesmer, Franz, 16
Meston, Cindy, 453
method of loci, 299, 299*f*

3,4-methylenedioxy-N-methylamphetamine (MDMA), 217
1-methyl-4-phenyl-1,2,3,6-tetrahydropyridine (MPTP), 57, 58
midbrain, 104, 105–106, 105*f*
    as relay station between sensory and motor areas, 105–106
    substantia nigra, 106
Milgram, Stanley, 546, 547, 548
Milgram obedience experiments, 546–548
    variations on, 548
Miller, George, 275
Miller, Zell, 30, 38
Milner, Brenda, 284
mimicry, 534–535
    implicit and ingrained, 535
    social benefits of, 535
    social norms and, 534, 535
mindfulness-based cognitive therapy (MBCT),
    decentring experience in, 673
    for social and generalized anxiety disorders, 673
mindfulness-based cognitive therapy (MCBT), 672
    emotional security in, 672
mindfulness-based stress reduction (MBSR), 606
    brain activity during, 606
    goals of, 606
mind over matter, 42
mind-wandering, 203
    about the future, 204, 204*f*
    effects on attention and memory, 203
    benefits of, 204
    brain activity and, 203–204
    connected to default mode network, 203–204
    description of, 203
    frequency of, 203
    studying effects of, 203
minimal group paradigm, 556–557
minimally conscious state (MCS), 209
Minnesota Study of Twins Reared Apart, 509
Mishkin, Mortimer, 151
misinformation effect, 307
    children and, 307
M'Naughten, Daniel, 622
mnemonics, 298–299
    acronyms in, 299
    as aid for rote memorization, 300
    dual coding premise for, 299–300
    first-letter technique, 299, 299*f*
    method of loci technique in, 299
Molaison, Henry (neurological patient H.M.), 284–285
Moniz, Antonio, 682
monoamine oxidase inhibitors (MAOIs), 677
    side effects, 678
monozygotic (identical) twins, 76
    personality and genetics research, 509

Monroe, Marilyn, 450
Monster (movie), 624
Montessori system, 406
Montreal Neurological Institute, 21, 101, 444
mood-dependent memory, 294–295
    limitations of, 294–295
mood disorders, 634, 639–641
    bipolar disorder, 639
    major depression, 639
    sociocultural and environmental influences on, 641
    suicide as outcome from, 641–642
mood stabilizers, 680
    lithium, 680
moral development, stage model of, 422–423, 423t
    sexes in, 423
moral dilemmas, 423
moral reasoning, stage model of,
    conventional level of, 423, 423t
    critiques of, 423
    postconventional level of, 423, 423t
    preconventional level of, 423, 423t
moral treatment (of mental illness), 616
morphine, 214, 214f
Morris Water Maze, 117–118, 117f
mortality salience, 469
    in political elections, 469–470
Motion Picture Association of America, 267
motivation,
    achievement, 465–467, 470–472
    affiliation, 467
    cultural differences in, 473–474
    as essential to survival, 441
    extrinsic, 472
    hierarchy of needs and, 466–467
    intrinsic, 472
    for love, 467–468
    physical factors in, 442
    psychological factors in, 442
    self-efficacy and, 471
    sexual, 452
    social, 465–468
motor development,
    in infancy, 396–397
    reflexes as set of infant innate responses, 396, 397t
    stages, 396–397, 398f
movement disturbances, 194–195
    see also sleep disorders
    restless legs syndrome, 194
    sexomnia (sleep sex), 195
    somnambulism (sleepwalking), 194–195
Mozart effect, 30, 32, 34
    replication of, 38
MPPP (synthetic drug), 57
Muir, Leilani, 350, 351
Müller, Johannes, 127
multimodal experiences, 168
    autonomous sensory meridian response (ASMR) and, 177
multimodal integration, 176–177

form of problem-solving by the brain, 176–177
    McGurk effect, 177
    synesthesia (blended perceptions) and, 177
multiple intelligences, 365, 369–370, 369t
    controversies and, 370–371
    differences in male and female cognitive skills, 372
multiple personality disorder, 630
multiple sclerosis,
    myelin breaks down in, 91
music perception, 162
    brain imaging studies to show brain areas for, 162
    links between beats/rhythms and movement systems in brain, 163
myelin, 91

N

naive realism, 555
narcissism, 496, 497
narcissistic personality disorder (NPD), 625t, 626
    psychological factors in, 629
Narcissus, 497, 626
narcolepsy, 196, 383
    causes, 196
    medications for, 196
    ways it differs from typical sleep, 196
narcotics. See opiates (narcotics)
Nash, John, 644, 646
National Association of Attorneys General (U.S.), 581
national character, 505
National Football League (NFL), 370
National Hockey League (NHL), 119, 256
National Institute of Mental Health (NIMH), 656
naturalistic observations, 45–46
    occurrence of anywhere behaviours are, 46
    operational definitions in, 46
    specific variables in, 46
    strengths and limitations of, 50–51, 50t
    unobtrusive, 45
natural selection, 13, 79, 356
    evolution through, 80, 80f
nature and nurture relationships, 17
    heritability and, 77
Necker cube, 126, 127f
negative affectivity, 604
negative political attack advertising, 239
    effects of, 240–241
    classical conditioning in, 239
    produce negative of one to produce positive of the other, 240
    use of evaluative conditioning in, 239–241
negative punishment, 248
negative reinforcement, 247

avoidance learning category of, 247
    escape learning category of, 247–248
Neisser, Ulric, 23, 302
nervous system,
    central nervous system (CNS) division, 102, 102f
    organization of, 102–103, 102f
    peripheral nervous system (PNS) division, 102, 102f
neurodevelopmental hypothesis, 649–650
    evaluation of research, 650
    research on, 650
neurogenesis, 90
neuroimaging (brain imaging), 116, 119
    computerized tomography (CT scan), 119, 119f
    diffusion tensor imaging (DTI), 119f, 120
    electroencephalogram (EEG), 120–121, 121f
    functional, 120–121, 123t
    functional magnetic resonance imaging (fMRI), 122, 122f
    magnetic resonance imaging (MRI), 119–120, 120f
    magnetoencephalography (MEG), 121
    positron emission tomography (PET), 121
    structural, 119
    structural compared to functional, 120
neurons, 89, 89f
    action potential in, 92
    all-or-none potential of, 92
    axon component of, 89f, 90
    axon hillock component of, 89f, 90
    cell body (soma) component of, 89, 89f
    dendrites component of, 89, 89f
    electrical system of, 91–92, 91f
    glial cells as insulators of axons of, 91
    myelin from glial cells in, 91
    neurotransmitters component of, 89f, 90
    postsynaptic, 93
    presynaptic, 92, 93
    refractory period, 91
    resting potential in, 91–92
    stimulating, 92
    structure and function varies in brain, 90
    synapses between nerve cells, 92
    synaptic cleft, 93
neuroplasticity of the brain, 112–113
    critical evaluation of, 114
neuroticism, 515
neurotransmitters,
    acetylcholine as most widespread, 94t, 95
    agonist drug effects on, 95
    antagonist drug effects on, 96
    as component of neurons, 90

neurotransmitters, (*Cont.*)
dopamine as monoamine, 94*t*, 95
functions of major, 94, 94*t*
gamma-amino butyric acid (GABA)
as primary inhibitory, 94–95, 94*f*
glutamate as most common
excitatory, 94, 94*t*
monoamine class of, 95
norepinephrine as monoamine, 94*t*,
95
serotonin as monoamine, 94*t*, 95
work with receptors, 93, 93*f*
Newborn Individualized
Developmental Care and
Assessment Program (NIDCAP),
393
Newsweek, 462
New York Post, The, 324
New York Times, The, 541
nicotine, 225
nociception, 169
cognitive, sensory and emotional
factors in, 170, 171*f*
nomothetic approach to personality
measurement, 492
non-declarative (implicit) memories,
282, 282*f*, 283
procedural memory, 283
nootropic substances, 383
ethics of uses of, 383
long-term effects of, 383
normal behaviour, 617
cultural diversity and, 617
Norman, Geoffrey, 320
Nun study, 604
nutrition,
intelligence and, 380–381

O

Obama, Barack, 239, 572
obedience to authority, 546–549
Milgram obedience experiments,
546–548
power of dissent, 548
obesity,
body mass index (BMI) as
measurement of, 583
children's rates of, 585
cognitive-behavioural therapy
(CBT) for, 674
ethnicity factors in, 585
factors in, 583
genes and set point, 584
genetics and, 584
growing concerns regarding, 583
impact on brain of, 585
metabolism and, 584
negative health consequences of,
583
rates of, 582–583
sedentary lifestyle factor in, 584–585
social factors in, 585
sociocultural influences and, 585
socioeconomic factors in, 585
sugar tax and, 579
television viewing and rates of, 584

objective measurements,
as foundation of scientific methodology, 31
objectivity, 31
object relations therapy, 666
observational learning, 262–264
ability to reproduce process in, 263,
264–265
attention in classical conditioning
and, 263
attention in operant conditioning
and, 263
attention process in, 263
customs exist because of, 263
imitation as primary mechanism
in, 265
memory process in, 263, 264
motivation process in, 263, 265
processes involved in, 263–264, 263*f*
punishment in, 265
observation in scientific research, 34
obsessive-compulsive disorder (OCD),
619, 637–638
bacterial streptococcal infections
and, 633
prevalence of symptoms of, 637,
637*t*
Oedipus complex, 519, 524, 525, 528
Oedipus Rex (Sophocles), 524
olfactory system,
function of smell, 175–176, 175*f*
olfactory bulb, 175
olfactory epithelium in nasal cavity,
175–176, 175*f*
One Flew Over the Cuckoo's Nest
(movie), 654, 683
Open Science Collaboration (OSC), 38
operant chambers (Skinner boxes),
246–247, 246*f*, 248
operant conditioning, 245
applied behaviour analysis as
application of., 248
biological explanations for, 249–251
compared to classical conditioning,
245, 245*t*, 251*t*
contingency concept in, 245
discrimination and generalization
in, 250
dopamine and, 250
fixed schedule, 253
interval schedule in, 253
punishers in, 247
ratio schedule in, 253
reinforcement and punishment
principles of, 245–246, 245*f*
reinforcers in, 246
role of in superstition, 256
slot machines and, 254–255
as stimulus-response relationships,
245
variable schedule, 253
operational definitions, 32
opiates (narcotics), 221–222
fentanyl, 221
heroin, 221
methadone, 222

morphine, 221
treating addiction to, 221–222
opponent-process theory, 144–145,
145*f*
optimism, 603
connected to better health than pessimism, 604
orienting responses, 128
orthography, 339
outgroups, 556
over-justification effect, 473
Owen, Adrian, 207
oxycodone (OxyContin), 212, 223
abuse of, 222, 223
as pain reliever, 223
OxyContin. *See* oxycodone
(OxyContin)
oxytocin, 595–596

P

Pacioretty, Max, 116, 119, 122
pain perception, 169–170, 170*f*
empathy influences on, 171–172
gate-control theory, 169–170
influenced by the experiences of
others, 172
phantom limb sensations, 172, 172*f*
related to emotions, 170
Palmer, John, 306, 307
Panel of Research Ethics, Government
of Canada, 54
panic disorder,
panic attacks as key feature of, 635
parasympathetic nervous system,
maintains homeostatic balance, 103
parenting,
adolescents, 425
adopting and, 509
in adulthood, 432–433
attachment and, 414
children's personality development
and, 509
inductive discipline approach, 415
operant rewards and, 414
use of conditional approaches, 414
Parkinson's disease, 57, 58
basal ganglia malfunction and
movement disorders, 106
damage to basal ganglia in
sufferers, 163
family gene in, 75
gene expression to treat, 78
neurogenesis and, 90
partial (intermittent) reinforcement,
253
patriarchy, 460–461
pattern recognition, 134
Pavlov, Ivan, 19, 20, 229, 230, 231, 233,
234, 245, 262
Pavlovian conditioning, 229, 230*f*, 231
Pearl Harbor attack (1941), 302
peer groups, 425–426
peer pressure,
eating disorders and, 449
Penfield, Dr. Wilder, 21, 101
Pennebaker, James, 602, 609

perception,
blended, 167
bottom-up processing, 135
brain and processes of, 538–539
compared to sensation, 126
deals with sensed stimuli, 127, 127t
depth, 152, 154
divided attention, 136
experience influence on adaptation
to sensory stimuli, 128
face, 148
Gestalt principles of, 133, 133f
inattentional blindness, 136–137
of music, 162
of musical beats/rhythms, 162–163
selective attention, 136
sound, 157–160
stimulus thresholds, 129
from stimulus to, 12–128, 128f
subliminal, 131–132
top-down processing, 135
perceptual constancy, 150
influence of previous experience on,
150–151, 151f
perceptual illusions, 133, 133f
perceptual set, 135–136
peripheral nervous system (PNS),
autonomic system division of,
102–104, 103f
somatic system division of, 102–103,
103f
peripheral route to persuasion, 566, 566f
belief in communicators we like,
572
consistency in, 573
effective use of, 572–573
reciprocity in, 572–573
social validation in, 572
use of experts in, 572
personality,
analytical psychology and, 527–528
animal behaviour as evolutionary
roots of, 511
behaviourist perspective of,
501–502, 502f
biological perspectives, 514–516
brain anatomy and measurements
of, 515, 515f
brain and extroversion and
extraversion traits, 514–515
brain-imaging technology and, 515
brain systems and, 514
cross-cultural work on, 506–507
culture and, 506–509
details of dwellings to measure,
491–492
development of from interaction
between person and
environment, 502
differences in human psyche and,
521
estimation of overall heritability of
traits, 509–510
evolutionary roots of, 511
Freudian structure of, 520–521, 520f
multicultural understanding of, 506

possibility of changing traits over
lifespan, 500
projection and relationship to, 526
psychodynamic perspective of,
519–520
reciprocal determinism and, 502,
502f
research studies into genes and, 510
self-definition differences and, 507
social and cultural factors in, 528
social cognitive approach to, 502,
502f
specific genes in, 510
stability in over the lifespan,
499–500, 500f
stress and, 598
temperaments as innate biological
foundation for, 499
twin studies to examine influence of
genetic factors on, 509
personality disorders (PDs), 619
antisocial personality disorder
(APD), 625t, 626–627
biological factors in, 629
biopsychosocial approach to,
629–631
borderline personality disorder
(BPD), 625–626, 625t
children with conduct disorders, 629
classification of, 625
cluster A, 625, 625t
cluster B, 625, 625t
cluster C, 625, 625t
definition of, 625
histrionic personality disorder
(HPD), 625t, 626
narcissistic personality disorder
(NPD), 625t, 626
psychological factors in, 629
sociocultural factors in, 629
personality measurement, 491–493
idiographic approach, 492
nomothetic approach to, 492
trait perspectives, 492–493
personality psychology, 24, 491–500
ego component, 39
female psychology and, 24–25
id component, 39
superego component, 39
personality trait, 492–493
person-centred therapy. See client-
centred therapy (person-centred
therapy)
person perception, 552–553
schemas in, 552
persuasion,
central route to, 565, 566f
elaboration-likelihood model (ELM)
of persuasive communication,
565
making the most of tools of, 569
peripheral route to, 566, 566f
through communication, 565
Perunovic, Elaine, 473
pessimism, 603
pessimistic explanatory style, 603–604

phallic stage (of psychodynamic
theory), 523–524, 523t
phantom limb sensations, 172, 172f
mirror box treatment for, 172, 172f,
173f
pharmacotherapy, 677
combination of drugs in, 681
drug safety and, 680–681
evaluation of, 681
Phelps, Elizabeth, 560
phenomenological approach (to
psychotherapy), 667
phobias,
also from no personal scary
experience, 635
factors in development of, 636
as a result of a frightening
experience, 635
social, 635
specific, 635, 635t
Phonological and Strategy Training
(PHAST) program, 339
phonological loop, 280
phonology, 339
phrenology, 15, 15f, 514
physical exercise, 608
psychological benefits of, 608
short-term effects and lifelong
benefits of, 608
Physicians for a Smoke-Free Canada,
581
Piaget, Jean, 401, 402, 403, 404, 405,
406, 422
Pinel, Philippe, 616
Pink Floyd, 134
placebo effect, 37, 131
plasticity (brain), 390
Playboy, 462
playing the race card, 558
pluralistic ignorance, 542–543
Polgár, Lázló, 275
political correctness, 558
polygraph, 484
polysomnography, 184
pornography, 461
positive psychology, 26, 603
positive punishment, 248
positive reinforcement, 247
positron emission tomography (PET),
121, 123t
of brain activity in consciousness
levels, 209f
of brain death, 206f
radioactivity of, 121
shows metabolic brain activity, 121
post-traumatic growth, 605
post-traumatic stress, 605
post-traumatic stress disorder (PTSD),
621
cultural differences in treatments
for, 621
differences in cognitive and
emotional symptoms in different
groups of sufferers, 621
virtual reality exposure (VRE) for,
670

poverty, 586
  as risk factor for depression, 641
Powell, James, 40
power analysis, 69
"Power of Vulnerability, The" (TED
  lecture), 654
pragmatics, 340
pregnancy,
  alcohol consumption during,
    391–392
  cigarette smoking during, 392
prejudice,
  contact hypothesis for combating,
    562
  effects of on health, 587
  implicit measures of, 559
  implicit *vs.* explicit processes, 559
  overcoming implicit, 652
  political correctness and, 558
  roots of, 557
  social-cognitive definition of, 558
prenatal stage of development,
    388–389, 388*t*
  embryonic stage, 388, 389*t*
  fetal stage, 388, 389*t*
  germinal stage, 388, 389*t*
preterm infants, 393
  developmental interventions to
    help, 393
primary mental abilities, 365
primary reinforcers, 249
priming (activation of individual
    concepts in LTM), 318
  in advertising, 319
  as factor in junk food eating, 446
  testing for through reaction time
    measurements, 318
  variations in strengths of, 318–319
priming (previous exposure to a
    stimulus), 131–132
principle of parsimony, 9
  alien abductions and, 9
Principles of Psychology, The (James,
    1890), 18
probability, 62
  problem solving and, 328–329
problem solving strategies, 325–326
  cognitive obstacles to, 326, 326*f*
  functional fixedness in, 327
  humour and, 327
  intuitive approach, 325
  logical approach, 325
problem solving techniques, 325–326
procedural memory, 283
processing fluency, 571
Progressive Conservative Party, 240,
    241
projective tests, 525
  criticisms of, 526
  perception of others as, 526
  problems with, 527
  Rorschach inkblot test, 525, 525*f*,
    526, 527
  Thematic Apperception Tests (TAT),
    525, 525*f*
Project MKUltra, 53

prosopagnosia (face blindness), 148,
    149
prototypes, 315–316
pseudoscience, 4
psilocybin (magic) mushrooms, 211,
    218
  therapeutic benefits of, 211
psychedelic drugs, 211
psychiatric hospitals, 616
psychiatrists,
  compared to psychologists, 657–658
psychics, 4
psychoactive drugs,
  hallucinogenics, 217–218
  stimulants, 215–217
psychoanalysis, 16, 21, 519
  compared to humanistic
    psychology, 21
  core ideas in, 665–666, 665*t*
  dream analysis strategy in, 665
  exploration of unconscious in, 665
  free association strategy in, 665
  to make unconscious conscious in,
    665
  repression in, 310
  resistance strategy in, 665–666
  transference strategy in, 666
psychodynamic theory, 519–520
  anal stage of, 523, 523*t*
  analytical psychology as alternative
    to, 527
  assumptions, 519–520
  criticisms of personality
    development and, 525
  defence mechanisms in, 521–522,
    522*t*
  genital stage of, 523*t*, 524–525
  latency stage of, 523*t*, 524
  phallic stage of, 523–524, 523*t*
  psyche in, 520–521
  psychosexual stage of, 522–523, 523*t*
  social psychology as challenge to,
    534
  unconscious processes, 520, 520*f*
psychodynamic therapies, 665
  contrast of psychoanalytic and
    humanistic views, 666, 666*t*
  object relations therapy as variation
    of, 666
Psychological Care of Infant and Child
    (Watson, 1928), 235
psychological disorders,
  see also mental disorders; mental
    illness
  diagnosis of, 617–618
  diathesis-stress model of, 640–641
  lack of perfect test for identification
    of, 622
  normalization of, 655
  technological and surgical methods
    for, 682–683
psychological perspective of human
    behaviour, 5, 5*f*
psychological treatment,
  barriers to receiving, 655
psychologists,

clinical, 658
  compared to psychiatrists, 657–658
  counselling, 658
psychology,
  biopsychosocial model of, 5–6, 5*f*
  definition, 3
  determinism origin of, 12
  empiricism origin of, 12
  establishment of as independent
    field, 18
  goals of, 3
  major events in history of, 13, 14*f*
  science of, 3
  as study of individual as product of
    multiple influences, 5–6, 5*f*
  of women, 24–25
psychoneuroimmunology, 598
psychopathy, 27, 236, 496, 497
psychophysics, 13, 15*f*, 129
psychosexual stage (of
    psychodynamic theory), 522–523
  fixation in, 523
psychosocial development, 425
  adolescence and identity *vs.* role
    confusion, 425, 428, 430*t*
  adulthood and generativity *vs.*
    stagnation, 430*t*, 431
  aging and ego integrity *vs.* despair,
    430*t*
  development across the lifespan
    and, 412–413
  parenting and prosocial behaviour,
    413–414
  stages of, 430*t*
  young adulthood and intimacy *vs.*
    isolation, 430*t*, 431
psychosomatic medicine, 16
psychotropic drugs, 677
  mechanisms of action, 677, 677*f*
  pathways to brain, 677*f*
puberty, 418
punishment (in operant conditioning),
    245–246, 245*f*
  applications, 256–257
  compared to reinforcement,
    245–246, 245*f*
  corporal, 257
  effective when combined with
    reinforcement, 257
  positive and negative, 247–248, 247*t*

Q

qualitative research, 43
quantitative research, 43
quasi-experimental research, 50–51
Queen, 134
Queen's University, 27, 123, 395, 420,
    486

R

R. v. Sharpe, 2001, 461
R. v. Trochym, 2007, 202
racism, 558–559
radical behaviourism, 20–21
Raichle, Marcus, 203
randomness, 610

Raonic, Milos, 139
Raven, John, 355, 357, 368
Raven's Progressive Matrices, 355, 355f
Rayner, Rosalie, 235
Read, Don, 134, 135
reading,
  phonemes, morphemes and semantics in, 339
Real Men, Real Depression campaign, 656
reciprocal determinism,
  personality and, 502, 502f
recognition memory, 292
recovered memory, 310
recovered memory controversy, 310
Redbook, 462
rehearsal for remembering, 279
reinforcement (in operant conditioning), 245–246, 245f
  compared to punishment, 245–246, 245f
  compared to superstition, 255–256
  continuous, 253
  delayed, 251
  learning without, 261, 261f
  partial (intermittent), 253
  positive and negative, 247–248, 247t
  schedules of, 252–253, 253f
  study of systematic relationship between behaviour and, 246
reinforcers (in operant condition), 246
  primary, 249
  secondary, 249
reliability in scientific measurement, 32–33
  alternate-forms, 32, 33f
  inter-rater, 33
  test-retest, 32, 33f
REM behaviour disorder, 181
  as potentially dangerous condition, 1985
Rembrandt van Rijn, 153
Remote Associates Task, 473
repetitive transcranial magnetic stimulation (rTMS), 683–684
  advantages of, 683
replication of a scientific study, 38
  publication bias in, 38
2011 Report of the Federal/Provincial/Territorial Heads of Prosecutions Subcommittee on the Prevention of Wrongful Convictions, 308
reproduction suppression hypothesis, 449
research designs, 42–44
  benefits and limitations of models, 50–51, 50t
  between-subjects experimental, 50
  case studies, 43–45
  data characteristic in, 43
  descriptive data in, 43
  influences of on investigators, 42–43
  naturalistic observations, 45–46

operational definitions
  characteristics in, 43
  self-reporting, 46
  surveys and questionnaires, 46
  variables characteristic in, 43
  within-subjects experimental, 50
research ethics board (REB), 54, 58
  to monitor animal research, 59
  as third party, 55
residential treatment centres, 659
  low-level, 659
  medium- to high-level, 659
resilience, 604–605
resistance (as strategy in psychoanalysis), 665–666
retrieval of memory, 290–291
  recall memory, 290
  recognition memory, 290
retrograde amnesia, 286, 286f
reverse anorexia, 449
reward devaluation, 251–252
ribosomal DNA, 78
Rice, Anne, 203
Right-Wing Authoritarianism (RWA) personality, 497–498
  emphasis on self-importance, 497
  group level characteristics, 497–498
  tendencies of, 497
Rogers, Carl, 21, 528, 667
Rorschach inkblot test, 525, 525f
Rosenham, David, 620
Rosenman, Ray, 598
Rotman Research Institute, Toronto, 37, 684
Rotman School of Management, 492
Rule, Nicholas, 553
Rumsfeld, Donald, 532
Rutherford, Beth, 310
Ryerson University, 575

S
salvia divinorum, 219
  dissociative experiences from taking, 219
sampling techniques, 33
  convenience, 33
  random, 33
Sandy Hook Elementary School shootings (2012), 568
sanity,
  measurement of, 622
Sarmiento, Nerlin, 622
satiation, 444
savant, 362, 364
scaffolding, 405
  different ways of exercising, 405–406
Scared Straight program, 664
Schachter, Stanley, 481
schedules of reinforcement, 252–253
  fixed-interval, 252f, 254
  fixed-ratio, 252f, 253
  partial reinforcement effect, 255
  types of, 253f, 254
  variable-interval, 252f, 254
  variable-ratio, 252f, 253

schemas, 303–304, 552
  see also self-schemas
  biasing effect in, 306
  brain-imaging studies and, 304
  children and adult dependence upon, 307
  choice of for guiding judgments, 554
  critical evaluation of concept of, 304
  memory and, 303–304, 304f
  ourselves as, 554
Schiavo, Terri, 205
Schimel, Jeff, 469
schizophrenia, 57, 391, 644
  active phase of, 645
  brain chemistry changes in, 649
  catatonic subtype, 647
  cognitive functioning difficulties with, 646
  combined drug therapy for, 681
  culture and, 651
  delusions as symptom of, 645
  different brain functions in, 649, 649f
  disorganized behaviour symptom of, 646
  disorganized subtype, 647
  environmental and social influences on, 650–651
  genetic explanations for, 648, 648f
  hallucinations as symptom of, 645
  negative symptoms of, 645
  nervous system explanations for, 648–649
  neurodevelopmental hypothesis and, 649–650
  no single gene responsible for, 76
  paranoid subtype, 646
  positive symptoms of, 645
  prodromal phase of, 645
  research into prevention of, 650
  residual phase of, 645
  residual subtype, 647
  social interaction difficulties and, 646
  stigma attached to, 647
  stress and social support impacts on, 561
  undifferentiated subtype, 647
  variety in terms of progression of, 645
  widely understood term, 647
Schwartz, Barry, 333
Schwarz, Norman, 570, 571
Science, 38
scientific explanation stage of scientific literacy model, 6, 6f
  laboratory-based studies compared to real world, 7
scientific literacy model, 6, 6f
  critical thinking stage, 6, 6f
  demand characteristics, 35–36
  knowledge application stage, 6, 6f
  knowledge gathering stage, 6, 6f
  scientific explanation stage, 6, 6f
  working the, 7

scientific method, 3–4, 3f
  communication of findings from objective experiments, 37–38
  definition, 3
  as dynamic interaction, 3, 3f
  falsifiable precision of hypothesis in, 4
  hypothesis testing in, 3, 3f
  objective measurements in, 31
  reliability in scientific measurements, 32–33
  theory construction, 3, 3f
  validity in scientific measurements, 32–33
scientific misconduct, 59–60
scientific research,
  all participants must provide informed consent, 55, 55f, 56
  anecdotal evidence as characteristic of poor, 39
  animal welfare in, 56
  appeals to authority as characteristic of poor, 39, 40
  appeals to common sense as characteristic of poor, 39, 40
  biased data as characteristic of poor, 39, 40, 40f
  bias reduction techniques as criteria for quality, 31, 34–37
  ethics of, 54
  ethics of data collection, 59
  ethics of data reporting, 59
  ethics of data storage, 59
  generalized criteria for quality, 31, 33–34
  mortality salience risk in, 54
  objective, valid and reliable measurements as criteria for quality, 31
  objectivity aspect of, 31
  operational definitions in, 32
  participant debriefing following, 56
  personal and/or sensitive information risk in, 54
  public criteria for quality, 31, 37–38
  replication criteria for quality, 31, 38–39
  researchers must only use volunteers, 55
  right to anonymity in, 56
  right to confidentiality in, 56
  stressful situations may have potential benefits for others, 55
  subjective vs objective in quality of, 32
  untestable hypotheses as characteristic of poor, 39
  use of deception in, 55–56
  variables that can be measured and described in, 31–32, 32f
  weak vs poor evidence in, 39
  weighing up risks in, 54
  writing about traumatic events as risk in, 54
Scoville, Dr. William, 284
secondary reinforcers, 249

release dopamine in rewards areas of bran, 250
sedatives, 222
  barbiturates, 222
  benzodiazepines, 222
  increase effects of gamma-aminobutyric acid (GABA), 222
seeing is believing, 12
selective attention, 136
selective serotonin reuptake inhibitors (SSRIs), 94, 678
  for depression, 676
  side effects of, 676
  suicidal thoughts and, 676
self, sense of, 305
  cross-cultural perspective of, 305
  projection of onto others, 554–555
  in social world, 554–555
self-actualization, 528
self-awareness, 409–410
  becomes more sophisticated with development, 409
  in development from birth, 410
self-concepts, 554
  false consensus effect in, 555
  naive realism and, 555
  projection of onto social world, 554–555
self-determination theory, 471–472
  continuum of, 472–473, 472f
  over-justification effect in, 473
self-efficacy, 471
  form from interactions with our environment, 502
self-esteem, 414
  belonging and, 468
  self-serving biases for, 555
self-fulfilling prophecies, 553–554
  effects of, 554
  diagnostic labelling and, 619
self-help treatments (for mental illness), 661–662
  availability of, 661
  effectiveness of, 661
self-referred effect, 290
self-reporting, 46
  face-to-face interviews, 46
  paper and pencil tests, 46
  phone surveys, 46
  web-based questionnaires, 46
self-schemas, 305
  depression and, 305
  psychological problems and, 305
self-serving biases, 555
  attributions and, 555–556
  better than average effect of, 555
  influence our understanding of behaviours by others, 555
  ingroups and outgroups, 556
  reinforce tendency to be biased against others, 556
Seligman, Martin, 609
Selye, Hans, 593
semantic network, 317, 317f
  priming in, 318
  usefulness of, 318

semantics, 339
sensation,
  compared to perception, 126
  first step in making world meaningful, 127
sense of touch, 168–170
  for information about texture, temperature and skin pressure, 168
  skin receptors transmit to somatosensory cortex in brain, 168
  two-point threshold device for measuring acuity, 168, 168f
sensory adaptation, 128–129
  disadvantages of, 128
  real-world example of, 128–129
sensory memory, 272, 273–274
  information held in, 273
  relationship to memory, 274, 274f
  test for iconic, 273, 273f
sensory receptors, 127, 127t
September 11, 2001 attacks, 297, 330
serial killers, 626–627
serial position effect, 277, 277f
  primacy effect, 277, 278
  proactive interference in, 277
  recency effect, 277, 278
  retroactive interference in, 277
  testing to evaluate, 277–278
set point theory, 584
  in nutrition, 584
sex differences,
  spatial memory and, 81–82
sexual behaviour, 452–453
  applying science to, 453
  cultural influences on, 460–462
  libido for, 452
  physiological influences, 455
  psychological influences on, 453–455
  sexual response cycle, 455–456
sexual education, 459
  sexual health information in, 459
sexual imagery,
  advertising and, 462
  explanations for success of in advertising, 462
sexual intercourse,
  differences in sex in, 456
sexual motivation, 452
  age factor in, 454
  cultural factors in, 460–461
  evolutionary purpose of reproduction, 453
  new technology and, 461–462
  personal factors in, 453
  physical factors in, 453
  psychological measures of, 453
  social factors in, 453, 460–461
sexual orientation, 426
  brain-imaging studies and, 457
  brain size and, 457
  definitions, 456
  differences in brain structure and, 457
sexual response cycle, 455–456

brain-imaging studies and hypothalamus in, 456
  phases in, 456
sexual scripts, 460
  ethnicity and, 461
  in homosexual relationships, 461
  religion and, 461
sexual selection,
  colour red and, 84
  evolutionary psychology and, 83–85
  intersexual, 83–84
  intrasexual, 83
Sexual Sterilization Act (Alberta, 1928), 350, 351, 357
shame-prone individuals, 426
shaping process, 248
Shiffrin, Richard, 272
short-term memory (STM), 272, 274–275
  behavioural differences between long-term memory (LTM) and, 277
  compared to long-term memory (LTM), 277
  as store with limited capacity and duration, 274–275
  working memory model of, 279
Sick Kids Hospital, Toronto, 339
Siegel, Dr. Daniel, 672
Siegel, Shepard, 241
Siffre, Michael, 183
signal detection theory, 130–131, 130*f*
  decision process in, 130
  factors involved in, 130–131
  outcomes of, 130
  sensory process in, 130
sign languages, 343
Simon, Theodore, 352
Simon Fraser University, 27, 214, 293
Simonides of Ceos, 288, 298, 299
Simpson, O. J., 297
Singer, Jerome, 481
single-blind study, 37
situational analysis, 533, 534
Skinner, B. F., 20, 21, 246, 256, 501
sleep, 181
  biological rhythms and, 182
  Circadian rhythms in, 182, 182*f*
  compared to hypnosis, 200
  effects of REM on learning new tasks, 192–193
  functions affected by REM, 192
  human sleep-dream cycle, 183–184, 183*f*
  non-REM, 185
  rapid eye movement (REM), 183, 184*f*, 185, 185*f*, 191
  REM effects on thinking, 192
  REM and dreaming help problem solving, 192
  REM rebound, 191
  requirements for animal species, 186
  variations in affects from REM, 192
sleep cycles,
  electroencephalogram (EEG) to define, 184–185, 184*f*
  order and duration of, 185, 185*f*

sleep deprivation, 186, 187–188
  caffeine consumption before bedtime as cause of, 189
  cognitive and coordination errors from, 189
  effects of, 188, 188*f*
  medical effects, 188–189
sleep disorders, 181
  see also movement disturbances
  insomnia, 193–194
  medications for, 196
  narcolepsy, 196
  nightmares, 194
  night terrors, 194
  nonpharmacological techniques for overcoming, 196, 196*t*
  overcoming, 196
  psychological interventions for, 196
  sleep apnea, 195–196, 195*f*
sleep displacement, 187, 189
  jet lag, 189
  shift work, 189
sleep theories, 186–187
  complementary, 186–187
  preserve and protect hypothesis, 186
  restore and repair hypothesis, 186
sleepwalking. *See* movement disturbances, somnambulism (sleepwalking)
Sleepwalk with Me (movie), 181
smell sensation, 175–176
Smith, Carlyle, 192
smoke-filled room study, 543
Smoke Free Movies, 581
Snyder, Kurt, 646
social acceptance, 467
  mental health effects of, 467
social anxiety disorder, 637
social approach to changing people's behaviour, 565–567
  awareness raising in, 565
  persuasion through communication, 565–566
social attuning, 395–396
social behaviour,
  hormones involved in, 596
social circuitry, 672
social-cognitive approach, to personality, 502, 502*f*
social-cognitive psychology, 552
  dual-process behaviour models, 552
social connectedness, 467
social contagion, 587–588
social Darwinism, 356
social desirability, 34
social exclusion, 425–426
social facilitation, 536
  explanation mechanisms for, 536
  social loafing as contrast to, 536
social influences, 537–538
  informational influence, 538
  normative influence, 538
social intuitionist model of morality, 423–424
social isolation, 587

social judgments,
  made instantaneously and on little information, 553
social loafing, 535–536
  belief of unimportance of contributions factor in, 535
  copying other loafers as factor in, 536
  low efficacy beliefs as factor in, 535
  non-identification with group as factor in, 536
  social facilitation as contrast to, 536
social networking, 417
  in adolescence, 425–426
social neuroscience, 26
social norms, 533
  definition, 535
  mimicry and, 534–535
social phobias, 635
social processing, 534–535
social psychology, 23–24, 533–536
  bystander effect in, 541–543
  chameleon effect, 534
  compared to behaviourism, 534
  compared to psychodynamic theory, 534
  group dynamics in, 535–536
  social roles in, 544–546
  World War II and, 544
Social Readjustment Rating Scale (SRRS), 591, 592*t*
social reality, 534
social rejection, 426
social resilience, 587
social roles, 544–545
  Stanford prison study and, 544–546
Society of Anthropology, Paris, 337
sociocultural perspective of human behaviour, 5, 5*f*, 23–24
socioeconomic status (SES), 85
  intelligence and, 380
  sexual selection and, 85
socioemotional selectivity theory, 433
sociology, 16, 17
somatic nervous system, 102–103
Sophocles, 524
sound perception, 157–160
  amplitude characteristic of sound waves, 157
  frequency characteristic of sound waves, 157
  frequency theory, 160–161
  place theory of hearing, 160
  primary auditory cortex in brain and, 161–162
  sound localization, 160
sound shadow, 160, 160*f*
spatial learning, 117–118
spatial location memory task, 83*f*
spatial memory,
  sex differences and, 81–82
Spearman, Charles, 363, 365
specific phobias, 635, 635*t*
Spelke, Elizabeth, 404
Sperling, George, 273
spiritualism, 607

split-brain studies, 111–112
Spurzheim, Johann, 15
St. Francis Xavier University, Nova
    Scotia, 443
St. John's wort, 679–680
    effectiveness of, 679
    studies of effects of on depression,
    679
St. Mary of Bethlehem ("bedlam"), 658
St. Mary's University, 27
stage models of human development,
    387
    role of in understanding continuity
    and change over time, 387
standard deviation, 65–66, 66f
Stanford-Binet Test, 352
Stanford University, 352, 544, 568
Star Wars: The Force Awakens (movie),
    156
state-dependent memory, 294
    limitations on, 294
states,
    compared to trait labels, 500–501
    situational factors and, 501
statistical significance, 67, 68
    critical evaluation of research
    testing, 68
    experimental hypothesis and, 68
    null hypothesis and, 68
    power analysis as alternative to, 69
    p-value in, 68
    science and, 68
statistics, 62
    analyzing the data, 63
    descriptive, 63–65
    number organization step in, 62
    probability as foundation of, 62
    test differences between groups as
    meaningful step in, 62
Statistics Canada, 244
stem cells, 90
stereotype,
    social-cognitive definition of, 558
stereotype threat, 358
stereotyping, 25, 552
    distinction between fluid and
    crystallized intelligence and, 368
    explicit *vs.* implicit processes, 559
    negative and positive aspects of, 558
    overcoming implicit, 562
Stern, William, 352
Sternberg, Robert, 368, 369
Stewart, Kristen, 580
stimulus-organism-response (S-O-R)
    psychologists, 262
stimulus-organism-response (S-O-R)
    theory of learning, 262
stimulus-response (S-R) theorists, 262
stimulus thresholds, 129
    limitations on the study of, 129–130
STM. *See* short-term memory (STM)
Strahan, Erin, 132
Strange Case of Dr. Jekyll and Mr. Hyde
    (Stevenson), 630
strange situation procedure, 407–408,
    408f

stress,
    effects on immune system and
    disease, 599–600
    age differences and, 591
    autonomic pathway, 594, 595f
    biofeedback for responses to, 605
    cancer progression and, 600
    causes of, 591
    changing levels of, 600
    cognitive appraisal theory of, 591,
    591f
    coping strategies, 602–604
    definition of, 97, 591
    evaluation of studies on hormones
    and, 596
    fight-or-flight response to, 593,
    594–595
    gender differences in reactions to,
    594–595
    high levels of and coronary heart
    disease, 598
    illness and, 598
    immigration and, 591
    immune system and, 597–598
    intelligence and effects of, 381
    from lack of control events, 609
    learned helplessness and, 609
    meditation and relaxation benefits
    from, 605–606
    motivational influence of, 442
    oxytocin role in, 595–596
    performance, 592–593
    personality characteristics and
    illness from, 598
    physiology of, 593–595
    pressure from, 590
    religion as coping strategy, 607
    shows nervous and endocrine
    systems at work, 97
    social relationships and, 596
    tend-and-befriend response to,
    594–595
    ulcers and, 599
    unhealthy foods and, 599
    in workplace, 591
stroke, 57
Stroop Task, 217f
structuralism, 18
subliminal perception, 131–132
    brain imaging studies, 132
    self-help products and, 131
sudden infant death syndrome (SIDS),
    392
suicide, 434
    bullying as risk factor in, 642
    gender differences and, 641
    helplines, 642
    as outcome from mood disorder,
    641
    social ostracism as risk factor in, 642
    warning signs of, 641–642, 642t
Sultan bin Salman Al-Saud, 562
Summers, Lawrence, 372
superstition, 255, 256
    performance outcomes and, 256
    prone to confirmation bias, 256

Supreme Court of Canada, 461
surveys and questionnaires, 46
    strengths and limitations of, 50t, 51
Suzuki, David, 436
Swarthmore College, Pennsylvania,
    333
sympathetic nervous system,
    fight-or-flight response from, 103
    stress effects on, 594
synapses,
    drug effects on, 96f
    between nerve cells, 92
    reuptakes at, 94, 94f
synaptic pruning, 398–399, 398f
synaptogenesis, 398
synesthesia (blended perceptions), 167
    multimodal integration and, 177,
    177f
    neuroimaging studies into, 177
syntax, 339–340, 340f
    meaning and, 340
    nouns and verbs as basic units of,
    340
systematic desensitization, 668–669
    barriers to effectiveness of, 669–670
    fear of public speaking and,
    668–669, 669t
    flooding process in, 669
systems perspective of human
    behaviour, 5–6, 5f

T

Talmi, Deborah, 277
taste aversion conditioning, 237–238,
    238f
    brain areas responsible for, 238
    characteristics of, 238–239
    development of, 238
    fear response and, 237–238
    latent inhibition explanation, 239
taste sensation, 173–175
    innate *vs.* learned taste preferences,
    174–175
    primary tastes, 173–174
    receptors on tongue surface, 174,
    174f
    registered primarily on the tongue,
    174
    supertasters, 174, 175f
Taylor, Shelley, 25, 594
teaching-like behaviour, 264
temperaments, 499
    inhibited type, 499
    as innate biological foundation for
    personality, 499
    under-controlled type, 499
    well-adjusted type of, 499
teratogens, 391
    alcohol as, 391–392
    thalidomide as, 391
    tobacco as, 391, 392
Terman, Lewis, 352, 356, 357, 358
terrorism, 533
terror management theory (TMT),
    468–469
    critical evaluation of studies of, 469

links to politics of, 469
studies of, 469
testing effect, 300
testosterone, 460
  effects on behaviour, 98
  aggression and, 97–98
  and dominance, 98
  increases in when perceived threat
    to status, 98
  involvement with social aggression,
    98, 99f
  related to social aggression, 98, 99f
Thackery, William M., 203
Thagard, Paul, 45
thalidomide, 391
Thematic Apperception Test (TAT),
  525, 525f, 526, 527
theories, 3, 3f, 4
  as built from hypotheses, 4
  compared to opinions and beliefs, 4
  definition, 4
  misconceptions about, 4
  plausibility of, 4
  quality of unrelated to number of
    believers, 4
theory of evolution, 13, 15, 18, 79
  early opposition to, 80
  human beings in, 80
  natural selection in, 79
  sexual selection and, 83–84
theory of mind, 410, 411f
  in development from birth, 410
therapeutic alliance, 660–661
therapy,
  barriers to receiving, 655–657
  changing attitudes towards, 655
  complex issues around, 660–661
  cultural differences in those
    seeking, 655
  gender differences in those seeking,
    655, 656
  pros and cons of major types of, 675t
  self-help options compared to in-
    person, 662
  settings, 657–658
  stigma associated with, 654
  virtual reality technologies for, 670
Theron, Charlize, 624
Thich Nnat Hanh, 433
thin slices of behaviour, 553
  social judgments made on, 553
third-variable problem, 378
Thorndike, Edward, 20, 246
Thorndike's puzzle box, 246, 246f
Thurstone, Louis, 365
Time, 462
tip-of-the-tongue (TOT) phenomenon,
  276
Titchener, Edward, 18
Todd, Amanda, 417
Tolman, Edward C., 261
top-down processing, 135
torture, 53, 532, 533, 534
Tourette's syndrome, 106
trait labels, 500
  compared to states, 500–501

trait perspectives, 492
  authoritarian personality, 496
  early research, 492–493
  Five Factor Model (FFM) of
    personality traits, 493–494, 494f
  personality scales for, 493
transcranial magnetic stimulation
  (TMS), 118, 118f
transduction,
  as brain process, 127, 128f
transference (as strategy in
  psychoanalysis), 666
transgender, 458, 459
  brain-based differences in, 458–459
transgenic animal, 377
transsexual, 458, 459
Trent University, 192
triarchic theory of intelligence,
  368–369
  analytical intelligence component,
    368
  creative intelligence component, 368
  practical intelligence component,
    368
trichromatic theory (Young-Helmholtz
  theory), 144, 144f, 145
Tri-Council Policy Statement: Ethical
  Conduct for Research Involving
  Humans, 54
tricyclic antidepressants, 678
  side effects, 678
trigger foods, 446
Triplett, Norman, 23, 536
Trudeau, Justin, 239, 241
Trudeau, Pierre Elliott, 572
Trump, Donald, 453
twin and adoption studies, 75–76
  to examine influence of genetic
    factors on personality, 509
  genetic factors in differences in
    intelligence and, 376
  genetics of intelligence and, 375
Twitmyer, Edwin, 19
two-factor theory of emotion, 481
  criticisms of, 483
  scientific explanations for, 481–482,
    482f
Type A personality, 598
Type B personality, 598

U

ultradian rhythms, 182
umami (savouriness), 174
unconscious mind, 520
  collective unconscious, 527
  personal unconscious, 527
  projective tests to explore, 525
  techniques for exploring, 525
Ungerleider, Leslie, 151
unhealthy lifestyles, 580
United Nations (UN), 565
universal needs, 471
  autonomy, 471
  competence, 471
  life control in, 471
  relatedness, 471

self-determination theory and,
    471–472
Université de Montréal, 156, 593
university counselling services, 659
university mental health services, 659
University of Alberta, 27, 203, 437, 469,
  648
University of British Columbia, 187,
  203, 333, 341, 414, 461, 473, 483,
  492, 496, 506
University of California, Los Angeles
  (UCLA), 594
University of Guelph, 27, 429
University of Leipzig, 18
University of Lethbridge, 134, 512
University of Manitoba, 123, 257, 462,
  497
University of New Brunswick, 459
University of Ottawa, 453
University of Toronto, 184, 271, 277,
  290, 484, 553, 606
University of Victoria, 27, 309, 564
University of Waterloo, 27, 45, 132,
  255, 306, 575, 586
U.S. Federal Drug Administration, 461
U.S. National Heart Institute, 588
U.S. National Science Board, 40
U.S. Supreme Court, 205
U.S. Veterans Affairs Normative Aging
  Study, 604
Useful Field of View (UFOV) Speed of
  Processing training, 435

V

vaccinations,
  autism and, 394
  measles, mumps, and rubella
    (MMR), 394
validity in scientific measurement,
  32–33
values approach to communication,
  570
  attitude inoculation, 570
  one-sided message in, 570
  sounding preachy in, 570
  two-sided messages compared to
    one-sided, 570
Vance, James, 126
vegetative state,
  assessment of consciousness in, 207
  evaluating studies of consciousness
    in, 207–208
  explanations for consciousness in,
    207
  permanent, 206, 207
  persistent, 205–206, 207
  using fMRI to communicate with
    someone in, 208f
Vernon, Tony, 364
vestibular system, 164–165, 164f
  brain and, 165
  and links to other senses, 165
  as part controller of our sense of
    balance, 164
  semicircular canals, 164, 164f
  vestibular sacs in, 164, 164f

Vicary, James, 131
virtual reality exposure (VRE), 670, 670f
  evaluation of, 670
  post-traumatic stress disorder
    (PTSD) and, 670
virtual reality therapies, 669
visual disorders,
  colour blindness, 145
  hyperopia (farsightedness), 145, 145f
  myopia (nearsightedness), 145, 145f
visual system,
  human eye, 140–142
visuospatial sketchpad, 280
Vokey, John, 134, 135
volley principle, 161
voluntarism, 18
von Helmholtz, Hermann, 144
Vygotsky, Lev, 405

W

Wagar, Brandon, 45
Wakefield, Andrew, 59, 60
Walker, Dr. Lawrence, 492
Watson, John B., 20, 21, 235
Watts, Dr. James, 682
weapons of mass destruction
  (WMDs), 537
Weber, Ernst, 129
Weber's Law, 129
Wechsler, David, 353
Wechsler Adult Intelligence Scale
  (WAIS), 353, 353f, 355, 378

Wechsler Memory Scales, 278
weight loss, 585–586
  challenges to retaining, 586
  positive image and, 586
Werker, Janet, 341
Wernicke, Carl, 16, 337
Wernicke's aphasia, 337
Wernicke's area, 337, 344, 346
Wertheimer, Max, 132
Western, Educated, Industrialized,
    Rich, and Democrat (WEIRD),
  506
Western cultural dominance, 356
Western University, London, Ontario,
    42, 151, 162, 207, 364
Whiten, Andrew, 260
Whorfian hypothesis, 322
Wiesel, Torsten, 146
Wilfrid Laurier University, 450
Williams, John, 156
Witelson, Sandra, 378
womb envy, 528
Women's Rights Movement,
  460–461
Wonderlic Personnel Test, 370
working memory, 279–281
  central executive, 281
  compared to the Atkinson-Shiffrin
    model, 279
  components, 279, 279f
  episodic buffer in short-term
    memory (STM), 279, 281

  nuanced model of short-term
    memory (STM), 279
  phonological loop in short-term
    memory (STM), 279, 280
  visuospatial sketchpad in short-term
    memory (STM), 279, 280–281
  workings of, 281
World Health Organization (WHO), 617
World War I,
  IQ testing during, 356
World War II, 23, 53, 544
Wundt, Wilhelm, 18, 20, 23
Wuornos, Aileen, 624, 626

Y

Yale University, 548
Yerkes, Robert, 592
yoga, 607
York University, 344, 492, 562
Young, Thomas, 144
Young-Helmholtz theory. *See*
  trichromatic theory (Young-
  Helmholtz theory)

Z

zeitgeist (spirit of the times), 13, 18
Zimbardo, Dr. Philip, 533, 534, 544,
  545, 548
zone of proximal development, 405
  scaffolding and, 405–406
Zuroff, David, 512
zygote, 388